EMPLOYMENT LAW

ASPEN SELECT SERIES

EMPLOYMENT LAW

Fourth Edition

Richard Carlson
South Texas College of Law

Scott A. Moss
University of Colorado School of Law

Published by Wolters Kluwer in New York.

Wolters Kluwer Legal & Regulatory U.S. serves customers worldwide with CCH, Aspen Publishers, and Kluwer Law International products. (www.WKLegaledu.com)

To contact Customer Service, e-mail customer.service@wolterskluwer.com, call 1-800-234-1660, fax 1-800-901-9075, or mail correspondence to:

Wolters Kluwer
Attn: Order Department
PO Box 990
Frederick, MD 21705

Printed in the United States of America.

1 2 3 4 5 6 7 8 9 0

ISBN 978-1-4548-9265-6

Library of Congress Cataloging-in-Publication Data

Names: Carlson, Richard R. (Richard Ray), 1954- author. | Moss, Scott A., 1973- author.
Title: Employment law / Richard Carlson, South Texas College of Law; Scott A. Moss, University of Colorado School of Law.
Description: Fourth edition. | New York : Wolters Kluwer, [2019] | Series: Aspen casebook series | Includes index.
Identifiers: LCCN 2018034377 | ISBN 9781454892656
Subjects: LCSH: Labor laws and legislation--United States. | LCGFT: Casebooks (Law)
Classification: LCC KF3457 .C37 2019 | DDC 344.7301--dc23
LC record available at https://lccn.loc.gov/2018034377

Certified Chain of Custody
Promoting Sustainable Forestry

www.sfiprogram.org
SFI-01347

About Wolters Kluwer Legal & Regulatory U.S.

Wolters Kluwer Legal & Regulatory U.S. delivers expert content and solutions in the areas of law, corporate compliance, health compliance, reimbursement, and legal education. Its practical solutions help customers successfully navigate the demands of a changing environment to drive their daily activities, enhance decision quality and inspire confident outcomes.

Serving customers worldwide, its legal and regulatory portfolio includes products under the Aspen Publishers, CCH Incorporated, Kluwer Law International, ftwilliam.com and MediRegs names. They are regarded as exceptional and trusted resources for general legal and practice-specific knowledge, compliance and risk management, dynamic workflow solutions, and expert commentary.

To my wife Lena, and to my children, Helen, Elsa, Darina, Greta, and Alexander

To Marianna, Piper, and Enrico Moss

SUMMARY OF CONTENTS

TABLE OF CONTENTS

PREFACE

There are many possible strategies for presenting the seemingly fragmented subject of employment law. One approach is to offer two separate courses addressing the deepest government interventions in employment relations: collective bargaining law (or "labor law" as it is known in many law school curriculums) and employment discrimination law. This two-part approach treats the remainder of employment law as a residue banished to the periphery. In contrast, this book is designed for a broad survey of employment law that accounts more effectively for important topics beyond collective bargaining and discrimination, including disputes over individual contract rights, statutory regulation of compensation and benefits, work-related injury and safety, conflicts between the demands of employment and the demands of family or the public interest, post-employment competition, and the resolution of disputes between employers and individual employees.

Collective bargaining and discrimination are not omitted. Both topics are themes that run substantial courses through this book. It is assumed, however, that students wishing a deeper understanding of collective bargaining or employment discrimination will take additional courses in these topics. This survey course stands either independently or as a third pillar in the employment law curriculum. It could appeal to either of two groups of students. First, students who might never take another course in employment law will find this course provides the widest exposure to a subject that, in one way or another, can affect nearly any other area of the law. Second, for students who plan to take or have already taken more specialized courses in employment discrimination or collective bargaining, this survey will complete the employment law picture.

One may wonder whether it is possible to present employment law as a single course without a principal legal regimen such as collective bargaining or antidiscrimination law as a gravitational core. The question is no different for employment law than it is for other broad subject areas of the curriculum, such as family law or business organizations. Indeed, as a survey course, employment law bears a particularly strong resemblance to family law. Each deals with human relationships that are fundamental in modern life. Just as our families define us, we are further defined by our work and our position in the workplace. Employment offers sustenance at the very least and potentially much more, but it can also present grave risks because of frequent imbalances of power, the parties' respective needs to rely on each other, and the difficulties of accounting for life or business-altering contingencies over the long term. A unifying theme for an employment law course is the need for legal rules that make employment a fulfilling and not unduly dangerous or unfair relationship.

Thus, this book is organized according to certain stages, contexts, and problems in the employment relationship, rather than by statutes or other sources of law. For example, after two introductory chapters about the historical development of employee relations and the distinctive characteristics of employment, Chapter 3 addresses the selection and hiring of employees, and the chapters that follow address successive aspects and stages of the relationship. From one chapter to the next, a few laws are ubiquitous.

Naturally, antidiscrimination law and the potential for collective bargaining permeate every aspect of employment with complexity that deserves the opportunity for further study in more specialized courses. But it is impossible to isolate these topics from examination of any other part of employment law, and a course that purported to do so would hardly serve as a representative survey. This book solves the problem by presenting a foundation of basic principles in antidiscrimination law and collective bargaining at the earliest appropriate stages and building on these early foundations in the various contexts and problem areas that follow. For example, employment discrimination laws make their first important appearance in Chapter 3, which presents the problem of discrimination and the basic theories of discrimination law in the context of employee selection. Students who have not studied employment discrimination law before this course will learn enough in Chapter 3 to work their way through the additional contexts examined in the subsequent chapters, including compensation and benefits, work-related safety and injury, supervision (including sexual harassment), work-family conflicts, and termination. By concentrating on one context or problem area at a time, students will have an opportunity to consider the contextual goals, needs, and circumstances of the parties, and to learn the interrelationships among different employment statutes, common law rules, and constitutional rules.

Richard Carlson and Scott Moss

March 2018

ACKNOWLEDGMENTS

Professor Richard Carlson is grateful to a number of persons whose support made this and prior editions of this book possible. His research assistant Natalie Sweeney discovered and collected many of the cases that fill this book. Two other students, GaryWinters and Stephanie Briggs, did much of the proofreading and editing. Professor Carlson's secretary Cheri Lange acted as the first line supervisor and converted the work for the first edition into a presentable format. Cindi Lowrimore provided secretarial support for this third edition. At Aspen Publishers, Richard Mixter and John Devins provided guided and advice at different stages along the way from the first proposal to the first edition. Professor Moss is grateful to his research assistants, Kimberly Jones (University of Colorado Law School, class of 2013), Maureen Chu (class of 2018), and Caitlin Stover (class of 2019,for their extensive work researching the diverse case law of numerous states on varied employment law topics.

Professors Carlson and Moss are grateful for grants of permission to reproduce excerpts from the following materials:

Gillian Lester, *Restrictive Covenants, Employee Training, and the Limits of Transaction- Cost Analysis*, 76 Ind. L. J. 49 (2001). Copyright © 2001 by the Trustees of Indiana University; Gillian Lester. Reprinted by permission.

National Academy of Social Insurance, *Workers' Compensation: Benefits, Coverage, and Costs, 2009* (August 2011). Copyright © 2011 National Academy of Social Insurance. Reprinted by permission of the National Academy of Social Insurance.

Stewart J. Schwab, *Life-Cycle Justice: Accommodating Just Cause and Employment at Will*, 92 Mich. L. Rev. 8 (1993). Copyright © 1993 by the Michigan Law Review Association; Stewart J. Schwab. Reprinted by permission of the Michigan Law Review Association and Stewart J. Schwab.

Emily A. Spieler, *Perpetuating Risk? Workers' Compensation and the Persistence of Occupational Injuries*, 31 Hou. L. Rev. 119 (1994). Copyright © 1994 by the Houston Law Review; Emily A. Spieler. Reprinted by permission of the Houston Law Review.

EMPLOYMENT LAW

CHAPTER 1

An Overview of Employment and the Law

A. THE CHANGING NATURE OF WORK IN AMERICA

1. *The Changing Workforce*

The nature of work, its management and organization, and the composition of the American workforce have changed radically over the last 200 years. Legal institutions for regulating working relationships have struggled to keep pace with these changes.

The most profound change, and the genesis of nearly any other important historical trend in employment, has been the relentless shift from agrarian and small-scale craft work to large-scale industrial, transportation, and commercial activity employing and organizing hundreds or thousands of workers in one workplace or enterprise. At the start of the nineteenth century the vast majority of Americans were employed, self-employed, or enslaved in agrarian work. As of 1820, about 80 percent of laborers were in agricultural work. By 1870, the balance between agricultural and nonagricultural workers was roughly even as the effects of industrial revolution took hold in the United States. *See* Deborah Ballam, *The Traditional View of the Origins of the Employment-at-Will Doctrine: Myth or Reality*, 33 Am. Bus. L.J. 1, 6 (1995). Today, less than 2 percent of the workforce is employed in agriculture, including self-employed farmers and unpaid family members. Bureau of Labor Statistics, Current Population Survey: Characteristics of the Employed: Employed Persons in Agriculture and Nonagricultural Industries, Table 15 (2016), at https://www.bls.gov/cps/cpsa2016.pdf. The decline in agriculture has been matched by a decline in small craft shops and the rise of large-scale industry and commerce.

The trend toward complex industrial and commercial activity has had profound consequences for relations between employers and employees. At the start of the eighteenth century, relations between a "master" and workers on the farm, in the household, or in the workshop were direct and personal, although this did not necessarily mean the relations were humane. The workplace was often an extension of the master's home, and all or part of a worker's compensation might include shelter, food, and other necessities. U.S. Dep't of Labor, History of Wages in the United States from Colonial Times to 1928, pp. 13-16 (1934). In some regions of the United States, a majority of workers labored as slaves. Even in non-slave states, significant numbers of workers were tied to masters in indentured servitude or peonage until the early nineteenth century. That relations were personal meant among other things that an employer or master rarely needed any intermediate hierarchy or bureaucracy to manage the work, apart from the employment of an overseer to supervise other employees, servants, or slaves. In such a setting, the employer was well acquainted with each worker, and that relationship may have extended beyond work. Indeed, legal scholars of the eighteenth century viewed employment as a family relation more than a business relation. For example, early legal treatises included the law of "master and servant" as part of the law of domestic relations. *See, e.g.*, James Schouler, Law of the Domestic Relations, Embracing Husband and Wife, Parent and Child, Guardian and Ward, Infancy, and Master and Servant (1905); Irving Browne, Elements of the Law of Domestic Relations and of Employer and Employed (1883).

Slaves, of course, were separated from their masters by an impenetrable wall of color, economic status, and social class, but indentured servants and free laborers could inspire themselves with the prospect that someday they would be self-employed and might even become "masters" of their own employees. A journeyman or apprentice might take the learning and experience acquired in the master's shop and open his or her own shop. An indentured servant who had fulfilled a term or a free laborer might travel west to establish his own farm.

The industrial revolution marked a dramatic end to the servant-to-master cycle for many workers. The reorganization of work into factories, where large numbers of workers shared the use of labor-saving but expensive equipment and other major capital investments, meant the death of less efficient craft shops. In the factory setting, however, the odds of a worker becoming his or her own master dimmed. Increasingly, members of each trade divided into a distinctly separate small group of factory owners and much larger group of wage earners.

Relations between the new class of factory owners and their employees became more impersonal and competitive as their long-term goals and expectations began to diverge. Direct supervision of employees by a master was replaced by hierarchy, bureaucracy, and the continuing invention of new ways of organizing work. To manage complex industrial and commercial operations required the development of a third group: administrative and managerial employees to supervise, count, record, design, buy, sell, pay, and collect. Government bureaucracy and independent professions such as the law, engineering, accounting, and marketing also flourished with the growth of industry and commerce. Industrial production, having long ago surpassed agriculture as a source of employment, was itself surpassed by the new white collar occupations during the twentieth century. Today, a category of workers the Bureau of Labor Statistics describes as "management, professional, and related occupations" constitutes more than 39 percent of the workforce. Bureau of Labor Statistics, Current Population Survey: Employed Persons by Occupation, Sex, and Age (2017), at http://www.bls.gov/cps/cpsaat09.htm. "Service occupations" constitute another 18 percent. *Id.* "Production, transportation, and material moving occupations" now constitute less than 12 percent of the workforce. *Id.*

Within categories of workers, changes in technology and consumer demands produce an endless stream of new work and job titles. The Bureau of Labor Statistics collects statistics for all occupations. One of its challenges is to identify new occupations absent from earlier surveys; in a 2001 survey, it identified 65 new occupations. Jerome Pikulinski, *New and Emerging Occupations*, published in Dep't of Labor, OCCUPATIONAL EMPLOYMENT AND WAGES, May 2003, p. 14 (Sept. 2004), https://www.bls.gov/oes/bulletin_2003.pdf. Important changes are also reflected in the Department of Labor's list of fastest growing occupations for the future. Of the 20 expected to grow fastest between 2010 and 2018, 10 were in health care, and 2 were in information technology. Bureau of Labor Statistics, 2010-11 Edition of the Occupational Outlook Handbook, at http://www.bls.gov/oco/oco2003.htm#occupation_d. In contrast, employment in farming, fishing and forestry was expected to decline 2.8 percent by 2016, and employment in "production" (mainly manufacturing) was expected to decline 4.9 percent. Bureau of Labor Statistics, Tomorrow's Jobs (Jan. 2008).

These changes in the profile of the American workforce have challenged the legal system in many ways. A legal system designed for agrarian slaves, indentured servants, and apprentices is hardly suited for relations between an information technology corporation and a software engineer. The goals, expectations, and needs of the parties, and risks of accident, miscalculation, oppression, or destructive opportunism by either party, vary tremendously according to the type of work. These differences occur not only in the passage of time from one generation to the next, but also within an era from one occupation or industry to the next. For example, even in the age of information technology, there are still significant numbers of agrarian workers who have needs not unlike those of workers in similar work 200 years ago. Unlike their eighteenth-century predecessors, however, modern agrarian workers are more likely to be highly mobile "migrant" workers whose work takes them from one part of the continent to another each year, and they are controlled chiefly by a labor contractor instead of a landowner. Any law or rule that fails to account for such differences, and for the likelihood of more change in the future, is likely to fail its purpose.

A second major change in the American workforce has been its integration across race and gender lines. The American workforce has always been diverse, but until the late twentieth century, legal and societal rules tended to separate workers into different jobs by race and gender. Black Americans, for example, remained in largely segregated communities and occupations long after the emancipation of the slaves, because society and the legal system continued to embrace or at least condone vestiges of slavery, such as the exclusion of black Americans from the best jobs. Women have always been important participants in the workforce but not in equal numbers with men in income-producing work, and social conventions prohibited their training or work in many of the most desirable occupations. On the other hand, some occupations, including nursing and secretarial work, were once reserved almost exclusively for women. Changes in the law, starting particularly with the Civil Rights Act of 1964, began a gradual process of racial and gender integration in the workforce, a process that continues. In 1930, only 24 percent of women were in the labor force. Today, the rate exceeds 57 percent. Bureau of Labor Statistics, Women in the Labor Force: A Databook, p. 1 (December 2014), http://www.bls.gov/opub/reports/womens-databook/archive/women-in-the-labor-force-a-databook-2014.pdf.

The integration of the workforce has exacerbated some old problems and created some new ones. Discrimination that was once a matter of express or official policy now takes subtle forms that are much more difficult to prove and remedy. Racial and ethnic integration of a workforce sometimes requires employers to deal with conflict between racial and ethnic groups or harassment by one group against another. Sexual harassment has undoubtedly always been a problem, but legally enforced integration of male and female workers raised awareness of the problem.

The legal community seldom viewed sexual harassment as a matter for legal recourse until the 1970s when courts began to see sexual harassment as an impediment to integration and gender equality. Gender integration of the workforce has also resulted in a growing number of employees who are primary or joint caretakers of children or other dependents. Unlike the stereotypical male worker of the past, today's worker is more likely to face caretaking demands that are difficult to reconcile with the demands of an employer.

2. *The Changing Workplace*

No single model has ever sufficed to describe all work relationships and methods of organizing work, and employers and employees have been quite creative in inventing new ways of forming their relationships according to the nature of the work and needs and goals of the parties. As described in the preceding section, employers developed the factory system in the nineteenth century as one way of organizing employees and their work. This more regimented way of organizing and coordinating work led to more impersonal working relations and to the growth of a business bureaucracy.

The factory system also exacerbated a number of conflicts between owners and workers. A factory depended on the coordination of activities of a large number of employees — hundreds of employees in some very large factories. Whether employees could work together effectively and efficiently depended in part on synchronization: a uniform schedule of working and nonworking days, established beginning and ending times each day, and scheduled breaks. The transition from the casual manner of agrarian or traditional craft work to the highly regimented manner of factories was not always smooth. Workers frequently chafed at the loss of autonomy they enjoyed in simpler, less organized workplaces.

Other conflicts arose from the factory owners' drive for greater productivity from workers. From an owner's point of view, squeezing more production from each worker meant higher profits and a direct benefit to the owner. From a worker's point of view, however, greater productivity might mean nothing more than harder work. Greater productivity did not necessarily mean higher wages. Greater productivity might actually *depress* wages for a number of reasons.

First, if the labor supply was plentiful and other potential workers were eager to accept work at existing wage rates, an owner might see no reason to raise wages no matter how high his profits. As each worker became more productive, an owner might need fewer workers, and the reduced demand for labor might cause a general wage reduction. Workers might ultimately reap benefits from greater productivity if it increased labor demand and reduced the cost of consumer goods, but no single worker or group of workers could be certain they would share in these gains. An employee fired for failing to maintain a proper pace at work, or laid off because of redundancy, would not be consoled at the thought that other workers would enjoy lower prices for his employer's goods.

Second, some of the factory system's productivity gains were the result of "deskilling," a process of reducing the skills required of employees assigned to the work. An individual shoemaker in his own shop required years of training and experience to make a shoe from beginning to end, but in a factory setting an owner could delegate each step in the process to a different worker who possessed few if any of the skills for making an entire shoe by himself. Deskilling required rigorous control and organization of the work, but if the process succeeded the employer could hire lower skilled workers at lower wages.

The net effect of improved efficiency and deskilling was quite complex for the workforce as a whole. Some workers lost jobs and others found their skilled crafts eliminated altogether by new factory methods, but factories also created new categories of skilled occupations — especially for the administrative, managerial, and professional workforce. Educational expectations for work have generally increased for the workforce as a whole over the last 200 years. In the nineteenth century, a benchmark of education was literacy. According to the 1880 U.S. Census, at least 17 percent of the population over age ten could not write, and 13.4 percent could not read. U.S. Census Bureau, Statistics in Brief (2004), at http://www.census.gov/statab/www/part2.html. Even in 1910, 23.8 percent of the population had fewer than five years of elementary school education, and only 2.7 percent had attended four or more years of college. By 2002, less than 1.6 percent of the population had failed to complete more than five years of elementary school, but more than 84 percent of the population had completed at least four years of high school, and more than 26 percent had completed at least four years of college. U.S. Census Bureau, Statistical Abstract of the United States (2003). Today, most of the fastest growing occupations require a high level of education. The Bureau of Labor Statistics reports that a bachelor's degree is required for 10 of the 20 fastest growing occupations. Bureau of Labor Statistics, Occupational Outlook Handbook (December 17, 2015), https://www.bls.gov/ooh/fastest-growing.htm. Heightened expectations for worker skill are also reflected in the pervasive use of computers in the workplace. Over 53 percent of the workforce used a computer at work in 2001. Bureau of Labor Statistics, Computer and Internet Use at Work in 2001 (Oct. 23, 2002), https://www.bls.gov/opub/mlr/2003/02/art2full.pdf.

Another result of the centralization of work in factories in the eighteenth century was to strengthen employers' relative bargaining power. An employer corporation that had consolidated a local industry under a single roof could more easily dictate the terms of employment by exercising its "monopsony" power, i.e., the power it gained by being the only buyer of labor in a particular labor market. Employees sometimes responded with their own system of organization: the labor union. Unions sought to match employer bargaining power by controlling the supply of labor. If an employer failed to accede to the union's demands, union members collectively withheld their labor and engaged in other tactics such as picketing to deter other workers from performing the work.

Unions enjoyed only limited success in organizing employees during the nineteenth century and the first part of the twentieth century. The hostility of employers, the legal establishment, and local communities kept unions at bay in most industries. Courts often viewed labor strikes, picketing, and other collective employee activities as unlawful civil conspiracies and were generally unhelpful in enforcing any collective bargaining agreements unions negotiated with employers. Moreover, the law offered employees no protection against employer retaliation. In Coppage v. Kansas, 236 U.S. 1 (1915), the U.S. Supreme Court struck down a state law prohibiting employers from firing union members, holding that such an imposition on the right to select and discharge employees violated employers' freedom of contract. *See also* Adair v. United States, 208 U.S. 161 (1908) (invalidating similar federal law). Unions prevailed, if at all, by superior economic force, but their occasional superior economic position was often fleeting in the fast-changing demographic and economic landscape of nineteenth-century America. Unions achieved some important legislative victories in the early twentieth century, including the Railway Labor Act of 1926 (regulating railroad-union collective bargaining) and the Norris-LaGuardia Act of 1930 (restricting federal courts from issuing injunctions in labor disputes). Still, as of 1933 union density (the ratio of union membership to the nonagricultural workforce) was only about 13 percent. Paul C. Weiler, *Promises to Keep: Securing Workers' Rights to Self-Organization Under the NLRA*, 96 Harv. L. Rev. 1769, 1771 (1983).

The position of unions changed radically under the Roosevelt Administration in the 1930s. In 1935, Congress enacted the National Labor Relations Act (the NLRA, also known as the Wagner Act) to promote, protect, and facilitate the selection of collective bargaining representatives and the process of collective bargaining. The NLRA's immediate effect was a dramatic growth in union membership and collective bargaining. By 1954, unions represented 35 percent of the nonagricultural workforce. The mid-1950s, however, marked the high point for unions in the private sector and were followed by persistent decline and eventual return to pre-Wagner Act levels. Today, only 6.4 percent of private sector employees are union members. The decline in private sector unionization has been offset somewhat by an increase in public sector unionization, which now stands at 34.4 percent of the government workforce. Bureau of Labor Statistics, Union Members Summary (January 26, 2017), https://www.bls.gov/news.release/union2.nr0.htm. Yet even in the public sector, unions have failed to maintain growth in the recent years. The number of government employees who are union members is no greater today than in 1983. Unionization varies widely by geography. In New York, 24.2 percent of workers are union members. In South Carolina, only 1.6 percent are. *Id.*

There are many reasons for the decline of collective bargaining in the private sector: employer opposition, employee opposition or disinterest, ineffectiveness of laws protecting of collective bargaining process, competition from nonunion firms in the United States, the availability of competitive labor outside the United States, the failure of many labor organizations to represent their members effectively or to adapt to changes in business and the economy, the decline of industries with traditionally high unionization rates, and the rise of new industries in which employees proved difficult to unionize. Still, unions remain an important force, powerful in many traditional industries where they first became strong, such as the railroad industry. Moreover, much of what nonunion employers do to improve working conditions is a reaction to the risk that employees might otherwise organize a union. Unions are also an important voice for employee interests in Congress, state legislatures, and city councils.

A number of other recent innovations in the organization of work are mainly the result of unilateral initiatives of employers. Among these are the deliberate use of "contingent" or alternative employment arrangements, including "staffing service" arrangements, to achieve certain personnel management purposes.

The contingent workforce is an amorphous group whose membership varies depending on how one defines a "contingent" worker. The Bureau of Labor Statistics defines "contingent" workers as "persons who do not have an implicit or explicit contract for ongoing employment." Bureau of Labor Statistics, Contingent and Alternative Employment Arrangements (May 24, 2001), at http://www.bls.gov/news.release/conemp.nr0.htm. In other words, contingent workers understand that their jobs are temporary and will not continue indefinitely. *Id.* A "temporary employee" assigned by a staffing service for the short term is one example of a contingent worker. A related group, treated separately by the bureau for statistical purposes, consists of persons in "alternative work arrangements," including some "part time" workers and "independent contractors." Independent contractors have become a particularly important alternative workforce because they are beyond the protection of many employment laws. Like contingent workers, true independent contractors are likely hired for a specific task or project, and they ordinarily lack an expectation of ongoing employment. However, independent contractors frequently resemble employees, and might actually be employees misclassified as independent contractors, if they lack genuine and substantial businesses of their own, if their employment relationships are long term, and if their relationships substantially limit or exclude the possibility of concurrent service for other parties.

There have always been contingent and alternative workers, but by most measures the numbers of such workers grew rapidly toward the end of the twentieth century, especially in the types of workplaces that previously depended mainly on regular, permanent employees. For example, the number of workers employed by "temporary agencies" to work in short-term assignments for client-employers doubled in a single decade, growing from 518,000 in 1980 to 1,032,000 in 1989. *See* Stone, *supra*, at 540. In 2005, contingent workers constituted from 1.8 to 4.1 percent of the workforce (depending on definition). Bureau of Labor Statistics, Contingent and Alternative Employment Arrangements (Feb. 2005), at http://bls.gov/pub/news.release/pdf/conemp.pdf. Independent contractors constituted 7.4 percent of the workforce in 2001. However, some studies of the labor market suggest that the contingent workforce may have reached 15 percent of the workforce by 2015 (depending on definition). William G. Gale, Sarah E. Holmes, and David C. John, *Retirement Plans for Contingent Workers: Issues and Options*, p. 5 (September 23, 2016), https://www.brookings.edu/wp-content/uploads/2016/08/rsp923paper1.pdf.

There are also alternative employment arrangements that preserve long-term employment relationships and are not "contingent," but delegate of some employer responsibilities to other parties. In an "employee leasing" arrangement, an employer might transfer all or part of its workforce to the payroll of a staffing service acting as the "employer" for certain purposes. The leasing arrangement need not have any effect on the employment duration; employees might not even be aware that they have been "leased" by one employer to another.

There are many reasons some employers have turned to alternative working relations for work formerly performed by "regular" employees. First, the increasing complexity and bureaucratization of employee relations has spawned an independent staffing and personnel service industry. Many smaller employers that cannot efficiently provide for their own human resources administration have contracted out some human resources functions to independent providers. The delegation of human resources functions sometimes blurs the relationships of the parties and can create issues about who is the real employer.

Second, even many larger employers are attracted by the flexibility some contingent or alternative working relationships seem to offer. An employer that lays off regular employees due to a decline or change in business faces certain legal responsibilities to laid-off employees, risks of wrongful discharge litigation, higher unemployment compensation tax rates (which base on the employer's "experience rating"), demoralization of the employees who remain, and adverse publicity. An employer might believe, rightly or wrongly, it can avoid some or all of these problems by hiring a contingent workforce during peaks in the business cycle, and terminating mainly contingent workers when business declines.

Third, the medical conditions, lifestyle choices, or family demands of some workers make them prime candidates for the contingent workforce. Contingent workers tend to be young. They are more than twice as likely as noncontingent workers to be under the age of 25, and they may see contingent employment as a way to earn a living while they keep their options open and search for the "permanent" job of their choice. Workers with personal limitations or family caregiver responsibilities are another group that might accept contingent employment as a matter of choice. In this regard, the growing number of working women during the latter part of the twentieth century was undoubtedly an important factor in the growth of some types of alternative working arrangements, because women still tend to bear a greater responsibility for caregiving than men.

Finally, regular employees can create a demand for contingent workers when they exercise a statutory or contractual right to a medical or caregiving "leave of absence." An employer cannot permanently replace a leave-protected absent employee. It must assign the work to existing employees or hire a temporary employee to perform the work until the absent employee returns.

One reason to be concerned about the size and growth of the contingent and alternative workforces is that employment is an important basis for social welfare benefits such as medical insurance and pensions, but employers frequently design their benefits plans to exclude part-time, contingent and alternative workers. The Affordable Care Act creates strong incentives for employers to offer medical insurance plans for full-time employees, but not for part-time employees, independent contractors or other contingent workers. As of 2012, about 86.4 percent of full-time employees were covered by employer-provided medical insurance but only 23.7 percent of part-time employees were covered by medical insurance. There is no law that requires employers to offer pension plans for employees. When employers do offer such plans, the plans tend to be reserved for regular full-time employees. About half of regular employees, but only a fifth of contingent workers, were eligible for employer-provided pensions as of 2001. Bureau of Labor Statistics, Contingent and Alternative Employment Arrangements (Feb. 2001), at http://bls.gov/pub/news.release/contemp.txt.

3. *Changing Employee Expectations*

a. Compensation and Fringe Benefits

As discussed in the preceding section, employers sometimes use alternative working arrangements to make distinctions between workers who are eligible for certain fringe benefits and workers who are not. Eligibility for employee benefits is an important issue for employees, because employees often expect that employment will provide more than cash wages. It will also provide for their retirement and health insurance needs.

Change in worker longevity is one reason why employees have come to rely on employers to provide for retirement. Two hundred years ago workers worked until they died, or until they became disabled by age, illness, or injury. In the latter case, death usually followed quickly. A worker who lived for an extended period of disability, but who had failed to accumulate substantial savings, might well be reduced to begging or peddling as a means of support in his old age. Steven Erlanger, The Colonial Worker in Boston, 1775, pp. 10-11 (U.S. Dep't of Labor 1976). A leisurely retirement was simply not part of the normal life cycle for most workers. Even as late as 1900, the average life expectancy was a mere 47.3 years— far short of an age most modern workers would regard as a "retirement age."

Today, average life expectancy for a child is about 78 years and rising, and workers generally assume their lives will include several years of retirement. U.S. Census Bureau, 2012 Statistical Abstract, Table 104, Expectation of Life at Birth (2012), at http://www.census.gov/compendia/statab/2012/tables/12s0104.pdf. The prolonged life expectancy and productive years of modern workers have created two types of issues. First, should the employer (or a union) defer part of an employee's compensation until retirement as a means of assuring the employee will have adequate savings for retirement? Second, is there an age at which retirement should be mandatory regardless of an individual's ability to work?

The earliest welfare benefit plans for workers disabled by old age were "mutual benefit societies" established by trade unions, and pension plans created by a handful of major employers in the late nineteenth and early twentieth century. By 1929 about 10 percent of nonagricultural workers were covered by pension plans, but many of these plans became insolvent during the Great Depression, leaving elderly workers who had relied on these plans without any pension at all. Peter Wiedenbeck & Russell Osgood, Cases and Materials on Employee Benefits, 72-73 (1996). The Social Security Act of 1935 established a public system of mandatory retirement benefits for most employees. However, the act was designed to provide only a minimum level of retirement income, and benefits are far short of the amount of income retirees need for the lifestyle they have come to expect.

Employee demand for employer-sponsored retirement plans was one important factor in the growth of such plans after the Great Depression, but it is questionable whether employers would have accepted responsibility for creating such plans without a number of government incentives and the competition presented by unions. The growth of employer-sponsored pension plans was particularly rapid during World War II as a result of federal tax measures and other wartime incentives. In a two-year period from September 1942 to December 1944, the Internal Revenue Service approved 4,208 pension plans, in comparison with only 1,360 approvals during the previous 12 years. Today, about 54 percent of employees in the civilian workforce participate in employer-provided retirement plans. Bureau of Labor Statistics, Economic News Release, Employee Benefits in the U.S, Table A (July 22, 2016). http://www.bls.gov/news.release/ebs2.htm.

The longer life expectancy of workers and the greater promise of medical care in preserving worker health have also created a need for health care insurance, and employer-sponsored health insurance plans have grown in tandem with pension plans. In early America, a master might owe a duty to provide minimal care and support for a disabled slave or indentured servant, but a free laborer who became sick or disabled depended on his own resources or community charity. An employer's legal responsibility for the health of its employees was limited to negligence-based liability for work-related injuries. After the Civil War, some employers began to employ company doctors to treat workers for work-related injuries or to maintain a supply of healthy labor in remote areas where employee illness or injury might severely affect operations. A few employers experimented with "welfare capitalism" and provided general medical care for employees to assure a stable and loyal supply of labor or because of genuine concern for employee welfare. Employers became strictly liable for work-related injuries under state-enacted workers' compensation laws in the early twentieth century. However, it is only recently that employers have assumed a key role in providing general medical insurance for illness or injury of any cause. Today, 54 percent of workers participate in health insurance plans associated with their work. Bureau of Labor Statistics, Economic News Release, Employee Benefits in the U.S. (July 26, 2011), at http://www.bls.gov/news.release/ebs2.t02.htm. Many others are covered as spouses or dependents of other workers whose employers provide insurance.

As life expectancy and medical costs increase, so do employer costs for pensions and health insurance. On average, benefits costs (including social security and medicare contributions) now constitute more than 17 percent of the total cost of compensation. Medical insurance costs are by far the fastest growing component of compensation and benefits. In 1960, health benefits constituted only 14.4 percent of benefits costs; today, they are 43.5 percent of benefits costs. Employee Benefits Research Institute, Facts from EBRI: Employer Spending on Benefits (May 2004), at http://www.ebri.org/facts/0504fact.pdf.

b. Tenure and Career Advancement

The U.S. labor market has been characterized by comparatively high labor mobility and turnover for most of its history. Turnover was especially high in the later stages of the industrial revolution, when the annual turnover rate in some industries was well over 100 percent. *See* Mathew Finken, *The Bureaucratization of Work: Employer Policies and Contract Law*, 1986 Wis. L. Rev. 733, 737-38 (1986). The ease with which American employers and employees have terminated their relations is due in part to a presumption in contract law that either party in employment can terminate the relationship "at will."

The right to terminate employment at will can be advantageous to either party in a rapidly changing environment, but high turnover can be a source of insecurity for an employer who needs a reliable and stable workforce, or an employee who faces at least a temporary loss of income and shortage of attractive alternative opportunities. The ideal contract for either party preserves that party's right to terminate but restricts the other party's. Thus, employers and employees have often attempted to restrict the opposite side's right to terminate, either by express contract or by some theory of contract, tort, or property law.

Slavery, indentured servitude, and apprenticeship were among the earliest and most substantial employer strategies to prevent loss of workers, but none of these strategies persisted much beyond the Civil War. In the late nineteenth and early twentieth centuries, employers experimented with fixed-term contracts or contracts requiring advance notice of resignation, enforcing such contracts by the forfeiture of substantial deferred pay. Finken, *supra*, at 737. When contractual solutions proved inadequate, employers sometimes resorted to "blacklists" to prevent competition for employees by other employers in their industry. Today, employers are more likely to rely on more subtle employee retention strategies such as covenants not to compete or benefit plans incentivizing long-term service.

Employees were not as quick as employers to seek contractual solutions to the instability of employment. Labor shortages were chronic in America until the later stages of the industrial revolution, and in this state of affairs employees generally benefitted from employment at will. During the twentieth century, however, changes in labor markets, business organization, and employee lifestyle made job-hopping or migration less attractive and longevity within a single enterprise more rewarding. Employee goals and expectations began to change.

Like the indentured servants, apprentices, and journeymen craftsmen of the eighteenth and nineteenth centuries, today's employees often see work as a rung on a ladder for advancement. Instead of the old servant-to-master cycle, however, the more likely model for many employees of the twentieth century has been long-term employment and advancement within a single employer organization.

One modern model of job security and advancement is an outgrowth of collective bargaining among blue collar workers. Unions have consistently sought and obtained contractual protection against discharge without just cause, which has limited the arbitrary exercise of power by employers and their supervisors. In addition, unions frequently negotiate contractual rewards for longevity, usually in the form of seniority that protects the most senior employees from layoffs and grants them a preference for various work opportunities.

A second modern model of job security and advancement evolved for many nonunion white collar employees after the Great Depression and World War II. During a period of prosperous and nearly uncontested economic growth following the war, many U.S. enterprises and their employees adopted a culture of lifetime commitment. One aspect of this model was that an employer hired young employees at an entry level and developed their skills by a series of promotions according to an established career ladder. Another aspect of this model was that the employer reserved higher managerial positions for internal candidates in the appropriate career ladder. The reciprocal commitments of the parties could be expressed as a quid pro quo: The employer provided training, experience, and opportunity, and the employees provided loyal and devoted service. This implicit bargain offered advantages to both sides. Employees gained job security and the possibility of fulfilling their ambitions. Employers gained a secure, stable, and loyal workforce. But the bargain also exposed the parties to some risks. Employers, having committed to long-term employment and limited pools of future management candidates, became increasingly focused on better, more predictive means of selecting promising entry-level employees. Employees, having committed to a career with a single employer, faced a risk that opportunities for advancement would be less than expected or that an employer would be unable or unwilling to abide by its loosely stated promise of job security.

By the end of the twentieth century, the white collar and blue collar models of lifetime employment had been shaken by the consolidation of major industries, outright failure of major corporations, deregulation of industries such as transportation and utilities, decline in collective bargaining, global competition, and transition to an economy and culture according less value to stability and security. *See* Stephen Befort, *Revisiting the Black Hole of Workplace Regulation: A Historical and Comparative Perspective of Contingent Work*, 24 Berkley J. Emp. & Lab. L. 153, 155-156 (2003); Katherine V.W. Stone, *The New Psychological Contract: Implications of the Changing Workplace for Labor and Employment Law*, 48 UCLA L. Rev. 519, 529-538 (2001). Since the Bureau of Labor Statistics began measuring job tenure in 1983, median tenure for U.S. workers has been 3.4-4.4 years; it was 4.2 in 2016. Bureau of Labor Statistics, Employee Tenure in 2016 (Sept. 22, 2016), at http://www.bls.gov/news.release/pdf/tenure.nr0.pdf. Unsurprisingly, tenure tends to increase with age. Half of all employees over age 55 have been with their current employer for at least 10 years. The median tenure for public sector employees is about double that of the private sector, though part of this difference is due to the relatively older age of public employees. Managerial and professional employees have the longest median tenure by occupation; employees in the service sector, which includes a large, unstable food service workforce, have the lowest median tenure.

B. ALTERNATIVE LEGAL SYSTEMS FOR REGULATING EMPLOYMENT RELATIONS

1. *Individual Contract*

From the beginning of European settlement in America, working relationships (with the exception of master-slave relationships and convict labor) initiated by contract. One common type of employment contract in the colonial era was the contract for indentured service, which established the terms of employment and financed the transatlantic passage of many European immigrants to America:

> British law required that all British subjects emigrating as servants should, before sailing, execute indentures stipulating the number of years of service entered into, and whether the labor to be performed was a definite trade or any kind of work required by the other party to the contract. The master, in consideration of his right to the servant's labor, agreed to provide food, clothing, and lodging for the stated period of time, and generally to allow additional compensation in the nature of provisions, clothing, and equipment upon the expiration of the term. This allowance came to be

> known as "freedom dues" and sometimes, particularly in the beginning, included land. These indentures were similar in form; in fact a printed form came into use as the system developed.

U.S. Dep't of Labor, History of Wages in the United States from Colonial Times to 1928, p. 27 (1934). Like a slave, the indentured servant was subject to resale from one master to another without the servant's consent for the duration of the term. At the expiration of the term, however, the servant was liberated and could seek other work as a free laborer at prevailing wages. Wages and maintenance (e.g., shelter and food) were usually subject to negotiation despite frequent but generally unsuccessful efforts of early lawmakers to restrict the wage demands of free laborers during periods of labor shortage. *Id.* at 7-11.

Today, contract remains the primary basis for determining the terms and conditions of employment, and as work has become more complex so too has the potential complexity of employment contracts. For example, in order to spur employee productivity and loyalty, employers have often adopted incentive and deferred compensation plans that make pay much less straightforward than it was in the days of simple cash wages and in-kind maintenance. Compensation also now includes a wide range of fringe benefits, including pensions, medical insurance, vacation pay, and sick leave.

Employers and employees can also agree to express contract terms about job security, but in the absence of any express agreement they are subject to a default rule: employment at will, which means that either party may terminate the employment at any time with or without good cause. The implicit bargain of lifetime employment described earlier might override the presumption of "at-will" employment in some states, but not in others. In any event, it appears that the great majority of workers whose job security is subject to individual negotiation are employed at will and are subject to discharge even for arbitrary or unfair reasons. There are some important exceptions to an employer's freedom to discharge employees at will. An employer must not discriminate or retaliate for reasons that are prohibited by federal and state antidiscrimination laws, and in most states the courts have recognized additional tort and public policy-based restrictions on an employer's right to discharge. For example, in most states an employer cannot lawfully discharge an employee for disobeying an order to commit a criminal act. These very specific restrictions, however, leave employers with a wide range of discretion in continuing or terminating an "at-will" employment relationship.

The lack of job protection in individual contracts of employment may be the result of several shortcomings in the process of individual negotiation. First, most employees simply lack the skill and sophistication necessary to secure the kinds of contract terms that would better protect their interests and reduce their risks. Employees also lack information about the nature and magnitude of many of the risks their prospective employment might involve. In the case of job security, for example, it is difficult for an individual employee to calculate the risk of discharge or an appropriate wage concession to accept in return for job security. Other risks present even more daunting challenges for the individual employee in bargaining. In comparison with the employer, an individual job applicant has very poor access to information about industrial illnesses and injuries associated with the work.

Again, even if the applicant is aware of the risks, he probably possesses little information useful for determining the magnitude of the risk.

Second, the bureaucratization and standardization of modern personnel practices present other obstacles to individual negotiation of employment terms. Some important aspects of compensation are not open for negotiation because they are offered in a "plan" that must, as a practical matter, be uniform for all employees. As in consumer-merchant or consumer-lender settings, employers unavoidably must present some terms on a take-it-or-leave-it basis, but employer can also use standardization to their advantage to weaken employees' bargaining position and to include various terms that may be oppressive to employees.

Third, individual bargaining often fails to achieve employee goals for "public goods," which are conditions, services, or facilities that, if obtained at all, will be shared by all. An individual employee might wish to bargain for a cleaner, healthier work environment. The employer might be willing to grant that request, but only if the employee allows some compensatory reduction in wages. Employees who agree will earn less than co-workers, but the co-workers will enjoy the cleaner, healthier workplace without having paid for it.

Finally, an individual employee might have long-term objectives difficult to secure in an individual contract. For example, an employee might want the employer's promise that he or she will be allowed a certain amount of maternity leave, will have equal opportunity for promotion, or will be accommodated in the event of future physical limitations caused by age, illness, or injury. Promises such as these are difficult to negotiate, draft, and implement for the long term. If employment is "at will" or for a series of limited but renewable terms, an employer's promises might be illusory, because it can terminate the employment at any time. Even if the employer intends to abide by such promises, drafting and implementing some long-term promises might require standardization of terms and administration that cannot be achieved by individual bargaining.

2. *Collective Bargaining*

Collective bargaining offers an alternative and a solution to some of the problems of individual bargaining. Unions can provide more experienced and informed negotiation and drafting, and they can increase the bargaining power enjoyed by employees. Unions can also solve part of the "public goods" problem because, through unions, employees can collectively seek and pay for goods they collectively desire. Collective bargaining has also produced a highly developed tradition and system for the administration of uniform terms of employment, including grievance and arbitration procedures that reduce the cost of resolving the many disputes that can arise during the course of a complex employment contract.

Collective bargaining requires a fairly elaborate legal code to protect employees from employer retaliation, to validate the selection of employee representatives, to require the employer to participate in the process of collective bargaining, to set limits on the ways employers and unions exert pressure against each other in support of their respective demands, and to assure the legitimacy and enforceability of collective bargaining agreements. Indeed, collective bargaining is such a complex area of the law that a complete treatment of this field is best reserved to a course devoted to collective bargaining. Nevertheless, the survey of employee law presented by this book frequently touches on the subject of collective bargaining and the ways it affects other aspects of employment law. Therefore, a brief overview of collective bargaining law is essential.

The most important law regulating the process of collective bargaining is the National Labor Relations Act, 29 U.S.C. §§ 151 et seq. Among its key features are a system for determining the validity of a union's claim to represent a group of employees, and a system for choosing between unions if there is more than one candidate. Employees decide whether to accept union representation by majority vote, typically in a secret ballot conducted by the National Labor Relations Board. If a union wins that election, the NLRB will certify the union, and the act requires the employer to bargain with the union in "good faith." The act prohibits employers from discriminating against or otherwise "interfering" with employees who support unions, try to organize unions, or engage in reasonable activity in support of collective bargaining. An employer may not "discharge" employees engaged in legitimate strike activity to support collective bargaining, but may permanently "replace" such employees, and replaced strikers might not be able to return to their jobs until new openings arise in the future.

Tradition and NLRB rules steer an employer and union toward a contract with a three-year term. A contract ordinarily prohibits employees from striking during the term of the contract. However, employees can seek remedies for alleged employer breaches of the contract by presenting their grievances for informal resolution by union and management representatives, and ultimately by arbitration.

The NLRB enforces the law by "unfair labor practice" proceedings. If an employee believes an employer has discriminated because of his or her support for a union, the employee can file a charge with the NLRB, and the regional office will investigate the charge. If the NLRB determines that the charge has merit, it will issue a complaint against the employer, which will be tried before an administrative law judge. If the ALJ finds that the employer has committed an unfair labor practice, and if the NLRB and subsequent judicial review upholds that finding, the ALJ can award back pay and reinstate the employee or restore him to the position he would have held but for the employer's discrimination.

Collective bargaining in the public sector is subject to different laws — federal laws for federal employees, and state laws for state and local government employees. The collective bargaining process can be quite different in the public sector, because the law often prohibits public employees from striking. Instead, unionized public sector employees often can invoke "interest arbitration" in which a neutral third party resolves differences in the parties' bargaining positions.

3. *Statutory Protection of Employees*

Statutory regulation of employment has a long history, beginning with the unsuccessful efforts of colonial authorities to fix wages during the chronic labor shortages of that era. Today, employment statutes are more often an effort to protect employees and maintain minimum standards of employment.

Legislative protection of employees has come in three waves, beginning with early efforts to deal with occupational injury and illness at the beginning of the twentieth century. A primary example of this first wave of legislation was the development of workers' compensation law, mainly at the state level, creating systems for employer-financed insurance against work-related injury and disease. Workers' compensation laws were not the only type of employment legislation in the first wave, but most other efforts to regulate employment were curtailed by courts during the "*Lochner* era" of constitutional law. In Lochner v. New York, 198 U.S. 45 (1905), the U.S. Supreme Court held that a state law limiting bakers' hours of work per day and week violated the Fourteenth Amendment. "The right to purchase or to sell labor," the Court declared, "is part of the liberty protected by this amendment, unless there are circumstances which exclude the right." *Id.* at 53.

The *Lochner* era ended in the latter years of the Great Depression when the Court finally approved vital pieces of the Roosevelt Administration's "New Deal" package of legislation. These laws included the second wave of statutory regulation of employment. The National Labor Relations Act (or the Wagner Act) was the most revolutionary of the employment laws in this wave, because it validated and promoted collective bargaining against strong employer opposition. The NLRA also substantially raised the threshold for determining what might constitute a permissible level of government interference in private employment relations. For example, the NLRA established a precedent for laws prohibiting job discrimination, in this case discrimination against union activists. The second wave of employment legislation also included the Fair Labor Standards Act, which established a minimum compensation for employees and required additional "overtime" compensation for hours in excess of 40 in any workweek.

The third wave of employment legislation began in 1964 with Title VII of the Civil Rights Act. Borrowing from the antidiscrimination example of the NLRA, Title VII prohibited job discrimination based on a number of other protected traits, including race, color, national origin, sex, and religion. Like the NLRA, Title VII established an independent administrative agency, the Equal Employment Opportunity Commission, to provide an administrative procedure for resolving disputes. Title VII marked the beginning of the largest wave of employment legislation, which included laws against discrimination, such as the Age Discrimination in Employment Law and the Americans with Disabilities Law; occupational safety laws such as the Occupational Safety and Health Act; benefits laws such as the Employee Retirement Income and Security Act; laws securing the right to unpaid leave (and in some states, paid leave) for personal illness or to care for dependents; and a long list of statutes protecting employees who engage in "whistleblowing" or other actions in the public interest.

Employment discrimination law is particularly complex. Like collective bargaining law, a complete treatment of the area requires a separate course. Nevertheless, employment discrimination touches nearly every other aspect of employment law and establishes important precedents for other laws, such as proof of unlawful employer intent. Therefore, this book includes a brief overview of employment discrimination mainly in Chapter 3, Selection of Employees, and returns to this subject periodically to explore the relationship between employment discrimination and other employment laws.

4. *The Law of the Public Workplace*

In nearly any issue under employment law, an initial point of departure might be whether the employer in question is a public sector employer or a private sector employer. The distinction is important because public sector employers, as governmental entities, are subject to the limits of the U.S. and state constitutions, but private sector employers generally are not subject to these limits. When a public sector employer makes a decision affecting an employee, it must not violate the employee's constitutional rights.

Among the constitutional rights that public employees frequently assert are the First Amendment, which prohibits the government from interfering with an individual's right of free speech and religion even when the individual is a government employee. Another constitutional right affecting public employment relations is the Fourteenth Amendment right to due process when the government seeks to deprive an employee of a property interest (such as a contractual right to job security) or a liberty interest (such as an employee's right not to be falsely stigmatized in his career). Finally, an employee might assert the Fourteenth Amendment right to equal protection. The Equal Protection Clause prohibits many unjustifiable forms of discrimination by the government, such as when the government discriminates arbitrarily as an employer in selecting employees.

Public sector employees also frequently enjoy protection under statutes that apply only to public employment, not private employment. For example, many public employees enjoy job security under civil service laws that provide for administrative review and possibly judicial review of adverse employment actions. The terms and conditions of employment of public employees may be set by statute, rather than contract. On the other hand, some of the most important employment laws, such as ERISA, do not apply to public employees.

C. COMPLICATIONS CREATED BY EMPLOYMENT FOR AN INDEFINITE DURATION

Most employment is for an indefinite duration. This is especially true of employment at will, which is the default rule in employment and which leaves either party free to discontinue the relationship at any time. It is also true to some extent in employment for renewable fixed terms, because either party remains free not to renew the employment even if the other party wishes to continue it. The indefinite duration of employment is a necessary result of the difficulty of planning for the long term and of the parties' reluctance to bind themselves to a relationship given changing circumstances, opportunities, and personal goals. However, a wholly nonbinding relationship makes it difficult to form commitments about any aspect of the relationship. It also has important implications for the parties' abilities to protect their respective long-term interests in the employment, and for the effectiveness of law in protecting employee rights.

IN RE HALLIBURTON CO.

80 S.W.3d 566 (Tex. 2002)

Chief Justice PHILLIPS delivered the opinion of the court.

We are once again asked to decide whether mandamus should issue to enforce an arbitration provision, in this instance between an employer and an at-will employee. . . . James D. Myers has been an at-will employee of Brown & Root Energy Services, now a subsidiary of Halliburton Company, for approximately thirty years. In November 1997, Halliburton sent notice to all employees of Halliburton companies that it was adopting a Dispute Resolution Program. As part of that program, binding arbitration was designated as the exclusive method for resolving all disputes between the company and its employees. The notice informed employees that by continuing to work after January 1, 1998, they would be accepting the new program.

Myers does not dispute that he received this notice, but he claims that he did not fully understand it. Nevertheless, he continued working for Halliburton after January 1, 1998. Sometime in 1998, Halliburton demoted him from his position as a General Welding Foreman. Although he was told this demotion was due to "a lack of interpersonal skills," Myers alleges that the real reason was discrimination based on his race and age. In October 1999, Myers brought this suit in district court alleging wrongful demotion in violation of the Texas Commission on Human Rights Act, Tex. Lab. Code § 21.001. Halliburton asked the trial court to compel arbitration under the Program and to either stay or dismiss the lawsuit. The trial court denied the motion, and the court of appeals denied Halliburton's petition for writ of mandamus.

. . . In Hathaway v. General Mills, Inc., 711 S.W.2d 227 (Tex. 1986), we outlined the manner in which an employer may change the terms of an at-will employment contract. We held that the party asserting a change to an at-will employment contract must prove two things: (1) notice of the change, and (2) acceptance of the change. *Id.* at 229. We stated that "to prove notice, an employer asserting a modification must prove that he unequivocally notified the employee of definite changes in employment terms." *Id.* Yet we made clear that when an employer notifies an employee of changes to the at-will employment contract and the employee "continues working with knowledge of the changes, he has accepted the changes as a matter of law." *Id.*

Here, it is undisputed that Halliburton notified Myers of the proposed changes. The notice explained the Program, stated its effective date, and explained that by working after that date an employee would indicate that he or she accepted the provision. Myers argues that he only briefly looked at the documents and that he did not understand them. The materials, however, unequivocally notified him that his employment terms would be changing . . . :

> While both you and Halliburton retain all substantive legal rights and remedies under this Program, you and Halliburton are both waiving all rights which either may have with regard to trial by jury for employment related matters in state or federal court.

The accompanying materials set forth that adopting the new Program meant that

> if you accept or continue your employment after January 1, 1998, you will agree to resolve all legal claims against Halliburton through this process instead of through the court system.

After receiving this notice, Myers continued to work for Halliburton after January 1, 1998, thus accepting the changes as a matter of law.

This is not a case in which the written notice was contradicted by other written or oral communications between the employer and the employee. *See Hathaway*, 711 S.W.2d at 229. On this record we conclude that Halliburton's offer was unequivocal and that Myers' conduct was an acceptance of that offer.

The court of appeals held that Halliburton's promises were illusory, and therefore could not constitute consideration for Myers' promise to arbitrate. . . . The court relied on Light v. Centel Cellular Co., 883 S.W.2d 642 (Tex. 1994), for the proposition that because an at-will employer and employee may not contract to limit the ability of either to terminate the employment at-will, a promise by either which is dependent on a period of continued employment is illusory and thus insufficient to support a bilateral contract because it would fail to bind the promisor who always retains the option of discontinuing employment . . . .

This is a correct statement of the law, but it does not apply . . . . In *Light*, we considered the validity of a covenant not to compete between an at-will employee and her employer. . . . We held that certain promises made by the employer in the covenant were illusory because they were dependent on the at-will employee's continued employment. *Id.* at 645-46. The employer could avoid performance simply by terminating the employment relationship, while the employee was bound whether she stayed or left. *Id.* at 645. By contrast, the Program is not dependent on continuing employment. Instead, it was accepted by the employee's continuing employment. When Myers reported for work after January 1, 1998, he accepted Halliburton's offer; both Myers and Halliburton became bound to arbitrate any disputes between them. Even if Myers' employment had ended shortly thereafter, the promise to arbitrate would have been binding and enforceable on both parties. In *Light*, the employer was bound only while the employee continued to work. Thus, following Myers' acceptance, the Program was not dependent on continuing employment and was not illusory. . . .

Myers also asserts that Halliburton's promises were illusory because the company retained the right to modify or discontinue the Program. But the Program also provided that "no amendment shall apply to a Dispute of which the Sponsor [Halliburton] had actual notice on the date of amendment." As to termination, the plan stated that "termination shall not be effective until 10 days after reasonable notice of termination is given to Employees or as to Disputes which arose prior to the date of termination." Therefore, Halliburton cannot avoid its promise to arbitrate by amending the provision or terminating it altogether. Accordingly, the provision is not illusory.

. . . Finally, Myers argues that this provision should not be enforced because it is unconscionable. Unconscionability includes two aspects: (1) procedural unconscionability, which refers to the circumstances surrounding the adoption of the arbitration provision, and (2) substantive unconscionability, which refers to the fairness of the arbitration provision itself. *See* Southwestern Bell Tel. Co. v.

DeLanney, 809 S.W.2d 493, 498-99 (Tex. 1991) (Gonzalez, J., concurring). . . . [C]ourts may consider both procedural and substantive unconscionability of an arbitration clause in evaluating the validity of an arbitration provision.

Myers first asserts that the provision is procedurally unconscionable as there was gross disparity in bargaining power between the parties because Myers had no opportunity to negotiate; Halliburton told him to accept the Program or leave. But in *Hathaway*, we recognized that an employer may make precisely such a "take it or leave it" offer to its at-will employees. *Hathaway*, 711 S.W.2d at 228-29. Because an employer has a general right under Texas law to discharge an at-will employee, it cannot be unconscionable, without more, merely to premise continued employment on acceptance of new or additional employment terms. *See also* Smith v. H.E. Butt Grocery Co., 18 S.W.3d 910, 912 (Tex. App. — Beaumont 2000, pet. denied) (rejecting the argument that an arbitration provision is unconscionable merely because the parties did not negotiate its terms).

Myers also argues that the arbitration plan is so unfair to employees that the Program is substantively unconscionable. But Myers has failed to make such a showing here. The Program has several terms that provide protection to the employee in the process. For example, the company agreed to pay all the expenses of an arbitration except a $50 filing fee. Both parties are to participate in the selection of the neutral arbitrator. The Program provides up to $2,500 for an employee to consult with an attorney. The rules provide for prearbitration discovery under the Federal Rules of Civil Procedure. All remedies the employee could have pursued in the court system are available in the arbitration. And the arbitrator may award reasonable attorneys fees to an employee who receives a favorable award regardless of whether such an award would be available in court. . . . Myers has failed to carry his burden to show that the Program is unconscionable.

. . . Myers clearly had notice of the proposed changes to his at-will employment contract and accepted them by continuing to work after January 1, 1998. We also conclude that Myers has failed to show that the arbitration provision is unconscionable. Because the arbitration provision is otherwise enforceable under general contract principles, a valid arbitration provision exists between Myers and Halliburton, and the trial court should have granted Halliburton's motion to compel arbitration. Mandamus relief is appropriate because Halliburton has no adequate remedy by appeal. . . .

NOTES AND QUESTIONS

1. The Halliburton arbitration program was much more generous to employees than many other employer-mandated arbitration programs. For example, it provided an attorney consultation benefit of up to $2,500, and Halliburton bore all arbitration expenses except a $50 filing fee the employee paid. Why might Mr. Myers have resisted submitting his claim to arbitration?

2. Arbitration of contractual employment disputes is a long-established collective bargaining practice. Nearly all contracts between unions and employers provide for resolution of contractual disputes through grievance and arbitration proceedings. The Halliburton program was different in two ways: (1) it was an arbitration program for individual employees, who accepted it as part of their

individual employment contracts; and (2) it applied to claims involving statutory as well as contract rights. Are these differences a cause of concern? Arbitration of individual employment disputes is addressed further in Chapter 10.

3. Could Mr. Myers have avoided "accepting" the arbitration program or negotiated specialized arbitration terms for himself? If he "rejected" the program, how would he have conveyed his rejection? Is it relevant to procedural unconscionability that Mr. Myers was employed with the company for 30 years?

4. If Mr. Myers had stated his rejection of the arbitration program, it appears that Halliburton could have discharged him from employment without violating any of Mr. Myers' contract rights. In general, neither an employer nor an employee is under any duty to continue indefinite employment or renew employment for a term unless the parties agreed to such a duty. This doctrine of "employment at will" is covered in detail in Chapter 8.

5. When employment is at will, *Halliburton* suggests an employer can change employment terms any day just by announcing the change, and employees "accept" by continuing to work, at least if the employer was clear that continuing to work constitutes acceptance of the new terms. But if the employer's terms require a promise by the employee (such as a promise to arbitrate, or not to compete), the employee's promise is not binding unless the employer provides "consideration." Consideration for an employee's promise might be a promise by the employer, or something else. In classic contract law, a promise for a promise results in a "bilateral" contract in which each party is bound by a promise. In contrast, a "unilateral" contract is a promise in return for performance (such as a promise of a "reward" for some action), and one party is bound by a promise and the other is not. Could an employee, having promised to submit claims to arbitration, be bound by a unilateral contract if the employer provides employment "at will" in return? *Compare* Ex parte McNaughton, 728 So. 2d 592 (Ala. 1998) (yes), *with* Gibson v. Neighborhood Health Clinics, Inc., 121 F.3d 1126 (7th Cir. 1997) (no). The problem with unilateral contract analysis in this context is that an employee at will might end up with much less employment than expected in return for the promise. The employer might fire the next day. The usual rule in contract law is that courts do not weigh adequacy of consideration. Yet in employment, courts sometimes hold an employee not bound by a unilateral contract unless and until the employer has provided a reasonable amount of employment. *See, e.g.*, Cent. Adjustment Bureau, Inc. v. Ingram, 678 S.W.2d 28 (Tenn. 1984) (enforcing employee promise not to compete after employment termination).

6. On the other hand, consideration for an employee's promise to arbitrate might be the employer's promise to submit to and be bound by arbitration—a bilateral contract. The usual contract law rule is that a promise is not consideration if it is "illusory" — not really binding on the promisor (e.g., "I will pay you a bonus at the end of the year if I want"). Did Halliburton's promise pass this test? *Compare* J. M. Davidson, Inc. v. Webster, 128 S.W.3d 223 (Tex. 2003) (employer reservation of right to modify arbitration policy might have rendered illusory its promise to submit to and be bound by arbitration, if reservation was unqualified and operated retroactively as well as prospectively as to any dispute).

7. In at least one type of employment arrangement, it is not so easy for an employer to change employment terms. If Mr. Myers and Halliburton had agreed

to a renewable fixed term, the contract would have fixed the essential employment conditions for the term. Halliburton, though, might have insisted on agreement to arbitration as a condition for renewing the employment for another term.

8. The fact that the duration of employment is completely or partially at will is important to nearly every other aspect of employment law.

9. First, the indefinite duration of employment tends to distinguish employees from other providers of personal services, such as independent contractors. An independent contractor typically agrees to perform a particular task, and that task will mark the beginning and end of the relationship unless the parties agree to a new task. In contrast, employees typically expect employment to continue for the indefinite future, whether the initial agreement is for a renewable term or an indefinite term. Moreover, while an employee's job may be described to some degree by his title, his engagement with the employer is not for a specific task and there is no specific task that marks the beginning and end of the contract. Instead, the engagement is open-ended and might include many tasks that can change from day to day, at least within the vague limits of the employee's title or job description. The problems and consequences of determining employee versus independent contractor status are a major topic in Chapter 2 of this book.

10. Second, although an employer and employee might expect their relationship to continue for many years, it may be impossible for them to make binding promises about many of their long-term expectations and aspirations. Is there any guarantee, for example, that Halliburton will not change the arbitration program in the future and make it even less attractive to Mr. Myers?

11. Third, the right to terminate "at will" can contribute to a significant imbalance in bargaining power, which passage of time may accentuate. As *Halliburton* illustrates, a long-term employee like Mr. Myers may have little practical choice but to agree to any new terms the employer wishes to impose.

12. Finally, an employer's power to discharge or discontinue employment without cause affects a wide range of personal and public interests if it results in the employee's loss of employment for reasons that are arbitrary, discriminatory, or predatory. Moreover, an employer's right to discharge can undermine personal and public interests even before the employer exercises its right. In *Halliburton*, for example, the employer used an implicit threat to terminate employees to demand their acceptance of an arbitration program that affected the enforcement of laws against unlawful discrimination. If an employer's exercise of its greater bargaining power is unrestricted, it might force employees to accept oppressive working conditions or relinquish important statutory rights.

13. An employer might use its right to threaten discharge to require an employee to violate the law or cooperate in a conspiracy to do so. To the extent that effective regulation of business practices depends on employee willingness to report wrongdoing or cooperate with regulators, an employer's ability to retaliate against employees is a major complication for law enforcement. Moreover, regulations targeting the employment relation itself, such as minimum wage laws, workplace safety standards, or workers' compensation laws, are effective only if employees can assert their rights without fear of reprisal.

CHAPTER 2

Who Is an Employee and Who Is the Employer?

A. THE EMPLOYEE/INDEPENDENT CONTRACTOR PROBLEM

Employee status is a basis for coverage of many civil rights, labor relations, and tax laws. For example, the National Labor Relations Act, 29 U.S.C. §§ 157 – 169, protects the right of "employees" to engage in collective bargaining; federal antidiscrimination laws prohibit discrimination in "employment," *e.g.*, 42 U.S.C. § 2000e-2, and the Internal Revenue Code requires withholding of income taxes on wages paid to "employees." 26 U.S.C. § 3403. However, not all individuals who perform services for others are employees. Millions perform work as nonemployees. Individual "independent contractors" form the largest and most important group of nonemployee workers.

The importance of distinguishing employees from independent contractors is illustrated by Vizcaino v. Microsoft, 120 F.3d 1006 (9th Cir. 1997), which describes the complications Microsoft faced after misclassifying many of its workers as independent contractors. Thinking the workers were not employees, Microsoft had failed for years to withhold taxes from the workers' wages, to pay the employer share of FICA taxes, or to allow the workers to participate in employee benefit plans. The Internal Revenue Service eventually determined that the workers were in fact employees, requiring Microsoft to make substantial payments of back taxes. *Vizcaino* was a class action on behalf of hundreds of misclassified workers for the recovery of benefits the workers claimed Microsoft owed based on their "employee" status.

The consequences of misclassification can be severe, but statutes that apply to employees seldom provide useful guidance for determining who is an employee and who is not. Consider for example the Fair Labor Standards Act, which defines "employee" as "any individual *employed* by an *employer*," and defines "employer" as a person "acting . . . in the interest of an *employer* in relation to an *employee*." 29 U.S.C. § 203(d) (emphasis added). Congress and state legislatures have adopted the same circular definition in numerous other federal and state laws regulating employment relations and protecting employees. Thus, the job of developing a useful definition has fallen largely to the courts.

The courts have struggled to distinguish employees or "servants" from other workers, particularly independent contractors, since at least the early nineteenth century, long before modern employment or tax statutes. A reliable test of status has remained elusive because there is no characteristic common to all employees that makes them different from all independent contractors. Moreover, the nature and organization of work do not stand still. Parties tend to re-invent their relationships in myriad, ever-changing ways that belie the courts' latest generalizations about categories of workers.

Judge Richard Posner has described the difference between "employees" and "independent contractors" as follows:

> Contrast two methods of organizing production. In the first, the entrepreneur contracts with one person to supply component parts, with another to assemble them, and with a third to sell the finished product. In the second, he hires them to perform these tasks as his employees under his direction. The first method of organizing production is the traditional domain of contract law, the second of master-servant law. The essence of the first method is that the entrepreneur negotiates with each of the three producers an agreement specifying the price, quantity, quality, delivery date, credit terms, and guarantees of the contractor's performance. The essence of the second method is that the entrepreneur pays the producers a wage — a price not for a specific performance but for the right to direct their performance.

Richard Posner, Economic Analysis of Law, 391 (1992). *See also* R. Carlson, *Employees, Independent Contractors, and the Theory of the Firm*, ___ ARK L. REV. ___ (2018) (forthcoming).

Why choose one method rather than the other? First, consider the difficulty of negotiating a contract with an independent firm versus employing one's own employees. Contracting with independent contractors or other independent firms requires careful negotiation of and commitment to many details in advance. Modifying the relationship in the face of changed circumstances or goals might not be easy. In contrast, hiring employees to perform the same work avoids the costs and restrictions of advance negotiation because the employer reserves the right to direct performance and decide or change the details as the work progresses.

Second, there are cost considerations in choosing to engage an independent firm or contractor versus employing one's own employees. If an employer's need for specialized work is episodic rather than continuous, then the occasional engagement of an independent contractor may be more efficient than employing a "permanent" workforce. If the work requires an investment in expensive equipment and supplies, then an independent contractor may operate more efficiently by spreading the cost of this investment among many different clients and assignments. Hiring employees may be more efficient if the employer has a continuous need for their work, but only if the employer can also effectively *manage* their work. Effective management can be crucial to whether the employer saves costs by hiring of employees because employees earning "wages" or "salaries" may have little incentive to control the costs of their work or to boost their output without the employer's substantial supervision and oversight — perhaps much more than the employer wants or is able to exercise. Contracting out, on the other hand, permits an employer to solicit bids from competing firms, and competition will force these firms to keep labor costs low. Posner, *supra*, at 391-92. An independent contractor may also do a superior job self-managing its own specialized work.

The outcome of an employer's decision and the status of workers performing the work will be clear if the work is performed by an independent firm having its own substantial investments in equipment and independent management. But a "contractor" might not be a "firm." The contractor might be an *individual*, and the terms or manner of his engagement might make his status ambiguous. Knowing his status would be unimportant if it not for important legal consequences of "employee" status. Indeed, a vexing question has been whether an employer can legitimately claim that an *individual worker* — particularly a *lower skilled* worker — can be an independent contractor if the work requires little investment or "self-management" by the worker in comparison with the employer's management and oversight of operations of which the work is a part.

The courts' effort to develop a test of employee status initially was driven by developments in tort law. Under the doctrine of *respondeat superior*, a plaintiff could hold a "master" or employer accountable for the negligence of a "servant" or employee without evidence of any personal negligence of the employer. There were several possible rationales for imputing a worker's negligence to the person he served. One was that the employer selected the worker and had the right and responsibility to supervise and control the work to see that it was done properly. Another was that the employer was in the best position to bear the risk. A third was that the employer should not be permitted to avoid the inherent risks and liabilities of his enterprise by delegating the riskiest parts of the work to less financially responsible parties. Whatever the rationale, not all working relationships were equally appealing for the application of *respondeat superior*. An employer might not have the practical means to supervise a worker, especially if the worker had special skills beyond the employer's knowledge. Not every employer was better able to bear risks than each of his workers, especially if the work was outside the employer's usual business or was not for any business purpose at all. Sometimes a court might reasonably have viewed a worker as being in his own business or "independent occupation" even if he performed the work with his own hands.

Nineteenth-century courts identified a number of "factors" for distinguishing employees, whose negligence is appropriately imputed to an employer, from independent contractors, who are self-employed and solely responsible for their own accidents. Among these factors are the scope and duration of the employment. Employees tend to work in relationships of long or indefinite duration, and to perform a series of tasks of comparatively open-ended definition as directed by the employer. Independent contractors, on the other hand, perform discrete tasks that mark the beginning and end of each engagement. Employees are also more likely paid for their time rather than for the completion of a specific task. In contrast, self-employed independent contractors are more likely paid a fee for completing a specific task, and completion of the task will be the end of the relationship. Unfortunately, these generalizations are not reliable in every setting. Even clearly independent providers of services sometimes serve in long-term relationships of indefinite scope and duration, and some employees work for very short terms or are paid a piece rate, commission, or some other task-based rate.

A more important factor identified by nineteenth-century courts was supervisory control of the details of work. If an employer exercised actual control, or if the parties understood the employer *could* exercise control, the worker was more likely an employee and not an independent contractor. Of course, employer control is not an easily measurable or quantifiable feature, especially when either party's power to control the work emanates from sources other than the contract terms. Nevertheless, the parties' relative control served as an attractive test of status in tort cases because control was the most widely articulated rationale for imputing a worker's negligence to his employer. Thus, evidence of an employer's actual supervision or right to control the work not only justified *respondeat superior*, it became the "primary" factor distinguishing employees from independent contractors. By the late nineteenth century, the so-called common law control test was the dominant method for identifying employees.

By the end of the nineteenth century, a variety of new laws to protect employees from abusive or careless employers made the question of worker status important for purposes other than *respondeat superior*. The control test was a well-known and readily available tool to determine coverage under the new laws for "employees." However, not all judges believed a control test designed for *respondeat superior* was equally suitable for determining coverage under a statute enforcing an employee's right to payment of wages, regulating employee working conditions, or requiring compensation for an employee's work-related injuries.

Nearly a century before the *Microsoft* case, Judge Learned Hand confronted the problem of worker status in a case involving a coal mining company's scheme to treat miners as independent contractors in order to deny them benefits under an early workers' compensation law. The company had granted the miners at least a veneer of self-management and independence. But in Lehigh Valley Coal Co. v. Yensavage, 218 F. 547 (2d Cir. 1914), Judge Hand focused on the employer's exercise of economic power to dominate its relationship with the miners, and on the integration of the miners in the employer's core business. He also gave great weight to the purpose of the statute before the court:

> It is true that the statute uses the word "employed," but it must be understood with reference to the purpose of the act, and where all the conditions of the relation require protection, protection ought to be given.

Id. at 552. The statute in question was designed to protect those "at an economic disadvantage" by creating a right to protection against hazardous work. Coal miners, regardless of common law status, were the exact sort of workers for whom the law was enacted. *Id.* Thus, the miners were employees for purposes of this law.

Lehigh Valley Coal Co. is among one group of decisions that looked beyond employer supervisory control to consider the economic context of the working relationship and the purpose of the legislative scheme. Most courts continued to regard control of the work as the most important indication of employee status. However, when evidence of control was mixed or uncertain, even proponents of the common law control test permitted considering additional factors, including the parties' comparative investment in tools and equipment and the worker's opportunity for profit or loss. Including such factors tended to lessen the difference between the control test and Judge Hand's freewheeling contextual approach.

Distinctions in worker status became more important with each new act of Congress or the state legislatures regulating employment. By the mid-twentieth century, employee status had long ceased to be a mere rule of tort law for the occasional *respondeat superior* case. Employee status now determined a wide range of employer obligations and employee rights across the entire span of the relationship. The case that follows involves the Wagner Act, then the most radical and far-reaching regulation of employment relations in U.S. history. Among other things, the Wagner Act created the National Labor Relations Board and authorized the board to certify unions to represent employees in designated units for collective bargaining. The act also required employers to recognize certified unions as the representatives of their employees, and to bargain with such unions in good faith. But the act created these rights and obligations only with respect to "employees."

NATIONAL LABOR RELATIONS BOARD v. HEARST PUBLICATIONS, INC.

322 U.S. 111 (1944)

Mr. Justice RUTLEDGE delivered the opinion of the Court.

These cases arise from the refusal of respondents, publishers of four Los Angeles daily newspapers, to bargain collectively with a union representing newsboys who distribute their papers on the streets of that city. Respondents' contention that they were not required to bargain because the newsboys are not their "employees" within the meaning of that term in the National Labor Relations Act, 29 U.S.C.A. § 152,[1] presents the important question which we granted certiorari to resolve.

[The National Labor Relations Board found that the newsboys were "employees." After an election to determine the newsboys' preferences, the board found that Los Angeles Newsboys Local Industrial Union No. 75 was the newsboys' collective bargaining representative. The respondents refused to recognize the union, and the board issued a further order requiring them to bargain with the union.] The Circuit Court of Appeals, one judge dissenting, set aside the Board's orders. Rejecting the Board's analysis, the court independently examined whether the newsboys are employees within the act, decided that the statute imports common-law standards, and held the newsboys are not employees. . . .

The newsboys work under varying terms and conditions. . . . The units which the Board determined to be appropriate are composed of those who sell fulltime at established spots. Those vendors, misnamed boys, are generally mature men, dependent upon the proceeds of their sales for their sustenance, and frequently supporters of families. Working thus as news vendors on a regular basis often for a number of years, they form a stable group with relatively little turnover, in contrast to schoolboys and others who sell as bootjackers, temporary and casual distributors.

Over-all circulation and distribution of the papers are under the general supervision of circulation managers. But for purposes of street distribution each paper has divided metropolitan Los Angeles into geographic districts. Each district is under the direct and close supervision of a district manager. His function in the mechanics of distribution is to supply the newsboys in his district with papers . . . and to turn over to the publisher the receipts which he collects from their sales. . . .

The newsboys' compensation consists in the difference between the prices at which they sell the papers and the prices they pay for them. The former are fixed by the publishers and the latter are fixed either by the publishers or, in the case of

[1] Section 2(3) of the act provides that "The term 'employee' shall include any employee, and shall not be limited to the employees of a particular employer, unless the act explicitly states otherwise. . . ."

the News, by the district manager. In practice the newsboys receive their papers on credit. They pay for those sold either sometime during or after the close of their selling day, returning for credit all unsold papers. Lost or otherwise unreturned papers, however, must be paid for as though sold. Not only is the "profit" per paper thus effectively fixed by the publisher, but substantial control of the newsboys' total "take home" can be effected through the ability to designate their sales areas and the power to determine the number of papers allocated to each. While as a practical matter this power is not exercised fully, the newsboys' "right" to decide how many papers they will take is also not absolute. In practice, the Board found, they cannot determine the size of their established order without the cooperation of the district manager. And often the number of papers they must take is determined unilaterally by the district managers.

In addition to effectively fixing the compensation, respondents in a variety of ways prescribe, if not the minutiae of daily activities, at least the broad terms and conditions of work. This is accomplished largely through the supervisory efforts of the district managers, who serve as the nexus between the publishers and the newsboys. The district managers assign "spots" or corners to which the newsboys are expected to confine their selling activities. Transfers from one "spot" to another may be ordered by the district manager for reasons of discipline or efficiency or other cause. Transportation to the spots from the newspaper building is offered by each of respondents. Hours of work on the spots are determined not simply by the impersonal pressures of the market, but to a real extent by explicit instructions from the district managers. Adherence to the prescribed hours is observed closely by the district managers or other supervisory agents of the publishers. Sanctions, varying in severity from reprimand to dismissal, are visited on the tardy and the delinquent. By similar supervisory controls minimum standards of diligence and good conduct while at work are sought to be enforced. However wide may be the latitude for individual initiative beyond those standards, district managers' instructions in what the publishers apparently regard as helpful sales technique are expected to be followed. Such varied items as the manner of displaying the paper, of emphasizing current features and headlines, and of placing advertising placards, or the advantages of soliciting customers at specific stores or in the traffic lanes are among the subjects of this instruction. Moreover, newsboys are furnished with sales equipment, such as racks, boxes and change aprons, and advertising placards by the publishers. In this pattern of employment the Board found that the newsboys are an integral part of the publishers' distribution system and circulation organization. And the record discloses that the newsboys and checkmen feel they are employees of the papers and respondents' supervisory employees, if not respondents themselves, regard them as such.

In addition to questioning the sufficiency of the evidence to sustain these findings, respondents point to a number of other attributes characterizing their relationship with the newsboys. . . .[17]

---

[17] E.g., that there is either no evidence in the record to show, or the record explicitly negatives, that respondents carry the newsboys on their payrolls, pay "salaries" to them, keep records of their sales or locations, or register them as "employees" with the Social Security Board, or that the newsboys are covered by workmen's compensation insurance of the California Compensation Act. Furthermore, it is urged the record shows that the newsboys all sell

I.

The principal question is whether the newsboys are "employees." Because Congress did not explicitly define the term, respondents say its meaning must be determined by reference to common-law standards. In their view "common-law standards" are those the courts have applied in distinguishing between "employees" and "independent contractors" when working out various problems unrelated to the Wagner Act's purposes and provisions.

The argument assumes that there is some simple, uniform and easily applicable test which the courts have used, in dealing with such problems, to determine whether persons doing work for others fall in one class or the other. Unfortunately this is not true. Only by a long and tortuous history was the simple formulation worked out which has been stated most frequently as "the test" for deciding whether one who hires another is responsible in tort for his wrongdoing. But this formula has been by no means exclusively controlling in the solution of other problems. And its simplicity has been illusory because it is more largely simplicity of formulation than of application. Few problems in the law have given greater variety of application and conflict in results than the cases arising in the borderland between what is clearly an employer-employee relationship and what is clearly one of independent entrepreneurial dealing. This is true within the limited field of determining vicarious liability in tort. It becomes more so when the field is expanded to include all of the possible applications of the distinction. . . . With reference to an identical problem, results may be contrary over a very considerable region of doubt in applying the distinction, depending upon the state or jurisdiction where the determination is made; and that within a single jurisdiction a person who, for instance, is held to be an "independent contractor" for the purpose of imposing vicarious liability in tort may be an "employee" for the purposes of particular legislation, such as unemployment compensation. *See, e.g.*, Globe Grain & Milling Co. v. Industrial Commn., 91 P.2d 512. In short, the assumed simplicity and uniformity, resulting from application of "common-law standards" does not exist.

II.

Whether, given the intended national uniformity, the term "employee" includes such workers as these newsboys must be answered primarily from the history, terms and purposes of the legislation. The word "is not treated by Congress as a word of art having a definite meaning. . . ." Rather "it takes color from its surroundings . . . (in) the statute where it appears," United States v. American Trucking Associations, Inc., 310 U.S. 534, 545, and derives meaning from the context of that statute, which "must be read in the light of the mischief to be corrected and the end to be attained." South Chicago Coal & Dock Co. v. Bassett, 309 U.S. 251, 259. Congress, on the one hand, was not thinking solely of the immediate technical relation of employer and employee. It had in mind at least

---

newspapers, periodicals and other items not furnished to them by their respective publishers, assume the risk for papers lost, stolen or destroyed, purchase and sell their "spots," hire assistants and relief men and make arrangements among themselves for the sale of competing or left-over papers.

some other persons than those standing in the proximate legal relation of employee to the particular employer involved in the labor dispute. It cannot be taken, however, that the purpose was to include all other persons who may perform service for another or was to ignore entirely legal classifications made for other purposes. Congress had in mind a wider field than the narrow technical legal relation of "master and servant," as the common law had worked this out in all its variations, and at the same time a narrower one than the entire area of rendering service to others...

It will not do, for deciding this question as one of uniform national application, to import wholesale the traditional common-law conceptions or some distilled essence of their local variations. . . . Congress was not seeking to solve the nationally harassing problems with which the statute deals by solutions only partially effective. It rather sought to find a broad solution, one that would bring industrial peace by substituting, so far as its power could reach, the rights of workers to self-organization and collective bargaining for the industrial strife which prevails where these rights are not effectively established. Yet only partial solutions would be provided if large segments of workers about whose technical legal position such local differences exist should be wholly excluded from coverage by reason of such differences. . . . The consequences would be ultimately to defeat, in part at least, the achievement of the statute's objectives. Congress no more intended to import this mass of technicality as a controlling "standard" for uniform national application than to refer decision of the question outright to the local law.

The Act, as its first section states, was designed to avert the "substantial obstructions to the free flow of commerce" which result from "strikes and other forms of industrial strife or unrest" by eliminating the causes of that unrest. It is premised on explicit findings that strikes and industrial strife themselves result in large measure from the refusal of employers to bargain collectively and the inability of individual workers to bargain successfully for improvements in their "wages, hours, or other working conditions" with employers who are "organized in the corporate or other forms of ownership association." Hence the avowed and interrelated purposes of the Act are to encourage collective bargaining and to remedy the individual worker's inequality of bargaining power by "protecting . . . full freedom of association, self-organization, and designation of representatives of their own choosing, for the purpose of negotiating the terms and conditions of their employment or other mutual aid or protection." 29 U.S.C.A. § 151.

The mischief at which the Act is aimed and the remedies it offers are not confined exclusively to "employees" within the traditional legal distinctions separating them from "independent contractors." Myriad forms of service relationship, with infinite and subtle variations in the terms of employment, blanket the nation's economy. Some are within this Act, others beyond its coverage. Large numbers will fall clearly on one side or on the other, by whatever test may be applied. But intermediate there will be many, the incidents of whose employment partake in part of the one group, in part of the other, in varying proportions of weight. And consequently the legal pendulum, for purposes of applying the statute, may swing one way or the other, depending upon the weight of this balance and its relation to the special purpose at hand.

Unless the common-law tests are to be imported and made exclusively controlling, without regard to the statute's purposes, it cannot be irrelevant that the particular workers in these cases are subject, as a matter of economic fact, to the evils the statute was designed to eradicate and that the remedies it affords are appropriate for preventing them or curing their harmful effects in the special situation. Interruption of commerce through strikes and unrest may stem as well from labor disputes between some who, for other purposes, are technically "independent contractors" and their employers as from disputes between persons who, for those purposes, are "employees" and their employers. *Cf.* Milk Wagon Drivers' Union Local No. 753 v. Lake Valley Farm Products, Inc., 311 U.S. 91. Inequality of bargaining power in controversies over wages, hours and working conditions may as well characterize the status of the one group as of the other. The former, when acting alone, may be as "helpless in dealing with an employer," as "dependent . . . on his daily wage" and as "unable to leave the employ and to resist arbitrary and unfair treatment" as the latter. For each, "union . . . (may be) essential to give . . . opportunity to deal on equality with their employer."[25] And for each, collective bargaining may be appropriate and effective for the "friendly adjustment of industrial disputes arising out of differences as to wages, hours, or other working conditions."[26] 29 U.S.C.A. § 151. In short, when the particular situation of employment combines these characteristics, so that the economic facts of the relation make it more nearly one of employment than of independent business enterprise with respect to the ends sought to be accomplished by the legislation, those characteristics may outweigh technical legal classification for purposes unrelated to the statute's objectives and bring the relation within its protections.

To eliminate the causes of labor disputes and industrial strife, Congress thought it necessary to create a balance of forces in certain types of economic relationships. . . . [The term *employee*], like other provisions, must be understood with reference to the purpose of the Act and the facts involved in the economic relationship. "Where all the conditions of the relation require protection, protection ought to be given."[33] . . .

[T]he Board concluded that the newsboys are employees. The record sustains the Board's findings and there is ample basis in the law for its conclusion. . . .

NOTES AND QUESTIONS

1. Contemporaneously with *Hearst*, the Court also considered the meaning of "employee" in the Social Security Act and the Fair Labor Standards Act. In United States v. Silk, 331 U.S. 704 (1947), the Court reiterated the importance of statutory purpose in determining a worker's status as an employee, but it also

[25] American Steel Foundries Co. v. Tri-City Central Trades Council, 257 U.S. 184, 209.

[26] The practice of self organization and collective bargaining to resolve labor disputes has for some time been common among such varied types of "independent contractors" as musicians, actors, and writers and such atypical "employees" as insurance agents, artists, architects and engineers (*see e.g.*, Proceedings of the 2d Convention of the UOPWA, C.I.O. (1938); Proceedings of the 3d Convention of the UOPWA, C.I.O. (1940); Handbook of American Trade Unions (1936); Bureau of Labor Statistics, Bull. No. 618, 291-293; Constitution and By-Laws of the IFTEAD of the A.F.L., 1942.)

[33] Lehigh Valley Coal Co. v. Yensavage, 2 Cir., 218 F. 547, 552.

emphasized that true independent contractors were necessarily beyond the reach of laws that, by their terms, applied only to employees. 331 U.S. at 714. Employer control over a worker's performance was still a key factor, the Court stated, but control was to be viewed in relation to the economic realities of the parties' relationship. Under this economic realities approach some of the workers before the Court were employees, but a group of delivery drivers were properly deemed to be independent contractors:

> These driver-owners are small businessmen. They own their own trucks. They hire their own helpers. In one instance they haul for a single business, in the other for any customer. The distinction, though important, is not controlling. It is the total situation, including the risk undertaken, the control exercised, the opportunity for profit from sound management, that marks these driver-owners as independent contractors.

331 U.S. at 718-719. On the same day, the Court also decided Rutherford Food Corp. v. McComb, 331 U.S. 722, 722 (1947), following the same approach and finding that "boners" employed by a meat processing firm were employees subject to coverage under the Fair Labor Standards Act.

2. As *Hearst*, *Silk*, and *Rutherford* suggest, an employer might control a worker's performance by virtue of the terms of a contract, or by virtue of surrounding circumstances including the employer's economic advantages over the worker. Indeed, most employees lack any written contract to specify the allocation of authority over the performance of the work, but if they reject their employer's supervision they might be discharged for insubordination.

An employer's control over the details of the work may also depend on its capacity for supervision of the worker. For example, an employer might hire a professional to perform work of such skill or expertise that the employer cannot, as a practical matter, review or guide the work. At one time, many courts took the view that professionals such as physicians could not be "employees" because their expertise and skill placed them beyond the possibility of supervision. *See, e.g.*, Virginia Iron, Coal & Coke Co. v. Odle's Admin., 105 S.E. 107, 109 (Va. 1920); Schloendorff v. Soc'y of New York Hosp., 105 N.E. 92 (N.Y. 1914). Today, however, it is widely accepted that professionals and other workers performing specialized work difficult to "supervise" might be sufficiently under employer control to qualify as "employees" under certain circumstances. *See Health Care Employees: Independent Union Certified as Agent for Emergency Doctors at Austin Hospitals*, Daily Labor Report, p. A-1 (March 21, 2000) (reporting the NLRB's certification of a bargaining unit of physician employees). *But see* AmeriHealth Inc./AmeriHealth HMO, 329 NLRB No. 76 (1999) (finding that primary care and specialty physicians were independent contractors and not employees).

3. The Court's decision in *Hearst* and *Silk* provoked an angry response in Congress. The House Report accompanying the 1947 amendments to the National Labor Relations Act stated as follows:

> An "employee," according to all standard dictionaries, according to the law as the courts have stated it, and according to the understanding of almost everyone, with the exception of members of the National Labor Relations Board, means someone who works for another for hire. But in ... *Hearst* ...,

> the Board expanded the definition of the term "employee" beyond anything that it ever had included before, and the Supreme Court, relying on the theoretic "expertness" of the Board, upheld the Board. . . . It must be presumed that when Congress passed the Labor Act, it intended words it used to have the meanings that they had when Congress passed the act, not new meanings that, 9 years later, the Labor Board might think up. . . . To correct what the Board has done, and what the Supreme Court, putting misplaced reliance upon the Board's expertness, has approved, the bill excludes "independent contractors" from the definition of "employee."

House Committee on Education and Labor, H.R. Rep. No. 245, on H.R. 3020, 80th Cong., 1st Sess. 18 (1947). The 1947 amendment altered section 2(3) of the act to provide that "the term 'employee' . . . shall not include . . . any individual having the status of an independent contractor." 29 U.S.C. § 152(3).

Did Congress overrule *Hearst*? In what respect?

4. Congress also responded to the Court's decision in *Silk* by amending the Social Security Act. As a result of amendments in 1948, the act now provides that the term *employee* does not include "any individual who, *under the usual common-law rules* applicable in determining the employer-employee relationship, has the status of an independent contractor." 26 U.S.C. § 3121(d).

5. For nearly half a century after *Hearst*, some lower courts applying other employment laws continued to supplement the "control" test with consideration of statutory purpose and the "economic realities" of the parties' relationships. In Darden v. Nationwide Mutual Ins. Co., 796 F.2d 701 (4th Cir. 1986), for example, the U.S. Court of Appeals for the Fourth Circuit considered the employee status of an insurance agent under the Employee Retirement Income and Security Act (ERISA). The court considered, among other things, ERISA's purpose and the disparity in bargaining power between the defendant insurance company and agents such as the plaintiff. After further proceedings the case finally reached the Supreme Court on the issue whether the plaintiff was an employee or an independent contractor. Nationwide Mut. Ins. Co. v. Darden, 503 U.S. 318 (1992). The Supreme Court rejected the Fourth Circuit's statutory purpose analysis.

Recalling Congress's rejection of the *Hearst* decision half a century earlier, the Court declared that statutory purpose was no longer an appropriate basis for determining worker status. It dismissed *Hearst* and *Silk* as "feeble precedents for unmooring the term [*employee*] from the common law." *Id.* at 324. But the Court endorsed a modern, multi-factored version of the common law test that included consideration of "the source of the instrumentalities and tools; . . . the location of the work; . . . the duration of the relationship"; and "whether the work is part of the regular business of the hiring party. . . ." It also cited Section 220 of the Restatement (Second) of Agency, which lists, among other things, "whether or not the one employed is engaged in a distinct occupation or business." RESTATEMENT (SECOND) OF AGENCY, § 220(2)(b) (1958). Finally, it cited a 20-point checklist used by the Internal Revenue Service, which adds, among other things, "the integration of the worker's services in the business operations of the employer; . . . the possibility of profit or loss for the worker; . . . the worker's freedom to work for other persons"; and "the availability of the worker's services to the general public." Rev. Rul. 87-41, 1987-1 Cum. Bull. 296, 298-99.

Although the Fourth Circuit had expressed doubt whether Darden would be an employee under the common law test, the Supreme Court remanded for further proceedings to determine his status under the Court's new description of the test.

6. The Restatement of Employment Law defines employee status in a potentially expansive manner. First, it presents the control and economic realities tests as *alternative* bases for employee status: a worker is an employee either if "the employer controls the manner and means by which the individual renders service" *or* if "the employer otherwise effectively prevents the individual from rendering those services as an *independent businessperson*." RESTATEMENT OF THE LAW, EMPLOYMENT LAW § 1.01 (emphasis added). An individual worker is an "independent business person" if he or she "exercises entrepreneurial control over important business decisions, including whether to hire and where to assign assistants, whether to purchase and where to deploy equipment, and whether and when to provide service to other customers." *Id.*

7. Were the newsboys in *Hearst* employees or independent contractors under the test described in *Darden* or the Restatement of Employment Law?

8. The status of some types of workers is especially likely to be ambiguous. Among these are sales representatives, taxi drivers, and truck drivers. *See* Lowen Corp. v. United States, 1993 WL 245960 (D. Kan. 1993) (sales); Farmers Ins. Co., 209 NLRB 1163 (1974) (sales); Locations, Inc. v. Hawaii Dep't of Labor & Indus. Relations, 900 P.2d 784 (Haw. 1995) (sales); Hemmerling v. Happy Cab Co., 530 N.W.2d 916 (Neb. 1995) (taxi drivers); C&H Taxi Co. v. Richardson, 461 S.E.2d 442 (W. Va. 1995) (taxi drivers); Nat'l Freight, 146 NLRB 144 (1964) (truck drivers).

The latest wave of employee v. independent contractor litigation involves the status of package or parcel delivery drivers and workers in the "sharing" economy who use their own vehicles to offer "ride-sharing" arranged by a central internet-based dispatching system. The fact that the workers have invested in vehicles points toward self-employed or independent contractor status, but an alleged employer's management and standardization of many details of the operation point toward employee status. Case law regarding the status of these workers is far from uniform because of differences in state and federal law common law regarding the definition of "employee," the different ways judges or tribunals understand or apply the law, different statutory definitions in state and federal regulations, and differences in the details of an employer's relationship with workers from one location to another or from one period of time to the next. Many of these cases have been or will be decided by private arbitrators as a result of arbitration clauses in the underlying contracts of service, but an arbitrator's decision is not always public and does not have the effect of judicial precedent. *See* Carlson v. FedEx Ground Package Sys., Inc., 787 F.3d 1313 (11th Cir. 2015); Mumin v. Uber Techs., Inc., 239 F. Supp. 3d 507 (E.D.N.Y. 2017) (describing New York case); Ben Hancock, *Uber Driver Is Independent Contractor, Arbitrator Rules*, THE RECORDER, Jan. 11, 2017 (describing California case), http://www.therecorder.com/id=1202776655398/Uber-Driver-Is-Independent-Contractor-Arbitrator-Rules?slreturn=20170502173952.

Federal Tax Laws

Congress has been a little clearer about the method for determining employee status for federal tax purposes. The key lies in sections 3101 and 3121 of the Federal Insurance Contributions Act (FICA). Section 3101 requires an employer to pay social security taxes on "wages" paid because of "employment," which is "any service . . . performed by an *employee* for the person employing him. . . ." 26 U.S.C. § 3121(b) (emphasis added). As noted above, the post-*Silk* amended act defines "employee" as "any individual who, *under the usual common law rules* applicable in determining the employer-employee relationship, has the status of an employee." 26 U.S.C. § 3121(d) (emphasis added). The Internal Revenue Service has described the common law test with a non-exhaustive, 20-factor checklist — the same checklist the Supreme Court endorsed in *Darden*. Rev. Rul. 87-41, 1987-1 C.B. 296.

The Federal Unemployment Tax Act (FUTA) (which imposes a tax to finance the unemployment compensation system) adopts section 3121's common law definition of "employee" by reference. 26 U.S.C. § 3306(i). Federal income tax withholding law lacks any direct reference to the common law test, *see* 26 U.S.C. §§ 3403, 3401(c), but the Internal Revenue Service, which enforces all three laws, follows the same 20-factor checklist in each case. Thus, a worker who is an employee for FICA purposes is also an employee for FUTA and federal income tax withholding purposes.

The picture is actually more complicated because Congress has enacted special rules under each tax law for a long list of occupations and situations. Some workers, such as corporate officers, certain "homeworkers," and certain sales and delivery persons, are "statutory employees," regardless of their status under the common law. 26 U.S.C. §§ 3121(d), 3306(i), § 3401(c). Some are excluded from treatment as employees, regardless of their status under the common law. These include, for example, certain real estate agents (and of course newspaper sales and delivery persons!). 26 U.S.C. §§ 3121(b), 3306(c), 3401(a), 3506, 3508. Still others are treated as employees only if they satisfy the common law test *and* the employer has paid them a minimum amount of money. These include domestic service workers, casual workers who perform services not in the ordinary course of the employer's business, and certain agricultural laborers and home workers. 26 U.S.C. §§ 3121(a)(7)-(10), 3306(a) & (c), 3401(a).

Safe Harbor Provisions. Misclassification of workers can result in substantial liability, including back taxes for employees an employer mistakenly treated as independent contractors. Congress has alleviated the risk somewhat by granting a good faith defense for FICA and FUTA purposes. If the employer satisfies certain conditions, such as consistency in its past treatment of a worker as a nonemployee and consistency in treatment of other workers in substantially similar positions, the worker in question will be deemed *not* to have been an employee (even though he *was* an employee under the usual rules) "unless the [employer] had no reasonable basis for not treating such individual as an employee." 26 U.S.C. § 3401 note § 530(a)(1) Pub. L. No. 95-600, as amended. The defense works only retrospectively. Once the Internal Revenue Service has determined that the worker is an employee, the employer must treat the worker as an employee from that point forward.

Other Potential Federal Tax Issues. A worker's classification as an independent contractor has important tax consequences for the worker as well as for the employer. An independent contractor whose compensation does not qualify as "wages" will be responsible for paying his income and social security taxes without the advantages of employer withholding. On the other hand, the independent contractor enjoys certain advantages with regard to various business expenses, which are deductible by an independent contractor but not necessarily by an employee. *See, e.g.,* Alford v. United States, 116 F.3d 334 (8th Cir. 1997) (minister was independent contractor and not employee, and was entitled to deduct certain business expenses); Ware v. United States, 67 F.3d 574 (6th Cir. 1995) (insurance agent was independent contractor and not employee, and was therefore entitled to deduct full amount of unreimbursed business expenses from gross income).

State Tax Laws and the "ABC" Test

Employers pay a state payroll tax in addition to FUTA taxes to support the unemployment compensation system, and the definition of "employee" varies from one state tax law to the next, but federal law sets the baseline for coverage. Nearly every state has a standard provision that if an employer is required to pay federal FUTA taxes with respect to certain service by a worker, the worker is to be regarded as covered under state law notwithstanding any provision to the contrary. This standard rule allows the employer and the state to take advantage of the fact that FUTA taxes must be paid in any event with respect to the worker, and additional state taxes will be largely offset by a state tax credit the employer will enjoy against FUTA taxes.

But some states have decided to extend the security of the unemployment compensation scheme to a broader class of workers. These states expand the definition of employee indirectly by a particularly narrow definition of "independent contractor." Thus, it is possible that some workers whose compensation is not taxable under FUTA (because they are independent contractors under the common law test) are "employees" whose compensation *is* subject to taxation under state unemployment tax law.

States that have opted for wider coverage generally do so by adopting the so-called ABC test of independent contractor status. *See* Carpet Remnant Warehouse, Inc. v. New Jersey Dep't of Labor, 593 A.2d 1177, 1183-1187 (N.J. 1991) (discussing the development of the ABC test and its application); In re BKU Enter., 513 N.W.2d 382, 384 & n.1 (N.D. 1994) (noting that persons who were "employees" under the ABC test might be independent contractors under an amended law that replaced the ABC test with the common law test).

A typical version of the ABC test begins with a standard broad definition of employment, which is "service . . . performed for remuneration under any contract of hire, written or oral, express or implied." E.g., N.J. Stat. Ann. § 43:21-19(i)(1)(A). Standing alone, this definition could encompass independent contractors as well as employees. However, the ABC test takes its name from an exemption it creates for persons who satisfy all three parts (A, B, and C) of a test of independent contractor status. The burden of proof with respect to each part of the test is usually on an employer asserting that a worker is an independent contractor. Carpet Remnant Warehouse, 593 A.2d at 1184-1185. Part A of the ABC test essentially restates the common law requirement that the worker "has been and will continue to be free from control or direction over the performance of such services." E.g., N.J. Stat. Ann. § 43:21-19(i)(6)(A). However, even if this "control" requirement is satisfied, the worker is not an independent contractor unless he also satisfies parts B and C.

Part B of the test is that the services are performed outside the employer's usual course of business, *or* that the service is performed outside of all the employer's places of business. E.g., N.J. Stat. Ann. § 43:21-19(i)(6)(B). The common law test of employment, in contrast, would have considered these alternative factors as relevant but not decisive in determining employee status. *See* Restatement (Second) of Agency § 220(e), (h) (1958). Some courts have interpreted the "place of business" factor in a way that makes it especially difficult for an employer to overcome the presumption of employee status. *See, e.g.,* Vermont Inst. of Cmty. Involvement, Inc. v. Dep't of Employment Sec., 436 A.2d 765, 767 (Vt. 1981) ("An employer's place of business includes not only the location of its offices, but also the entire area in which it conducts the business. . . .").

Part C requires proof that the worker is engaged in an independently established trade, occupation, profession, or business, often with the further requirement that the business must involve services of the same nature as the service as to which exemption is sought, e.g., N.J. Stat. Ann. § 43:21-19(i)(6)(C). It is not enough that the worker performs an identifiable or traditionally recognized occupation. McGuire v. Dep't of Employment Sec., 768 P.2d 985 (Utah App. 1989) (nurses did not have "independently established" trade, occupation, profession or business, despite proof that they held professional licenses). Part C looks not only to the distinct character of the worker's occupation, but also to the stability and continuity of the worker's business apart from his relationship with the particular employer challenging coverage. Midland Atlas Co. v. S. Dakota Dep't of Labor, 538 N.W.2d 235 (S.D. 1995) ("whether or not she is unemployed is solely a function of market forces and the demand for her skills, not the response of her master to similar economic realities"). In other words, if termination of the relationship would leave the worker "unemployed," he is likely to be an employee. If he will continue to have a business apart from his work for the employer, he is likely to be an independent contractor. *See* Carpet Remnant Warehouse, 593 A.2d at 1187. *See also* In re Bourbeau Custom Homes, Inc., 171 A.3d 40 (Vt. 2017) (carpenters who worked as individuals for general contractor were general contractor's "employees" for purposes of unemployment compensation, but one carpenter who worked as sole owner and sole employee of his own corporation was not an "employee").

NOTES AND QUESTIONS

1. Employers enjoy so many legal advantages in hiring independent contractors that there is cause for concern that employers will shift a great deal of work from employees to independent contractors or simply misclassify employees as independent contractors. Indeed, independent contractors now constitute a substantial part of the "contingent workforce" that labors outside the usual protections and securities of regular employment. U.S. Government Accountability Office, *Contingent Workforce: Size, Characteristics, Earnings, and Benefits* (April 20, 2015), http://www.gao.gov/assets/670/669766.pdf. By one estimate, "independent contractors" and "self-employed" workers appear to constitute about 12 percent of the labor force, but such estimates depend partly on precise definition

and partly on the accuracy of an employer's classification of its workers.

Not surprisingly, the legal tests of worker status and the vigor with which regulatory authorities investigate classification of workers have become prominent employment policy issues for the executive and legislative branches. Pro-labor administrations tend to favor greater scrutiny of employer classification of workers and might tilt in favor of employee status in any questionable case. Pro-business administrations are more likely to defer to employer classification of workers. Federal authorities during the Obama administration adopted a comparatively restrictive description of "independent contractor" status. See U.S. Dep't of Labor, Interpretation No. 2015-1 (emphasizing that an independent contractor has his or her own "business"). However, the Trump administration withdrew this interpretation, an action widely interpreted as a signal that the government would be more willing to defer to an employer's classification of its workers. U.S. Dep't of Labor, News Release (June 7, 2017).

2. One worker's status as an employee or independent contractor may affect the rights of other workers employed by the same employer. Many employment laws cover only employers of a certain size, as measured by the number of "employees" in their workforce. The principal federal employment discrimination laws, for example, apply only to employers with at least 15 employees. *See, e.g.*, Title VII of the Civil Rights Act of 1964, 42 U.S.C. § 2000e(b) (defining "employer" as "a person . . . who has fifteen or more employees in each working day in each of twenty or more calendar weeks in the current or preceding calendar year").

Independent contractors do not count. Thus, the status of some workers as independent contractors might prevent the employer's "employee" workforce from reaching the required number. In that case, all the workers, employees and independent contractors alike, are removed from the protection of several federal employment laws. *See* EEOC, Enforcement Guidance: Application of EEO Laws to Contingent Workers Placed by Temporary Employment Agencies and Other Staffing Firms (Dec. 8, 1997), at http://www.eeoc.gov/policy/guidance.html.

3. There are times when an employer might prefer a worker to be an employee and not an independent contractor. For example, an employer is in the best position to claim ownership of a worker's work-related ideas, inventions, and creations if the worker is an employee. An independent contractor is more likely to retain ownership of what he invents and creates in the course of his work for the employer. *See* Cmty. for Creative Non-Violence v. Reid, 490 U.S. 730 (1989); Natkin v. Winfrey, 111 F. Supp. 2d 1003 (N.D. Ill. 2000); Efremov v. GeoSteering, LLC, 2017 WL 976072 (Tex. App.—Houston [1st Dist.] 2017) (employer's ownership of and access to software source code depended on whether the worker who created the code was an employee or an independent contractor). An employer might also prefer a worker to be an employee in the event of a work-related accident. If the worker is an employee, the worker's right to sue the employer will be severely limited by the "exclusive remedy" defense of workers' compensation law. If the worker is an independent contractor and the employer's negligence caused the worker's personal injuries, the worker can sue the employer under traditional tort law without the limitations of workers' compensation law.

4. Obviously, the statutory and judicial tests for distinguishing employees

from independent contractors do not always lead to clear, predictable, or consistently correct results. Can you imagine a better test? Consider Oregon's solution, Or. Rev. Stat. § 670.600, which requires, among other things, evidence of a separate and independent business, such as separate registration and licensing of the business, separate office and telephone numbers, or business cards. *See* Comment, *Oregon's Independent Contractor Statute: A Legislative Placebo for Employers*, 31 Willamette L. Rev. 647 (1995).

5. Can a worker be an independent contractor for some purposes, but an employee of the same employer for other purposes? In Hathcock v. Acme Truck Lines, Inc., 262 F.3d 522 (5th Cir. 2001), the plaintiff was a truck driver for an employer, but like many drivers in the transportation industry he owned the vehicle he was driving and he "leased" the vehicle to the employer. The plaintiff's compensation had two components: (1) driver compensation and (2) leasing fees for the use of the vehicle. The plaintiff received a separate check for each component of his compensation, but the check for leasing fees included deductions (in accordance with the contract) for the employer's share of certain payroll taxes (FUTA, FICA, and state unemployment compensation taxes). Ordinarily, an employer may not charge its share of these taxes to an employee. Nevertheless, the court held that the employer had not acted illegally. In his capacity as a driver, the plaintiff was an "employee," and not an independent contractor, and therefore his compensation was subject to the usual employee payroll taxes. On the other hand, in his capacity as owner/lessor of the truck, the plaintiff was not an employee but a lessor, and, according to the court, the lease agreement lawfully permitted the employer to deduct labor costs, including payroll taxes, from the rental payments.

PROBLEM

Dan Driver is suing Hale, Inc. under a state law that prohibits an "employer" from taking deductions from the "wages" of an "employee, unless the deductions satisfy certain conditions. Hale's defense is that Hale was an independent contractor and not its employee.

The evidence shows that Driver provided transportation for paying riders by arrangement through Hale. To arrange such transportation, Hale provides a "driver application" for drivers like Driver to use with their smartphones, and a "rider application" for riders to use with their smartphones. Drivers are connected to nearby willing riders when each party uses Hale's applications. Hale charges each rider a fare. Then, once a week, it distributes a portion of the fare for each rider to the appropriate driver's bank account by direct deposit.

Driver owned and operated the vehicle he used to transport riders arranged by Hale. It was the same vehicle Driver used for personal purposes. Driver bore all the costs of maintaining the vehicle and buying fuel, but Hale provided insurance coverage for Driver's commercial operation of his vehicle. Hale did not treat Driver as an employee. It did not include him in any employee benefit plan, pay or withhold any amount for social security or Medicare taxes, or withhold income taxes. Hale sent Driver a 1099 form, not a W-2, to report payments for each tax year. Driver remained responsible for the all of the 15.3 % "self-employment" tax that takes the place of social security taxes for independent contractors.

When Driver entered into this arrangement, he signed a contract stating "I hereby agree I am an independent contractor and not an employee." The contract also stated that every trip arranged through Hale is a "separate contractual engagement," and that Driver is "entitled to accept, reject, and select" transportation requests as he sees fit, has no obligation to accept any request," and is "free to set his own schedule and determine what locations he will serve."

Before Driver entered into this contract, Hale conducted a background check and required Driver to submit information about his vehicle, registration, license, and insurance. Hale required Driver to verify that his vehicle was no more than ten years old.

Hale did not require Driver to display Hale's name, trademark or any kind of sign on or in his vehicle. Hale did not require Driver to dress in any particular way. Driver remained free to offer his transportations services through other intermediaries similar to and competitive with Hale.

Hale did not directly evaluate or supervise Driver, but Driver's passengers could rate him on a scale ranging from one to five stars and enter comments. Under Driver's contract with Hale, if his rating fell below a level determined by Hale in its discretion or if customer comments warranted investigation in Hale's view, Hale could contact Driver through its "Driver Coordinator" to engage in "performance review and enhancement." If a Driver's ratings continued below a level determined by Hale in its discretion, Hale could "deactivate" Driver's account. Hale also maintains data on the frequency and duration of each driver's availability for service. Drivers with better records of availability are favored in the allocation of service opportunities.

Is Driver an employee of Hale, or an independent contractor?

For one court's view based on similar facts, see McGillis v. Department of Economic Opportunity, 210 So.3d 220 (Fla. App. 2017)

Other Nonemployees

Owners and Officers. Independent contractors are the most important group of nonemployee workers, but not the only group. Other workers who may or may not be "employees" include owners, partners, major shareholders, corporate officers, and members of the board of directors. In Clackamas Gastroenterology Assocs., P.C. v. Wells, 538 U.S. 440, 123 S. Ct. 1673, 155 L. Ed. 2d 615 (2003), the U.S. Supreme Court considered whether a professional corporation's four physician shareholders, who also constituted the board of directors, were employees. Shareholders, corporate officers, and directors are not employees as such. However, the four shareholder/directors in this case also performed physician services for the corporation. The question of their status was important because if they were employees, the corporation would have enough employees to be a covered "employer" under the Age Discrimination in Employment Act, 29 U.S.C. §§ 621 et seq. The Court adopted the position of the Equal Employment Opportunity Commission, which looks to "whether the individual acts independently and participates in managing the organization, or whether the individual is subject to the organization's control." 538 U.S. at 448, citing EEOC Compliance Manual § 605:0009. The EEOC lists six factors for this purpose:

1. whether the organization can hire or fire the individual or set the rules and regulations of the individual's work;
2. whether and, if so, to what extent the organization supervises the individual's work;
3. whether the individual reports to someone higher in the organization;
4. whether and, if so, to what extent the individual is able to influence the organization;
5. whether the parties intended that the individual be an employee, as expressed in written agreements or contracts; and
6. whether the individual shares in the profits, losses, and liabilities of the organization.

Id. The Court remanded the case for further examination of the director/shareholders' status under this test. Justice Ginsburg dissented, joined by Justice Breyer:

> The Equal Employment Opportunity Commission's approach, which the Court endorses, it is true, "excludes from protection those who are most able to control the firm's practices and who, as a consequence, are least vulnerable to the discriminatory treatment prohibited by the Act." Brief for United States et al. as Amici Curiae 11; see 42 U.S.C. §§ 12111(8), 12112(a) (only "employees" are protected by the ADA). As this dispute demonstrates, however, the determination whether the physician-shareholders are employees of Clackamas affects not only whether they may sue under the ADA, but also — and of far greater practical import — whether employees like bookkeeper Deborah Anne Wells are covered by the Act. Because the character of the relationship between Clackamas and the doctors supplies no justification for withholding from clerical worker Wells federal protection against discrimination in the workplace, I would affirm the judgment of the Court of Appeals [treating the shareholder/directors as employees for purposes of determining "employer" coverage].

538 U.S. at 454-455.

Volunteers. "Volunteers" form yet another group of service providers who are like employees for some purposes but not others. For *respondeat superior* and related tort purposes, the courts have usually treated volunteers the same as employees if the employer was aware of and accepted their services, and they were subject to the employer's control. *See, e.g.*, Restatement (Second) of Agency § 225 ("One who volunteers services without an agreement for or expectation of reward *may* be a servant of the one accepting such services.") (emphasis added); Hatcher v. Bellevue Volunteer Fire Dep't, 628 N.W.2d 685 (Neb. 2001) (volunteer firefighters acting in the scope of their employment entitled to official immunity as public employees). *But see* Munoz v. City of Palmdale, 75 Cal. App. 4th 367, 89 Cal. Rptr. 2d 229 (1999) (city not liable in *respondeat superior* for negligence of volunteer, regardless of city's control over volunteer's services).

For most statutory purposes, volunteers are generally not employees. *See, e.g.*, Jacob-Mua v. Veneman, 289 F.3d 517 (8th Cir. 2002) (volunteer not an employee under federal employment discrimination law); Spradlin v. Cox, 247 Cal. Rptr. 347 (Cal. App. 1988) (remanding to determine if plaintiff was a volunteer or employee for purposes of workers' compensation law).

Under some laws, a key test of "employee" versus "volunteer" status appears to be whether work serves mainly an employer's own interests or a civic or charitable purpose. *See Ex-AOL Volunteers File Lawsuit*, N.Y. Times, May 25, 1999. In the AOL case, a class of volunteers who helped lead chat rooms, reported rule violations, and answered user questions, sued for unpaid minimum wages under the Fair Labor Standards Act; AOL reportedly settled for $15 million. Lauren Kirchner, *AOL Settled with Unpaid "Volunteers" for $15 Million*, Columbia Journalism Rev., Feb. 10, 2011, at http://www.cjr.org/the_news_frontier/aol_settled_with_unpaid_volunt.php?page=all.

Student Athletes. If a student intern might be an "employee" entitle at least to the minimum wage, what about a student athlete whose participation in a school team yields valuable economic benefits for the school? In Berger v. National Collegiate Athletic Association, 843 F.3d 285 (7th Cir. 2016), former student athletes sued the University of Pennsylvania alleging that their participation in NCAA sports was employment, that the University and the NCAA were employers, and that the athletes were entitled to the minimum wage. "Appellants liken student athletes to interns and contend that we should use the Second Circuit's test set forth in *Glatt* to determine whether student athletes are employees under the FLSA," the court wrote. "We disagree." *Id.* at 290.

> As the Supreme Court has noted, there exists "a revered tradition of amateurism in college sports." Nat'l Collegiate Athletic Ass'n v. Bd. of Regents of Univ. of Okla., 468 U.S. 85, 120 (1984). That long-standing tradition defines the economic reality of the relationship between student athletes and their schools. To maintain this tradition of amateurism, the NCAA and its member universities and colleges have created an elaborate system of eligibility rules. We have held that these rules "define what it means to be an amateur or a student-athlete, and are therefore essential to the very existence of" collegiate athletics. Agnew v. Nat'l Collegiate Athletic Ass'n, 683 F.3d 328, 343 (7th Cir. 2012). The multifactor test proposed by Appellants here simply does not take into account this tradition of amateurism or the reality of the student-athlete experience. In short, it "fail[s] to capture the true nature of the relationship" between student athletes and their schools and is not a "helpful guide." Vanskike, 974 F.2d at 809.

Id. at 291.

"Salts" and Testers. Finally, there are so-called salts and testers, who seek or accept employment with an ulterior motive to serve some party or purpose other than the employer. Testers frequently operate in pairs of minority applicants and equally or less qualified nonminority applicants. If the employer agrees to interview or hire the nonminority applicants but not the minority applicants, this difference in treatment may be compelling evidence of unlawful discrimination. The issue whether testers may sue for unlawful discrimination usually arises as a matter of standing rather than employee status, because a tester who has no intention of accepting a job offer arguably has suffered no injury. *But see* Kyles v. J.K. Guardian Sec. Servs., Inc., 222 F.3d 289 (7th Cir. 2000) (testers had standing to sue for unlawful job discrimination under Title VII of the Civil Rights Act of 1964, but not under 42 U.S.C. § 1981).

A salt is employed and compensated by a union to accept work with a nonunion employer in order to organize the employer's workforce from the inside. In NLRB v. Town & Country Elec., Inc., 516 U.S. 85 (1995), an employer charged with discriminating unlawfully against salts argued before the Supreme Court that salts are not employees protected by the act. The Court upheld that part of the NLRB's order finding that salts may be employees:

> The Board's decision is consistent with the broad language of the Act itself — language that is broad enough to include those company workers whom a union also pays for organizing. The ordinary dictionary definition of "employee" includes any "person who works for another in return for financial or other compensation." American Heritage Dictionary 604 (3d ed. 1992). . . . The Board's broad, literal interpretation of the word "employee" is consistent with several of the Act's purposes, such as protecting "the right of employees to organize for mutual aid without employer interference," Republic Aviation Corp. v. NLRB, 324 U.S. 793, 798 (1945); see also 29 U.S.C. § 157 (1988 ed.); and "encouraging and protecting the collective-bargaining process." Sure-Tan, Inc. v. NLRB, *supra*, at 892.

516 U.S. at 91. In any event, the Court also found that the salts in *Town & Country Elec., Inc.* qualified as common law employees. In response to the employer's argument that the salts were not employees because they were compensated and controlled by the union, the Court stated:

> The Restatement's hornbook rule (to which the quoted commentary is appended) says that a "person may be the servant of two masters . . . at one time as to one act, if the service to one does not involve abandonment of the service to the other." Restatement (Second) of Agency § 226, at 498 . . . . The Board, in quoting this rule, concluded that service to the union for pay does not "involve abandonment of . . . service" to the company. 309 N.L.R.B., at 1254. And, that conclusion seems correct. Common sense suggests that as a worker goes about his or her ordinary tasks during a working day, say, wiring sockets or laying cable, he or she is subject to the control of the company employer, whether or not the union also pays the worker. The company, the worker, the union, all would expect that to be so. And, that being so, that union and company interests or control might sometimes differ should make no difference. . . . Moreover, union organizers may limit their organizing to nonwork hours . . . . If so, union organizing, when done for pay but during nonwork hours, would seem equivalent to simple moonlighting, a practice wholly consistent with a company's control over its workers as to their assigned duties.

516 U.S. at 94-95.

As *Town & Country Elec., Inc.* illustrates, the "statutory purpose" rule Congress seemed to overrule after *Hearst* is not entirely dead. Congress's action, as interpreted by the Court in *Darden*, precludes the courts from extending "employee" protection to common law independent contractors on grounds of statutory purpose. However, statutory purpose remains a permissible consideration when a court must choose between employee status and some other type of nonemployee status.

Interns and Trainees. Related to the problem of volunteers is the problem of "unpaid interns," typically college or graduate students who serve an employer as part of their "education" or to gain exposure, familiarity, and contracts within a particular firm, industry, or profession. If an intern performs basic office work or other service typically performed by paid employees, is the employer's failure to pay for the intern's service a violation of the FLSA?

SCHUMANN v. COLLIER ANESTHESIA, P.A.

803 F.3d 1199 (11th Cir. 2015)

ROBIN S. ROSENBAUM, Circuit Judge

Former student registered nurse anesthetists ("SRNAs" or "Students") who attended a master's degree program at Wolford College, LLC, with the goal of becoming certified registered nurse anesthetists ("CRNAs") … participated in a clinical curriculum, which, under Florida law, was a prerequisite to their master's degrees. Through this legal action, the students sought unpaid wages and overtime under the FLSA for their clinical hours….[T]he district court determined that the SRNAs were not "employees" of Defendants and entered summary judgment….

To obtain a CRNA license under Florida law, a person must graduate from an accredited program…. Defendant Wolford College is a for-profit college owned by Defendant Lynda Waterhouse and several anesthesiologists who also have an ownership interest in Defendant Collier Anesthesia, P.A., a Florida corporation that provides anesthesia…. Waterhouse serves as the executive director of Collier Anesthesia. Wolford College offers one of 113 accredited CRNA programs in the country, a 28-month curriculum that culminates in a Master of Science in Nurse Anesthesia. While classroom learning dominates the first three semesters, the last four semesters consist mainly of clinical experience—a requirement that Florida law and the National Board of Certification mandate….

Accredited schools must require a minimum of 550 clinical cases in a variety of surgical procedures…. Among other tasks that must be mastered during the clinical phase of training, SRNAs must learn to complete preoperative forms; set up equipment; draw proper medications; monitor patients; stock and re-stock carts; prepare rooms; and serve "on call." In Wolford College's clinical phase of education, each course has an instructor and a syllabus. Every day, the supervising CRNA or anesthesiologist must grade the student in several areas…. Clinical courses also require end-of-semester evaluations….

In this case the Students obtained some, if not all, of their clinical education at facilities where Collier Anesthesia practices. But the Students viewed their clinical efforts as more than just education; they filed suit alleging that they served as "employees" of Defendants for purposes of the FLSA and that Defendants unlawfully failed to compensate them with wages and overtime pay…. The Students claimed that Collier benefited financially by using their services in place of licensed CRNAs. Although Wolford's curriculum contemplated 40 hours per week, Collier routinely scheduled SRNAs in excess of 40 hours. They further presented testimony that they were scheduled at Collier-staffed facilities 365 days per year, including weekends, holidays, and between semesters. And, although Wolford and Collier represented that their shifts would be eight hours long, the

Students stated that they were required to arrive in advance of their scheduled shifts. Consequently, the Students indicated, an eight-hour shift actually required … 8.75 to 10 hours.… Barbara Rose, [a former Collier employee responsible for CRNA and SRNA scheduling at Collier's sites], indicated that in preparing the daily schedule, she strived to use SRNAs to reduce the number of CRNAs needed. Collier removed CRNAs from the schedule in favor of SRNAs and, in Rose's opinion, if the SRNAs had not been scheduled, Collier would have needed CRNAs to cover shifts.… The Students argued that the displacement of CRNAs allowed Collier to save money in running its practice.…

Defense expert Dr. Daniel Janyja, an anesthesiologist at Collier, … provided evidence that … Collier was capable of meeting its obligations with existing personnel, without the Students.… Dr. Janyja viewed the Students as more of a burden than a benefit because, among other reasons, the learning process impedes the actual delivery of anesthesia. Defendants also presented evidence … that it is sometimes difficult to place students in a clinical environment. Certain surgeons and hospital locations refuse to allow students in the operating room. Patients also sometimes decline student participation.…[A]llowing a student to participate … creates an added stress that would not otherwise be present. Moreover, student participation can slow down the administration of anesthesia because the CRNA may need to respond to questions. Or a student may attempt a procedure, fail, and require the CRNA to complete the procedure. . . . Wolford also requires the anesthesiologist or CRNA supervising students to complete paperwork pertaining to each student's presence, including daily evaluations. This paperwork detracts time from the CRNA or anesthesiologist's day.

The Students responded … that, under what is known as the [Medicare] "Revised Teaching Rule," Collier could receive reimbursement for student activities.… Collier was able to use one CRNA to obtain 100% of the CRNA fee for two cases at the same time with one student assigned to each. And, following [the adoption of the Revised Rule], Wolford and Collier decided to institute a two-to-one SRNA-to-CRNA ratio. The Students argued that made teaching "more advantageous" because Collier was reimbursed for two students where only one CRNA provided supervision.

Collier acknowledged that it … billed Medicare for some of its patients' procedures using the Revised Teaching Rule. According to Collier, however, … the number of CRNAs and Collier's payroll remained "substantially unchanged" despite fluctuations in the number of students that it used in the clinical program.…

[T]he district court granted summary judgment in favor of Defendants, finding that the Students were not employees under the FLSA, so they were not entitled to a minimum wage or overtime pay.…

In [*Walling v. Portland Terminal Co.*, 330 U.S. 148 (1947)], the seminal case involving whether trainees are "employees" for purposes of the FLSA, the defendant railroad company offered a practical-training course for prospective yard brakemen. While participants were not guaranteed a job upon completion of the course, they were required to successfully finish the course to be eligible to serve as brakemen for the railroad. On average, the course lasted seven or eight days. During training, a yard crew instructed and supervised the trainees, gradually allowing them to perform actual work under close scrutiny. The trainees' work did not displace any regular employees, who continued to do most of the work themselves. Nor did the trainees' work expedite company business. In fact, at times, it impeded it. In holding that the trainees were not "employees" ... , the Supreme Court reasoned, ... "[t]he Fair Labor Standards Act was not intended to penalize railroads for providing, free of charge, the same kind of instruction at a place and in a manner which would most greatly benefit the trainees." *Id.* at 153.

Since *Portland Terminal*, courts ... have focused on the Supreme Court's language describing the program at issue in that case as having "most greatly benefit[ed]" the trainees. As a result, these courts have, for the most part, concentrated on evaluating the "primary beneficiary" of the training or school program to determine whether participants constituted "employees" under the FLSA, generally concluding that such an approach reveals the "economic reality" of the situation. In doing so, they have considered the entirety of the circumstances, balancing a variety of factors that often entail comparing the facts of the case to the facts in *Portland Terminal* or to the six factors that the DOL sets forth ....

[T]he training involved in *Portland Terminal* was not a universal requirement for a particular type of educational degree or for professional certification or professional licensure in the field. Instead, the *Portland Terminal* training was offered by a company for its own, specific purposes, to create a ready labor pool for itself.... [T]he training at issue in *Portland Terminal* and in the case under review have similarities ... [but] longer-term, intensive modern internships that are required to obtain academic degrees and professional certification and licensure in a field are just too different from the short training class offered by the railroad in *Portland Terminal* for the purpose of creating its own labor pool.

As exemplified by the facts of the pending case, modern internships can play an important—indeed critical—role in preparing students for their chosen careers. Imagine if a CRNA could report to work on her first day and be allowed unsupervised to conduct the induction, maintenance, and emergence phases of anesthesia administration, having only ever read about or watched someone else perform them. The potential danger and discomfort to the patient under such circumstances is self-evident and startling..

Nevertheless, we recognize the potential for some employers to maximize their benefits at the unfair expense and abuse of student interns. And that is a problem.

So our dilemma arises in determining how to discern the primary beneficiary where both the intern and the employer may obtain significant benefits. We think that the best way to do this is to focus on the benefits to the student while still considering whether the manner in which the employer implements the internship program takes unfair advantage of or is otherwise abusive towards the student. This allows for student internships to accomplish their important goals but still accounts for congressional concerns in enacting the FLSA....

The Second Circuit's articulation of "a non-exhaustive set of considerations" ... in determining the "primary beneficiary" ... goes far towards fulfilling this function.... No one factor is dispositive, and courts must engage in a weighing and balancing including, where appropriate, other considerations not in the seven factors. In particular, the Second Circuit has identified the following factors:

1. The extent to which the intern and the employer clearly understand that

there is no expectation of compensation....

2. The extent to which the internship provides training that would be similar to that which would be given in an educational environment, including the clinical and other hands-on training provided by educational institutions.
3. The extent to which the internship is tied to the intern's formal education program by integrated coursework or the receipt of academic credit.
4. The extent to which the internship accommodates the intern's academic commitments by corresponding to the academic calendar.
5. The extent to which the internship's duration is limited to the period in which the internship provides the intern with beneficial learning.
6. The extent to which the intern's work complements, rather than displaces, the work of paid employees while providing significant educational benefits to the intern.
7. The extent to which the intern and the employer understand that the internship is conducted without entitlement to a paid job at the conclusion of the internship.

Glatt, 791 F.3d at 384. Under the Second Circuit's approach, "[n]o one factor is dispositive and every factor need not point in the same direction for the court to conclude that the intern is not an employee...." *Id.* Rather, courts must engage in a "weighing and balancing [of] all of the circumstances," including, where appropriate, other considerations not expressed in the seven factors. *Id.*...

To allow the district court to apply these factors, we remand.... But first we provide some guidance on applying some of the factors.

The fourth factor focuses on the extent to which the internship accommodates the intern's academic commitment by corresponding to the academic calendar. In a case like this, where the clinical training and the academic commitment are one and the same, this consideration must account for whether a legitimate reason exists for clinical training on days when school is out of session.

As for the fifth factor—the extent to which the duration is limited to the period in which the internship provides beneficial learning—this consideration must recognize the goals of the internship and determine whether the duration is necessary to accomplish them.... The court should consider whether the duration of the internship is grossly excessive in comparison to the period of beneficial learning. As part of this consideration, the court should also evaluate the extent to which the nature of the training requires the daily schedule that the intern must endure. In this case, graduation, certification and licensure requirements all demanded that students participate in at least 550 cases.... It does not seem that the four-semester duration would have been excessive.... But if the reason the SRNAs completed well in excess of 550 cases was because they were made to work grossly excessive hours, that would be an indication that the employer may have unfairly taken advantage of or otherwise abused the SRNAs and that they should be regarded as "employees" under the FLSA.

The sixth factor evaluates the extent to which the intern's work complements, rather than displaces, the work of paid employees while providing significant educational benefits.... The Students assert that CRNAs each worked fewer hours than they would in the absence of the SRNAs, meaning that the SRNAs displaced CRNA hours.... The Revised Teaching Rule allowed Collier to be reimbursed by Medicare for anesthesia in two rooms while having to pay only a single CRNA—something Collier could not have done if the SRNAs were not there....

[But] we do not think that such a fact, in and of itself, would resolve which party this factor favors.... a Medicare rule ... contemplates the use of two SRNAs to assist one CRNA in two rooms simultaneously.... The [Medicare Rule's]u existence and endorsement suggests there was nothing wrong with scheduling two SRNAs overseen by a single CRNA.... Of course, to the extent that CRNA hours may have been displaced by SRNA hours for reasons other than the Rule, the court should evaluate those circumstances....

Applying the factors to ascertain the primary beneficiary ... may not necessarily be an all-or-nothing determination. That is, we can envision a scenario where a portion of the student's efforts constitute a *bona fide* internship that primarily benefits the student, but the employer also takes unfair advantage of the student's need to complete the internship by making the internship implicitly or explicitly contingent on performance of tasks or working of hours well beyond what could fairly be expected to be part of the internship.

Finally, we do not take a position at this time regarding whether the Students in this case were "employees" for purposes of the FLSA.

... We vacate the district court's entry of summary judgment for Defendants and remand for further proceedings consistent with this opinion.

NOTES AND QUESTIONS

1. *Schumann* and the *Portland Terminal* case described in *Schumann* exemplify two very different internship programs: one formally connected with an accredited school, and another formed independently by an employer without connection to a separate educational institution. *Portland Terminal* suggests that it is possible for an employer to establish an internship or training program without connection to an accredited school and without formal academic credit. However, the "factors" described in *Schumann* make more likely that an employer lacking a legitimate school partner is employing "employees," not just training "interns."

2. For interns who are not employees, there might still be good reason to grant some of the protections of employment law. Consider, for example, the problem of sexual harassment. Employees are protected from sexual harassment by federal and state laws that prohibit sex discrimination in employment. If an intern is not an employee, does this mean that managers have a license to engage in sexual harassment that stops short of an actionable tort? *See* Tex. Lab. Code § 21.065 (prohibiting "sexual harassment" of a non-employee intern). Are there other employment protections that ought to be extended to non-employee interns?

3. Employers sometimes require new hires to undergo a period of training and orientation. Even after a new hire becomes an employee, the employer might require the employee to attend additional training or instruction programs in the capacity of a trainee. The U.S. Department of Labor regards training and instructional meetings as work time in employment unless (1) the program is outside regular work hours, (2) participation is voluntary, (3) the program is not

"directly" related to the trainee's employment with the employer, and (4) the trainee does not perform any "productive" work for the employer during the training or instruction. 29 C.F.R. § 785.27. *See also* McLaughlin v. Ensley, 877 F.2d 1207 (4th Cir. 1989) (pre-hire trainees in orientation program were employees during orientation for purposes of minimum wage law).

B. WHO IS THE EMPLOYER?

"No servant can serve two masters" (Luke 16:13), but an employee might have two employers, even with respect to a single job, in the book of employment law. The fact that one party is an employee's "employer" does not preclude the possibility that some other party is also the employee's "employer" with respect to the same work. One party might act as a nominal employer—the employer in name—with the other party acting as an employer in fact. Two or more employers can share or allocate different employer functions with respect to the same workforce, such as selection and hiring, record-keeping (including keeping track of working time), payroll management, management of benefits, and supervising, with each employer bearing some or all employer liability for a certain function.

A multiple employer setting illustrated in the *Black* case below involves "employee leasing." In many employee leasing arrangements, a workforce is transferred from the employer to a leasing agency (also known as a "staffing service" or, in some jurisdictions, a "professional employer organization"). The leasing agency becomes the nominal employer in the sense that a contract between the employers designates the leasing agency as the "employer," the leasing agency manages the payroll and issues checks under its own name, and the leasing agency identifies itself as the employer to third parties such as tax authorities and insurance companies. However, the transferred workers continue work under the control and for the benefit of their old employer. A number of states have enacted special laws regulating and sometimes licensing employee leasing agencies. *See, e.g.*, Ark. Code Ann. §§ 23-92-401 et seq.; Fla. Stat. Ann. § 468.520; Idaho Code §§ 44-2401 et seq.; Mont. Code Ann. §§ 39-8-101 et seq.; N.H. Rev. Stat. §§ 277-B:5 et seq.; N.M. Stat. Ann. §§ 16-13A-1 et seq.; S.C. Code Ann. §§ 40-68-10 et seq.; Tenn. Code Ann. §§ 62-43-101 et seq.; Tex. Lab. Code Ann. §§ 91.001 et seq.; Utah Code Ann. § 31a-40-101; Vt. Stat. Ann. tit. 21, §§ 1031-1043.

Employee leasing might be one more way of excluding a class of workers from participation in the lessee employer's benefits plans. *See* Burrey v. Pacific Gas & Electric Co., 159 F.3d 388 (9th Cir. 1998); Bronk v. Mountain States Telephone and Telegraph, Inc., 140 F.3d 1335 (10th Cir. 1998); Abraham v. Exxon Corp., 85 F.3d 1126 (5th Cir. 1996). Employee leasing might also be a way to use the leasing agency's expertise and resources to manage payroll or secure insurance. But employee leasing has sometimes been used to obscure the true rate of accidental injury or "experience rating" of a workforce, which is the usual basis for calculating an employer's workers' compensation insurance premium. *See* Texas Workers' Compensation Ins. Facility v. Personnel Servs., Inc., 895 S.W.2d 889 (Tex. App. 1995) (remanding for further proceedings claim of Texas insurance agency that employee leasing companies improperly used leasing arrangements to conceal true "experience rating" for client workforces). For a legislative solution to this problem, see Tex. Lab. Code § 91.042(b), (e).

BLACK v. EMPLOYEE SOLUTIONS, INC.

725 N.E.2d 138 (Ind. App. 2000)

NAJAM, Judge

Central States Xpress, Inc. ("CSX") was a trucking company with operations in several Midwestern states, including Indiana. . . . In early 1996, CSX was operating without worker's compensation coverage. In an effort to secure coverage, CSX approached ESI, an employee leasing company that provides a variety of employment-related services. On March 17, 1996, CSX and ESI entered into a Service Agreement whereby ESI would provide worker's compensation coverage and would hire CSX's employees and lease them back to CSX.

ESI began processing the CSX payroll. CSX would supply ESI with a computer printout containing the names and gross earnings for each person. ESI would then calculate the deductions and net pay, issue payroll checks and send the checks to CSX, where they would be distributed. Both CSX's and ESI's names appeared on each check. CSX would then reimburse ESI for the payroll plus ESI's service fee.

CSX did not pay ESI's invoices as agreed. ESI then terminated the contract on May 3, 1996, the same day CSX permanently ceased operations. CSX entered Chapter 7 bankruptcy. The Employees filed claims for unpaid wages and benefits with the bankruptcy court, but there were insufficient assets to pay the claims.

On January 8, 1998, the Employees filed suit against ESI asserting state law wage claims under the Indiana Wage Payment Statute, Indiana Code Section 22-2-5-1 et seq. Although there were no agreements between the Employees and ESI, the Employees alleged they were employees of ESI and sought unpaid wages earned prior to May 3, 1996. . . . The trial court granted summary judgment for ESI. . . .

The Wage Payment Statute is a limited purpose statute providing employees the right to receive wages in a timely fashion. The Statute does not create a right of payment in itself. The Employees' right to maintain an action is contingent upon whether ESI was their employer under the common law. . . .

The determination whether an employer-employee relationship exists is a complex matter involving many factors. Rensing v. Indiana State Univ. Bd. of Trustees, 444 N.E.2d 1170, 1173 (Ind. 1983). When the claim is based on the existence of a contract, the primary consideration is whether there was an intent that a contract of employment, either express or implied, did exist. *Id.* In other words, there must be a mutual belief that there was an employer-employee relationship. *Id.* However, where as in this case the claim is based on a statutory right, the parties' contractual agreement is significant but not dispositive. *Mortgage Consultants*, 655 N.E.2d at 496. Instead, we look at the totality of the circumstances to determine whether the alleged employee is entitled to statutory benefits. *Id.* Applying these principles, we conclude that as a matter of law ESI was not an employer of the Employees.

A. INTENT TO CREATE AN EMPLOYMENT RELATIONSHIP

The Employees assert that the intent of the parties to create an employment relationship could "hardly be more clear" from the language of the Service Agreement. They cite two provisions in support of their contention: that ESI "has in its employ qualified personnel and desires to supply drivers, mechanics and clerical personnel whose services Customer [CSX] may use" and that ESI "is the employer of personnel supplied to Customer [CSX]." We cannot agree.

Generally, where the intent of the parties can be clearly ascertained from language of the contract, courts recognize and enforce the parties' agreement. *Mortgage Consultants*, 655 N.E.2d at 496. In *Mortgage Consultants*, . . . our supreme court stated that the language of the contract was not determinative of the parties' intent to create an employment relationship and that the totality of the circumstances must be taken into account. *Id.* at 496-97.

Likewise, in this case, the language of the Service Agreement between CSX and ESI is not dispositive of the parties' intent. The Agreement stated that ESI is an "employer," but it also provided that each CSX employee assigned to ESI "will be a party to an agreement" with ESI. While the Service Agreement contemplated an employment relationship, it is undisputed that the Employees were neither parties to that Agreement nor to any other agreement with ESI.

The parties disagree whether ESI was required to enter into an agreement with each CSX employee as a condition precedent to an employment relationship. The Employees note that, as a general rule, a condition precedent must be explicitly stated in a contract to be enforceable. *See* Scott-Reitz Ltd. v. Rein Warsaw Assoc., 658 N.E.2d 98, 103 (Ind. Ct. App. 1995). We think the language of the Service Agreement is sufficiently explicit.

The requirement that each employee assigned to ESI "will be party to an agreement" must be a condition precedent because a mutual belief between ESI and the Employees that an employer-employee relationship existed is required as a matter of law. *Rensing*, 444 N.E.2d at 1173. Indeed, even in the absence of an explicit provision requiring an agreement between the parties, mutual assent is a prerequisite to the creation of a contractual relationship. *See* Jay County Rural Elec. Membership Corp. v. Wabash Valley Power Ass'n, 692 N.E.2d 905, 912 (Ind. Ct. App. 1998), *trans. denied.* While the contract of employment out of which the relationship of employer and employee arises may be express or implied, one may not unilaterally bind another to a contract of employment. Moore v. Review Bd. of Indiana Employment Sec. Div., 406 N.E.2d 325, 327 (Ind. Ct. App. 1980); Kirmse v. City of Gary, 51 N.E.2d 883, 884 (Ind. App. 1944).

. . . As we have stated, there were no individual agreements between ESI and the Employees. . . . In essence, therefore, the Employees acknowledge they were given no reason to believe that ESI was their employer. . . . The evidence does not show a mutual intent of the parties to establish an employer-employee relationship.[2]

B. Control over the Employees

Even if contractual intent were a genuine issue, the intent of the parties is not determinative in a statutory wage claim. The Wage Payment Statute does not

---

[2] The Employees direct us to several W-2 forms prepared by ESI which show ESI as the employer. We decline to hold that a W-2 form is sufficient to create a genuine issue of material fact absent any evidence of mutual intent and where, as here, the evidence is undisputed that ESI did not pay the Employees' wages.

suggest that intent is even a primary consideration that should be given greater weight than the hiring party's ability to control the hired party. *Mortgage Consultants*, 655 N.E.2d at 497. An employer either controls or has the right to control the conduct of his agent. Dague v. Fort Wayne Newspapers, Inc., 647 N.E.2d 1138, 1140 (Ind. Ct. App. 1995), *trans. denied*. . . . Here, there is no evidence that as of May 3, 1996, ESI had either exercised or had the right to exercise any control over the manner in which the Employees performed their work. The undisputed evidence shows that ESI clerical staff issued payroll checks from offices located in Angola, Indiana, and Coldwater, Michigan, several hundred miles from the CSX headquarters in Minneapolis, Minnesota. CSX would fax or mail to ESI a listing of the gross wages to be paid each individual, and ESI would issue checks after calculating the appropriate deductions. It would overnight the checks to CSX which would distribute them to their employees. ESI would then invoice CSX for reimbursement. That was the extent of ESI's involvement with the Employees.

There is no evidence that ESI scheduled, directed or supervised the Employees in any manner. Nor is there any evidence that ESI created or maintained original business records. Instead, ESI merely processed payroll data submitted by CSX. In sum, the Employees failed to present any evidence that ESI was anything more than a payroll agent and conduit for money supplied by CSX.

CONCLUSION

There is no evidence of mutual assent to an employment relationship between ESI and the Employees. There is no evidence that ESI and the Employees had agreed on the terms of employment or that ESI either controlled or had the right to control the conduct of the Employees. The evidence shows only that ESI was CSX's payroll agent. On these undisputed material facts, we hold as a matter of law that there was no employment relationship between ESI and the Employees and, hence, no factual basis to support the Employees' statutory wage claim. . . .

NOTES AND QUESTIONS

1. The court's opinion in *Black* notes that employer status can arise either by contract or statute. Employment is a contractual relationship, and *contract* duties are limited to those persons who are parties to the contract in question. *Statutory* employer duties are another matter. As *Black* suggests, a party can be an "employer" of a worker for statutory purposes in the absence of a contract with the worker. To be an employer for a statutory purpose, a party must exercise an employer responsibility relevant to the statutory duty in question. "Control" of an employee's work has been an especially important employer function for most statutory employer duties. In this regard, the solutions to an issue of employer status resemble the solutions for distinguishing "employees" from "independent contractors." However, in multiple employer problems, there is typically no dispute that a set of workers are "employees." The dispute is over the "employer" status of one or more parties who exercised some control over the employment.

2. Employee leasing is just one of many arrangements that lead to multiple employer problems. Another is a "temporary" staffing arrangement in which workers are recruited and selected by a staffing service that assigns the workers to

positions with client employers for short term labor needs, such as the temporary replacement of a regular employee on a medical leave of absence. In some cases, however, a "temp" worker and client employer are not strangers to each other when the staffing service becomes the nominal employer and "assigns" the temp to the client, and the assignment might continue for more than just a few weeks. In this situation the difference between temporary employment and employee leasing might be negligible for many purposes. For example, in the *Vizcaino* case described at the beginning of this chapter, Microsoft attempted to repair its misclassification of some employees as "independent contractors" by discharging them and re-employing them as "temps" through outside staffing services. Some of these temps then sued Microsoft, alleging that the arrangement with the staffing service was a sham reclassification to deprive them of their rights to certain employee benefits. *See* Vizcaino v. U.S. Dist. Court for Western Dist. of Washington, 173 F.3d 713 (9th Cir. 1999).

Introduction to Butler v. Drive Automotive

The plaintiff in the case below had at least one undisputed "employer." Why might the plaintiff want or need to name an additional party as the "employer?" The undisputed employer might not be liable to the plaintiff because the alleged harasser was not an agent of the undisputed employer. The alleged harasser was an agent of the putative employer. The plaintiff's right of recovery might therefore depend on proof that the putative employer was a joint employer in fact.

BUTLER v. DRIVE AUTOMOTIVE INDUSTRIES OF AMERICA, INC.

793 F.3d 404 (4th Cir. 2015)

FLOYD, Circuit Judge:

Brenda Butler seeks to recover for sexual harassment she allegedly experienced while working at a Drive Automotive Industries (Drive) factory. Drive argued that Butler was actually employed by a temporary staffing agency, ResourceMFG, and therefore Drive was not an "employer" subject to Title VII liability. Although the district court acknowledged that in some instances an employee can have multiple "employers" for Title VII purposes, it concluded that in this case ResourceMFG was Butler's sole employer . . . [and] granted summary judgment to Drive on Butler's claims....

I.

Appellant Brenda Butler was hired by ResourceMFG, a temporary employment agency, to work at Drive Automotive Industries in Piedmont, South Carolina. Drive manufactures doors, fenders, and other parts for automotive companies. The company hires some employees directly and employs others through temporary employment agencies.

Drive and ResourceMFG each exercised control over various aspects of Butler's employment. For example, Butler wore ResourceMFG's uniform, was paid by ResourceMFG, and parked in a special ResourceMFG lot. ResourceMFG also had ultimate responsibility for issues related to discipline and termination. Drive, however, determined Butler's work schedule and arranged portions of Butler's training. Drive employees supervised Butler while she worked on the factory floor. Butler said she was told by ResourceMFG that she worked for "both" Drive and ResourceMFG.

Butler claims that one of her Drive supervisors, John Green, verbally and physically harassed her throughout her time at Drive. Specifically, Butler alleges that Green made repeated comments about Butler's physical features, such as "You sure do have a big old ass"; "I wish my girlfriend had a big old ass like yours"; "Boy, I love women with big old asses"; and calling her a "big booty Judy." Green also rubbed his crotch against Butler's buttocks. Butler reported Green's conduct to ResourceMFG's on-site representative, Ryan Roberson, and to Green's supervisor at Drive, Lisa Gardner Thomas. According to Butler, however, neither took any action to curb the harassment.

The harassment culminated on December 19, 2010, when Green directed Butler to work on a particular machine called "the laser." Butler refused, saying she was tired from working overtime the night before. Green said that his supervisor had said "hell no." Green continued, "You have to run it. If you can't fucking run it, take your ass home.... [Y]our assignment has ended." He also called her "big booty Judy" again. When Butler objected to Green's language, he informed her that she was a temp and could be easily fired.

When Butler informed Thomas of the encounter, Thomas asked another supervisor at Drive that Butler be terminated. The request was then sent to ResourceMFG. A few days later, Green called Butler and implied that he could save her job by performing sexual favors for him. Butler refused. A ResourceMFG supervisor then called her to tell her she had been terminated from Drive....

III.

An entity can be held liable in a Title VII action only if it is an "employer" of the complainant.... The parties do not dispute that ResourceMFG employed Butler. The dispositive question on appeal is whether Drive also employed Butler for Title VII purposes. In answering this question, we first must consider the threshold issue of whether an employee can have multiple "employers" under Title VII....

A.

... Although this Circuit has never expressly adopted the joint employment doctrine in the Title VII context, ... [t]he joint employment doctrine is wholly consistent with our precedent. We have repeatedly used the joint employment doctrine in cases involving analogous statutes to resolve similar difficulties in defining "employer" and "employee." *See* Schultz v. Capital Int'l Sec., Inc., 466 F.3d 298, 305–06 (4th Cir.2006) (Fair Labor Standards Act); Howard v. Malcolm, 852 F.2d 101, 102, 104–05 (4th Cir.1988) (Migrant and Seasonal Agricultural Worker Protection Act); NLRB v. Jewell Smokeless Coal Corp., 435 F.2d 1270, 1271 (4th Cir.1970) (per curiam) (National Labor Relations Act). Nothing suggests a different treatment is warranted here.

Second, the doctrine's emphasis on determining which entities actually exercise control over an employee is consistent with Supreme Court precedent interpreting Title VII's definitions. The Supreme Court has held that "the common-law element of control," drawn from the law of agency, "is the principal guidepost" to be followed when construing an analogous claim under the Americans with Disabilities Act. Clackamas Gastroenterology Assocs., P.C. v. Wells, 538 U.S. 440, 448 (2003). Likewise, the Fourth Circuit has consistently focused on control, especially in the comparable instance where the status of the plaintiff as an employee or independent contractor is at issue. *See, e.g., Cilecek*, 115 F.3d at 260. The joint employment doctrine captures instances in which multiple entities control an employee.

Third, the joint employer doctrine serves Title VII's purpose of eliminating "discrimination in employment based on race, color, religion, sex, or national origin." Title VII should be liberally construed in light of its remedial purpose.

Finally, the joint employment doctrine also recognizes the reality of changes in modern employment, in which increasing numbers of workers are employed by temporary staffing companies that exercise little control over their day-to-day activities. The joint employment doctrine thus prevents those who effectively employ a worker from evading liability by hiding behind another entity, such as a staffing agency. Given Title VII's remedial intent, employers should not be able to "avoid Title VII by affixing a label to a person that does not capture the substance of the employment relationship." Schwieger v. Farm Bureau Ins. Co. of Neb., 207 F.3d 480, 484 (8th Cir.2000).

Consequently, we hold that multiple entities may simultaneously be considered employers for the purposes of Title VII.

IV.

We turn next to whether the court correctly applied the joint employment doctrine in this case. The object of the joint employment doctrine is to determine whether a putative employer "exercise[s] significant control over the same employees." *Bristol*, 312 F.3d at 1218 (quoting Graves, 117 F.3d at 727). The question then is how to determine the extent to which an employer "controls" an employee.

Courts have formulated at least three tests that could be used in the joint employment context: the economic realities test, the control test, and the hybrid test. All three tests aim to determine, in a highly fact-specific way, whether an entity exercises control over an employee to the extent that it should be liable under Title VII.

A.

We will briefly review the three tests . . . Drive contends that this Circuit should adopt the "control" test, which is drawn solely from basic principles of agency law. Some other circuits and district courts in this Circuit use the control test.

Courts in the Third Circuit, for example, have used three factors to determine whether an entity exercises sufficient control over an employee for Title VII liability:

1) authority to hire and fire employees, promulgate work rules and

assignments, and set conditions of employment, including compensation, benefits, and hours;

2) day-to-day supervision of employees, including employee discipline; and
3) control of employee records, including payroll, insurance, taxes and the like.

Butterbaugh v. Chertoff, 479 F.Supp.2d 485, 491 (W.D.Pa.2007) (quoting Cella v. Villanova Univ., No. CIV.A.01–7181, 2003 WL 329147, at *7 (E.D. Pa. Feb. 12, 2003))…. The control test is somewhat formal in that it tends to look to the legal parameters of employment such as hiring and firing, supervision and from where an employee receives his or her paychecks.

Butler, by contrast, argues, that the economic realities test applies. This test differs from the control test in that it focuses on "degree of economic dependence of alleged employees on the business with which they are connected that indicates employee status." EEOC v. Zippo Mfg. Co., 713 F.2d 32, 37 (3d Cir.1983) (brackets and ellipsis omitted) (quoting Usery v. Pilgrim Equip. Co., 527 F.2d 1308, 1311 (5th Cir.1976)). In other words, the economic realities test focuses less on the legal parameters of employment, but more on the entity (or entities) on which the employee relies on for work and remuneration—irrespective of who is actually writing the paychecks and determining work status. An entity that is a mere front might be an employer under the control test, but it would not be under the economic realities test….

Finally, below and on appeal, neither Butler nor Drive argued in favor of the hybrid test, even though we have consistently adopted it in analogous Title VII cases. The hybrid test combines aspects of the economic realities and control tests. In *Garrett v. Phillips Mills, Inc.*, we adopted the hybrid test in an ADEA [Age Discrimination in Employment Act] independent contractor case, describing the test as "analyzing the facts of each employment relationship under a standard that incorporates both the common law test derived from principles of agency and the so-called 'economic realities' test." 721 F.2d 979, 981 (4th Cir.1983). We noted that "the test applied in Title VII cases was appropriate for resolving employee status issues in ADEA cases." *Id.*

The *Garrett* court adopted a list of factors (the "*Spirides* factors") to evaluate along with the entity's degree of control:

(1) the kind of occupation, with reference to whether the work usually is done under the direction of a supervisor or is done by a specialist without supervision;

(2) the skill required in the particular occupation;

(3) whether the "employer" or the individual in question furnishes the equipment used and the place of work;

(4) the length of time during which the individual has worked;

(5) the method of payment, whether by time or by the job;

(6) the manner in which the work relationship is terminated; i.e., by one or both parties, with or without notice and explanation;

(7) whether annual leave is afforded;

(8) whether the work is an integral part of the business of the "employer";
(9) whether the worker accumulates retirement benefits;
(10) whether the "employer" pays social security taxes; and
(11) the intention of the parties.

Id. at 982 (quoting Spirides v. Reinhardt, 613 F.2d 826, 832 (D.C.Cir.1979)). Under the hybrid test, "control is still the most important factor to be considered, but it is not dispositive." *Id.*

A decade later, we implicitly adopted the hybrid test in a Title VII case to determine whether a plaintiff was an independent contractor or an employee. *Haavistola*, 6 F.3d at 219–20. Referencing Garrett, we remarked that "the operative language in ADEA is identical to the operative language in Title VII, so the analysis utilized under either act is interchangeable." *Id.* at 219 n. 2. We further described "a standard that incorporates both the common law test derived from principles of agency and the so-called 'economic realities' test," which asks whether employees "as a matter of economic reality are dependent upon the business to which they render service." *Id.* at 220 (citations omitted)....

Guided by these decisions, we conclude that the hybrid test best captures the fact-specific nature of Title VII cases, such as the one before us. The hybrid test also allows for the broadest possible set of considerations in making a determination of which entity is an employer. Moreover, it best captures the reality of modern employment in which "control" of an employee may be shared by two or more entities. The hybrid test correctly bridges the control test and the economic realities test.

Accordingly, we adopt the hybrid test. We find, however, that our previous statements of the hybrid test, involving the analogous but legally distinct independent contractor context, do not adequately capture the unique circumstances of joint employment. The factors used in Spirides and Cilecek include considerations that are irrelevant to the joint employment context. Drawing on our existing precedent and joint employment cases in other circuits, we now articulate a new set of factors for courts in this Circuit to use in assessing whether an individual is jointly employed by two or more entities:

(1) authority to hire and fire the individual;
(2) day-to-day supervision of the individual, including employee discipline;
(3) whether the putative employer furnishes the equipment used and the place of work;
(4) possession of and responsibility over the individual's employment records, including payroll, insurance, and taxes;
(5) the length of time during which the individual has worked for the putative employer;
(6) whether the putative employer provides the individual with formal or informal training;
(7) whether the individual's duties are akin to a regular employee's duties;
(8) whether the individual is assigned solely to the putative employer; and

(9) whether the individual and putative employer intended to enter into an employment relationship.

We note that none of these factors are dispositive and that the common-law element of control remains the "principal guidepost." ... [C]onsistent with our opinion in *Cilecek*, courts can modify the factors to the specific industry context.

Three factors are the most important. The first factor, which entity or entities have the power to hire and fire the putative employee, is important to determining ultimate control. The second factor, to what extent the employee is supervised, is useful for determining the day-to-day, practical control of the employee. The third factor, where and how the work takes place, is valuable for determining how similar the work functions are compared to those of an ordinary employee. When applying the joint employment factors, however, "no one factor is determinative, and the consideration of factors must relate to the particular relationship under consideration." *Cilecek*, 115 F.3d at 260.... Control remains the principal guidepost for determining whether multiple entities can be a plaintiff's joint employers.

B.

... Under the set of factors we state above, the district court inappropriately discounted several considerations that militate in favor of finding that Drive and ResourceMFG are joint employers of Butler. Most importantly, Drive exhibited a high degree of control over the terms of Butler's employment (factor 1). The uncontradicted evidence shows that a Drive employee sent an e-mail to Roxanne Lombard, an ResourceMFG employee, directing that Butler be "add[ed] to the list for replacement." ResourceMFG then, after a delay, terminated Butler. Although ResourceMFG was the entity that formally fired Butler, Drive had effective control over Butler's employment. Charlie Sanders, the ResourceMFG branch manager in Greenville, South Carolina, could not recall an instance when Drive requested an ResourceMFG employee to be disciplined or terminated and it was not done.

Second, Drive employees supervised both sets of workers (factor 2). Indeed, Drive—specifically Green and Thomas—handled the day-to-day supervision of Butler on the factory floor.

Third, Drive and ResourceMFG employees worked "side by side," performed the same tasks, and used the same equipment (factor 3). Although Butler wore a ResourceMFG uniform on the factory floor, there was little or no effective difference between the work performed by the two sets of employees.

Fourth, Butler's labor was not tangential or peripheral to Drive. Instead, she performed the same tasks as Drive employees and produced goods that were Drive's core business (factor 7).

The hybrid test, as we have articulated it, specifically aims to pierce the legal formalities of an employment relationship to determine the loci of effective control over an employee, while not discounting those formalities entirely. Otherwise, an employer who exercises actual control could avoid Title VII liability by hiding behind another entity. Here, although ResourceMFG disbursed Butler's paychecks, officially terminated her, and handled employee discipline, it did not prevent Drive from having a substantial degree of control over the circumstances of Butler's employment. Accordingly, we reverse the district court and hold, as a matter of law, that Drive and ResourceMFG are Butler's joint employers.

... Because we reverse the district court's finding that Drive was not an employer of Butler, the district must now consider the merits of Butler's claims...

NOTES AND QUESTIONS

1. Under most workers' compensation laws, an employer can assert the "exclusive remedy" defense against an employee's common law personal injury claim if workers' compensation covers the injury. But in arrangements such as those in *Black and Butler,* who is an "employer" for purposes of the exclusive remedy defense? *See* Frank v. Hawaii Planning Mill Found., 963 P.2d 349 (1998) (employer that leased injured worker from staffing agency could assert exclusive remedy defense). *Accord* Ghersi v. Salazaar, 883 P.2d 1352 (Utah 1994). A number of states have now answered the question by statute, usually allowing *both* the staffing agency and the client employer to enjoy the protection of the exclusive remedy defense. *See, e.g.*, Tex. Lab. Code Ann. § 91.042(c). This approach finds supportive precedent in some variations of the "borrowed servant rule," an old doctrine of workers' compensation law for situations in which one employer's worker is under the temporary direction and control of a "borrowing" employer. *See generally* 3 Arthur Larson, Larson's Workers' Compensation Law §§ 67, 68 (2001 ed.).

2. Similar issues arise with respect to the payment of unemployment compensation taxes, which are based in part on an employer's experience rating (a figure that depends on benefit claims by former employees). Employee leasing might be a way of delegating the administrative burden of paying taxes, or it might be a way of obscuring an employer's true experience rating. *See* Cameron v. Dep't of Labor and Indus., 699 A.2d 843 (Pa. Commw. Ct. 1997) (tax rate should be based on client employer's experience rating). On the other hand, discharging employees and then leasing them back, or switching leasing agencies, might count as termination for purposes of an employee's experience rating, resulting in a *higher* rate. *But see* Clark Printing Co. v. Mississippi Emp. Sec. Comm., 681 So. 2d 1328 (Miss. 1996) (switching leasing firms was not termination of the employees for this purpose). Many states now address these complications by statute. *See, e.g.*, Colo. Rev. Stat. § 8-70-114(2).

3. A staffing agreement often provides that the staffing service will withhold and pay taxes with respect to the paychecks it issues to employees. Does this relieve the client employer of its responsibility to pay taxes, if the staffing agency fails to do so? *See* Sunshine Staff Leasing, Inc. v. Earthmovers, Inc., 199 B.R. 62 (M.D. Fla. 1996), *vacated and dismissed as moot*, 242 B.R. 49 (M.D. Fla. 1999); United States v. Garami, 184 B.R. 834 (M.D. Fla. 1995) (even if client employer forwarded funds to staffing agency for wages and taxes, client employer remained responsible for taxes until payment was actually made to United States).

4. Employees owe common law, and sometimes contractual, duties not to compete with their employer during their employment. See Chapter 9, *infra.* To whom do leased employees owe this duty? *See* Constr. Mat'ls, Ltd. v. Kirkpatrick Concrete, Inc., 631 So. 2d 1006 (Ala. 1994) (lessee employer lacked standing to enforce noncompete agreement between leased employee and leasing company).

5. The size of an employer's workforce determines "employer" coverage and limitations on damages under some employment statutes. *See, e.g.*, 42 U.S.C.

§§ 1981a(b)(3), 2000e(b) ("'employer' means a person . . . who has fifteen or more employees. . . ."). Do temps and leased employees count for purposes of determining whether an employer is subject to the law? *See* Trainor v. Apollo Metal Specialties, 318 F.3d 976 (10th Cir. 2002) (fact issues regarding "employee" status of temps precluded summary judgment as to employer coverage); Burdett v. Abrasive Eng'g & Tech., Inc., 989 F. Supp. 1107 (D. Kan. 1997) (temps who were subject to client employer's direction and control should be counted as employees for purposes of determining whether client employer was subject to Title VII).

6. Whether or not a staffing agency is an "employer" of a particular worker, the agency is still subject to some employment laws in its capacity as a staffing service or employment agency. *See, e.g.*, 42 U.S.C. § 2000e-2(b) (prohibiting discrimination by an "employment agency," defined as "any person regularly undertaking with or without compensation to procure employees for an employer or to procure for employees opportunities to work for an employer. . . .").

Joint Employer Issues in Purchasing, Outsourcing and Subcontracting

You are not an "employer" of a worker simply because you receive the worker's work product from the business that hires the worker, controls his work and charges you for the work. Thus, for example, even if an Uber driver works as Uber's "employee," your receipt of and payment for his services does not make you a "joint employer." Nor is a business necessarily a "joint employer" of workers employed by a supplier or subcontractor to fill the business's regular orders. Most purchasing, subcontracting or outsourcing happens for the simple reason that a buyer firm does not have the capacity to efficiently perform desired work itself. It must buy the work from someone else. *See* R. Carlson, *Employment by Design: Employees, Independent Contractors and the Theory of the Firm*, ___ ARK. L. REV. ___, (2018) (forthcoming). However, some subcontracting or outsourcing arrangements can lead to plausible joint employer relations, especially if the buyer exercises an unusual amount of control over the work.

ZHENG v. LIBERTY APPAREL CO.

355 F.3d 61 (2d Cir. 2003)

JOSE A. CABRANES, Circuit Judge:

This case asks us to decide whether garment manufacturers who hired contractors to stitch and finish pieces of clothing were "joint employers" within the meaning of the Fair Labor Standards Act of 1938 ("FLSA"), 29 U.S.C. § 201 et seq., and New York law. . . . Plaintiffs-Appellants are 26 non-English-speaking adult garment workers who worked in a factory at 103 Broadway in New York's Chinatown. They brought this action against both (1) their immediate employers, six contractors doing business at 103 Broadway ("Contractor Corporations") and their principals (collectively, "Contractor Defendants"), and (2) Liberty Apparel Company, Inc. ("Liberty") and its principals, Albert Nigri and Hagai Laniado (collectively, "Liberty Defendants"). Because the Contractor Defendants either could not be located or have ceased doing business, plaintiffs have voluntarily dismissed their claims against those defendants with prejudice. Accordingly, plaintiffs now seek damages only from the Liberty Defendants.

Liberty, a "jobber" in the parlance of the garment industry, is a manufacturing company that contracts out the last phase of its production process. That process, in broad terms, worked as follows: First, Liberty employees developed a pattern for a garment, . . . purchased the necessary fabric from a vendor, and the vendor delivered the fabric to Liberty's warehouse. There, the fabric was graded and marked, spread out on tables, and, finally, cut by Liberty employees.

After the fabric was cut, Liberty did not complete the production process on its own premises. Instead, Liberty delivered the cut fabric, along with other essential materials, to various contractors for assembly. The assemblers, in turn, employed workers to stitch and finish the pieces, a process that included sewing the fabrics, buttons, and labels into the garments, cuffing and hemming the garments, and, finally, hanging the garments. The workers, including plaintiffs, were paid at a piece rate for their labor.

From March 1997 through April 1999, Liberty entered into agreements with the Contractor Corporations under which the Contractor Corporations would assemble garments to meet Liberty's specifications. During that time period, Liberty utilized as many as thirty to forty assemblers, including the Contractor Corporations. Liberty did not seek out assemblers; instead, assemblers came to Liberty's warehouse looking for assembly work. In order to obtain such work, a prospective assembler was required by Liberty to sign a form agreement. . . .

The parties do not dispute that Liberty employed people to monitor Liberty's garments while they were being assembled. However, the parties dispute the extent to which Liberty oversaw the assembly process. Various plaintiffs presented affidavits to the District Court stating that two Liberty representatives — a man named Ah Sen and "a Taiwanese woman" — visited the factory approximately two to four times a week for up to three hours a day, and exhorted the plaintiffs to work harder and faster. In their affidavits, these plaintiffs claim further that, when they finished working on garments, Liberty representatives — as opposed to employees of the Contractor Corporations — inspected their work and gave instructions directly to the workers if corrections needed to be made. One of the plaintiffs also asserts that she informed the "Taiwanese woman" that the workers were not being paid for their work at the factory.

Albert Nigri, on the other hand, avers that Liberty's quality control person made brief visits to assemblers' factories and was instructed to speak only with Lai Huen Yam, a co-owner of the Contractor Corporations, or with his wife. . . .

. . . [P]laintiffs alleged that both the Liberty Defendants and the Contractor Defendants violated 29 U.S.C. § 206 and N.Y. Lab. Law § 652(1) ("§ 652(1)"), which require an employer to pay employees . . . a legally mandated minimum wage. Plaintiffs alleged further that all of the defendants, including Liberty and its principals, violated 29 U.S.C. § 207 and N.Y. Comp. Codes R. & Regs. tit. 12, § 142-2.2 ("§ 142-2"), which require employers to compensate employees at one-and-one-half times the regular rate when an employee works in excess of 40 hours per week. . . . Finally, plaintiffs alleged that, in violation of N.Y. Lab. Law § 345-a ("§ 345-a") — a statutory provision that applies to the apparel industry only — Liberty Defendants entered into contracts with the Contractor Corporations even though they knew, or should have known, that the Contractor Corporations failed to comply with the provisions of New York law that govern the payment of wages.

. . . . [T]he District Court granted Liberty Defendants' motion for summary judgment and dismissed every federal and state claim in the complaint on the merits except the claim arising under N.Y. Lab. Law § 345-a, which does not require an employment relationship. The District Court determined that Liberty Defendants were not joint employers under the FLSA because, based on the plaintiffs' own admissions, these defendants did not (1) hire and fire the plaintiffs, (2) supervise and control their work schedules or conditions of employment, (3) determine the rate and method of payment, or (4) maintain employment records. . . . The District Court then declined to exercise pendent jurisdiction over the surviving claim under N.Y. Lab. Law § 345, and dismissed the complaint. . . .

As noted above, the relevant provision of the FLSA, 29 U.S.C. § 203(g), defines "employ" as including "to suffer or permit to work." This is "'the broadest definition [of "employ"] that has ever been included in any one act,' " United States v. Rosenwasser, 323 U.S. 360, 363 n.3 (1945) (quoting 81 Cong. Rec. 7657 (1937) (statement of Sen. Hugo L. Black)), and it encompasses "working relationships, which prior to [the FLSA], were not deemed to fall within an employer-employee category," Walling v. Portland Terminal Co., 330 U.S. 148, 150-51 (1947). Measured against the expansive language of the FLSA, the four-part test employed by the District Court is unduly narrow, as it focuses solely on the formal right to control the physical performance of another's work. That right is central to the common-law employment relationship, *see* Restatement of Agency § 220(1) (1933), and, therefore, the four-factor test may approximate the common-law test for identifying joint employers. However, the four-factor test cannot be reconciled with the "suffer or permit" language in the statute, which necessarily reaches beyond traditional agency law. . . .

Rutherford [Food Corp. v. McComb, 331 U.S. 722 (1947)] confirmed that the definition of "employ" in the FLSA cannot be reduced to formal control over the physical performance of another's work. In *Rutherford*, the Supreme Court held that a slaughterhouse jointly employed workers who de-boned meat on its premises, despite the fact that a boning supervisor — with whom the slaughterhouse had entered into a contract — directly controlled the terms and conditions of the meat boners' employment. Specifically, the supervisor, *rather than the slaughterhouse*, (i) hired and fired the boners, (ii) set their hours, and, (iii) after being paid a set amount by the slaughterhouse for each one hundred pounds of de-boned meat, paid the boners for their work. *Rutherford*, 331 U.S. at 726, 730.

In determining that the meat boners were employees of the slaughterhouse notwithstanding the role played by the boning supervisor, the Court examined the "circumstances of the whole activity," *id.* at 730, but also isolated specific relevant factors that help distinguish a legitimate contractor from an entity that "suffers or permit[s]" its subcontractor's employees to work. First, the Court noted that the boners "did a specialty job on the production line"; that is, their work was "a part of the integrated unit of production" at the slaughterhouse. *Id.* at 729-30. The Court noted also that responsibility under the boning contracts passed from one boning supervisor to another "without material changes" in the work performed at the slaughterhouse; that the slaughterhouse's premises and equipment were used for the boners' work; that the group of boners "had no business organization that could or did shift as a unit from one slaughterhouse to another"; and that the managing official of the slaughterhouse, in addition to the boners' purported employer, closely monitored the boners' performance and productivity. *Id.* Based on its analysis of these factors, the Court imposed FLSA liability on the slaughterhouse.

. . . The factors we find pertinent in these circumstances, listed in no particular order, are whether Liberty's premises and equipment were used for the plaintiffs' work; whether the Contractor Corporations had a business that could or did shift as a unit from one putative joint employer to another; the extent to which plaintiffs performed a discrete line-job that was integral to Liberty's process of production; whether responsibility under the contracts could pass from one subcontractor to another without material changes; the degree to which the Liberty Defendants or their agents supervised plaintiffs' work; and whether plaintiffs worked exclusively or predominantly for the Liberty Defendants. *See Rutherford*, 331 U.S. at 724-25, 730.

These particular factors are relevant because, when they weigh in plaintiffs' favor, they indicate that an entity has functional control over workers even in the absence of the formal control measured factors. Thus, in *Rutherford*, by looking beyond the boning supervisor's formal prerogatives, the Supreme Court determined, based principally on the factors listed above, that the slaughterhouse dictated the terms and conditions of the boners' employment. First, although it did not literally pay the workers, the slaughterhouse *de facto* set the workers' wages, because the boners did no meat boning for any other firm and shared equally in the funds paid to the boning supervisor. *See Rutherford*, 331 U.S. at 726, 730. The slaughterhouse also controlled employee work schedules, both because the boners' hours were dependent on the number of cattle slaughtered, and also because the slaughterhouse manager was constantly "after" the boners about their work. *See Rutherford*, 331 U.S. at 726. Finally, the slaughterhouse effectively "controlled the [boners'] . . . conditions of employment," *Carter*, 735 F.2d at 12, because the boners worked for the slaughterhouse as an in-house boning unit on the slaughterhouse's premises, *see id.* at 730.

In sum, the relationship between the slaughterhouse and the successive boning supervisors who managed the boners had no substantial, independent economic purpose; instead, it was most likely a subterfuge meant to evade the FLSA or other labor laws.

The first two factors derived from *Rutherford* require minimal discussion. The first factor — namely, whether a putative joint employer's premises and equipment are used by its putative joint employees — is relevant because the shared use of premises and equipment may support the inference that a putative joint employer has functional control over the plaintiffs' work. Similarly, the second factor — namely, whether the putative joint employees are part of a business organization that shifts as a unit from one putative joint employer to another — is relevant because a subcontractor that seeks business from a variety of contractors is less likely to be part of a subterfuge arrangement than a subcontractor that serves a single client. Although neither shared premises nor the absence of a broad client base is anything close to a perfect proxy for joint employment (because they are both perfectly consistent with a legitimate subcontracting relationship), the factfinder can use these readily verifiable facts as a starting point in uncovering the economic realities of a business relationship.

The other factors we have pointed out are less straightforward. *Rutherford* considered the extent to which plaintiffs performed a line-job that is integral to the putative joint employer's process of production. Interpreted broadly, this factor could be said to be implicated in *every* subcontracting relationship, because all subcontractors perform a function that a general contractor deems "integral" to a product or a service. However, we do not interpret the factor quite so broadly. . . . On one end of the spectrum lies the type of work performed by the boners in *Rutherford* — i.e., piecework on a producer's premises that requires minimal training or equipment, and which constitutes an essential step in the producer's integrated manufacturing process. On the other end of the spectrum lies work that is not part of an integrated production unit, that is not performed on a predictable schedule, and that requires specialized skills or expensive technology. In classifying business relationships that fall in between these two poles, we are mindful of the substantial and valuable place that outsourcing, along with the subcontracting relationships that follow from outsourcing, have come to occupy in the American economy. *See, e.g.*, *The Outing of Outsourcing*, The Economist, Nov. 25, 1995, at 57, 57 (noting that outsourcing "is part and parcel of the way American companies of all sizes do business"). We are also mindful that manufacturers, and especially manufacturers of relatively sophisticated products that require multiple components, may choose to outsource the production of some of those components in order to increase efficiency. *See, e.g.*, Ravi Venkatesan, *Strategic Sourcing: To Make or Not to Make*, Harv. Bus. Rev., Nov./Dec. 1992, at 98 (arguing that manufacturers should outsource the production of components to maximize efficiency). Accordingly, we resist the temptation to say that any work on a so-called production line — no matter what product is being manufactured — should attract heightened scrutiny. Instead, in determining the weight and degree of factor (3), we believe that both industry custom and historical practice should be consulted. Industry custom may be relevant because, insofar as the practice of using subcontractors to complete a particular task is widespread, it is unlikely to be a mere subterfuge to avoid complying with labor laws. At the same time, historical practice may also be relevant, because, if plaintiffs can prove that, as a historical matter, a contracting device has developed in response to and as a means to avoid applicable labor laws, the prevalence of that device may, in particular circumstances, be attributable to widespread evasion of labor laws. Ultimately, this factor, like the other *Rutherford* factors, is not independently determinative of a defendant's status, because the mere fact that a manufacturing job is not typically outsourced does not necessarily mean that there is no substantial economic reason to outsource it in a particular case. However, as *Rutherford* indicates, the type of work performed by plaintiffs can bear on the overall determination as to whether a defendant may be held liable for an FLSA violation.

The fourth factor the Court considered in *Rutherford* is whether responsibility under the contracts could pass from one subcontractor to another without material changes. That factor is derived from the *Rutherford* Court's observation that "[t]he responsibility under the boning contracts without material changes passed from one boner to another." *Rutherford*, 331 U.S. at 730. In the quoted passage . . . the Supreme Court was referring to the fact that, even when the boning supervisor abandoned his position and another supervisor took his place (as occurred several times), the *same* employees would continue to do the *same* work in the *same* place. Under *Rutherford*, therefore, this factor weighs in favor of a determination of joint employment when employees are tied to an entity such as the slaughterhouse rather than to an ostensible direct employer such as the boning supervisor. In such circumstances, it is difficult *not* to draw the inference that a subterfuge arrangement exists. Where, on the other hand, employees work for an entity (the purported joint employer) only to the extent that their direct employer is hired by that entity, this factor does not in any way support the determination that a joint employment relationship exists.

The fifth factor listed above—namely, the degree to which the defendants supervise the plaintiffs' work—also requires some comment, as it too can be misinterpreted to encompass run-of-the-mill subcontracting relationships. Although *Rutherford* indicates that a defendant's extensive supervision of a plaintiff 's work is indicative of an employment relationship, . . . *Rutherford* indicates also that such extensive supervision weighs in favor of joint employment only if it demonstrates effective control of the terms and conditions of the plaintiff's employment, *see Rutherford*, 331 U.S. at 726 (suggesting slaughterhouse owner's close scrutiny of the boners' work played a role in setting the boners' schedule). By contrast, supervision with respect to contractual warranties of quality and time of delivery has no bearing on the joint employment inquiry, as such supervision is perfectly consistent with a typical, legitimate subcontracting arrangement.

Finally, the *Rutherford* Court considered whether the purported joint employees worked exclusively or predominantly for the putative joint employer. . . . In [this] situation[ ], the joint employer may *de facto* become responsible, among other things, for the amount workers are paid and for their schedules, which are traditional indicia of employment. On the other hand, where a subcontractor performs merely a majority of its work for a single customer, there is no sound basis on which to infer that the customer has assumed the prerogatives of an employer.

In sum, by looking beyond a defendant's formal control over the physical performance of a plaintiff 's work, the "economic reality" test — which has been distilled into a nonexclusive and overlapping set of factors — gives content to the broad "suffer or permit" language in the statute. *See* 29 U.S.C. § 203(g) (stating that an entity "employs" an individual for purposes of the FLSA if it "suffer[s] or permit[s]" that individual to work). However, by limiting FLSA liability to cases in which defendants, based on the totality of the circumstances, function as employers of the plaintiffs rather than mere business partners of plaintiffs' direct employer, the test also ensures that the statute is not interpreted to subsume typical outsourcing relationships. The "economic reality" test, therefore, is intended to expose outsourcing relationships that lack a substantial economic purpose, but it is manifestly not intended to bring normal, strategically-oriented contracting schemes within the ambit of the FLSA.

We intimate no view as to whether plaintiffs, under a proper application of the economic reality test derived from *Rutherford*, will have presented sufficient evidence to survive a renewed motion for summary judgment on remand. . . . [T]he

District Court's conclusion that, in the present circumstances, the record cannot support summary judgment in plaintiffs' favor, remains undisturbed . . . . Should the District Court, on remand, deny summary judgment in favor of defendants, it will be incumbent upon the Court to conduct a trial. . . .

[The court reinstated the plaintiffs' claims under New York minimum wage and overtime law, which, like the FLSA, defines "employ" as "suffer or permit."]

As a final matter, we reiterate that plaintiffs have not challenged the dismissal of their claims under N.Y. Labor Law §§ 191 and 193 [requiring weekly payment of wages and restricting deductions], which are governed by a narrower definition of employment applicable to Article 6 of New York's labor statute. *See* N.Y. Labor Law § 190 (defining "employer" and "employee" without using the "suffer or permit" language). Accordingly, we need not address those claims, the disposition of which remains undisturbed. . . .

NOTES AND QUESTIONS

1. On remand, a jury rendered a verdict for the employees for $556,566.76. The Second Circuit's decision upholding that verdict reveals that the workers averaged 85 hours per week. When they were paid (and they were not always paid) they received less than the minimum wage and overtime rates required by law. Zheng v. Liberty Apparel Co., 617 F.3d 182 (2d Cir. 2010).

2. The garment industry is only one industry in which essential functions of an operation are regularly assigned to subcontractors under circumstances possibly supporting a joint employer theory. The issue of joint employer status also arises frequently in farming with respect to a "grower's" responsibility to a labor contractor's workforce that harvests the grower's fields. *See, e.g.*, Torres-Lopez v. May, 111 F.3d 633 (9th Cir. 1997); Ricketts v. Vann, 32 F.3d 71 (4th Cir. 1994). The issue also arises for retailers who contract out routine cleaning and maintenance work. *See, e.g.*, Zavala v. Wal-Mart Stores, Inc., 393 F. Supp. 2d 295 (D.N.J. 2005); Flores v. Albertsons, Inc., 2002 WL 1163623 (C.D. Cal. 2002).

Could a retailer be liable as a "joint employer" for the employment conditions of the suppliers whose goods are on the retailer's shelves? *See* Doe v. Wal-Mart, 572 F.3d 677 (9th Cir. 2009) (not in this case).

3. In *Zheng,* how important is it to the manufacturer's joint employer status that the plaintiffs asserted their claims under the FLSA, with its "suffer or permit" standard of employment? Only a few other employment laws include this definition of "employ." *See also* 29 U.S.C. § 1802(5) (Migrant and Seasonal Agricultural Worker Protection Act). Note that the plaintiffs did not appeal from summary judgment against their claims under New York wage payment statutes that required a common law employment relationship.

The Policy Debate Over Potential, Indirect and Aggregated "Control" of Work

During the Obama administration, the National Labor Relations Board, the Department of Labor and a number of courts took a broad view of the joint employer theory. *See* Bowning-Ferris Indus. of Calif., Inc., 362 NLRB No. 186 (2015); Dep't of Labor, Administrator's Interpretation No. 2016-1 (Jan. 20, 2016);

Hall v. DirectTV, L.L.C. 846 F.3d 757 (4th Cir. 2017); Ocampo v. 455 Hospitality LLC, 2016 WL 4926204 (S.D.N.Y. 2016). The NLRB and DOL emphasized two particular arguments that suggested a more aggressive application of the joint employer doctrine to certain business arrangements.

First, the NLRB and Department of Labor highlighted the importance of an alleged joint employer's *potential* power to control work even when the alleged joint employer has not actually exercised such control. An unexercised *right* to control work was a basis for employer status even under the early common law test of employer status, but the *Bowning-Ferris* and the Department of Labor interpretation suggested an intention to pursue joint employer claims in some new settings, such as franchise arrangements in which the franchisor retains sufficient control over a franchisee's business practices to significantly affect employment standards. An alleged joint employer's potential control could be particularly important in the collective bargaining setting if a labor contract will have little value without the alleged joint employer's mandatory participation in bargaining.

Second, *Browning-Ferris* and the Department of Labor interpretation emphasized the relevance of "indirect" control a putative joint employer might exercise over work. Consideration of "indirect" control is consistent with most versions of the "economic realities" test, but the agencies' emphasis on indirect control seemed to confirm an intention to pursue the joint employer status of franchisors and others similarly affiliated to a primary employer.

During the same time frame, some courts adopted a third theory important to employee and employer classification: aggregated control of work. *See* Hall v. DirectTV, L.L.C., 846 F.3d 757 (4th Cir. 2017). The aggregated control theory is important when there is an issue whether a worker is an independent contractor or an employee of two or more alleged joint employers. In analyzing a worker's freedom from control, the court considers the aggregate control of all the alleged joint employers over the worker. If the worker is sufficiently controlled in the aggregate to be an "employee," the court then determines whether each of the alleged employers is in fact a joint employer.

One of the first major policy actions of the Department of Labor under the Trump administration was to withdraw the Obama era interpretation regarding potential and indirect control. Dep't of Labor, OPA News Release, June 7, 2017. As of this writing the Department of Labor has not issued a substitute interpretation, but the withdrawal of the Obama era interpretation suggests a less vigorous pursuit of joint employer claims. Private litigants and courts remain free pursue their own interpretations of the law.

In Congress, at least one bill, H.R. 3441, proposes to amend federal employment laws to limit the application of joint employer doctrine. A few state legislatures have already enacted such laws with respect to franchisors for purposes of state employment law. *See, e.g.,* Tex. Lab. Code § 61.0031.

Beyond the Joint Employer Doctrine: Alternative Bases for Extending Responsibility

Even if a manufacturer or general contractor is not a "joint employer" under the common law or a statutory concept of employment, it might nevertheless bear liability based on some other concept of responsibility. Under the Restatement (Second) of Torts § 414, "one who entrusts work to an independent contractor, but who retains the control of any part of the work" is liable to persons harmed because of that person's failure to exercise control with care. In Read v. Scott Fetzer Co., 990 S.W.2d 732 (Tex. 1998), a court relied on this provision in holding that a manufacturer of vacuum cleaners was liable for an independent distributor's negligent hiring practices that led to a door-to-door salesman's sexual assault of a customer. Although the manufacturer was not the salesman's employer, it required the in-home sales strategy that heightened the risk of such torts, and its control over distributors made it possible for it to require greater care in hiring.

If a business's "control" and knowledge with respect to an independent contractor can make it liable to non-employee third parties hurt by the contractor's employment practices, could it also be liable on the same basis to the contractor's *workers* injured by the contractor's employment practices? In thinking about this problem, consider the following excerpt from Edward Hegstrom, *Local Homebuilders "Mixed" Over Immigrant Proposal*, Houston Chronicle, Jan. 12, 2004, regarding the employment of undocumented aliens in the building industry:

> Typically, a contractor will bid on a job, then call in Penny as the subcontractor to do the framing. But Penny doesn't hire the workers himself. He hires another man, a sub-contractor, who is typically a legal immigrant from Mexico. That man hires the workers. "I know the guy I pay is bullet-proof," Penny said, meaning that he knows that man has a legal work visa. "But who works for him — it doesn't matter." Penny admits that this practice limits his liability. If a worker gets injured, or in the unlikely event that the immigration service conducts a raid, the sub-contractor would be the one held liable.

If the subcontractor can be found. Authorized and unauthorized workers hired under these circumstances are frequent victims of wage theft by subcontractors. See Renee C. Clark, *Workers Demand Justice for Wage Theft*, Houston Chronicle (November 17, 2011), at http://www.chron.com/news/houston-texas/article/Workers-confront-employers-for-back-wages-2275330.php

There are also some statutory alternatives to the joint employer doctrine. One of the plaintiffs' claims in *Zheng* was under a New York statute that imposes employer-like responsibility in the absence of an employment relationship. Under N.Y. Labor Law § 345-a, "A manufacturer or contractor who contracts or subcontracts with another manufacturer or contractor for the performance of any apparel industry service . . . and who *knew or should have known* with the exercise of reasonable care or diligence of such other manufacturer's or contractor's failure to comply [with certain New York wage payment statutes] in the performance of such service shall be liable for such failure" (emphasis added). Consider also the following California statute of somewhat broader coverage:

> A person or entity may not enter into a contract or agreement for labor or services with a construction, farm labor, garment, janitorial, or security guard contractor, *where the person or entity knows or should know* that the contract or agreement does not include funds sufficient to allow the contractor to comply with all applicable local, state, and federal laws or regulations governing the labor or services to be provided.

Cal. Lab. Code § 2819 (emphasis added). *See also* Sanders Constr. Co. v. Cerda, 95 Cal.Rptr.3d 911 (Cal. App. 2009) (applying California law that makes a general contractor liable for wage obligations of an unlicensed subcontractor).

Finally, in a number of cases during the last two decades, foreign workers have sued transnational corporations in U.S. federal courts under the Alien Tort Claims Act (ATCA), 28 U.S.C. § 1350, based on alleged employment practices violating "the law of nations." *See, e.g.*, Doe v. Unocal Corp., 395 F.3d 932 (9th Cir. 2002), dismissed on stipulated motion to dismiss, 403 F.3d 708 (9th Cir. 2005); Sarei v. Rio Tinto, PLC, 671 F.3d 736 (9th Cir. 2011). However, in Kiobel v. Royal Dutch Petroleum Co., 569 U.S. 108 (2013), the Supreme Court held that the ATCA does not apply to violations of the law of nations within territories of sovereigns other than the United States. Of course, most employment occurs in some territory of some sovereign—unless it occurs on the high seas.

Corporate Families and the "Single Employer" Theory

Using the "joint employer" doctrine described above, courts and administrative agencies sometimes find an employee had two employers for the same job. Joint employers, however, are generally regarded as separate "persons." Each must be served with process separately, each must be judged separately with respect to their alleged violations of employment law, and a judgment against one is effective and enforceable only against that one and not the other. Moreover, each of the joint employers must qualify separately for purposes of statutory coverage. Even if one qualifies as a statutory "employer" based on its number of employees, or its nature or volume of business, the other might not qualify. They cannot be combined as one for purposes of satisfying workforce or volume-of-business qualifications.

A different doctrine, the "single employer" rule, allows courts and administrative agencies to treat two separate entities as one person for statutory coverage and certain other purposes in employment law. The "single employer" doctrine resembles, but is distinct from, the rules for "piercing the corporate veil."

The National Labor Relations Board was one of the first tribunals to invoke the single employer theory, and the Supreme Court endorsed the theory in Radio and Television Broadcast Technicians Local Union 1264 v. Broadcast Serv. of Mobile, Inc., 380 U.S. 255 (1965). In that case, the issue was whether a labor dispute at a radio station was subject to federal collective bargaining law. The NLRB had adopted a rule that it would decline to assert jurisdiction over an enterprise having annual receipts of less than $100,000, in effect leaving the labor disputes of such small enterprises to state law. The radio station in question had annual receipts of less than $100,000 but it was affiliated with separately incorporated stations with combined annual receipts exceeding the jurisdictional threshold. The Court held that the radio stations were properly treated as one employer subject to federal collective bargaining law:

> [I]n determining the relevant employer, the Board considers several nominally separate business entities to be a single employer where they comprise an integrated enterprise. The controlling criteria, set out and elaborated in Board decisions, are interrelations of operations, common management, centralized control of labor relations and common ownership.

> The record below is more than adequate to show that all these factors are present in regard to the Holt enterprise. . . .

Id. at 256-257.

Over the years the NLRB has used the single employer theory for a variety of other purposes under federal collective bargaining law. Following the NLRB's lead, other administrative agencies and courts have also applied the single employer theory in cases involving other employment laws. Richard Carlson, *The Small Firm Exemption and the Single Employer Doctrine in Employment Discrimination Law*, 80 St. John's L. Rev. 1197, 1217-1222 (2006).

The single employer doctrine is useful mainly to extend the reach of statutory coverage over an employer who might otherwise to be too small, or to combine the workforces of separate entities for purposes of collective bargaining. *See* S. Prairie Constr. Co. v. Local No. 627, 425 U.S. 800 (1982). Its usefulness for other purposes is less certain. Application of the doctrine does not necessarily result in the merger of two entities into one "person" if it would not otherwise be proper for a court to pierce the corporate veil. Carlson, *supra*, at 1258. *Compare* Papa v. Katy Industries, Inc., 166 F.3d 937 (7th Cir. 1999) (declining to apply the doctrine to satisfy Title VII requirement for employer coverage, in absence of proof of intent to evade coverage) *with* Knowlton v. Teltrust Phones, Inc., 189 F.3d 1177 (10th Cir. 1999) (jury properly found that parent corporation and its subsidiary were a single employer, and that parent was liable for subsidiary's violations); Story v. Vae Nortrak, Inc., 214 F. Supp. 2d 1209 (N.D. Ala. 2001) (applying the doctrine with respect to a statute that limits compensatory and punitive damages according to the size of an employer's workforce); *and* Jarred v. Walters Industries, Inc., 153 F. Supp. 2d 1095 (W.D. Mo. 2001) (applying the doctrine to treat a plaintiff's administrative EEOC charge against one defendant as a charge against another).

The problem of identifying the "employer" from among a number of interrelated or affiliated entities is not limited to the private sector. The problem can also arise with respect to public entities. In Lyes v. City of Riviera Beach, 166 F.3d 1332 (11th Cir. 1999), the court considered whether the traditional four-part single employer test was useful for determining whether the workforces of a city government and a community redevelopment agency (CRA) should be combined for purposes of satisfying the minimum workforce threshold (15 employees) for coverage under Title VII. The court noted that two of the traditional four factors, "common ownership or financial control," and "common management," would frequently be inappropriate grounds for treating multiple public entities as if they were one. *Id.* at 1343. The court regarded the other two factors, "interrelation of operations and centralized control of labor relations," as much more relevant to single employer status in the public sector. However, the court concluded that considerations of federalism required "great deference" to state law in determining whether two public entities were separate. *Id.* at 1344-1345. Applying this deferential test to the facts before it, the court found that the city and the CRA were not a single employer. A substantial overlap in membership of the respective governing boards, the CRA's use of certain city personnel forms, and regular consultation between CRA and city officials were insufficient to overcome the presumption of separateness created by the clear terms of Florida statutes authorizing the creation of agencies such as the CRA. *Id.* at 1346-1347.

PROBLEM

Value-Shop is a nationwide discount retailer. Until recently, it relied on its own regular employees assigned to the custodial staff at its Metro City store to perform general cleaning and maintenance work. It paid its custodial staff at the store at least $3.00 per hour more than the statutory minimum wage. Value-Shop found that it needed to pay custodial workers at least $3.00 per hour more than the minimum wage in order to attract and retain employees. Employees were eligible to participate in a group health insurance plan, and Value-Shop also contributed to a retirement plan for employees. Value-Shop's annual contribution to both plans for each employee was about 15 percent of the employee's regular earnings.

Value-Shop recently eliminated its custodial staff for the Metro City store as a result of a new arrangement with Custodial Services, Inc. (CSI), a separately owned and managed company formed by a former manager of custodial services for Value-Shop. CSI approached Value-Shop with an offer to provide custodial services for the Metro City store at a cost that was 20 percent less than the amount Value-Shop estimated it spent to maintain its own custodial staff. When Value-Shop terminated its custodial staff, it offered the employees transfers to other Value-Shop stores or the opportunity to apply for employment with CSI to work at the same store. Former Value-Shop custodial employees complained to an associate manager of the store that CSI was offering reduced pay and fewer benefits, and none of the former custodial employees accepted work with CSI.

Under CSI's arrangement with Value-Shop, CSI's regional supervisor visits the store at least once every evening to check on the CSI workers assigned to the store, but the CSI supervisor is elsewhere (visiting other Valu-Shop stores) during most of the evening shift when CSI's workers perform their work. While the CSI supervisor is away, the on-duty Value-Shop manager (who is at the store to supervise inventory and stocking at night) can observe the CSI workers and direct them to specific problems needing attention. Value-Shop's night shift personnel have noticed that no CSI workers speak English very well, and some seem to speak no English at all. Value-Shop's managers might also have noticed that the CSI workers frequently work seven days a week and more than eight hours an evening.

The CSI supervisor regularly consults with the Value-Shop store managers to make sure they are satisfied with the work of the CSI workers. On some occasions, CSI has discharged or disciplined its workers based on reports it received from Value-Shop's store managers.

A Department of Justice investigation has now determined that several CSI workers recently assigned to the Value-Shop store are aliens who are not authorized to work in the United States. The workers, who are about to be deported, have hired a lawyer to sue CSI and Value-Shop for various violations of the FLSA (the federal minimum wage and overtime law) and local wage laws. Assuming that CSI clearly violated these laws, could Value-Shop also be liable to the workers?

C. WHO CAN BE EMPLOYED?

1. Children

Federal child labor laws regulate employment of children in three ways. First, employing a child under age 14 is unlawful, except for employment by a parent or person standing in the place of a parent. Second, employing a child between ages 14 and 16 is unlawful except in accordance with Department of Labor regulations restricting the hours of work (so as not "to interfere with their schooling") and the types of such employment (so as not to "interfere with their health and wellbeing"). Finally, employing a child between ages 16 and 18 is lawful except in occupations the Department of Labor deems "hazardous." 29 U.S.C. § 203(l).

Child labor issues frequently overlap with issues of "volunteer" or "intern" or "trainee" status. In Reich v. Shiloh True Light Church of Christ, 1996 WL 228802 (4th Cir. 1996) (unpublished), a church created the Shiloh Vocational Training Program (SVTP) to engage children in work in the church's residential construction operations. At first the SVTP paid the children, clearly treating them as construction employees. However, after a first Department of Labor citation for illegal child labor, the SVTP reconfigured its relationship with the children to treat them as trainees. Under the new arrangement, children under 16 no longer received "wages." Instead, SVTP occasionally paid the children lump sum "gifts. SVTP also granted young children "imaginary" wages or credits for work done. SVTP used a child's accumulated "imaginary wages" to determine the child's beginning "wage" rate when the child turned 16. SVTP did not "charge" its customers for the value of labor performed by unpaid children. However, it did encourage customers to make a donation to the church in an amount based on the unpaid children's labor. The Department of Labor initiated a second set of proceedings against the SVTP for child labor violations. The SVTP's principal defense was that the children were students, trainees or perhaps volunteers for the church in construction work. However, the SVTP's various work inducements such as gifts and work credits were inconsistent with volunteer status. Nor was the arrangement consistent with training or instruction. The record showed that children receiving imaginary wages were simply performing the same work performed by older wage-earning employees. Finally, while the children may have benefited from the work experience, the primary beneficiary of their work was the SVTP. Thus, the SVTP's use of children to perform labor was illegal per se with respect to some children, and the SVTP owed back pay for minimum wage violations for all unpaid children.

NOTES AND QUESTIONS

1. Much illegal child labor would not take place but for the demands, encouragement or condonation of parents. *See, e.g.*, Doty v. Dep't of Labor and Indus. of State, 185 Wash. App. 1057 (2015) (father unlawfully employed his children in hazardous construction work and allowed them to operate hazardous equipment with no supervision). *See also* Steven Greenhouse, *Take Daughters to Work? Union Offers Another Idea*, N.Y. Times, Apr. 23, 1997, at B3 (describing the common practice of garment workers in bringing their children to work and relying on their children for help in the work). For many of these low-paid workers,

there may be few if any alternatives to this practice if there is no suitable day care for the children. If the employer knows a child is helping her parent and that the parent's "piece rate" earnings are augmented by the child's labor, is the employer violating child labor laws or minimum wage laws?

Child labor laws do not address a *parent*'s responsibility for the illegal employment of her children, except when the parent is the employer. Even then, federal child labor laws grant parents a special exemption to employ their own children in non-hazardous work under circumstances when employment by others would be illegal. *See* 29 U.S.C. § 203(l); 29 C.F.R. § 570.32. However, a parent's responsibility as a parent in employing her own children or permitting them to work for others might be addressed under laws regarding child abuse or neglect. *See, e.g.*, Interests of Sarah, 1998 WL 531826 (Conn. Super. 1998) (unpublished) (proceedings for termination of parent-child relationship triggered in part by law officers' discovery that parents used young children to help them deliver newspapers beginning as early as 3 a.m.).

2. Could an employer avoid a violation of child labor laws by hiring children as independent contractors? The Fair Labor Standards Act defines "employ" as to "suffer or permit to work." 29 U.S.C. § 203(g). In Nationwide Mut. Ins. Co. v. Darden, 503 U.S. 318 (1992), the Supreme Court observed that this definition had its origin in early state child labor statutes, and encompassed more than the common relation of employer/employee. Thus, the Court suggested that the FLSA is one federal employment law that extends its coverage beyond the common law test of employee status. 503 U.S. at 326. *See also* Clark v. Arkansas Democrat Co., 413 S.W.2d 629 (Ark. 1967) (state child labor law applied to employment as independent contractor); Northwest Advancement, Inc. v. Bureau of Labor, 772 P.2d 934 (Or. App. 1989) (children engaged in door-to-door sales were employees within meaning of state and federal law).

3. If a child is illegally employed and suffers a workplace injury, a court might regard the child as a covered "employee" for purposes of workers' compensation law, or it might find he is a nonemployee, beyond the coverage of workers' compensation law. In Lemmerman v. A.T. Williams Oil Co., 350 S.E.2d 83 (N.C. 1986), the court held that the child was an employee under workers' compensation law. This result allows the child to collect workers' compensation benefits without proof of employer negligence, and regardless of the child's contributory negligence. On the other hand, the benefits provided by workers' compensation are limited, and workers' compensation law bars an employee from seeking a more generous award of damages in a common law negligence action against the employer. *See* Chapter 5. An alternative approach is illustrated by Whitney-Fidalgo Seafoods, Inc. v. Beukers, 554 P.2d 250 (Alaska 1976), where the court held that an illegally employed child has an option of choosing workers' compensation benefits or a common law remedy. The court also held that the child's earlier receipt of workers' compensation benefits was not proof of his conscious election between remedies. *See also* Ewert v. Georgia Casualty & Surety Co., 548 So. 2d 358 (La. App. 1989).

Which approach is more appropriate? Should it matter whether the employer knew it was employing a minor or knew it had violated the child labor laws? What if the employer lawfully employed a child of age to perform nonhazardous work during restricted hours, but the child was injured when he exceeded his usual hours or performed an unlawfully hazardous task? *See* Dugan ex rel. Dugan v. Gen'l Servs. Co., 799 So. 2d 760 (La. App. 2001) (parent's negligence action against child's employer barred by the exclusive remedy of workers' compensation; child legally employed but was performing illegal work at time of accident).

4. If a child or his representatives or survivors are allowed to sue the employer for common law negligence, should the employer be permitted to assert the common law defense of contributory negligence? *See, e.g.*, Pitzer v. M.D. Tomkies & Sons, 67 S.E.2d 437 (W.Va. 1951) (defense of contributory negligence not available against unlawfully employed child). What of the parents' contributory negligence in consenting to the child's illegal labor? *See* Strain v. Christians, 438 N.W.2d 783 (S.D. 1992) (parents not barred from recovering in wrongful death action against deceased child's employer).

Exemptions and the Lawfully Employed Child

Federal child labor law allows plenty of opportunity for lawful child labor, especially for children over the age of 16, who may work in any occupation not deemed hazardous by the Department of Labor. But employment of younger children may also be lawful in some circumstances. One of the most important exemptions from the child labor laws is for parents, who may lawfully employ their own children at any age, except in mining, manufacturing, or other designated "hazardous" occupations. 29 U.S.C. § 203(l); 29 C.F.R. § 570.32. Another set of exemptions applies to agricultural labor in particular. 29 U.S.C. § 213(c). For example, the Secretary of Labor may grant an employer's application to waive the prohibition against child labor with respect to children as young as 10 years of age employed in harvesting work under certain circumstances. 29 C.F.R. § 575.1. *See generally* D. Curtiss, *The Fair Labor Standards Act and Child Labor in Agriculture*, 20 J. Corp. L. 303 (1995).

If the continued existence of these exemptions is based on a belief in the comparative safety or healthfulness of farming or family business, data collected by the Department of Labor raise some important questions. According to a recent report, "youths aged 15 to 17 who have jobs in agriculture had a risk of a fatality that was more than 4.4 times as great as the average worker aged 15 to 17." Department of Labor, Bureau of Statistics, *Report on the Youth Labor Force* 58 (2000). The same report observed that "youths who were self-employed or working in a family business had a risk of an occupational fatality that was at least 4 times as great as that of other youths, regardless of industry." *Id.* If the family farm or family business is not, in fact, comparatively safe or wholesome, what reasons might explain the persistence of these exemptions?

Some state child labor laws establish their own standards for determining what child labor is permitted. *See* Prince v. Commonwealth of Massachusetts, 321 U.S. 158 (1944) (upholding conviction of parent for furnishing magazines to her child, knowing he would sell them on the street). But many state laws merely adopt the same exemptions and rules of coverage as the Fair Labor Standards Act. *See, e.g.*, 40 Tex. Admin. Code §§ 817.4 to 817.7. For a more thorough examination of the persistence and potential harm of lawful child labor in the U.S., *see* Seymour

Moskowitz, *Malignant Indifference: The Wages of Contemporary Child Labor in the United States*, 57 Okla. L. Rev. 465 (2004).

The legal status of lawfully employed children differs from that of lawfully employed adults in at least one important way: They are still minors whose contracts might be voidable on grounds of incapacity. *See* RESTATEMENT (SECOND) OF CONTRACTS § 14. In the past, the right to disaffirm an employment contract was of little practical significance; children rarely made the sort of promises an employer might enforce against an adult worker. *But see* Career Placement of White Plains, Inc. v. Vaus, 354 N.Y.S.2d 764 (N.Y. Sup. Ct. 1974) (applying the "salutory" rule favoring enforcement or a restrictive covenant against a minor, because "infants would not be employed in businesses having trade secrets and their ilk unless employers were permitted to bind infants to restrictive covenants as security for their endeavors"). *See also* Scott Eden Mgmt. v. Kavovit, 563 N.Y.S.2d 1001 (N.Y. Sup. Ct. 1990) (granting agent's right to commissions based on child's earnings, to prevent unjust enrichment).

The question of a minor's right to disaffirm has gained importance recently because of employer demands for employee promises to submit disputes to arbitration. *Compare* Traylor, 56 Cal.Rptr.3d 140 (Cal. App. 2007), *and* In re Mexican Restaurants, Inc., 2004 WL 2850151 (Tex. App. 2004) (minors could disaffirm their agreements to arbitrate claims), *with* Berg v. Douglass v. Pflueger Hawaii, Inc.,135 P.3d 129 (Haw. 2006) *and* Sheller by Sheller v. Frank's Nursery & Crafts, Inc., 957 F. Supp. 150 (N.D.Ill.1997) (laws permitting employment of minors implicitly authorize their agreements to arbitrate claims). *See also* Cross v. Carnes, 724 N.E.2d 828 (Ohio App. 1998), (parent had authority to consent to arbitration agreement with respect to child's employment).

The International Child Labor Problem

Not surprisingly, unhealthful child labor of the sort that would clearly violate U.S. law is much more common in poorer nations. The International Labor Organization's Bureau of Statistics estimates that at least 144 million children younger than 14 are employed throughout the world. International Labour Organization, Global Child Labor Trends 2008 to 2012, p. x (2013). Many of these and older children are employed in very dangerous work. The ILO estimates that more than 85 million children below the age of 18 are employed in hazardous activities of the sort that would violate U.S. labor standards. Id. at 12.

Oppressive child labor is a blight on the future of affected children and the nations in which they work. To the extent that child labor occurs in lieu of education, a child's current earnings come at a substantial cost to the long-term productivity of the individual child, his family, and the nation. International Labor Affairs Bureau, Dep't of Labor, *An Economic Consideration of Child Labor*, By the Sweat and Toil of Children, vol. 6, ch. II (2000). Moreover, many children in developing nations are enslaved in criminal enterprises such as prostitution or the distribution of illegal drugs, where they are exposed to death, serious injury, or illness at an early age. Even lawful work that might not be unreasonably dangerous for adults can be quite hazardous for children, who tend to be more accident-prone, and who are more sensitive to the effects of labor and an industrial environment.

Children are also particularly susceptible to physical, sexual, and emotional abuse at the hands of their employers. The result for working children is a very significant and well-documented exposure to life-long serious health problems. For good reason, the ILO describes oppressive child labor as "the single most important source of child exploitation and child abuse in the world today." ILO Report at p. 5.

Oppressive child labor has a supply side and a demand side. On the supply side, desperate poverty is certainly a strong motivation for many families who require or permit their children to work. Indeed, in some parts of the world it is not unusual for families to accept a loan or advance payment for their children's labor, and to deliver their children, bonded in servitude to the employer. ILO Report at p. 13. But why might an employer prefer child labor when there is an abundance of relatively cheap, unemployed adult labor in developing nations? First, children generally work for lower wages than adults, although part of the difference in wage rates is offset by the fact that children are generally less capable and efficient than adults. International Labor Affairs Bureau, Dep't of Labor, *An Economic Consideration of Child Labor*, By the Sweat and Toil of Children, vol. 6, ch. III, pt. D (2000). Second, and possibly more important in the long run, children are more easily managed than adults.

> Children are often described as more compliant than adults in the workplace. They are less likely to complain about poor working conditions or to organize to improve them. Insomuch as this reduces an employer's expenditure on workplace conditions, employment of children may be less costly. This argument suggests that even if children are equally productive, children will be paid less than adults. Another factor worth consideration is that absenteeism among child workers tends to be lower than among adults. These factors increase incentives for firms or employers to hire children, but they also demonstrate the inherent danger to children of being exploited....

Id.

Oppressive child labor is already illegal in nearly every nation. *See* Dep't of Labor 2002 Findings on the Worst Forms of Child Labor (2003), available at http://www.dol.gov/ILAB/media/reports/iclp/tda2002/overview.htm. Its persistence raises important questions about the efficacy of simple legislative reform in each nation.

International legal institutions have made limited progress in establishing or enforcing international labor standards. Considering the difficulty of finding a consensus on many employment standards even within the United States, it might come as no surprise that consensus is frequently unattainable in any forum that combines developed nations such as the United States with developing nations such as Bangladesh. Child labor, however, is one matter as to which consensus might seem possible. Article 32 of the United Nations Convention on the Rights of the Child declares a child's right to be "protected from economic exploitation and from performing any work that is likely to be hazardous or to interfere with the child's education, or to be harmful to the child's health or physical, mental, spiritual, moral or social development." 1577 U.N.T.S. 3, 54 (1989). A NAFTA side agreement, the North American Agreement on Labor Cooperation (NAALC), Can.-Mex.-U.S., 32 I.L.M. 1499 (1993), commits the United States, Canada, and Mexico to "promote" certain principles, including "the establishment of restrictions on the employment of children and young persons" to protect their safety, their physical and moral development, and their access to school. NAALC, Annex 1. However, neither the U.N. Convention nor the NAALC prescribes specific minimum standards, and the NAALC preserves each signatory's freedom to establish and enforce its own standards as national law. NAALC, Art. 3.

More specific child labor standards are included in two widely ratified conventions of the International Labor Organization. *See Convention Concerning Minimum Age for Admission to Employment*, ILO Convention 138, ILO Gen. Conf., 58th Sess., preamble (1973); Convention No. 182, *Prohibition and Immediate Action for the Elimination of the Worst Forms of Child Labor*, 38 I.L.M. 1207 (1999). Convention 138, art. 2, the more specific of the two conventions, establishes a minimum employment age of 15 (or older, depending on each nation's compulsory schooling laws), but it also allows a nation to reduce its age limit to 14 years if its "economy and educational facilities are insufficiently developed." Convention 182 addresses the "worst forms" of child labor, including "hazardous" employment as determined by each nation in consultation with employer and worker organizations.

The United States unilaterally projects its own child labor laws across international borders in at least two ways. First, U.S. law prohibits the importation of goods made by "forced or indentured child labor." 19 U.S.C. § 1307. Second, Executive Order 13126 (June 12, 1999) requires federal contractors to take certain steps to assure that the goods they supply the federal government are not made from "forced or indentured child labor." These two measures are quite limited in scope. They do not address many of the worst forms of child labor unless a child's labor was involuntary and "exacted . . . under the menace of any penalty for its nonperformance," or "performed . . . pursuant to a contract the enforcement of which can be accomplished by process or penalties." E.O. 13126, § 6. In other words, neither the statute nor the executive order would bar goods made by a child of any age, no matter how hazardous the work, if the laboring child was free to resign at will under the home nation's law, and if his resignation was not prevented by "menace of penalty."[1] Moreover, enforcement of the law depends to some extent on the executive branch's ability and willingness to identify goods made from proscribed labor. Diplomacy, limited investigatory resources, and the practical difficulties of investigating labor practices overseas have greatly limited the U.S. government's accomplishments in identifying suspect goods. However, as of 2016, the Bureau of International Labor Affairs of the Department of Labor has compiled a long list of products ranging from cocoa to pornography made by child labor in about in 75 nations around the world. Bureau of International Labor Affairs, Dep't of Labor, List of Goods Produced by Child Labor or Forced Labor (2016), at https://www.dol.gov/sites/default/files/documents/ilab/reports/child-labor/findings/TVPRA_Report2016.pdf. *See also* Sarah H. Cleveland, *Norm Internationalization and U.S. Economic Sanctions*, 26 Yale J. Intl. L. 1 (2001).

U.S. child labor standards are also projected abroad by private initiative. The Apparel Industry Partnership is one private industry association that has

[1] In addition, Executive Order 13126 exempts contracts subject to certain nondiscrimination in procurement provisions of other international laws and treaties.

promulgated a workplace code of conduct which, among other things, prohibits the employment of children under the age of 15. Participation in the partnership is voluntary. *See* Robert Liubicic, *Corporate Codes of Conduct and Product Labeling Schemes: The Limits and Possibilities of Promoting International Labor Rights Through Private Initiatives*, 30 Law & Pol'y Int'l Bus. 111 (1998). Violation of the code is not subject to any formal sanction, other than expulsion from or denial of membership in the partnership. A more important informal sanction is the possibility of a consumer boycott of suspect goods. *See also* Kasky v. Nike, Inc., 27 Cal. 4th 939, 45 P.3d 243, 119 Cal. Rptr. 2d 296 (2002) (remanding for further proceedings a private attorney general action against Nike, Inc. for alleged misrepresentations to the public regarding labor practices in overseas factories); International Labor Affairs Bureau, Dep't of Labor, By the Sweat and Toil of Children, vols. III (1996), IV (1997), at http://www.dol.gov/ILAB/media/reports/iclp/main.htm.

Some U.S. corporations have included labor standards in contracts with overseas suppliers. In Doe v. Wal-Mart, 572 F.3d 677 (9th Cir. 2009), the court rejected an argument of a foreign supplier's workers that they were third-party beneficiaries of the supplier's labor standards duties in its contracts with Wal-Mart. The court also held that Wal-Mart's contractual *right* to inspect the supplier's operations was not a *duty* to inspect.

2. *Aliens*

For the first century after U.S. independence, immigration to the U.S. was without restriction. Persons became lawful residents simply by entering the country by whatever means they could. There was no "illegal" immigration. U.S. law did not restrict the entry of aliens seeking residence until 1882 when Congress enacted the Chinese Exclusion Act, an overtly racist law that excluded only Chinese from immigrating to the U.S. 22 Stat. 58 (1882) (repealed in 1943). From that point forward Congress regularly added or removed various qualifications for immigration and lawful residence, such as certain political or health requirements. A system of quotas limiting the number of immigrants by nation of origin (usually based on the estimated ethnic composition of the U.S. in particular census years) began with the Emergency Quota Act of 1921. 42 Stat. 5 (1921).

Enforcement authorities were only partly effective in preventing unauthorized immigration. Hope of employment or shelter from oppressive conditions has been a strong magnet for immigration even for those who do not qualify to immigrate legally. Moreover, until 1986, an employer was not required to verify the immigration status of its workers, and an employer did not violate the law by knowingly hiring unauthorized immigration status. This state of the law changed significantly with enactment of the Immigration Reform and Control Act of 1986.

COLLINS FOOD INT'L, INC. v. IMMIGRATION AND NATURALIZATION SERVICE

948 F.2d 549 (9th Cir. 1991)

CANBY, Circuit Judge:

Collins Foods International ["Sizzler"] appeals from the decision of an

Administrative Law Judge (ALJ) holding Collins Foods subject to a civil penalty for hiring an alien, knowing him to be unauthorized to work in the United States, in violation of 8 U.S.C. § 1324a(a)(1)(A).[3] The ALJ found that Collins Foods had constructive knowledge of the alien's status, and that this constructive knowledge was sufficient to establish the knowledge element of section 1324a(a)(1).

We reverse.

Ricardo Soto Gomez (Soto), an employee at a Phoenix Sizzler Restaurant, is authorized to hire other Sizzler employees for that location. Soto extended a job offer to Armando Rodriguez in a long-distance telephone conversation; Soto was in Phoenix and Rodriguez was in California. Rodriguez said nothing in the telephone conversation to indicate that he was not authorized to work in the United States. Rodriguez was working for Sizzler in California at the time Soto extended the offer of employment in Phoenix.

When Rodriguez came to Phoenix, he reported to Sizzler for work. Before allowing Rodriguez to begin work, Soto asked Rodriguez for evidence of his authorization to work in the United States. Rodriguez informed Soto that he did not have the necessary identification with him. At that point, Soto did not let Rodriguez begin work, but sent him away with the understanding that he would return with his qualifying documents.

Rodriguez returned with a driver's license and what appeared to be a Social Security card. Soto looked at the face of the documents and copied information from them onto a Form I-9.[4] Soto did not look at the back of the Social Security card, nor did he compare it with the example in the INS handbook. After Soto completed the necessary paperwork, Rodriguez began work at the Sizzler in Phoenix. Rodriguez, it turned out, was an alien not authorized to work in the United States, and his "Social Security card" was a forgery.

The INS charged Collins Foods with one count of hiring an alien, knowing him to be unauthorized to work in the United States, in violation of 8 U.S.C. § 1324a(a)(1)(A). Upon receiving INS' Notice of Intent to Fine, Collins Foods requested a hearing. Inasmuch as it was uncontroverted that Rodriguez was unauthorized to work in the United States, the only issue to be decided at the hearing was whether Collins Foods knew that Rodriguez was unauthorized at the time of hire. The ALJ declined to decide that Collins Foods had actual knowledge of the fact that Rodriguez was an illegal alien, but decided instead that it had "constructive knowledge." The ALJ based his "constructive knowledge" conclusion on two facts: first, that Soto offered the job to Rodriguez over the telephone without having seen Rodriguez' documentation; and, second, that Soto failed to compare the back of the Social Security card with the example in the INS manual.[7] While we do not disturb the factual determinations made by the ALJ, we

---

[3] Section 1324a(a)(1) provides:

It is unlawful for a person or other entity —

(A) to hire . . . for employment in the United States an alien knowing the alien is an unauthorized alien . . . with respect to such employment. . . .

[4] A Form I-9 is an INS Employment Eligibility Verification Form.

[7] The ALJ determined that a look at the back of the Social Security card would not necessarily have revealed its lack of authenticity, but that a comparison of the language on the back of the

hold that these two facts cannot, as a matter of law, establish constructive knowledge under 8 U.S.C. § 1324a(a)(1)(A).

I. Job Offer Prior to Verification of Documents

The first of these facts, as a matter of law, cannot support a finding of constructive knowledge. Nothing in the statute prohibits the offering of a job prior to checking the documents; indeed, the regulations contemplate just such a course of action.

The statute that Collins Foods is charged with violating prohibits "a person or other entity [from] hir[ing] for employment" an alien not authorized to work. 8 U.S.C. § 1324a(a)(1)(A). The Regulations define "hiring" as "the actual commencement of employment of an employee for wages or other remuneration." 8 C.F.R. § 274a.1(c). As Rodriguez had not commenced employment for wages at the time Soto extended a job offer to him over the telephone, Rodriguez was not yet "hired" for purposes of section 1324a. Soto was therefore not required to verify Rodriguez' documentation at that time.

Another regulation addresses the issue of the timeliness of verification, and it suggests the same result. Under 8 C.F.R. § 274a.2(b)(ii), employers are required to examine an employee's documentation and complete Form I-9 "within three business days of the hire."[8] Because Soto had examined Rodriguez' documents and completed the necessary paperwork by the time Rodriguez began work for wages, Soto was not delinquent in verifying Rodriguez' documentation.

There are additional, highly cogent reasons for rejecting the ALJ's reliance on the fact that Soto "told Rodriguez he would be hired long before Soto ever saw, or had any opportunity to verify, any evidence of Rodriguez' work authorization." To hold such a failure of early verification against the employer, as the ALJ did, places the employer in an impossible position. Pre-employment questioning concerning the applicant's national origin, race or citizenship exposes the employer to charges of discrimination if he does not hire that applicant. The Equal Employment Opportunity Commission has held that pre-employment inquiries concerning a job applicant's race, color, religion, national origin, or citizenship status "may constitute evidence of discrimination prohibited by Title VII." EEOC, Pre-Employment Inquiries (1981), reprinted in 2 Employment Practices Guide ¶4120, 4163 (CCH 1985). An employer who makes such inquiries will have the burden of proving that the answers to such inquiries "are not used in making hiring and placement decisions in a discriminatory manner prohibited by law." *Id.* ¶4120 at 4166. For that reason, employers attempting to comply with the Immigration

---

card to that on the back of the example in the INS handbook would have. The ALJ stated:

> At a glance, the face of the card might not necessarily appear to be false. Both the genuine and the false card have large letters reading "SOCIAL SECURITY" across the top. . . . Had Soto taken the time to make a comparison, he would have found that the printing on the reverse side of the card did not contain all of the language found on the Social Security card example provided in the INS Handbook. He further would have found that every Social Security card is considered void if laminated.

[8] In the Supplementary Information to the regulations, INS states that "the Service wishes to stress that verification may be completed either at the time of an individual's acceptance of an offer of employment or at the time employment actually commences." 52 Fed. Reg. 16216, 16218 (May 1, 1987).

Reform and Control Act of 1986 ("IRCA"), are well advised not to examine documents until after an offer of employment is made. . . .

The ultimate danger, of course, is that many employers, faced with conflicting commands from the EEOC and the INS, would simply avoid interviewing any applicant whose appearance suggests alienage. The resulting discrimination against citizens and authorized aliens would frustrate the intent of Congress embodied in both Title VII of the Civil Rights Act of 1964, 42 U.S.C. § 2000e et seq., and the 1986 Immigration Reform Act itself. We discuss below some of the legislative history of the latter Act. The legislative history cannot be squared with the ruling of the ALJ regarding Soto's telephone offer of employment to Rodriguez.

Soto complied with the statute and regulations, and followed the course of action recommended by the EEOC, in waiting until the day Rodriguez began work to verify Rodriguez' authorization to work and to complete the Form I-9. Soto's offer of employment prior to that verification cannot serve to establish that Collins Foods had constructive knowledge of Rodriguez' unauthorized work status.

II. Verification of Documents

The portion of the statute that Collins Foods allegedly violated prohibits the hiring of an alien while "knowing" the alien is not authorized to work. 8 U.S.C. § 1324a(a)(1)(A). The statute also prohibits the hiring of an individual without complying with the verification requirements outlined in the statute at section 1324a(b)(1)(A). 8 U.S.C. § 1324a(a)(1)(B)(i). These two actions, failing properly to verify an employee's work-authorization documents, and hiring an alien knowing him to be unauthorized to work, constitute separate offenses under the IRCA.[9] Nevertheless, the INS argues, and the ALJ held, that Collins Foods' failure to comply with the verification provisions of the statute establishes the knowledge element of subsection (a)(1)(A), hiring an alien knowing him to be unauthorized. We need not decide, however, whether a violation of the verification requirement establishes the knowledge element of section (a)(1)(A); Collins Foods complied with the verification requirement.[11]

The statute, at 8 U.S.C. § 1324a(b)(1)(A), provides that an employer will have satisfied its verification obligation by examining a document which "reasonably appears on its face to be genuine." Soto examined the face of both Rodriguez' false

[9] The two provisions under 8 U.S.C. § 1324a(1) are not completely distinct. The statute provides in section 1324a(a)(3) that a person who has complied in good faith with the verification requirements has established an affirmative defense to the violation contained in paragraph (a)(1)(A), knowingly hiring an unauthorized alien. The House Judiciary Committee Report states, however, that the affirmative defense of good faith raises only a rebuttable presumption. H.R. Rep. No. 99-682 (Part 1), 99 Cong. 2d Sess. 56-57 (1986). The presumption is rebutted if the INS can establish, inter alia, that the documents did not reasonably appear on their face to be genuine. *Id.* at 57.

[11] Although an employer may still be found in violation of subsection (a)(1)(A), knowingly hiring an unauthorized alien, when he has complied with the verification requirements, such a finding would require other evidence of the employer's knowledge. Here, however, the ALJ's constructive knowledge finding rested on a factual finding that Collins' verification was inadequate.

Social Security card[12] and his genuine driver's license,[13] but failed to detect that the Social Security card was invalid. But as the ALJ acknowledged, even though Rodriguez was spelled "Rodriquez" on the front of the social security card, at a glance the card on its face did not appear to be false.

Although the verification requirement of the statute requires only that the document "reasonably appear[] on its face to be genuine," *id.*, the ALJ held that Collins Foods did not satisfy its verification obligation because Soto did not compare the back of Rodriguez' social security card with the example in the INS handbook. We can find nothing in the statute that requires such a comparison. Moreover, even if Soto had compared the card with the example, he still may not have been able to discern that the card was not genuine. The handbook contains but one example of a Social Security card, when numerous versions exist.[14] The card Rodriguez presented was not so different from the example that it necessarily would have alerted a reasonable person to its falsity.[15] Collins Foods, through its employee Soto, did all that it was required to do by statute to satisfy its verification obligation.

Moreover, the legislative history of section 1324a indicates that Congress intended to minimize the burden and the risk placed on the employer in the verification process. The Judiciary Committee Report on the statute shows that Congress did not intend the statute to cause employers to become experts in identifying and examining a prospective employee's employment authorization documents. The Judiciary Committee Report states that "[i]t is not expected that employers ascertain the legitimacy of documents presented during the verification process." H.R. Rep. No. 99-682 (Part 1), 99 Cong. 2d Sess. 61 (1986). The Report goes on to say that "[t]he 'reasonable man' standard is to be used in implementing this provision and the Committee wishes to emphasize that documents that reasonably appear to be genuine should be accepted by employers without requiring further investigation of those documents." *Id.* at 62. The primary enforcement threat in the legislation is directed at the unauthorized alien presenting the false documentation; the statute provides criminal penalties against that party. *Id.*

Congress carefully crafted section 1324a to limit the burden and the risk placed on employers. The ALJ's holding in this case places on employers a verification obligation greater than that intended by Congress and beyond that outlined in the narrowly-drawn statute. In addition, the ALJ's holding extends the

---

[12] The statute includes social security cards in its list of documents that "evidenc[e] employment authorization." 8 U.S.C. § 1324a(b)(1)(C)(i).

[13] The statute lists a driver's license as a document that "establish[es] identity of individual." 8 U.S.C. § 1324a(b)(1)(D)(i).

[14] In fact, there are 16 valid versions of the Social Security card currently in circulation. General Accounting Office, Immigration Control: A New Role for the Social Security Card, 11, 15 (Mar. 1988). The GAO points to this failure to include all versions of acceptable documents to substantiate its finding that employers are not in a position to verify documents, and the GAO specifically notes the inadequacy of the Handbook's "information on the characteristics or security features of acceptable documents." *Id.* at 14, 15. To require a match of a document with the example included in the Handbook would result in employers excluding many individuals authorized to work.

[15] Also unpersuasive is the ALJ's comment that Soto should have known the Social Security card was not genuine because it was laminated. The information that Social Security cards are invalid if laminated is rather obscurely presented: it is found on the reverse side of the example in the INS handbook.

constructive knowledge doctrine far beyond its permissible application in IRCA employer sanction cases. IRCA, as we have pointed out, is delicately balanced to serve the goal of preventing unauthorized alien employment while avoiding discrimination against citizens and authorized aliens. The doctrine of constructive knowledge has great potential to upset that balance, and it should not be expansively applied. The statute prohibits the hiring of an alien "*knowing* the alien is an unauthorized alien . . . with respect to such employment." 8 U.S.C. § 1324a(a)(1)(A) (emphasis added). Insofar as that prohibition refers to actual knowledge, as it appears to on its face, any employer can avoid the prohibited conduct with reasonable ease. When the scope of liability is expanded by the doctrine of constructive knowledge, the employer is subject to penalties for a range of undefined acts that may result in knowledge being imputed to him. To guard against unknowing violations, the employer may, again, avoid hiring anyone with an appearance of alienage. To preserve Congress' intent in passing the employer sanctions provisions of IRCA, then, the doctrine of constructive knowledge must be sparingly applied.

Indeed, the only federal cases we have found that have allowed constructive knowledge to satisfy the knowledge element of section 1324a(a)(1)(A) are two recent decisions of this court. A comparison of those cases with the one before us illustrates why constructive knowledge cannot be found here. In Mester Mfg. Co. v. INS, 879 F.2d 561 (9th Cir. 1989), the INS had visited the employer's plant and obtained a list of employees. It then notified the employer that certain employees were suspected unlawful aliens, and if their green cards matched the numbers listed in the INS' letter to the employer, then they were using false cards or cards belonging to someone else. The employer did not take any corrective action, and continued to employ the unlawful aliens. We found constructive knowledge.

New El Rey Sausage Co. v. INS, 925 F.2d 1153 (9th Cir. 1991), is essentially the same case. The INS visited the employer to inspect paperwork. After running checks on the alien registration numbers of the workers, the INS found several using improper or borrowed numbers. The INS then hand-delivered a letter to the employer reciting the results of its investigation and saying: "Unless these individuals can provide valid employment authorization from the United States Immigration and Naturalization Service, they are to be considered unauthorized aliens, and are therefore not authorized to be employed in the United States. Their continued employment could result in fine proceedings. . . ." *Id.* at 1155. The employer simply accepted the word of the aliens as to their legal status, and continued to employ them. We found constructive knowledge.

These cases lead us to conclude that a finding of constructive knowledge under the hiring violation statute requires more than the ALJ found to exist here. Failure to compare the back of a Social Security card with the example in the INS handbook, when neither statute nor regulation requires the employer to do so, falls far short of the "willful blindness" found in *Mester* and *New El Rey Sausage*.[17] To expand the

[17] Both *Mester* and *New El Rey Sausage* relied on United States v. Jewell, 532 F.2d 697, 698 (9th Cir.), *cert. denied*, 426 U.S. 951 (1976), for its application of the constructive knowledge standard. In *Jewell*, the constructive knowledge finding was based upon "a mental state in which the defendant is aware that the fact in question is highly probable but consciously avoids enlightenment," *id.* at 704, or the defendant evidenced willful blindness.

concept of constructive knowledge to encompass this case would not serve the intent of Congress, and is certainly not required by the terms of ICRA.

CONCLUSION

Collins Foods did not have the kind of positive information that the INS had provided in *Mester* and *New El Rey Sausage* to support a finding of constructive knowledge. Neither the failure to verify documentation before offering employment, nor the failure to compare the back of the applicant's Social Security card with the example in the INS manual, justifies such a finding. There is no support in the employer sanctions provisions of IRCA or in their legislative history to charge Collins Foods, on the basis of the facts relied on by the ALJ here, with constructive knowledge of Rodriguez' unauthorized status. Accordingly, we reverse.

NOTES AND QUESTIONS

1. Note that an employer must verify the status of *every* new employee under IRCA, without regard to the employer's certainty that an individual is a resident, citizen, or otherwise authorized to work. Failing to follow the verification procedure for applicants the employer believes are certainly authorized would fail to satisfy the absolute verification requirements of 8 U.S.C. § 1324a(b). Moreover, the employer's selective verification might also violate prohibitions against discrimination on the basis of national origin or citizenship. *See* 8 U.S.C. § 1324b; 42 U.S.C. § 2000e-2.

2. If an employer is not necessarily liable for accepting an employee's forged documents, what other facts might prove an employer's "constructive knowledge" of an employee's unauthorized status? In considering this question, remember that an employer must not violate the prohibitions against national origin or citizenship discrimination.

Arguably, one way an employer might gain constructive knowledge of a worker's unauthorized status is by its receipt of a so-called "no-match" letter from the Social Security Administration (SSA), indicating that the worker's name does not match the social security number transmitted by the employer in connection with the payment of income and payroll taxes. *See* Anica v. Wal Mart Stores, Inc., 119 Wash. App. 1072 (Wash. App. 2004) (employer's receipt of such a notice was a lawful and nondiscriminatory reason for its decision to discharge the plaintiff).

The effect of an employer's receipt of a no-match letter is not as straightforward as it might seem. A no-match letter is issued by the SSA, but the laws prohibiting employment of unauthorized aliens are enforced mainly by a separate agency, currently the Department of Homeland Security (DHS). A third agency, the Immigrant and Employee Rights Section (IERS) of the Department of Justice, investigates national origin or citizenship discrimination including discrimination that is the result of overreaction to a no-match notice. Over the years these three agencies have struggled to coordinate their policies and to provide clear and consistent guidance to employers. The most controversial question has been whether these agencies should specifically advise an employer that a no-match constitutes constructive notice that continued employment of a worker is unauthorized. Such a warning is controversial because of the risk that it may precipitate hasty or discriminatory action by employers.

A no-match is not necessarily because of a worker's unauthorized status. The worker's failure to report a name change, or a typographical error by the worker, employer or government officials are common causes of a no-match. Nevertheless, the SSA began to include a warning of possible unauthorized employment in its no-match letters in 2007. About the same time, the DHS issued regulations stating that a no-match letter could constitute constructive notice of a worker's unauthorized status, exposing the employer to sanctions if it continued the worker's employment. 72 Fed. Reg. at 45611, 45623-24 (August 15, 2007). But the SSA's no-match letter and the DHS's regulations did not require or advise a worker's immediate termination. Instead, they advised the employer to check its own records for errors, and to grant a worker up to 90 days to resolve the discrepancy with the SSA. Nevertheless, a U.S. district court quickly enjoined the new regulations in American Federation of Labor v. Chertoff, 552 F. Supp. 2d 999, 1002 (N.D. Cal. 2007). A principal basis for that decision was that significant errors in the SSA matching system and delays in the process for curing errors would cause hardship for many workers wrongly implied to be unauthorized.

While the "no-match" letter rules were on hold, the DHS refined and expanded its own procedure — E-Verify — for assisting employers in verifying employment authorization. E-Verify is DHS's internet-based process for quickly comparing a worker's I-9 information with SSA and immigration data. Federal contractors are required to use E-Verify at the hiring stage, but E-Verify remains voluntary for all other employers. 48 C.F.R. § 22.1802. An employer who chooses not to access the DHS's E-Verify system might still receive a no-match letter from the SSA, and in April 2011 the SSA resumed its warning about possible unauthorized employment status of workers whose names do not match their SS numbers. Thus, employers must still confront the issue whether a no-match constitutes "constructive notice" of unauthorized employment, regardless of whether notice comes from the DHS or the SSA.

The current approach of the DHS, SSA and IERS is designed to better protect workers from hasty employer action, discourage discrimination, and account for the sometimes lengthy process required to correct a worker's official records. The IERS, for example, advises employers to recognize that a no-match might be the result of an administrative error, and to follow the same procedure regardless of a worker's national origin or citizenship. The IERS also states that an employer may continue the employment and should allow the worker a "reasonable time" (up to 120 days, not the SSA's old 90 day time limit) to cure an error in official records. Firing a worker without allowing this opportunity to cure may constitute unlawful discrimination, especially if a worker's actual or perceived national origin or citizenship are factors. Department of Justice, Office of Special Counsel for Immigration Related Unfair Employment Practices, *Frequently Asked Questions About Name/Social Security Number "No Matches,"* http://www.justice.gov/crt/about/osc/pdf/publications/SSA/FAQs.pdf (last visited on December 21, 2011).

3. A few states have now adopted employment authorization laws of their own. For example, Arizona enacted a law requiring all employers to use E-Verify and providing for revocation of an employer's business license for knowingly

employing an authorized worker. In Chamber of Commerce of the U.S. v. Whiting, 563 U.S. 582 (2011), the Supreme Court rejected the Chamber of Commerce's argument that the federal law preempted the Arizona statute.

4. Does an employer owe any duty to *accept* an applicant's valid documentation of status? *See* Burgess v. Jaramillo, 914 S.W.2d 246 (Tex. App. 1996) (county human resources director was protected by official immunity from defamation claim based on rejection of plaintiff applicant's alien registration card). IRCA and other laws prohibit discrimination on the basis of national origin and citizenship. Thus, an employer who rejects an applicant's documentation might be unlawfully discriminating, if it would have accepted the documentation but for the applicant's real or perceived national origin or citizenship.

5. Could an employer obtain the benefit of an unauthorized alien's services without violating the law by hiring the alien as an independent contractor? *See* 8 U.S.C. § 1324a(a)(4).

6. Despite the Immigration Reform and Control Act, unauthorized workers still constitute a significant if immeasurable part of the U.S. workforce. As of 2016, the estimated number of unauthorized immigrants living in the U.S. was over 11 million. As of 2014, the estimated number of unauthorized immigrant workers was about 8 million. Pew Research Center, 5 Facts About Illegal Immigration in the U.S., online at http://www.pewresearch.org/fact-tank/2017/04/27/5-facts-about-illegal-immigration-in-the-u-s/.

HOFFMAN PLASTIC COMPOUNDS, INC. v. NLRB

535 U.S. 137 (2002)

Chief Justice REHNQUIST delivered the opinion of the Court.

The National Labor Relations Board (Board) awarded backpay to an undocumented alien who has never been legally authorized to work in the United States. We hold that such relief is foreclosed by federal immigration policy, as expressed by Congress in the Immigration Reform and Control Act of 1986 (IRCA).

Petitioner Hoffman Plastic Compounds, Inc. (petitioner or Hoffman), custom-formulates chemical compounds for businesses that manufacture pharmaceutical, construction, and household products. In May 1988, petitioner hired Jose Castro to operate various blending machines that "mix and cook" the particular formulas per customer order. Before being hired for this position, Castro presented documents that appeared to verify his authorization to work in the United States. In December 1988, the United Rubber, Cork, Linoleum, and Plastic Workers of America, AFL-CIO, began a union organizing campaign at petitioner's production plant. Castro and several other employees supported the organizing campaign and distributed authorization cards to co-workers. In January 1989, Hoffman laid off Castro and other employees engaged in these organizing activities.

Three years later, in January 1992, respondent Board found that Hoffman unlawfully selected four employees, including Castro, for layoff "in order to rid itself of known union supporters" in violation of § 8(a)(3) of the National Labor Relations Act (NLRA).[1] To remedy this violation, the Board ordered that Hoffman

[1] Section 8(a)(3) of the NLRA prohibits discrimination "in regard to hire or tenure of

. . . offer reinstatement and backpay to the four affected employees. *Id.*, at 107-108. Hoffman entered into a stipulation with the Board's General Counsel and agreed to abide by the Board's order.

In June 1993, the parties proceeded to a compliance hearing before an Administrative Law Judge (ALJ) to determine the amount of backpay owed to each discriminatee. On the final day of the hearing, Castro testified that he was born in Mexico and that he had never been legally admitted to, or authorized to work in, the United States. He admitted gaining employment with Hoffman only after tendering a birth certificate belonging to a friend who was born in Texas. *Ibid.* He also admitted that he used this birth certificate to fraudulently obtain a California driver's license and a Social Security card, and to fraudulently obtain employment following his layoff by Hoffman. *Ibid.* Neither Castro nor the Board's General Counsel offered any evidence that Castro had applied or intended to apply for legal authorization to work in the United States. *Ibid.* Based on this testimony, the ALJ found the Board precluded from awarding Castro backpay or reinstatement as such relief would be contrary to Sure-Tan, Inc. v. NLRB, 467 U.S. 883 (1984), and in conflict with IRCA, which makes it unlawful for employers knowingly to hire undocumented workers or for employees to use fraudulent documents to establish employment eligibility. In September 1998, four years after the ALJ's decision, and seven years after Castro was fired, the Board reversed with respect to backpay . . . . [T]he Board determined that "the most effective way to accommodate and further the immigration policies embodied in [IRCA] is to provide the protections and remedies of the [NLRA] to undocumented workers in the same manner as to other employees." The Board thus found that Castro was entitled to $66,951 of backpay, plus interest. It calculated this backpay award from the date of Castro's termination to the date Hoffman first learned of Castro's undocumented status, a period of 3½ years.

Hoffman filed a petition for review of the Board's order in the Court of Appeals. A panel of the Court of Appeals denied the petition for review. After rehearing the case en banc, the court again denied the petition for review and enforced the Board's order. We granted certiorari, and now reverse.

This case exemplifies the principle that the Board's discretion to select and fashion remedies for violations of the NLRA, though generally broad, . . . is not unlimited. . . . [W]e have consistently set aside awards of reinstatement or backpay to employees found guilty of serious illegal conduct in connection with their employment. In *Fansteel*, the Board awarded reinstatement with backpay to employees who engaged in a "sit down strike" that led to confrontation with local law enforcement officials. We set aside the award, saying: "We are unable to conclude that Congress intended to compel employers to retain persons in their employ regardless of their unlawful conduct, to invest those who go on strike with an immunity from discharge for acts of trespass or violence against the employer's property, which they would not have enjoyed had they remained at work." 306 U.S., at 255.

Though we found that the employer had committed serious violations of the NLRA, the Board had no discretion to remedy those violations by awarding

---

employment or any term or condition of employment to encourage or discourage membership in any labor organization." 49 Stat. 452, as added, 61 Stat. 140, 29 U.S.C. § 158(a)(3).

reinstatement with backpay to employees who themselves had committed serious criminal acts. . . . [I]n *Southern S.S. Co., supra*, the Board awarded reinstatement with backpay to five employees whose strike on shipboard had amounted to a mutiny in violation of federal law. We set aside the award, saying: "It is sufficient for this case to observe that the Board has not been commissioned to effectuate the policies of the Labor Relations Act so single-mindedly that it may wholly ignore other and equally important [c]ongressional objectives." 316 U.S., at 47. . . .

Our decision in *Sure-Tan* followed this line of cases and set aside an award closely analogous to the award challenged here. There we confronted for the first time a potential conflict between the NLRA and federal immigration policy, as then expressed in the Immigration and Nationality Act (INA), 66 Stat. 163, as amended, 8 U.S.C. § 1101 et seq. Two companies had unlawfully reported alien-employees to the INS in retaliation for union activity. Rather than face INS sanction, the employees voluntarily departed to Mexico. The Board investigated and found the companies acted in violation of §§ 8(a)(1) and (3) of the NLRA. The Board's ensuing order directed the companies to reinstate the affected workers and pay them six months' backpay.

We affirmed the Board's determination that the NLRA applied to undocumented workers, reasoning that the immigration laws "as presently written" expressed only a "'peripheral concern' " with the employment of illegal aliens. 467 U.S., at 892 (quoting De Canas v. Bica, 424 U.S. 351, 360 (1976)). "For whatever reason," Congress had not "made it a separate criminal offense" for employers to hire an illegal alien, or for an illegal alien "to accept employment after entering this country illegally." *Sure-Tan, supra*, at 892-893. Therefore, we found "no reason to conclude that application of the NLRA to employment practices affecting such aliens would necessarily conflict with the terms of the INA." 467 U.S., at 893.

With respect to the Board's selection of remedies, however, we found its authority limited by federal immigration policy. *See id.*, at 903. . . . For example, the Board was prohibited from effectively rewarding a violation of the immigration laws by reinstating workers not authorized to reenter the United States. *Sure-Tan*, 467 U.S., at 903. Thus, to avoid "a potential conflict with the INA," the Board's reinstatement order had to be conditioned upon proof of "the employees' legal reentry." *Ibid.* "Similarly," with respect to backpay, we stated: "[T]he employees must be deemed 'unavailable' for work (and the accrual of backpay therefore tolled) during any period when they were not lawfully entitled to be present and employed in the United States." *Ibid.* "In light of the practical workings of the immigration laws," such remedial limitations were appropriate even if they led to "[t]he probable unavailability of the [NLRA's] more effective remedies." *Id.*, at 904. . . .

It is against this decisional background that we turn to the question presented here. The parties and the lower courts focus much of their attention on *Sure-Tan*, particularly its express limitation of backpay to aliens "lawfully entitled to be present and employed in the United States." 467 U.S., at 903. All agree that as a matter of plain language, this limitation forecloses the award of backpay to Castro. Castro was never lawfully entitled to be present or employed in the United States, and thus, under the plain language of *Sure-Tan*, he has no right to claim backpay.

The Board takes the view, however, that read in context, this limitation applies only to aliens who left the United States and thus cannot claim backpay without lawful reentry . . . . [W]e think the question presented here better analyzed through a wider lens, focused as it must be on a legal landscape now significantly changed.

The *Southern S.S. Co.* line of cases established that where the Board's chosen remedy trenches upon a federal statute or policy outside the Board's competence to administer, the Board's remedy may be required to yield. Whether or not this was the situation at the time of *Sure-Tan*, it is precisely the situation today. In 1986, two years after *Sure-Tan*, Congress enacted IRCA, a comprehensive scheme prohibiting the employment of illegal aliens in the United States. § 101(a)(1), 100 Stat. 3360, 8 U.S.C. § 1324a. As we have previously noted, IRCA "forcefully" made combating the employment of illegal aliens central to "[t]he policy of immigration law." INS v. National Center for Immigrants' Rights, Inc., 502 U.S. 183, 194, and n.8 (1991). It did so by establishing an extensive "employment verification system,"§ 1324a(a)(1), designed to deny employment to aliens who (a) are not lawfully present in the United States, or (b) are not lawfully authorized to work in the United States, § 1324a(h)(3). . . . This verification system is critical to the IRCA regime. To enforce it, IRCA mandates that employers verify the identity and eligibility of all new hires by examining specified documents before they begin work. § 1324a(b). If an alien applicant is unable to present the required documentation, the unauthorized alien cannot be hired. § 1324a(a)(1).

Similarly, if an employer unknowingly hires an unauthorized alien, or if the alien becomes unauthorized while employed, the employer is compelled to discharge the worker upon discovery of the worker's undocumented status. § 1324a(a)(2). Employers who violate IRCA are punished by civil fines, § 1324a(e)(4)(A), and may be subject to criminal prosecution, § 1324a(f)(1). IRCA also makes it a crime for an unauthorized alien to subvert the employer verification system by tendering fraudulent documents. § 1324c(a). It thus prohibits aliens from using or attempting to use "any forged, counterfeit, altered, or falsely made document" or "any document lawfully issued to or with respect to a person other than the possessor" for purposes of obtaining employment in the United States. §§ 1324c(a)(1)-(3). Aliens who use or attempt to use such documents are subject to fines and criminal prosecution. 18 U.S.C. § 1546(b). There is no dispute that Castro's use of false documents to obtain employment with Hoffman violated these provisions.

Under the IRCA regime, it is impossible for an undocumented alien to obtain employment in the United States without some party directly contravening explicit congressional policies. Either the undocumented alien tenders fraudulent identification, which subverts the cornerstone of IRCA's enforcement mechanism, or the employer knowingly hires the undocumented alien in direct contradiction of its IRCA obligations. The Board asks that we overlook this fact and allow it to award backpay to an illegal alien for years of work not performed, for wages that could not lawfully have been earned, and for a job obtained in the first instance by a criminal fraud. We find, however, that awarding backpay to illegal aliens runs counter to policies underlying IRCA, policies the Board has no authority to enforce or administer. Therefore, as we have consistently held in like circumstances, the award lies beyond the bounds of the Board's remedial discretion.

The Board contends that awarding limited backpay to Castro "reasonably accommodates" IRCA, because, in the Board's view, such an award is not "inconsistent" with IRCA. Brief for Respondent 29-42. The Board argues that because the backpay period was closed as of the date Hoffman learned of Castro's illegal status, Hoffman could have employed Castro during the backpay period without violating IRCA. *Id.*, at 37. The Board further argues that while IRCA criminalized the misuse of documents, "it did not make violators ineligible for back pay awards or other compensation flowing from employment secured by the misuse of such documents." *Id.*, at 38. This latter statement, of course, proves little: The mutiny statute in *Southern S.S. Co.*, and the INA in *Sure-Tan*, were likewise understandably silent with respect to such things as backpay awards under the NLRA. What matters here, and what sinks both of the Board's claims, is that Congress has expressly made it criminally punishable for an alien to obtain employment with false documents.

There is no reason to think that Congress nonetheless intended to permit backpay where but for an employer's unfair labor practices, an alien-employee would have remained in the United States illegally, and continued to work illegally, all the while successfully evading apprehension by immigration authorities. . . . Far from "accommodating" IRCA, the Board's position, recognizing employer misconduct but discounting the misconduct of illegal alien employees, subverts it. Indeed, awarding backpay in a case like this not only trivializes the immigration laws, it also condones and encourages future violations. The Board admits that had the INS detained Castro, or had Castro obeyed the law and departed to Mexico, Castro would have lost his right to backpay . . . . Castro thus qualifies for the Board's award only by remaining inside the United States illegally. *See, e.g., A.P.R.A. Fuel Buyers Group*, 134 F.3d, at 62, n.4 ("Considering that NLRB proceedings can span a whole decade, this is no small inducement to prolong illegal presence in the country") (Jacobs, J., concurring in part and dissenting in part). Similarly, Castro cannot mitigate damages, a duty our cases require, see *Sure-Tan*, 467 U.S., at 901, without triggering new IRCA violations, either by tendering false documents to employers or by finding employers willing to ignore IRCA and hire illegal workers. The Board here has failed to even consider this tension. *See* 326 N.L.R.B., at 1063, n.10 (finding that Castro adequately mitigated damages through interim work with no mention of ALJ findings that Castro secured interim work with false documents).

We therefore conclude that allowing the Board to award backpay to illegal aliens would unduly trench upon explicit statutory prohibitions critical to federal immigration policy, as expressed in IRCA. It would encourage the successful evasion of apprehension by immigration authorities, condone prior violations of the immigration laws, and encourage future violations. However broad the Board's discretion to fashion remedies when dealing only with the NLRA, it is not so unbounded as to authorize this sort of an award.

Lack of authority to award backpay does not mean that the employer gets off scot-free. The Board here has already imposed other significant sanctions against Hoffman — sanctions Hoffman does not challenge. These include orders that Hoffman cease and desist its violations of the NLRA, and that it conspicuously post a notice to employees setting forth their rights under the NLRA and detailing its prior unfair practices. Hoffman will be subject to contempt proceedings should it fail to comply with these orders. NLRB v. Warren Co., 350 U.S. 107, 112-113

(1955). We have deemed such "traditional remedies" sufficient to effectuate national labor policy regardless of whether the "spur and catalyst" of backpay accompanies them. *Sure-Tan*, 467 U.S., at 904. *See also id.*, at 904, n.13) . . . . As we concluded in *Sure-Tan*, "in light of the practical workings of the immigration laws," any "perceived deficienc[y] in the NLRA's existing remedial arsenal," must be "addressed by congressional action," not the courts. *Id.*, at 904. In light of IRCA, this statement is even truer today.[6]

The judgment of the Court of Appeals is reversed.

Justice BREYER, with whom Justice STEVENS, Justice SOUTER, and Justice GINSBURG join, dissenting.

I cannot agree that the backpay award before us "runs counter to," or "trenches upon," national immigration policy. Ante, at 1282, 1283 (citing the Immigration Reform and Control Act of 1986 (IRCA)). As all the relevant agencies (including the Department of Justice) have told us, the National Labor Relations Board's limited backpay order will not interfere with the implementation of immigration policy. Rather, it reasonably helps to deter unlawful activity that both labor laws and immigration laws seek to prevent. . . .

Without the possibility of the deterrence that backpay provides, the Board can impose only future-oriented obligations upon law-violating employers . . . . And in the absence of the backpay weapon, employers could conclude that they can violate the labor laws at least once with impunity. . . .

Where in the immigration laws can the Court find a "policy" that might warrant taking from the Board this critically important remedial power? Certainly not in any statutory language. The immigration statutes say that an employer may not knowingly employ an illegal alien, that an alien may not submit false documents, and that the employer must verify documentation. *See* 8 U.S.C. §§ 1324a(a)(1),1324a(b); 18 U.S.C. § 1546(b)(1). They provide specific penalties, including criminal penalties, for violations. *Ibid.*, 8 U.S.C. §§ 1324a(e)(4), 1324a(f)(1). But the statutes' language itself does not explicitly state how a violation is to effect the enforcement of other laws, such as the labor laws.

Nor can the Court comfortably rest its conclusion upon the immigration laws' purposes. For one thing, the general purpose of the immigration statute's employment prohibition is to diminish the attractive force of employment, which like a "magnet" pulls illegal immigrants towards the United States. H.R. Rep. No. 99-682, pt. 1, p. 45 (1986), U.S. Code Cong. & Admin. News 1986, p. 5649. To permit the Board to award backpay could not significantly increase the strength of this magnetic force, for so speculative a future possibility could not realistically influence an individual's decision to migrate illegally. . . .To deny the Board the power to award backpay, however, might very well increase the strength of this magnetic force. That denial lowers the cost to the employer of an initial labor law

---

[6] Because the Board is precluded from imposing punitive remedies, Republic Steel Corp. v. NLRB, 311 U.S. 7, 9-12 (1940), it is an open question whether awarding backpay to undocumented aliens, who have no entitlement to work in the United States at all, might constitute a prohibited punitive remedy against an employer. Because we find the remedy foreclosed on other grounds, we do not address whether the award at issue here is "'punitive' and hence beyond the authority of the Board." *Sure-Tan, supra*, at 905, n.4.

violation (provided, of course, that the only victims are illegal aliens). . . .

The immigration law's specific labor-law-related purposes also favor preservation, not elimination, of the Board's backpay powers. As I just mentioned and as this Court has held, the immigration law foresees application of the Nation's labor laws to protect "workers who are illegal immigrants." *Id.*, at 891-893; H.R. Rep. No. 99-682, *supra*, at 58, U.S. Code Cong. & Admin. News 1986, pp. 5649, 5662. And a policy of applying the labor laws must encompass a policy of enforcing the labor laws effectively. Otherwise, as Justice Kennedy once put the matter, "we would leave helpless the very persons who most need protection from exploitative employer practices." NLRB v. Apollo Tire Co., 604 F.2d 1180, 1184 (C.A.9 1979) (concurring opinion). That presumably is why those in Congress who wrote the immigration statute stated explicitly and unequivocally that the immigration statute does not take from the Board any of its remedial authority. H.R. Rep. No. 99-682, *supra*, at 58, U.S. Code Cong. & Admin. News 1986, pp. 5649, 5662 (IRCA does not "undermine or diminish in any way labor protections in existing law, or . . . limit the powers of federal or state labor relations boards . . . to remedy unfair practices committed against undocumented employees"). . . .

NOTES AND QUESTIONS

1. Note that the Court did not overrule its holding in *Sure-Tan* that unauthorized aliens are still "employees" within the meaning of the NLRA. What is the significance of this fact? If a majority of the employees vote for a union, and the employer then proves that some of the workers are unauthorized aliens (and they are subsequently deported by the INS and replaced by new "authorized" workers), should the Board hold the election invalid? *Cf.* NLRB v. Curtin Matheson Scientific, Inc., 494 U.S. 775 (1990) (upholding board's presumption that employees hired to replace strikers support the union, for purposes of determining whether union continues to represent a majority of employees). Prior to *Hoffman Plastic Compounds*, the board and at least one court had held that the validity of an election would not be affected by the participation of unauthorized aliens. NLRB v. Kolkka, 170 F.3d 937 (9th Cir. 1999).

2. One issue between the majority and the dissent in *Hoffman Plastic Compounds* is whether limiting or denying individual remedies to unauthorized employees will encourage employers to *favor* the hiring of unauthorized employees to avoid liability for illegal employment standards and practices. Will penalties other than "back pay" suffice to discourage illegal employer conduct? In general, penalties—as opposed to compensatory damages—tend to be relatively mild for violations of employment laws.. The National Labor Relations Act, for example, authorizes primarily remedial or "make whole" relief such as "back pay." *See* 29 U.S.C. § 160(c). The NLRB lacks the power to assess penalties, but if it has ordered an employer to "desist" from a particular violation, it can petition a U.S. court of appeals to enter a court order against a recalcitrant employer. . 29 U.S.C. § 160(e). If the employer subsequently violates the *court*'s order by a further violation, the court may hold the employer in contempt. However, NLRB and judicial proceedings are likely to take many years—even decades—to reach such a point, and time tends to be on the side of the employer in any battle over the union's right

to represent employees. Some employment laws are more potent than the NLRA in providing for punitive remedies against offenders. *See, e.g.*, 29 U.S.C. §§ 215, 216 (providing for fines and imprisonment in the case of "willful" violations of minimum wage and overtime rules). Should courts or administrative agencies consider the unavailability of remedial relief for unauthorized workers as a factor favoring the assessment of a larger penalty against an employer?

3. If an unauthorized employee does report an employer's violations or otherwise asserts rights, the employer might retaliate by calling immigration authorities and seeking the employee's deportation. Such retaliation might expose the employer to liability other than back pay, depending on the wording or judicial interpretation of various anti-retaliation provisions in different employment laws. In Arias v. Raimondo, 860 F.3d 1185 (9th Cir. 2017), the employer and its attorney sought to avoid liability for retaliation by having a *non*-employer—the employer's attorney—investigate and report or threaten to report claimant employees to the immigration authorities. One such employee, the plaintiff in *Arias*, quickly settled a minimum wage and overtime claim under threat of deportation, but then he sued the employer's attorney for retaliation under the Fair Labor Standards Act. The plaintiff sought damages for "emotional distress." The district court dismissed the claim on the grounds that the attorney was not an "employer" under the FLSA, but the court of appeals reinstated the claim. The FLSA prohibits retaliation by a "person," whether or not that person is an "employer." *See* 29 U.S.C. § 215(a)(3).

4. As the *Arias* case suggests, even after *Hoffman Plastics* unauthorized employees might still seek remedies including damages *other than* back pay for work not done because of a wrongful discharge. An award of damages for emotional distress, where available, is one possibility. However, the risk of deportation often makes the assertion of employee rights and claims impractical. Even if the named or lead plaintiff in a multi-party or class action has nothing to fear, the threat of deportation for other members of the plaintiff class can lead to complications and conflict. And an employer can exhibit the threat of deportation merely by its normal use of the judicial discovery process. An interrogatory or deposition question about birth place or resident status can have a chilling effect.

In Rivera v. Nibco, Inc., 364 F.3d 1057 (9th Cir. 2004), the Ninth Circuit considered whether a district court had properly granted a protective order barring a defendant employer from using the discovery process to determine the immigration status of plaintiffs in a national origin discrimination lawsuit. Upholding the protective order, the Ninth Circuit stated that "We seriously doubt" that *Hoffman Plastic* precludes an award of backpay in actions under Title VII.

> First, the NLRA authorizes only certain limited private causes of action, while Title VII depends principally upon private causes of action for enforcement. The NLRA is enforced primarily through actions of the NLRB — private actions are available only in exceptional circumstances .... Title VII, by contrast, depends almost entirely upon individual workers — private attorneys general — to achieve the deterrent purposes of the statute.
>
> Second, Congress has armed Title VII plaintiffs with remedies designed to punish employers who engage in unlawful discriminatory acts, and to deter future discrimination both by the defendant and by all other employers. Title VII's enforcement regime includes not only traditional

> remedies for employment law violations, such as backpay, frontpay, and reinstatement, but also full compensatory and punitive damages. 42 U.S.C. § 1981a .... This full complement of remedies accords with the longstanding notion that Title VII requires courts to remedy instances of discrimination by sending strong messages to would-be discriminators ....
>
> Third, ... *Hoffman* held that the NLRB possesses only the discretion to "select and fashion remedies for violations of the NLRA," and that this discretion, "though broad, is not unlimited." 535 U.S. at 142-43 (citations omitted). The Court held that, given the strong policies underlying IRCA and the Board's limited power to construe statutes outside of its authority, the NLRB's construction of the NLRA was impermissible. This limitation on the Board's authority says nothing regarding a federal court's power to balance IRCA against Title VII if the two statutes conflict. A district court has the very authority to interpret both Title VII and IRCA that the NLRB lacks.

Id. at 1066-68. The Ninth Circuit suggested that, on remand, the district court might bifurcate the proceedings into separate liability and remedies phases, and that a final decision regarding the applicability of *Hoffman Plastic* would not be reached until the remedies phase. The Circuit later denied a petition for rehearing en banc over the vigorous dissent of four judges. 384 F.3d 822 (9th Cir. 2004).

5. What if an employer illegally employs an unauthorized alien and pays him less than the statutory minimum wage? Can the Department of Labor, which enforces the minimum wage law, require the employer to compensate the unauthorized alien for the amount of the underpayment? Or does *Hoffman Plastics* foreclose such a remedy? Reacting to the *Hoffman Plastics* case, the Department of Labor described the minimum wage and overtime laws it enforces as "core labor protections" and it adopted the following enforcement policy for these laws:

> The Department's Wage and Hour Division will continue to enforce the FLSA and MSPA without regard to whether an employee is documented or undocumented. Enforcement of these laws is distinguishable from ordering back pay under the NLRA. In *Hoffman Plastics*, the NLRB sought back pay for time an employee *would* have worked if he had not been illegally discharged, under a law that permitted but did not require back pay as a remedy. Under the FLSA or MSPA, the Department (or an employee) seeks back pay for hours an employee has *actually worked*, under laws that require payment for such work. The Supreme Court's concern with awarding back pay "for years of work not performed, for wages that could not lawfully have been earned," does not apply to work actually performed. Two federal courts already have adopted this approach. *See* Flores v. Albertson's, Inc., 2002 WL 1163623 (C.D. Cal. 2002); Liu v. Donna Karan Int'l, Inc., 2002 WL 1300260 (S.D.N.Y. 2002).

DOL Fact Sheet #48, Application of U.S. Labor Laws to Immigrant Workers: Effect of *Hoffman Plastics* decision on laws enforced by the Wage & Hour Div. (Jan. 13, 2002), at https://www.dol.gov/whd/regs/compliance/whdfs48.htm.

6. A common issue in proceedings under nearly any federal employment law is whether a defendant employer is entitled to discovery of a claimant's immigration status. Facts that might limit a claimant's right to reinstatement or backpay are clearly relevant at some stage, depending on what remedies the

claimant demands. On the other hand, discovery of immigration status at the outset of a proceeding might deter employees from seeking any remedy at all. Variations of the "bifurcated" approach proposed by the Ninth Circuit in *Rivera* (note 4, *supra*) have been widely adopted by courts and administrative agencies. Thus, if immigration law would not bar all remedies available to an unauthorized alien worker under a particular law, a court might bar discovery of the worker's immigration status during the liability phase, but permit such discovery during the remedy phase. *See, e.g.,* Galaviz-Zamora v. Brady Farms, Inc., 230 F.R.D. 499 (W.D. Mich. 2005); Liu v. Donna Karan Int'l, Inc., 207 F. Supp. 2d 191 (S.D.N.Y. 2002); NLRB Gen. Couns. Memo 02-06, Part E (July 19, 2002).

7. Are state courts and legislatures bound to follow *Hoffman Plastic Compounds* when they enact or enforce their own laws? Here is the California Legislature's response to *Hoffman Plastic Compounds*, for purposes of state law:

> (a) All protections, rights, and remedies available under state law, except any reinstatement remedy prohibited by federal law, are available to all individuals regardless of immigration status who have applied for employment, or who are or who have been employed, in this state.
>
> (b) For purposes of enforcing state labor and employment laws, a person's immigration status is irrelevant to the issue of liability, and in proceedings or discovery undertaken to enforce those state laws no inquiry shall be permitted into a person's immigration status except where the person seeking to make this inquiry has shown by clear and convincing evidence that the inquiry is necessary in order to comply with federal immigration law.

Cal. Lab. Code § 1171.5. Another provision of California law defines "employee" to include "every person in the service of an employer . . . whether lawfully or unlawfully employed." Cal. Labor Code § 3351. In Farmers Brothers Coffee v. Workers' Compensation Appeals Board, 35 Cal. Rptr. 3d 23 (Cal. App. 2005), the court held that federal immigration law does not preempt these statutes insofar as their application in a workers' compensation case.

8. Workers' compensation laws mandate employer-funded insurance for work-related injuries and illnesses. For most industries, workers' compensation is governed by state, not federal law. Before *Hoffman Plastic*, state legislatures and courts took a variety of approaches to the question whether an illegally employed undocumented alien is entitled to benefits for a work-related injury or illness. *Hoffman Plastic* did not clearly answer this question, given its allowance that an undocumented alien might still constitute an "employee" for some legal purposes.

The issue of workers' compensation protection for unlawfully employed aliens really involves two separate questions. First is the question of statutory coverage. A workers' compensation law may or may not include unlawfully employed aliens within the definition of "employee." Many but not all state workers' compensation laws do extend coverage to unlawfully employed aliens. *Compare* Va. Code 65.02-101 (defining "employee" to include "aliens . . . whether lawfully or unlawfully employed") *with* Wy. Stat. 27-14-102 ("employee" includes "aliens authorized to work by the United States Department of Justice").

Second, if an unlawfully employed alien qualifies as an "employee," his immigration status might still affect his entitlement to some benefits, particularly disability benefits as distinguished from benefits for medical expenses. States that extend employee coverage to unlawfully employed aliens generally hold that the injured or ill alien is entitled to coverage for the cost of medical treatment. *See, e.g.,* AMS Staff Leasing, Inc. v. Arreola, 976 So. 2d 612 (Fla. App. 2008) (upholding award of benefits for cost of alien's continued medical treatment in Mexico for injury he suffered in course of unlawful U.S. employment).

On the other hand, state courts and legislatures remain particularly divided over the question whether an alien who is not authorized to work in the U.S. is entitled to disability benefits compensating for lost income or lost ability to work. *Compare* Curiel v. Env'tl Mgmt. Servs., 655 S.E.2d 482 (S.C. 2007) (alien unlawfully employed at time of injury was entitled to disability benefits) *with* Ramroop v. Flexo-Craft Printing, Inc., 896 N.E.2d 69 (N.Y. 2008) (denying benefits for impairment of earning capacity).

Should the answer to such questions depend on the employer's own culpability in employing unauthorized aliens? In other words, should the law be most generous in favor of an unauthorized alien if the employer knowingly or purposely violated federal immigration law?

9. Federal law now prohibits unemployment compensation benefits for aliens not authorized to work in the United States. 26 U.S.C. § 3304(a)(14).

10. *Hoffman Plastic* also has implications for a worker's personal injury and lost earnings claims against a non-employer defendant, such as the maker or provider of the equipment that caused the worker's injury. *Compare* Veliz v. Rental Serv. Corp. USA, 313 F. Supp. 2d 1317 (M.D. Fla. 2003) (acknowledging that Florida law allows workers' compensation benefits for undocumented aliens, but denying claim for lost wages in products liability case based on undocumented alien's work-related death) *with* Madeira v. Affordable Hous. Found., Inc., 469 F.3d 219 (2d Cir. 2006) (federal immigration law did not preempt award of lost wages to injured undocumented worker in his tort action under New York law).

If a court grants the undocumented worker a tort claim for lost wages, how should the court calculate the amount of lost earnings? Should it rely on U.S. wage rates or wage rates in the worker's homeland? In the *Madeira* case, *supra*, the court held that federal law did not preempt an award of lost wages based on U.S. rates.

CHAPTER 3

Selection of Employees

A. OVERVIEW

An employer is generally free to hire whomever it wishes, according to any test or set of qualifications it wishes, provided it does not make its decision based on race, sex, age, or other specific traits protected by law.[1] In fact, the employer can be wholly arbitrary in selecting employees. In Price v. City of Chicago, 251 F.3d 656 (7th Cir. 2001), for example, the employer used employee birthdate as the tie-breaking factor in making certain employee selection decisions. The court held that the employer's method was not unlawful. There simply is no general duty to be "fair" to job applicants in the selection process. *See also* Womack v. Runyon, 147 F.3d 1298 (11th Cir. 1998) (employer's alleged favoritism toward paramour was not unlawful, even if rejection of plaintiff was unfair). *See generally* Mark Rothstein, *Wrongful Refusal to Hire*, 24 Conn. L. Rev. 97 (1991).

An employer may hope its selection methods will identify the best candidate for each position. Indeed, the success of its business may depend in part on its ability to assemble a good workforce. However, the employer's selection goals may be constrained by limited time and resources, uncertainty as to which test or set of qualifications best reveals an applicant's competence, or a shortage or overabundance of applicants seeking work. If there are few applicants and an employer's needs are immediate, the employer may be resigned to accept any applicant who satisfies minimum qualifications. If there are more applicants than the employer could possibly consider on a careful and individualized basis, the employer may need to reduce the size of the pool of applicants by some arbitrary measure (e.g., only the first 100 persons) to achieve a smaller and more manageable pool. Even then, the carefulness of its selection process will depend on the resources

[1] The Supreme Court once deemed an employer's right to select employees to be so fundamental that laws restricting this right were deemed a violation of substantive due process. In Coppage v. Kansas, 236 U.S.1 (1915), for example, the Court struck down a law prohibiting employers from refusing to employ union members, stating as follows:

> Included in the right of personal liberty and the right of private property — partaking of the nature of each — is the right to make contracts for the acquisition of property. Chief among such contracts is that of personal employment, by which labor and other services are exchanged for money or other forms of property. If this right be struck down or arbitrarily interfered with, there is a substantial impairment of liberty in the long-established constitutional sense. The right is as essential to the laborer as to the capitalist, to the poor as to the rich; for the vast majority of persons have no other honest way to begin to acquire property, save by working for money. An interference with this liberty so serious as that now under consideration, and so disturbing of equality of right, must be deemed to be arbitrary, unless it be supportable as a reasonable exercise of the police power of the state.

1236 U.S. at 13. The Court's subsequent approval of a number of New Deal era laws, including the National Labor Relations Act, "completely sapped" *Coppage* of its authority. NLRB v. Phelps Dodge Corp., 313 U.S. 177, 187 (1941).

it can reasonably devote to interviewing, testing, or background checking.

Regardless of the effort an employer can devote to employee selection, there is no guaranteed method of determining who is "best." The selection of criteria and their priority (e.g., is intelligence most important, or character?)[2] and the methods for measuring the candidates' qualities are subject to dispute in most cases. Some qualities such as honesty or integrity probably cannot be tested in advance by any reliable method. An applicant's past is one important consideration, but a fair and complete investigation of an applicant's past may be impossible, and the limited amount of personal history available to an employer might not be an accurate reflection of future conduct. Medical or physiological tests can yield some potentially important information, but the most accurate tests used by employers usually tell very little (e.g., a urinalysis test revealing whether the applicant has used certain drugs within a limited past time frame). Tests designed to tell the most about an applicant (e.g., personality tests) are of very doubtful accuracy.

The general rule is that an employer's errors in hiring are business mistakes of no legal consequence to disappointed applicants or the public at large. But careless, irrational, or unfair selection practices sometimes create special risks for the public. An employer of truck drivers, for example, risks injury to the public if he hires obviously dangerous drivers. Discrimination against a minority class, especially if practiced by a large number of employers, may cause or perpetuate the impoverishment of that class and lead to social division and upheaval. Thus, there are some important limits to an employer's right to hire whomever it chooses.

B. DUTIES TO THIRD PARTIES IN THE SELECTION OF EMPLOYEES

The common law of torts includes a few important rules for an employer's methods of selecting employees. Recall that an employer risks liability in *respondeat superior* for the torts of its employees. *See* Chapter 2.A, *supra*. Employees selected for jobs for which they are not competent might be expected to cause more accidents and expose the employer to greater liability to injured third parties. A delivery service, for example, might be especially concerned about the driving record of its applicants, because the delivery service will be liable if the employee/driver negligently injuries a third party while making a delivery. Prodding employers to be careful was a goal courts frequently cited in first adopting the rule of *respondeat superior*. *See, e.g.*, McCafferty v. The Spuyten Duyvil, 61 N.Y. 178, 181 (1874).

Are *respondeat superior* and the employer's self-interest in promoting efficiency sufficient incentives to deter careless hiring practices harmful to the public? An employer might assume (perhaps miscalculating) that quickly hired and poorly paid employees are still less expensive than highly paid employees of

---

[2] In one recent survey, 46 percent of responding employers believed "job-related knowledge" was the "most important" factor in selecting job applicants. "Personality or attitude" was most important to 26 percent, "communication or social skills" was most important to 12 percent, and "general intelligence" was most important to 7 percent. Nine percent believed "your gut feeling" was the most important. HRhero.com Monthly Survey Results (July 18, 2003), at *http://www.HRhero.com/survey/hiring_results.*

proven competence and temperament. Moreover, *respondeat superior* does not necessarily impute liability for an employee's *intentional* torts. This shortcoming stems from the fact that *respondeat superior* applies only to torts in the scope of the employee's employment. It is not hard to see that an employee's negligent performance of his work is within the scope of his employment, but an *intentional* tort, such as an assault or battery motivated by personal outrage or passion, may have little or no connection with the employer's business. Courts often pause to hold an employer liable for an employee's intentional tort even if the employee committed the tort against a customer or fellow employee during working hours and on the employer's premises. *See* Restatement (Third) of Agency § 7.07 (2006) ("An employee's act is not within the scope of employment when it occurs within an independent course of conduct not intended by the employee to serve any purpose of the employer.").

Physical intentional torts are particularly unlikely to be in the scope of employment, except when the use of force is expected in or incidental to an employee's work and might further the employer's business interest. *Compare* Mason v. Sportsman's Pub., 702 A.2d 1301 (N.J. Super. 1997) (bouncer's assault against customer was in the scope of employment) *with* Stephens v. A-Able Rents Co., 654 N.E.2d 1315 (Ohio App. 1995) (employee's rape of plaintiff was outside scope of employment because "it did not facilitate or promote [employer's] rental business").[3] An employee's intentional tort in a business transaction or communication — such as fraud, misrepresentation or defamation — might be imputed to the employer if the employee acted as an "agent" on the employer's behalf with respect to the transaction or communication. *See* Restatement of Agency (Third) § 2.04, *comment b* (2006). The employer might also be liable for an employee's intentional tort against a third party if the employer owed a special duty to protect the third party and the employer delegated responsibility for such protection to the employee. *Id.* § 7.05(2). According to the Restatement, "such relationships include a common carrier with its passengers, an innkeeper with its guests, a school with its students, and a custodian with those in its custody when the custodian is required by law or voluntarily takes custody of a person in circumstances in which the custodian has a superior ability to protect the other." *Id.* § 7.05, *comment e*.

Even when an employer is liable for actual damages caused by an employee's intentional tort, it does not always follow that the employer is liable for *punitive* damages. Under the Restatement (Second) of Torts, an employer is liable for punitive damages based on an employee's tort only if the employer authorized "the doing and the manner of the act," the employer ratified or approved the act, the employee was a manager acting in the scope of employment, or the employer was "reckless" in hiring or retaining the employee. Restatement (Second) of Torts § 909 (1965).

---

[3] California is one state that imputes an employee's intentional tort to the employer on a wider basis. *See* Flores v. Autozone W., Inc., 74 Cal. Rptr. 3d 178 (2008) (employer liable for employee assault against customer who complained about employee's work; assault was an "outgrowth" of employee's work even he did not intend to advance employer's business).

WISE v. COMPLETE STAFFING

56 S.W.3d 900 (Tex. App. 2001)

Opinion by Chief Justice CORNELIUS.

McKinley and Yolanda Wise appeal from a take-nothing summary judgment rendered in their suit against Complete Staffing Services, Inc. (Staffing). They sued, alleging that McKinley, while working at Mrs. Baird's Bakery, was attacked and severely injured by a temporary worker, Meredith Turner, who had been provided by and was actually employed by Staffing. McKinley Wise (Wise) was a supervisor at Mrs. Baird's, and Staffing provided Turner to Mrs. Baird's to do unskilled manual labor. Wise alleged that Staffing was negligent and grossly negligent in employing Turner because it did not sufficiently investigate his criminal background, and that Staffing had a "special relationship" with Turner and failed to adequately supervise his activities and adequately check his credentials. Wise also alleged that because of the special relationship with Turner, Staffing had a duty to discover and warn Mrs. Baird's about Turner's criminal background.

. . . Wise argues that Mrs. Baird's had a duty, and that Staffing placed itself in Mrs. Baird's shoes by volunteering or undertaking to meet that duty. Thus, we first determine whether Mrs. Baird's had a duty to investigate Turner's background.

The basis of liability under the doctrine of negligent hiring is the master's own negligence in hiring or retaining in his employ an incompetent servant whom the master knows, or by the exercise of reasonable care should have known, was incompetent or unfit, thereby creating an unreasonable risk of harm to others. Estate of Arrington v. Fields, 578 S.W.2d 173, 178 (Tex. Civ. App. — Tyler 1979, writ ref'd n.r.e.). An employer owes a duty to its other employees and to the general public to ascertain the qualifications and competence of the employees it hires, especially when the employees are engaged in occupations that require skill or experience and that could be hazardous to the safety of others. Texas & Pac. Ry. Co. v. Johnson, 89 Tex. 519, 35 S.W. 1042, 1044 (1896).

. . . The decision to impose a legal duty involves complex considerations of public policy, including social, economic, and political questions and their application to the particular facts at hand. In deciding whether to impose a duty on a particular defendant, courts weigh the risk, foreseeability, and likelihood of injury against the social utility of the actor's conduct, the magnitude of the burden of guarding against the injury, and the consequences of placing that burden on the actor.. Other proper considerations include whether one party would generally have superior knowledge of the risk or a right to control the actor who caused the harm. Of these, the foremost consideration is the foreseeability of the risk..

We first address Wise's claim of negligent hiring. The issue here is whether the employee was placed in a situation that foreseeably created a risk of harm to others because of his employment duties. It is therefore unlike the situation in Estate of Arrington v. Fields. In *Arrington*, the employer was found liable for negligently hiring someone as an armed security guard when he had a long criminal record. *Id.* at 184. The court concluded that it was more foreseeable that a customer might be harmed when the employee is armed and charged with performing a hazardous job that requires skill or experience. *See id.* at 178.

This case is closer on its facts to Guidry v. Nat'l Freight, Inc., 944 S.W.2d 807 (Tex. App. — Austin 1997, no writ). In *Guidry,* while making a delivery by truck, a driver stopped to "stretch his legs," wandered to an apartment complex, and sexually assaulted a woman. The victim sued the trucking company for the negligent hiring, supervision, and retention of the driver. Guidry argued that the company had a duty to check the driver's criminal background and that such an investigation would have revealed a history of sexually predatory behavior, thereby making foreseeable a risk of his injuring Guidry. The court held that although the company had a duty to the driving public to employ competent drivers, the duty did not require the company to conduct independent investigations into its employees' nonvehicular criminal backgrounds. *Id.* The court recognized that while the company could foresee that the driver might stop to stretch, it could not foresee the risk that the driver would commit a sexual assault while on duty, and because that type of conduct was unforeseeable, the company owed no legal duty to the victim of the driver's criminal conduct. *Id.* at 812.

The holding in *Guidry* is in line with the general negligent hiring rule, which is aimed, not at avoiding a general propensity for bad acts, but to protect the public and fellow employees from workers who are unsafe or dangerous on the job. Estate of Arrington v. Fields, 578 S.W.2d at 178. The incompetency must, in some manner, be job-related. Dieter v. Baker Serv. Tools, 739 S.W.2d 405, 407 (Tex. App. — Corpus Christi 1987, writ denied). Turner did not injure Wise as a result of his incompetence or unfitness for the job, but by an intervening criminal act. Under this analysis, Mrs. Baird's had no duty to check the criminal histories of its employees unless it was directly related to the duties of the job at hand. Thus, Staffing also had no such duty.

Wise argues that because Staffing voluntarily undertook to perform such a duty, it had a duty to perform it without negligence. It is uncontested that Staffing did perform a criminal history check on Turner. It limited its check, however, to Harris County, where Turner had lived for the last four years. It did not seek information from any other area. The summary judgment evidence shows that Turner was a repeat employee of Staffing, that his application showed he was working between college semesters, and that Staffing had contacted his prior employers and received good reports about him.

... In summary, Staffing did undertake to perform a service, but the scope of that service is not clearly stated. Staffing's representatives contend that the background check was limited to Harris County, while Turner's prior criminal record was from Fort Bend County. Wise contends that a portion of Houston is in Fort Bend County, and because Staffing represented that it conducted a "thorough" background check, it negligently performed its undertaking by limiting it to Harris County.

The summary judgment evidence does not conclusively show that Mrs. Baird's agreed that Staffing's background check would cover only Harris County . . . [and] it does not contradict Wise's evidence . . . that such a limited check constituted negligence in itself. Because a fact issue exists on whether Staffing negligently performed its investigation of Turner's criminal history, summary judgment on the negligent hiring issue was not proper.

Wise also argues that because there were special circumstances with respect to Staffing's relationship with Turner, it had a heightened level of duty. This argument concerning special circumstances is abstracted from the exception to the rule that, generally, there is no duty to control the conduct of third persons. See Greater Houston Transp. Co. v. Phillips, 801 S.W.2d 523, 525 (Tex. 1990). . . . Such situations include what is generally described as potential contact with particularly vulnerable individuals. Golden Spread Council of Boy Scouts v. Akins, 926 S.W.2d 287 (Tex. 1996) (organization held negligent for recommending scoutmaster despite rumors of his past sexual deviancy); Scott Fetzer Co. v. Read, 945 S.W.2d 854, 866 (Tex. App. — Austin 1997), *aff'd*, 990 S.W.2d 732 (Tex. 1998) (imposing duty on company to check salesmen who demonstrated products only in homes); Porter v. Nemir, 900 S.W.2d 376 (Tex. App. — Austin 1995, no writ) (a psychologically fragile victim was sexually assaulted by a drug counselor); Doe v. Boys Clubs of Greater Dallas, Inc., 868 S.W.2d 942 (Tex. App. — Amarillo 1994), *aff'd*, 907 S.W.2d 472 (Tex. 1995) (employer whose function is to care for and educate children owed a higher duty to its patrons to exercise care in the selection of its employees than would other employers); Deerings W. Nursing Ctr. v. Scott, 787 S.W.2d 494, 495 (Tex. App. — El Paso 1990, writ denied) (nursing home was sued for negligence in hiring an unlicensed nurse-employee who assaulted an elderly visitor). In the *Golden Spread Council of Boy Scouts* case, the court held that liability is imposed when the entity brings into contact or association with the vulnerable person an individual whom the entity knows or should know is particularly likely to commit intentional misconduct, under circumstances which afford a peculiar opportunity or temptation for such misconduct. Golden Spread Council of Boy Scouts v. Akins, 926 S.W.2d at 291, *citing* Restatement (Second) Of Torts § 302B, cmt. e (1965).

Cases finding no special relationship sufficient to impose a duty include: Boyd v. Texas Christian Univ., Inc., 8 S.W.3d 758, 760 (Tex. App. — Fort Worth 1999, no pet.) (relationship between a private university and its adult students is not recognized by Texas law as a special relationship); Houser v. Smith, 968 S.W.2d 542, 546 (Tex. App. — Austin 1998, no pet.) (customer not part of a specially protected group, even though sexual assault occurred on the work premises); Guidry v. Nat'l Freight, Inc., 944 S.W.2d at 810 (third party not part of specially protected group when truck driver leaves his truck and commits rape).

Wise has directed us to no authority imposing an expanded duty on an employer or suggesting that an employee under this type of allegation of harm is a part of a specially protected group. Further, the social implications of requiring an unlimited background check of all employees, and then imposing liability if an employee is harmed by the criminal actions of a co-worker, are beyond what we believe would be appropriate. Thus, Wise has not demonstrated that the trial court erred by rendering summary judgment on this basis.

. . . Wise's claim for negligent performance of Staffing's undertaking to check Turner's criminal background is severed from the other claims; the summary judgment as to that claim is reversed and the cause remanded for trial. The trial court's judgment as to Wise's other claims is affirmed.

NOTES AND QUESTIONS

1. *Wise* is a bit of an anomaly as a negligent hiring case in that the plaintiff

Wise and the tortfeasor Turner appeared to be fellow employees of Mrs. Baird's. Ordinarily, when an employee sues a fellow employee or the employer for work-related personal injuries, his claim will be subject to the "exclusive remedy" of workers' compensation law. *See* Chapter 5.B. Thus, the Wises' remedy against Mrs. Baird's for negligent hiring would be limited to the benefits provided by workers' compensation law. Their tort claim against Mrs. Baird would be barred. How did the Wises avoid the workers' compensation barrier? They sued Complete Staffing, the staffing agency that supplied Turner as a "temp," rather than Mrs. Baird's.

Workers' compensation law generally does not bar an *intentional* tort claim against an employer or fellow employee. The Wises' might have sued Turner in tort for assault, but Turner's intentional tort would not have been imputed to Mrs. Baird's because the assault was likely outside the scope of Turner's employment.

2. If Mrs. Baird's owed no duty to the Wises to conduct a criminal background check of Turner, on what basis did the court remand the Wises' claim against Complete Staffing? If the potential basis for Complete Staffing's liability was its "undertaking" to conduct a criminal background check, would negligence in that undertaking be a breach of duty to the Wises? Or would it breach a duty only to Mrs. Baird's?

3. As the court suggests in *Wise*, a plaintiff is most likely to persuade a court that an employer owed a heightened duty of care in hiring if there was a "special relationship" between the plaintiff and the employer or the plaintiff was especially vulnerable to the hired employee. Such cases frequently involve health, security, or dependent care services.

In Wilson N. Jones Mem. Hosp. v. Davis, 553 S.W.2d 180 (Tex. App. 1977), the court considered a hospital's alleged negligence in hiring an orderly who injured the plaintiff in the course of improperly removing a catheter. In hiring the orderly the hospital violated its normal procedures, which required the hospital to obtain four employment references and three personal references. Due to a "critical need for orderlies," the hospital failed to complete the usual reference checks. Had the hospital conducted the usual investigation, it would have learned that the orderly lacked the training he claimed, because he had been expelled from the Navy Medical Corps School after only one month's training. The hospital also might have learned the orderly had a record of drug abuse and a criminal record.

The orderly in *Wilson N. Jones Memorial Hospital* was evidently negligent and acting within the scope of his employment when he injured the plaintiff. *Respondeat superior* would have imputed simple negligence to the hospital. However, the plaintiff sought and the jury awarded punitive damages against the hospital based on the hospital's own gross negligence in hiring. The court of appeals affirmed. "[T]he hiring of [the orderly] Mr. Looman was the result of conscious indifference to the rights, welfare and safety of the patients in the hospital. In short, the Hospital was so interested in filling the jobs that they consciously jeopardized the health, welfare, and safety of their patients, which included Plaintiff. . . . " *Id.* at 183.

4. *Wilson* illustrates a second reason why a plaintiff might invoke the doctrine of negligent hiring: To hold the employer directly liable for *punitive* damages. Liability for punitive damages is not ordinarily imputed to an employer by *respondeat superior*. Thus, an employer's liability for punitive damages based

on the act of an employee often depends on the employer's *own* "gross", "willful" or "reckless" negligence in hiring, depending on local law. *See, e.g.*, Ala. Code § 6-11-27; Cal. Civ. Code § 3294; Fla. Stat. Ann. § 768.72; Nev. Rev. Stat. § 42.007; Tex. Civ. Prac. & Rem. Code Ann. § 41.005.

5. The scope of the employment is a limit on an employer's imputed liability for employee conduct under the doctrine of *respondeat superior*. But what if the employer was negligent by its own conduct in hiring the employee? What limits an employer's liability for the torts of another person who happens to be the employer's negligently hired employee? Negligent hiring can make an employer liable for employee torts outside the scope of employment, but there must still be some causal link between the hiring or employment relation and the tort.

In TGM Ashly Lakes, Inc. v. Jennings, 590 S.E.2d 807 (Ga. App. 2003), a maintenance employee of a management company for an apartment complex murdered a resident in her apartment. The murdered woman's parents sued the management company based on *respondeat superior* and negligent hiring. The trial court dismissed the plaintiffs' *respondeat superior* claim, evidently accepting the management company's argument that the employee acted outside the scope of his employment when he unlawfully entered the deceased woman's apartment and assaulted her. Nevertheless, the trial court allowed the plaintiffs to go forward on their negligent hiring claim, and it eventually entered judgment in favor of the plaintiffs after a jury verdict. The management company appealed, arguing that if the employee's torts were outside the scope of his employment, the company could not be liable on any basis, including negligent hiring. The court rejected this argument and affirmed judgment for the plaintiffs:

> It has long been the law of this state that a negligent hiring and retention claim can be based on a tort that occurred outside of the scope of employment:
>
> The question is not whether the servant was acting within the scope of his authority, but whether in view of his known characteristics such an injury by him was reasonably to be apprehended or anticipated by the proprietor.

Henderson, 184 Ga. at 736, 193 S.E. 347. With regard to tortious conduct, a claim of negligent hiring and retention is very similar to a claim of premises liability. "'The presence of a mischievous human being on premises may constitute the danger against which the law requires of the occupant reasonable care to protect his invitee.'" *Id.* Thus, it is the dangerous nature of the person in general, not simply the person acting within the scope of his duties, that is a concern . . . .

> In [Lear Siegler, Inc. v. Stegall, 184 Ga. App. 27, 360 S.E.2d 619 (1987)], this Court attempted to define the outer limits of liability for negligent hiring and retention for torts committed by the employee on the public in general. In that case, an employee had a car accident under the influence of alcohol during his morning commute to work, and a question was raised as to whether the employer should have known of the employee's past bad driving record. This Court held that the theory of negligent hiring was "conceptually inapplicable" because a review of the case law showed that in each prior case involving negligent hiring, "at the very least the tortious act occurred during the tortfeasor's working hours or the employee was acting under the color of employment." *Id.* at 28, 360 S.E.2d 619. The Court concluded,

> We decline to extend the parameters of the cause of action for negligent hiring so as to require every business whose employees drive to work to investigate those employees' driving records before hiring, or expose themselves to liability.

Id. at 28-29, 360 S.E.2d 619. In other words, without more, an employee's regular commute is not considered to be under color of employment, and therefore, the cause of action does not extend to torts committed on members of the public during an employee's commute.

> . . . [T]he limitation found in *Lear Siegler* simply shields employers from liability for torts that their employees commit on the public in general, that is to say, people who have no relation to or association with the employer's business. *See Harvey Freeman*, 189 Ga. App. at 257(1), 375 S.E.2d 261. In *Harvey Freeman* it was held that where there is a relationship, such as landlord-tenant, between the employer and the tort victim, the theory of negligent hiring does apply to employers whose employees commit torts outside the scope of employment. *Id.* That is so because an employer's duty extends to all persons who come into contact with the employee/tortfeasor as a result of their relationship to the employer. *Id.* The cases of *Lear Siegler* and *Harvey Freeman* establish the sound principle that even for employers who should have known of the dangerous propensities of an employee, they will not be liable if the employee acts on those propensities in a setting or under circumstances wholly unrelated to his employment.

590 S.E.2d at 814-16. *See also* Malorney v. B&L Motor Freight, Inc., 496 N.E.2d 1086 (Ill. App. 1986) (remanding for trial claim that employer negligently hired truck driver who raped hitchhiker).

6. Negligent hiring is a particularly important alternative to *respondeat superior* when the defendant employer is a local government and the plaintiff alleges a violation of federal constitutional rights. There is no *respondeat superior* liability for local governments under federal civil rights law. Monell v. Dep't of Soc. Servs., 436 U.S. 658 (1978). Thus, negligent hiring is an especially important way of holding a local government employer liable for the civil rights violations of its employees. *See, e.g.*, Young v. City of Providence, 404 F.3d 4 (1st Cir. 2005).

7. The Internet makes a criminal background check even easier, at least in states that make such information easily accessible. If an Internet-based criminal background check costs as little as $5 (perhaps much less for a regular subscriber to some services), should a criminal background check be routine for *every* hiring decision? Many states *do* require criminal background checks for certain types of employees, especially those whose job duties would include responsibility for children, the elderly, or medical patients. *See, e.g.*, Ark. Code Ann. §§ 20-33-203, 21-15-102; Del. Code Ann. tit. 16, § 1141.8.

Even with the Internet, there are still many impediments to a complete and accurate criminal background check. However, many states facilitate criminal background checks for employers hiring persons for occupations in which the personal safety and security of customers or the general public may be at stake. *See, e.g.*, Colo. Rev. Stat. Ann. § 24-33.5-415.4 (employers may submit fingerprints of security guards for purpose of national criminal history record check). Moreover, a federal law, the National Child Protection Act of 1993, 42

U.S.C. § 5119, facilitates nationwide criminal background checks by child care or child placement services. *See also* Mass. Gen. Laws Ann. ch. 6 §1781 (authorizing release of sex offender information to any person who seeks the information "for the protection of a child . . . or another person for whom the requesting person has responsibility, care or custody").

8. If an employer discovered or should have discovered an employee's criminal record, is the employer necessarily negligent in hiring the employee? To put the issue differently, under what circumstances does an employer's duty to the public preclude hiring an ex-convict, and when might hiring the ex-convict still be reasonable?

Consider the opinion of Judge Welch of the Appellate Court of Illinois, in Bryant v. Livigni, 619 N.E.2d 550 (Ill. App. 1993). In that case, the plaintiff, a four-year-old child, sued the employer of a store manager, Livigni, for assault and battery. Livigni had attacked the child in an intoxicated rage after another child had urinated against an outside wall of the store. The majority upheld an award of compensatory and punitive damages against the store. Judge Welch concurred as to the employer's *respondeat superior* liability, but dissented from the court's judgment with respect to the employer's liability for willfully negligent hiring and retention, which was the basis for punitive damages:

> [T]he majority opinion places an unreasonable investigative burden upon the employer by forcing the employer to discover, retain, and analyze the criminal records of its employees. Is not the majority's opinion then at cross-purposes with the established public policy and laws of Illinois protecting the privacy of citizens and promoting the education and rehabilitation of criminal offenders? *See* Ill. Rev. Stat.1991, ch. 68, par. 2-103 (making it a civil rights violation to ask a job applicant about an arrest record); *see also* Ill. Rev. Stat.1991, ch. 38, par. 1003-12-1 et seq. (concerning correctional employment programs whose function is to teach marketable skills and work habits and responsibility to Illinois prisoners).

Id. at 560-561. Consider also that about 65 million Americans have either an arrest or a criminal conviction record. In the age of the Internet, it is increasingly difficult for such persons to find new employment. *See* Erica Goode, Internet Lets a Criminal Past Catch Up Quicker, New York Times (April 28, 2010), at http://www.nytimes.com/2011/04/29/us/29records.html?scp=1&sq=erica%20goode%20criminal%20past&st=cse.

9. Concern for the implications of a large, potentially unemployable class of persons with tainted records has led some states to *restrict* criminal background checks for most employment purposes. Massachusetts law restricts the release of criminal conviction records by making some but not all information accessible to the public, depending on such factors as the degree of the offense and the passage of time. Mass. Gen. Laws ch. 6, §§ 167-178. Some types of employers, such as those responsible for the care of children or the elderly, are granted much greater access than others. *Id.* An employer might simply ask an applicant whether he has been convicted of a crime, but some states limit the questions an employer can ask about such matters. For example, California prohibits an employer from asking about certain types of convictions (such as possession of marijuana), or from asking about convictions more than a certain number of years in the past. Cal. Labor Code §

432.7. *But see* 21 U.S.C. § 830 (Combat Methamphetamine Epidemic Act provision that may preempt state laws limiting employer inquiries regarding past drug convictions for some occupations).

A few states take a step farther and prohibit discrimination on the basis of a criminal conviction. A New York law, for example, provides as follows:

> No application for any license or employment . . . shall be denied by reason of the applicant's having been previously convicted of one or more criminal offenses, or by reason of a finding of lack of "good moral character" when such finding is based upon the fact that the applicant has previously been convicted of one or more criminal offenses, unless:
>
> (1) there is a direct relationship between one or more of the previous criminal offenses and the specific license or employment sought; or
>
> (2) the issuance of the license or the granting of the employment would involve an unreasonable risk to property or to the safety or welfare of specific individuals or the general public.

Corrections Law § 752. *See also* N.Y. Exec. Law § 296, par. 15; N.J. Stat. Ann. 2A:168A-1; Wis. Stat. Ann. §§ 111.321, 111.335. How should an employer determine whether hiring a person with a criminal conviction record poses an "unreasonable risk"? *See* Arrocha v. Board of Ed. of the City of New York, 712 N.E.2d 669 (N.Y. 1999) (listing factors licensing agency properly considered in finding that applicant's criminal record posed an unreasonable risk); Shimose v. Hawaii Health Systems Corp., 345 P.3d 145 (Haw. 2015) (finding issues of fact whether employer's rejection of applicant was supported by "rational relationship" between applicant's conviction for possession of controlled substance with intent to distribute and "core" duties of radiological technician position).

10. The variety of approaches states take to investigating and considering criminal convictions can create headaches for employers who use a single application form or hiring process for more than one state. *See, e.g.*, Starbucks Corp. v. Superior Court, 86 Cal.Rptr.3d 482 (Cal. App. 2008) (employer's application form requiring disclosure of convictions but listing various states in which certain types of information was not required, was not sufficiently clear, and thus violated California law).

11. The Equal Employment Opportunity Commission (EEOC), which enforces federal laws against employment discrimination, has warned employers that an across the board rejection of any applicant with a criminal record may constitute illegal disparate impact discrimination on the basis of race or national origin. EEOC Enforcement Guidance on the Consideration of Arrest and Conviction Records in Employment Decisions (April 25, 2012). The theory of disparate impact discrimination is discussed in part C.4 of this chapter.

12. To what extent should state policies prohibiting discrimination or favoring rehabilitation of ex-convicts affect the issue whether it is negligent to hire a person with a criminal record? *Compare* Givens v. New York City Hous. Auth., 671 N.Y.S.2d 479 (N.Y. App. Div. 1998) (housing authority, which was prohibited from discriminating on the basis of criminal conviction, was not negligent in hiring caretaker with robbery conviction record) *with* Nigg v. Patterson, 276 Cal. Rptr. 587 (Cal. App. 1991) (law creating program for rehabilitation of convicts did not

protect employer against liability for hiring employee from such a program).

13. Arrest records should be distinguished from conviction records, because many arrestees are innocent and eventually exonerated. An employer who decides not to hire an applicant because of an arrest that did *not* result in a conviction is at even greater risk of liability under a theory of disparate impact discrimination based on race, color, national origin or disability. See part C.4 of this chapter. Some state laws expressly prohibit an employer from asking an applicant about arrest records. A Massachusetts law provides for the sealing of arrest and prosecution records in certain cases not resulting conviction, and the law further provides:

> An application for employment used by an employer which seeks information concerning prior arrests or convictions of the applicant shall include . . . the following statement: "An applicant for employment with a sealed record on file with the commissioner of probation may answer 'no record' with respect to an inquiry herein relative to prior arrests or criminal court appearances."

Mass. Gen. Laws ch. 276, § 100C. *See also* Cal. Lab. Code § 432.7

14. What if Looman, the negligent orderly in *Wilson N. Jones Memorial Hospital, supra* Note 3, was or worked for an independent contractor? Would his status as a non-employee of the hospital immunize the hospital from liability? The employer of an independent contractor is not subject to imputed liability for the contractor's torts under *respondeat superior*. However, if the contractor serves as an "agent" for the employer as to a particular matter, such as by representing the employer in dealing with third parties about certain business, the employer may be vicariously liable for the agent's torts within the scope of the agency. Restatement (Third) of Agency § 7.03(b). Moreover, employers can sometimes be directly liable for failing to exercise care in selecting independent contractors. *See* Bagley v. Insight Comm'ns Co., 658 N.E.2d 584 (Ind. 1995) (describing situations in which employer might be liable for negligence in selecting of independent contractor); Restatement (Second) of Torts § 411 (1965); Restatement (Third) of Agency § 7.03(a).

15. In *Wilson N. Jones Memorial Hospital*, *supra*, the hospital called one of Looman's former employers before hiring Looman. However, the former employer refused to provide any information about Looman's employment record, other than the dates of his employment and his job classification. The court found that the hospital should have been on notice that the former employer might have something to hide. What motivations might an employer have in not releasing information about a former employee? For a discussion of an employer's liability to a former employee or prospective employers for disclosing incorrect or incomplete information about the former employee, see Chapter 8.D.1a.

C. STATUTORY PROHIBITIONS AGAINST EMPLOYMENT DISCRIMINATION

1. *Background*

As explained in the preceding section, hiring the wrong person can lead to employer liability if the negligently hired person injures a third party. What if the employer *fails* to hire the *right* person? Sometimes an employer's reason for rejecting an applicant not only is unfair to the applicant, but also poses a significant danger to community harmony, security, and prosperity. Suppose, for example, that an employer automatically rejects African Americans, women, and Jews because he assumes that African Americans are lazy, women are weak, and Jews are unscrupulous. A hiring practice that excludes African Americans, women, and Jews risks enormous social and economic harm to not only the rejected individuals but the public at large, especially if many other employers have the same prejudices.

Although the general rule is that an employer owes no duty to hire any particular individual and can hire whomever it chooses, federal and state laws frequently invade this prerogative to prohibit the most pernicious forms of employment discrimination. The best known law, and the model for many others, is Title VII of the Civil Rights Act of 1964, 42 U.S.C. §§ 2000e et seq. (Title VII).

The enactment of Title VII in 1964 was a major threshold in employment law, but it was not the first congressional effort to remedy the effects of invidious discrimination. Nearly 100 years earlier, the Reconstruction era Congress enacted the Civil Rights Acts of 1866 and 1871 to eliminate the vestiges of antebellum slavery and bring an end to the institutionalized oppression of African Americans. Several provisions of these nineteenth-century laws offered protection for African Americans and other minorities against discrimination. One provision relevant to employment discrimination, now codified as 42 U.S.C. § 1981, provides that "*All persons . . . shall have the same right . . . to make and enforce contracts*, to sue, be parties, give evidence, and to the full and equal benefit of all laws and proceedings for the security of persons and property *as is enjoyed by white citizens* . . ." (emphasis added). Since employment is a kind of contract, section 1981 as originally enacted prohibited the denial of rights of African Americans to enforce their employment contracts or to obtain remedies for the breach of employment contracts.

Discrimination against African Americans remained pervasive despite section 1981 and the other Reconstruction era laws. There are several reasons why section 1981 was ineffective in remedying race discrimination, especially in employment. First, section 1981 as originally enacted was ambiguous as to whether it prohibited discrimination by employers in *choosing* parties with whom to make contracts. Was the right "to make and enforce contracts" nothing more than a grant of legal *capacity* to make and seek judicial enforcement of contracts, invalidating state laws that denied legal capacity to African Americans? Or did it include a right against discrimination by employers or other parties offering contracts? Second, whether or not section 1981 prohibited discrimination, did it apply to the actions of private parties, or only to those of state and local governments and officials?

In regard to the last question, federal courts restricted the application of section 1981 and other civil rights laws to actions "under color" of state law almost from the beginning until the mid-twentieth century. *See, e.g.*, Kerr v. Enoch Pratt Free Library of Baltimore City, 54 F. Supp. 514 (D. Md. 1944), *rev'd on other grounds*, 149 F.2d 212 (4th Cir. 1945). The conclusion that section 1981 and related Reconstruction era laws did not reach private action was reinforced by the Supreme Court's initial view that Congress lacked power, even under the Fourteenth Amendment, to prohibit discrimination by private parties. *See* Hurd v. Hodge, 334 U.S. 24 (1948); Reuben Hodges v. United States, 203 U.S. 1 (1906); The Civil Rights Cases, 109 U.S. 3, 16 (1883). Under these interpretations, a plaintiff might challenge a local law prohibiting employers from hiring African Americans, a local government's policy denying employment to African Americans, or a local government's refusal to enforce an African-American employee's contractual right to earned wages, but could not challenge race discrimination in employment by a privately owned business. Eventually, modern judicial interpretation, amendments to section 1981, and a new section 1981a clarified that the law does apply to private action, and that it does prohibit an employer's refusal to make an employment contract on the basis of race. But these measures to strengthen section 1981 did not occur until a century after the original enactment.

Even within the limited range of protection granted by section 1981, the law was an unlikely remedy for the victims of race discrimination. Local attorneys willing to confront the segregationist establishment were rare. *See* J. Greenberg, Crusaders in the Courts 37-41 (1994). Attorneys might also have been deterred by the frequent poverty of prospective clients and the unlikelihood of recovering even the cost of the litigation. The defendant's right to trial by jury and widespread discrimination against African Americans in the selection of jurors made it likely that an African-American plaintiff and his attorney would face an all-white and generally unsympathetic or even hostile jury. *Id.* at 459-460. It is not surprising, in retrospect, that section 1981 was ineffective in achieving equal opportunity in public or private employment.

A century later, Congress enacted the Civil Rights Act of 1964 as a broad attack against discrimination and segregation in employment, housing, voting, and public services and accommodations. The employment section of the act, Title VII, included the following key features:

1. clear prohibition against private sector employment discrimination "because of [an] individual's race, color, religion, sex, or national origin";
2. enforcement power in the Department of Justice (later assigned to the Equal Employment Opportunity Commission (EEOC)), to bring lawsuits on behalf of the victims of discrimination;
3. investigatory power for the EEOC to provide a preliminary determination of the merits of a complainant's belief that he was the victim of discrimination, so that the strength of the claim could be tested before the filing of a lawsuit;
4. authorization for "equitable relief," including "equitable" awards of back pay, which a court could grant without a jury (because claims for equitable relief are not subject to the Seventh Amendment right to trial by jury);[4] and
5. authorization for an award of attorneys' fees.

Amendments to Title VII in 1972 and 1991 extended the act's protection to public sector employees and authorized awards of compensatory and punitive damages.

The accessibility of Title VII and related federal laws as remedies for discrimination is evidenced by the magnitude of litigation under these laws. In

[4] Harkless v. Sweeny Indep. Sch. Dist., 427 F.2d 319 (5th Cir. 1970). In 1991, Congress rewrote the law to permit either party in a Title VII action to demand a trial by jury if the plaintiff seeks compensatory damages. *See* Pub. L. No. 102-166, Title I, § 102, 105 Stat. 1072, codified at 42 U.S.C. § 1981a(c).

2011, the EEOC received about 100,000 administrative charges of discrimination. The EEOC filed only about 300 lawsuits based on charges of discrimination, but complaining parties filed another 17,000 lawsuits on their own. EEOC, Enforcement and Litigation Statistics, at http://www.eeoc.gov/eeoc/statistics/enforcement/index.cfm; Administrative Office of the U.S. Courts, Federal Judicial Caseload Statistics 2001, Table C-2, at http://www.uscourts.gov/Statistics/FederalJudicialCaseloadStatistics.aspx. The total number of all employment discrimination charges filed and lawsuits initiated during 2011 is probably much higher, because individual plaintiffs often seek relief in state agencies and courts under local laws modeled after Title VII, or they submit their claims to an arbitrator by agreement with the employer.[5]

The foremost problem targeted by Title VII was discrimination on the basis of race or color, particularly (though not exclusively) discrimination against African Americans. However, Title VII also prohibited discrimination on the basis of sex, religion, and national origin. By a process of interpretation and amendment, Congress and the courts have extended the prohibition against sex discrimination to include prohibitions against sexual harassment and discrimination on the basis of pregnancy. In 1967, Congress enacted the Age Discrimination in Employment Act, 29 U.S.C. §§ 621 et seq., prohibiting age discrimination in employment against persons who are more than 40 years old. In 1990, Congress prohibited disability discrimination with the Americans with Disabilities Act, 42 U.S.C. §§ 12101 et seq.

States have enacted their own employment discrimination laws. Many of these laws are modeled after the federal discrimination laws, but some state laws protect additional traits not protected by federal law. *See, e.g.*, Conn. Gen. Stat. Ann. § 46a-60 (prohibiting, among other things, discrimination on the basis of marital status); Del. Stat. tit. 19 § 711 (genetic information); D.C. Stat. § 1-2512 (personal appearance, family responsibilities, matriculation, political affiliation); Haw. Stat. § 368-1 (sexual orientation); Mass. Stat. ch. 151B § 3 (parenthood); Mich. Comp. Laws Ann. § 37.2202 (height and weight); Minn. Stat. Ann. § 363.03 (status with regard to public assistance). Together, these laws constitute the most important exception to the rule that an employer need not be "fair" in selecting employees.

2. *Proving Discriminatory Intent*

When Title VII was enacted in 1964, many employers still had express or fairly obvious policies of not hiring women or minorities for certain positions. *See, e.g.*, Griggs v. Duke Power Co., 401 U.S. 424 (1971) (company with pre-1965 policy of excluding African Americans from certain positions); Teamsters v. United States, 431 U.S. 324 (1977) (employer that hired only one African-American regular "line driver" among hundreds before being sued). As recently as 1981, Southwest

[5] Other developments resuscitated section 1981 as a parallel enforcement scheme for race discrimination in employment cases. First, the Supreme Court reversed a century of law by holding that Congress *did* have the power, under the Thirteenth Amendment, to prohibit discrimination by private parties, and that Congress intended to exercise this power in some of the early civil rights laws (including, by implication, section 1981). Jones v. Alfred H. Mayer Co., 392 U.S. 409 (1968). Second, Congress confirmed this ruling by amending section 1981 to state clearly that this provision prohibits employment discrimination by private parties. *See* 42 U.S.C. § 1981(c).

Airlines maintained an express policy of hiring only women for flight attendant positions. *See* Wilson v. Sw. Air. Co., 517 F. Supp. 189 (N.D. Tex. 1981).

Proving employer intent to discriminate is fairly simple if discrimination is an official policy or deeply ingrained in the organizational culture. But discrimination frequently takes more subtle forms. An employer who knows discrimination is illegal is not likely to announce his bias as a matter of corporate policy. Moreover, bias might affect one supervisor or manager but not others, so that the effect of the bias is not reflected in overall employment statistics for the entire company. Bias might affect hiring in an irregular fashion, because race or gender frequently act as negative factors in a decision, not as absolute or categorical qualifications. For example, an employer might require an African-American or female applicant to present much stronger credentials to overcome the employer's presumption that they are not qualified. Such an employer might hire some women and African Americans, but not as many as if the employer were color- and gender-blind. Moreover, the prejudice of one individual in a group of decision-makers might be enough to prevent the hiring of one minority candidate but not others.

One of the most challenging problems in the enforcement of antidiscrimination laws is to identify those employment decisions actually affected by prejudice, and to *prove* that the decision maker allowed prejudice to affect the decision. Proof that a normally lawful action such as rejecting a job applicant was actually motivated by illegal intent is difficult for a number of reasons. First, there is nothing inherently suspicious in an employer's decision not to hire an individual. Second, the employer need not and frequently will not explain its decision to a rejected applicant, leaving the applicant to guess. A woman or minority applicant with past personal experiences of discrimination might suspect that race or gender affected the decision, but suspicion alone proves nothing.

If the employer does not have an express policy of discriminating, the evidence of discriminatory intent usually will have to be circumstantial. Again, the mere suspicion that illegal discrimination taints many employment actions is not enough to prove that any particular action was affected by discrimination. For plaintiffs who hope to proceed with their claims in the absence of direct evidence of illegal intent, there are a series of important questions: (1) how can the plaintiff force the employer to explain its decision, so that the plaintiff can subject the employer's explanation to the sort of rigorous examination that might yield evidence of intent; (2) how much circumstantial evidence is necessary to justify a trial and avoid a summary judgment for the employer; and (3) how much circumstantial evidence is necessary to support a court (or jury's) ultimate conclusion that the employer discriminated unlawfully?

MCDONNELL DOUGLAS v. GREEN

411 U.S. 792 (1973)

Mr. Justice POWELL delivered the opinion of the Court.

The case before us raises significant questions as to the proper order and nature of proof in actions under Title VII of the Civil Rights Act of 1964, 78 Stat. 253, 42 U.S.C. § 2000e et seq. Petitioner, McDonnell Douglas Corp., is an aerospace and aircraft manufacturer headquartered in St. Louis, Missouri, where it employs over 30,000 people. Respondent, a black citizen of St. Louis, worked for petitioner as a mechanic and laboratory technician from 1956 until August 28, 1964 when he was laid off in the course of a general reduction in petitioner's work force.

Respondent, a long-time activist in the civil rights movement, protested vigorously that his discharge and the general hiring practices of petitioner were racially motivated. As part of this protest, respondent and other members of the Congress on Racial Equality illegally stalled their cars on the main roads leading to petitioner's plant for the purpose of blocking access to it at the time of the morning shift change. . . .

On July 2, 1965, a "lock-in" took place wherein a chain and padlock were placed on the front door of a building to prevent the occupants, certain of petitioner's employees, from leaving. Though respondent apparently knew beforehand of the "lock-in," the full extent of his involvement remains uncertain.

Some three weeks following the "lock-in," on July 25, 1965, petitioner publicly advertised for qualified mechanics, respondent's trade, and respondent promptly applied for re-employment. Petitioner turned down respondent, basing its rejection on respondent's participation in the "stall-in" and "lock-in." Shortly thereafter, respondent filed a formal complaint with the Equal Employment Opportunity Commission, claiming that petitioner had refused to rehire him because of his race and persistent involvement in the civil rights movement, in violation of §§ 703(a)(1) and 704(a) of the Civil Rights Act of 1964, 42 U.S.C. §§ 2000e-2(a)(1) and 2000e-3(a). The former section generally prohibits racial discrimination in any employment decision while the latter forbids discrimination against applicants or employees for attempting to protest or correct allegedly discriminatory conditions of employment. . . .

The critical issue before us concerns the order and allocation of proof in a private, non-class action challenging employment discrimination. The language of Title VII makes plain the purpose of Congress to assure equality of employment opportunities and to eliminate those discriminatory practices and devices which have fostered racially stratified job environments to the disadvantage of minority citizens. Griggs v. Duke Power Co., 401 U.S. 424, 429 (1971); Castro v. Beecher, 459 F.2d 725 (CA1 1972); Chance v. Board of Examiners, 458 F.2d 1167 (CA2 1972); Quarles v. Philip Morris, Inc., 279 F. Supp. 505 (E.D. Va. 1968). As noted in *Griggs, supra*:

> Congress did not intend by Title VII, however, to guarantee a job to every person regardless of qualifications. In short, the Act does not command that any person be hired simply because he was formerly the subject of discrimination, or because he is a member of a minority group. Discriminatory preference for any group, minority or majority, is precisely and only what Congress has proscribed. What is required by Congress is the removal of artificial, arbitrary, and unnecessary barriers to employment when the barriers operate invidiously to discriminate on the basis of racial or other impermissible classification. *Id.*, 401 U.S., at 430-431.

There are societal as well as personal interests on both sides of this equation. The broad, overriding interest, shared by employer, employee, and consumer, is efficient and trustworthy workmanship assured through fair and racially neutral employment and personnel decisions. In the implementation of such decisions, it is abundantly clear that Title VII tolerates no racial discrimination, subtle or otherwise. . . .

The complainant in a Title VII trial must carry the initial burden under the statute of establishing a prima facie case of racial discrimination. This may be done by showing (i) that he belongs to a racial minority; (ii) that he applied and was qualified for a job for which the employer was seeking applicants; (iii) that, despite his qualifications, he was rejected; and (iv) that, after his rejection, the position remained open and the employer continued to seek applicants from persons of complainant's qualifications.[13] In the instant case, we agree with the Court of Appeals that respondent proved a prima facie case. 463 F.2d 337, 353. Petitioner sought mechanics, respondent's trade, and continued to do so after respondent's rejection. Petitioner, moreover, does not dispute respondent's qualifications and acknowledges that his past work performance in petitioner's employ was "satisfactory."

The burden then must shift to the employer to articulate some legitimate, nondiscriminatory reason for the employee's rejection. We need not attempt in the instant case to detail every matter which fairly could be recognized as a reasonable basis for a refusal to hire. Here petitioner has assigned respondent's participation in unlawful conduct against it as the cause for his rejection. We think that this suffices to discharge petitioner's burden of proof at this stage and to meet respondent's prima facie case of discrimination.

. . . Petitioner's reason for rejection thus suffices to meet the prima facie case, but the inquiry must not end here. While Title VII does not, without more, compel rehiring of respondent, neither does it permit petitioner to use respondent's conduct as a pretext for the sort of discrimination prohibited by 703(a)(1). On remand, respondent must, as the Court of Appeals recognized, be afforded a fair opportunity to show that petitioner's stated reason for respondent's rejection was in fact pretext. Especially relevant to such a showing would be evidence that white employees involved in acts against petitioner of comparable seriousness to the "stall-in" were nevertheless retained or rehired. Petitioner may justifiably refuse to rehire one who was engaged in unlawful, disruptive acts against it, but only if this criterion is applied alike to members of all races. Other evidence that may be relevant to any showing of pretext includes facts as to the petitioner's treatment of respondent during his prior term of employment; petitioner's reaction, if any, to respondent's legitimate civil rights activities; and petitioner's general policy and practice with respect to minority employment. On the latter point, statistics as to petitioner's employment policy and practice may be helpful to a determination of whether petitioner's refusal to rehire respondent in this case conformed to a general pattern of discrimination against blacks. Jones v. Lee Way Motor Freight, Inc., 431 F.2d 245 (CA10 1970); Blumrosen, *Strangers in Paradise:* Griggs v. Duke Power Co., *and the Concept of Employment Discrimination*, 71 Mich. L. Rev. 59, 91-94 (1972).[19] In short, on the retrial respondent must be given a full and fair opportunity

---

[13] The facts necessarily will vary in Title VII cases, and the specification above of the prima facie proof required from respondent is not necessarily applicable in every respect to differing factual situations.

[19] The District Court may, for example, determine, after reasonable discovery that "the (racial)

to demonstrate by competent evidence that the presumptively valid reasons for his rejection were in fact a coverup for a racially discriminatory decision.

In sum, respondent should have been allowed to pursue his claim under § 703(a)(1). If the evidence on retrial is substantially in accord with that before us in this case, we think that respondent carried his burden of establishing a prima facie case of racial discrimination and that petitioner successfully rebutted that case. But this does not end the matter. On retrial, respondent must be afforded a fair opportunity to demonstrate that petitioner's assigned reason for refusing to re-employ was a pretext or discriminatory in its application. If the District Judge so finds, he must order a prompt and appropriate remedy. In the absence of such a finding, petitioner's refusal to rehire must stand.

The cause is hereby remanded to the District Court for reconsideration in accordance with this opinion.

NOTES AND QUESTIONS

1. The *McDonnell Douglas* inference of discrimination based on a minimum of circumstantial evidence accomplishes at least three things: (1) it identifies the type of discrimination being alleged (e.g., race discrimination) by requiring the plaintiff to state the protected group of which he is member (e.g., a racial minority); (2) it identifies the adverse action (e.g., refusal to hire) of which the plaintiff complains; and (3) it presents facts that negate the most obvious nondiscriminatory reasons for the adverse action and that are consistent with the possibility of discrimination. For example, some obvious nondiscriminatory reasons an employer might have for failing to hire a plaintiff are that the plaintiff failed to file an application, the plaintiff lacked the minimum qualifications, or the employer had already filled the position when the plaintiff applied. In *McDonnell Douglas*, the plaintiff negated these possibilities by showing he filed an application, he satisfied the minimum qualifications, and the position was open and remained open even after the employer rejected him. Do these facts, standing alone, lead to the conclusion that it is more likely than not that the employer had an illegal motive in rejecting the plaintiff's application?

In *McDonnell Douglas* the plaintiff's prima facie case may have been bolstered by the additional fact, stated by the Court but not included in the four-part formula, that "discriminatory practices and devices . . . have fostered racially stratified job environments to the disadvantage of minority citizens." In other words, a plaintiff's negation of the other obvious reasons for rejection leaves race discrimination as the next possibility, given the prevalence of race discrimination in our society. *See* Burdine v. Texas Dep't of Cmty. Affairs, 450 U.S. 248, 252 (1981); Furnco Constr. Corp. v. Waters, 438 U.S. 567, 577 (1978). At the very least, the possibility of race discrimination is strong enough that an employer should be required to explain itself and expose its explanation to the scrutiny of a trial.

Would the same four-part proof work equally well for a white applicant

---

composition of defendant's labor force is itself reflective of restrictive or exclusionary practices." *See* Blumrosen, *supra*, at 92. We caution that such general determinations, while helpful, may not be in and of themselves controlling as to an individualized hiring decision, particularly in the presence of an otherwise justifiable reason for refusing to rehire.

alleging race discrimination against an employer with a predominantly white force? *See* Taken v. Oklahoma Corp. Comm., 125 F.3d 1366 (10th Cir. 1997):

> [B]ecause plaintiffs are members of a historically favored group [whites], they are not entitled to the *McDonnell Douglas* presumption . . . unless they demonstrate the existence of "background circumstances that support an inference that the defendant is one of those unusual employers who discriminates against the majority. . . ."

Id. at 1369.

2. The fourth part of the plaintiff's formula for an inference of discrimination in *McDonnell Douglas* was that the position in question remained open after the employer rejected the plaintiff. What if the employer filled the position simultaneously with rejecting the plaintiff? In that case, the fourth part of the formula might be that the employer filled the position from the opposite class (e.g., in a race discrimination case, the employer rejected an African-American plaintiff and filled the position with a white candidate). *See, e.g.*, Walker v. Mortham, 158 F.3d 1177, 1184-1193 (11th Cir. 1998).

If the employer selected another applicant at the same time it rejected the plaintiff, is it not reasonable to assume the employer believed the successful candidate was better qualified than the plaintiff? Should the plaintiff be required to negate that possibility in his case in chief by presenting evidence of his own equal or superior qualifications? The Eleventh Circuit Court of Appeals considered this view in *Walker* but noted that the formula adopted in *McDonnell Douglas* was based less on the force of a logical inference than on policy and pragmatism. An applicant ordinarily has no way of knowing the facts of the employer's decision-making process. Thus, in *Walker*, the court held that a plaintiff need only prove that the successful candidate was from outside the plaintiff's protected category. The burden of production then shifts to the employer, and the employer must explain the basis for its decision.

3. The *McDonnell Douglas* prima facie evidence rule applies with appropriate modification to a variety of fact situations, adverse actions, and types of discrimination. In a discriminatory discharge case, for example, discrimination might be inferred from the facts that the plaintiff was a member of a protected class, was qualified for his job, was discharged, and was replaced by a person from outside the same class. *See, e.g.*, St. Mary's Honor Ctr. v. *Hicks*, 509 U.S. 502, 506 (1993). The formula is useful under nearly any of the other federal antidiscrimination laws. Thus, in an age discrimination case under the ADEA, the plaintiff alleges membership in the protected age group and the other elements of the *McDonnell Douglas* formula. Reeves v. Sanderson Plumbing Prods., Inc., 530 U.S. 133 (2000).

State courts have also applied the same *McDonnell Douglas* approach in deciding a variety of discrimination cases under state employment laws. *See, e.g.*, Colorado Civil Rights Comm'n v. Big O Tires, Inc., 940 P.2d 397 (Colo. 1997); DeBrow v. Century 21 Greta Lakes, Inc., 620 N.W.2d 836 (Mich. 2001); Reynolds v. Planut Co., 748 A.2d 1216 (N.J. Super. 2000); General Electric v. Pennsylvania Human Relations Comm'n, 365 A.2d 649 (Pa. 1976); Carpenter v. Central Vermont Med. Ctr., 743 A.2d 692 (Vt. 1999).

4. Is the four-part *McDonnell Douglas* test simply one set of facts

permitting an inference of discrimination, or is it a list of the essential elements of a cause of action for discrimination? The issue is especially important when a plaintiff presents some other set of facts arguably evidencing discrimination, but he cannot show the employer selected or preferred someone from outside the "protected class" with respect to a particular job. Suppose, for example, an employer hoping to hire a man is disappointed that all the best qualified candidates are women, so it rejects all candidates and suspends hiring, possibly forfeiting business or subcontracting the work a new employee might otherwise have performed. Is it possible for a rejected applicant to state a cause of action? *See* Carson v. Bethlehem Steel Corp., 82 F.3d 157 (7th Cir. 1996):

> The question . . . is whether the plaintiff has established a logical reason to believe that the decision rests on a legally forbidden ground. That one's replacement is of another race, sex, or age may help to raise an inference of discrimination, but it is neither a sufficient nor a necessary condition. Any demonstration strong enough to support a judgment in the plaintiff's favor if the employer remains silent will do, even if the proof does not fit into a set of pigeonholes.

82 F.3d at 158-159. *See also* O'Connor v. Consol. Coin Caterers Corp., 517 U.S. 308 (1996) (in age discrimination case, plaintiff is not required to prove employer preferred someone from outside the protected class of persons over 40); Cordova v. State Farm Ins. Cos., 124 F.3d 1145 (9th Cir. 1997) (other evidence may substitute for the *McDonnell Douglas* formula). Other possible sources of evidence might include statements by decision makers revealing discriminatory attitudes, statistical analysis of an employer's hiring practices, or other means of comparing an employer's treatment of persons within and outside the protected group. *See* Hazelwood Sch. Dist. v. United States, 433 U.S. 299 (1977); Abdu-Brisson v. Delta Air., 239 F.3d 456, 466-468 (2d Cir. 2001).

5. If the plaintiff presents prima facie evidence of discrimination, the burden of production shifts to the employer. The employer must present, by admissible evidence, a nondiscriminatory explanation for its action, and the plaintiff gains an opportunity to challenge the employer's credibility. Texas Dep't of Cmty. Affairs v. Burdine, 450 U.S. 248, 254-256 (1981). "[T]he factual inquiry proceeds to a new level of specificity," *id.* at 255, namely, whether the employer rejected the plaintiff because of discriminatory intent or because of the asserted nondiscriminatory reason. Put differently, the issue whether the employer's explanation is truthful becomes a proxy for the issue whether the employer intended to discriminate. If the employer appears to be hiding something, it might be reasonable to suppose it is hiding discrimination. However, "[t]he ultimate burden of persuading the trier of fact that the defendant intentionally discriminated against the plaintiff remains at all times with the plaintiff." *Id.* at 253.

Suppose the plaintiff presents nothing more than a set of facts *McDonnell Douglas* describes for a permissible inference of discrimination. The employer then "articulates" its reason for the adverse action. After argument on a motion for summary judgment or at the end of the trial, however, it becomes evident that the employer's explanation is wrong. If the *truthfulness* of the employer's explanation is a "proxy" for this issue of employer intent to discriminate, does the factfinder's rejection of the employer's explanation mean that the plaintiff is entitled to judgment as a matter of law? That issue is presented by the next case.

ST. MARY'S HONOR CTR. v. HICKS

509 U.S. 502 (1993)

Justice SCALIA delivered the opinion of the Court.

We granted certiorari to determine whether, in a suit against an employer alleging intentional racial discrimination in violation of § 703(a)(1) of Title VII of the Civil Rights Act of 1964, 42 U.S.C. § 2000e-2(a)(1), the trier of fact's rejection of the employer's asserted reasons for its actions mandates a finding for the plaintiff.

I

Petitioner St. Mary's Honor Center (St. Mary's) is a halfway house operated by the Missouri Department of Corrections and Human Resources (MDCHR). Respondent Melvin Hicks, a black man, was hired as a correctional officer at St. Mary's in August 1978 and was promoted to shift commander, one of six supervisory positions, in February 1980.

In 1983 MDCHR conducted an investigation of the administration of St. Mary's, which resulted in extensive supervisory changes in January 1984. Respondent retained his position, but John Powell became the new chief of custody (respondent's immediate supervisor) and petitioner Steve Long the new superintendent. Prior to these personnel changes respondent had enjoyed a satisfactory employment record, but soon thereafter became the subject of repeated, and increasingly severe, disciplinary actions. He was suspended for five days for violations of institutional rules by his subordinates on March 3, 1984. He received a letter of reprimand for alleged failure to conduct an adequate investigation of a brawl between inmates that occurred during his shift on March 21. He was later demoted from shift commander to correctional officer for his failure to ensure that his subordinates entered their use of a St. Mary's vehicle into the official log book on March 19, 1984. Finally, on June 7, 1984, he was discharged for threatening Powell during an exchange of heated words on April 19. [Respondent Hicks sued the petitioners under Title VII for alleged race discrimination in discharging him].

II

. . . With the goal of "progressively . . . sharpen[ing] the inquiry into the elusive factual question of intentional discrimination," Texas Dep't of Community Affairs v. Burdine, 450 U.S. 248, 255, n.8 (1981), our opinion in McDonnell Douglas Corp. v. Green, 411 U.S. 792 (1973), established an allocation of the burden of production and an order for the presentation of proof in Title VII discriminatory-treatment cases....Petitioners do not challenge the District Court's finding that respondent satisfied the minimal requirements of such a prima facie case ... by proving (1) that he is black, (2) that he was qualified for the position of shift commander, (3) that he was demoted from that position and ultimately discharged, and (4) that the position remained open and was ultimately filled by a white man....

Thus, the *McDonnell Douglas* presumption places upon the defendant the burden of producing an explanation to rebut the prima facie case—i.e., the burden of "producing evidence" that the adverse employment actions were taken "for a legitimate, nondiscriminatory reason." *Burdine*, 450 U.S., at 254. ...It is important to note, however, that although the *McDonnell Douglas* presumption shifts the burden of production to the defendant, "[t]he ultimate burden of persuading the trier of fact that the defendant intentionally discriminated against the plaintiff remains at all times with the plaintiff." 450 U.S., at 253. . . .

Respondent does not challenge the District Court's finding that petitioners sustained their burden of production by introducing evidence of two legitimate, nondiscriminatory reasons for their actions: the severity and the accumulation of rules violations committed by respondent. Our cases make clear that at that point the shifted burden of production became irrelevant: "If the defendant carries this burden of production, the presumption raised by the prima facie case is rebutted," *Burdine*, 450 U.S., at 255, and "drops from the case," *id.*, at 255, n.10. The plaintiff then has "the full and fair opportunity to demonstrate," through presentation of his own case and through cross-examination of the defendant's witnesses, "that the proffered reason was not the true reason for the employment decision," *id.*, at 256, and that race was. He retains that "ultimate burden of persuading the [trier of fact] that [he] has been the victim of intentional discrimination." *Ibid.*

The District Court, acting as trier of fact in this bench trial, found that the reasons petitioners gave were not the real reasons for respondent's demotion and discharge. It found that respondent was the only supervisor disciplined for violations committed by his subordinates; that similar and even more serious violations committed by respondent's co-workers were either disregarded or treated more leniently; and that Powell manufactured the final verbal confrontation in order to provoke respondent into threatening him. It nonetheless held that respondent had failed to carry his ultimate burden of proving that his race was the determining factor in petitioners' decision first to demote and then to dismiss him.[2] In short, the District Court concluded that "although [respondent] has proven the existence of a crusade to terminate him, he has not proven that the crusade was racially rather than personally motivated."

The Court of Appeals set this determination aside on the ground that "[o]nce [respondent] proved all of [petitioners'] proffered reasons for the adverse employment actions to be pretextual, [respondent] was entitled to judgment as a matter of law." 970 F.2d, at 492. ...

> Because all of defendants' proffered reasons were discredited, defendants were in a position of having offered no legitimate reason for their actions. In other words, defendants were in no better position than if they had remained silent, offering no rebuttal to an established inference that they had unlawfully discriminated against plaintiff on the basis of his race.

Ibid.

That is not so. By producing evidence (whether ultimately persuasive or not)

---

[2] Various considerations led it to this conclusion, including the fact that two blacks sat on the disciplinary review board that recommended disciplining respondent, that respondent's black subordinates who actually committed the violations were not disciplined, and that "the number of black employees at St. Mary's remained constant" . . . .

of nondiscriminatory reasons, petitioners sustained their burden of production, and thus placed themselves in a "better position than if they had remained silent." . . .

If . . . the defendant has succeeded in carrying its burden of production, the *McDonnell Douglas* framework — with its presumptions and burdens — is no longer relevant. To resurrect it later, after the trier of fact has determined that what was "produced" to meet the burden of production is not credible, flies in the face of our holding in *Burdine* that to rebut the presumption "[t]he defendant need not persuade the court that it was actually motivated by the proffered reasons." 450 U.S., at 254. The presumption, having fulfilled its role of forcing the defendant to come forward with some response, simply drops out of the picture. *Id.*, at 255. The defendant's "production" (whatever its persuasive effect) having been made, the trier of fact proceeds to decide the ultimate question: whether plaintiff has proven "that the defendant intentionally discriminated against [him]" because of his race, *id.*, at 253. The factfinder's disbelief of the reasons put forward by the defendant (particularly if disbelief is accompanied by a suspicion of mendacity) may, together with the elements of the prima facie case, suffice to show intentional discrimination. Thus, rejection of the defendant's proffered reasons will permit the trier of fact to infer the ultimate fact of intentional discrimination,[4] and the Court of Appeals was correct when it noted that, upon such rejection, "[n]o additional proof of discrimination is required." But the Court of Appeals' holding that rejection of the defendant's proffered reasons compels judgment for the plaintiff ... ignores our repeated admonition that the Title VII plaintiff at all times bears the "ultimate burden of persuasion." *See, e.g.*, Postal Service Bd. of Governors v. Aikens, 460 U.S. 711 (1983). . . .

IV

... What appears to trouble the dissent more than anything is that, in its view, our rule is adopted "for the benefit of employers who have been found to have given false evidence in a court of law," whom we "favo[r]" by "exempting them from responsibility for lies." ... [T]here is no justification for assuming (as the dissent repeatedly does) that those employers whose evidence is disbelieved are perjurers and liars. . . . Even if these were typically cases in which an individual defendant's sworn assertion regarding a physical occurrence was pitted against an individual plaintiff's sworn assertion regarding the same physical occurrence, surely it would be imprudent to call the party whose assertion is (by a mere preponderance of the evidence) disbelieved, a perjurer and a liar. And in these Title VII cases, the defendant is ordinarily not an individual but a company, which must rely upon the statement of an employee—often a relatively low-level employee—as to the central fact; and that central fact is not a physical occurrence, but rather that employee's state of mind. To say that the company which in good faith introduces such testimony, or even the testifying employee himself, becomes a liar and a perjurer when the testimony is not believed, is nothing short of absurd.

---

[4] ... [T]here is nothing whatever inconsistent between this statement and our later statements that (1) the plaintiff must show "both that the reason was false, and that discrimination was the real reason," and (2) "it is not enough . . . to disbelieve the employer." Even though (as we say here) rejection of the defendant's proffered reasons is enough at law to sustain a finding of discrimination, there must be a finding of discrimination.

Respondent contends that "[t]he litigation decision of the employer to place in controversy only . . . particular explanations eliminates from further consideration the alternative explanations that the employer chose not to advance." The employer should bear, he contends, "the responsibility for its choices and the risk that plaintiff will disprove any pretextual reasons *and therefore prevail.*" (emphasis added). It is the "therefore" that is problematic. Title VII does not award damages against employers who cannot prove a nondiscriminatory reason for adverse employment action, but only against employers who are proven to have taken adverse employment action by reason of (in the context of the present case) race. That the employer's proffered reason is unpersuasive, or even obviously contrived, does not necessarily establish that the plaintiff's proffered reason of race is correct. That remains a question for the factfinder to answer . . . .

The judgment of the Court of Appeals is reversed, and the case is remanded for further proceedings consistent with this opinion.

NOTES AND QUESTIONS

1. The truthfulness of an employer's articulated reason for an adverse action sometimes serves as a "proxy" for the issue of discriminatory intent, but as *St. Mary's* makes clear, being *wrong* about what happened should not be confused with *intending* to discriminate.

2. The significance of the rule in *St. Mary's* might arise at various points in litigation, assuming that the plaintiff has presented the basis for a *McDonnell Douglas* inference of discrimination and the employer has articulated a legitimate nondiscriminatory reason for the adverse action. First, at the summary judgment stage, the plaintiff might present irrefutable evidence that the employer's explanation is wrong, and argue for summary judgment in the plaintiff's favor. Second, the plaintiff might argue at the conclusion of trial that the employer's explanation is so unworthy of belief that the court should grant the plaintiff a directed verdict or judgment notwithstanding the verdict. Third, the plaintiff might seek a jury instruction or argue to the jury that they *must* find in the plaintiff's favor if they reject the employer's explanation. Finally, the plaintiff might argue on appeal that judgment for the plaintiff should be affirmed, or judgment for the employer should be reversed, because there is no reasonable dispute that the employer's explanation was pretextual. However, after *St. Mary's* it is clear that rejection of an employer's explanation does not in itself preclude a material issue of fact regarding discriminatory intent. The judge or jury might find that while the employer's explanation was wrong, the employer did not intend to discriminate.

3. To understand the ruling and operation of *St. Mary's* it is helpful to consider that not all prima facie cases are equal, not all failed explanations are equally bad, and every case has potentially significant facts outside the circle of a *McDonnell Douglas* inference and the employer's explanation. Imagine, for example, that a plaintiff uses the *McDonnell Douglas* model to establish an inference that the employer rejected his job application because of his national origin: Canadian. The interviewer is gone by the time of trial or does not remember the plaintiff or why he rejected the plaintiff because he interviews so many applicants. The employer's attorney guesses, wrongly, that the interviewer rejected

the plaintiff because the plaintiff performed poorly in the interview. At trial, the plaintiff presents himself so well that no juror can believe the plaintiff would perform poorly in an interview. The jury also notes the employer's chief executive is Canadian. Even if the jury rejects the employer's explanation for what happened, the jury might still reasonably find that the employer did not intend to discriminate on the basis of Canadian national origin.

4. Parts of Justice Scalia's opinion in *St. Mary's* opened the door for employers to advocate a theory known as "pretext plus": that once the employer fulfills its burden of production by articulating a legitimate nondiscriminatory reason for an adverse action, a *McDonnell Douglas* inference of discriminatory intent drops from the case and has no further legal significance—even if the employer's explanation proves wrong. Thus, if a judge or jury ultimately finds the employer's explanation wrong, the plaintiff still has *no* evidence of discriminatory intent unless the plaintiff has something *more* than the now ineffectual *McDonnell Douglas* inference. As long as the employer presents even a failed explanation for its adverse action, the plaintiff loses *as a matter of* law unless there is *additional* evidence of discriminatory intent. In other words, the plaintiff must prove "pretext" (the employer's explanation is wrong) "plus" present additional evidence of discriminatory intent. The Supreme Court rejected the "pretext plus" theory in *Reeves v. Sanderson Plumbing Products, Inc.*, 530 U.S. 133 (2000):

> In appropriate circumstances, the trier of fact can reasonably infer from the falsity of the explanation that the employer is dissembling to cover up a discriminatory purpose.... Moreover, once the employer's justification has been eliminated, discrimination may well be the most likely alternative explanation, especially since the employer is in the best position to put forth the actual reason for its decision. . . . Thus, a plaintiff's prima facie case, combined with sufficient evidence to find that the employer's asserted justification is false, may permit the trier of fact to conclude that the employer unlawfully discriminated.
>
> This is not to say that such a showing by the plaintiff will always be adequate to sustain a jury's finding of liability. Certainly there will be instances where, although the plaintiff has established a prima facie case and set forth sufficient evidence to reject the defendant's explanation, no rational factfinder could conclude that the action was discriminatory. For instance, an employer would be entitled to judgment as a matter of law if the record conclusively revealed some other, nondiscriminatory reason for the employer's decision, or if the plaintiff created only a weak issue of fact as to whether the employer's reason was untrue and there was abundant and uncontroverted independent evidence that no discrimination had occurred.

Id. at 147-148. In sum, when the truth of the employer's reason is a proxy for the issue of discriminatory intent, the employer does not earn a free pass to judgment just by articulating a nondiscriminatory reason, and the plaintiff does not earn a free pass to judgment just by proving that the employer's explanation is wrong.

Mixed Motives v. Single Motive

One shortcoming of the *McDonnell Douglas* model of proof is its assumption that employers select or choose between employees for one reason or another reason, and not for both reasons. In the real world, employers often make decisions based on several motives. In fact, given the decline of categorical discrimination (absolute policies against hiring minorities), the more likely situation is an employer that leans by degrees against minorities. Such a decision-maker's bias will be most important if there is a convenient lawful excuse to reject or terminate a minority. A mixture of motives is even more likely if there is more than one decision-maker, which is true whenever a decision is by a committee or other collective body. Some members of the body might be free of bias while others are not.

The U.S. Supreme Court first recognized the possibility of a "mixed motive" discrimination case in Price Waterhouse v. Hopkins, 490 U.S. 228 (1989), one of the most important cases in the law of discrimination for a multitude of reasons. In *Price Waterhouse*, the plaintiff applied for but was rejected for promotion from associate to partner of an accounting firm. By its express terms, Title VII applies only to discrimination against an "employee" or applicant for employment. However, the opportunity for elevation to partnership is part of the package of rights and benefits of employment in some firms. In a law firm, for example, it is often understood that an associate (an "employee") gains the opportunity to apply for and compete for partnership according to a particular process. In this situation, Title VII does apply to the firm's selection of partners from its associates. See Hishon v. King & Spalding, 467 U.S. 69 (1984).

The firm in *Price Waterhouse* did not categorically exclude women. It did consider Hopkins' partnership application but was troubled by her record of abrasiveness and lack of interpersonal skills, which were lawful, nondiscriminatory reasons. However, some voting partners were clearly influenced by *stereotypes* about how a woman should behave in comparison with a man:

> One partner described her as "macho;" another suggested that she "overcompensated for being a woman;" a third advised her to take "a course at charm school." Several partners criticized her use of profanity; in response, one partner suggested that those partners objected to her swearing only "because it's a lady using foul language." Another supporter explained that Hopkins "ha[d] matured from a tough-talking somewhat masculine hard-nosed mgr to an authoritative, formidable, but much more appealing lady ptr candidate." But it was the man who, as Judge Gesell found, bore responsibility for explaining to Hopkins the reasons for the Policy Board's decision ... who delivered the coup de grace: in order to improve her chances for partnership, Thomas Beyer advised, Hopkins should "walk more femininely, talk more femininely, dress more femininely, wear make-up, have her hair styled, and wear jewelry."

Id. at 235. The Court found that this sex stereotyping evidenced the employer's illegal discriminatory intent. The Court's effort to sort out the mixture of legal motives (e.g., lack of interpersonal skills) v. illegal motive (unlawful sex stereotyping) led to a debate that culminated in the Civil Rights Act of 1991, which amended Title VII to specifically address the problem of "mixed motive" cases.

As amended, Title VII provides that a plaintiff establishes the employer's violation and liability for discrimination by proving the employer was motivated by race, sex or other unlawful bias. 42 U.S.C. § 2000e-2(m). However, the employer can limit its liability—avoiding back pay or an order to hire or reinstate— by proving an affirmative defense: that it would have taken the same action regardless of the illegal bias. *Id.* § 2000e-5(g)(1)(B). A plaintiff who would have suffered the same adverse action anyway and is not entitled to back pay or the job might still be entitled to damages for emotional distress, a judicial declaration that the employer violates Title VII, an injunction against continued discriminatory practices, and attorneys' fees.

QUIGG v. THOMAS COUNTY SCHOOL DISTRICT

814 F.3d 1227 (11th Cir. 2016)

WILSON, Circuit Judge:

Linda Quigg claims that the Thomas County School District (School District) ... discriminated and retaliated against her, in violation of Title VII of the Civil Rights Act of 1964, 42 U.S.C. § 2000e et seq., and 42 U.S.C. § 1983, by refusing to renew her employment contract and filing an ethics complaint against her. The district court granted summary judgment to the School District....

On appeal, Quigg argues, inter alia, that the district court erred because the summary judgment framework the court applied to her discrimination claims—the *McDonnell Douglas* framework—is not the proper framework for evaluating mixed-motive claims that rely on circumstantial evidence. Applying the proper mixed-motive framework to Quigg's discrimination claims, we hold that the district court erred in granting summary judgment ....

I. BACKGROUND

Quigg served as the Assistant Superintendent of the School District from 1998 to 2007. In 2007, she became the Superintendent The School Board appoints superintendents through term contracts, which are subject to renewal. The School Board consists of seven members, and a majority vote is required to renew a superintendent's contract....

Given that Quigg's superintendent contract was set to expire in mid-2011, the School Board agreed to meet in February 2011 for a renewal vote on the contract. Prior to the vote, School Board members Morgan and Nesmith encouraged Quigg to reorganize her administration to provide for an assistant superintendent. Morgan and Nesmith told Quigg that she needed a tough "hatchet man" to address school policy implementation—a "guy" she could send to individual schools to "handle" things. Morgan and Nesmith recommended a specific male employee.... Quigg suggested a female employee.... Morgan replied: "We have no males in the school system?" [and] stated to Quigg: "[W]hat about a guy in this position? ... I'm just being honest about that, you know, a guy will—and I was just thinking from the standpoint of an offset." However, following these comments, Morgan named a female school employee as a possible candidate....

Nesmith [also] spoke to a parent of a School District student prior to the renewal vote .... Referring to the position of superintendent, the proposed assistant superintendent position, or alternatively, the office of the superintendent more generally, Nesmith told the parent: "[I]t is time to put a man in there." ...

At the beginning of the February 2011 renewal vote meeting, Quigg rejected

Morgan's and Nesmith's assistant superintendent proposal. Instead, Quigg proposed a reorganization plan providing for various "directors" to oversee different aspects of her administration. The School Board then voted five-to-two against renewing Quigg's contract.... [Board Member] Hiers told a School District employee that she voted against Quigg because Quigg "needed a strong male to work under her to handle problems, someone who could get tough."

... Quigg filed a complaint with the Equal Employment Opportunity Commission (EEOC).... [I]n February 2012 the School District lodged a complaint against Quigg with the Georgia Professional Standards Commission (PSC) ... partly based on the documents the School Board sent to the PSC in 2010. The PSC ... recommended suspension of Quigg's teaching license....

[T]he court held that Quigg presented only circumstantial evidence of discrimination and, applying the *McDonnell Douglas* framework, concluded that no triable issues of discrimination exist. The court also found that Quigg's various retaliation claims were without merit [and] granted summary judgment to the School District and School Board members on all of Quigg's claims....

III. TITLE VII AND § 1983 DISCRIMINATION CLAIMS

We first address Quigg's Title VII and § 1983 mixed-motive sex discrimination claims... Discrimination claims brought under Title VII and § 1983 are typically categorized as either mixed-motive or single-motive claims. An employee can succeed on a mixed-motive claim by showing that illegal bias, such as bias based on sex or gender, "was a motivating factor for" an adverse employment action, "even though other factors also motivated" the action. 42 U.S.C. § 2000e–2(m); see also *Mt. Healthy City Sch. Dist. Bd. of Educ. v. Doyle*, 429 U.S. 274 (1977). In contrast, single-motive claims—which are also known as "pretext" claims—require a showing that bias was the true reason for the adverse action.

Single-motive and mixed-motive discrimination claims can be established with either direct or circumstantial evidence. See *Desert Palace, Inc. v. Costa*, 539 U.S. 90, 99–102 (2003); *Wilson v. B/E Aerospace, Inc.*, 376 F.3d 1079, 1085 (11th Cir.2004). Here, Quigg's claims are based on circumstantial evidence—the evidence "suggests, but does not prove, a discriminatory motive." *Id.* at 1086.

A. The Proper Summary Judgment Framework for Evaluating Mixed-Motive Claims Based on Circumstantial Evidence

1. Relevant Legal Developments

In *Price Waterhouse v. Hopkins*, 490 U.S. 228 (1989), the Supreme Court held, for the first time, that an adverse employment action motivated by both legal and illegal reasons constitutes actionable discrimination under Title VII. In a concurring opinion, Justice O'Connor agreed that an employee can prove discrimination under a mixed-motive theory, but she concluded that the employee must offer direct evidence in support thereof.

A few years after *Price Waterhouse*, Congress amended Title VII by passing 42 U.S.C. § 2000e–2(m). Section 2000e–2(m) "responded to Price Waterhouse by setting forth standards applicable in mixed-motive cases." See *Desert Palace*, 539 U.S. at 94.

... [F]ollowing the passage of § 2000e–2(m), our circuit and several of our sister circuits relied on Justice O'Connor's *Price Waterhouse* concurrence to hold that direct evidence is required to prove a mixed-motive claim under the section. In light of this "direct evidence" requirement, employees relying on circumstantial evidence of discrimination could not bring Title VII mixed-motive claims.... In *Desert Palace*, the Supreme Court rejected [the] "direct evidence" requirement and held that an employee can prove a mixed-motive case with direct or circumstantial evidence. 539 U.S. at 101–02. In doing so, the Court opened the door to claims like Quigg's. Yet, Desert Palace did not resolve the question of the appropriate summary judgment framework for such claims....

2. An Examination of *McDonnell Douglas*

Our court has primarily used the *McDonnell Douglas* framework to evaluate circumstantial evidence-based discrimination claims at summary judgment. [W]e must first consider whether this approach resolves the question before us. It does not. *McDonnell Douglas* is inappropriate for evaluating mixed-motive claims because it is overly burdensome when applied in the mixed-motive context.

[The *McDonnell-Douglas*] framework is fatally inconsistent with the mixed-motive theory of discrimination because the framework is predicated on proof of a single, "true reason" for an adverse action.... [A]n employee can only meet her burden under *McDonnell Douglas* by showing the employer's purported legitimate reasons "never motivated the employer ... [or] did not do so in a particular case." See *Price Waterhouse*, 490 U.S. at 270 (O'Connor, J., concurring). Thus, if an employee cannot rebut her employer's proffered reasons for an adverse action but offers evidence demonstrating that the employer also relied on a forbidden consideration, she will not meet her burden. Yet, this is the exact type of employee that the mixed-motive theory of discrimination is designed to protect. In light of this clear incongruity between the *McDonnell Douglas* framework and mixed-motive claims, it is improper to use that framework to evaluate such claims at summary judgment....

3. Identifying the Appropriate Framework

Given that *McDonnell Douglas* is not appropriate for examining mixed-motive claims at summary judgment, we adopt the framework put forth ...in *White v. Baxter Healthcare Corp.*, 533 F.3d 381 (6th Cir. 2008). That framework requires a court to ask only whether a plaintiff has offered "evidence sufficient to convince a jury that: (1) the defendant took an adverse employment action against the plaintiff; and (2) [a protected characteristic] was a motivating factor for the defendant's adverse employment action." 533 F.3d at 400 (internal quotation marks omitted). [T]he court must determine whether the "plaintiff has presented sufficient evidence for a reasonable jury to conclude, by a preponderance of the evidence, that [her protected characteristic] was a motivating factor for [an] adverse employment decision." *Id.* at 401 (quoting *Desert Palace*, 539 U.S. at 101)....

[T]he framework identified in ... *White* aligns with the mixed-motive theory of discrimination because it directly incorporates the "motivating factor" language used in Price Waterhouse and § 2000e–2(m) to describe mixed-motive claims. It also does not call for the unnecessary burden-shifting required by *McDonnell*

Douglas, nor does it suffer from *McDonnell Douglas*'s pitfall of demanding that employees prove pretext....

Although we primarily have relied on *McDonnell Douglas* when considering circumstantial evidence-based claims at summary judgment, . . . *McDonnell Douglas* is not "the sine qua non for a plaintiff to survive a summary judgment motion in an employment discrimination case." See *Smith v. Lockheed-Martin Corp.*, 644 F.3d 1321, 1328 (11th Cir. 2011). Rather, the crux of the analysis at the summary judgment stage is whether the plaintiff has offered sufficient evidence to establish a genuine issue of discrimination. Accordingly, "the plaintiff will always survive summary judgment if [s]he presents circumstantial evidence that creates a triable issue concerning the employer's discriminatory intent." *Id.* The framework we adopt from *White* requires the same analysis emphasized in these precedents—a straightforward inquiry into whether the plaintiff has presented sufficient evidence of mixed-motive discrimination to establish a jury issue. . . .

B. Title VII and § 1983 Claims Against the School District

Quigg asserts the School District is liable for sex discrimination under Title VII and § 1983 because the School Board's decision not to renew her contract was based on her sex and gender. The School District responds that the Board's decision not to renew Quigg's contract was solely based on legitimate, nondiscriminatory reasons. The School District also argues that, even assuming a triable issue of mixed-motive discrimination exists, it is entitled to partial summary judgment on Quigg's § 1983 claims and complete summary judgment on her Title VII claims because the Board would have made the "same decision" regardless of her sex....

1. Quigg Has Established a Triable Issue of Mixed-Motive Discrimination

... An employee challenging a decision made by a board can succeed on a mixed-motive claim if she demonstrates that "discriminatory input," such as sex or gender-based bias, factored into the board's "decisional process." *Price Waterhouse*, 490 U.S. at 272 (O'Connor, J., concurring). Statements by the board's members or others involved with the board's decisional process that suggest bias can serve as evidence of discrimination. See *id.* at 251 (plurality opinion) (explaining that "stereotyped remarks can certainly be evidence that gender played a part" in an adverse employment action). However, "[r]emarks at work that are based on sex stereotypes do not inevitably prove that gender played a part in a particular employment decision." *Price Waterhouse*, 490 U.S. at 251. When an employee raising a mixed-motive claim relies solely on remarks that indirectly evidence discrimination, the employee must show the circumstances surrounding the remarks create a genuine issue of material fact that the employer "actually relied on her [sex or] gender in making its decision." *Id.*

Quigg offers the following statements by Nesmith, Morgan, and Hiers as evidence of discrimination: (1) Nesmith's statement to a school parent that "it is time to put a man in there"; (2) Morgan's and Nesmith's recommendation to Quigg that she hire a tough "hatchet man" to serve as assistant superintendent; (3) Morgan's statement to Quigg that she should consider a male assistant superintendent because it is important to achieve gender balance in the school administration; and (4) the comment by Hiers shortly after the renewal vote that she voted against Quigg because Quigg "needed a strong male to work under her to handle problems, someone who could get tough."

These statements indicate that Nesmith, Morgan, and Hiers preferred men—or, at the least, individuals with masculine characteristics—for positions within the office of the superintendent. As such, the statements are circumstantial evidence of discrimination. Moreover, a jury could find that the circumstances surrounding the statements prove this bias played a role in Nesmith's, Morgan's, and Hiers's votes against Quigg. The statements were far from stray remarks at the workplace based on sex stereotypes. Rather, Nesmith, Morgan, and Hiers made the statements (1) during conversations about whether to renew Quigg's contract, (2) in relative temporal proximity to the vote, and (3) specifically referring to the composition of the office of the superintendent. Accordingly, … the statements establish a jury issue as to whether sex or gender-based bias was a motivating factor in the School Board's decision not to renew her contract.

2. The School District's "Same Decision" Defense Fails

The School District asserts that it has successfully raised an affirmative defense to Quigg's claims—the "same decision" defense.… Title VII provides that if an employer can demonstrate it "would have taken the same action in the absence of the impermissible motivating factor, the court ... shall not award damages" or certain equitable relief. 42 U.S.C. § 2000e–5(g)(2)(B)…. This defense is also available under § 1983; however, under § 1983 the defense serves as a complete bar to liability….

The School District claims it has presented evidence showing that all five Board members who voted against renewal—Streets, Evans, Hiers, Nesmith, and Morgan—would have done so regardless of Quigg's sex or gender. We agree with the School District with respect to Streets, Evans, and Hiers, but hold that a triable issue exists as to whether Nesmith and Morgan would have made the same decision absent bias….

Streets and Evans never made any comments suggesting illegal bias; their deposition testimony and performance evaluations of Quigg show that they felt her performance was inadequate; and their and Quigg's deposition testimony demonstrate ongoing personal animosity between them and Quigg, including tension resulting from Quigg's negative attitude towards them and her attempt to remove them from the School Board during the 2010 election. Likewise,…. Hiers rated Quigg as "unacceptable" in several categories on her individual performance evaluation of Quigg in 2010 and testified that Quigg created a toxic atmosphere….

Regarding Nesmith and Morgan, we reach a different conclusion. According to the School District, Nesmith and Morgan would have voted against Quigg regardless of her sex or gender because she refused to adopt their reorganization plan. However, the only evidence the School District offers in direct support of this claim is self-serving testimony from Morgan and Nesmith.… Taking the evidence in the light most favorable to Quigg, a jury could conclude that the reorganization plan proposed by Morgan and Nesmith was motivated by sex or gender-based bias given the plan's emphasis on a tough, "hatchet man" assistant superintendent.... Therefore, a showing that Nesmith and Morgan voted against Quigg because she rejected their plan would not provide sufficient evidentiary support that their decisions were made without regard to sex….

[T]he district court erred in dismissing her Title VII and § 1983 mixed-motive claims …. [We] remand for proceedings consistent with this opinion.

NOTES AND QUESTIONS

1. How much circumstantial evidence is necessary for a case to be a "mixed motive" rather than "single motive" or "pretext" case? The question is important because the mixed motive rule effectively shifts the burden of proof on the issue of causation to the employer. If illegal motive was a proven factor, the *employer* must prove it would have taken the same action anyway. The jury must be instructed accordingly, and the judge reviewing the evidence in support of a verdict for the plaintiff has much less leeway to reject the verdict.

Not much evidence is necessary for a case to require mixed motive analysis according to Desert Palace, Inc. v. Costa, 539 U.S. 90 (2003). In that case, the Court suggested that the plaintiff is entitled to a mixed motive analysis by the court and a mixed motive instruction for the jury whenever the plaintiff has enough for a prima facie case—including one based on nothing more than a *McDonnell Douglas* inference of discrimination and doubt about the employer's explanation:

> We have often acknowledged the utility of circumstantial evidence in discrimination cases. For instance, in Reeves v. Sanderson Plumbing Products, Inc., 530 U.S. 133 (2000), we recognized that evidence that a defendant's explanation for an employment practice is "unworthy of credence" is "one form of *circumstantial evidence* that is probative of intentional discrimination." *Id.*, at 147 (emphasis added). The reason for treating circumstantial and direct evidence alike is both clear and deep rooted: "Circumstantial evidence is not only sufficient, but may also be more certain, satisfying and persuasive than direct evidence." Rogers v. Missouri Pacific R. Co., 352 U.S. 500, 508, n. 17 (1957)….
>
> In order to obtain an instruction under § 2000e–2(m), a plaintiff need only present sufficient evidence for a reasonable jury to conclude, by a preponderance of the evidence, that "race, color, religion, sex, or national origin was a motivating factor for any employment practice."

539 U.S. at 99-101.

2. The *Price Waterhouse* rule that sex stereotyping is evidence of illegal motive is especially significant in the current debate regarding whether Title VII's prohibition against sex discrimination applies to discrimination on the basis of sexual orientation or identity. Is it illegal for an employer to require applicants or employees to adhere to gender stereotypes? If an employer discriminates against a man for behaving effeminately, is the employer engaged in a type of sex discrimination described by *Price Waterhouse*? The theory that Title VII does apply to discrimination on the basis of sexual orientation, identity or gender stereotypes was boosted to some degree by another U.S. Supreme Court decision, Oncale v. Sundowner Offshore Servs., Inc., 523 U.S. 75 (1998). In *Oncale*, the Court held that male a plaintiff pleaded a case of sex discrimination by alleging that other male employees targeted and "harassed" him because of his sex—male. Justice Scalia, writing for the Court, observed that "sex discrimination" can occur even when the

discriminator and the injured party are of the same sex. The essence of "sex discrimination" is difference in treatment because of sex. Justice Scalia continued:

> Courts and juries have found the inference of discrimination easy to draw in most male-female sexual harassment situations, because the challenged conduct typically involves explicit or implicit proposals of sexual activity; it is reasonable to assume those proposals would not have been made to someone of the same sex. The same chain of inference would be available to a plaintiff alleging same-sex harassment, if there were credible evidence that the harasser was homosexual. But harassing conduct need not be motivated by sexual desire to support an inference of discrimination on the basis of sex. A trier of fact might reasonably find such discrimination, for example, if a female victim is harassed in such sex-specific and derogatory terms by another woman as to make it clear that the harasser is motivated by general hostility to the presence of women in the workplace. A same-sex harassment plaintiff may also, of course, offer direct comparative evidence about how the alleged harasser treated members of both sexes .... Whatever evidentiary route the plaintiff chooses to follow, he or she must always prove that the conduct at issue was not merely tinged with offensive sexual connotations, but actually constituted "discrimina[tion] ... because of ... sex."

523 U.S. at 80-81. This passage in Justice Scalia's opinion did not necessarily address whether *all* differences in treatment associated with sex are illegal under Title VII. Many lower courts continue to hold that an employer can require applicants and employees to adhere to some traditional gender norms. *See, e.g.*, Jespersen v. Harrah's Operating Co., 444 F.3d 1104 (9th Cir. 2006) (requirement that female employees wear makeup was not illegal sex discrimination).

3. During the Obama administration, the EEOC, substantially relying on *Price Waterhouse* and *Oncale*, announced that it would treat discrimination on the basis of sexual orientation or identity as illegal sex discrimination. *See* Baldwin v. Fox, EEOC App. No. 0120133080, 2015 WL 4397641 (July 15, 2015). But EEOC interpretations of the law are non-binding upon, and subject to review by, the federal courts. The Trump administration has taken the position that Title VII does *not* prohibit discrimination based on sexual orientation or identity. In Zarda v. Altitude Express, Inc. (pending in the United States Court of Appeals for the Second Circuit), the Department of Justice urged the court to reject the theory that Title VII prohibits discrimination on the basis of sexual orientation. The Trump administration's nominees for new Commissioners of the EEOC have left some doubt about their own views regarding LGBT rights under Title VII. . *Trump's EEOC Nominees "Wishy Washy" on LGBT Workplace Rights*, Washington Blade (Sept. 25, 2017), http://www.washingtonblade.com/2017/09/25/trumps-eeoc-nominees-wishy-washy-on-lgbt-workplace-rights/. Thus, it remains ultimately for the courts to determine whether discrimination on the basis of sexual identity or orientation is illegal "sex discrimination."

EVANS v. GEORGIA REGIONAL HOSPITAL

850 F.3d 1248 (11th Cir. 2017)

MARTINEZ, District Judge:

Jameka Evans appeals the sua sponte dismissal of her employment discrimination complaint, filed pursuant to 42 U.S.C. § 2000e et seq., in which she alleged that she was discriminated against because of her sexual orientation and gender non-conformity, and retaliated against after she lodged a complaint with her employer's human resources department.... For the reasons set forth below, we affirm the district court's dismissal order in part, and vacate and remand in part.

Evans filed a pro se complaint against Georgia Regional Hospital ("Hospital"), Chief Charles Moss, Lisa Clark, and Senior Human Resources Manager Jamekia Powers, alleging employment discrimination under Title VII in her job as a security officer at the Hospital. Evans also moved for leave to proceed in forma pauperis before the district court, and for appointment of counsel. In her complaint, Evans alleged the following facts, which this Court accepts as true.

Evans worked at the Hospital as a security officer from August 1, 2012, to October 11, 2013, when she left voluntarily. During her time at the Hospital, she was denied equal pay or work, harassed, and physically assaulted or battered. She was discriminated against on the basis of her sex and targeted for termination for failing to carry herself in a "traditional woman[ly] manner." Although she is a gay woman, she did not broadcast her sexuality. However, it was "evident" that she identified with the male gender, because of how she presented herself—"(male uniform, low male haircut, shoes, etc.")....

[Evans filed suit against the Hospital under Title VII alleging sex discrimination. The district court granted the Hospital's motion for summary judgment, rejecting Evans' argument that discrimination on the basis of sexual orientation is "sex discrimination" under Title VII].

First, Evans argues that the district court erred in dismissing her claim that she was discriminated against for failing to conform to gender stereotypes, because an LGBT person may bring a separate discrimination claim for gender nonconformity. She contends that her status as a lesbian supports her claim of sex discrimination, because discrimination against someone for her orientation often coincides with discrimination for gender non-conformity. Evans further asserts that discrimination based on gender stereotypes is a broad claim that encompasses more than just her appearance, but also provides for suits based on various other stereotypes, such as family structure....

Discrimination based on failure to conform to a gender stereotype is sex-based discrimination. Glenn v. Brumby, 663 F.3d 1312, 1316 (11th Cir. 2011) (citing Price Waterhouse v. Hopkins, 490 U.S. 228 (1989). Specifically, in Glenn, we held that discrimination against a transgender individual because of gender-nonconformity was sex discrimination. In that decision, we stated that "[a]ll persons, whether transgender or not, are protected from discrimination on the basis of gender stereotype," and we reasoned that, because those protections apply to everyone, a transgender individual could not be excluded. Id. at 1318-19. We hold that the lower court erred because a gender non-conformity claim is not "just another way to claim discrimination based on sexual orientation," but instead, constitutes a separate, distinct avenue for relief under Title VII.

Accordingly, we vacate the portion of the district court's order dismissing Evans's gender non-conformity claim with prejudice and remand with instructions to grant Evans leave to amend such claim.

Evans next argues that she has stated a claim under Title VII by alleging that she endured workplace discrimination because of her sexual orientation. She has not. Our binding precedent forecloses such an action. Blum v. Gulf Oil Corp., 597 F.2d 936, 938 (5th Cir. 1979) ("Discharge for homosexuality is not prohibited by Title VII ..."). Evans and the EEOC also argue that ... Price Waterhouse v. Hopkins, 490 U.S. 228 (1989), and Oncale v. Sundowner Offshore Servs., Inc., 523 U.S. 75 (1998), support a cause of action for sexual orientation discrimination under Title VII. Again, we disagree. The fact that claims for gender non-conformity and same-sex discrimination can be brought pursuant to Title VII does not permit us to depart from *Blum. Price Waterhouse* and *Oncale* are neither clearly on point nor contrary to *Blum.* These Supreme Court decisions do not squarely address whether sexual orientation discrimination is prohibited by Title VII.

Finally, even though they disagree with the decisions, Evans and the EEOC acknowledge that other circuits have held that sexual orientation discrimination is not actionable under Title VII. *See, e.g.*, Higgins v. New Balance Athletic Shoe, Inc., 194 F.3d 252, 259 (1st Cir. 1999); Simonton v. Runyon, 232 F.3d 33, 36 (2d Cir. 2000); Bibby v. Phila. Coca Cola Bottling Co., 260 F.3d 257, 261 (3d Cir. 2001); Vickers v. Fairfield Med. Ctr., 453 F.3d 757, 762 (6th Cir. 2006); Hamner v. St. Vincent Hosp. & Health Care Ctr., Inc., 224 F.3d 701, 704 (7th Cir. 2000); Williamson v. A.G. Edwards & Sons, Inc., 876 F.2d 69, 70 (8th Cir. 1989) ("Title VII does not prohibit discrimination against homosexuals."); Rene v. MGM Grand Hotel, Inc., 305 F.3d 1061, 1063-64 (9th Cir. 2002); Medina v. Income Support Div., 413 F.3d 1131, 1135 (10th Cir. 2005). Evans and the EEOC question these decisions, in part, because of *Price Waterhouse* and *Oncale.* Whether those Supreme Court cases impact other circuit's decisions, many of which were decided after *Price Waterhouse* and *Oncale*, does not change our analysis that Blum is binding precedent that has not been overruled by a clearly contrary opinion of the Supreme Court or of this Court sitting en banc. Accordingly, we affirm the portion of the district court's order dismissing Evan's sexual orientation claim....

PRYOR, Circuit Judge, concurring:

I concur in the majority opinion, but I write separately to explain the error of the argument of the Equal Employment Opportunity Commission and the dissent that a person who experiences discrimination because of sexual orientation necessarily experiences discrimination for deviating from gender stereotypes. Although a person who experiences the former will sometimes also experience the latter, the two concepts are legally distinct....

Like any other woman, Evans can state a claim that she experienced, for example, discrimination for wearing a "male haircut" if she includes enough factual allegations. But just as a woman cannot recover under Title VII when she is fired because of her heterosexuality, neither can a gay woman sue for discrimination based on her sexual orientation. Deviation from a particular gender stereotype may correlate disproportionately with a particular sexual orientation, and plaintiffs who allege discrimination on the basis of gender nonconformity will often also have experienced discrimination because of sexual orientation. But under Title VII, we ask only whether the individual experienced discrimination for deviating from a gender stereotype.

... The Commission and the dissent would have us hold that sexual orientation discrimination always constitutes discrimination for gender nonconformity. They contend, for example, that all gay individuals necessarily engage in the same behavior. But that argument stereotypes all gay individuals in the same way that the Commission and the dissent allege that the Hospital stereotyped Evans.

By assuming that all gay individuals behave the same way or have the same interests, the Commission and the dissent disregard the diversity of experiences of gay individuals. Some gay individuals adopt what various commentators have referred to as the gay "social identity" but experience a variety of sexual desires.... A gay individual may establish with enough factual evidence that she experienced sex discrimination because her behavior deviated from a gender stereotype held by an employer, but our review of that claim would rest on behavior alone.

ROSENBAUM, Circuit Judge, concurring in part and dissenting in part:

A woman should be a "woman." She should wear dresses, be subservient to men, and be sexually attracted to only men. If she doesn't conform to this view of what a woman should be, an employer has every right to fire her.

That was the law in 1963—before Congress enacted Title VII of the Civil Rights Act of 1964. But that is not the law now. And the rule that Title VII precludes discrimination on the basis of every stereotype of what a woman supposedly should be—including each of those stated above—has existed since the Supreme Court issued Price Waterhouse v. Hopkins, 490 U.S. 228 (1989), 28 years ago.

Yet even today the panel ignores this clear mandate. To justify its position, the panel invokes 38-year-old precedent—issued ten years before *Price Waterhouse* necessarily abrogated it—and calls it binding precedent that ties our hands. I respectfully disagree.

Plain and simple, when a woman alleges, as Evans has, that she has been discriminated against because she is a lesbian, she necessarily alleges that she has been discriminated against because she failed to conform to the employer's image of what women should be—specifically, that women should be sexually attracted to men only. And it is utter fiction to suggest that she was not discriminated against for failing to comport with her employer's stereotyped view of women. That is discrimination "because of ... sex," 42 U.S.C. § 2000e-2(a)(1), and it clearly violates Title VII under *Price Waterhouse*.

So I dissent from Part IV of the panel's opinion. On remand, Evans should be allowed to amend her complaint to state such a claim....

We in the Eleventh Circuit heard the Supreme Court's message loud and clear. In Glenn v. Brumby, 663 F.3d 1312 (11th Cir. 2011), the employer fired Glenn, a transgender woman, because the employer learned that Glenn intended to proceed with gender transition. In fact, the employer testified that he terminated Glenn's employment "based on 'the sheer fact of the transition.'"

We relied on *Price Waterhouse's* reasoning to find that the employer's testimony "provide[d] ample direct evidence ... that [the employer] acted on the basis of Glenn's gender non-conformity." For this reason, we concluded that the employer had violated Title VII. So we applied prescriptive-stereotyping theory to hold that discrimination against a transgender employee merely because the employee fails to conform to the employer's view of what a member of the employee's birth-assigned sex should be violates Title VII.

Price Waterhouse and *Glenn* likewise demand the conclusion that discrimination because an employee is gay violates Title VII's proscription on discrimination "because of ... sex." By definition, a gay employee is sexually attracted to members of her own sex. *See* Gay, The American Heritage Dictionary (5th ed. 2011) ("Of, relating to, or having a sexual orientation to persons of the same sex."). So when an employer discriminates against an employee solely because she is a lesbian, the employer acts against the employee only because she is sexually attracted to women, instead of being attracted to only men, like the employer prescriptively believes women should be. This is no different than when an employer discriminates against an employee because she is an aggressive or "macho" woman or solely because she is a transgender woman. In all cases, the employer discriminates against the employee because she does not conform to the employer's prescriptive stereotype of what a person of that birth-assigned gender should be [a]nd so ... discriminates against the employee "because of ... sex." ...

I am not the first person to conclude that discrimination against an employee because of her sexual orientation is discrimination against an employee "because of ... sex." In recent years in particular, numerous district courts, including two in our Circuit, have also reached this conclusion. See, e.g., Winstead v. Lafayette Cty. Bd. of Cty. Comm'rs, 197 F. Supp. 3d 1334 (N.D. Fla. June 20, 2016); Isaacs v. Felder Servs., LLC, 143 F. Supp. 3d 1190 (M.D. Ala. 2015); Videckis v. Pepperdine Univ., 150 F. Supp. 3d 1151 (C.D. Cal. 2015); Terveer v. Billington, 34 F. Supp. 3d 100, 116 (D.D.C. 2014); Heller v. Columbia Edgewater Country Club, 195 F. Supp. 2d 1212 (D. Or. 2002).

And the U.S. Equal Employment Opportunity Commission has taken the same position as these district courts, both in a recent administrative decision, see Baldwin v. Foxx, EEOC Appeal No. 0120133080, 2015 WL 4397641 (July 15, 2015), and in this litigation in the capacity as an amicus curiae. It is time that we as a court recognized that Title VII prohibits discrimination based on an employee's sexual orientation since that is discrimination "because of ... sex."

Presidential-Medal-of-Freedom recipient Marlo Thomas has expressed the sentiment that "[i]n this land, every girl grows to be her own woman." Title VII codifies the promise that when she does, she will not be discriminated against on the job, regardless of whether she conforms to what her employer thinks a woman should be. Because the panel does not read Title VII to fulfill that promise, I respectfully dissent.

NOTES AND QUESTIONS

1. Less than a month after the Eleventh Circuit decided *Evans*, the Seventh Circuit, *en banc*, held the opposite, espousing many of the arguments in Judge Rosenbaum's dissent in *Evans*:

> For many years, the courts of appeals ... understood the prohibition against sex discrimination to exclude discrimination on the basis of a person's sexual orientation. The Supreme Court, however, has never spoken to that question. In this case, we have been asked to take a fresh look at our position in light of developments at the Supreme Court extending over two decades. We have done so, and we conclude today that discrimination on the basis of sexual orientation is a form of sex discrimination.

Hively v. Ivy Tech Cmty. Coll. of Ind., 853 F.3d 339, 340-41 (7th Cir. 2017).

The law continues to develop even as this book goes to publication. In EEOC v. R.G.&G.R. Harris Funeral Homes, Inc., 884 F.3d 560 (6th Cir. 2018), the court held that illegal "sex discrimination" includes discrimination on the basis of a person's transitioning from one sex to the other. Thus, the employer's "decision to fire [the plaintiff] because [the plaintiff] was no longer going to represent himself as a man' and 'wanted to dress as a woman,' falls squarely within the ambit of sex-based discrimination that Price Waterhouse ... forbid[s]."

2. Whether or not Title VII prohibits employment discrimination based on sexual orientation or identity, many states have enacted laws against such discrimination. Movement Advancement Project, *Non-Discrimination Laws*, http://www.lgbtmap.org/equality-maps/non_discrimination_laws. In states lacking such laws, some local governments have enacted anti-discrimination ordinances, but some states responded by prohibiting such local ordinances. *Id.*

3. *Discriminatory Inquiries*

An employer's discriminatory intent might be evidenced by the way it describes an opening or by the questions it asks of applicants. Before Title VII, for example, it was not uncommon for an employer to advertise job openings in separate "help wanted — men" and "help wanted — women" columns of the classified section of a newspaper. An employer could also indicate its preference for one gender or the other in the way it described the position, seeking, for example, "girl Friday" or "career-minded men." Title VII now prohibits employer advertising "indicating any preference, limitation, specification, or discrimination based on race, color, religion, sex or national origin. . . . " 42 U.S.C. § 2000e-3.

Employer questions about personal status on an application form or in a job interview present a more complicated problem. The answers to some questions might provide information that is not otherwise obvious to the interviewer and that could lead to illegal discrimination. For example, if an interviewer asks a female applicant about her children, his purpose might be innocent conversation, or it might be to discriminate against women who have young children because of his belief that mothers are too easily distracted by family responsibilities. Depending on the circumstances, any interview or application question that could lead to discrimination might be prima facie evidence of discriminatory intent. *See, e.g.*, Doe v. Syracuse Sch. Dist., 508 F. Supp. 333 338 n.4 (N.D.N.Y. 1981); Sheriff's Dep't v. State Dep't of Human Rights, 514 N.Y.S.2d 779 (N.Y. App. Div. 1987).

Are there some questions an employer simply should not ask? Could an employer's question to an applicant be unlawful *per se*, even if the applicant's answer or reaction was not the cause of the applicant's rejection? The Americans with Disabilities Act provides that an employer "*shall not* conduct a medical examination or make inquiries of a job applicant as to whether such applicant is an individual with a disability or as to the nature or severity of such disability." 42 U.S.C. § 12112(d)(2) (emphasis added). However, an employer "may make preemployment inquiries into the ability of an applicant to perform job-related functions." Once an employer offers employment, the rules change. Subject to certain limitations, an employer can make an offer contingent on a medical examination and can conduct medical examinations of current employees if the employer follows certain rules set out in the act. 42 U.S.C. §§ 12112(d)(3), (4).

GRIFFIN v. STEELTEK, INC.
261 F.3d 1026 (10th Cir. 2001)

SEYMOUR, Circuit Judge.

In this case a jury returned a verdict in favor of defendant-appellee Steeltek, Inc., on plaintiff-appellant Randy D. Griffin's suit for damages alleging violation of § 12112(d)(2)(A) of the Americans With Disabilities Act of 1991 ("ADA"), 42 U.S.C. §§ 12101-12213. Mr. Griffin appeals from the district court's order denying his post-trial motion for judgment as a matter of law on the issue of nominal damages, denying his motion for new trial on the issue of punitive damages, and denying his motion for attorney's fees. . . . [W]e affirm.

I.

. . . Mr. Griffin raises three issues on appeal: (1) whether violation of § 12112(d)(2)(A)'s prohibition against asking preemployment questions regarding medical history or condition necessarily constitutes a compensable injury that must, at a minimum, result in an award of nominal damages; (2) whether punitive damages may be awarded independently of an award of actual or nominal damages for this technical violation . . . ; and (3) whether a nonprevailing plaintiff who has proved that an employer technically violated § 12112(d)(2)(A) but then discontinued the prohibited practice after suit was filed is entitled to attorney's fees and costs solely by virtue of that proof. . . under a "catalyst for change" theory. We answer all three questions in the negative.

II.

We address Mr. Griffin's first two claims of error together. . . . Steeltek asked two questions on its employment application: "Have you received Worker's Compensation or Disability Income payments? If yes, describe." and "Have you physical defects which preclude you from performing certain jobs? If yes, describe." *Griffin*, 160 F.3d at 592. Mr. Griffin answered the first question, but not the second. Mr. Griffin alleges that he was entitled to an award of nominal damages as a matter of law and to a jury determination on the issue of punitive damages because the two prohibited questions undisputedly violate § 12112(d)(2)(A).

The district court found that "merely being ask[ed] the impermissible question is not sufficient, by itself, to inflict a cognizable injury." . . . [T]he jury had concluded in a special interrogatory . . . that Mr. Griffin had not suffered an injury as a result of being asked the questions. The court held that, absent an injury, Mr. Griffin was not entitled to either nominal or punitive damages. We agree.

Mr. Griffin's theory of the case . . . was twofold. First, he claimed that having to answer the prohibited questions caused him emotional and mental distress because he had filed worker's compensation claims that he would either have to reveal, perhaps to his detriment, or lie about. Second, he claimed that Steeltek actually discriminated against him by refusing to hire him because of his answer to (and/or failure to answer) the prohibited questions. Steeltek, however, presented testimony that the questions played no part in its hiring decision and that its hiring manager did not interview Mr. Griffin because the face of his application did not indicate that he had the requisite experience. . . . The manager also testified that he instead rehired an experienced individual who had been recently laid off after working for the company for two years. . . . On this evidence, the jury concluded that Mr. Griffin suffered no injury from being asked the prohibited questions. . . .

Nominal damages are a token award, compensatory in nature. . . . Compensatory damages are available under the ADA, however, only if the plaintiff establishes that the employer not only technically violated § 12112(d)(2)(A) by asking a prohibited question, but also that by doing so it actually "engaged in unlawful intentional discrimination." 42 U.S.C. § 1981a(a)(2); § 12117(a) (adopting the remedies available for violations of Title VII set out at 42 U.S.C. § 2000e-5); *see also* Tice v. Ctr. Area Transp. Auth., 247 F.3d 506, 520 (3d Cir. 2001) (holding that ADA claimant must present evidence of actual harm arising from technical violation of § 12112(d)). . .

Punitive damages require proof that the defendant engaged in "a discriminatory practice... with malice or with reckless indifference to the federally protected rights of an aggrieved individual," 42 U.S.C. § 1981a(b)(1), which the Supreme Court has interpreted as knowingly discriminating "'in the face of a perceived risk that its action will violate federal law.'" *Wal-Mart Stores*, 187 F.3d at 1245 (quoting Kolstad v. Am. Dental Ass'n, 527 U.S. 526, 536 (1999)). Because Mr. Griffin failed to establish injury by intentional discrimination, he was not entitled to an award of either nominal or punitive damages.

III.

Mr. Griffin was entitled to attorney's fees and costs only if he was the prevailing party . . . . [A] plaintiff who has failed to secure a judgment on the merits or by court-ordered consent decree in an ADA suit is not entitled to attorney's fees even if the pursuit of litigation has caused a desired and voluntary change in the defendant's conduct. Buckhannon Bd. & Care Home, Inc. v. W. Va. Dep't of Health & Human Res., 121 S. Ct. 1835, 1838 & 1843 (2001). The district court therefore did not abuse its discretion in refusing to grant attorney's fees and costs to Mr. Griffin or in granting costs to Steeltek as the prevailing party.[2]

We affirm the judgment of the United States District Court . . . .

---

[2] Mr. Griffin cites Parham v. Southwestern Bell Telephone Co., 433 F.2d 421 (8th Cir. 1970), as authority for awarding attorney's fees under a "catalyst" theory. However, as the Supreme Court has pointed out, "*Parham* stands for the proposition that an enforceable judgment permits an award of attorney's fees." Buckhannon Bd. & Care Home, 121 S. Ct. at 1842 n.9. Mr. Griffin has no enforceable judgment on which to base attorney's fees, thus *Parham* affords him no aid.

NOTES AND QUESTIONS

1. Griffin failed to obtain an award of individual relief or attorney's fees. Would he have been entitled to attorney's fees if he had sought and obtained declaratory or injunctive relief against the employer's unlawful inquiries? Reread the section on *Mixed Motives v. Single Motive* preceding the *Quigg* case. The ADA adopts the same "remedies" and "procedures" as certain parts of Title VII, including 42 U.S.C. § 2000e-5. *See* 42 U.S.C. § 12117(a). Mr. Griffin evidently argued that while he did not obtain injunctive or declaratory relief, his lawsuit was a "catalyst" for Steeltek's discontinuation of unlawful practices, and therefore he "prevailed." The court's answer is in footnote 2 of its opinion.

2. Unlike the Americans with Disabilities Act, Title VII and the ADEA do not specifically prohibit an employer from asking applicants about protected characteristics such as race, color, national origin, gender, religion, or age. However, not long after Title VII was enacted, the Equal Employment Opportunity Commission warned that some questions by an employer in its job applications or interviews might constitute or be evidence of illegal race, sex, or other discrimination. *See, e.g.*, Equal Opportunity Commission Decision No. 75-S-68, 21 Fair Empl. Prac. Cas. [BNA] 1766 (1974). Here is what the Equal Employment Opportunity Commission currently says in its sex discrimination regulations:

> A pre-employment inquiry may ask "Male . . . , Female . . . "; or "Mr. Mrs. Miss," provided that the inquiry is made in good faith for a nondiscriminatory purpose. Any pre-employment inquiry in connection with prospective employment which expresses directly or indirectly any limitation, specification, or discrimination as to sex shall be unlawful unless based upon a bona fide occupational qualification.

29 C.F.R. § 1604.7. The EEOC cautions employers similarly in its age discrimination regulations:

> A request on the part of an employer for information such as "Date of Birth" or "State Age" on an employment application form is not, in itself, a violation of the Act. But because the request that an applicant state his age may tend to deter older applicants or otherwise indicate discrimination based on age, employment application forms which request such information will be closely scrutinized to assure that the request is for a permissible purpose and not for purposes proscribed by the Act. That the purpose is not one proscribed by the statute should be made known to the applicant, either by a reference on the application form to the statutory prohibition in language to the following effect: "The Age Discrimination in Employment Act of 1967 prohibits discrimination on the basis of age with respect to individuals who are at least 40 years of age," or by other means.

29 C.F.R. § 1625.5.

3. At least one state takes a stronger position against employer inquiries in the hiring process. A West Virginia statute provides that it is unlawful

> [f]or any employer, employment agency or labor organization, prior to the employment or admission to membership, to . . . [e]licit any information or make or keep a record of or use any form of application or application blank containing questions or entries concerning the race, religion, color, national

origin, ancestry, sex or age of any applicant for employment or membership.

W. Va. Stat. § 5-11-9(2)(A); *see also* N.J. Stat. Ann. § 10:5-12, prohibiting employers from asking about draft status or marital status.

4. Should employers ever be *required* to record the race, gender, age, or national origin of their applicants? Employers who do business with or receive funds from the federal government are often required to adopt "affirmative action plans" that include gathering information about the number of women and minorities in the labor market, the applicant pool, and the workforce. The rules for federal contractors also require an employer to obtain and preserve information about each applicant's gender or minority status. *See, e.g.*, 29 C.F.R. §§ 1607.4, 1608.3. Can these rules be reconciled with other rules that discourage preemployment inquiries related to gender and minority status? Affirmative action is discussed further in Section C.5 of this chapter, *infra*.

5. Employment applications often warn prospective employees that any misrepresentation on the application or in the interview could be grounds for termination. Suppose an employer asks the sort of question it might use to discriminate, such as "are you pregnant?" or "do you have young children?" If the applicant misrepresents that she is not pregnant and does not have young children, can the employer later discharge her for "misrepresentation" when it discovers she is, in fact pregnant? Some courts treat a false response to a potentially discriminatory inquiry differently from an *unsolicited* misrepresentation of fact. Under this approach, the former is not a permissible ground for discharge; the latter is. *See* Lysak v. Selier Corp., 614 N.E.2d 991 (Mass. 1993) (employer lawfully discharged employee when it discovered she had misrepresented she had no plans to have another child, when in fact she was pregnant).

"Concealment" is another problem. In Lopez v. River Oaks Imaging 542 F. Supp. 2d 653 (S.D. Tex. 2008), an applicant who intended to become a female, but was still male, dressed as a female at his job interview. The employer offered a job, but it withdrew its offer when it learned the applicant was male, not female. In the applicant's sex discrimination lawsuit, the employer moved for summary judgment on the ground that it had lawfully withdrawn its offer based on the applicant's misrepresentation or concealment of gender. The court denied the motion. Among other things, the court noted that the employer had not *asked* about gender. The court also held that there is no duty to disclose one's gender.

PROBLEM

The law firm of Click & Flash is sending two of its attorneys to a local law school to interview law students for associate positions. They hope to interview about 30 students over two days, and to select five from this group for follow-up interviews. One of the interviewers proposes to take a camera with him to photograph each of the interviewees, and to use the photos as an aid for recalling each interviewee. He has asked you, the firm's employment law expert, whether such use of a camera is permissible. How would you advise him?

4. *Disparate Impact*

GRIGGS v. DUKE POWER CO.

401 U.S. 424 (1971)

Mr. Chief Justice BURGER delivered the opinion of the Court.

We granted the writ in this case to resolve the question whether an employer is prohibited by the Civil Rights Act of 1964, Title VII, from requiring a high school education or passing of a standardized general intelligence test as a condition of employment in or transfer to jobs when (a) neither standard is shown to be significantly related to successful job performance, (b) both requirements operate to disqualify Negroes at a substantially higher rate than white applicants, and (c) the jobs in question formerly had been filled only by white employees as part of a longstanding practice of giving preference to whites.[1]

Congress provided, in Title VII of the Civil Rights Act of 1964, for class actions for enforcement of provisions of the Act and this proceeding was brought by a group of incumbent Negro employees against Duke Power Company. All the petitioners are employed at the Company's Dan River Steam Station, a power generating facility located at Draper, North Carolina. At the time this action was instituted, the Company had 95 employees at the Dan River Station, 14 of whom were Negroes; 13 of these are petitioners here.

The District Court found that prior to July 2, 1965, the effective date of the Civil Rights Act of 1964, the Company openly discriminated on the basis of race in the hiring and assigning of employees at its Dan River plant. The plant was organized into five operating departments: (1) Labor, (2) Coal Handling, (3) Operations, (4) Maintenance, and (5) Laboratory and Test. Negroes were employed only in the Labor Department where the highest paying jobs paid less than the lowest paying jobs in the other four "operating" departments in which only whites were employed. Promotions were normally made within each department on the basis of job seniority. Transferees into a department usually began in the lowest position.

In 1955 the Company instituted a policy of requiring a high school education for initial assignment to any department except Labor, and for transfer from the Coal Handling to any "inside" department (Operations, Maintenance, or Laboratory). When the Company abandoned its policy of restricting Negroes to the Labor Department in 1965, completion of high school also was made a

---

[1] The Act provides:

§ 703. (a) It shall be an unlawful employment practice for an employer —

(2) to limit, segregate, or classify his employees in any way which would deprive or tend to deprive any individual of employment opportunities or otherwise adversely affect his status as an employee, because of such individual's race, color, religion, sex, or national origin.

(h) Notwithstanding any other provision of this title, it shall not be an unlawful employment practice for an employer... to give and to act upon the results of any professionally developed ability test provided that such test, its administration or action upon the results is not designed, intended or used to discriminate because of race, color, religion, sex or national origin.

42 U.S.C. § 2000e-2.

prerequisite to transfer from Labor to any other department. From the time the high school requirement was instituted to the time of trial, however, white employees hired before the time of the high school education requirement continued to perform satisfactorily and achieve promotions in the "operating" departments. Findings on this score are not challenged.

The Company added a further requirement for new employees on July 2, 1965, the date on which Title VII became effective. To qualify for placement in any but the Labor Department it become necessary to register satisfactory scores on two professionally prepared aptitude tests, as well as to have a high school education. Completion of high school alone continued to render employees eligible for transfer to the four desirable departments from which Negroes had been excluded if the incumbent had been employed prior to the time of the new requirement. In September 1965 the Company began to permit incumbent employees who lacked a high school education to qualify for transfer from Labor or Coal Handling to an "inside" job by passing two tests — the Wonderlic Personnel Test, which purports to measure general intelligence, and the Bennett Mechanical Comprehension Test. Neither was directed or intended to measure the ability to learn to perform a particular job or category of jobs. The requisite scores used for both initial hiring and transfer approximated the national median for high school graduates.[3]

The District Court had found that while the Company previously followed a policy of overt racial discrimination in a period prior to the Act, such conduct had ceased. The District Court also concluded that Title VII was intended to be prospective only and, consequently, the impact of prior inequities was beyond the reach of corrective action authorized by the Act.

The Court of Appeals was confronted with a question of first impression, as are we, concerning the meaning of Title VII. After careful analysis a majority of that court concluded that a subjective test of the employer's intent should govern, particularly in a close case, and that in this case there was no showing of a discriminatory purpose in the adoption of the diploma and test requirements. On this basis, the Court of Appeals concluded there was no violation of the Act.

. . . The objective of Congress in the enactment of Title VII is plain from the language of the statute. It was to achieve equality of employment opportunities and remove barriers that have operated in the past to favor an identifiable group of white employees over other employees. Under the Act, practices, procedures, or tests neutral on their face, and even neutral in terms of intent, cannot be maintained if they operate to "freeze" the status quo of prior discriminatory employment practices.

. . . The Court of Appeals' opinion, and the partial dissent, agreed that, on the record in the present case, "whites register far better on the Company's alternative requirements" than Negroes.[6] . . . Because they are Negroes, petitioners have long

[3] The test standards are thus more stringent than the high school requirement, since they would screen out approximately half of all high school graduates.

[6] In North Carolina, 1960 census statistics show that, while 34% of white males had completed high school, only 12% of Negro males had done so. U.S. Bureau of the Census, U.S. Census of Population: 1960, Vol. 1, Characteristics of the Population, pt. 35, Table 47. Similarly, with respect to standardized tests, the EEOC in one case found that use of a battery of tests, including the Wonderlic and Bennett tests used by the Company in the instant case, resulted in 58% of whites passing the tests, as compared with only 6% of the blacks. Decision

received inferior education in segregated schools. . . . Congress did not intend by Title VII, however, to guarantee a job to every person regardless of qualifications. In short, the Act does not command that any person be hired simply because he was formerly the subject of discrimination, or because he is a member of a minority group. Discriminatory preference for any group, minority or majority, is precisely and only what Congress has proscribed. What is required by Congress is the removal of artificial, arbitrary, and unnecessary barriers to employment when the barriers operate invidiously to discriminate on the basis of racial or other impermissible classification.

. . . The Act proscribes not only overt discrimination but also practices that are fair in form, but discriminatory in operation. The touchstone is business necessity. If an employment practice which operates to exclude Negroes cannot be shown to be related to job performance, the practice is prohibited.

On the record before us, neither the high school completion requirement nor the general intelligence test is shown to bear a demonstrable relationship to successful performance of the jobs for which it was used. Both were adopted, as the Court of Appeals noted, without meaningful study of their relationship to job-performance ability. Rather, a vice president of the Company testified, the requirements were instituted on the Company's judgment that they generally would improve the overall quality of the work force. The evidence, however, shows that employees who have not completed high school or taken the tests have continued to perform satisfactorily and make progress in departments for which the high school and test criteria are now used.[7] The promotion record of present employees who would not be able to meet the new criteria thus suggests the possibility that the requirements may not be needed even for the limited purpose of preserving the avowed policy of advancement within the Company. In the context of this case, it is unnecessary to reach the question whether testing requirements that take into account capability for the next succeeding position or related future promotion might be utilized upon a showing that such long range requirements fulfill a genuine business need. In the present case the Company has made no such showing.

The Court of Appeals held that the Company had adopted the diploma and test requirements without any "intention to discriminate against Negro employees." 420 F.2d at 1232. We do not suggest that either the District Court or the Court of Appeals erred in examining the employer's intent; but good intent or absence of discriminatory intent does not redeem employment procedures or testing mechanisms that operate as "built-in headwinds" for minority groups and are unrelated to measuring job capability.

The Company's lack of discriminatory intent is suggested by special efforts to help the undereducated employees through Company financing of two thirds the cost of tuition for high school training. But . . . Congress directed the thrust of the Act to the consequences of employment practices, not simply the motivation. More than that, Congress has placed on the employer the burden of showing that any

---

of EEOC, CCH Empl. Prac. Guide, 17,304.53 (Dec. 2, 1966).

[7] For example, between July 2, 1965, and November 14, 1966, the percentage of white employees who were promoted but who were not high school graduates was nearly identical to the percentage of nongraduates in the entire white work force.

given requirement must have a manifest relationship to the employment in question. The facts of this case demonstrate the inadequacy of broad and general testing devices as well as the infirmity of using diplomas or degrees as fixed measures of capability. History is filled with examples of men and women who rendered highly effective performance without the conventional badges of accomplishment in terms of certificates, diplomas, or degrees. Diplomas and tests are useful servants, but Congress has mandated the commonsense proposition that they are not to become masters of reality.

The Company contends that its general intelligence tests are specifically permitted by § 703(h) of the Act.[8] That section authorizes the use of "any professionally developed ability test" that is not "designed, intended *or used* to discriminate because of race. . . ." (Emphasis added.)

The Equal Employment Opportunity Commission, having enforcement responsibility, has issued guidelines interpreting § 703(h) to permit only the use of job-related tests.[9] . . . Since the Act and its legislative history support the Commission's construction, this affords good reason to treat the guidelines as expressing the will of Congress.

. . . Nothing in the Act precludes the use of testing or measuring procedures; obviously they are useful. What Congress has forbidden is giving these devices and mechanisms controlling force unless they are demonstrably a reasonable measure of job performance. Congress has not commanded that the less qualified be preferred over the better qualified simply because of minority origins. Far from disparaging job qualifications as such, Congress has made such qualifications the controlling factor, so that race, religion, nationality, and sex become irrelevant. What Congress has commanded is that any tests used must measure the person for the job and not the person in the abstract.

The judgment of the Court of Appeals is, as to that portion of the judgment appealed from, reversed.

NOTES AND QUESTIONS

1. Plaintiffs have used the "disparate impact" theory described in *Griggs* to attack an assortment of employee selection practices that exclude a disproportionate number of minorities or women. *See, e.g.*, Dothard v. Rawlinson, 433 U.S. 321

---

[8] Section 703(h) applies only to tests. It has no applicability to the high school diploma requirement.

[9] EEOC Guidelines on Employment Testing Procedures, issued August 24, 1966, provide:

> The Commission accordingly interprets "professionally developed ability test" to mean a test which fairly measures the knowledge or skills required by the particular job or class of jobs which the applicant seeks, or which fairly affords the employer a chance to measure the applicant's ability to perform a particular job or class of jobs. The fact that a test was prepared by an individual or organization claiming expertise in test preparation does not, without more, justify its use within the meaning of Title VII.

The EEOC position has been elaborated in the new Guidelines on Employee Selection Procedures, 29 CFR § 1607, 35 Fed. Reg. 12333 (Aug. 1, 1970). These guidelines demand that employers using tests have available "data demonstrating that the test is predictive of or significantly correlated with important elements of work behavior which comprise or are relevant to the job or jobs for which candidates are being evaluated." *Id.*, at § 1607.4(c).

(1977) (minimum height and weight requirement for prison guards had illegal disparate impact against women); Albermarle Paper Co. v. Moody, 422 U.S. 405 (1975) (use of Revised Beta Examination and Wonderlic Test caused illegal disparate impact); Walker v. Jefferson County Home, 726 F.2d 1554 (11th Cir. 1984) (experience requirement had unlawful disparate impact).

The key advantage of disparate impact theory from the plaintiff's point of view is that discriminatory intent is not a necessary element of the cause of action. However, the plaintiff must prove that the challenged employment practice significantly and disproportionately excludes persons of the protected class. One frequently applied rule of thumb is that an employment practice does not have significant disparate impact unless the resulting selection rate for the plaintiff's class is less than four-fifths (or 80 percent) of the selection rate for the allegedly preferred class. 29 C.F.R. §§ 1607.1, 1607.4(D). For example, if half of all white applicants satisfied a certain qualification, the qualification would have significant disparate impact against black applicants if fewer than 40 percent of black applicants satisfied the qualification.

2. Aside from discrediting the plaintiff's statistics or otherwise denying disparate impact, the employer's usual defense in a disparate impact case is that the job qualification in question is truly predictive of success on the job — e.g., that a test score correlates with a job ability — and that use of the qualification is therefore justified by "business necessity." 42 U.S.C. § 2000e-2(k)(1)(i). The Civil Rights Act of 1991 allocates the burden of proof on this issue to the employer in Title VII cases. *Id.* §§ 2000e-2(k)(1)(i), 2000e(m). The Americans with Disabilities Act uses the same approach for disability discrimination. 42 U.S.C. § 12112(b)(6). *But see* Meacham v. Knolls Atomic Power Lab., 554 U.S. 84 (2008) (describing different rules for disparate impact under Age Discrimination in Employment Act)

The EEOC and the courts generally require an employer to prove business necessity by empirical evidence that its test or job qualification is "predictive of or significantly correlated with important elements of job performance." 29 C.F.R. §§ 1607.5, 1607.6. One way to provide such empirical evidence is to run an experiment in which the employer administers the test to the current workforce and compares individual test results with actual performance on the job. *See, e.g.*, Clady v. County of Los Angeles, 770 F.2d 1421 (9th Cir. 1985). Courts have been especially demanding of such proof in the case of paper and pencil tests that are not obviously or intuitively predictive of success on the job. Courts appear on the whole to be less demanding in the case of some job qualifications that appeal to "common sense." *See, e.g.*, Briggs v. Anderson, 796 F.2d 1009 (8th Cir. 1986) (upholding requirement of college degree in psychology for counselor position). They are especially deferential to employers with respect to jobs involving a high degree of responsibility for public safety. *See, e.g.*, Spurlock v. United Airlines, Inc., 475 F.2d 216 (10th Cir. 1972) (approving airline's experience requirement for airline pilots). Nevertheless, it is risky for an employer to assume its job qualification is "obviously" necessary or predictive without first conducting a validation study, and the EEOC still maintains a strong preference for empirical validation of any selection procedure that has disparate impact. 29 C.F.R. § 1607.6.

3. The laws against race, color, national origin or disability discrimination and the doctrine of disparate impact may limit the way an employer inquires about

and considers an applicant's arrest or criminal conviction record. A practice of rejecting persons with criminal arrest records might have disparate impact in communities where minorities or the disabled are subject to a higher rate of "suspicion" arrests because of profiling and prejudice. *See* Gregory v. Litton Sys., Inc., 316 F. Supp. 401 (C.D. Cal. 1970), *aff'd and vacated in part on other grounds*, 472 F.2d 631 (9th Cir. 1972). An employer might respond that an arrest record negatively correlates with law-abiding behavior, which is a necessary qualification for employment. But an arrest standing alone does not equate with guilt. A *conviction* does equate with a judicial determination of guilt, and therefore courts have generally accepted an employer's assertion of "business necessity" for rejecting employees with *conviction* records. *See, e.g.*, Davis v. City of Dallas, 777 F.2d 205 (5th Cir. 1985). However, even a conviction does not always reflect a violent or dishonest disposition, especially, for example, if the conviction was because of civil disobedience arising out of political action.

In 2012, the EEOC issued a new enforcement guidance describing that agency's view that an employer's disqualification of applicants based on criminal conviction or arrest records might cause disparate impact on the basis of race or national origin. However, rejection of an applicant with a criminal record might often be justified by business necessity. Thus, the EEOC recommends that an employer develop a policy for individualized assessment to consider (at a minimum) the nature of an applicant's crime, the amount of time that has passed since the crime, and the nature of the job the applicant seeks. EEOC Enforcement Guidance on the Consideration of Arrest and Conviction Records in Employment Decisions (April 25, 2012). It is also important to remember that a few states regard criminal record as a protected characteristic in itself, aside from disparate impact against minorities. *See* notes following Wise v. Complete Staffing, *supra.*

4. Another issue of recent interest to the EEOC is whether an employer's practice of rejecting applicants who are unemployed, or who have been out of work for more than a certain length of time, may have disparate impact against minorities. *See* EEOC Press Release, Out of Work? Out of Luck, February 16, 2011, at http://www.eeoc.gov/eeoc/newsroom/release/2-16-11.cfm

5. If an employer carries its burden of proving a job qualification or test has a significant correlation with job performance, the plaintiff might still prevail by proving there is an alternative selection method that would serve the employer's purposes with less adverse impact, but the employer has refused to use the alternative. *See* 42 U.S.C. § 2000e-2(k)(1)(A)(ii). Not many reported cases have reached this stage of disparate impact analysis. However, with the growing number of carefully validated and reduced-impact tests available for some occupations (generated in no small part because of Title VII and *Griggs*), this "alternative test" claim could be potentially decisive. *See, e.g.*, Anderson v. Zubieta, 180 F.3d 329 (D.C. Cir. 1999); Brown v. City of Chicago, 8 F. Supp. 2d 1095 (N.D. Ill. 1998).

PROBLEM

Fun Land Park owns and operates amusement parks around the United States. Most of its employees are seasonal or part-time. Most employees below the level of "department manager" are between the ages of 17 and 22.

Fun Land was recently sued as a result of an incident in which an 18-year-old maintenance employee assaulted a park guest who was accompanying the employee's former girlfriend. The guest filed a lawsuit against Fun Land based on *respondeat superior* and negligent hiring. Discovery in the lawsuit revealed that the maintenance employee had been charged with assault two years earlier, that he had received a deferred adjudication under the local "first offender" program, and that the court dismissed the assault charge after the employee had satisfied the conditions of the deferred adjudication.

Fun Land won summary judgment in the lawsuit described above. Nevertheless, Fun Land is greatly distressed by the publicity that attended the lawsuit, and it is worried about future liability. Among other things, Fun Land is contemplating a revision of its application form. Fun Land has always asked applicants, "Have you ever been convicted of a crime?" The application provides applicants an opportunity to explain. Fun Land's proposed revised application changes the question to read as follows:

> Have you ever been convicted of a crime, or have you ever received deferred adjudication under a first offender program? If so, explain.

Fun Land wants to know whether this question is lawful and whether the revised question could lead to other legal difficulties. How would you advise it?

5. *Affirmative Action*

Merely desisting from discrimination might not be enough to establish equal employment opportunity for women and minorities. An employer's choice of methods for attracting and selecting applicants, and the vestiges of past discrimination might perpetuate the preexisting gender, racial, and ethnic composition of the workforce. For example, if the employer recruits from a segregated neighborhood, the applicant pool might be exclusively or predominantly white. Despite a corporate-wide edict not to discriminate, individual supervisors and managers might consciously or subconsciously continue their preference for similarly colored subordinates. The biases of individual decision makers might be masked by the subjectiveness of the decision-making process. And minorities may continue to be deterred from seeking employment because of their sense of insecurity in a setting where there are few minorities and no established culture of diversity.

Recognizing that Title VII might not be sufficient to overcome the effects of centuries of discrimination, President Lyndon Johnson issued the first of a series of executive orders, starting in 1965, requiring "affirmative action" by employers who provide goods, services, or construction work under a contract with the federal government.[6] By virtue of these orders, persons entering into such contracts with the federal government promise to take affirmative action to ensure that employment decisions are without regard to protected characteristics and to achieve equal employment opportunity.

The duty of affirmative action is more than a duty not to discriminate. It

[6] Executive Order No. 11246 (1965). Other "affirmative action" obligations are in section 503 of the Rehabilitation Act of 1973, 29 U.S.C. § 793 (disabled persons) and section 402 of the Vietnam Era Veterans' Readjustment Assistance Act of 1972, 38 U.S.C. §§ 4211-4212.

requires an employer to develop an affirmative action plan (AAP), which among other things requires a written analysis of the gender and minority composition of the employer's workforce in comparison with the relevant labor market. 41 C.F.R. § 60.2-11. The AAP also includes an analysis of the employer's hiring, assignment, and promotion practices that may have disparate impact. 41 C.F.R. §§ 60-1.40(b), -2.23, -2.24. Finally, the AAP outlines steps the employer will take to broaden the reach of its hiring practices to include a more representative sampling of the available labor force, such as by recruiting in neighborhoods, schools, or universities with a greater representation of minorities than the employer's traditional hiring grounds. 41 C.F.R. §§ 60.13(f), -2.24. Affirmative action obligations are backed by the threat of debarment. If an employer fails in its duty, it may be disqualified from federal contract work. Exec. Order No. 11246, § 209(a)(6) (1965); 41 C.F.R. §§ 60-1.4(a), -1.26 to .27, -250.28, -741.28.

The affirmative action that federal contractors undertake as a contractual duty is not the only type of affirmative action. Employers who are not federal contractors might be required to engage in affirmative action as part of a court-ordered remedy following a lawsuit by private individuals, or as a result of a conciliation or settlement agreement with the EEOC or other enforcement agencies. *See* 29 C.F.R. §§ 1608.6-1608.8. If an employer's discrimination is "systemic" or part of a "pattern practice," a court order or settlement might require the employer to take specific steps to increase the likelihood that it will hire more women or minorities in the future. Finally, an employer might engage in "voluntary" affirmative action, even though it is not a federal contractor and is not subject to a court order or settlement agreement. One motive for adopting a voluntary affirmative action plan might be to prevent charges of discrimination in the future. Other possible motives, especially in the case of government employers, might be a sense of civic duty or a response to political or community pressure.

The preparation and implementation of an AAP undoubtedly requires a certain amount of "color-consciousness." Could the existence of an AAP and the employer's collection of data about employee race, gender, and ethnicity be some evidence of illegal "reverse" discrimination against non-minorities? What if the plan includes a "goal" of achieving a representative workforce? *See* 29 C.F.R. §§ 1608.5, 1608.10 (for EEOC purposes, creating a safe harbor for federal contractor affirmative action plans "adopted in good faith reliance on these Guidelines"); 29 C.F.R. §§ 1608.3, 1608.4 (describing circumstances and methods for a lawful voluntary affirmative action plan); EEOC Dec. 81-26 (July 17, 1981), 27 Fair Empl. Prac. Cas. [BNA] 1823, 1981 WL 17717 (finding no reasonable cause to believe employer used Characteristic Survey Sheet, identifying applicants by sex, age, and race, to discriminate unlawfully, where employer used the survey sheet as part of its affirmative action plan and to facilitate completion of its EEO-4 report); 29 C.F.R. § 1607.17 (regarding the circumstances under which state and local governments may lawfully engage in affirmative action, and listing methods for lawfully promoting equal employment opportunity).

When a court orders an employer to engage in affirmative action after finding the employer guilty of systemic discrimination, a race-conscious "goal" or even quota might be justified as a necessary remedy to undo the employer's wrongdoing. United States v. Paradise, 480 U.S. 149 (1987); Firefighters Local 93 v. City of

Cleveland, 478 U.S. 501 (1986). But an employer's *voluntary* adoption of a race-conscious goal in the absence of a court order has been particularly controversial. In United Steelworkers v. Weber, 223 U.S. 193 (1979), the Supreme Court approved an employer's voluntary adoption of a one-for-one racial quota in admission of trainees for a new job training program. Arguably, the employer plan in *Weber* was not really voluntary, because the Office of Federal Contract Compliance Programs, which enforces the federal contractor affirmative action requirements, had threatened to debar the employer if it failed to increase its number of skilled minority employees. 223 U.S. at 222-223. However, no government agency had instructed the employer to remedy its workforce racial disparity in any particular fashion, and the Court treated Kaiser's action as "voluntary." 223 U.S. at 201.

Writing for the Court in *Weber*, Justice Brennan emphasized a number of facts in favor of upholding Kaiser's plan. First, he noted that Kaiser and the United Steelworkers had designed the plan in the face of disturbing statistics. Prior to the creation of the new training program, only 1.83 percent of Kaiser's skilled craftworkers were African American although the surrounding labor force was 39 percent African American. 223 U.S. at 198-199. Second, conceding there were limits to race-conscious affirmative action, Justice Brennan noted redeeming features of Kaiser's training program quota:

> The purposes of the plan mirror those of [Title VII]. Both were designed to break down old patterns of racial segregation and hierarchy. . . . At the same time, the plan does not unnecessarily trammel the interests of the white employees. The plan does not require the discharge of white workers and their replacement with new black hirees. Nor does the plan create an absolute bar to the advancement of white employees; half of those trained in the program will be white. Moreover, the plan is a temporary measure; it is not intended to maintain racial balance, but simply to eliminate a manifest racial imbalance. Preferential selection of craft trainees at the Gramercy plant will end as soon as the percentage of black skilled craftworkers in the Gramercy plant approximates the percentage of blacks in the local labor force.
>
> We conclude . . . that the adoption of the Kaiser-USWA plan for the Gramercy plant falls within the area of discretion left by Title VII to the private sector voluntarily to adopt affirmative action plans designed to eliminate conspicuous racial imbalance in traditionally segregated job categories.

123 U.S. at 208-209 (footnotes and citations omitted).

The *Weber* case left many unanswered questions. What are the minimum facts necessary to justify an employer's race-conscious employment action? Is it enough that the employer has discovered a significant racial disparity between its workforce and the available labor market? Or must the employer acknowledge its own discrimination to justify a self-imposed remedy? Other unanswered questions pertained to the appropriate character of race-conscious employee selection. *Weber* upheld a strict, one-for-one race-based quota for admission to an employer-sponsored job training program, but Justice Brennan was careful to note that the program did not result in the discharge of any of Kaiser's nonminority employees. To what extent might an employer treat race, gender, or any other protected trait as a determinative factor in *hiring*, as part of an affirmative action plan?

JOHNSON v. TRANSPORTATION AGENCY

480 U.S. 616 (1987)

Justice BRENNAN delivered the opinion of the Court.

Respondent, Transportation Agency of Santa Clara County, California, unilaterally promulgated an Affirmative Action Plan applicable, inter alia, to promotions of employees. In selecting applicants for the promotional position of road dispatcher, the Agency, pursuant to the Plan, passed over petitioner Paul Johnson, a male employee, and promoted a female employee applicant, Diane Joyce. The question for decision is whether in making the promotion the Agency impermissibly took into account the sex of the applicants in violation of Title VII of the Civil Rights Act of 1964, 42 U.S.C. § 2000e et seq. . . . [2]

I

A

In December 1978, the Santa Clara County Transit District Board of Supervisors adopted an Affirmative Action Plan (Plan) for the County Transportation Agency. The Plan implemented a County Affirmative Action Plan, which had been adopted, declared the County, because "mere prohibition of discriminatory practices is not enough to remedy the effects of past practices and to permit attainment of an equitable representation of minorities, women and handicapped persons." Relevant to this case, the Agency Plan provides that, in making promotions to positions within a traditionally segregated job classification in which women have been significantly underrepresented, the Agency is authorized to consider as one factor the sex of a qualified applicant.

In reviewing the composition of its work force, the Agency noted in its Plan that women were represented in numbers far less than their proportion of the County labor force in both the Agency as a whole and in five of seven job categories. Specifically, while women constituted 36.4% of the area labor market, they composed only 22.4% of Agency employees. Furthermore, women working at the Agency were concentrated largely in EEOC job categories traditionally held by women: women made up 76% of Office and Clerical Workers, but only 7.1% of Agency Officials and Administrators, 8.6% of Professionals, 9.7% of Technicians, and 22% of Service and Maintenance Workers. As for the job classification relevant to this case, none of the 238 Skilled Craft Worker positions was held by a woman. The Plan noted that this underrepresentation of women in part reflected the fact that women had not traditionally been employed in these positions, and that they had not been strongly motivated to seek training or employment in them "because of the limited opportunities that have existed in the past for them to work in such classifications." . . .

The Agency stated that its Plan was intended to achieve "a statistically

---

[2] No constitutional issue was either raised or addressed in the litigation below. We therefore decide in this case only the issue of the prohibitory scope of Title VII. Of course, where the issue is properly raised, public employers must justify the adoption and implementation of a voluntary affirmative action plan under the Equal Protection Clause. *See* Wygant v. Jackson Board of Education, 476 U.S. 267 (1986).

measurable yearly improvement in hiring, training and promotion of minorities and women throughout the Agency in all major job classifications where they are underrepresented." As a benchmark by which to evaluate progress, the Agency stated that its long-term goal was to attain a work force whose composition reflected the proportion of minorities and women in the area labor force. Thus, for the Skilled Craft category in which the road dispatcher position at issue here was classified, the Agency's aspiration was that eventually about 36% of the jobs would be occupied by women. The Plan acknowledged that a number of factors might make it unrealistic to rely on the Agency's longterm goals in evaluating the Agency's progress in expanding job opportunities for minorities and women. Among the factors identified were low turnover rates in some classifications, the fact that some jobs involved heavy labor, the small number of positions within some job categories, the limited number of entry positions leading to the Technical and Skilled Craft classifications, and the limited number of minorities and women qualified for positions requiring specialized training and experience. As a result, the Plan counseled that shortrange goals be established and annually adjusted to serve as the most realistic guide for actual employment decisions. . . .

The Agency's Plan thus set aside no specific number of positions for minorities or women, but authorized the consideration of ethnicity or sex as a factor when evaluating qualified candidates for jobs in which members of such groups were poorly represented. One such job was the road dispatcher position that is the subject of the dispute in this case.

B

On December 12, 1979, the Agency announced a vacancy for the promotional position of road dispatcher in the Agency's Roads Division. Dispatchers assign road crews, equipment, and materials, and maintain records pertaining to road maintenance jobs. The position requires at minimum four years of dispatch or road maintenance work experience for Santa Clara County. The EEOC job classification scheme designates a road dispatcher as a Skilled Craft Worker.

Twelve County employees applied for the promotion, including Joyce and Johnson. Joyce had worked for the County since 1970, serving as an account clerk until 1975. She had applied for a road dispatcher position in 1974, but was deemed ineligible because she had not served as a road maintenance worker. In 1975, Joyce transferred from a senior account clerk position to a road maintenance worker position, becoming the first woman to fill such a job. During her four years in that position, she occasionally worked out of class as a road dispatcher.

Petitioner Johnson began with the County in 1967 as a road yard clerk, after private employment that included working as a supervisor and dispatcher. He had also unsuccessfully applied for the road dispatcher opening in 1974. In 1977, his clerical position was downgraded, and he sought and received a transfer to the position of road maintenance worker. He also occasionally worked out of class as a dispatcher while performing that job.

Nine of the applicants, including Joyce and Johnson, were deemed qualified for the job, and were interviewed by a two-person board. Seven of the applicants scored above 70 on this interview, which meant that they were certified as eligible for selection by the appointing authority. The scores awarded ranged from 70 to 80.

Johnson was tied for second with a score of 75, while Joyce ranked next with a score of 73. A second interview was conducted by three Agency supervisors, who ultimately recommended that Johnson be promoted. Prior to the second interview, Joyce had contacted the County's Affirmative Action Office because she feared that her application might not receive disinterested review. The Office in turn contacted the Agency's Affirmative Action Coordinator, whom the Agency's Plan makes responsible for, inter alia, keeping the Director informed of opportunities for the Agency to accomplish its objectives under the Plan. At the time, the Agency employed no women in any Skilled Craft position, and had never employed a woman as a road dispatcher. The Coordinator recommended to the Director of the Agency, James Graebner, that Joyce be promoted.

Graebner, authorized to choose any of the seven persons deemed eligible, thus had the benefit of suggestions by the second interview panel and by the Agency Coordinator in arriving at his decision. After deliberation, Graebner concluded that the promotion should be given to Joyce. As he testified: "I tried to look at the whole picture, the combination of her qualifications and Mr. Johnson's qualifications, their test scores, their expertise, their background, affirmative action matters, things like that. . . . I believe it was a combination of all those."

The certification form naming Joyce as the person promoted to the dispatcher position stated that both she and Johnson were rated as well qualified for the job. The evaluation of Joyce read: "Well qualified by virtue of 18 years of past clerical experience including 3 1/2 years at West Yard plus almost 5 years as a [road maintenance worker]." The evaluation of Johnson was as follows: "Well qualified applicant; two years of [road maintenance worker] experience plus 11 years of Road Yard Clerk. Has had previous outside Dispatch experience but was 13 years ago." Graebner testified that he did not regard as significant the fact that Johnson scored 75 and Joyce 73 when interviewed by the two-person board.

. . . The District Court found that Johnson was more qualified for the dispatcher position than Joyce, and that the sex of Joyce was the "determining factor in her selection." . . . The Court of Appeals for the Ninth Circuit reversed, holding that . . . [t]he Agency Plan had been adopted . . . to address a conspicuous imbalance in the Agency's work force, and neither unnecessarily trammeled the rights of other employees, nor created an absolute bar to their advancement.

II

. . . [P]etitioner bears the burden of establishing the invalidity of the [P]lan. . . . Once a plaintiff establishes a prima facie case that race or sex has been taken into account in an employer's employment decision, the burden shifts to the employer to articulate a nondiscriminatory rationale for its decision. The existence of an affirmative action plan provides such a rationale. If such a plan is articulated as the basis for the employer's decision, the burden shifts to the plaintiff to prove that the employer's justification is pretextual and the plan is invalid. As a practical matter, of course, an employer will generally seek to avoid a charge of pretext by presenting evidence in support of its plan. That does not mean, however, as petitioner suggests, that reliance on an affirmative action plan is to be treated as an affirmative defense requiring the employer to carry the burden of proving the validity of the plan. The burden of proving its invalidity remains on the plaintiff.

The assessment of the legality of the Agency Plan must be guided by our decision in [United Steelworkers v. Weber, 223 U.S. 193 (1979)]. In that case, . . . [w]e upheld the employer's decision to select less senior black applicants over the white respondent, for we found that taking race into account was consistent with Title VII's objective of "break[ing] down old patterns of racial segregation and hierarchy." *Id.*, at 208. . . . As Justice Blackmun's concurrence made clear, *Weber* held that an employer seeking to justify the adoption of a plan need not point to its own prior discriminatory practices, nor even to evidence of an "arguable violation" on its part. *Id.*, at 212. Rather, it need point only to a "conspicuous . . . imbalance in traditionally segregated job categories." *Id.*, at 209. Our decision was grounded in the recognition that voluntary employer action can play a crucial role in furthering Title VII's purpose of eliminating the effects of discrimination in the workplace, and that Title VII should not be read to thwart such efforts. *Id.*, at 204.

[W]e must first examine whether that decision was made pursuant to a plan prompted by concerns similar to those of the employer in *Weber*. Next, we must determine whether the effect of the Plan on males and nonminorities is comparable to the effect of the Plan in that case.

The first issue is therefore whether consideration of the sex of applicants for Skilled Craft jobs was justified by the existence of a "manifest imbalance" that reflected underrepresentation of women in "traditionally segregated job categories." *Id.*, at 197. In determining whether an imbalance exists that would justify taking sex or race into account, a comparison of the percentage of minorities or women in the employer's work force with the percentage in the area labor market or general population is appropriate in analyzing jobs that require no special expertise, see Teamsters v. United States, 431 U.S. 324 (1977), or training programs designed to provide expertise, see Steelworkers v. Weber, 443 U.S. 193 (1979). Where a job requires special training, however, the comparison should be with those in the labor force who possess the relevant qualifications. *See* Hazelwood School District v. United States, 433 U.S. 299 (1977). The requirement that the "manifest imbalance" relate to a "traditionally segregated job category" provides assurance both that sex or race will be taken into account in a manner consistent with Title VII's purpose of eliminating the effects of employment discrimination, and that the interests of those employees not benefitting from the plan will not be unduly infringed.

A manifest imbalance need not be such that it would support a prima facie case against the employer, as suggested in Justice O'Connor's concurrence, since we do not regard as identical the constraints of Title VII and the Federal Constitution on voluntarily adopted affirmative action plans. Application of the "prima facie" standard in Title VII cases would be inconsistent with *Weber*'s focus on statistical imbalance, and could inappropriately create a significant disincentive for employers to adopt an affirmative action plan. A corporation concerned with maximizing return on investment, for instance, is hardly likely to adopt a plan if in order to do so it must compile evidence that could be used to subject it to a colorable Title VII suit.

It is clear that the decision to hire Joyce was made pursuant to an Agency plan that directed that sex or race be taken into account for the purpose of remedying underrepresentation. The Agency Plan acknowledged the "limited opportunities that have existed in the past" for women to find employment in certain job classifications "where women have not been traditionally employed in significant numbers." As a result, observed the Plan, women were concentrated in traditionally female jobs in the Agency, and represented a lower percentage in other job classifications than would be expected if such traditional segregation had not occurred. . . . The Plan sought to remedy these imbalances through "hiring, training and promotion of . . . women throughout the Agency in all major job classifications where they are underrepresented."

As an initial matter, the Agency adopted as a benchmark for measuring progress in eliminating underrepresentation the long-term goal of a work force that mirrored in its major job classifications the percentage of women in the area labor market. Even as it did so, however, the Agency acknowledged that such a figure could not by itself necessarily justify taking into account the sex of applicants for positions in all job categories. For positions requiring specialized training and experience, the Plan observed that the number of minorities and women "who possess the qualifications required for entry into such job classifications is limited." The Plan therefore directed that annual short-term goals be formulated that would provide a more realistic indication of the degree to which sex should be taken into account in filling particular positions. The Plan stressed that such goals "should not be construed as 'quotas' that must be met," but as reasonable aspirations in correcting the imbalance in the Agency's work force. These goals were to take into account factors such as "turnover, layoffs, lateral transfers, new job openings, retirements and availability of minorities, women and handicapped persons in the area work force who possess the desired qualifications or potential for placement." . . .

As the Agency Plan recognized, women were most egregiously underrepresented in the Skilled Craft job category, since none of the 238 positions was occupied by a woman. In mid-1980, when Joyce was selected for the road dispatcher position, the Agency was still in the process of refining its short-term goals for Skilled Craft Workers in accordance with the directive of the Plan. This process did not reach fruition until 1982, when the Agency established a short-term goal for that year of 3 women for the 55 expected openings in that job category — a modest goal of about 6% for that category.

We reject petitioner's argument that, since only the long-term goal was in place for Skilled Craft positions at the time of Joyce's promotion, it was inappropriate for the Director to take into account affirmative action considerations in filling the road dispatcher position. The Agency's Plan emphasized that the long-term goals were not to be taken as guides for actual hiring decisions, but that supervisors were to consider a host of practical factors in seeking to meet affirmative action objectives, including the fact that in some job categories women were not qualified in numbers comparable to their representation in the labor force.

By contrast, had the Plan simply calculated imbalances in all categories according to the proportion of women in the area labor pool, and then directed that hiring be governed solely by those figures, its validity fairly could be called into question. This is because analysis of a more specialized labor pool normally is necessary in determining underrepresentation in some positions. If a plan failed to take distinctions in qualifications into account in providing guidance for actual employment decisions, it would dictate mere blind hiring by the numbers . . . .

Given the obvious imbalance in the Skilled Craft category, and given the Agency's commitment to eliminating such imbalances, it was plainly not unreasonable for the Agency to determine that it was appropriate to consider as one factor the sex of Ms. Joyce in making its decision.[14] The promotion of Joyce thus satisfies the first requirement enunciated in *Weber*, since it was undertaken to further an affirmative action plan designed to eliminate Agency work force imbalances in traditionally segregated job categories.

We next consider whether the Agency Plan unnecessarily trammeled the rights of male employees or created an absolute bar to their advancement. In contrast to the plan in *Weber*, which provided that 50% of the positions in the craft training program were exclusively for blacks, and to the consent decree upheld last Term in Firefighters v. Cleveland, 478 U.S. 501 (1986), which required the promotion of specific numbers of minorities, the Plan sets aside no positions for women. The Plan expressly states that "[t]he 'goals' established for each Division should not be construed as 'quotas' that must be met." Rather, the Plan merely authorizes that consideration be given to affirmative action concerns when evaluating qualified applicants. As the Agency Director testified, the sex of Joyce was but one of numerous factors he took into account in arriving at his decision. . . . [T]he Agency Plan requires women to compete with all other qualified applicants. No persons are automatically excluded from consideration; all are able to have their qualifications weighed against those of other applicants.

In addition, petitioner had no absolute entitlement to the road dispatcher position. Seven of the applicants were classified as qualified and eligible, and the Agency Director was authorized to promote any of the seven. Thus, denial of the promotion unsettled no legitimate, firmly rooted expectation on the part of petitioner. Furthermore, while petitioner in this case was denied a promotion, he retained his employment with the Agency, at the same salary and with the same seniority, and remained eligible for other promotions.[15]

Finally, the Agency's Plan was intended to attain a balanced work force, not to maintain one. The Plan contains 10 references to the Agency's desire to "attain" such a balance, but no reference whatsoever to a goal of maintaining it. The Director testified that, while the "broader goal" of affirmative action, defined as "the desire to hire, to promote, to give opportunity and training on an equitable, non-discriminatory basis," is something that is "a permanent part" of "the Agency's operating philosophy," that broader goal "is divorced, if you will, from specific numbers or percentages." The Agency acknowledged the difficulties that it would confront in remedying the imbalance in its work force, and it anticipated only gradual increases in the representation of minorities and women. It is thus

[14] In addition, the Agency was mindful of the importance of finally hiring a woman in a job category that had formerly been all male. The Director testified that, while the promotion of Joyce "made a small dent, for sure, in the numbers," nonetheless "philosophically it made a larger impact in that it probably has encouraged other females and minorities to look at the possibility of so-called 'non-traditional' jobs . . . ."

[15] Furthermore, from 1978 to 1982 Skilled Craft jobs in the Agency increased from 238 to 349. The Agency's personnel figures indicate that the Agency fully expected most of these positions to be filled by men. Of the 111 new Skilled Craft jobs during this period, 105, or almost 95%, went to men. As previously noted, the Agency's 1982 Plan set a goal of hiring only 3 women out of the 55 new Skilled Craft positions projected for that year, . . . about 6%. . . .

unsurprising that the Plan contains no explicit end date, for the Agency's flexible, case-by-case approach was not expected to yield success in a brief period of time. Express assurance that a program is only temporary may be necessary if the program actually sets aside positions according to specific numbers. *See, e.g., Firefighters, supra*, 478 U.S., at 510; *Weber*, 443 U.S., at 199. . . . [T]he Agency has sought to take a moderate, gradual approach to eliminating the imbalance in its work force, one which establishes realistic guidance for employment decisions, and which visits minimal intrusion on the legitimate expectations of other employees. Given this fact, as well as the Agency's express commitment to "attain" a balanced work force, there is ample assurance that the Agency does not seek to use its Plan to maintain a permanent racial and sexual balance. . . .

We therefore hold that the Agency appropriately took into account as one factor the sex of Diane Joyce in determining that she should be promoted to the road dispatcher position. The decision to do so was made pursuant to an affirmative action plan that represents a moderate, flexible, case-by-case approach to effecting a gradual improvement in the representation of minorities and women . . . . Such a plan is fully consistent with Title VII, for it embodies the contribution that voluntary employer action can make in eliminating the vestiges of discrimination. . . [T]he judgment of the Court of Appeals is Affirmed.

[Concurring opinion of Justice STEVENS omitted.]

Justice O'CONNOR, concurring in the judgment.

. . . In my view, the proper initial inquiry in evaluating the legality of an affirmative action plan by a public employer under Title VII is no different from that required by the Equal Protection Clause. In either case, . . . the employer must have had a firm basis for believing that remedial action was required. An employer would have such a firm basis if it can point to a statistical disparity sufficient to support a prima facie claim under Title VII by the employee beneficiaries of the affirmative action plan of a pattern or practice claim of discrimination.

. . . While employers must have a firm basis for concluding that remedial action is necessary, neither *Wygant* nor *Weber* places a burden on employers to prove that they actually discriminated. . . . A requirement that an employer actually prove that it had discriminated in the past would also unduly discourage voluntary efforts to remedy apparent discrimination. . . . Evidence sufficient for a prima facie Title VII pattern or practice claim against the employer itself suggests that the absence of women or minorities in a work force cannot be explained by general societal discrimination alone and that remedial action is appropriate.

[Dissenting opinion of Justice WHITE omitted.]

Justice SCALIA, with whom THE CHIEF JUSTICE joins, and with whom Justice WHITE joins in Parts I and II, dissenting.

. . . [T]oday's decision goes well beyond merely allowing racial or sexual discrimination in order to eliminate the effects of prior societal discrimination. The majority opinion often uses the phrase "traditionally segregated job category" to describe the evil against which the plan is legitimately (according to the majority) directed. As originally used in Steelworkers v. Weber, 443 U.S. 193 (1979), that phrase described skilled jobs from which employers and unions had systematically and intentionally excluded black workers — traditionally segregated jobs, that is, in the sense of conscious, exclusionary discrimination. *See id.*, at 197-198. But that is assuredly not the sense in which the phrase is used here. It is absurd to think that the nationwide failure of road maintenance crews, for example, to achieve the Agency's ambition of 36.4% female representation is attributable primarily, if even substantially, to systematic exclusion of women eager to shoulder pick and shovel. It is a "traditionally segregated job category" not in the *Weber* sense, but in the sense that, because of longstanding social attitudes, it has not been regarded by women themselves as desirable work. . . . And it is the alteration of social attitudes, rather than the elimination of discrimination, which today's decision approves as justification for state-enforced discrimination . . . .

. . . The majority emphasizes, as though it is meaningful, that "No persons are automatically excluded from consideration; all are able to have their qualifications weighed against those of other applicants." . . . Johnson was indeed entitled to have his qualifications weighed against those of other applicants — but more to the point, he was virtually assured that, after the weighing, if there was any minimally qualified applicant from one of the favored groups, he would be rejected.

Similarly hollow is the Court's assurance that we would strike this plan down if it "failed to take distinctions in qualifications into account," because that "would dictate mere blind hiring by the numbers." For what the Court means by "taking distinctions in qualifications into account" consists of no more than eliminating from the applicant pool those who are not even minimally qualified for the job. Once that has been done, once the promoting officer assures himself that all the candidates before him are "M.Q.'s" (minimally qualifieds), he can then ignore, as the Agency Director did here, how much better than minimally qualified some of the candidates may be, and can proceed to appoint from the pool solely on the basis of race or sex, until the affirmative-action "goals" have been reached. . . .

. . . This Court's prior interpretations of Title VII, especially the decision in Griggs v. Duke Power Co., 401 U.S. 424 (1971), subject employers to a potential Title VII suit whenever there is a noticeable imbalance in the representation of minorities or women in the employer's work force. Even the employer who is confident of ultimately prevailing in such a suit must contemplate the expense and adverse publicity of a trial, because the extent of the imbalance, and the "job relatedness" of his selection criteria, are questions of fact to be explored through rebuttal and counterrebuttal of a "prima facie case" consisting of no more than the showing that the employer's selection process "selects those from the protected class at a 'significantly' lesser rate than their counterparts." B. Schlei & P. Grossman, Employment Discrimination Law 91 (2d ed. 1983). If, however, employers are free to discriminate through affirmative action, without fear of "reverse discrimination" suits by their nonminority or male victims, they are offered a threshold defense against Title VII liability premised on numerical disparities. Thus, after today's decision the failure to engage in reverse discrimination is economic folly, and arguably a breach of duty to shareholders or taxpayers, wherever the cost of anticipated Title VII litigation exceeds the cost of hiring less capable (though still minimally capable) workers. . . .

NOTES AND QUESTIONS

1. The employer in *Johnson* was a public agency. Although the plaintiff challenged the validity of the agency's affirmative action plan under Title VII, he might also have challenged it under the Fourteenth Amendment's Equal Protection Clause. Wygant v. Jackson Bd. of Educ., 476 U.S. 276 (1986). The analysis for determining the validity of a public employer's affirmative action under the Fourteenth Amendment resembles the majority's in *Johnson*. First, the plan must be "justified by a compelling governmental interest," which, for affirmative action, means that the plan must be based on evidence of prior discrimination. *Id.* at 274-277. In the words of Justice O'Connor, concurring in *Wygant*, "the public employer must have a firm basis for determining that affirmative action is warranted," but "a contemporaneous or antecedent finding of past discrimination by a court or other competent body is not a constitutional prerequisite." *Id.* at 289, 292. Second, the plan must be "narrowly tailored to the achievement" of the public employer's legitimate interests. *Id.* at 274. A plan that is unduly intrusive against the interests of nonminority employees and applicants is unlawful. *Id.*

2. Concurring in *Johnson*, Justice Stevens suggested an employer might have legitimate reasons for affirmative action other than to remedy its own or societal discrimination. 480 U.S. at 642-646. For example, a school system might seek to hire more minority teachers to improve minority students' self-esteem and academic performance, or a local government might hire more minorities to improve relations with a minority community or avert racial tension. *Id.*, citing Sullivan, *The Supreme Court – Comment, Sins of Discrimination: Last Term's Affirmative Action Cases*, 100 Harv. L. Rev. 78, 96 (1986). Are there other potentially legitimate reasons for affirmative action in employment?

In Grutter v. Bollinger, 539 U.S. 306 (2003), the Court held that a law school's consideration of race in admitting students did not violate the Fourteenth Amendment, where race was but one of many "soft variables" designed to "achieve that diversity which has the potential to enrich everyone's education and thus make a law school class stronger than the sum of its parts." *Id.* at 315. The Court agreed that the school "has a compelling interest in attaining a diverse student body." Diversity promotes "'cross-racial understanding,' helps to break down racial stereotypes and 'enables [students] to better understand persons of different races.' " Furthermore, "classroom discussion is livelier, more spirited, and simply more enlightening and interesting" if students have the "greatest possible variety of backgrounds." *Id.* at 330; *see also* Fisher v. Univ. of Tex., ___ U.S. ___, 136 S. Ct. 2198 (2016) (re-affirming and applying the principles of *Grutter* to evaluate lawfulness of university admissions program).

If diversity is a legitimate goal for schools selecting students, could an employer use affirmative action in hiring for no reason other than workplace diversity? *See* Petit v. City of Chicago, 352 F.3d 1111, 1115 (7th Cir. 2003) (police department "had compelling interest in a diverse population at the rank of sergeant in order to set the proper tone in the department and to earn the trust of the community, which in turn increases police effectiveness in protecting the city").

6. *Reasonable Accommodation*

"Equal" treatment can be a barrier to some groups whose personal characteristics or religious practices prevent them from performing a job exactly as the employer has located, described, or scheduled the job. Consider, for example, a person who can move about only with the aid of a wheelchair and cannot climb stairs. If the best jobs require work and travel between the second, third, and fourth floors, equal access to the stairs is not much use to such a person.

Not all barriers are physical. Members of a religion that proscribes working after the sun goes down are unable to accept jobs requiring regular or occasional work on the night shift, or they risk being discharged whenever their religious practices conflict with their employer's demands. Similarly, persons whose religious convictions require a head cover or other religious attire might find their religious practices incompatible with an employer's nondiscriminatory dress code or company uniform. Under what circumstances should an employer be compelled to make a special exception or bear a burden (such as the cost of an elevator) simply to benefit one or more members of a minority?

OPUKU-BOATENG v. STATE OF CALIFORNIA

95 F.3d 1461 (9th Cir. 1996)

REINHARDT, Circuit Judge:

This is a case involving an employer's obligation to accommodate a worker's religious beliefs and, in particular, the commitment to observe the Sabbath. Kwasi Opuku-Boateng . . . sought permanent employment with the [California Department of Food and Agriculture]. He was selected for a permanent position but, when he advised the Department that he was unable to work on Saturdays because of his religious beliefs, the Department terminated the hiring process. Opuku-Boateng sued the State of California and several Department officials ("the State"), claiming that the State denied him a position on the basis of his religion, in violation of Title VII . . . . The district court concluded that Opuku-Boateng had established a prima facie case of discrimination but that the State had demonstrated that accommodating his religious beliefs would have caused undue hardship. Accordingly, it entered judgment in favor of the State. We reverse.

BACKGROUND

Opuku-Boateng is a devout member of the Seventh Day Adventist Church. The Church teaches its members to observe the Sabbath from sundown Friday to sundown Saturday and to refrain from engaging in secular work during that period. It further teaches that repeated violations of the Sabbath observance imperil one's salvation. Opuku-Boateng, adhering to the tenets of his faith, . . . has never worked on the Sabbath and refuses to do so under any circumstances.

. . . [Opuku-Boateng] applied for numerous positions, including Plant Quarantine Inspector ("Plant Inspector"). . . . On October 18, 1982, Opuku-Boateng received an appointment as a Plant Inspector to the border-inspection station in Yermo, California, to begin on November 2. The Yermo station employed a total of 15 inspectors, including 5 supervisors. It operated seven days a week, twenty-four hours a day, and maintained three eight-hour shifts — day, evening, and night. The size of the staff and the number of shifts would increase, however, during certain times of the year, such as the summer months. Departmental policy required that work assignments be made as equitably as possible. As the district court found, all employees at the Yermo station were required to work "an equal number of undesirable weekend, holiday, and night shifts." Departmental policy further required that employees be assigned varying schedules to avoid the possibility of collusion between inspectors and "the travelling public or trucking industry," and to expose inspectors to the various commodities that were transported through the station at different times.

. . . On October 28, Opuku-Boateng visited the station, accompanied by the local Adventist pastor. He reviewed the posted work schedule and learned that he was scheduled to work on an upcoming Saturday, November 14. He informed the acting supervisor, William Whitacre, that his religious beliefs precluded him from working on his Sabbath. Whitacre advised Opuku-Boateng that unless he was willing to work on Saturdays, his appointment would not be processed.

. . . Over the next week, Opuku-Boateng and representatives of the local Adventist parish negotiated with various Department representatives in an attempt to find a solution. Opuku-Boateng offered to work undesirable non-Sabbath shifts (i.e., Sundays, nights and holidays) in place of the Sabbath assignments he would ordinarily receive; to trade shifts with other employees; or to transfer to another station or another position . . . . Howard Ingham, a Program Supervisor for the Department, instructed a supervisor in the Yermo station, whose identity he no longer recalls, to conduct a poll of the staff to determine whether voluntary trading of shifts to accommodate Opuku-Boateng would be feasible. According to the district court, "[a]lthough one or two employees said they would be willing to do so on rare occasions, none were willing to accommodate [Opuku-Boateng] permanently."

Ingham stated that he was told that none of the Yermo station employees was willing to accommodate Opuku-Boateng on a regular basis. . . . Whitacre recalled the poll but said that he could not state what question was asked or how many employees were contacted. Lozano recalled that when asked whether she would be willing to accommodate Opuku-Boateng, she said that she was willing to trade shifts but not on a permanent basis. However, Lozano also recalled being told that the accommodation would involve three days per week, Friday, Saturday, and Sunday.

By letter dated November 1, Ingham informed Opuku-Boateng that his request for an accommodation . . . was not considered reasonable, and advised Opuku-Boateng that if he wanted to be employed as a Plant Inspector, he would be "expected to work assigned shifts as scheduled." [The state subsequently rejected Opuku-Boateng's application for the Plant Inspector position.]

. . . Opuku-Boateng filed an action claiming that the denial of his appointment violated Title VII. Following trial, the district court entered judgment in favor of the State. It concluded that although Opuku-Boateng established a prima facie case of religious discrimination, the State had demonstrated that it could not reasonably have accommodated his religious beliefs without suffering undue hardship.

Discussion

Title VII of the Civil Rights Act of 1964 prohibits an employer from discriminating on the basis of religion. It defines the term "religion" to include "all aspects of religious observance and practice, as well as belief," and imposes a duty of reasonable accommodation on employers. 42 U.S.C. § 2000e(j). It is therefore unlawful "for an employer not to make reasonable accommodations, short of undue hardship, for the religious practices of his employees and prospective employees." Trans World Airlines, Inc. v. Hardison, 432 U.S. 63, 74 (1977).

We assess Title VII religious discrimination claims using a two-part analysis. Heller v. EBB Auto Co., 8 F.3d 1433, 1438 (9th Cir. 1993). First, the employee must establish a prima facie case of religious discrimination. *Id.*[9] Second, if the employee does so, the burden shifts to the employer to show that it "'negotiate[d] with the employee in an effort reasonably to accommodate the employee's religious beliefs.' " *Id.* (quoting EEOC v. Hacienda Hotel, 881 F.2d 1504, 1513 (9th Cir. 1989)). Where the negotiations do not produce a proposal by the employer that would eliminate the religious conflict, the employer must either accept the employee's proposal or demonstrate that it would cause undue hardship were it to do so. EEOC v. Townley Eng'g & Mfg. Co., 859 F.2d 610, 615 (9th Cir. 1988), *cert. denied*, 489 U.S. 1077 (1989). Only if the employer can show that no accommodation would be possible without undue hardship is it excused from taking the necessary steps to accommodate the employee's religious beliefs.

Prima Facie Case

The State concedes that Opuku-Boateng established a prima facie case of discrimination. First, he established that observance of his Sabbath is a bona fide religious practice and that it conflicts with the employment duty to be available to work on Saturdays. Second, he demonstrated that he notified the State upon learning of the conflict between his religious beliefs and the employment duty. Last, he proved that the failure to hire him was a result of the conflict.

Reasonable Accommodation and Undue Hardship

Because Opuku-Boateng established a prima facie case of discrimination, the State was required to establish that it did not violate the statutory duty to accommodate his observance of the Sabbath. . . .

Whether a proposed accommodation would cause undue hardship must be determined in the particular factual context of the case. *See* American Postal Workers Union v. Postmaster Gen., 781 F.2d 772, 775 (9th Cir. 1986). Ordinarily, the employer must show that the accommodation would cause "'undue hardship on the conduct of the business.'" *Townley Eng'g*, 859 F.2d at 615 (quoting 42 U.S.C. § 2000e(j)). "An accommodation causes an 'undue hardship' when it results

---

[9] In order to establish a prima facie case of religious discrimination, a plaintiff . . . must establish that "(1) he had a bona fide religious belief, the practice of which conflicted with an employment duty; (2) he informed his employer of the belief and conflict; and (3) the employer threatened him or subjected him to discriminatory treatment . . . because of his inability to fulfill the job requirements." *Heller*, 8 F.3d at 1438. The employee need not be penalized with discharge to establish a prima facie case. *Townley*, 859 F.2d at 614 n.5. ("The threat of discharge (or other adverse employment practices) is a sufficient penalty.")

in more than a de minimis cost to the employer." *Heller*, 8 F.3d at 1440.[11] However, an employer may also show hardship on the plaintiff's coworkers. It is less clear what type of impact on coworkers, apart from a significant discriminatory impact, constitutes an undue hardship.

Here, the district court concluded that the State entered into good-faith negotiations for the purpose of arriving at an accommodation of Opuku-Boateng's religious beliefs. The court based its conclusion on the fact that the State engaged in negotiations with Opuku-Boateng's representatives and conducted a poll of the Yermo station employees before determining that an accommodation was not feasible. Without relying on the evidence regarding the poll, we agree that the State "'negotiate[d] with the employee in an effort reasonably to accommodate the employee's religious beliefs.'" *Heller,* 8 F.3d at 1438 (citation omitted). This is clearly not a case in which the employer did not make an effort to negotiate with the employee. Indeed, it appears that as a result of weeklong negotiations, a church elder arrived at a tentative agreement with the State but that the arrangement later fell through. While the nature of the understanding has been lost with the death of the elder and the failure of the state, for whatever reason, to produce a witness from its side of the discussions, we nevertheless conclude that the State satisfied the first requirement. The threshold for satisfying this requirement is low because, while a negative conclusion results in a violation of the statute, an affirmative conclusion serves only to move the analysis to the next issue: whether the various potential accommodations would all have resulted in undue hardship.

Although the State negotiated in good faith, there is no evidence that it ever made any proposal to Opuku-Boateng. Therefore, the next issue is whether Opuku-Boateng's proposed accommodations would have resulted in undue hardship to the State or his co-workers. . . . [P]roposed accommodations included excusing him from Sabbath work and scheduling him instead for other equally undesirable shifts, adopting a system of voluntary or mandatory shift trades, employing a combination of the above procedures, arranging a transfer to another department, and making a temporary accommodation, which would have allowed the State to experiment with the various proposals while permitting both it and Opuku-Boateng to make efforts to find him other employment with the Department or another State agency. The district court rejected all of these proposed accommodations on the ground that each would have resulted in undue hardship both to his coworkers and the Department. . . .

SCHEDULING ARRANGEMENT AND/OR SHIFT TRADES

The district court concluded that although scheduling Opuku-Boateng to be off every Sabbath was mathematically possible, it constituted an unreasonable

[11] The Supreme Court has made it clear that an accommodation that imposes more than a de minimis cost to the employer constitutes an undue hardship. *See Ansonia*, 479 U.S. at 66-68 (stating that in *Hardison*, the Court held that "an accommodation causes 'undue hardship' whenever that accommodation results in 'more than a de minimis cost' to the employer."). As we have stated, "The statute . . . posits a gain-seeking employer exclusively concerned with preserving and promoting its economic efficiency." *Townley Eng'g*, 859 F.2d at 616. Accordingly, additional costs in the form of lost efficiency or higher wages may constitute undue hardships. *Hardison*, 432 U.S. at 84.

accommodation "because it would have had a discriminatory impact on other employees and more than a de minimis impact on the operation of the Yermo station." Specifically, the district court determined that accommodating Opuku-Boateng in this manner would have required a number of other employees to work more than their fair share of Friday night and Saturday day and evening shifts, hampered the Department's ability to accommodate other employees' scheduling needs, resulted in substantial morale problems and additional requests for accommodations, and violated Departmental policy. With respect to a system of voluntary shift trades, which could have been employed either by itself or in combination with modifications to the scheduling system, the district court concluded that any such arrangement was infeasible because the other station employees were unwilling to trade shifts with Opuku-Boateng on a regular basis.

In determining that the proposed accommodations would result in discriminatory treatment of other employees, the court relied principally on Trans World Airlines v. Hardison, 432 U.S. 63 (1977). We have not read *Hardison* so broadly as to proscribe all differences in treatment. . . . Instead, we have read it to bar "preferential treatment of employees." *Tooley*, 648 F.2d at 1243.

In *Hardison*, the proposed accommodation would have conflicted with the contractually-established seniority system, thus violating an employee's seniority rights under the collective bargaining agreement by denying him his shift preferences. *Hardison*, 432 U.S. at 80. By contrast, in this case, the scheduling of shifts was not governed by any collective bargaining agreement, and the proposed accommodation would not have deprived any employee of any contractually-established seniority rights or privileges, or indeed of any contractually-established rights or privileges of any kind. More important, unlike in *Hardison,* there is no evidence that the proposed shift-scheduling arrangement would, in the end, have granted Opuku-Boateng a privilege or imposed more than a de minimis burden on other employees. In *Hardison*, not all TWA employees were required to work weekends. Those employees who had worked in a department the longest had first preference to take weekends off. . . . Requiring another employee with greater seniority to substitute for Hardison on Saturday would have afforded Hardison the privilege of not working Saturday, and imposed the burden of working that day on the other employee, "according to religious beliefs." *Hardison*, 432 U.S. at 85.

In this case, . . . all employees at the Yermo station were required to work "an equal number of undesirable weekend, holiday, and night shifts." So long as Opuku-Boateng worked that equal number of "undesirable shifts," being assigned a holiday, Sunday, or night shift for every shift he missed to observe the Sabbath, he would not have been granted any preferential treatment, nor would any cognizable burden have been imposed on other employees who simply were assigned one undesirable shift instead of another. . . . Therefore, the State failed to carry its burden of demonstrating that Opuku-Boateng's practice of observing the Sabbath could not have been accommodated through scheduling arrangements without affording him preferential treatment.

Opuku-Boateng also proposed an alternative means by which the State could accommodate his religious practices without affording him preferential treatment or discriminating against his coworkers. This alternative, voluntary shift trades, could have been implemented by itself or in combination with the proposed scheduling arrangement discussed above. For example, the State could have prepared a six-month or year-long schedule in advance, determined how many Sabbath shifts Opuku-Boateng would ordinarily be assigned, and then determined how many of those shifts his coworkers would be willing to accept in exchange for undesirable Sunday, holiday, or night shifts that they would otherwise have had to work. It is not unreasonable to assume that other employees would have been willing to trade for many, if not all, of Opuku-Boateng's Sabbath shifts in exchange for shifts that they were assigned and might have found even more undesirable. By preparing a tentative schedule, the State might well have determined that voluntary shift trades would completely eliminate the hypothetical difficulty resulting from the need to accommodate . . . .

. . . The State contends that the district court relied not only on the results of the poll, as recounted by Ingham, but also on "independent" testimony that the Yermo station employees were not willing to accommodate Opuku-Boateng. . . . The State draws our attention to Maria Lozano's testimony. Her testimony, however, substantially undermines the reliability of the poll itself. Lozano testified that when she was asked whether she would be willing to trade shifts with Opuku-Boateng, it was her belief that he would be unable to work three days per week, not just one twenty-four-hour period. Her belief was not simply a mistake on her part. Lozano stated that various supervisors had told her that accommodating Opuku-Boateng's request would involve three days per week. Without any evidence to the contrary, we can only assume that the other employees were polled about a three-day accommodation as well. Accordingly, we fail to see how the evidence suggests, let alone establishes, that the Yermo station employees were collectively unwilling to accommodate Opuku-Boateng by trading shifts.

The State conducted a vague and ambiguous poll that was not capable of producing reliable results regarding the question whether an accommodation was practicable. The issue was not, as the question asked of Lozano, and presumably other employees, implied, whether any one employee would be willing to accommodate Opuku-Boateng's religious beliefs by trading for all of his Sabbath shifts. Instead, the issue was whether over the course of a year (or any other fixed period of time) there would be a sufficient number of employees in the station who would agree to work one or more of Opuku-Boateng's Sabbath shifts in exchange for his working one or more shifts assigned to them that they found equally undesirable. . . . The State failed to conduct the type of inquiry into the feasibility of trading shifts that would have been necessary to answer that question one way or the other, and thus to enable it to carry its burden.

. . . Having addressed the district court's conclusions regarding the impact the proposed accommodations would have had on Opuku-Boateng's coworkers, we now consider . . . their potential impact on the operation of the station. . . .

The district court determined that even though Opuku-Boateng proposed to work additional Sunday, holiday, and night shifts in exchange for not working on his Sabbath, such an accommodation was nonetheless infeasible because it would have resulted in his working a more predictable schedule, in violation of departmental policy. Although the Department had a legitimate interest in varying the work schedules of its border station employees in order to discourage bribery or dishonesty, there is no probative evidence that suggests that accommodating

Opuku-Boateng's religious beliefs would have resulted in a schedule that was so predictable . . . that it would have jeopardized the Department's security interests.

The district court also concluded that the Department's ability to accommodate the scheduling needs of other employees would have been affected and that morale problems with a significant impact could have arisen. We find this conclusion clearly erroneous as well.... [E]vidence introduced by the State as to its ability (or lack thereof) to accommodate other employees' scheduling desires was wholly inadequate. . . . [H]ypothetical morale problems are clearly insufficient to establish undue hardship. "Even proof that employees would grumble about a particular accommodation is not enough to establish undue hardship." Anderson v. General Dynamics Convair Aerospace Div., 589 F.2d 397, 402 (1978) . . . .[24] Likewise, the mere possibility that there would be an unfulfillable number of additional requests for similar accommodations by others cannot constitute undue hardship. *See Burns*, 589 F.2d at 407 (rejecting contention that "accommodating [the plaintiff] would open the gate to excusing vast numbers of persons who claimed to share [the plaintiff's] beliefs," where the record established that only three of the union's members were Seventh Day Adventists). Far more concrete undue hardship is required before an employer can be said to have met its burden....

Thus, we conclude that the district court erred in determining that the proposed scheduling arrangement, voluntary trade shifts, or a combination of the two, would have resulted in undue hardship.

Temporary Accommodation and Transfer

Finally, Opuku-Boateng proposed a temporary or trial accommodation that would have allowed the Department to experiment with the proposed accommodations and permitted both parties to investigate the possibility that Opuku-Boateng could be employed in another job in the Department or some other State agency, should the accommodations prove infeasible in practice. . . . At the very least, the State should have either temporarily scheduled Opuku-Boateng not to work on the Sabbath or sought to obtain voluntary shift trades for him on a short- or long-term basis. Then, certainly by the end of his probationary term, it would have been able to determine what actual hardships, if any, would result. Had the State followed this course, it would have placed itself on far firmer ground to argue that Opuku-Boateng could not reasonably be accommodated. . . .

Conclusion

Opuku-Boateng established a prima facie case of religious discrimination and that the State failed to demonstrate that he could not be reasonably accommodated without undue hardship. . . . [T]he judgment of the district court is reversed and the case is remanded to the district court for the award of appropriate relief.

KING, Senior District Judge, dissenting:

I would affirm the district court for the reasons stated by the district judge.

---

[24] . . . "If relief under Title VII can be denied merely because the majority of employees, who have not been discriminated against, will be unhappy about it, there will be little hope of correcting the wrongs to which the Act is directed." . . .

NOTES AND QUESTIONS

1. The "de minimis" standard of "undue hardship," which is the most the law requires of an employer to accommodate employee religious practices, has its source in the Supreme Court's decision in Trans World Airlines, Inc. v. Hardison, 432 U.S. 63, 84 (1977). The de minimis standard prevents an employer from arbitrarily denying an accommodation that involves no real and substantial hardship, but it also relieves the employer of any duty to bear significant costs or burdens. Had the Supreme Court in imposed a greater burden on employers, it might have confronted a difficult question whether Title VII's religious accommodation rules violate the Establishment Clause of the First Amendment. *See* 432 U.S. at 70 n.4. The de minimis burden of religious accommodation has easily survived constitutional challenge. *See, e.g.*, Protos v. Volkswagen of America, Inc., 797 F.2d 129, 135-136 (3d Cir. 1986).

2. The Americans with Disabilities Act is another law that imposes a duty to accommodate. The ADA defines the term *discriminate* to include "not making reasonable accommodations to the known physical or mental limitations of an otherwise qualified individual with a disability" unless the employer "can demonstrate that the accommodation would impose an undue hardship on the operation of the . . . [employer's] business." 42 U.S.C. § 12112(b)(5)(A). Unconstrained by First Amendment concerns, Congress imposed a duty to accommodate disability that is much greater than the de minimis duty to accommodate religion.

EEOC regulations offer the following nonexclusive list of accommodations the act might require of employers, depending on burdensomeness:

> Reasonable accommodation may include but is not limited to:
>
> (i) Making existing facilities used by employees readily accessible to and usable by individuals with disabilities; and
>
> (ii) Job restructuring; part-time or modified work schedules; reassignment to a vacant position; acquisition or modifications of equipment or devices; appropriate adjustment or modifications of examinations, training materials, or policies; the provision of qualified readers or interpreters; and other similar accommodations for individuals with disabilities.

29 C.F.R. § 1630.2(o)(2).

How much burden must an employer bear to accommodate disability? The answer might depend on factors and circumstances unique to each employer or workplace. The Americans with Disabilities Act lists the following factors as relevant to whether a proposed accommodation would impose an undue hardship:

> (i) the nature and cost of the accommodation needed under this chapter;
>
> (ii) the overall financial resources of the facility or facilities involved in the provision of the reasonable accommodation; the number of persons employed at such facility; the effect on expenses and resources, or the impact otherwise of such accommodation upon the operation of the facility;
>
> (iii) the overall financial resources of the covered entity; the overall size of

the business of a covered entity with respect to the number of its employees; the number, type, and location of its facilities; and

(iv) the type of operation or operations of the covered entity, including the composition, structure, and functions of the workforce of such entity; the geographic separateness, administrative, or fiscal relationship of the facility or facilities in question to the covered entity.

42 U.S.C. § 12111(10).

Note that these factors look to the cost of the accommodation relative to the size and resources of the employer and the particular facility. They do not include consideration of the "benefits" to the claimant (e.g., improved salary or job satisfaction) or the number of additional job opportunities the accommodation might create for other disabled applicants. Thus, it is the EEOC's position that "cost-benefits" analysis is inappropriate for determining undue burden:

> Neither the statute nor the legislative history supports a cost-benefit analysis to determine whether a specific accommodation causes an undue hardship. Whether the cost of a reasonable accommodation imposes an undue hardship depends on the employer's resources, not on the individual's salary, position, or status (e.g., fulltime versus part-time, salary versus hourly wage, permanent versus temporary).

EEOC Enforcement Guidance: Reasonable Accommodation and Undue Hardship Under the Americans with Disabilities Act (Oct. 2000), at http://www.eeoc.gov/policy/docs/accommodation.html#undue.

Many courts take the opposing view that cost-benefit analysis is implicitly included in the act's requirement of "reasonable" accommodation, even if not included in the act's list of "undue burden" factors, 42 U.S.C.§ 12112(b)(5). In Borkowski v. Valley Cent. Sch. Dist., 63 F.3d 131 (2d Cir. 1995), the court stated:

> We would not, for example, require an employer to make a multi-million dollar modification for the benefit of a single individual with a disability, even if the proposed modification would allow that individual to perform the essential functions of a job that she sought. In spite of its effectiveness, the proposed modification would be unreasonable because of its excessive costs. In short, an accommodation is reasonable only if its costs are not clearly disproportionate to the benefits that it will produce.

Id. at 138.

Assuming the cost of accommodation should be weighed against the benefits to be attained, how should the benefits be measured? By the savings enjoyed by society, which would otherwise pay disability benefits? By the value of the wages and benefits the disabled person would earn? By the disabled person's personal and noneconomic valuation of the career? By the number of opportunities an accommodation might create for other disabled persons?

3. A proposed accommodation of an applicant's disability might leave the applicant short of 100 percent capacity to perform all the usual functions of the job. For example, an accommodation might make it possible for a disabled applicant to perform most tasks of a desk job, but he might still be unable to perform a few incidental tasks, such as lifting an occasional 25 lb. box, If the applicant cannot perform every single task even after accommodation, should the

employer be allowed to reject the applicant as "unqualified"?

The answer depends on whether the tasks the applicant cannot perform are "essential." The ADA prohibits only discrimination against a "*qualified* individual with a disability." 42 U.S.C. § 12112(a) (emphasis added). "Qualified" requires consideration of what the individual can do with reasonable accommodation. A disabled person who still cannot perform every task after reasonable accommodation might still be "qualified" if able to perform every "essential" function. The employer cannot justify rejection of a disabled person simply for inability to perform some peripheral or incidental task. *Compare* Conneen v. MBNA Am. Bank, N.A., 334 F.3d 318 (3d Cir. 2003) (arriving by 8 A.M. was not an "essential function" of job) *with* Darby v. Bratch, 287 F.3d 673 (8th Cir. 2002) (employee disabled by depression not able to perform all essential functions of job if she could not satisfy minimum attendance requirements).

4. Note the discussion of whether the State "negotiated" with Opuku-Boateng regarding possible accommodation. Finding the right accommodation depends on each party's willingness to share information, particularly because each has important information the other lacks. The employer has the best information about its business needs; the employee has the best information about the demands of his religion or disability. In E.E.O.C. v. Sears, Roebuck & Co., 417 F.3d 789 (7th Cir. 2005), the court described this "interactive process" as follows: If the employer participates in the process in good faith, it will be relieved of liability if the failure to find an accommodation was due to the *employee's* refusal to communicate or provide important information. On the other hand, if the employee requests an accommodation, the employer may not reject the accommodation out of hand without explaining the reason for rejection, offering alternatives or otherwise expressing a willingness to search for a different solution. *Id.* at 806-807.

D. BEYOND DISCRIMINATION: INACCURACY AND INTRUSION

1. *Overview*

Discrimination laws prohibit employers from making arbitrary employment decisions based on protected characteristics, and they certainly encourage employers to be cautious in general to avoid allegations of discrimination. But discrimination law goes only so far. Employers might be arbitrary and unfair in ways that do not violate discrimination laws. For example, the manager who makes the final decision might favor a family relative, paramour, or friend over a better-qualified individual. Or the manager might discriminate based on an unprotected characteristic, such as height, attractiveness, or personality. If the employer's unfairness or negligence in hiring the wrong person causes personal injury or property damage to another employee, a customer or other third party, the injured party might sue under the doctrines of *respondeat superior* or negligent hiring. However, an employer breaches no duty in *failing* to hire the *right* person. In particular, the employer owes no duty of care or fairness to applicants in hiring decisions. The injury a disappointed applicant feels is simply not one for which the common law offers any remedy. This rule is so widely assumed that there are almost no reported cases challenging it. See section A of this chapter, *supra. See also* Holder v. City of Raleigh, 867 F.2d 823 (4th Cir. 1989) (employer's preference for hiring relatives did not violate federal discrimination law).

The harm suffered by rejected applicants because of arbitrary, eccentric, or misguided hiring decisions might be an unavoidable consequence of the inherently subjective quality of judgments employers and employees make in choosing each other. Choosing a person with whom you will work is somewhat like choosing a friend or a spouse. It might not be a matter of purely "objective" qualifications and values. If a court sought to correct an employer's hiring decisions, the court would have to make its own subjective judgment as to the "best" candidate, and the court's judgment might not be any better than the employer's. Moreover, even if it were possible to identify the "wrong" and "right" hiring decisions, the harm suffered by a rejected individual is highly speculative. Thus, discrimination law tends to target only those misguided employer prejudices likely to cause great social and economic harm — such as race discrimination.

Nevertheless, there are at least two situations in which there might be special grounds to complain about hiring methods that do not violate any of the usual laws against discrimination. The first is when the harm of an unfair or misguided selection method is compounded because so many other employers have adopted the same method. The harm might be especially objectionable if it falls disproportionately on a group of employee/applicants who share some common characteristic. The rejected group might begin to suffer in employment much like other groups of traditional discriminatees. For example, if every employer disqualifies any applicant who has ever been convicted of a crime, all persons with such a record will be unemployable.

A second troubling situation is when a hiring method violates the employee/applicant's dignity by invading her privacy or otherwise causing embarrassment. Laws against discrimination provide some protection against employers' prying into facts that might reveal an applicant's protected characteristics, such religion or disability. But some questions are simply embarrassing, demeaning, or disrespectful of an individual's desire for privacy. In this case, the selection process might cause harm regardless of its outcome. Even the winning candidate might have a complaint.

Both problems are compounded and interrelated by modern technology that augments an employer's ability to investigate facts an employee might wish to remain private. It is increasingly easy, and therefore increasingly more likely, for employers to investigate many facts about an applicant's background, such as his criminal record, health, financial situation, life history and family, without needing to ask the applicant directly and without relying on the applicant's word. Information technology makes much of this information immediately available at comparatively little cost. By using certain medical tests, it is even possible for an employer to learn more about an individual applicant than the applicant knew about himself. Thus, we may be nearing a day when every job application is both a confessional and an unexpected experience in self-discovery.

a. Inaccuracy

DOE v. SMITHKLINE BEECHAM CORP.

855 S.W.2d 248 (Tex. App. 1993)

CARROLL, Chief Justice.

This case involves liability of an employer and a testing lab in connection with a pre-employment drug-screening test. Appellant, Jane Doe, the prospective employee, appeals from an adverse summary judgment. We will affirm the summary judgment in part and reverse and remand in part.

BACKGROUND

The Quaker Oats Company ("Quaker") offered Doe, a Master of Business Administration student, a job as a marketing assistant in its Chicago office at a starting salary of $49,000 plus a bonus of $4,000. The offer did not state a definite term of employment. Quaker's employment offer was conditioned on Doe . . . satisfactorily completing a drug-screening examination as required by Quaker policy. . . . Doe had previously signed a "Pre-Employment Consent to Drug Screening" form required by Quaker. Quaker furnished Doe with a drug "testing package" that directed her to the Austin Occupational Health Center ("AOHC") where she completed the enclosed forms, including a questionnaire on recent medication use, and provided a urine sample. The only medication Doe listed on the pretesting questionnaire was her prescribed birth-control pills.[3] AOHC forwarded Doe's sample to SmithKline Beecham Clinical Laboratories, Inc. ("SmithKline"), the drug testing laboratory with which Quaker had contracted for its pre-employment screening.

Doe's sample tested positive for the presence of opiates.[5] SmithKline so informed Quaker, which, through its representatives, notified Doe by telephone that her employment offer had been rescinded because "she had tested positive for narcotics." Doe denied any illegal drug use and requested an opportunity to submit a second test sample. She was informed that, according to Quaker policy, the offer had been automatically rescinded and that her only recourse was to reapply for the position in six months.

During one of several telephone conversations between Doe and Quaker representatives, as a possible explanation for the positive test result, Doe stated that she had taken one of her roommate's prescription painkillers. She later retracted this statement and accounted for the fabrication regarding the painkillers as made "under extreme duress" and when she was "completely, essentially out of [her] mind." When Doe reapplied with Quaker, she was not hired for the stated reason of her misrepresentation of taking someone else's prescription medication.

Doe asserts that her positive test for opiates was the result of her consumption of several poppy seed muffins in the days before she provided her urine sample. It

---

[3] The pretesting questionnaire inquired about general types of prescription and nonprescription medications; it did not inquire about food intake or poppy seed consumption.

[5] Doe does not dispute that the test was conducted by proper technical procedures and by a valid two-step testing methodology — Enzyme Multiplied Immunoassay Test ("EMIT") screening with a confirmatory gas chromatography, mass spectrometry ("GC/MS") test.

is undisputed that for several years before Doe's test, scientific literature on drug testing reported that ordinary poppy seed consumption could produce positive test results for opiates. Neither the pretesting forms nor any representative of Quaker, AOHC, or SmithKline inquired about Doe's consumption of poppy seed products or warned her to abstain from them before the test.

Doe initially brought suit against SmithKline . . . for negligence in the manner in which the drug test was conducted. After Quaker declined her reapplication, Doe added Quaker as a defendant. Doe alleged negligence on the part of SmithKline and Quaker in their: (1) failure to warn of the poppy seed danger, to inform her to refrain from poppy seed consumption before the test, or to inquire about consumption of poppy seeds on the pretesting questionnaire; (2) failure to review properly her test results or conduct additional tests to determine whether they indicated poppy seed consumption rather than illegal drug use; and (3) failure to retain and return her urine sample properly. Doe also urged that Quaker breached the employment contract by failing to provide her a reasonable opportunity to pass the drug test. . . . The trial court granted summary judgment and ordered that Doe take nothing by her claims against Quaker and SmithKline. . . . Doe appeals . . . from the take-nothing judgment. . . .

Discussion and Holding

Breach of Contract

Doe's first point of error argues that summary judgment was not proper because the summary-judgment proof supports a cause of action against Quaker for breach of contract. . . .

Quaker offered Doe employment for an indeterminate period. As such, the offer was for employment at will. Under the "employment at will" doctrine, absent an express contract term to the contrary, Quaker could terminate Doe's employment at any time with or without cause and without liability. Winters v. Houston Chronicle Publishing Co., 795 S.W.2d 723 (Tex. 1990). . . .

Assuming that a contract existed between Quaker and Doe, Quaker was entitled, without risk of liability, to fire Doe without a reason or for an arbitrary reason. If Doe had failed a drug test, for whatever reason, after starting her job, Quaker would be within its rights and would not breach the contract by terminating Doe. We see no reason to place greater contractual duties on Quaker in a pre-employment situation. Moreover, the summary-judgment proof shows that Quaker had grounds to withdraw its offer to Doe, because, as discussed previously, she admitted having lied to Quaker representatives about taking her roommate's prescription medication. Accordingly, under the employment-at-will doctrine, Quaker is not liable for any breach simply because it revoked its offer or decided not to hire Doe on her reapplication.

Doe argues that Quaker was obligated by an implied term of the offer to provide a reasonable opportunity to pass the drug test. By failing to provide safeguards to prevent a so-called "poppy seed positive," Doe argues Quaker breached that obligation. Quaker's written offer to Doe merely stated that she must satisfactorily complete the drug test "per company policy." Texas courts have refused to imply a duty of good faith and fair dealing in employment contracts.

Lumpkin v. H & C Communications, Inc., 755 S.W.2d 538, 540 (Tex. App. — Houston [1st Dist.] 1988, writ denied). We decline to imply the good faith and fair dealing or any other implied contractual obligations to the immediate situation.

. . . We overrule Doe's first point of error.

Negligence

[In another portion of the opinion, the court upheld summary judgment against Doe's negligence claim against Quaker because "[i]n order to impose a tort duty upon parties to a contract, the court must find that a special relationship exists between the parties. Some contracts do involve a special relationship that may give rise to duties enforceable as torts. An employment situation governed by the employment-at-will doctrine is not such a situation" (citations omitted).]

Doe's second point of error alleges that the trial court erred in rendering summary judgment because the summary-judgment proof supports a cause of action against SmithKline for negligence. SmithKline argued on summary judgment that it was not liable under negligence because it owed no duty, did not breach any duty owed to Doe, and did not proximately cause any damage . . . .

The Texas Supreme Court has described the existence of a "duty" as follows: "[I]f a party negligently creates a situation, then it becomes his duty to do something about it to prevent injury to others if it reasonably appears or should appear to him that others in the exercise of their lawful rights may be injured thereby." Buchanan v. Rose, 138 Tex. 390, 159 S.W.2d 109, 110 (1942). More recent cases have described duty as a function of several interrelated factors — the risk, foreseeability, and likelihood of injury weighed against the social utility of the actor's conduct — of which the foremost and dominant consideration is the foreseeability of the risk. Corbin v. Safeway Stores, Inc., 648 S.W.2d 292, 296 (Tex. 1983). If a risk is foreseeable, it gives rise to a duty of reasonable care.

SmithKline argues that Doe's cause of action is only for a failure to act or "nonfeasance" which is not actionable under Texas law. This argument relies on the case law holding that innocent bystanders are under no legal duty to act. *Buchanan*, 159 S.W.2d at 110. As stated in *Otis*, "[c]hanging social conditions lead constantly to the recognition of new duties." *Otis*, 668 S.W.2d at 310. If an individual has "at least partially created the danger" in issue, he is under an affirmative duty to act. *El Chico*, 732 S.W.2d at 306. We conclude that SmithKline is not merely an innocent bystander, but rather, it partially created a dangerous situation. As information services become more prevalent in our economy and society, the information providers should be held accountable for the information they provide. Such information should be complete and not misleading. Credit-reporting agencies have long been held to the exercise of due care in securing and distributing information concerning the financial standing of individuals, firms, and corporations. *See, e.g.*, Bradstreet Co. v. Gill, 72 Tex. 115, 9 S.W. 753, 757 (1888). By making representations that implied the infallibility of its tests and by failing to provide any information to its customers on the possible implications of the raw test results, SmithKline created a possibility of misinterpretation of the information it provides.

SmithKline marketed its services to employers as "the largest and most quality-conscious network of clinical laboratories in North America" and "the most accurate, dependable and cost-effective substance-abuse testing on the market." SmithKline represented to Quaker that "a positive result from [SmithKline] can be accepted with virtual certainty as evidence of drug use." By these statements, SmithKline invited employers such as Quaker to rely on SmithKline's superior knowledge and resources in the area of drug testing and to rely on the test results as authoritative.[6] It is foreseeable that employers would interpret a raw result showing a positive opiate test result as exclusively indicating illegal or illicit drug use and would not consider the possibility of poppy seed consumption or other anomalies. It is also foreseeable that the lack of full disclosure of all possible implications of a positive opiate test result could lead an employer to dismiss an employee or to revoke a pending offer.

Doe has claimed negligence not only from SmithKline's failure to act. Doe alleged negligence by an affirmative act of SmithKline — destroying her urine sample contrary to her instructions and before it could be tested by an independent laboratory. Based on the above analysis, we conclude that SmithKline has failed to conclusively demonstrate that it owed no duty to Doe.

Proximate cause consists of cause-in-fact and foreseeability. *El Chico*, 732 S.W.2d at 313; Exxon Corp. v. Quinn, 726 S.W.2d 17, 21 (Tex. 1987). . . . Construing all disputed facts and inferences in favor of Doe, we conclude that "but for" SmithKline's failure to provide some safeguards or additional information, Doe failed her drug test because she consumed poppy seeds, and but for Doe's positive test result, Quaker would not have withdrawn its offer. Quaker's policy required an automatic revocation of an offer on a positive test. As discussed above, the fact that the testing SmithKline conducted could adversely affect the employees of its customers was foreseeable. We conclude that SmithKline has not conclusively demonstrated the absence of proximate cause.

SmithKline argues that it only provides raw test results and is forbidden by Illinois law from making any interpretation of those results. *See* Ill. Ann. Stat. ch. 111 1/2, para. 627-102 (Smith-Hurd 1991). We do not find this argument persuasive. We find reasonable Doe's assertion that to most individuals and many employers, a positive drug test result exclusively indicates illegal drug use by the subject. The record evidence indicates that, in fact, this was Quaker's perception of drug testing. We believe that SmithKline is obligated to provide sufficient information on possible test anomalies to prevent this misleading perception. We do not believe that providing such information would run afoul of Illinois law. By requiring such information on a general basis, the law does not require that SmithKline interpret individual results; the law requires that sufficient information be provided on a general basis to prevent the potential misleading interpretation of the information it provides. For the above reasons, we sustain Doe's second point of error. . . .

Conclusion

We affirm the portions of the trial court's judgment granting Quaker a summary

---

[6] An employer's high level of reliance on the expertise of testing labs is supported by the testimony of the Quaker officials who supervised its pre-employment drug screening program that Quaker officials contacted SmithKline for information on the viability of Doe's explanations for her positive test.

judgment on all Doe's claims. . . . We reverse the portions of the trial court's judgment granting SmithKline a summary judgment on Doe's claims for negligence. . . . We remand for further proceedings consistent with this opinion.

NOTE

Doe did not appeal the Court of Appeal's decision affirming summary judgment against her claims against the prospective employer, Quaker. However, the laboratory SmithKline appealed the Court of Appeal's reinstatement of Doe's claims against SmithKline.

SMITHKLINE BEECHAM CORP. v. DOE

903 S.W.2d 347 (Tex. 1994)

HECHT, Justice.

Increasingly within the past decade, the policy of employers in this country has been to screen employees and prospective employees for drug usage. Employers frequently retain independent laboratories to perform drug screening tests. This case requires us to begin to define these laboratories' legal responsibility to persons tested.

[The facts are set forth in the court of appeals opinion in Doe v. SmithKline Beecham, *supra*.]

. . . We assume for present purposes that Doe's positive test result was due not to any use of drugs but to her ingestion of poppy seeds, which she would not have eaten had she known of their effect on the test. There is no dispute that a person's ingestion of poppy seeds in sufficient quantities will result in the presence of morphine and codeine in his or her urine for a few hours. . . . SBCL was aware of this and knew that its test could not distinguish between poppy seed ingestion and drug use. SBCL did not convey this information to Quaker or Doe. SBCL and Doe never communicated with each other before her test results were reported to Quaker. Quaker would have considered the information important and might have investigated Doe's result more fully if it had known, but its ultimate decision to withdraw Doe's offer consistent with its policy might have been the same. Of the more than 4,000 persons Quaker has had screened for drugs, none besides Doe has ever claimed a positive result due to ingestion of poppy seeds.

Doe sued SBCL and its parent, SmithKline Beecham Corp. (together, SmithKline), for negligence . . . and tortious interference with a prospective contract. . . . The trial court granted summary judgment for SmithKline. . . . The court of appeals reversed the summary judgment for SmithKline on Doe's negligence and tortious interference claims. 855 S.W.2d at 248. . . .

II

A

. . . We first consider whether SmithKline owed Doe a duty to warn her or Quaker of the effect that ingestion of poppy seeds can have on a drug test. Doe has not cited, and we are not aware of, a single decision of any court in the United States which recognizes the legal duty for which she argues. The United States Court of Appeals for the Fifth Circuit and intermediate courts of appeals in Illinois and Louisiana have held that a drug testing laboratory owes persons tested a duty to perform its services with reasonable care. Willis v. Roche Biomedical Lab., 21 F.3d 1368, 1372-1375 (5th Cir. 1994) (Texas law requires a laboratory to use reasonable care in conducting drug tests, citing the court of appeals' opinion in the case now at bar); Stinson v. Physicians Immediate Care, Ltd., 646 N.E.2d 930, 932-934 (1995) (laboratory owes prospective employee a duty not to contaminate sample and report a false result); Nehrenz v. Dunn, 593 So. 2d 915, 917-918 (La. Ct. App. 1992) (laboratory owes employee a duty to perform test in a competent manner); Elliott v. Laboratory Specialists, 588 So. 2d 175, 176 (La. Ct. App. 1991), *writ denied*, 592 So. 2d 415 (La. 1992) (laboratory owes employee a duty to perform test in a scientifically reasonable manner); Lewis v. Aluminum Co. of Am., 588 So. 2d 167, 170 (La. Ct. App. 1991), *writ denied*, 592 So. 2d 411 (La. 1992) (laboratory owes employee a duty to perform tests in a competent, nonnegligent manner). *But see* Herbert v. Placid Ref. Co., 564 So. 2d 371, 374 (La. Ct. App. 1990) (laboratory owed employee no duty to properly analyze test sample). Whether a laboratory is responsible to persons tested for negligently performing drug tests is not the issue before us. Doe does not complain that SmithKline failed to perform her drug test with reasonable care; she concedes that the test accurately identified opiates in her urine. Doe's complaint — her principal one, at least — is that SmithKline did not warn her and Quaker of the effects of eating poppy seeds on drug tests. No court has imposed a duty on drug testing laboratories to warn test subjects about the possible influences on results.

Even on the issue addressed in the cases cited, the law is in a nascent stage. No court of last resort has spoken. There appears to be some disagreement among the intermediate courts of Louisiana. *Compare Nehrenz*, *Elliott* and *Lewis* with *Herbert*. And *Willis* is based solely, and erroneously, on the court of appeals' decision in the case now before us. The issues in the two cases are simply not the same. (Curiously, the Fifth Circuit did not regard this Court's having agreed to review the court of appeals' decision as relevant in evaluating its precedential value. *Willis*, 21 F.3d at 1374.)

In a different but somewhat related context, a few courts have applied a reasonable care standard to conducting polygraph tests when the results would be a factor in hiring and firing decisions. Ellis v. Buckley, 790 P.2d 875, 877 (Colo. Ct. App. 1989), *cert. denied*, 498 U.S. 920 (1990); Lawson v. Howmet Aluminum Corp., 449 N.E.2d 1172, 1177 (Ind. Ct. App. 1983); Zampatori v. United Parcel Serv., 479 N.Y.S.2d 470, 473-474 (N.Y. Sup. Ct. 1984); *see* Lewis v. Rodriguez,, 759 P.2d 1012, 1014-1016 (1988). However, the only court of last resort in any American jurisdiction to clearly consider the issue has held that no tort duty to use reasonable care should be imposed on polygraph test operators. Hall v. United Parcel Serv. of Am., , 555 N.E.2d 273, 276-278 (N.Y. 1990).

Absent any direct authority in this State or any other state for creating a duty to warn, we look to general tort principles for guidance. . . . While we can find no direct authority in this State or elsewhere, either in specific decisions or in general principles, for recognizing the duty Doe seeks in this case, this Court could recognize a new common law duty based on "several interrelated factors, including the risk, foreseeability, and likelihood of injury weighed against the social utility of the actor's conduct, the magnitude of the burden of guarding against the injury, and the consequences of placing the burden on the defendant." *Greater Houston Transp.*, 801 S.W.2d at 525. We therefore examine these factors in the context of this case.

We assume that there is some significant likelihood, which SmithKline could and did foresee, that a person will have a positive drug test due to having eaten poppy seeds (although Quaker asserts that it has tested more than 4,000 people with only one such complaint). Foreseeability alone, however, is not sufficient to create a new duty. *Bird*, 868 S.W.2d at 769. We must consider the other factors as well.

The duty Doe seeks cannot be readily defined. It would require SmithKline to inform each test subject not only of the possible effect of poppy seeds but of all possible causes of positive results other than using drugs. Doe's own research, for example, suggests that a positive drug test may also result from using an over-the-counter inhaler, or from inhaling second-hand marijuana smoke. The more possibilities that must be suggested to the person tested, the more excuses the person will have for positive results. Moreover, the duty Doe seeks would charge SmithKline with responsibility that belongs to its clients. In this case, for example, SmithKline recommended to Quaker that test subjects be asked to disclose before the test any medications being used, and that positive results be interpreted in light of such disclosure. It was Quaker's responsibility, however, to decide whether and how to implement such recommendations. SmithKline should be allowed to perform only the service it chose to offer and Quaker chose to procure — testing for the presence of drugs in the body. Finally, placing a duty on SmithKline in these circumstances impinges on the liability of other professionals for services rendered. A simple duty to warn of the possibilities that information may be misinterpreted is unworkable.

Without precedent and without the support of our own jurisprudence, we decline to recognize the duty Doe alleges in this case. We agree with a federal district court that has written:

> Although it may be true . . . that the increasing use of drug testing for employment purposes raises serious questions concerning the duties owed by entities seeking and using the tests to current or prospective employees subjected thereto, the fact that there are reasons to be concerned about the uses, potential misuses or abuses of drug test results does not justify imposing additional and unprecedented duties upon a laboratory with the sole function of analyzing a sample and returning a report, particularly when such report is factually accurate.

Caputo v. Compuchem Lab., 1994 WL 100084, at *4 (E.D. Pa., Feb. 23, 1994), *aff'd*, 37 F.3d 1485 (3d Cir. 1994), *cert. denied*, 513 U.S. 1082 (1995). In *Caputo*, a case with facts very similar to this one, the court declined to impose a duty on a drug testing laboratory to perform followup testing on weak positive test samples or assure competent medical interpretation of test results absent a laboratory's contractual duty to do so. *Id.*

For the reasons we have explained, we hold that SmithKline had no duty to disclose to either Quaker or Doe any information about the effect of eating poppy seeds on a positive drug test result. . . .

D

. . . [W]e have not considered whether a drug testing laboratory like SBCL has a duty to use reasonable care in performing tests and reporting the results. Doe does not claim such a duty in this case. Our consideration of the responsibility of drug testing laboratories is limited to the issues presented in this case. . . .

Accordingly, we modify the judgment of the court of appeals to affirm summary judgment as to SmithKline on Doe's claims for negligence. . . .

[Dissenting opinion of Justice GAMMAGE, joined by Justices HIGHTOWER and SPECTOR, omitted.]

NOTES AND QUESTIONS

1. Would the outcome in *SmithKline Beecham* have been different if Doe had alleged and proved that SmithKline not only failed to explain the "poppy seed" problem, it negligently performed the test and reported an erroneous result? *See* Calbillo v. Cavender Oldsmobile, Inc., 288 F.3d 721 (5th Cir. 2002) (relying on *SmithKline Beecham* and holding that independent polygraph examiner hired by employer owes no duty of care to employee/examinee under Texas law); Mission Petroleum Carriers, Inc. v. Solomon, 106 S.W.3d 705 (Tex. 2003) (no cause of action for employer's own alleged negligence in performing the test).

On the other side of the issue is Duncan v. Afton, 991 P.2d 739 (Wyo. 1999). There, the Wyoming Supreme Court rejected the Texas court's *SmithKline Beecham* decision and held "that a collection company owes a duty of care to an employee when collecting, handling, and processing urine specimens for the purpose of performing substance abuse testing." In that case the plaintiff alleged the defendant failed to follow standard testing protocol for measuring the temperature of the sample, and improperly recorded the chain of custody. In finding liability based on simple negligence, the court reasoned as follows:

> Companies like Afton provide services that present a risk of harm great enough to hold them accountable. The particular services provided demand adequate protection of employees' interests to prevent future harm, and the imposition of a duty to act reasonably will reduce the likelihood of injury.... [O]ur ruling that Afton owes a duty places a burden upon Afton to act in a "scientifically reasonable manner" and guard against human error; however, Afton is in the best position to guard against employee injury arising from its collection and handling procedures. Because Afton is paid for its services, it is better able to bear the burden financially than the individual wrongly maligned by a false positive report.

Id. at 745; *see* Sharpe v. St. Luke's Hosp., 821 A.2d 1215 (Pa. 2003) (hospital mishandling of sample); Ellis v. Buckley, 790 P.2d 875, 877 (Colo. Ct. App. 1989) (negligent administration of polygraph); Stinson v. Physicians Immediate Care, Ltd., 646 N.E.2d 930, 932-934 (Ill. App. 1995) (contamination of sample).

2. Employers frequently rely on third-party contractors to test or gather information about applicants. Disappointed applicants tend to have more success suing third parties than suing employers. *Duncan* (note 1, *supra*) suggests one basis for holding an independent professional or laboratory but not an employer liable

for negligent administration of a test. Another approach is offered by Ishikawa v. Delta Air Lines, Inc., 149 F. Supp. 2d 1246 (D. Or. 2001). In that case, the plaintiff alleged that she was the third party beneficiary of a contract between her employer and the testing laboratory, and that the laboratory breached the contract by negligently mischaracterizing the test results to the employer.

> The Oregon courts have examined several types of professional relationships, including relationships involving a nongratuitous supplier of information and the duty of care owed to an intended third-party beneficiary of a contractual, professional or employment relationship. *See id.* For example, the Oregon Court of Appeals has held that the plaintiff buyers of a house were intended beneficiaries of the contract between the sellers and the defendant inspector to inspect the roof. Meininger v. Henris Roofing & Supply of Klamath County, Inc., 905 P.2d 861 (1995). The plaintiff buyers relied on the inspection report in deciding to buy the house. When the roof leaked, the plaintiff buyers sued the defendant inspector for misrepresentation. The court concluded that the plaintiff buyers were the intended third-party beneficiaries to the contract between the sellers and the defendant inspector because the purpose of the inspection report was to provide an opinion about the condition of the roof to potential buyers of the house and because the inspection report would be used in part to further the economic interests of the plaintiff buyers. *Id.*
>
> The facts of this case are analogous. Delta entered into a contract with LabOne for the professional service of drug testing of Delta employees. Under Oregon law, employees like plaintiff would be intended beneficiaries to that sort of contract because employees have an economic interest in accurate drug testing and reporting of test results. LabOne was acting, at least in part, to further the economic interests of Delta's employees, because an inaccurate report that an employee failed a drug test would have significant adverse economic consequences to an employee. Similarly, an accurate report that an employee did not use drugs would act, at least in part, to further that employee's economic interest in maintaining his or her job with Delta. In this case, the evidence shows that LabOne knew that the test reports would be used in Delta's employment decisions and that inaccurate reports could result in the termination of an employee.

149 F. Supp. 2d at 1250-51 (denying summary judgment). Plaintiff won a verdict against LabOne, which was affirmed. *Ishikawa*, 343 F.3d 1129 (9th Cir. 2003).

3. If the defendant in a negligent testing or data collection case is not the employer but an independent firm, should it matter whether that firm overstated the accuracy of its methods to the employer? Recall that SmithKline represented that "a positive result from [SmithKline] can be accepted with *virtual certainty* as evidence of drug use" (emphasis added). The Texas Supreme Court avoided the employee's argument that SmithKline had negligently misrepresented the accuracy of its test to Quaker, because the plaintiff failed to raise the issue in the trial court. 903 S.W.2d at 354-355; *see also* Chapman v. LabOne, 460 F. Supp. 2d 989 (S.D. Iowa 2006) (rejecting negligent misrepresentation claim under Iowa law).

4. While most courts hold an employer owes no common law duty to an applicant to be careful in testing, background checking, or data evaluation, an employer's duty to *current employees* may be another matter. Current employees

may enjoy rights to job security by virtue of contract or other rules of "wrongful discharge" depending on the strength of the employment at will doctrine in the jurisdiction in question. Moreover, a court might be more sympathetic to a current employee who suffers the loss of his job and becomes unemployed with a troubling mark on his employment record. Indeed, prevailing plaintiffs in reported negligent testing cases are more often discharged employees than disappointed applicants. The job security rights of current employees are addressed in Chapter 6.

5. Does the employer or agent who collects or evaluates data about an applicant or employee owe any duty to disclose the results to the applicant/employee? What if the examination reveals important information about which the examinee is likely unaware, such as disparaging comments on the Internet, a low credit score, or alarming data from a physical examination? *See* Eaton v. Continental Gen. Ins. Co., 147 F. Supp. 2d 829 (N.D. Ohio 2001), *aff'd*, 59 Fed. Appx. 719, 2003 WL 857330 (6th Cir. 2003) (laboratory had no duty to inform examinee he was HIV positive); Dubose v. Workers' Medical, P.A., 117 S.W.3d 916 (Tex. App. 2003) (doctor who performed examination as part of employer's pre-employment test had no duty to inform examinee/applicant that her X-ray results were "patently abnormal").

b. Intrusion

Whether or not the test in *SmithKline* was "fair" or "accurate," it was at least somewhat intrusive. Drug tests involve the indignity of urinalysis and a possible revelation of substance abuse. And the accuracy of testing or data collection is often inversely related to its invasiveness. In drug testing accurate interpretation of test results requires investigation of an examinee's eating habits and prescription medications. Thus, it would seem reasonable — even if it not required by law — to inquire about such personal matters before or after the test. But inquiries about medications might reveal medical conditions such as depression, epilepsy, or high blood pressure. This information not only is potentially embarrassing, but might cause the employer to discriminate. *See* Harrison v. Benchmark Elec. Huntsville, Inc., 593 F.3d 1206 (11th Cir. 2010) (supervisor's knowledge of plaintiff's answers to questions about prescription medications possibly affecting drug test result was some evidence of intent to discriminate because of disability). Thus, the intrusiveness of a test raises issues because even an accurate and fair test might be objectionably intrusive to even a successful candidate.

NORMAN-BLOODSAW v. LAWRENCE BERKELEY LAB.

135 F.3d 1260 (9th Cir. 1998)

REINHARDT, Circuit Judge:

This appeal involves the question whether a clerical or administrative worker who undergoes a general employee health examination may, without his knowledge, be tested for highly private and sensitive medical and genetic information such as syphilis, sickle cell trait, and pregnancy. . . .

Plaintiffs . . . are current and former administrative and clerical employees of defendant Lawrence Berkeley Laboratory ("Lawrence"), a research facility operated by the appellee Regents of the University of California pursuant to a contract with the United States Department of Energy (the Department). . . .

The Department requires federal contractors such as Lawrence to establish an occupational medical program. Since 1981, it has required its contractors to perform "preplacement examinations" of employees as part of this program, and until 1995, it also required its contractors to offer their employees the option of subsequent "periodic health examinations." The mandatory preplacement examination occurs after the offer of employment but prior to the assumption of job duties. The Department actively oversees Lawrence's occupational health program, and, prior to 1992, specifically required syphilis testing as part of the preplacement examination.

With the exception of Ellis, who was hired in 1968 and underwent an examination after beginning employment, each of the plaintiffs received written offers of employment expressly conditioned upon a "medical examination," "medical approval," or "health evaluation." All accepted these offers and underwent preplacement examinations, and Randolph and Smith underwent subsequent examinations as well. In the course of these examinations, plaintiffs completed medical history questionnaires and provided blood and urine samples. The questionnaires asked, inter alia, whether the patient had ever had any of sixty-one medical conditions, including "[s]ickle cell anemia,"[3] "[v]enereal disease," and, in the case of women, "[m]enstrual disorders."[4]

The blood and urine samples given by all employees during their preplacement examinations were tested for syphilis; in addition, certain samples were tested for sickle cell trait; and certain samples were tested for pregnancy. Lawrence discontinued syphilis testing in April 1993, pregnancy testing in December 1994, and sickle cell trait testing in June 1995.

. . . Plaintiffs allege that the testing of their blood and urine samples for syphilis, sickle cell trait, and pregnancy occurred without their knowledge or consent, and without any subsequent notification that the tests had been conducted. They also allege that only black employees were tested for sickle cell trait and assert the obvious fact that only female employees were tested for pregnancy. Finally, they allege that Lawrence failed to provide safeguards to prevent the dissemination of the test results. They contend that they did not discover that the disputed tests had been conducted until approximately January 1995. . . . Plaintiffs do not allege that the defendants took any subsequent employment-related action on the basis of their test results, or that their test results have been disclosed to third parties.

On the basis of these factual allegations, plaintiffs contend that the defendants

---

[3] Sickle cell anemia is a physical affliction in which a large proportion or majority of an individual's red blood cells become sickle-shaped. Webster's Third New International Dictionary 2111 (1976). Sickle cell trait is a genetic condition in which an individual carries the gene that causes sickle cell anemia. *Id.* The sickle cell gene is only semi-dominant: if the carrier of the gene is heterozygous (meaning that the gene is paired with a non-sickle cell gene), some of his or her red blood cells may sickle, but usually not to a sufficient degree to result in actual sickle cell anemia. *Id.*

[4] The section of the questionnaire also asks women if they have ever had abnormal pap smears and men if they have ever had prostate gland disorders.

violated the ADA by requiring, encouraging, or assisting in medical testing that was neither job-related nor consistent with business necessity. Second, they contend that the defendants violated the federal constitutional right to privacy by conducting the testing at issue, collecting and maintaining the results of the testing, and failing to provide adequate safeguards against disclosure of the results. Third, they contend that the testing violated their right to privacy under Article I, § 1 of the California Constitution. Finally, plaintiffs contend that Lawrence and the Regents violated Title VII by singling out black employees for sickle cell trait testing and by performing pregnancy testing on female employees generally.

DISCUSSION

I. STATUTE OF LIMITATIONS

The district court dismissed all of the claims on statute of limitations grounds because it found that the limitations period began to run at the time the tests were taken, in which case each cause of action would be time-barred. . . . [T]he general federal rule is that "a limitations period begins to run when the plaintiff knows or has reason to know of the injury which is the basis of the action." Trotter v. International Longshoremen's & Warehousemen's Union, 704 F.2d 1141, 1143 (9th Cir. 1983) . . . .

Plaintiffs' declarations clearly state that at the time of the examination they did not know that the testing in question would be performed, and they neither saw signs nor received any other indications to that effect. The district court had three possible reasons for concluding that plaintiffs knew or should have expected the tests at issue: (1) they submitted to an occupational preplacement examination; (2) they answered written questions as to whether they had had "venereal disease," "menstrual problems," or "sickle cell anemia"; and (3) they voluntarily gave blood and urine samples. . . .

The question of what tests plaintiffs should have expected or foreseen depends in large part upon what preplacement medical examinations usually entail, and what, if anything, plaintiffs were told to expect. The record strongly suggests that plaintiffs' submission to the exam did not serve to afford them notice of the particular testing involved. The letters that plaintiffs received informed them merely that a "medical examination," "medical approval," or "health evaluation" was an express condition of employment. These letters did not inform plaintiffs that they would be subjected to comprehensive diagnostic medical examinations that would inquire into intimate health matters bearing no relation to their responsibilities as administrative or clerical employees.

The record, indeed, contains considerable evidence that the manner in which the tests were performed was inconsistent with sound medical practice. Plaintiffs introduced before the district court numerous expert declarations by medical scholars roundly condemning Lawrence's alleged practices and explaining, inter alia, that testing for syphilis, sickle cell trait, and pregnancy is not an appropriate part of an occupational medical examination and is rarely if ever done by employers as a matter of routine; that Lawrence lacked any reasonable medical or public health basis for performing these tests on clerical and administrative employees such as plaintiffs; and that the performance of such tests without explicit notice and informed consent violates prevailing medical standards. These experts further agreed that "generally accepted standards of occupational medicine" require employers to inform their employees of the tests to be performed, to specify whether the tests are a condition of employment, and to provide notification of the results. Defendants counter that the "tests [for sickle cell trait] were consistent with good medical practices," . . . and that testing for syphilis in a preventive health exam is an accepted practice. These factual disagreements over the objective medical reasonableness of the specific tests can be resolved only at trial. For summary judgment purposes, foreseeability cannot be established on the ground that the plaintiffs were required to submit to a general medical examination.

The district court also appears to have reasoned that plaintiffs knew or had reason to know of the tests because they were asked questions on a medical form concerning "venereal disease," "sickle cell anemia," and "menstrual disorders," and because they gave blood and urine samples. The fact that plaintiffs acquiesced in the minor intrusion of checking or not checking three boxes on a questionnaire does not mean that they had reason to expect further intrusions in the form of having their blood and urine tested for specific conditions that corresponded tangentially if at all to the written questions. First, the entries on the questionnaire were neither identical to nor, in some cases, even suggestive of the characteristics for which plaintiffs were tested. For example, sickle cell trait is a genetic condition distinct from actually having sickle cell anemia, and pregnancy is not considered a "menstrual disorder" or a "venereal disease." Second, and more important, it is not reasonable to infer that a person who answers a questionnaire upon personal knowledge is put on notice that his employer will take intrusive means to verify the accuracy of his answers. There is a significant difference between answering on the basis of what you know about your health and consenting to let someone else investigate the most intimate aspects of your life. Indeed, a reasonable person could conclude that by completing a written questionnaire, he has reduced or eliminated the need for seemingly redundant and even more intrusive laboratory testing in search of highly sensitive and non-job-related information.

Furthermore, if plaintiffs' evidence concerning reasonable medical practice is to be credited, they had no reason to think that tests would be performed without their consent simply because they had answered some questions on a form and had then, in addition, provided bodily fluid samples: Plaintiffs could reasonably have expected Lawrence to seek their consent before running any tests not usually performed in an occupational health exam—particularly tests for intimate medical conditions bearing no relationship to their responsibilities or working conditions as clerical employees. The mere fact that an employee has given a blood or urine sample does not provide notice that an employer will perform any and all tests on that specimen that it desires, — no matter how invasive — particularly where, as here, the employer has yet to offer a valid reason for the testing. . . .

Because the question of what testing, if any, plaintiffs had reason to expect turns on material factual issues that can only be resolved at trial, summary judgment on statute of limitations grounds was inappropriate with respect to the causes of action based on an invasion of privacy in violation of the Federal and California Constitutions, and also on the Title VII claims.

II. FEDERAL CONSTITUTIONAL DUE PROCESS RIGHT OF PRIVACY

. . . While acknowledging that the government had failed to identify any "undisputed legitimate governmental purpose" for the three tests, the district court concluded that no violation of plaintiffs' right to privacy could have occurred because any intrusions arising from the testing were de minimis in light of (1) the "large overlap" between the subjects covered by the medical questionnaire and the three tests and (2) the "overall intrusiveness" of "a full-scale physical examination." We hold that the district court erred.

The constitutionally protected privacy interest in avoiding disclosure of personal matters clearly encompasses medical information and its confidentiality. Doe v. Attorney General of the United States, 941 F.2d 780, 795 (9th Cir. 1991). Although cases defining the privacy interest in medical information have typically involved its disclosure to "third" parties, rather than the collection of information by illicit means, it goes without saying that the most basic violation possible involves the performance of unauthorized tests — that is, the non-consensual retrieval of previously unrevealed medical information that may be unknown even to plaintiffs. These tests may also be viewed as searches in violation of Fourth Amendment rights that require Fourth Amendment scrutiny. The tests at issue in this case thus implicate rights protected under both the Fourth Amendment and the Due Process Clause of the Fifth or Fourteenth Amendments.

Because it would not make sense to examine the collection of medical information under two different approaches, we generally "analyze[ ] [medical tests and examinations] under the rubric of [the Fourth] Amendment." *Id.* at 871 & n.12. Accordingly, we must balance the government's interest in conducting these particular tests against the plaintiffs' expectations of privacy. *Id.* at 873. Furthermore, "application of the balancing test requires not only considering the degree of intrusiveness and the state's interests in requiring that intrusion, but also 'the efficacy of this [the state's] means for meeting' its needs." *Id.* (quoting Vernonia Sch. Dist. 47J v. Acton, 515 U.S. 646, 660 (1995)).

The district court erred in dismissing the claims on the ground that any violation was de minimis, incremental, or overlapping. The latter two grounds are actually just the court's explanations for its adoption of its "de minimis" conclusion. They are not in themselves reasons for dismissal. Nor if the violation is otherwise significant does it become insignificant simply because it is overlapping or incremental. We cannot, therefore, escape a scrupulous examination of the nature of the violation, although we can, of course, consider whether the plaintiffs have in fact consented to any part of the alleged intrusion.

One can think of few subject areas more personal and more likely to implicate privacy interests than that of one's health or genetic make-up. Furthermore, the facts revealed by the tests are highly sensitive, even relative to other medical information. With respect to the testing of plaintiffs for syphilis and pregnancy, it is well established in this circuit "that the Constitution prohibits unregulated, unrestrained employer inquiries into personal sexual matters that have no bearing on job performance." Schowengerdt v. General Dynamics Corp., 823 F.2d 1328, 1336 (9th Cir. 1987). The fact that one has syphilis is an intimate matter that pertains to one's sexual history and may invite tremendous amounts of social stigma. Pregnancy is likewise, for many, an intensely private matter, which also may pertain to one's sexual history and often carries far-reaching societal implications. Finally, the carrying of sickle cell trait can pertain to sensitive information about family history and reproductive decisionmaking. . . .

As discussed above, with respect to the question of the statute of limitations, there was little, if any, "overlap" between what plaintiffs consented to and the testing at issue here. Nor was the additional invasion only incremental. In some instances, the tests related to entirely different conditions. In all, the information obtained as the result of the testing was qualitatively different from the information that plaintiffs provided in their answers to the questions, and was highly invasive. That one has consented to a general medical examination does not abolish one's privacy right not to be tested for intimate, personal matters involving one's health — nor does consenting to giving blood or urine samples,[13] or filling out a questionnaire. As we have made clear, revealing one's personal knowledge as to whether one has a particular medical condition has nothing to do with one's expectations about actually being tested for that condition. Thus, the intrusion was by no means de minimis. . . .

Lawrence further contends that the tests in question, even if their intrusiveness is not de minimis, would be justified by an employer's interest in performing a general physical examination. This argument fails because issues of fact exist with respect to whether the testing at issue is normally part of a general physical examination.[15] There would of course be no violation if the testing were authorized, or if the plaintiffs reasonably should have known that the blood and urine samples they provided would be used for the disputed testing and failed to object. However, . . . material issues of fact exist as to those questions. . . .

III. Right to Privacy under Article I, § 1 of the California Constitution

[For many of the same reasons discussed above, the Court of Appeals held that the District Court erred in dismissing the plaintiffs' right to privacy claims under the California Constitution.]

IV. Title VII Claims

The district court also dismissed the Title VII counts on the merits on the ground that plaintiffs had failed to state a claim because the "alleged classifications, standing alone, do not suffice to provide a cognizable basis for relief under Title VII" and because plaintiffs had neither alleged nor demonstrated how these classifications had adversely affected them.

. . . It is well established that Title VII bars discrimination not only in the "terms" and "conditions" of ongoing employment, but also in the "terms" and

[13] Indeed, the Supreme Court has recognized that while the taking of a bodily fluid sample implicates one's privacy interests, "[t]he ensuing chemical analysis of the sample to obtain physiological data is a *further* intrusion of the tested employee's privacy interests." Skinner v. Railway Labor Executives' Ass'n, 489 U.S. 602, 616 (1989) (emphasis added).

[15] Lawrence has not identified a single interest in performing the tests in question other than that they are part of generally accepted medical practice. Thus, on the present record, if the plaintiffs were to prevail on the statute of limitations issue, they would also prevail with respect to the federal privacy claim.

"conditions" under which individuals may obtain employment. Thus, for example, a requirement of preemployment health examinations imposed only on female employees, or a requirement of preemployment background security checks imposed only on black employees, would surely violate Title VII.

[T]he term or condition for black employees was undergoing a test for sickle cell trait; for women it was undergoing a test for pregnancy. It is not disputed that the preplacement exams were, literally, a condition of employment: the offers of employment stated this explicitly. Thus, the employment of women and blacks at Lawrence was conditioned in part on allegedly unconstitutional invasions of privacy to which white and/or male employees were not subjected. An additional "term or condition" requiring an unconstitutional invasion of privacy is, without doubt, actionable under Title VII. Furthermore, even if the intrusions did not rise to the level of unconstitutionality, they would still be a "term" or "condition" based on an illicit category as described by the statute and thus a proper basis for a Title VII action. Thus, the district court erred in ruling on the pleadings that the plaintiffs had failed to assert a proper Title VII claim. . . .

The district court also erred in finding as a matter of law that there was no "adverse effect" with respect to the tests. . . . The unauthorized obtaining of sensitive medical information on the basis of race or sex would in itself constitute an "adverse effect," or injury, under Title VII. Thus, it was error to rule that as a matter of law no "adverse effect" could arise from a classification that singled out particular groups for unconstitutionally invasive, non-consensual medical testing. . . .

V. The ADA Claims

. . . The complaint alleges that defendants violated the ADA by requiring medical examinations and making medical inquiries that were "neither job related nor consistent with business necessity." (citing 42 U.S.C. § 12112(c)(4)). . . . Plaintiffs do not allege that defendants made use of information gathered in the examinations to discriminate against them on the basis of disability. . . .

The ADA creates three categories of medical inquiries and examinations by employers: (1) those conducted prior to an offer of employment ("preemployment" inquiries and examinations); (2) those conducted "after an offer of employment has been made" but "prior to the commencement of . . . employment duties" ("employment entrance examinations"); and (3) those conducted at any point thereafter. It is undisputed that the second category, employment entrance examinations, as governed by § 12112(d)(3), are the examinations and inquiries to which [some plaintiffs] were subjected. Unlike examinations conducted at any other time, an employment entrance examination need not be concerned solely with the individual's "ability to perform job-related functions,"§ 12112(d)(2); nor must it be "job-related or consistent with business necessity,"§ 12112(d)(4). Thus, the ADA imposes no restriction on the scope of entrance examinations; it only guarantees the confidentiality of the information gathered, § 12112(d)(3)(B), and restricts the use to which an employer may put the information. Because the ADA does not limit the scope of such examinations to matters that are "job-related and consistent with business necessity," dismissal of the ADA claims was proper. . . .

NOTES AND QUESTIONS

1. For what reasons might an employer want the information Lawrence Berkeley Laboratory collected in *Norman-Bloodsaw*? Might it be reasonable to collect such information from at least *some* employees working in *some* settings?

Lawrence Berkeley Laboratory was founded by Ernest Lawrence in the 1930s. It housed Lawrence's famous particle-smashing cyclotron in the "Rad House" in Berkeley. Its early work focused on nuclear energy, which required handling uranium and plutonium. During the 1970s, its research branched into other areas, but nuclear physics remained its best known and most successful area. Lawrence Berkeley Laboratory, An Historical Perspective, online at http://www.lbl.gov/Publications/75th/files/04-lab-history-pt-1.html

2. Were the employees *injured* by the collection of the information? In what way? Whether an applicant/employee asserts a claim under the Constitution or tort law, proving damages can be challenging if an intrusion did not cause employment loss. A court cannot award damages simply for lost value of constitutional rights. Memphis Cmty. Sch. Dist. v. Stachura, 477 U.S. 299 (1968). Whether a plaintiff can recover damages for emotional distress under tort or civil rights law depends on the provable severity of the distress. Punitive damages will likely depend on the willfulness of the defendant's conduct. Thus, in some cases the plaintiff's only substantial remedy might be declaratory or injunctive relief. If Lawrence Berkeley had discontinued its challenged practices by the time of the lawsuit, what declaratory or injunctive relief might the plaintiffs have sought?

3. As *Norman-Bloodsaw* illustrates, employment issues frequently involve an intersection of multiple sources of law. Constitutional and tort law rights of privacy are often augmented or superseded by a variety of federal and state statutes, such as the Americans with Disabilities Act.

i. Constitutional Rights of Privacy in Public Sector Employment

In *Norman-Bloodsaw*, the plaintiffs asserted two different but closely related rights of privacy based on the U.S. Constitution. The first was the right against unreasonable "search and seizure" based on the Fourth Amendment, and the second was a right of "informational privacy" based partly on the Fourth Amendment and partly on other provisions of the Constitution.

Fourth Amendment search and seizure rights. The standard analysis for employee selection was established in two Supreme Court cases decided the same day, Skinner v. Railway Labor Executives' Ass'n 489 U.S. 602 (1989), and National Treasury Employees Union v. Von Raab, 489 U.S. 656 (1989). The *Skinner* case confirmed that an employer's drug and alcohol testing of applicants and employees is a "search" under the Fourth Amendment. 489 U.S. at 616. While the Fourth Amendment ordinarily restricts only government action, *Skinner* illustrates that there are some circumstances in which a private sector applicant or employee might also be able to invoke the protection of the Fourth Amendment. In particular, if a private sector employer's testing is *required* by government action (e.g., by statute or regulation), affected applicants and employees might challenge the government action that is the source of the private employer's duty to test.

In *Skinner*, U.S. Department of Transportation regulations required private railroads to test for employees for drug and alcohol in certain instances, and authorized such tests in other instances (overriding state laws and contracts that might prohibit such tests). The starting point for determining whether such a "search" violates the Fourth Amendment is to evaluate the reasonableness of the claimant's "expectation of privacy." *Id.* at 616-17. The Court agreed that a claimant might have an expectation of privacy against collecting a physical sample and extracting information from it. *Id.* However, even if a claimant has a "reasonable expectation of privacy," the government intrusion might be "reasonable" given some legitimate public interest as well as the nature and circumstances of the search. The Court ultimately upheld the drug testing regulations after balancing the plaintiffs' Fourth Amendment privacy interests against the public's interest in transportation safety. Similarly, in *National Treasury Employees Union*, the Court upheld Customs Service drug testing of applicants for positions involving interdiction of illegal drugs, given the special dangers and temptations to which agents might be exposed, and the Service's precautions to minimize the intrusiveness of the tests. *Id.* at 677. Outside of public safety jobs, across-the-board drug testing has not been as quickly upheld. *See* Chandler v. Miller, 520 U.S. 305 (1997) (Georgia requirement of urinalysis for all candidates for public office violated Fourth Amendment; alleged state interests did not outweigh candidates' privacy interests).

Of course, forcibly or surreptitiously taking a person's physical specimen with neither consent nor warrant would be a battery and a likely violation of the Fourth Amendment. When a public employer engages in a "search" such as a drug test, the examinee will ordinarily have consented by knowing that the test is about to occur and not resisting it. Moreover, public employers normally obtain written permission for a test. Arguably, the examinee's consent to and failure to resist testing diminishes any expectation of privacy, and possibly waives any later objection. A public employer's express or implicit threat to deny or terminate employment does not necessarily render an examinee's consent void or render the intrusion unlawful. In *National Treasury Employees Union*, the Court approved mandatory drug testing of applicants for certain positions without discussing whether applicants' consent was voluntary. "Duress" or involuntariness appears neither to have been argued nor considered by the Court. Whether or not applicants retained their pre-consent expectation of privacy or a right to challenge the intrusion, the government's reasons for conducting the tests were reasonable. In a later case, the Court seemed to downplay the difficulty of a job applicant's dilemma in choosing whether to allow a test that was a mandatory condition of employment. *See Ferguson, supra*, 532 U.S. at 78. *Cf.* Vernonia Sch. Dist. 47J v. Acton, 515 U.S. 646, 657 (1995) (student athlete consent to drug test was voluntary, even though test was mandatory condition of sports participation, because sports participation was voluntary, and student athletes had reason to expect certain loss of personal privacy). However, courts have tended to be skeptical of public employer arguments that *all* expectations of privacy or rights to challenge intrusions are extinguished by consent that the employer demanded as a condition for employment. *See, e.g.*, Kallstrom v. City of Columbus, 136 F.3d 1055, 1063 & n.3 (6th Cir. 1998).

Thus, while consent obtained by a threat to deny employment does not bar a Fourth Amendment challenge, consent does weaken the challenge, if only because the examinee has a lesser expectation of privacy. *See* Kerns v. Chalfont-New Britain Twp. Joint Sewage Auth., 263 F.3d 61 (3d Cir. 2001); Carroll v. City of Westminster, 233 F.3d 208 (4th Cir. 2000) (Fourth Amendment). However, as *Norman-Bloodsaw* illustrates, consent is limited by the scope of an employer's advance disclosures about the nature, direction, and depth of an examination. In blood or urinalysis testing, or even some paper and pencil testing, the employer's extraction and evaluation of information from a sample voluntarily given might improperly exceed the scope of what the employer described in a consent form.

Informational privacy rights. The right to informational privacy is not clearly established under the Fourth Amendment. In NASA v. Nelson, 562 U.S. 134, 152 (2011), the Court assumed arguendo that a public employer might intrude upon a right of informational privacy with applicant interview questions and interviews of the applicant's associates and acquaintances about the applicant's drug use. However, the Court held the inquiries were "reasonable" and furthered the government's interests "in managing its internal operations." Other cases appear to agree that if there is a Fourth Amendment-based right of informational privacy in employment or other contexts, it is quite limited. *See* Wolfe v. Schaefer, 619 F.3d 782, 784-86 (7th Cir. 2010) (surveying Supreme Court decisions). Lower courts frequently have held that public employer gathering of information by interviewing applicants/employees, or third-party acquaintances is not a Fourth Amendment "search." *See, e.g.*, Nelson v. NASA, 530 F.3d 865, 876-77 (9th Cir. 2008), *rev'd on other grounds sub nom* NASA v. Nelson, 562 U.S. 134 (2011).

Beyond the Fourth Amendment, the Supreme Court has held that the "constitutionally protected 'zone of privacy'" includes "the individual interest in avoiding disclosure of personal matters." *Whalen v. Roe*, 429 U.S. 589, 598-99 (1977). Based on that caselaw, *Norman-Bloodsaw* held that the "constitutionally protected privacy interest in avoiding disclosure of personal matters clearly encompasses medical information and its confidentiality," 135 F.3d at 1269. Yet the Supreme Court repeatedly has rejected claims of infringements of that right, as Judge Posner noted in *Wolfe v. Schaefer*, 619 F.3d 782 (7th Cir. 2010):

> [*Whalen*] held that "liberty" includes "privacy." But ... the Court in the decades since has confined the label "privacy" mainly to sexual and reproductive rights .... [T]he right to conceal information ... is recognized by the Supreme Court only when anonymity is sought in order to protect freedom of expression .... [*Whalen*] suggest[ed] that there might be a due process right to the nondisclosure of certain private information, though it upheld the law challenged .... *Nixon v. Administrator of General Services* [1977] ... , was more explicit about the existence of a constitutional right of privacy in personal papers, but again the plaintiff lost ....
>
> [Appeals] courts ... have interpreted *Whalen* to recognize a constitutional right to the privacy of medical, sexual, financial, and perhaps other ... highly personal information .... The Supreme Court, in contrast, has seemed more interested in limiting the right of informational privacy than in its recognition and enforcement. It has held that reputation is not part of the liberty that the due process clauses protect, *Paul v. Davis* [1976] ... , even though concern with reputation is one of the principal reasons people don't want personal information [disclosed] .... It has held that the First Amendment forbids a

> state to punish broadcasting the name of a murdered rape victim if her name is in judicial records open to public inspection. *Cox Broadcasting Corp. v. Cohn* [1975] .... [P]ublicizing of highly personal information that is not in a record open to public inspection is privileged if there is a public interest in access.... *Bartnicki v. Vopper* [2001] ....
>
> The rejection in *Paul v. Davis* of a liberty or property interest in reputation ... casts doubt on any effort to limit the public disclosure of personal information .... But the Court has not ... extinguished state-law protections, whether common law or statutory, against publication of intimate details of people's private lives ....

Id. at 784-786.

ii. Private Sector Employees: Common Law and Other State Law Privacy Rights

Neither the Fourth Amendment right against unreasonable search nor a possible multi-based right of informational privacy protect an applicant or employee against intrusive investigation by a *private* sector employer. Thus, if the employer in *Norman-Bloodsaw* were privately owned, the plaintiffs would have needed some other source of protection for their alleged right of privacy. The *Norman-Bloodsaw* plaintiffs also alleged a claim under Article I, Section 1 of the California Constitution, which is unique among state constitutions in possibly extending a constitutional right of privacy to the private sector. Outside of California, however, applicants and employees of private sector employers must rely on a common law or statutory right of privacy.

The analysis for a claim based on the common law right of privacy is similar but not identical to the analysis of a Fourth Amendment "search" claim. *Compare* Luedtke v. Nabors Alaska Drilling, Inc., 768 P.2d 1123, 1133-1135 (Alaska 1989) (looking to Fourth Amendment cases as precedent for the common law of privacy) *with* Wilcher v. City of Wilmington, 139 F.3d 366 (3d Cir. 1998) (state courts might interpret the common law to be more protective than the Fourth Amendment, and dismissal of Fourth Amendment claim did not necessarily require dismissal of common law claim). As in a case under the Fourth Amendment, the starting point for a tort claim is to evaluate the claimant's privacy interest—the interest against which the defendant has intruded.

The new Restatement of Employment Law divides privacy interests into two types relevant to applicants. Although these Restatement provisions speak only of "employees," the commentary and illustrations that follow make clear that they apply to applicants as well. *See, e.g.,* RESTATEMENT OF THE LAW, EMPLOYMENT LAW §§ 7.03, comment c, illustration 1. On the other hand, some commentators and courts have concluded that a certain amount of examination is so routine in the hiring phase that applicants have a much diminished expectation of privacy as compared with current employees. *Id.*, Reporter's Notes on comment c; *see also, e.g.*, Baughman v. Wal-Mart Stores, Inc., 592 S.E.2d 824 (W. Va. 2003).

The first relevant privacy interest the Restatement of Employment Law recognizes is in an employee's or applicant's "physical person, bodily functions, and personal possessions." RESTATEMENT OF THE LAW, EMPLOYMENT LAW §§

7.03(a). Second, an applicant or employee has a privacy interest in "information relating to the employee [or applicant] that is of a personal nature and that the employee [or applicant] has made reasonable efforts to keep private." *Id.* 7.04. The Restatement is clear in recognizing informational privacy, and in this regard the protection it grants private sector applicants and employees is more certain than Constitutional protection for public sector applicants and employees.

Not every intrusion against these privacy interests is unlawful. An intrusion is tortious only if it would be "highly offensive to a reasonable person under the circumstances." *Id.* § 7.06. The question whether an intrusion is "highly offensive" is quite similar to an inquiry whether government intrusion is unreasonable under the Fourth Amendment. The employer's need or reason for the intrusion is the key. "An intrusion is highly offensive ... if the nature, manner, and scope of the intrusion are clearly unreasonable when judged against the employer's legitimate business interests or the public's interests in intruding." *Id.*

As in Fourth Amendment cases, a frequent obstacle for an applicant or employee is the problem of consent. The examinee either will have seemed to consent by failing to resist the intrusion, or will have signed a written consent. Voluntary consent normally bars a tort claim for invasion of privacy. RESTATEMENT OF TORTS (SECOND) §§ 652B, 892. Might private sector employees and applicants argue that consent to a particular intrusion was involuntary if it was necessary to obtain or keep a job? For an applicant, threatened loss of a mere job *opportunity* is not likely to constitute duress. *Current* employees are another matter. A current employee may argue that the prospective loss of an *existing* job is particularly coercive. Whether mandatory intrusion under threat of employee *discharge* is duress invalidating consent is addressed in Chapter Six, part B.4.

2. *Background Investigations*

Even the simplest employee selection process will likely involve some inquiry into an applicant's background. An employer can seek some of this information directly from the applicant in a resume, an application form, or a personal interview. Arguably, whatever "private" information the applicant supplies is voluntary and not the result of a nonconsensual intrusion. Nevertheless, applicants have sometimes asserted the Constitutional right of informational privacy against highly intrusive interview or application questions, especially in the public sector. NASA v. Nelson, 562 U.S. 134 (2011) (allowing employer's questions about drug use); McKenna v. Fargo, 451 F. Supp. 1355, 1380-81 (D.N.J. 1978), *aff'd*, 601 F.2d 575 (3d Cir. 1979) (disallowing employer's questions about social and religious beliefs); Fraternal Order of Police, Lodge No. 5 v. City of Philadelphia, 812 F.2d 105 (3d Cir. 1987) (allowing police department's questions about gambling, alcohol consumption, and criminal records of relatives). Moreover, questions that might yield evidence of an employee's protected status (e.g., religion, disability, arrest record, union membership) might violate antidiscrimination laws or constitute evidence of an intent to discriminate. See section C.3 of this chapter, *supra*. States that prohibit discrimination on the basis of political activity or affiliation might also prohibit questions tending to reveal one's political outlook or personal values. *See, e.g.*, Cal. Lab. Code §§1101, 1102. A few states have adopted very specific laws against certain questions by an employer. California, for example, not only prohibits inquiries about arrests, it also prohibits inquiries about certain marijuana-related *convictions*. Cal. Lab. Code §§ 432.7, 432.8 (also prohibiting employer from seeking the same information from any other source). See also section C.3 of this chapter.

Direct questioning of an applicant also has significant practical limitations. The applicant is hardly an objective judge of his own qualifications or character. Resume and application fraud is a problem widely discussed among human resources professionals, although its significance is difficult to gauge and appears to vary substantially from one industry or profession to another. *See, e.g.*, J. Olian, *Resume Fraud in the Corner Office,* Smeal College of Business News (Nov. 2001), at http://www.smeal.psu.edu/news/releases/nov02/resume.html (describing studies indicating that 24 to 27 percent of job applicants had misrepresented some aspect of their backgrounds).

An employer can verify some of the information an applicant supplies by contacting the applicant's prior employers. *See Hiring*, HRhero.com Monthly Survey Results (July 18, 2003), at http://www.HRhero.com/survey/hiring_results/ (reporting that 85 percent of respondents contact prior employers before hiring an applicant for a "typical job opening"). However, past employers may be very guarded about what they disclose. Even a former employer who fired the applicant might be sympathetic and hopeful that the applicant will "land on his feet," or it might be fearful of a defamation lawsuit.

A prospective employer might also call non-employer references listed by the applicant. *Hiring*, HRhero.com, *supra* (reporting that 75 percent of respondents contact an applicant's listed references before hiring an applicant for a "typical job opening"). References, however, are selected by the applicant and might be no more objective than the applicant himself.

A background check might therefore explore some of the "objective" records of an applicant's personal history, including criminal record, financial history and credit record, driving record, education, and litigation. A criminal background check is particularly likely. *Hiring*, HRhero.com, *supra* (reporting that 59 percent of respondents perform a criminal background check before accepting an applicant for a "typical job opening"). For an employer to gather such information by itself is laborious. However, it can quickly and easily obtain a great deal of information from the same private data collection services that provide lenders with data about prospective borrowers. Such "consumer credit reporting" services can provide an employer with information about an applicant's employment history, financial record, and criminal conviction record, all at relatively little cost.

Collecting and transmitting personal data by background-checking services is hardly foolproof. There may be errors in the public or private records on which the service relies, confusion about identity (particularly if the applicant has been the victim of identity theft), mistakes in interpretation of the data, or errors in the summation or transmission of the data to the employer. Congress attempted to address these concerns in 1970 when it enacted the Fair Credit Reporting Act (FCRA). 15 U.S.C. §§ 1681-1681x. The act's title might suggest it applies only to background investigations and reports in the consumer credit context. In fact, the act also applies to an employer's use of third-party investigations and reports about job applicants and employees. Among other things, the act regulates the practices of certain data collection and reporting agencies, requires employers to notify applicants and employees in advance before obtaining reports from such agencies, and provides a procedure for applicants and employees to correct errors.

By some estimates, 35 percent of employers obtain consumer credit reports as part of a background check of some or all prospective employees. The rate is probably much higher for large employers with sophisticated human resources offices. *See* Employment Law Counselor, No. 247, March 2011, p. 3 (West 2011) (quoting 2010 Society for Human Resource Management survey showing six in ten reporting employers conduct credit checks on applicants). Yet even after the enactment of the FCRA, consumer credit reports frequently contain significant errors or omissions. Studies show that nearly 30 percent of such reports contain the sort of errors that might adversely affect the ability to obtain credit. Note: *Rethinking the Fair Credit Reporting Act: When Requesting Credit Reports for "Employment Purposes" Goes Too Far*, 91 Iowa L. Rev. 1593, 1598-1599 (2006).

OBABUEKI v. INTERNATIONAL BUSINESS MACHINES CORP.

145 F. Supp. 2d 371 (S.D.N.Y. 2001), *aff'd*, 319 F.3d 87 (2d Cir. 2003)

SCHWARTZ, District Judge.

This diversity action arises out of the withdrawal of an employment offer to plaintiff Abel Obabueki by defendant International Business Machines Corp. Plaintiff alleges that IBM improperly considered his dismissed misdemeanor conviction in making its decision to withdraw the offer, and failed to properly inform plaintiff of its intent to withdraw the offer, in violation of the New York State Human Rights Law . . . , and the Fair Credit Reporting Act ("FCRA"), 15 U.S.C. §§ 1681 et seq. Plaintiff asserts claims against defendant Choicepoint, Inc. under the FCRA . . . as a result of Choicepoint's allegedly improper provision of information related to the conviction to IBM. Currently before the Court are cross-motions for summary judgment on plaintiff's claims against each defendant. . . .

I. Factual Background

A. The Parties and Plaintiff's 1995 Conviction

Plaintiff, a citizen of Connecticut, has a Ph.D. in Materials Science and Engineering and a Master of Business Administration from Stanford University. . . . In 1995, plaintiff was arrested and charged with fraud in obtaining welfare aid.[3] He entered a plea of nolo contendere, was ordered to pay restitution for the amount he illegally obtained, was fined $100, served 13 days in jail, and was placed on two years' probation. On January 27, 1997, plaintiff's conviction was "vacated" and "dismissed" pursuant to California Penal Code § 1203.4.[4] The Order disposing

---

[3] According to plaintiff, his wife had been receiving welfare benefits under the federal Aid to Families with Dependent Children program. Plaintiff's conviction apparently arose out of his failure to properly report a change in income status to the government when he was a paid summer intern between his first and second year at Stanford Business School. . . .

[4] Section 1203.4 provides in pertinent part:

(a) In any case in which a defendant has fulfilled the conditions of probation . . . the

of his case (the "California Order") stated that plaintiff was convicted of a misdemeanor offense, and . . . further directed that "plea, verdict, or finding of guilt . . . be set aside and vacated and a plea of not guilty be entered; and that the complaint be, and hereby is, dismissed." . . .

B. PLAINTIFF'S APPLICATION FOR EMPLOYMENT AT IBM

At IBM, once a decision is made to make a conditional offer of employment to a candidate, the individual is asked to complete an application form. An applicant must also complete a Security Data Sheet ("SDS"), which requests, inter alia, that he identify whether he has pleaded guilty or "no contest" to a crime or other offense within the last seven years. However, the applicant is expressly requested not to include "arrests without convictions" or "convictions or incarcerations for which a record has been sealed or expunged." Both the application form and SDS provide that "any misrepresentation or deliberate omission of a fact . . . will justify terminating consideration" of the application for employment. Further, IBM policy states that the mere identification of a conviction on the SDS will not subject an applicant to disqualification. Rather, the policy requires that the company perform an analysis of whether the crime is related to the position for which the applicant has applied. Specifically, the policy provides that "when reviewing information listed on the SDS (i.e. criminal record history) of a potential employee," the Human Resources unit responsible for hiring must perform an analysis of the crime in relation to the job being offered to determine whether placing the applicant in the position would create a risk to the safety or property of others.

In April 1999, Olwyn Spencer, IBM's Program Director for Market Management, identified the need for a marketing manager position for the company's JAVA Company Software group. . . . In September 1999, plaintiff interviewed with Spencer for the marketing manager position. Spencer rated plaintiff an outstanding candidate for the job, and he was given a conditional offer of employment subject to a background check. Plaintiff then completed the IBM application form and SDS. In response to the question regarding prior convictions that were neither "expunged" nor "sealed," plaintiff checked "no."

IBM retained Choicepoint to perform the background check on plaintiff, pursuant to a longstanding agreement whereby Choicepoint renders "background Verification Services" to IBM. . . . On or about October 5, 1999, IBM received a report from Choicepoint, . . . which reflected plaintiff's welfare fraud conviction (the "First Report"). However, the report failed to mention the dismissal of the conviction pursuant to Section 1203.4. Upon receiving the First Report, [IBM] contacted plaintiff and advised him of its contents. Plaintiff responded that the conviction had been vacated and the case dismissed, and provided [IBM] with a copy of the California Order. However, plaintiff did not explicitly state that the conviction had been "expunged" or "sealed."

Several IBM employees then reviewed plaintiff's candidacy in light of the

defendant shall . . . be permitted by the court to withdraw his or her plea of guilty or plea of nolo contendere and enter a plea of not guilty . . . and . . . the court shall thereupon dismiss the accusations or information against the defendant and except as noted below, he or she shall thereafter be released from all penalties and disabilities resulting from the offense of which he or she has been convicted. . . .

First Report and the California Order. Each of them concluded that plaintiff should have disclosed his conviction on the SDS. . . . The underlying facts concerning plaintiff's former conviction were not discussed or factored into the decision; IBM contends that the job offer was withdrawn because plaintiff lied on his employment application. . . . By letter dated October 13, 1999, IBM informed plaintiff that it "intend[ed] not to employ [him] based in part on information contained in [the First Report]." . . . By letter dated October 18, 1999, IBM informed plaintiff that the offer was formally withdrawn. . . .

Following the withdrawal of the employment offer, and as a result of plaintiff's complaint to Choicepoint, Choicepoint obtained his California court file, and, upon review of the file, issued an amended report to IBM (the "Second Report"). The Second Report, which IBM received on October 20, 1999, contains no mention of plaintiff's conviction, and reflects a clear record. However, IBM did not re-offer the marketing manager position to plaintiff. . . .

II. Discussion

B. NYSHRL Claims Against IBM

. . . [The court found that the plaintiff had established a prima facie case of unlawful discrimination because of a criminal conviction. *See* N.Y. Exec. Law § 296(15). However, IBM articulated a lawful, nondiscriminatory reason for rejecting him. According to IBM, it rejected the plaintiff because it believed he had lied when he answered "no" to the question whether he had ever been convicted of a crime (New York law prohibits unjustifiable discrimination on the basis of a criminal record, but it does not prohibit an employer from inquiring and making a case-by-case decision in accordance with statutory criteria). IBM's application did not require disclosure of a "sealed" or "expunged" conviction. However, the plaintiff's California conviction was "vacated," and IBM's decision makers did not believe or understand that a "vacated" California conviction might be an "expunged" conviction. The plaintiff argued that his "vacated" conviction was "expunged" within the meaning of IBM's application form. See description of Cal. Pen. Code § 1203.4, fn. 4, *supra*. Nevertheless, the court held that the plaintiff lacked sufficient evidence to rebut that IBM's decision makers truly believed the plaintiff lied by failing to disclose a "vacated" conviction. Accordingly, the court granted summary judgment in favor of IBM with respect to the plaintiff's discrimination claim under section 296(15).]

C. FCRA Claims Against IBM

Plaintiff alleges that IBM violated the FCRA, [15 U.S.C. § 1681b(b)(3), by] withdrawing plaintiff's conditional offer of employment without first providing him with a copy of the First Report and a description of rights under the Act. . . .

Section 1681b(b)(3) requires that, "in using a consumer report for employment purposes, before taking any adverse action based in whole or in part on the report, the person intending to take such adverse action shall provide to the consumer to whom the report relates (a) a copy of the report; and (b) a description in writing of the rights of the consumer under this subchapter, as prescribed by the Federal Trade Commission . . . ." Plaintiff claims that such procedures were not properly followed because IBM had already "taken adverse action" by October 13,

1999, the day plaintiff received the letter from IBM's Human Resources department stating that the company intended to withdraw its conditional offer of employment. Plaintiff points to facts . . . indicating that IBM's internal decision-making process had been completed by October 12. . . .

Because plaintiff misinterprets the statute and misconstrues the underlying purpose of its requirements, his contention is unavailing. An internal decision to rescind an offer is not an adverse action. The FCRA defines "adverse action," inter alia, as the "denial of employment or any other decision for employment purposes that adversely affects any current or prospective employee." 15 U.S.C. § 1681a(k)(1)(B)(ii). Clearly, plaintiff did not suffer any adverse effect until his offer of conditional employment was withdrawn on October 18, 1999. IBM's internal discussions had no impact on plaintiff; only when its staff acted by letter did IBM take any action. . . . Moreover, the statute expressly allows for the formation of an intent to take adverse action before complying with Section 1681b(b)(3), as it states that "the person intending to take" adverse action must provide the report and description of rights. 15 U.S.C. § 1681b(b)(3). After all, how can an employer send an intent letter without having first formed the requisite intent?

After receipt of the intent letter, plaintiff could have come forward with information responding to the First Report that showed he had not lied on his application. He attempted to do so by asking Choicepoint to reexamine his records. Such opportunity to discuss and dispute the report is exactly the scenario envisioned by the FCRA. . . . Because plaintiff's position that forming an intent to withdraw an employment offer is an adverse action is legally unsupportable, the Court denies his motion, and grants IBM's motion for summary judgment as to his FCRA claim under Section 1681b(b)(3).

Plaintiff also argues that IBM violated the FCRA because "before using a report, IBM must certify to Choicepoint that it will comply with the FCRA and the State Human Rights Laws." [29 U.S.C. § 1681b(b)(1)(A)]. . . . IBM argues, based on the plain language of the statutory provision, that only the consumer reporting agency may be held liable under this subsection, not the user of the reports. The Court agrees. . . . Section 1681b(b)(1) . . . sets forth obligations that an agency must satisfy before furnishing a consumer report. The plain language of the provision states that "*a consumer reporting agency may furnish a consumer report for employment purposes only if* . . . " certain certifications are obtained from the user of such report. 15 U.S.C. § 1681b(b)(1). . . . Moreover, another section of the FCRA, 15 U.S.C. § 1681e(a), contains an analogous requirement: the section obligates the agency to obtain certain certifications from the user and to make sure the report will be used for the purposes listed in Section 1681b. . . . [W]hile plaintiff may assert a claim against Choicepoint under Section 1681b(b)(1)(A), *see infra*, he has no standing to assert a claim against IBM under this section. Accordingly, plaintiff's claim under this section must be dismissed as against IBM.

D. FCRA Claims Against Choicepoint

1. Section 1681b(b)(1)(A)

Plaintiff alleges that Choicepoint violated 15 U.S.C. § 1681b(b)(1)(A) because it furnished a credit report to IBM concerning plaintiff without first obtaining the required certification.

. . . [T]he Court finds that Choicepoint has failed to demonstrate that there is any issue of material fact as to their failure to obtain the required certification before providing the First Report to IBM. The Court finds that such failure constitutes negligent, as opposed to wilful conduct, for while the record reflects that Choicepoint neglected to obtain proper certification documents from IBM, there is nothing in the record to suggest that it did so intentionally. Accordingly, the Court grants summary judgment to plaintiff on this claim.

2. Section 1681k

15 U.S.C. § 1681k sets forth public record obligations which apply specifically in the employment context. This section requires a credit reporting agency furnishing information that is a matter of public record and which is likely to have an adverse impact on the applicant, to either (1) notify the applicant of the fact that public record information is being reported along with the name and address of the person who requested the report, *or* (2) maintain "strict procedures" designed to insure that any such reported information is "complete and up to date." 15 U.S.C. § 1681k (emphasis added). For purposes of the section, "items of public record relating to arrests, indictments, convictions, suits, tax liens, and outstanding judgments shall be considered up to date if the current public record status of the item at the time of the report is reported." *Id.* In this case, the threshold requirements for the application of this section are clearly met, as the information concerning plaintiff was reported for employment purposes, was a matter of public record, and was certainly likely to have an adverse impact on him. In addition, it is undisputed that Choicepoint did not notify plaintiff that his criminal record information was being reported to IBM.

Accordingly, plaintiff alleges that Choicepoint violated Section 1681k because the information that it provided to IBM was neither complete nor up to date, and Choicepoint "has no procedures — let alone strict procedures — designed to ensure that such information is complete and up to date." . . . The record reflects that, in this case, the information provided to IBM by Choicepoint was neither complete nor up to date. Rather, the First Report, dated October 1, 1999, reflected plaintiff's 1995 conviction, but not its subsequent dismissal in 1997 under Section 1203.4. Leaving aside whether the omission of the information was the fault of Choicepoint's contractor or some other entity (e.g. the court), and whether the conviction itself should have been disclosed given the disposition under 1203.4, the information provided to IBM was clearly deficient because the dismissal was not mentioned. Similarly, while this information reflected one entry in the "current public record" with regard to plaintiff's criminal record in Santa Clara County, it was not up to date because it did not provide the most current information with regard to that entry, i.e., the Section 1203.4 dismissal. . . .

Nevertheless, on the current record, the Court declines to find that Choicepoint failed to "maintain strict procedures" designed to insure that the information concerning plaintiff was complete and up to date, thereby making Choicepoint liable for a violation of Section 1681k as a matter of law. Likewise, the Court cannot find that Choicepoint clearly maintained such strict procedures, in order to warrant an award of summary judgment to Choicepoint. Rather, there are issues of fact related to Choicepoint's investigatory procedures which would affect the determination of whether Choicepoint violated Section 1681k in the conduct of their investigations. The deposition testimony of Choicepoint's record manager, Andrew Klaer, reflects that, generally: (i) Choicepoint contracts with various "suppliers" to conduct searches, who are either "researchers," internal Choicepoint employees, or independent contractors; (ii) Choicepoint selects the low cost supplier if multiple suppliers are available; (iii) Choicepoint assumes the accuracy of the search performed by the supplier; (iv) if there is a "hit," i.e. if a person is found to have a criminal record, the only verification provided is a check by someone at Choicepoint's employment service center in order to make sure the person on the report is identical to the person about whom the employer requested; if the identities match, Choicepoint forwards the report to the employer; (v) certain investigatory procedures are provided in a training manual provided to internal Choicepoint employees, but nothing is provided to the outside contractors; (vi) third party suppliers have an "implied" instruction to be accurate; (vii) Klaer does not know if Choicepoint has a policy or procedure with regard to reporting convictions that have been dismissed; and, as noted *supra*, (viii) when an individual complains, in generating an amended report, it is "Choicepoint's practice to favor the consumer if anything is disputed."

Based on this information and on the limited facts in the record surrounding the contractor's search and Choicepoint's report in this case, the Court concludes that there are questions of fact relating to the specifics of, and hence the reasonableness of, [Choicepoint's] procedures. . . . Moreover, assuming that such procedures would not meet the standard for strictness required under Section 1681k, there are questions as to whether, based on the procedures used to investigate plaintiff's criminal record in this case, Choicepoint intentionally maintained substandard procedures, or knew or should have known that its procedures would not meet the standard. Accordingly, the Court declines to grant summary judgment to either party on this claim. . . .

3. Section 1681e(b)

15 U.S.C. §1681e(b) requires that "[w]henever a consumer reporting agency prepares a consumer report *it shall follow reasonable procedures to assure maximum possible accuracy* of the information concerning the individual about whom the report relates." 15 U.S.C. § 1681e(b) (emphasis added). Plaintiff alleges that Choicepoint violated this section because it neither provided "maximally accurate" information to IBM nor has "reasonable procedures" designed to ensure such accuracy. Similar to Section 1681k, and in accordance with one of the FCRA's central purposes, Section 1681e(b) is intended to ensure the accuracy of reports generated by credit reporting agencies. . . . However, under Section 1681e(b), the agency is held to the less specific standard of "maximal accuracy" rather than the "complete and up to date" requirement of Section 1681k, and requires that the agency only have "reasonable procedures" to ensure such accuracy, rather than the "strict" procedures required under Section 1681k. . . .

[T]he disposition of plaintiff's respective claims under these sections are parallel in this case. Specifically, the Court finds that the information provided to IBM was not maximally accurate under Section 1681e(b), given Choicepoint's failure to report the Section 1203.4 dismissal. The Court also finds that, for the reasons enumerated *supra* with respect to plaintiff's Section 1681k claim, issues of fact exist with regard to the nature of Choicepoint's investigatory procedures as applied to the instant case so as to prevent a judgment as a matter of law as to their reasonableness. Moreover, even assuming they are unreasonable, the jury must determine whether Choicepoint intentionally maintained such unreasonable procedures, or knew or should have known this to be the case. The Court therefore denies the parties' respective summary judgment motions on plaintiff's Section 1681e(b) claim. . . .

NOTES AND QUESTIONS

1. State "first offender" laws are common. Unfortunately, there is no uniform terminology or the practical effect for a local procedure seeming to "erase" an offender's record.
2. As in the case of testing or examination of applicants, a disappointed applicant's best remedy is more likely to be against the third party background-checker, not the employer.

FCRA Coverage and Obligations in the Employment Context

As *Obabueki* illustrates, an employer's reliance on a third party for information about an applicant or employee may trigger important provisions of the FCRA. However, not all third-party reports to an employer are subject to the act. There are three key terms to bear in mind in determining the applicability of the FCRA in the employment context. First, if an employer obtains information about an employee or applicant from a third party, the third party might be a "consumer reporting agency." 15 U.S.C. § 1681a(e). Second, if a consumer reporting agency sends an employer (or other party) a "consumer report," as defined by 15 U.S.C. § 1681a(e), the act imposes a number of duties on the agency and the recipient. Third, the agency might provide a special "investigative consumer report," as defined by 15 U.S.C. § 1681a(e), resulting in an additional set of duties.

At the outset, one must determine whether the third party supplying information about an applicant qualifies as a "consumer reporting agency." The act does not apply to many transfers of information an employer receives from other parties because of the act's restrictive definition of "consumer reporting agency." To qualify as a consumer reporting agency, a party must (1) *regularly* assemble or evaluate information on individuals (2) for the purpose of furnishing consumer reports *to third parties* (3) in return for a monetary *fee or dues*, or on a nonprofit cooperative basis. 15 U.S.C. § 1681a(e). Many parties who supply information to an employer are not consumer reporting agencies, because they supply the information on a purely incidental basis as a courtesy and without any fee or cooperative arrangement. Thus, an applicant's former employer is not acting as a consumer reporting agency when it supplies information to a prospective employer. On the other hand, if a group or association of employers agreed to share information about employees on a "cooperative basis," this arrangement might constitute a consumer reporting agency.

Another reason most information supplied by third parties to an employer is not covered by the act is that the information does not constitute a "consumer report." The act defines "consumer report" to include information about a broad range of subjects, including "credit worthiness, . . . character, general reputation, personal characteristics, or mode of living," but the act adds an important exemption: a report is not a consumer report if it involves "information solely as to transactions or experiences between the [subject person] and the person making the report." 15 U.S.C. § 1681a(d)(2). In other words, a former employer who provides information about its former employee is not making a consumer report (even if it qualifies as a consumer reporting agency) if it is describing only its own relationship and experience with the employee. For the same reason, many agencies conducting polygraph, urinalysis, or personality examinations of job applicants are not consumer reporting agencies because they are reporting only their own direct observations. Hodge v. Texaco U.S.A., 764 F. Supp. 424 (W.D. La. 1991); Chube v. Exxon Chem. Am., 760 F. Supp. 557 (M.D. La. 1991).

If an employer seeks a consumer report from a consumer reporting agency for an employment purpose, the employer must (1) provide a "clear and conspicuous disclosure" in a separate writing that it might obtain a consumer report about the applicant or employee; and (2) obtain the applicant/employee's written authorization for the report. 15 U.S.C. § 1681b(b)(2)(A).

If the employer, having obtained a consumer report, takes an "adverse action based in whole or in part on the report," the employer will have an additional set of duties. The employer must provide the affected applicant/ employee (1) a copy of the report; and (2) a written description of her rights under the act. 15 U.S.C. § 1681b(b)(3). If the consumer reporting agency has satisfied its own obligations under the act, which include providing the employer with a written description of rights, the employer will have the necessary description on hand to supply to a rejected, discharged, or otherwise adversely affected applicant or employee. Otherwise, an FTC-approved description of rights is available from the FTC. 15 C.F.R. pt. 601, Appendix A, http://www.ftc.gov/os/statutes/2summary.htm. The rights listed in the notice pertain primarily to rights against the consumer reporting agency for the purpose of correcting inaccurate or outdated information.

The act does not prohibit an employer from discriminating against an applicant or employee based on a report that later proves inaccurate as long as the employer satisfied its own duties to obtain advance authorization and provide the requisite notices to the applicant/employee. However, a rejected or discharged applicant/employee may have important remedies against the consumer reporting agency. At the very least, an applicant/employee may invoke a procedure for correcting inaccurate or outdated information, such as information that is older than permitted under act. 25 U.S.C. §§ 1681c. If the report is inaccurate because the agency violated one of its FCRA duties, the applicant/employee may recover damages against the agency. *See* 15 U.S.C. §§ 1681n, 1681o.

The act imposes additional duties in connection with an "investigative consumer report," which is a report containing information about character, general reputation, personal characteristics, or mode of living, based on personal interviews of persons having information about the applicant or employee, including her neighbors, friends, associates, or other acquaintances. 15 U.S.C. §§ 1681a(e). An investigative report might also in include an examination of information displayed on social media or other Internet sources. Letter of Mineesha Mithal on behalf of

Federal Trade Commission, May 9, 2011, available online at http://ftc.gov/os/closings/110509socialintelligenceletter.pdf. Again, if the employer performs this sort of investigation itself, the investigation is not subject to the act because the employer is not acting as a consumer reporting agency and it is collecting the information for its own use, not for a third party. But if the employer obtains such a report from a consumer reporting agency, the act imposes additional notice and authorization requirements on the employer, and it requires the agency to take "reasonable steps to ensure the maximum possible accuracy" of the information. *Id.*; 15 U.S.C. §§ 1681d, 1681*l*. What might such "reasonable steps" be, in the case of information gleaned from a Facebook page?

NOTES AND QUESTIONS

1. How far back in time should an employer or consumer credit reporting agency be permitted to look in investigating a job applicant's background? Under the FCRA, a consumer reporting agency's report must not include certain bankruptcy data older than ten years; arrest records, civil suits, or civil judgments older than seven years; or "any other adverse item of information, other than records of convictions of crimes" older than seven years. 15 U.S.C. § 1681c(a).

The FRCA provides no limits on the age of criminal convictions that might be included in a consumer report. Moreover, none of the time limits described above apply to "the employment of any individual at an annual salary which equals, or which may reasonably be expected to equal $75,000, or more." *Id.* § 1681c(b).

2. A consumer report will typically include any record of personal bankruptcy (subject to the time limits described above), but federal law prohibits a private sector employer from discriminating against a person "who is or has been . . . a debtor or bankrupt under the Bankruptcy Act." 11 U.S.C.A. § 525.

3. The FCRA preempts some state laws and causes of action an applicant might otherwise invoke if she is harmed by inaccurate or outdated information. *See* 15 U.S.C. § 1681h(e) (consumer may not bring action "in the nature [of] defamation, invasion of privacy or negligence" with respect to a report subject to the act). The FCRA does not appear to preempt a wrongful discharge claim under state law against an employer whose illegal procurement or use of a credit report causes a loss of employment or employment opportunity. *See e.g.*, Ohle v. Neiman Marcus Group, 65 N.E.3d 850 (Ill. App. 2016) (describing and applying Illinois law prohibiting employment discrimination on basis of credit report).

State law remedies might also be available with respect to reports that fall outside the scope of the FCRA, such as a former employer's report to a prospective employer. In fact, the FCRA permits the states to enact their own fair credit reporting laws not "inconsistent" with the FCRA. 15 U.S.C. § 1681t. A number of states have adopted such laws, and at least one state — California — has enacted a law that appears to go much farther than the federal FCRA. Perhaps most importantly, the California law extends its protections to an employer's own background investigation of employees or applicants without the use of a third-party consumer reporting agency. If an employer obtains information from a "public record" about a person's "character, general reputation, personal characteristics, or mode of living," the California law requires the employer to disclose its information to that person. Thus, for example, under California law an applicant has a right to disclosure of criminal record information the employer used even if the employer obtained this information on its own and not from a consumer reporting agency. *See* Cal. Civ. Code § 1786.53.

4. Congress enacted the FCRA in 1970, when a thorough and accurate background check could be expensive, tedious, or impractical. For a reasonably complete background check, an employer had little choice but to turn to one of a few established consumer reporting agencies. Today, the Internet presents an employer with a wide range of options for conducting a background check. How does this FCRA address Internet-based background checking strategies? Although Congress has amended the FCRA many times since 1970, the Act still does not clearly and directly address the problem of background checking on the Internet.

Suppose, for example, an employer uses the Internet to engage in its own background check, by using a common search engine, visiting social media webpages or blogs, or inspecting courthouse or other public records that might now be available online at little or no cost. As long as the employer does not rely on the sort of third party who might qualify as a "consumer reporting agency," the employer's actions are simply not subject to the FCRA as an agency or as an employer. Thus, the FCRA does not require the employer to take any steps to assure the accuracy of the data it collects. Considering the quantity and quality of personal data now available on the Internet, the lack of any duty of care on the employer's part might be troubling to an applicant. Moreover, the FCRA does not require the employer to give the applicant notice of the search or of the existence of data that caused an adverse employment action. There may be no way to know whether an employer rejected a candidate because of erroneous data that is still on the Internet, and an employer's discriminatory purpose may be easier to hide.

5. An employer can also conduct a relatively inexpensive and current Internet background check by requiring an applicant to grant access to his or her Facebook page or other social media, such as by "friending" the interviewer. An applicant's refusal to grant such access might lead to automatic rejection. Social media access provides the employer with more than current social activity and posted personal information. It also supplies the employer with a list of the applicant's Facebook "friends" and "family." And if the employer hires the applicant, Facebook access provides a means for the employer to monitor off-duty conduct and posted comments that may offend or disparage the employer. *See* Manuel Valdes (Associated Press), *Job Seekers Getting Asked for Facebook Passwords* (March 20, 2012), at http://finance.yahoo.com/news/job-seekers-getting-asked-facebook-080920368.html

6. Even with the Internet, an employer seeking a reasonably complete background check that covers public records in many different states is likely to rely on a third-party agent to gather, monitor and present the data. The Internet seems to have spawned a large number of such agencies. They are far more numerous than the small handful of agencies Congress confronted in 1970. Typically, a background checking agency operating through an Internet portal offers easy, low-cost, and fast access to public records and other data the agency may have in its own database. Does the FCRA apply to such Internet-based reporting agencies? In general, yes. An agency that deals with customers through a website could still

satisfy the definition of a "consumer reporting" agency, and the data it delivers over the Internet could still satisfy the definition of a "consumer report." Moreover, if the agency also delivers data gleaned from social media, blogs, and message boards, its collection and delivery of the data might constitute an "investigative consumer report" as to which the FCRA applies special rules. Letter of Mineesha Mithal on behalf of Federal Trade Commission, May 9, 2011, available online at http://ftc.gov/os/closings/110509socialintelligenceletter.pdf

7. Is the FCRA adequate to deal with background checking services sold and delivered over the Internet? There are at least two reasons for concern. First, the new generation of Internet-based services are so inexpensive that they have drawn a very wide range of customers. Some customers are searching for information about spouses, family members, dating partners, neighbors and other social relations, as opposed to business or employment relations. The FCRA might not apply to background reports issued for many of these social and family purposes. *See* 15 U.S.C. §1681a(d)(1). Internet-based agencies frequently market their services for *both* FCRA covered and *non*-covered purposes. Typically, a customer identifies itself as one kind of user or the other at the time it purchases services online. If the customer indicates it seeks data for a non-FCRA purpose, such as investigating a dating partner, the agency might not take any steps to assure that the customer complies with employer FCRA duties. And the agency might assume its own data collection methods are not governed by the FCRA for purposes of that report. In short, the FCRA's safeguards depend at least in part on the honesty of the customer.

8. Another reason for concern about the new generation of background checking agencies relates to their storage of data. Agencies that collect, assemble and report data on job candidates, and then store the data for future customers, may be preserving the data indefinitely. Thus, information or comments posted on the Internet by or about an individual might be preserved in a credit reporting agency's database long after an individual's information was deleted or corrected on the Internet. *See* Linda Criddle, *Civil Rights Get Trampled in Internet Background Searches*, iLookBothWays, http://ilookbothways.com/2011/07/27/civil-rights-get-trampled-in-Internet-background-checks/.

PROBLEM

Joe Sibley filed an application for employment with the Green Valley Police Department, where he hoped to find employment as a police officer. The application required him to list parents, brothers, spouses, and children, and it included the following questions: "Have you or any member of your family (including your parents, siblings, spouse or children) ever been arrested?" and "If so, what were the circumstances, and what was the outcome (conviction or acquittal)?" These questions were followed by statement that

> [y]ou will not be automatically disqualified as a result of your own arrest or conviction or the arrest or conviction of any family member. Green Valley Police Department will consider each case based on all the facts.

Sibley completed the application and answered "no" to the question whether he or any family member had ever been arrested. The department accepted his application and enrolled him in its officer training program, "subject to a criminal background check."

A week after Sibley's enrollment in the training program, the instructor informed Sibley that the department was dismissing him from the program because he had failed to disclose that his younger brother Larry Sibley had been arrested for drug possession in 2001 and had pleaded "nolo contendere." Joe was surprised to learn of his brother's arrest. When he confronted Larry about the matter, Larry admitted he had been arrested, and he explained that he pleaded nolo to qualify for dismissal of the charge under the local first offender program.

Joe Sibley has come to you to see if he can sue Green Valley for violating his rights. How would you advise him?

3. *Drug Testing*

By some estimates, nearly two-thirds of all employers engage in drug testing of at least some applicants and employees. However, in comparison with testing of *current* employees after an accident or in an investigation of misconduct — a major topic in Chapter Six — the need for and usefulness of drug testing of *applicants* might be particularly suspect. Whether drug testing is accurate for *hiring* decisions depends on the question the employer is asking and the manner in which the test is conducted. Assuming a test is reasonably fair and accurate, is it sufficiently important to justify this intrusion at the hiring stage? Federal regulations *require* drug testing of some job candidates — particularly in the transportation industry. Beyond these regulations for specially regulated industries, there is no federal statute to determine when such testing is appropriate or how an employer should conduct tests. Thus, the answers to these questions depend on the Constitution in the case of public sector job opportunities, tort law in the case of private sector job opportunities, and local statutes in states that expressly regulate drug testing.

When the U.S. Supreme Court considered a Fourth Amendment challenge to drug testing of job candidates in National Treasury Employees Union v. Von Raab, 489 U.S. 656 (1989), it upheld the reasonableness of the testing after weighing the government's reasons for testing against the intrusiveness of the testing. With respect to the government's reasons for testing, the Court noted that customs officers were exposed to special dangers of violence by drug dealers, bribes by dealers and the temptations of vast amounts of government seized contraband. These circumstances gave the Customs Service a "compelling interest" in determining the integrity and judgment of its officers. 489 U.S. at 670. Even in the case of officers not involved in drug interdiction but required to carry a firearm, the Court agreed "that the public should not bear the risk that employees who may suffer from impaired perception and judgment will be promoted to positions where they may need to employ deadly force." 489 U.S. at 670.

The Court was unpersuaded by the plaintiffs' argument that testing was unnecessary in light of evidence that only 5 of 3,600 employees had tested positive for drugs. The purpose of testing was not only to detect drug users but also to *deter* others from using drugs. 489 U.S. at 674. The Court found useful analogies in this regard in suspicionless housing code inspections and searches of passengers of commercial airlines. *Id.*

The Court also found that the intrusiveness of drug testing was not so severe as to outweigh the government's safety and security concerns. The Court noted the following safeguards to minimize intrusiveness: (1) only those persons tentatively accepted for the positions in question were tested; (2) applicants knew at the outset that a drug test would be required; (3) they were notified well in advance of the scheduled testing, thus reducing any "unsettling show of authority" associated with the intrusion; (4) there was no direct observation of the act of urination; (5) urine samples were examined only for specified drugs and not for any other purpose; (6) the tests were highly accurate, assuming proper procedures; and (7) an examinee was not required to disclose personal medical information unless his test result was positive, and in that event a disclosure was to a physician. 489 U.S. at 673 & n.2.

The Court did not approve drug testing across the board. The Court remanded the case for further proceedings with respect to some job classifications as to which the need for testing was less certain. Thus, *National Treasury Employees Union* does not necessarily support wholesale suspicionless drug testing of all applicants in the face of a Fourth Amendment challenge. By negative implication, the Court's opinion suggests that a public employer's drug testing program must be supported by some special need beyond the employer's usual interest in management and efficiency. *Cf.* Chandler v. Miller, 520 U.S. 305 (1997) (overruling Georgia's requirement that all candidates for public office must take a drug test).

LODER v. CITY OF GLENDALE

14 Cal. 4th 846, 927 P.2d 1200, 59 Cal. Rptr. 2d 696 (1997)

GEORGE, Chief Justice.

In this case we address a challenge to an employment-related drug testing program adopted by the City of Glendale in 1986. Under the program in question, all individuals who conditionally have been offered new positions with the city (both newly hired persons and current city employees who have been approved for promotion to a new position) are required to undergo urinalysis testing for a variety of illegal drugs and alcohol as part of a preplacement medical examination that the city traditionally has conducted prior to hiring or promotion. The drug testing requirement applies to all of the city's employment positions, and is imposed without regard to whether the city has any basis for suspecting that a particular applicant for employment or promotion currently is abusing drugs or alcohol. . . . We granted review to determine the validity of the city's drug testing program under the statutory and constitutional provisions relied upon by plaintiff. As we shall explain, we conclude that the across-the-board drug testing program here at issue is invalid as applied to current employees who have been conditionally approved for promotion, but is valid as applied to job applicants.

. . . From 1983 to 1985, the city's personnel department observed an increase in the number of city employee disciplinary cases in which substance abuse appeared to be a significant factor, as well as an increase in the number of city employees who voluntarily referred themselves for treatment for substance abuse. In response, the city instituted a two-month pilot project (beginning in November 1985) under which drug testing was conducted on all applicants for city employment. Of the 48 applicants who were tested during the pilot project, 10 (approximately 21 percent) tested positive for drugs. Thereafter, in mid-1986, the city's civil service commission adopted the drug and alcohol screening program that is challenged in this case.

For at least 10 years prior to the 1986 adoption of the program, the city had required every applicant who had been conditionally approved for hiring or promotion to undergo a preplacement medical examination paid for by the city and conducted at the medical offices of a city-designated physician. As part of the preplacement medical examination, applicants were required to provide a urine sample for analysis for various medical conditions. In adopting the drug and alcohol testing program here at issue, the civil service commission approved the addition of a drug and alcohol screening component to this preexisting preplacement medical examination process.

The record discloses that the medical examination and drug and alcohol screening process operates in the following manner. Applicants for employment or promotion are notified in the city's employment bulletin (which announces job openings) that, as part of the selection process, a medical examination, including drug and alcohol screening, is required of all applicants. After an applicant has completed the initial, substantive portion of the application process (consisting, typically, of written and/or oral examinations, performance tests, background and reference checks, etc.), and has been selected by the city for employment or promotion, the applicant is notified that his or her hiring or promotion is conditioned upon successful completion of a preplacement medical examination that includes a drug and alcohol screening component. . . .

The medical examination and drug and alcohol screening are conducted at Dr. Newhouse's medical offices. When an applicant arrives at the offices, he or she is asked by a medical employee to sign a written form, consenting to a medical examination and to drug and alcohol testing, and authorizing the release of the test results to the city. The form also asks the applicant to list all medications and drugs that he or she currently is taking, and informs the applicant that a positive result on the drug or alcohol screening test, absent a valid legal explanation for the presence of such drug or alcohol, will result in disqualification from the hiring or promotion process. Applicants who refuse to sign the consent form or to undergo the screening process are considered medically disqualified for employment or promotion, and are advised that the disqualification will remain in effect for the applicant's entire period of eligibility for the position in question.

After the consent form has been completed and signed, the testing process begins. At the time the city added the drug testing component, it instituted a number of measures designed to prevent fraud or adulteration in the drug testing procedure. First, the applicant is provided a hospital gown to wear and is asked to undress down to his or her underwear. A medical employee then furnishes the applicant an empty, sealed, sterile container, and the seal is broken in the presence of the applicant. Thereafter, a medical employee accompanies the applicant to a restroom and stands in a cubicle next to the applicant's cubicle while the applicant provides a urine sample; the medical employee does not visually observe the urination process. As additional safeguards against potential fraud, blue colored water is used in the toilet bowl to prevent adulteration of the urine sample, and the medical employee checks the temperature of the sample that the applicant has provided. If the urine sample is cold, the applicant is requested to provide another sample.

After the applicant has given the urine sample to the medical employee, the sample is tested (in the applicant's presence), using a "dipstick," to determine the presence of blood, sugar, or protein in the urine, as a screen for medical problems. Thereafter, the container is closed and sealed with evidence tape, and the applicant and medical employee both sign a "chain of custody" slip that is placed in a laboratory envelope along with the sample. The applicant subsequently undergoes the remainder of the medical examination, which generally consists of at least the taking of a complete medical history from the applicant, a general physical examination, audiometric testing, and tuberculosis skin testing.

. . . At the laboratory, the urine sample is tested for the following substances: (1) amphetamines and methamphetamines (including "speed" and "crystal"), (2) benzodiazepines (including Valium, Librium, Oxazepam, Serex, and Dalmane), (3) barbiturates (including Amobarbital, Butabarbital, Pentobarbital, Phenobarbital, Secobarbital), (4) cocaine, (5) methadone, (6) methaqualone (i.e., Quaalude), (7) opiates (including codeine, heroin, morphine, hydromorphone, hydrocodone), (8) phencyclidine (PCP); (9) "THC" (marijuana), and (10) alcohol. The sample initially is tested by an enzyme immunoassay (EMIT) test. If that test discloses a positive finding, the sample is tested by a gas chromatography/mass spectrometry (GCMS) test. If the second test is negative, the overall test result is considered negative and reported as such by the laboratory. Any sample that has tested positive is retained by the laboratory for 12 months, to permit retesting in connection with any administrative appeal the applicant may file. . . . All test results, like all other medical records, are treated as confidential and kept in a confidential medical file. The director of personnel testified that the information is not disclosed to any law enforcement agency.

If the test reveals the presence of drugs for which the applicant has no legitimate medical explanation, the applicant is disqualified from hiring or promotion, and remains ineligible for the period during which the "eligibility list" for the job in question is in force. A disqualified promotional applicant, currently employed by the city in another position, is referred to a mandatory assistance program that includes group counseling and a wide variety of educational programs.

[The court's findings with respect to *current* employees are omitted.] Although the United States Supreme Court has not yet spoken on the issue, we conclude that when, as in the case before us, the drug screening program is administered in a reasonable fashion as part of a lawful preemployment medical examination that is required of each job applicant, drug testing of all job applicants is constitutionally permissible under the Fourth Amendment even though similar drug testing of current employees seeking promotion is not. . . . [I]n evaluating the "reasonableness" of a drug testing program for purposes of the Fourth Amendment, it is necessary to weigh the importance or strength of the governmental interest supporting suspicionless drug testing against the intrusion on reasonable expectations of privacy imposed by such testing. As we explain, we conclude that an employer has a significantly greater need for, and interest in, conducting suspicionless drug testing of job applicants than it does in conducting similar testing of current employees, and also that a drug testing requirement imposes a lesser intrusion on reasonable expectations of privacy when the drug test is conducted as part of a lawful preemployment medical examination that a job applicant is, in any event, required to undergo. Because of these significant differences in both the strength of the interest supporting preemployment drug testing and in the diminished intrusion upon reasonable expectations of privacy implicit in the testing, we conclude that in the preemployment context, unlike the prepromotional context, such drug testing is reasonable, and hence constitutionally permissible, under the Fourth Amendment.

We begin with a consideration of the interest supporting suspicionless drug testing of all job applicants. In light of the well documented problems that are associated with the abuse of drugs and alcohol by employees — increased absenteeism, diminished productivity, greater health costs, increased safety problems and potential liability to third parties, and more frequent turnover[14] — an employer, private or public, clearly has a legitimate (i.e., constitutionally permissible) interest in ascertaining whether persons to be employed in any position currently are abusing drugs or alcohol. Although this interest logically could support drug testing of current employees as well as job applicants, an employer generally need not resort to suspicionless drug testing to determine whether a current employee is likely to be absent from work or less productive or effective as a result of current drug or alcohol abuse: an employer can observe the employee at work, evaluate his or her work product and safety record, and check employment records to determine whether the employee has been excessively absent or late. If a current employee's performance and work record provides some basis for suspecting that the employee presently is abusing drugs or alcohol, the employer will have an individualized basis for requesting that the particular employee undergo drug testing, and current employees whose performance provides no reason to suspect that they currently are using drugs or abusing alcohol will not be compelled to sustain the intrusion on their privacy inherent in mandatory urinalysis testing. (*See* 4 LaFave, *supra,* § 10.3(e), pp. 498-500.)

When deciding whether to hire a job applicant, however, an employer has not had a similar opportunity to observe the applicant over a period of time. Although the employer can request information regarding the applicant's performance in past jobs or in nonemployment settings, an employer reasonably may lack total confidence in the reliability of information supplied by a former employer or other references. And although an employer will, of course, obtain the opportunity to make its own observations after it has hired the applicant, the hiring of a new employee frequently represents a considerable investment on the part of an employer, often involving the training of the new employee. Furthermore, once an applicant is hired, any attempt by the employer to dismiss the employee generally will entail additional expenses, including those relating to the hiring of a replacement. In view of these considerations, we believe that an employer has a greater need for, and interest in, conducting suspicionless drug testing of job applicants than it does in conducting such testing of current employees. (*See* 4

[14] *See, generally*, National Research Council, Under the Influence: Drugs and the American Work Force (1994) pages 129-169, 227; United States Dep't of Health and Human Services, Drugs in the Workplace: Research and Evaluation Data, volume II (1990) pages 11, 228, 231; Larson, Employment Screening, *supra*, sections 1.03, 3.06, pages 1-4 to 1-9, 3-56 to 3-59.

LaFave, *supra*, § 10.3(e), p. 504.)

Turning to the degree of the intrusion on reasonable expectations of privacy imposed by the city's drug testing program, we believe that the intrusion on privacy is significantly diminished because the drug testing urinalysis in this case was administered as part of a preemployment medical examination that the job applicant, in any event, would have been required to undergo. Although, as the [Skinner v. Railway Labor Executives' Ass'n, 489 U.S. 602 (1989)] and [National Treasury Employees Union v. Von Raab, 489 U.S. 656 (1989)] decisions indicate, a requirement that an individual submit to a monitored urinalysis test ordinarily represents a significant intrusion on individual privacy . . . , neither *Skinner* nor *Von Raab* considered whether the intrusion on privacy rises to that level when such drug testing is not administered as a separate procedure (as it was in *Skinner* and *Von Raab*) but rather is conducted as part of a comprehensive medical examination that already includes a urinalysis component.

We believe that, from a realistic standpoint, requiring an individual to undergo a complete medical examination generally entails a significantly greater intrusion on privacy than simply requiring him or her to provide a urine sample for drug testing. After all, a medical examination, in itself, ordinarily requires the individual not only to submit a urine sample but in addition to provide a medical history and to undergo a physical examination that entails an intrusive touching of one's body by a physician. . . . Although in this case the city's addition of the drug screening test to its preexisting medical examination procedure was accompanied by the institution of several new security measures (such as the aural monitoring of the urinalysis process) that entailed some additional intrusion on the applicant's privacy with regard to provision of the urine sample, the incremental intrusion on privacy attributable to these new measures appears rather minor when viewed in the context of a complete medical examination.[17]

Of course, if requiring a job applicant to undergo a preemployment medical examination itself would constitute an unconstitutional intrusion on privacy, the circumstance that the addition of a drug testing component to a medical examination represents only a minimal incremental intrusion on privacy would provide an inadequate basis for finding the intrusive effect of the drug test to be minimal for constitutional purposes. Plaintiff in this case, however, has not contended that the city's examination procedure is unlawful insofar as it requires all job applicants who have been offered employment to submit to a medical examination as a condition of their hiring, and plaintiff has not cited, and our independent research has not revealed, any authority suggesting it is impermissible for an employer to require all job applicants to submit to medical examinations

---

[17] In addition to the aural monitoring feature, the city required applicants to undress to their underwear and put on a hospital gown, and added blue dye in the toilet water to prevent adulteration of the urine sample. The addition of the dye obviously did not intrude on the applicant's interest in privacy. Requiring the applicant partially to disrobe and wear a gown also did not significantly increase the invasion of privacy inherent in the required medical examination, because a physical examination by a physician ordinarily would involve a comparable degree of disrobing. Similarly, although the drug testing program required the applicant to disclose, on the drug screening authorization form, the medications that he or she currently was taking, the required medical examination itself included taking a medical history from the applicant, which ordinarily would include the disclosure of current medications.

without regard to the nature of the position in question.

In this respect, the position of job applicants appears to differ from that of current employees. As we have noted above in connection with the discussion of plaintiff's statutory claim, the recently enacted federal ADA [Americans with Disabilities Act] contains a number of provisions addressing the circumstances under which an employer may require a job applicant or a current employee to undergo a medical examination. Under the ADA, an employer is prohibited from requiring any applicant to submit to a medical examination before the employer has made an offer of employment to the applicant, but once an employer has made a conditional offer of employment the ADA specifically provides that the employer may require the applicant to undergo a medical examination and may condition its offer of employment on the results of the examination so long as all entering employees are required to undergo such an examination. 42 U.S.C. § 12112(d)(2), (3). Furthermore, under the ADA, preemployment, post-offer "[m]edical examinations . . . do not have to be job-related and consistent with business necessity." 29 C.F.R. § 1630.14(b)(3) (1996). By contrast, once an employee has been hired and has begun working, the ADA provides that an employer "shall not require a medical examination . . . unless such examination . . . is shown to be job-related and consistent with business necessity." 42 U.S.C. § 12112(d)(4)(A).

. . . Although the current provisions of the ADA are not, of course, determinative of the scope of a job applicant's reasonable expectation of privacy (for Fourth Amendment purposes) with regard to medical examinations, we believe the statute does accurately reflect the general societal understanding that a requirement that all job applicants submit to a medical examination prior to hiring does not violate a job applicant's reasonable expectation of privacy. As one federal court has observed: "Pre-employment physical examination, including urinalysis, is simply too familiar a feature of the job market on all levels to permit anyone to claim an objectively based expectation of privacy in what such analysis might disclose." Fowler v. New York City Dep't of Sanitation (S.D.N.Y. 1989) 704 F. Supp. 1264, 1270. . . . [19]

Thus, we conclude that an employer has a significantly greater interest in conducting suspicionless drug testing of job applicants than it does in testing current employees seeking promotion, and that the imposition of a urinalysis drug testing requirement on job applicants as part of a lawful preemployment medical examination involves a lesser intrusion on reasonable expectations of privacy than does testing conducted independently of such an examination. In balancing an employer's interest in suspicionless drug testing in this context against the intrusion on a job applicant's reasonable expectation of privacy, we conclude that

[19] Our conclusion with regard to job applicants' reasonable expectations of privacy in relation to medical examinations does not depend upon the circumstances that, in the present case, the city notified job applicants at the outset that a medical examination and drug screening were part of the hiring process and the applicants applied for positions with knowledge of the screening requirement. As the court explained in Nat. Federation of Fed. Employees v. Weinberger (D.C. Cir. 1987) 818 F.2d 935, 943: "[A] search otherwise unreasonable cannot be redeemed by a public employer's exaction of a 'consent' to the search as a condition of employment. . . . Advance notice of the employer's condition, however, may be taken into account as one of the factors relevant to the employees' legitimate expectations of privacy."

the city's urinalysis drug testing of job applicants, administered as part of a lawful preemployment medical examination, is "reasonable" within the meaning of the Fourth Amendment. We believe that this is one of the "limited circumstances," referred to in *Skinner*, "where the privacy interests implicated by the search are minimal, and where an important governmental interest furthered by the intrusion would be placed in jeopardy by a requirement of individualized suspicion. . . ."*Skinner, supra*, 489 U.S. at 624.

In sum, we conclude that the city's across-the-board urinalysis drug testing program . . . does not violate the Fourth Amendment as applied to job applicants.

NOTES AND QUESTIONS

1. A few weeks after *Loder*, the U.S. Supreme Court decided Chandler v. Miller, 520 U.S. 305 (1997), holding that Georgia lacked a sufficient justification to require drug testing of all candidates for public office. The State conceded that the law was not based on any fear or suspicion of actual drug use by public officials. In fact, the Court concluded, the record showed that the requirement served only to display the State's "commitment to the struggle against drug abuse." 520 U.S. at 321. This "symbolic" purpose was insufficient to justify even Georgia's "relatively noninvasive" testing procedure. *Id.* The Court added, however, "Georgia's singular drug test for candidates is not part of a medical examination designed to provide certification of a candidate's general health, and we express no opinion on such examinations." 520 U.S. at 323.

Is *Loder* still good law after *Chandler*? *See also* Lanier v. City of Woodburn, 518 F.3d 1147 (9th Cir. 2008), where the court held that a city's across-the-board testing of library pages was insufficiently justified to survive a Fourth Amendment challenge. The court observed, "While a demonstrated problem of drug abuse might 'shore up' an assertion of special need, Woodburn's showing of an impact on job performance consists of unspecified difficulty with employees under the influence experienced by a few department heads over the years, and one library employee in 23 years who had to undergo rehabilitation on a couple of occasions. . . ." *Id.* at 1151.

2. A key premise of *National Treasury Employees Union* and *Loder* is that drug testing can be accurate with minimally intrusive safeguards against "cheating." *See* 489 U.S. at 676. Is this assumption correct? There is some evidence that it might not be.

A quick Internet search for terms such as "drug test" reveals the easy availability of products purporting to be effective in defeating a drug test. Most of these products are probably worthless and hazardous to the user. Naturally, there is no regulatory agency to validate the effectiveness or safety of anti-drug test products. Nevertheless, the possible effectiveness of some products led the Department of Transportation to amend its regulations in 2008 to require much more intrusive drug testing procedures in the transportation industry. Among other things, the regulations now *require* "partial disrobing" and "direct observation" of urination in certain situations. In BNSF Ry. Co. v. U.S. Dep't of Transp., 566 F.3d 200 (D.C. Cir. 2009), the U.S. Court of Appeals for the District of Columbia upheld the Department's new, much more intrusive method of testing as to *current* employees who are already subject to a drug-related *disciplinary* action.

Job applicants may be in a particularly good position to "cheat" because they are more likely to know exactly when and where a test is to be conducted. Does the possible effectiveness of cheating undermine the value and defensibility of across-the-board testing at the hiring stage? Would an employer be entitled to adopt the highly intrusive disrobing procedure validated in *BNSF Ry.* if it were testing job applicants rather than current employees?

3. Another complication for employment-based drug testing is that the use of marijuana is now lawful under some state laws, sometimes only for medicinal purposes and sometimes for recreational purposes as well. Some job applicants and employees have sued employers for adverse employment actions based on positive test results for marijuana use even when the use of marijuana was not illegal under local law. In general, the courts have held that employers are still free to reject applicants or employees based on marijuana use, either because employment is at will and discrimination against marijuana users is not illegal, or because marijuana use is still illegal under federal law. *See Statutory Protection for "Off-Duty" Conduct* in Chapter 6.A, *infra*.

4. Still another complication for employment-based drug testing is purposeful or inadvertent detection of prescription medications that reveal disabilities, such as pain-killers, psychological medications, and medicines for lawful treatment of addiction. The Americans with Disabilities Act limits the use of medical examinations in employee selection, 42 U.S.C. § 12112(d), but it also provides that a test to determine the "*illegal*" use of drugs is not a "medical examination" for purposes of that law. 42 U.S.C. § 12114(d) (emphasis added). However, it may be impossible to distinguish legal use of some disability-revealing medications from the illegal use of drugs without a careful interview of the applicant or employee about disabilities. This complication makes it even more important for an employer to rely on an independent drug-testing service to conduct the testing, and to postpone the testing until after a conditional offer of employment when ADA restrictions on medical examinations and inquiries are more relaxed. 42 U.S.C. § 12112(d)(3). In any event, an employer cannot discriminate on the basis of a physical or mental disability unless the condition renders the employee unable to perform the essential requirements of the job even with reasonable accommodation or would lead to a "direct threat to the health and safety of other individuals in the workplace. 42 U.S.C. § 12113(a), (b).

5. *Loder* and *National Treasury Employees' Union* do not address tort law implications of drug testing of applicants in the private sector. However, assuming a private sector job applicant could overcome the problem of consent to a drug test, the analysis of a tort claim is likely to be very similar to the analysis of a Fourth Amendment claim. *See* Baughman v. Wal-Mart Stores, Inc., 592 S.E.2d 824 (W. Va. 2003) (rejecting a tort claim against testing of private sector applicants). This similarity of analysis is especially likely in California where the state constitution is the source of a right of privacy that extends to the private sector. *See* Kaslawsky v. Upper Deck Co., 65 Cal. Rptr. 2d 297 (Cal. App. 1997).

6. An applicant might object that drug testing is not only intrusive, it is inaccurate. There are many possible causes of "false positives," and some types of tests are more prone to yielding false positives than others. Drug tests do not search

for drugs, they search for the byproducts of drug use — drug metabolites. However, a drug test might fail to distinguish between metabolites of illegal drugs and metabolites of legal substances, such as decongestants and poppy seeds. Not surprisingly, less expensive tests such as immunoassay screening are less accurate than more expensive tests, such as gas chromatography/mass spectrometry tests. Hair tests are subject to an additional objection: The problem of passive exposure, especially to drugs that are smoked. Finally, there is the possibility of human error in the handling of the sample, the performance of the test, and the communication of the result. The risk of error is compounded when an employer relies on its own regular personnel to perform the sample collection or testing process, and the risk is greatest if the employer uses one of several widely marketed do-it-yourself onsite drug testing kits, such as "oral" tests based on an examinee's saliva. *See generally* Mark A. Rothstein, *Drug Testing in the Workplace: The Challenge to Employment Relations and Employment Law*, 63 Chi.-Kent L. Rev. 683 (1987); Mark A. Rothstein, *Workplace Drug Testing: A Case Study in the Misapplication of Technology*, 5 Harv. J.L. & Tech. 65 (1991); American Civil Liberties Union, Drug Testing: A Bad Investment (1999), at http://archive.aclu.org/issues/worker/drugtesting1999.pdf.

7. Whether or not a laboratory or employer has been negligent in conducting or interpreting a drug test, an examinee is usually in a poor position to challenge the test, identify and prove negligence, or prove that negligence was the cause of a "false" positive, At the outset, the examinee must prove by a preponderance of the evidence that he did not use drugs and that the test result was a *false* positive. Is it possible to prove such a negative proposition, other than by one's own sworn denial of drug use?

In Mission Petroleum Carriers, Inc. v. Solomon, 106 S.W.3d 705 (Tex. 2003), the plaintiff alleged his employer negligently performed a urinalysis test, and he evidently persuaded the jury that the test result that led to his discharge was a false positive. Among other things, the plaintiff introduced evidence of the negative result of a hair test conducted after his discharge.[8] The plaintiff also pointed to the employer's general mismanagement of its drug testing program. To save money, the employer had conducted its own on-site collection of urine samples. Moreover, the manager who received the plaintiff's sample was subject to a deferred adjudication for an unspecified offense, and the terms of his probation required random drug testing. A Texas court of appeals upheld a jury verdict in favor of the plaintiff, but the Texas Supreme Court reversed.

The Court noted that the employer's drug testing program was pursuant to U.S. Department of Transportation regulations providing for the administration of drug tests. The Department's regulations allowed the plaintiff a number of "avenues of redress." 106 S.W.3d at 713. For example, the plaintiff could have immediately challenged the chain of custody with respect to his test sample, or he could have filed an administrative protest challenging the defendant carrier's testing procedure. If the plaintiff had followed these procedures, and if the Federal Highway Administration had agreed that the defendant carrier's testing procedure

---

[8] This and some other important facts of the case are described in the lower court's opinion, Mission Petroleum Carriers, Inc. v. Solomon, 37 S.W.3d 482 (Tex. App. 2001).

was faulty, the FHA might have granted relief designed to "assure that the complainant is not subject to harassment, intimidation, disciplinary action, discrimination, or financial loss." 106 S.W.3d at 714, quoting 49 C.F.R. § 386.12. The court concluded, "the DOT regulations strike the appropriate balance between the need for efficient drug testing and the requirement that each employee have the means to insist on the integrity of the process.... We therefore decline to impose a common law duty on employers who conduct in-house urine specimen collection under the DOT regulations."106 S.W.3d 714-715.

8. Assuming an applicant/employee's common law negligence claim is not superseded by administrative regulations or local statutes, his claim against the party who actually performed the test is more likely to be viable than his claim against an employer who merely relied on the results of the test. See section D.1.a of this chapter, *supra*.

9. The problem of "consent," the practical difficulty of proving negligence and causation, and the lack of an employer duty to be "fair" in "employment at will," severely limit the effectiveness of the common law as a source of protection against intrusive or mismanaged drug testing. Statutory regulation might be a better answer. As noted above, the Department of Transportation regulates drug testing in the transportation industry and provides a procedure for administrative appeals. *See* Omnibus Transportation Employee Testing Act, 49 U.S.C. §§ 20140, 31306 and 45101-45106. In addition, many states have adopted statutes to regulate drug and alcohol testing by employers. However, these statutes and regulations also tend to endorse drug testing. Indeed, these laws arguably serve the interests of employers more than employees, because they specifically authorize testing in a wide range of circumstances, supersede the common law, and bar employee lawsuits against employers who comply with prescribed procedures. Ariz. Rev. Stat. Ann. §§ 23-493.01 to .09; Ark. Code Ann. §§ 11-14-101 to -112; Neb. Rev. Stat. § 48-1910. Some states even encourage drug testing by offering a reduction in workers' compensation insurance premiums for employers who adopt drug testing polices. *See, e.g.*, Ark. Code Ann. §§ 11-14-106, -112.

Drug and alcohol testing laws frequently allow testing in a much wider range of circumstances for applicants than for current employees. *See, e.g.*, Ark. Code Ann. §§ 11-14-102, -106 (permitting testing of all applicants but restricting testing of current employees); Conn. Gen. Stat. Ann. § 31-51v, -51x (same); Me. Rev. Stat. Ann. § 684 (same); Minn. Stat. Ann. § 181.951; R.I. Gen. Laws Ann. § 28-6.5-2. They also frequently distinguish applicants from employees with respect to the substances for which testing is permitted: testing for alcohol impairment is frequently reserved for current employees and limited to occasions when the employer has reason to believe the employee is under the influence of alcohol. *See, e.g.*, Ariz. Rev. Stat. Ann. §§ 23-493.01; Or. Rev. Stat. § 659.225.

Laws that authorize testing typically require some mixture of the following safeguards for applicants and employees:

— Advance notification or written policies regarding testing. *See, e.g.*, Ariz. Rev. Stat. Ann. § 23-493.04; Ark. Code Ann. §§ 11-14-105; Conn. Gen. Stat. Ann. § 31-51v; Me. Rev. Stat. Ann. § 683; Minn. Stat. Ann. § 181.951; Vt. Stat. Ann. § 514.

— Limiting tests of job applicants to those who have already received conditional offers of employment. Minn. Stat. Ann. § 181.951; R.I. Gen. Laws Ann. § 28-6.5-2.

— Rules regarding disrobing or visual monitoring of persons subjected to testing. Me. Rev. Stat. Ann. § 683; R.I. Gen. Laws Ann. § 28-6.5-2.

— Testing only by certified or licensed laboratories. *See, e.g.*, Ariz. Rev. Stat. Ann. § 23-493.03; Me. Rev. Stat. Ann. § 683; Minn. Stat. Ann. § 181.951; Neb. Rev. Stat. § 48-1903; Vt. Stat. Ann. § 514.

— Precautions against contamination or misidentification. *See, e.g.*, Ariz. Rev. Stat. Ann. § 23-493.03; Ark. Code Ann. §§ 11-14-107; Me. Rev. Stat. Ann. § 683; Minn. Stat. Ann. § 181.953; Vt. Stat. Ann. § 514.

— Limitations on the purposes for which test may be conducted or the substances for which testing may be conducted. *See, e.g.*, Ariz. Rev. Stat. Ann. § 23-493.09; Me. Rev. Stat. Ann. § 683; Vt. Stat. Ann. § 514.

— Secondary or confirmation testing for applicants and employees who test "positive" in an initial test. *See, e.g.*, Ariz. Rev. Stat. Ann. § 23-493.03; Ark. Code Ann. §§ 11-14-107; Conn. Gen. Stat. Ann. § 31-51u; Me. Rev. Stat. Ann. § 685; Minn. Stat. Ann. § 181.953; Neb. Rev. Stat. § 48-1903; R.I. Gen. Laws Ann. § 28-6.5-2; Vt. Stat. Ann. § 514.

— Provisions for appealing or challenging the results of a test. Ark. Code Ann. §§ 11-14-105; Me. Rev. Stat. Ann. § 683.

— Provisions for an employee's right of access to test results or samples. *See, e.g.*, Ariz. Rev. Stat. Ann. § 23-493.09; Me. Rev. Stat. Ann. § 683; Minn. Stat. Ann. § 81.953; Vt. Stat. Ann. § 514.

— A current employee's right to participate in a drug rehabilitation program at the employee's expense, before disciplinary action. Minn. Stat. Ann. § 181.953.

— Precautions to protect the confidentiality of test results. *See, e.g.*, Ariz. Rev. Stat. Ann. § 23-493.04, .09; Me. Rev. Stat. Ann. § 685; Minn. Stat. Ann. § 181.954.

— Nondiscrimination rules, including requirements that all compensated employees (including, e.g., officers, directors, and supervisors) must be subject to the same uniform policy. *See, e.g.*, Ariz. Rev. Stat. Ann. § 23-493.04; Minn. Stat. Ann. § 181.951.

10. Whether or not an employer chooses to implement a drug testing policy, many employers must establish a workplace drug policy by virtue of the Drug-Free Workplace Act of 1988, 41 U.S.C. §§ 701 et seq. An employer is subject to the act if it has a federal contract in excess of $25,000. The act does not require drug testing. Nor does it permit an employer to conduct testing that would be illegal under any other law. The employer must simply adopt and distribute a policy prohibiting illegal drug-related activities in the workplace, providing penalties for violations, and establishing a program to educate employees about the dangers of drugs and the availability of rehabilitation and counseling services.

4. *Polygraph Examinations and Other Tests of Honesty and Character*

VEAZEY v. COMMUNICATIONS & CABLE OF CHICAGO, INC.

194 F.3d 850 (7th Cir. 1999)

[The facts and other parts of the court's opinion are reproduced at Chapter 6, Part B(3), note 8, *infra.*]

The polygraph is composed of a combination of devices which measure certain, specified physical data.[3] In 1895, an Italian psychiatrist and criminologist named Cesare Lombroso made the unprecedented claim that he could "detect lies" by monitoring a person's blood pressure and "reading" the changes in it. *See* Michael Tiner & Daniel J. O'Grady, *Lie Detectors in Employment*, 23 Harv. C.R.-C.L. L. Rev. 85, 85-86 (1988). Lombroso asserted that by understanding the typical criminal responses and physical characteristics he could distinguish "criminal types" from the rest of society. *See id.* Over a hundred years later, his claims continue to shape society's perceptions of polygraphs and account for their popularity. [A] 1978 survey of four hundred major U.S. corporations found that more than fifty percent of the commercial banks and retailers that had responded to the survey used polygraphs. *See* Belt & Holden, *Polygraph Usage Among Major U.S. Corporations*, 51 Personnel J. 80, 86 (February 1978). The survey also noted that these companies were more likely to test all job applicants and employees than to conduct random sampling. *See id.*

As polygraph machines gained popularity in the American business world, many researchers and defense lawyers began to question the accuracy of the machine that was dictating numerous peoples' employment fate. Several studies concerning polygraph validity were published in the late 1970's and early 1980's, and contributed greatly to the understanding of the lie detector's limitations.[4]

---

[3] The standard polygraph has three components: a blood pressure cuff, a galvanic skin response indicator, and a pneumatic chest tube. The blood pressure cuff is attached to a person's upper arm to record changes in blood pressure. The galvanic skin response indicator measures changes in the skin's electrical conductivity, which increases when a person perspires. It consists of two electrodes which are attached to the index and second fingers of one hand. The pneumatic chest tube is strapped around the chest to measure alterations in breathing patterns. Other components can be added to the standard polygraph. Some polygraphs include a pneumatic tube which is stretched around a person's throat to gauge swallowing, contractions of the throat, and voice muscle tension. The more "sophisticated" polygraphs may also be connected to chairs which have seats and armrests wired to monitor muscle pressure and body movements.

[4] To this day, the scientific community remains skeptical and has grave doubts about the reliability of polygraph techniques. *See* 1 D. Faigman, D. Kaye, M. Saks, & J. Sanders, *Modern Scientific Evidence* 565, n.14-2.0, and § 14-3.0 (1997); 1 P. Giannelli & E. Imwinkelried, *Scientific Evidence* § 8-2(C), pp. 225-27 (2d ed.1993); 1 J. Strong, McCormick on Evidence § 206, p. 909 (4th ed. 1992). Even ignoring the basic debate about the reliability of polygraph technology itself, the controversy remains over the efficacy of countermeasures, and the fact that examinees may deliberately adopt strategies that provoke physiological responses that will obscure accurate readings and thus "fool" the polygraph machine and the examiner. *See* Iacono & Lykken, The Scientific Status of Research on Polygraph Techniques: The Case Against Polygraph Tests, in 1 Modern Scientific Evidence § 14-3.0 (1997).

FIELD STUDIES

1. Benjamin Kleinmuntz & Julian J. Szucko, *On the Fallibility of Lie Detection*, 17 L. & Soc'y Rev. 85 (1982)

In 1982, Kleinmuntz and Szucko obtained the charts of one hundred polygraph examinations which were performed by the then well-known Reid Polygraph Agency . . . [on] fifty charts that had been verified as deceptive by the subsequent confessions of the examinees and fifty charts that had been verified as truthful by the subsequent confessions of other people. Polygraphers from the well recognized Reid agency then independently rescored all one hundred charts, incorrectly classifying 39% of the verified innocent examinees as guilty.

2. Frank Horvath, The Effect of Selected Variables on Interpretation of Polygraph Records, 62 J. Applied Psychol. 127 (1977)

In 1977, Horvath published a polygraph validity study using fifty-six polygraph examination charts — all of which had been verified by using subsequent confessions made to police. Ten polygraphers then independently rescored the examination charts. Of the now established innocent examinees, only 51% were correctly scored as truthful when denying their guilt — hardly better than simply flipping a coin. . . .

4. Congressional Office of Technology Assessment (O.T.A.) Summary of Studies (1983)

The O.T.A. reviewed ten field studies of polygraph validity and found that the results of these studies varied widely. *See* Congressional Office of Technology Assessment, Scientific Validity of Polygraph Testing: A Research Review and Evaluation (A Technical Memorandum), OTA-TMH-15, 98th Cong., 1st Sess. 5 (1983). O.T.A. summarized its findings as follows:

1. false negatives (incorrectly classifying a deceptive person as truthful) varied from 29.4% to 0%;
2. false positives (incorrectly classifying a truthful individual as deceptive) varied from 75% to 0%;
3. inconclusive results varied from 25% to 0%;
4. correct guilty detections varied from 98.6% to 70.6%;
5. correct innocent detections varied from 94.1% to 12.5%.

The significance of a 90%, 80%, or 70% polygraph validity rate cannot be fully understood unless one understands what that figure means to an individual seeking employment or facing criminal charges. In fact, O.T.A. determined that the mathematical chance of false positives is greatest when polygraphs are used randomly to test large numbers of employees because, according to O.T.A., only a small percentage of screened individuals are actually guilty. For example, if one out of one thousand people is actually guilty and we posit that a polygraph will be 99% accurate in determining truthful statements, then the law of probability would dictate that not only would one person be correctly identified as guilty but so would ten innocent people. . . .

Armed with these studies . . . , the [Employee Polygraph Protection Act of 1987] was enacted, prohibiting private employers, in most situations, from subjecting job applicants or employees to lie detector tests.

[The court's decision is continued on pp. 591-92, *infra.*]

Polygraph Examinations and the EPPA

The Employee Polygraph Protection Act of 1987 (EPPA), 29 U.S.C. §§ 2001-2009, strictly prohibits an employer's use of a "lie detector" in some situations, and strictly regulates the use of such a device in other situations. The act defines "lie detector" as a "polygraph, deceptograph, voice stress analyzer, psychological stress evaluator or any other similar device (whether mechanical or electrical) that is used, or the results of which are used, for the purpose of rendering a diagnostic opinion regarding the honesty or dishonesty of an individual." *Id.* § 2001(3).

In general, the act deals separately with two different employer uses of a lie detector: (1) screening job applicants, and (2) investigation of current employees suspected of specific wrongdoing. The act absolutely prohibits the use of lie detectors for screening job applicants by employers subject to the act (i.e., nearly all private sector employers). On the other hand, the act permits the use of a "polygraph" (which is one type of "lie detector") to investigate current employees suspected of specific wrongdoing, subject to important restrictions. The distinguishing feature of a "polygraph," in comparison with other "lie detectors," is that it records an examinee's "cardiovascular, respiratory, and electrodermal" responses to a question. *Id.* § 2001(4).

Congress evidently believed the polygraph — but not other lie detectors — has some usefulness as an investigatory tool for specific incidents of wrongdoing, despite questions about its accuracy and fears that it will stigmatize innocent employees. Why then the complete ban against polygraphs or other lie detectors for screening job applicants? For purposes of comparison, recall that legal regulation of drug testing is usually lightest in the hiring phase.

There appears to be widespread agreement, even by many leading proponents of the polygraph, that the polygraph is least effective as a tool for testing the character or job aptitude of applicants for employment. When used to screen job applicants without reference to the investigation of a particular incident, the polygraph examination usually takes the form of the so-called relevant-irrelevant question test in which the examiner asks questions that are "relevant" to some subject matter (such as the applicant's job qualifications), and "neutral" questions that are not relevant. There is little or no scientific evidence that this use of the polygraph is effective for testing deceptiveness or other character traits or aptitudes. *See* Senate Committee on Labor and Human Resources, Senate Report 100-284, *The Polygraph Protection Act of 1987*, pp. 41-43 (Feb. 11, 1988). Nevertheless, before the EPPA, job applicant screening was by far the most common setting for more than two million polygraph examinations conducted every year. *Id.* at 41, 46. Some employers who used or still use the polygraph to screen applicants maintain that they do not care whether it is truly accurate. Instead, they use the polygraph because it encourages applicants to be honest. *See* Charles Honts, *The Emperor's New Clothes: Application of Polygraph Tests in the American Workplace,* Forensic

Reports, vol. 9, pp. 91, 97-98 (1991).

One might attempt to improve the accuracy of the test by using the same methodology traditionally used in criminal investigations, the so-called control question test. One example of the control question method in the employment context was described by the court in Woodland v. City of Houston, 918 F. Supp. 1047 (S.D. Tex. 1996), *vacated pursuant to agreement of the parties*, 1996 WL 752803 (5th Cir. 1996). The district court found that the employer police department had administered applicant screening polygraph examinations that included questions about sexual relations with wives, other married women, girlfriends, and animals; sexual activities including homosexual behavior, masturbation, and sexual positions; criminal activity as an adult or as a child (including, for example, taking money from a mother's purse without permission as a child); drug use; and membership in "radical" organizations. Polygraph examiners often include such unsettling questions because they serve as the "control questions" in the control question method. The examiner assumes all or most people have committed one or more of these transgressions, and he compares the examinee's reaction to such questions with the examinee's reaction to other questions that are the real purpose of the examination. *See* Honts, *supra*, at 91-116.

Whether or not this method of examination is any more accurate, it is potentially much more invasive. If questioning a person about his or her private sexual activities or other embarrassing matters in the course of a personal interview would ordinarily be deemed offensive, is such questioning any less offensive as a control question in the course of a professionally administered polygraph examination? Or is it potentially *more* unsettling and threatening?

For some individual examinees, the experience of being connected to a machine and being exposed to the often intimidating and embarrassing interrogation of the examiner may be emotionally damaging regardless of whether there is much to hide. In at least one case, a court upheld a bank teller's claim that she suffered severe distress as a consequence of an employer-administered polygraph examination in the course of an investigation of theft. *See* Kamrath v. Suburban Natl. Bank, 363 N.W.2d 108 (Minn. Ct. App. 1985). Persons applying for police or security positions might be expected to take the process in stride. However, the same cannot be said for many job applicants seeking positions involving nothing more than the usual employer interest in honesty and integrity.

The potentially wide-ranging scope of an examination and its control questions lead to additional risks: employer misuse and mishandling of personal information. An examinee's response to control questions might reveal much more information than the employer would have sought in a normal interview or application form. If the examiner reveals these answers to the employer, the employer might find new reasons to discriminate based on personal lifestyle. The damage to the examinee might be compounded if the examiner or the employer fail to safeguard this information to prevent its misuse or disclosure to other parties. *Compare* Hester v. City of Milledgeville, 777 F.2d 1492 (11th Cir. 1985) (approving use of control questions, based on lack of evidence of employer's misuse of data from control questions) with Texas State Employees' Union v. Texas Dep't of Mental Health & Mental Retardation, 746 S.W.2d 203 (Tex. 1987) (control questions violated constitutional right of privacy of public employees).

NOTES AND QUESTIONS

1. The EPPA prohibits the use of any lie detector for employee selection, but not in the case of certain exempt industries and professions. Most important, the act does not apply to federal, state, and local government employers (although some states have enacted their own laws for public employees). 29 U.S.C. § 2006(a). The Senate Report accompanying the act states that "the legislation does not apply in situations where a government is the employer, primarily because the Constitution does." Senate Committee on Labor and Human Resources, Senate Report 100-284, *The Polygraph Protection Act of 1987*, pp. 41-43 (Feb. 11, 1988).

Does the Constitution limit a public employer's administration of a lie detector test? The U.S. Constitution creates at least two types of privacy arguably applying to a lie detector test administered to job applicants. The first is the Fourth Amendment's prohibition against an unreasonable "search." Is it a "search" to attach sensing devices to an examinee's body in order to measure and record the examinee's physiological responses to a series of questions? In Greenawalt v. Indiana Dep't of Corrections, 397 F.3d 587 (7th Cir. 2005), the court answered "no." The essence of a lie detector test, the court reasoned, is interrogation, but asking questions does not constitute a Fourth Amendment "search," even if the questioner uses a device to measure the examinee's physiological response.

A second possible source of protection under the Constitution is the right of informational privacy, which might apply to questions an employer asks whether or not the employer uses a lie detector. *See* sections D.1.b & D.2 of this chapter, *supra*. Whether employer questions violate a job applicant's informational right of privacy depends on whether the questions are unreasonably intrusive or degrading. 397 F.3d at 592. Employer use of a lie detector makes a violation more likely if only because the examiner is more likely to ask intrusive "control" questions.

In any event, courts that have entertained such claims have not always barred the use of lie detectors to screen applicants for public jobs, especially when the employer is hiring police officers or other personnel responsible for matters of public security. *See, e.g.*, Chesna v. Dep't of Def., 850 F. Supp. 110 (D. Conn. 1994) (revocation of security clearance); O'Hartigan v. Dep't of Pers., 821 P.2d 44 (Wash. 1991) (word processor position with state patrol); Flood v. City of Suffolk, 820 F. Supp. 709 (E.D.N.Y. 1993); Bd. of Trustees of Miami Twp. v. Fraternal Order of Police, 690 N.E.2d 1262 (Ohio 1998) (police officer position).

2. The EPPA exempts private sector employers providing security services or engaged in manufacture, sale, or distribution of certain controlled substances, 29 U.S.C. § 2006(e), (f), and it exempts the federal government's administration of tests to private sector job applicants of contractors with certain agencies, such as the Department of Defense. *Id.* §§ 2006(b), (c). These exemptions may additionally preempt state laws limiting lie detectors. *See* Stehney v. Perry, 101 F.3d 925 (3d Cir. 1996) (EPPA preempted New Jersey polygraph law that might have prohibited national security clearance examination that EPPA permitted).

3. The EPPA's definition of "lie detector" is broad. It preemptively regulates employer use of *any* lie detecting "device" (other than a polygraph for investigatory purposes), whether it exists today or is invented and marketed in the future. Senate Committee on Labor and Human Resources, Senate Report 100-

284, *The Polygraph Protection Act of 1987*, p. 47 (Feb. 11, 1988).

Honesty and Personality Tests

Not all techniques for testing "honesty" or character rely on a "mechanical or electrical" device or instrument. Some employers use a paper and pencil variety of "honesty" or personality testing, or even "handwriting analysis" in an attempt to reveal an applicant's true character. The EPPA does not apply to these tests, nor do many state laws that regulate the use of lie detectors in the employment context. *See, e.g.*, State v. Century Camera, Inc., 309 N.W.2d 735 (Minn. 1981); Pluskota v. Roadrunner Freight Systems, Inc., 524 N.W.2d 904 (Wis. App. 1994), *rev. denied*, 531 N.W.2d 325 (Wis. 1995). An incidental effect of the EPPA may have been to turn employers away from mechanical or electrical "lie detector" examination toward these alternative paper and pencil methods.

Empirical support for the effectiveness of paper and pencil tests of honesty and other personality traits is mixed, at best. *See* Susan Stabile, *The Use of Personality Tests as a Hiring Tool: Is the Benefit Worth the Cost?* 4 U. Pa. J. Lab. & Emp. L. 279 (2002); David Yamada, *The Regulation of Pre-Employment Honesty Testing: Striking a Temporary(?) Balance Between Self-Regulation and Prohibition*, 39 Wayne L. Rev. 1549, 1555-1562 (1993). Such tests are suspect not only because of the doubtfulness of identifying personality traits by a paper and pencil test, but also because answers to some questions might be scored as evidence of "dishonesty" when they just as likely represent other character traits. One review of honesty tests available to employers concluded that "the most consistent finding was that open-minded people fail honesty tests." *Id.* at 1561, quoting Guastello & Rieke, *A Review and Critique of Honesty Test Research*, Behavioral Sci. & L. 501, 513 (1991).

One potential legal obstacle for paper and pencil "honesty" or "personality" tests is the Americans with Disabilities Act, which prohibits an employer's use of medical inquiries or examinations until after an offer of employment, and which greatly restricts the use of medical examinations or inquiries after hiring. *See* Section C.3 of this chapter. Whether the ADA restricts the use of a paper and pencil test depends on whether the test qualifies as a "medical examination."

In Karraker v. Rent-A-Center, Inc., 411 F.3d 831 (7th Cir. 2005), three brothers sued Rent-A-Center (RAC) because RAC had required them to take a paper and pencil test of mental acumen and "personality" to qualify for promotion into to management. The test included questions from the Minnesota Multiphasic Personality Inventory (MMPI), which was designed in part to measure traits such as depression, hypochondriasis, hysteria, paranoia, and mania. Elevated scores for some traits can be used to diagnose psychiatric disorders. Any applicant who had more than 12 "weighted deviations" was disqualified. All three of the Karraker brothers were disqualified by the test. In their ADA lawsuit against the employer, they alleged that the MMPI was a medical examination and that it was unlawful to use the MMPI in selecting employees for promotion.

To answer the question whether the MMPI was a medical examination, the court first looked to EEOC regulations interpreting the ADA. The EEOC defines "medical examination" as "a procedure or test that seeks information about an individual's physical or mental impairments or health." *ADA Enforcement*

Guidance: Preemployment Disability-Related Questions and Medical Examinations (1995). For purposes of determining whether any "test" is a medical examination, relevant factors include :

(1) whether the test is administered by a health care professional;

(2) whether the test is interpreted by a health care professional;

(3) whether the test is designed to reveal an impairment of physical or mental health;

(4) whether the test is invasive;

(5) whether the test measures an employee's performance of a task or measures his/her physiological responses to performing the task;

(6) whether the test normally is given in a medical setting; and

(7) whether medical equipment is used.

Id. Just one of these factors may be enough to determine that a test is "medical." *Id.* The central inquiry, however, is whether the test is "designed to identify a mental *disorder or impairment*" (a "medical examination") or whether it is "designed to measure *personality traits* such as honesty, preferences, and habits" (not a "medical examination"). *Id.*

RAC argued that it had not *used* the MMPI as a medical examination because it had not employed a psychologist to interpret the results, it used the "vocational" protocol for scoring the test (as opposed to the "clinical" protocol used by doctors), and it *used* the test only to identify "personality" characteristics. The court rejected this argument.

The mere fact that a psychologist did not interpret the MMPI is not, however, dispositive. The ... practical effect of the use of the MMPI is similar no matter how the test is used or scored—that is, whether or not RAC used the test to weed out applicants with certain disorders, its use of the MMPI likely had the effect of excluding employees with disorders from promotions.

[RAC's expert witness] Dr. Koransky claims, for example, that the Pa scale "does not diagnose or detect any psychological disorders," but that "an elevated score on the Pa scale is one of several symptoms which may contribute" to a diagnosis of paranoid personality disorder. We accept Dr. Koransky's contention that a high score on the Pa scale does not necessarily mean that the person has paranoid personality disorder. But it also seems likely that a person who does, in fact, have paranoid personality disorder, and is therefore protected under the ADA, would register a high score on the Pa scale. And that high score could end up costing the applicant any chance of a promotion. Because it is designed, at least in part, to reveal mental illness and has the effect of hurting the employment prospects of one with a mental disability, we think the MMPI is best categorized as a medical examination. . . .

The Karrakers also sued for public disclosure of private facts under Illinois tort law. However, the court upheld dismissal of this claim because the Karrakers could not prove that RAC disclosed or allowed disclosure of their test results to the public or any person with whom the Karrakers had a special relationship.

NOTES AND QUESTIONS

1. In an earlier proceeding at the district court in the same case, 239 F. Supp. 2d 828 (C.D. Ill. 2004), the court held that the plaintiffs had standing to assert "examination" claims under the ADA even though they were not disabled. First, the court relied on the terms of the ADA medical examination provision, 29 U.S.C. § 12112(d), which among other things prohibits medical examination of "applicants," apparently without regard to whether an applicant is disabled. Second, the court found that granting standing to non-disabled examinees was consistent with the purpose of the act. The court reasoned, "[i]t makes little sense to require an employee to demonstrate that he has a disability to prevent his employer from inquiring as to whether or not he has a disability." 239 F. Supp. 2d at 835, quoting Roe v. Cheyenne Mountain Conf. Resort, Inc., 124 F.3d 1221, 1229 (10th Cir. 1997). Nevertheless, the issue whether non-disabled persons have standing to challenge testing that might violate the ADA continues to divide the courts. *See* Psychological Testing of Employee or Job Applicant as Violation of Americans with Disabilities Act or Rehabilitation Act, 24 A.L.R.3d art. 1 (2017).

2. If a personality test or psychological evaluation could be a "medical examination" for purposes of the ADA, what about "counseling" an employer requires for an employee based on the employer's belief that the employee is suffering from depression? *See* Kroll v. White Lake Ambulance Auth., 691 F.3d 809 (6th Cir. 2012) (finding issue of fact as to whether employer's request that employee seek psychological counseling constituted a violation of the ADA).

3. If administration of a personality or psychological test is a "medical examination" under the ADA, an employer's use of such testing might still be lawful if the test is sufficiently "job related" and supported by job necessity. For example, an employer might be able to prove a certain test score is significantly correlated with success on the job. Proving such a correlation is not easy, and the correlation, if any, might be insignificant for the job in question. Note that the employer in *Karraker* made no attempt to prove a correlation between test score and performance on the job. However, courts tend to grant employers considerable leeway in requiring psychological testing to identify possible mental illness as part of an investigation of *current* employees based on *actual and observed* behavioral problems. Under these circumstances the courts have not required scientific proof of a test's predictive value for performance in a particular job. *See* Psychological Testing of Employee or Job Applicant as Violation of Americans with Disabilities Act or Rehabilitation Act, 24 A.L.R.3d art. 1 (2017).

4. Depending on the types of questions included in a personality test, it might provoke other types of discrimination claims. In Soroka v. Dayton Hudson Corp., 1 Cal. Rptr. 2d 77 (Cal. App. 1991), the employer required applicants for security guard (SSO) positions at its Target stores to take a "Psychscreen" test. The court described the test as follows:

> The Psychscreen is a combination of the Minnesota Multiphasic Personality Inventory and the California Psychological Inventory. Both of these tests have been used to screen out emotionally unfit applicants for public safety positions such as police officers, correctional officers, pilots, air traffic controllers and nuclear power plant operators. The test is

> composed of 704 true-false questions. At Target, the test administrator is told to instruct applicants to answer every question.
>
> The test includes questions about an applicant's religious attitudes, such as: "[¶] 67. I feel sure that there is only one true religion.... [¶] 201. I have no patience with people who believe there is only one true religion.... [¶] 477. My soul sometimes leaves my body.... [¶] 483. A minister can cure disease by praying and putting his hand on your head.... [¶] 486. Everything is turning out just like the prophets of the Bible said it would.... [¶] 505. I go to church almost every week. [¶] 506. I believe in the second coming of Christ.... [¶] 516. I believe in a life hereafter.... [¶] 578. I am very religious (more than most people).... [¶] 580. I believe my sins are unpardonable.... [¶] 606. I believe there is a God.... [¶] 688. I believe there is a Devil and a Hell in afterlife."
>
> The test includes questions that might reveal an applicant's sexual orientation, such as: "[¶] 137. I wish I were not bothered by thoughts about sex .... [¶] 290. I have never been in trouble because of my sex behavior.... [¶] 339. I have been in trouble one or more times because of my sex behavior.... [¶] 466. My sex life is satisfactory.... [¶] 492. I am very strongly attracted by members of my own sex.... [¶] 496. I have often wished I were a girl. (Or if you are a girl) I have never been sorry that I am a girl.... [¶] 525. I have never indulged in any unusual sex practices.... [¶] 558. I am worried about sex matters.... [¶] 592. I like to talk about sex.... [¶] 640. Many of my dreams are about sex matters."
>
> An SSO's completed test is scored by the consulting psychologist firm of Martin-McAllister. The firm interprets test responses and rates the applicant on five traits: emotional stability, interpersonal style, addiction potential, dependability and reliability, and socialization — i.e., a tendency to follow established rules. Martin-McAllister sends a form to Target rating the applicant on these five traits and recommending whether to hire the applicant.

Id. at 79. The court of appeals held that the employer's use of the test constituted unlawful discrimination based on religion, because many of the questions inquired about religious beliefs, as well as sexual orientation discrimination. *Id.* at 87-88.

5. Like the *Karraker* plaintiffs, the *Soroka* plaintiffs claimed an employer's administration of the test constituted an invasion of privacy. The *Soroka* plaintiffs, however, were more successful because of unique features of California privacy law. First, California's constitutional right of privacy applies to the private sector in much the same way it applies to the public sector. *Id.* at 82. Second, under California law as interpreted by the court in *Soroka*, an applicant enjoys the same right to privacy as a current employee, and an applicant's "consent" to a test does not foreclose a privacy claim. *Id.* at 82-85. Third, the *Soroka* plaintiffs established that the Psychscreen included intrusive questions; thus, the employer had to satisfy the "compelling interest" standard applicable to a public institution's intrusion. *Id.* at 85-86. The court held that an employer has a compelling interest in using such a test if it proves a "nexus" between test results and job performance. However,

> Target . . . did no more than to make generalized claims about the Psychscreen's relationship to emotional fitness and to assert that it has seen an overall improvement in SSO quality and performance since it

> implemented the Psychscreen. This is not sufficient to constitute a compelling interest, nor does it satisfy the nexus requirement.

Id. at 86.

6. In *Soroka*, the court of appeals reversed the trial court's denial of a temporary injunction against the employer's continued use of the Psychscreen. The California Supreme Court initially granted review of the *Soroka* case, but later dismissed review on the grounds that the parties' settlement agreement rendered the case moot. Soroka v. Dayton Hudson Corp., 862 P.2d 148 (Cal. 1993). The settlement agreement was reported to have included payment of $1.3 million to about 2,500 applicants to whom Target administered the test. *See* W. Camara & P. Merenda, *Using Personality Tests in Preemployment Screening: Issues Raised in Soroka v. Dayton Hudson Corp.*, 6 Psychol., Pub. Pol'y L. 1164, 1167 & n.2 (2000).

7. At least two states, Massachusetts and Rhode Island, have enacted statutes prohibiting or limiting the use of personality tests in employee selection. Mass. Gen. Laws Ann. ch. 149, § 19B (prohibiting lie detector tests, including those by any "written instrument," for employee selection purposes); R.I. Gen. Laws §§ 28-6.1-1 to 28.6.1-4 (prohibiting the use of an honesty test as a "primary basis for an employment decision," but otherwise allowing such tests).

8. Suppose a state prohibits employer discrimination against persons convicted of nonviolent offenses more than ten years before the date of prospective employment. Would an employer violate such a law by administering an "honesty" test with the yes/no question, "I have never stolen anything from my employer?" *See* Stanton Corp. v. Dep't of Labor, 561 N.Y.S.2d 6 (N.Y. App. Div. 1990) (raising, but declining to decide an analogous issue).

9. What if test results suggest a dangerous character trait, but the employer hires the applicant anyway? Thatcher v. Brennan, 657 F. Supp. 6 (S.D. Miss. 1986), *aff'd mem.*, 816 F.2d 675 (5th Cir. 1987) (negligent hiring claim rejected; test result indicating "high aggression" did not mean employee was "violent").

PROBLEM

Your client, an employer, has used a paper and pencil test to screen applicants at its retail stores across the country. The test was designed by a psychologist and marketed to the employer as a way to predict whether an applicant is service-oriented and will be good at dealing with customers. It asks questions like, "I talk to strangers (a) all the time; (b) sometimes; (c) almost never; (d) never." The test is scored by software the employer had installed on its computers. The employer began using this test a few years ago because it was unhappy with its store managers' hiring decisions; there were reports of nepotism, favoritism of friends and associates, discrimination, and generally poor judgment in employee selection. Now the employer has learned of the *Karraker* case, and it is wondering what to do. Is its test necessarily unlawful? Should it cease using the test and return to the old procedure of personal interviews and decisions by each store manager?

5. Genetic Screening: Is the Future Now?

Advances in genetic science make it possible to categorize individuals according to their genetic codes. Some genetic information might also be useful to make predictions about whether individuals are predisposed to certain behavior, or whether they have or are predisposed to certain diseases or medical conditions.

Might an employer use such information in employee selection? The most likely and effective employer use of genetic screening would be to eliminate applicants predisposed to medical conditions that could burden the employer's health benefits plan, or who are particularly susceptible to certain occupational injuries or illnesses. Such genetic screening by employers appears to be extremely rare. In a widely publicized case, Burlington Northern Santa Fe Railway allegedly collected blood samples for genetic analysis of employees who had made claims for carpel tunnel syndrome. The EEOC sued the railway on the ground that genetic screening was an illegal medical examination under the Americans with Disabilities Act. The lawsuit eventually settled, with the railway agreeing to pay 2.2 million and to cease genetic testing. *See* W. Corbett, *The Need for a Revitalized Common Law of the Workplace*, 69 Brook. L. Rev. 91, 109 (2003).

In 2008, Congress enacted the Genetic Information Nondiscrimination Act (GINA). Pub. L. 110-223, 122 Stat. 881 (2008). Title II of GINA, codified at 42 U.S.C. §§ 2000ff *et seq.*, prohibits an employer from discriminating against an employee "because of genetic information with respect to the employee." *Id.* § 2000ff-1(a). GINA also makes it unlawful for an employer to "request, require or purchase genetic information with respect to an employee or a family member of the employee" except in limited circumstances. *Id.* § 2000ff-1(b). One important exception is that an employer may provide a "wellness program" that includes an employee's voluntary submission of genetic information to a health care professional or genetic counselor. *Id.* § 2000ff-1(b)(2). Another exception is that the employer may collect genetic information, voluntarily provided by the employee, as part of a program required by law to monitor the effects of toxic substances in the workplace. *Id.* § 2000ff-1(b)(5).

Even before GINA, it was widely assumed that the ADA might prohibit some collection of genetic data or discrimination on that basis, and some states had enacted their own laws against genetic information discrimination. *See, e.g.,* Tex. Lab. Code §§ 21.401 et seq. GINA does not preempt or supersede such laws to the extent they provide equal or greater employee protection. 42 U.S.C. §§ 2000ff-8.

CHAPTER 4

Compensation and Benefits

A. WAGES AND THE LABOR MARKET

TODD v. EXXON CORP.

275 F.3d 191 (2d Cir. 2001)

SOTOMAYOR, Circuit Judge.

Plaintiff-appellant Roberta Todd appeals from an order of the United States District Court for the Southern District of New York (Sprizzo, J.) granting defendants-appellees' motion to dismiss the complaint for failure to state a claim pursuant to Fed. R. Civ. P. 12(b)(6). We hold that plaintiff adequately alleges a § 1 Sherman Act violation for an unlawful information exchange. Plaintiff's complaint alleges a plausible product market, a market structure that is susceptible to collusive activity, a data exchange with anticompetitive potential, and antitrust injury. We therefore vacate and remand.

Plaintiff brought this action against fourteen major companies in the integrated oil and petrochemical industry, collectively accounting for 80-90% of the industry's revenues and ... workforce. On behalf of herself and all other similarly situated current and former Exxon employees (the putative class), plaintiff alleges that defendants violated § 1 of the Sherman Act by regularly sharing detailed information regarding compensation paid to nonunion managerial, professional, and technical ("MPT") employees and using this information in setting the salaries of these employees at artificially low levels. ...

Accepting the allegations in the complaint as true, ... Defendants instituted a system whereby they periodically conducted surveys comparing past and current MPT salary information and participated in regular meetings at which current and future salary budgets were discussed. The data exchanges were also accompanied by assurances that the information would be used in setting the salaries of MPT employees. Defendants' "Job Match Survey" created a common denominator to facilitate the comparison of MPT salaries. The survey used certain jobs at defendant Chevron as benchmarks. The other defendants would submit detailed information regarding the jobs at their companies that were most comparable to the Chevron benchmark jobs so that they could be matched. . . . Chevron and Unocal each would meet with half of the other companies involved to develop matches to the benchmarks, and then would gather the information before submitting it to a third-party consultant, Towers Perrin. Towers Perrin compiled the information, then analyzed, refined, and distributed it to the defendants. . . .

. . . Plaintiff contends that defendants' arrangement ... had the purpose and effect of depressing MPT salaries paid by defendants. The arrangement reduced the incentive for defendants to bid up salaries in order to attract experienced MPT employees or to retain employees who might be lured to other firms. . . .

II. THE RULE OF REASON

Section 1 of the Sherman Act prohibits "[e]very contract, combination in the form of trust or otherwise, or conspiracy, in restraint of trade or commerce among the several States, or with foreign nations." 15 U.S.C. § 1. Traditional "hard-core" price fixing remains per se unlawful under the seminal case United States v. Socony-Vacuum Oil Co., 310 U.S. 150 (1940), and its progeny. If the plaintiff in this case could allege that defendants actually formed an agreement to fix MPT salaries, this per se rule would likely apply. Furthermore, even in the absence of direct "smoking gun" evidence, a horizontal price-fixing agreement may be inferred on the basis of conscious parallelism, when such interdependent conduct is accompanied by circumstantial evidence and plus factors such as defendants' use of facilitating practices. *See, e.g.,* Interstate Circuit, Inc. v. United States, 306 U.S. 208 (1939). Information exchange is an example of a facilitating practice that can help support an inference of a price-fixing agreement.

There is a closely related but analytically distinct type of claim, also based on § 1 of the Sherman Act, where the violation lies in the information exchange itself– as opposed to merely using the information exchange as evidence upon which to infer a price-fixing agreement. . . . In United States v. Container Corp. of America, the Supreme Court held that information exchange itself could constitute a § 1 violation, upholding the sufficiency of a complaint charging "an exchange of price information but no agreement to adhere to a price schedule." 393 U.S. 333 (1969). The Court found that under the market conditions present in that case, and in light of the nature of the information disseminated, the data exchange caused a stabilization of prices and thus had an anticompetitive effect on the market for corrugated containers. . . .

. . . United States v. Citizens & Southern National Bank[] clarif[ied] that "the dissemination of price information is not itself a per se violation of the Sherman Act." 422 U.S. 86, 113 (1975). In United States v. United States Gypsum Co., the Court explained its reasoning: "The exchange of price data and other information among competitors does not invariably have anticompetitive effects; indeed such practices can in certain circumstances increase economic efficiency and render markets more, rather than less, competitive." 438 U.S. 422, 441 n. 16 (1978). The Court then set out the basic framework for the rule of reason inquiry in this context: "A number of factors including most prominently the structure of the industry involved and the nature of the information exchanged are generally considered in divining the procompetitive or anticompetitive effects of this type of interseller communication." *Id.*

As plaintiff does not allege an actual agreement among defendants to fix salaries, we analyze plaintiff's complaint solely as to whether it alleges unlawful information exchange pursuant to this rule of reason.

III. MARKET POWER

A. The Relevant Market

An important factor to analyze in a *Gypsum* data exchange case is the market power of the defendants. One traditional way to demonstrate market power is by defining the relevant product market and showing defendants' percentage share of that market. Plaintiff argues that the relevant market in this case is the market for "the services of experienced, salaried, non-union, managerial, professional and technical (MPT) employees in the oil and petrochemical industry, in the continental United States and various submarkets thereof." If the market is defined in this way, defendants would have a substantial market share of 80-90%. . . .

The traditional horizontal conspiracy case involves an agreement among sellers with the purpose of raising prices to supracompetitive levels. The Sherman Act, however, also applies to abuse of market power on the buyer side–often taking the form of monopsony or oligopsony. ... There is thus no reason to doubt that a *Gypsum* data exchange claim — a close cousin of traditional price fixing — can be brought against a group of buyers.

The fact that this case involves a buyer-side conspiracy affects how the market is defined. Normally, the market "is composed of products that have reasonable interchangeability for the purposes for which they are produced-price, use and qualities considered." AD/SAT v. Associated Press, 181 F.3d 216, 227 (2d Cir. 1999). "In economists' terms, two products or services are reasonably interchangeable where there is sufficient cross-elasticity of demand. Cross-elasticity of demand exists if consumers would respond to a slight increase in the price of one product by switching to another product." *Id.* Thus, the inquiry is whether a "hypothetical cartel" would be "substantially constrain[ed]" from increasing prices by the ability of customers to switch to other producers. *AD/SAT*, 181 F.3d at 228.

... These factors are reversed in the context of a buyer-side conspiracy. . . . In such a case, "the market is not the market of competing sellers but of competing buyers ... who are seen by sellers as being reasonably good substitutes." A greater availability of substitute buyers indicates a smaller quantum of market power on the part of the buyers . . . .

[The court turned to the question whether employers in the oil and petrochemical industry constituted the relevant market for MPT employees. — ED.] Plaintiff claims that MPT employees accumulate industry-specific knowledge that renders them more valuable to employers in the oil and petrochemical industry than to employers in other industries. Plaintiff supports this contention by arguing that "[w]orkers receive compensation for skills that are specific to a set of firms that produce similar products," and thus MPT employees would "suffer large wage losses if they switch industries." According to the complaint, "[a]s the employees gain experience, the only practical outlets to sell their services at an amount reflecting the value of their experience are the integrated oil and petrochemical companies, i.e., Defendants."

. . . It may well be that the availability of employment in alternative industries places some constraints on the ability of the alleged conspirators to limit salary increases. Market definition is generally a matter of degree. Even a monopolist is subject to limitations on how far it can increase price. *See* Donald F. Turner, *Antitrust Policy and the Cellophane Case*, 70 Harv. L. Rev. 281, 308-10 (1956). In accordance with this Court's formulation in *AD/SAT*, 181 F.3d at 227-28, plaintiff is simply alleging that a slight decrease in salary by a hypothetical oligopsonist cartel in the oil/petrochemical industry would not cause MPT employees to leave the industry because they would have difficulty finding compensation fully reflecting the value of their experience elsewhere. At trial, plaintiff would have to prove this theory with economic evidence regarding the cross-industrial elasticity of MPT employees. Evidence could include information regarding, for example, the extent to which decreases in oil/petrochemical industry salaries, or increases that do not keep pace with increases in other industries, cause MPT employees to leave the industry; whether MPT employees who leave or are displaced from the oil/petrochemical industry suffer pay cuts upon switching industries; and whether it takes longer for MPT employees who leave or are displaced from oil/petrochemical industry jobs to find employment in other industries than within the same industry.

. . . It remains to be seen whether every category of MPT employee in the plaintiff class can demonstrate the requisite degree of inelasticity. We find only that the allegation of a market limited to employers in the oil and petrochemical industry is plausible on its face.

B. Anticompetitive Effect as an Indication of Market Power

Plaintiff's alleged product market would support the 80-90% market share figure for defendants. Market power defined as a percentage market share, however, is not the only way to demonstrate defendants' ability to depress salaries. . . . If a plaintiff can show that a defendant's conduct exerted an actual adverse effect on competition, this is a strong indicator of market power. In fact, this arguably is more direct evidence of market power than calculations of elusive market share figures. . . . On remand, therefore, the court should consider whether plaintiff has demonstrated anticompetitive effects as part of the court's assessment of defendants' market power.

IV. SUSCEPTIBILITY OF THE MARKET

A. Concentration

. . . Generally speaking, the possibility of anticompetitive collusive practices is most realistic in concentrated industries. If the relevant market in this case is defined as the plaintiff contends, the defendants would control collectively a 80-90% market share. While this is an extremely high market share by any measure, the district court contends that the alleged market "is not, as plaintiff contends, so clearly oligopolistic." The district court points out that there are fourteen defendants in this case. . . .

The Supreme Court has found that data exchange can be unlawful despite a relatively large number of sellers. In *Container Corp.*, the Court used the oft-cited language that the industry was "dominated by relatively few sellers." 393 U.S. at 337. But in fact, the defendants in *Container Corp.* were eighteen firms controlling 90% of the market, defined as the sale of cardboard cartons in the Southeast. The Court nonetheless found the market sufficiently concentrated … [T]he reason the Court reached its holding despite the multiplicity of sellers was the specific anticompetitive characteristics of the information exchange. Given that the market concentration in this case is not radically different from that in *Container Corp.*, … we do not think that fourteen companies sharing an 80-90% market share is so unconcentrated as to warrant a Rule 12(b)(6) dismissal … . We also find it unsurprising that data exchange cases may involve a number of participants that begins to push the boundaries of oligopoly. These players are most in need of such data exchange arrangements in order to facilitate price coordination; a very small handful of firms in a more highly concentrated market may be less likely to require the kind of sophisticated data dissemination alleged in this case.

B. Fungibility

. . . Fungibility is relevant . . . because it is less realistic for a cartel to establish and police a price conspiracy where it is difficult to compare the products being sold. In contrast, "[f]ungible products facilitate coordination of pricing in a concentrated industry because it is easier to determine and monitor a consensus on some competitive variable." Brian R. Henry, *Benchmarking and Antitrust*, 62 Antitrust L.J. 483, 496 (1994). The question in this case is whether jobs at the various oil and petrochemical companies were comparable, or fungible enough so that the defendants could have used the exchanged information as part of a tacit conspiracy to depress salaries. . . .

Plaintiff alleges that the information exchanged by defendants related to specific job categories — not to MPT employment in general. Therefore, the fact that a job as an attorney and one as a geologist are not comparable does not bear on the ability of defendants to coordinate salaries. Rather, the relevant question is whether jobs within each category are fungible enough across the oil and petrochemical industry to allow for such coordination.

. . . Services generally tend not to be fungible or susceptible to standardization, and it is unlikely that these fourteen different companies would have positions with job descriptions that precisely match one another. Even this argument, however, is complicated by the specific facts of this case, coupled with the policy rationale behind the fungibility inquiry.

Plaintiff's complaint alleges in detail the sophisticated techniques defendants used to "achieve a common denominator" with respect to the compensation paid to their MPT employees. Defendants developed the Job Match Survey because they "realized it was not functionally efficient simply to know what each others' employees were being paid unless they were able to horizontally match the various job classifications." The survey revolved around certain benchmark jobs provided by Chevron. . . . Plaintiff alleges that, during the relevant time period, Exxon was able to match 70-80% of its jobs to the 155 Chevron benchmark positions. Furthermore, because not all jobs could be matched precisely, the defendants agreed upon certain "offsets" reflecting the specific differences between jobs as a percentage figure. . . . Defendants even devised a formula to enhance the comparability of non-cash benefits afforded to MPT employees in their Long Term Incentive Survey.

Plaintiff is thus on solid ground when she argues that defendants "made their own employees' positions 'fungible' for comparison purposes with those of their competitors." The jobs in question may not be inherently fungible, but since the purpose of the fungibility inquiry is to test whether defendants would be able to compare the positions for coordination purposes, the sophisticated techniques employed by defendants to account for the differences among jobs are extremely telling.

C. *Inelastic Demand*

. . . This part of the inquiry, easily confused with the cross-elasticity and interchangeability analysis that is used to define the relevant market, traditionally asks whether demand is inelastic because "buyers place orders only for immediate, short-run needs." *Container Corp.*, 393 U.S. at 337. In other words, the question is whether it is economically feasible for buyers to abstain from purchasing the product for some period of time.

Here again, we reverse the equation in the context of an oligopsony. Where market power is exercised by buyers, it is the elasticity of the sellers' supply that is at issue. Sellers' supply could be elastic if, for example, they have "the option of withholding some output from the market in hopes of higher prices in future years." Blair & Harrison, *supra*, at 313. If, however, the goods are perishable, short-run supply may be quite inelastic. In this case, the supply at issue is the labor of the MPT employees. "Labor is an extremely perishable commodity–an hour not worked today can never be recovered." *Id.* at 314. As a result, "[c]ollusion among employers can drive the wage down to the individual's reservation wage." *Id.* . . .

In sum, the pleadings support the contention that the market was susceptible to tacit coordination by the defendant companies: The market is sufficiently concentrated under *Container Corp.*; the defendants have in effect manufactured a form of fungibility through sophisticated comparison techniques; and the supply of labor has an inherently inelastic quality.

V. THE NATURE OF THE INFORMATION EXCHANGED

Alongside the "structure of the industry involved," the other major factor for courts to consider in a data exchange case is the "nature of the information exchanged." *Gypsum*, 438 U.S. at 441 n. 16. …There are certain well-established criteria used to help ascertain the anticompetitive potential of information exchanges. . . .

The first factor to consider is the time frame of the data. The Supreme Court has made clear that "[e]xchanges of current price information, of course, have the greatest potential for generating anti-competitive effects and although not per se unlawful have consistently been held to violate the Sherman Act." *Gypsum*, 438 U.S. at 441 n. 16. The exchange of past price data is greatly preferred because current data have greater potential to affect future prices and facilitate price conspiracies. By the same reasoning, exchanges of future price information are considered especially anticompetitive.

Plaintiff's complaint alleges that defendants exchanged past and current salary information, as well as future salary budget information. It claims that there has been an:

> exchange among Defendants of massive amounts of extremely detailed information concerning job classifications, salaries, bonuses, and benefits paid, or to be paid, to categories of employees within the different job classifications; starting salaries of new employees; "signing bonuses"; relocation expenses, stock options; and related information. . . . Updated information on salaries is exchanged in oral and written communications throughout the year.
>
> . . . Defendants also attended meetings at least three times per year at which

various types of salary information were discussed. "Among the information exchanged at these meetings [were] current and future increases in Defendants' salary budgets."

... [A]nother factor courts look to is the specificity of the information. Price exchanges that identify particular parties, transactions, and prices are seen as potentially anticompetitive because they may be used to police a secret or tacit conspiracy to stabilize prices. *See, e.g., Container Corp.*, 393 U.S. at 334-38. Courts prefer that information be aggregated in the form of industry averages, thus avoiding transactional specificity.

Two aspects of the information exchange at issue are problematic in this regard. First, although the salary information was aggregated and distributed by a third-party consulting firm, companies participating in the Job Family Survey received compensation data broken down to subsets consisting of as few as three competitors. Plaintiff alleges that these periodically updated data sets were used by each defendant to determine whether the announced budgets of its competitors had in fact been implemented so that each could consider what adjustments should be made to coordinate salaries. This practice, plaintiff argues on appeal, made "deviations from previously announced salary levels easily and quickly detectable." Second, at their meetings defendants discussed current and future salary budgets, including "company-specific" information, such that "all participants learn where each other participant is going with its salary budget for the upcoming year" ....

Another important factor ... is whether the data are made publicly available. Public dissemination is a primary way for data exchange to realize its procompetitive potential. For example, in the traditional oligopoly (seller-side) context, access to information may better equip buyers to compare products, rendering the market more efficient while diminishing the anticompetitive effects of the exchange. A court is therefore more likely to approve a data exchange where the information is made public. *Maple Flooring*, 268 U.S. at 573-74.

In the instant case, dissemination of the information to the employees could have helped mitigate any anticompetitive effects of the exchange and possibly enhanced market efficiency by making employees more sensitive to salary increases. No such dissemination occurred, however. The information was not disclosed to the public nor to the employees whose salaries were the subject of the exchange. Plaintiff alleges that "[t]he confidential treatment of the information exchanged impedes the ability of employees to bargain intelligently and competitively with the members of the information exchange."

A final troubling aspect of the arrangement at issue is the fact that the defendants allegedly participated in frequent meetings to discuss the salary information, accompanied by assurances that the participants would primarily use the exchanged data in setting their MPT salaries. Meetings, of course, are not inherently unlawful but in this context they have the potential to enhance the anticompetitive effects and "likelihood of . . . uniformity" caused by information exchange. VI Areeda, *supra*, ¶1435b, at 224. Meanwhile, the frequency of the meetings ... tends to facilitate the policing of price conspiracies.

In sum, the "nature of the information exchanged" weighs against the motion to dismiss. The characteristics of the data exchange in this case are precisely those that arouse suspicion of anticompetitive activity under the rule of reason.

VI. EFFECT ON COMPETITION AND ANTITRUST INJURY

An antitrust plaintiff must allege not only cognizable harm to herself, but an adverse effect on competition market-wide. . . . Plaintiff specifically alleges that salary levels across the integrated oil and petrochemical industry have been artificially depressed because the information exchange has reduced competitive incentives. Moreover, Exxon has supposedly used the information to reduce its competitive factor from 6.5% in 1991 to 0% in 1995, to reduce its salaries 4.1% between 1987 and 1994 in comparison to the Six Majors, and to reduce its salary index in relation to the competition from 110.7% in 1987 to 107.0% in 1993. . . . In all, plaintiff alleges that with Exxon's total salary budget at $800 million, the conduct described in the complaint had the effect of lowering Exxon's MPT salaries by a total of $20 million per year. Whether this is so is a question of fact that cannot be resolved on this Rule 12(b)(6) motion. . . .

CONCLUSION

. . . [W]e vacate the district court's grant of defendants' Rule 12(b)(6) motion to dismiss and remand for proceedings consistent with this opinion.

NOTES AND QUESTIONS

1. The Judicial Panel on Multidistrict Litigation transferred *Todd* to the District Court for the District of New Jersey to be consolidated with a number of related cases. In re Compensation of Managerial, Professional and Technical Employees Antitrust Litigation, 206 F.Supp.2d 1374 (Jud. Pan. Mult. Lit. 2002). There, the district court twice denied the plaintiffs' motion to certify a class action. In short, the court found that a putative class of 40,000 employees in 4,000 different occupations was not sufficiently cohesive to satisfy the requirements of Rule 23, especially because the "interchangeability" of employment opportunities was likely to vary significantly for each particular occupation. In re Compensation of Managerial, Professional and Technical Employees Antitrust Litigation, 2006 WL 38937 (D.N.J. 2006). Eventually, the court granted summary judgment for the defendants against the plaintiffs' individual claims, on the ground that the plaintiffs had failed to produce evidence of employer market power within a defined labor market for their particular occupations. Compensation of Managerial, Professional and Technical Employees Antitrust Litigation, 2008 WL 3887619 (D.N.J. 2008).

2. Economists distinguish between internal and external labor markets. An external labor market is the set of forces that determine the wage an employer will pay newly hired employees. An internal labor market is the set of forces that determine wages for incumbent employees who continue their employment with the same employer. For a variety of reasons employees in the internal labor market might not earn as much as they could if they competed in the external labor market by looking for employment with a new employer. One reason is that an employer or its incumbent employees might not be sure what the external labor market would pay. Could information sharing by employers actually benefit incumbent employees in this situation?

3. An employer might attempt to restrain the internal labor market by preventing employees from sharing information about their wages. In fact, it is not unusual for an employer to prohibit an employee from disclosing or discussing his wage rate with other employees. For reasons discussed in section B.2 of this chapter, such an employer policy is unlawful.

4. If employees of the defendant corporations in *Todd* organized into an association not only to share information but also to set the wage members could accept for initial or continued employment, would they be violating laws against price or wage fixing? At one time, many U.S. courts would have answered "yes." Indeed, during the nineteenth century some courts held that labor organizations striving to maintain or raise wages were guilty of common law criminal conspiracy, even in the absence of any statute prohibiting price or wage fixing.

The danger of being charged with criminal conspiracy may have been the least of an early labor organization's problems. A larger problem was enforcing member solidarity in demanding the prescribed wage rate. Even if a nineteenth-century court declined to find the labor organization's conduct criminal, it would certainly refuse to enforce the organization's rules or contract with members. Whether or not an agreement to fix wages was criminal, it was against "public policy," void and unenforceable by legal process. *See* R. Carlson, *The Origin and Future of Exclusive Representation in American Labor Law*, 30 Duquesne L. Rev. 779, 783-808 (1992). In this regard, labor organizations seeking to raise wages were at a distinct disadvantage in dealing with employer organizations. Employer organizations had relatively few members, and the benefits of cooperation might have been enough to keep a few members in line without judicial enforcement. In contrast, labor organizations needed the cooperation of hundreds or thousands of individual laborers who were often divided at the outset by race, ethnicity, religion, their attitude toward collective bargaining, or their need for current wages. Without the benefit of judicial enforcement, labor organizations resorted to extra-judicial measures, including "patrolling," picketing, "shunning," and even tortious or criminal acts against defectors. *Id.*

5. The end of the nineteenth century and the beginning of the twentieth century brought two important developments. The first was the enactment of the Sherman Act, 15 U.S.C. §§ 1 et seq., specifically prohibiting agreements to restrain competition. The second was the enactment of laws authorizing, protecting and facilitating the formation of labor unions and collective bargaining, even though the usual purpose of collective bargaining is to prevent wage competition. *See* 15 U.S.C. § 17, 29 U.S.C. §§ 52, 101-115. Thus, if the employers in *Todd* had formed an association to bargain collectively with an organization of their employees, neither side would have violated the laws prohibiting agreements in restraint of trade. Collective bargaining is usually the subject of a separate labor law or collective bargaining course, and a more complete description of this body of law is beyond the scope of this book.

6. Another way employers might attempt to restrain the labor market is by a "no poaching" agreement, in which each employer party to the arrangement agrees not to hire the others' employees. Such an agreement might include a promise to report employees who are inquiring about new job opportunities. The Department of Justice has issued a guidance for employers and human resources

managers to remind them that such agreements can violate federal antitrust laws. Antitrust Division, Department of Justice, ANTITRUST GUIDANCE FOR HUMAN RESOURCE PROFESSIONALS (Oct. 2016), online at http://src.bna.com/jMS. Here is a sample from the DOJ's guidance:

> ***Question***: I work as an HR professional in an industry where we spend a lot of money to recruit and train new employees. At a trade show, I mentioned how frustrated I get when a recent hire jumps ship to work at a competitor. A colleague at a competing firm suggested that we deal with this problem by agreeing not to recruit or hire each other's employees. She mentioned that her company had entered into these kinds of agreements in the past, and they seemed to work. What should I do?
>
> ***Answer***: What that colleague is suggesting is a no-poaching agreement. That suggestion amounts to a solicitation to engage in serious criminal conduct. You should refuse her suggestion and consider contacting the Antitrust Division's Citizen Complaint Centeror the Federal Trade Commission's Bureau of Competition to report the behavior of your colleague's company. If you agree not to recruit or hire each other's employees, you would likely be exposing yourself and your employer to substantial criminal and civil liability.

7. Still another way employers might try to limit or depress wages is to expand the labor supply by accepting or even recruiting undocumented alien workers, who are more likely to accept lower wages and less likely to assert their rights under protective employment laws. In Williams v. Mohawk Indus., Inc., 465 F.3d 1277 (11th Cir. 2006), the Eleventh Circuit held that the representatives of a proposed plaintiff class stated a claim under the Racketeer Influenced and Corrupt Practices Act, 18 U.S.C. 1961-1968 (RICO) against the defendant corporation and its agents for knowingly employing and harboring illegal workers. The proposed class included workers who suffered a loss of individual or collective bargaining power with a resulting loss of wages.

8. An employer could also expand the labor supply by hiring "guestworkers" under the H-2A, H2-B or other special visa program, but only if it persuades the Department of Labor that the local labor force is inadequate. In Perez-Farias v. Global Horizons, Inc., 2008 WL 833055 (E.D. Wash. 2008), a class of resident workers sued an employer who recruited guestworkers from Thailand under the H-2A program. The plaintiffs alleged that the availability of local workers was not inadequate, and that employer's hiring of guestworkers constituted illegal race discrimination and violated other local laws pertaining to farm labor. The court entered judgment based on a jury verdict for the plaintiffs, awarding damages that included $300,000 in punitive damages.

Guestworker visa programs are a continuing point of conflict between employer groups seeking to expand and such programs and labor organizations seeking to curtail them. *See* Julia Preston, *La. Business Owners Sue Over New Rules for Guest Workers*, New York Times (September 11, 2011), at http://www.nytimes.com/2011/09/12/us/12alligator.html?scp=3&sq=preston%20and%20guest%20workers&st=cse.

B. CONTRACTUAL RIGHTS

1. Individual Bargaining

Employee compensation is more than a simple agreed payment of money for services. The basic issue (what is the right price for the employee's service?) requires some thought about the best formula for or unitization of the price. Will the employer pay the employee for time or for output? If payment is for time, how will the parties measure time? Will the employer pay the employee daily, biweekly, or annually? Will compensation consist only of cash wages, or will it include in-kind goods such as a company car, or benefits such as a pension or health insurance? Which of the parties will bear the cost of tools, occupational licenses, "entertainment of clients," or other expenses the employee's work might incur?

It may seem that employee compensation has become more complex in recent times because of stock options, profit-sharing plans, and employer-sponsored group insurance plans. In general, however, the basic questions employers and employees face about compensation are no different from the questions they faced two or three hundred years ago. In the colonial era, workers often found it convenient to accept part of their compensation in the form of room and board or other facilities (sometimes including an allotment of wine or other alcoholic beverages). Dep't of Labor, History of Wages in the U.S. from Colonial Times to 1928, pp. 15-16 (1934). Both an employer and an employee could gain from this arrangement if the employer's cost in providing facilities was less than what a third party would charge the employee. However, "in-kind" benefits can be difficult to value and compare, and in a long-term relationship the employee might be at the mercy of the employer's good faith and generosity as to the quality and quantity of the benefits.

Issues relating to the timing or deferral of compensation also have a long history. In early America employers often deferred payment of all or most wages for as long as possible. An employee who received none of his cash wages until the end of an agreed term was less likely to abandon the job before the end of the term. Deferral of payment was a particularly important strategy for a master of an indentured servant who, unlike an African-American slave, could easily escape and disappear among the free workforce of another community. Deferral of pay could also be useful to the employee as a means to save for independence. Indentured servants, for example, received "freedom dues" at the end of their terms. Freedom dues might include land and other facilities for establishing a farm or shop. *Id.* at 38-39. On the other hand, deferral of any part of compensation presented a risk for the employee or servant. He might work for months (or years in the case of an indentured servant) only to find that his employer was insolvent or unwilling to pay what the employee expected.

If compensation has become more complicated in modern times, this is partly because employers have relied on their control over compensation to strengthen their control over complex work within very complex organizations. As production has moved from small farms and shops to large factories and commercial enterprises of global scale, employers have used various compensation schemes to strengthen their management of the work and their enforcement of work rules. For example, employers experiment with pay schemes designed to boost productivity by tying compensation to output or results. For manual laborers, "incentive" compensation might be a "piece rate" based on easily measurable output such as units of fruit a worker has picked. Incentive compensation is necessarily more complicated for white collar employees whose output and work quality can be difficult to measure. Other factors making compensation more complicated in the modern world include the lengthening work-life of the average employee (which makes deferral of compensation more problematic) and widespread employee dependency on employment for health care, pension, and other welfare benefits that are not easily described by a simple formula or unit.

Despite the importance of these issues, the parties' agreements about them are seldom reduced to a single written and "integrated" contract. Employers and employees tend to have many partially integrated and collateral agreements rather than one final and exclusive integration of their terms. To they may have integrated any set of terms, integration bars only an attempt to prove inconsistent prior or contemporaneous terms. *See* RESTATEMENT OF CONTRACTS (SECOND) § 215. Integration does not prevent proof of a *subsequent* modification of the terms of employment. Regular modification is typical in an ongoing relationship like employment. Moreover, while employers and employees normally bargain explicitly and carefully over base compensation, their discussions about other benefits are often oral, vague, incomplete or a matter of unwritten custom.

MARTIN v. MANN MERCHANDISING, INC.

570 S.W.2d 208 (Tex. Civ. App. 1978)

MCCLOUD, Chief Justice.

This is a summary judgment case. Plaintiff, Gordon Martin, sued defendant, Mann Merchandising, Inc., plaintiff's former employer, seeking severance and vacation pay. Plaintiff alleged that defendant represented to him that its policy was to pay one week's severance pay for each year of service and two weeks' vacation in the event his employment with defendant was terminated. Plaintiff pleaded he had been employed under an oral agreement for a period of more than eleven years and upon termination he was paid only one half of the severance and vacation pay he was entitled to receive. The trial court granted defendant's motion for summary judgment and plaintiff has appealed. We reverse and remand.

Severance pay is usually associated with termination of the employment relationship for reasons generally beyond the control of the employee, and its purpose is to assure a worker whose employment has terminated certain funds while he seeks another job. 40 A.L.R.2d 1045. Plaintiff stated in his affidavit . . . :

> . . . I never thought I was going to be fired, but certainly from my knowledge of their company policy and my knowledge that other sales managers received their severance pay, I believe that I would receive such same as the others and knowing that I must have and did consciously rely upon receiving same. I did all my work and I expected the company to perform all its obligation. Everyone who left the company before me received at least 1 week's severance pay for every year of service, and I was the only one who did not receive same.

By deposition plaintiff testified that no officer or anyone with the company ever orally told him he would receive one week's severance pay for each year he worked. Plaintiff answered that he did not discuss it with anyone because he never planned on leaving. This testimony establishes that there was no express contract but plaintiff urges there was a contract implied in fact.

Plaintiff stated he first learned of the alleged severance pay policy after he became a regional manager. This was about a year or a year and a half before he was terminated. While being questioned about two regional managers who had received severance pay after being terminated by defendant, plaintiff stated he did not personally know how their severance pay was calculated, but one of the managers told him it was "very, very generous." Immediately following this answer, plaintiff was asked the following questions and he gave the following answers:

Q: That didn't have anything to do with your decision to take the job as Regional Manager?

A: No; this happened after I had been Regional Manager.

Q: Didn't have anything to do with whether you stayed on as Regional Manager, did it?

A: No. . . . When I go to work for a company, I plan on staying 'til I'm dead.

Defendant contends the answers by plaintiff conclusively establish that he did not rely upon the alleged offer of severance pay. We disagree. Plaintiff clearly stated in his affidavit he did so rely. Plaintiff's answers, if contradictory, created a fact issue. Moreover, we think "reliance" by the employee is not significant in a case of this nature. We find no Texas case in point, however, in Anthony v. Jersey Central Power & Light Co., 143 A.2d 762 (1958), when confronted with the argument there was no evidence that the employees relied upon the promise of severance pay in continuing their employment, the court, after holding that reliance was presumed, stated:

As was said in a different context in Diamond v. Davis, 62 N.Y.S.2d 181, 194 (Sup. Ct. 1945):

> Employees have the right to place reliance upon the full performance of every authorized act and plan for employee benefit and welfare, such as group life insurance, retirement allowance, bonus, managers shares, and any other incentive offers. Every benefit firmly offered or authoritatively fixed for an employee or official which in the course of fair dealing and reasonable conduct should be rightfully expected may be regarded as part of or a just increment to the compensation payable for the work, labor or service performed or to be performed in a specified period.

The employer obviously cannot evade liability for one of the proffered items of compensation after the employee has performed his labor by showing that the employee would have taken the job without the particular benefit in question and therefore cannot be said to have relied upon it in doing the work. It makes no difference that the severance pay plan was promulgated after the plaintiffs had been employed for some time by defendant. Since the employment was always at will, any announcement of a change in or addition to the compensation of the employees of any form followed by the continuance of the employees in employment constituted an effective and binding agreement [as] the new terms for the service rendered thereafter. Consequently, once defendant improved the terms of compensation for plaintiffs' work by announcing the institution of the severance pay plan it must be assumed that plaintiffs were thereafter working for that benefit as much as for any other benefit or item of compensation held out to them as compensation by the employer.

Suppose, instead of the institution of the severance pay plan, the employer had of its own volition announced a 10% increase in the salary of the plaintiffs. Could the defendant have thereafter repudiated its assumed obligation for the increase at the end of a pay period by the argument that plaintiffs had not relied thereon because they would have continued in their jobs even if the increase had not been announced? The question answers itself and also the defendant's contention here.

. . . Defendant has failed to conclusively establish that no contract implied in fact existed between the parties as urged by plaintiff.

The judgment of the trial court is reversed and the cause is remanded.

NOTES AND QUESTIONS

1. Must an employee prove he "relied" on a particular benefit when he accepted or continued his employment? The court's conclusion in *Martin* is in accord with most modern descriptions of contract law. For purposes of finding "consideration" for a promise, the focus is usually on the existence of a "bargained for" exchange, not "detrimental reliance." RESTATEMENT (SECOND) OF CONTRACTS §§ 71, 79(a). The question is not whether the promisee relied in fact on a promise, but whether is reasonable to view the promise as part of the promisor's package of consideration offered to the promisee in a bargain. Thus, enforcement is not limited to the particular terms that were decisive in inducing the promisee's acceptance. *Id.* § 81(2) ("The fact that a promise does not of itself induce a performance or return promise does not prevent the performance or return promise from being consideration for the promise"). In other words, it is no defense against the enforcement of a promise that the promisee would have accepted the same contract without that particular promise or with a less valuable promise. Anderson v. Douglas & Lomason Co., 540 N.W.2d 277, 284 (Iowa 1995). In contrast, promissory estoppel—a theory frequently invoked in the absence of bargained for exchange—requires proof of actual detrimental reliance. RESTATEMENT (SECOND) OF CONTRACTS, *supra*, § 90.

2. While an employee needs no proof of reliance to enforce a particular promise as a matter of contract, he must still prove he knowingly accepted or assented to the set of terms of which the promise was a part. *Id.* § 51, cmt. a ("it is ordinarily essential to the acceptance of the offer that the offeree know of the proposal made"); Anderson v. Douglas & Lomason Co., 540 N.W.2d 277, 283-284 (Iowa 1995) (employee could not have accepted handbook as a contract unless employer "communicated" the handbook to the employee). If all the terms of employment were presented in a single, integrated package, such as a handbook or formal contract, the employee might accept the entire package just by accepting the job and starting or continuing to work with some general awareness or

acknowledgment of the package. Under bargained-for exchange theory, an employee who manifests acceptance of the package of terms by beginning or continuing employment can enforce any promise in the package without proving he was aware of that particular promise. *Id.* It is possible, for example, that the employee only learned of a promise of severance pay when, after receiving a layoff notice, he checked the employee handbook for the first time.

But what if the promise was not within a handbook or any other attempted integration of employment terms? Some employment terms arise and evolve piecemeal in separate communications, and an employer might make a promise to one employee or set of employees but not others. A court might therefore require an employee to prove the employer made the promise *to* the employee, and that the employee manifested acceptance by starting or continuing to work after becoming at least vaguely aware of the promise or the document with the promise. As *Martin* suggests, an employee might assert he learned of the "promise" indirectly, perhaps from other employees. On remand, Martin might also be required to prove the employer made the promise *to him* or to a class of employees that included him.

3. In the absence of explicit bargaining or an unambiguous assent to and acceptance of terms, lawyers and judges who resolve an employment dispute sometimes turn to the idea of "detrimental reliance," which is the basis for promissory estoppel. *See* RESTATEMENT (SECOND) OF CONTRACTS § 90. Promissory estoppel would require the employee to prove he relied on a promise, such as by continuing his employment, even if the employer was not "bargaining" in making the promise. However, a court might require a more particularized knowledge of the promise than is ordinarily required for a bargained for contract. It might not be enough for an employee to have been vaguely aware of a handbook or memorandum that contained the promise. To prove reliance, an employee must prove sufficient knowledge of and familiarity with a particular promise to support his claim that he acted a certain way because of that promise. Compare *Martin* with Bulman v. Safeway, Inc., 27 P.3d 1172, 1175 (Wash. 2001), where the plaintiff sought to prove a company "guide" limited the employer's right to terminate the employment. The court stated, "[A]n employee seeking to enforce promises an employer made in an employee handbook must prove . . . [that] the employee justifiably relied on any of these promises. . . ." In *Bulman*, the court summarized the facts with respect to the issue of "reliance" as follows:

> When asked whether he even had a copy of the guide in which the policy appeared, [plaintiff] responded, "It would've been probably in my — one of my file cabinets." Asked whether he periodically used the guide, he responded, . . . "I had no reason to. I mean, if there's a question that I wanted an answer to, I would've asked [my secretary] Darlene and she would go get me an answer, but for me to sit down and thumb through it, I was fortunate in having Darlene."

27 P.3d 1172, 1177-1178. The court found the evidence of reliance insufficient to support a verdict in favor of the plaintiff. Would the facts described in *Bulman* have precluded the employee's claim under a bargained-for contract theory?

4. In relational contracts in which performance continues over a long period, it is not unusual for one party to assert that an unwritten custom or practice

has become part of the contract. *See* 66 A.L.R.3d 1075 (3d ed. 2001) (collecting cases deciding whether past practice of paying a bonus had become a contractual obligation). In employment, however, repeated actions that might seem to form a pattern are not just between two fixed parties. The actions might be between the employer and many employees under separate and individual contracts. Is a practice between the employer and one employee or set of employees a "custom" on which other employees may rely? Do employees have a contractual right to be treated equally or consistently? In *Martin*, would a judge or jury be authorized to find that the employer did *not* breach the contract by offering severance pay to every employee *except* Martin? *Cf.* Anderson v. Douglas & Lomason Co., 540 N.W.2d 277 (Iowa 1995) (handbook should be "interpreted wherever reasonable as treating alike all those similarly situated, without regard to their knowledge or understanding of the standard terms").

In Krossa v. All Alaskan Seafoods, Inc., 37 P.3d 411 (Alaska 2001), an employee claimed the employer failed to calculate compensation in accord with the contract. When the employer disputed the employee's contract interpretation, the employee noted that his interpretation was supported by the result in Narte v. All Alaskan Seafoods, Inc., a lawsuit by a different employee against the same employer based on the same contract language. The court, however, rejected the employee's argument that collateral estoppel barred the employer from asserting a different interpretation of the contract: "[T]hat case determined only the meaning of the term as understood by the particular parties in that case. . . . *Narte* did not address the reasonable expectations of the parties in this case. . . ." *Id.* at 418.

5. Claims for deferred compensation frequently fail because the amount promised is too indefinite. *See, e.g.*, G.D. Douglass v. Panama, Inc., 504 S.W.2d 776 (Tex. 1974) (statement to employee, "do a good job and you will get a good bonus," was too indefinite to be enforced as a promise). *But see* Guggenheimer v. Bernstein Litowitz & Grossman, L.L.P. 810 N.Y.S.2d 880 (N.Y. Sup. Ct. 2006) (amount of promised bonus proved by evidence of firm's usual practice).

In Uphoff v. Wachovia Securities, 30 IER Cases 138 (S.D. Fla. 2009), the court held that an employer's alleged promise of a "meaningful" retention bonus (a bonus for an employee's continued service in the face of an impending reduction in force) was too vague to be enforced as a matter of contract obligation. However, the court held that the employee did state a claim under a theory of promissory estoppel because he alleged he relied on the promise by turning down offers of bonuses from competing employers. Note that under Section 90 of the Restatement (Second) of Contracts, the remedy for promissory estoppel might be either an award of the employee's expectation interest (the amount promised) or the employee's reliance interest (the amount "lost" in reliance on the promise).

6. Employee expectations might be disappointed not because the employer failed to keep its promises, but because the amount of compensation is based on facts the employer misrepresented. For example, an employer may have overstated its profits in recruiting an employee whose compensation is based in part on a profit-sharing bonus. There are few "truth in hiring" laws analogous to those for consumer transactions. *See, e.g.*, Cal. Lab. Code § 96 (Labor Commissioner to receive claims for misrepresentation of the conditions of employment). However, employees have sometimes succeeded in suing employers for tortious misrepresentation or fraud in

the hiring process. *See, e.g.*, Columbia/HCA Healthcare Corp. v. Cottey, 72 S.W.3d 735 (Tex. App. 2002) (employer misrepresented profit-sharing plan by failing to explain that the plan was subject to termination at any time); Marsland v. Family Heritage Life Ins. Co., 2001 WL 100190 (Tex. App. 2001) (unpublished) (employer representation that plaintiff could expect commissions of more than $50,000 in first year was a statement of opinion and could not be the basis for a claim of fraud). *See also* Chapter 8.B.4.b.

RUSSELL v. BOARD OF COUNTY COMMISSIONERS, CARTER COUNTY

1997 Okla. 80, 952 P.2d 492 (1997)

OPALA, Justice.

Ten deputy sheriffs of Carter County . . . commenced a breach-of employment-contract action against the Board of County Commissioners . . . to recover overtime pay alleged to be due them under an at-will employment arrangement with the county. . . . The trial court gave summary judgment to the Board, and the deputies appealed. The Court of Civil Appeals reversed. . . . The Board seeks our review by certiorari. The deputies argue that the commissioners, sitting as a personnel board, adopted a personnel policy manual, which provides that county employees — including "law enforcement officers" — shall be compensated for overtime hours and receive holiday work pay. The deputies argue they are law enforcement officers within the meaning of the county's personnel policy. . . .

These written policies, the deputies urge, which codified the prior practice of paying overtime wages to county employees, have become a part of the at-will employment arrangement. According to the deputies, when they accepted the county's offer (in the handbook) of compensation for overtime worked, the county became contractually bound to pay according to the promised wage regime. . . . Moreover, they submit that the county is bound by the doctrine of promissory estoppel and cannot now deny the overtime wages after they have performed the work.

. . . The Board contends it never intended to create, by the text of the handbook, an employment contract that modified the at-will employment status or authorized overtime pay for deputy sheriffs. Its intent, the Board argues, is clearly expressed in a disclaimer placed on the front of the handbook. The pertinent language states:

> THESE POLICIES ARE NOT TO BE CONSIDERED AN EMPLOYMENT CONTRACT WITH ANY EMPLOYEE

The handbook is not a contract, the Board sums up, and cannot, as a matter of law, create any contractual obligations.

THE HANDBOOK AS THE BASIS OF AN IMPLIED CONTRACT

The question pressed by the deputies regarding their alleged contract claim calls for an analysis of the principles that govern the legal efficacy of employee personnel handbooks (or manuals).

Oklahoma jurisprudence recognizes that an employee handbook may form the basis of an implied contract between an employer and its employees if four traditional contract requirements exist: (1) competent parties, (2) consent, (3) a legal object and (4) consideration. Two limitations on the scope of implied contracts via an employee handbook stand identified by extant caselaw: (1) the manual only alters the at-will relationship with respect to accrued benefits and (2) the promises in the employee manual must be in definite terms, not in the form of vague assurances. Although the existence of an implied contract generally presents an issue of fact, if the alleged promises are nothing more than vague assurances the issue can be decided as a matter of law. This is so because in order to create an implied contract the promises must be definite.

While an employer may deny (or disclaim) any intent to make the provisions of a personnel manual part of the employment relationship, the disclaimer must be clear. An employer's conduct — i.e., representations and practices — which is inconsistent with its disclaimer may negate the disclaimer's effect. . . .

We cannot, on this record, decide the contractual efficacy of the handbook as a matter of law. While the manual states that its purpose is "to provide a working guide" to county officials and that the personnel policies do not represent an "employment contract," conflicting inferences may be drawn from other statements made in the same handbook. The manual's "overtime" provisions state that county employees "who are not exempt, law enforcement personnel or emergency medical personnel, *shall be entitled* to overtime payment." Under the "general statement" section, the employer offers "paid holidays" for "full-time employees of the county." The deputies' evidentiary materials indicate that other personnel in the sheriff's office have received overtime pay in accordance with these written personnel policies. Because they are law enforcement personnel and county employees, the deputies urge, they should receive the same benefits and stand on the same footing with others. The deputies' evidentiary materials raise a material fact question whether the effectiveness of the Board's written disclaimer is negated by inconsistent employer conduct.

If the disclaimer is found to be ineffective, there remains a material fact issue whether deputy sheriffs (a) are included in the category of law enforcement personnel eligible for overtime pay or (b) fall within the exempt classification that is excluded from these benefits. The manual fails to identify the county employees that fall within these categories. The Board's explanation (by affidavits attached to its summary judgment response) that deputy sheriffs were not intended to be included within the manual's overtime pay classifications points out an ambiguity in the handbook that must be clarified by extrinsic evidence.

THE HANDBOOK'S BINDING EFFECT AS DECLARED POLICY UNDER THE THEORY OF PROMISSORY ESTOPPEL

The deputies argue that the county is liable for overtime pay under the theory of promissory estoppel. Promissory estoppel, which is grounded in the Restatement (Second) of Contracts § 90, has been incorporated into Oklahoma common law. . . . The elements necessary to establish promissory estoppel are: (1) a clear and unambiguous promise, (2) foreseeability by the promisor that the promisee would rely upon it, (3) reasonable reliance upon the promise to the promisee's detriment and (4) hardship or unfairness can be avoided only by the promise's enforcement.

According to the deputies, they relied on two separate promises in the manual which entitle them to relief under the theory of promissory estoppel — (a) § 5-3, which constitutes a promise that they would be given overtime compensation as law enforcement officers, and (b) § 6-1, which promises that full-time county employees will receive compensation for holidays worked. As discussed [above], the manual is ambiguous. It neither specifies what categories of sheriff's employees are designated "law enforcement personnel" nor identifies those who are exempted from the overtime pay requirements.

We hold that whether the county is liable under the doctrine of promissory estoppel—i.e., on the notion of the deputies' detrimental reliance on the personnel manual's provision for overtime or holiday pay (or compensatory time off)—tenders a material fact in dispute. It is yet to be determined. An examination of the evidentiary materials submitted in opposition to the county's quest for summary adjudication reveals that opposite inferences may be drawn from the facts presented.

. . . [T]he trial court's summary judgment reversed and the cause remanded for further proceedings consistent with today's pronouncement.

NOTES AND QUESTIONS

1. The county subsequently settled its dispute with the ten plaintiffs in *Russell* for $50,000. Russell v. Bd. of County Comm'rs, 1 P.3d 442 (2000).

2. Both *Martin* and *Russell* involved alleged employer "policies" the employees sought to enforce as contractual promises. What is the ordinary meaning and effect of a "policy"? If an employer describes a workplace rule or practice as a "policy," should employees understand that the policy is part of their contract, or is a policy something less than a contract? Compare the following excerpts from cases in which employees sought to enforce employer "policies":

> If there were any doubt about it . . . the name of the manual dispels it, for it is nothing short of the official policy of the company, it is the Personnel Policy Manual. As every employee knows, when superiors tell you "it's company policy," they mean business.

Woolley v. Hoffman-LaRoche, Inc., 491 A.2d 1257, 1265 (N.J. 1985).

> The very definition of "policy" negates a legitimate expectation of permanence. In other words, a "policy" is commonly understood to be a flexible framework for operational guidance, not a perpetually binding contractual obligation.

In re Certified Question (Bankey v. Storer Broadcasting Co.), 443 N.W.2d 112 (Mich. 1989).

Are these two statements necessarily inconsistent?

The policies in question in *Woolley* and *Bankey* related to disciplinary action and termination from employment, rather than compensation. The enforceability of employer policies relating to discipline and termination are examined in greater depth in Chapter 8.

3. Why would an employer create and distribute a "handbook" or "policy manual" like the one in *Russell* if it does not want employees to regard the handbook as a binding contract? If the document was not a contract between the employer and its employees, what was it? Consider this passage from Judge Posner

in Workman v. United Parcel Service, Inc., 234 F.3d 998 (7th Cir. 2000), upholding the effect of a disclaimer clause similar to the one in *Russell*:

> One might wonder what function an employee handbook serves if it does not create enforceable obligations. The answer is that it conveys useful information to the employee. And more — for to the extent that it does contain promises, even if not legally binding ones, it places the employer under a moral obligation, or more crassly gives him a reputational incentive, to honor those promises.

Id. at 1000-1001. According to Judge Posner, promises in a handbook subject to a disclaimer "may not be worth as much to the promisee as a promise that the law enforces, but they are worth more than nothing," because the employer's aversion to demoralizing its workforce acts as a self-enforcing mechanism. *Id.* In other words, the employer stakes his reputation, but not his legal liability, on the terms of the handbook. For more on a theory of self-enforcing workplace promises that are not legally binding, *see* W. Kamiat, *Labor and Lemons, Efficient Norms in the Internal Labor Market and the Possible Failures of Individual Contracting,* 144 U. Pa. L. Rev. 1953 (1996); E. Rock & M. Wachter, *The Enforceability of Norms and the Employment Relationship*, 144 U. Pa. L. Rev. 1913 (1996).

4. Consider the court's statement in *Russell* that "an employer's conduct — i.e., representations and practices — which is inconsistent with its disclaimer may negate the disclaimer's effect." Does this mean an employer's pattern of behavior adhering to a "nonbinding" policy transforms the policy into a binding contract? Does consistent adherence to policy, standing alone, manifest intent to be bound?

5. Another possible explanation for a disclaimer clause is that the employer simply wants to reserve the right unilaterally to change the terms of employment in the future. In fact, disclaimers are frequently accompanied by words to the effect that the employer might modify or revoke any of its policies at any time. Is a reservation of right to modify necessarily inconsistent with the idea that the document could be a contract?

In an employment relationship "at will," the employer makes most of the promises. Both parties probably understand, at least implicitly, that the employer might change the terms and conditions of employment. Employment at will is frequently described as a "unilateral" contract in which an employer offers or promises certain compensation and benefits and an employee accepts and provides consideration by his performance. Viewing employment at will in this way preserves the employer's freedom to make prospective changes, subject to the employee's right to resign..

Sometimes employees also make promises. For example, in the *Halliburton* case in Chapter 1, the plaintiff employee promised to submit disputes to arbitration. What if an arbitration policy is part of a handbook that includes a disclaimer clause denying that the handbook is a contract? *See* Walker v. Air Liquide Am. Corp., 113 F. Supp. 2d 983 (M.D. La. 2000) (handbook arbitration provision was unenforceable; handbook included a disclaimer of contract).

7. Not all courts would agree with the court's conclusion in *Russell* that a disclaimer, effective against a contract claim, can be circumvented by promissory estoppel. *See Workman*, *supra*, where Judge Posner stated:

> A disclaimer that is effective against a claim of breach of contract is also effective, we believe, against a claim of promissory estoppel . . . . A promise can be legally binding because it is supported by consideration or because it induces reasonable reliance, but in either case the promisor is free by a suitable disclaimer to deny any legally binding effect . . . . [C]onsideration or reliance is a necessary but not a sufficient condition of the enforceability of a promise. Another necessary condition is that the promise be worded consistently with its being intended to be enforceable.

234 F.3d at 1001.

2. *Collective Bargaining*

Instead of negotiating individually, employees can exercise their rights under the National Labor Relations Act to negotiate collectively by authorizing a union to represent all employees in a designated "bargaining unit" (a group of employees defined by their employer, job classifications, geographic location, or other criteria). *See* 29 U.S.C. §§ 157, 158, 159. Collective action can strengthen the employees' bargaining power, and the agreement a union negotiates will probably be better drafted and more comprehensive than the usual individual contract. Collective bargaining agreements also empower employees to forcefully assert contract rights by protecting employees against retaliatory discharge "without cause" (a provision of nearly all collective bargaining agreements) and by providing a relatively quick and inexpensive means to assert contract claims through binding grievance and arbitration proceedings.

In the prevailing model of collective bargaining in the United States, a union gains the *exclusive* right to represent all employees in the bargaining unit. 29 U.S.C. § 159(a). Individual employees in the bargaining unit may decline to become union members. However, all are represented by the union regardless of membership, and all are subject to the agreement the union negotiates.

J. I. CASE CO. v. NLRB

321 U.S. 332 (1944)

Mr. Justice JACKSON delivered the opinion of the Court.

This cause was heard by the National Labor Relations Board on stipulated facts which so far as concern present issues are as follows:

The petitioner, J. I. Case Company, at its Rock Island, Illinois, plant, from 1937 offered each employee an individual contract of employment. The contracts were uniform and for a term of one year. The Company agreed to furnish employment as steadily as conditions permitted, to pay a specified rate, which the Company might redetermine if the job changed, and to maintain certain hospital facilities. The employee agreed to accept the provisions, to serve faithfully and honestly for the term, to comply with factory rules, and that defective work should not be paid for. About 75% of the employees accepted and worked under these agreements.

According to the Board's stipulation and finding, the execution of the contracts was not a condition of employment, nor was the status of individual employees affected by reason of signing or failing to sign the contracts. It is not found or contended that the agreements were coerced, obtained by any unfair labor practice, or that they were not valid under the circumstances in which they were made.

While the individual contracts executed August 1, 1941 were in effect, a C.I.O. union petitioned the Board for certification as the exclusive bargaining representative of the production and maintenance employees. On December 17, 1941 a hearing was held, at which the Company urged the individual contracts as a bar to representation proceedings. The Board, however, directed an election, which was won by the union. The union was thereupon certified as the exclusive bargaining representative of the employees in question in respect to wages, hours, and other conditions of employment. The union then asked the Company to bargain. It refused, declaring that it could not deal with the union in any manner affecting rights and obligations under the individual contracts while they remained in effect. It offered to negotiate on matters which did not affect rights under the individual contracts, and said that upon the expiration of the contracts it would bargain as to all matters. Twice the Company sent circulars to its employees asserting the validity of the individual contracts and stating the position that it took before the Board in reference to them.

The Board held that the Company had refused to bargain collectively, in violation of § 8(5) of the National Labor Relations Act, 29 U.S.C.A. § 158(5); and that the contracts had been utilized, by means of the circulars, to impede employees in the exercise of rights guaranteed by § 7 of the Act, 29 U.S.C.A. § 157, with the result that the Company had engaged in unfair labor practices within the meaning of § 8(1) of the Act. It ordered the Company to cease and desist from giving effect to the contracts, from extending them or entering into new ones, from refusing to bargain and from interfering with the employees; and it required the Company to give notice accordingly and to bargain upon request.

The Circuit Court of Appeals, with modification not in issue here, granted an order of enforcement. The issues are unsettled ones important in the administration of the Act, and we granted certiorari. In doing so we asked counsel, in view of the expiration of the individual contracts and the negotiation of a collective contract, to discuss whether the case was moot. In view of the continuing character of the obligation imposed by the order we think it is not, and will examine the merits.

Contract in labor law is a term the implications of which must be determined from the connection in which it appears. Collective bargaining between employer and the representatives of a unit, usually a union, results in an accord as to terms which will govern hiring and work and pay in that unit. The result is not, however, a contract of employment except in rare cases; no one has a job by reason of it and no obligation to any individual ordinarily comes into existence from it alone. The negotiations between union and management result in what often has been called a trade agreement, rather than in a contract of employment. Without pushing the analogy too far, the agreement may be likened to the tariffs established by a carrier, to standard provisions prescribed by supervising authorities for insurance policies, or to utility schedules of rates and rules for service, which do not of themselves establish any relationships but which do govern the terms of the shipper or insurer or customer relationship whenever and with whomever it may be established.

Indeed, in some European countries, contrary to American practice, the terms of a collectively negotiated trade agreement are submitted to a government department and if approved become a governmental regulation ruling employment in the unit.

After the collective trade agreement is made, the individuals who shall benefit by it are identified by individual hirings. The employer, except as restricted by the collective agreement itself and except that he must engage in no unfair labor practice or discrimination, is free to select those he will employ or discharge. But the terms of the employment already have been traded out. There is little left to individual agreement except the act of hiring. This hiring may be by writing or by word of mouth or may be implied from conduct. In the sense of contracts of hiring, individual contracts between the employer and employee are not forbidden, but indeed are necessitated by the collective bargaining procedure.

But, however engaged, an employee becomes entitled by virtue of the Labor Relations Act somewhat as a third party beneficiary to all benefits of the collective trade agreement, even if on his own he would yield to less favorable terms. The individual hiring contract is subsidiary to the terms of the trade agreement and may not waive any of its benefits, any more than a shipper can contract away the benefit of filed tariffs, the insurer the benefit of standard provisions, or the utility customer the benefit of legally established rates.

. . . Care has been taken in the opinions of the Court to reserve a field for the individual contract, even in industries covered by the National Labor Relations Act, not merely as an act or evidence of hiring, but also in the sense of a completely individually bargained contract setting out terms of employment, because there are circumstances in which it may legally be used, in fact, in which there is no alternative. Without limiting the possibilities, instances such as the following will occur: Men may continue work after a collective agreement expires and, despite negotiation in good faith, the negotiation may be deadlocked or delayed; in the interim express or implied individual agreements may be held to govern. The conditions for collective bargaining may not exist; thus a majority of the employees may refuse to join a union or to agree upon or designate bargaining representatives, or the majority may not be demonstrable by the means prescribed by the statute, or a previously existent majority may have been lost without unlawful interference by the employer and no new majority have been formed. As the employer in these circumstances may be under no legal obligation to bargain collectively, he may be free to enter into individual contracts.

Individual contracts no matter what the circumstances that justify their execution or what their terms, may not be availed of to defeat or delay the procedures prescribed by the National Labor Relations Act looking to collective bargaining, nor to exclude the contracting employee from a duly ascertained bargaining unit; nor may they be used to forestall bargaining or to limit or condition the terms of the collective agreement. "The Board asserts a public right vested in it as a public body, charged in the public interest with the duty of preventing unfair labor practices." National Licorice Co. v. National Labor Relations Board, 309 U.S. 350. Wherever private contracts conflict with its functions, they obviously must yield or the Act would be reduced to a futility. It is equally clear since the collective trade agreement is to serve the purpose contemplated by the Act, the individual contract cannot be effective as a waiver of any benefit to which the employee otherwise would be entitled under the trade agreement. The very purpose of providing by statute for the collective agreement is to supersede the terms of separate agreements of employees with terms which reflect the strength and bargaining power and serve the welfare of the group. Its benefits and advantages are open to every employee of the represented unit, whatever the type or terms of his pre-existing contract of employment.

But it is urged that some employees may lose by the collective agreement, that an individual workman may sometimes have, or be capable of getting, better terms than those obtainable by the group and that his freedom of contract must be respected on that account. We are not called upon to say that under no circumstances can an individual enforce an agreement more advantageous than a collective agreement, but we find the mere possibility that such agreements might be made no ground for holding generally that individual contracts may survive or surmount collective ones. The practice and philosophy of collective bargaining looks with suspicion on such individual advantages.

Of course, where there is great variation in circumstances of employment or capacity of employees, it is possible for the collective bargain to prescribe only minimum rates or maximum hours or expressly to leave certain areas open to individual bargaining. But except as so provided, advantages to individuals may prove as disruptive of industrial peace as disadvantages. They are a fruitful way of interfering with organization and choice of representatives; increased compensation, if individually deserved, is often earned at the cost of breaking down some other standard thought to be for the welfare of the group, and always creates the suspicion of being paid at the long-range expense of the group as a whole. Such discriminations not infrequently amount to unfair labor practices. The workman is free, if he values his own bargaining position more than that of the group, to vote against representation; but the majority rules, and if it collectivizes the employment bargain, individual advantages or favors will generally in practice go in as a contribution to the collective result. We cannot except individual contracts generally from the operation of collective ones because some may be more individually advantageous. Individual contracts cannot subtract from collective ones, and whether under some circumstances they may add to them in matters covered by the collective bargain, we leave to be determined by appropriate forums under the laws of contracts applicable, and to the Labor Board if they constitute unfair labor practices.

It also is urged that such individual contracts may embody matters that are not necessarily included within the statutory scope of collective bargaining, such as stock purchase, group insurance, hospitalization, or medical attention. We know of nothing to prevent the employee's, because he is an employee, making any contract provided it is not inconsistent with a collective agreement or does not amount to or result from or is not part of an unfair labor practice. But in so doing the employer may not incidentally exact or obtain any diminution of his own obligation or any increase of those of employees in the matters covered by collective agreement.

Hence we find that the contentions of the Company that the individual contracts precluded a choice of representatives and warranted refusal to bargain during their duration were properly over-ruled. It follows that representation to the employees by circular letter that they had such legal effect was improper and could properly be prohibited by the Board. . . .

[The court amended the board's order to prohibit negotiation or enforcement of any individual contract "to forestall collective bargaining or deter self-organization."]

As so modified the decree is Affirmed.

NOTES AND QUESTIONS

1. Why might a union object to one employee's agreement with the employer for a more generous wage rate for that employee?

2. Contract formation is very different when employees form a union for the purpose of collective bargaining. So is contract enforcement. The usual collective bargaining agreement provides a process for grievance adjustment and arbitration to resolve contractual disputes. An employee can file his own grievance about any perceived employer breach of contract. It will be up to the union, however, to decide whether to pursue the grievance, how to present the grievance, whether to "trade" that grievance in exchange for the employer's concession on some other matter, whether to demand arbitration, and how to present the grievance in arbitration.

An employee might prefer to speak or sue for himself. Although a certified or lawfully recognized union has the exclusive right to negotiate terms and conditions of employment, the National Labor Relations Act reserves some opportunity for individual self-representation. Section 9(a), 29 U.S.C. § 159(a), provides

> any individual employee or group of employees shall have the right at any time to present grievances to their employer and to have such grievances adjusted, without the intervention of the bargaining representative, as long as the adjustment is not inconsistent with the terms of a collective bargaining contract or agreement then in effect: *Provided further*, That the bargaining representative has been given opportunity to be present at such adjustment.

Obviously, the rule that any "adjustment" gained by the employee must not be "inconsistent" with the collective bargaining agreement is an important limitation on the "right" of individual self-representation. Another important limitation is that the employee cannot compel an employer to listen to his grievance. The employer may insist that it will consider only grievances processed through the union, with which the employer has an enforceable duty to bargain. 29 U.S.C. § 158(a)(5). Indeed, the most important effect of the individual employee's "right" under section 9(a) might be the defense it creates for the employer. If the employer chooses to deal directly with the employee, it can assert the section 9(a) proviso as a defense against the union's charge that the employer has ignored the union's exclusive authority to negotiate for employees. *See* Emporium Capwell Co. v. Western Addition Community Org., 420 U.S. 50, 61 & n.12, (1975).

If the union chooses not to pursue an employee's grievance, or if the employee is unhappy with the union's efforts or results, he is bound nonetheless by the results of the contractual dispute resolution process. A court will not entertain the employee's own breach of contract lawsuit unless the employee is able to prove (1) the employer breached the agreement; and (2) the union's actions in rejecting or processing the grievance were "arbitrary, discriminatory or in bad faith," in violation of its duty of fair representation. Vaca v. Sipes, 386 U.S. 171 (1967). The employee's "hybrid" breach of contract/duty of fair representation lawsuit (in which the union might be joined as a defendant with the employer) is subject to federal court jurisdiction under 29 U.S.C. § 185, and to the six-month statute of limitations for actions based on a union's breach of duties under the National Labor Relations Act. 29 U.S.C. § 160. *See* DelCostello v. Teamsters, 462 U.S. 151 (1983).

Beyond Collective Bargaining: Other Protected "Concerted Activities"

Even when employees do not form unions or bargain collectively in the usual sense, they might act together in other ways to improve their terms and conditions. For example, they might share information with each other about their respective wage rates. Employers, on the other hand, often prefer to keep individual wage information confidential. An employer could have many reasons for keeping employees in the dark about what each person is earning, but one possible reason is that employees are more likely to underestimate their worth if they do not know what the employer pays other individuals for the same work.

While employer rules against disclosure of pay rates appear to be quite common, employee discussions about wages and employee sharing of wage information are protected in most instances by the same law that protects the right of collective bargaining. Section 7 of the National Labor Relations Act, 29 U.S.C. § 157, states as follows (emphasis added):

> Employees shall have the right to self-organization, to form, join, or assist labor organizations, to bargain collectively through representatives of their own choosing, and to engage in *other concerted activities for the purpose of* collective bargaining or *other mutual aid or protection*. . . .

A discussion between two employees is a "concerted activity," and it might be for "mutual aid or protection" if the purpose or effect is to strengthen their quest for higher wages. Thus, the NLRB has consistently held that an employer interferes with its employees' section 7 rights by prohibiting employees from discussing wages or disclosing wage rates to each other. *See, e.g.*, Koronis Parts, Inc., 324 NLRB 675 (1997). At least one state, California, also prohibits employers from punishing employees for disclosing or discussing wages. *See* Cal. Lab. Code § 232. *See also* Grant-Burton v. Covenant Care, Inc., 122 Cal. Rptr. 2d 204 (Cal. App. 2002) (applying California law to an employee discussion about bonuses).

The frequent employer argument that a confidentiality rule is necessary to prevent "jealousies and strife among employees" has swayed neither the board nor the courts. As the court explained in Jeannette Corp. v. NLRB, 532 F.2d 916, 919 (3d Cir. 1976):

> [D]issatisfaction due to low wages is the grist on which concerted activity feeds. Discord generated by what employees view as unjustified wage differentials also provides the sinew for persistent concerted action. The possibility that ordinary speech and discussion over wages on an employee's own time may cause "jealousies and strife among employees" is not a justifiable business reason to inhibit the opportunity for an employee to exercise section 7 rights.

532 F.2d at 919.

There are, however, limits of reasonableness to the protection section 7 offers concerted activities. An employer can restrict employee activities, including conversation, that interfere with productive work during working time, and an employer can prohibit employees from stealing or copying confidential business documents. *See* NLRB v. Brookshire Grocery Co., 919 F.2d 359 (5th Cir. 1990) (employer lawfully discharged employee who secretly removed, copied and disseminated wage records and performance evaluations from supervisor's office).

In MasTec Advanced Technologies, 357 NLRB No. 17 (2011), the NLRB considered whether employees engaged in protected concerted activity when they took their pay dispute to the local media. The employees were satellite TV installation technicians whose compensation was affected by a new employer rule reducing their compensation whenever they failed to persuade a customer to accept a telephone line hookup, which involved additional service and products non-essential to the satellite connection.

After several meetings at which the employees expressed their displeasure with the rule to their employer, the employees took their problem to a local TV station. The resulting story broadcast on the local TV news was about both the pay dispute *and* certain sales techniques to which the pay dispute was connected. For example, one part of an interview aired on the TV news was as follows: *Interviewer*: "So you've basically been told to lie to customers [about the need for the phone hookup]?" *Technician*: "Yeah."

When the employer saw the story on the TV news, he fired several of the employees. The employees filed charges with the NLRB alleging that the employer had interfered with their right to engage in concerted activity, and the Board agreed with the employees.

The Board cited established law that "[e]mployee communications to third parties in an effort to obtain their support are protected where the communication indicated it is related to an ongoing dispute between the employees and the employers and the communication is not so disloyal, reckless or maliciously untrue as to lose the Act's protection." The employee communications in this case were admittedly related to their pay dispute. Thus, the principal issues were whether the employees' statements on TV were (1) "maliciously untrue;" or (2) "disloyal."

The Board found that the statements were not "maliciously untrue." "Indeed," the Board found, "for the most part, the statements were accurate representations of what the Respondents had instructed the technicians to tell customers." In fact, "the technicians *were* essentially told to lie." For example, the employer had "advised technicians to say that the hookup to the phone was 'a mandatory part of the installation' and needed 'for the equipment to function correctly.' " In fact, the hookup was optional and was not necessary for the equipment to function. And although the employees' broadcast statements were not complete and accurate in every detail, "[a]ny arguable departures from the truth were no more than good-faith misstatements or incomplete statements, not malicious falsehoods justifying removal of the Act's protection."

The Board also found that the employees' actions were not "disloyal" and did not constitute "reckless disparagement" of the employer's services. An employee's public criticisms of an employee are not so "disloyal" as to lose the protection of

Section 7 unless the criticisms are "wholly incommensurate with any grievances which [the employees] might have." In this case, the employees went to the local media only after several efforts to resolve their pay dispute directly with the employer. The resulting newscast "shed unwelcome light on certain deceptive business practices, but it was nevertheless directly related to [a] pay policy [the employees] believed forced them to mislead customers." Moreover, "while the technicians may have been aware that some consumers might cancel the Respondents' services after listening to the newscast, there is no evidence that they intended to inflict such harm on the Respondents, or that they acted recklessly without regard for the financial consequences to the Respondents' businesses.

Concerted Action on the Internet

The Internet has become another major forum for employee discussions about wages and other working conditions. A discussion between employees or a call for concerted action with respect to their working conditions does not lose its protection under Section 7 simply because it occurs on the Internet rather than at work. However, the fact that employee communications occur on the Internet leads to two special problems. First, discussions occurring on the Internet are easily broadcast to a very wide audience, including customers, investors, and the general public. The employer might feel even more threatened by such communications than it would if employees were talking only among themselves at the workplace. Second, it may be relatively easy for the employer to monitor employee internet communications in comparison with its monitoring of other forms of communication.

The following memorandum is by the General Counsel of the National Labor Relations Board. The General Counsel's office investigates possible violations of the National Labor Relations Act, decides whether to issue a complaint, and prosecutes the action in an administrative enforcement proceeding. This memorandum does not carry the same weight as a final adjudicatory decision of the National Labor Relations Board or of a court, but it does set forth the General Counsel's approach in deciding whether to issue a complaint in circumstances involving employee use of the Internet as a forum.

OFFICE OF THE GENERAL COUNSEL, NATIONAL LABOR RELATIONS BOARD

Memorandum OM 11-74 (August 18, 2011)

. . . This report presents recent case developments arising in the context of today's social media. Social media include various online technology tools that enable people to communicate easily via the internet to share information and resources. These tools can encompass text, audio, video, images, podcasts, and other multimedia communications. Recent developments in the Office of the General Counsel have presented emerging issues concerning the protected and/or concerted nature of employees' Facebook and Twitter postings . . . and the lawfulness of employers' social media policies and rules . . . . All of these cases were decided upon a request for advice from a Regional Director . . . .

Employees' Facebook Postings About Tax Withholding Practices Were Protected Concerted Activity

We also considered a case in which the Employer — a sports bar and restaurant — discharged and threatened to sue two employees who participated in a Facebook conversation initiated by a former coworker about the Employer's tax withholding practices. This case also raised issues concerning the Employer's Internet/blogging policy that prohibited "inappropriate discussions." We found that the discharges, threats of legal action, and the Internet policy were unlawful.

In early 2011, several of the Employer's former and current employees discovered that they owed state income taxes for 2010, related to earnings at the Employer. After this discovery, at least one employee brought the issue to the Employer's attention and requested that the matter be placed on the agenda for discussion at an upcoming management meeting with employees.

Thereafter, on February 1, a former employee posted on her Facebook page a statement, including a short-hand expletive, that expressed dissatisfaction with the fact that she now owed money. She also asserted that the Employer's owners could not even do paperwork correctly. One employee — Charging Party A — responded to this posting by clicking "Like." That same day, a series of statements related to the initial posting followed. Two other employees commented that they had never owed money before, and one of them referred to telling the Employer that we will discuss this at the meeting. Two of the Employer's customers joined in the conversation, as did Charging Party B, who asserted that she also owed money and referred to one of the Employer's owners as "[s]uch an asshole."

The Charging Parties were not working on the day of the Facebook conversation. When Charging Party B reported back to work on February 2, she was told that her employment was terminated due to her Facebook posting and because she was not "loyal enough" to work for the Employer anymore. The following day, Charging Party A reported to work and was confronted by the Employer about the Facebook conversation. He was terminated and told that he would be hearing from the Employer's attorney.

Thereafter, Charging Party B received a letter dated February 5 from the Employer's attorney stating that legal action would be initiated against her unless she retracted her "defamatory" statements regarding the Employer and its principals published to the general public on Facebook.

As noted, under the *Meyers* cases, [Meyers Industries (*Meyers I*), 268 NLRB 493 (1984), *revd. sub nom* Prill v. NLRB, 755 F.2d 941 (D.C. Cir. 1985), *cert. denied* 474 U.S. 948 (1985), *on remand* Meyers Industries (*Meyers II*), 281 NLRB 882 (1986), *affd. sub nom* Prill v. NLRB, 835 F.2d 1481 (D.C. Cir. 1987), *cert. denied* 487 U.S. 1205 (1988)], the Board's test for concerted activity is whether activity is "engaged in with or on the authority of other employees, and not solely by and on behalf of the employee himself." Concerted activity also includes "circumstances where individual employees seek to initiate or to induce or to prepare for group action" and where individual employees bring "truly group complaints" to management's attention. *Meyers II*, 281 NLRB at 887.

Here, the February 1 conversation on Facebook related to employees' shared concerns about a term and condition of employment — the Employer's administration of income tax withholdings. Moreover, prior to the Facebook conversation, this shared concern had been brought to the Employer's attention by at least one employee who specifically noted on Facebook that she had requested it be discussed at an upcoming management meeting with employees. Thus, the conversation that transpired on Facebook not only embodied "truly group complaints" but also contemplated future group activity.

We found that the Charging Parties' statements did not lose protection either under *Atlantic Steel* or, as the Employer asserted, because they were defamatory.

Applying *Atlantic Steel*, [245 NLRB 814 (1979) (a leading precedent for determining whether an employee's public outbursts against a supervisor can be regarded as part of protected concerted activity)], we found that the Charging Parties' statements related to a core concern protected under Section 7. Moreover, the comments were initiated outside of the workplace during the Charging Parties' nonworking time, and neither disrupted operations nor undermined supervisory authority. Furthermore, although the activity was not provoked by any unfair labor practice committed by the Employer, the nature of the Charging Parties' postings was much less offensive than other behavior found protected by the Board.

With regard to the Employer's allegation of defamation, an alleged defamatory statement will not lose its protected status unless it is not only false but maliciously false. [NLRB v. Electrical Workers Local 1229 (*Jefferson Standard*), 346 U.S. 464 (1953)]. Here, Charging Party A merely indicated that he "liked" the initial Facebook posting by his former coworker, which accused the Employer's owners of not being able to do paperwork correctly. Charging Party B's posting was limited to a factually correct statement that she had an outstanding tax obligation, and her opinion that one of the Employer's owners was "[s]uch an asshole." The Charging Parties' Facebook postings, to the extent that they constituted statements of fact that could be alleged as defamatory, were not even false, much less maliciously false under the Board's standard.

We also concluded that the Employer's threats to sue the Charging Parties for engaging in protected concerted activity violated Section 8(a)(1). It is well established that an employer's threat to sue employees for engaging in Section 7 activity violates the Act because it would reasonably tend to interfere with the exercise of Section 7 rights. The Board has historically distinguished the threat of a lawsuit from the actual filing of a lawsuit and has rejected employers' attempts to extend the First Amendment protection accorded to lawsuits to threats to sue where those threats, as here, were not incidental to the actual filing of a suit. Thus, we found that the Employer's threats to sue the Charging Parties were unlawful, even if there was a reasonable basis for potential legal action.

We also considered the lawfulness of the Employer's Internet/blogging policy. This policy, included in the Employer's employee handbook, provided that the employer supported the free exchange of information and camaraderie among employees. The policy went on to state that when internet blogging, chat room discussions, e-mail, text messages, or other forms of communication extend to employees revealing confidential and proprietary information about the employer, or engaging in inappropriate discussions about the company, management, and/or coworkers, the employee may be violating the law and is subject to disciplinary action, up to and including termination.

An employer violates Section 8(a)(1) of the Act through the maintenance of a work rule if that rule would "reasonably tend to chill employees in the exercise of their Section 7 rights." Lafayette Park Hotel, 326 NLRB 824, 825 (1998), *enf'd.* 203 F.3d 52 (D.C. Cir. 1999). The Board uses a two-step inquiry to determine if a work rule would have such an effect. Lutheran Heritage Village–Livonia, 343 NLRB 646, 647 (2004). First, a rule is unlawful if it explicitly restricts Section 7 activities. If the rule does not explicitly restrict protected activities, it is unlawful only upon a showing that: (1) employees would reasonably construe the language to prohibit Section 7 activity; (2) the rule was promulgated in response to union activity; or (3) the rule has been applied to restrict the exercise of Section 7 rights.

Applying these standards here, we concluded that the provision of the Employer's policy stating that employees are subject to discipline for engaging in "inappropriate discussions" about the company, management, and/or coworkers could reasonably be interpreted to restrain Section 7 activity. This policy utilized broad terms that would commonly apply to protected criticism of the Employer's labor policies, treatment of employees, and terms and conditions of employment. Moreover, the policy did not define what was encompassed by the broad term "inappropriate discussions" by specific examples or limit it in any way that would exclude Section 7 activity. Absent such limitations or examples of what was covered, we concluded that employees would reasonably interpret the rule to prohibit their discussion of terms and conditions of employment among themselves or with third parties . . . .

Bartender Who Posted Facebook Message About Employer's Tipping Policy Was Not Engaged in Concerted Activity

This case concerned an employee — a bartender — who was discharged for posting a message on his Facebook page that referenced the Employer's tipping policy in response to a question from a nonemployee. We found that the employee was not engaged in concerted activity.

The Employer operates a restaurant and bar. It maintains an unwritten policy that waitresses do not share their tips with the bartenders even though the bartenders help the waitresses serve food.

Sometime in the fall of 2010, the employee had a conversation with a fellow bartender about this tipping policy. He complained about the policy, and she agreed that it "sucked." However, neither they nor any other bartender ever raised the issue with management.

In February 2011, the employee had a conversation on Facebook with a relative. Responding to her query as to how his night at work had gone, he complained that he hadn't had a raise in five years and that he was doing the waitresses' work without tips. He also called the Employer's customers "rednecks" and stated that he hoped they choked on glass as they drove home drunk. He did not discuss his posting with any of his coworkers, and none of them responded to it.

About a week later, the Employer's night manager told the employee that he was probably going to be fired over it. In May, the employee received a Facebook message from the Employer's owner informing him that his services were no longer required, and the next day, the Employer's day manager left him a voice message stating that he was fired for his Facebook posting about the Employer's customers.

As noted above, under the *Meyers* cases, the Board's test for concerted activity is whether activity is "engaged in with or on the authority of other employees, and not solely by and on behalf of the employee himself." We found no evidence of concerted activity here. Although the employee's Facebook posting addressed his terms and conditions of employment, he did not discuss the posting with his coworkers, and none of them responded to the posting. There had been no employee meetings or any attempt to initiate group action concerning the tipping policy or raises. We also found that this internet "conversation" did not grow out of the employee's conversation with a fellow bartender months earlier about the tipping policy . . . .

NOTES AND QUESTIONS

1. As the cases described in the General Counsel's memorandum illustrate, employees can engage in protected "concerted activity" even in the absence of a union or a practice of collective bargaining.

2. Does the distinction between "concerted activity" versus purely individual activity make sense? Has the NLRB employed the right set of tests for distinguishing protected concerted activity from unprotected concerted activity? If not, how would you rewrite the law?

Wage Bargaining Practices and Race or Sex Discrimination

Race and sex discrimination in employment are illegal under Title VII of the Civil Rights Act of 1964, and sex discrimination in pay is further prohibited by the Equal Pay Act. But minorities and women still tend to earn less than white men for the same work. Some of the disparity might be the result of intentional or subconscious bias of employers, and some might be the result of the ways white men "bargain" as compared with women or minorities. Stephanie Boraas & William M. Rodgers III, *How Does Gender Play a Role in the Earnings Gap? An Update*, Monthly Lab. Rev. (Mar. 2003). Whatever the causes, the persistence of disparities might be enabled by the unavailability of wage data to applicants employees. The National Labor Relations Act protects the rights of covered employees to discuss wages and share information among themselves, but many salaried managerial employees are not protected by the National Labor Relations Act and have no "right" to discuss their comparative rates. Employees who are protected by the NLRA have a right but no duty to respond or disclose, and many employees prefer to keep their compensation confidential from other employees. Employers generally do not post comparative earnings or provide any means for the accurate collection and distribution of wage information for nonunion employees.

In 2016 during the Obama Administration, the EEOC proposed to amend its regulations to require certain employers to disclose wage rates by race and sex in annual reports to the EEOC. Such reports would have made the existence of disparities in a workplace obvious—at least to the EEOC. The EEOC intended to use the information to target industries or employers for further investigation and possible charges of discrimination. 81 Fed. Reg. 5113 (Feb. 1, 2016).

The following year the Trump Administration froze a number of the Obama Administration's still-pending proposals including the EEOC's proposed pay disclosure rule. The Trump Administration's first set of nominees for the EEOC have indicated they will either rescind the pay disclosure proposal or amend it to limit its reach and effect. Josh Eidelson, *Trump Appointees Expected to Reorient Equal Employment Commission*, Insurance Journal (Oct. 10, 2017), https://www.insurancejournal.com/news/national/2017/10/10/466901.htm.

C. STATUTORY MINIMUMS AND REMEDIES

1. *Minimum Wage and Overtime Laws: Basic Requirements*

a. The Rates

Government regulation of personal earnings has an ancient and varied lineage. In early America, wage regulation was mainly to protect employers from the "unreasonable" demands of workers during periods of labor shortage. Department of Labor, History of Wages in the United States from Colonial Times to 1928, pp. 9-11 (1934). In modern times regulation has more often protected workers by establishing "minimum" rates of pay. *But see* Fry v. United States, 421 U.S. 542 (1975) (upholding injunction against officials of State of Ohio to prevent them from granting raises to public employees in violation of Nixon-era price and wage controls); Tex. Lab. Code § 408.221 (regulating the fee an attorney may earn in a workers' compensation matter).

The most important example of wage regulation today is the Fair Labor Standards Act (FLSA) and its requirement of a "minimum wage." Section 6 of the act states the minimum wage as an hourly rate, which is $7.25 per hour as of 2012. 29 U.S.C. § 206. Section 6 does not require that an employer must actually pay an *hourly* rate. An employer could pay according to a weekly salary, commission, or other rate or method of calculating earnings. However, the earnings an employee receives in a workweek, divided by hours of work in that week, must equal the minimum wage. *See* 29 C.F.R. §§ 778.113, 778.114.

Congress adjusts the minimum wage from time to time by amending the FLSA, though not always in close step with inflation. Moreover, today's minimum wage appears to be significantly below the prevailing market rate for any occupation identified by the Department of Labor. According to wage data collected by the Bureau of Labor Statistics for 2016, the median hourly wage of workers in the U.S. is $17.81. The median hourly wage for the lowest-paid non-farm occupation, fast-food preparation and service, is $9.35 per hour. For housekeeping workers the median rate is $10.49 per hour. Cashiers earn a median rate of $9.70 per hour. Farmworkers earn a median rate of $10.58 per hour. Bureau of Labor Statistics, National Occupational Employment and Wage estimates (May 2016), at http://www.bls.gov/oes/current/oes_nat.htm#00-0000. Of course, many workers earn much less than these median rates. In fact, the Bureau of Labor Statistics estimates that during 2014, there were about 1.3 million workers earning exactly the minimum wage of $7.25 per hour, and there were 1.7 million earning *less* than the minimum wage. Bureau of Labor Statistics, Characteristics of Minimum Wage Workers: 2014 (April 2015), at https://www.bls.gov/opub/reports/minimum-wage/archive/characteristics-of-minimum-wage-workers-2014.pdf

How could so many employees be earning less than the statutory minimum wage? Most of these sub-minimum wage employees work outside the coverage of the act or in exempt occupations or industries. But the reported number of employees earning less than the minimum wage is probably understated. Workers misclassified as "self-employed" independent contractors are excluded. *Id.* at p. 4 Note. Moreover, some low paid "salaried" workers dip below the minimum hourly rate during weeks when they work more than forty hours, but the Bureau's report looks only at hourly rated employees. *Id.* at p. 17. Congress has repeatedly rejected proposed FLSA amendments for an "indexed" minimum wage that would increase automatically with the cost of living. *See* William Quigley, *A Fair Day's Pay for a Fair Day's Work: Time to Raise and Index the Minimum Wage*, 27 St. Mary's L.J. 513 (1996). In contrast, a series of laws applicable only to work under certain federal government contracts requires payment of "prevailing" rates, determined administratively and regularly adjusted by the Department of Labor. *See, e.g.*, Davis-Bacon Act, 40 U.S.C. §§ 276-276a-7 (certain public works and construction contracts); Walsh-Healey Act, 41 §§ 35-45 (certain contracts for supplies); Service Contract Act, 41 U.S.C. §§ 351-358 (certain service contracts).

The need for periodic adjustment of the minimum wage sustains a debate whether minimum wage laws lift underpaid workers from poverty or cause greater poverty by increasing the cost of labor and discouraging employers from hiring or retaining low-wage workers? Empirical data is mixed. *See generally* J. Addison, M. Blackburn & C. Cotti, *Minimum Wage Increases Under Straightened Circumstances* (October 2011), online at http://papers.ssrn.com/sol3/papers.cfm?abstract_id=1948032##; D. Card & A. Krueger, Myth and Measurement: The New Economics of the Minimum Wage (Princeton Univ. Press 1995); C. Brown, C. Gilroy & A. Kohen, *The Effect of the Minimum Wage on Employment and Unemployment*, 20 J. Econ. Lit. 487 (1982).

States are free to enact higher minimum wages, 29 U.S.C. § 218, and some have done so. The U.S. Department of Labor maintains an interactive online map displaying information about current state minimum wage laws at http://www.dol.gov/whd/minwage/america.htm#Washington. As of 2017, the District of Columbia had the highest minimum wage at $12.50 per hour, followed by the State of Washington at $11.00 per hour. However, many states have either adopted whatever rate is currently in force under the FLSA, or have adopted no state minimum wage at all. Some municipal governments have higher minimum wages, frequently under the title of "living wage" ordinances, for work performed within their jurisdictions. Whether these laws are valid exercises of municipal power depends on state law. *See, e.g.*, New Orleans Campaign for a Living Wage v. City of New Orleans, 825 So. 2d 1098 (La. 2002). The recent adoption of local minimum wage rates by some cities has served as an opportunity for further investigation into the actual effect of minimum wage hikes on employment and earnings. See Noam Scheiber, *How a Rising Minimum Wage Affects Jobs in Seattle*, New York Times (June 26, 2017), https://nyti.ms/2taxiCJ.

Another basic FLSA requirement is the payment of premium wages for hours in excess of 40 in a single workweek. 29 U.S.C. § 207. The overtime rate depends on an employee's "regular" hourly rate. In general, an employee's overtime rate is one and one half times his regular rate. An employee's entitlement to overtime pay is determined separately for each workweek. The act does not permit an employer to "average" the number of hours an employee has worked over two or more workweeks. Nor does the act permit an employer to fulfill its overtime pay obligation by granting "compensatory time-off," except in the case of state and local government employers under certain circumstances. 29 U.S.C. § 207(o).

Again, the states are free to adopt more protective overtime requirements. For example, a state might require the payment of premium pay for any hours in excess of eight in a single day. *See, e.g.*, Cal. Lab. Code § 510. However, most states with overtime laws have adopted the 40 hours per week standard.

OVERNIGHT MOTOR TRANSPORT CO. v. MISSEL

316 U.S. 572 (1942)

Mr. Justice REED delivered the opinion of the Court.

This case involves the application of the overtime section of the Fair Labor Standards Act of 1938 to an employee working irregular hours for a fixed weekly wage. Respondent, Missel, was an employee of the petitioner, Overnight Motor Transportation Company, a corporation engaged in interstate motor transportation as a common carrier. He acted as rate clerk and performed other incidental duties, none of which were connected with safety of operation. The work for which he was employed involved wide fluctuations in the time required to complete his duties. . . . Until November 1, 1938, his salary was $25.50 per week and thereafter $27.50. Time records are available for only a third of the critical period, and these show an average workweek of 65 hours, with a maximum of 80 for each of two weeks in the first year of the Act's operation and a maximum of 75 hours in each of three weeks in the second year. Nothing above the weekly wage was paid. . . .

Respondent brought a statutory action to recover alleged unpaid overtime compensation in such sum as might be found due him, an additional equal amount as liquidated damages, and counsel fee. The trial court, refusing to hear evidence on the precise amount claimed, decided in favor of the petitioner on the ground that an agreement for a fixed weekly wage for irregular hours satisfied the requirements of the Act. Under such circumstances the court was of the view that pay would be adequate which amounted to the required minimum for the regular hours and time and a half the minimum for overtime. The Circuit Court of Appeals reversed with directions to enter judgment for the plaintiff in accordance with its opinion, an order which we interpret as authorizing a hearing in the trial court as to the amounts due. As the questions involved were important in the administration of the Fair Labor Standards Act, we granted certiorari. 315 U.S. 791.

Petitioner renews here its contentions that the private right to contract for a fixed weekly wage with employees in commerce is restricted only by the requirement that the wages paid should comply with the minimum wage schedule of the Fair Labor Standards Act, section 6, 29 U.S.C.A. § 206, with overtime pay at time and a half that minimum. . . .

The petitioner attacks the basic conceptions upon which the Circuit Court of Appeals determined that the compensation paid by the respondent violated section 7(a) of the act. That court felt that "one of the fundamental purposes of the act was to induce worksharing and relieve unemployment by reducing hours of work." (126 F.2d 98, 103.) We agree that the purpose of the act was not limited to a scheme to raise substandard wages first by a minimum wage and then by increased pay for overtime work. Of course, this was one effect of the time and a half provision, but another and an intended effect was to require extra pay for overtime work by those covered by the act even though their hourly wages exceeded the statutory minimum.

The provision of section 7(a) requiring this extra pay for overtime is clear and unambiguous. It calls for 150% of the regular, not the minimum, wage. By this requirement, although overtime was not flatly prohibited, financial pressure was applied to spread employment to avoid the extra wage and workers were assured additional pay to compensate them for the burden of a workweek beyond the hours fixed in the act. In a period of widespread unemployment and small profits, the economy inherent in avoiding extra pay was expected to have an appreciable effect in the distribution of available work. Reduction of hours was a part of the plan from the beginning. "A fair day's pay for a fair day's work" was the objective stated in the Presidential message which initiated the legislation. That message referred to a "general maximum working week," "longer hours on the payment of time and a half for overtime" and the evil of "overwork" as well as "underpay." The message of November 15, 1937, calling for the enactment of this type of legislation referred again to protection from excessive hours. Senate Report No. 884 just cited, page 4, the companion House Report and the Conference report all spoke of maximum hours as a separately desirable object. Indeed, the form of the act itself in setting up two sections of standards, Section 6 for wages and Section 7 for hours, emphasizes the duality of the Congressional purpose.

The existence of such a purpose is no less certain because Congress chose to use a less drastic form of limitation than outright prohibition of overtime. We conclude that the act was designed to require payment for overtime at time and a half the regular pay, where that pay is above the minimum, as well as where the regular pay is at the minimum.

We now come to the determination of the meaning of the words "the regular rate at which he is employed." . . . The wages for minimum pay are expressed in terms of so much an hour. § 6(a)(1) — "Not less than 25 cents an hour" with raises for succeeding years or by order of the Administrator under § 8. Neither the wage, the hour nor the overtime provisions of sections 6 and 7 on their passage spoke specifically of any other method of paying wages except by hourly rate. But we have no doubt that pay by the week, to be reduced by some method of computation to hourly rates, was also covered by the act. It is likewise abundantly clear from the words of section 7 that the unit of time under that section within which to distinguish regular from overtime is the week. "No employer shall . . . employ any of his employees . . . (1) for a workweek longer than forty-four hours. . . ."

No problem is presented in assimilating the computation of overtime for employees under contract for a fixed weekly wage for regular contract hours which are the actual hours worked, to similar computations for employees on hourly rates. Where the employment contract is for a weekly wage with variable or fluctuating hours the same method of computation produces the regular rate for each week. As that rate is on an hourly basis, it is regular in the statutory sense inasmuch as the rate per hour does not vary for the entire week, though week by week the regular rate varies with the number of hours worked. It is true that the longer the hours the less the rate and the pay per hour. This is not an argument, however, against this method of determining the regular rate of employment for the week in question. Apart from the Act if there is a fixed weekly wage regardless of the length of the workweek, the longer the hours the less are the earnings per hour. This method of computation has been approved by each circuit court of appeals which has considered such problems. *See* Warren Bradshaw Drilling Co. v. Hall, 5 Cir., 124 F.2d 42, 44; Bumpus v. Continental Baking Co., 6 Cir., 124 F.2d 549, 552. It is this quotient which is the "regular rate at which an employee is employed" under contracts of the types described and applied in this paragraph for fixed weekly compensation for hours, certain or variable.

Petitioner invokes the presumption that contracting parties contemplate compliance with law and contends that accordingly there is no warrant for construing the contract as paying the employee only his base pay or "regular rate," regardless of hours worked. It is true that the wage paid was sufficiently large to cover both base pay and fifty per cent additional for the hours actually worked over the statutory maximum without violating section six. But there was no contractual limit upon the hours which petitioner could have required respondent to work for the agreed wage, had he seen fit to do so, and no provision for additional pay in the event the hours worked required minimum compensation greater than the fixed wage. Implication cannot mend a contract so deficient in complying with the law. This contract differs from the one in Walling v. A. H. Belo Corp., 316 U.S. 624, decided today, where the contract specified an hourly rate and not less than time and a half for overtime, with a guaranty of a fixed weekly sum, and required the employer to pay more than the weekly guaranty where the hours worked at the contract rate exceeded that sum. . . .

Affirmed.

NOTES AND QUESTIONS

1. Do overtime laws necessarily encourage an employer to hire more workers to avoid overtime costs? The answer depends on a number of factors. For example, the cost of an expensive benefit, such as health care insurance, does not fluctuate with hours of work (as long as too much overtime does not affect an employee's health). Thus, when an employer decides whether to work an incumbent employee more hours or to hire an additional employee, the employer might consider that the cost of adding another employee to the health plan could be just as expensive as paying the incumbent employee for overtime. An employer might also find it can offset overtime premium costs by reducing the regular rate, reassigning the work to a new, lower-paid workforce if necessary. For more discussion of these issues, see S. Rabin-Margalioth, *Cross-Employee Redistribution Effects of Mandated Employee Benefits*, 20 Hofstra Employment L.J. 311 (2003); and S. Trejo, *Does the Statutory Overtime Premium Discourage Long Workweeks?* 56 Indus. & Lab. Rel. Rev. 530 (2003).

2. As *Overnight Motor Transport* suggests, the rules requiring payment of minimum wages and overtime do not mean that an employer must pay a simple hourly rate. For purposes of the minimum wage, the law simply requires that an

employee's total compensation for a week, however determined, equals at least the minimum wage when divided by the hours the employee worked. For example, if an employee earns a commission, and assuming he is subject to the minimum wage requirement, the employer must pay him at least the minimum wage times the number of hours he worked, regardless of whether the employee actually earned any commissions for that week. However, as long as the method of determining pay yields an amount equal to the statutory minimum when converted to an hourly rate, the purpose of the minimum wage law is satisfied.

3. Complying with overtime requirements is more complicated, and there may be more than one way of satisfying the law in any given situation. Consider first a salaried employee such as the one in *Overnight Motor Transport*. If the employee works more than 40 hours in a week, the employer must first calculate a "regular" hourly rate that will be the basis for calculating the additional overtime pay. To convert the salary to an hourly rate, however, one must first ask whether the salary was designed to pay for a *variable* number of hours per week (the usual understanding if compensation is a true "salary"), or a *fixed* number of hours (40 or some other specific number) per week. The answer to this question affects the way the regular rate is calculated and it determines whether the employer can claim that an employee is already partly compensated for overtime by virtue of his base salary.

For example, a weekly salary paid for a fixed workweek of 40 (or fewer) hours does not include any compensation for overtime hours. In this case, the employer must divide the salary by 40 hours (or the number of hours for which the employee is regularly employed at that salary) to yield the regular rate, and the employer must pay one and half times this regular rate for each overtime hour. *See generally* 29 C.F.R. § 778.322.

In contrast, if the salary is for a variable or "fluctuating" workweek and compensates the employee for all hours whatever their number, then calculating statutory overtime pay is very different. *See* 29 C.F.R. § 778.114. Every week, the employer must divide the salary by the total hours worked (including overtime hours) that week to yield the "regular rate" for that week. Note that the regular rate may change from week to week, and the more hours an employee works, the smaller his "regular rate." For example, if the employee works 45 hours and the weekly salary is $450, the regular rate is $10, but if the employee works 50 hours his regular rate will be only $9. Moreover, since his salary is intended to cover all hours, including overtime hours, the employer satisfies the statutory overtime requirement by paying an additional *one half* that week's regular rate for each overtime hour (an extra $5 per overtime hour when he worked 5 overtime hours, or an extra $4.50 per overtime hour when he worked 10 overtime hours). Although this method results in significantly lower overtime pay, it is lawful provided the employer can prove a clear written agreement with the employee authorizing this method. Moreover, the employer must be consistent. If it pays an employee a fixed salary for a variable workweek, then it must pay the same salary even in weeks in which the employee works fewer than 40 hours.

For still other types of salaries and overtime calculations for nonexempt employees, see 29 C.F.R. pt. 778.

4. A nonexempt employee might also be paid a "piece rate" for each unit of work produced. This too can be converted week by week to a regular hourly rate

by totaling all compensation from piece rates and other sources for the week, and by then dividing that number by the number of hours worked that week. The employee is entitled to an additional *one-half* the regular rate for each overtime hour (his regular piece rate earnings have already compensated him at the regular rate for overtime hours). *See* 29 C.F.R. § 778.111. Alternatively, the parties could agree to a premium piece rate for work done after the 40th hour. In other words, the employee earns his regular piece rate for work during the first 40 hours, and one and a half times that piece rate for work done after the 40th hour. 29 U.S.C. § 207(g); 29 C.F.R. § 778.418.

5. Many commissioned salespersons are exempt from the overtime rules, but some are not. For a nonexempt employee compensated all or in part by commissions, the employer must include commission earnings in the calculation of the regular rate for the week in which the commission was earned. In some cases, this may require the employer to make the overtime payment much later if commission earnings cannot be determined by the payday for the week in which commissions were earned. *See* 29 C.F.R. § 778.117.

PROBLEMS

In each of the following problems, assume that the employer and employees are subject to the minimum wage and overtime requirements of the FLSA.

1. Time Management, Inc. pays its employee Sally Reed a "salary" of $400 per week. Time has told Reed, and she understands, that she is to work 40 hours per week (8 to 5 each day with an hour for lunch). Reed is not required to punch a time clock, but if she misses time during the week she is required to make up the time during lunch or by staying late.

a. In one workweek, Reed missed some time because of illness and worked only 30 hours. She has not made up this time. What must Time pay Reed?

b. In the next week, Reed worked 50 hours. What must Time pay Reed?

2. Time Management, Inc. pays another employee, Wayne Cash, a "salary" of $400 per week. Cash's written agreement with Time says his salary is for a "variable" workweek, and he is not required to keep track of his time.

a. In one workweek, Cash missed some of his usual working time to go to a parent-teacher conference for his son. As a result, he worked only 38 hours for that week. What must Time pay Cash?

b. The next workweek, Cash worked 50 hours. What must Time pay Cash?

3. Time Management, Inc. pays another employee, Dexter Hand, a "piece rate" of $1 for every timepiece he inspects as a quality assurance worker on the assembly line.

a. During Hand's first week of employment he spent many hours in orientation and training and only a little time working. In a week that included 30 hours of training and 10 hours of actual inspection work, Hand inspected 200 timepieces. What must Time pay Hand?

b. The next week, Hand worked for 50 hours and inspected 1,000 timepieces. What must Time pay Hand?

b. Exempt vs. Nonexempt

The FLSA includes numerous exceptions to the minimum wage and overtime rules in its definitions of "employee" and covered "enterprise," in provisos to the minimum wage and overtime rules, and in the act's principal "exemptions" provision, section 213. A complete treatment of these special rules is not possible in this brief overview. In general, it is always a good idea to review the act and the Department of Labor's regulations for special rules that might apply to any particular type of activity, employee or employer.

One important exemption available to many small employers — especially in the retail and services industries — is based on a gross sales threshold for "enterprise" coverage. An employer is not a covered "enterprise engaged in commerce" unless it has gross sales of $500,000. 29 U.S.C. § 203. However, this "enterprise" coverage rule does not provide a complete exemption. If a small enterprise has any employee whose work involves the production of goods for interstate commerce, or who is otherwise engaged in "commerce" (such as by transportation or shipping of goods across state lines), the minimum wage and overtime requirements might still apply to compensation for that employee. *Id.* §§ 206(a), 207(a). Thus, a small professional services office, restaurant, or construction service might escape coverage under the FLSA for all or most of its employees if its business serves an essentially intrastate market. On the other hand, nearly any manufacturing facility — even a very small one — remains subject to coverage as to workers producing goods for interstate commerce.

On the other hand, even if an employer or some of its employees are sufficiently in interstate commerce, the FLSA exempts some workers from all or part of the minimum wage or overtime requirements. These exemptions include

> any employee employed in a bona fide *executive*, *administrative*, or *professional* capacity (including any employee employed in the capacity of academic administrative personnel or teacher in elementary or secondary schools), . . . as such terms are defined and delimited from time to time by regulations of the Secretary. . . .

29 U.S.C. § 213(a)(1) (emphasis added). An employer need not record work hours or pay overtime to such workers, although, as noted below, the employer generally must pay such workers a minimum *salary*. In 1996, Congress amended the act to include a similar exemption for "a computer systems analyst, computer programmer, software engineer, or other similarly skilled worker." *See Id.* § 213(a)(17). Department of Labor regulations define in detail what constitutes exempt work. *See generally* 29 C.F.R. pt. 541. In a dispute over whether an employees is exempt, the employer bears the burden of proving an exemption applies. Lederman v. Frontier Fire Prot'n, 685 F.3d 1151, 1158 (10th Cir. 2012).

The white collar exemptions look to the actual work an employee performs, not his job title. 29 C.F.R. § 541.2. According to the Department of Labor, the white collar exemptions

> do not apply to manual laborers or other "blue collar" workers who perform work involving repetitive operations with their hands, physical skill and energy. . . . Thus, for example, non-management production-line employees and non-management employees in maintenance, construction and similar

> occupations such as carpenters, electricians, mechanics, plumbers, iron workers, craftsmen, operating engineers, longshoremen, construction workers and laborers . . . are not exempt under the regulations in this part no matter how highly paid they might be.

Id. § 541.3. This rough distinction between primarily manual versus non-manual work is not always easy to apply. For one thing, some arguably exempt workers perform a mixture of exempt and nonexempt work. For example, a manager in sole charge of a restaurant and its employees frequently spends some time performing the same work subordinates perform, such as serving customers, cooking, and cleaning. Not surprisingly, a frequent issue in litigation involving the white collar exemptions is whether an employee performed primarily exempt white collar work or primarily nonexempt work. *E.g.*, Donovan v. Burger King Corp., 675 F.2d 516 (2d Cir. 1982) (employer properly treated some assistant managers as exempt, but some performed too much nonexempt work and should have received overtime pay as nonexempt employees); *see also* 29 C.F.R. § 541.106 ("whether an employee meets the requirements [for an exemption] when the employee performs concurrent duties is determined on a case-by-case basis").

Each of the white collar exemptions includes a "primary duty" test, which varies by exemption. The primary duty of an **executive employee** is "management of the enterprise in which the employee is employed or of a customarily recognized department or subdivision thereof." 29 C.F.R. § 541.100(a)(2). An executive employee also must "customarily and regularly" direct the work of two or more other employees (or any number of part time employees working 80 hours per week) and must either have "authority to hire or fire other employees," or make "suggestions and recommendations" the employer gives "particular weight" with respect to hiring or changes of status of other employees. *Id.* §§ 541.100(a)(2), 541.105; *see, e.g.*, Sec'y of Labor v. Daylight Dairy Prods., 779 F.2d 784, 787 (1st Cir. 1985) ("[T]he equivalent of two full-time employees working 40-hour weeks is any number of part-time employees, as long as the total . . . hours supervised exceeds 80.").

The primary duty of an **administrative employee** is "the performance of office or non-manual work directly related to the management or general business operations of the employer or the employer's customers." 29 C.F.R. § 541.200(a)(2). Unlike an executive employee, an administrative employee does not manage a particular department or supervise other employees. However, his management or business operations work "includes the exercise of discretion and independent judgment with respect to matters of significance." *Id.* § 541.200(a)(3). Exempt administrative work can relate to matters such as finance, insurance, quality control, procurement, marketing, research, safety, human resources, public relations, and regulatory compliance. *Id.* §§ 541.201(b), 541.203.

The primary duty of a **professional employee** is work that fits within either of two categories. First, the employee might perform work "requiring knowledge of an advanced type in a field of science or learning customarily acquired by a prolonged course of specialized intellectual instruction." 29 C.F.R. § 541.300(a)(2)(i). A "prolonged" course of "intellectual" instruction means the training required for some occupations is not enough. For various medical technology occupations, for example, regulations offer the following standard for professional work: "three academic years of pre-professional study in an accredited college or university plus a fourth year of professional course work in a school of medical technology approved by the Council of Medical Education of the American Medical Association." *Id.* § 541.301(e).

A second type of professional employee is one who performs work "requiring invention, imagination, originality or talent in a recognized field of artistic or creative endeavor." 29 C.F.R. § 541.300(a)(2)(ii). A performer or artist may qualify regardless of education. However, an employee whose work is not truly creative or artistic, such as a "copyist," an "animator" of motion-picture cartoons, or a "retoucher" of photographs, might fail to qualify as a creative or artistic professional. 29 C.F.R. § 541.302(c). Writers can be exempt creative professionals, but not if they "only collect, organize and record information that is routine or already public, or if they do not contribute a unique interpretation or analysis to a news product." 29 C.F.R. § 541.302(d). Computer systems analysts, computer programmers, and software engineers may be exempt professionals, or they may be exempt under the separate statutory provision for such occupations.

For employees arguably within any of these white collar exemptions, a very high rate of pay is some evidence in favor of an exemption. In fact, the regulations provide a relaxed test for a "highly compensated" white collar employee earning at least $134,004 per year. 29 C.F.R. § 541.601(a). This "highly compensated" salary level will be updated to account for inflation beginning in 2020. *Id.* A highly compensated employee may be exempt under one of the white collar exemptions described above if he performs exempt work "customarily and regularly," even if executive, administrative, or professional work is not his "primary" duty or his work fails to satisfy some other usual requirement for a particular exemption. However, even for a highly compensated employee, an employer claiming an exemption must identify and prove a "primary duty" that includes "office or non-manual work." *Id.* § 541.601(d).

All of these white collar exemptions have an additional requirement: The employee must earn a "salary" (or in some cases, a "fee") that, calculated on a weekly basis, yields at least $455 per week as of 2017. 29 C.F.R. § 541.602. Even a highly compensated employee earning over $134,004 per year must earn at least part of his compensation on the basis of a true salary of at least $455 per week. *Id.* § 541.601(b). This minimum weekly salary yields an annual salary of about $23,660, which might seem surprisingly low for an "executive" or other white collar employee. The minimum salary at this level therefore adds little to the requirements for executive, administrative or professional employees.

In 2016 during the Obama Administration, the Department of Labor amended its regulations to double the minimum salary to $913 per week (or $47,476 per year), which would have affected approximately 4 million workers. Employers of the affected employees would have been required either to raise the affected employees' salaries to at least the new minimum or to begin paying additional overtime pay for hours in excess of forty in any workweek. However, a district court issued a temporary injunction against enforcement of the regulation just before its effective date. The Trump Administration's Department of Labor subsequently announced an indefinite suspension of the regulation.

The minimum salary requirement, whatever its level, is more than a guarantee of minimum total weekly compensation for an exempt white collar employee. The exempt employee's pay must be in the form of a true salary. The essence of a salary is "a predetermined amount constituting all or part of the employee's compensation, which amount is not subject to reduction because of variations in the quality or quantity of the work performed." 29 C.F.R. § 541.602(a). The white collar regulations require that an exempt employee's salary must cover at least a week. Therefore, an exempt salaried employee who has worked during a week generally must receive the full weekly pay "without regard to the number of days or hours worked" that week. *Id.* § 541.602(a). Deductions from a salary to reflect the actual number of hours worked in a week might mean the employee is hourly rated and not salaried. *Id.* § 541.602(a). However, some deduction types are consistent with the idea of a weekly salary.

In general, if an employee misses work for *personal* reasons, the employer can deduct pay for *whole*-day absences, but not partial-day absences. *See* 29 C.F.R. §§ 541.602(b)(1), (2), (7) (detailing rules for absence due to sickness or disability, and a special rule for leave under the Family and Medical Leave Act).

Absences for the *employer's* reasons are another matter. If a salaried employee is ready, willing, and able to work, the employer must not deduct for "absences occasioned by the employer or by the operating requirements of the business." 29 C.F.R. § 541.602(a).

If an employee is not really salaried under these rules, he is not exempt, regardless of his performance of white collar work (unless he falls within some other exemption). Such an employee might be entitled to overtime pay for any week in which he worked more than 40 hours. A persistent issue has been whether a deduction inconsistent with the idea of "salary" necessarily disqualifies an employee from a white collar exemption for *all* the weeks he has been employed (subject to the statute of limitations) or only for the week in which the improper deduction occurred. A related issue is whether an improper deduction from one employee's salary disqualifies *all employees* in the same class, exposing the employer to potentially massive overtime claims by the entire class.

The Department of Labor addressed these and other issues connected to the idea of a "salary" when it revised its regulations in 2004. Among other things, the revised regulations make it less likely an employer will lose a white collar exemption simply because of one improper deduction. The revised regulations also recognize a new category of permissible salary deduction that takes the form of an unpaid disciplinary suspension. The department's announcement of the new rules, set forth below, summarizes the debate that led to this set of revisions.

WAGE AND HOUR DIVISION, DEPARTMENT OF LABOR, FINAL RULE: DEFINING AND DELIMITING THE EXEMPTIONS FOR EXECUTIVE, ADMINISTRATIVE, PROFESSIONAL, OUTSIDE SALES AND COMPUTER EMPLOYEES

69 Fed. Reg. 22122-01 (Apr. 23, 2004)

SALARY BASIS

In its proposal, the Department retained the requirement that, to qualify for the executive, administrative or professional exemption, an employee must be paid on a "salary basis." Proposed section 541.602(a) set forth the general rules for determining whether an employee is paid on a salary basis, which were retained virtually unchanged from the existing regulation. Under this subsection (a), an employee must regularly receive a "predetermined amount" of salary, on a weekly or less frequent basis, that is "not subject to reduction because of variations in the quality or quantity of the work performed." With a few identified exceptions, the employee "must receive the full salary for any week in which the employee performs any work without regard to the number of days or hours worked." Subsection (a) also provides that an "employee is not paid on a salary basis if deductions from the employee's predetermined compensation are made for absences occasioned by the employer or by the operating requirements of the business. If the employee is ready, willing and able to work, deductions may not be made for time when work is not available." Exempt employees, however, "need not be paid for any workweek in which they perform no work."

Proposed subsection (b) included several exceptions to the salary basis rules that are in the existing regulations. An employer may make deductions from the guaranteed pay: when the employee is "absent from work for a full day for personal reasons, other than sickness or disability"; for absences of a full day or more due to sickness or disability, if taken in accordance with a bona fide plan, policy or practice providing wage replacement benefits; for any hours not worked in the initial and final weeks of employment; for hours taken as unpaid FMLA leave; as offsets for amounts received by an employee for jury or witness fees or military pay; or for penalties imposed in good faith for "infractions of safety rules of major significance." The proposed subsection (b) also added a new exception to the salary basis rule for deductions for "unpaid disciplinary suspensions of a full day or more imposed in good faith for infractions of workplace conduct rules," such as rules prohibiting sexual harassment or workplace violence. Such suspensions must be imposed "pursuant to a written policy applied uniformly to all workers." ...

Many commenters ... support the proposed new exception to the salary basis rule for "unpaid disciplinary suspensions of a full day or more imposed in good faith for infractions of workplace conduct rules." These commenters note that this additional exception will permit employers to apply the same progressive disciplinary rules to both exempt and nonexempt employees, and is needed in light of federal and state laws requiring employers to take appropriate remedial action to address employee misconduct. . . . In contrast, [other] commenters ... oppose the new exception, arguing that the current rule properly recognizes that receiving a salary includes not being subject to disciplinary deductions of less than a week. These commenters argue that employers have other ways to discipline exempt employees without violating the salary basis test.

The final rule includes the exception to the salary basis requirement for deductions from pay due to suspensions for infractions of workplace conduct rules. The Department believes that this is a common-sense change that will permit employers to hold exempt employees to the same standards of conduct as that required of their nonexempt workforce. At the same time, as one commenter notes, it will avoid harsh treatment of exempt employees — in the form of a full-week suspension — when a shorter suspension would be appropriate. It also takes into account that a growing number of laws governing the workplace have placed increased responsibility and risk of liability on employers for their exempt employees' conduct. *See* Burlington Industries, Inc. v. Ellerth, 524 U.S. 742 (1998). At the same time, the Department does not intend that the term "workplace conduct" be construed expansively. As the term indicates, it refers to conduct, not performance or attendance, issues. Moreover, consistent with the examples included in the regulatory provision, it refers to serious workplace misconduct like sexual harassment, violence, drug or alcohol violations, or violations of state or federal laws....

Some [c]ommenters ... urge the Department to delete the proposed requirement that any pay deductions for workplace conduct violations must be imposed pursuant to a "written policy applied uniformly to all workers." These commenters question the need for the policy to be in writing, and are concerned that the uniform application requirement would breed litigation and diminish employer flexibility to take individual circumstances into account. . . . The Department has decided to retain the requirement that the policy be in writing, on the assumption that most employers would put (or already have) significant conduct rules in writing, and to deter misuse of this exception. This provision is a new exception to the salary basis test, and the Department does not believe restricting this new exception to written disciplinary policies will lead to changes in current employer practices regarding such policies. However, the written policy need not include an exhaustive list of specific violations that could result in a suspension, or a definitive declaration of when a suspension will be imposed. The written policy should be sufficient to put employees on notice that they could be subject to an unpaid disciplinary suspension. We have clarified the regulatory language to provide that the written policy must be "applicable to all employees," which should not preclude an employer from making case-by-case disciplinary determinations. Thus, for example, the "written policy" requirement for this exception would be satisfied by a sexual harassment policy, distributed generally to employees, that warns employees that violations of the policy will result in disciplinary action up to and including suspension or termination....

EFFECT OF IMPROPER DEDUCTIONS FROM SALARY

... Proposed subsection 541.603(a) contained the general rule regarding the effect of improper deductions from salary on the exempt status of employees: "An employer who makes improper deductions from salary shall lose the exemption if the facts demonstrate that the employer has a pattern and practice of not paying employees on a salary basis." Many commenters ... express concern that the phrase "pattern and practice of not paying employees on a salary basis" in proposed subsection 541.603(a) was ambiguous and would engender litigation and perhaps result in unintended consequences. The final rule clarifies that the central inquiry to determine whether an employer who makes improper deductions will lose the exemption is whether "the facts demonstrate that the employer did not intend to pay employees on a salary basis." The final subsection (a) replaces the proposed "pattern and practice" language with the phrase "actual practice," and also states that an "actual practice of making improper deductions demonstrates that the employer did not intend to pay employees on a salary basis." ...

Most commenters support the listed factors in subsection (a) for determining when an employer has an actual practice of making improper deductions.... [T]he final rule states that the number of improper deductions should be considered "particularly as compared to the number of employee infractions warranting discipline." . . . Thus, it is the ratio of deductions to infractions that is most informative, rather than simply the number of deductions, because the total number of deductions is significantly influenced by the size of the employer. . . .

Final subsection 541.603(b), as in the proposal, addresses which employees will lose the exemption, and for what time period, if an employer has an actual practice of making improper deductions. The proposal provided that the exemption would be lost "during the time period in which improper deductions were made for employees in the same job classification working for the same managers responsible for the improper deductions." . . .

The final regulation also retains the language that employees in different job classifications or who work for different managers do not lose their status as exempt employees. Any other approach, on the one hand, would provide a windfall to employees who have not even arguably been harmed by a "policy" that a manager has never applied and may never intend to apply, but on the other hand, would fail to recognize that some employees may reasonably believe that they would be subject to the same types of impermissible deductions made from the pay of similarly situated employees.

. . . We disagree . . . with those comments arguing that only employees who suffered an actual deduction should lose their exempt status. An exempt employee who has not suffered an actual deduction nonetheless may be harmed by an employer docking the pay of a similarly situated co-worker. An exempt employee in the same job classification working for the same manager responsible for making improper deductions, for example, may choose not to leave work early for a parent-teacher conference for fear that her pay will be reduced, and thus is also suffering harm as a result of the manager's improper practices. Because exempt employees in the same job classification working for the same managers responsible for the actual improper deductions may reasonably believe that their salary will also be docked, such employees have also suffered harm and therefore should also lose their exempt status . . . . [S]ubsection (a) provides that "whether the employer has a clearly communicated policy permitting or prohibiting improper deductions" is one factor to consider when determining whether the employer has an actual practice of not paying employees on a salary basis . . . .

Final subsection (c) contains language taken from proposed subsection 541.603(a) and the existing "window of correction" in current subsection 541.118(a)(6) regarding the effect of "isolated" or "inadvertent" improper deductions. . . . Inadvertent deductions are those taken unintentionally, for example, as a result of a clerical or time-keeping error. Whether deductions are "isolated" is determined by reference to the factors set forth in final subsection 541.603(a).. . . We agree with commenters who state that employees whose salary has been improperly docked should be reimbursed, even if the improper deductions were isolated or inadvertent. Thus, final subsection (c) provides: "Improper deductions that are either isolated or inadvertent will not result in loss of the exemption for any employees subject to such improper deductions, if the employer reimburses the employees for such improper deductions." The Department continues to adhere to current law that reimbursement does not have to be made immediately upon the discovery that an improper deduction was made. . . . The safe harbor provision applies regardless of the reason for the improper deduction — whether improper deductions were made for lack of work or for reasons other than lack of work. . . .

NOTES AND QUESTIONS

1. Before its 2004 revision of the white collar exemptions, the Department of Labor had taken the position that a disciplinary suspension without pay for less than a full week was inconsistent with the meaning of a weekly salary. In Auer v. Robbins, 519 U.S. 452 (1997), the U.S. Supreme Court deferred to the department's interpretation of the law in this regard, finding that the department's position was not "unreasonable." Is the department's 180 degree turn on this issue also not "unreasonable"? Does an employer need the possibility of a partial week suspension for effective disciplinary control of salaried workers?

2. The new regulations might make it important for any employer, large or small, to amend its "policies" to include a "no-deductions" rule for salaried employees and a complaint procedure for reporting possible violations. What are the consequences of failing to adopt such a policy?

3. The white collar exemptions are part of a long list of exemptions or special rules for specific occupations, activities, employers, or collective bargaining situations, ranging from agriculture to "wreathmaking." *E.g.,* 29 U.S.C. §§ 203(e), (r), (s); 206(e), (f), (g); 207(b), (f)-(q); 213; 214. Here are a few others:

a. **Outside salesperson.** A sales employee might qualify as an exempt outside salesperson if his primary duty is "making sales . . . or obtaining orders or contracts for services or for the use of facilities for which a consideration will be paid by the client or customer." However, a salesperson is not an exempt outside salesperson unless he is "customarily and regularly engaged away from the employer's place or places of business in performing such primary duty." 29 C.F.R. § 541.500. Unlike exempt executive, administrative, or professional employees, an exempt outside salesperson need not receive a salary. For example, an exempt outside salesperson might earn commissions and no salary.

b. **Commission-paid employee of a retail or service establishment.** Many sales employees do not qualify for the "outside" salesperson exemption because they spend most of their time on the employer's premises. However, a special rule might apply to a retail or service establishment's "inside" salesperson. The employer need not pay overtime if more than half the employee's compensation consists of commissions, and the weekly earnings yield a regular rate that is one and a half times the minimum wage. 29 U.S.C. § 213(i).

c. **Employee in the computer technology field.** If the employee is a "computer systems analyst, computer programmer, software engineer, or similarly skilled worker," and her work satisfies other requirements, the employer need not pay for overtime. In contrast with the administrative, executive, or professional exemptions, this exemption requires no minimum salary, only compensation that, when converted to an hourly rate, yields $27.63 per hour. *Id.* § 213(a)(17).

4. State and local government employees are not exempt, but are subject to

a different set of overtime rules. The general rule for private sector employees is that an employer cannot satisfy its overtime obligation by granting compensatory time off. In other words, overtime in one workweek cannot be offset by reduced hours or time off in another week. For state and local governments, however, Congress enacted section 207(o), permitting such employers to adopt a "compensatory time" plan. The requirements for such a plan are less than straightforward and have been the source of considerable litigation. *See* Christensen v. Harris County, 529 U.S. 576 (2000) (county could require employees to use accrued compensatory time when it reached a certain amount, rather than allow it to accumulate indefinitely); Moreau v. Klevenhagen, 508 U.S. 22 (1993).

2. *What Compensation Counts?*

Work has many potential rewards. Which count as credits toward the minimum wage, and how do they affect overtime liability? If an employer provides free parking and computer training, or if the employee receives and keeps customer "tips," do any of these items constitute "wages" for FLSA purposes?

An employer might claim it pays the minimum wage partly in cash and partly in noncash benefits. Accordingly, it might subtract the value of a uniform it provides from the minimum wage, and pay the employee the difference in cash. The employee, however, might argue that a uniform should not count as "wages" because it is for the *employer's* benefit: it identifies the employee as a representative of the employer. Moreover, a uniform does not provide the kind of sustenance the minimum wage is designed to assure.

But there are some noncash items that do count as wages for FLSA purposes. The FLSA defines "wage" to include "the reasonable cost . . . to the employer of furnishing . . . board, lodging, or other facilities, if such board, lodging or other facilities are customarily furnished by such employer to his employees." 29 U.S.C. § 203(m). *See also* 29 C.F.R. § 531.27. A "reasonable cost" is not more than the actual cost (without any profit) to the employer. 29 C.F.R. § 531.3.

"Board" and "lodging" might be clear enough, but what are "other facilities"? The Department of Labor states as follows:

> "Other facilities," as used in this section, must be *something like board or lodging*. The following items have been deemed to be within the meaning of the term: Meals furnished at company restaurants or cafeterias or by hospitals, hotels, or restaurants to their employees; meals, dormitory rooms, and tuition furnished by a college to its student employees; housing furnished for dwelling purposes; general merchandise furnished at company stores and commissaries (including articles of food, clothing, and household effects); fuel (including coal, kerosene, firewood, and lumber slabs), electricity, water, and gas furnished for the noncommercial personal use of the employee; transportation furnished employees between their homes and work where the travel time does not constitute hours worked compensable under the act and the transportation is not an incident of and necessary to the employment.

29 C.F.R. § 531.32 (emphasis added).

The department's regulations also clarify two other important requirements. First, "it is essential that [the employee's] acceptance of the facility be *voluntary and uncoerced.* 29 C.F.R. § 531.30 (emphasis added). Second, board, lodging, and facilities may not serve as credits toward the minimum wage if they are *primarily for the convenience of the employer*. *Id.* Thus, if an employer provides lodging because it is necessary for the employee's work to live or sleep on the premises, the value of the lodging does not count as a credit against the minimum wage. *See also* Brennan v. Modern Chevrolet Co., 363 F. Supp. 327, 333 (N.D. Tex. 1973), *aff'd*, 491 F.2d 1271 (5th Cir. 1974) (employee's use of an automobile was primarily for the benefit of the employer even though 90 percent of mileage was for personal use).The fact that an employer is not entitled to a credit toward the minimum wage does not necessarily prevent the employer from charging the employee for the item in question in some other manner. The problem of employer charges against wages is discussed in Part C.4 of this chapter, *infra*. .

"Tips" are another benefit for which an employer might wish to claim a credit. Although tips are paid by a customer and not the employer, the act permits the employer to claim a limited credit toward its minimum wage obligation for tips the employee actually receives and is permitted to retain. *See* 29 U.S.C. § 203(m); 29 C.F.R. § 779.17.

From the employer's point of view, credits for noncash items and tips might seem an attractive means of satisfying the minimum wage. But what if a tipped employee works overtime? Tips and other items for which the employer has claimed a credit might be part of the "regular rate" for purposes of calculating *overtime* pay. *See* 29 C.F.R. § 531.60.

MCCOMB v. SHEPARD NILES CRANE & HOIST CORP.

171 F.2d 69 (2d Cir. 1948)

AUGUSTUS N. HAND, Circuit Judge.

This action was begun in October, 1945, by the Administrator of the Wage and Hour Division to enjoin violation of the overtime provisions of the Fair Labor Standards Act of 1938, 29 U.S.C.A. § 201 et seq. The Administrator moved for summary judgment based upon the complaint, the answer, and a stipulation of facts. The defendant filed affidavits in opposition to the motion, and the District Court denied the motion and dismissed the complaint.

The defendant is a corporation engaged in the manufacture and sale of electric cranes, hoists and allied products, and has about 450 employees who are admittedly covered by the Act. Beginning August 29, 1940, and until shortly before the institution of this suit, the defendant made bonus payments to its employees at approximately three months intervals. These bonus payments were in addition to other hourly and incentive earnings of the employees. They generally followed a resolution of the defendant's board of directors making provision for the payments "as additional compensation for services rendered." These bonus payments were at all times based upon the straight-time hourly rates of the employees, but the amounts paid were changed three times: April, 1942; July, 1942; and December, 1944.

The defendant always deducted social security taxes from the bonus payments, included them as "Salary and Wages" in its income tax returns, and also included them in computing the premium on its workman's compensation insurance and unemployment insurance. Likewise, it included them in Victory and withholding tax deductions. The defendant did not, however, include the bonus payments in computing the regular rate of pay under the Fair Labor Standards Act.

On August 23, 1943, the Defendant applied to the National War Labor Board for approval of its practice of making bonus payments. In a letter accompanying the application, the defendant company recited that during the year 1942 it had paid four bonuses to its hourly rate employees which "were paid about every three months and were at the exclusive discretion of the employer." It said that the amounts of the bonuses were increased principally because of the increased cost of living, and that it wished to continue them at the amounts which had been paid on October 1 and December 17, 1942. It added in the letter that "certain key men" received additional sums that were paid on April 2, July 2, October 1, and December 17.

Just prior to an election held in December, 1943, to determine the collective bargaining agent of defendant's employees, the company sent a letter to each of its employees together with a payroll slip indicating the total payments from the company to the individual employee during the first nine months of 1943. This included all the earnings paid to the employee, whether as bonuses or otherwise.

It is stipulated that some of the employees who had received the payments here described if called to testify at a trial would say that "they expected to continue to receive these bonus payments and assumed that they would continue to be made and that they regarded these bonus payments as an integral part of the total earnings received for the work performed for the defendant; and further that this expectation and assumption was predicated on the fact that the bonus payments had been made at recurrent intervals as described in this stipulation over a substantial period of time." Subsequent to the stipulation and the motion for summary judgment affidavits of six employees were filed, which stated that the latter considered the bonus payments as "gifts from the company and not part of the regular wages." Likewise an affidavit of the defendant's President and General Manager was filed that the bonuses "were paid as an exercise of arbitrary discretion on the part of the board which would in each case decide to reward the employees in any amount it felt was reasonable at the particular moment."

Upon the record we have described the District Court held that the bonus payments were not part of the regular rates of compensation of the defendant's employees in that they were not paid under a promise that any bonus payment would be made at any future time, or under any plan or formula determining bonus payments that was ever communicated to the employees, and further that the payments did not conform to the description of bonuses as published by the Wage and Hour administrator in his Interpretive Bulletin released February 5, 1945. Accordingly, the District Court denied the Administrator's application for an injunction and dismissed his complaint.

Section 7(a) of the Fair Labor Standards Act provides that no employer shall employ any employee engaged in commerce or the production of goods for commerce for more than forty hours per week "unless such employee receives compensation for his employment in excess of the hours above specified at a rate not less than one and one-half times the regular rate at which he is employed." . . . The question before us is whether the bonus payments which were based on the employee's hourly rates of pay and at least since 1941 were paid at regularly recurring intervals should be regarded as a part of the employee's regular rate of pay within the meaning of Section 7(a). We think this question must be answered in the affirmative under the two recent decisions of this court in Walling v. Richmond Screw Anchor Co., 2 Cir., 154 F.2d 780, *certiorari denied* 328 U.S. 870, 66 S. Ct. 1383, 90 L. Ed. 1640; and Walling v. Garlock Packing Co., 2 Cir., 159 F.2d 44, *certiorari denied* 331 U.S. 820. In both of those cases there was a "plan" for awarding bonuses which had been announced to the employees in advance with, however, the right of the company to deny a bonus at any time if its board of directors so determined. Moreover, in Walling v. Garlock Packing Co., *supra*, the receipt of a bonus was dependant upon a vote of a dividend to stockholders by the board of directors, a feature which added a further uncertainty as to the receipt of any bonus. We see no tenable distinction between an announcement of a bonus in advance when that bonus might at any time be withdrawn and a regular payment of a bonus at recurrent intervals, for in either event the expectation and reliance of the employee would be the same. This would certainly be true as of October, 1945, when the present action was brought, for long prior to that time there had been recurrent payments of bonuses at substantially equal intervals.

In *Richmond Screw Anchor* case, as in the case at bar, employees furnished affidavits that they did not regard the bonuses as part of their salary and knew that the company had the right at any time to withhold them. Nevertheless, Judge Frank in his opinion held that no issue of fact existed, saying that (154 F.2d 784):

> We take it as admitted that the company was not legally obligated to pay the bonuses, that the employees knew the payments were not contractual, and that the company would have discontinued them "if and when the company finances indicated an unhealthy condition." But the undenied, crucial fact here is that in fact they were regularly paid. Although the employees knew they could not legally compel the company to make those payments, no one can doubt that the employees assumed that, in the normal course of events, the employees would receive them. That seems to us to be enough to constitute them part of "the regular rate at which" the men were employed.

We may add that the affidavits submitted by the employees did not bear upon their expectations of the payment of bonuses but only upon their right to receive them if the company chose to withhold payment — a right which clearly did not exist. The basis for an expectation of bonuses in the case at bar was well established and the affidavits created no issue as to their expectation.

In Walling v. Frank Adam Electric Co., 163 F.2d 277, the Court of Appeals for the Eighth Circuit declined to include bonuses for the purpose of computing the regular rate of pay on the ground that no plan had been promulgated by the company in advance and that the bonuses were all voted at the end of the different periods without any obligation for continuance. The court adverted to the distinction between such a situation and one where an antecedent plan existed and observed that in Walling v. Garlock Packing Co., *supra*, Judge Clark had referred to this fact as a possible distinction between the *Garlock* case and the holding of the District Court in Walling v. Frank Adam Electric Co., 66 F. Supp. 811. But, as we have already said, we can see no distinction between a "plan" capable of withdrawal at any time and an arrangement which the employee had every reason to suppose would be continued in the absence of some change of circumstances. Were this distinction made significant and controlling, it would afford a ready means for a company to obtain discriminatory rights in paying overtime.

. . . For the foregoing reasons, the judgment of the District Court dismissing the complaint should be reversed and a judgment entered enjoining the defendant from violating the provisions of Section 15(a)(1) and 15(a)(2) of the Fair Labor Standards Act by failing to include the bonus payments in computing amounts due to its employees for overtime.

NOTES AND QUESTIONS

1. In 1949 Congress amended the Fair Labor Standards Act to clarify when fringe benefits and deferred compensation must be included in the "regular rate" for purposes of determining overtime. Act of Oct. 26, 1949, ch. 736, § 7, 63 Stat. 912, codified at 29 U.S.C. § 207(e). As amended, the FLSA currently provides:

> [T]he "regular rate" at which an employee is employed shall be deemed to include *all remuneration for employment* paid to, or on behalf of, the employee, but shall not be deemed to include . . . sums paid as gifts; payments in the nature of gifts made at Christmas time or on other special occasions, as a reward for service, the amounts of which are not measured by or dependent on hours worked, production, or efficiency. . . .

29 U.S.C. § 207(e)(1) (emphasis added). Also excluded from the regular rate are:

> Sums paid in recognition of services performed during a given period if . . . both the fact that payment is to be made and the amount of the payment are determined at the sole discretion of the employer at or near the end of the period and not pursuant to any prior contract, agreement, or promise causing the employee to expect such payments regularly. . . .

29 U.S.C. § 207(e)(3). How do these provisions compare with the result in *Shepard Niles Crane & Hoist*?

2. Also excluded from "regular rates" are certain other deferred compensation and benefits, such as "payments for occasional periods when no work is performed," such as vacation, holidays, or sick leave, 29 U.S.C. § 207(e)(2); "payments . . . pursuant to a bona fide profit-sharing plan or trust or bona fide thrift or savings plan" meeting the requirements of the Department of Labor (and in general such payments must not depend on "hours of work, production, or efficiency"), *id.* § 207(3)(b); "contributions irrevocably made by an employer to a trustee or third person pursuant to a bona fide plan for providing old-age, retirement, life, accident, or health insurance or similar benefits for employees," *id.* § 207(e)(4), and "any value or income derived from" stock option or employee stock purchase plans (with certain requirements). *Id.* § 207(e)(2)-(4), (8).

3. Most extra payments or "wage augments" for particular tasks must be counted as employee remuneration in a weekly recalculation of the "regular rate" for overtime purposes. On the other hand, actual or estimated reimbursements for an employee's travel or other business expenses are not remuneration for work. *See* Newman v. Advanced Tech. Innovation Corp., 749 F.3d 33 (1st Cir. 2014) ("per diem" payments could not be excluded from regular rate of pay when calculating overtime, because the per diem amount was "tied to hours worked in a

week and thus, in reality, was a shadow wage"; per diem payments are excludable from a regular rate only if they are "actually used to offset expenses an employee incurs due to time spent away on the employer's business" and thus are akin to estimated expense reimbursements); Murphy v. Town of Natick, 516 F. Supp. 2d 153 (D. Mass. 2007) (for police officer overtime, "regular rate" does not include training stipends that served as reimbursement for out-of-pocket expenses, but otherwise includes all wage "augments," including longevity pay, "community service" and "crimetracking technology" bonuses, and "assignment differentials" providing extra pay for special work such as detective duties).

4. An employment contract might go farther than the FLSA by defining a regular workweek to be fewer than 40 hours, by requiring premium pay for hours in excess of eight hours in a day, or by requiring premium pay for hours worked during a holiday or weekend. Subject to certain conditions, an employer may exclude these payments from the regular rate for overtime purposes. *See* 29 U.S.C. § 207(e)(5), (6) and (7), and § 207(h).

5. An employer offers a union a series of annual "lump sum" payments to employees in lieu of a wage increase. Under the proposal, every employee will receive the same lump sum each year, provided she is actively employed for a certain number of weeks before the payment but without regard to the number of hours worked. The union accepts the proposal. Must the employer include these lump sum payments in calculating the regular rate for purposes of overtime? *See* Minizza v. Stone Container Corp., 842 F.2d 1456 (3d Cir. 1988) (lump sum payments properly excluded from regular rate; with dissenting opinion).

3. *What Hours Count? Allocating the Cost of Unproductive Time*

The fact that an employee earns an hourly wage or other time-based rate does not mean that all periods of work are equal. Some periods of service are more productive than others, and some are more burdensome to the employee than others. For example, a salesperson might perform very little productive "work" while she is waiting for customers on a "slow day." On the other hand, she works especially hard the day before Christmas. Should the employer pay the same hourly rate for these periods? As a matter of contract, the parties could agree to different hourly rates for different periods of time. As a matter of contract, the parties could abandon time-based pay and choose compensation based on actual productivity. In fact, as a matter of contract, the parties might agree to any rule of compensation they want. *See, e.g.*, Dove v. Rose Acre Farms, Inc., 434 N.E.2d 931, 931 (Ind. App. 1982) (describing a compensation system that depended in part on whether an employee wore a silver feather).

Whatever the parties' private agreement, the FLSA requires that non-exempt employees receive the minimum wage and overtime for each workweek. As a practical matter, this means the employer must count time even for non-exempt employees whose contract rate is not based on time. And regardless of how the parties have agreed to count time or not count time for purposes of a contract rate, the FLSA imposes its own rules for determining whether time is "compensable" for minimum wage or overtime purposes. Tennessee Coal, Iron & R. Co. v. Muscoda Local No. 123, 321 U.S. 590, 602 (1944) ("The Fair Labor Standards

Act was not designed to codify or perpetuate those customs and contracts which allow an employer to claim all of an employee's time while compensating him for only a part of it"). *See also* 29 C.F.R. § 778.318.

One of the most difficult issues under the FLSA has been whether time in activity preparing for work at the work site (such waiting in line to clock in, "donning" work clothes and reaching an assigned work station) or disengaging from work (such as "doffing" work clothes and clocking out) should be counted as compensable for purposes of the overtime rule. A decade after enacting the FLSA, Congress passed the Portal to Portal Act of 1947, the title reflecting an issue whether underground miners are entitled to compensation for time traveling from the portal of a mine to a location of productive work. According to the Portal to Portal Act, in the absence of a contrary contract or custom an employer is not required to count time an employee spends in activities "preliminary to or postliminary to" an employee's "principle activities." 29 U.S.C. § 254(a). The act specifically excludes preliminary and postliminary activities such as "walking, riding or traveling to and from the actual place of performance of the principal activity or activities." 29 U.S.C. § 254(a)(1).

From the start, the concepts of preliminary, principal, and postliminary activity were very vague, and sixty years of enforcement experience sharpened these concepts only a little. Finally, in IBP, Inc. v. Alvarez, 546 U.S. 21 (2005), the Supreme Court gave some clarity to the Portal to Portal Act in a case involving employee time spent *waiting* to "don" or "doff" special protective clothes on the employer's premises, actually donning and doffing such clothes, walking from the dressing area to the work area and vice versa, and waiting for productive work to begin. The court's opinion may be summarized as follows. In effect, the Portal to Portal Act divides the day into three time periods: preliminary, principal, and postliminary. Knowing which of these periods was in effect at the time of questioned activity is important because some nonproductive activities, such as walking and waiting, are presumed *not* to be compensable during the preliminary and postliminary periods, but *are* presumed to be compensable during the period of principal activity. The period of principal activity begins when an employee first engages in activity that is (a) the very activity for which the employer employs the employee, *or* (b) "integral and indispensable" to the principal activity. *Id.* For example, a worker's time spent dressing in *special protective gear* on the employer's premises may be within the period of principal activity, even though dressing is not in itself a principle activity (it is not the reason for which the employer employs the worker), if dressing in such gear is "integral and indispensable" to performing a principle activity, as it was in *IBP*.

In *IBP*, the Court held that time spent *waiting* to don special protective gear was not compensable because the waiting occurred during the preliminary activity period. On the other hand, *actually* donning special protective gear was compensable because it was integral to the employees' principal activity and it marked the beginning of the period of principal activity. Waiting to begin productive work after donning special gear was also presumably compensable because the period of principal activity had already begun. Later in the day, the time employees spent *waiting* to doff their gear was still within the period of principal activity and was presumably compensable. The period of principal activity was not over until the employees finished their last principal activity: the actual doffing of their gear. Only then did the non-compensable period of postliminary activity begin. 546 U.S. at 37-41.

INTEGRITY STAFFING SOLUTIONS, INC. v. BUSK
546 U.S. 21 (2014)

Justice THOMAS delivered the opinion of the Court.

… Integrity Staffing Solutions, Inc., provides warehouse staffing to Amazon.com …. Jesse Busk and Laurie Castro worked as hourly employees …. [T]hey retrieved products from the shelves and packaged those products for delivery to Amazon customers. Integrity Staffing required … a security screening before leaving the warehouse at the end of each day. … [E]mployees removed items such as wallets, keys, and belts … and passed through metal detectors.

In 2010, Busk and Castro filed a putative class action … for the time spent waiting to undergo and actually undergoing the security screenings. They alleged that such time amounted to roughly 25 minutes each day and that it could have been reduced to a *de minimis* amount by adding more security screeners or by staggering the termination of shifts … They also alleged that the screenings were conducted "to prevent employee theft" and thus occurred "solely for the benefit of the employers and their customers."

At issue here is the [Portal to Portal Act] exemption for "activities … preliminary to or postliminary to … principal activity or activities."

This Court has consistently interpreted "the term 'principal activity or activities' [to] embrac[e] all activities which are an 'integral and indispensable part of the principal activities.' " *IBP, Inc. v. Alvarez,* 546 U.S. 21, 29-30 (2005) (quoting *Steiner v. Mitchell,* 350 U.S. 247, 252-253 (1956)). Our prior opinions used those words in their ordinary sense. The word "integral" means "[b]elonging to or making up an integral whole; constituent, component; *spec*[*ifically*] necessary to the completeness or integrity of the whole; forming an intrinsic portion or element, as distinguished from an adjunct or appendage." 5 Oxford Eng. Dictionary 366 (1933) (OED); … *see also* Webster's New Int'l Dictionary 1290 (2d ed. 1954) (Webster's Second) ("[e]ssential to completeness; constituent, as a part"). And, when used to describe a duty, "indispensable" means a duty "[t]hat cannot be dispensed with, remitted, set aside, disregarded, or neglected." 5 OED 219 …. An activity is therefore integral and indispensable to the principal activities that an employee is employed to perform if it is an intrinsic element of those activities and one with which the employee cannot dispense if he is to perform his principal activities. …

Our precedents have identified several activities that satisfy this test. For example, we have held compensable the time battery-plant employees spent showering and changing clothes because the chemicals in the plant were "toxic to human beings" and … "the clothes-changing and showering activities of the employees [were] indispensable to the performance of their productive work and integrally related thereto." *Steiner, supra,* at 249, 251. And we have held compensable the time meatpacker employees spent sharpening their knives because dull knives would "slow down production" on the assembly line, "affect the appearance of the meat as well as the quality of the hides," "cause waste," and lead to "accidents." *Mitchell v. King Packing Co.,* 350 U.S. 260, 262 (1956). By contrast, we have held noncompensable the time poultry-plant employees spent *waiting* to don protective gear because such waiting was "two steps removed from the productive activity on the assembly line." *IBP, supra,* at 42 (editor's emphasis)

The Department of Labor's regulations are consistent with this approach. *See* 29 CFR § 790.8(b) (2013). … [T]hose regulations explain that the time spent … in a chemical plant changing clothes would be compensable if he "c[ould not] perform his principal activities without putting on certain clothes" but would not be … if "changing clothes [were] merely a convenience to the employee and not directly related to his principal activities." § 790.8(c).… "[W]hen performed under the conditions normally present," activities including "checking in and out and waiting in line to do so, changing clothes, washing up or showering, and waiting in line to receive pay checks" are "'preliminary'" or "'postliminary' " activities. § 790.7(g).

The security screenings at issue here are noncompensable postliminary activities. To begin with, the screenings were not the "principal activity or activities which [the] employee is employed to perform." 29 U.S.C. § 254(a)(1). Integrity Staffing did not employ its workers to undergo security screenings, but to retrieve products from warehouse shelves and package those products for shipment to Amazon customers.

The security screenings also were not "integral and indispensable" to … duties as warehouse workers. … [A]ctivity is not integral and indispensable to … principal activities unless it is an intrinsic element of those activities and one with which the employee cannot dispense …. The screenings were not an intrinsic element of retrieving products from warehouse shelves or packaging them for shipment. And Integrity Staffing could have eliminated the screenings altogether without impairing the employees' ability to complete their work.…

The Court of Appeals erred by focusing on whether an employer *required* a particular activity. The integral and indispensable test is tied to the productive work that the employee is *employed to perform*.… If the test could be satisfied merely by the fact that an employer required an activity, it would sweep into "principal activities" the very activities … the Portal-to-Portal Act was designed to address. The employer in *Anderson* … required its employees to walk "from a timeclock near the factory gate to a workstation" so that they could "begin their work," "but ... the Portal-to-Portal Act evinces Congress' intent to repudiate *Anderson's* holding that such walking time was compensable …." *IBP, supra,* at 41. A test that turns on whether the activity is for the benefit of the employer is similarly overbroad.

Finally, we reject the employees' argument that … waiting to undergo the security screenings is compensable under the FLSA because Integrity Staffing could have reduced that time to a *de minimis* amount. The fact that an employer could conceivably reduce the time … on any preliminary or postliminary activity does not change the nature of the activity …. These arguments are properly presented to the employer at the bargaining table, not to a court ….

[A]ctivity is integral and indispensable to the principal activities that an employee is employed to perform – and thus compensable under the FLSA – if it is an intrinsic element of those activities and one with which the employee cannot dispense if he is to perform his principal activities. … [W]aiting to undergo and undergoing Integrity Staffing's security screenings does not meet these criteria ….

Justice SOTOMAYOR, with whom Justice KAGAN joins, concurring.

I … write separately only to explain my understanding of the standards the Court applies…. First, the Court confirms that compensable "'principal'" activities "'includ[e] ... closely related activities which are indispensable to … performance,'" and … security screenings ... were not "integral and indispensable" to another principal activity the employees were employed to perform…. [A]ctivity is "indispensable" to another, principal activity only when an employee could not dispense with it without impairing his ability to perform the principal activity safely and effectively. Thus, although a battery plant worker might … perform his principal activities without donning proper protective gear, he could not do so safely, *see Steiner*; likewise, a butcher might be able to cut meat without having sharpened his knives, but he could not do so effectively, see *Mitchell*. Here, … [t]he screenings may … have been in some way related to the work that the employees performed … , but the employees could skip the screenings altogether without the safety or effectiveness of their principal activities being substantially impaired ….

Second, the Court holds also that the screenings were not themselves "'principal'"…. [T]he Portal-to-Portal Act … is primarily concerned with defining *the beginning and end of the workday*. It distinguishes between activities that are essentially part of the ingress and egress process … and activities that constitute the actual "work of consequence" …. The searches were part of the process by which the employees egressed … , akin to checking in and out and waiting in line to do so—activities that Congress clearly deemed to be preliminary or postliminary. ...

PEREZ v. CITY OF NEW YORK

832 F.3d 120 (2d Cir. 2016)

ROBERT SACK, Circuit Judge:

… Assistant Urban Park Rangers ("AUPRs") employed by the City's Department of Parks & Recreation ("Parks Department") … perform a range of public services in the City's parks … : "providing directions and other information to persons seeking to use parks or pools; providing assistance to those persons involved in accidents or those who may be victims of unlawful activity and investigating … such accidents or activity; implementing crowd control procedures at special events; providing safety and educational information to the public; and issuing summonses to or making arrests of persons suspected of unlawful conduct"…. AUPRs are required to wear uniforms comprising both professional clothing and equipment. The professional clothing includes "olive drab" pants and jacket, "'Smokey the Bear' style hats," and various Parks Department insignias, while the equipment includes a bulletproof vest and a utility belt holding handcuffs, gloves, a radio, a flashlight, a baton, a can of mace, a summons book, and a tape recorder. … The plaintiffs' estimates of the time needed to don and doff those uniforms each day (that is, to put them on before a shift and take them off afterward) range from approximately five to thirty minutes.

The plaintiffs claim that the defendants … provided inadequate compensation … by failing to pay wages for compensable activities … immediately before and after their regularly scheduled shifts, including donning and doffing their uniforms

.... [T]he district court concluded as a matter of law that the plaintiffs' donning and doffing of uniforms were not compensable activities .... We vacate the district court's decision .... Absent another appeal or additional motions by the parties that dispose of the action ... , the case should then proceed to trial.

The FLSA generally mandates compensation for "the principal activity or activities which [an] employee is employed to perform," 29 U.S.C. § 254(a)(1), including tasks—even those completed outside a regularly scheduled shift—that are "an integral and indispensable part of the principal activities," *IBP, Inc. v. Alvarez*, 546 U.S. 21, 30 (2005) (quoting *Steiner v. Mitchell*, 350 U.S. 247, 256 (1956)). But the FLSA does not require payment for time spent on "activities which are preliminary to or postliminary to" ... principal activities. 29 U.S.C. § 254(a)(2). The parties dispute which standard applies to the plaintiffs' donning and doffing ....

"[T]he more the pre- or post-shift activity is undertaken for the employer's benefit, the more indispensable it is to the primary goal of the employee's work, and the less choice the employee has in the matter, the more likely such work will be found to be compensable." *Reich v. N.Y.C. Transit Auth.*, 45 F.3d 646, 650 (2d Cir. 1995). Relatedly, an employer's requirement that pre- or post-shift activities take place at the workplace may indicate that the activities are integral and indispensable to an employee's duties. *See Alvarez v. IBP, Inc.*, 339 F.3d 894, 903 (9th Cir.2003) (... donning and doffing of protective gear were integral and indispensable ... in part because they had to be performed at the workplace), *aff'd*, 546 U.S. 21 (2005) ....

Applying those principles, this Court and others have concluded that ... *pre- and post-shift preparation of items* used to perform principal activities can qualify as integral and indispensable. In *[Mitchell v.] King Packing*, ... the Supreme Court held that a slaughterhouse employee's knife sharpening was integral and indispensable to the principal activity of butchering. ... [I]n *Kosakow v. New Rochelle Radiology Associates, P.C.*, 274 F.3d 706 (2d Cir. 2001), we concluded that a reasonable factfinder might classify a radiological technician's powering up and testing of an x-ray machine as integral and indispensable to the principal activity of taking x-rays. And in *Reich*, we decided that a K-9 officer's feeding, walking, and training of his dog was integral and indispensable to his principal law enforcement activities. All of these activities occurred before or after regularly scheduled shifts, or during lunch breaks.

Courts have also concluded that ... *pre- and post-shift efforts to protect against heightened workplace dangers* can qualify as integral and indispensable. In *Steiner*, the Supreme Court decided that employees ... in a battery plant should be compensated ... for the time ... showering and changing clothes at the workplace after a shift. Those tasks ... were integral and indispensable ... because they prevented lead poisoning, an acute danger attendant to work in the plant. ... [I]n *Alvarez*, the Ninth Circuit concluded that slaughterhouse employees' donning and doffing of protective equipment, including "metal-mesh gear," qualified as integral and indispensable to ... butchering.... *Gorman v. Consol. Edison Corp.*, 488 F.3d 586, 591 (2d Cir. 2007)... acknowledged that ... efforts to protect against "workplace dangers that transcend ordinary risks" may qualify as integral and indispensable, although we concluded that employees at a nuclear power plant did not protect against such heightened dangers merely by donning and doffing "generic" helmets, safety glasses, and steel-toed boots.

With those precedents in mind, … we think that a reasonable factfinder could conclude that the plaintiffs' donning and doffing of uniforms are integral and indispensable to their principal activities as AUPRs.

… [D]onning and doffing of an AUPR's uniform are … "undertaken for the employer's benefit," with no choice on the employee's behalf. *Reich*, 45 F.3d at 650. The Parks Department prescribes … the uniform in painstaking detail, and AUPRs may be disciplined for non-compliance.… [The] Department requires AUPRs to don and doff … at the workplace, another factor that suggests those tasks may qualify as integral and indispensable. *Alvarez*, 339 F.3d at 903.

More fundamentally, the uniforms appear … vital to "the primary goal[s] of … work" during a shift. *See Reich*, 45 F.3d at 650. … [A]n AUPR's utility belt holds items used to perform law-enforcement duties. A summons book is … necessary for the issuance of summonses. A baton, mace, and handcuffs … may be critical in effecting an arrest. And a radio and flashlight may prove crucial in tracking suspects and coordinating with other … employees. We … classify these items as tools of an AUPR's trade, arguably analogous to a butcher's knife, a radiological technician's x-ray machine, or a K-9 officer's dog. In keeping with *King Packing*, *Kosakow*, and *Reich*, … a reasonable factfinder could conclude that the donning and doffing of an AUPR's utility belt are integral and indispensable tasks.

An AUPR's bulletproof vest more closely resembles the type of protective gear analyzed in *Gorman* and *Alvarez*. Like the helmets, safety glasses, and metal mesh at issue in those decisions, the vest is not a tool used to perform principal activities; … it functions solely to protect against risks collateral to those activities. We recognized in *Gorman* that the use of such protective gear may be integral and indispensable to … principal activities where it guards against "workplace dangers that transcend ordinary risks." … Under *Gorman*, therefore, the donning and doffing of an AUPR's bulletproof vest also may qualify as integral and indispensable. …

Professional clothing appears … comparably essential to an AUPR's work. Uniforms … identify employees to others, and for many jobs (waiting tables, for example) that function may be a mere convenience. In the case of law-enforcement … , however, identification to the public is more fundamentally intertwined with the objectives of employment. … [I]t is professional Parks Department clothing … that not only attracts citizens in need of assistance but also establishes an AUPR's authority to investigate violations, issue summonses, make arrests, and … intervene in emergency situations. Without such a visible signal of authority, an AUPR's efforts to instruct the public and enforce park rules, perhaps with force, could be ineffective and even perilous—the AUPR might be mistaken for a citizen breaking the law rather than a government official enforcing it. … Parks Department supervisors frequently tell AUPRs that [their] role is to be a highly visible uniformed presence in New York City. That instruction blurs the distinction between wearing the uniform and performing the job. … [D]onning and doffing of an AUPR's professional clothing, no less than her equipment, could reasonably be viewed as integral and indispensable to her principal activities.…

[The district court] characterized the protective elements of an AUPR's uniform as comparably "generic" to the helmets, safety glasses, and steel-toed boots … in *Gorman*. Those items qualified as generic because they were widely available to the public and commonly worn in a range of settings. The same cannot be said of an AUPR's bulletproof vest, baton, mace, or handcuffs ....

Compounding those errors, the district court misconstrued *Gorman* as establishing that generic protective gear is *never* integral and indispensable.... *Gorman* did not endorse any such categorical rule. The Court there held that nuclear power plant employees' donning and doffing of helmets, safety glasses, and steel-toed boots did not qualify as integral and indispensable because the items ... guarded against only routine workplace risks. The generic nature of the items may have pointed toward that ... conclusion, because generic equipment is more likely than specialized equipment to address workplace conditions that are commonplace. But the items' generic nature did not *establish* ... that they guarded against only routine risks. As *Steiner* demonstrates, items as generic as a shower and a change of clothes can, in certain circumstances, neutralize extreme threats.... [C]ourts always must determine whether the gear—however generic or specialized—guards against "workplace dangers" that accompany ... principal activities and "transcend ordinary risks." ... This inquiry requires a fact-intensive examination of the gear at issue, the ... principal activities, and the relationship between them. ...

NOTES AND QUESTIONS

1. An important underlying principal of *Integrity Staffing* and *Perez* is that an employee's first and last principal or integral activity marks the beginning and end of the period when other related activities are presumed to be compensable. Related activities outside that time zone are presumed not to be compensable. Consider, for example, routine travel from home to the workplace and back again. Such commuting takes place before the first principal/integral activity or after the last principal/integral activity and is thus presumed non-compensable. 29 C.F.R. § 785.34, .35. However, a presumption is rebuttable. Travel time back to work on an "emergency" call might count, depending on the circumstances. 29 C.F.R. § 785.36. Travel from home to work on a special short-term assignment at a remote location away from the regular workplace might count depending on the circumstances. 29 C.F.R. § 785.37, .39. Travel from one job site to another also counts. 29 C.F.R. § 785.38.

2. Time spent in many non-productive activities between the first and last principal/integral activities are presumed to be compensable if they are sufficiently related to the work.

a. **Rest and meal breaks.** The Department of Labor views short rest periods as integral to work because "[t]hey promote the efficiency of the employee and are customarily paid for as working time." 29 C.F.R. § 785.18. Thus, the employer must count rest periods (at least those of no more than 20 minutes in duration). *Id.* However, a "bona fide" meal break does not count. In order for a meal break to be bona fide, "[t]he employee must be completely relieved from duty for the purposes of eating," and except in "special situations" a bona fide meal break must be at least 30 minutes in duration. If the employer requires the employee to eat at his desk or other work station, the meal break counts as work time. 29 C.F.R. § 785.19(a); *see, e.g.*, Reich v. S. New England Telecom. Corp., 121 F.3d 58 (2d Cir. 1996) (half-hour lunch breaks must be compensated where employer required telephone repair and maintenance crew workers to remain "at or near the work site" to keep the area secure and safe). *But see* 29 C.F.R. § 785.19(b) ("It is not necessary that an employee be permitted to leave the premises if he is otherwise completely freed from duties during the meal period").

b. **Workplace accidents/medical attention.** If an employee receives medical attention at the workplace or at the employer's direction during normal working hours, the time the employee spends waiting for and receiving the medical attention counts. 29 C.F.R. § 785.43.

c. **Meetings and training.** Whether time in meetings and training is compensable depends not only on when the activity occurred but also why it occurred. The Department of Labor has a four-part test for determining whether an employee's time at a meeting or in training counts. The employer need not count the time if "(a) Attendance is outside of the employee's regular working hours; (b) Attendance is in fact voluntary; (c) The course, lecture, or meeting is not directly related to the employee's job; and (d) The employee does not perform any productive work during such attendance." 29 C.F.R. § 785.28. *See also* 29 C.F.R. § 785.29 (regarding whether training is directly related to an employee's job); 29 C.F.R. § 785.31 (special situations). The FLSA caselaw has been highly fact-specific as to what meeting or training time must be counted. *See also Jimenez v. Board of County Commissioners*, 697 Fed. Appx. 597 (10th Cir. 2017) (*pre-shift* briefings providing plaintiff information integral and indispensable to principal activity was compensable; *post-shift* briefings plaintiff provided to worker who relieved her were not compensable because plaintiff could have left notes rather than staying late perform an in-person briefing).

d. **Waiting for work**. An employee might spend time "waiting" for work either before the beginning of a shift or during a shift. Waiting on the employer's premises for the beginning of a shift is presumed noncompensable. Waiting for the next task in the middle of a shift, on the other hand, is presumed to be compensable. What about "on call" employees who are at home and engaged in personal activity but not completely disengaged from work because they must "wait" for a possible urgent call to duty? The treatment of "on call" time is the subject of the next case.

DINGES v. SACRED HEART ST. MARY'S HOSPITALS, INC.

164 F.3d 1056 (7th Cir. 1999)

EASTERBROOK, Circuit Judge.

Working more than 40 hours per week draws premium pay under the Fair Labor Standards Act, 29 U.S.C. § 207. Should hours spent "on call" be treated as work? According to the Supreme Court, the answer depends on whether one has been "engaged to wait" or is "waiting to be engaged." Compare Armour & Co. v. Wantock, 323 U.S. 126 (1944), with Skidmore v. Swift & Co., 323 U.S. 134 (1944). That evocative distinction rarely decides a concrete case; on-call time readily can be characterized either way. For most purposes it is best to ask what the employee can do during on-call periods. Can the time be devoted to the ordinary activities of private life? If so, it is not "work." Even a functional approach produces close calls, however; this is one.

Sacred Heart St. Mary's Hospitals operates a hospital in rural Tomahawk, Wisconsin. The Hospital's ambulance department has two "emergency medical technicians" (EMTs) in-house during the day (and recently for an evening shift), but after hours the Hospital relies on standby crews. Two EMTs serve as the "first-out" crew and two more as the "second-out" crew, which will be called to duty if the first-out crew is in the field when the Hospital must dispatch an ambulance. An EMT on first-out status must arrive at the Hospital within 7 minutes of receiving a page. Members of the first-out crew receive $2.25 per hour of on-call time, plus pay at time-and-a-half for all hours devoted to handling a medical emergency. The Hospital credits them with at least two hours' work (and thus they receive three hours' wages) for each emergency call, even if they are back home in less — as they usually are. When calls take more than two hours, they are paid for actual time. Members of the second-out crew have 15 rather than 7 minutes to reach the Hospital. The schedule of a first-out EMT over a two-week period includes 7 days of duty at the Hospital (on 8 or 10 hour shifts) plus 7 evenings and nights of on-call time. It also has three 48-hour periods when the EMT is neither working nor on call. When the Hospital had only one shift per day of EMTs on the premises, and the on-call period correspondingly lasted 14 to 16 hours, a first-out EMT could expect to receive an average of 0.65 calls per period. Because medical emergencies sometimes occur in bunches, the probability of receiving at least one call to work during a given 14 to 16 hour period is lower, approximately one in two.

Garrett Dinges and Christine Foster asked for and were assigned first-out status. Now, in this suit, they contend that the rewards should have been even greater than those the Hospital promised and delivered — that the entire 14 to 16 hour on-call period should be treated as working time, so it would produce 21 to 24 hours' wages even if they did not receive any emergency call. Both Dinges and Foster live within 7 minutes' drive from the Hospital — indeed, the entire City of Tomahawk is within the 7-minute radius — so they can and do pass the on-call time at home or at other activities in or near the City. Plaintiffs observe that during on-call time their options are restricted:

- They can't travel outside Tomahawk. Each has spent holidays at home rather than with relatives, and has been unable to attend weddings, family reunions, parties, and other events. While on call, Dinges cannot assist in operation of the family business, located 20 miles from the Hospital. Hunting, fishing, boating, camping, and other recreational activities are restricted to what is possible near the Hospital (and near a car, so that the Hospital can be reached quickly).
- They cannot engage in activities such as using a power lawn mower or snowmobiling whose loud noise would prevent them from hearing a page; correspondingly they cannot attend concerts, where pagers must be turned off, or go swimming.
- They are forbidden to drink alcohol.
- Foster has a babysitter on hand during on-call hours, because she may be called away from her children at any time. She cannot go bike riding with the children or attend school events with them, because responding to a call would take too long.

- Shopping is curtailed because retail outlets in Tomahawk are open shorter hours, and carry fewer goods, than stores in larger population centers outside the 7-minute radius from the Hospital.

The Hospital responds by emphasizing what EMTs can do during on-call hours — cook, eat, sleep, read, exercise, watch TV and movies, do housework, care for pets, family, and loved ones at home. Many things in the vicinity of home also are compatible with first-out status. For example, Foster watches her children participate in sports, attends dance recitals, and goes to restaurants and parties. Moreover, the Hospital adds, most of the things that can't be done on first-call status, such as camping and attending events out of town, also are foreclosed by the 15-minute response time of the second-call team, or for that matter by a one-hour response time. But attending special events such as out-of-town weddings could be arranged, even if the weddings were scheduled during on-call time, if an EMT swapped duty periods with another member of the staff. The Hospital has a flexible swap policy. Because swaps require finding another EMT willing to trade, they are hard to arrange for holidays (few EMTs are anxious to work on Thanksgiving or Christmas and give up their own family get-togethers) but easier to arrange for occasional events such as parties and weddings. The district judge concluded that the extensive list of things EMTs can do during first-out time is the legally important one — because time is not "work" if it can be used effectively for personal pursuits — and granted summary judgment to the Hospital.

The district court's emphasis on the fact that the EMTs can stay at home while on call, and can do many things while there, has the support of the Department of Labor's implementing regulations.

> An employee who is not required to remain on the employer's premises but is merely required to leave word at home or with company officials where he or she may be reached is not working while on call. Time spent at home on call may or may not be compensable depending on whether the restrictions placed on the employee preclude using the time for personal pursuits. Where, for example, a firefighter has returned home after the shift, with the understanding that he or she is expected to return to work in the event of an emergency in the night, such time spent at home is normally not compensable. On the other hand, where the conditions placed on the employee's activities are so restrictive that the employee cannot use the time effectively for personal pursuits, such time spent on call is compensable.

29 C.F.R. § 553.221(d). *See* Auer v. Robbins, 519 U.S. 452 (1997) (courts should defer to the Secretary's definitions of terms). The regulatory question is whether the employee can "use the time effectively for personal pursuits" — not for all personal pursuits, but for many. But then there is that weasel word "effectively." An employee who can remain at home while on call, but is called away every few hours, can't use the time "effectively" for sleeping, and probably not for many other activities. Plaintiffs, however, experience less than a 50% chance that there will be any call in a 14- to 16-hour period, so their time may be used effectively for sleeping, eating, and many other activities at home and around Tomahawk. (Over 338 on-call periods, Dinges had 184 pass without a call. Thus Dinges responded to at least one call only 46% of the time. Foster's experience was similar.)

Plaintiffs make a great deal of the 7-minute response limit, which they say is below the shortest period that any appellate court has deemed compatible with "effective" use of time for personal pursuits. Maybe so; the cases are not easy to classify. [citations omitted]. But we do not think that response time is dispositive. It sets a limit on the distance an EMT may live from the Hospital, but a person who lives nearby may have ample time to respond. A person who lived well outside Tomahawk would find a 20-minute response time as constraining as plaintiffs find a 7-minute time, while someone who lived next door to the hospital would think 7 minutes generous.

Both plaintiffs live where they did before they asked for first-out status and do not say that they would have moved farther away if the time were longer; the response time has not affected residential choices. Tomahawk is rural and traffic jams are rare. A 7-minute response limit in Milwaukee would not be compatible with effective use of time for personal pursuits; things are otherwise in the countryside. Plaintiffs do not contend that the 7-minute time interferes with sleeping or the care of children. It is long enough to wake up (or finish changing a diaper) and still get to the Hospital on time. Seven minutes may be the lower limit, for it takes time to shake off the cobwebs when awakening and to jump into clothes, but we need not explore the question further.

To the extent there is uncertainty — and the open-ended regulatory standard, combined with the Supreme Court's oracular "test," ensures uncertainty — we must take account of the arrangement plaintiffs themselves chose. They sought first-out status because it created the best earnings opportunity, and they agreed to a combination of hourly pay for on-call hours plus time-and-a-half for actual emergency calls. The prospect of being paid for spending time at home (even time asleep) must have been attractive. Although the FLSA overrides contracts, in close cases it makes sense to let private arrangements endure — for the less flexible statutory approach has the potential to make everyone worse off. Suppose we were to hold that time the EMTs spend on call counts as "work." That would produce a windfall for Dinges and Foster today, but it would lead the Hospital to modify its practices tomorrow. If the EMTs are "working" 24 hours a day, then the Hospital will abolish the on-call system and have EMTs on its premises 24 hours a day, likely hiring additional EMTs so that it can limit the premium pay for overtime. This is what St. Mary's already has done at its hospital in Rhinelander, Wisconsin. The Hospital will pay more in the process, but EMTs such as Dinges and Foster will receive less, spend more time at the Hospital (and less at home), or both. Ambulatory statutory and regulatory language permits labor and management to structure their relations so that each side gains. That is what the Hospital has done in Tomahawk, and we do not think that the FLSA compels a different arrangement.

NOTES AND QUESTIONS

1. There are other types of activities that cannot be categorized by the usual division into time zones of preliminary, principal/integral and postliminary activity. Another example is time engaged in volunteer activity organized by or encouraged by the employer. Whether an employer must count an employee's time in volunteer activities and community or charitable service depends on whether the work was truly voluntary, whether it was predominantly for the employee's benefit (including

to serve the employee's humanitarian or social urges), whether the volunteer employee's activity displaces a paying work opportunity for another employee, whether the activity is outside the employee's normal hours of work, whether the activity is insubstantial in relation to the employee's regular hours, and whether the activity is of the same type of service for which the employee ordinarily receives compensation. 29 C.F.R. § 785.44; Wage & Hour Division, Department of Labor, Opinion Letter, 1996 WL 1005197 (Apr. 21, 1996). In the case of public employees, it may be especially difficult to distinguish public spirited volunteerism from normal work. See Congress's solution to this problem in 29 U.S.C. § 203(e)(4).

2. *"Gap time" claims*. The FLSA and a private employment *contract* frequently disagree as to whether certain time periods are compensable. Suppose a nonexempt employee attends a mandatory but "unpaid" training session that would clearly constitute compensable time under the FLSA. Assuming the *contract* does not require payment for this time, does the FLSA nevertheless require payment for this time if the employee works no more than 40 compensable hours and still receives at least the minimum wage after counting the training time? The weight of authority says "no." *See, e.g.*, United States v. Klinghoffer Bros. Realty Corp., 285 F.2d 487 (2d Cir. 1960).

4. *Allocating Expenses and Losses*

a. The Employment Contract and the FLSA

Work is expensive, and not only in terms of an employee's time and physical or mental effort. At the very least there is the additional expense of travel to and from work. Clothes, uniforms, occupational licenses, tools, equipment, materials and day care are other potential expenses. There are also risks of liability to the employer or a third party for personal or property injuries caused by the work (the risk of the employee's own personal injury is the subject of the next chapter). As a matter of contract, the employer and employee might allocate such costs to either party. *See, e.g.*, Diaz v. Silver Bay Logging, Inc., 55 P.3d 732 (Alaska 2002) (contract allowed employer to charge employee for food and lodging at remote logging camp); Mytych v. May Dep't Stores Co., 260 Conn. 152, 793 A.2d 1068 (2002) (contract allowed employer to charge each sales employee a pro rata share of "unidentified" customer returns).

Contract law might impose limits on employers shifting costs to employees. In Gutierrez v. Hachar's Dep't Store, 484 S.W.2d 433 (Tex. Civ. App. 1972), the plaintiff sued her employer for "malicious withholding" from her paycheck. The deduction was for $124.99 missing from the plaintiff's cash drawer. The plaintiff had agreed in advance, apparently as a condition of employment, "that my employer, or any of his representatives, has the authority to withhold all or any part of my salary earned by me in order to pay in full any debts that I may owe [the employer]." *Id.* at 436 n.3. The court of appeals reversed a summary judgment for the employer and remanded for trial with the following comments:

> The summary judgment evidence before us does not establish as a matter of law that plaintiff owed defendant a debt of $124.99, or that defendant, as matter of law, was authorized to withhold this sum from plaintiff's pay

> check. The agreement signed by plaintiff did not make her a guarantor of all shortage which might be discovered in such cash drawer, such as loss from theft by others, vandalism, fire, arson, or other acts beyond the control of plaintiff. Plaintiff, by signing such statement, did not become responsible for losses or shortages in such cash drawer arising through acts entirely beyond the control of plaintiff.

Id. at 436.

Would or should it have made a difference if the agreement in *Gutierrez* had more clearly stated that the employee was a "guarantor of all shortage" in her cash drawer? In Kobus v. Jefferson Ice Co., 2 Ill. App. 3d 458, 276 N.E.2d 725 (1971), the plaintiff argued that an employment contract making him responsible for "any and all shortages" during his shift was unconscionable. The court avoided the unconscionability issue by deciding in his favor on another ground: "If the plaintiff was to be responsible for losses incurred during the hours he worked, the defendant had the obligation to provide some suitable method to allocate the losses to those hours he was on duty." *Id.* at 727. Having breached this duty, the employer was foreclosed from enforcing the agreement as to shortages.

The FLSA imposes another limit on allocation of costs to the employee with the "free and clear" rule. 29 C.F.R. §§ 531.28, .35. Not only must the employer pay the minimum wage, it must pay this amount free and clear of withholding, deductions, or credits not otherwise permitted by the act. Some deductions are permitted against the minimum wage because they are required by law, such as withholding for income taxes and social security taxes, and obeying a court order of garnishment or family support wage assignment, subject to other laws that limit the amount of such deductions. 29 C.F.R. § 531.39; *see also* 15 U.S.C. §§ 1671-1677 (restrictions on garnishment). But deductions *not* required by law *might* violate the free and clear rule if they reduce the employee's earnings to less than the minimum wage for any particular week. 29 C.F.R. §§ 531.38, .39. This rule also applies to the overtime component of a nonexempt employee's compensation. *Id.* § 531.37. Thus, the amount an employer may lawfully deduct is the same in a 40-hour week (no overtime) as in a 50-hour week (10 hours overtime). In the case of white collar exempt employees, the free and clear rule applies to the applicable minimum salary. *Id.* §§ 541.117, .211, .311.

The "free and clear" rule preserves the employee's right to receive and manage the disposition of at least his statutory minimum compensation for every workweek. Thus, the rule does not limit all types of deductions — only those that deny the employee his right to receive and manage disposition of his compensation. If a deduction is merely a credit based on the employee's earlier receipt of an advance payment of wages, the "deduction" is not subject to the free and clear rule . Brennan v. Veterans Cleaning Serv., Inc., 482 F.2d 1362, 1369 (5th Cir. 1973). Similarly, the rule does not apply to the employee's voluntary assignment of wages directing the employer to send part of his wages to a third party to pay for goods, services, or benefits (such as insurance) the employee has received for his own benefit. 29 C.F.R. § 531.40.

ARRIAGA v. FLORIDA PACIFIC FARMS, L.L.C.
305 F.3d 1228 (11th Cir. 2002)

KRAVITCH, Circuit Judge:

The plaintiffs-appellants are migrant farm workers from Mexico (the "Farmworkers") employed by the defendants-appellees Florida Pacific Farms, L.L.C. and Sleepy Creek Farms, Inc. (the "Growers") during the 1998-1999 strawberry and raspberry seasons. The Farmworkers sued the Growers, alleging a failure by the Growers to comply with the minimum wage provisions of the Fair Labor Standards Act ("FLSA"), 29 U.S.C. §§ 203(m) & 206(a), and the terms of the work contracts. Specifically, the FLSA claim asserted that the Growers' failure to reimburse the Farmworkers' travel, visa, and recruitment costs at the end of the first workweek pushed their first week's wages below the minimum wage. The contract claim contended that the Growers violated the work contract by not reimbursing the Farmworkers for the cost of transportation to and from their home villages to the Mexican point of hire.

The parties filed cross motions for summary judgment, which were based upon an agreed statement of undisputed facts. The district court granted the Growers' motion and denied the Farmworkers' motion. . . .

I. BACKGROUND

A. H-2A PROGRAM OVERVIEW

[The court described the H-2A visa program administered by the Department of Labor under the Immigration Reform and Control Act of 1986 (IRCA), Pub. L. No. 99-603, 100 Stat. 3359 (codified in scattered sections of 8 U.S.C.), to authorize the temporary agricultural employment of nonimmigrant aliens. In addition to requiring payment of at least the FLSA minimum wage, the program requires a contract providing for reimbursement of inbound transportation and subsistence costs if and when the worker completes 50 percent of his contract work period. If the employee completes the contract work period, he is entitled to reimbursement of his outbound transportation and subsistence costs.]

B. FACTS

. . . In its efforts to locate Mexican workers willing to accept the approved H-2A visas and to arrange for their transportation to Florida, the Growers used the services of [Florida Fruit and Vegetable Association (FFVA)], which utilized Florida East Coast Travel Service Inc. ("Florida East Coast Travel") and Berthina Cervantes. Cervantes maintained an office in Monterrey, Mexico, and assembled the group of workers through several means. . . .

. . . The workers . . . paid Cervantes the following amounts: $100 for the visa; $45 for the visa application fee; and $130 for transportation ($20 bus fare from Monterrey to Laredo, Texas, and $110 bus fare from Laredo to Florida). Some workers also were required to pay a recruitment fee to Cervantes's assistant, Maria Del Carmen Gonzalez-Rodriguez. This occurred without the knowledge of Cervantes, Florida East Coast Travel, FFVA, or the Growers; this fee was contrary to directions given by Florida East Coast Travel, FFVA, and the Growers, who were paying Cervantes $50 per worker for her services and who had directed her not to charge the workers a fee. The workers also were required to pay $6 to the U.S. Immigration Service at the border for the issuance of their entry document.

At the conclusion of the 50 percent period of the contract, the Growers reimbursed workers still on the job $130 for transportation from Monterrey to Florida. When the contract period ended, the Growers provided the workers with a bus ticket to Laredo, Texas, and $20 to be used toward a bus ticket to Monterrey, or any destination in Mexico. The Growers did not pay any of the workers the costs for transportation from their homes to Monterrey, visa costs, the entry document fee, or any payments made to local contact persons or Gonzalez-Rodriguez.

II. Discussion

A. FLSA Claim

. . . The Growers contend that the FLSA was satisfied because the Farmworkers' hourly wage rate was higher than the FLSA minimum wage rate and deductions were not made for the costs the Farmworkers seek to recover. The district court correctly stated that there is no legal difference between deducting a cost directly from the worker's wages and shifting a cost, which they could not deduct, for the employee to bear. An employer may not deduct from employee wages the cost of facilities which primarily benefit the employer if such deductions drive wages below the minimum wage. *See* 29 C.F.R. § 531.36(b). This rule cannot be avoided by simply requiring employees to make such purchases on their own, either in advance of or during the employment. *See id.* § 531.35; Ayres v. 127 Rest. Corp., 12 F. Supp. 2d 305, 310 (S.D.N.Y. 1998).

An employer is allowed to count as wages the reasonable cost "of furnishing [an] employee with board, lodging, or other facilities, if such board, lodging, or other facilities are customarily furnished by such employer to his employees." 29 U.S.C. § 203(m). Although the FLSA does not define "other facilities," DOL has promulgated regulations dedicated to this term which identify circumstances when an employer may claim a wage credit or deduction for the provision of "other facilities." *See* 29 C.F.R. § 531.32. One of the DOL regulations states that "the cost of furnishing 'facilities' which are primarily for the benefit or convenience of the employer will not be recognized as reasonable and may not therefore be included in computing wages." *Id.* § 531.32(c). For guidance in applying this test, DOL regulations provide "a list of facilities found by the Administrator to be primarily for the benefit [or] convenience of the employer," which includes tools and uniforms. *Id.* § 531.3(d)(2). The expenses which are primarily for the benefit of the employee, and therefore constitute other facilities, include: meals; dormitory rooms; housing; merchandise from company stores such as "food, clothing, and household effects"; and fuel, electricity, water and gas "furnished for the noncommercial personal use of the employee." *Id.* § 531.32(a).

If an expense is determined to be primarily for the benefit of the employer, the employer must reimburse the employee during the workweek in which the expense arose. *See* 29 C.F.R. § 531.35.[10] Situations in which items such as required

---

[10] For example, if it is a requirement of the employer that the employee must provide tools of the trade which will be used in or are specifically required for the performance of the employer's

tools or uniforms were purchased before the first workweek are not explicitly covered by the regulations. However, there is simply no legal difference between an employer requiring a worker to have the tools before the first day of work, requiring the tools to be purchased during the first workweek, or deducting the cost of the tools from the first week's wages. Compliance with the FLSA is measured by the workweek. *See id.* § 776.4. Workers must be reimbursed during the first workweek for pre-employment expenses which primarily benefit the employer, to the point that wages are at least equivalent to the minimum wage.[11] *Cf.* Marshall v. Root's Rest., 667 F.2d 559, 560 (6th Cir. 1982) (affirming district court finding that defendants required waitresses to wear uniforms at work and that the cost of uniforms therefore pushed first week pay below minimum wage).

The costs in dispute are de facto deductions which, if not permissible, drove the Farmworkers' pay below the FLSA minimum wage. We thus must analyze whether the transportation, visa, and recruitment costs incurred by the Farmworkers are primarily for the benefit or convenience of the employer. If so, the Growers must reimburse the Farmworkers up to the point that their wages satisfy the FLSA minimum wage.

1. Transportation Costs

The Farmworkers paid $130 for bus transportation from Monterrey, Mexico, to the farms in Florida. To determine whether or not this cost is "primarily for the benefit or convenience of the employer," we begin with the DOL regulations, §§ 531.3 and 531.32. Transportation costs are twice mentioned, and in each situation the regulation states that where such transportation is "an incident of and necessary to the employment," it does not constitute "other facilities." 29 C.F.R. § 531.32(a) & (c).

. . . The district court and the Growers primarily rely on Vega v. Gasper, 36 F.3d 417 (5th Cir. 1994), which held that time spent traveling to and from work is not compensable under the "Portal-to-Portal Act," 29 U.S.C. § 251 *et seq.* The Growers assert that the appropriate standard should be drawn from *Vega*: only items which are directly connected or integral to the performance of the employee's principal activity are primarily for the benefit and convenience of the employer. In *Vega*, seasonal farmworkers asserted that the defendant farm labor contractor's failure to compensate them for their time traveling to and from work constituted a violation of the FLSA. 36 F.3d at 423. Under the Portal-to-Portal Act, however, an employer is not liable under the FLSA for certain employee activities. *See* 29 U.S.C. § 254(a). If the time spent traveling to and from work daily is a

---

particular work, there would be a violation of the Act in any workweek when the cost of such tools purchased by the employee cuts into the minimum or overtime wages required to be paid under the Act. 29 C.F.R. § 531.35.

[11] An example may clarify confusion in this terminology. Suppose a worker is required to bring to work tools which cost $100. In his first workweek, he works 40 hours at a rate of $7 per hour. If only given pay for the hours worked, which would be $280, the FLSA would be violated. This is so because the cost of the tools, which has been imposed on the worker prior to employment, reduces the wages to $180; when $180 is divided by 40 hours, the hourly rate drops below the minimum wage of $5.15. However, the FLSA does not require the employer to add the cost of the tools onto the regular wages, but only to reimburse the worker up to the point that the minimum wage is met. To satisfy the FLSA, the employer would need to pay this worker $306 the first workweek: $100 for the tools plus $206 (40 hours multiplied by $5.15).

"principal activity" of the employee, the employees would be due FLSA minimum wages. *See Vega*, 36 F.3d at 424; 29 U.S.C. § 254(a). The court construed the term "principal activity" to include "activities performed as part of the regular work of the employees in the ordinary course of business," where the "work is necessary to the business and is performed by the employees, primarily for the benefit of the employer[.]" *Vega*, 36 F.3d at 424 (internal quotations and citations omitted). The district court in this case stated that the Farmworkers' claim turns on the same language as the *Vega* plaintiffs — whether the travel primarily benefits the employer — although it noted that the Farmworkers here are claiming travel costs whereas the workers in *Vega* sought wages for travel time. Basing its decision on *Vega*, the district court found that the travel expenses incurred by the Farmworkers were not costs that primarily benefit the employer.

The district court erred in its reliance on *Vega* for two reasons. . . . First, the district court failed to note that in *Vega*, the type of travel under evaluation was fundamentally different than the nature of the travel here. The workers in *Vega* spent at least four hours daily traveling to and from work; although this is a long trip, the court found that this "was just an extended home-to-work-and-back commute." *Id.* at 424-25. According to the court, this time "was indisputably ordinary to-work or from-work travel and not compensable." *Id.* at 425. Here, by contrast, the Farmworkers' petition for transportation costs derived from a one-time bus ride from Monterrey, Mexico, to Florida. This is not a minor factual distinction, but rather a fundamental difference making *Vega* inapposite.

Second, *Vega* involves the Portal-to-Portal Act rather than the FLSA. Because the Farmworkers do not seek to be compensated for their time spent traveling, the Portal-to-Portal Act does not apply. Although *Vega* employs the same language as the DOL regulations interpreting the FLSA — "primarily for the benefit of the employer" — the language is being applied to statutes with different concepts and different purposes. Section 531.32 uses this language to determine "other facilities" whereas the *Vega* test defines "principal activity." The FLSA prevents improper deductions from reducing the wages of a worker below the minimum wage, *see* 29 C.F.R. § 531.35 (wages must be "free and clear" of improper deductions), whereas the Portal-to-Portal Act prevents courts from construing the term "work" too widely. *See* Reich v. N.Y. City Transit Auth., 45 F.3d 646, 649 (2d Cir. 1995) (stating that the Portal-to-Portal Act "represented an attempt by Congress to delineate certain activities which did not constitute work"). The standard urged by the Growers is inappropriate to import into the FLSA.

c. *Analysis*

We return to the actual language of the DOL regulations in our effort to determine whether or not the transportation costs at issue constitute "other facilities." Clearly, § 531.32 considers expenses related to commuting between home and work — like that in *Vega* — to be primarily for the benefit of the employee and thus they would constitute "other facilities." *See* 29 C.F.R. § 531.32(a) ("transportation furnished employees between their homes and work where the travel time does not constitute hours worked compensable under the Act" is primarily for the benefit or convenience of the employee). Other transportation costs, such as the bus fare at issue here or travel from one job site to another, may or may not be considered "other facilities," depending on whether the travel is "an incident of and necessary to the employment." 29 C.F.R. § 531.32(a); *see also* 29 C.F.R. § 531.32(c) ("transportation charges where such transportation is an incident of and necessary to the employment (as in the case of maintenance-of-way employees of a railroad)" are "primarily for the benefit or convenience of the employer"). If the transportation charge falls into this category, it does not constitute "other facilities" and may not be counted as wages; the employer therefore would be required to reimburse the expense up to the point the FLSA minimum wage provisions have been met.[17]

The Growers hired the Farmworkers — nonimmigrant aliens allowed to perform seasonal or temporary agricultural work — pursuant to the H-2A visa program. In choosing to participate in this program, the Growers understood that certain regulations would be imposed on them. Nonimmigrant alien workers employed pursuant to this program are not coming from commutable distances; their employment necessitates that one-time transportation costs be paid by someone. We hold that this transportation cost is "an incident of and necessary to the employment" of H-2A workers. . . . Transportation charges are an inevitable and inescapable consequence of having foreign H-2A workers employed in the United States; these are costs which arise out of the employment of H-2A workers. When a grower seeks employees and hires from its locale, transportation costs that go beyond basic commuting are not necessarily going to arise from the employment relationship. Employers resort to the H-2A program because they are unable to employ local workers who would not require such transportation costs; transportation will be needed, and not of the daily commuting type, whenever employing H-2A workers.

The "incident of and necessary to the employment" language is not the only part of the DOL regulations that supports the conclusion that these long distance transportation costs are primarily for the benefit of the employer. When evaluating expenses that are directly or indirectly related to employment, the examples in § 531.32 show a consistent line being drawn between those costs arising from the employment itself and those that would arise in the course of ordinary life. Section 531.32(a) begins by stating that "'other facilities,' as used in this section, must be something like board or lodging." Transportation costs — aside from regular commuting costs — are nothing like board or lodging. *See* Shultz v. Hinojosa, 432 F.2d 259, 267 (5th Cir. 1970) . . . ("We conclude that as used in the statute, the words 'other facilities' are to be considered as being in pari materia with the preceding words 'board and lodging.' "). In the list of examples which fall under "other facilities," costs that "primarily benefit the employee" are universally

[17] The Growers assert that the transportation costs borne by the Farmworkers are not primarily for the benefit of the employer because they were incurred prior to the commencement of employment. Again, the Growers have borrowed a standard from the Portal-to-Portal Act, *see* 29 U.S.C. § 254(a)(2) (employers do not have to pay minimum wage for time spent on activities which are preliminary to the principal activity), and attempt to impose it onto the FLSA. Even assuming that the transportation expense occurred prior to the employment relationship, this would not permit the Growers to avoid this expense if it is determined to be primarily for their benefit. Such a position would permit employers to avoid expenses primarily for their benefit simply by making them a requirement to employment, which would allow an end-run around the FLSA.

ordinary living expenses that one would incur in the course of life outside of the workplace.

Certain costs — for example, food for employees[20] and safety equipment used by employees[21] — categorically are either for the benefit of the employee or the employer. Other categories are more nuanced; the costs are primarily for the benefit of the employer or the employee depending on the specific facts. By looking at items classified by the regulations as "other facilities," it is apparent that the line is drawn based on whether the employment-related cost is a personal expense that would arise as a normal living expense.

Uniforms provide an illustration of this dividing line. "Charges for rental uniforms," when required by the employment, are considered to be primarily for the benefit of the employer. 29 C.F.R. § 531.32(c). Costs such as drycleaning, ironing, or other special treatment must be reimbursed by the employer when such expenses reduce wages below the minimum wage, and such uniform maintenance is required by the nature of the work. *See* 29 C.F.R. § 531.3(d)(2) (stating that "the cost of uniforms and of their laundering, where the nature of the business requires the employee to wear a uniform," is an expense primarily for the benefit of the employer). As to the question of what constitutes a required uniform, DOL has taken a practical approach; if the employer "merely prescribes a general type of ordinary basic street clothing to be worn while working and permits variations in details of dress[,] the garments chosen would not be considered uniforms . . . ." Ayres v. 127 Rest. Corp., 12 F. Supp. 2d 305, 310 (S.D.N.Y. 1998) (quoting DOL Wage & Hour Field Operations Handbook § 30c12(f)). As such attire would be considered "ordinary street clothing" rather than a uniform, the expense of purchasing and maintaining such clothing is an expense an employee would encounter as a normal living expense, and is therefore not primarily for the benefit of the employer.

2. *Visa Costs*

The Farmworkers' FLSA claim also demands reimbursement for their visa costs, visa application fees, and immigration fees for the entry documents, again up to the amount needed to comply with the minimum wage laws. The visa costs here were necessitated by the Growers' employment of the Farmworkers under the H-2A program. Unlike food, boarding, or commuter expenses, these fees are not costs that would arise as an ordinary living expense. When an employer decides to utilize the H-2A program these costs are certain to arise, and it is therefore incumbent upon the employer to pay them. Although immediate reimbursement is not necessary, payment may be required within the first week if the employees' wages, once the costs are subtracted, are below minimum wage. If so, the employer must provide reimbursement up to the point where the minimum wage is met. H-2A workers are nonimmigrant alien workers who obviously require visas; in fact, the Growers applied to the DOL for the admission of H-2A workers and then sought to locate workers willing to accept the H-2A visas. Furthermore, the visas restricted the workers to the work described on the clearance order; at the

---

20 "[M]eals are always regarded as primarily for the benefit and convenience of the employee." 29 C.F.R. § 531.32(c).

21 "Safety caps, explosives, and miners' lamps (in the mining industry)" are "primarily for the benefit or convenience of the employer." 29 C.F.R. § 531.32(c).

conclusion of the work period specified in the clearance order or upon termination of the worker's employment (which ever occurred first), the H-2A visas required the workers to return to Mexico. . . . By participating in the H-2A program, the Growers created the need for these visa costs, which are not the type of expense they are permitted to pass on to the Farmworkers as "other facilities."

3. *Recruitment Fees*

Like the travel and visa expenses, the Farmworkers contend that the recruitment fees charged by some of the village recruiters and Gonzalez-Rodriguez should be reimbursed to the Farmworkers under the FLSA. The district court held that the Growers are not responsible for payment of recruitment fees. . . . To be reimbursable, (1) these fees must not constitute "other facilities" and (2) there must be authority to hold the Growers liable for the unauthorized acts of their agents. Because the principles of agency law do not hold the Growers responsible for the recruitment fees, we need not discuss whether the recruitment fees are "other facilities." . . . The agreed statement of undisputed facts includes no words or conduct of the Growers which, reasonably interpreted, could have caused the Farmworkers to believe the Growers consented to have the recruitment fees demanded on their behalf. . . . Because the Farmworkers have failed to allege facts to support the creation of apparent authority, the Growers are not liable for the recruitment fees.

B. Clearance Order Contract Claim

[The court agreed with the farmworkers that the clearance order work contracts entitled them to reimbursement for the cost of transportation between their home villages and Monterrey. Therefore, the court reversed the district court's dismissal of the farmworkers' contract claims for these expenses.]

III. Conclusion

We AFFIRM the district court's entry of summary judgment for the Growers as to the Farmworkers' FLSA claim for recruitment fees; we REVERSE the entry of summary judgment as to the Farmworkers' FLSA claim for transportation costs, visa expenses and immigration fees, as well as the Farmworker's contract claim. This case is REMANDED to the district court for further proceedings consistent with this opinion.

NOTES AND QUESTIONS

1. Not long after *Arriaga* and in the last days of the Bush Administration, the Department of Labor issued a new interpretation of the FLSA stating the Department's disagreement with *Arriaga. See Labor Certification Process and Enforcement for Temporary Employment in Occupations Other Than Agriculture or Registered Nursing in the United States (H-2B Workers), and Other Technical Changes*, 73 Fed. Reg. 78020, 78041 (Dec. 19, 2008). The Department's view in this interpretation was that pre-employment transportation expenses of non-immigrant workers are primarily for the workers' own benefit.

Three months later, after the transition to the Obama Administration, the

Department issued a notice withdrawing its December 18 interpretation. *Withdrawal of Interpretation of the Fair Labor Standards Act Concerning Relocation Expenses Incurred by H-2A and H-2B Workers*, 74 Fed. Reg. 13261, 13262 (Mar. 26, 2009). The March 2009 notice stated that the Department "believes that this issue warrants further review. Consequently . . . [the Department] withdraws the [December 19, 2008,] interpretation . . . for further consideration and the interpretation may not be relied upon as a statement of agency policy . . .").

Subsequently, the U.S. Court of Appeals for the Fifth Circuit addressed the issue of pre-employment transportation, visa and recruitment expenses for H-2B workers in *Castellanos-Contreras v. Decatur Hotels, LLC*, 576 F.3d 274 (5th Cir. 2009). In that case, an agent recruited workers in Mexico to serve in New Orleans hotels in the aftermath of Hurricane Katrina, and the workers later sued the hotel for reimbursement of their travel and visa expenses. In an interlocutory appeal from the denial of summary judgment for the hotel, the Fifth Circuit reversed and ordered a summary judgment in favor of the hotel. The Fifth Circuit specifically rejected *Arriaga* and adopted an analysis generally consistent with the Department of Labor's withdrawn December 2008 interpretation.

2. The FLSA's protection against cost shifting goes no further than the minimum wage and overtime requirements of the act. An employer might be able to shift any of the costs disallowed in *Arriaga* if the employee's net earnings, after these costs, are still in excess of the minimum wage and statutory overtime. Alternatively, the employer could satisfy its FLSA obligations by managing the rate at which deductions or costs are borne by an employee, e.g., taking smaller deductions over a greater number of weeks, so as never to decrease net weekly earnings below the statutory minimum. Is this consistent with the Department of Labor's view that the act was designed partly to prevent "profiteering or manipulation" by employers? *See* 29 C.F.R. § 531.28.

3. Theft, unexplained shortages, accidents, and other risks of damage or loss are also costs an employer might try to shift to the employee. For example, a restaurant employer might deduct cash "shortages," "walkouts" (customers leaving without paying), or "spills" from the paycheck of the employee deemed "responsible." Again, cost shifting may violate the act if the effect is to reduce earnings for any week below the minimum wage. *See, e.g.*, Marshall v. Newport Motel, Inc., 24 Wage & Hour Cas. [BNA] 497, 1979 WL 15529 (S.D. Fla. 1979).

Should it make any difference that the employer truly believes and can prove the employee was a thief ? *See* Mayhue's Super Liquor Stores, Inc. v. Hodgson, 464 F.2d 1196 (5th Cir. 1972): "In such a case there would be no violation of the 'act' because the employee has taken more than the amount of his wage and the return could in no way reduce his wage below the minimum . . . ."

4. An employer must pay the minimum wage and overtime in cash or a cash equivalent (such as a check drawn on a bank account) subject to some non-cash credits described above. See 29 C.F.R. § 531.27. Some employers now pay employees by debit card. A debit card might qualify as a cash equivalent for purposes of the FLSA. *But see* Siciliano v. Mueller, 149 A.3d 863 (Pa. 2016) (debit card was not a "cash equivalent" for purposes of state law because it resulted in bank fees charged to employees). If bank fees reduce an employee's net earnings below the minimum wage and overtime requirements, the employer's payment of wages

by debit card might violate the FLSA. Whether or not payment by debit card violates the FLSA, it might violate other regulations enforced by the Consumer Finance Protection Board. See Consumer Financial Protection Bureau, Bulletin 2013-10; Payroll Card Account (Regulation E) (September 12, 2013) (employer may not require employees to receive wage payment by payroll card unless employer provides at least one alternative permissible option for receipt of wages), online at http://files.consumerfinance.gov/f/201309_cfpb_payroll-card-bulletin.pdf.

b. State Wage Payment and Deduction Laws

State law is often more important and far reaching than federal law when it comes to the regulation of wage deductions. While federal law protects only statutory minimum compensation, state law frequently has the effect of barring a deduction in its entirety, regardless of the amount of an employee's residual wages. In general, the states fall into three categories on this point.

The least protective states have no wage deduction statute but apply the common law rule that an employee is entitled to payment of the full amount of his earned wages when due, subject only to deductions required or permitted by law or by the employee's consent. *See, e.g.*, Georgia R. Co. v. Gouedy, 36 S.E. 691 (Ga. 1900) (employer had no right to deduct amount of loss allegedly caused by employee, where there was no contract or employer policy that permitted the deduction); Brown v. Navarre Chevrolet, Inc., 610 So. 2d 165 (La. App. 1992) (employer could not deduct amount of customer's failure to pay for certain repairs, where employment agreement did not authorize such a deduction). Absent employee consent or statutory authorization, the common law approach might still permit an employer to deduct from wages to collect employee debts from advances or losses due to the employee's breach of some obligation. *See, e.g.*, Cramer v. Coastal States Life Ins. Co., 292 S.E.2d 112 (Ga. App. 1982) (employer entitled to offset amount of employee's indebtedness against commissions owed at time of termination); Puritan Fashions Corp. v. Naftel, 226 S.E.2d 305 (Ga. App. 1976) (in employee's claim for unpaid commissions, jury properly offset amount employee owed employer for samples not returned). However, if a court or administrative agency later finds the employee owed less than the employer claimed, the employer might be subject to penalties under local wage payment statutes.

Most states have now joined a second group with statutes or regulations requiring express employee consent to deductions. *See, e.g.*, Neb. Rev. Stat. § 48-1230 (consent must be in writing); Duffy v. Gainey Transp. Serv., Inc., 484 N.W.2d 7 (Mich. App. 1992), *app. den.*, 487 N.W.2d 426 (Mich. 1992) (interpreting Michigan law to require separate authorization for each specific debt and for each paycheck subject to deduction). In some states an employee's authorization for a deduction is not valid unless it is free of any threat of disciplinary discharge. *See, e.g.*, Mich. Comp. Laws § 408.477(1). *But see* Coast Hotels & Casinos, Inc. v. Nevada State Labor Comm'n, 34 P.3d 546 (Nev. 2001) (in absence of statute to contrary, employer may make authorization for deductions a condition of employment). Moreover, in some states an employer might be liable for wrongful discharge if it terminates an employee for refusing to authorize a deduction. *Compare* Lockwood v. Professional Wheelchair Transp., Inc., 654 A.2d 1252 (Conn. App. 1995) (recognizing public policy cause of action for discharge in retaliation for refusing to pay for cost not properly assessed against employee) *with* Batteries Plus, LLC v. Mohr, 628 N.W.2d 364 (Wis. 2001) (no cause of action where employer discharged employee for refusing to repay prior overpayment of wages).

The third and most protective group of states prohibits any deductions *regardless of employee consent*, except for deductions required by law or for the employee's benefit (such as to direct money to an employee savings or benefit plan).

NOTES AND QUESTIONS

1. States that regulate deductions frequently confront issues about what constitutes a "deduction." The issue arises most often in cases of incentive compensation, which may be based on a formula that takes account of the same types of costs or losses targeted by wage deduction laws. For example, if an employee's bonus is a percentage of the net profits of the unit he manages, an inventory shortage will reduce his compensation. Is the reduction in compensation the rough equivalent of a deduction? *Compare* Jacobs v. Macy's East, Inc., 693 N.Y.S.2d 164 (N.Y. App. Div. 1999) (possibly, depending on whether commissions were "earned" under contract *before* or *after* accounting for losses); *with* Dean Witter Reynolds, Inc. v. Ross, 429 N.Y.S.2d 653 (N.Y. App. Div. 1980) (no, because employee did not "earn" incentive compensation until employer completed calculations that accounted for losses).

Consider also Zarnott v. Timken-Detroit Axle Co., 13 N.W.2d 53 (Wis. 1944), where the court interpreted and applied a Wisconsin statute restricting wage deductions for defective workmanship. The employer in *Zarnott* paid the employee a piece rate, but credited only those pieces approved by the employee's supervisor. The employee argued that the system of crediting or rejecting pieces was a wage deduction without his consent, and the court agreed. Thus, the employer was required to pay the employee for every piece, except pieces the employee agreed were defective, or pieces found defective under an administrative dispute resolution system set forth in the statute.

2. An employer might attempt to evade a "no deduction" law by paying an employee in full but demanding the employee to compensate the employer by "separate transaction": writing a check or handing cash back to the employer. For example, if the employer believes the employee is responsible for an inventory shortage, the employer might pay the employee's usual paycheck but insist on the employee's payment back to the employer, under threat of discharge. New York is one state that has treated such a "separate transaction" as the equivalent of a deduction, and the employer's demand might be illegal if the employee's payment is not for an employee benefit that would make a deduction lawful. *See* Hudacs v. Frito Lay, Inc., 683 N.E.2d 322 (N.Y. 1997) (describing New York law but holding that the employer's system for allocating inventory losses under circumstances of that case was not an illegal deduction or separate transaction).

3. Laws prohibiting deductions regardless of employee consent appear to be motivated by at least two different concerns. One is that an employer should not be permitted to shift to the employee the sorts of risks or costs that are inherent in business and not the result of an employee's gross negligence or criminal conduct.

See Guepet v. Int'l Tao Sys., 443 N.Y.S.2d 321, 322-323 (N.Y. Sup. Ct. 1981). In California, for example, an employer must not take a deduction from employee wages "unless it can be shown that the shortage, breakage, or loss is caused by a dishonest or willful act, or by the gross negligence of the employee." Cal. Admin. Code Regs. tit. 8 § 11010, ¶8. Under that rule, even employee authorization for a deduction for inventory or cash shortages might be ineffective, unless accompanied by a voluntary confession of theft or negligence. *See also* Colo. Rev. Stat. § 8-4-105(1)(c); Okla. Admin. Code § 380:30-1-7(d)(5); Wis. Stat. § 103.455.

The second concern is that the employer should not wield a unilateral and self-serving authority to decide that the employee must pay for a loss. *See* Dempsey Bros. Dairies, Inc. v. Blalock, 325 S.E.2d 410 (Ga. App. 1984) (upholding punitive damages where employer charged employee for inventory shortage not reasonably attributable to employee, employer relied on inaccurate records, and on one occasion deduction was without any notice to employee). In the *Hudacs* case described in the preceding note, the employer avoided the problem of the self-serving adjudicator by allowing a disputed loss to be resolved by grievance proceedings with a union leading where necessary to arbitration.

A law that prohibits an employer from taking a deduction does not necessarily deny the employer any remedy if it believes the employee is a thief or is responsible for the loss of or damage to property. The employer could sue the employee. A lawsuit is certainly less convenient than a wage deduction and might not be practical at all. Moreover, if the employer must sue to recover a loss, a court rather than the employer will decide who must bear the loss. For more on whether an employer may sue an employee for losses caused by the employee's breach of duty, see Part C.5.b and the end of Part C.5.c of this chapter, *infra*.

3. Neither the FLSA nor state deduction laws would limit an employer in requiring an employee to dress "nicely" and to pay for his or her own clothes, if the employer's dress code does not prescribe a "uniform." But what if an employer, such as a clothing retailer, requires employees to purchase their clothing from one of the employer's own shops? In a series of lawsuits in California beginning in 2002, employees of The Gap, Abercrombie & Fitch, and Polo Ralph Lauren sued their employers, alleging that company policies unlawfully required employees to buy clothes from company stores and wear those clothes on the job. Boylen v. Gap, Inc., Cal. Super. Ct., No. CGC-03-417075; Stevenson v. Abercrombie & Fitch Co., Cal. Super. Ct., No. CGC-03-417074; Young v. Polo Retail LLC, N.D. Cal. No. C02-4546. The statutes and regulations that were the bases for their claims included 8 Cal. Admin. Code. § 11070, which prohibits an employer from shifting the cost of "uniforms" to its employees, and which defines "uniform" to include "apparel and accessories of distinctive design." Another basis for their claim was a "company store" law, Cal. Lab. Code § 450. Many states enacted company store laws a century or more ago to prohibit employers from requiring workers to buy goods at company-owned stores under terms that resulted in a kind of servitude. Cal. Lab. Code § 450, for example, provides that "No employer . . . may compel or coerce any employee, or applicant for employment, to patronize his or her employer, or any other person, in the purchase of any thing of value." At least one of the California cases described above ended in a court-approved settlement. Young v. Polo Retail, LLC, 2007 U.S. Dist. LEXIS 27269 (N.D. Cal. 2007).

5. *Enforcement and Remedies*

An employee who asserts a contract or statutory right to compensation faces at least three obstacles. First, he risks employer retaliation if he is still employed. Second, the amount of his claim may be relatively small in comparison with the cost of a lawsuit or subsequent unemployment. Third, if the employee failed to challenge the employer's pay practices during his employment, a court might find that he waived his claim. The FLSA and state wage payment laws are designed to overcome these obstacles in a variety of ways.

a. FLSA

The FLSA provides employees with two separate tracks for enforcement. First, enforcement might be through the Department of Labor. *See* 29 U.S.C. §§ 216, 217. The department's Wage and Hour Division conducts some investigations on its own initiative, but most of its investigations are initiated by an employee complaint. The act protects complainants by prohibiting an employer from discharging or otherwise discriminating against any employee who has "instituted or caused to be instituted a proceeding" or has testified in a proceeding under the act. 29 U.S.C. § 215(a)(3).

If the department determines that the employer may have violated the act, it can sue the employer for injunctive relief and to collect backpay on behalf of all affected employees. 29 U.S.C. §§ 216, 217. An employer's settlement of claims directly with employees and without the supervision of the department is generally ineffective against either the department or the employees if the settlement was for less than what the employer owed under the act. Lynn's Food Stores, Inc. v. United States, 679 F.2d 1350 (11th Cir. 1982).

An employee can file his own lawsuit without the involvement of the department, but the department might preempt his right to sue if it files a lawsuit encompassing the same claim. 29 U.S.C. § 216(a), (c). Given the department's limited enforcement resources, this second track for enforcement by private cause of action is an important feature of the FLSA, and the act eases the way for employee lawsuits in a number of other ways. Again, the act protects the employee from employer retaliation for having filed a complaint against the employer. 29 U.S.C. § 215(a)(3). Moreover, neither the employee's alleged prior consent to a pay practice nor his alleged waiver of rights by continued employment will bar his claim. Tho Dinh Tran v. Alphonse Hotel Corp., 281 F.3d 23 (2d Cir. 2002). The employee (or the department) can seek back pay going back two years from the date of the complaint, and the period of limitations extends to three years if the employer's violations were "willful." 29 U.S.C. § 255.

In many cases the amount at stake for a single employee might seem small in comparison with the cost and effort of a private lawsuit. Three additional features of the FLSA may make a private lawsuit more attractive. First, in any successful lawsuit under the FLSA (whether by the department or a private individual), a court will award liquidated damages, in effect doubling the amount of backpay the employer owes. 29 U.S.C. § 216(b). Second, the court "shall" award attorneys' fees to a prevailing plaintiff. 29 U.S.C. § 216(b). Third, the employee could combine other employee claims with his own by means of a "collective action," which resembles a class action. 29 U.S.C. § 216(b). However, "No employee shall be a party plaintiff to any such action unless he gives his consent in writing to become a party and such consent is filed with the court in which the action is brought." *Id.* Thus, in contrast with a class action, an FLSA collective action requires specific action by prospective members: they must "opt in" to join the action.

Given the complexity of the FLSA and the department's regulations, one might expect that many employer violations are due to ignorance, inadvertence, or misunderstanding. The Portal to Portal Act granted employers a set of "good faith" affirmative defenses that might reduce or eliminate liability. 29 U.S.C. §§ 258-260. However, in this context "good faith" relates to an employer's reasonable reliance on the department's formal, written interpretations of the law, or the employer's effort to understand the law. *See, e.g.*, Thomas v. Howard Univ. Hosp., 39 F.3d 370 (7th Cir. 1994) ("Even if, through no fault of management, the payroll department blundered, the employer must still make the undercompensated employee whole").

b. State Wage Payment Laws

Most states have special wage collection laws to overcome the practical obstacles individual employees face when they assert claims based on an employer's underpayment of compensation. These state laws are especially important when an employee's claim is based on contract or other state law and exceeds the amount of any claim under the FLSA. One typical statutory solution is to create an administrative scheme for the enforcement of wage claims. In Texas, for example, an employee may file a wage claim with an agency that will prosecute the claim against the employer on the employee's behalf. Tex. Lab. Code §§ 61.051 et seq. *See also* Cal. Lab. Code §§ 90 et seq. With or without such an administrative enforcement scheme, many states also allow the state or the employee to seek additional damages as a penalty against the employer in the event the agency or a court upholds the claim. *See, e.g.*, Tex. Lab. Code § 61.053 (penalty based on bad faith); Cal. Lab. Code § 203 (penalty based on employer's willful violation). A few states prohibit retaliatory discharge of an employee who has filed a wage claim. *See, e.g.*, Cal. Lab. Code § 98.6; N.Y. [Labor] Law § 215.

Not surprisingly wage disputes are particularly common when employment terminates, especially if an employee demands deferred pay (such as a bonus or cash in lieu of vacation), or the employer withholds wages to offset some loss it alleges the employee has caused. The employer's temptation to withhold wages may be particularly strong at the end of the employment, because the employer might think that the same "cause" for discharge is also grounds for a claim against the employee, or it might simply believe it has little to lose by antagonizing the employee by denying payment. The consequence of a wage dispute may be disproportionately severe to an unemployed worker whose sustenance depends on the regular receipt of wages. Thus, in addition to relatively modern laws for the administrative enforcement of wage claims, most states retain a much older variety of laws, "payment upon discharge" statutes, which require an employer to issue the last paycheck for all amounts due within a certain number of days after the termination of employment. *See, e.g.,* 820 Ill. Comp. Stat. Ann. § 115/5; Or. Rev.

Stat. § 652.140. A violation may expose the employer to a penalty and liability for the employee's attorneys' fees.

Payment upon discharge statutes are frequently accompanied by a requirement that if the employer disputes what it owes in good faith, the employer must pay at least the amount it agrees is due. The employee's acceptance of this amount will not constitute a waiver of his claim for the greater amount. *See, e.g.,* 820 Ill. Comp. Stat. Ann. § 115/9 (also requiring employer to notify local agency of any wage dispute, so as to trigger investigation); Or. Rev. Stat. § 652.160.

NOTES AND QUESTIONS

1. State wage collection laws are not necessarily reserved for low or even average wage earning workers. In Miller v. Meisel, 183 Or. App. 148, 51 P.3d 650 (2002), a general manager sued his former employer under a local payment upon discharge law, alleging that the employer breached a promise to pay a bonus of 20 percent of the "value" he added to the business. A jury awarded $1.36 million as the amount due. On appeal, the employer argued that a sizeable bonus did not constitute "wages" within the meaning of the statute, but the court disagreed. The statute defined "wages" as "all compensation for performance of services by an employee," and an incentive bonus however large fit within this definition. *Contra* Thomas v. H&R Block Eastern Enterprises, Inc., 630 F.3d 659 (7th Cir. 2011) ("end of season" bonus was not "wages" under law regarding payment within 10 days after wage earned; reasoning that deferred compensation is not a "wage" if by its nature it is difficult to calculate within ten days).

2. What does an employee gain, particularly in a case like *Miller*, described above, by being able to sue under a wage collection statute instead of the contract law? Unlawful withholding of or deduction from wages is usually a *per se* violation of a wage collection statute, even if the employer can prove a reason that would suffice under contract law for a failure to pay wages. In *Miller*, for example, the employer argued that it withheld the bonus because of a dispute over Miller's alleged breach of duty as an employee. While the employer could have sued or counterclaimed for Miller's alleged indebtedness, the employer's withholding of "wages" was a per se violation of the statute. The result of a per se violation in many states is a penalty and award of attorney's fees. In Massachusetts, for example, an employer must pay treble damages for any wage violation. Mass. Gen. Laws ch. 149 § 27H. In *Miller*, the plaintiff manager recovered nearly half a million dollars in attorneys' fees under Oregon law.

3. Wage collection statutes generally protect only "employees" and not independent contractors. *See* Baltimore Harbor Contractors, Ltd. v. Ayd, 780 A.2d. 303 (Md. 2001). On the other hand, some statutes, particularly older ones, address payment of "workers." These worker payment laws may benefit some independent contractors. *See, e.g.*, Tex. Lab. Code § 58.001 (statutory lien for any "worker" including, but not limited to, any "employee").

c. Class and Collective Wage Actions

Wage claims are sometimes suitable for Rule 23 class action or, in the case of alleged violations of the FLSA, a Section 216 "collective action." An FLSA

Section 216 collective action resembles a class action but with some important procedural differences. For example, in a Rule 23 class action, class members become and remain members of the class unless they take action to "opt *out*." In a collective action under Section 216, however, no employee becomes a member of the class unless they opt *in*.

Whether an action is a Rule 23 class action or a Section 216 collective action, the plaintiffs must describe a question of fact or law common to members of the class with respect to the defendant. In the context of a pay dispute, this requirement ordinarily means that the plaintiffs must identify a particular employer pay practice, classification scheme or policy that affected all members of the class. Plaintiffs face a different set of challenges depending on whether their claims are based on state contract or wage payment law, for which Rule 23 applies, or minimum wage or overtime rules of the FLSA, for which Section 216 applies.

The following case is a so-called "gap time" case under state law. Gap time cases generally arise out of circumstances in which the employer is in compliance with the FLSA, perhaps because wages are substantially in excess of the minimum wage and the employer has controlled working hours to prevent any possibility of overtime work by any employee (e.g., by scheduling only 38 or 39 hours of work per week, with an extra hour cushion against the possibility of exceeding 40 hours). Employees might still complain that the employer does not count certain periods of time as working time. However, if the additional time claimed by employees would not place them above the 40 hour overtime limit, their claim cannot be based on the FLSA. It must be based on contract law or some other wage payment law.

CLAUSNITZER v. FEDERAL EXPRESS CORP.
248 F.R.D. 647 (S.D. Fla. 2008)

CECILIA M. ALTONGA, District Judge.

Plaintiffs, a group of hourly employees of Federal Express Corporation ("FedEx"), brought the instant action against FedEx alleging the company engaged in a pervasive and long-standing policy of failing to pay hourly employees for all time worked. Plaintiffs style their suit as a class action and purport to represent a class of individuals consisting of hourly, non-exempt FedEx employees employed in every state and the District of Columbia, with the exclusion of California. The proposed class includes all such employees whose claims are not barred by the applicable statutes of limitations.

Plaintiffs allege two causes of action: (1) breach of contract for non-payment of wages owed; and (2) a claim in quantum meruit for services rendered. Class certification is sought only with respect to the claim for breach of contract. According to Plaintiffs, FedEx breached its contractual obligation to compensate them by failing to pay for three categories of time worked: (1) time worked between arriving at a FedEx facility and the scheduled start time; (2) time worked between the scheduled stop time and leaving a FedEx facility; and (3) time worked during unpaid breaks....Each potential member of the class signed an employment agreement upon beginning the employment application process with FedEx. . . . Every employment agreement contains a clause specifying that the nature of the employment relationship between FedEx and the employee is at-will. There were a number of different versions of the employment agreement signed by employees over the years; most material terms were consistent. . . .

FedEx also provided employees copies, or gave them access to, various company employment manuals, including an "Employment Handbook" and a "People Manual." Both the Employment Handbook and the People Manual explicitly disclaim that their respective terms create contractual rights. Employees also signed a receipt accompanying the Employee Handbook acknowledging that the Handbook does not create a contract. Section 3-92 of both the Employee Handbook and the People Manual states, "[i]t is the policy of FedEx Express to compensate employees for all time worked in accordance with applicable state and federal laws." In the People Manual, the following sentence states, "[e]xcept for certain approved preliminary and post-liminary activities, no employee should perform work 'off the clock' for any reason, whether on their own initiative or at the request of management." . . .

According to Plaintiffs, it was FedEx's corporate policy that employees were required to perform certain work functions during the "gap periods" between punching in and the scheduled start time, and between the scheduled end time and punching out for the day. Thus, Plaintiffs assert that employees were required to perform work during time periods when they were not being paid. The activities allegedly performed during these unpaid periods vary according to the job function of the particular employee and include gathering equipment and supplies, finishing paperwork, and completing closing procedures. . . .

Plaintiffs have also submitted the affidavits of statistician, Dr. Richard Drogin, who reviewed and analyzed a sample of employee time data obtained from FedEx. Dr. Drogin . . . found that, on average, each employee's records reflected an 8.1 minute gap period each day. Plaintiffs claim all gap periods of every class member constitute unpaid work.

The record does not contain any evidence of an explicit FedEx policy requiring employees to work during gap periods. To the contrary, FedEx's policies explicitly prohibited employees from performing work off-the-clock.

FedEx notes that there were many individualized reasons unrelated to the completion of work why employees may have arrived at the facility before the scheduled start time or left the facility after the scheduled end time....

Plaintiffs assert that working during breaks was a regular occurrence at FedEx. They state that by comparing the various reports the company was able to discover that employees were working during breaks, and thus FedEx had knowledge of the work, approved it, and permitted it to continue. . . . To prove the frequency of this work, Plaintiffs again offer the study of Dr. Drogin. Dr. Drogin's analysis compared a sample of time records from the FAMIS database with records of package and stop scans and concluded that 17.6% of unpaid breaks were interrupted by scans.

FedEx argues that employees were explicitly told not to work during unpaid breaks and cites documentation of this policy. The company also points to statements of employees and named Plaintiffs indicating they did not work during unpaid breaks and that they understood the company policy prohibited such work ....

CLASS CERTIFICATION ANALYSIS

. . . A plaintiff seeking certification of a claim for class treatment must propose an adequately defined class that satisfies the requirements of Rule 23, Federal Rules of Civil Procedure. . . . Rule 23(a) provides that class certification is only appropriate where:

> (1) the class is so numerous that joinder of all members is impracticable, (2) there are questions of law or fact common to the class, (3) the claims and defenses of the representative parties are typical of the claims or defenses of the class, and (4) the representative parties will fairly and adequately protect the interests of the class.

The plaintiff class must also satisfy one of the three additional requirements of Rule 23(b). . . . Plaintiffs assert that the proposed class is certifiable under either Rule 23(b)(1) or 23(b)(3). Under Rule 23(b)(1), the court may certify if "prosecuting separate actions . . . would create a risk of inconsistent or varying adjudications . . . that would establish incompatible standards of conduct for the party opposing the class." Fed. R. Civ. P. 23(b)(1)(A). The final type of sustainable class requires the court to find "that the questions of law or fact common to class members predominate over any questions affecting only individual members, and that a class action is superior to other available methods for fairly and efficiently adjudicating the controversy." Fed. R. Civ. P. 23(b)(3). . . .

A. PLAINTIFFS FAIL TO ADEQUATELY DEFINE THE CLASS

. . . Plaintiffs propose a class consisting of "[a]ll employees of FedEx in the DGO and AGFS Divisions, in all states and the District of Columbia, except California, who were paid on an hourly basis." Plaintiffs propose limiting the class "from the maximum time period preceding the filing of th[e] complaint, as permitted by the applicable statute of limitation, until such time as the Class period closes." The issue of the applicable statutes of limitations is relevant not only to the amount of damages recoverable, but also impacts the definition of the class. Obviously potential class members will be included or excluded depending on whether the limitations period on each claim has run. Therefore, in order for the class to be defined in a way that will be manageable for purposes such as providing notice to potential members, the applicable limitations period or periods must be specifically identified.

In an effort to address this issue, Plaintiffs filed the compendium of state statutes, which includes information with respect to the limitations periods in each of the fifty jurisdictions to be included in the potential class. Plaintiffs point out that courts in other multi-state class actions have addressed issues of varying state law by certifying subclasses. Plaintiffs suggest that jurisdictions with identical limitations periods could be grouped together in a subclass. The statutory limitations periods laid out by Plaintiffs in their compendium range from three to twenty years. Aside from their assurances at oral argument that dividing the class into subclasses would serve to rectify class definition problems, Plaintiffs have not presented a proposed subclass scheme.

FedEx correctly points out that in addition to the issue of varying limitations periods for each jurisdiction, there are also employees whose employment agreements included an express limitations period. The employment agreements signed by certain employees limit the time for filing suit to six months. While some states recognize contractual provisions that create limitations periods shorter than the statutory period, other states refuse to give effect to such provisions. A proper examination of the limitations period applicable to potential class members with six-month provisions in their agreements would accordingly require a determination as to which jurisdiction's law governs the agreement. Such an inquiry would entail examination of state choice of law rules, which might also include consideration of where the contract was entered into, the employee's residence, and where the breach occurred, among other factors. This inquiry is necessarily individualized, and is not addressed by Plaintiffs' definition of the proposed class.

It is difficult to imagine how Plaintiffs could correct the defects with respect to their definition of the proposed class. Because Plaintiffs fail to satisfy any of the Rule 23(b) requirements, however, the undersigned does not invite a request by Plaintiffs to seek to rectify the inadequate class definition.

B. PLAINTIFFS' PROPOSED CLASS SATISFIES THE REQUIREMENTS OF RULE 23(A)

[Considering the requirements of subpart (a) of Rule 23, the court found that the proposed class satisfied the requirement of numerosity, that there were at least some common issues for the class, that the representatives' claims were "typical" of the class claims, and that the proposed class representatives could provide adequate representation. — ED.]

C. THE PROPOSED CLASS DOES NOT SATISFY THE REQUIREMENTS OF RULE 23(B)

1. Certification under Rule 23(b)(3)

. . . . In a properly certified Rule 23(b)(3) class, "'the issues in the class action that are subject to generalized proof, and thus applicable to the class as a whole, must predominate over those issues that are subject only to individualized proof.' " Jackson v. Motel 6 Multipurpose, Inc., 130 F.3d 999, 1005 (11th Cir. 1997). . . .

a. Common Issues Of Law Do Not Predominate

Plaintiffs assert that certification is proper under Rule 23(b)(3) because FedEx's breach of the alleged employment contracts is a predominating issue of law common to all class members. As described, Plaintiffs contend that the basic tenets of contract law — namely what constitutes a breach of contract — are the same in every jurisdiction included in the proposed class. Plaintiffs endeavor to characterize the contracts as simply as possible: FedEx promised to pay for all time worked; we performed work for which we were not paid. There is little doubt that Plaintiffs oversimplify the issues of law necessary to adjudicate the claims of individual members of the proposed class. The legal questions particular to individual members will predominate over those common among the class, thus precluding certification under Rule 23(b)(3).

Adjudication of a claim for breach of contract necessarily requires clear identification of the operative contracts. Plaintiffs sue for breach of contracts consisting of the employment agreement in conjunction with Section 3-92 of the People Manual, which states FedEx's policy to pay for all time worked. Plaintiffs' reference to the People Manual gives rise to the first of several issues that present individual questions.

In most jurisdictions, provisions of an employment manual standing alone will not create rights contractually enforceable by employees.... Many jurisdictions covered by the proposed class reject the proposition that any of the policies in the People Manual form the basis for a breach of contract claim. Others, such as Florida, require specific proof that the parties intended the manual to create enforceable rights.

Determining which jurisdictions permit a contractual claim based on the People Manual provision is a question that must be addressed on an individual basis, or at the very least, by the creation of subclasses. The issue of law Plaintiffs suggest predominates — that FedEx breached its contractual obligation — cannot predominate over individual questions of law where the very terms of the contracts are an open question given the different treatment accorded to employee manuals by the fifty jurisdictions included in the proposed class.

The issue of the applicability of the People Manual is further complicated by the clause explicitly disclaiming the creation of contractual rights. The effect of this provision on the breach of contract claim also may vary within those jurisdictions that do recognize contractually enforceable employment manuals. Whether the People Manual provisions are part of the alleged contracts is a question that will devolve into individual inquiries into the contract law of every jurisdiction covered by the proposed class.

Even assuming that the contracts as described by Plaintiffs are recognized in every jurisdiction, the terms of People Manual Section 3-92 present further issues preventing a finding of predominance of common issues of law. Section 3-92 states that FedEx pays for all time worked "in accordance with applicable state and federal laws." This provision declares FedEx's policy to comply with the wage and hour laws of individual states as well as the federal Fair Labor Standards Act ("FLSA"). Plaintiffs have failed to demonstrate that this reference to state and federal wage and hour laws will not pose individual questions. FedEx has aptly noted that, at least with respect to the calculation of overtime and damages, state wage and hour laws may cause the action to become unmanageable.

Additionally, Section 3-92 provides that employees are not to work "off the clock" except for certain approved preliminary and post-liminary activities. Plaintiffs have not explained the impact of this provision on their breach of contract claim. Given that Plaintiffs assert 3-92 is part of the contracts, it would appear relevant to the analysis of their claim to consider whether Plaintiffs themselves violated this term of their contracts by performing work off-the-clock. The interpretation of this clause may present individual inquiries into whether a given class member knew of the contract and knew of the prohibition. Furthermore, Plaintiffs have not provided a definition of what constitutes compensable work under the contracts. There is a distinct possibility that the various rules of contract interpretation in the fifty jurisdictions would not treat these questions similarly and spurn further individualized legal inquiries. Without an exhaustive analysis prior to certification, which the parties have not done, the undersigned has no way of knowing the answer....

b. Common Issues of Fact Also Do Not Predominate

Plaintiffs contend that the issue of whether FedEx had a company-wide policy of not compensating hourly employees for all time worked is a common question of fact that predominates over individual inquiries. However, as noted by FedEx, the time records produced by FedEx as well as the statistical analysis completed by Dr. Drogin do not indicate whether employees were actually working during gap periods. Indeed, testimony from employees, including named Plaintiffs, supports the conclusion that employees may have been engaged in a variety of non-work related activities during some of the gap periods. With respect to work during unpaid breaks, FedEx has shown many individual reasons why a scan could have occurred while the employee was recording a break code, and has also shown that such scans were not frequent among a substantial majority of employees. Many employees, including named Plaintiffs, stated they did not work during unpaid breaks, although their time records indicate scans occurring during breaks. These scans could be evidence that work was being performed during the break, but could also have been caused by the after-the-fact entry of break codes into the electronic time system. Moreover, in the event an employee did work during unpaid breaks, individual inquiries would be necessary to determine the amount of time actually spent. . . . However, the time records produced by FedEx and studied by Plaintiffs' expert to develop his opinion only show the number of scans that occurred during a break, not how long the employee was allegedly working when the scan occurred. . . .

c. Class Treatment Is Not Superior to Other Methods of Adjudication.

In light of the determination that individual issues of law and fact predominate over issues common among class members, the class procedure is not superior to other methods of adjudication. . . . Engaging in such inquiries will cause the adjudication of the over 100,000 potential employees' claims to become unmanageable, burdensome, and would unreasonably tax scarce judicial resources. Due to these individual differences, proceeding with this case as a class action is not the superior vehicle for litigating potential class members' claims.

2. Certification under Rule 23(b)(1)(A)

. . . Under Rule 23(b)(1)(A), the proponents of certification must establish that prosecuting individual actions would create the risk of inconsistent adjudications causing incompatible standards of conduct for the party opposing certification. [I]n cases seeking compensatory damages the risk of "inconsistent standards for future conduct [is] not created because a defendant might be found liable to some plaintiffs and not to others." Dennis Greenman Sec. Litig., 829 F.2d 1539, 1545 (11th Cir.1987). Instead, certification under this section is generally appropriate "only [in] actions seeking declaratory or injunctive relief. . . ." *Id.*

Plaintiffs seek compensatory damages for FedEx's alleged breach of contract. If Plaintiffs individually pursued their claims against FedEx it is quite possible that FedEx might be found liable to some and not to others, but these divergent outcomes would likely result from the particular facts and law underlying each employee's contract claims. This result would not create incompatible standards of conduct for FedEx because each claim is fact specific.

III. CONCLUSION

. . . Plaintiffs' Motion for Class Certification is DENIED.

NOTES AND QUESTIONS

1. The same attorneys who filed *Clausnitzer* also filed a class action lawsuit in California for FedEx employees in that state. Foster v. FedEx, Case No. BC 282300 (Cal. Sup. Ct.). The *Foster* complaint was based on similar facts but it added claims specific to California law and an allegation that FedEx managers had intentionally altered time records. In contrast with *Clausnitzer*, the *Foster* case did result in certification of a *state*wide class of hourly employees.

2. As the *Foster* case described above suggests, plaintiffs seeking certification of class actions for violations of state wage laws have fared best in California, where the law is especially aggressive in protecting employees. *See, e.g.*, Amaral v. Cintas Corp. No. 2, 78 Cal. Rptr. 3d 572 (Cal. App. 2008) (class action against employer for claims based partly on employer's requirement that employees bear cost of laundering their uniforms); Bell v. Superior Court, 69 Cal. Rptr. 3d 328 (Cal. App. 2007) (reversing denial of class certification as to some claims, including those relating to improper calculation of vacation time); Estrada v. FedEx Ground Package Sys., Inc., 64 Cal. Rptr. 3d 327 (Cal. App. 2007) (certifying class of drivers who sought reimbursement of driving expenses); Parris v. Lowe's HIW, Inc., 2007 WL 2165375 (Cal. App. 2007) (reversing denial of class certification for alleged "off the clock" work). *But see* Brinker Restaurant Corp. v. Superior Ct., 80 Cal. Rptr. 3d 781 (Cal. App. 2008) (rejecting certification of class of restaurant employees alleging violation of local rest and meal break laws).

3. As discussed in *Clausnitzer*, one of the requirements for class action certification under federal and most state laws is that class action is "superior" to other methods of adjudication. Is it relevant that a state provides administrative wage dispute resolution at little or no cost to an employee?

ANSOUMANA v. GRISTEDE'S OPERATING CORP.
201 F.R.D. 81 (S.D.N.Y. 2001)

Plaintiffs are unskilled immigrants who have been working as delivery workers, delivering to customers of New York City supermarket and drugstore chains . . . 60 to 84 hours per week, six or seven days each week, and . . . paid only one to two dollars per hour without overtime . . . . The supermarket and drugstore chains considered the Plaintiffs independent contractors, not employees, and the labor agents who gathered and assigned them also considered them independent contractors . . . .

Plaintiffs sue under the Federal Fair Labor Standards Act ("FLSA"), 29 U.S.C. §216, and under the New York Minimum Wage Act, N.Y. Lab. L. §§650 et seq., to recover unpaid compensation . . . . Section 216(b) of the FLSA allows individuals to become parties to a collective action under the FLSA by filing consents. Approximately 350 . . . have filed such consents. Plaintiffs also . . . have filed a motion for class certification pursuant to Rule 23 of the Federal Rules . . . to pursue their state-law claims . . . .

[FLSA] §216(b) provides that "[n]o employee shall be a party plaintiff . . . unless he gives his consent in writing to become such a party and such consent is filed in the court in which such action is brought." This opt-in requirement thus restricts the right of recovery under the federal law to those who affirmatively file consents . . . . The federal action thus is a collective action under Section 216(b) of the FLSA, not a class action brought under Rule 23 . . . There is no opt-in requirement . . . under the New York Minimum Wage Act, N.Y. Lab. L. § 650 et seq. Accordingly, Plaintiffs seek class certification under Rule 23 with respect to their state law Minimum Wage Act claims . . . .

Section 216(b) . . . does not instruct . . . how and to what extent those filing consents may participate and control the litigation and be bound by any settlement or trial, or what kinds of notice, if any, they are entitled to receive. However, the tasks that I will have to perform in order to manage these . . . claims are essentially the same as those required for class actions generally, and considerable guidance exists in the developed jurisprudence for class actions under Rule 23. As with members of a Rule 23 class, district judges must oversee the fairness and sufficiency of notice to those who have become parties by their filed consents. The district judge must be assured that counsel are competent and responsive to all for whom they act, that there be no discrimination among the parties, [and] that settlements be fair . . . . The protections of Rule 23, although directed to class actions, can be easily adapted to . . . a collective action under section 216(b) of the FLSA . . . . [Rule] 16, providing for the "just, speedy, and inexpensive disposition" of all civil cases . . . , gives me ample discretion to supervise these proceedings and to take wisdom from the entire body of Civil Procedure, including Rule 23, to accomplish those goals . . . .

[A] class action is superior to other available methods for the fair and efficient adjudication of the controversy. The interest of the class as a whole to litigate the predominant common questions substantially outweighs any interest by individual members to bring and prosecute separate actions. These common questions are best litigated in a single forum, and the proceedings already undertaken cause any separate actions in this and other forums to be wasteful and inefficient. Finally, the difficulties likely to be encountered in the management of the class portion of this action are not likely to be different or greater than in the management of the collective portion of this action. Thus, the specific considerations set out in Rule 23(b)(3)(A) through (D) are satisfied . . . . Certifying a Rule 23(b)(3) class is appropriate . . . to allow members to be fully advised of their rights and options in a notice approved by the court, and thereafter to opt-out . . . .

Having decided that common questions of law and fact predominate . . . , that my management of the class action of the Minimum Wage Act claims is consistent with my management of the collective action of the FLSA claims, and that there is a substantial judicial interest to avoid additional and unnecessary lawsuits . . . in other state and federal courts, I must now decide whether I have jurisdiction to hear the Plaintiffs' state law claims. The issue is one of supplemental jurisdiction: whether the claims under the FLSA and under the Minimum Wage Act are "so related . . . that they form part of the same case or controversy under Article III of the United States Constitution;" 28 U.S.C. §1367(a) . . . . A basic argument made by Defendants is that the longer period of limitations under New York's Minimum Wage Act (six years, compared to two year under the FLSA (three years for willful violations) . . . would cause the state law claims to predominate over the federal claims, and that I should therefore exercise my discretion to dismiss the state claims and allow them to be filed in the New York courts . . . .

Defendants' argument of predominance is not persuasive. If Plaintiffs are able to show that they were employees, not independent contractors, during their most recent two years of employment, they probably will prevail as well for earlier years. . . . The essential facts and issues are likely to be the same, and pre-trial proceedings are not likely to be materially more burdensome, nor is it likely that a trial will be materially prolonged, if supplemental jurisdiction is exercised over the related Minimum Wage Act claims. The existence of a longer statute of limitations in a related state claim is not a unique phenomenon, and district courts commonly exercise supplemental jurisdiction in such circumstances . . . . [T]he common federal and state issues predominate, and the class action device is superior to the alternatives of numerous actions in a number of courts, or a loss of guaranteed rights because many Plaintiffs will not have the ability or means to file individual suits. This case presents the ideal factual scenario supporting the exercise of supplemental jurisdiction . . . .

If the related FLSA and Minimum Wage Act claims were to be litigated in parallel [federal and state] court[s] . . . , there would be great potential for confusion of issues; considerable unnecessary costs; inefficiency and inconsistency of proceedings and results; . . . differing rulings by multiple courts with respect to discovery, relevance and privilege; . . . and the difficulties of managing joint trials even where multiple courts agree jointly to manage complex litigations. Congress enacted Section 1367 to avoid such problems.

NOTES AND QUESTIONS

1. Because employees must "opt in" to a Section 216 collective action, the most common preliminary step for the court in a collective action is to grant "conditional" class certification for purposes of issuing notice to potential members of their right to opt in. *See* Bowens v. Atlantic Maintenance Corp., 546 F. Supp. 2d 55, 80-84 (E.D.N.Y. 2008). At this stage, proposed collective action members have what some courts call a "minimal burden" of establishing the viability of a class, although a court might later deny certification based on the results of the opt in notice and a closer examination of the case. Sobczak v. AWL Industries, Inc., 540 F. Supp. 2d 354, 362 (E.D.N.Y. 2007). The requirement of a certification process for Section 216(b) collective actions is not universally accepted, however. *See* Scott A. Moss & Nantiya Ruan, *The Second-Class Action: How Courts Thwart Wage Rights by Misapplying Class Action Rules*, 61 Amer. U. L. Rev. 523 (2012) (arguing that given the express FLSA authorization for similarly situated workers to join collective actions simply by filing consent forms, no judicial "certification" inquiry that might deny such a right is authorized, so joinder is of right until and unless the defendant files and prevails upon a "misjoinder" motion).

2. It is not clear whether it is easier to satisfy the FLSA Section 216 "similarly situated" standard than Rule 23 standards. Courts entertaining final

certification of private collective actions under Section 216 still tend to use much the same analysis as they do under Rule 23. Thus, plaintiffs proposing a Section 216 collective action are most likely to succeed if they can prove that alleged violations resulted from a policy or regularly followed organization-wide practice. *Compare* Resendiz-Ramirez v. P & H Forestry, LLC, 515 F. Supp. 2d 937 (W.D. Ark. 2007) (granting conditional certification of class action based on alleged company policy) *with* Seever v. Carrols Corp., 528 F. Supp. 2d 159, 174 (W.D.N.Y. 2007) (denying conditional certification because evidence showed only "unilateral" acts of a few "rogue" managers).

3. Minimum wage or overtime claims stated under state law might not have the advantage of a local state version of Section 216. Nevertheless, the trend is to allow class certification of state minimum wage or overtime claims under Rule 23 or an equivalent state class action rule, provided the plaintiffs can satisfy the Rule 23 requirement of "commonality." *See, e.g.*, *Myers v. Hertz Inc.*, 624 F.3d 53, 549 (2d Cir. 2010) (plaintiffs, who the employer treated as exempt from overtime rules, established common issues regarding their qualification for the exemption); *Ross v. RBS Citizens, N.A.*, 667 F.3d 900, 909-910 (7th Cir. 2012) (alleged misclassification of employees was based on company-wide policy).

Employee Liability to an Employer for Business and Property Losses

Should an employee be liable for any and all loss resulting from his dereliction of duty? An employee is not an insurer of property under his control or management, absent a clear agreement to the contrary. Gutierrez v. Hachar's Dep't Store, 484 S.W.2d 433 (Tex. Civ. App. 1972); Carmichael v. Lavengood, 144, 44 N.E.2d. 177, 180 (Ind. App. 1942). However, if an employee is unable to account for money or goods the employer entrusted to him, he might be required to bear the loss because he cannot carry his burden of proving he delivered it to his employer or disposed of it in accordance with his job duties. RESTATEMENT (SECOND) OF AGENCY § 382 (1958). *See also* Schulstad v. Hudson Oil Co., 637 P.2d 1334 (Or. App. 1981), *rev. denied*, 648 P.2d 849 (Or. 1982). Moreover, most courts appear to agree that an employee is liable for any loss caused by his negligence. *See* RESTATEMENT (SECOND) OF AGENCY § 379 (1958).

The rule that an employee might be liable for all sorts of business losses, even those disproportionately large in relation to his compensation, has not gone unchallenged. One widely recognized exception limits the liability of corporate managers for errors in judgment within the range of their managerial discretion. *See, e.g.*, Brown v. United Cerebral Palsy/Atlantic & Cape May, Inc., 650 A.2d 848, 852 (N. J. Super. 1994). Moreover, an employer must still show proximate cause, and many business losses, especially lost profits, are affected by so many different factors that an employer is unable to prove its loss would not have occurred but for the manager's negligence. *Id. See also* Weymer v. Belleplaine Broom Co., 132 N.W. 27 (Iowa 1911). But the managerial discretion rule and the practical difficulties of proving the cause of business failure do not protect a non-managerial employee whose accident and simple negligence may cause a major loss to the employer.

In *Brown*, *supra*, the court moved halfway toward a broader employee defense applicable to managers and non-managers alike:

> Prior to 1961, New Jersey appeared to accept "as a fundamental rule in the law of agency that an agent or employee is generally liable to his principal or employer for loss sustained by the latter due to the former's negligence or defalcation." . . . In 1961, the New Jersey Supreme Court suggested that such a rule was "anachronistic" insofar as it permitted an employer, liable to a third party for the negligence of an employee under the doctrine of respondent superior, to recoup the loss from the negligent employee. Eule v. Eule Motor Sales, 34 N.J. 537, 540, 170 A.2d 241 (1961). The *Eule* Court, quite clearly, if not explicitly, rejected the general rule, at least in the context of liability incurred as the result of negligence in operating a motor vehicle. It opined that the liability of the employer to third parties is derived from the doctrine of respondent superior which in turn "rests on a public policy that the employer bear the burden as an expense of the operation he expends through the employment of others." The employee should not, therefore, be required to bear that cost by way of indemnification to the employer.
>
> . . . Such a rule is consistent with the approach that New Jersey has taken in requiring a business entity to assume the costs attendant on the conduct of that business. It is analogous to our rule prohibiting an employer from seeking indemnification from a co-employee who negligently injures an employee to whom the employer is liable under our workers' compensation laws. N.J.S.A. 34:15-8 . . . . .
>
> This rationale suggests that the *Eule* rejection of employee liability to an employer for indemnification of third party claims should not be limited to automobile negligence. An employer's business necessarily and foreseeably will involve acts of negligence on the part of an employee. As a matter of policy then, the employer, not the negligent employee, should bear the cost of loss occasioned in the conduct of the employer's business. Accordingly, I have no hesitation in determining that our law prohibits an employer from recouping from an employee any sums the employer may be required to pay to a third party as a result of the employee's negligence.
>
> . . . It is not clear why corporate losses sustained as a result of a third party claim should be treated differently from losses sustained as the result of an employee's negligent injury to corporate property without third party involvement. Nevertheless, the cases treat the situations differently and it would be improper for a trial court to anticipate a change in the law without a clear indication from an appellate court that such a change is appropriate.

650 A.2d at 849-850. Based on this reasoning, the court granted summary judgment against the employer's negligence claim for damages stemming from losses suffered by third parties, but it denied summary judgment with respect to damages stemming from losses suffered by the employer itself. *Id.* at 850-853.

PROBLEM

Harry Rassler is a salaried, exempt (a white collar "executive") restaurant supervisor of Fast Food, Inc. One of his employees accused him of sexual harassment. Although the facts were disputed (Rassler denied the charges), Fast Food decided to discipline Rassler by fining him the equivalent of one day's pay.

Fast Food collected the fine by withholding it from Rassler's paycheck. Discuss whether Fast Food may have violated any rights of Rassler.

D. DEFERRED AND CONTINGENT COMPENSATION

1. *The Risk of Forfeiture*

In comparison with true independent contractors, employees are not risk takers. In general, their right to compensation does not depend on the success of the enterprise. *Cf.* Zaremba v. Miller, 169 Cal. Rptr. 688 (Cal App. 1980) (rejecting employer's argument that employee's right to payment was subject to a condition that the employer must first receive payment from its client). Nevertheless, some parts of an employee's compensation might be deferred and contingent in ways that do expose the employee to all sorts of business risks.

To a certain extent, even an employee's basic wages are deferred and contingent. Employees generally must work before they are paid, and part of an employee's compensation might be deferred for many weeks, months, or even years. The custom that an employer need not pay until the employee completes a certain amount of service is consistent with the traditional rule of contract law that "where the performance of only one party under such an exchange requires a period of time, his performance is due at an earlier time than that of the other party, unless the language or the circumstances indicate the contrary." RESTATEMENT (SECOND) OF CONTRACTS § 234.

Deferral of compensation presents some risk for the employee, because he must serve in reliance on employer good faith and creditworthiness. The risk of nonpayment is compounded by any express condition that no amount of payment is due unless and until the employee completes all of a certain unit of service.

At one time, it was not uncommon for an employer to hire an employee for a one-year term and to withhold *all* wages until the employee completed the term. This arrangement was typically combined with room and board to provide the employee his basic sustenance during the term of the agreement. The condition of a completed year of service secured the employee's devotion to his tasks by denying him an entire year's wages if he failed to complete the term. *See, e.g.*, Stark v. Turner, 19 Mass. (2 Pick.) 267 (1824). But even the most devoted employee might suffer a forfeiture of pay under this arrangement. For example, the employee might fail to complete the term because of disability or death. *See, e.g.*, Cutter v. Powell, 6 T.R. 320, 101 Eng. Rep. 573 (K.B. 1795) (denying employee's widow any recovery for services performed before employee's death). An early judicial solution to such oppressive results was to grant the employee an extra-contractual remedy, *quantum meruit*, measured by the value of service actually performed, subject to reduction by any damages the employer could prove. *See* Britton v. Turner, 6 N.H. 481 (1834).

An early legislative solution still found in nearly every state is to require an employer to pay wages on a biweekly, semimonthly, or other short-term basis. *See, e.g.*, Cal. Lab. Code § 204; N.J. Stat. Ann. § 34:11-4.2; N.Y. Lab. Law § 191; Tex. Lab. Code § 61.011. Thus, an employee is never at risk for more than half a month's pay unless he continues to work even after the employer has "missed" a scheduled wage payment.

Statutes scheduling the payment of current "wages" generally do not apply to many forms of deferred compensation, such as commissions, bonuses, profit-sharing, vacation pay, severance pay, and retirement benefits, which by their nature must be deferred for longer than half a month. *See, e.g.*, Thomas v. H&R Block Eastern Enters., Inc., 630 F.3d 659 (7th Cir. 2011). Legitimately deferred compensation may also be subject to a condition, such as employment for a specific duration or on a particular date. But what if the employee was not employed on the required date only because the employer discharged the employee?

TWISS v. LINCOLN TEL. & TEL. CO.

136 Neb. 788, 287 N.W. 620 (Neb. 1939)

ROSE, Justice.

Plaintiff, Marjorie Twiss, an employee of the Lincoln Telephone & Telegraph Company, defendant, demanded in her petition pension benefits under the latter's pension plan and recovered in her action therefor a judgment for $1,272.95. On appeal defendant insists the trial court erred in overruling motions to direct a verdict in its favor.

Plaintiff contends that defendant's pension plan constitutes a binding contract between employer and employee; that the evidence supports the verdict on the issue that plaintiff was wrongfully discharged and that her vested pension rights were then $1,272.95.

Defendant issued a 23-page pamphlet, effective January 1, 1917, entitled "Plan for Employees' Pensions, Disability Benefits and Death Benefits." The plan is described in the pamphlet. Plaintiff makes no claim for disability or death benefits. The redress sought by her in this cause of action is limited to pension benefits which depend on the plan and terms described in the pamphlet. The trust fund for the payment of pensions is created solely by defendant. Plaintiff contributed nothing thereto. Nothing was taken from her compensation to augment the trust fund. She was employed by defendant for telephone service at Louisville, August 1, 1917, and in some capacity was continuously an employee there until she was discharged by defendant July 19, 1935, at the age of 38 years, after approximately 18 years of service.

[A slander claim plaintiff also asserted suggests the reason for her discharge: "on or about the 19th day of July, 1935, the defendant . . . said in substance that plaintiff 'had been having beer parties with men in the office' and that plaintiff 'asked a traveling man from Kansas City to stay all night with her. . . .'"]

. . . When plaintiff was employed in 1917, an officer of defendant explained to her the pension plan described in the pamphlet and she understood the terms on which pensions were to be granted. Under section 4 of the pension plan plaintiff, after 20 or more years of service, having reached the age of 55 years, would have a right to a pension of $30 a month for life. Her position is that she entered the service of defendant and continued therein, relying on her vested pension rights under her contract of employment, until she was wrongfully discharged July 19, 1935, and that she is entitled to the present worth of her pension benefits for the entire 18-year period of her service, which an actuary figured at $1,272.95, the amount of the verdict on this claim.

. . . Section 8 of the pamphlet, under "General Provisions," referring to section 4 . . . thereof, is as follows:

> (1) Neither the action of the board of directors in establishing this plan for employees' pensions, disability benefits and death benefits, nor any action hereafter taken by the board or the committee shall be construed as giving to any officer, agent or employee a right to be retained in the service of the company or any right to claim to any pension or other benefit or allowance after discharge from the service of the company, unless the right to such pension or benefit has accrued prior to such discharge. No employee shall have any right to a service pension by reason of service less than that specified in . . . section 4 of these regulations, nor shall any employee have any right in the pension fund unless a service pension authorized by the committee under the plan has not been paid. No employee shall have any right against the company to any benefit under the plan except for the amount to which the employee has theretofore become entitled and which the committee has directed be paid to that employee under the plan.

Under plan and conditions needing no interpretation, plaintiff did not qualify for a pension. Her term of service was not 20 years and she had not reached the age of 55 years. "No employee shall have any right to a service pension by reason of service less than that specified in paragraph 1(a) and 1(b) of section 4 of these regulations," says the pamphlet. If plaintiff, as she contends, has a vested right to pension benefits from the time she was employed to the end of her service, those rights would be unaffected by her discharge. There is no right to a pension after the discharge of any employee, unless it previously accrued. Defendant provided the trust fund for pensions voluntarily and gratuitously and was at liberty to prescribe the conditions on which they are granted. The trust fund contributed alone by defendant for pensions is protected by the provision that an employee can acquire no right to a pension for a term of service shorter than that specified in the plan. The trust fund for pensions is also protected by the provision that the plan confers on an employee no right to remain in the service of defendant or any right to a pension after discharge, unless the right to a pension previously accrued. The allowance of plaintiff's claim for a shorter period than that specified in the plan would, to that extent, divert the trust fund from the purposes for which it was created and impair the rights of employees legally qualified for pensions under the plan adopted by defendant.

Decisions of courts are not in point in cases where employee contributed part of the trust fund for pensions, where the employee had been qualified by service and age, and where bonuses became part of the compensation of employee. . . . Plaintiff did not make a case for pension benefits in any amount. The judgment for pension benefits is therefore reversed and the action therefor dismissed.

NOTES AND QUESTIONS

1. *Twiss* illustrates the usual rule in contract law that a promisee's right to performance of a promise may be subject to a condition, and a failure of the condition bars the promisee's right to enforce the promise. Courts have followed

this rule for many types of deferred compensation conditioned on employment on a particular date. *See* Shaw v. J. Pollock & Co., 612 N.E.2d 1295 (Ohio App.1992) (denying claim under profit-sharing plan); Foreman v. E. Foods, Inc., 393 S.E.2d 695 (Ga. App. 1990) (denying claim under employee stock purchase plan); Feola v. Valmont Indus., Inc., 304 N.W.2d 377 (Neb. 1981) (denying claim under bonus plan). A contract might promise a bonus, commission or retirement benefit only if the employee is still employed on a particular date. The usual contract rule is that if a condition is not fulfilled according to its terms, the promise to pay is excused. RESTATEMENT (SECOND) OF CONTRACTS §§ 224, 225.

2. Deferred compensation might be conditioned on something other than continued employment. Disability pay, for example, is contingent on disability. Severance pay is contingent on involuntary termination.

In Dove v. Rose Acre Farms, Inc., 434 N.E.2d 931 (Ind. App. 1982), the employer had a practice of offering incentive bonuses subject to rather eccentric conditions, such as a condition that an employee must wear a silver feather for a period of time. The employer was also known for its strict attitude toward attendance. The employer promised the plaintiff Dove and some coworkers a bonus of $6,000 *provided* they completed a project by a deadline and had *perfect* attendance for a period of time. The employer required 12 weeks of perfect attendance for most of the employees, but required only 10 weeks of perfect attendance for Dove so he could begin his fall semester in law school as planned. But during the tenth week Dove became ill with strep throat. He reported to the job site with a temperature of 104° but explained he was unable to work. The employer warned Dove that if he left he would forfeit the bonus, but the employer also offered to permit Dove to stay on a couch, even to sleep during work that day, and still earn the bonus. Alternatively, the employer offered to permit Dove to make up his time on the next Saturday and Sunday. Nevertheless, Dove left the worksite to seek medical attention. The employer denied the bonus.

Dove sued, arguing he was entitled to the bonus because the project was completed on time and the employer had "got what it bargained for." Nevertheless, the court ruled in favor of the employer: "[T]he bonus rules at Rose Acre were well known to Dove when he agreed to the disputed bonus contract. . . . If the conditions were unnecessarily harsh or eccentric, and the terms odious, he could have shown his disdain by simply declining to participate, for participation in the bonus program was not obligatory or job dependent." *Id.* at 935.

3. In *Twiss,* the plaintiff failed to fulfill the condition of her deferred compensation because she was *involuntarily discharged* by the employer. The employer had the right to discharge her because she was apparently an employee "at will" *See* section 8 of the pamphlet quoted by the court. Was the reason for her discharge nevertheless relevant to her claim for retirement benefits? The Restatement provides that a failure of a condition will not discharge an obligor's duty if the failure of the condition "is the result of a breach by the obligor of his duty of good faith and fair dealing." RESTATEMENT (SECOND) OF CONTRACTS § 230. Some courts apply a variation of this rule in the employment context, holding that an employee terminated lawfully but "without good cause" is entitled to a "pro rata" share of deferred compensation despite an express condition of continued employment. *See, e.g.*, Seidler v. FKM Advertising Co., 763 N.E.2d 1266 (Ohio

App. 2001); Klondike Indus. v. Gibson, 741 P.2d 1161 (Alaska 1987); Fortune v. Nat'l Cash Register Co., 364 N.E.2d 1251 (Mass. 1977); Miller v. Riata Cadillac Co., 517 S.W.2d 773 (Tex. 1974).

Involuntary discharge is not the only reason a condition of continued employment might fail. Employees also become sick or die, or other events beyond their control interfere with their fulfillment of a condition. Assuming an employer is *not* at fault in causing the failure of a condition of continued employment, could a court still excuse a failure of the condition in the interest of justice? *See* RESTATEMENT (SECOND) OF CONTRACTS § 229 ("To the extent that the non-occurrence of a condition would cause disproportionate forfeiture, a court may excuse the non-occurrence of that condition unless its occurrence was a material part of the agreed exchange"). Whether the forfeiture is disproportionate requires a comparison of the amount of the forfeited compensation with the value or importance of the failed condition to the promisor. *See. e.g.*, Capistrant v. Lifetouch Nat'l Sch. Studios, Inc., 899 N.W.2d 84 (Minn. App. 2017) (under circumstances of parties and termination of employment, deferred compensation promise was enforceable despite alleged failure of condition of timely returning employer property). If the condition was simply to reserve the employer's discretion to arbitrarily deny promised compensation, and the employer's denial of compensation was in fact arbitrary or unconscionable, forfeiture of significant earned but deferred compensation is likely to be disproportionate. Would application of this rule have changed the result in *Dove*, discussed in note 2 above?

4. For yet another approach, *see* Camillo v. Wal-Mart Stores, Inc., 582 N.E.2d 729 (Ill. App. 1991). The employer discharged the plaintiff at the end of the busiest season (Christmas) but just short of the date he would have qualified for an annual bonus. The court found a statutory solution. Like most other states, Illinois has a "payment upon discharge" statute that requires an employer to pay an employee all earned compensation within a few days of termination. Such statutes provide special remedies for employees seeking to collect wages an employer might withhold after termination as an act of retribution, spite, or opportunism. But in *Camillo* the court held that the statute, requiring final payment of "earned bonuses" among other things, prohibited the employer from conditioning incentive compensation on employment on any particular date. Without addressing the question whether the plaintiff employee was discharged "for cause," the court ordered the employer to pay the pro rata share of the bonus. *See also* Medex v. McCabe, 811 A.2d 297 (Md. 2002) (Maryland payment upon discharge statute overrode contractual condition of continued employment with respect to incentive compensation).

5. A "commission" based on an employee's success in arranging sales is a particularly common form of deferred compensation. Commissions must ordinarily be deferred for practical reasons, because it will likely take time for the employer to account for sales, assign the benefit of a sale to a particular employee, and make sure the sale did not fail because of a customer return or nonpayment. In many instances, therefore, an employer makes the commission payable with a particular paycheck at the end of a calendar quarter or other period. If the employee resigns or is discharged after arranging a sale but before the end of the accounting period, has a "condition" (being employed and receiving a paycheck at the end of

a designated period) failed?

The Restatement of Employment Law says that the issue is to be decided "in accordance with the parties' agreement." RESTATEMENT OF THE LAW, EMPLOYMENT LAW § 3.01, cmt. d. But the Restatement adds two protections for commissioned employees. First, if the parties' agreement is unclear, an employee *is entitled* to a commission if a transaction in question closed, the commission is "determinable," and the employee produced "a ready, willing and able purchaser." Second, if the commissioned employee brought a customer who "did not accept" the offered sale until after the employee's employment terminated, the employee is still entitled to the commission. Finally, even if the contract fails to support the commissioned employee's claim, the employee might have a claim for quantum meruit (restitution) if it would be inequitable for the employer not to pay the disputed compensation.

6. Vacation pay is a form of deferred compensation that is a frequent point of contention. A typical vacation policy might have one or more of three typical conditions. First, an employee does not earn a block of vacation time unless he completes a full year of service. Second, he must use each earned vacation day within one year of the date he earned the vacation. Third, the employee will not receive vacation pay unless he is employed on the day *before* the vacation and the first day *after* the vacation.

If the employment terminates before the employee has used all his accrued vacation time, there are at least two potential issues: (1) does the employee have a right to cash in lieu of accrued but unused vacation time? and (2) if the employer discharges the employee without cause, is the employee entitled to a pro rata share of the vacation benefits he would have earned during the current year for use in the following year? To some courts, the answer to either question depends strictly on the terms of the contract. *See, e.g.*, Chester v. Jones, 386 S.W.3d 544 (Tex. Civ. App. 1965). Other courts have applied rules of equity, good faith, or statutory construction to award vacation pay to terminated employees. *See, e.g.*, Golden Bear Family Restaurants, Inc. v. Murray, 144 Ill. App. 3d 616, 494 N.E.2d 581 (1986) (applying payment upon discharge law to require payment of vacation pay); Elec. Data Sys. Corp. v. Attorney Gen'l, 907 N.E.2d 635 (Mass. 2009) (applying payment upon discharge law); Henry v. Amrol, Inc., 272 Cal. Rptr. 134 (Cal App. 1990) (applying California law prohibiting "use it or lose it" vacation policies).

7. In promising deferred compensation, an employer might reserve "discretion" as to the amount of the deferred compensation or whether to pay the compensation at all. A reservation of discretion, however, raises the issue whether the "promise" was really a promise after all. For example, a statement of intent to pay a bonus might be unenforceable if a court finds the bonus was "discretionary." *See, e.g.*, Jackson v. Ford, 555 S.E.2d 143 (Ga. App. 2001); Kaplan v. Capital Co. of Am. LLC, 747 N.Y.S.2d 504 (N.Y. App. Div. 2002).

Some early employer-established retirement plans reserved the employer's discretion whether to continue the plan or whether to pay a pension to any particular employee, and some plans were conditioned on an employer's financial situation at the time of an employee's retirement. Such a reservation of discretion could produce a particularly nasty surprise for an employee who had worked for decades until his old age, believing he was earning a right to a pension. If the plan included a discretion clause, a court might find the plan unenforceable despite the obvious hardship to the worker and the public interest in securing retirement benefits for retirees. *See, e.g.*, Hughes v. Encyclopedia Britannica, Inc., 108 F. Supp. 303 (E.D. Ill. 1952); Crawford v. Peabody Coal Co., 181 N.E.2d 369 (Ill. App. 1962); Dolan v. Heller Bros. Co., 104 A.2d 860 (N. J. Super. 1954). Even public employees sometimes found that long-term deferred benefits provided under the laws of their government employers were subject to modification or even repeal. *See* Pennie v. Reis, 132 U.S. 464 (1889) (upholding California Legislature's amendment changing qualifications for death benefits).

Forfeiture of retirement income is profoundly more serious than the forfeiture of a bonus, vacation or other deferred pay. Fortunately, by the second half of the twentieth century most courts came to view retirement benefits as a special case. An Ohio court's 1960 decision in Cantor v. Berkshire Life Ins., 171 N.E.2d 518 (Ohio 1960), is representative:

> The concept of employees' rights and of the place of the so-called fringe benefits in relationship to employees' remuneration has undergone a substantial change in recent years. Due perhaps to the increased span of life, retirement benefits have assumed a more important role in the consideration of an employee when he accepts employment. Management has recognized this fact and, to encourage career service and to minimize labor turnover which is so costly to industry, has inaugurated retirement programs in addition to Social Security. . . .
>
> There has been, however, in recent years a gradual trend away from the gratuity theory of pensions. The courts, recognizing that a consideration flows to an employer as a result of such pension plans, in the form of a more stable and a more contented labor force, have determined that such arrangements will give rise to contractual rights enforceable by the employee who has complied with all the conditions of the plan, even though he has made no actual monetary contribution to the fund. . . .
>
> Therefore, whether a retirement plan is contributory or noncontributory *and even though the employer has reserved the right to amend or terminate the plan*, once an employee, who has accepted employment under such plan, has complied with all the conditions entitling him to participate in such plan, his rights become vested and the employer cannot divest the employee of his rights thereunder.

171 N.E.2d at 520-522 (emphasis added). *See also* Psutka v. Michigan Alkali Co., 264 N.W. 385 (Mich. 1936) (discretionary language in death benefit plan did not defeat claim for benefit that had already accrued by virtue of employee's death).

8. The risk of forfeiture of earned retirement benefits is substantially reduced by modern federal legislation described in the section that follows.

2. *Retirement and Welfare Benefits: ERISA and Related Federal Laws*

a. Securing the Right to Benefits

Retirement and welfare benefits are a significant part of employee compensation and employer labor costs. As of 2008, benefit costs, including the employer's share of mandatory social security and Medicare benefits, constituted more than 30 percent of total compensation. Bureau of Labor Statistics, Employer Costs for Employee Compensation Summary (accessed June 11, 2008), at http://www.bls.gov/news.release/ecec.t02.htm. Unfortunately, "employee benefits" is an amorphous concept. The Bureau of Labor Statistics includes vacation, holiday and premium pay (such as extra pay for a late shift), as "benefits" rather than as wages or salary. As of 2008, the bureau's figures did *not* include stock options, either as benefits or as wages and salary. *Id*

Benefits differ from current pay in a number of ways. First, benefits frequently serve an insurance or long-term savings function, so that an employee's receipt of benefits is necessarily deferred and might be subject to the employer's future solvency or contractual conditions. Thus, as in the case of other forms of deferred compensation, there is no guarantee the employee will actually receive what has accrued. Second, in contrast with current wages or salary, welfare and retirement benefits are more likely paid according to a "plan" the employer has established for a defined class of persons rather than by individual negotiation and contract, especially if the benefits are designed to serve an insurance function. The concept of a "plan" is important to the way courts determine the existence and meaning of this part of the "contract" of employment.

MOELLER v. BERTRANG

801 F. Supp. 291 (D.S.D. 1992)

DONALD J. PORTER, Senior District Judge.

Defendant operates an auto repair business in Watertown, South Dakota under the name, Bernie's Body Shop. In 1965, at age 21 years, plaintiff began employment at the Body Shop. His employment continued almost twenty-five years.

Conditions of employment established by defendant at his business were: (1) an employee who worked for defendant at least five consecutive years would receive a lump sum upon retirement at age 62 years; (2) when an employee reached the fifth year of employment, defendant would credit the employee with $5,000 for the first five years and $1,000 per year for each year of employment thereafter, until the employee reached age 62.

To date, one employee, Carl Matteson, has received a payment pursuant to the conditions of employment. Matteson worked for defendant for eleven years until his retirement, upon which defendant paid him $11,000. Several other employees, including defendant's son, have worked at defendant's business over the years and have left for a variety of reasons. None of these employees has received a payment pursuant to defendant's conditions of employment.

The conditions of employment were not reduced to writing and do not appear in any other agreement. Defendant did not keep written records of the agreement nor did he make annual reports concerning retirement benefits paid. No part of the paychecks of any employee were withheld as a contribution to the retirement plan.

Defendant contends that the promise to pay retirement benefits was based on two conditions. First, the employee had to abstain from "moonlighting," that is, working for pay at a location other than Bernie's Body Shop in a capacity that is substantially similar to that of the employee at Bernie's Body Shop.

Defendant contends another condition of receiving retirement benefits was that an employee could not quit the term of employment with defendant before the retirement age of 62 years. According to defendant, if an employee left Bernie's Body Shop before such time, the employee forfeited all rights to the lump sum payment. There is no evidence that a person who quit employment before the retirement age of 62 years received payments pursuant to defendant's plan.

Defendant cancelled the plan after plaintiff left his employment. Defendant said at trial that he did so because he found out "everybody was moonlighting."

That defendant made a promise to his employees to pay retirement benefits is not contested. Instead, the essential dispute is whether plaintiff's promise is enforceable under the Employee Retirement Income Security Act of 1974 (ERISA), 29 U.S.C. §§ 1001-1401. In contesting the applicability of ERISA to this case, defendant argues that under all of the surrounding facts, defendant's retirement scheme is not an ERISA plan.

II. DISCUSSION

A. THE ERISA CLAIM

1. "Plan, Fund, or Program"

ERISA was enacted to "protect working men and women from abuses in the administration and investment of private retirement plans and employee welfare plans." Donovan v. Dillingham, 688 F.2d 1367, 1370 (11th Cir. 1982). In enacting ERISA, Congress was primarily concerned with:

> assuring employees that they would not be deprived of their reasonably-anticipated pension benefits; an employer was to be prevented from "pulling the rug out from under" promised retirement benefits upon which his employees had relied during their long years of service. There was public concern "that despite the enormous growth [in employee benefit plans] many employees with long years of employment [were] losing anticipated retirement benefits owing to the lack of vesting provisions in such plans."

Amato v. Western Union Int'l Inc., 773 F.2d 1402, 1409 (2d Cir. 1985), *cert. dismissed*, 474 U.S. 1113 (1986). While the decision to adopt a plan rests with the employer, once the decision is made to establish a plan, an employee is entitled to any vested benefits that arise under the plan. Williams v. Wright, 927 F.2d 1540, 1543 (11th Cir. 1991). In order to determine whether plaintiff is entitled to recover retirement benefits from defendant, the question is whether defendant established or maintained an ERISA plan.

There are two types of plans under ERISA, "employer welfare benefit plans" and "employee pension benefit plans." 29 U.S.C. §§ 1002(1), 1002(2)(A). At issue here is the employee pension benefit plan which is defined in 29 U.S.C. § 1002(2)(A) as:

> [A]ny plan, fund, or program which was heretofore or is hereafter established or maintained by an employer or by an employee organization, or by both, to the extent that by its express terms or as a result of surrounding circumstances such plan, fund, or program —

> (i) provides retirement income to employees, or
>
> (ii) results in a deferral of income by employees for periods extending to the termination of covered employment or beyond,
>
> regardless of the method of calculating the contributions made to the plan, the method of calculating the benefits under the plan or the method of distributing benefits from the plan.

Thus, in order to invoke ERISA, a "plan, fund, or program" must be "established or maintained" by an employer. Hansen v. Continental Ins. Co., 940 F.2d 971, 977 (5th Cir. 1991).

Courts have set out the prerequisites for a finding that an employer "established or maintained" a plan for purposes of ERISA. It is clear that more is required than merely an employer's decision to provide an employee pension benefits. Donovan v. Dillingham, 688 F.2d 1367, 1373 (11th Cir. 1982). "[I]t is the reality of a plan, fund or program and not the decision to extend certain benefits that is determinative." 688 F.2d at 1373. In discussing the point at which a plan, whether in writing or not, becomes a reality, the *Donovan* court stated:

> [A] court must determine whether from the surrounding circumstances a reasonable person could ascertain the intended benefits, beneficiaries, source of financing, and procedures for receiving benefits. Some essentials of a plan, fund or program can be adopted, explicitly or implicitly, from sources outside the plan, fund, or program . . . but no single act in itself necessarily constitutes the establishment of the plan, fund, or program.

Id.

The circumstances surrounding defendant's retirement plan are such that a reasonable person could ascertain the intended benefits and beneficiaries. Defendant's plan unambiguously provided each employee $1,000 for each year of employment for defendant until retirement. . . . [E]ach employee who worked for defendant was intended to be a member of the class of beneficiaries at least to the extent that the employee worked for defendant for five years and thereby reached the vesting period. Section 29 U.S.C. § 1053 requires pension plans to provide an employee who has completed at least five years of service with a nonforfeitable right to all of the employee's accrued benefit. . . . That defendant's retirement plan substantially mirrored the vesting requirements of 29 U.S.C. § 1053 is additional evidence that an ERISA plan was in existence.

Although less clear, defendant's source of financing is ascertainable. Defendant did not make contributions to any trust in order to insure adequate funding for the employees' retirement benefits. It appears the source of financing for the retirement plan was the general assets of Bernie's Body Shop. "Although, with some exceptions, it is true that the assets of employee benefit plans are required to be held in trust, . . . it is equally true that an employer's failure to meet an ERISA requirement does not exempt the plan from ERISA coverage. (citation omitted). '[A]n employer . . . should not be able to evade the requirements of the statute merely by paying . . . benefits out of general assets.' " Williams v. Wright, 927 F.2d at 1544 (quoting Fort Halifax Packing Co., Inc. v. Coyne, 482 U.S. 1, 18 (1987)). Defendant's refusal to maintain separate funding for the retirement benefits, therefore, cannot defeat the existence of an ERISA plan.

Finally, with respect to the plan's procedures, defendant admitted at trial that an employee who worked for defendant for five years would receive credit in the amount of $1,000 for each of the first five years of employment. After working for defendant for five years, the employee would receive $1,000 for each year employed by defendant until the retirement age of 62 years. Defendant promised to pay to the employee a lump-sum in the amount of the employee's accrued retirement benefit when the employee reached the retirement age of 62 years. Although defendant's retirement scheme was simple, such simplicity does not preclude the existence of a plan under ERISA. The procedures under the scheme are sufficiently ascertainable to establish an ERISA plan. *See Wright*, 927 F.2d at 1544.

. . . [D]efendant argues that a naked promise cannot constitute a pension plan covered by ERISA. The mere fact that an agreement is oral, however, does not necessarily prevent the agreement from becoming an ERISA plan. Courts have consistently held that ERISA does not require a formal, written plan. Scott v. Gulf Oil Corp., 754 F.2d 1499, 1503 (9th Cir. 1985); Donovan v. Dillingham, 688 F.2d 1367, 1372 (11th Cir. 1982) . . . . The writing requirement becomes important only when it is determined that ERISA covers a plan, because it is this point in time that plan administrators and fiduciaries are charged with various fiduciary and reporting responsibilities. . . . "[I]t would be incongruous for persons establishing or maintaining informal or unwritten employee benefit plans, or assuming the responsibility of safeguarding plan assets, to circumvent the act merely because an administrator or other fiduciary failed to satisfy reporting or fiduciary standards." *Id.* Where, as here, an employee relies on representations made by an employer regarding retirement benefits, the absence of a writing is insignificant.

This result is consistent with the equitable principles underlying ERISA. While an employer may rely upon a written plan to protect itself from oral modifications and amendments, its agents may not, before producing a written plan, make false representations to employees with regard to coverage, and only after a claim is filed or relevant event occurs rely upon a later-composed, conveniently inconsistent version of the "plan" to deny benefits to employees. Lipscomb v. Transac, Inc., 749 F. Supp. 1128, 1135 (M.D. Ga. 1990). Similarly, in Armistead v. Vernitron Corp., 944 F.2d 1287 (6th Cir. 1991), the court, despite the absence of a writing, upheld the district court's decision allowing plaintiffs to recover retirement benefits because plaintiffs relied on the employer's representations that such benefits would be forthcoming. Defendant here cannot avail himself of the fact that he has failed to comply with the writing requirement. . . .

Plaintiff's claim is based on more than a mere oral promise. Defendant's payment to Carl Matteson provides independent and reliable proof of the existence of defendant's retirement plan. There is no indication in the record the payment to Carl Matteson was gratuitous. The more reasonable conclusion is that the payments were made to Matteson obligatorily. . . . [T]he $11,000 lump-sum payment to Matteson conformed exactly to the formula outlined in defendant's retirement scheme and could not have come to Matteson as a surprise. . . . Plaintiff here was not only told he would receive a pension upon retirement, plaintiff was told the precise amount the pension would annually accrue. In addition, defendant told his employees that his retirement plan compared favorably to that of his nearby competitor. While "no single act in itself necessarily constitutes the establishment of the plan, fund, or program," *Dillingham*, 688 F.2d at 1373, the nongratuitous payment to Matteson, in conjunction with the highly specific promises defendant made to plaintiff, is sufficient to constitute a plan under ERISA.

Defendant at trial . . . claimed plaintiff violated the conditions of the promise by moonlighting and quitting employment under defendant. . . . [But] plaintiff's right to the accrued benefits vested after the fifth year of employment with defendant. Defendant's plan, which he himself designed, provided that after five years of employment, an employee's retirement benefit would be credited $1,000 for each of the five years. This arrangement, known as "cliff-vesting," *see* 29 U.S.C. § 1053(a)(2)(A), provided plaintiff with a nonforfeitable right to retirement benefits when he reached the age of 62 years. This right is not affected on this record by the fact that plaintiff left defendant's employment before reaching the age of 62 years. . . .

Unless an employee's rights to his accrued pension benefits are nonforfeitable, he has no assurance that he will ultimately receive a pension. Thus, pension rights which have slowly been stockpiled over many years may suddenly be lost if the employee leaves or loses his job prior to retirement. Quite apart from the resulting hardships, . . . such losses of pension rights are inequitable, since the pension contributions previously made on behalf of the employee may have been made in lieu of additional compensation or some other benefit.

2. Damages under ERISA

Defendant's plan promised a lump-sum retirement benefit in the amount of $1,000 per year of employment subject to the five year vesting requirement. Plaintiff was duly employed by defendant for 24 years. Plaintiff is entitled to the accrued amount of his fully vested benefits. 29 U.S.C. § 1002(23). . . . Thus, Plaintiff is entitled to the present value of $24,000 in the year of Plaintiff's normal retirement age under the plan, determined as of April 24, 1990, the date Plaintiff left Defendant's employment and was entitled to the present value of his future retirement benefits. . . . The Court recognizes that defendant's promise to pay retirement benefits to an employee was in the form of a lump sum payment made to the employee when the employee reached the age of 62 years. In accordance with this promise, plaintiff may elect to receive a lump sum amount of $24,000 when plaintiff reaches the age of 62 years in lieu of receiving the present value of that amount plus interest.

B. STATE LAW CONTRACT CLAIM

ERISA preempts "any and all State laws insofar as they may now or hereafter relate to any employee benefit plan" covered by ERISA. 29 U.S.C. § 1144(a). Having found defendant's plan is covered by ERISA, plaintiff's common law contract claim is preempted. Harper v. R.H. Macy & Co., Inc., 920 F.2d 544 (8th Cir. 1990). . . .

III. CONCLUSION

Damages will . . . be entered in favor of the plaintiff, together with interest at the rate of 12% from April 24, 1990, or, if plaintiff elects, defendant shall pay plaintiff $24,000 when plaintiff reaches the age of 62 years.

NOTES AND QUESTIONS

1. The Employee Retirement and Income Security Act (ERISA) applies to any "plan" that provides certain benefits to employees and that was "established or maintained" by an employer or a union. 29 U.S.C. § 1003(a). Is the idea of a plan established or maintained by an employer different from the usual idea of a contract of employment?

The idea of a plan is important chiefly for statutory purposes, because ERISA and related federal laws apply to plans but not to simple contracts for providing benefits. *See* Gresham v. Lumbermen's Mut. Casualty Co., 404 F.3d 253 (4th Cir. 2005) (employer's promise to employee of severance terms different from the terms of plan for the general workforce was not an ERISA plan, and state contract law claim based on the promise was not preempted by ERISA). However, ERISA does not define "plan." It merely requires that if an employer establishes or maintains a plan, the employer should put the plan in writing and follow a number of other requirements. 29 U.S.C. § 1102(b). As *Moeller* illustrates, ERISA's requirement of a writing is not a statute of frauds. An oral plan is still enforceable, and the employer may have violated ERISA by failing to put the plan in writing.

If an employer's promise of benefits constitutes the establishment or maintenance of a plan subject to ERISA, most questions relating to the plan will be decided by federal law rather than state law by virtue of ERISA's preemption provision, and ERISA grants federal court jurisdiction for actions relating to ERISA or an ERISA plan. 29 U.S.C. §§ 1132, 1144.

2. One other difference between a plan and a contract is that federal law treats a plan as a separate, artificial person that can sue and be sued. 29 U.S.C. § 1132(d). This is true even though a plan may lack the formal organizational features of a corporation or other business organization.

3. An employer's payment of benefits, standing alone, does not necessarily mean the employer has an ERISA plan. In Fort Halifax Packing Co. v. Coyne, 482 U.S. 1 (1987), an employer challenged a Maine plant closing statute requiring a one-time severance payment to laid-off employees. The employer argued that payment of benefits under the statute would constitute an "employee benefit plan" subject to ERISA, and that ERISA preempts any state law mandating an employee benefit plan because ERISA grants an employer *discretion* whether to create a benefit plan. The Court held that ERISA did not preempt the plant closing law because the law did not require an employer to establish or maintain a "plan."

First, the Court rejected the employer's argument that the plant closing law necessarily required creating a plan if it required paying a benefit: "The words 'benefit' and 'plan' are used separately throughout ERISA, and nowhere in the statute are they treated as the equivalent of one another. Given the basic difference between a 'benefit' and a 'plan,' Congress' choice of language is significant in its pre-emption of only [state laws regulating] the latter." *Id.* at 8.

Second, the Court distinguished the simple act of making a payment to employees from the creation of an ongoing scheme for such payments. The "focus of [ERISA] is on the administrative integrity of benefit plans — which presumes that some type of administrative activity is taking place." *Id.* at 15. In contrast,

> [t]he requirement of a one-time, lump-sum payment triggered by a single

> event requires no administrative scheme whatsoever to meet the employer's obligation. The employer assumes no responsibility to pay benefits on a regular basis, and thus faces no periodic demands on its assets that create a need for financial coordination and control. Rather, the employer's obligation is predicated on the occurrence of a single contingency that may never materialize. The employer may well never have to pay the severance benefits. To the extent that the obligation to do so arises, satisfaction of that duty involves only making a single set of payments to employees at the time the plant closes. To do little more than write a check hardly constitutes the operation of a benefit plan. Once this single event is over, the employer has no further responsibility. The theoretical possibility of a one-time obligation in the future simply creates no need for an ongoing administrative program for processing claims and paying benefits.

Id. at 12 (footnotes omitted). This is not to say severance payments are never pursuant to a plan; an employer might establish a severance plan that will be subject to ERISA. *See* Firestone Tire & Rubber Co. v. Bruch, 489 U.S. 101 (1989).

4. Another set of employer practices that resemble plans, but usually are not, are vacation pay, holiday pay, and sick leave pay policies. Payments under such policies could be regarded as "welfare" benefits. *See* 29 U.S.C. § 1002(1) (plan providing benefits for "sickness" or "vacation" is a "welfare plan"). However, the Department of Labor takes the view that a "plan" does not include a mere "payroll practice" of retaining an employee on the payroll as if she is working even though she is not. 29 C.F.R § 2510.3-1. *See also* Bassiri v. Xerox Corp., 463 F.3d 927 (9th Cir. 2006) (policy of continuing employee's compensation during period of disability might constitute a "payroll" practice exempt from treatment as a benefit plan). On the other hand, an employer could establish an ERISA plan for vacation, holiday, or sick leave pay, as employers frequently do when they contribute to a fund created by a multiemployer collective bargaining agreement to make such benefits available to workers not permanently attached to a single employer.

Yet another type of payroll practice that might look like a plan, but is not, is an employer's periodic deduction from employee paychecks to pay the cost of insurance that employees may purchase at their option, provided the employer serves as nothing more than a conduit for the insurance company to collect premiums from the employees. *See* 29 C.F.R § 2510.3-1(j).

5. Some benefit schemes that have all the necessary features of a plan are nevertheless exempt from coverage under ERISA. One important exemption is for a "governmental plan" established by a federal, state, or local government employer. *See* 29 U.S.C. §§ 1002(32), 1003(b). This exemption leaves many public employees without equivalent accrual, vesting, or anti-forfeiture rules. *See*, e.g., Crosby v. City of Gastonia, 635 F.3d 634 (4th Cir. 2011) (retirees lacked cause of action against city with respect to the failure of pension plan). Other exemptions are for "church" plans, plans subject to the Railroad Retirement Act, plans maintained outside the United States primarily for nonresident aliens, and so-called excess benefit plans. 29 U.S.C. § 1003(b).

6. In *Moeller*, could the employer have avoided the creation of an enforceable plan or contract by making the pension subject to his own absolute discretion, or by leaving the terms of the pension vague and uncertain? Would such

a promise be illusory and unenforceable?

A traditional rule of contracts law is that a promise is not enforceable unless its terms are sufficiently clear and definite for a court to determine whether the promisor breached the promise and to determine what remedy would enforce the promise. *See* RESTATEMENT OF CONTRACTS (SECOND) § 33. In Donovan v. Dillingham, 688 F.2d 1367 (11th Cir. 1982), the court took a similar approach with an ERISA plan: "In determining whether a plan . . . (pursuant to a writing or not) is a reality a court must determine whether from the surrounding circumstances a reasonable person could ascertain the intended benefits, beneficiaries, source of financing, and procedures for receiving benefits." *Id.* at 1373.

Even under this test, an employer might omit many details in announcing a benefits policy and still create a plan for purposes of ERISA. For some missing terms, ERISA provides default rules. *See, e.g.*, 29 U.S.C. § 1002(16)(A) (if the plan fails to identify its administrator, the administrator is the plan sponsor (usually the employer or a union)). Moreover, an employer's reservation of discretion as to important matters in the administration of benefits will not prevent a court from recognizing the existence of a plan if the plan is otherwise reasonably ascertainable. It would undermine a principal purpose of ERISA — protecting employee expectations — if an employer could prevent enforcement of benefit rights by reserving discretion or being unclear, incomplete, or evasive in describing benefits. Moreover, employer discretion in some aspects of benefits administration is perfectly compatible with the concept of an ERISA plan. Indeed, courts have sometimes viewed an employer's reservation or exercise of discretion in administering benefits as a factor *supporting* the existence of an ERISA plan. *See, e.g.*, Tinoco v. Marine Chartering Co., 311 F.3d 617, 621 (5th Cir. 2002); Cassidy v. Akzo Nobel Salt, Inc., 308 F.3d 613, 616 (6th Cir. 2002)).

PROBLEM

Reconsider the allegations in Martin v. Mann Merchandising, Inc., *supra* part B.1. If these facts are true, did the employer establish an ERISA benefit plan?

An Introduction to ERISA, COBRA, and HIPAA: Protection Against Loss or Interruption of Benefits

Enacted in 1974, ERISA was preceded by a series of much more limited and generally ineffectual federal laws regulating employee benefits plans. The early laws were generally of three types: laws addressing the tax consequences of pension and welfare benefits; laws loosely regulating benefit funds administered by unions; and laws with reporting and disclosure requirements designed to bring transparency to benefit fund administration. The shortcomings of these early laws were revealed by a number of shocking and sometimes scandalous pension fund failures in which an employer's insolvency resulted in the loss of pensions funded by the employer's general revenues. There were also widely publicized cases in which employees and their families lost expected benefits because of an employer's arbitrary denial of what the employer deemed to be a mere "gratuity."

Less well publicized but equally troubling for employees was the risk of losing a pension because of the failure of a condition. For example, employees might lose their pensions if their employment terminated — even for reasons beyond their control — and they failed to fulfill a condition of continued service until "retirement age" or they violated a condition of "loyalty" by serving a competing enterprise. Conditions of continued service and loyalty could cause harm even when employees fulfilled the conditions because such conditions suppressed labor market competition and impeded the mobility of labor.

ERISA's solution to the problems of financial insecurity and forfeiture begins with a division of benefit plans into two types: "pension plans" and "welfare plans." A pension plan provides "retirement income to employees, or results in deferral of income by employees for periods extending to the termination of covered employment or beyond." 29 U.S.C. § 1002(2)(A). A welfare plan provides "medical, surgical, or hospital care or benefits, or benefits in the event of sickness, accident, disability, death or unemployment, or vacation benefits, apprenticeship or other training programs, or day care centers, scholarship funds, or prepaid legal services. . . ." 29 U.S.C. § 1002(1). The distinction between pension plans and welfare plans is important. While many ERISA rules apply to both types of plans, ERISA's accrual, vesting, and funding rules apply only to pension plans, not welfare plans. 29 U.S.C. §§ 1051, 1081.

i. *Securing Benefits Against the Risk of Employment Termination*

One goal of ERISA and its subsequent amendments has been to make benefits reliable and "portable" and to allow employees to move from one employer to another without losing medical insurance or forfeiting pension benefits they "earned" with the first employer. However, the problems posed by pension benefits on the one hand and medical insurance on the other are so different that legislative solutions have evolved quite differently for each.

Pension Benefits. The reliability and portability of an employee's right to pension benefits results from a combination of participation, vesting, accrual, and anti-cutback rules.

First, a pension plan generally cannot restrict employee eligibility to participate in the plan beyond the *later* of an employee's completion of one year of service or 21st birthday. 29 U.S.C. § 1052.

Second, ERISA's minimum vesting standards for pension plans provide that an employee's rights to accrued benefits based on his own contributions to the plan are "nonforfeitable." As for accrued benefits based on the *employer's* contributions, the employer can adopt a vesting schedule that requires a minimum period of service before an employee's rights vest and become nonforfeitable. However, the schedule must satisfy ERISA's minimum standards. For most plans, ERISA requires complete vesting within five years or vesting in phases over a period of no more than seven years. 29 U.S.C. § 1053(a).

Third, ERISA's benefit accrual provisions restrict (but do not entirely prohibit) "backloading" of benefits, in which an employee's accrued benefits accumulate only a little until the later years of his employment, making it impossible to earn a significant pension without remaining with the same employer for a prolonged period of time. *See* 29 U.S.C. § 1054. The effect of these accrual provisions, in combination with participation and vesting requirements, is to make it more likely that an employee will begin to earn a vested, nonforfeitable pension benefit early in his career, provided he works for employers that provide pension plans.

The fact that accrued benefits are vested and nonforfeitable means the employee is still entitled to these benefits even if he resigns or the employment terminates for any other reason before the employee's retirement. In this way, ERISA strengthens the reliability and security of retirement benefits and encourages labor mobility.

The anti-forfeiture rule also prohibits other conditions an employer might impose on an employee's receipt of otherwise vested retirement benefits. For example, an employer might hope to discourage an employee from resigning to work for a competitor, by providing that benefits are forfeited if the employee accepts employment with a competitor. ERISA prohibits such a forfeiture to the extent the employee's benefits have vested under ERISA's minimum vesting schedule. Thus, in *Moeller*, the court negated the employer's alleged condition that an employee would forfeit his pension benefits if he engaged in competitive activity. *But see* Nationwide Mut. Ins. Co. v. Darden, 503 U.S. 318 (1992) ("independent contractor" might not be protected by anti-forfeiture rules of ERISA); Noell v. American Design, Inc. Profit Sharing Plan, 764 F.2d 827, 831 (11th Cir. 1985) (benefits in excess of ERISA's minimum vesting requirements were subject to forfeiture in accordance with terms of plan). *See also* Mary F. Radford, *Implied Exceptions to the ERISA Prohibitions Against the Forfeiture and Alienation of Retirement Plan Interests*, 1990 Utah L. Rev. 685 (1990).

Finally, ERISA protects a participant or beneficiary from changes in a pension plan that might diminish the value of benefits. An employer is not required to continue a pension plan in the same form indefinitely. It can modify or even terminate the plan and pay out accumulated benefits. However, ERISA's "anti-cutback" rules generally prohibit amendments that reduce "accrued benefits." 29 U.S.C. § 1054(g), (h). If the employer terminates the plan, accrued pension benefits become nonforfeitable and ERISA provides a procedure for distributing benefits to beneficiaries and participants. 26 U.S.C. § 411(d)(3), 29 U.S.C. §§ 1341, 1344.

Medical Insurance Benefits. Medical insurance benefits present a distinctly different problem because the benefit—medical care—is enjoyed currently and is not deferred to retirement, and because the cost of medical care is unpredictable and highly variable from one employee to the next. The operation and effect of the rules for medical insurance benefits remain a matter of heated political debate following the adoption of the Patient Protection and Affordable Care Act of 2010 (the "PPACA").

A key feature of the U.S. health care system is that most insurance is offered — and is frequently only affordable — through employers to their employees and to dependents of employees. However, before the PPACA employers were not required to offer insurance, and many individuals — employed or otherwise — were uninsured. Moreover, even individuals who had employer-provided insurance had no guarantee that their insurance would continue. Medical and other welfare benefits generally do not accrue in the fashion of pension benefits, and ERISA's vesting and accrual requirements do not apply to welfare plans. 29 U.S.C. § 1051(1). *See also* Sutton v. Weireton Steel Div. of Nat'l Steel, 724 F.2d 406 (4th Cir. 1983) (right to unfunded, contingent benefits do not "vest"). An employer seeking to modify or terminate an existing medical insurance or other welfare plan must simply follow ERISA's amendment procedures. Under the PPACA, however, employers with 50 or more employees are encouraged to maintain or establish medical insurance plans by virtue of a "pay or play" rule: a covered employer must offer a minimum form of medical insurance *or* it must pay an assessment based on the number of its employees. 26 U.S.C. § 4980H. Individuals left without coverage under an employer plan will be required to obtain their own insurance or pay a penalty. 26 U.S.C. § 5000A.

An employee or dependent might still lose existing insurance coverage if an employer elects to terminate a medical insurance plan or the employee's coverage ceases because of employment termination. The consequences of losing employer-provided insurance could be especially severe if the employee or a dependent has a health condition that makes individual insurance prohibitively expensive or that is subject to the next insurer's "preexisting condition" exclusion. The PPACA and a series of amendments to ERISA offer three solutions to these problems.

First, for most group health plans subject to ERISA, the Consolidated Omnibus Budget Reconciliation Act of 1986 (COBRA) requires "continuation coverage" for beneficiaries who might otherwise lose their basis for coverage under certain circumstances. *See* 29 U.S.C. § 1163 (defining "qualifying events" causing a loss of coverage under an employer's plan but triggering rights under COBRA). COBRA preserves a bridge of insurance from one employer's health plan to the next, although the employer may charge the cost of this insurance bridge to the beneficiary based on the "cost" of covering "similarly situated" beneficiaries. 29 U.S.C. §§ 1162(3), 1164.

The rights COBRA creates belong to "beneficiaries," not just "employees," because many of the persons covered under a health plan are not employees but are members of an employee's family. Thus, "spouses" and dependent children have their own separate rights under COBRA, and there are some situations (such as divorce) when a spouse or child will assert these rights separately from the employee. 29 U.S.C. § 1167(3). When a qualifying event occurs, the plan administrator must provide a beneficiary with notice of her continuation coverage rights. *Id.* § 1166. *See* McDowell v. Krawchison, 125 F.3d 954 (6th Cir. 1997) (oral notice of COBRA rights to employee husband, and husband's apparent decision not to accept continuation coverage, was ineffective to defeat wife's COBRA rights). In some cases, the burden of providing notice actually begins with the employee. For example, if the employee divorces a beneficiary-spouse, it is the employee's duty to inform the administrator of that fact so the administrator can provide notice to the beneficiary-spouse. 29 U.S.C. § 1166; *see* Kiedo v. Kiedo, 1995 WL 643807 (Ohio App. 1995) (unpublished) (holding husband liable to wife, apparently for failing to safeguard wife's COBRA rights). The beneficiary then has a limited time to elect to purchase continued coverage or forgo continued coverage under the employer's plan. 29 U.S.C. § 1165. The period for which coverage continues depends on the nature of the qualifying event and the beneficiary's success in gaining new coverage. If the qualifying event is termination from employment or reduction in hours, coverage continues for no more than 18 months, or until she is covered under another plan, whichever is first. *Id.* § 1162(2). For most other qualifying events, the period of continued coverage may be as long as 36 months.

Id. If one qualifying event follows another (e.g., an employee spouse's termination from employment, followed by her death), the period of continued coverage is 36 months from the first event. *Id.*

Standing alone, COBRA is an imperfect solution to the loss of employer-provided insurance: an unemployed beneficiary might not be able to bear the cost charged by the employer, and there is no guarantee that a beneficiary will find new employer-provided insurance for future and *existing* medical conditions before COBRA rights expire. Two other laws amending ERISA — the PPACA and the Health Insurance Portability and Accountability Act of 1996 (HIPAA) — provide controversial solutions for these problems. Under the PPACA, it is more likely that a beneficiary's future employer will offer medical insurance because of the penalty employers pay if they do not provide employees insurance. For individuals who remain unemployed or accept employment without insurance benefits, the PPACA requires the purchase of individual insurance but also creates an insurance marketplace, supported by subsidies, to make individual coverage more affordable than it was before the PPACA. Both the PPACA and HIPAA include additional measures to prevent or limit the impact of preexisting condition clauses that would otherwise deny coverage for illness, injury or pregnancy that occurred before enrollment in a new plan. 29 U.S.C. § 1181.

ii. Securing Benefits Against the Risk of Insolvency

Another risk to plan participants and beneficiaries, particularly with respect to pension benefits, is that the plan will become insolvent. A plan might fail because of mismanagement of assets, poor investment performance of assets, or the financial insolvency of the employer that funds the plan. ERISA addresses these risks by imposing certain reporting and disclosure requirements on plans, regulating the management of plan assets, and by providing a system of insurance against pension plan failure. A pension plan subject to ERISA must satisfy certain minimum funding standards designed to assure the plan's ability to fulfill its obligations to beneficiaries. 29 U.S.C. §§ 1081-1084. However, these funding requirements do not apply to welfare benefit plans.

To the extent that a plan has assets (such as the funds a retirement plan holds for the future payment of benefits), ERISA requires that the assets must be held in trust, and "the assets of a plan shall never inure to the benefit of any employer and shall be held for the exclusive purposes of providing benefits to participants and their beneficiaries and defraying reasonable expenses of administering the plan." 29 U.S.C. §§ 1103(a), (c). ERISA protects against mismanagement of plan assets by regulating plan transactions and imposing fiduciary duties on trustees, administrators, and certain other persons involved in the management of the plan. *Id.* §§ 1101-1114. A plan must file an annual report with the Secretary of Labor providing information about the plan's operations and finances. *Id.* § 1103.

For pension benefits, ERISA provides another important source of security: the Pension Benefit Guaranty Corporation (PBGC), a government corporation that insures against insolvency of "defined benefit" plans and certain multiemployer plans. 29 U.S.C. §§ 1301-1461 A defined benefit plan promises a level of retirement income according to a formula, typically based on years of service and history of compensation (in contrast with a defined benefit plan creating individual employee accounts into which the employer periodically deposits fixed contributions). The PBGC collects premiums from employers who sponsor covered defined benefit pension plans (but not defined contribution plans), oversees voluntary or involuntary termination of such plans, and, when necessary, provides benefits to retirees of insured plans that are insolvent or underfunded.

iii. Securing Benefits Against Alienation

To prevent a participant's dissipation of pension benefits even before his retirement, a pension plan must provide that benefits "may not be assigned or alienated." 29 U.S.C. § 1056; *see also* Patterson v. Shumate, 504 U.S. 753 (1992) (participant's interest in "ERISA-qualified" plan excluded from bankruptcy estate). By its terms, the rule against assignment clearly applies to a participant's or beneficiary's voluntary assignment of undistributed benefits, and courts have interpreted the rule to apply to involuntary assignments as well. *See, e.g.*, Tenneco Inc. v. First Virginia Bank of Tidewater, 698 F.2d 688 (4th Cir. 1983). The anti-assignment rule does not apply to benefits a plan has already paid a retiree. Guidry v. Sheet Metal Workers Int'l Ass'n, 39 F.3d 1078 (10th Cir. 1994, en banc).

There are a number of important exceptions to the rule against assignment or alienation. First, a participant's pension benefits may be subject to a "qualified domestic relations order" (QDRO), which is an order of a state court for the payment of alimony, marital property interests, or child support. 29 U.S.C. § 1056(d)(3). Second, if a benefit is in pay status, a participant may assign up to 10 percent of any benefit payment. 29 U.S.C. § 1056(d)(2). Third, a plan loan to a participant may be secured by the participant's accrued vested benefits, provided the transaction satisfies certain requirements. 29 U.S.C. § 1056(d)(2). Finally, a participant's benefits may be subject to an offset for amounts the participant is required to pay the plan under a conviction or civil judgment involving the plan or a violation of a fiduciary duty with respect to the plan. 29 U.S.C. § 1056(d)(4).

Unlike pension benefits, welfare benefits are not protected by a statutory prohibition against assignment or alienation. To the contrary, some welfare benefits, especially medical, are intended to satisfy the beneficiary's obligation to third parties such as health care providers. On the other hand, a welfare benefit plan could include a provision restricting the assignment or alienation of benefits. Davidowitz v. Delta Dental Plan of Cal., 946 F.2d 1476 (9th Cir. 1991).

b. Deciding Benefit Claims: Ensuring Fairness and Accountability

FIRESTONE TIRE & RUBBER CO. v. BRUCH

489 U.S. 101 (1989)

Justice O'CONNOR delivered the opinion of the Court.

This case presents two questions concerning the Employee Retirement Income Security Act of 1974 (ERISA), 88 Stat. 829, as amended, 29 U.S.C. § 1001 et seq. First, we address the appropriate standard of judicial review of benefit determinations by fiduciaries or plan administrators under ERISA. Second, we determine which persons are "participants" entitled to obtain information about benefit plans covered by ERISA.

I

Late in 1980, petitioner Firestone Tire and Rubber Company (Firestone) sold, as going concerns, the five plants composing its Plastics Division to Occidental Petroleum Company (Occidental). Most of the approximately 500 salaried employees at the five plants were rehired by Occidental and continued in their same positions without interruption and at the same rates of pay. At the time of the sale, Firestone maintained three pension and welfare benefit plans for its employees: a termination pay plan, a retirement plan, and a stock purchase plan. Firestone was the sole source of funding for the plans and had not established separate trust funds out of which to pay the benefits from the plans. All three of the plans were either "employee welfare benefit plans" or "employee pension benefit plans" governed (albeit in different ways) by ERISA. By operation of law, Firestone itself was the administrator, 29 U.S.C. § 1002(16)(A)(ii), and fiduciary, § 1002(21)(A), of each of these "unfunded" plans. At the time of the sale of its Plastics Division, Firestone was not aware that the termination pay plan was governed by ERISA, and therefore had not set up a claims procedure, § 1133, nor complied with ERISA's reporting and disclosure obligations, §§ 1021-1031, with respect to that plan.

Respondents, six Firestone employees who were rehired by Occidental, sought severance benefits from Firestone under the termination pay plan. In relevant part, that plan provides as follows:

> If your service is discontinued prior to the time you are eligible for pension benefits, you will be given termination pay if released because of a reduction in work force or if you become physically or mentally unable to perform your job.
>
> The amount of termination pay you will receive will depend on your period of credited company service.

. . . Firestone denied respondents severance benefits on the ground that the sale of the Plastics Division to Occidental did not constitute a "reduction in work force" within the meaning of the termination pay plan. . . .

Respondents then filed a class action on behalf of "former, salaried, nonunion employees who worked in the five plants that comprised the Plastics Division of Firestone." The action was based on § 1132(a)(1), which provides that a "civil action may be brought . . . by a participant or beneficiary [of a covered plan] . . . (A) for the relief provided for in [§ 1132(c) and] (B) to recover benefits due to him under the terms of his plan." In Count I of their complaint, respondents alleged that they were entitled to severance benefits because Firestone's sale of the Plastics Division to Occidental constituted a "reduction in work force" within the meaning of the termination pay plan. . . . The District Court granted Firestone's motion for summary judgment.

[T]he District Court held that Firestone had satisfied its fiduciary duty under ERISA because its decision not to pay severance benefits to respondents under the termination pay plan was not arbitrary or capricious. . . . The Court of Appeals reversed the District Court's grant of summary judgment. . . . [T]he Court of

Appeals acknowledged that most federal courts have reviewed the denial of benefits by ERISA fiduciaries and administrators under the arbitrary and capricious standard. *Id.* It noted, however, that the arbitrary and capricious standard had been softened in cases where fiduciaries and administrators had some bias or adverse interest. The Court of Appeals held that where an employer is itself the fiduciary and administrator of an unfunded benefit plan, its decision to deny benefits should be subject to *de novo* judicial review . . . [and] deference is unwarranted given the lack of assurance of impartiality . . . .

II

. . . Respondents' action asserting that they were entitled to benefits because the sale of Firestone's Plastics Division constituted a "reduction in work force" within the meaning of the termination pay plan was based on the authority of § 1132(a)(1)(B). That provision allows a suit to recover benefits due under the plan, to enforce rights under the terms of the plan, and to obtain a declaratory judgment of future entitlement to benefits under the provisions of the plan contract. The discussion which follows is limited to the appropriate standard of review in § 1132(a)(1)(B) actions challenging denials of benefits based on plan interpretations. . . .

A

. . . ERISA does not set out the appropriate standard of review for actions under § 1132(a)(1)(B) challenging benefit eligibility determinations. To fill this gap, federal courts have adopted the arbitrary and capricious standard developed under, 29 U.S.C. § 86(c), a provision of the Labor Management Relations Act, 1947 (LMRA).. . . . In light of Congress' general intent to incorporate much of LMRA fiduciary law into ERISA, . . . and because ERISA, like the LMRA, imposes a duty of loyalty on fiduciaries and plan administrators, Firestone argues that the LMRA arbitrary and capricious standard should apply to ERISA actions. A comparison of the LMRA and ERISA, however, shows that the wholesale importation of the arbitrary and capricious standard into ERISA is unwarranted.

. . . 29 U.S.C. § 186(c) authorizes unions and employers to set up pension plans jointly and provides that contributions to such plans be made "for the sole and exclusive benefit of the employees . . . and their families and dependents." The LMRA does not provide for judicial review of the decisions of LMRA trustees. Federal courts adopted the arbitrary and capricious standard both as a standard of review and, more importantly, as a means of asserting jurisdiction over suits under § 186(c) by beneficiaries of LMRA plans who were denied benefits by trustees. *See* Van Boxel v. Journal Co. Employees' Pension Trust, 836 F.2d 1048, 1052 (CA7 1987) ("[W]hen a plan provision as interpreted had the effect of denying an application for benefits unreasonably, or as it came to be said, arbitrarily and capriciously, courts would hold that the plan as 'structured' was not for the sole and exclusive benefit of the employees, so that the denial of benefits violated [§ 186(c)])." Unlike the LMRA, ERISA explicitly authorizes suits against fiduciaries and plan administrators to remedy statutory violations, including breaches of fiduciary duty and lack of compliance with benefit plans. *See* 29 U.S.C. §§ 1132(a), 1132(f). . . .

Thus, the *raison d'etre* for the LMRA arbitrary and capricious standard —

the need for a jurisdictional basis in suits against trustees — is not present in ERISA. Without this jurisdictional analogy, LMRA principles offer no support for the adoption of the arbitrary and capricious standard insofar as § 1132(a)(1)(B) is concerned.

B

ERISA abounds with the language and terminology of trust law. *See, e.g.*, 29 U.S.C. §§ 1002(7) ("participant"), 1002(8) ("beneficiary"), 1002(21)(A) ("fiduciary"), 1103(a) ("trustee"), 1104 ("fiduciary duties"). ERISA's legislative history confirms that the Act's fiduciary responsibility provisions, 29 U.S.C. §§ 1101-1114, "codif[y] and mak[e] applicable to [ERISA] fiduciaries certain principles developed in the evolution of the law of trusts." H.R. Rep. No. 93533, p. 11 (1973). Given this language and history, we have held that courts are to develop a "federal common law of rights and obligations under ERISA-regulated plans." Pilot Life Ins. Co. v. Dedeaux, *supra*, at 56. In determining the appropriate standard of review for actions under § 1132(a)(1)(B), we are guided by principles of trust law. *Central States, Southeast and Southwest Areas Pension Fund v. Central Transport, Inc.*, 472 U.S. 559, 570 (1985).

Trust principles make a deferential standard of review appropriate when a trustee exercises discretionary powers. *See* RESTATEMENT (SECOND) OF TRUSTS § 187 (1959) ("[w]here discretion is conferred upon the trustee with respect to the exercise of a power, its exercise is not subject to control by the court except to prevent an abuse by the trustee of his discretion"). *See also* G. Bogert & G. Bogert, Law of Trusts and Trustees § 560, pp. 193-208 (2d rev. ed. 1980). A trustee may be given power to construe disputed or doubtful terms, and in such circumstances the trustee's interpretation will not be disturbed if reasonable. *Id.*, § 559, at 169-171. Whether "the exercise of a power is permissive or mandatory depends upon the terms of the trust." 3 W. Fratcher, Scott on Trusts § 187, p. 14 (4th ed. 1988). Hence, over a century ago we remarked that "[w]hen trustees are in existence, and capable of acting, a court of equity will not interfere to control them in the exercise of a *discretion vested in them by the instrument* under which they act." Nichols v. Eaton, 91 U.S. 716 (1875) (emphasis added). Firestone can seek no shelter in these principles of trust law, however, for there is no evidence that under Firestone's termination pay plan the administrator has the power to construe uncertain terms or that eligibility determinations are to be given deference.

Finding no support in the language of its termination pay plan for the arbitrary and capricious standard, Firestone argues that as a matter of trust law the interpretation of the terms of a plan is an inherently discretionary function. But other settled principles of trust law, which point to *de novo* review of benefit eligibility determinations based on plan interpretations, belie this contention. As they do with contractual provisions, courts construe terms in trust agreements without deferring to either party's interpretation. "The extent of the duties and powers of a trustee is determined by the rules of law that are applicable to the situation, and not the rules that the trustee or his attorney believes to be applicable, and by the terms of the trust as *the court may interpret them*, and not as they may be interpreted by the trustee himself or by his attorney." 3 W. Fratcher, Scott on Trusts § 201, at 221 (emphasis added). A trustee who is in doubt as to the interpretation of the instrument can protect himself by obtaining instructions from the court. Bogert & Bogert, *supra*, § 559, at 162-168. . . . The terms of trusts created by written instruments are "determined by the provisions of the instrument as interpreted in light of all the circumstances and such other evidence of the intention of the settlor with respect to the trust as is not inadmissible." RESTATEMENT (SECOND) OF TRUSTS § 4, Comment d (1959).

The trust law *de novo* standard of review is consistent with the judicial interpretation of employee benefit plans prior to the enactment of ERISA. Actions challenging an employer's denial of benefits before the enactment of ERISA were governed by principles of contract law. If the plan did not give the employer or administrator discretionary or final authority to construe uncertain terms, the court reviewed the employee's claim as it would have any other contract claim — by looking to the terms of the plan and other manifestations of the parties' intent. . . .

Despite these principles of trust law pointing to a *de novo* standard of review for claims like respondents', Firestone would have us read ERISA to require the application of the arbitrary and capricious standard to such claims. ERISA defines a fiduciary as one who "exercises any discretionary authority or discretionary control respecting management of [a] plan or exercises any authority or control respecting management or disposition of its assets." 29 U.S.C. § 1002(21)(A)(i). A fiduciary has "authority to control and manage the operation and administration of the plan,"§ 1102(a)(1), and must provide a "full and fair review" of claim denials, § 1133(2). From these provisions, Firestone concludes that an ERISA plan administrator, fiduciary, or trustee is empowered to exercise *all* his authority in a discretionary manner subject only to review for arbitrariness and capriciousness. But the provisions relied upon so heavily by Firestone do not characterize a fiduciary as one who exercises *entirely* discretionary authority or control. Rather, one is a fiduciary to the extent he exercises any discretionary authority or control.

ERISA was enacted "to promote the interests of employees and their beneficiaries in employee benefit plans," Shaw v. Delta Airlines, Inc., 463 U.S. 85, 90 (1983), and "to protect contractually defined benefits," Massachusetts Mutual Life Ins. Co. v. Russell, 473 U.S., at 148, 105 S. Ct., at 3093. . . . Adopting Firestone's reading of ERISA would require us to impose a standard of review that would afford less protection to employees and their beneficiaries than they enjoyed before ERISA was enacted. Nevertheless, Firestone maintains that congressional action after the passage of ERISA indicates that Congress intended ERISA claims to be reviewed under the arbitrary and capricious standard. At a time when most federal courts had adopted the arbitrary and capricious standard of review, a bill was introduced in Congress to amend § 1132 by providing *de novo* review of decisions denying benefits. *See* H.R. 6226, 97th Cong., 2d Sess. (1982), *reprinted in* Pension Legislation: Hearings on H.R. 1614 et al. before the Sub-committee on Labor-Management Relations of the House Committee on Education and Labor, 97th Cong., 2d Sess., 60 (1983). Because the bill was never enacted, Firestone asserts that we should conclude that Congress was satisfied with the arbitrary and capricious standard. We do not think that this bit of legislative inaction carries the day for Firestone. Though "instructive," failure to act on the proposed bill is not conclusive of Congress' views on the appropriate standard of review. Bowsher v. Merck & Co., 460 U.S. 824, 837, n.12 (1983). The bill's demise may have been the result of events that had nothing to do with Congress' view on the propriety of *de novo* review. Without more, we cannot ascribe to Congress any acquiescence in the arbitrary and capricious standard. "[T]he views of a subsequent Congress form a hazardous basis for inferring the intent of an earlier one." United States v. Price, 361 U.S. 304, 313 (1960).

Firestone and its amici also assert that a *de novo* standard would contravene the spirit of ERISA because it would impose much higher administrative and litigation costs and therefore discourage employers from creating benefit plans. *See, e.g.*, Brief for American Council of Life Insurance et al. as Amici Curiae 10-11. Because even under the arbitrary and capricious standard an employer's denial of benefits could be subject to judicial review, the assumption seems to be that a *de novo* standard would encourage more litigation by employees, participants, and beneficiaries who wish to assert their right to benefits. Neither general principles of trust law nor a concern for impartial decisionmaking, however, forecloses parties from agreeing upon a narrower standard of review. Moreover, as to both funded and unfunded plans, the threat of increased litigation is not sufficient to outweigh the reasons for a *de novo* standard that we have already explained.

As this case aptly demonstrates, the validity of a claim to benefits under an ERISA plan is likely to turn on the interpretation of terms in the plan at issue. Consistent with established principles of trust law, we hold that a denial of benefits challenged under § 1132(a)(1)(B) is to be reviewed under a *de novo* standard unless the benefit plan gives the administrator or fiduciary discretionary authority to determine eligibility for benefits or to construe the terms of the plan. Because we do not rest our decision on the concern for impartiality that guided the Court of Appeals, *see* 828 F.2d, at 143-146, we need not distinguish between types of plans or focus on the motivations of plan administrators and fiduciaries. Thus, for purposes of actions under § 1132(a)(1)(B), the *de novo* standard of review applies regardless of whether the plan at issue is funded or unfunded and regardless of whether the administrator or fiduciary is operating under a possible or actual conflict of interest. Of course, if a benefit plan gives discretion to an administrator or fiduciary who is operating under a conflict of interest, that conflict must be weighed as a "facto[r] in determining whether there is an abuse of discretion." Restatement (Second) of Trusts § 187, Comment d (1959). . . .

III

[The Court also addressed whether Firestone unlawfully denied the plaintiffs' request for a copy of a writing describing or establishing the plan under 29 U.S.C. § 1024(b)(4). Whether or not the plaintiffs prevailed on their underlying claim for severance benefits, they might be entitled to an award of up to $100 per day for a wrongful refusal to provide the requested documentation. 29 U.S.C. § 1132(c). However, only a "participant or beneficiary" is entitled to such documentation, and Firestone argued that the plaintiffs were neither beneficiaries nor participants because they were no longer employees and not entitled to severance benefits under the plan. The Court held that the term "participant" includes a former employee who has "a *colorable* claim that (1) he or she will prevail in a suit for benefits, or that (2) eligibility requirements will be fulfilled in the future." (emphasis added). The Court expressed no opinion whether the plaintiffs qualified as having a colorable claim.]

. . . [T]he decision of the Court of Appeals is affirmed in part and reversed in part, and the case is remanded for proceedings consistent with this opinion.

NOTES AND QUESTIONS

1. As *Firestone* illustrates, ERISA establishes federal court jurisdiction for claims under the act. For most types of ERISA claims, federal court jurisdiction is exclusive and state courts are without jurisdiction. There is one very important exception. If a plaintiff asserts a claim for the denial of benefits, and his claim is based on the terms of the plan, not statutory ERISA rights, a state court will have concurrent jurisdiction, subject to removal to federal court. 29 U.S.C. § 1132(e). Whether the action proceeds in federal or state court, federal substantive law will apply to the claim. Metro. Life Ins. Co. v. Taylor, 481 U.S. 58 (1987).

2. ERISA includes a number of measures in addition to judicial review to assure fairness and accountability in a plan's decisions regarding claims for benefits. First, if the plan denies a claim, it must give the participant or beneficiary a written notice of the denial and the reasons for the denial. 29 U.S.C. § 1133(1). Second, the plan must provide a "reasonable opportunity" for a "full and fair review" of the denied claim. 29 U.S.C. § 1133(2). *See also* 29 C.F.R. §§ 2560.503-1(b) through 1(m) (describing detailed requirements for plan claims procedures). The requirement of an internal appeal procedure is designed to provide a relatively quick and inexpensive way to challenge the denial of a claim, but the courts have also viewed it as a limitation on access to judicial review. Before filing suit challenging the denial of a claim, the claimant must first exhaust plan procedures. Amato v. Bernard, 618 F.2d 559 (9th Cir. 1980).

If a plan fails to provide the internal appeals procedure required by the act, the claimant may file suit as soon as the plan's initial denial of the claim. 29 C.F.R. § 2560.503-1(*l*). Moreover, if the plan provides for an internal appeal but suggests an appeal is permissive, at least some courts have refused to apply the exhaustion requirement. Watts v. BellSouth Telecom., Inc., 316 F.3d 1203 (11th Cir. 2003). *Contra* Baxter v. C.A. Muer Corp., 941 F.2d 451 (6th Cir. 1991).

3. Since *Firestone Tire & Rubber*, many employers have written or amended their benefit plans to grant discretionary authority to an administrator in deciding benefit claims. How clear must a plan be in granting discretion to limit judicial review under *Firestone Tire & Rubber*? Diaz v. Prudential Ins. Co., 424 F.3d 635 (7th Cir. 2005), suggests "safe harbor" language: "Benefits under this plan will be paid only if the plan administrator decides in his discretion that the applicant is entitled to them." However, the *Diaz* court stated it would accept language less clear than the safe harbor language if it "gives the employee adequate notice that the plan administrator . . . has the latitude to shape the application, interpretation, and content of the rules in each case." *Id.* at 637-639.

4. Why does ERISA permit a self-interested employer to appoint one of its own managers to serve as the administrator, especially with "discretion," to decide whether to pay claims for benefits? Is the potential conflict of interest noted in *Firestone Tire & Rubber* sufficiently serious that Congress should require claim determinations by an independent administrator?

Remember that an employer is not required to provide any pension or welfare benefits at all. An employer might be more willing to offer such benefits if it can retain some oversight of the process of administering benefits, and administration by regular staff is often less expensive than contracting with a truly independent administrator (except for very complex benefits such as health care, for which an employer typically contracts with an insurance company). Moreover, there are practical and legal constraints against bad faith decisions by the employer's own administrator. First, an employer will want to avoid decisions that alienate employees, because the purpose of establishing a plan is to gain and preserve employee goodwill. Second, ERISA requires any administrator to "discharge his duties . . . in accordance with the documents and instruments governing the plan," and to observe a "duty of loyalty" to the plan, participants, and beneficiaries. 29 U.S.C. § 1104(a)(1). Thus, the administrator must exercise any discretion "solely in the interest of the participants and beneficiaries" (and not, one might add, in the interest of the employer). *Id.* A violation of this duty exposes the administrator to personal liability and penalties under the act. *Id.* §§ 1109, 1132(*l*).

5. Another reason not to require an independent administrator — such as an insurance company — is that an independent administrator may be subject to a conflict of interest similar to that of an "in house" administrator. *See* J. Langbein, *Trust Law as Regulatory Law: The UNUM/Provident Scandal and Judicial Review of Benefit Denials Under ERISA*, 101 Nw. L. Rev. 1315 (2007). The Supreme Court addressed this problem in Metropolitan Life Insurance Co. v. Glenn, 554 U.S. 105 (2008). An insurance company, MetLife, argued that, as an independent administrator, it did not labor under the same "conflict of interest" as an employer administrator, and therefore was entitled to even greater judicial deference. According to MetLife, an independent administrator like an insurance company has "greater incentive than a self-insuring employer to provide accurate claims processing . . . because the insurance company typically charges a fee that attempts to account for the cost of claims payouts, with the result that paying an individual claim does not come to the same extent from the company's own pocket." MetLife also asserted that the market will "punish an insurance company when its products," such as claims processing, fall "below par when it seeks a biased result, rather than an accurate one." *Id.* at 114. The Court rejected MetLife's arguments and applied the same general standard as for employer administrators:

> [F]or ERISA purposes a conflict exists. For one thing, the employer's own conflict may extend to its selection of an insurance company to administer its plan. An employer choosing an administrator in effect buys insurance for others and consequently (when compared to the marketplace customer who buys for himself) may be more interested in an insurance company with low rates than in one with accurate claims processing . . . . Finally, a legal rule that treats insurance company administrators and employers alike in respect to the existence of a conflict can nonetheless take account of the circumstances to which MetLife points so far as it treats those, or similar, circumstances as diminishing the significance or severity of the conflict in individual cases.

Id. at 115.

6. In *Glenn*, the Court also clarified how to weigh the conflict of interest

"factor." For an administrator with discretionary authority, the standard of review remains "abuse of discretion," not de novo, despite an appearance of conflict. *Id.* Because nearly any benefit decision by an employer administrator or independent administrator is subject to a potential conflict, a rule elevating the standard of review for a conflict "could bring about near universal review by judges de novo — i.e., without deference — of the lion's share of ERISA plan claims denials." *Id.* Instead, the Court reaffirmed its loose, multi-factored approach:

> We believe that *Firestone* means what the word "factor" implies, namely, that when judges review the lawfulness of benefit denials, they will often take account of several different considerations of which a conflict of interest is one. This kind of review is no stranger to the judicial system. Not only trust law, but also administrative law, can ask judges to determine lawfulness by taking account of several different, often case-specific, factors, reaching a result by weighing all together.
>
> In such instances, any one factor will act as a tiebreaker when the other factors are closely balanced, the degree of closeness necessary depending upon the tiebreaking factor's inherent or case-specific importance. The conflict of interest . . . should prove more important (perhaps of great importance) where circumstances suggest a higher likelihood that it affected the benefits decision, including, but not limited to, cases where an insurance company administrator has a history of biased claims administration. It should prove less important (perhaps to the vanishing point) where the administrator has taken active steps to reduce potential bias and to promote accuracy, for example, by walling off claims administrators from those interested in firm finances, or by imposing management checks that penalize inaccurate decisionmaking irrespective of whom the inaccuracy benefits.

Id.. at 116-17.

7. Benefit claims often depend on interpretation of plan terms, which involves many of the same problems that attend interpretation of a contract, but with a few additional wrinkles. First, ERISA requires not one but two separate types of documents describing a plan. One is the "written instrument" that ERISA requires for the establishment of a plan and that serves as the basis for administering the plan. 29 U.S.C. § 1102(b). The employer need not distribute this document but it must make it available to participants and beneficiaries on demand. *Id.* § 1024(b)(4). The other required document is the "summary plan document" (SPD), which an employer furnishes to participants and beneficiaries but which presents only the central facts about a plan in a manner "calculated to be understood by the average plan participant." *Id.* §§ 1021(a), 1022(b), 1024(b). The SPD must be "sufficiently accurate and comprehensive to reasonably apprise . . . participants and beneficiaries of their rights and obligations under the plan." *Id.* § 1022(a); *see also* 19 U.S.C. § 1022(b) (listing information SPD must include).

Occasionally there is a conflict between the SPD and the document establishing the plan, and a court must decide which document prevails to determine a claimant's rights under the plan. In CIGNA Corp. v. Amara, 563 U.S. 421 (2011), the Supreme Court held that SPDs "provide communication with beneficiaries *about* the plan," but SPDs "do not themselves constitute the *terms* of the plan" for purposes of an action to recover benefits due under the plan. *Id.* at 438-39. Thus, under *Amara*, an SPD cannot add to or override the "written instrument" establishing the plan. However, *Amara* does not necessarily preclude a claim against an employer or administrator for misrepresentation in an SPD.

8. Another difference between interpreting a basic contract and an ERISA plan is that a contract might be modified by subsequent oral or written statements of the parties (subject to the statute of frauds and the preexisting duty rule), but a plan is much more difficult to change because it is designed to apply uniformly to all participants and beneficiaries. If a plan could be amended by an alleged oral statement of a manager or supervisor to one or a few employees, the task of administering the plan uniformly and predictably for all employees might become impossible. *See* 29 U.S.C. §§ 1024(b), 1102(b) (requiring plan to be in writing, procedure for plan amendments, and reporting and disclosure of amendments). Unsurprisingly, courts have been inhospitable to claims that a plan was modified by an alleged oral statement made to one or a few employees. *See*, *e.g.*, Straub v. W. Union Tel. Co., 851 F.2d 1262 (10th Cir. 1988). Courts have also rejected employers' defenses based on alleged oral amendments to plans. Confer v. Custom Eng'g Co., 952 F.2d 41 (3d Cir. 1991). On the other hand, extrinsic evidence is admissible to aid in interpreting ambiguous plan terms, just as under contract law. Sprague v. Gen'l Motors Corp., 133 F.3d 388 (6th Cir. 1998).

Finally, a participant or beneficiary might claim that a plan administrator or employer sponsor is estopped from acting contrary to an alleged promise or misrepresentation, or is liable for a participant's or beneficiary's detrimental reliance, even though the promise or misrepresentation is inconsistent with plan terms. 1998. Black v. TIC Inv. Corp., 900 F.2d 112 (7th Cir. 1990) (describing estoppel theory under ERISA). But estoppel is not based on a claimant's rights under plan. Instead, the basis for estoppel and associated remedies appears to be ERISA's "fiduciary duties" provisions. *See* CIGNA Corp. v. Amara, 563 U.S. 421 (U.S. 2011) (discussing estoppel and equitable doctrine of "surcharge"). ERISA fiduciary duties are described in Part D.2.c of this chapter, *infra*.

9. If the administrators of a plan consistently follow an unwritten rule with respect to some recurrent issue in deciding claims for benefits, does the failure to include the rule in the SPD or plan document violate ERISA?

In Pompano v. Michael Schiavone & Sons, Inc., 680 F.2d 911 (2d Cir. 1982), a plan provided that a retiree could receive his pension in a lump sum with "approval" of the pension committee, but the committee withheld approval of a lump-sum payout for the plaintiff. The plaintiff sued, alleging that the committee had followed an unwritten rule for the denial of a lump-sum payment for any long-term employee, and that this unwritten rule violated the requirement that an SPD must delineate the "circumstances which may result in disqualification, ineligibility, or denial or loss of benefits." 29 U.S.C. § 1022(b). A majority of the court rejected the argument that ERISA barred an administrator from following a rule or considering a factor unenumerated in the SPD. The majority also noted that the committee appeared to have made its decision in good faith, with sound financial reasons for denying a lump sum that would be very large (as it ordinarily would be for a long-term employee). Judge Mansfield dissented:

> The issue before us . . . is not the soundness of the Committee's exercise of

> discretion. Nor is the economic basis or wisdom of a policy against lump sum payments being challenged. The issue is whether the Schiavone plan summary complied with ERISA's express requirement that it be materially accurate. The answer is that the summary, by failing to disclose an "unwritten general rule" against lump sum payments to long-term retirees, which was found by the district court to exist and is not disputed by the majority, was misleading and therefore violated the act.

Id. at 917.

Does the majority's approach leave participants and beneficiaries without fair access to information about the plan's actual terms? Or would the dissent's approach unduly hinder a plan in the development of its own common law? If the dissent is correct, what is the appropriate remedy? A reversal of the committee decision? Or a remand to the committee for reconsideration of a lump sum payout?

10. Benefit claims often depend on issues of fact rather than plan interpretation. For example, whether a beneficiary is completely or partially "disabled" may be entirely an issue of fact. If the plan grants the administrator discretion in deciding benefit claims, should a reviewing court apply the same "abuse of discretion" standard of judicial review to the administrator's fact findings? The courts have generally assumed the answer is "yes." If so, should an administrator's "discretion" in deciding "facts" be limited by a duty to conduct a "reasonable" investigation of the facts before reaching a conclusion? In Vega v. National Life Ins. Servs., 188 F.3d 287 (5th Cir. 1999), the Fifth Circuit rejected a proposed duty of reasonable investigation, at least to the extent that it would require the administrator to seek evidence not supplied by the claimant. *Id.* at 298. Yet courts have generally considered unfairness or neglect in the administrator's method or process for receiving and reviewing evidence to be important factors showing abuse of discretion. Capone v. Aetna Life Ins. Co., 592 F.3d 1189 (11th Cir. 2010); Pinto v. Reliance Standard Life Ins., 214 F.3d 377 (3d Cir. 2000).

PROBLEM

Benny Fisher has come to your office with the following story. His father, a long-time employee of the Life Assurance Co., retired about a year ago but has very recently died. Several years before the father's retirement he first received an employee handbook that included a summary plan description of the company's group life insurance benefits. The life insurance plan provided coverage at an amount equal to an employee's annual salary. The employer bore the entire cost of this insurance. The plan also provided continued life insurance coverage after an employee's retirement, as follows (emphasis added):

> If you retire at 65 or older with 10 or more years of service, or at age 55 or older with 20 or more years of service, your life insurance will be reduced by 10 percent on your retirement date, and by an equal amount on each of the next four anniversaries of your retirement date. Thereafter, 50 percent of your life insurance coverage *will remain in force for the rest of your life, at no cost to you*. For more details of the plan, refer to the Life Insurance Plan Statement available in the Human Resources Office.

The Life Insurance Plan Statement, the plan document establishing the life insurance plan, designated the company's vice president of human resources as the administrator of the plan. The plan document stated, among other things, that "the administrator shall interpret the plan in his sole discretion." The plan also stated that "the Company reserves the right to terminate or amend the plan at any time."

Fisher's father retired at age 65, having named Fisher, now a freshman in college, as the life insurance beneficiary. When Fisher's father died, Fisher contacted the company's human resources office about the life insurance proceeds. He received a letter from the vice president of human resources stating as follows:

> I am very sorry to hear about your father's death. He was a wonderful person and a loyal employee. Unfortunately, we recently terminated the life insurance plan for retirees. I've attached a copy of the letter we mailed to all our retirees several months ago.

The attached letter, written and signed by that vice president, addressed to Fisher's father, and dated about a year earlier, stated "The Company regrets to inform its retirees that it will be terminating its life insurance coverage for retirees."

Discuss whether Benny Fisher may have a viable argument that the plan has improperly rejected his claim for benefits.

c. Fiduciaries and Fiduciary Duties

ERISA imposes a number of duties on anyone performing the functions of a fiduciary with respect to a plan, including a duty of loyalty, which means a fiduciary must perform duties with respect to a plan "solely in the interest of the participants and beneficiaries." 29 U.S.C. § 1104(a)(1). This duty of loyalty is also sometimes described as the "exclusive benefit rule." It might seem that the duty of loyalty relates primarily to financial management and integrity of a plan, as where it prohibits misuse of plan assets for improper purposes. Yet the duty of loyalty has other important aspects for plan fiduciaries, particularly with respect to the sorts of information fiduciaries must or may provide to plan participants and beneficiaries.

Every ERISA plan has at least one fiduciary: the administrator, responsible for managing the plan and paying benefits. Since plan assets must be held in trust, a plan might also have one or more trustees who are fiduciaries. But there could be other fiduciaries; ERISA recognizes that the complexity of benefit plans frequently requires delegating a variety of discretionary functions to others. 29 U.S.C. § 1105(c). For example, an investment advisor to the plan might be a fiduciary. *Id.* § 1002(21)(A). Fiduciaries include any other person who "exercises discretionary authority or discretionary control respecting management of such plan or . . . any authority or control respecting management or disposition of its assets, . . . [or] discretionary authority or discretionary responsibility in [plan] administration." *Id.* § 1002(21)(A). A person is a fiduciary only to the extent of the discretionary authority or control exercised. 29 C.F.R. § 2509.75-8, at FR-16. Those performing purely ministerial functions are not fiduciaries.

In general, an employer is not a fiduciary of a plan it established. When an employer establishes, amends, or terminates a plan, it is not acting as a fiduciary, and its motivations in those actions might lawfully base on self-interest. Curtiss-Wright Corp. v. Schoonejongen, 514 U.S. 73, 78 (1995). Nor are managers or supervisors fiduciaries except to the extent they exercise discretionary authority or control as to the plan. However, an employer could be a fiduciary for at least some purposes. First, the employer might appoint itself to serve as the plan administrator — and remember that the employer is the default administrator in the absence of an express appointment of any other administrator. 29 U.S.C. § 1002(16). If the employer is the administrator, it is a fiduciary like any other administrator with respect to any action it takes as an administrator. Second, whether or not the employer is the administrator, an employer might be a fiduciary to the extent it actually performs one of the functions of a fiduciary.

VARITY CORP. v. HOWE

516 U.S. 489 (1996)

Justice BREYER delivered the opinion of the Court.

A group of beneficiaries of a firm's employee welfare benefit plan, protected by the Employee Retirement Income Security Act of 1974 (ERISA), 88 Stat. 832, as amended, 29 U.S.C. § 1001 et seq. (1988 ed.), have sued their plan's administrator, who was also their employer. They claim that the administrator, through trickery, led them to withdraw from the plan and to forfeit their benefits. They seek, among other things, an order that, in essence, would reinstate each of them as a participant in the employer's ERISA plan. The lower courts entered judgment in the employees' favor, and we agreed to review that judgment.

I

. . . Charles Howe, and the other respondents, used to work for Massey-Ferguson, Inc., a farm equipment manufacturer, and a wholly owned subsidiary of the petitioner, Varity Corporation. (Since the lower courts found that Varity and Massey-Ferguson were "alter egos," we shall refer to them interchangeably.) These employees all were participants in, and beneficiaries of, Massey-Ferguson's self-funded employee welfare benefit plan — an ERISA-protected plan that Massey-Ferguson itself administered. In the mid-1980's, Varity became concerned that some of Massey-Ferguson's divisions were losing too much money and developed a business plan to deal with the problem.

The business plan — which Varity called "Project Sunshine" — amounted to placing many of Varity's money-losing eggs in one financially rickety basket. It called for a transfer of Massey-Ferguson's money-losing divisions, along with various other debts, to a newly created, separately incorporated subsidiary called Massey Combines. The plan foresaw the possibility that Massey Combines would fail. But it viewed such a failure, from Varity's business perspective, as closer to a victory than to a defeat. That is because Massey Combines' failure would not only eliminate several of Varity's poorly performing divisions, but it would also eradicate various debts that Varity would transfer to Massey Combines, and which, in the absence of the reorganization, Varity's more profitable subsidiaries or divisions might have to pay.

Among the obligations that Varity hoped the reorganization would eliminate were those arising from the Massey-Ferguson benefit plan's promises to pay medical and other nonpension benefits to employees of Massey-Ferguson's money-losing divisions. Rather than terminate those benefits directly (as it had retained the right to do), Varity attempted to avoid the undesirable fallout that could have accompanied cancellation by inducing the failing divisions' employees to switch employers and thereby voluntarily release Massey-Ferguson from its obligation to provide them benefits (effectively substituting the new, self-funded Massey Combines benefit plan for the former Massey-Ferguson plan). Insofar as Massey-Ferguson's employees did so, a subsequent Massey Combines failure would eliminate — simply and automatically, without distressing the remaining Massey-Ferguson employees — what would otherwise have been Massey-Ferguson's obligation to pay those employees their benefits.

To persuade the employees of the failing divisions to accept the change of employer and benefit plan, Varity called them together at a special meeting and talked to them about Massey Combines' future business outlook, its likely financial viability, and the security of their employee benefits. The thrust of Varity's remarks . . . was that the employees' benefits would remain secure if they voluntarily transferred to Massey Combines. As Varity knew, however, the reality was very different. Indeed, the District Court found that Massey Combines was insolvent from the day of its creation and that it hid a $46 million negative net worth by overvaluing its assets and underestimating its liabilities.

After the presentation, about 1,500 Massey-Ferguson employees accepted Varity's assurances and voluntarily agreed to the transfer. (Varity also unilaterally assigned to Massey Combines the benefit obligations it owed to some 4,000 workers who had retired from Massey-Ferguson prior to this reorganization, without requesting permission or informing them of the assignment.) Unfortunately for these employees, Massey Combines ended its first year with a loss of $88 million, and ended its second year in a receivership, under which its employees lost their nonpension benefits. . . .

After trial, the District Court found, among other things, that Varity and Massey-Ferguson, acting as ERISA fiduciaries, had harmed the plan's beneficiaries through deliberate deception. The court held that Varity and Massey-Ferguson thereby violated an ERISA-imposed fiduciary obligation to administer Massey-Ferguson's benefit plan "solely in the interest of the participants and beneficiaries" of the plan. [29 U.S.C. § 1104.] The court added that [29 U.S.C. § 1132(a)(3)] gave the former Massey-Ferguson employees a right to "appropriate equitable relief . . . to redress" the harm that this deception had caused them individually. Among other remedies the court considered "appropriate equitable relief" was an order that Massey-Ferguson reinstate its former employees into its own plan (which had continued to provide benefits to employees of Massey-Ferguson's profitable divisions). The court also ordered certain monetary relief which is not at issue here. The Court of Appeals later affirmed . . . .

II

. . . [ERISA] fiduciary duties draw much of their content from the common law of trusts, the law that governed most benefit plans before ERISA's enactment. We also recognize, however, that trust law does not tell the entire story. After all, ERISA's standards and procedural protections partly reflect a congressional determination that the common law of trusts did not offer completely satisfactory protection. *See* [29 U.S.C. § 1001]. . . . [T]he law of trusts often will inform, but will not necessarily determine the outcome of, an effort to interpret ERISA's fiduciary duties. In some instances, trust law will offer only a starting point, after which courts must go on to ask whether, or to what extent, the language of the statute, its structure, or its purposes require departing from common-law trust requirements. And, in doing so, courts may have to take account of competing congressional purposes, such as Congress' desire to offer employees enhanced protection for their benefits, on the one hand, and, on the other, its desire not to create a system that is so complex that administrative costs, or litigation expenses, unduly discourage employers from offering welfare benefit plans. . . .

A

[A] "person is a fiduciary with respect to a plan," and therefore subject to ERISA fiduciary duties, "to the extent" that he or she "exercises any discretionary authority or discretionary control respecting management" of the plan, or "has any discretionary authority or discretionary responsibility in the administration" of the plan. [29 U.S.C. § 1002(21)(A).]

Varity was both an employer and the benefit plan's administrator, as ERISA permits. But, obviously, not all of Varity's business activities involved plan management or administration. Varity argues that when it communicated with its Massey-Ferguson workers about transferring to Massey Combines, it was not administering or managing the plan; rather, it was acting only in its capacity as an employer and not as a plan administrator.

The District Court, however, held that when the misrepresentations regarding employee benefits were made, Varity was wearing its "fiduciary," as well as its "employer," hat. . . . We believe that the factual findings (which Varity does not challenge) adequately support the District Court's holding that Varity was exercising "discretionary authority" respecting the plan's "management" or "administration" when it made these misrepresentations . . . .

The relevant factual circumstances include the following: In the spring of 1986, Varity summoned the employees of Massey-Ferguson's money-losing divisions to a meeting at Massey-Ferguson's corporate headquarters for a 30-minute presentation. The employees saw a 90-second videotaped message from Mr. Ivan Porter, a Varity vice president and Massey Combines' newly appointed president. They also received four documents: (a) a several-page, detailed comparison between the employee benefits offered by Massey-Ferguson and those offered by Massey Combines; (b) a question-and-answer sheet; (c) a transcript of the Porter videotape; and (d) a cover letter with an acceptance form. . . . The District Court concluded that the basic message conveyed to the employees was that transferring from Massey-Ferguson to Massey Combines would not significantly undermine the security of their benefits. And, given this view of the facts, we believe that the District Court reached the correct legal conclusion, namely, that Varity spoke, in significant part, in its capacity as plan administrator.

To decide whether Varity's actions fall within the statutory definition of "fiduciary" acts, we must interpret the statutory terms which limit the scope of fiduciary activity to discretionary acts of plan "management" and "administration." [29 U.S.C. § 1002(21)(A)]. . . . The ordinary trust law understanding of fiduciary "administration" of a trust is that to act as an administrator is to perform the duties imposed, or exercise the powers conferred, by the trust documents. *See* Restatement (Second) of Trusts § 164 (1957). The law of trusts also understands a trust document to implicitly confer "such powers as are necessary or appropriate for the carrying out of the purposes" of the trust. 3 A. Scott & W. Fratcher, Law of Trusts § 186, p. 6 (4th ed. 1988). Conveying information about the likely future of plan benefits, thereby permitting beneficiaries to make an informed choice about continued participation, would seem to be an exercise of a power "appropriate" to carrying out an important plan purpose. After all, ERISA itself specifically requires administrators to give beneficiaries certain information about the plan. *See, e.g.*, [29 U.S.C. §§ 1022, 1024(b)(1), 1025(a)]. And administrators, as part of their administrative responsibilities, frequently offer beneficiaries more than the minimum information that the statute requires — for example, answering beneficiaries' questions about the meaning of the terms of a plan so that those beneficiaries can more easily obtain the plan's benefits. To offer beneficiaries detailed plan information in order to help them decide whether to remain with the plan is essentially the same kind of plan-related activity.

Moreover, as far as the record reveals, Mr. Porter's letter, videotape, and the other documents came from those within the firm who had authority to communicate as fiduciaries with plan beneficiaries. Varity does not claim that it authorized only special individuals, not connected with the meeting documents, to speak as plan administrators. *See* [29 U.S.C. § 1102(b)(2)] (a plan may describe a "procedure under the plan for the allocation of responsibilities for the operation and administration of the plan").

Finally, reasonable employees, in the circumstances found by the District Court, could have thought that Varity was communicating with them both in its capacity as employer and in its capacity as plan administrator. Reasonable employees might not have distinguished consciously between the two roles. But they would have known that the employer was their plan's administrator and had expert knowledge about how their plan worked. The central conclusion ("your benefits are secure") could well have drawn strength from their awareness of that expertise, and one could reasonably believe that the employer, aware of the importance of the matter, so intended.

We conclude, therefore, that the factual context in which the statements were made, combined with the plan-related nature of the activity, engaged in by those who had plan-related authority to do so, together provide sufficient support for the District Court's legal conclusion that Varity was acting as a fiduciary.

Varity raises three contrary arguments. First, Varity argues that it was not engaged in plan administration because neither the specific disclosure provisions of ERISA, nor the specific terms of the plan instruments, required it to make these statements. But that does not mean Varity was not engaging in plan administration in making them. . . . There is more to plan (or trust) administration than simply complying with the specific duties imposed by the plan documents or statutory regime; it also includes the activities that are "ordinary and natural means" of achieving the "objective" of the plan. Bogert & Bogert, *supra*, § 551, at 41-52. . . .

Second, Varity says that when it made the statements that most worried the

District Court — the statements about Massey Combines' "bright future" — it must have been speaking only as employer (and not as fiduciary), for statements about a new subsidiary's financial future have virtually nothing to do with administering benefit plans. But this argument parses the meeting's communications too finely. The ultimate message Varity intended to convey — "your benefits are secure" — depended in part upon its repeated assurances that benefits would remain "unchanged," in part upon the detailed comparison of benefits, and in part upon assurances about Massey Combines' "bright" financial future. Varity's workers would not necessarily have focused upon each underlying supporting statement separately, because what primarily interested them, and what primarily interested the District Court, was the truthfulness of the ultimate conclusion that transferring to Massey Combines would not adversely affect the security of their benefits. And, in the present context, Varity's statements about the security of benefits amounted to an act of plan administration. That Varity intentionally communicated its conclusion through a closely linked set of statements (some directly concerning plan benefits, others concerning the viability of the corporation) does not change this conclusion. . . .

Third, Varity says that an employer's decision to amend or terminate a plan (as Varity had the right to do) is not an act of plan administration. *See Curtiss-Wright Corp.,* 514 U.S., at 78-81. How then, it asks, could conveying information about the likelihood of termination be an act of plan administration? While it may be true that amending or terminating a plan (or a common-law trust) is beyond the power of a plan administrator (or trustee) — and, therefore, cannot be an act of plan "management" or "administration" — it does not follow that making statements about the likely future of the plan is also beyond the scope of plan administration. As we explained above, plan administrators often have, and commonly exercise, discretionary authority to communicate with beneficiaries about the future of plan benefits.

B

The second question — whether Varity's deception violated ERISA-imposed fiduciary obligations — calls for a brief, affirmative answer. ERISA requires a "fiduciary" to "discharge his duties with respect to a plan solely in the interest of the participants and beneficiaries." [29 U.S.C. § 1104(a).] To participate knowingly and significantly in deceiving a plan's beneficiaries in order to save the employer money at the beneficiaries' expense is not to act "solely in the interest of the participants and beneficiaries." As other courts have held, "[l]ying is inconsistent with the duty of loyalty owed by all fiduciaries and codified in section 404(a)(1) of ERISA," Peoria Union Stock Yards Co. v. Penn Mut. Life Ins. Co., 698 F.2d 320, 326 (C.A.7 1983). *See also Central States,* 472 U.S., at 570-571 (ERISA fiduciary duty includes common-law duty of loyalty). Because the breach of this duty is sufficient to uphold the decision below, we need not reach the question whether ERISA fiduciaries have any fiduciary duty to disclose truthful information on their own initiative, or in response to employee inquiries. . . .

C

The remaining question before us is whether or not the remedial provision of

ERISA that the beneficiaries invoked, [29 U.S.C. § 1132(a)(3)], authorizes this lawsuit for individual relief. That subsection is the third of six subsections contained within ERISA's "Civil Enforcement" provision . . . :

> . . . A civil action may be brought —
>
> > . . . (3) by a participant, beneficiary, or fiduciary (A) to enjoin any act or practice which violates any provision of this title or the terms of the plan, or (B) to obtain other appropriate equitable relief (i) to redress such violations or (ii) to enforce any provisions of this title or the terms of the plan. . . . 29 U.S.C. § 1132(a) (1988 ed.).

. . . Varity concedes that the plaintiffs satisfy most of this provision's requirements, namely, that the plaintiffs are plan "participants" or "beneficiaries," and that they are suing for "equitable" relief to "redress" a violation of [29 U.S.C. § 1104(a)], which is a "provision of this title." Varity does not agree, however, that this lawsuit seeks equitable relief that is "appropriate."

. . . ERISA's basic purposes favor a reading of the third subsection that provides the plaintiffs with a remedy. The statute itself says that it seeks

> to protect . . . the interests of participants . . . and . . . beneficiaries . . . by establishing standards of conduct, responsibility, and obligation for fiduciaries . . . and . . . providing for appropriate remedies . . . and ready access to the Federal courts. [29 U.S.C. § 1001(b).]

[29 U.S.C. § 1104(a)], in furtherance of this general objective, requires fiduciaries to discharge their duties "solely in the interest of the participants and beneficiaries." Given these objectives, it is hard to imagine why Congress would want to immunize breaches of fiduciary obligation that harm individuals by denying injured beneficiaries a remedy.

. . . *Amici* supporting Varity find a strong contrary argument in an important, subsidiary congressional purpose — the need for a sensible administrative system. They say that holding that the Act permits individuals to enforce fiduciary obligations owed directly to them as individuals threatens to increase the cost of welfare benefit plans and thereby discourage employers from offering them. Consider a plan administrator's decision not to pay for surgery on the ground that it falls outside the plan's coverage. At present, courts review such decisions with a degree of deference to the administrator, provided that "the benefit plan gives the administrator or fiduciary discretionary authority to determine eligibility for benefits or to construe the terms of the plan." *Firestone, supra*, at 115. But what will happen, ask *amici*, if a beneficiary can repackage his or her "denial of benefits" claim as a claim for "breach of fiduciary duty"? Wouldn't a court, they ask, then have to forgo deference and hold the administrator to the "rigid level of conduct" expected of fiduciaries? . . .

The concerns that *amici* raise seem to us unlikely to materialize, however, for several reasons. First, a fiduciary obligation, enforceable by beneficiaries seeking relief for themselves, does not necessarily favor payment over nonpayment. The common law of trusts recognizes the need to preserve assets to satisfy future, as well as present, claims and requires a trustee to take impartial account of the interests of all beneficiaries. *See* Restatement (Second) of Trusts § 183 (discussing duty of impartiality); id., § 232 (same).

Second, characterizing a denial of benefits as a breach of fiduciary duty does not necessarily change the standard a court would apply when reviewing the administrator's decision to deny benefits. After all, *Firestone*, which authorized deferential court review when the plan itself gives the administrator discretionary authority, based its decision upon the same common-law trust doctrines that govern standards of fiduciary conduct. *See* Restatement (Second) of Trusts § 187 ("Where discretion is conferred upon the trustee with respect to the exercise of a power, its exercise is not subject to control by the court, except to prevent an abuse by the trustee of his discretion") (as quoted in *Firestone*, 489 U.S., at 111).

Third, the statute authorizes "appropriate" equitable relief. We should expect that courts, in fashioning "appropriate" equitable relief, will keep in mind the "special nature and purpose of employee benefit plans," and will respect the "policy choices reflected in the inclusion of certain remedies and the exclusion of others." *Pilot Life Ins. Co.*, 481 U.S., at 54. [W]here Congress elsewhere provided adequate relief for a beneficiary's injury, there will likely be no need for further equitable relief, in which case such relief normally would not be "appropriate."

But that is not the case here. . . . We are not aware of any ERISA-related purpose that denial of a remedy would serve. Rather, we believe that granting a remedy is consistent with the literal language of the statute, the Act's purposes, and pre-existing trust law. For these reasons, the judgment of the Court of Appeals is Affirmed.

NOTES AND QUESTIONS

1. The availability of a "breach of fiduciary duty" claim against an employer might help to fill an otherwise troubling gap in ERISA remedies for plan beneficiaries. ERISA largely supplants and supersedes common law tort and contract remedies, but the substitute statutory remedies ERISA offers in Section 502, codified at 29 U.S.C. § 1132, ERISA are not necessarily as comprehensive as the common law. The appropriate remedy for a beneficiary seeking benefits denied by a plan administrator is a Section 502(a)(1)(B) action for "benefits due" under the terms of the plan. 29 U.S.C. § 1132(a)(1)(B). An action for "benefits due" is roughly analogous to a breach of contract action, except that it is based on a "plan," not a "contract." But winning a judicial award of benefits due may not fully compensate the beneficiary for consequential losses caused by an administrator's denial of benefits. Moreover, some administrator or employer wrongs that are "related" to a plan do not involve the usual simple denial of "benefits due." For example, the plaintiffs in *Varity* could not have sued for "benefits due" because they had no rights under the Massey-Ferguson plan — they had ceased to be participants, and there were no "benefits due" for them under the terms of that plan. The wrong of which they complained was roughly analogous to a tort, like misrepresentation or fraud, but Section 502 does not clearly provide for such cause of action.

What other causes of action does Section 502 authorize for a participant or beneficiary? A second possibility, after an action for "benefits due," is an action "for appropriate relief" to require a "fiduciary" "make good *to such plan* any losses to the plan" caused by the fiduciary, or "to restore *to such plan* any profits" the fiduciary has unlawfully gained by his use of plan assets (emphasis added). 29 U.S.C. § 1132(a)(2) (referencing § 1109). Such a cause of action is particularly suited for a case in which a fiduciary has misappropriated plan assets. But it is *the plan* for which the plaintiff seeks a remedy. In a case like *Varity*, such relief is useless to plaintiffs who are seeking compensation for their own personal losses. *Compare* Massachusetts Mut. Life Ins. Co. v. Russell, 473 U.S. 134 (1985) (participant cannot obtain personal relief under this provision) *with* LaRue v. DeWolff, Boberg & Assoc., 552 U.S. 248 (2008) (this provision does authorize recovery for fiduciary breaches that impair the value of assets in a participant's individual defined contribution retirement account).

The third possibility is the very cause of action the plaintiffs asserted in *Varity*: an action for "other appropriate *equitable* relief" to redress violations or enforce provisions of ERISA or the terms of an ERISA plan. 29 U.S.C. § 1132(a)(3). This provision appears to be the only ERISA provision for individual relief other than "benefits due," but its usefulness depends on what constitutes "equitable relief." Historically, the term "equitable relief" has suggested something other than "money damages."

2. In *Varity* the district court awarded the plaintiffs "equitable relief" in the form of an order that Massey-Ferguson reinstate the plaintiffs in its own plan. Reinstatement did not in itself result in an award of any money or "damages" to the plaintiffs; it simply made them eligible for benefits in accordance with the terms of the plan. The plaintiffs did seek damages in the lower courts, and the jury's verdict included an award of $36 million in punitive damages. However, the district court set this part of the verdict aside because punitive damages are not "equitable relief." The Eight Circuit affirmed this part of the district court's decision. Howe v. Varity Corp., 36 F.3d 746, 752 (8th Cir. 1994). The district court also declined to award compensatory damages, again because "compensatory damages are not "equitable relief." However, the district did award monetary relief it termed "restitution," an equitable remedy, to "restore [the plaintiffs] to the position they would have occupied if the misrepresentations described in this opinion had never occurred." The Eight Circuit affirmed on this point as well, finding that restitution under these circumstances qualified as "equitable relief." The issues whether this award of monetary relief was properly viewed as "restitution," and whether it qualified as "equitable relief," were not presented to the Supreme Court on appeal. *But see* Great-West Life & Annuity Ins. Co. v. Knudson, 534 U.S. 204 (2002) (monetary relief unavailable under section 1132(a)(3), where claim was not "restitution" but was essentially a claim for money due).

3. A number of employer "misrepresentation" cases following *Varity* grow out of some variation of the following scenario: An employer seeking to reduce its workforce offers early retirement or severance benefits to encourage employees to accept voluntary resignation or retirement. The employer leads employees to believe that the early retirement plan will not get any better and might get worse, and some of the employees decide to resign immediately in return for these benefits. Unfortunately, the employer finds that not enough employees have accepted early retirement, and so it amends the plan to sweeten its offer. Naturally, those who retired before the plan amendment are upset to learn they could have received a better deal had they waited. They sue the employer under ERISA,

alleging the employer breached a fiduciary duty by misleading them about prospective changes in the plan.

The plaintiffs in these actions have achieved mixed results. *Compare* Bins v. Exxon, 220 F.3d 1042 (9th Cir. 2000) (employer accurately stated to employee that it did not plan to amend early retirement program, and it had no duty to update employee as soon as its intention changed), *and* Pocchia v. NYNEX Corp., 81 F.3d 275, 278-279 (2d Cir. 1996) (employer had no duty to disclose to employees that it intended to amend plan to improve benefits in the future), *with* Vartanian v. Monsanto Co., 131 F.3d 264 (1st Cir. 1997) (if employee asks, employer must disclose change that is under "serious consideration").

4. In another scenario, an employee makes a job or benefits decision he would not have made had he better understood the terms of his benefits. When he discovers his error, he sues the employer and alleges that the employer breached its fiduciary duty by failing to provide more or better information or advice. In Watson v. Deaconess Waltham Hospital, 298 F.3d 102 (1st Cir. 2002), for example, the plaintiff Watson made poorly informed job decisions that had the effect of disqualifying him from receiving long-term disability benefits.

As a full-time employee, Watson qualified for long-term disability benefits under his employer's plan. When Watson began to suffer serious, progressive, and incurable health problems, he faced a decision whether to resign or to strive to continue his active employment. On the recommendation of a supervisor, Watson switched to "part-time" status and continued active employment at a reduced workload, However, switching to part-time status eventually disqualified Watson from participating in the long-term disability plan. Watson might have preserved his eligibility for benefits if he had claimed disability when it first became evident that he could no longer work full-time. When Watson's condition deteriorated to the point of severe disability, he discovered his mistake.

Watson sued the employer under ERISA. Watson's claim was not for "benefits due," because he was clearly ineligible for benefits under the terms of the plan. Instead, he sued for "equitable relief" under 29 U.S.C. § 1132(a)(3), alleging the employer breached its fiduciary duty by failing to properly inform him about his benefits or to warn him about the consequences of his employment decisions. The court, in rejecting this claim, summarized the law as follows:

> There are two limitations on the imposition of an affirmative fiduciary duty to inform beneficiaries of material facts about the plan. First, a duty only arises if there was some particular reason that the fiduciary should have known that his failure to convey the information would be harmful. A failure to inform is a fiduciary breach only where the fiduciary "knew of the confusion [detrimental to the participant] generated by its misrepresentations or its silence." UAW v. Skinner Engine Co., 188 F.3d 130, 148 (3d Cir. 1999). . . .
>
> Second, fiduciaries need not generally provide individualized unsolicited advice. *See, e.g., Griggs*, 237 F.3d at 381. It is "uncontroversial . . . that a fiduciary does not have to regularly inform beneficiaries every time a plan term affects them." [citing Harte v. Bethlehem Steel Corp., 214 F.3d 446, 454 (3d Cir. 2000)].
>
> As to the first limitation, there is insufficient evidence in the record to

> suggest that any of the Human Resources employees knew or should have known that Watson was likely to need LTD benefits [during the time he switched to part-time status and during the time he remained part-time]. . . .
>
> As to the second limitation, [none of the employer's officials] . . . violated any fiduciary duty by failing to conduct a sua sponte personalized benefits assessment for Watson. There is no evidence that [the employer or its officials] . . . had any reason to think that Watson was unaware of his benefits and the basic eligibility requirements for them.
>
> . . . Watson . . . has not introduced evidence that the information he was given was in any way misleading, either directly or by omission. *See Varity Corp.*, 516 U.S. at 506. Further, Watson could have discovered the existence of the plan if he had attended the annual benefit fair, or if he had asked for a full listing of all benefits for which he was eligible.

Id. at 114-116.

5. Watson also alleged that his employer breached its fiduciary duty by failing to provide him with a "summary plan description" within 90 days after he became a plan participant, and by failing to notify him of changes in the plan. 29 U.S.C. §§ 1021, 1024. Although the employer did owe Watson a duty to provide him with this documentation, the court held that the employer's "technical" violation of ERISA's notice and disclosure requirements did not, standing alone, constitute a breach of fiduciary duty.

6. Remember that if a beneficiary's claim is not for "benefits due" under the terms of a plan, his or her only other ERISA remedy appears to be for "equitable relief." If Watson had proved a breach of fiduciary duty by the employer, what "equitable relief" might he have obtained? In *Watson*, the employer argued that Watson's claim was essentially one for money damages — not equitable relief. The court noted the "uncertainty . . . whether a claim for reinstatement of beneficiary status or equitable restitution of past due benefits can be classified as a request for equitable relief or a request for money damages." *Id.* at 110 n.8. Having found other reasons to dismiss Watson's claim, the court declined to decide this issue.

d. Interference and Retaliation

An employer can wear two hats under ERISA: One as an "employer," the other as a plan "administrator" or other fiduciary. The distinction is important because ERISA does not impose fiduciary duties on an employer when it acts as an "employer." The employer acts an "employer" when it takes basic employment actions, such terminating, transferring, or otherwise changing employee status. Such actions are not, per se, actions to manage or administer a benefit plan, even though they can indirectly affect employee qualification for benefits. Other types of "employer" actions related to creation and form of benefit plans, such as establishing, amending, or terminating plans, directly impact benefits. Nevertheless, these are still "employer," not "fiduciary," actions. When an employer takes any of these "employer" actions, it need not act "solely in the interest" of employees or other beneficiaries. It can act in its own interest.

ERISA does impose some limits on an employer's actions as an employer. If it did not, an employer could defeat the purposes of ERISA by threatening, discharging or otherwise retaliating against employees simply to prevent their assertion of legitimate claims to benefits. ERISA's most important limit on an employer's conduct as an employer is its anti-interference provision, "section 510" (29 U.S.C. § 1140), which states in pertinent part:

> It shall be unlawful for any person to discharge, fine, suspend, expel, discipline, or discriminate against a participant or beneficiary for exercising any right to which he is entitled under the provisions of an employee benefit plan . . . [or ERISA], or for the purpose of interfering with the attainment of any right to which such participant may become entitled under the plan [or ERISA].

As the courts have said, "§ 510 helps to make promises credible" by preventing an employer from using various employment actions as a pretext for breaching a promise of benefits. Inter-Modal Rail Employees Ass'n v. Atchison, Topeka & Santa Fe Ry. Co., 520 U.S. 510 (1997). Thus, while the fiduciary duty provisions of ERISA govern an employer's behavior as a plan administrator, section 510 governs the employer's behavior as an employer.

An employer might violate section 510 in two ways: (1) *retaliating* against an employee for seeking benefits or exercising other ERISA rights, or (2) *interfering* with the employee's attainment of rights, such as by impeding his application for benefits or discharging him to prevent the vesting of his pension benefits.

"Retaliation" claims tend to be straightforward: Did the employee's use of a benefit plan or exercise of ERISA rights cause the employer to discharge or otherwise retaliate against him or her? The fact that benefit claims cost money might well motivate an employer to retaliate under some circumstances. However, an employee seeking to prove retaliation must show more than a discharge and a past claim for benefits. *Compare* Larimer v. Int'l Bus. Mach. Corp., 370 F.3d 698 (7th Cir. 2004) (employee's recent claim for benefits was insufficient, standing alone, to create issue of fact whether discharge was retaliatory); *with* Conners v. SpectraSite Comm'ns, Inc., 465 F. Supp. 2d 834 (S.D. Ohio 2006) (close nexus in time was some evidence of intent).

"Interference" cases can be much more complex. In general, interference involves an employer's action prior to the employee's accessing or "attainment" of benefits, and the employer's intent is to prevent attainment of benefits. The simplest interference cases include those in which an employer *threatened* an employee with retaliation to discourage the employee from accessing benefits. Garratt v. Walker, 164 F.3d 1249 (10th Cir. 1998) (en banc) (employer told employee that if he participated in pension, his pay would be cut to offset the increased benefits cost to the employer). A somewhat more complex group of "interference" cases are those in which an employer is alleged to have prevented an employee's qualification for, vesting in, or continued use of a benefit plan by terminating or changing the employee's status. Targeting an employee for adverse employment action simply to disqualify that employee from benefits or to interfere with the vesting of benefits appears to be a clear violation of section 510. Seaman v. Arvida Realty Sales, 985 F.2d 543 (11th Cir. 1993). On the other hand, an employer is under no obligation to change an employee's existing status to another status simply to make the employee eligible for benefits. *See* Rush v. McDonald's Corp., 760 F. Supp. 1349, 1364 (S.D. Ind. 1991), *aff'd*, 966 F.2d 1104 (7th Cir. 1992). The difference between taking adverse action to disqualify an employee, versus failing to change the status of an employee to gain qualification, is not always clear cut. *See, e.g.,* Becker v. Mack Trucks, Inc., 281 F.3d 372 (3d Cir. 2002) (section 510 does not apply to hiring decisions, and therefore employer did not violate section 510 by refusing to rehire former employees who, by reason of prior credited service, would have earned greater pension benefits than applicants without past service).

The problem of alleged "interference" is particularly complex when the employer's action was a business reorganization, consolidation, transfer of ownership, or other business change that led to the layoff or other major change in status for a group or class of employees. *See* Pickering v. USX Corp., 809 F. Supp. 1501 (D. Utah 1992) (employer violated ERISA by failing to recall employees and by idling plant in order to interfere with accrual of pension benefits). If the employer's motivation was to reduce costs, and benefits costs were one part of the equation, can it be said that the employer's motive was to interfere with its employees' attainment of rights to benefits, in violation of ERISA?

In Nemeth v. Clark Equip. Co., 677 F. Supp. 899 (W.D. Mich. 1987), the employer closed one facility and transferred production to another more efficient facility. The employer also laid-off many of its employees at the first facility, and some of these laid-off employees sued the employer, alleging it had acted to interfere with their rights to benefits in violation of ERISA. The employer had embarked on this consolidation in the face of serious business difficulty — it had lost $234 million in one year and feared bankruptcy. The employer decided it must close one of two plants — either Benton Harbor, Michigan or Asheville, North Carolina — and consolidate production in the remaining plant. The employer determined that operating costs at Benton Harbor were much greater than at Asheville. Approximately one-fifth of this difference in cost was due to the higher benefits costs of the Benton Harbor workforce. A Benton Harbor manager was heard to say "the pension costs were killing us." The employer chose Benton Harbor for shutdown. While the employer offered affected employees transfer rights to Asheville, the offer was limited to "able-bodied" employees not previously laid off. Employees who accepted transfer had to report within 14 days and lost all seniority for purposes of job bidding or layoff protection. Evidently, the restrictions were not designed to ration a shortage of jobs in Asheville. A year after Benton Harbor closed, the employer still relied on temporary employees to fill positions in Asheville because there were not enough transferees.

The court found that this evidence constituted a prima facie case of discrimination and interference in violation of ERISA. However, the court also found that the employer had established a legitimate, nondiscriminatory reason for its actions. The employer contended, and the court found, that "pension costs were one of many considerations in their decision, and that no single factor standing alone motivated or dominated [the] decision to close the Benton Harbor plant." *Id.* at 905. Indeed, the court concluded, the employer would have made the same decision regardless of comparative pension costs. However:

> Had plaintiffs been able to prove that the increased cost associated with

> operating the Benton Harbor plant was attributable solely, or in large part, to the cost of its pension plan, the Court would have no choice but to find in favor of the plaintiffs. If Clark had made the decision based primarily on the costs of the pension plan, Clark would have acted with the purpose of interfering with plaintiffs' rights under that plan.

Id. at 906-909. As to the employer's denial of broader, more generous transfer rights to Benton Harbor employees, the court again agreed with the employer that the evidence showed a nondiscriminatory motive. According to the employer's witnesses, the purpose of a restrictive transfer policy was "to protect both the seniority and the pension rights of workers at the Asheville plant." Had large numbers of Benton Harbor employees made the transfer, their likely retirement within a few years would have upset an assumption underlying the Asheville plan that few employees would collect benefits for many more years. *Id.* at 910.

Even if the *Nemeth* plaintiffs had proven the plant closing or other employer actions violated section 510, it is not clear what remedy might have been available. In Millsap v. McDonnell Douglas Corp., 162 F. Supp. 2d 1262 (N.D. Okla. 2001), the plaintiffs successfully proved the employer's decision to close their plant, and not some other plant, was discriminatory in violation of section 510. However, in an appeal from the remedies portion of the case, the Tenth Circuit left the plaintiffs empty-handed. Millsap v. McDonnell Douglas Corp., 368 F.3d 1246 (10th Cir. 2004). The *Millsap* case and remedy problems under section 510 are explained in the Notes and Questions following the next case.

Aside from the section 510 claim, the employees also claimed age discrimination, and a jury returned a verdict for the plaintiffs on this claim. 677 F. Supp. at 902. On what basis might the jury have found age discrimination?

LESSARD v. APPLIED RISK MANAGEMENT

307 F.3d 1020 (9th Cir. 2002)

BETTY B. FLETCHER, Circuit Judge.

Plaintiff-Appellant Lessard appeals a grant of summary judgment on her claim that Defendants Appellees Applied Risk Management, Inc. ("ARM"), its successor, Professional Risk Management ("PRM"), and the parent of PRM, MMI Companies, Inc. ("MMI"), violated section 510 of the Employee Retirement Income Security Act of 1974 ("ERISA"), 29 U.S.C. § 1140, when Lessard's medical benefits were terminated following the sale of ARM's assets to PRM and Lessard was subsequently denied benefits under the new plan established by PRM/MMI. Because we find that the Asset Sale Agreement ("Agreement") between the defendants facially discriminated against persons on disability and medical leave, we reverse the decision of the district court and remand for judgment and an award of damages in favor of the Plaintiff-Appellant.

I. FACTUAL BACKGROUND

Denice Lessard began working as a workers' compensation analyst for ARM in February 1996. In the course of her employment with ARM, Lessard enrolled in a self-funded employee welfare benefits plan, the Group Benefit Plan ("Plan"), administered by ARM. As a Plan participant, Lessard was entitled to participate in the medical portion of the Plan. Following a work-related injury to her spine, Lessard left active employment in October 1996 on workers' compensation leave while maintaining her coverage under the Plan. She has not returned to active employment status since May 1997, and she has not sought employment since her spinal fusion surgery in January 1998.

On February 1, 1999, ARM entered into an agreement with PRM, a subsidiary of MMI, for the sale of ARM's assets to PRM/MMI. Under the Agreement, ARM was required to continue funding the Plan through February 28, 1999, when its Plan was finally terminated. Pursuant to conditions that are the subject of this lawsuit, ARM employees were automatically transferred to active employment with PRM/MMI coincident with the execution of the sale. Transfer of the seller's labor force permitted the purchaser to acquire the seller's assets without a break in business operations. ARM employees transferred to employment with the new company were covered under its welfare benefits plan without an interruption in coverage since they were covered under the new plan upon the termination of the ARM plan.

In the Agreement, ARM and PRM/MMI attached one condition to each employee's automatic transfer to employment with the latter company: In order to be eligible for transfer, the employee had to be actively employed by ARM (i.e., "at work") on the day of the sale or on non-medical, nonextended leave from active employment. However, the Agreement excepted from the condition employees who were on vacation or who had taken a personal day and thus were not "at work" on February 1. If an employee was on medical, disability, workers' compensation or other extended leave at the time of the sale, such employee would become eligible for transfer only "if and when he or she returns to active employment." Section 7.2(a) of the Agreement in fact provided a separate transfer "schedule" for employees, such as Lessard, who were on medical or other extended leave on the day of the sale. ARM automatically transferred roughly 250 employees to PRM/MMI with the rest of its business assets, leaving only six employees to conform to the requirements of this special schedule: three, including Lessard, on workers' compensation leave; two on maternity leave; and one on leave of absence to prepare for a bar examination.

PRM/MMI has stipulated that if any of these employees were to return to work, that employee would be given a position with PRM including full medical benefits. Lessard understood that she could become an employee of PRM/MMI if she were released to work. However, as of September 29, 2000, Lessard still had not been released to return to work by any physician, and the prognosis for her future return to full-time employment is poor.

[Lessard initially sued under the Americans with Disabilities Act, a claim the district court dismissed for failure to exhaust administrative remedies. Lessard proceeded with an ERISA § 510 claim, but the district court granted the defendants' motion for summary judgment, and Lessard appealed. — ED.]

III. ANALYSIS

The purpose of section 510 is to "prevent persons and entities from taking actions which might cut off or interfere with a participant's ability to collect present or future benefits or which punish a participant for exercising his or her rights under an employee benefit plan." Tolle v. Carroll Touch, Inc., 977 F.2d 1129, 1134 (7th Cir. 1992). . . . The Supreme Court has described an employer's discharge of an employee, who had worked for the company for over nine years, four months before his pension would have vested as the "prototypical" type of claim that Congress intended to cover under section 510. Ingersoll-Rand Co. v. McClendon, 498 U.S. 133, 143 (1990). With respect to non-vesting welfare benefits, we follow a general rule that "[e]mployers or other plan sponsors are generally free under ERISA, for any reason at any time, to adopt, modify, or terminate welfare plans." Curtiss-Wright Corp. v. Schoonejongen, 514 U.S. 73 (1995). However, as the Supreme Court stated in Inter-Modal Rail Employees Ass'n v. Atchison, Topeka & Santa Fe Ry. Co., 520 U.S. 510 (1997), the "right that an employer or plan sponsor may enjoy in some circumstances to unilaterally amend or eliminate its welfare benefit plan does not. . . justify a departure from § 510's plain language." *Id.* at 515.

The facts of this case are not typical since both a buyer and a seller are involved. There would be no question of ARM's liability if, without selling its assets to PRM/MMI, ARM had simply decided to retain the plan but terminate six of its employees absent for reasons of injury or illness on February 1, 1999, terminate their benefits, and attach as a condition of the reinstatement of their benefits that they return to full-time, active employment. As section 510 clearly states, it is a violation of federal law for an employer to "discharge" an employee or otherwise to "discriminate against a participant or beneficiary for exercising any right to which he is entitled under the provisions of an employee benefit plan." 29 U.S.C. § 1140. ARM and PRM/MMI excluded the six employees who were on extended leave from the normal, or automatic, transfer schedule that included the vast majority of former ARM employees and placed them on a separate, deferred schedule. Once placed on this deferred schedule, these employees were presumptively discharged unless and until they complied with the companies' express condition that they return to active employment. ARM acting alone would not have been permitted to terminate the benefits of a select group of employees — most of whom were high-rate users of the company's Plan — because those employees were on medical leave and to offer those employees reinstatement of benefits only on the condition that they return to work. Nor would ARM have been permitted to terminate benefits in a way that guaranteed that employees with the worst disabilities would get the worst deal. It could not structure an agreement whose foreseeable effect is that an employee who took a leave of absence because of a bad flu could return to work with only minor difficulty and thereby resume coverage, but an employee with a major health problem could not. The same single action, jointly agreed upon and executed by the two companies, just as certainly constitutes a violation of section 510.

Defendants argue that the asset sale was in itself a neutral action, and that the injury of which Lessard complains was caused by her own refusal or inability to return to work. In short, defendants deny that Lessard has put forth sufficient evidence to establish their "specific intent to interfere with [her] benefit rights." Ritter v. Hughes Aircraft Co., 58 F.3d 454, 457 (9th Cir. 1995). . . .

Here, Lessard's proof of discrimination is direct and uncontroverted. Section 7.2(a) of the Agreement facially discriminates against employees who were on disability, workers' compensation, and any other form of extended leave, explicitly excepting from its separate schedule for conditional transfer any employee who was absent from work due to vacation, holiday, or personal reasons. At the time the companies executed the Agreement, they knew that five of the six employees placed on the deferred schedule were on some form of medical leave or disability-related leave. We find that this conduct constitutes discrimination on its face.

The fact that Lessard, by returning to work, could have reinstituted her coverage under the new PRM/MMI plan is of no moment. Whether Lessard or defendants are more liable for the permanence of her predicament does not change the fact that she was placed in this predicament by the defendants' conduct. Whether there were any other former employees of ARM who were high-rate users of Plan benefits before the sale and who were automatically transferred to work for PRM/MMI is also inconsequential, because the fact that defendants may not have discriminated against other high-rate users of Plan benefits does not excuse their intentional discrimination against Lessard. Again, Lessard's case does not rely upon circumstantial evidence from which a causal connection must be deduced. Absence from work due to disability or medical leave is a clear, even if incomplete, proxy for high rate of use of health benefits. The fact that the companies could have been more inclusive in their targeting of high-rate users does not make them any less liable here.

. . . The only question that remains is the extent of each defendant's liability. Ordinarily "a corporation which purchases the assets of another corporation does not thereby become liable for the selling corporation's obligations." Harry G. Henn & John R. Alexander, Laws of Corporations 967 (3d ed. 1983). However, courts make exceptions for corporate mergers fraudulently executed to avoid the predecessor's liabilities, *id.*, or for transactions where the purchaser has specified which liabilities it intends to assume, *see* Chaveriat v. Williams Pipe Line Co., 11 F.3d 1420, 1425 (7th Cir. 1993). On remand, the district court is directed to award judgment in favor of Lessard, the extent of each defendant's liability and the amount of damages to be determined in further proceedings.

NOTES AND QUESTIONS

1. Imagine some other ways ARM and PRM might have structured this transaction. First, suppose ARM sold its assets to PRM and terminated its plan without making any particular arrangement for the continued employment of the workforce. PRM then hired its own workforce, inviting former ARM employees to file job applications on the same basis as non-ARM applicants. PRM hired only applicants ready to work within the next week, and rejected applicants like Lessard (if she applied) who were unable to work that week. Would ARM or PRM have violated ERISA? Would either company have violated the Americans with Disabilities Act? Whether this arrangement would be a wise, aside from the requirements of ERISA or the ADA, would depend on the importance of continuity and morale of the workforce in an ongoing business. Moreover, across the board termination of employees (subject to the possibility of rehire on an individual basis) may create problems for the buyer and seller of a business under the WARN Act. See Chapter 8, Section D.3.b.

2. Alternatively, suppose ARM sold its business to PRM, and Lessard recovered in time to qualify for a job with PRM. PRM, however, chose not to offer medical insurance or disability benefits. Would this arrangement have violated ERISA? Consider West v. Greyhound Corp., 813 F.2d 951 (9th Cir. 1987), holding, "a purchaser of assets is under no obligation to hire employees of a predecessor and is free to set the initial terms of employment for these employees should it decide to hire them." *Id.* at 955. Again, whether the denial of benefits to all employees across the board would be a wise business decision would depend on the effect of such an action on employee morale and retention.

3. Suppose ARM decided not to sell the business but to reduce benefit costs by amending its plan in a way that affected Lessard more than any other employee — perhaps by excluding coverage for the particular medical condition she suffered. Would such an action have violated ERISA?

Consider McGann v. H&H Music Co., 946 F.2d 401 (5th Cir. 1991), where the employer, upon learning its employee McGann had AIDS, amended its plan to limit AIDS coverage. McGann alleged that the amendment constituted discrimination and interference under section 510. The court rejected his claim:

> Although we assume . . . a connection between the benefits reduction and either McGann's filing of claims or his revelations about his illness, there is nothing in the record to suggest that defendants' motivation was other than as they asserted, namely to avoid the expense of paying for AIDS treatment (if not, indeed, also for other treatment), no more for McGann than for any other . . . beneficiary who might suffer from AIDS. McGann concedes that the reduction in AIDS benefits will apply equally to all employees filing AIDS-related claims and that the effect of the reduction will not necessarily be felt only by him. He fails to allege that the coverage reduction was otherwise specifically intended to deny him particularly medical coverage except "in effect." He does not challenge defendants' assertion that their purpose in reducing AIDS benefits was to reduce costs.
>
> . . . To adopt McGann's contrary construction of . . . section 510 would mean that an employer could not effectively reserve the right to amend a medical plan to reduce benefits respecting subsequently incurred medical expenses, as H & H Music did here, because such an amendment would obviously have as a purpose preventing participants from attaining the right to such future benefits as they otherwise might do under the existing plan absent the amendment. But this is plainly not the law, and ERISA does not require such "vesting" of the right to a continued level of the same medical benefits once those are ever included in a welfare plan.

946 F.2d at 404-405. In response to McGann's argument that the amendment was designed to discriminate on the basis of AIDS, the court replied:

> Section 510 does not mandate that if some, or most, or virtually all catastrophic illnesses are covered, AIDS (or any other particular catastrophic illness) must be among them. It does not prohibit an employer from electing not to cover or continue to cover AIDS, while covering or continuing to cover other catastrophic illnesses, even though the employer's decision in this respect may stem from some "prejudice" against AIDS or its victims generally. . . . That sort of "discrimination" is simply not

addressed by section 510.

Id. at 408.

One might well ask whether discrimination not prohibited by ERISA might be illegal under some other law, such as the Americans with Disabilities Act or the Age Discrimination in Employment Act. The effect of these and other laws on an employer's discrimination in providing benefits is the subject of Section D.2.f.

4. As noted earlier, ERISA requires a plan to have a benefits review procedure. The courts have generally required that if a plan creates such a procedure, the participant or beneficiary must exhaust this procedure before seeking judicial review of the plan's denial of a benefit claim. Should this requirement of exhaustion of internal plan remedies apply to a claim under section 510, even if it involves discharge from employment? *See* Counts v. American General Life and Acc. Ins. Co.,111 F.3d 105 (11th Cir. 1997) (holding "yes," but describing contrary view of other courts).

5. The usual remedies for unlawful retaliatory or discriminatory discharge under other employment laws are back pay, other compensatory damages and, if the plaintiff wants, reinstatement. In the case of section 510, however, the remedies for unlawful discharge are uncertain. Section 510 does not state any particular remedies. Instead, it says that the provisions of 29 U.S.C. § 1132 "shall be applicable in the enforcement of this section." But section 1132 deals primarily with enforcement of rights with to benefits. It says nothing directly about unlawful discharge or other adverse employment actions. If an employee lost benefits because of an unlawful employment action, he might seek "benefits due" under section 1132(a)(1). If he lost his job, he might seek reinstatement under section 1132(a)(3), which authorizes an action for "appropriate *equitable* relief." But the availability of compensatory damages or punitive damages is uncertain because section 1132 does not specifically authorize individual monetary relief except in the form of "benefits" due or as an "equitable" remedy,

Millsap v. McDonnell Douglas Corp., 368 F.3d 1246 (10th Cir. 2004) illustrates the problem for section 510 plaintiffs. In *Millsap*, the district court found that the employer's decision to close the plant where the plaintiffs worked was discriminatory under section 510. On appeal, the Tenth Circuit held that ERISA provided no remedy for the plaintiffs. The lower court had found, and the plaintiffs evidently had conceded, that injunctive relief was not appropriate to reopen the plant or to require the plaintiffs' reinstatement. The plaintiffs sought only back pay. Whether the plaintiffs were entitled to back pay depended on whether back pay is "appropriate equitable relief." The court held that back pay is a form of damages, not equitable relief. The court conceded that an equitable remedy such as reinstatement might include back pay, based on a principle that an award of damages is sometimes intertwined with and part of an equitable remedy. In this case, however, the plaintiffs conceded they were not seeking reinstatement or any equitable remedy aside from back pay. Thus, despite the employer's violation, the act offered the plaintiffs no remedy.

PROBLEM

Waiverly Disposal, Inc., established a severance pay plan funded general company assets. The plan provided that "employees involuntarily terminated without cause will receive one week's pay for every year of employment."

Starting about two years ago Waiverly began experiencing a severe business downturn. With little prospect of business conditions improving in the short term, Waiverly decided to begin laying off employees. Waiverly selected employees for layoff according to a mixture of factors including job performance evaluations and seniority (recently hired employees were more likely to be laid off). Laid-off employees received severance benefits under the severance pay plan, but most of the employees Waiverly selected were those with only a few years of tenure, and the severance payments they received were not large. Regrettably, this round of layoffs was not sufficient to return Waiverly to profitability.

Al Middleton had worked for Waiverly Disposal for over 30 years when the first round of layoffs occurred. Over the years, his performance evaluations ranged from "satisfactory" to "exceeds expectations." In the past two years all his evaluations have been "satisfactory," a middle rating. When the layoffs began, he believed his long tenure would protect him. However, at Middleton's most recent job review with his supervisor, the supervisor informed Middelton that the company was going to terminate his employment for "substandard employment" based on the last six months of work. "In this business environment," the supervisor explained, "we just can't keep employees who are barely marginal."

The supervisor escorted Middleton to the human resources office, where a human resources manager made him an offer: "There's no severance pay for employees discharged for cause. However, if you'll sign a release of claims against the company, we'll treat this as a layoff. Then you can get severance pay, which for you is 30 weeks' pay — $30,000 — plus accrued vacation."

The human resources manager presented him a release of claims stating that "employee hereby acknowledges that he is not entitled to any severance pay under the company's severance pay plan," and that "in consideration for the company's payment of $30,000, employee hereby waives any and all claims arising out of his employment with the company." Middleton didn't think his performance was that bad and pleaded for reconsideration. The human resources manager, however, stood firm. Although Middleton believed he was being treated unfairly, he also feared he would be unable to make ends meet if he rejected the offer. He signed the waiver and accepted the severance pay check.

Middleton came to your office two days later for advice and to see whether he has any rights. He believes the company may have discriminated against him based on his age (55) and wonders if the waiver can really stop him from suing. Considering only what you learned in this chapter, what advice should you give?

e. Discrimination in Benefits

i. ERISA's Nondiscrimination Rules

Tax-supported public welfare benefit systems such as Social Security, Medicare, and unemployment compensation provide broad, mandatory coverage for the vast majority of workers, but offer a minimal level of benefits. Access to greater benefits sufficient to support a worker's lifestyle upon retirement, disability, or a medical crisis depends mainly on private insurance or financial services. Most workers depend on employers for access such benefits, but employers need not offer them (subject to implementation, as to health insurance, of the Patient Protection and Affordable Care Act for many employers).

In the absence of a benefit mandate, why do some employers provide pension benefits? Why not simply pay employees the cash value of benefits and leave it to employees to purchase what they desire in the outside market? From the employer's point of view, providing benefits can be more expensive than paying additional wages because of the cost of managing a plan and complying with ERISA. Administrative overhead costs might be particularly significant for small employers who cannot easily spread these costs over a large number of plan participants. Thus, it might seem as if the employer and its employees would be better off simply paying and receiving cash wages.

Nevertheless, there are a variety of reasons why employers first began to adopt benefits plans for employees beginning over a century ago. Some employers might first have adopted benefits plans out of paternalistic concern for employees, fearing employees might otherwise neglect to obtain adequate insurance against old age or illness. Some employers might have offered benefits to persuade employees that labor unions were unnecessary to provide pensions and insurance. And some may have offered benefits to circumvent war-time wage controls that prohibited wage increases but not benefit increases. Today, an employer might establish a welfare plan to attract or retain certain kinds of employees or to induce certain behavior. Stable, family-oriented employees might be more likely to accept employment with an employer who provides family medical insurance, disability insurance, and life insurance. Women might be more likely to accept employment with an employer with generous parental leave policies. A generous pension plan might encourage older workers to retire voluntarily to make way for a new generation of employees.

None of these historical motivations, standing alone, would likely suffice to cause the fairly broad pension and medical insurance coverage enjoyed by employees in the private sector in modern times. A more powerful and likely set of incentives, in the absence of mandated coverage, have been tax advantages.

Tax advantages begin with the simple fact that the value of qualified benefits is not subject to payroll taxes for social security or unemployment compensation insurance. Thus, if an employer can choose between paying an employee an additional $1,000 in salary or $1,000 in medical insurance, the employer and employee might observe that the additional salary will be subject to payroll taxes of around $200, but the value of additional insurance will not.

Second, medical insurance benefits are not included in an employee's taxable income. In other words, medical insurance benefits are a form of tax-free income to the employee, but the employer is still entitled to deduct the cost of insurance, just as it deducts the cost of any other employee compensation.

Third, income taxes are deferred on pension benefits. Instead of paying taxes when the employee "accrues" or the employer contributes such benefits, the employee ordinarily pays taxes only when he retires and actually receives the benefits, The deferral of taxation can be especially advantageous if the employee or the plan is able to reinvest fund earnings during the period of deferral, or if the employee's taxable income and rate of taxation are lower after retirement.

One might ask why an employer is so strongly motivated to establish benefit plans if the tax advantages are enjoyed predominantly by employees and not by the employer. One answer is that employees who are the employer's decision makers may want these tax advantages for themselves. The decision makers, who are also likely to be the most highly compensated employees, stand to gain the most from benefit plans. However, in the case of pension benefits, a plan is not qualified for tax advantages unless the plan complies with a "nondiscrimination" in coverage rule, IRC § 410(b), and a nondiscrimination in contributions or benefits rule, IRC § 401(a)(4). These nondiscrimination rules operate in a distinctly different manner than other employment discrimination laws. The rules are designed to discourage discrimination that favors "highly compensated employees" in comparison with "non-highly compensated employees," but they do not prohibit intentional discrimination per se. Instead, the nondiscrimination rules depend on tests that resemble a theory of disparate impact. In essence, a qualified pension plan must pass a series of statistical tests to determine whether highly compensated employees enjoy a disproportionate benefit in comparison with non-highly compensated employees. If a pension plan fails these tests, it will not qualify for favorable tax treatment and there may be other adverse consequences.

Nondiscrimination in Coverage. Compliance with the nondiscrimination in coverage rule requires a comparison of highly compensated employees with those who are not highly compensated. A highly compensated employee is one who (1) was a 5 percent or greater owner during the year in question or the preceding year; *or* (2) received a certain minimum compensation (indexed for inflation), and, if the employer elects, was among the top 20 percent of employees ranked by compensation for the year in question. IRC § 414(q).

A pension plan is qualified under the nondiscriminatory coverage rule if it satisfies either of two separate tests. The "ratio percentage test" is the simplest. A plan's "ratio percentage" is the proportion of non-highly compensated employees who benefit under the plan, divided by the proportion of highly compensated employees who benefit under the plan. The ratio percentage must be at least 70 percent. IRC § 410(b)(1)(B); 26 C.F.R. § 1.410(b)-2. For example, if a plan covers 100 percent of the employer's highly compensated employees, it must cover at least 70 percent of non-highly compensated employees. If a plan covers 50 percent of highly compensated employees, it must cover at least 35 percent of non-highly compensated employees. If a pension plan fails to satisfy the ratio percentage test, it might nevertheless qualify under the much more complicated "average benefits percentage test," which considers a number of additional factors. IRC § 410(b)(2).

The nondiscrimination in coverage rule is one more reason why an employer might classify some low paid workers as something other than "employees," in order to prevent their inclusion in the tests of discriminatory coverage. Thus, the employer might classify some low paid workers as "independent contractors" who do not count under the nondiscrimination rules (unless they are misclassified and are really "employees"). Alternatively, an employer might "lease" low paid workers from a staffing service. However, leasing employees does not necessarily place them outside the employer's workforce for purposes of the nondiscrimination rules. The rules provide that leased employees still count as employees of the lessee employer *unless* they receive a certain level of benefits from the staffing service (in which case they are the employees of the staffing service and not of the lessee employer. IRC § 414(n)(1),

Nondiscrimination in Contributions or Benefits. Even if a pension plan satisfies the nondiscrimination rules with respect to coverage, the plan might still discriminate with respect to the *amount* of benefits paid to different types of employees. Therefore, a separate set of tests limits discrimination with respect to the level of benefits paid to highly compensated employees versus non-highly compensated employees. IRC § 401(a)(4). Again, the details of these tests are quite complex and are summarized here only in very general terms.

The simplest way for an employer to satisfy the nondiscrimination rules is to make contributions to each employee's pension account based on the same percentage of compensation, the same dollar amount, or the same dollar amount per uniform unit of service. 26 C.F.R. § 1.401(a)(4)-2(b)(2). For pension plans not based on employer contributions to individual accounts, there are alternative but much more complex tests of nondiscrimination. And finally, no matter what kind of pension plan an employer establishes, participant rights, plan amendments and plan terminations must be nondiscriminatory.

An important limitation of the nondiscrimination rules is that they do not apply to welfare benefits, such as medical insurance. Thus, an employer can offer medical insurance to highly compensated employees and deny these benefits to other employees. However, the Patient Protection and Affordable Care Act of 2010 will operate in some ways like a nondiscrimination rule if and when certain provisions take effect in 2014. Under the PPACA, employers will be required to offer a minimum level of medical insurance to all "full-time employees" and their "dependents" in order to avoid the imposition of certain fees. 26 U.S.C. § 4980H. The PPACA will permit an employer to offer all or some employees more than the minimum benefits required by the PPACA, but such "excess" benefits may be subject to an excise tax. 26 U.S.C. § 4980I.

ii. The Other Employment Discrimination Laws

An employer might seem to offer equal benefits for all employees but discriminate in subtle ways, particularly with respect to the conditions or events covered by a plan, or with respect to the treatments or services for which the plan offers reimbursement. The exclusion of a condition, event or service may affect one group of employees more than another. However, even if an exclusion seems unfair, remember that ERISA does not require an employer to put the interests of employees ahead of its own business interests. An employer is not a fiduciary with respect to its design and establishment of a plan, and it might lawfully exclude certain conditions or services simply to save money.

The problem of discriminatory exclusion of conditions or services is illustrated by McGann v. H&H Music Co., 946 F.2d 401 (5th Cir. 1991), where the employer amended a medical insurance plan to restrict benefits for the treatment of AIDS. The *McGann* case is described in greater detail in part D.2.e of this chapter. Managers who approve such an exclusion might be biased against the affected group, or might simply believe that the excluded condition is not one they will suffer and that it is better to conserve funds for other conditions that worry them personally. In general, ERISA does not prohibit discriminatory exclusions except as to certain maternity and newborn care, mental health and addiction services, and reconstructive surgery following a mastectomy. 29 U.S.C. §§1185-1185b.

Three other employment discrimination laws limit discrimination in employee benefits: (1) Title VII, particularly its prohibition against "sex discrimination," which includes pregnancy discrimination; (2) the Age Discrimination in Employment Act, and (3) the Americans with Disabilities Act. Of these three, Title VII has the most important effect on benefit plan coverage.

These three laws once formed the main bulwark against discriminatory exclusion of benefits that were based on membership in a protected class or that disproportionately and adversely affected a protected class (such as a denial of coverage for birth control pills). Since 2014, however, the Patient Protection and Affordable Care Act (PPACA) has served as the broadest and most important protection against discriminatory coverage of medical insurance plans. The PPACA provides that an employer's provision of health benefits will not satisfy the requirements of the act unless it includes an "essential health benefits package" as determined by the Secretary of Health and Human Services. 42 U.S.C. §§18021-18024; *see also* 29 U.S.C. § 1185 (standards relating to benefits for mothers and newborns); § 1185a (parity in application of certain limits to mental health benefits); § 1185b (required coverage for reconstructive surgery after mastectomy).

In this way the PPACA has mooted many of the issues regarding what constitutes illegal discrimination in an employer's *medical insurance* plan for employees. Tovar v. Essentia Health, 857 F.3d 771 (8th Cir. 2017) (employee stated claim under Patient Protection and Affordable Care Act for denial of coverage of dependent child's sex reassignment surgery even if denial of coverage did not constitute "sex discrimination"). But Title VII, the Age Discrimination in Employment Act, and the Americans with Disabilities Act still serve a vital function in preventing discrimination in *other* types of benefit plans and policies.

Title VII (Sex and Pregnancy Discrimination). An employer would clearly violate Title VII if it simply excluded women or any other protected group from participation in a plan. An employer would also violate Title VII if it segregated employees into separate risk pools based on protected characteristics, such as by offering women smaller pensions or requiring them to contribute more earnings to account for the longer expected lifespan of women. *See* City of Los Angeles Dep't of Water & Power v. Manhart, 435 U.S. 702 (1978). A more complicated question is whether an employer can lawfully exclude coverage of conditions or services that might be more important to women than to men, or vice versa.

In an early Title VII sex discrimination case, General Electric Co. v. Gilbert, 429 U.S. 125 (1976), the Supreme Court considered whether an employer discriminated on the basis of sex by offering disability benefits that excluded disability caused by pregnancy. The court concluded that the denial of disability benefits for pregnancy did not constitute illegal sex discrimination. "For all that appears," the Court concluded, "pregnancy-related disabilities constitute an additional risk, unique to women, and the failure to compensate them for this risk does not destroy the presumed parity of the benefits, accruing to men and women alike, which results from the facially evenhanded inclusion of risks." 429 U.S. at

139. In other words, under *General Electric* an employer's benefit plan could lawfully exclude coverage of risks or conditions unique to women.

Congress acted quickly to overrule *General Electric* with the Pregnancy Discrimination Act of 1978. First, the PDA amended Title VII to provide that prohibited discrimination "because of sex" includes discrimination "because of or on the basis of pregnancy, childbirth, or related medical conditions." 42 U.S.C. § 2000e(k). Thus, any distinction based on pregnancy is unlawful. But proving discrimination often requires a comparison between the employer's treatment of persons with the protected trait and persons without the protected trait. Comparison is problematic in the case of benefits and exclusions from benefits. With what should "pregnancy, childbirth, or related medical conditions" be compared, for purposes of determining whether coverage or exclusion of pregnancy is illegally discriminatory? The PDA offers the following solution: "women affected by pregnancy, childbirth, or related medical conditions shall be treated the same for all employment-related purposes, including receipt of benefits under fringe benefit programs, as other persons not so affected but similar in their ability or inability to work. . . ." In sum, a disability plan such as the one in *General Electric* is unlawful if it denies benefits for persons disabled by pregnancy while providing benefits for persons "similar in their ability or inability to work."

Surprisingly, the first important case to test the meaning of the PDA involved a claim by *male* employees. In Newport News Shipbuilding & Dry Dock Co. v. EEOC, 462 U.S. 669 (1983), the employer's health benefits plan provided full coverage for pregnancy-related medical costs of employees (necessarily female employees) but provided only limited coverage for pregnancy-related medical costs of *spouses* of employees (necessarily male employees). The Court held that the plan violated Title VII: "[P]etitioner's plan unlawfully gives married male employees a benefit package for their dependents that is less inclusive than the dependency coverage provided to married female employees." *Id.* at 684. The Court also held that *General Electric* was legislatively overruled by the PDA. Thus, it might be enough to prove sex discrimination simply to show that a benefit plan or policy makes distinctions related to conditions unique to one sex or offers benefits more inclusive or generous for one sex as a class than the other. Proving sex discrimination in this way might be important in a case that does not qualify as "pregnancy" discrimination. *See* In re Union Pac. R.R. Employment Practices Litig., 479 F.3d 936 (8th Cir. 2007) (majority holding that denial of contraception coverage is not "pregnancy" or "sex discrimination;" dissent arguing that denial of coverage was "sex discrimination" even if it was not "pregnancy discrimination").

The Age Discrimination in Employment Act. Age discrimination can be another issue in the design of benefits plans, particularly because the costs of some benefits are so closely associated with the age of the beneficiary, and because the needs of older workers may be very different from the needs of younger workers. For example, life insurance for a 75-year-old employee is very expensive and usually unnecessary. Life insurance for a 30-year-old employee is much less expensive, and her needs for insurance could be much greater. If an employer could not provide life insurance benefits for the young employee without providing equal benefits for the older employee, it might well choose to provide no benefits at all. The Older Workers' Benefit Protection Act, amending the Age Discrimination in

Employment Act, addresses this problem by providing that it shall not constitute unlawful age discrimination for an employer "to observe the terms of a bona fide employee benefit plan . . . where, for each benefit or benefit package, the actual amount of payment made or cost incurred on behalf of an older worker is no less than that made or incurred on behalf of a younger worker. . . ." 29 U.S.C. § 623(f)(2); *see also* 29 C.F.R. § 1625.10; 29 U.S.C. §§ 623(*l*)(2), (3) (permitting reduction of severance pay and disability benefits for employees receiving retirement benefits).

The Americans with Disabilities Act. A health plan's exclusion for some medical conditions but not others might be viewed as discrimination on the basis of disability if an excluded condition is a protected disability under the Americans with Disabilities Act. However, the ADA provides that "[T]his act shall not be construed to prohibit or restrict . . . a person or organization covered by this chapter from establishing, sponsoring, observing or administering the terms of a bona fide benefit plan that are based on *underwriting risks, classifying risks, or administering such risks* that are based on or not inconsistent with State law. 42 U.S.C. § 12201(c) (emphasis added). The act further states that this provision "shall not be used as a subterfuge to evade the purposes" of the act. 42 U.S.C. § 12201(c).

The extent to which this inscrutable provision authorizes disability-based distinctions in coverage remains a matter in dispute. One thing is certain. If an employer's health plan denies an employee participation or coverage because the employee has a protected disability (e.g., the plan does not include any person who has AIDS), or the plan admits such an employee but charges that employee a higher premium or subjects that employee to other discriminatory terms because of the employee's disability, the plan violates the ADA. *See* EEOC Compliance Manual, Chapter Three, *Employee Benefits: ADA Issues* (Transmittal Date Oct. 2000), at http://www.eeoc.gov/policy/compliance.html; *see also* 29 U.S.C. § 1182 (HIPAA provision prohibiting discrimination based on "health status").

The disagreement between the EEOC and some courts relates to a separate question: Assuming a plan provides all employees coverage regardless of disability, can it deny coverage or limit benefits for certain conditions? For example, could it deny coverage of medical expenses related to AIDS or diabetes? This issue has been mooted and possibly preempted to a significant degree by enactment of the PPACA, which, as noted above, requires insurance policies to provide minimum coverages and prohibits most discriminatory exclusions.

3. Retirement and Welfare Benefits: State Law Rights and Remedies

Some federal employment laws establish minimum standards for the protection of employees but allow the states to enact duplicate laws or laws providing a higher standard of protection and additional remedies. *See, e.g.*, Fair Labor Standards Act, 29 U.S.C. § 218 (permitting states to enact higher minimum wages or shorter maximum workweeks). Not ERISA. ERISA is broadly preemptive of state law. Subject to a few exceptions, ERISA "shall supersede any and all State laws insofar as they may now or hereafter *relate to* any [nonexempt] employee benefit plan. . . ." 29 U.S.C. § 1144 (emphasis added).

ERISA's "relate to" rule of preemption bars the application of a wide variety of state laws in circumstances involving ERISA plans. . State laws of general application for contracts, property, family relations, or torts may be preempted by ERISA insofar as any party asserts the law in connection with the administration of an ERISA plan. *See, e.g.*, Pilot Life Ins. Co. v. Dedeaux, 481 U.S. 41 (1987) (ERISA preemption barred plaintiff's complaint alleging various state tort law claims, including "tortious breach of contract," based on defendant insurer's failure to pay benefits allegedly due under disability benefits plan); Egelhoff v. Egelhoff, 532 U.S. 141 (2001) (state law automatically revoking, upon divorce, designation of spouse as beneficiary, was preempted insofar as it applied to ERISA plans); Boggs v. Boggs, 520 U.S. 833 (1997) (ERISA preempted state community property laws to the extent they would allow participant's first wife to make testamentary transfer of her interest in survivor's annuity).

Ironically, ERISA's preemption provision can have the effect of negating some misguided state efforts to avoid conflict between state law and ERISA. In Macky v. Lanier Collection Agency & Serv., Inc., 486 U.S. 825 (1988), for example, the Court found that ERISA preempted a provision of state garnishment law that *exempted* ERISA plan benefits from garnishment orders. The Court held that neither ERISA in general nor the preemption provision in particular prevented the garnishment of plan benefits. Thus, the state law went too far in granting special rights or protection with respect to ERISA plan benefits.

Still, the Supreme Court has warned that the phrase "relate to" in 29 U.S.C. § 1144 does not extend preemption "to the furthest stretch of its indeterminacy." New York State Conf. of Blue Cross & Blue Shield Plans v. Travelers Ins. Co., 514 U.S. 645 (1995) Otherwise, "for all practical purposes pre-emption would never run its course." *Id.* Thus, ERISA does not preempt a state law "if the state law has only a tenuous, remote, or peripheral connection with covered plans." Dist. of Columbia v. Greater Wash. Bd. of Trade, 506 U.S. 125, 130 n.1 (1992).

ERISA's broad rule of preemption is bolstered by a particularly forceful application of the procedure for removing ERISA-related lawsuits from state court to federal court. If a plaintiff files an ERISA claim in a state court, the defendant may remove the action to a federal court pursuant to the usual "federal question" removal law. 28 U.S.C. § 1441(b). Removal is possible even as to a claim for which a state court has concurrent jurisdiction, such as a claim for "benefits due" under an ERISA plan. *Id.* § 1132(e)(1). But what if a plaintiff's complaint states a claim exclusively under state law or otherwise avoids a clear connection with ERISA? Under the usual "well-pleaded complaint" rule, a defendant may not remove a case to federal court unless a federal question appears on the face of the plaintiff's complaint, even if federal preemption is a likely defense. Franchise Tax Bd. v. Constr. Laborers Vacation Trust, 463 U.S. 1, 10 (1983). However, ERISA's strong preemption provision results in the application of an important exception to the well-pleaded complaint rule: the "complete preemption" doctrine, which allows a federal court to deem a state law claim to be a federal claim for purposes of removal if the claim relates to a matter as to which Congress intended complete preemption. Metro. Life Ins. Co. v. Taylor, 481 U.S. 58 (1987). Thus, a federal court need only find that a state court action is "within the scope" of ERISA's enforcement provisions to grant a defendant's request to remove the action to federal court. Metro. Life Ins. Co. v. Massachusetts, 471 U.S. 724 (1985).

AETNA HEALTH INC. v. DAVILA

542 U.S. 200 (2004)

Justice THOMAS delivered the opinion of the Court.

In these consolidated cases, two individuals sued their respective health maintenance organizations (HMOs) for alleged failures to exercise ordinary care in the handling of coverage decisions, in violation of a duty imposed by the Texas Health Care Liability Act (THCLA), Tex. Civ. Prac. & Rem. Code Ann. §§ 88.001-88.003 (2004 Supp. Pamphlet). . . .

I

. . . Respondent Juan Davila is a participant, and respondent Ruby Calad is a beneficiary, in ERISA-regulated employee benefit plans. Their respective plan sponsors had entered into agreements with petitioners, Aetna Health Inc. and CIGNA Healthcare of Texas, Inc., to administer the plans. Under Davila's plan . . . Aetna reviews requests for coverage and pays providers, such as doctors, hospitals, and nursing homes, which perform covered services for members; under Calad's plan sponsor's agreement, CIGNA is responsible . . . .

Respondents both suffered injuries allegedly arising from Aetna's and CIGNA's decisions not to provide coverage for certain treatment and services recommended by respondents' treating physicians. Davila's treating physician prescribed Vioxx to remedy Davila's arthritis pain, but Aetna refused to pay for it. Davila did not appeal or contest this decision, nor did he purchase Vioxx with his own resources and seek reimbursement. Instead, Davila began taking Naprosyn, from which he allegedly suffered a severe reaction that required extensive treatment and hospitalization. Calad underwent surgery, and although her treating physician recommended an extended hospital stay, a CIGNA discharge nurse determined that Calad did not meet the plan's criteria for a continued hospital stay. CIGNA consequently denied coverage for the extended hospital stay. Calad experienced postsurgery complications forcing her to return to the hospital. She alleges that these complications would not have occurred had CIGNA approved coverage for a longer hospital stay.

Respondents brought separate suits in Texas state court against petitioners. Invoking THCLA § 88.002(a), respondents argued that petitioners' refusal to cover the requested services violated their "duty to exercise ordinary care when making health care treatment decisions," and that these refusals "proximately caused" their injuries. Petitioners removed the cases to Federal District Courts, arguing that respondents' causes of action fit within the scope of, and were therefore completely pre-empted by, ERISA § 502(a). The respective District Courts agreed, and declined to remand the cases to state court. Because respondents refused to amend their complaints to bring explicit ERISA claims, the District Courts dismissed the complaints with prejudice. [Davila and Calad appealed to the United States Court of Appeals for the Fifth Circuit, which held that ERISA did not preempt the respondents' claims because they sought remedies under Texas law that did not duplicate or fall within the scope of ERISA's remedies.] . . .

II

. . . The purpose of ERISA is to provide a uniform regulatory regime over employee benefit plans. To this end, ERISA includes expansive pre-emption provisions, *see* ERISA § 514, 29 U.S.C. § 1144, which are intended to ensure that employee benefit plan regulation would be "exclusively a federal concern." Alessi v. Raybestos-Manhattan, Inc., 451 U.S. 504, 523 (1981).

ERISA's "comprehensive legislative scheme" includes "an integrated system of procedures for enforcement." [Massachusetts Mut. Life Ins. Co. v. Russell, 473 U.S. 134, 147 (1985).] . . . As the Court said in Pilot Life Ins. Co. v. Dedeaux, 481 U.S. 41 (1987):

> [T]he detailed provisions of § 502(a) set forth a comprehensive civil enforcement scheme that represents a careful balancing of the need for prompt and fair claims settlement procedures against the public interest in encouraging the formation of employee benefit plans. The policy choices reflected in the inclusion of certain remedies and the exclusion of others under the federal scheme would be completely undermined if ERISA-plan participants and beneficiaries were free to obtain remedies under state law that Congress rejected in ERISA. . . .

Therefore, any state-law cause of action that duplicates, supplements, or supplants the ERISA civil enforcement remedy conflicts with the clear congressional intent to make the ERISA remedy exclusive and is therefore pre-empted. The pre-emptive force of ERISA § 502(a) is still stronger. . . . [T]he ERISA civil enforcement mechanism is one of those provisions with such "extraordinary pre-emptive power" that it "converts an ordinary state common law complaint into one stating a federal claim for purposes of the well-pleaded complaint rule." *Metropolitan Life*, 481 U.S., at 65-66. Hence, "causes of action within the scope of the civil enforcement provisions of § 502(a) [are] removable to federal court." *Id.*, at 66.

III

A

ERISA § 502(a)(1)(B) provides:

> A civil action may be brought — (1) by a participant or beneficiary — . . . (B) to recover benefits due to him under the terms of his plan, to enforce his rights under the terms of the plan, or to clarify his rights to future benefits under the terms of the plan. 29 U.S.C. § 1132(a)(1)(B).

This provision is relatively straightforward. If a participant or beneficiary believes that benefits promised to him under the terms of the plan are not provided, he can bring suit seeking provision of those benefits. A participant or beneficiary can also bring suit generically to "enforce his rights" under the plan, or to clarify any of his rights to future benefits. Any dispute over the precise terms of the plan is resolved by a court under a de novo review standard, unless the terms of the plan "giv[e] the administrator or fiduciary discretionary authority to determine eligibility for benefits or to construe the terms of the plan." Firestone Tire & Rubber Co. v. Bruch, 489 U.S. 101 (1989).

It follows that if an individual brings suit complaining of a denial of coverage for medical care, where the individual is entitled to such coverage only because of the terms of an ERISA-regulated employee benefit plan, and where no legal duty (state or federal) independent of ERISA or the plan terms is violated, then the suit falls "within the scope of" ERISA § 502(a)(1)(B). *Metropolitan Life, supra,* at 66. In other words, if an individual, at some point in time, could have brought his claim under ERISA § 502(a)(1)(B), and where there is no other independent legal duty that is implicated by a defendant's actions, then the individual's cause of action is completely pre-empted by ERISA § 502(a)(1)(B).

To determine whether respondents' causes of action fall "within the scope" of ERISA § 502(a)(1)(B), we must examine respondents' complaints, the statute on which their claims are based, and the various plan documents. Davila alleges that Aetna provides health coverage under his employer's health benefits plan. Davila also alleges that after his primary care physician prescribed Vioxx, Aetna refused to pay for it. The only action complained of was Aetna's refusal to approve payment for Davila's Vioxx prescription. Further, the only relationship Aetna had with Davila was its partial administration of Davila's employer's benefit plan.

Similarly, Calad alleges that she receives, as her husband's beneficiary under an ERISA-regulated benefit plan, health coverage from CIGNA. She alleges that she was informed by CIGNA, upon admittance into a hospital for major surgery, that she would be authorized to stay for only one day. She also alleges that CIGNA, acting through a discharge nurse, refused to authorize more than a single day despite the advice and recommendation of her treating physician. Calad contests only CIGNA's decision to refuse coverage for her hospital stay. And, as in Davila's case, the only connection between Calad and CIGNA is CIGNA's administration of portions of Calad's ERISA-regulated benefit plan.

It is clear, then, that respondents complain only about denials of coverage promised under the terms of ERISA-regulated employee benefit plans. Upon the denial of benefits, respondents could have paid for the treatment themselves and then sought reimbursement through a § 502(a)(1)(B) action, or sought a preliminary injunction.

Respondents contend, however, that the complained-of actions violate legal duties that arise independently of ERISA or the terms of the employee benefit plans at issue in these cases. Both respondents brought suit specifically under the THCLA, alleging that petitioners "controlled, influenced, participated in and made decisions which affected the quality of the diagnosis, care, and treatment provided" in a manner that violated "the duty of ordinary care set forth in §§ 88.001 and 88.002." Respondents contend that this duty of ordinary care is an independent legal duty. . . . Because this duty of ordinary care arises independently of any duty imposed by ERISA or the plan terms, the argument goes, any civil action to enforce this duty is not within the scope of the ERISA civil enforcement mechanism.

The duties imposed by the THCLA in the context of these cases, however, do not arise independently of ERISA or the plan terms. The THCLA does impose a duty on managed care entities to "exercise ordinary care when making health care treatment decisions," and makes them liable for damages proximately caused by failures to abide by that duty. § 88.002(a). However, if a managed care entity correctly concluded that, under the terms of the relevant plan, a particular treatment was not covered, the managed care entity's denial of coverage would not be a proximate cause of any injuries arising from the denial. Rather, the failure of the plan itself to cover the requested treatment would be the proximate cause. More significantly, the THCLA clearly states that "[t]he standards in Subsections (a) and (b) create no obligation on the part of the health insurance carrier, health maintenance organization, or other managed care entity to provide to an insured or enrollee treatment which is not covered by the health care plan of the entity." § 88.002(d). Hence, a managed care entity could not be subject to liability under the THCLA if it denied coverage for any treatment not covered by the health care plan that it was administering.

Thus, interpretation of the terms of respondents' benefit plans forms an essential part of their THCLA claim, and THCLA liability would exist here only because of petitioners' administration of ERISA-regulated benefit plans. Petitioners' potential liability under the THCLA . . . , then, derives entirely from the particular rights and obligations established by the benefit plans. . . .

[R]espondents bring suit only to rectify a wrongful denial of benefits promised under ERISA-regulated plans, and do not attempt to remedy any violation of a legal duty independent of ERISA. We hold that respondents' state causes of action fall "within the scope of" ERISA § 502(a)(1)(B), and are therefore completely pre-empted by ERISA § 502 and removable to federal district court. . . .

NOTES AND QUESTIONS

1. The Texas law in *Aetna* authorizes the same remedies typically associated with a tort action. *See, e.g.*, CIGNA Healthcare of Texas, Inc. v. Pybas, 127 S.W.3d 400 (Tex. App. 2004) (upholding award of $3 million for pain and suffering from insurer's failure to arrange for certain medical treatment). In contrast, the prevailing view is that punitive damages and damages for emotional distress, injury to reputation, humiliation, and embarrassment are not available under ERISA. Zimmerman v. Sloss Equipment, Inc., 72 F.3d 822 (10th Cir. 1995).

2. Preemption of state tort law may leave a gap in the regulation of benefits if ERISA fails to provide any federal right or remedy to take the place of state tort law. Should federal courts fill this gap by fashioning a federal "common law" of rights and remedies not specifically enumerated by ERISA? The Supreme Court has sometimes characterized ERISA as "comprehensive" and "carefully integrated," and it has warned that courts should not "tamper with an enforcement scheme crafted with such evident care as the one in ERISA." Massachusetts Mut. Life Ins. v. Russell, 473 U.S. 134 (1985). On the other hand, Firestone Tire & Rubber Co. v. Bruch, 489 U.S. 101 (1989), announced that federal courts should develop a "federal common law" of ERISA. 489 U.S. at 109..

3. One example of a remedy the federal courts have recognized to fill a perceived gap in the text of ERISA is the doctrine of estoppel, for cases in which the employer has misled a beneficiary to his detriment about the terms of a benefit plan. ERISA provides no express provision for the doctrine of estoppel, and preemption bars the application of state rules of estoppel. Nevertheless, some courts have applied a federal law version of estoppel based on ERISA's imposition of "fiduciary duties" on plan administrators. *See, e.g.*, CIGNA Corp. v. Amara,

563 U.S. 421 (2011). *See generally* part D.2.d of this Chapter.

4. Another gap in ERISA's omission of a statement of remedies for employer "interference" in violation of section 510, 29 U.S.C. § 1140, such as by discharging an employee in retaliation for asserting rights under ERISA or preventing the employee's attainment of benefit rights. Back pay would be the usual remedy to make an unlawfully discharged employee whole. ERISA does not expressly authorize "back pay." Instead, it authorizes "appropriate equitable relief," and there is some question as to when back pay qualifies as equitable relief instead of compensatory damages. See part D.2.e of this Chapter, *supra*.

5. An important exception to ERISA preemption is that "nothing in this subchapter [ERISA] shall be construed to exempt or relieve any person from any law of any State which regulates insurance, banking, or securities." Thus, if a plan provides benefits by purchasing insurance or by investing assets with a financial institution, the insurer or financial institution remains within the normal reach of state insurance, banking or securities law. Of course, nearly any benefits plan resembles a form of insurance or financial investment. The allowance for state regulation might have swallowed the whole preemption provision but for a proviso also known as the "deemer clause" that "[n]either [a nonexempt] . . . employee benefit plan . . . nor any trust established under such a plan, shall be deemed to be an insurance company or other insurer, bank, trust company, or investment company or to be engaged in the business of insurance or banking for purposes of any law of any State purporting to regulate insurance companies, insurance contracts, banks, trust companies, or investment companies." 29 U.S.C. § 1144(b)(2)(A). In other words, only the insurance company or financial institution that sells insurance or financial investments to the plan, and not the plan itself, is subject to state regulation. An employer can avoid the application of state insurance regulation altogether by "self-insuring" instead of purchasing insurance, even if the employer employs an independent insurance company to serve as the administrator by receiving and deciding claims for benefits.

6. Another important exception to ERISA coverage or preemption is for a "plan maintained solely for the purpose of complying with applicable workmen's compensation laws. . . ." 29 U.S.C. § 1003(b)(3). Like a health plan, workers' compensation insurance provides coverage for medical expenses; and like a disability insurance plan, workers' compensation insurance replaces income an employee loses as the result of disability. However, workers' compensation covers only medical expenses and disabilities caused by a work-related accident. ERISA's exception for traditional workers' compensation plans leaves such plans within the domain of state law. Workers' compensation is a subject of Chapter 5.

7. Divorce frequently touches on interests in ERISA plans. It may not be possible for a court to divide marital property without some division of one spouse's interests in an ERISA plan, but doing so necessarily "relates to" an ERISA plan. Thus, ERISA allows one more important exception to the usual rule of ERISA preemption of state law: A state court may issue a "qualified domestic relations order" (QDRO) effectuating a division of benefit plan assets, and a plan administrator must abide by the terms of the QDRO in distributing benefits. 29 U.S.C. § 1056(d)(3). The prevailing view is that an action to enforce a QDRO is "within the scope" of ERISA's causes of actions for plan participants and

beneficiaries. Thus, such an action is subject to the concurrent jurisdiction of state and federal courts, and subject to removal from state to federal court. Jones v. Am. Air., Inc., 57 F. Supp. 2d 1224 (D. Wyo. 1999). Other state law claims asserted in connection with a QDRO are likely preempted. Callahan v. Callahan, 247 F. Supp. 2d 935 (S.D. Ohio 2002) (removing and dismissing petition to hold ex-spouse in contempt under state law for failure to comply with QDRO)

CHAPTER 5

Workplace Safety and Health

A. WORKPLACE SAFETY AND HEALTH AT THE BEGINNING OF THE MODERN REGULATORY ERA

JUDSON MACLAURY, *GOVERNMENT REGULATION OF WORKERS' SAFETY AND HEALTH* 1877-1917[1]

From 1902 to 1907, The Factory Inspector, unofficial journal of the International Association of Factory Inspectors, regularly published accounts gathered by state labor bureaus of industrial accidents. The steel industry produced some of the most violent accidents that this journal reported. At a steel mill in Butler, Pennsylvania, a heavy pot of hot metal spilled molten steel onto wet sand, causing a huge explosion which destroyed part of the plant. Streams of hot metal poured down on the workmen, engulfing and literally cooking some of them. Four men died and 30 more were injured. The explosion shook buildings in the town and caused panic among the populace. . . . Two employees at a steel plant in Youngstown, Ohio were sent to clean out the dust underneath the blast furnaces. Suddenly there was a slippage of tons of molten fuel and ore inside the furnace, causing large amounts of very hot dust to fall on them. One of the men was completely buried in it and died in great agony. The other escaped with severe burns.

Less spectacular but more frequent were the individual tragedies reported in The Factory Inspector resulting from unprotected machinery in a variety of industries. A machinist got his arm caught in a rapidly moving belt. It was jerked from its socket, and he fell 50 feet to the floor. His fellow workers, aghast at the man's shrieks, ran in panic from the shop. A young boy working in a coffin plant was decapitated and had both arms and both legs torn off when he was caught on shafting rotating at 300 revolutions per minute. A worker in a brick-making factory was caught in a belt and had most of his skin torn off. A sawmill worker fell onto a large, unguarded circular saw and was split in two. When a worker got caught in the large flywheel of the main steam power plant of a navy yard, his arms and legs were torn off and the lifeless trunk was hurled against a wall 50 feet away. . . .

The steel industry had come under intense public scrutiny with the formation of the U.S. Steel Corp. and several muckrakers also turned their attention to this industry. . . . Writer William B. Hard . . . estimated that each year 1,200 men were killed or injured out of a work force of about 10,000. He described an accident in which a man was roasted alive by molten slag that spilled from a giant ladle when a hook from an overhead crane carrying it slipped. The ladle lacked proper lugs and the hook had been attached precariously to the rim. Hard argued that U.S. Steel

[1] Available online at http://www.dol.gov/asp/programs/history/mono-regsafeintrotoc.htm.

had ample ability to reduce accidents but lacked strong incentive to do so. When a man was killed on the job, there was only one chance in five that the company would ever have to pay compensation to his survivors. . . .

Immigrant steelworkers were generally willing to put up with the long hours, hard work, and bad conditions as long as they had steady employment. They were usually stuck with the dirtiest, hottest, most hazardous jobs. Steelmaking, dangerous enough for experienced workers, was even more so for these unseasoned peasants. From 1906 to 1910, the accident rates for immigrants at the South Works were double those for English-speakers. Each year, about one-fourth of the immigrant workers were killed or injured on the job. . . .

Crystal Eastman's Work Accidents and the Law, published in 1910[,] . . . [was based] on data gathered on all industrial deaths in the Pittsburgh area for one year [and] accidents for three months, over a thousand cases in all. Investigators tracked down data on the nature of each accident — the cause, who was at fault, economic effects on families, and so on. Mines and railroads were included, but steel mills constituted the largest manufacturing sector. Eastman hoped to find the answers to two questions: what was the true distribution of blame for accidents between workers and employers; and, who bore the brunt of the economic burden of work accidents.

The answer to the second question was fairly clear. Of the 526 deaths in the year of the Pittsburgh Survey, 235 involved survivors. Of those, 53 percent received $100 or less from the employer. Of the 509 workmen injured in a three month period, employers paid hospital costs for 84 percent of them, but only 37 percent received any benefits beyond that, according to Eastman. "In over one-half of the deaths and injuries . . . employers assumed absolutely no share of the inevitable income loss." ... Eastman wrote:

> In work accidents we have a peculiar kind of disaster, by which . . . only wage earners are affected, and which falls upon them in addition to all the disasters that are the common lot.. . . [They] endure not only all the physical torture that comes with injury, but also almost the entire economic loss which inevitably follows it.

. . . At that time, employers commonly believed that around 95 percent of all accidents were due to workers' carelessness. Eastman challenged this conviction with figures showing that, of the 377 accidents covered in the Survey for which fault could be determined, 113, or 30 percent, of them were solely the employers' fault. Further, at most, only 44 percent could be even partially blamed on the victim or fellow workmen.

Shifting the statistical focus somewhat, Eastman made a strong case that even those accidents due to "carelessness" were not very clear-cut. Of the 132 deaths which were found to be the victim's fault, 47 involved very young or inexperienced workers, or those with physical conditions that made them vulnerable. That left 85 experienced, able-bodied victims of "carelessness":

> For the heedless ones, no defense is made. For the inattentive we maintain that human powers of attention, universally limited, are in their case further limited by the conditions under which the work is done — long hours, heat, noise, intense speed. For the reckless ones we maintain that natural

inclination is in their case encouraged and inevitably increased by an occupation involving constant risk.

Regarding the workman who was reckless, not on impulse but in a deliberate effort to cut corners, Eastman wrote in their defense:

> If a hundred times a day a man is required to take necessary risks, it is not in reason to expect him to stop there and never take an unnecessary risk. Extreme caution is as unprofessional among the men in dangerous trades as fear would be in a soldier.

. . . It was difficult under common law principles to prove to a jury that the employer was at fault, and the size of awards varied enormously. As juries became more sympathetic to injured workers, and states, under pressure from organized labor, passed laws making it easier to prove an employer was at fault in an accident, the size and frequency of jury awards to workers increased. To avoid the possibly ruinous injury claims, many companies took out expensive employers' liability insurance. . . .

In 1908 the federal government established a very limited compensation system for its employees which, in combination with the growing movement for compensation as a preventive measure, helped spur the states to action. In May 1911 Wisconsin became the first state to establish a workmen's compensation system. . . . By 1921, 46 jurisdictions had workmen's compensation laws . . . .

B. COMPENSATION FOR WORK-RELATED INJURIES

1. *Introduction: The Workers' Compensation Scheme*

NEW YORK CENTRAL RAILROAD CO. v. WHITE

243 U.S. 188 (1917)

Mr. Justice PITNEY delivered the opinion of the Court:

A proceeding was commenced by [White] before the Workmen's Compensation Commission of the State of New York, established by the Workmen's Compensation Law of that state, to recover compensation from the New York Central & Hudson River Railroad Company for the death of her husband, Jacob White, who lost his life September 2, 1914, through an accidental injury arising out of and in the course of his employment under that company. The Commission awarded compensation in accordance with the terms of the law; its award was affirmed … by the court of appeals . . . .

The errors specified are based upon these contentions: . . . that to award compensation to defendant in error under the provisions of the Workmen's Compensation Law would deprive [the employer] of its property without due process of law, and deny to it the equal protection of the laws, in contravention of the 14th Amendment.

The Workmen's Compensation Law of New York . . . requires every employer subject to its provisions to pay or provide compensation according to a prescribed schedule for the disability or death of his employee resulting from an accidental personal injury arising out of and in the course of the employment, without regard to fault as a cause, except where the injury is occasioned by the wilful intention of the injured employee to bring about the injury or death of himself or of another, or where it results solely from the intoxication of the injured employee while on duty, in which cases neither the injured employee nor any dependent shall receive compensation.

By § 11 the prescribed liability is made exclusive, except that, if an employer fail to secure the payment of compensation as provided in § 50, an injured employee, or his legal representative, in case death results from the injury, may, at his option, elect to claim compensation under the act, or to maintain an action in the courts for damages, and in such an action it shall not be necessary to plead or prove freedom from contributory negligence, nor may the defendant plead as a defense that the injury was caused by the negligence of a fellow servant, that the employee assumed the risk of his employment, or that the injury was due to contributory negligence. Compensation under the act is not regulated by the measure of damages applied in negligence suits, but, in addition to providing surgical, or other like treatment, it is based solely on loss of earning power, being graduated according to the average weekly wages of the injured employee and the character and duration of the disability, whether partial or total, temporary or permanent; while in case the injury causes death, the compensation is known as a death benefit, and includes funeral expenses, not exceeding $100, payments to the surviving wife (or dependent husband) during widowhood (or dependent widowerhood) of a percentage of the average wages of the deceased, and if there be a surviving child or children under the age of eighteen years an additional percentage of such wages for each child until that age is reached.

Provision is made for the establishment of a Workmen's Compensation Commission with administrative and judicial functions, including authority to pass upon claims to compensation . . . . The award or decision of the Commission is made subject to an appeal, on questions of law only. . . .

A fund is created, known as "the state insurance fund," for the purpose of insuring employers against liability under the law, and assuring to the persons entitled the compensation thereby provided. The fund is made up primarily of premiums received from employers, at rates fixed by the Commission in view of the hazards of the different classes of employment, and the premiums are to be based upon the total pay roll and number of employees in each class . . . .

The scheme of the act is so wide a departure from common-law standards respecting the responsibility of employer to employee that doubts naturally have been raised respecting its constitutional validity. The adverse considerations urged or suggested in this case and in kindred cases submitted at the same time are: (a) That the employer's property is taken without due process of law, because he is subjected to a liability for compensation without regard to any neglect or default on his part or on the part of any other person for whom he is responsible, and in spite of the fact that the injury may be solely attributable to the fault of the employee; (b) that the employee's rights are interfered with, in that he is prevented from having compensation for injuries arising from the employer's fault commensurate with the damages actually sustained, and is limited to the measure of compensation prescribed by the act; and (c) that both employer and employee are deprived of their liberty to acquire property by being prevented from making such agreement as they choose respecting the terms of the employment.

In support of the legislation, it is said that the whole common-law doctrine of employer's liability for negligence, with its defenses of contributory negligence, fellow servant's negligence, and assumption of risk, is based upon fictions, and is inapplicable to modern conditions of employment; that in the highly organized and hazardous industries of the present day the causes of accident are often so obscure and complex that in a material proportion of cases it is impossible by any method correctly to ascertain the facts necessary to form an accurate judgment, and in a still larger proportion the expense and delay required for such ascertainment amount in effect to a defeat of justice; that, under the present system, the injured workman is left to bear the greater part of industrial accident loss, which, because of his limited income, he is unable to sustain, so that he and those dependent upon him are overcome by poverty and frequently become a burden upon public or private charity; and that litigation is unduly costly and tedious, encouraging corrupt practices and arousing antagonisms between employers and employees. . . .

The common law bases the employer's liability for injuries to the employee upon the ground of negligence. . . . The fault may be that of the employer himself, or — most frequently — that of another for whose conduct he is made responsible according to the maxim respondeat superior. . . . The immunity of the employer from responsibility to an employee for the negligence of a fellow employee is of comparatively recent origin, it being the product of the judicial conception that the probability of a fellow workman's negligence is one of the natural and ordinary risks of the occupation. . . . . It needs no argument to show that such a rule is subject to modification or abrogation by a state upon proper occasion.

The same may be said with respect to the general doctrine of assumption of risk. By the common law the employee assumes the risks normally incident to the occupation in which he voluntarily engages. . . . Plainly, these rules, as guides of conduct and tests of liability, are subject to change in the exercise of the sovereign authority of the state. So, also, with respect to contributory negligence. Aside from injuries intentionally self-inflicted, for which the statute under consideration affords no compensation, it is plain that the rules of law upon the subject . . . are subject to legislative change. . . .

The statute under consideration sets aside one body of rules only to establish another system in its place. If the employee is no longer able to recover as much as before in case of being injured through the employer's negligence, he is entitled to moderate compensation in all cases of injury, and has a certain and speedy remedy without the difficulty and expense of establishing negligence or proving the amount of the damages. Instead of assuming the entire consequences of all ordinary risks of the occupation, he assumes the consequences, in excess of the scheduled compensation, of risks ordinary and extraordinary.

On the other hand, if the employer is left without defense respecting the question of fault, he at the same time is assured that the recovery is limited, and that it goes directly to the relief of the designated beneficiary. And just as the employee's assumption of ordinary risks at common law presumably was taken into account in fixing the rate of wages, so the fixed responsibility of the employer, and the modified assumption of risk by the employee under the new system, presumably will be reflected in the wage scale. . . .

Reduced to its elements, the situation to be dealt with is this: . . . In the nature of things, there is more or less of a probability that the employee may lose his life through some accidental injury arising out of the employment, leaving his widow or children deprived of their natural support; or that he may sustain an injury not mortal, but resulting in his total or partial disablement, temporary or permanent, with corresponding impairment of earning capacity. . . .

[I]t is not unreasonable for the state, while relieving the employer from responsibility for damages measured by common-law standards and payable in cases where he or those for whose conduct he is answerable are found to be at fault, to require him to contribute a reasonable amount, and according to a reasonable and definite scale, by way of compensation for the loss of earning power incurred in the common enterprise, irrespective of the question of negligence, instead of leaving the entire loss to rest where it may chance to fall, — that is, upon the injured employee or his dependents. . . .

In excluding the question of fault as a cause of the injury, the act in effect disregards the proximate cause and looks to one more remote — the primary cause, as it may be deemed — and that is, the employment itself. . . .

Viewing the entire matter, it cannot be pronounced arbitrary and unreasonable for the state to impose upon the employer the absolute duty of making a moderate and definite compensation in money to every disabled employee . . . , in lieu of the common-law liability confined to cases of negligence. . . .

NOTES AND QUESTIONS

1. The essential features of the workers' compensation system described in *New York Central Railroad* remain, although there are variations in important details from state to state. The system represents a kind of compromise: strict liability of the employer or its workers' compensation insurer for injuries in the course of employment, without regard to negligence; a limited measure of liability designed to compensate the employee and his family for medical expenses and lost earning capacity; and mandatory insurance or other financial arrangements to assure payment of benefits. The employer gains the "exclusive remedy" defense, which bars nearly any common law tort claim against the employer, thereby limiting the employer's liability to the cost of workers' compensation.

Not all workers' compensation law is state law. Federal law governs work-related injuries in certain industries, including maritime, railroad, coal mining, and nuclear weapons development. Employees of the federal government are covered by the Federal Employees' Compensation Act, 5 U.S.C. §§ 8101 et seq.

2. State workers' compensation laws frequently exclude domestic servants and farm laborers from coverage. *See Note, Workers' Compensation and the Agricultural Exemption: An American Tragedy for Farmers and Injured Farmhands*, 4 Drake J. Ag. L. 491 (1999). However, under some state laws, an employer may elect to submit his employment of a domestic servant or agricultural laborer to the workers' compensation system. *See, e.g.*, Mass. Gen. L. Ann. 152 § 1.

3. Another frequently excluded category of workers is "casual laborers," who work on a very short-term basis. *See, e.g.*, Ala. Code 1975 § 25-5-50; Ariz.

Rev. Stat. § 23-901; Ark. Code Ann. § 11-9-102; Colo. Rev. Stat. Ann. §§ 8-40-202, -302; Con. Gen. Stat. Ann. § 31-2; Del Stat. tit. 19 § 2301. The precise definition of "casual" varies from state to state. However, a typical defining feature of casual work is that it is "not in the ordinary course" of the employer's business. Thus, depending on local law, a day laborer might not qualify as a casual worker if he performs the same work regular employees perform.

4. Workers' compensation laws generally do not apply to workers who are independent contractors, not employees. However, independent contractor status is not always to an injured worker's disadvantage under workers' compensation law. Sometimes the employer claims the worker was an employee, and the worker claims independent contractor status. When might the parties take such positions?

5. One reason some employers engage in staffing arrangements with employee "leasing" services or "professional employer organizations" is to rely on the leasing service or PEO to obtain workers' compensation insurance and other benefits at a better price. The premium any "employer" pays for workers' compensation is based on its claims history. The more accident-prone the employer, the higher its premium. Does employee leasing pose any risk to the workers' compensation system in this regard? See the introduction to Chapter Two, Part B.

NATIONAL ACADEMY OF SOCIAL INSURANCE, *WORKERS' COMPENSATION: BENEFITS, COVERAGE, AND COSTS, 2009*

pp. 7-9 (October 2016)

Types of Workers' Compensation Benefits

There are three basic types of workers' compensation claims: (1) medical-only, (2) temporary disability, and (3) permanent disability, which are determined by the severity of injury and whether or not the claim involves an injury-related work absence. Medical-only claims are the most common, but permanent disability claims impose the greatest costs.

Medical-only claims. Most workers' compensation claims do not involve lost work time in excess of the waiting period for cash benefits, so only medical benefits (and not cash benefits) are paid for these claims. "Medical-only" claims are the most common type of workers' compensation claim, but they represent only a small share of overall payments. According to the National Council on Compensation Insurance (NCCI), between 1994 and 2012, medical-only claims accounted for 75 percent of all workers' compensation claims, but only 7 percent of total benefit payments, in the 37 states where NCCI is licensed.

Temporary disability claims. Temporary total disability (TTD) benefits are paid when a work-related injury or illness temporarily prevents a worker from returning to their pre-injury job or to another job for the same employer. Temporary total disability claims accounted for more than 61 percent of all claims involving cash benefits but less than 30 percent of cash benefits paid in 2012.... The benefits replace approximately two-thirds of the worker's gross, pre-injury weekly earnings from the time-of-injury employer....

Compensation for temporary disability is subject to maximum and minimum benefit levels that vary from state to state. As of January 2016, the maximum weekly TTD benefit ranged from a high of $1,628 in Iowa to a low of $469 in Mississippi. The minimum weekly benefit ranged from a high of $585 in North Dakota to a low of $20 in Arkansas and Florida.

Most workers who receive TTD benefits fully recover and return to work, at which time benefits end. In many cases, however, employers make accommodations allowing injured workers to return to work before they are physically able to resume some or all of their former job duties. In these cases, a worker may be assigned to restricted duties or shorter hours at lower wages. When injured workers return to work at less than their pre-injury wage, they may be eligible for temporary partial disability (TPD) benefits.

Permanent disability claims. Some injured workers experience work-related injuries or illnesses that result in permanent impairments. These workers may be entitled to either permanent partial or permanent total disability benefits. Eligibility for permanent disability benefits is determined after the injured worker reaches maximum medical improvement (the point at which further medical intervention is no longer expected to improve functional capacity or provide further healing). Permanent total disability (PTD) benefits are paid to workers who are considered legally unable to work at all because of a work-related injury or illness. Permanent partial disability (PPD) benefits are paid to workers whose injuries result in permanent impairments, even though they are able to work in some capacity. The amount of permanent disability benefits may be determined by reduced earning capacity or by some measure of physical loss to the body.

The bulk of cash benefits for workers' compensation go to permanent disability claims, of which permanent partial disability claims are more common. In 2012, PPD claims accounted for less than 38 percent of claims involving cash benefits but more than 53 percent of cash benefits paid.... Permanent total disability claims accounted for 0.2 percent of claims involving cash benefits and 6.8 percent of cash benefits paid. Fatality claims occurred in only 0.4 percent of claims and represented 2.6 percent of cash benefits. Permanent total disability and fatality claims are relatively rare, accounting for less than 1 percent of claims involving cash benefits and 7-13 percent of total payments in the period 1994-2012....

NOTES AND QUESTIONS

1. Workers' compensation is not the only benefit an injured employee might receive after a work-related accident or illness. She might submit her claim for medical expenses to personal medical insurance or a regular employer-sponsored medical plan. If unable to work for a relatively short time, she might use existing paid sick leave or vacation time instead of filing a workers' compensation claim for temporary disability (which in any event would not pay for the first few days). For long-term disability, employer-provided disability insurance or Social Security disability benefits may be comparable to or better than workers' compensation long-term disability benefits. The existence of alternative benefits may be one factor in the surprising number of cases in which employees do not file workers' compensation claims. According to one estimate, only about 55 percent of employees with work-related injuries serious enough to cause lost work time file workers' compensation claims. Biddle, J. E., and K. Roberts, *Claiming Behavior in*

Workers' Compensation, 70 J. of Risk & Ins. 759 (2003).

However, the relationship between workers' compensation claims behavior and the availability of alternative benefits is complex and surprising. For example, injured employees are *more likely* to file workers' compensation claims when their *own* employers also provide health insurance. D. Lakdawalla, R. Reville, & S. Seabury, *How Does Health Insurance Affect Workers Compensation Filing?* 45 Economic Inquiry 286 (April 2007). The most likely explanation for this fact is that employers who provide medical insurance to their employees are less likely to engage in behaviors that tend to discourage the filing of workers' compensation claims. For more on this problem, see Section B.5 of this Chapter, *infra*.

2. Roughly a century after the start of workers' compensation law, some commentators have wondered whether the it is still a good bargain for employees. Would employees fare better in the modern tort system? The difference between workers' compensation and tort recoveries by employees against negligent third parties (who cannot claim the exclusive remedy defense) is revealing. In one 1970s study, 120,000 permanently disabled employees recovered an average of $4,000 in workers' compensation benefits. Approximately 30,000 also asserted personal injury claims against third parties and recovered additional damages averaging nearly $40,000. P. Weiler, *Workers' Compensation and Product Liability: The Interaction of a Tort and a Non-Tort Regime*, 80 Ohio St. L.J. 825, 830 (1989).

There are several reasons for this disparity. Tort recoveries often include damages for pain and suffering. Workers' compensation benefits do not. And workers' compensation disability benefits replace only between one-half and two-thirds of pre-injury earning. *See* Haas, *On Reintegrating Workers' Compensation and Employers' Liability*, 21 Ga. L. Rev. 843, 847 n.20 (1987). Still, the more generous awards of the tort system are available only to those able to prove that another party's negligence caused their injuries. For employees who cannot prove employer fault, a limited workers' compensation award is unquestionably better than the alternative, especially for those who lack any other form of medical or disability insurance. Moreover, workers' compensation benefits are paid faster and without the tort system's delays and risks of employer insolvency.

The Texas "Opt-Out" Model: Return to the Common Law?

A unique feature of the Texas workers' compensation system is its "opt-out" provision. Any employer or any individual employee may opt out of the system and return to a modified version of the common law negligence-based system. Tex. Lab. Code §§ 406.002, 406.034. An employer who opts out is known as a "nonsubscriber" and is liable to injured employees only if its negligence caused the injury. The rule of negligence for nonsubscriber employers is a modern version, not the nineteenth-century version. The old defenses of contributory negligence, fellow servant, and assumption of risk are abrogated. Tex. Lab. Code § 406.033.

Shorn of the old common law defenses, negligence is still an important limit on employer liability. If an employee injures his back by lifting an unexceptional load, the employee will recover nothing from the employer for his medical expenses or disability if a court determines that the employer was not negligent in any way that caused the accident. In Werner v. Colwell, 909 S.W.2d 866 (Tex.

1995), the court described the law as follows:

> In Great Atlantic & Pac. Tea Co. v. Evans, 175 S.W.2d 249 (1943), a grocery clerk injured himself while carrying a 100 pound sack of potatoes. We held that when the employee was doing the same character of work that he had always done and that other employees in other stores were required to do, there was no negligence. When there is no evidence that the lifting involved is unusual or poses a threat of injury, plaintiff has failed to establish a prima facie case. . . . Dr. LaPerriere, an expert for Colwell, simply stated that lifting objects is a common cause of back injury. The doctor did not differentiate the risk of injury from lifting a large rump roast, a bag of frozen meat or an entire side of beef. Such a broad generalization is no evidence that Colwell's activities on October 8 involved an increased risk of injury.

175 S.W.2d at 869.

The return to negligence as the basis for employer liability comes with a price for the employer. If the employer is liable, damages are calculated in the same fashion, and include all the same elements (e.g., pain and suffering) as in any other personal injury action. This is one likely reason why most employers in Texas have not opted out of workers' compensation. Nonsubscribers frequently deal with this problem in the following fashion.

First, some nonsubscribers offer alternative accidental injury insurance to its employees. Establishing an accidental injury insurance plan resembles a privatized version of workers' compensation, because such a plan provides benefits for injuries in the course of employment without regard to employer negligence. However, even if a nonsubscriber provides such benefits, benefits need not be comparable to those provided by regular workers' compensation. In fact, benefits provided by nonsubscribers tend to be significantly less than benefits paid by workers' compensation. Jason Ohana, *Texas Elective Workers' Compensation: A Model of Innovation?* Wm. & Mary Bus. L. Rev. 323, 341 (2011). Moreover, a nonsubscriber plan replaces the usual administrative procedure of workers' compensation law with something entirely different. A nonsubscriber's accidental injury benefits plan constitutes an ERISA plan and is not subject to the ERISA exemption for workers' compensation. Hernandez v. Jobe Concrete Products, Inc., 282 F.3d 360 (5th Cir. 2002). Thus, a nonsubscriber plan has an "administrator," probably an insurance company, and the plan may grant the administrator "discretion" in deciding benefit claims. Decisions of an administrator with such authority are subject to an "abuse of discretion" standard of judicial review.

Second, a nonsubscriber may seek an employee's agreement to arbitrate any personal injury claim as a condition of enrollment in the accidental injury plan. Tex. Lab. Code § 406.033. Enrollment does not constitute an effective waiver of the employee's right to sue in tort. *Id.* However, nonsubscribers frequently demand an injured employee's waiver of his right to sue or seek additional damages in return for the receipt of benefits under a nonsubscriber accidental benefit plan.

2. *Accidental Injury*

Eliminating negligence as the basis for employer liability avoids some difficult issues of causation and duty, but workers' compensation adds its own issues. First, under most statutory formulations, the employer or its insurer is liable for an accidental injury that "(1) arose out of *and* (2) in the course of employment." The first requirement—that the accident arose out of the employment—suggests some causal connection between employment and the accident. The second requirement—that the accident was in the course of employment—can be broken down into three dimensions: (a) time; (b) place; and (c) activity. In other words, did the accident occur at work, during work, and in the course of work activity? An accident may fulfill one requirement but not the other. The typical workers' compensation statute presents the test in the conjunctive. An accident is not covered unless it "arose out of" *and* was "in the course of" employment. Whether an injury is covered by workers' compensation could be especially important if the employee has no other source of benefits (disability, life, etc.).

LFI PIERCE, INC. v. CARTER

829 So.2d 158 (Ala. 2001)

YATES, Presiding Judge.

Patricia Ann Carter, as the mother and next friend of Nathan Luvell Carter, a minor; and Kenya Foster, as the mother and next friend of Jemisha Foster, a minor, sued Treesmith, Inc., and LFI Pierce, Inc., d/b/a Labor Finders, seeking to recover workers' compensation death benefits … arising from the death of the children's father, Phillip Lee Mahan, Jr. The case proceeded to trial on stipulated facts. On November 8, 2000, the trial court entered an order awarding the children death benefits pursuant to § 25-5-60. Labor Finders appeals.

Mahan was employed by Labor Finders, a temporary labor provider, which placed him on a job with Treesmith. Pursuant to its contract with Treesmith, Labor Finders was responsible for providing workers' compensation coverage for Mahan. On the day of the accident, Mahan and others were working to remove storm debris from a steep slope on a residential lot on Lake Tuscaloosa. Dennis Robertson, a Treesmith employee, supervised and directed all work on the job site. There were 13 workers on the job site; some of them were regular Treesmith employees, and some, like Mahan, were furnished by Labor Finders.

Mahan and the other employees began removing the debris from the lot at approximately 7:30 a.m. on the date in question. The lot on which Mahan and the others were working contained 160 steps that were built into the slope leading from the house down to the lake. Mahan was required to carry heavy trees and other debris to the top of the slope. The temperature on that date ranged from 98° to 100° F., with a high level of humidity. Because of the extreme and oppressive conditions, the crew was given a 15-minute break every 45 minutes.

Mahan and the crew took a break at approximately 3:00 p.m.; Mahan and the other employees had at least one to two more hours of work remaining at that time. At the beginning of the break, Robertson (Mahan's supervisor) and others walked to the pier at the bottom of the slope and jumped into the lake to cool off. Robertson testified in his deposition that before jumping into the lake he stated that "it would be a pretty good cooling off time." Mahan first climbed the slope for a drink of water from the water cooler located at the top of the hill and then he descended the slope to the pier. Mahan followed the other employees into the lake; he drowned.

Robertson testified that he had jumped into the lake for the purpose of cooling off and not for a recreational swim. Robertson stated that in his judgment, given the heat and humidity and the kind of work he and the others were performing, they were getting into the lake just to cool off.

Matthew Smith, the president of Treesmith, … questioned Robertson after the drowning …. Robertson had thought going into the water was a good idea because it was hot and the crew was fatigued and wanted to cool off. Smith stated that Robertson did not call it a swim but rather described it as "[jumping] in, [washing] the sweat and sawdust off and [climbing] right back out."

. . . [F]or Mahan's death to be compensable, it must have been caused by an accident "arising out of" and "in the course of" his employment with Labor Finders. §§ 25-5-31 and 25-5-51, Ala. Code 1975. The phrase "arising out of" requires a causal connection between the injury and the employment. The phrase "in the course of" refers to the time, place, and circumstances under which the accident occurred. It is not contested that Mahan's conduct was "in the course of" his employment with Labor Finders; rather, the question is whether the accident causing Mahan's death was one "arising out of" his employment. …

> "When an employee deliberately and substantially steps outside of his employment, this conduct constitutes a substantial deviation from his employment. If an employee is injured while substantially deviating from his employment, the employee's injury is not a compensable injury because the injury does not arise out of and in the course of his employment. It is necessary to determine whether the employee's activity so deviated from his business purpose that he went beyond his course of employment by leaving his business purpose to carry out a personal purpose or objective."

Kewish v. Alabama Home Builders Self Insurers Fund, 664 So.2d 917, 922 (Ala. Civ. App.1995) (citations omitted). This court has also stated:

> "It is well settled that work-connected activity goes beyond the direct services performed for the employer and includes at least some ministration to the personal comfort and human wants of the employee. Such acts which are necessary to the life, comfort, and convenience of the employee while at work, though strictly personal to himself, and not acts of service are incidental to the service. Therefore, an injury sustained in the performance thereof is deemed to have arisen out of the employment."

Gold Kist, Inc. v. Jones, 537 So.2d 39, 41 (Ala.Civ.App.1988) (citations omitted). However, the method or manner of seeking the personal comfort must not be unreasonably dangerous or unconventional. *Id.*

Considering the particular facts of this case and keeping in mind the beneficent purpose of the Act, we conclude that Mahan did not substantially deviate from his employment by jumping into the lake to cool off. Mahan simply followed his supervisor and others into the lake for a few minutes in order to escape the oppressive heat and humidity and conditions of his employment, to which he had been exposed for approximately seven and one-half hours. Mahan's entering the lake did have a causal connection with his employment, and it falls within those incidental acts described in *Gold Kist, supra.* … [T]he judgment is … affirmed.

MURDOCK, Judge, concurring specially.

. . . Our Supreme Court long ago recognized that . . ."'[I]n the course of his employment' refers to the time, place and circumstances under which the accident took place." Massey v. United States Steel Corp., 86 So.2d 375, 378 (1955). "An injury to an employee arises in the course of his employment when it occurs [(1)] within the period of his employment, [(2)] at a place where he may reasonably be and [(3)] while he is reasonably fulfilling the duties of his employment or engaged in doing something incident to it. 86 So.2d at 378. "It is well settled that work-connected activity goes beyond the direct services performed for the employer and includes at least some ministration to the [employee's] personal comfort and human wants…." Gold Kist, Inc. v. Jones, 537 So.2d 39, 41 (Ala.Civ.App.1988) (citing 1A A. Larson, The Law of Workmen's Compensation, § 20.10 (1985)).

For an act that is not in reasonable fulfillment of the duties of employment to be considered "in the course of" employment, it must be reasonably incidental to the duties of employment, themselves. Thus, an injury is compensable under the Act "if, when the injury was received, the employee was either doing the work or performing the service he was engaged to do or perform, or was engaged in an act or service naturally related thereto, such as a reasonable judgment would refer either to the express or the implied elements of the contract of employment, such as a reasonable conception would conclude to be a natural incident of the employee's engagement." *Massey*, 86 So.2d 375. In this regard, this court has stated that "the method or manner of seeking personal comfort may be unreasonably dangerous or unconventional and in that instance may not be considered incidental to the work normally within the course of the employment." *Gold Kist*, 537 So.2d at 41 (citing 1A A. Larson, The Law of Workmen's Compensation, § 21.10 (1985)).

However, we need not resolve the issue of whether Mahan's drowning arose in the course of his employment because that issue was not argued on appeal.

... I agree that Mahan's death did "arise out of" his employment. "[I]t is usually said that the phrase 'arise out of' employment refers to employment as the cause and source of the accident." Massey, 86 So.2d at 378. "The rational mind must be able to trace the resulting injury to a proximate cause *set in motion by the employment* and not by some other agency." *Id.* (emphasis added and citations omitted).

Mahan entered the lake ... to obtain relief from the severe conditions of his employment, including physical exertion and the extremely high heat and humidity. . . . I conclude that his entering the lake did have a causal connection with his employment and, therefore, his death did "arise out of" that employment....

THOMPSON, Judge, dissenting.

... The record . . . indicates that the work crew engaged in manual labor and that, because of the heat, the work crew took a 15-minute break every 45 minutes. During those breaks, the crew sat in the shade and had drinks from a water cooler. Thus, the employer had provided a method by which its work crew periodically could "cool off." The trial court specifically found that the 15 minute breaks "facilitated getting the work done" and served a business or employment purpose. In other words, those breaks were incidental to the employees' work duties….

I cannot conclude that it might "reasonably be assumed" that Mahan's jumping into the lake to "cool off" provided some benefit or advantage to the employer, especially where the employer had provided alternative and conventional methods of cooling off, and the employee had taken advantage of them. Rather, . . .the employee's actions, and his method of seeking personal comfort, were unconventional, and . . . should not be considered incidental to his employment. . . . Mahan's jumping into the lake was not an act "arising out of" his employment . . . and was not incidental to the duties of his employment. . . .

TECHNICAL TAPE CORP. v. THE INDUSTRIAL COMM'N

58 Ill. 2d 226, 317 N.E.2d 515 (1974)

WARD, Justice:

This is a direct appeal . . . by the employer-respondent, Technical Tape Corporation, from a judgment of the circuit court of Jackson County, which affirmed an award of the Industrial Commission in favor of the employee claimant, Terry Crain, for temporary disability, partial incapacity and permanent disfigurement under the Workmen's Compensation Act . . . .

On January 31, 1969, Terry Crain, who was working on the three-to-eleven p.m. shift at the Technical Tape Corporation, was told to clean the residue from a glue churn. The churn was five feet long, five feet wide, and three feet deep. It had a capacity of approximately 200 gallons and was completely enclosed except for a small opening on the top. The ingredients of the glue included toluene, which is a solvent, resins, and rubber.

When the claimant came out of the churn at 10:45 P.M., after working in it for over a half hour, he testified he felt a burning sensation in his feet and legs. He also felt nauseated. The record shows that after leaving the plant at the completion of his shift the claimant drove his car erratically for about five miles and then ran a stop sign and collided with another car. He suffered a disfigurement of his left ear, a fractured skull, and a partial loss of the use of his right foot.

The only witnesses at the hearing before the arbitrator were the claimant and his father, George Crain, who also was employed at the Technical Tape Corporation. The father testified he saw Terry as he was coming out of the churn after cleaning it. He noticed that there were "two big red streaks on both sides of Terry's neck." He said that he admonished Terry for doing that work because it was his experience that employees who worked in such churns would "get so drunk (they could) hardly get out of them." He testified that at that time Terry told him that he was dizzy and felt ill. Because he was concerned about his son's condition, George Crain attempted to see Terry again before he left for home. However, upon reaching the parking lot he heard the motor of Terry's auto roar "as loud as it would go" and saw him speed out of the parking lot. He got into his car and began to follow Terry. He said Terry drove through a four-way stop intersection without stopping and minutes later narrowly missed hitting a railroad-crossing gate that was being lowered. Terry's car would have struck the gate if the crossing guard had not quickly raised it. The gate was re-lowered and the father had to wait for a crossing train to pass. When it did he continued his pursuit of Terry. He drove about five miles and came upon the scene of the collision.

Terry Crain testified that he hardly remembered climbing from the churn. He testified that the last thing he recalled the night of the accident was "clocking out of the plant" shortly after 11 P.M. He said he did not recall anything until he awakened in a hospital two weeks later. The employer did not offer any evidence at the hearing before the arbitrator. The arbitrator found in favor of the claimant and entered an award for 20 3/7 weeks of temporary total compensation, 6 weeks of compensation for the permanent disfigurement of the left ear, 60 weeks of compensation for a fracture of the skull and 85¼ weeks of compensation representing 55% permanent loss of the use of the right foot.

Upon the filing of a petition for review by the employer with the Industrial Commission, the deposition of Dr. Host Von Paleske, who specializes in orthopedic surgery, was admitted into evidence in behalf of the claimant. Dr. Von Paleske stated that when he examined the claimant shortly before midnight on the night of the accident it was obvious that the claimant had been exposed to a large amount of toluene, because the odor of toluene came not only from his nostrils and mouth but from his skin and hair as well. He said that exposure to toluene for a long period of time could cause dizziness and "almost a drunken-type feeling." Dr. Von Paleske said that toluene produced an effect similar to that caused by alcohol.

An injury must "arise out of" and "in the course of" employment to be compensable under the Workmen's Compensation Act. . . . While the phrase "in the course of employment" relates to the time, place and circumstances of the injury, the phrase "arising out of the employment" refers to the requisite causal connection between the injury and the employment. . . . In order for an injury to "arise out of" employment it must have had its origin in some risk connected with, or incidental to, the employment, so that there is a causal connection between the employment and the injury. . . .

Professor Larson, in The Law of Workmen's Compensation . . . comments:

> [I]n Workmen's Compensation the controlling event is something done To, not By, the employee, and since the real question is whether this something was an industrial accident, the Origin of the accident is crucial, and the moment of manifestation should be immaterial. . . . [The Act] does not say that the injury must "occur" or "be manifested" or "be consummated" in the course of employment. It merely says that it must "arise . . . in the course of employment." "Arising" connotes origin, not completion or manifestation. If a strain occurs during employment hours which produces no symptoms, and claimant suffers a heart attack as a result sometime after working hours, the injury is compensable.

1 A. Larson, The Law of Workmen's Compensation, sec. 29.22. . . .

The evidence showed that the claimant's intoxication was a result of his cleaning the churn and that the injuries sustained in the collision had their origin in the intoxication. It cannot be reasonably said that the Commission's finding that the claimant's injuries arose out of and in the course of his employment was contrary to the manifest weight of the evidence.

NOTES AND QUESTIONS

1. Were the employee in *Technical Tape Corp.* and the surviving children in *LFI Pierce* better off or worse off because of the substitution of workers'

compensation for tort law?

2. Alabama and Illinois, the jurisdictions for the preceding cases, have adopted the prevailing rule of coverage for injuries due to accidents "arising out of *and* in the course of employment." A few states have adopted a *one* part rule of coverage that requires only that the accident was in the *course* of employment. Remember that the "course of employment" requirement involves three dimensions: (a) time; (b) place; and (c) activity. The effect of a one-part "course of employment" test is illustrated by a Pennsylvania case, Stillman v. Workers' Compensation Board, 569 A.2d 983 (Pa. Cmmw. 1990). In that case, an employee whose job was to service portable toilets and who traveled from location to location in his truck stopped at home for his lunch break. He used his home garden hose to begin filling the water tank on his truck while his wife prepared a sandwich. A yellow jacked landed on or crawled into the sandwich as he took a bite, and stung him on the tongue. Stillman was allergic to bee stings, and he died from the sting. His widow sought workers' compensation death benefits. The Pennsylvania Workers' Compensation Appeal Board denied the claim, as might well be expected if the law required proof that the accident *arose out of* the employment. After all, being stung on the tongue while eating a sandwich at home is not a risk connected with or caused by employment. On appeal, however, the court reversed and remanded. Pennsylvania does not require that the accident arose out of the employment. All that is required is that the accident occurred during the course of employment. As a roving employee, Stillman's workplace was not limited to a single location, and there was at least some evidence that the accident occurred during work time and while Stillman was engaged in work activity by refilling his tank with water from the garden hose. Applying Pennsylvania's one part "course of employment" test, the court held that there was an unresolved question whether Stillman was in the course of employment at the time of the accident that caused his death, and it remanded the case for further proceedings.

3. The result of applying the "course of employment" test might depend on how one defines the "accident." Did Crain's accident in *Technical Tape* happen in the course of employment? Did it happen during employment, at work, and in the activity of working? The answer depends on which occurrence was "the accident."

4. The additional requirement in most states that a compensable accident must "arise out of" the employment can lead to very different results depending on how a court chooses to apply this requirement. Larson has identified a number of possible approaches to the "arising out of employment" requirement:

- *Peculiar Risk.* The risk must be peculiar to the employment and not a risk shared by the general public. Under this rule, a court might deny benefits to an employee struck by lightning while he was working, if lightning is a risk shared by the public and not a risk "peculiar" to the employment. *See, e.g.*, Sheeler v. Greystone Homes, Inc., 6 Cal. Rptr. 3d 683 (Cal. App. 2003).
- *Increased Risk.* The nature or particulars of the employment increased the risk, even if the risk or hazard is shared by others outside of the employment. This appears to be the majority rule. Thus, an employee struck by lightning might recover benefits if his work required him to remain outdoors and exposed him to a heightened risk. *See, e.g.*, Simmons v. City of Charleston, 562 S.E.2d 476 (S.C. 2002).

- *Positional Risk.* A "but for" test of causation, which leads to compensability if the injury would not have occurred but for the employment. An employee struck by lightning is likely to receive benefits if the lightning would not have struck him but for the fact that his employment placed him in that spot. *See, e.g.*, Montgomery County v. Smith, 799 A.2d 406 (Md. App. 2002).

See 1 A. Larson, Larson's Workers' Compensation Law §§ 3.02-3.05 (2002).

5. Neither the "course of employment" nor "arising out of employment" test is completely adequate to deal with certain classes of accidents. Cases involving transportation to and from work constitute one problem area. It could be argued that an accident during commuting "arises out of" employment because employment requires commuting and increases the risk of an accident. However, commuting to and from work is not in the course of employment because work has either not begun or is finished. In many jurisdictions, this exclusion of coverage of accidents during commuting is also known as the "going and coming rule." Poole v. Westchester Fire Ins. Co., 830 S.W.2d 183 (Tex. App. 1992).

But the going and coming rule has many exceptions due to the many ways work can blend with "personal" time or activity. For example, work-related stops or errands between home and the office might be enough to qualify a commute as "in the course of employment" in the view of some courts. *See, e.g.*, R.C.A. Serv. Co. v. Liggett, 394 P.2d 675 (Alaska 1964); Johnson v. Skelly Oil Co., 288 N.W.2d 493 (1980) (automobile accident was in the course of employment because employee was carrying employer's mail to deposit in a mailbox on the way home). If the employee takes work home, "commuting" might be viewed as "roving" between workplaces, like the employee's roving in *Stillman*. McKeever v. N.J. Bell Tel. Co., 430 A.2d 247 (N.J. Super. 1981) (lawyer who took work home was in the course of employment while driving home from work). If the employee "roves," simply walking out his front door at the beginning of the day might be regarded as the beginning of his work. *Compare* Black River Dairy Prods., Inc. v. Dep't of Indus., Lab. and Human Relations, 207 N.W.2d 65 (Wis. 1973) (delivery driver who slipped while walking out front door of his home on his way to his truck was covered) *with* Jellico Grocery Co. v. Hendrickson, 110 S.W.2d 333 (Tenn. 1937) (denying coverage for salesman injured on steps of his home after returning from sales calls, despite evidence he was carrying paperwork to finish at home).

6. So-called "personal comfort" cases such as *LFI Pierce* are another problem area for coverage of work-related accidents. Again, the essence of the problem is the blending of "personal" action with work. In the personal comfort cases, an accident was during working hours and at the workplace, but the employee was arguably engaged in a "personal" matter rather than a work matter. Many states have adopted some variation of the "personal comfort doctrine" described in *LFI Pierce*, which allows coverage if an accident was during or caused by a "reasonable activity designed for personal comfort" during or incidental to work, such a stretching or using the restroom. Costley v. Nevada Indus. Ins. Com., 296 P. 1011 (Nev. 1931). The "personal comfort doctrine" treats non-work activity as work activity for purposes of the "course of employment" requirement, or avoids the need for a clear causal connection with work for purposes of the "arising out of" requirement. The premise of the personal comfort doctrine is that employees must attend to personal and natural needs such as eating during work

hours, and attending to these personal needs makes continuing work possible and inures to the employer's benefit. Johme v. St. John's Mercy Healthcare, 366 S.W.3d 504, 507 n. 5 (Mo. 2012). On the other hand, coverage is denied for accidents caused by or arising out of unreasonable, unnecessary, or extraordinary deviations from normal personal activity incidental to work — such as horseplay. Some states reject the personal comfort doctrine.. *See*, e.g., Johme v. St. John's Mercy Healthcare, 366 S.W.3d 504, 507 n. 5 (Mo. 2012). However, even in states rejecting the personal comfort doctrine, an accident occurring in the course of "personal comfort" activity might still be covered if the accident was because of a condition or risk of the work or the workplace and the employee's activity was arguably essential to or inextricable from working or continuing to work. Rio All Suite Hotel & Casino v. Phillips, 240 P.3d 2, 4-5 (Nev. 2010) ("slips and falls that are due to employment risks include tripping on a defect at employer's premises or falling on uneven or slippery ground at the work site").

7. Employment can also blend with social and recreational activities. In Ezzy v. Workers' Compensation App. Bd., 194 Cal. Rptr. 90 (Cal. App. 1983), a summer law clerk was injured in a softball game her law firm sponsored. Partners of the firm had made it clear that they wanted the claimant to join the team because the team played in a coed league, and they might have forfeited the game if they lacked enough women. The firm also provided tee shirts and refreshments for the game. The court upheld coverage because participation in the game was a "reasonable expectancy" of the claimant's employment. *See also* Smith v. University of Idaho, 170 P.2d 404 (Id. 1946) (upholding coverage of accident of university housemother who slipped on ice on her way to shop for decorations at an off-campus store, because some of her purchases benefitted the employer because they would have contributed to the dormitory's congenial atmosphere).

8. What are the implications of workers' compensation law for the growing number of telecommuters and their employers? *See* Tovish v. Gerber Elec., 630 A.2d 136 (Conn. App. 1993) (granting benefits to sales employee who maintained an office at his home and who suffered heart attack while shoveling snow from driveway to prepare to leave for first sales call); American Red Cross v. Wilson, 519 S.W.2d 60 (Ark. 1975) (granting benefits to employee who worked at home and fell down stairs when going to answer phone).

DALLAS INDEPENDENT SCHOOL DISTRICT v. PORTER

759 S.W.2d 454 (Tex. App. 1988)

McKAY, Justice.

This is an appeal from a judgment against the Dallas Independent School District (DISD) in favor of Mattie Porter for death benefits under the Texas Workers' Compensation Act. Mattie Bell Porter is the widow of Woodrow Porter, Jr. (Porter).

Porter was employed by DISD as a janitor at Dunbar Elementary School in Dallas. He resided directly across the street from the school. From the statement of facts we glean that on April 26, 1978, Porter was on duty at the school when he noticed a child near his automobile which was parked at his residence. Believing that the child was vandalizing his car, Porter left the school premises, confronted the child in front of Porter's residence, and spanked the child. After the spanking, the child left and Porter returned to the school.

Later on that same day, the grandmother of Mondell Washington, the child who was spanked, arrived at the Dunbar School and asked to see Porter. Porter was called to the office by his supervisor, and he and the grandmother began discussing the spanking incident. The meeting turned into an argument and then into loud yelling. The supervisor directed Porter to return to his post on another floor in the school. At this point, Porter left the office and the supervisor remained behind to talk with the grandmother. However, as the grandmother left the school office, she came upon Porter who had not yet returned to his post. The argument again heated up whereupon the grandmother took a pistol from her purse and shot and killed Porter.

In its first point of error, DISD complains that there was no evidence that the injury which caused Porter's death was sustained in the course of his employment. . . . For an employee or his statutory beneficiaries to recover workers' compensation benefits, the claimant must show that the employee sustained an injury in the course of his employment. Tex. Rev. Civ. Stat. Ann. art. 8306, §§ 1, 3b (Vernon 1967). . . . Thus, for a claimant to recover under our statute he must meet two requirements. First, the injury must have occurred while the claimant was engaged in or about the furtherance of his employer's affairs or business. Second, the claimant must show that the injury was of a kind and character that had to do with and originated in the employer's work, trade, business or profession. Texas Employers Insurance Association v. Page, 553 S.W.2d 98, 99 (Tex. 1977). . . .

In addition to imposing these two requirements, article 8309, § 1 specifically excludes from the definition of an injury sustained in the course of employment:

> (2) An injury caused by an act of a third person intended to injure the employee because of reasons personal to him and not directed against him as an employee, or because of his employment.

Tex. Rev. Civ. Stat. Ann. art. 8309, § 1 (Vernon 1967). In Nasser v. Security Insurance Co., 724 S.W.2d 17 (Tex. 1987), the supreme court recently addressed this "personal animosity exception." In *Nasser*, Izzat Nasser, an assistant manager of a restaurant, was stabbed by Victor Daryoush. Daryoush, who had recently been released from a mental hospital, was the former boyfriend of Marianne Dawes, a frequent customer at Nasser's restaurant. When Dawes was eating at the restaurant, Nasser would sometimes sit and talk with her. Daryoush apparently saw them together and became jealous. He went to the restaurant and, when Nasser was called from his office to see him, stabbed Nasser.

The jury found that Nasser's injury was sustained in the course of his employment, and the trial court entered judgment in Nasser's favor. Concluding that Nasser's injury fell squarely within the "personal animosity" exception, the court of appeals held that there was no evidence to sustain the jury's finding and reversed. The supreme court reversed the court of appeals. The supreme court observed that Nasser had testified that being nice to customers was part of his job and that he frequently sat down with customers dining alone. The court further observed that Nasser stated that when he was called from his office to see Daryoush, he assumed that he was needed to deal with a customer's problem.

Dealing with customer problems was also part of his job. Finally the court noted that Nasser would never have talked with Dawes if she had not been a customer of the restaurant. The court held that these factors represented some evidence to support the jury's finding that Nasser was injured in the course of his employment.

In the present case, however, there are no similar factors to support the jury's finding. Only two facts support the jury finding: the fact that the grandmother went to the school to pursue her grievance against Porter and the fact that Porter was called to speak to her by his supervisor. These factors alone are not sufficient to support the jury finding. *See* Texas Indemnity Insurance Co. v. Cheely, 232 S.W.2d 124, 126 (Tex. Civ. App.-Amarillo 1950, writ ref'd) (proof that the injury occurred while the employee was engaged in the furtherance of his employers' business is not alone sufficient); A. Larson, The Law of Workmen's Compensation § 11.21 (1985) (positional risk test inapplicable to privately motivated assault). The undisputed evidence showed that Porter's duties did not include disciplining children. When Porter left the school property to discipline Washington, he was not acting in pursuit of his duties as an employee or in furtherance of his employer's business. Thus, unlike Nasser, the injury in this case was the result of a dispute which had been transported from Porter's private life into his place of employment. This is precisely the type of injury which the "personal animosity exception" is intended to exclude. *Nasser*, 724 S.W.2d at 19. . . . [T]here is no evidence that Porter's injuries were sustained in the course of his employment. . . . The judgment of the trial court is reversed, and judgment is here rendered for appellant.

NOTES AND QUESTIONS

1. Does the "personal animosity" rule necessarily follow from the requirement that an accidental injury or death is not covered unless it arose out of and in the course of employment? Whether it follows or not, many state legislatures have confirmed the personal animosity rule with statutes like the Texas provision described in *Porter*.

2. If the personal animosity rule results in the denial of workers' compensation benefits for an employee or survivor, might the employee or survivor sue the employer or a fellow employee in tort (e.g., based on the employer's negligence in failing to provide adequate security, or a fellow employee's intent to cause harm in assaulting the claimant)? Or does the exclusive remedy defense still bar the tort claim? The possibility of tort claims by employees or their survivors is addressed in Part B.6 of this Chapter.

PROBLEM

Foreman was an assistant supervisor at a 24-hour retail store. He loved practical jokes. He played them against other employees mainly for fun, but when others complained, he often defended his actions by saying the jokes built comradery and taught employees to think on their feet and deal with shocks and surprises. Just before the incident described below, higher management counseled him to act more professionally and stop engaging in pranks on company time.

One night when Foreman was off-duty, he and another employee decided to play a joke on Vicky, the employee on duty at the cash register that evening.

Foreman and his accomplice put masks over their faces, entered the store at 2 a.m., and yelled "This is a robbery! Give us your cash or we'll shoot!" Foremen poked used his finger underneath his jacket to create the impression of a concealed handgun aimed at Vicky. Vicky fainted and fell to the floor, hitting and injuring her head on a shelf. She incurred substantial medical expenses that were not covered by her medical insurance because of a high deductible. She also lost several weeks of work but lacked her own disability insurance for this loss. Might she have a claim for workers' compensation benefits?

3. *Occupational Disease and Other Progressive Injuries*

Not all injury is the result of an "accident." What if an employee who has worked for years in a job that requires heavy lifting begins to experience disabling back pain? Early workers' compensation law focused on "accidental" injury, but limiting coverage to "accidental" injuries meant that a claimant was required to show that her injury could be traced to a definite time, place, and cause and that the cause was an "accident" and not simply the natural, progressive effect of normal work. Normal lifting in the course of work is not an "accident." Moreover, progressive injuries that result from work over years rather than one precise action cannot be tied to a definite place and time.

By the middle of the twentieth century, some courts and administrative agencies had begun to rebel against the requirement of a clear-cut "accident." One typical way of seeming to satisfy the requirement of an "accident" was to regard the *injury* rather than the cause as the "accident." *See, e.g.*, Bernier v. Cola-Cola Bottling Plants, Inc., 250 A.2d 820, 822 (Me. 1969) ("an internal injury that is itself sudden, unusual, and unexpected is none the less accidental because its external cause is a part of the victim's ordinary work"); Dawes v. Wittrock Sandblasting & Painting, Inc., 667 N.W.2d 167 (Neb. 2003) (injury might be accidental if the injury "materializes" at an identifiable point in time, even if the event that caused it did not occur at an identifiable point in time).

The question whether progressive injuries are compensable "accidental injuries" has been mooted to a large extent by legislative amendments acknowledging the compensability of "repetitive stress" injuries and "occupational diseases." The result is a two track system: An injury might be compensable because it is the result of an accident, or the injury might be compensable because it is the result of repetitive work stress or occupational disease.

BRUNELL v. WILDWOOD CREST POLICE DEPARTMENT

822 A.2d 576 (2003)

LONG, J.

These consolidated appeals present the issue of whether Post Traumatic Stress Disorder (PTSD) is an "accidental injury" or an "occupational disease" under the workers' compensation statute. We conclude that the condition may qualify, depending on the circumstances, as either and that when the facts of a case straddle both categories, a worker is entitled to file both claims. Finally, we hold that in the narrow band of accident cases that result in latent or insidiously progressive injury, the accident statute of limitations does not begin to run until the worker knows or should know that he has sustained a compensable injury.

I

A

Brunell v. Wildwood Crest Police Department

In 1995, Petitioner Diana Brunell was employed by respondent Wildwood Crest Police Department as a civilian police dispatcher. On June 2, she dispatched Officer Eugene Miglio to the scene of a vehicle stop. A scuffle ensued, during which the suspect struck Miglio on the chest. As a result, Miglio suffered a cardiac arrest and died later that night. Although Brunell did not witness the incident directly, in addition to sending Miglio to the scene of his death, she called for medical assistance, informed and consoled other members of the police department, and arranged for notification of Officer Miglio's widow. Immediately after the incident, Brunell suffered "symptoms of anxiety, depression, nightmares, irritability, fatigue, insomnia, and exaggerated startle response." She became more tense as time passed.

In June 1999, Brunell began to experience difficulty at work, including disagreements with co-workers and other "emotional problems." As a result, she was suspended for a week. . . . On August 20, 1999, Brunell was diagnosed with PTSD as the direct result of Officer Miglio's death in 1995. . . .

On January 6, 2000, Brunell filed a claim petition seeking workers' compensation. In the petition, she declared that the date of her accident or occupational exposure was June 2, 1995, and that she suffered from delayed onset PTSD as a result of Officer Miglio's death. . . .

B

Stango v. Lower Township Police Department

Petitioner Samuel Stango was a uniformed patrolman for the Lower Township Police Department for nine years, prior to his honorable resignation in 2000. On February 18, 1994, Stango and a fellow officer, David Douglass, responded to the scene of a domestic dispute. When they arrived, the officers split up and took separate routes around the property. As Stango approached the backyard, he heard what sounded like gunshots. Stango found Douglass lying on the ground, the victim of a shooting in the throat. Stango held Douglass, who was bleeding from the mouth and ears, and watched him die. Following the incident, Stango noticed an increased anxiety level and began "having problems with awakening at night with panic feelings, anxiety and sweats, coupled with flashbacks and bad dreams."

In February 2000, Stango . . . was carrying balloons into his house for his twin daughters' birthday party when one of the balloons burst. The "pop" sound triggered a flashback that was "extremely intense and anxiety provoking." . . . On April 5, 2000, Stango discussed his troubles with his lieutenant who relieved him of his duties, requested the surrender of his service weapon, and referred him to an Employee Assistance Program.

On April 13, 2000, Stango filed two claim petitions for Workers' Compensation, one alleging that the date of his accident or occupational exposure was February 13, 2000 (the date of the balloon-popping flashback), and the other identifying the date as February 18, 1994 (the initial shooting incident). . . .

C

. . . [B]ecause Brunell and Stango raised many of the same legal issues, . . . the two cases were consolidated and argued together . . . . The judge granted the motions to dismiss because neither petition was filed within two years of the "accident." The Appellate Division affirmed. . . .

III

[T]he New Jersey Workers' Compensation Act [of 1911]. . initially swept in only typical industrial accidents; however, "it rapidly became apparent that the new law failed to cover many of the developing hazards of industrial production, specifically the hazards of occupational disease resulting from exposure to toxic substances." Suzanne Nussbaum & James Boskey, *The Consumers League of New Jersey and the Development of Occupational Disease Legislation*, 4 Seton Hall Legis. J. 101, 110-11 (1979).

In 1924, the Legislature amended the compensation statutes to include toxic exposure . . . . [A] worker was covered for specifically delineated diseases[1] but only if the disability was reported within five months of the last exposure and the claim was filed within one year thereof. *Ibid*. Because "many of these diseases could manifest years after exposure, the limitations posed a serious problem." Nussbaum & Boskey, *supra*, 4 Seton H. Legis. J. at 124. It was not until 1948 that the Legislature loosened the statute of limitations for occupational diseases by adding a two-year discovery rule, although maintaining an absolute five-year statute of repose[, then] . . . amended the section to cover all occupational diseases. . . . [I]n 1974, in recognition of the insidious nature and delayed onset of many occupational diseases and the difficulty in pinpointing the exact date the disease process began, the five-year statute of repose was repealed, leaving only the discovery rule. . . .

IV

As indicated, our workers' compensation scheme provides a remedy to an employee who suffers injury "arising out of and in the course of employment" either by accident, N.J.S.A. 34:15-7, or by contracting a compensable occupational disease, N.J.S.A. 34:15-34. . . .

A

. . . The statute does not define "by accident"; however, it has been held that an accident "is an unlooked for mishap or an untoward event which is not expected or designed." Klein v. New York Times Co., 721 A.2d 29 (App. Div.1998). . . . Obviously, it is not the mere mishap that triggers the compensation statute, but the mishap in combination with the statutory requirement of "personal injuries." N.J.S.A. 34:15-7. To be an accident, what must be present is an "unintended or

[1] Compensable occupational diseases were limited to "anthrax; lead poisoning; mercury poisoning; arsenic poisoning; phosphorous poisoning; poisoning from benzene and its homologues, and all derivatives thereof; wood alcohol poisoning; chrome poisoning; caisson disease; mesothorium or radium poisoning." L. 1924, c. 124, § 1(22b).

unexpected occurrence which produces hurt or loss." Spindler v. Universal Chain Corp., 93 A.2d 171 (1952). . . .

Indeed, the entire workers' compensation law is based on disability caused by injury. . . . A worker simply has no claim unless he can demonstrate either temporary or permanent disability. . . . That principle is underscored by the statute, which denominates "the occurrence of the injury" as the trigger for an employee to notify the employer. N.J.S.A. 34:15-17. That provision serves to insulate employers from having to investigate an onslaught of passing incidents that do not result in injury and therefore do not constitute accidents under the statute. . . . Further, an accident claim cannot be filed unless the "injury" and its "extent and character" are described, thus obviating the possibility of filing a claim when injury is absent. N.J.S.A. 34:15-51.

A "second ingredient" that has been added to the notion of injury by accident in most jurisdictions is that the injury must be traceable, within reasonable limits, to a definite time, place, occasion or cause. Larson, *supra*, § 42.02 at 42-4. . . . When an untoward event occurring at a definite time causes a definite injury, Larson observes that "one has the clearest example of a typical industrial accident, in the colloquial sense: collisions, explosions, slips, falls, and the like, leading to obvious traumatic injuries." Larson, *supra*, § 42.02 at 42-6.

B

> N.J.S.A. 34:15-31 defines "compensable occupational disease" as including all diseases arising out of and in the course of employment, which are due in a material degree to causes and conditions which are or were characteristic of or peculiar to a particular trade, occupation, process or place of employment.

By "characteristic of or peculiar to" is meant conditions that one engaged in that particular employment would view as creating a likely risk of injury. Those conditions must "cause" the disease as a natural incident of either the occupation in general or the place of employment. Walck v. Johns-Mansville Prods. Corp., 267 A.2d 508 (1970). In other words, there is attached to that job a hazard that distinguishes it from the usual run of occupations. . . .

In differentiating between accidental injury and occupational disease, Larson observes that the basic "unexpectedness" ingredient of accident is absent in an occupational disease:

> The cause is characteristic harmful conditions of the particular industry. The result is a kind of disability which is not unexpected if work under these conditions continues for a long time. And the development is usually gradual and imperceptible over an extended period.

[Larson, *supra*, § 42.02 at 42-6.]

C

In most instances, when a worker is hurt on the job the claim is easily classifiable. For example, a worker who loses a finger due to a malfunctioning machine clearly has suffered an untoward or unexpected event resulting in hurt or loss. That is an accidental injury. Conversely, a worker who has developed emphysema, over time, due to continued toxic exposure in a chemical plant, plainly has experienced an occupational disease.

In a narrow band of cases, however, the denomination of exactly what the worker has suffered and when he has suffered it is less clear. According to Larson, those are the cases that fall somewhere between the two extremes and constitute a fruitful source of litigation. Larson, *supra*, § 42.02 at 42-6. This is one of them.

V

The Diagnostic and Statistical Manual of Mental Disorders, Fourth Edition, states:

> The essential feature of Posttraumatic Stress Disorder is the development of characteristic symptoms following exposure to an extreme traumatic stress or involving direct personal experience of an event that involves actual or threatened death or serious injury, or other threat to one's physical integrity; or witnessing an event that involves death, injury, or a threat to the physical integrity of another person; or learning about unexpected or violent death, serious harm, or threat of death or injury experienced by a family member or other close associate.

[American Psychiatric Association, Diagnostic and Statistical Manual of Mental Disorders 463 (4th ed. 2000) (DSM-IV).]

. . . Symptoms may present quickly and last less than three months, in which case the PTSD is denominated as "acute." If symptoms last more than three months, the condition is called "chronic." Schiraldi, *supra*, at 6; Mann & Neece, *supra*, 8 Behav. Sci. & L. at 49 (noting that after police officer witnesses traumatic event, PTSD symptoms may last days or several years). Although the symptoms may appear immediately after a traumatic event, they also may remain dormant until at least six months or more have passed, in which case the PTSD is specified as "with delayed onset." Schiraldi, *supra*, at 6. In short, PTSD is a catchall phrase for an array of reactions to stress that can arise in various employment settings.

VI

There is no question but that PTSD is cognizable under the workers' compensation statutes. With the passage of time, our courts have come to recognize legitimate mental stress claims as a compensable psychiatric disability. . . . That result also has been reached by a number of our sister states that provide workers' compensation for purely mental injuries. *See generally* George Chamberlain, Psychiatric Claims in Workers' Compensation and Civil Litigation 27-48 (Supp. 2002). The majority of those states have compensated PTSD as an accidental injury. Generally, each case has involved PTSD that resulted in proximity to one or two traumatic events. [citations omitted].

None of the cited cases addressed the cognate issue of whether PTSD also could qualify as an occupational disease, presumably because none of the injured workers in fact made such a claim and because PTSD was not a condition that naturally was regarded as incident to the work in question. That issue, however, has been answered by the courts of Colorado, Maryland, North Carolina, and Virginia. Those courts have concluded that, depending on the facts, PTSD may be either an occupational disease or an accidental injury. . . . Generally speaking, each of those cases found PTSD to be an occupational disease when it developed over time from multiple stressors unique to the employment. . . .

We think the cases that have concluded that PTSD can qualify either as an accidental injury or an occupational disease, depending on the facts, are closest to the mark. . . . [T]he majority of out-of-state cases correctly recognized a worker's accidental injury claim for PTSD when the condition arose from a single traumatic event that generated immediate symptoms and was not caused by the peculiar conditions of the employment. Colorado, Maryland, North Carolina and Virginia likewise correctly recognized PTSD as an occupational disease when it arose out of recurrent traumatic events experienced by policemen, firemen and rescue workers, the conditions of whose employment compelled regular exposure to such traumas with expectable consequences. . . .

Any pigeonholing of PTSD into one or the other of the statutory categories would have the effect of excluding whole classes of workers from coverage. For example, classifying PTSD as exclusively "accidental" would eliminate from coverage all workers who did not suffer an identifiable traumatic event but developed PTSD over time from multiple stressors. Similarly, classifying PTSD as exclusively "occupational" would exclude workers who developed PTSD in the myriad of everyday jobs that do not bear a special hazard that would qualify under the occupational disease statute. . . .

. . . The dividing line is that in order to prove an occupational disease, the worker must establish that his condition was not unexpected but that it was "due in material degree to causes and conditions which are or were characteristic of or peculiar to the particular trade, occupation, process or place of employment." N.J.S.A. 34:15-31. . . . [A] worker who fell short on proof that his injury resulted from the unique hazard of his job, nevertheless might have proved that he sustained an accidental injury as a result of an unexpected event. . . .

VII

Part and parcel of determining the nature of the claims will be the issue of the timeliness of the filings. As we have indicated, different notice and claim provisions apply, depending upon how the worker's claim is characterized.

An employee claiming an occupational disease must notify his employer within ninety days after the employee "knew or ought to have known the nature of his disability and its relation to his employment," N.J.S.A. 34:1533. Likewise, he must file a claim petition within two years after he "knew the nature of the disability and its relation to the employment." N.J.S.A. 34:15-36. In the occupational disease context, "knowledge of the 'nature' of [the] disability connotes knowledge of the most notable characteristics of the disease, sufficient to bring home substantial realization of its extent and seriousness." Earl v. Johnson & Johnson, 158 N.J. 155, 163, 728 A.2d 820 (1999). . . .

With respect to accidental injury, an employee must give notice to the employer within ninety days of the occurrence "of the injury," N.J.S.A. 34:15-17, and must file a claim petition within two years of the date the "accident" occurred, N.J.S.A. 34:15-51. . . . There is usually very little problem in calculating the notice and claim limitations periods for accidental injury because in classic industrial accident cases, the injury and the unexpected traumatic event are simultaneous.

That is not the case with delayed onset PTSD or any other latent or progressive condition, for that matter. . . . Indeed, to be diagnosed with delayed onset PTSD, an employee cannot begin to suffer the symptoms of injury until at least six months or longer have passed since the trauma. PTSD is an example of an insidious disease process of which the worker is unaware at the time of the original traumatic event. The question presented is how, in those circumstances, to calculate the notice and claim provisions in the accident statute.

The Departments contend that *Schwarz, supra*, 108 A.2d 417, provides the answer. There, the employee, while performing his job, was struck in the groin by a falling transom locker. 108 A.2d 417. . . . Despite intermittently missing work due to pain and being informed within the statutory period by his private physician that his testicle might have to be removed, Schwarz did not file a claim until long after the two-year statute expired, when testicular cancer was diagnosed. 108 A.2d 417. The court held Schwartz's claim barred because our statute requires the filing within two years of the accident regardless of when the exact "seriousness" of the harm becomes manifest. 108 A.2d 417. . . . *Schwarz* reflects the basic rule that when there is an unexpected traumatic event leading to an injury that results in lost wages, the incurring of medical bills, and a diagnosis of possible future surgery, and the worker knows he has suffered a compensable injury for workers' compensation purposes, the filing clock begins to run and the employee cannot put off filing until the full extent of his injury is determined. . . .

Here, and presumably in other delayed onset and insidious development cases, ascertainable disease symptoms emerge long after the time of the traumatic event. On the date of the initial incident, the worker is completely ignorant of an injury of which to notify the employer or with respect to which to file a claim. Indeed, it is theoretically possible for PTSD and other diseases with a quiescent period to remain dormant until more than two years after the traumatic event. If the statute is read to time the notice and the filing of a claim from the traumatic event, a worker's right could expire before there was any evidence whatsoever that he had been injured. . . .

Because the Workers' Compensation Act does not contemplate notice or the filing of a claim in the absence of injury, those time periods do not begin to run until the worker is, or reasonably should be, aware that he has sustained a compensable injury. . . . As noted in Part IV, *supra*, there is no accident for the purpose of filing a claim without an injury. Likewise, we think that is the reason why filing a claim requires the description of the injury. . . . It is simply inconceivable to us that the Legislature contemplated knowledge of injury as a trigger for notifying the employer but not for filing a claim. . . . Obviously, it is notice that should precede filing . . . [otherwise] the right to file a claim would expire before notice was required in many latency cases.

We are, therefore, satisfied that in the limited class of cases in which an unexpected traumatic event occurs and the injury it generates is latent or insidiously progressive, an accident . . . has not taken place until the signs and symptoms are such that they would alert a reasonable person that he had sustained a compensable injury. . . .

Notice and claim limitations in classic industrial accidents involving simultaneous traumatic event and injury will continue to be calculated from the date of the traumatic event. It is only in the narrow band of accident cases involving latency and insidious onset diseases that we think the Legislature would have intended the kind of leeway it developed to avoid a legitimately injured worker losing an occupational claim to be equally applicable to latent injury accidents. . . .

Finally, we note that our analysis of the timeliness issue will be critical not only to the claimants here, but also to the many workers in ordinary occupations who develop insidious onset diseases from a trauma and cannot invoke the occupational disease statute. Without it, those workers, who the Legislature clearly intended to be the beneficiaries of the Workers' Compensation Act, would otherwise lose their claims two years from the traumatic event even if, at that point, they were totally unaware that they had sustained an injury. We therefore hold that an accidental injury for reporting and filing purposes has not occurred until the point at which a reasonable person would know he had sustained a compensable injury. . . .

We reverse . . . and remand . . . the cases to the Division of Workers' Compensation for consideration of the substance and timeliness of the claimants' contentions under the standards to which we have adverted. . . .

NOTES AND QUESTIONS

1. Applying the court's newly announced rules to the facts it described, what result do you predict for each claimant? Are their claims best viewed as "accidental injuries," "occupational disease" (or under some laws, "repetitive stress"), or both? When did the time for reporting and filing begin to run for each claim?

2. The problem of multiple causes is a familiar one in tort law, and it is a regular feature of workers' compensation cases involving occupational disease or repetitive stress. If an employee suffers from a disabling emotional disorder, evidence of work-related stress may be mixed with evidence of family-related stress or preexisting conditions. If an employee suffers a respiratory disease after years of exposure to a work environment likely to cause such a disease, is it relevant that the employee has smoked cigarettes for years? In Fry's Food Stores v. Industrial Comm'n, 866 P.2d 1350 (Ariz. 1994), the court granted full benefits for an employee's "baker's lung" claim, based on exposure to flour, even though 85 percent of his impairment was due to smoking:

> [C]laimant's disability, or loss of earning capacity, did not occur until after he was exposed to flour dust. Thus, the evidence supports the ALJ's finding that the baker's lung was "the straw that broke the camel's back."

Id. at 1353. There are a variety of other approaches to the problem of multiple causes in workers' compensation law. Benefits might be apportioned to the extent that work aggravated a preexisting disability. *See id.* at 1352-1353 (denying such apportionment because claimant was not "disabled" until he began to suffer the additional effects of baker's lung). Still another approach is to change the standard of causation for occupational diseases. In some states, a claimant cannot recover for an occupational disease unless he proves that the disease was due "in material degree" to causes that characterize an employee's occupation and that substantially contribute to development of the disease. *See, e.g.*, N.J. Stat. Ann. § 34:15-31; Foxbilt Elec. v. Stanton, 583 So. 2d 720 (Fla. App. 1991) (occupational injury cases require "clear evidence" of causation).

3. What if an employee develops an occupational disease after working for a series of different employers in the same industry? It may be difficult to prove that

an employee's exposure at any single employer's workplace was sufficient in itself to produce the occupational disease. If the disease is covered, how should a court apportion liability for benefits? Many states have "last injuriously exposed" rules, which place the full liability on the employer with whom the claimant was last injuriously exposed. *See, e.g.*, Ariz. Rev. Stat. § 23-901.02; Colo. Rev. Stat. Ann. § 8-41-304; Fla. Stat. Ann. § 440.151; Ga. Code Ann. § 34-9-284; Iowa Code Ann. § 85A.10; Kan. Stat. §§ 44-5a06, 342.316; Md. Lab. & Empl. Code § 9-502; Tenn. Code Ann. § 50-6-304; Tex. Lab. Code Ann. § 406.031.

4. As *Brunell* illustrates, psychic injury might be traceable to a precise event or "accident," or it might be the result of repetitive stress. But even if psychic injury is clearly the result of an accident or repetitive stress, it is not always compensable to the same extent as physical injury. State courts and legislatures have provided a variety of approaches to the problem of "psychic injury." While most jurisdictions permit an award of benefits for psychic injury caused by physical injury, many draw the line at "pure" psychic injury. *See, e.g.*, Biasetti v. City of Stamford, 735 A.2d 321 (Conn. 1999); Rambaldo v. Accúrate Die Casting, 603 N.E.2d 975 (Ohio 1992); Andolsek v. City of Kirkland, 650 N.E.2d 911 (1994); Osborne v. City of Okla. City Police Dep't, 882 P.2d 75 (Okla. 1994); Seitz v. L & R Indus., 437 A.2d 1345 (R.I. 1981).

States that do not completely reject compensation for a pure psychic injury sometimes limit such claims by distinguishing accidental psychic injuries from repetitive stress psychic injuries: The former is compensable but not the latter. *See, e.g.*, Gatlin v. City of Knoxville, 822 S.W.2d 587, 591-592 (Tenn. 1991) (PTSD not compensable unless it arises out of sudden, unexpected incident, and mental injury resulting from stress over a period of time is not compensable). Another possible limit derives from the usual definition of occupational disease, which requires proof that "the employment exposed the employee to an identifiable condition of employment that is not common and necessary to all or a great many occupations." Chicago Bd. of Educ. v. Indus. Commn., 523 N.E.2d 912, 918 (Ill. App.), *app. denied,* 530 N.E.2d 241 (Ill. 1988).

5. Some aspects of employment are naturally stressful, like losing a promotion, or being reprimanded or fired. Could a stressful reprimand or discharge be an "accident" causing psychic injury? If so, should there be an exception for psychic injury resulting from "normal" employment actions? *See* Cigna Prop. & Cas. Ins. Co. v. Sneed, 772 S.W.2d 422 (Tenn. 1989) (not compensable); Brown & Root Constr. Co. v. Duckworth, 475 So. 2d 813 (Miss. 1985) (compensable). Some state legislatures have responded by amending their laws expressly to preclude benefits for stress resulting from personnel actions. *See, e.g.*, Mass. Gen. Laws ch. 152 § 29; Tex. Lab. Code § 408.006.

6. Work-related mental stress might lead to physical injury, such as a heart attack or cardiovascular illness. Many states have now adopted special cardiovascular injury rules that increase the burden of proof for a claimant or otherwise limit the compensability of such claims. *See, e.g.,* Ariz. Rev. Stat. § 23-1043.01; Ark. Code Ann. § 11-9-114; Colo. Rev. Stat. Ann. § 8-41-302; Ga. Code Ann. § 34-9-280; La. Stat. Ann. §§ 23:1021, 23:1031.1; Okla. Stat. Ann. tit. 85, § 3; Tex. Lab. Code Ann. § 408.008. Some states that do not otherwise limit compensability of cardiovascular injuries have enacted special rules for police

officers, firefighters, and other public safety personnel.

7. If an employee's psychic injury claim is not compensable under workers' compensation law, is a negligence-based tort claim against the employer still barred by the exclusive remedy defense? The possibility of tort claims by employees or their survivors is addressed in Part B.6 of this Chapter.

8. Statutes of limitations present a potentially serious obstacle for any latent injury claim. A statute of limitations might run from the date of the first exposure, the last exposure, or the last day of employment. Under any of these versions a claimant may lose a claim before he knows he has one. In *Brunell*, the New Jersey court avoided this result by holding that the period of limitations for notice or filing with respect to an accidental injury runs from the date "a reasonable person would know he had sustained a compensable injury." In the case of occupational disease, New Jersey law already provided a similar rule. N.J. Stat. Ann. § 34:15-33. Courts and legislatures in many other states agree that the period of limitations runs from the date of the employee's "discovery" of his claim. Unfortunately for latent disease victims, some states still apply statutes of limitations that may begin to run long before the employee discovers the claim. *See, e.g.*, Cable v. Workmen's Compensation App. Bd., 664 A.2d 1349 (Pa. 1995); Tisco Intermountain v. Indus. Comm'n, 744 P.2d 1340 (Utah 1987).

9. The suspicion and reality of fraud by claimants has been part of the workers' compensation debate from the start. The so-called "Monday effect" refers to the greater number of claims filed on Monday than on any other day. One possible explanation is that some employees injured at home on Saturday or Sunday falsely claim that accidents occurred on Monday and were work-related. Granting compensation for occupational diseases and "repetitive stress" injuries appears to have increased the potential for fraud. *See* M. McCluskey, *The Illusion of Efficiency in Workers' Compensation "Reform,"* 50 Rutgers L. Rev. 657 (1998); G. Schwartz, *Waste, Fraud, and Abuse in Workers' Compensation: The Recent California Experience*, 52 Md. L. Rev. 983 (1993). The significance of claimant fraud remains a matter of debate. *See* Benjamin Hansen, *The "Monday Effect" in Workers' Compensation: Evidence from the California Reforms* (2008), available at http://ssrn.com/abstract=1940142.

10. The lack of personal medical insurance coverage might be an important factor leading some injured or ill workers' to file workers' compensation claims that have no real connection or a doubtful connection to work. Health care insurance reforms that expand coverage to previously uninsured workers might reduce the number of questionable claims and shift some costs currently borne by the workers' compensation system to the general health care insurance system. Bronchetti, Erin Todd and McInerney, Melissa, *Does Increased Access to Health Insurance Impact Claims for Workers' Compensation? Evidence from Massachusetts Health Care Reform* (June 30, 2017). Upjohn Institute Working Paper 17-277. Available at SSRN: https://ssrn.com/abstract=3000944.

4. *Disqualification*

Workers' compensation law eliminates negligence as a basis for or defense against compensation, but that elimination introduces the problem of moral hazard: Will a no-fault approach encourage negligence or unreasonable risk-taking by either party? Wholly aside from the question of whether the no-fault approach actually affects behavior, are there some forms of employee or employer behavior that are so intolerable that it is unacceptable to require the other party to bear any part of the cost of the loss? Should some behavior be "punished" by the denial of benefits or the denial of the exclusive remedy defense? Finally, are some accidents not "work-related" in that the causative behavior far exceeded the normal or expected range of carelessness that makes work activity more dangerous than not working?

In this section we look at one angle of the problem, employee misbehavior. Later, we will consider the other angle, employer misbehavior.

CAREY v. BRYAN & ROLLINS

49 Del. 387, 117 A.2d 240 (1955)

HERRMANN, J.

The Industrial Accident Board awarded workmen's compensation to the claimant for injuries sustained by him when a pickup truck, which he was driving, ran off the road and struck a telephone pole. According to the uncontroverted testimony of the claimant, he was driving in a 50 mile per hour zone at a speed of "better than fifty-five; 55, 65, something like that." While driving at that speed, the claimant attempted to light a cigarette and, in so doing, the cigarette dropped to the seat or the floor of the truck. The claimant reached down to search for and recover the cigarette, lost control of the vehicle and ran off the road into the pole. . . .

The portion of the Workmen's Compensation Statute involved here, being 19 Del. C. § 2353(b) derived from 1935 Code ¶6106, provides as follows:

> (b) If any employee be injured as a result of his intoxication, or because of his deliberate and reckless indifference to danger, or because of his wilful intention to bring about the injury or death of himself, or of another, or because of his wilful failure or refusal to use a reasonable safety appliance provided for him, or to perform a duty required by statute, he shall not be entitled to recover damages in an action at law, or compensation or medical, dental, optometric or hospital service under the compensatory provisions of this chapter. The burden of proof under the provisions of this subsection shall be on the employer.

. . . The word "willful" is the key word in this case. That word, as used in the subsection of the Statute here involved, was considered by this Court in Lobdell Car Wheel Co. v. Subielski, 2 W.W. Harr. 462, 125 A. 462, 464 . . . :

> The word "willful" may be defined with a reasonable degree of satisfaction, although the definitions vary in some respects, depending somewhat upon the meaning intended to be conveyed by its use with other words. In the present statute we believe it was used to define an act done intentionally, knowingly, and purposely, without justifiable excuse, as distinguished from an act done carelessly, thoughtlessly, heedlessly or inadvertently.

There is no evidence in this case that the claimant intentionally and deliberately exceeded the speed limit or drove recklessly, knowingly and purposely, without justifiable excuse. The employer has the burden of proof under the forfeiture provisions of the Workmen's Compensation Statute. *See* 19 Del. C. § 2353(b). The employer has not been able to point to anything in the evidence which would compel the inference that the actions of the claimant were intentional, deliberate and "wilful." Most operators of motor vehicles have, at one time or another, found themselves driving at 60 or 65 miles per hour on the open highway carelessly, thoughtlessly and inadvertently, without conscious intention to exceed the speed limit. While an inference of wilfulness might be the only reasonable inference to be drawn from such speed within city or town limits, no such inference is created where, as here, the speed limit was 50 miles per hour.

Similarly, no inference of deliberation or intention, or conscious indifference to consequences, is compelled by the fact that, while driving along the open highway, the claimant reached down to recover the cigarette he had started to light. It is common knowledge that drivers often do this as a matter of reflex action and impulse, carelessly and thoughtlessly but without conscious intention, to prevent burns to the person, clothing or upholstery. This may be folly and negligence when driving at 60 miles per hour but, as a matter of law, it does not constitute "wilful" reckless driving in the absence of some evidence of deliberation.

The employer contends that a violation of a penal statute, such as the motor vehicle statute prohibiting speeding and reckless driving, in and of itself constitutes a "wilful failure to perform a duty required by statute" and a forfeiture of compensation rights under the provisions of § 2353(b). The employer places principal reliance upon Aetna Life Ins. Co. v. Carroll, 169 Ga. 333, 150 S.E. 208, 211. In that case, the Supreme Court of Georgia held that violation of a penal statute, such as the motor vehicle speed law, in and of itself constituted "willful misconduct" and "willful failure . . . to perform a duty required by statute" so as to bar rights under the Georgia Workmen's Compensation Statute.

The ratio decidendi of the case is that an employer should not be compelled to compensate an employee for his injury, or his dependents for his death, caused by the employee's violation of a criminal statute. I find the rule of the *Carroll* case to be unacceptable for the following reasons: (1) That case deals with the construction of the words "willful misconduct" which do not appear in the Delaware statute although, in other respects, the pertinent provision of the Georgia statute is almost identical with ours. (2) In Delaware, violation of a penal motor vehicle statute, without more, constitutes negligence per se. It is settled that negligence alone will not defeat recovery of workmen's compensation. (3) There is such conflict and confusion among the various statutes and decisions relating to this phase of the law of workmen's compensation, precedents from other jurisdictions are of little value. . . . The only reasonable course, therefore, is to confine ourselves to the precise language of our Statute and an attempt to determine the intention of our Legislature. (4) I find the rule of the *Carroll* case to be unacceptably harsh when considered in the light of the humanitarian purposes of the Workmen's Compensation Law. It does not seem consonant with the spirit of such legislation to hold that a forfeiture of all rights of compensation may result from an inadvertent and unintentional violation of a traffic law. . . .

It is held that violation of a penal motor vehicle statute does not, per se, constitute a "wilful failure to perform a duty required by statute" and forfeiture under 19 Del. C. § 2353(b) and that, in order to invoke the forfeiture provisions of the Workmen's Compensation Law, the employer has the burden of proving by a preponderance of the evidence that the violation of the statute was "wilful," i.e., intentional and deliberate and not just careless and inadvertent. In the instant case, the employer was unable to make such a showing . . . .

NOTES AND QUESTIONS

1. What are some distinguishing features of willfulness or recklessness that make these states of mind observably different from mere negligence? In thinking about this question, consider the facts in Chandler Telecom, LLC v. Burdette, 797 S.E.2d 93 (Ga. 2017). The employee technician in *Chandler Telecom* suffered serious injuries when he fell during a "controlled descent" from a cell phone tower.

> [P]rior to their shift that day, the supervisor over Burdette's six-person crew instructed them to climb down the towers and not to use controlled descent.... When their work was almost complete, Prejean [the lead worker for the crew] instructed Burdette to climb down the tower, but Burdette responded that he wanted to use controlled descent instead.
>
> Prejean's account of his conversation with Burdette just before Burdette's descent (and fall) is as follows:
>
> > I told him no, man, just climb down. Might as well just climb down.... [W]e don't have a safety rope up here for you to grab. He told me he had done this so many times. I was like, dude, they're going to be mad if you do it. [Our supervisor] will be mad if you do it and, ... you might not have a job or you might, you know, have to deal with the consequences if you don't listen....
>
> Nevertheless, even after Prejean instructed Burdette to climb down the tower two or three more times, Burdette prepared his equipment and began controlled descent. Shortly thereafter, Burdette fell a great distance from the tower and landed on an "ice bridge," which caused serious injuries.... Prejean testified that Burdette's fall was the result of "user error," rather than any equipment malfunction. He further noted that, while Burdette had the required equipment for climbing down, he did not have all of the necessary equipment for controlled descent.

Id. at 627-28.

2. If an employee's willfulness in violating a statute, work rule, or other duty could be cause for disqualification, then the employer's own conduct in permitting, encouraging, or profiting from the employee's willfulness might also become an issue. *See, e.g.*, Perry v. State, 134 P.3d 1242 (Wyo. 2006) (describing Wyoming law that employee's violation of safety rule is grounds for disqualification provided employer did not accept benefit of the violation).

3. Willfulness and recklessness are mainly associated with "accidents" that occur during a moment of bad behavior. But willfulness or recklessness can also be the cause of occupational disease or repetitive stress that occurs over time and not in a single moment. For example, an employee's persistent and willful refusal to wear a respirator may lead to lung disease. If an employee's "willful" self-exposure to a hazard is persistent, it may be particularly difficult to deny the employer's corresponding fault in failing to manage the problem. Thus,

occupational disease or repetitive stress injury requires a more nuanced approach to disqualification. *See, e.g.*, N.J. Stat. Ann. § 34:15-30.

> [N]o compensation shall be payable when the injury or death by occupational disease is caused by willful self-exposure to a known hazard or by the employee's willful failure to make use of a reasonable and proper guard or personal protective device furnished by the employer which has been clearly made a requirement of the employee's employment by the employer and which an employer can properly document that despite repeated warnings, the employee has willfully failed to properly and effectively utilize.

4. In addition to general disqualifications based on "willfulness" or "recklessness," workers' compensation laws in most states add disqualifications based on specific misconduct. A typical example is disqualification if an accident was because of a claimant's use of alcohol or drugs. *See, e.g.*, Ark. Code Ann. § 11-9-102(4)(B)(iv). At least one state takes an even harder approach. In Texas, the claimant is disqualified if his injury "*occurred while* the employee was in a state of intoxication." *See, e.g.*, Tex. Lab. Code § 406.032 (emphasis added).

What if the employee's job entails consuming alcohol? *Compare* Balk v. Austin Ford Logan Inc., 633 N.Y.S.2d 675 (N.Y. App. Div. 1995) (upholding disqualification of sales employee whose intoxication caused accident after he left a sales meeting); *with* Beneficiaries of McBroom v. Chamber of Commerce, 713 P.2d 1095 (Or. App. 1986) (granting benefits to survivors of employee whose body was found in whirlpool in hotel where he attended employer's conference despite blood alcohol level of .40 at time of death); *and* W. Florida Distrib. v. Laramie, 438 So. 2d 133 (Fla. App. 1983) (employer could not assert intoxication defense because employer impliedly represented that employee liquor salesman would not be deprived of his job or compensation if he became intoxicated on the job).

5. Another type of disqualification for specific misconduct is based on the claimant's own "horseplay." *See, e.g.*, Utah Code Ann. § 35-1-45. Of course, even without a specific statutory ground for disqualification, denial of benefits on the grounds of horseplay might be based on an argument that horseplay accidents do not arise out of employment. Still, the regularity and acceptance of horseplay in the workplace may be a matter over which the employer exercises some control. Thus, employer supervision is sometimes an issue determining whether horseplay disqualifies a claimant. *See* Prows v. Industrial Comm'n, 610 P.2d 1362 (Utah 1980); A. Larson, The Law of Workmen's Compensation, vol. 1A, § 23.20 (1979).

5. *Employer Interference with Access to Benefits*

An employer could undermine the purpose of the workers' compensation scheme if it could exercise the right of "employment at will" to discipline, discharge, or threaten to discharge an employee for filing a workers' compensation claim. The threat of discharge might mean little to a severely injured or permanently disabled employee who has little to lose by seeking benefits. However, an employee who suffers a less serious injury and expects to return to her job has much to fear from a vindictive employer. She might therefore fail to report an accident even if this means going without medical care or bearing the cost on her own.

For years after the enactment of workers' compensation systems, employment at will doctrine permitted an employer to exercise its economic power to discourage the reporting of accidents or the filing of claims. *See* E. Spieler, *Perpetuating Risk? Workers' Compensation and the Persistence of Occupational Injuries*, 31 Hous. L. Rev. 119, 220-225 (1994). In Frampton v. Central Indiana Gas Co., 297 N.E.2d 425 (Ind. 1973), the Supreme Court of Indiana recognized a public policy-based exception to the employment-at-will doctrine:

> Retaliatory discharge for filing a workmen's compensation claim is a wrongful, unconscionable act and should be actionable in a court of law. . . . [A]n employee who alleges he or she was retaliatorily discharged for filing a claim pursuant to the Indiana Workmen's Compensation Act . . . has stated a claim upon which relief can be granted. . . . [U]nder ordinary circumstances, an employee at will may be discharged without cause. However, when an employee is discharged solely for exercising a statutorily conferred right an exception to the general rule must be recognized.

Id. at 428.

Frampton led the way to similar reforms in nearly all states. Today, workers' compensation statutes or antidiscrimination statutes in many states specifically prohibit retaliating or discriminating against workers' compensation claimants. *See, e.g.*, Tex. Lab. Code Ann. § 541.001. In states without specific legislation, courts often adopt the *Frampton* public policy approach under common law. *See, e.g.,* Martin Marietta Corp. v. Lorenz, 823 P.2d 100, 108 (Colo. 1992) (common law discharge in violation of public policy claim).

A practical problem in enforcing rules against retaliation is that alleged retaliatory motive frequently springs from a series of interconnected events, some of which are perfectly lawful motivations for adverse actions. Accidents that cause injury might be the result of employee negligence. Negligence does not disqualify the employee from receiving benefits, but can subject the employee to legitimate discipline. Moreover, negligent or not, an employee has no right to a job he cannot perform. Thus, if the injury or illness leaves the employee unable to work for any length of time, the employer can lawfully terminate the employee and hire a replacement if the employer's business need, and not retaliation, is the motivation.

SWEARINGEN v. OWENS-CORNING FIBERGLAS CORP.

968 F.2d 559 (5th Cir. 1992)

GOLDBERG, C. J.:

. . . The Texas legislature created a narrow exception to the Texas common law employment-at-will doctrine when it enacted article 8307c of the workers' compensation laws. [A]rticle 8307c protects employees who file workers' compensation claims, hire attorneys to represent them in workers' compensation claims, assist in filing workers' compensation claims or testify at hearings concerning workers' compensation claims from discrimination by employers.

In this appeal, we decide whether an employer that terminates an employee for an excessive absence from work pursuant to an absence control policy after the employee experienced a job-related injury violates article 8307c. . . . [B]ecause the employee cannot prove that the employer terminated her for one of the four reasons prohibited by the statute, we affirm the . . . judgment for the defendant employer.

I. Background

. . . Vergie Swearingen sustained a work-related injury while employed by Owens-Corning Fiberglas Corporation ("OCF") at its plant. . . . Swearingen then applied for and received workers' compensation benefits. Swearingen could not return to work for medical reasons for about four years.

As an employee of OCF, Swearingen belonged to the collective bargaining unit represented by the Glass, Pottery, Plastics and Allied Workers International Union ("Union"). The collective bargaining agreement between OCF and the Union contained an "absence control provision," which stated that "[a]n employee will lose seniority rights . . . [i]f off work . . . twenty-four consecutive months." On September 26, 1988, the Personnel Manager at OCF wrote Swearingen a letter referencing the absence control provision and terminating Swearingen effective that day because her absence on medical leave exceeded twenty-four months. Swearingen attempted to return to work at OCF in the spring of 1990, after her physician released her to return to work with certain restrictions. Swearingen then discovered that, under the absence control provision of the collective bargaining agreement, she had lost her seniority rights and that OCF had terminated her . . . .

Swearingen . . . claim[s] that OCF retaliated against her for filing a workers' compensation claim in violation of article 8307c. The court [entered] a take-nothing judgment against plaintiff Swearingen. Swearingen now appeals . . . [and] has filed a motion requesting this Court to certify the issue . . . to the Texas Supreme Court.

II. Article 8307c

Article 8307c is a statutory exception to the Texas common law employment at-will doctrine. Thurman v. Sears, Roebuck & Co., 952 F.2d 128, 131 (5th Cir. 1992). . . . The statute provides that

> [n]o person may discharge or in any other manner discriminate against any employee because the employee has in good faith filed a claim, hired a lawyer to represent [her] in a claim, instituted, or caused to be instituted, in good faith, any proceeding under the Texas Workmen's Compensation Act, or has testified or is about to testify in any such proceeding.

Tex. Rev. Civ. Stat. Ann. art. 8307c, § 1 (Vernon Supp. 1992). Through article 8307c, the Texas legislature generally expressed "'the state's public policy of protecting its important interest in insuring that its work[ers'] compensation law can function to the benefit of its intended beneficiaries, employees, without coercion or unjust treatment from their employers as a result of exercising their rights under that law.'" *Roadway Express*, 931 F.2d at 1090 (*quoting* Carnation Co. v. Borner, 588 S.W.2d 814, 819 (Tex. Civ. App.1979), *aff'd*, 610 S.W.2d 450 (Tex. 1980)). . . .

The employee bears the initial burden of establishing a causal link between the "discharge and [the] claim for workers' compensation." *Roadway Express*, 931 F.2d at 1090. . . . The employee only needs to prove that the workers' compensation claim represented a "determining factor" in the discharge, not that the employer discharged her solely because of the claim. *Roadway Express*, 931 F.2d at 1090. . . . Retaliation, then, only needs to be "a reason" for discharge to permit an employee to recover under 8307c. *Id.*; Hunt v. Van Der Horst Corp., 711 S.W.2d

77, 79 (Tex. App. — Dallas 1986, no writ); *see also* Santex, Inc. v. Cunningham, 618 S.W.2d 557, 559 (Tex. Civ. App. — Waco 1981, no writ) ("even if there are other reasons," an employer cannot use the filing of a workers' compensation claim "as a reason to discharge or otherwise discriminate against an employee"). Once the employee establishes the causal link, "the employer must rebut [the alleged discrimination] by showing a legitimate reason for the discharge." *Roadway Express*, 931 F.2d at 1090 (citing *Hughes*, 624 S.W.2d at 599). . . .

The district court concluded that OCF did not retaliate against Swearingen for one of the reasons listed in 8307c (filing a claim, hiring a lawyer, assisting in filing a claim or testifying at a proceeding), but that OCF terminated Swearingen because her absence exceeded the 24-month period permitted by the collective bargaining agreement. Our holding today is simple: Swearingen cannot demonstrate the requisite causal link between her discharge and any of the four activities protected in article 8307c. Swearingen has offered no evidence that the filing of her claim constituted a "determining factor" in her discharge. *See id.* at 265. . . . No evidence shows that Swearingen's termination was motivated, even in part, by the filing of a workers' compensation claim. Swearingen "cannot hope to prove this link" between her termination and her claim for workers' compensation benefits, for she admitted that she has no evidence to do so. *American Red Cross*, 752 F. Supp. at 739. Instead, Swearingen conceded in her deposition testimony that OCF terminated her for one reason: violation of the absence control policy. Violation of a neutrally-applied absence control policy is not one of the circumstances safeguarded by article 8307c. Unless one of the four specific circumstances listed in article 8307c motivated the employer in discharging or discriminating against an employee, that employee cannot prevail in an action based on article 8307c. For this reason, we conclude that Swearingen's article 8307c claim of retaliatory discharge fails as a matter of law. . . .

NOTES AND QUESTIONS

1. The Texas Supreme Court confirmed the Fifth Circuit's interpretation of Texas law in. Contin. Coffee Prods., Inc. v. Casarez, 937 S.W.2d 444 (Tex. 1996).

2. An employer's absence control policy must also comply with another important law, the Family and Medical Leave Act, which requires an employer to grant an employee unpaid leave of up to 12 weeks for medical and certain other purposes. Thus, while a policy such as the one in *Swearingen* might not violate workers' compensation law, it will violate the FMLA if the employer does not observe the employee's right to return to his job within the time guaranteed by the FMLA. See Chapter 7, *infra*. An employer's refusal to extend a worker's medical leave might also violate the duty reasonably to accommodate an employer's disability under the Americans with Disabilities Act. See Holly v. Clairson Indus., L.L.C., 492 F.3d 1247 (11th Cir. 2007); Watt v. County, 210 F.Supp.3d 1078 (E.D. Wis. 2016) (employer policy denying return to work until employee is "100% healed might violate a duty to accommodate the disabled).

3. Suppose Swearingen, having fully recovered, filed an application for employment with her former employer. The employer rejected her application because of its policy of not rehiring any former employee. Should a court hold that the employer has violated a law against "discrimination" against an employee who

has filed a workers' compensation claim? *Compare* Warnek v. ABB Combustion Eng'g Servs., Inc., 972 P.2d 453 (Wash. 1999) (no) *with* Ill. Comp. Stat. tit. 820, § 305/4(h) and N.M. Stat. Ann. § 52-1-50.1 (specifically prohibiting retaliatory refusal to rehire or recall). *See also* Gonzalez-Centeno v. North Cent. Kansas Regional Juvenile Detention Facility, 101 P.3d 1170 (Kan. 2004) (employee concurrently employed by two employers stated claim against one employer who discharged him because of his claim against the other employer).

4. Could an employer ask applicants whether they have ever filed a workers' compensation claim? See Chapter Three, Part C.3, *supra*. Is such a question necessarily for the purpose of discriminating? If there is any legitimate nondiscriminatory reason for the question, is there any way for the employer to obtain this information without violating the laws against discrimination?

5. Aside from potential retaliation liability, it is *not* necessarily in an employer's interest to discharge a partially or temporarily disabled employee who has filed a claim. Depending on the circumstances, reassignment or rehabilitation may be less expensive than disability payments. Many employers try to control workers' compensation costs by assigning partially disabled employees to "light duty" and funding additional rehabilitation services. But if the employer provides accommodations only for employees disabled by work-related injuries and denies accommodations for employees disabled by pregnancy, the employer might face a claim of pregnancy discrimination. *See* Young v. United Parcel Serv., Inc., 135 S. Ct. 1338 (2015), and Chapter 7.C.4.

6. Could an employer lawfully discharge a partially and temporarily disabled employee for failing to participate in or cooperate with a job rehabilitation program?

7. Despite laws against "retaliation," a significant number of employees still do not file claims for qualified injuries. According to some surveys, only about 55 percent of employees file claims after suffering a work-related injury serious enough to cause lost time. D. Lakdawalla, R. Reville & S. Seabury, *How Does Health Insurance Affect Workers Compensation Filing?* 45 Economic Inquiry 286 (April 2007). A significant factor appears to be the existence of the employer's own medical insurance plan. According to one theory, an employer that has established its own regular medical insurance plan is more likely to encourage employees to file workers' compensation claims, because the employer will ultimately bear some part of the cost whether the injury is work-related or not.

PROBLEMS

1. Henry Stoick was a factory worker for Nimble Manufacturing. Nimble had a safety incentive program that awarded a bonus to every employee in a department if the department had an above average accidental injury record for the year. One day Stoick strained his back while lifting a box in the course of his employment. He reported his injury to his supervisor Les Cash, and Cash reminded him that the department needed "to avoid any more accidents" to win an annual safety bonus. Cash agreed to give Stoick "light duty" the rest of the day, and Stoick went back to work without making any official report of his injury. Stoick hoped his back would get better and he returned to work each day the next week. Cash

continued to assign Stoick to light duty. Nevertheless, Stoick's back pain persisted.

After Stoick's doctor advised him to take two weeks off work, Stoick called Cash and said he wanted to file a workers' compensation claim. "Can't you just take a couple of weeks of sick leave or vacation?" Cash queried in an exasperated tone. "We might miss our bonus if we file one more claim." But Stoick didn't want to use his vacation time or sick leave, especially because he didn't know how long his injury might last. He filed a claim.

Stoick eventually returned to work after some much-needed rest for his back. When he returned, Cash informed him that the department would not be getting its annual safety bonus. "I guess we all know why," he said pointedly to Stoick.

Did Nimble violate the rights of Stoick and other employees in the same department by denying them the safety bonus?

2. Suppose that after Stoick filed his claim, Nimble discharged him under another safety policy for the termination of "accident-prone" employees. The policy required termination of any employee who caused more than three "serious" accidents in a year. The policy defined "serious accident" as one leading to the injury or death of any person, or leading to property damage of over $500. Did Nimble lawfully discharge Stoick based on the safety policy?

6. *Preserved Tort Claims*

a. Third-Party Liability: Who's an Employee and Who's the Employer?

The workers' compensation compromise — compensation for work-related injuries without regard to fault in exchange for limited employer liability — is a compromise only among and between an employer and its employees. The employer or fellow employee can assert the "exclusive remedy" defense against an employee's common law tort claim based on any injury covered by workers' compensation law. However, there is no such compromise between an employee and "third parties" outside the employment relationship, such as a manufacturer of equipment that, by reason of defect, may have caused the employee's injury.[2] Not surprisingly, employees injured in their work frequently sue third parties in the hope of recovering damages in addition to their workers' compensation benefits.

Distinguishing a third party from the employer or a fellow employee is not always easy. Suppose, for example, one worker negligently causes injury to another. The exclusive remedy defense protects the negligent worker from tort liability if he and the injured worker are both "employees" of the same "employer." However, the injured worker might try to prove that the negligent worker is really a "third party," such as an independent contractor or an employee of a different employer. If the negligent worker is an employee of a different employer, the injured employee might also sue the other employer under the doctrine of *respondeat superior* or

[2] Nor are other injured parties with claims derivative of the employee's claim necessarily bound by the compromise with respect to their separate claims against the employer. *See, e.g.*, Hitachi Chem. Electro-Prods., Inc. v. Gurley, 466 S.E.2d 867 (1995) (children who sought damages for prenatal injuries caused by parent-employees' exposure to hazardous chemicals were not subject to employer's exclusive remedy defense).

negligent hiring. *See, e.g.*, Wise v. Complete Staffing, 56 S.W.3d 900 (Tex. App. 2001), portions of which are set forth in Chapter Three, Part B.

Whether an alleged tortfeasor is an "employer" or a third party can also be uncertain when the alleged tortfeasor is affiliated with the admitted employer. An employer's negligence is generally not imputed to its owner, parent or subsidiary. Great Atl. & Pac. Tea Co. v. Imbraguglio, 346 Md. 573, 697 A.2d 885 (1997); Mitchell v. Burrillville Racing Ass'n, 673 A.2d 446 (R.I. 1996). But what if the parent or subsidiary caused the accident by its own active negligence, perhaps because it controlled the worksite or participated in the work? Can the owner, parent, or subsidiary assert the employer's exclusive remedy defense? In answering this question, the courts often resort to the same analysis they use under other employment laws when a plaintiff employee seeks to treat two defendant corporate entities as one "employer." See Chapter 2, Part B, *supra*. However, in "third-party" negligence cases it is typically the *defendants* who argue they should be regarded as a "single employer" for the exclusive remedy defense. *See, e.g.*, Clark v. United Tech. Auto., Inc., 594 N.W.2d 447 (Mich. 1999); Hall v. Fanticone, 730 A.2d 919 (N.J. Super. 1999); Gunderson v. Harrington, 632 N.W.2d 695 (Minn. 2001). The claimant's typical response to the "single employer" theory is the *dual persona* or dual capacity theory: A separate but affiliated entity is not entitled to the employer's exclusive remedy defense if the affiliated entity's negligent action was in some non-employer capacity. *See* Tatum v. Med. Univ. of S. Carolina, 552 S.E.2d 18 (S.C. 2001); Thomeier v. Rhone-Poulenc, Inc., 928 F. Supp. 548 (W.D. Pa. 1996).

The problem of third-party liability is especially severe at a construction site where many different and independent employers and workforces work side by side, and employees are often mixed with individual independent contractors. In many states, special rules provide that the general contractor of a project is or may be deemed the employer of all employees of all subcontractors for purposes of workers' compensation law. *See, e.g.*, Entergy Gulf States, Inc. v. Summers, 282 S.W.3d 433 (Tex. 2009) (also allowing premises owner to assert exclusive remedy defense); Ioerger v. Halverson, 902 N.E.2d 645 (Ill. 2008) (employer's co-venturer in construction project could assert exclusive remedy defense). Depending on the terms of local law and the agreements between the parties, independent contractors on the site might also be deemed employees of the general contractor for purposes of workers' compensation law. What reasons might lawmakers have for treating the general contractor and all subcontractors and their employees as if they are part of a single employer entity, for purposes of the exclusive remedy defense?

Another rule that extends the scope of the exclusive remedy defense is the "borrowed" or "loaned" employee doctrine. Under this rule, a worker employed by one employer might become the "borrowed" employee of another employer while the borrowing employer is actually directing the employee's work. The doctrine has its origins in general tort law, where it extended an employer's *respondeat superior* liability or barred an employee's tort claim under the fellow servant rule. *See, e.g.*, Delory v. Blodgett, 69 N.E. 1078 (Mass. 1904). The effect of the borrowed employee doctrine in workers' compensation cases might be to hold the borrowing employer or its insurer liable for workers' compensation benefits, to bar the borrowed employee's tort claim against the borrowing employer, or to bar an employee's *respondeat superior* claim against a negligent worker's lending employer. *See generally* Appeal of Longchamps Elec., Inc., 137 N.H. 731, 634 A.2d 994 (1993); Pace v. Cummins Engine Co., 905 P.2d 308 (Utah App. 1995).

Third-party staffing situations provide a likely setting for borrowed employee issues if local legislation fails to supply answers. If a staffing service holds itself out as the "employer" of employees it assigns to a client under a leasing or temporary employment arrangement, a court might apply the borrowed servant doctrine to treat the client as the employer for purposes of the exclusive remedy defense, even if the staffing service obtains and pays for workers compensation insurance. *See, e.g.*, Candido v. Polymers, Inc., 687 A.2d 476 (Vt. 1996); Chapa v. Koch Refining Corp., 985 S.W.2d 158 (Tex. App. 1998) (permitting both lessor employer and lessee employer to assert exclusive remedy defense against leased employee).

b. Employer Liability

As noted earlier in connection with the problem of employee misconduct, a no-fault approach raises a question of moral hazard: Will eliminating fault as a basis for benefits encourage risky behavior? Apart from the problem of moral hazard, are some actions so likely to cause injury that they are not "accidents" as to which workers' compensation law should apply? In this section, we consider the *employer* misconduct side of these problems.

MEAD v. WESTERN SLATE, INC.
848 A.2d 257 (Vt. 2004)

JOHNSON, J.

Defendants Western Slate, Inc. and Jeffrey N. Harrison appeal from . . . a jury verdict finding them liable for injuries to their employee, plaintiff Martin Mead, Jr., under the intentional-injury exception to the workers' compensation law. Defendants contend the court erred in ruling that the exception could be satisfied by a showing that they knew to a "substantial certainty" their conduct would result in plaintiff's injury. . . .

Plaintiff Martin Mead had worked for defendant Western Slate, Inc. as a mechanic, sawyer, and driller for several years prior to the accident. . . . He had extensive experience working in Western's slate quarry pit, and also had prior work experience in the quarry of another employer. Defendant Jeffrey N. Harrison is the co-owner of Western. He is an experienced slate quarry operator and was generally in charge of mining operations at the time of incident. On the morning of August 17, 1999, Harrison directed plaintiff to prepare a "pillar" — or area of stone — below the northeastern high wall for excavation. Plaintiff spent much of the day in the pit drilling holes along the butt and grain of the rock for the insertion of packing material and explosives.

The next morning, plaintiff returned to the area to complete the drilling. Upon arrival, however, he observed fresh debris in the area — indicating a recent rock fall. Plaintiff sent two co-workers, his brother Richard Mead and Leonard

Andrews, to inform Harrison about the situation, and then commenced to complete the drilling. Plaintiff recalled that when the two returned, Richard reported that Harrison had instructed them to load the explosives and packing material in their truck, return to the pit, and finish the drilling, loading, and firing. Harrison had also indicated that he needed to go to the store to buy parts, and would return shortly to inspect the area. . . . Plaintiff then completed the drilling and was in the process of loading the holes with explosives when he was struck by a rock fall, sustaining multiple fractures and lacerations.

Plaintiff applied for and received workers' compensation benefits. He also filed a personal injury action against Harrison and Western, alleging that they had committed an intentional tort by failing to order him to cease operations and leave the area after the initial rock fall, resulting in a substantial certainty of injury. *See* Kittell v. Vt. Weatherboard, Inc., 417 A.2d 926, 927 (1980) (workers' compensation provides exclusive remedy for work-related injury absent "specific intent to injure"). Plaintiff also sued Harrison under a separate co-employee claim that Harrison had committed affirmative acts of negligence by ordering plaintiff to work in the pit after Harrison had been informed of the initial rock fall. *See* Gerrish v. Savard, 739 A.2d 1195, 1198 (1999) (workers' compensation exclusivity does not prohibit employee's action against co-worker for negligence outside parameters of employer's non-delegable duty to maintain safe workplace).

. . . At the close of plaintiff's case in chief, and again at the conclusion of all the evidence, defendants moved for judgment as a matter of law. . . . The court denied both motions, finding that the evidence was sufficient to raise a jury question as to whether defendants had knowledge to a "substantial certainty" that their actions would result in plaintiff's injuries. . . .

[T]he court then instructed the jury that it was plaintiff's burden to prove that defendants had the "specific intent to injure him," but that such intent could be established in one of two ways: that defendants either "had the purpose or desire to cause him injury or that although the Defendants lack[ed] such purpose or desire they knew to a substantial certainty that their actions would bring about his injury." . . . The jury returned a special verdict in favor of plaintiff, finding that although neither defendant had a specific purpose or desire to injure him, both knew to a substantial certainty that their actions or inactions would injure plaintiff. . . .

We turn first to defendants' contention that the court erred by allowing plaintiff to prove a "specific intent" to injure based on a showing that defendants knew to a "substantial certainty" their conduct would result in injury to plaintiff.

. . . Subject to certain limited exceptions, Vermont's workers' compensation statute provides the exclusive remedy for workplace injuries. . . . Like most other jurisdictions, we have recognized an exception to the exclusivity rule for intentional injuries committed by the employer. *See Kittell*, 417 A.2d at 927. . . . We stressed in *Kittell*, however, that the policy trade-off underlying the workers' compensation law was "best served by allowing the remedial system which the Legislature has created a broad sphere of operations." *Kittell*, 417 A.2d at 927. Hence, we held that "nothing short of a specific intent to injure falls outside the scope of the Act." *Id.* . . . Under *Kittell*, even "wilful and wanton conduct leading to a sudden but foreseeable injury" is within the scope of the Act. 417 A.2d at 926.

A growing number of jurisdictions have broadened the definition of specific intent beyond those in *Kittell*, to include instances where an employer not only intends to injure the worker, but engages in conduct knowing that it is substantially certain to cause injury or death. *See generally*, Davis v. CMS Continental Natural Gas, Inc., 23 P.3d 288, 292-95 (2001) (collecting cases); A. Larson & L. Larson, 6 Larson's Workers' Compensation Law §§ 103.04[2][a]-103.04[2][e] at 103-12-103-20.1 (2003). On the continuum of tortious conduct, substantial certainty has been described as just below the most aggravated conduct where the actor intends to injure the victim; it is more than "mere knowledge and appreciation of a risk," Pariseau v. Wedge Products, Inc., 522 N.E.2d 511, 514 (Ohio 1988) (quoting Prosser & Keeton, The Law of Torts 36 (5th ed. 1984)), "beyond gross negligence," Birklid v. Boeing Co., 904 P.2d 278, 284 (Wash. 1995), and more egregious than even "mere recklessness" in which the actor knows or should know that there is a strong probability that harm may result. *Pariseau*, 522 N.E.2d at 513 n.1 (quoting RESTATEMENT OF THE LAW (SECOND) TORTS, § 8A cmt. b(19)); *see* RESTATEMENT OF THE LAW (SECOND) TORTS, § 500 cmt. f (differentiating reckless conduct, which requires "strong probability" of harm, from substantial certainty). Thus, the substantial certainty standard has been variously described as "tantamount to an intentional tort," Woodson v. Rowland, 407 S.E.2d 222, 228 (N.C. 1991), a "surrogate state of mind for purposefully harmful conduct," Suarez v. Dickmont Plastics Corp., 639 A.2d 507, 518 (Conn. 1994) (Borden, J; concurring and dissenting), and "a substitute for a subjective desire to injure." Millison v. E.I. DuPont de Nemours & Co., 501 A.2d 505, 514 (N.J. 1985).

The standard is not uniform. Some states that have modified their specific intent exception have opted for a stricter test than substantial certainty, requiring a showing of knowledge by the employer that injury is "certain" or "virtually certain" to occur. *See, e.g., Millison*, 501 A.2d at 514; Zimmerman v. Valdak Corp., 570 N.W.2d 204, 209 (N.D. 1997); Fryer v. Kranz, 616 N.W.2d 102, 106 (S.D. 2000); *Birklid*, 904 P.2d at 285. Other states have enacted specific statutes codifying relatively stringent intent-to-injure exceptions in response to more expansive court decisions. *See, e.g.*, Mich. Comp. Laws § 418.131 (intentional tort exception applies where employer "has actual knowledge that an injury was certain to occur and willfully disregarded that knowledge").

A number of state courts have also rejected invitations to adopt the "substantial certainty" standard, choosing instead to retain the strict requirement that the employer harbor "a specific intent to injure an employee." Fenner v. Municipality of Anchorage, 53 P.3d 573, 577 (Alaska 2002); *see also* Limanowski v. Ashland Oil Co., 655 N.E.2d 1049, 1052-53 (Ill. App. Ct. 1995); Davis v. United States Employers Council, Inc., 934 P.2d 1142, 1150 (Or. 1997); Lantz v. National Semiconductor Corp., 775 P.2d 937, 940 (Utah Ct. App. 1989). Courts adopting the substantial certainty standard have also drawn harsh criticism from some commentators for "alter[ing] the balance of interests within the workers' compensation system," Note, *The Intentional-Tort Exception to the Workers' Compensation Exclusive Remedy Immunity Provision: Woodson v. Rowland*, 70 N.C. L. Rev. 849, 880 (1992), employing a "vague" and "ill-defined" standard, J. Burnett, *The Enigma of Workers' Compensation Immunity: A Call to the Legislature for a Statutorily Defined Intentional Tort Exception*, 28 Fla. St. U. L. Rev. 491, 493, 517 (2001), and impinging upon the policy prerogatives of the legislative branch. *See, e.g.*, Note, *Ohio's "Employment Intentional Tort:" A Workers' Compensation Exception, Or the Creation of an Entirely New Cause of Action*, 44 Cleve. St. L. Rev. 381, 404 (1996) . . . .

Even those courts that have adopted the substantial-certainty test have stressed that it is intended to operate as a "very narrow exception," *Suarez*, 639 A.2d at 516, intended for the most "egregious employer conduct," *Millison*, 501 A.2d at 511, and hence is "to be strictly construed." Sorban v. Sterling Eng. Corp., 830 A.2d 372, 377 (Conn. App. Ct. 2003). As the New Jersey Supreme Court in *Millison*, 501 A.2d at 514, explained, "the dividing line between negligent or reckless conduct on the one hand and intentional wrong on the other must be drawn with caution, so that the statutory framework of the Act is not circumvented simply because a known risk later blossoms into reality."

Viewed in light of this standard, the evidence shows — at most — that Harrison directed plaintiff and his co-workers to continue to work in the quarry knowing that a rock fall had recently occurred and that it represented a dangerous situation that required attention. Plaintiff's expert, a former inspector for the federal Mine Safety and Health Administration, also opined that another fall was substantially certain to follow the first, and that allowing the drilling to proceed violated at least two federal safety regulations. He offered no testimony, however, tying a second rock fall to any particular time-frame. All that the evidence shows, therefore, is a substantial risk of second fall, but there is no evidence that it was substantially certain to occur within a few hours, or a day, or a month. Nor was there any evidence presented of prior falls leading to injuries under similar circumstances at the Western quarry or elsewhere within defendants' knowledge. Thus, the evidence cannot support a reasonable inference that defendants knew to a substantial certainty that the decision directing plaintiff to continue to work until Harrison returned from his errand would result in plaintiff's injury. Indeed, neither Harrison nor anyone else on site — including plaintiff — expected the accident to occur. Even as he waited for word from Harrison as to how to proceed, plaintiff — an experienced quarry worker in his own right — voluntarily commenced to complete the drilling that he had started the day before, and later expressed surprise at the occurrence of the second fall. The evidence thus belies any rational inference that Harrison knew to a substantial certainty that directing plaintiff to work until he returned to inspect the area would result in plaintiff's injury.

This is not a case where an employer, for example, knowingly orders workers to expose themselves to dangerous fumes or toxic materials that are a constant and unavoidable presence in the workplace, *see, e.g.*, *Millison*, 501 A.2d at 508-509, or instructs an employee, over his objection and at the risk of termination if he refused, to operate a table-saw knowing that other employees had previously suffered injuries because of the lack of a safety guard which the employer had willfully removed to improve production speed. Mandolis v. Elkins Indus., Inc., 246 S.E.2d 907, 914-15 (1978). Here, there is little doubt that defendants were negligent in exposing plaintiff to the known risk of a subsequent rock fall, but unlike these other cases there is no evidence from which a jury could reasonably infer that defendants knew the injury to plaintiff was substantially certain . . . .

While their standards may vary, decisions from other states that have adopted the substantial certainty test uniformly hold that the exception must be reserved for the exceptional case, where it can be said that the employee's injury — viewed in light of the risks known to the employer at the time — was not truly an accident. This is not such a case. We hold, therefore, that the evidence was insufficient as a matter of law to support the jury's finding that defendants knew to a substantial certainty their actions would result in injury to plaintiff. Accordingly, the judgments in favor of plaintiff and against defendants must be reversed.

NOTES AND QUESTIONS

1. In some states there is an additional related exception for a wrongful death action by an employee's survivors. In Texas, survivors may sue for wrongful death caused by the employer's "gross negligence" or intentional tort. Tex. Lab. Code § 408.001. Of course, distinguishing recklessness or "gross" negligence from simple negligence in this context presents the same problems that attend the disqualification of employee claimants based on their reckless misconduct.

2. Most intentional or reckless conduct claims against employers are based on employer actions or omissions that caused the employee's accident or occupational disease. In Johns-Manville Products Corp. v. Contra Costa Superior Court, 612 P.2d 948 (Cal. 1980), however, heirs of a deceased employee alleged that the employer had fraudulently concealed the fact of the employee's asbestosis from the employee, his doctor, and government agencies. The court held that the plaintiffs had stated a cause of action for *aggravation* of the disease even though the exclusive remedy defense would bar any claim as to *contracting* the disease. *See also* Palestini v. Gen'l Dynamics Corp., 120 Cal. Rptr. 2d 741 (Cal App. 2002).

3. An employer might also be a merchant, a manufacturer, a landlord, a medical services provider, or a neighbor with respect to an employee. If the employer is negligent in one of these nonemployer capacities and its negligence causes injury to the employee, should the employer still be able to claim the benefit of the exclusive remedy defense? Consider first the situation in which an employer negligently injures an employee *outside* the course of employment. In this case workers' compensation law might not apply to the accident at all. For example, if an employee is driving home from work (not in the course of employment) and by coincidence collides with a truck owned and negligently operated by the employer, the employee's injury is outside the coverage of workers' compensation. He is not entitled to workers' compensation benefits, but neither is the employer entitled to assert the exclusive remedy defense. *See* Krasevic v. Goodwill Indus. of Cent. Pennsylvania, Inc., 764 A.2d 561 (Pa. Super. 2000) (upholding judgment against employer for negligent supervision where plaintiff was sexually assaulted on employer's premises but not in the course of her employment).

4. A more controversial case for denying the employer the exclusive remedy defense is where the employer, acting other than as the employer, negligently injures the employee in the course of the employee's employment. In most states, if an employee's accident occurs in the course of his employment, it makes no difference whether the employer negligently caused the accident as an employer or in some nonemployer capacity. The employer may assert the exclusive remedy defense. *See, e.g.*, Barrett v. Rodgers, 562 N.E.2d 480 (Mass. 1990) (owner of dog that bit plaintiff in course of plaintiff's employment was also plaintiff's employer

and was entitled to assert exclusive remedy defense). A few states, however, recognize a "dual capacity" doctrine, according to which the employee might sue the employer for negligence in a non-employer capacity — such as manufacturing a defective tool or malpractice in providing health care — regardless of whether the employee was injured in the course of employment. *See* Suburban Hosp., Inc. v. Kirson, 763 A.2d 185 (Md. 2000) (explaining dual capacity theory but rejecting it); Mercer v. Uniroyal, Inc., 361 N.E.2d 492 (Ohio App. 1976) (applying dual capacity theory where employer made the defective tire that caused employee's accident in the course of employment as a truck driver).

5. Employees can also be in a dual capacity. For example, if an employee's accident is witnessed by and causes psychic injury to a parent who is also an employee, the parent employee might sue in tort for his or her psychic injuries in tort as a parent, rather than as an employee. *See* Collins v. COP Wyoming, 366 P.3d 521 (Wyo. 2016) (parent employee's tort claim not subject to exclusive remedy defense).

6. What if an employee is injured in a clearly work-related accident, but his injuries are the sort for which workers' compensation law provides no benefits, such as psychic injury unaccompanied by physical injury? If the employer asserts that the injuries are not compensable under workers' compensation law, can it also assert the exclusive remedy defense as a bar against any common law remedy? The employee might argue that to deny any workers' compensation benefits while barring the common law claim is not the "compromise" intended by workers compensation. *Compare* Smothers v. Gresham Transfer, Inc., 23 P.3d 333 (Or. 2001) (exclusive remedy defense did not apply to occupational disease claim that was not compensable under workers' compensation), GTE Sw., Inc. v. Bruce, 998 S.W.2d 605, 620 (Tex. 1999) (exclusive remedy defense did not bar common law claim because repetitive mental trauma injuries were not compensable under workers' compensation), *and* Collins v. COP Wyoming, 366 P.3d 521 (Wyo. 2016), *with* Livitsanos v. Super. Ct., 828 P.2d 1195 (Cal. 1982) (exclusive remedy defense barred tort claim as to emotional injuries not compensable under workers' compensation). *See also* Nassa v. Hook-SupeRx, Inc., 790 A.2d 368 (R.I. 2002) (exclusive remedy defense did not bar defamation claim because workers' compensation does not provide benefits for reputational injury.

7. The exclusive remedy defense has important implications for workplace violence cases. Workers' compensation laws typically deny compensation for intentional third-party torts (including intentional torts of fellow employees acting outside the scope of employment), if the tortfeasor acted for reasons "personal" to the injured employee. See Part B.2, *supra*. Should an injured employee, if not entitled to workers' compensation, be allowed to sue the employer for negligence, such as negligence in hiring, retaining, training, or supervising a fellow employee tortfeasor? *See* Butler v. S. States Cooperative, Inc., 620 S.E.2d 768 (Va. 2005) (rejecting exclusive remedy defense, permitting employee's negligent hiring tort claim against employer). *Compare* Tex. Labor Code §§ 406.032(1), 408.001(d) (extending exclusive remedy defense to any injury that "arose out of an act of a third person intended to injure the employee because of a personal reason and not directed at the employee as an employee or because of the employment").

PROBLEM

Reread the facts in the Problem following *Dallas Independent School District* in section B.2 of this chapter. Does Vicky have a tort claim against (a) the employer, or (b) Foreman?

C. PREVENTIVE REGULATION: OCCUPATIONAL SAFETY AND HEALTH LAW

1. *Overview*

EMILY A. SPIELER, *PERPETUATING RISK? WORKERS' COMPENSATION AND THE PERSISTENCE OF OCCUPATIONAL INJURIES*

31 Hous. L. Rev. 119 (1994)

In 1992, state and federal workers' compensation programs consumed over sixty-two billion dollars. . . . Not surprisingly, the dramatic and persistent increases in these costs in recent years have not been welcomed by employers (who must pay them), by politicians (who must confront the political pressure which accompanies them), or by workers and labor unions (who must defend benefit levels in the political arena).

At the same time, available data appear to indicate that injury rates, and in particular injuries which result in lost work time, have not declined during this period of exploding costs. . . . It would seem reasonable to expect that rising compensation costs would stimulate employers to engage in efforts to prevent occupational injury and disease. There is no persuasive evidence that this is so, however. Neither aggregate safety data nor more focused empirical studies give strong support to the notion that the high costs of workers' compensation in the aggregate, or enterprise-specific costs, have motivated large numbers of employers to take injury prevention activities seriously. This is remarkable, in view of the fact that empirical studies do show that enterprises with aggressive safety programs often exhibit lower, sometimes substantially lower, workers' compensation costs, and that the reduction in these costs more than offsets the cost of safety initiatives. . . .

Why then have these costs not motivated more employers to implement aggressive safety practices?

. . . Despite the high aggregate level of workers' compensation costs, the current methodology for the distribution of costs associated with occupational hazards fails to encourage improved safety practices among many employers for two reasons. First, costs are not spread in a manner which provide financial incentives to many employers to engage in primary prevention. . . . To the extent that insurance premiums are merit-based, the market would tend to reward low-risk employers with lower costs and penalize high-risk employers with higher costs. The particular nature of the pricing of workers' compensation premiums, however, tends both to attenuate the relationship between cost and risk for many employers, particularly smaller high risk employers, and to obfuscate the connection that does exist. . . . [N]ot all of an employer's experience "counts" in the calculation of modification factors. The extent to which an employer is rated as a result of its own experience depends on the credibility or predictive value of that employer's experience. As employers' total premium amounts grow, reflecting both larger payroll and the level of general hazard in the industry, the credibility of their past experience also grows. About ten to fifteen percent of firms, in which ninety percent of employees work, are experience rated. . . . Although manufacturing firms with as few as three to four employees may be experience rated, the size of the firm's workforce would have to be 1000 or more before the firm is fully experience rated. The result of this process is that relatively smaller employers' premium rates cluster around the manual rate; their rates can only change significantly as the experience of the entire class changes. . . .

[Furthermore], experience rating and the rate-making process in general can only effectively reflect the incidence of injuries and illnesses for which compensation is actually paid or approved. As a result, the process fails to reflect any injuries which have occurred but which have not appeared in the compensation system. In particular, occupational diseases, as a class, tend to be inadequately reflected in insurance rates. Because of long latency periods, uncertainty in diagnosis, and obstructions to eligibility found in many compensation systems, they may never be compensated at all. Moreover, because of their latency periods, the costs of many diseases cannot be charged against an employer in the period in which the exposure to the disease-causing agents occurred; if these diseases are ever reflected in the rates, their impact generally does not occur contemporaneously with the existence of hazard. . . .

[A second reason the workers' compensation system fails to encourage improved safety practices is that] despite the apparent internalization of costs, employers do not pay the full costs of injuries. . . . The underlying workers' compensation paradigm never intended that workers be fully compensated for the cost of their injuries. Because all occupational injuries are supposed to be compensated in this system — not only those that are the result of a wrong committed by the employer — workers simply have no fundamental legal claim to full compensation. Therefore, injured workers themselves, their families, and the public are expected to contribute to the costs of workplace injuries.

This sharing of costs occurs in numerous ways. [M]any occupational injuries and illnesses are simply never compensated at all. . . . [W]orkers do not receive compensation for many occupational illnesses. In addition, to the extent that injured workers are discouraged from filing claims for eligible injuries, or choose not to file them, they are, in effect, choosing to absorb directly the costs associated with the injury themselves. Obviously, costs associated with uncompensated occurrences are entirely externalized; workers or other social benefit programs absorb these costs. . . . [E]ven for those injuries and illnesses which are compensated, a worker's full pecuniary losses are not replaced by compensation benefits. To the extent that compensation is inadequate, and higher wages have not already provided compensation for the risk of injury at work, injured workers themselves absorb the costs of injuries. . . .

Moreover, despite the fact that the aggregate amount spent on permanent disability is high, permanent partial disability payments rarely approximate the full amount of loss in future wages. Permanent total disability benefits do not come close, in some states, to compensating for a family's loss of income. Fatalities are sometimes compensated least adequately. In essence, this means that more serious injuries and illnesses may be compensated less adequately than less serious ones. [N]onpecuniary losses are never compensated by workers' compensation programs. Benefits are plainly limited to wage-loss protection, loss of earning capacity, and rehabilitation costs and medical treatment. Pain and suffering is noncompensable in this system. Furthermore, family members are not compensated for any of their economic or other losses associated with a worker's injuries. . . .

NOTES AND QUESTIONS

1. Even when state legislatures were adopting the first workers' compensation laws at the beginning of the twentieth century, workplace safety advocates were not content to rely on the theoretical safety incentive generated by a system of accidental injury insurance. They also saw a need for mandatory preventive measures to stop accidents and occupational diseases before they happened. In New York, an early forerunner of today's regulatory job safety agencies was the Factory Investigating Commission, which emerged out of a particularly traumatic event for New York City, the Triangle Shirtwaist Factory fire.

> It all began on Saturday afternoon, March 25, 1911, when fire broke out in one of the crowded and littered workrooms of the Triangle Waist Company, a woman's shirtwaist manufacturer which occupied the top three floors of the ten stored [sic] Ash building near New York's fashionable Washington Square. Fed by waste containers which were full after the day's work, the fire spread quickly throughout the factory, panicking the largely female work force. Workers on the eighth and tenth floors were able to escape unharmed, but those on the ninth floor were not so lucky. There they jammed up at illegally locked exits, at doors blocked by machinery and at the elevator shaft with its single car. The fire department responded quickly, but its ladders reached only to the seventh floor. Many workers crowded by the windows and, as the flames became more intense and hopes of escape more feeble, some of them took the only way out and jumped to the street below. A United Press reporter who witnessed the scene told how he learned "a new sound — a more horrible sound than description can picture. It was the thud of a speeding, living body on a stone sidewalk." About forty young girls, some of them flaming human torches, crashed to the sidewalk and collapsed in broken heaps. None of these survived. Over a hundred more died in the building. According to the reporter, water pumped into the building by the firemen ran red in the gutter.
>
> . . . On April 5, 1911, over 100,000 people joined in a procession up Fifth Avenue to express their grief, as another 400,000 watched. Socialite and reformer Martha Bruere watched the procession go by her window for six hours and wrote "Never have seen a military pageant or triumphant ovation so impressive. . . . it is dawning on these thousands on thousands that such

things do not have to be!"

Judson MacLaury, Government Regulation of Workers' Safety and Health, 1877-1917, available online at http://www.dol.gov/asp/programs/history/mono-regsafeintrotoc.htm.

2. The Factory Investigating Commission broke new ground in the breadth and depth of its investigation of job safety and occupational disease in a number of industries. It proposed mandatory workplace safety rules, many of which the state legislature enacted into law. In the long run, however, state job safety initiatives such as the New York Commission were stymied by a shortage of public resources, business opposition, and fear that a strong and effective regulatory policy would drive employers into other states with weaker policies.

3. The federal government's first efforts at national regulation of job safety were limited to federal contractors and specific industries clearly affecting interstate commerce, such as the transportation industry. In 1936, Congress enacted the Walsh-Healey Public Contracts Act, which among other things established relatively mild safety standards for factories performing work pursuant to federal contracts. Congress enacted the Coal Mine Safety Act in 1952, and the Maritime Safety Act in 1958. Not until 1970 did Congress enact comprehensive national legislation, the Occupational Safety and Health Act (the "OSH Act"), 29 U.S.C. §§ 651-678. The Secretary of Labor is primarily responsible for rulemaking and enforcement under the act, and the Secretary has delegated these functions to the Occupational Safety and Health Administration (OSHA).

In contrast with earlier federal workplace safety legislation, the OSH Act applies to all employers in businesses "affecting commerce," and to all employees of such employers, 29 U.S.C. §§ 652(5), (6). There are, however, a few important exclusions. First, it does not apply to federal, state, or local government employers. *Id.* § 652(5). Second, although the act superseded some preexisting workplace safety rules under the Walsh-Healey Act and other federal laws, it left some preexisting rules intact — particularly rules for coal mines and the maritime and transportation industries. *Id.* § 653(b)(1). The act thus excludes from coverage "working conditions of employees with respect to which other Federal agencies . . . exercise statutory authority to prescribe or enforce standards or regulations affecting occupational safety or health." *Id.* § 653(b)(2).

4. The OSH Act regulates employers and employees only with respect to "working conditions" and "workplaces." It does not protect employees from risks they face as members of the general public, such as risks from an employer's air or water pollution in the surrounding community where employees live when they are not working. But what is a "workplace"? Could the workplace include the living quarters an employer provides to its employees? *See* Frank Diehl Farms v. Sec'y of Labor, 696 F.2d 1325 (11th Cir. 1983) (department lacks authority to regulate employer-provided housing for seasonal workers, unless the employer or practical necessity requires employees to live in such housing).

What about telecommuters who perform all or part of their work from home? If an employee makes a workplace of his home, is the employer liable under the OSH Act for conditions in the employee's home? *See* Note, *Working at Home at Your Own Risk: Employer Liability for Teleworkers Under the Occupational*

Safety and Health Act of 1970, 18 Ga. St. L.J. 955 (2002).

5. Much of what an employer does affects not only the safety and health of its own employees, but also of nonemployees or employees of other employers. Imagine, for example, a construction site at which one employer has failed properly to secure scaffolding or equipment. The employer's negligence might threaten every worker or visitor to the site, and the first person killed or injured might be someone other than the employer's employee. But the OSH Act is a preventive law, not a compensatory one, and the lack of an injury to any of the employer's own employees is immaterial. The hazard, not an injury, constitutes the violation. Therefore, it is enough for authorities to prove a violation if an "employee" was exposed to a hazard for which the employer was responsible. According to the view of some courts, it is not even necessary that the "employee" exposed to the hazard was the employer's employee — he might be the employee of another employer working at the same site. For more on the "multi-employer" workplace theory *see* IBP, Inc. v. Herman, 144 F.3d 861 (D.C. Cir. 1998).

6. The OSH Act preempts state occupational and safety law, except that a state may regulate a safety or health issue "with respect to which no [OSHA] standard is in effect." 29 U.S.C.§ 667(a). However, this proviso does not authorize states to "supplement" or increase protection of employees beyond what OSHA standards require for a particular matter. Gade v. Nat'l Solid Wastes Mgmt. Ass'n, 505 U.S. 88 (1992). Nor is an employer's compliance with a specific state law a defense against a complaint alleging the employer's violation of an OSHA standard. Puffer's Hardware, Inc. v. Donovan, 742 F.2d 12 (1st Cir. 1984).

An important exception from the preemptive effect of the OSH Act is for a "state plan," approved by the Secretary of Labor, in which the state regains jurisdiction over occupational safety and health matters within its borders. The secretary will approve a state plan if it provides standards and enforcement comparable to the OSH Act. 29 U.S.C. § 667(c). There are currently 22 such plans (not counting state plans that apply only to state and local government employees). *See* Occupational Safety and Health Administration, *State Occupational and Safety Plans*, at http://www.osha.gov/fso/osp/index.html (last visited July 20, 2012).

7. OSHA's investigation and enforcement responsibility is staggering. There are approximately 130 million workers at 8 million sites in the United States, but only 2,200 OSHA inspectors. Occupational Safety and Health Administration, Dep't of Labor, Commonly Used Statistics, at http://www.osha.gov/oshstats/commonstats.html. During fiscal year 2011, OSHA conducted 40,648 inspections (state agencies with approved plans conducted another 52,056). The vast majority of OSHA investigations (nearly 25,000) were pursuant to an annual "plan" randomly selecting employers in targeted industries with high accident or occupational disease rates. Other inspections aimed at employers with prior violations, with high accident rates, identified by employee complaints, or involved in recent fatalities. Occupational Safety and Health Administration, Dep't of Labor, OSHA Issues 2011 Annual Inspection Plan (September 9, 2011), at http://www.osha.gov/dep/2010_enforcement_summary.html.

8. The combination of workers' compensation laws and preventive laws such as the OSH Act have undoubtedly made work safer. Still, work remains dangerous, especially in persistently hazardous industries. In 2007, there were

5,488 fatal occupational injuries and 4 million non-fatal work-related injuries or illnesses. Bureau of Labor Statistics, *Latest Numbers: Fatal Work-Related Injuries*, at http://www.bls.gov/iif. At least 1,183,500 of these non-fatal injuries and illnesses (private sector alone) were serious enough to require time off work or reassignment to restricted duty. *Id.* The reported statistics probably understate the true magnitude of the problem, especially as to occupational illnesses. The statistics include only work-related illnesses recognized, diagnosed, and reported by an employer. Because of the long latency and uncertain causation of some illnesses, the actual number of occupational illnesses is likely to be much higher.

2. *Establishing Employer Duties*

The OSH Act regulates occupational safety and health in two distinctly different ways. First, the act authorizes the Secretary of Labor to issue "standards," which are quasi-legislative regulations prospectively binding on employers, and which establish specific rules for an employer's management of work and the workplace. 29 U.S.C. § 655. For example, a standard might require an employer to install a safety guard on a certain type of equipment, or it might require an employer to limit the level of an employee's exposure to a particular chemical.

Of course, promulgating a specific rule for every risk to which any employee might be exposed under current or future employment conditions is impossible. Moreover, when OSHA identifies a previously unknown or underappreciated risk, the process for drafting and adopting a new standard can take years. Thus, the act provides a second method of regulation for the myriad situations for which there are no specific standards. This second method of regulation begins with the act's establishment of a "general duty" of an employer to "furnish to each of his employees employment and a place of employment which are free from recognized hazards that are causing or are likely to cause death or serious physical harm to his employees." 29 U.S.C. § 654. Standing alone, the general duty clause does not tell an employer what hazards are unacceptable or what an employer can do to abate a hazard. Like the common law duty to provide a safe workplace, the act's general duty clause requires case-by-case adjudication to determine whether an employer permitted or caused a condition "likely to cause" serious injury or death, and whether the condition was a "recognized" hazard. The general duty clause is a versatile tool for dealing with the impossibility of drafting specific rules for every imaginable hazard. For example, OSHA recently relied on the general duty clause to issue a citation against a retailer whose employee was trampled to death by shoppers rushing through a store entrance at the opening of a major sale event. *OSHA Proposes $7,000 Fine for Wal-Mart After Shoppers Trampled Worker to Death*, Labor Relations Week [BNA], p. 902 (June 4, 2009).

Because the OSH Act is a preventive law, not a law of compensation, an employer might violate an OSH Act standard or the act's general duty clause whether or not the hazard in question caused the injury, illness, or death of any of that employer's employees. However, because many OSHA inspections are triggered by an employee's accidental injury or death, it is not unusual for an OSHA enforcement proceeding to follow an accident, and an employee's injury or death is certainly some evidence of the seriousness of a hazard.

An OSHA enforcement proceeding begins with the issuance of a citation alleging an employer's violation of the general duty clause or a specific standard. If the employer or another interested party contests the citation, OSHA issues a complaint and schedules a hearing before an administrative law judge (ALJ). 29 U.S.C. § 658. The ALJ decision can be appealed to the Occupational Safety and Health Review Commission (OSHRC), a panel of three members appointed by the President to provide independent review of OSHA enforcement proceedings. *Id.* § 661(a). A party aggrieved by the commission's decision may file a further appeal to the U.S. Court of Appeals for the District of Columbia or to a court of appeals for the circuit in which the alleged violation occurred. *Id.* § 660(a).

a. The General Duty Clause

NATIONAL REALTY & CONSTRUCTION CO. v. OSHRC
489 F.2d 1257 (D.C. App. 1973)

J. SKELLY WRIGHT, Circuit Judge:

We review here an order of the Occupational Safety and Health Review Commission which found National Realty and Construction Company, Inc. to have committed a "serious violation" of the "general duty clause" of the Occupational Safety and Health Act . . . . [A] civil fine of $300 was imposed. [W]e reverse.

I. THE PROCEEDINGS AND THE EVIDENCE

. . . [T]he Secretary cited National Realty for serious breach of its general duty in that an employee was permitted to stand as a passenger on the running board of an Allis Chalmers 645 front end loader while the loader was in motion. . . . The evidence is quickly restated.

[A]t a motel construction site operated by National Realty in Arlington, Virginia, O. C. Smith, a foreman with the company, rode the running board of a front-end loader driven by one of his subordinates, Clyde Williams. The loader suffered a stalled engine while going down an earthen ramp into an excavation and began to swerve off the ramp. Smith jumped from the loader, but was killed when it toppled off the ramp and fell on him. John Irwin, Smith's supervisor, testified that he had not seen the accident, that Smith's safety record had been very good, that the company had a "policy" against equipment riding, and that he — Irwin — had stopped the "4 or 5" employees he had seen taking rides in the past two years. The loader's driver testified that he did not order Smith off the vehicle because Smith was his foreman; he further testified that loader riding was extremely rare . . . . Another company employee testified that it was contrary to company policy to ride on heavy equipment. A company supervisor said he had reprimanded violators of this policy and would fire second offenders should the occasion arise. . . .

The hearing examiner dismissed the citation, finding that National Realty had not "permitted" O. C. Smith to ride the loader, as charged in the citation and complaint. The examiner reasoned that a company did not "permit" an activity which its safety policies prohibited unless the policies were "not enforced or effective." Such constructive permission could be found only if the hazardous activity were a "practice" among employees, rather than — as here — a rare occurrence. Upon reviewing the hearing record, the Commission reversed its examiner by a 2-1 vote, each commissioner writing separately.

Ruling for the Secretary, Commissioners Burch and Van Namee found inadequate implementation of National Realty's safety "policy" . . . [and] briefly suggested several improvements which National Realty might have effected in its safety policy: placing the policy in writing, posting no-riding signs, threatening riders with automatic discharge, and providing alternative means of transport at the construction site. In dissent, Commissioner Moran concluded that the Secretary had not proved his charge that National Realty had "permitted" either equipment riding in general or the particular incident. . . .

II. THE ISSUES

Published regulations of the Commission impose on the Secretary the burden of proving a violation of the general duty clause. When the Secretary fails to produce evidence on all necessary elements of a violation, the record will — as a practical consequence — lack substantial evidence to support a Commission finding in the Secretary's favor. . . . It may well be that National Realty failed to meet its general duty under the Act, but the Secretary neglected to present evidence demonstrating in what manner the company's conduct fell short . . . .

B. THE STATUTORY DUTY TO PREVENT HAZARDOUS CONDUCT BY EMPLOYEES

. . . Under the [general duty] clause, the Secretary must prove (1) that the employer failed to render its workplace "free" of a hazard which was (2) "recognized" and (3) "causing or likely to cause death or serious physical harm." The hazard here was the dangerous activity of riding heavy equipment. The record clearly contains substantial evidence to support the Commission's finding that this hazard was "recognized"[32] and "likely to cause death or serious physical harm."[33] The question then is whether National Realty rendered its construction site "free" of the hazard. In this case of first impression, the meaning of that statutory term must be settled before the sufficiency of the evidence can be assessed.

Construing the term in the present context presents a dilemma. On the one hand, the adjective is unqualified and absolute: A workplace cannot be just "reasonably free" of a hazard, or merely as free as the average workplace in the

---

[32] An activity may be a "recognized hazard" even if the defendant employer is ignorant of the activity's existence or its potential for harm. . . . The standard would be the common knowledge of safety experts who are familiar with the circumstances of the industry or activity in question. The evidence below showed that both National Realty and the Army Corps of Engineers took equipment riding seriously enough to prohibit it as a matter of policy. . . . [T]his is at least substantial evidence that equipment riding is a "recognized hazard."

[33] Presumably, any given instance of equipment riding carries a less than 50% probability of serious mishap, but no such mathematical test would be proper in construing this element of the general duty clause. If evidence is presented that a practice could eventuate in serious physical harm upon other than a freakish or utterly implausible concurrence of circumstances, the Commission's expert determination of likelihood should be accorded considerable deference by the courts. For equipment riding, the potential for injury is indicated on the record by Smith's death. . . .

industry. On the other hand, Congress quite clearly did not intend the general duty clause to impose strict liability: The duty was to be an achievable one. Congress' language is consonant with its intent only where the "recognized" hazard in question can be totally eliminated from a workplace. A hazard consisting of conduct by employees, such as equipment riding, cannot, however, be totally eliminated. A demented, suicidal, or willfully reckless employee may on occasion circumvent the best conceived and most vigorously enforced safety regime.[36] This seeming dilemma is, however, soluble within the literal structure of the general duty clause. Congress intended to require elimination only of preventable hazards. It follows, we think, that Congress did not intend unpreventable hazards to be considered "recognized" under the clause. Though a generic form of hazardous conduct, such as equipment riding, may be "recognized," unpreventable instances of it are not, and thus the possibility of their occurrence at a workplace is not inconsistent with the workplace being "free" of recognized hazards.

Though resistant to precise definition, the criterion of preventability draws content from the informed judgment of safety experts. Hazardous conduct is not preventable if it is so idiosyncratic and implausible in motive or means that conscientious experts, familiar with the industry, would not take it into account in prescribing a safety program. Nor is misconduct preventable if its elimination would require methods of hiring, training, monitoring, or sanctioning workers which are either so untested or so expensive that safety experts would substantially concur in thinking the methods infeasible.[37] All preventable forms and instances of hazardous conduct must, however, be entirely excluded from the workplace. To establish a violation of the general duty clause, hazardous conduct need not actually have occurred, for a safety program's feasibly curable inadequacies may sometimes be demonstrated before employees have acted dangerously. At the same time, however, actual occurrence of hazardous conduct is not, by itself, sufficient evidence of a violation, even when the conduct has led to injury. The record must additionally indicate that demonstrably feasible measures would have materially reduced the likelihood that such misconduct would have occurred.

C. DEFICIENCIES IN THIS RECORD

The hearing record shows several incidents of equipment riding, including the Smith episode where a foreman broke a safety policy he was charged with enforcing.[38] It seems quite unlikely that these were unpreventable instances of

---

[36] . . . An employer has a duty to prevent and suppress hazardous conduct by employees, and this duty is not qualified by such common law doctrines as assumption of risk, contributory negligence, or comparative negligence. The employer's duty is, however, qualified by the simple requirement that it be achievable. . . .

[37] This is not to say that a safety precaution must find general usage in an industry before its absence gives rise to a general duty violation. The question is whether a precaution is recognized by safety experts as feasible, not whether the precaution's use has become customary. . . . [A] precaution does not become infeasible merely because it is expensive. But if adoption of the precaution would clearly threaten the economic viability of the employer, the Secretary should propose the precaution by way of promulgated regulations, subject to advance industry comment, rather than . . . enforcement of the general duty clause. . . .

[38] The hearing examiner thought that National Realty owed its supervisory personnel a lesser duty of care than was owed to rank-and-file employees. This involves a double misconception.

hazardous conduct. But the hearing record is barren of evidence describing, and demonstrating the feasibility and likely utility of, the particular measures which National Realty should have taken to improve its safety policy. . . . Having the burden of proof, the Secretary must be charged with these evidentiary deficiencies.

The Commission sought to cure these deficiencies sua sponte by speculating about what National Realty could have done to upgrade its safety program. These suggestions, while not unattractive, came too late in the proceedings. An employer is unfairly deprived of an opportunity to cross-examine or to present rebuttal evidence and testimony when it learns the exact nature of its alleged violation only after the hearing. . . . To assure that citations issue only upon careful deliberation, the Secretary must be constrained to specify the particular steps a cited employer should have taken to avoid citation, and to demonstrate the feasibility and likely utility of those measures.

Because the Secretary did not shoulder his burden of proof, the record lacks substantial evidence of a violation . . . .

NOTES AND QUESTIONS

1. In most instances, an employer's primary cost for violating the act is not the penalty but the expense of "abating" (correcting) the violation. If the violation is "not serious," OSHA need not assess any fine, or it may assess a fine of up to $7,000. 29 U.S.C. § 666(c). As of fiscal year 2006, it appears that the average fine for a violation that was not serious was about $119. Occupational Safety and Health Administration, Department of Labor, OSHA Facts, at http://www.osha.gov/as/opa/oshafacts.html. If the violation is "serious," OSHA "shall" assess a fine of up to $7,000. 29 U.S.C. § 666(b). More punitive fines ranging up to $70,000 are possible in the case of "willful" or "repeated" violations. 29 U.S.C. § 666(a). If the violation is willful the fine must be at least $5,000. *Id.* The total amount of fines can be especially high if OSHA levies separate penalties for each separate "exposure" of an employee to a risk. *See, e.g.*, Nat'l Ass'n of Home Builders v. OSHA, 602 F.3d 464 (D.C. Cir. 2010) (upholding assessment of separate penalties for each employee affected by employer's failure to provide a respirator). OSHA issued its largest penalty to date, $81,340,000, against BP Products North America, Inc., for a refinery explosion that killed 15 employees in Texas City, Texas in 2005.

2. A willful violation that leads to the death of an employee can lead to criminal penalties, including imprisonment for up to six months. 29 U.S.C. § 666(e). However, OSHA rarely refers cases for criminal prosecution. In about 93 percent of willful violation cases involving an employee death, OSHA has declined to seek criminal prosecution. D. Barstow, *When Workers Die, U.S. Rarely Seeks Charges for Deaths in Workplace*, Dec. 22, 2003, N.Y. Times. On the other hand, the Act does not foreclose state and local law enforcement officials from prosecuting employers for negligent homicide under state law. *See, e.g.*, Sabine Consol., Inc. v. State of Texas, 806 S.W.2d 553 (Tex. Crim. App. 1991); People v. Chicago Magnet

---

Because the behavior of supervisory personnel sets an example at the workplace, an employer has — if anything — a heightened duty to ensure the proper conduct of such personnel. Second, the fact that a foreman would feel free to breach a company safety policy is strong evidence that implementation of the policy was lax.

Wire Corp., 534 N.E.2d 962 (Ill. 1989). *But see* Commonwealth v. Coll. Pro Painters (U.S.) Ltd., 640 N.E.2d 777 (Mass. 1994) (state scaffold safety standard providing criminal penalty was preempted by OSHA's construction industry standards).

3. The employer faces additional liability if it fails to abate a cited violation within the specified time limit after a final OSHA order. Failure to abate can lead to fines of up to $7,000 *per day*. 29 U.S.C. § 666(d). Even in failure to abate cases, however, it appears that the average fine OSHA levied in fiscal year 2006 was only about $3,628. Occupational Safety and Health Administration, Department of Labor, OSHA Facts, at http://www.osha.gov/as/opa/oshafacts.html.

4. In *National Realty & Construction*, OSHA levied a fine of only $300. Nevertheless, the employer decided to bear the expense of contesting the citation before an administrative law judge, OSHRC, and the U.S. Court of Appeals for the District of Columbia. What reasons might an employer have for contesting a citation when the penalty is so low and the cost of litigation so high?

The cost of abatement is frequently much more than the amount of the penalty for a violation. If the employer does not contest the citation, it must abate the violation within the time limits set out in the citation. However, if the employer contests the citation in "good faith," it need not abate the alleged violation until the entry of a final order. 29 U.S.C. § 659(b). How much might abatement have cost the employer in *National Realty & Construction* if it had implemented one of measures belatedly suggested by the commission?

There are other reasons an employer might choose to fight a citation involving little or no penalty. An employer with a record of violations is more likely to be inspected in the future, and future penalties for that employer are likely to be higher. An employee or other parties also may rely on an OSHA citation and final order for evidentiary or collateral estoppel effect on the question of the employer's fault in causing an accident. While the exclusive remedy defense of workers' compensation law ordinarily bars an employee's common law negligence claim against the employer, there are intentional and "willful tort" exceptions to this defense, and nonemployee workers and other third parties (such as a manufacturer seeking contribution in a state that permits such an action against an employer) might not be restricted by the exclusive remedy defense. See Part B.6.a,, *supra*. *Compare* Mark v. Mellott Mfg. Co., 666 N.E.2d 631 (Ohio App. 1995) (permitting introduction of OSHA citation into evidence) *with* Herson v. New Boston Garden Corp., 667 N.E.2d 907 (Mass. App. 1996) (OSHA standards are admissible to prove standard of care, but OSHA citations are not).

5. As *National Realty & Construction* illustrates, employee misconduct is a hazard in itself. An employer is not strictly liable for the employee misconduct, but *is* liable for employee misconduct the employer could have prevented. Naturally, even the best training and the best management and supervision of work will not stop some employees from misbehaving. OSHA has outlined the following four-part test for cases in which an employer argues that an accident or hazardous activity was the result of unpreventable employee misconduct: (1) the employer established work rules designed to prevent the violation; (2) it adequately communicated the rules to employees; (3) it took steps to discover violations; and (4) it effectively enforced the rules when it discovered violations. Jensen Constr. Co., 7 OSHRC 1477, 1979 OSHD ¶23,664 (1979). *See also* Danis-Shook Venture

XXV v. Sec'y of Labor, 319 F.3d 805, 812 (6th Cir. 2003) (applying OSHA's test).

6. Disciplinary action against employees who violate safety rules might range from informal reprimand to discharge. Wage deductions within limits and suspension without pay might be appropriate forms of disciplinary action against "nonexempt" employees (those entitled to overtime under the Fair Labor Standards Act), depending on local laws against wage deductions. In the case of "exempt" salaried workers, however, it might be argued that a deduction or a suspension for less than a week is inconsistent with "salaried" status under the FLSA, rendering the affected employee and perhaps an entire classification of employees "nonexempt" (and therefore entitled to overtime pay). The Department of Labor has addressed the matter of safety-based disciplinary deductions as follows:

> The prohibition against deductions from pay in the salary basis requirement is subject to the following exceptions: . . . Deductions from pay of exempt employees may be made for penalties imposed in good faith for infractions of safety rules of *major significance*. Safety rules of major significance include those relating to the prevention of serious danger in the workplace or to other employees, such as rules prohibiting smoking in explosive plants, oil refineries and coal mines.

29 C.F.R. § 541.602(b)(4) (emphasis added) (but deductions from pay must be in whole day increments). State laws regarding deductions from wages might impose additional restrictions on an employer's right to take disciplinary deductions from the pay otherwise earned by employees. See Chapter 4.B.4.b, *supra*.

7. Issuing, communicating and enforcing work rules is a crucial part of preventing employee accidents, but are these actions always enough? *See* Brennan v. Butler Lime & Cement Co., 520 F.2d 1011 (7th Cir. 1975) (remanding to OSHRC to determine sufficiency of employer rule instructing crane operator not to come within ten feet of live electrical wire, where employer failed to explain possibility of "arcing" current, and employee may have failed to appreciate purpose of clearance rule).

8. If an employer establishes a safety training program for employees, must the employer pay employees for their time in classes in the program? *See* Chao v. Tradesmen Int'l, Inc., 310 F.3d 904 (6th Cir. 2002) (rejecting argument that FLSA required employer to compensate employees for time in OSHA safety training course, because the course related to general occupational skills rather than employer's unique work practices or demands, and employer allowed employees 'reasonable time' after hiring within which to complete the program). For more on the problem of compensation for training time, see Chapter 4, Part C.3.

9. What if employees engage in particularly stiff and concerted resistance to an employer's safety instructions? In Atlantic & Gulf Stevedores v. OSHRC, 534 F.2d 541 (3d Cir. 1976), the employers defended their lack of compliance with OSHA's hardhat requirement by arguing that further efforts to enforce compliance with the rule would result in wildcat strikes and walkouts. The commission upheld the citation and the Third Circuit affirmed, holding that the employers could enforce the rule by refusing to employ anyone who failed to comply. As for the risk of a strike, the court observed that the employers had several ways to protect themselves. They could insist on the union's agreement in collective bargaining

that the employers had a right to enforce safety rules by disciplinary action, could seek an injunction against an illegal work stoppage, or could petition OSHA for a variance or extension of time to abate a violation. Having not attempted any such measures, the employers could not rely on a mere risk of a strike as a defense.

10. The deceased employee in *National Realty & Construction* was a foreman, whom the court evidently considered a supervisory employee. *See* n.38 of the court's opinion. Considering that the knowledge of supervisors is imputed to the employer in many other circumstances, why not simply say the employer was guilty of a "serious" violation because it *knew* of the misconduct and failed to prevent it? In W.G. Yates & Sons Const. Co. v. OSHRC, 459 F.3d 604 (5th Cir. 2006), the court considered a "serious" violation citation against an employer whose supervisor was observed working on a steep slope without fall protection required by OSHA standards. The court held that the supervisor's misconduct is imputed to the employer only if the supervisor's misconduct was "foreseeable."

> OSHA is not a strict liability statute; the mere fact that violative conduct occurred is not, of itself sufficient to establish employer liability; knowledge, actual or constructive, of the unsafe condition is an element of an employer violation. . . . [But] *a supervisor's knowledge of his own rogue conduct cannot be imputed to the employer*; and consequently the element of employer knowledge must be established, not vicariously through the violator's knowledge, but by either the employer's actual knowledge, or by its constructive knowledge based on the fact that the employer could, under the circumstances of the case, foresee the unsafe conduct of the supervisor. This rule places only the initial burden on the government to prove its alleged violation against the employer, which it can do by showing the inadequacy of the employer's program and/or its failed enforcement.

459 F.3d at 609 n.8. Note, however, that both *National Realty* and *W.G. Yates & Sons* involved citations for "serious" violations. A non-serious violation, for which a citation might carry no penalty at all, does not necessarily require the application of the same standard of employer "knowledge."

b. Standards

An essential aspect of the OSH Act's preventive strategy is to promulgate, by quasi-legislative means, rules for the safe management of work and workplaces. The Department of Labor has promulgated standards by three different means.

First, in the early days after the enactment of the OSH Act, the Department of Labor exercised its statutory authority to adopt "national consensus standards," which had their origin in the preexisting safety codes of many industry or professional associations and other federal agencies. *See* 29 U.S.C. § 652(9). The adoption of these codes, sometimes drafted by private organizations unaccountable to the public interest, solved the immediate problem of managing a quick transition from a near-complete absence of federal standards to a reasonably comprehensive set of federal standards. *See* 29 U.S.C. § 651(b). The department's authority to adopt standards in this manner has now expired, although some of the national consensus standards adopted in the OSH Act's earliest days remain in effect.

Second, the department continues the ongoing process of creating new and permanent standards, or revising or revoking old ones, by quasi-legislative means subject to the usual requirements of advance notice and comment procedures, with the possibility of judicial review under the Administrative Procedure Act. *See* 5 U.S.C. §§ 701 et seq. The department's rulemaking process frequently attracts considerable interest from industry and labor, both of which have important stakes in the outcome. Labor usually wants rules providing the best possible protection for employees, and labor organizations have sometimes sued to compel the department to develop and promulgate standards for particular hazards. *But see* UAW v. Chao, 361 F.3d 249 (3d Cir. 2004) (department's failure to adopt rule limiting exposure to metalworking fluids was not an abuse of discretion, given department's limited resources and attention to more pressing safety and health priorities). Industry, on the other hand, frequently opposes such rulemaking, arguing that a targeted risk is not significant or that compliance is infeasible.

If the department finds that employees are exposed to a "grave danger" from toxic substances or "new hazards," and that an "emergency" standard is necessary to protect employees, the department may exercise a third kind of rulemaking authority. It can issue an "emergency" standard without the usual rulemaking process. 29 U.S.C. § 655(c)(1). However, the department must then initiate a rulemaking procedure in the usual manner leading to a permanent standard superseding the emergency one. 29 U.S.C. § 655(c)(3).

A.F.L.-C.I.O. v. OCCUPATIONAL SAFETY AND HEALTH ADMINISTRATION

965 F.2d 962 (11th Cir. 1992)

FAY, Circuit Judge:

In 1989, the Occupational Safety and Health Administration ("OSHA"), a division of the Department of Labor, issued its Air Contaminants Standard, a set of permissible exposure limits for 428 toxic substances. . . . [P]etitioners representing various affected industries and the American Federation of Labor and Congress of Industrial Organizations ("AFL-CIO" or "the union") challenge . . . OSHA's findings on numerous specific substances included in the new standard. For the reasons that follow, we VACATE the Air Contaminants Standard and REMAND to the agency.

I. Background

The Occupational Safety and Health Act . . . authorizes the Secretary to issue occupational health and safety standards, *id.* § 655, with which each employer must comply. *Id.* § 654. Section 6(a) of the Act provided that in its first two years, OSHA should promulgate "start-up" standards, on an expedited basis and without public hearing or comment, based on "national consensus" or "established Federal standard[s]" that improve employee safety or health. *Id.* § 655(a). Pursuant to that authority, OSHA in 1971 promulgated approximately 425 permissible exposure limits ("PELs") for air contaminants, 29 C.F.R. § 1910.1000 (1971), derived principally from federal standards applicable to government contractors under the Walsh-Healey Act, 41 U.S.C. § 35. . . .

On June 7, 1988, OSHA published a Notice of Proposed Rulemaking for its Air Contaminants Standard. In this single rulemaking, OSHA proposed to issue new or revised PELs for over 400 substances. . . . There was an initial comment period of forty-seven days, followed by a thirteen-day public hearing. Interested parties then had until October 7, 1988 to submit post-hearing evidence and until October 31, 1988 to submit post-hearing briefs.

OSHA then issued its revised Air Contaminants Standard for 428 toxic substances on January 19, 1989. This standard, which differs from the proposal in several respects, lowered the PELs for 212 substances, set new PELs for 164 previously unregulated substances, and left unchanged PELs for 52 substances for which lower limits had originally been proposed. . . .

[I]ndustry groups, the AFL-CIO, and specific individual companies filed challenges to the final standard in numerous United States Courts of Appeals. . . .

II. Standard of Review

. . . "[D]eterminations of the Secretary shall be conclusive if supported by *substantial evidence in the record considered as a whole*." 29 U.S.C. § 655(f) (emphasis added). . . . Under this test, "we must take a 'harder look' at OSHA's action than we would if we were reviewing the action under the more deferential arbitrary and capricious standard applicable to agencies governed by the Administrative Procedure Act." Asbestos Info. Ass'n v. OSHA, 727 F.2d 415, 421 (5th Cir. 1984) (footnote omitted). Considering the record "as a whole" further requires that reviewing courts "take into account not just evidence that supports the agency's decision, but also countervailing evidence. . . . Yet this requirement does not alter the court's fundamental duty to uphold the agency's 'choice between two fairly conflicting views, even though the court would justifiably have made a different choice had the matter been before it de novo.'" AFL-CIO v. Marshall, 617 F.2d 636, 649 n.44 (D.C. Cir. 1979) (quoting *Universal Camera Corp.*, 340 U.S. at 488), *aff'd in relevant part*, *ATMI*, 452 U.S. 490 (1981). . . .

III. Discussion

A. "Generic" Rulemaking

Unlike most of the OSHA standards previously reviewed by the courts, the Air Contaminants Standard regulates not a single toxic substance, but 428 different substances. The agency explained its decision to issue such an omnibus standard in its Notice of Proposed Rulemaking:

> OSHA has issued only 24 substance-specific health regulations since its creation. It has not been able to review the many thousands of currently unregulated chemicals in the workplace nor to keep up with reviewing the several thousand new chemicals introduced since its creation. It has not been able to fully review the literature to determine if lower limits are needed for many of the approximately 400 substances it now regulates.
>
> Using past approaches and practices, OSHA could continue to regulate a small number of the high priority substances and those of greatest public interest. However, it would take decades to review currently used chemicals and OSHA would never be able to keep up with the many chemicals which will be newly introduced in the future.

53 Fed. Reg. at 20963. For this reason, "OSHA determined that it was necessary to modify this approach through the use of *generic* rulemaking, which would simultaneously cover many substances." 54 Fed. Reg. at 2333 (emphasis added).

"Generic" means something "common to or characteristic of a whole group or class; ... not specific or individual." Webster's Third New International Dictionary 945 (1966). Previous "generic" rulemakings by OSHA have all dealt with requirements that, once promulgated, could be applied to numerous different situations. . . . By contrast, the new Air Contaminants Standard is an amalgamation of 428 unrelated substance exposure limits. There is little common to this group of diverse substances except the fact that OSHA considers them toxic and in need of regulation. In fact, this rulemaking is the antithesis of a "generic" rulemaking. . . .

Nonetheless, we find nothing in the OSH Act that would prevent OSHA from addressing multiple substances in a single rulemaking. . . . However, we believe the PEL for each substance must be able to stand independently, i.e., that each PEL must be supported by substantial evidence [and] . . . adequate explanation. OSHA may not, by using such multi-substance rulemaking, ignore the requirements of the OSH Act. . . .

B. SIGNIFICANT RISK OF MATERIAL HEALTH IMPAIRMENT

Section 3(8) of the OSH Act defines "occupational health and safety standard" as "a standard which requires conditions, or the adoption or use of one or more practices, means, methods, operations, or processes, *reasonably necessary or appropriate* to provide safe or healthful employment and places of employment." 29 U.S.C. § 652(8) (emphasis added). The Supreme Court has interpreted this provision to require that, before the promulgation of any permanent health standard, OSHA make a threshold finding that a significant risk of material health impairment exists at the current levels of exposure to the toxic substance in question, *Benzene*, 448 U.S. at 614-15, 642;[13] "and that a new, lower standard is therefore 'reasonably necessary or appropriate to provide safe or healthful employment and places of employment.'" *Benzene*, 448 U.S. at 615. OSHA is not entitled to regulate any risk, only those which present a "significant" risk of "material" health impairment. *Id.* at 641-42. OSHA must therefore determine: (1) what health impairments are "material," *Texas Independent Ginners*, 630 F.2d at 407, and (2) what constitutes a "significant" risk of such impairment, *Benzene*, 448 U.S. at 641-42, 655. . . . OSHA must provide at least an estimate of the actual risk associated with a particular toxic substance, *see* Public Citizen Health Research Group v. Tyson, 796 F.2d 1479, 1502-03 (D.C. Cir. 1986), and explain in an understandable way why that risk is significant. *Benzene*, 448 U.S. at 646. In past rulemakings, OSHA has satisfied this requirement by estimating either the number of workers likely to suffer the effects of exposure or the percentage of risk to any

---

[13] In Industrial Union Dep't, AFL-CIO v. American Petroleum Inst., 448 U.S. 607 (1980), commonly referred to as the *Benzene* case, a plurality of the Supreme Court vacated OSHA's standard for benzene and set forth the appropriate analysis for reviewing a standard promulgated under the OSH Act. Since that time, the courts of appeals have generally considered that the plurality opinion in *Benzene* was implicitly adopted by a majority of the Court in American Textile Mfrs. Inst. v. Donovan, 452 U.S. 490, 505 n.25 (1981) (hereinafter "*ATMI*"). . . .

particular worker.[15] *See ATMI*, 452 U.S. at 503, 505 n.25.

Once OSHA finds that a significant risk of material health impairment exists at current exposure levels . . . , any standard promulgated to address that risk must comply with the requirements of section 6(b)(5) of the OSH Act. 29 U.S.C. § 655(b)(5). That section provides that the agency

> in promulgating standards dealing with toxic materials or harmful physical agents under this subsection, shall set the standard which *most adequately assures, to the extent feasible, on the basis of the best available evidence, that no employee will suffer material impairment of health or functional capacity* even if such employee has regular exposure to the hazard dealt with by such standard for the period of his working life. . . . In addition to the attainment of the highest degree of health and safety protection for the employee, other considerations shall be the latest available scientific data in the field, the feasibility of the standards, and experience gained under this and other health and safety laws. . . .

Id. (emphasis added). In other words, section 6(b)(5) mandates that the standard adopted "prevent material impairment of health to the extent feasible." *ATMI*, 452 U.S. at 512 (emphasis omitted).

1. *Material Impairment*

In this rulemaking, OSHA grouped the 428 substances into eighteen categories by the primary health effects of those substances, for example, neuropathic effects, sensory irritation, and cancer. Industry petitioners charge that for several categories of substances OSHA failed to adequately justify its determination that the health effects caused by exposure to these substances are "material impairments." We disagree.

Petitioners cite the category of "sensory irritation" as a particularly egregious example. At the beginning of the discussion for each category, the agency summarized the types of health effects within that category, and discussed why those effects constituted "material impairments." The "Description of Health Effects" for the "sensory irritation" category includes the following discussion:

> The symptoms of sensory irritation include stinging, itching, and burning of the eyes, tearing (or lacrimation), a burning sensation in the nasal passages, rhinitis (nasal inflammation), cough, sputum production, chest pain, wheezing, and dyspnea (breathing difficulty). . . .
>
> These effects may cause severe discomfort and can be seriously disabling, as is the case with dyspnea or wheezing. The tearing and eye irritation associated with exposure to sensory irritants are often severe and can be as disabling as the weeping caused by exposure to tear gas. In addition to these primary effects, workers distracted by material irritant effects are more likely than nonexposed workers to have accidents and thus

---

[15] The Court in *Benzene* gave an example, stating that "if the odds are one in a thousand that regular inhalation of gasoline vapors that are 2% benzene will be fatal, a reasonable person might well consider the risk significant and take appropriate steps to decrease or eliminate it." *Benzene*, 448 U.S. at 655. OSHA has apparently incorporated that example "as a policy norm, at least in the sense of believing that it must regulate if it finds a risk at the 1/1000 level." Int'l Union v. Pendergrass, 878 F.2d 389, 392 (D.C. Cir. 1989).

> to endanger both themselves and others. (These adverse health effects also clearly have substantial productivity impacts.) . . .
>
> OSHA concludes that exposure limits are needed for those substances for which PELs are being established in this rulemaking to protect against sensory irritant effects that result in objective signs of irritation, such as coughing, wheezing, conjunctivitis, and tearing. Such levels of mucous membrane irritation may require medical treatment, adversely affect the well-being of employees, and place the affected individuals at risk from increased absorption of the substance and decreased resistance to infection. Exposing workers repeatedly to irritants at levels that cause subjective irritant effects[17] may cause workers to become inured to the irritant warning properties of these substances and thus increase the risk of overexposure.

54 Fed. Reg. at 2444-45 (citations omitted).

We find this explanation adequate. OSHA is not required to state with scientific certainty or precision the exact point at which each type of sensory or physical irritation becomes a material impairment. Moreover, section 6(b)(5) of the Act charges OSHA with addressing all forms of "material impairment of health or functional capacity," and not exclusively "death or serious physical harm" or "grave danger" from exposure to toxic substances. *See* 29 U.S.C. §§ 654(a)(1), 655(c). . . . OSHA's determinations of what constitute "material impairments" are adequately explained and supported in the record.

2. *Significant Risk*

However, the agency's determination of the extent of the risk posed by individual substances is more problematic. "No one could reasonably expect OSHA to adopt some precise estimate of fatalities likely from a given exposure level, and indeed the Supreme Court has said that the agency has 'no duty to calculate the exact probability of harm.'" International Union, UAW v. Pendergrass, 878 F.2d 389, 392 (D.C. Cir. 1989) (quoting *Benzene*, 448 U.S. at 655). Nevertheless, OSHA has a responsibility to quantify or explain, at least to some reasonable degree, the risk posed by each toxic substance . . . . If each of these 428 toxic substances had been addressed in separate rulemakings, OSHA would clearly have been required to estimate in some fashion the risk of harm for each substance.

However, OSHA's discussions of individual substances generally contain no quantification or explanation of the risk from that individual substance. The discussions of individual substances contain summaries of various studies of that substance and the health effects found at various levels of exposure to that substance. However, OSHA made no attempt to estimate the risk of contracting those health effects. Instead, OSHA merely provided a conclusory statement that the new PEL will reduce the "significant" risk of material health effects shown to be caused by that substance. . . . However, OSHA did make a generic finding that the Air Contaminants Standard as a whole would prevent 55,000 occupational illnesses and 683 deaths annually.

Moreover, a determination that the new standard is "reasonably necessary or appropriate," 29 U.S.C. § 652(8), and that it is the standard that "most adequately

[17] Subjective irritants include, for example, itching and burning of the eye, nose, or throat. . . .

assures . . . that no employee will suffer material impairment of health or functional capacity," *id.* § 655(b)(5), necessarily requires some assessment of the level at which significant risk of harm is eliminated or substantially reduced. *See Benzene*, 448 U.S. at 653. Yet, with rare exceptions, the individual substance discussions in the Air Contaminants Standard are virtually devoid of reasons for setting those individual standards. In most cases, OSHA cited a few studies and then established a PEL without explaining why the studies mandated the particular PEL chosen. For example, the PEL for bismuth telluride appears to be based on a single study that showed almost no effects of any kind in animals at several times that concentration. . . . For some substances, OSHA merely repeated a boilerplate finding that the new limit would protect workers from significant risk of some material health impairment. . . .

OSHA . . . responds by noting that it incorporated "uncertainty" or "safety" factors into many PELs . . ."Studies are often of small size and, since there is a large variation in human susceptibility, a study because of its small size may not demonstrate an effect that actually exists. . . . For this reason, it is not uncommon to set a limit below that level which the study may have indicated showed no effect." [54 Fed. Reg.] at 2365. OSHA claims that use of such uncertainty factors "has been the standard approach for recommending exposure limits for non-carcinogens by scientists and health experts in the field for many years." *Id.* In this rulemaking, the difference between the level shown by the evidence and the final PEL is sometimes substantial. We assume, because it is not expressly stated, that for each of those substances OSHA applied a safety factor to arrive at the final standard. Nevertheless, the method by which the "appropriate" safety factor was determined for each of those substances is not explained in the final rule. . . .

The Supreme Court in *Benzene* did recognize that absolute scientific certainty may be impossible when regulating on the edge of scientific knowledge, and that "so long as they are supported by a body of reputable scientific thought, the Agency is free to use conservative assumptions in interpreting the data . . . , risking error on the side of overprotection rather than underprotection." *Id.* at 656. . . . The lesson of *Benzene* is clearly that OSHA may use assumptions, but only to the extent that those assumptions have some basis in reputable scientific evidence. If the agency is concerned that the standard should be more stringent than even a conservative interpretation of the existing evidence supports, monitoring and medical testing may be done to accumulate the additional evidence needed to support that more protective limit. *Benzene* does not provide support for setting standards below the level substantiated by the evidence. Nor may OSHA base a finding of significant risk at lower levels of exposure on unsupported assumptions using evidence of health impairments at significantly higher levels of exposure.

While OSHA has probably established that most or all of the substances involved do pose a significant risk at some level, it has failed to establish that existing exposure levels in the workplace present a significant risk of material health impairment or that the new standards eliminate or substantially lessen the risk.

C. FEASIBILITY

The Supreme Court has defined "feasibility" as "'capable of being done, executed, or effected,'" *ATMI*, 452 U.S. at 508-09, both technologically and economically. . .

. [T]he burden is on OSHA to show by substantial evidence that the standard is feasible, although OSHA need not prove feasibility with scientific certainty.

1. *Technological Feasibility*

. . . To show that a standard is technologically feasible, OSHA must demonstrate "that modern technology has at least conceived some industrial strategies or devices which are likely to be capable of meeting the PEL and which the industries are generally capable of adopting." *United Steelworkers*, 647 F.2d at 1266. Further, "the undisputed principle that feasibility is to be tested industry-by-industry demands that OSHA examine the technological feasibility of each industry individually." *Id.* at 1301. . . .

In this rulemaking, OSHA first identified the primary air contaminant control methods: Engineering controls are methods such as ventilation, isolation, and substitution.[25] Complementing the engineering controls are work practices and administrative reforms (e.g., housekeeping, material handling or transfer procedures, leak detection programs, training, and personal hygiene). Finally, personal protective equipment such as respirators and gloves may become necessary when these other controls are not fully effective.

OSHA then organized its discussion of technological feasibility by industry sector using the Standard Industrial Classification (SIC) groupings. The SIC codes classify by type of activity for purposes of promoting uniformity and comparability in the presentation of data. . . . For most of the SIC codes discussed, OSHA provided only a general description of how generic engineering controls might be used in a given sector. Then, relying on this generic analysis, OSHA concluded that existing engineering controls are available to reduce exposure levels to the new levels. . . . However, OSHA made no attempt to show the ability of technology to meet specific exposure standards in specific industries. . . .

OSHA correctly notes that all it need demonstrate is "a general *presumption* of feasibility for *an industry*." *United Steelworkers*, 647 F.2d at 1266 (second emphasis added). . . . However, as this quote indicates, "a general presumption of feasibility" refers to a specific industry-by-industry determination that a "typical firm will be able to develop and install engineering and work practice controls that can meet the PEL in most of its operations." *United Steelworkers*, 647 F.2d at 1272. OSHA can prove this "by pointing to technology that is either already in use or has been conceived and is reasonably capable of experimental refinement and distribution within the standard's deadlines." *Id.* Only when OSHA has provided such proof for a given industry does there arise "a presumption that industry can meet the PEL without relying on respirators, a presumption which firms will have to overcome to obtain relief in any secondary inquiry into feasibility." *Id.* . . . We find that OSHA has not established the technological feasibility of the 428 PELs in its revised Air Contaminants Standard.

---

[25] Ventilation involves the movement of air to displace or dilute the contaminants. Isolation, or process enclosure, involves the placement of a physical barrier between the hazardous operation and the worker. Substitution, or process change, involves the replacement of a toxic chemical in a particular process or work area with another, less toxic substance.

2. *Economic Feasibility*

Nor has OSHA adequately demonstrated that the standard is economically feasible. OSHA must "provide a reasonable assessment of the likely range of costs of its standard, and the likely effects of those costs on the industry," *United Steelworkers*, 647 F.2d at 1266, so as to "demonstrate a reasonable likelihood that these costs will not threaten the existence or competitive structure of an industry, even if it does portend disaster for some marginal firms," *id.* at 1272. The determination of economic feasibility is governed by the same principles as technological feasibility. It must be supported by substantial evidence and OSHA must demonstrate its applicability to the affected industries.

. . . OSHA ostensibly recognized its responsibility "to demonstrate economic feasibility for *an industry*" (emphasis added), . . . [but] nevertheless determined feasibility for each industry "sector" . . . , without explaining why such a broad grouping was appropriate. OSHA's economic feasibility determinations therefore suffer from the same faults as its technological feasibility findings. Indeed, it would seem particularly important not to aggregate disparate industries . . . .

. . . [A]verage estimates of cost can be extremely misleading in assessing the impact of particular standards on individual industries. Analyzing the economic impact for an entire sector could conceal particular industries laboring under special disabilities and likely to fail as a result of enforcement. Moreover, for some substances, OSHA failed even to analyze all the affected industry sectors. We find that OSHA has not met its burden of establishing that its 428 new PELs are either economically or technologically feasible. . . .

IV. CONCLUSION

Therefore, although we find that the record adequately explains and supports OSHA's determination that the health effects of exposure to these 428 substances are material impairments, we hold that OSHA has not sufficiently explained or supported its threshold determination that exposure to these substances at previous levels posed a significant risk of these material health impairments or that the new standard eliminates or reduces that risk to the extent feasible. OSHA's overall approach to this rulemaking is so flawed that we must . . . VACATE the revised Air Contaminants Standard, and REMAND to the agency.

NOTES AND QUESTIONS

1. If OSHA fears that current conditions or standards leave employees exposed to a "significant risk," how will it develop "substantial evidence" of this risk to support a new or revised standard? In Industrial Union Dep't, AFL-CIO v. American Petroleum Inst., 448 U.S. 607 (1980), the Court pointed to other important OSHA authority:

> [I]n setting a permissible exposure level in reliance on less-than-perfect methods, OSHA would have the benefit of a backstop in the form of monitoring and medical testing. Thus, if OSHA properly determined that the permissible exposure limit should be set at 5 ppm, it could still require monitoring and medical testing for employees exposed to lower levels. By doing so, it could keep a constant check on the validity of the assumptions

> made in developing the permissible exposure limit, giving it a sound evidentiary basis for decreasing the limit if it was initially set too high . . . .

Id. at 658; *see also* 29 U.S.C. § 655(b)(7) (authorizing required monitoring and physical examinations); Nat'l Cottonseed Prod. Ass'n v. Brock, 825 F.2d 482 (D.C. Cir. 1987) (OSHA need not find that current levels of cotton dust present significant risk before requiring medical surveillance of employees exposed); GAF Corp. v. OSHRC, 561 F.2d 913 (1977) (upholding OSHA's requirement that employer must provide medical examinations for any employee exposed to asbestos fibers, even if exposure is below the permissible exposure limit).

2. Could OSHA avoid the rigorous requirements for the establishment of specific standards by proceeding under the "general duty" clause? Reread footnotes 33 and 37 of *National Realty & Construction*. Once OSHA has issued a specific standard regarding a hazard, the standard tends to limit the extent of any duty OSHA might assert with respect to the same hazard. In general, OSHA may not cite an employer under the general duty clause unless there is no applicable standard. Brisk Waterproofing Co., 1 OSHRC 1263, 1973-74 OSHD ¶16,345 (1973). *But see* Int'l Union, UAW v. Gen'l Dynamics Land Sys. Div., 815 F.2d 1570 (D.C. Cir. 1987) (existence of specific standard no defense to citation under general duty clause, where employer knew the standard did not adequately reduce risks to employees).

From Feasibility to Cost-Benefit Analysis Under the OSH Act

In *National Realty & Construction, supra,* Judge Wright held that an employer's responsibility under the general duty clause to eliminate "recognized" hazards means, among other things, that an employer must eliminate "preventable" hazards. Conversely, the general duty clause does not require an employer to adopt hazard abatement methods if "safety experts would substantially concur in thinking the methods infeasible." Thus, in any citation under the general duty clause, OSHA must describe an abatement method and prove the feasibility of abatement. *See* Nelson Tree Serv. v. OSHRC, 60 F.3d 1207, 1211 (6th Cir. 1995).

When OSHA promulgates or enforces a specific standard, it is subject to a different set of OSH Act provisions that impose a similar requirement of feasibility. Section 3(8) of the act, 29 U.S.C. § 652(8), defines an "occupational safety and health standard" as a standard "reasonably necessary or appropriate" for the safety and health of employees. A more explicit requirement of feasibility is contained in section 6(b)(5), 29 U.S.C. § 655(b)(5), which is a special provision for standards dealing with "toxic materials or harmful physical agents." Such standards must achieve the act's goals "to the extent feasible."

In AFL-CIO v. OSHA, *supra,* the court described the two separate components of feasibility: technological feasibility and economic feasibility. Technological feasibility, which is usually the easiest to determine, simply means that "modern technology has at least conceived some industrial strategies or devices" to achieve compliance with the standard. The more troublesome component has been economic feasibility. Economic feasibility means that the costs of compliance "will not threaten the existence or competitive structure of an industry, even if it does portend disaster for some marginal firms."[3] In predicting

[3] The requirement of economic feasibility might take a somewhat different shape under the

the viability or competitive structure of an industry, OSHA has relied in part on a comparison of current prices for the industry's products with the higher prices the industry would need to charge to recover the cost of compliance with a proposed standard. *See* Pub. Citizen Health Res. Group v. U.S. Dep't of Labor, 557 F.3d 165 (3d Cir. 2009) (upholding OSHA's finding that electroplating industry's compliance with proposed hexavalent chromium PEL was economically infeasible, where "a price increase that would assure continued profitability for the entire industry would require almost tripling the annual nominal price increase").

What if a standard does not threaten an industry's existence, but its costs to employers will exceed the value of the expected improvement in employee health and safety? What if the standard would lead to industry decline, unemployment, and associated health and social problems exceeding any gains in the health and safety of working conditions? Does section 3(8) of the Act answer the question when it defines "occupational safety and health standard" as "a standard . . . *reasonably* necessary or *appropriate*" for employee safety and health?

The answer might depend in part on whether the standard in question is a "toxic materials standard" or a general standard. In American Textile Mfrs. Inst., Inc. v. Donovan (*ATMI* or the *Cotton Dust Case*), 452 U.S. 490 (1981), the Supreme Court considered the validity of an OSHA toxic materials standard limiting employee exposure to cotton dust, which over time can cause a respiratory condition known as byssinosis. For toxic materials standards, section 6(b)(5) requires the secretary to adopt the standard "which most adequately assures, *to the extent feasible* . . . that *no employee* will suffer material impairment of health or functional capacity even if such employee has regular exposure to the hazard dealt with by such standard for the period of his working life." (emphasis added). An industry association opposing the standard argued that sections 3(8) (the general "standard" definition) and 6(b)(5) (toxic materials standards), taken together require OSHA to demonstrate "a reasonable relationship between the costs and benefits associated with" a standard. 452 U.S. at 494. In contrast, OSHA argued that in the case of a toxic materials standard, section 6(b)(5) requires "the *most protective standard possible* to eliminate a significant risk of material health impairment, subject to the constraints of economic and technological feasibility." *Id.* at 495 (emphasis added). The Court agreed with OSHA, rejected the industry's "cost-benefit" argument and adopted the "most protective standard possible" rule:

> [Section] 6(b)(5) directs the Secretary to issue the standard that "most adequately assures . . . that no employee will suffer material impairment of health" limited only by the extent to which this is "capable of being done." In effect then, as the Court of Appeals held, Congress itself defined the basic relationship between costs and benefits, by placing the "benefit" of worker

---

general duty clause, because an enforcement proceeding seeking to impose a duty on a single employer under the general duty clause would probably lack an investigation or a record sufficient to determine the effect of such a duty on an entire industry. Moreover, an employer singled out to bear the burden of compliance ahead of its rivals might be placed at a fatal disadvantage. Thus, in *National Realty & Construction, supra,* Judge Wright suggested in footnote 37 that if there were a real issue of economic feasibility with respect to a proposed abatement duty, OSHA might be required to adopt a standard subject to the usual rulemaking process instead of asserting the duty in a general duty clause enforcement proceeding.

> health above all other considerations save those making attainment of this "benefit" unachievable. Any standard based on a balancing of costs and benefits by the Secretary that strikes a different balance than that struck by Congress would be inconsistent with the command set forth in § 6(b)(5). Thus, cost-benefit analysis by OSHA is not required by the statute because feasibility analysis is.

Id. at 509.

Thus, the act does not *compel* OSHA to balance costs against benefits in adopting a toxic materials standard, and OSHA need not prove that benefits outweigh costs in defending such a standard. On the other hand, the Court noted in dicta that the act might *authorize* OSHA to consider costs of a standard in comparison with benefits, especially in setting regulatory priorities. *Id.* at 509 & n.29. Indeed, not long after the *Cotton Dust Case,* OSHA began routinely to perform cost-benefit analyses of proposed regulations in accordance with an executive order of the Reagan Administration. *See* Viscusi, *The Structure and Enforcement of Job Safety Regulation*, 49 J.L. & Contemp. Prob. 127 (1986). However, even if OSHA engages in cost-benefit analysis in deciding whether to issue a toxic materials standard, the *Cotton Dust Case* suggests the Court will not require OSHA to prove that the standard is justified under such analysis.

The Supreme Court also qualified its holding in the *Cotton Dust Case* in one other important way. The standard at issue in the *Cotton Dust Case* was a toxic materials standard, and the strict feasibility rule adopted by the Court was based on specific language of section 6(b)(5). Standards not dealing with "toxic materials or harmful agents" and not subject to section 6(b)(5) are subject to the "reasonably necessary or appropriate" rule of section 3(8). In the *Cotton Dust Case,* the Court explicitly declined to decide whether section 3(8) might require cost-benefit analysis. 452 U.S. at 509 & n.29.

Following the *Cotton Dust Case*, a few courts have considered whether some form of cost-benefit analysis might be necessary for standards other than toxic materials standards. In National Grain & Feed Ass'n v. OSHA, 866 F.2d 717 (5th Cir. 1989), the Fifth Circuit held that the "reasonably necessary or appropriate" requirement for general standards establishes a middle path between a strict feasibility rule and a strict cost-benefit analysis rule. The intermediate approach described by the Fifth Circuit requires OSHA to prove that the benefits of a standard are "reasonably related" to its costs. *Id.* at 733; *see also* UAW v. OSHA, 37 F.3d 665 (D.C. Cir. 1994); Donovan v. Castle & Cooke Foods, 692 F.2d 641, 649 (9th Cir. 1982). For more on cost-benefit analysis under the OSH Act and other federal laws, *see* Cass Sunstein, *The Cost Benefit State: The Future of Regulatory Protection* (Am. Bar Ass'n 2002).

NOTES AND QUESTIONS

1. Could OSHA regulate employment terms linked only *indirectly* to safety and health? Section 3(8) of the act defines "safety and occupational health standard" broadly to include any rule requiring "practices" or "methods" for employee safety and health. Could a rule affecting hiring, assignment, or pay practices be within this definition? The reach of OSHA's authority to impose new

employer duties has been one element in the debate over "ergonomic" standards, which are designed to reduce the hazard of musculoskeletal injuries.

When an employee first begins to suffer a musculoskeletal injury, such as a back injury, the best cure might be temporary work avoidance. If the employer lacks an effective "light duty" or paid medical leave policy, an employee's dependence on the job might force a return to work too early, aggravating the injury. OSHA sought to address this problem in an ergonomic standard issued in 2001 during the last days of the Clinton Administration. Among other things, it required an employer to continue all or part of an employee's regular earnings during some period of rest or light duty after an injury. Opponents of the measure argued, among other things, that the rule improperly displaced workers' compensation laws. *See* 29 U.S.C. § 653(b)(4) ("Nothing in this chapter shall be construed to supersede or in any manner affect any workmen's compensation law"). The question whether OSHA exceeded its authority in adopting the rule never reached the courts because Congress quickly exercised its authority under the Congressional Review Act to rescind the entire ergonomic standard. *See* J. Parks, *Lessons in Politics: Initial Use of the Congressional Review Act*, 55 Admin. L. Rev. 187, 192-195 (2003). *But see* United Steelworkers of Am. v. Marshall, 647 F.2d 1189 (D.C. Cir. 1980) (upholding OSHA lead standard requiring that if an employee's blood-lead level reaches a certain point, the employer must remove the employee from the job that caused the exposure and continue to pay the employee for a limited period of time).

2. In the absence of a standard, OSHA can still rely on the general duty clause to cite employers for ergonomic hazards. *See, e.g.*, Pepperidge Farm, Inc., 1995-1997 OSHD (CCH) ¶31301, 17 OSH Cas. (BNA) 1993; Beverly Enters., Inc., 2000 WL 34235994 (OSHRC 2000). *See also* Occupational Safety and Health Administration, *Effective Ergonomics: Strategy for Success*, at http://www.osha.gov/SLTC/ergonomics/index.html.

3. Another problem area posing special challenges for OSHA is workplace violence. If OSHA set priorities based only on the number of injuries and fatalities caused by each particular hazard, workplace violence would surely rank near the top. During 2010, nearly 18 percent of all workplace fatalities were due to assaults or other violent acts. Bureau of Labor Statistics, Revisions to 2010 Census of Fatal Occupational Injuries, at http://www.bls.gov/iif/oshwc/cfoi/cfoi_revised10.pdf. For female workers, homicide is the leading cause of work-related fatality. National Institute for Occupational Safety and Health, Current Intelligence Bulletin 57, *Violence in the Workplace: Risk Factors and Prevention Strategies* (July 1996), at http://www.cdc.gov/niosh/violcont.html.

Workplace violence is not necessarily "unpreventable," and measures to reduce the risk are not necessarily infeasible. The NIOSH report offers a number of measures, some as simple as installing better lighting, to reduce the risk of workplace violence. Nevertheless, OSHA has taken little action in this area. *See* Megawest Financial, Inc., 17 OSHRC 1337, 1995 OSHD ¶30,798 (1995) (ALJ dismissing general duty clause citation alleging employer must employ security guard to protect apartment complex staff that had suffered series of criminal assaults, because workplace violence is not a "recognized" hazard).

4. OSHA does not appear to have taken any position with respect to the right of employees to possess firearms in the workplace. There are no specific

OSHA standards that relate to the possession of firearms at work. In at least one case, however, an employee filed a complaint with the state OSHA, arguing that her employer's failure to ban guns at the bar where she worked constituted a violation of the general duty clause. *Workplace Violence: Tennessee Bar Employee Files Complaint with OSHA Over Allowing Guns in Workplace*, Occupational Safety & Health Daily (September 2, 2010). The Tennessee OSHA (which enforces an approved OSH law), rejected the complaint. Subsequently, Tennessee adopted a law providing that an employer's decision to permit guns on its premises is not an occupational safety or health hazard. Tenn. Code Ann. § 50-3-201(d). *Workplace Violence: Tennessee Governor Signs Bill Protecting Handguns at Work*, Occupational Safety & Health Daily (September 2, 2010).

Some states have gone farther and prohibit an employer from interfering with an employee's right to store a firearm in his automobile in the employer's parking area. In Ramsey Winch, Inc. v. Henry, 555 F.3d 1199 (10th Cir. 2009), the court held that Oklahoma's law guaranteeing this right was not preempted by the OSH Act, in the absence of any position by the federal OSHA on the matter.

5. If OSHA *fails* to act in the face of substantial evidence that current conditions or standards leave employees significantly at risk of serious injury or death, could employees or a labor organization sue to compel OSHA to issue a new standard? *See* Pub. Citizen Health Research Group v. Chao, 314 F.3d 143 (3d Cir. 2002) (OSHA's nine-year delay in adopting new standard for hexavalent chromium was excessive and not justified by scientific uncertainty or competing OSHA priorities; therefore OHSA must propose new standard according to timetable determined by judicial mediation). *Cf.* Int'l Union, United Mine Workers of Am. v. U.S. Dep't of Labor, 358 F.3d 40 (D.C. Cir. 2004) (Mine Safety and Health Administration failed to provide adequate explanation for withdrawing proposed rule, making such withdrawal arbitrary and capricious).

6. Should an OSHA standard be admissible evidence to prove a requisite standard of care in a common law personal injury action based on a defendant's alleged negligence? The issue might be important if an employee sues his own employer under some exception to workers' compensation law, or if he sues a third party such as a different employer on a multi-employer worksite. *See* Elsner v. Ubeges, 34 Cal.4th 915, 22 Cal. Rptr. 3d 530 (2004) (OSHA regulations are admissible for the purpose of proving the negligence of a defendant who was not the plaintiff's employer); Supreme Beef Packers, Inc. v. Maddox, 67 S.W.3d 453 (Tex. App. 2002) (permitting proof of OSHA standard, but denying plaintiff's request for "negligence per se" jury instruction); York v. Union Carbide Corp., 586 N.E.2d 861 (Ind. App. 1992) (manufacturer was not liable for failure to warn, where it supplied data in conformity with OSHA hazard communication standard).

3. *Employee Self-Help*

a. Individual Employee Action

The OSH Act provides a number of opportunities for employees or their representatives to participate in enforcement of the act. An employee who believes a violation of the act threatens "physical harm" or poses an "imminent danger" may request OSHA to inspect the workplace, and OSHA must either conduct an inspection or provide the employee a written notice of its determination that there are "no reasonable grounds" to believe there is a violation. 29 U.S.C. § 657(f)(1). If employees have a "representative" such as a labor union, the representative may accompany an OSHA official in the inspection of the workplace. *Id.* § 657(e). If the employees have no representative, the OSHA official "shall consult with a reasonable number of employees concerning matters of health and safety in the workplace." *Id.* If OSHA issues a citation but an employee believes it permits the employer an "unreasonable" time to abate a hazard, the employee can contest the abatement period and obtain a hearing. *Id.* § 659(c). Employees frequently serve as witnesses in OSHA enforcement hearings, and their testimony may be crucial to OSHA's proof that some condition or employer practice is a violation. *See, e.g.*, Brennan v. Butler Lime & Cement Co., 520 F.2d 1011 (7th Cir. 1975).

Because none of these rights or opportunities would count for much if an employer were free to discipline or discharge an employee who exercised his rights, the OSH Act adds one more right: to be free from employer retaliation. Section 11(c)(1) of the act, 29 U.S.C. § 660(c)(1), provides:

> No person shall discharge or in any manner discriminate against any employee because such employee has filed any complaint or instituted or caused to be instituted any proceeding under or related to this Act or has testified or is about to testify in any such proceeding or because of the exercise by such employee on behalf of himself or others of any right afforded by this Act.

Encouraging employees to report violations and cooperate in OSHA inspections and enforcement proceedings is an important part of OSHA enforcement. In 2010, about 20 percent of OSHA inspections arose from complaints, most likely from employees. Occupational Safety and Health Admin., Dep't of Labor, OSHA Issues 2011 Annual Inspection Plan (September 9, 2011), at http://www.osha.gov/dep/2010_enforcement_summary.html. A survey of 1987-1993 citations showed that about 70 percent of employee complaints resulted in citations, and about half of all employee complaints revealed willful, repeat, or serious violations. Not surprisingly, employees at firms with poor labor-management relations were more likely to file complaints, but their complaints were less likely to be valid. OSHA Data, *With OSHA, Sometimes It's the Squeaky Hinge That Gets Oiled!* (1997), at http://www.oshadata.com/fsshgo.htm.

Reporting an employer's violation might eventually lead to abatement, but the inspection and enforcement process can take time, sometimes many years if the employer contests a citation. If a danger of death or serious injury is imminent, the Secretary of Labor has authority to seek a preliminary injunction. 29 U.S.C. §§ 662(a), (b). If the secretary fails to act in the face of imminent danger, an affected employee can sue to compel the secretary to initiate injunction proceedings, but only if the employee can persuade a court that the secretary's failure to seek an injunction was arbitrary or capricious. 29 U.S.C. § 662(d). In any event, injunction proceedings are no solution for an employee who is presently on the job and facing an immediate danger. If an employer orders an employee to perform work under conditions that are immediately and especially hazardous, the employee faces a difficult choice. Refusing to work is insubordination and possibly grounds for discharge, but continuing to work means the risk of death or injury.

WHIRLPOOL CORP. v. MARSHALL

445 U.S. 1 (1980)

Mr. Justice STEWART delivered the opinion of the Court.

The Occupational Safety and Health Act of 1970 (Act) prohibits an employer from discharging or discriminating against any employee who exercises "any right afforded by" the Act. [29 U.S.C. § 660(c)(1).] The Secretary of Labor (Secretary) has promulgated a regulation providing that, among the rights that the Act so protects, is the right of an employee to choose not to perform his assigned task because of a reasonable apprehension of death or serious injury coupled with a reasonable belief that no less drastic alternative is available.[3] The question presented in the case before us is whether this regulation is consistent with the Act.

I

The petitioner company maintains a manufacturing plant in Marion, Ohio, for the production of household appliances. Overhead conveyors transport appliance components throughout the plant. To protect employees from objects that occasionally fall from these conveyors, the petitioner has installed a horizontal wire-mesh guard screen approximately 20 feet above the plant floor. This mesh screen is welded to angle-iron frames suspended from the building's structural steel skeleton.

Maintenance employees of the petitioner spend several hours each week removing objects from the screen, replacing paper spread on the screen to catch grease drippings from the material on the conveyors, and performing occasional maintenance work on the conveyors themselves. To perform these duties, maintenance employees usually are able to stand on the iron frames, but sometimes find it necessary to step onto the steel mesh screen itself.

In 1973, the company began to install heavier wire in the screen because its safety had been drawn into question. . . . On June 28, 1974, a maintenance employee fell to his death through the guard screen in an area where the newer, stronger mesh had not yet been installed.[4] Following this incident, the petitioner effectuated some

---

[3] The regulation, 29 CFR § 1977.12 (1979), provides . . . :

(b)(2) [O]ccasions might arise when an employee is confronted with a choice between not performing assigned tasks or subjecting himself to serious injury or death arising from a hazardous condition at the workplace. If the employee, with no reasonable alternative, refuses in good faith to expose himself to the dangerous condition, he would be protected against subsequent discrimination. The condition causing the employee's apprehension of death or injury must be of such a nature that a reasonable person, under the circumstances then confronting the employee, would conclude that there is a real danger of death or serious injury and that there is insufficient time due to the urgency of the situation, to eliminate the danger through resort to regular statutory enforcement channels. In addition, in such circumstances, the employee, where possible, must also have sought from his employer, and been unable to obtain, a correction of the dangerous condition.

[4] As a result of this fatality, the Secretary conducted an investigation that led to the issuance

repairs and issued an order strictly forbidding maintenance employees from stepping on either the screens or the angle-iron supporting structure. An alternative but somewhat more cumbersome and less satisfactory method was developed for removing objects from the screen. This procedure required employees to stand on power-raised mobile platforms and use hooks to recover the material.

On July 7, 1974, two of the petitioner's maintenance employees, Virgil Deemer and Thomas Cornwell, met with the plant maintenance superintendent to voice their concern about the safety of the screen. The superintendent disagreed with their view, but permitted the two men to inspect the screen with their foreman and to point out dangerous areas needing repair. Unsatisfied with the petitioner's response to the results of this inspection, Deemer and Cornwell met on July 9 with the plant safety director. At that meeting, they requested the name, address, and telephone number of a representative of the local office of the Occupational Safety and Health Administration (OSHA). Although the safety director told the men that they "had better stop and think about what [they] were doing," he furnished the men with the information they requested. Later that same day, Deemer contacted an official of the regional OSHA office and discussed the guard screen.

The next day, Deemer and Cornwell reported for the night shift at 10:45 P.M. Their foreman, after himself walking on some of the angle-iron frames, directed the two men to perform their usual maintenance duties on a section of the old screen.[6] Claiming that the screen was unsafe, they refused to carry out this directive. The foreman then sent them to the personnel office, where they were ordered to punch out without working or being paid for the remaining six hours of the shift. The two men subsequently received written reprimands, which were placed in their employment files.

A little over a month later, the Secretary filed suit in the United States District Court for the Northern District of Ohio, alleging that the petitioner's actions against Deemer and Cornwell constituted discrimination in violation of § 11(c)(1) of the Act. As relief, the complaint prayed, inter alia, that the petitioner be ordered to expunge from its personnel files all references to the reprimands issued to the two employees, and for a permanent injunction requiring the petitioner to compensate the two employees for the six hours of pay they had lost by reason of their disciplinary suspensions.

Following a bench trial, the District Court found that the regulation in question justified Deemer's and Cornwell's refusals to obey their foreman's order on July 10, 1974. . . . The District Court nevertheless denied relief, holding that the Secretary's regulation was inconsistent with the Act and therefore invalid. Usery v. Whirlpool Corp., 416 F. Supp. 30, 32-34.

---

of a citation charging the company with maintaining an unsafe walking and working surface in violation of 29 U.S.C. § 654(a)(1). The citation required immediate abatement of the hazard and proposed a $600 penalty. Nearly five years following the accident, the Occupational Safety and Health Review Commission affirmed the citation, but decided to permit the petitioner six months in which to correct the unsafe condition. Whirlpool Corp., 1979 CCH OSHD ¶23,552. A petition to review that decision is pending in the United States Court of Appeals for the District of Columbia Circuit.

[6] This order appears to have been in direct violation of the outstanding company directive that maintenance work was to be accomplished without stepping on the screen apparatus.

The Court of Appeals for the Sixth Circuit reversed the District Court's judgment. 593 F.2d 715. . . . [It] disagreed with the District Court's conclusion that the regulation is invalid. *Id.*, at 721-736. . . .

II

The Act itself creates an express mechanism for protecting workers from employment conditions believed to pose an emergent threat of death or serious injury. Upon receipt of an employee inspection request stating reasonable grounds to believe that an imminent danger is present in a workplace, OSHA must conduct an inspection. 29 U.S.C. § 657(f)(1). In the event this inspection reveals workplace conditions or practices that "could reasonably be expected to cause death or serious physical harm immediately or before the imminence of such danger can be eliminated through the enforcement procedures otherwise provided by" the Act, 29 U.S.C. § 662(a), the OSHA inspector must inform the affected employees and the employer of the danger and notify them that he is recommending to the Secretary that injunctive relief be sought. § 662(c). At this juncture, the Secretary can petition a federal court to restrain the conditions or practices giving rise to the imminent danger. By means of a temporary restraining order or preliminary injunction, the court may then require the employer to avoid, correct, or remove the danger or to prohibit employees from working in the area. § 662(a).

To ensure that this process functions effectively, the Act expressly accords to every employee several rights, the exercise of which may not subject him to discharge or discrimination. An employee is given the right to inform OSHA of an imminently dangerous workplace condition or practice and request that OSHA inspect that condition or practice. 29 U.S.C. § 657(f)(1). He is given a limited right to assist the OSHA inspector in inspecting the workplace, §§ 657(a)(2), (e), and (f)(2), and the right to aid a court in determining whether or not a risk of imminent danger in fact exists. *See* § 660(c)(1). Finally, an affected employee is given the right to bring an action to compel the Secretary to seek injunctive relief if he believes the Secretary has wrongfully declined to do so. § 662(d).

In the light of this detailed statutory scheme, the Secretary is obviously correct when he acknowledges in his regulation that, "as a general matter, there is no right afforded by the Act which would entitle employees to walk off the job because of potential unsafe conditions at the workplace." By providing for prompt notice to the employer of an inspector's intention to seek an injunction against an imminently dangerous condition, the legislation obviously contemplates that the employer will normally respond by voluntarily and speedily eliminating the danger. And in the few instances where this does not occur, the legislative provisions authorizing prompt judicial action are designed to give employees full protection in most situations from the risk of injury or death resulting from an imminently dangerous condition at the worksite.

As this case illustrates, however, circumstances may sometimes exist in which the employee justifiably believes that the express statutory arrangement does not sufficiently protect him from death or serious injury. Such circumstances will probably not often occur, but such a situation may arise when (1) the employee is ordered by his employer to work under conditions that the employee reasonably believes pose an imminent risk of death or serious bodily injury, and (2) the employee has reason to believe that there is not sufficient time or opportunity either to seek effective redress from his employer or to apprise OSHA of the danger.

Nothing in the Act suggests that those few employees who have to face this dilemma must rely exclusively on the remedies expressly set forth in the Act at the risk of their own safety. But nothing in the Act explicitly provides otherwise. Against this background of legislative silence, the Secretary has exercised his rulemaking power under 29 U.S.C. § 657(g)(2) and has determined that, when an employee in good faith finds himself in such a predicament, he may refuse to expose himself to the dangerous condition, without being subjected to "subsequent discrimination" by the employer.

The question before us is whether this interpretative regulation constitutes a permissible gloss on the Act by the Secretary, in light of the Act's language, structure, and legislative history. Our inquiry is informed by an awareness that the regulation is entitled to deference unless it can be said not to be a reasoned and supportable interpretation of the Act. . . .

A

The regulation clearly conforms to the fundamental objective of the Act — to prevent occupational deaths and serious injuries. The Act, in its preamble, declares that its purpose and policy is "to assure so far as possible every working man and woman in the Nation safe and healthful working conditions and to *preserve* our human resources. . . ." 29 U.S.C. § 651(b). (Emphasis added.) To accomplish this basic purpose, the legislation's remedial orientation is prophylactic in nature. . . . The Act does not wait for an employee to die or become injured. It authorizes the promulgation of health and safety standards and the issuance of citations in the hope that these will act to prevent deaths or injuries from ever occurring. It would seem anomalous to construe an Act so directed and constructed as prohibiting an employee, with no other reasonable alternative, the freedom to withdraw from a workplace environment that he reasonably believes is highly dangerous.

Moreover, the Secretary's regulation can be viewed as an appropriate aid to the full effectuation of the Act's "general duty" clause. . . . As the legislative history of this provision reflects, it was intended itself to deter the occurrence of occupational deaths and serious injuries by placing on employers a mandatory obligation independent of the specific health and safety standards to be promulgated by the Secretary. Since OSHA inspectors cannot be present around the clock in every workplace, the Secretary's regulation ensures that employees will in all circumstances enjoy the rights afforded them by the "general duty" clause.

The regulation thus on its face appears to further the overriding purpose of the Act, and rationally to complement its remedial scheme. . . .

C

For these reasons we conclude that 29 CFR § 1977.12(b)(2) (1979) was promulgated by the Secretary in the valid exercise of his authority under the Act.

NOTES AND QUESTIONS

1. Note that in the days preceding Deemer's and Cornwell's refusal to

work, another employee's fatal accident in falling through the screen prompted OSHA to investigate and issue a citation alleging that the screen was an unsafe working surface. It is unclear whether OSHA issued its citation before or after Deemer's and Cornwell's refusal to work. However, OSHA evidently did not seek the preliminary injunctive relief the act authorizes in cases of "imminent danger." Why not?

According to the Supreme Court's description of the facts, immediately after the fatality Whirlpool "effectuated some repairs and issued an order strictly forbidding maintenance employees from stepping on either the screens or the angle-iron supporting structure." If so, why might a supervisor have ordered Deemer and Cornwell to work in clear violation of this policy, and why might the company have disciplined them for insisting on compliance with the policy?

2. If OSHA issued its citation before Deemer's and Cornwell's refusal to work, why did its proposed order to abate fail to protect Deemer and Cornwell? Ordinarily, a citation requires an employer to abate a violation within a specified time, sometimes immediately, and the failure to abate within the prescribed time limit is a violation in itself. However, if the employer contests the citation, it is not required to abate the alleged violation until the issue is resolved by a final order. Whirlpool did contest the citation. As the Supreme Court notes in footnote 3, the issue whether Whirlpool's screen violated the act was still pending before the U.S. Court of Appeals for the District of Columbia even as the Supreme Court was deciding the principal case. Seven years after the accident that caused the investigation, the Court of Appeals found that OSHA had failed to present substantial evidence of a feasible alternative to Whirlpool's protective screen, and it reversed and vacated OSHRC's order against Whirlpool. Whirlpool Corp. v. OSHRC, 645 F.2d 1096 (D.C. Cir. 1981). In view of the ultimate disposition of the citation, would Deemer and Cornwell be protected from discrimination under section 1977.12(b)(2) if they refused to work on the screen again?

3. Section 1977.12(b)(2) does not require an employer to pay for time an employee refuses to work. However, the employer must not "discriminate" against an employee who exercises his section 1977.12(b)(2) right not to perform a particular task. If an employee is still willing to perform other available work, an employer might be discriminating if it sends the employee home instead. The Supreme Court in *Whirlpool* offered no opinion as to whether OSHA could remedy Whirlpool's discrimination by requiring Whirlpool to compensate Deemer and Cornwell for lost wages. On remand, the employees won an award of back pay on the grounds that Whirlpool had sent them home without offering alternative work. Marshall v. Whirlpool Corp., OSH Dec. (CCH) ¶24,957 (N.D. Ohio 1980).

4. An employee seeking a remedy for alleged retaliation under the act faces some unusual procedural obstacles. First, he must file his complaint with OSHA within a mere 30 days after the alleged violation. 29 U.S.C. § 660(c). Second, the employee has no private cause of action. If OSHA decides not to initiate proceedings against the employer, the employee cannot file his own OSH Act retaliation lawsuit. George v. Aztec Rental Ctr. Inc., 763 F.2d 184 (5th Cir. 1985).

5. Could an employee alleging retaliatory discharge file a lawsuit in a state court based on state law, instead of or in addition to filing a complaint with OSHA? Despite the employment at will doctrine, many states allow a wrongful discharge

cause of action if an employer discharges an employee for reporting violations of the law or assisting in law enforcement. State courts disagree whether an employee should be limited to OSH Act remedies when the employee's claim is covered by the OSH Act. Some deny relief under state law because of the availability of relief under the OSH Act. Grant v. Butler, 590 So. 2d 254 (Ala. 1991); Burnham v. Karl & Gelb, P.C., 1997 WL 133399 (Conn. Super. Ct. 1997) (unreported). Others, noting the limitations of the OSH Act's anti-retaliation remedy, allow a cause of action under state law. The Kansas court's decision in Flenker v. Willamette Industries, Inc., 967 P.2d 295 (Kan. 1998) is representative of the latter group. In *Flenker*, the Tenth Circuit certified a question to the Kansas court whether it would deny a cause of action to an employee whose complaint stated a claim under the anti-retaliation provision of the OSH Act. The Kansas court answered no:

> The remedy under [OSH Act] § 11(c) . . . is the right to file a complaint with the Secretary of Labor . . . OSHA § 11(c) says that the Secretary "shall cause such investigation to be made *as he deems appropriate*," and "*[i]f upon such investigation, the Secretary determines that the provisions of this subsection have been violated*, he shall bring an action." (Emphasis added.) . . . [N]o guidance is given "as to what factors the Secretary must or may consider to constitute an investigation." . . . What would, in a common-law tort action, be the decision of the plaintiff and plaintiff's counsel is, under § 11(c), the decision of a government employee. The concerns of the government employee could range from budget constraints to political pressure. In addition the limitation period for filing an OSHA § 11(c) complaint is 30 days from discharge.
>
> The facts here illustrate the type of agency ruling for which the employee cannot receive redress. . . . Flenker filed his complaint with OSHA, . . . [and] was informed, presumably by an OSHA employee, that because he had fixed the machine in question, which had been a part of his section 11(c) claim, he no longer had a claim under OSHA. Section 11(c)(1) declares discharge in retaliation for filing a complaint to be a violation of OSHA. Fixing the defective equipment in question does not cancel the wrong of retaliatory discharge. The OSHA statute, however, does not appear to provide a second chance for Flenker to try to convince the agency to see things his way.
>
> The inadequacy of the OSHA remedy is not outweighed by the factors cited by Willamette. Willamette suggests that under OSHA (1) there is a lower burden of proof, (2) the Secretary of Labor has considerable resources and expertise in investigating the complaint, (3) the available federal discovery process is for gathering evidence for use at trial, and (4) the employee has the Secretary's experienced representation at trial without cost to the employee. If the complaint is only half-heartedly investigated, or a suit is not filed by the Secretary of Labor, the OSHA factors do not benefit the discharged employee at all. . . . [Furthermore], unless there is some kind of administrative appeal of OSHA's decision not to pursue the complaint, which neither party has suggested exists, an employee is limited to voting against an incumbent legislator or against the current administration. . . .
>
> We answer the certified question in the negative. . . . OSHA does not provide an adequate alternative remedy under the facts certified here.

Id. at 301-03; *see* Schweiss v. Chrysler Motors Corp., 922 F.2d 473 (8th Cir. 1990)

(OSHA retaliation section does not preempt Missouri wrongful discharge claim).

6. OSHA has two other rules for employee self-help. First, OSHA's Hazard Communication Standard (HCS) requires chemical manufacturers to provide warnings about dangerous products they sell. An employer is required to make the data it receives from a manufacturer available to its employees. 29 C.F.R. § 1910.1200. Second, OSHA has promulgated the Access to Exposure and Medical Records rule, which requires an employer to grant an employee access to any exposure and medical records the employer has for that employee. 29 C.F.R. § 1910.20. Such records could include personal medical records, environmental monitoring records, biological monitoring records, material safety data sheets, and other records disclosing toxic substances or harmful physical agents to which the employee might be exposed. In itself, this regulation does not require an employer to prepare any particular records, but an employer might be required to create records under other OSHA standards. *See* 29 U.S.C. § 657(c)(3).

b. Concerted Employee Action

Employees who organize or appoint a union for the purpose of collective bargaining gain some additional means for enforcing or augmenting their rights under the OSH Act. Unions have been active parties in the judicial review of OSHA rulemaking, either seeking to compel OSHA to raise the level of protection for employees or joining OSHA in the defense of its standards. Unions have the right to participate in OSHA workplace inspections and to participate as parties in enforcement proceedings. 29 U.S.C. §§ 659, 660. A union can negotiate with an employer to adopt contractual safety rules more protective than OSHA standards, establish safety committees to promote employee safety and health, and provide for regular safety inspections by union and employer officials.

A union might also negotiate a contractual version of OSHA's regulation granting employees a right to refuse to perform unreasonably dangerous work. Even in the absence of a specific "right of refusal" contract provision, an employee or his union might argue that a refusal to work in unreasonably dangerous conditions is not "good cause" for discharge under the usual job security provision of a collective bargaining agreement. *See, e.g.*, In re Arbitration Between Reynolds Elec. & Eng'g Co. and Las Vegas Joint Bd. of Culinary Workers and Bartenders, FMCS File No. 70A/8019 (Oct. 23, 1970) (available online in Westlaw's ARBIT database). The advantages of a contractual right of refusal are to eliminate any doubt whether an employee may refuse to work based on his own reasonable opinion of danger, and to assure the employee a contractual grievance and arbitration remedy that is likely to be speedier and may be more effective than the usual OSH Act remedy. *See* Marshall v. N.L. Indus., Inc., 618 F.2d 1220 (7th Cir. 1980) (arbitrator's award of reinstatement without back pay did not foreclose OSHA's later pursuit of judicial action seeking additional relief for employee).

A surprising additional advantage of an express contractual right of refusal is the possibility of a third remedy under the National Labor Relations Act, illustrated by NLRB v. City Disposal Sys., Inc., 465 U.S. 822 (1984). In *City Disposal Systems*, an employer discharged an employee who had invoked his contractual right to refuse to drive a truck he believed was unsafe. The union chose not to process the employee's grievance, marking the end of the employee's contractual remedy as a practical matter. The employee then filed a charge with the National Labor Relations Board, alleging that his exercise of a contractual right of refusal constituted protected conduct under section 7 of the National Labor Relations Act, 29 U.S.C. § 157. Section 7 provides that "[e]mployees shall have the right . . . to engage in . . . concerted activities for the purpose of collective bargaining or other mutual aid or protection." The Board found that the employer had violated the NLRA by discharging the employee, and the U.S. Supreme Court agreed. In sum, when an employee exercises a right created by a collective bargaining agreement, the employee is engaged in concerted activity "for the purposes of collective bargaining." Even though the employee acts alone, his action vindicates the collective bargaining process, and this is true despite a union's decision not to process the employee's discharge grievance.[4] The result is to grant unionized employees up to three remedies (OSH Act, collective bargaining agreement, and NLRA) in contrast with the single OSH Act remedy for nonunion employees.

Could nonunion employees also seek an NLRA remedy in support of a right not to work in dangerous conditions? Recall that employees can act "in concert" even if they do not organize or appoint a union. See Chapter 4, Part B.2, *supra*.

NLRB v. WASHINGTON ALUMINUM CO.

370 U.S. 9 (1962)

Mr. Justice BLACK delivered the opinion of the Court.

The Court of Appeals for the Fourth Circuit, with Chief Judge Sobeloff dissenting, refused to enforce an order of the National Labor Relations Board directing the respondent Washington Aluminum Company to reinstate and make whole seven employees whom the company had discharged for leaving their work in the machine shop without permission on claims that the shop was too cold to work in. Because that decision raises important questions affecting the proper administration of the National Labor Relations Act, we granted certiorari.

. . . The respondent company is engaged in the fabrication of aluminum products . . . . The machine shop in which the seven discharged employees worked was not insulated and had a number of doors to the outside that had to be opened frequently. An oil furnace located in an adjoining building was the chief source of heat . . . , although there were two gas-fired space heaters that contributed heat to a lesser extent. The heat produced by these units was not always satisfactory and, even prior to the day of the walkout involved here, several of the eight machinists who made up the day shift at the shop had complained from time to time to the company's foreman "over the cold working conditions."

January 5, 1959, was an extraordinarily cold day for Baltimore, with unusually high winds and a low temperature of 11 degrees followed by a high of 22. When the employees on the day shift came to work that morning, they found the shop bitterly cold, due not only to the unusually harsh weather, but also to the fact that the large

[4] *Compare* Meyers Indus., Inc., 268 NLRB 493 (1984) (employee was not engaged in protected concerted activity when he refused to drive allegedly unsafe truck, because he acted alone and was not asserting a contractual right of refusal).

oil furnace had broken down the night before and had not as yet been put back into operation. As the workers gathered in the shop just before the starting hour of 7:30, one of them, a Mr. Caron, went into the office of Mr. Jarvis, the foreman, hoping to warm himself but, instead, found the foreman's quarters as uncomfortable as the rest of the shop. As Caron and Jarvis sat in Jarvis' office discussing how bitingly cold the building was, some of the other machinists walked by the office window "huddled" together in a fashion that caused Jarvis to exclaim that "(i)f those fellows had any guts at all, they would go home."

When the starting buzzer sounded a few moments later, Caron walked back to his working place in the shop and found all the other machinists "huddled there, shaking a little, cold." Caron then said to these workers, " . . . Dave (Jarvis) told me if we had any guts, we would go home. . . . I am going home, it is too damned cold to work." Caron asked the other workers what they were going to do and, after some discussion among themselves, they decided to leave with him. One of these workers, testifying before the Board, summarized their entire discussion this way: "And we had all got together and thought it would be a good idea to go home; maybe we could get some heat brought into the plant that way." As they started to leave, Jarvis approached and persuaded one of the workers to remain at the job. But Caron and the other six workers on the day shift left practically in a body in a matter of minutes after the 7:30 buzzer.

When the company's general foreman arrived between 7:45 and 8 that morning, Jarvis promptly informed him that all but one of the employees had left because the shop was too cold. The company's president came in at approximately 8:20 a.m. and, upon learning of the walkout, immediately said to the foreman, " . . . if they have all gone, we are going to terminate them." After discussion "at great length" between the general foreman and the company president as to what might be the effect of the walkout on employee discipline and plant production, the president formalized his discharge of the workers who had walked out by giving orders at 9 A.M. that the affected workers should be notified about their discharge immediately, either by telephone, telegram or personally. This was done.

On these facts the Board found that the conduct of the workers was a concerted activity to protest the company's failure to supply adequate heat in its machine shop, that such conduct is protected under the provision of § 7 of the National Labor Relations Act [29 U.S.C. § 157] which guarantees that "Employees shall have the right . . . to engage in . . . concerted activities for the purpose of collective bargaining or other mutual aid or protection," and that the discharge of these workers by the company amounted to an unfair labor practice under § 8(a)(1) of the Act, [29 U.S.C. § 158(a)(1)] which forbids employers "to interfere with, restrain, or coerce employees in the exercise of the rights guaranteed in section 7." . . . [T]he Board then ordered the company to reinstate the discharged workers to their previous positions and to make them whole for losses resulting from what the Board found to have been the unlawful termination of their employment.

In denying enforcement of this order, the majority of the Court of Appeals took the position that because the workers simply "summarily left their place of employment" without affording the company an "opportunity to avoid the work stoppage by granting a concession to a demand," their walkout did not amount to a concerted activity protected by § 7 of the Act. On this basis, they held that there was no justification for the conduct of the workers in violating the established rules of the plant by leaving their jobs without permission and that the Board had therefore exceeded its power in issuing the order. . . .

We cannot agree that employees necessarily lose their right to engage in concerted activities under § 7 merely because they do not present a specific demand upon their employer to remedy a condition they find objectionable. The language of § 7 is broad enough to protect concerted activities whether they take place before, after, or at the same time such a demand is made. To compel the Board to interpret and apply that language in the restricted fashion suggested by the respondent here would only tend to frustrate the policy of the Act to protect the right of workers to act together to better their working conditions. Indeed, as indicated by this very case, such an interpretation of § 7 might place burdens upon employees so great that it would effectively nullify the right to engage in concerted activities which that section protects.

The seven employees here were part of a small group of employees who were wholly unorganized. They had no bargaining representative and, in fact, no representative of any kind to present their grievances to their employer. Under these circumstances, they had to speak for themselves as best they could. As pointed out above, prior to the day they left the shop, several of them had repeatedly complained to company officials about the cold working conditions in the shop. These had been more or less spontaneous individual pleas, unsupported by any threat of concerted protest, to which the company apparently gave little consideration and which it now says the Board should have treated as nothing more than "the same sort of gripes as the gripes made about the heat in the summertime." The bitter cold of January 5, however, finally brought these workers' individual complaints into concert so that some more effective action could be considered. Having no bargaining representative and no established procedure by which they could take full advantage of their unanimity of opinion in negotiations with the company, the men took the most direct course to let the company know that they wanted a warmer place in which to work. So, after talking among themselves, they walked out together in the hope that this action might spotlight their complaint and bring about some improvement in what they considered to be the "miserable" conditions of their employment. This we think was enough to justify the Board's holding that they were not required to make any more specific demand than they did to be entitled to the protection of § 7.

. . . The fact that the company was already making every effort to repair the furnace and bring heat into the shop that morning does not change the nature of the controversy that caused the walkout. At the very most, that fact might tend to indicate that the conduct of the men in leaving was unnecessary and unwise, and it has long been settled that the reasonableness of workers' decisions to engage in concerted activity is irrelevant to the determination of whether a labor dispute exists or not. Moreover, the evidence here shows that the conduct of these workers was far from unjustified under the circumstances. The company's own foreman expressed the opinion that the shop was so cold that the men should go home. This statement by the foreman but emphasizes the obvious — that is, that the conditions of coldness about which complaint had been made before had been so aggravated on the day of the walkout that the concerted action of the men in leaving their jobs seemed like a perfectly natural and reasonable thing to do.

Nor can we accept the company's contention that because it admittedly had an established plant rule which forbade employees to leave their work without permission of the foreman, there was justifiable "cause" for discharging these employees, wholly separate and apart from any concerted activities in which they engaged in protest against the poorly heated plant. Section 10(c) of the Act does authorize an employer to discharge employees for "cause" and our cases have long recognized this right on the part of an employer. But this, of course, cannot mean that an employer is at liberty to punish a man by discharging him for engaging in concerted activities which § 7 of the Act protects. And the plant rule in question here purports to permit the company to do just that for it would prohibit even the most plainly protected kinds of concerted work stoppages until and unless the permission of the company's foreman was obtained.

It is of course true that § 7 does not protect all concerted activities, but that aspect of the section is not involved in this case. The activities engaged in here do not fall within the normal categories of unprotected concerted activities such as those that are unlawful, violent or in breach of contract. Nor can they be brought under this Court's more recent pronouncement which denied the protection of § 7 to activities characterized as "indefensible" because they were there found to show a disloyalty to the workers' employer which this Court deemed unnecessary to carry on the workers' legitimate concerted activities. The activities of these seven employees cannot be classified as "indefensible" by any recognized standard of conduct. Indeed, concerted activities by employees for the purpose of trying to protect themselves from working conditions as uncomfortable as the testimony and Board findings showed them to be in this case are unquestionably activities to correct conditions which modern labor-management legislation treats as too bad to have to be tolerated in a humane and civilized society like ours.

We hold therefore that the Board correctly interpreted and applied the Act to the circumstances of this case and it was error for the Court of Appeals to refuse to enforce its order. The judgment of the Court of Appeals is reversed and the cause is remanded to that court with directions to enforce the order in its entirety.

NOTES AND QUESTIONS

1. When the employees walked off the job in *Washington Aluminum*, Congress had yet to enact the OSH Act, OSHA did not exist, and there was no right of refusal regulation, 29 C.F.R. § 1977.12(b)(2). Is the section 7 remedy described in *Washington Aluminum* now a mere duplication of OSHA's right of refusal regulation? If a group of employees walked off the job today in circumstances like those in *Washington Aluminum*, could they rely on their rights under OSHA's right of refusal regulation? Or would section 7 be the better remedy?

2. OSHA has issued a "fact sheet" recommending measures to protect employees from the cold, but there does not appear to be any specific OSHA safety standard dealing with a situation like the one in *Washington Aluminum*. *See* Fact Sheet No. OSHA 98-55, *Protecting Workers in Cold Environments* (Dec. 1998), at http://www.osha.gov. *But see* 29 C.F.R. § 1910.138 (requiring "appropriate hand protection when employees' hands are exposed to hazards such as . . . harmful

temperature extremes."). Could OSHA issue a general duty clause citation against an employer for failing to provide a reasonably warm workplace? *Cf.* Glass Molders, Plastic, Pottery and Allied Workers, Local 208, OSHRC Docket No. 88-348 (Apr. 21, 1992) ("although it was clear that temperatures near the machines were very hot and that working there was uncomfortable, the Secretary . . . failed to prove that the working conditions constituted a hazard").

3. The employees in *Washington Aluminum* were not represented by a union. If they were, the rules with respect to their "walk out" might be different. If an employer has a collective bargaining agreement with a union, that agreement is likely to include a "no-strike" provision prohibiting employees from engaging in a work stoppage during the term of the agreement. A work stoppage by employees in violation of the no-strike clause would be unprotected, meaning that the employer could lawfully discharge the employees. Even in the absence of a current no-strike clause, a walkout might be unprotected if it constituted a strike in violation of certain advance notice requirements. 29 U.S.C. § 158(d). However, under section 502 of the Taft Hartley Act of 1947, 29 U.S.C. § 143,"the quitting of labor by an employee or employees in good faith because of *abnormally dangerous* conditions for work at the place of employment of such employee or employees" is not a "strike." (emphasis added). If the employees in *Washington Aluminum* were subject to a collective bargaining agreement with a no-strike clause, would their walkout have been a strike in violation of the agreement?

4. *Employer Rights*

Workplace inspection is an important tool for the Department of Labor — acting through OSHA — to accomplish its mission of *preventing* accidents before they occur. Thus, the act authorizes the Secretary of Labor, "to enter without delay" and "to inspect and investigate during regular working hours and at other reasonable times, and within reasonable limits and in a reasonable manner, any . . . place of employment." 29 U.S.C. § 657(a). Inspection could be especially effective if it were by "surprise" and without any need for the consent of an employer. The threat of random, unannounced inspections might encourage better employer compliance. And inspection would be fast, easy and inexpensive if there were no requirement for a court's issuance of a warrant. Indeed, neither employer consent nor a warrant is required by the terms of section 657(a). However, an inspector's *unchecked* authority to enter and inspect private property would be at the expense of an employer's privacy interests, and it might lead to corruption and other abuses of official authority. The next case addresses the question whether the authority to inspect is limited to any degree by the Constitution.

MARSHALL v. BARLOW'S, INC.

436 U.S. 307 (1978)

Mr. Justice WHITE delivered the opinion of the Court.

Section 8(a) of the Occupational Safety and Health Act of 1970 [29 U.S.C. § 657(a)] (OSHA or Act) empowers agents of the Secretary of Labor (Secretary) to search the work area of any employment facility within the Act's jurisdiction. The purpose of the search is to inspect for safety hazards and violations of OSHA regulations. No search warrant or other process is expressly required under the Act.

On the morning of September 11, 1975, an OSHA inspector entered the customer service area of Barlow's, Inc., an electrical and plumbing installation business located in Pocatello, Idaho. The president and general manager, Ferrol G. "Bill" Barlow, was on hand; and the OSHA inspector, after showing his credentials, informed Mr. Barlow that he wished to conduct a search of the working areas of the business. Mr. Barlow inquired whether any complaint had been received about his company. The inspector answered no, but that Barlow's Inc., had simply turned up in the agency's selection process. The inspector again asked to enter the nonpublic area of the business; Mr. Barlow's response was to inquire whether the inspector had a search warrant. The inspector had none. Thereupon, Mr. Barlow refused the inspector admission . . . .

Three months later, the Secretary petitioned the United States District Court for the District of Idaho to issue an order compelling Mr. Barlow to admit the inspector. The requested order was issued on December 30, 1975, and was presented to Mr. Barlow on January 5, 1976. Mr. Barlow again refused admission, and he sought his own injunctive relief against the warrantless searches. . . .

I

The Secretary urges that warrantless inspections to enforce OSHA are reasonable within the meaning of the Fourth Amendment. Among other things, he relies on § 8(a) of the Act, 29 U.S.C. § 657(a), which authorizes inspection of business premises without a warrant . . . . Regrettably, we are unable to agree.

The Warrant Clause of the Fourth Amendment protects commercial buildings as well as private homes. . . . An important forerunner of the first 10 Amendments to the United States Constitution, the Virginia Bill of Rights, specifically opposed "general warrants, whereby an officer or messenger may be commanded to search suspected places without evidence of a fact committed." The general warrant was a recurring point of contention in the Colonies immediately preceding the Revolution. The particular offensiveness it engendered was acutely felt by the merchants and businessmen whose premises and products were inspected for compliance with the several parliamentary revenue measures that most irritated the colonists. "[T]he Fourth Amendment's commands grew in large measure out of the colonists' experience with the writs of assistance . . . [that] granted sweeping power to customs officials and other agents of the King to search at large for smuggled goods." United States v. Chadwick, 433 U.S. 1, 7-8 (1977). . . .

This Court has already held that warrantless searches are generally unreasonable, and that this rule applies to commercial premises as well as homes. In Camara v. Municipal Court, *supra*, 387 U.S., at 528-529, we held:

> [E]xcept in certain carefully defined classes of cases, a search of private property without proper consent is "unreasonable" unless it has been authorized by a valid search warrant.

On the same day, we also ruled:

> As we explained in *Camara*, a search of private houses is presumptively unreasonable if conducted without a warrant. The businessman, like the

> occupant of a residence, has a constitutional right to go about his business free from unreasonable official entries upon his private commercial property. The businessman, too, has that right placed in jeopardy if the decision to enter and inspect for violation of regulatory laws can be made and enforced by the inspector in the field without official authority evidenced by a warrant.

See v. City of Seattle, *supra*, 387 U.S., at 543.

These same cases also held that the Fourth Amendment prohibition against unreasonable searches protects against warrantless intrusions during civil as well as criminal investigations. . . .The Secretary urges that an exception from the search warrant requirement has been recognized for "pervasively regulated business[es]," United States v. Biswell, 406 U.S. 311 (1972), and for "closely regulated" industries "long subject to close supervision and inspection." Colonnade Catering Corp. v. United States, 397 U.S. 72, 74, 77 (1970). These cases are indeed exceptions, but they represent responses to relatively unique circumstances. Certain industries have such a history of government oversight that no reasonable expectation of privacy . . . could exist for a proprietor over the stock of such an enterprise. Liquor (*Colonnade*) and firearms (*Biswell*) are industries of this type; when an entrepreneur embarks upon such a business, he has voluntarily chosen to subject himself to a full arsenal of governmental regulation.

. . . [T]he closely regulated industry of the type involved in *Colonnade* and *Biswell* is the exception. The Secretary would make it the rule. Invoking the Walsh-Healey Act of 1936, 41 U.S.C. § 35 et seq., the Secretary attempts to support a conclusion that all businesses involved in interstate commerce have long been subjected to close supervision of employee safety and health conditions. But the degree of federal involvement in employee working circumstances has never been of the order of specificity and pervasiveness that OSHA mandates. . . .

. . . Employees are not being prohibited from reporting OSHA violations. What they observe in their daily functions is undoubtedly beyond the employer's reasonable expectation of privacy. The Government inspector, however, is not an employee. Without a warrant he stands in no better position than a member of the public. What is observable by the public is observable, without a warrant, by the Government inspector as well. The owner of a business has not, by the necessary utilization of employees in his operation, thrown open the areas where employees alone are permitted to the warrantless scrutiny of Government agents. That an employee is free to report . . . noncompliance with OSHA . . . furnishes no justification for federal agents to enter a place of business from which the public is restricted and to conduct their own warrantless search.

II

. . . The Secretary submits that warrantless inspections are essential . . . because they afford the opportunity to inspect without prior notice and hence to preserve the advantages of surprise. While the dangerous conditions outlawed by the Act include structural defects that cannot be quickly hidden or remedied, the Act also regulates a myriad of safety details that may be amenable to speedy alteration or disguise. The risk is that during the interval between an inspector's initial request to search a plant and his procuring a warrant following the owner's refusal of permission, violations of this latter type could be corrected and thus escape the inspector's notice. To the suggestion that warrants may be issued ex parte and executed without delay and without prior notice, thereby preserving the element of surprise, the Secretary expresses concern for the administrative strain that would be experienced by the inspection system, and by the courts, should ex parte warrants issued in advance become standard practice.

We are unconvinced, however, that requiring warrants to inspect will impose serious burdens on the inspection system or the courts, will prevent inspections necessary to enforce the statute, or will make them less effective. . . . In the first place, the great majority of businessmen can be expected in normal course to consent to inspection without warrant. . . . In those cases where an owner does insist on a warrant, the Secretary argues that inspection efficiency will be impeded by the advance notice and delay. . . . However, the Secretary has also promulgated a regulation providing that upon refusal to permit an inspector to enter the property or to complete his inspection, the inspector shall attempt to ascertain the reasons for the refusal and report to his superior, who shall "promptly take appropriate action, including compulsory process, if necessary." 29 CFR § 1903.4 (1977). The regulation represents a choice to proceed by process where entry is refused; and . . . the Act's effectiveness has not been crippled by providing those owners who wish to refuse an initial requested entry with a time lapse while the inspector obtains the necessary process. Indeed, the kind of process sought in this case and apparently anticipated by the regulation provides notice to the business operator. . . . Nor is it immediately apparent why the advantages of surprise would be lost if, after being refused entry, procedures were available for the Secretary to seek an ex parte warrant and to reappear at the premises without further notice to the establishment being inspected.

Whether the Secretary proceeds to secure a warrant or other process, with or without prior notice, his entitlement to inspect will not depend on his demonstrating probable cause to believe that conditions in violation of OSHA exist on the premises. Probable cause in the criminal law sense is not required. For purposes of an administrative search such as this, probable cause justifying the issuance of a warrant may be based not only on specific evidence of an existing violation but also on a showing that "reasonable legislative or administrative standards for conducting an . . . inspection are satisfied with respect to a particular [establishment]." Camara v. Municipal Court, 387 U.S., at 538. A warrant showing that a specific business has been chosen for an OSHA search on the basis of a general administrative plan for the enforcement of the Act derived from neutral sources such as, for example, dispersion of employees in various types of industries across a given area, and the desired frequency of searches in any of the lesser divisions of the area, would protect an employer's Fourth Amendment rights. . . .

Nor do we agree that the incremental protections afforded the employer's privacy by a warrant are so marginal that they fail to justify the administrative burdens that may be entailed. The authority to make warrantless searches devolves almost unbridled discretion upon executive and administrative officers, particularly those in the field, as to when to search and whom to search. A warrant, by contrast, would provide assurances from a neutral officer that the inspection is reasonable under the Constitution, is authorized by statute, and is pursuant to an administrative plan containing specific neutral criteria. Also, a warrant would then and there advise the owner of the scope and objects of the search, beyond which limits the inspector is not expected to proceed. These are important functions for a warrant to perform, functions which underlie the Court's prior decisions that the Warrant Clause applies to inspections for compliance with regulatory statutes. . . .

III

We hold that Barlow's was entitled to a declaratory judgment that the Act is unconstitutional insofar as it purports to authorize inspections without warrant or its equivalent and to an injunction enjoining the Act's enforcement to that extent.

NOTES AND QUESTIONS

1. After *Barlow's,* OSHA must have either a warrant or consent to enter and inspect an employer's property, but the requirement of a warrant is clearly less onerous than it is for a police officer. Consider the Court's statement that a warrant might be based on "a general administrative plan . . . derived from neutral sources." What might constitute such a "general administrative plan"? In National Eng'g & Contracting Co. v. OSHRC, 45 F.3d 476 (D.C. Cir. 1995), the local OSHA office selected the employer for inspection based on a process that began with a commercial publication listing current construction projects. The actual selection from this list was by a computer owned and maintained by the University of Tennessee's Construction Resources Analysis Department.

> The computer randomly selects worksites contained in the [list] that meet certain criteria specified by the director of each area office. The criteria include a minimum dollar value of the construction project, a minimum size in square feet, the length of time the project is likely to last, the completion stage of the project and the type of construction project.

Id. at 478 n.2. The inspector in *National Engineering & Contracting Co.* obtained an "anticipatory warrant" in advance of his visit to the worksite, based on his description of the selection process and his attestation that "the general contractor at the inspection worksite scheduled . . . has a stated and written policy forbidding government inspection of their worksites without a valid inspection warrant." *See* 29 C.F.R. § 1903.4 (regarding anticipatory warrants). The employer later challenged the validity of the warrant, but the court held that the selection process sufficiently complied with the requirements of *Barlow's*.

> It is not disputed that OSHA's inspection program is a neutral one. . . . National complains instead that the warrant application did not manifest how National in particular was chosen for inspection under the program. While we have not previously addressed this question, other circuits have concluded that OSHA establishes probable cause by simply attesting that the worksite fits within the program. [citations omitted]. We find these cases persuasive and fully consistent with the Supreme Court's reasoning. . . .

Id. at 480. The court also rejected the employer's argument that the warrant was invalid because the inspector had falsely represented that the employer had a written policy forbidding government inspection without a warrant. "We believe that Collier's mischaracterization of National's policy does not defeat the validity of the warrant because it does not undercut any of the attestations supporting a finding of administrative probable cause." *Id.* at 481.

2. If OSHA is not required to prove it has any reason to believe a workplace is in violation of the act, why require the issuance of a warrant at all?

3. OSHA usually has little difficulty in obtaining a warrant for a programmed inspection like the one in *National Eng'g & Contracting*. On the other hand, when OSHA seeks a warrant for an unprogrammed search, it faces traditional questions about what constitutes "probable cause." *Compare* Donovan v. Federal Clearing Die Casting Co., 655 F.2d 793 (7th Cir. 1981) (two newspaper articles describing industrial accident did not provide probable cause) *with* In re Establishment Inspection of Microcosm, 951 F.2d 121 (7th Cir. 1991) (anonymous letter purportedly written by a friend of an employee provided probable cause).

4. A warrant is not necessary in three instances: where an employer voluntarily consents to a search, where an OSHA official observes a violation in plain view, and where emergency circumstances made an application for a warrant impractical. *See, e.g.,* Designs Unlimited Contractors, 2002 OSHD (CCH) ¶32,671 (2003) (OSHA inspector observed violations while driving by employer's construction site); *Sarasota Concrete Co.*, 1981 OSHD (CCH) ¶25,360 (1981) (Cottine, Commissioner, dissenting) (describing the emergency and consent exceptions to the requirement of a warrant).

5. Whether there is "cause" to inspect is one thing. Whether the scope of the actual inspection is consistent with the "cause" is another. In the case of a programmed inspection, which by definition is not related to suspicion of any particular violation, an OSHA inspector has access to the entire worksite. But if a warrant is based on a complaint about a particular problem, the permissible scope of the inspection is much more limited. For a discussion of this issue, *see* Trinity Industries, Inc. v. OSHRC, 16 F.3d 1455 (6th Cir. 1994).

6. According to one survey, employers who refuse entry to an OSHA inspector without a warrant are cited for twice as many violations and end up paying twice the amount in penalties as employers who permit warrantless inspections. OSHA Data, *It's Confirmed — OSHA Inspectors are Human!* (1997), at http://www.oshadata.com/fsoihu.htm. The survey concedes, however, "it can be argued that employers who deny OSHA entry do so because they have more problems to hide. Unfortunately, this thesis can be neither confirmed nor denied."

5. *Employee Selection and Occupational Safety*

Some employees might naturally be "accident-prone" or naturally susceptible to injury or illness because of a specific physical, mental or genetic trait. Does an employer's OSH Act general duty require it to reject such job applicants? Or would such a selection policy violate other laws regulating employee selection?

In general, an employer might consider prospective job safety and health in employee selection or retention in either of two ways, and for each there is a different set of potential job discrimination issues. First, an employer might predict that some applicants or employees are more likely than others to have work-related accidents (i.e., they are accident-prone). Second, an employer might predict that some applicants or employees are more likely to suffer injury or illness even without an accident because of their sensitivity to repetitive stress or long-term exposure to workplace chemicals or physical agents.

a. The Accident-Prone Employee

Decisions of the courts and the OSHRC strongly endorse the view that an employer must discipline employees, even discharging them if necessary, to enforce safety rules required by OSHA standards or the general duty clause. However, discharging an employee merely for having an accident may be another matter. Not all accidents are because of an employee's negligence or violation of a safety rule. Moreover, if an employee's accident leads to a workers' compensation claim, it may be difficult to disentangle the employer's motivation to enforce a safety policy from a motivation to retaliate because of an expensive injury claim. Indeed, plaintiffs in workers' compensation retaliation cases frequently rely on the fact that they were discharged or criticized for having an accident as evidence of the employer's unlawful retaliatory intent.

An employer might also seek to prevent accidents by refusing to hire those with specific traits the employer believes make accidents more likely. However, courts and the OSHRC have been very guarded in suggesting that employers have an OSH Act duty to rely on factors other than training or education to predict which applicants are safe or accident-prone. *See, e.g.,* Donohue Indus., Inc., 2000 O.S.H.D. (CCH) ¶32076 (2000) (relying in part on evidence that employer hired electricians qualified by training, in finding that employer proved its defense of unpreventable employee misconduct). If an employer targeted a protected trait like age, believing that older workers are less alert, the employer's selection policy would violate the ADEA unless the employer could prove that youth is a "bona fide occupational qualification" (BFOQ). Similarly, a policy targeting pregnant women or all women would violate Title VII (unless being non-pregnant or a man is a BFOQ), and a policy targeting a particular disability might violate the ADA.

The possibility that age, gender, or non-pregnancy might be a BFOQ should not be regarded as a gaping loophole in discrimination law. Stereotypical assumptions about the abilities of older workers, women, or pregnant women to perform a job will not support a BFOQ defense. An employer must prove that *not* having a protected trait (e.g., not being a woman) is *essential* to performing a job. The difficulty of this proof is such that employers very rarely prevail in asserting a BFOQ defense. Among the few cases of successfully asserted BFOQs are those in which an employer persuaded a court that older or pregnant workers were inherently unable to perform a particular job safely because they were particularly subject to unpredictable disabling conditions in potentially catastrophic circumstances. *See, e.g.,* Harriss v. Pan Am. World Air., Inc., 649 F.2d 670 (9th Cir. 1980) (upholding pregnancy-based BFOQ for flight attendants with emergency evacuation responsibilities); Usery v. Tamiami Trail Tours, Inc., 531 F.2d 224 (5th Cir. 1976) (upholding age-based BFOQ for long distance bus drivers). In each of these cases, however, the courts have distinguished an employer's proper concern for the safety of *third parties* such as passengers from impermissible interference with an individual employee's right to weigh and accept a risk to *personal* safety.

A representative case is Dothard v. Rawlinson, 433 U.S. 321 (1977), in which the Supreme Court considered a claim that the Alabama state penitentiary system unlawfully discriminated by forbidding the employment of women as correctional counselors in positions involving contact with male prisoners. Alabama argued that for the jobs in question, male gender was a BFOQ. The Court agreed with Alabama that "[t]he environment in Alabama's penitentiaries is a peculiarly inhospitable one for human beings of whatever sex." *Id.* at 334-335. But the Court emphasized that if the personal safety of women was all that was involved, the State's discrimination would be unlawful. "In the usual case," the Court admonished, "the argument that a particular job is too dangerous for women may appropriately be met by the rejoinder that it is the purpose of Title VII to allow the individual woman to make that choice for herself." *Id.* Instead, the Court upheld Alabama's discrimination on the ground that the penitentiary system's mixture of male sex offenders among the general prison population made women inherently incapable of maintaining order. Women, because they were women, would provoke disorder, threatening not just their own safety but also the safety of other members of the prison community. "The employee's very womanhood would thus directly undermine her capacity to provide the security that is the essence of a correctional counselor's responsibility." 433 U.S. at 336.

b. The Injury/Illness-Prone Employee

Employees who are not accident prone might nevertheless suffer work-related injuries or illness because of their sensitivity to repetitive stress or long-term exposure to chemicals or physical agents. Thus, an employer might be tempted to consider the second type of OSH-based employee selection/retention policy: identifying and rejecting applicants or employees most likely to suffer a work-related injury or illness. For example, an employer might predict that applicants who suffer respiratory ailments are more likely to become ill as a result of exposure to airborne dust in the workplace. The OSH Act does not appear to require such a policy, but an employer may feel a powerful incentive for such a policy. An employee who suffers a work-related injury or illness may file an expensive workers' compensation claim. Even if the injury or illness is not compensable because of the nature of the injury or the uncertainty of causation, the employee might file an expensive claim with the employer's medical insurance plan.

If an employer believes or discovers evidence that workers of a particular race, gender, or age are more likely than others to suffer a work-related injury, could the employer lawfully discriminate against the high-risk group? Again, the answer depends on whether the employer can prove that a protected trait is a BFOQ, and whether the employer's concern is for the employee's personal safety or the safety of others. A representative case is UAW v. Johnson Controls, Inc., 499 U.S. 187 (1991), where the Court held that an employer violated the Pregnancy Discrimination Act, 42 U.S.C. § 2000e(k), by excluding fertile women from jobs involving exposure to lead. The Court reiterated that Title VII prohibits an employer from interfering with a woman's right to weigh and accept work-related risks to her personal safety or the safety of her unborn child The Court downplayed the employer's potential liability for birth defects, noting that the employer was in compliance with OSHA lead exposure standards, and speculating that federal preemption might override any state tort law making the employer liable for what Title VII required. However, even if an employer might ultimately bear liability for the harmful results of lead exposure, "[t]he extra cost of employing members of one sex . . . does not provide an affirmative Title VII defense for a discriminatory refusal to hire members of that gender," at least when the extra cost does not "threaten the survival of the employer's business." 499 U.S. at 210-211.

CHEVRON U.S.A. INC. v. ECHAZABAL

536 U.S. 73 (2002)

Justice SOUTER delivered the opinion of the Court.

A regulation of the Equal Employment Opportunity Commission authorizes refusal to hire an individual because his performance on the job would endanger his own health, owing to a disability. The question in this case is whether the Americans with Disabilities Act of 1990 permits the regulation. We hold that it does.

I

Beginning in 1972, respondent Mario Echazabal worked for independent contractors at an oil refinery owned by petitioner Chevron U.S.A. Inc. Twice he applied for a job directly with Chevron, which offered to hire him if he could pass the company's physical examination. *See* 42 U.S.C. § 12112(d)(3) (1994 ed.). Each time, the exam showed liver abnormality or damage, the cause eventually being identified as Hepatitis C, which Chevron's doctors said would be aggravated by continued exposure to toxins at Chevron's refinery. In each instance, the company withdrew the offer, and the second time it asked the contractor employing Echazabal either to reassign him to a job without exposure to harmful chemicals or to remove him from the refinery altogether. The contractor laid him off in early 1996.

Echazabal filed suit, ultimately removed to federal court, claiming, among other things, that Chevron violated the Americans with Disabilities Act (ADA or Act) in refusing to hire him, or even to let him continue working in the plant, because of a disability, his liver condition.[2] Chevron defended under a regulation of the Equal Employment Opportunity Commission (EEOC) permitting the defense that a worker's disability on the job would pose a "direct threat" to his health, *see* 29 CFR § 1630.15(b)(2) (2001). Although two medical witnesses disputed Chevron's judgment that Echazabal's liver function was impaired and subject to further damage under the job conditions in the refinery, the District Court granted summary judgment for Chevron. It held that Echazabal raised no genuine issue of material fact as to whether the company acted reasonably in relying on its own doctors' medical advice, regardless of its accuracy.

On appeal, the Ninth Circuit asked for briefs on a threshold question not raised before, whether the EEOC's regulation recognizing a threat-to-self defense exceeded the scope of permissible rulemaking under the ADA. The Circuit held

[2] Chevron did not dispute for purposes of its summary-judgment motion that Echazabal is "disabled" under the ADA, and Echazabal did not argue that Chevron could have made a "'reasonable accommodation.'"

that it did and reversed the summary judgment. . . .

II

Section 102 of the ADA, 42 U.S.C. § 12101 et seq., prohibits "discriminat[ion] against a qualified individual with a disability because of the disability . . . in regard to" a number of actions by an employer, including "hiring." 42 U.S.C. § 12112(a). The statutory definition of "discriminat[ion]" covers a number of things an employer might do to block a disabled person from advancing in the workplace, such as "using qualification standards . . . that screen out or tend to screen out an individual with a disability."§ 12112(b)(6). By that same definition as well as by separate provision, § 12113(a), the Act creates an affirmative defense for action under a qualification standard "shown to be job-related for the position in question and . . . consistent with business necessity." Such a standard may include "a requirement that an individual shall not pose a direct threat to the health or safety of other individuals in the workplace," § 12113(b), if the individual cannot perform the job safely with reasonable accommodation, § 12113(a). By regulation, the EEOC carries the defense one step further, in allowing an employer to screen out a potential worker with a disability not only for risks that he would pose to others in the workplace but for risks on the job to his own health or safety as well: "The term 'qualification standard' may include a requirement that an individual shall not pose a direct threat to the health or safety of the individual or others in the workplace." 29 CFR § 1630.15(b)(2) (2001).

Chevron relies on the regulation here, since it says a job in the refinery would pose a "direct threat" to Echazabal's health. In seeking deference to the agency, it argues that nothing in the statute unambiguously precludes such a defense. . . . Echazabal, on the contrary, argues that as a matter of law the statute precludes the regulation, which he claims would be an unreasonable interpretation even if the agency had leeway to go beyond the literal text.

A

As for the textual bar to any agency action as a matter of law, Echazabal says that Chevron loses on the threshold question whether the statute leaves a gap for the EEOC to fill. Echazabal recognizes the generality of the language providing for a defense when a plaintiff is screened out by "qualification standards" that are "job-related and consistent with business necessity" (and reasonable accommodation would not cure the difficulty posed by employment). 42 U.S.C. § 12113(a). Without more, those provisions would allow an employer to turn away someone whose work would pose a serious risk to himself. That possibility is said to be eliminated, however, by the further specification that "'qualification standards' may include a requirement that an individual shall not pose a direct threat to the health or safety of other individuals in the workplace." § 12113(b); *see also* § 12111(3) (defining "direct threat" in terms of risk to others). Echazabal contrasts this provision with an EEOC regulation under the Rehabilitation Act of 1973, 29 U.S.C. § 701 et seq., antedating the ADA, which recognized an employer's right to consider threats both to other workers and to the threatening employee himself. Because the ADA defense provision recognizes threats only if they extend to another, Echazabal reads the statute to imply as a matter of law that threats to the worker himself cannot count.

. . . Congress included the harm-to-others provision as an example of legitimate qualifications that are "job-related and consistent with business necessity." These are spacious defensive categories, which seem to give an agency (or in the absence of agency action, a court) a good deal of discretion in setting the limits of permissible qualification standards.

. . . Echazabal [also relies on] the EEOC's rule interpreting the Rehabilitation Act of 1973, 29 U.S.C. § 701 et seq., a precursor of the ADA. That statute excepts from the definition of a protected "qualified individual with a handicap" anyone who would pose a "direct threat to the health or safety of other individuals," but, like the later ADA, the Rehabilitation Act says nothing about threats to self that particular employment might pose. 42 U.S.C. § 12113(b). The EEOC nonetheless extended the exception to cover threat to self-employment, 29 CFR § 1613.702(f) (1990), and Echazabal argues that Congress's adoption only of the threat-to-others exception in the ADA must have been a deliberate omission of the Rehabilitation Act regulation's tandem term of threat-to-self, with intent to exclude it.

[However,] the congressional choice to speak only of threats to others [is] equivocal. Consider what the ADA reference to threats to others might have meant on somewhat different facts. If the Rehabilitation Act had spoken only of "threats to health" and the EEOC regulation had read that to mean threats to self or others, a congressional choice to be more specific in the ADA by listing threats to others but not threats to self would have carried a message. The most probable reading would have been that Congress understood what a failure to specify could lead to and had made a choice to limit the possibilities. The statutory basis for any agency rulemaking under the ADA would have been different from its basis under the Rehabilitation Act and would have indicated a difference in the agency's rulemaking discretion. But these are not the circumstances here. Instead of making the ADA different from the Rehabilitation Act on the point at issue, Congress used identical language, knowing full well what the EEOC had made of that language under the earlier statute. Did Congress mean to imply that the agency had been wrong in reading the earlier language to allow it to recognize threats to self, or did Congress just assume that the agency was free to do under the ADA what it had already done under the earlier Act's identical language? There is no way to tell. Omitting the EEOC's reference to self-harm while using the very language that the EEOC had read as consistent with recognizing self-harm is equivocal at best. No negative inference is possible.

[Finally], [w]hen Congress specified threats to others in the workplace, for example, could it possibly have meant that an employer could not defend a refusal to hire when a worker's disability would threaten others outside the workplace? If Typhoid Mary had come under the ADA, would a meat packer have been defenseless if Mary had sued after being turned away? *See* 42 U.S.C. § 12113(e)....

B

Since Congress has not spoken exhaustively on threats to a worker's own health, the agency regulation can claim adherence under the rule in *Chevron*, 467 U.S., at 843, so long as it makes sense of the statutory defense for qualification standards that are "job-related and consistent with business necessity." 42 U.S.C. § 12113(a).

Chevron's reasons for calling the regulation reasonable are unsurprising: moral concerns aside, it wishes to avoid time lost to sickness, excessive turnover from medical retirement or death, litigation under state tort law, and the risk of violating the national Occupational Safety and Health Act of 1970, 29 U.S.C. § 651 et seq.

Echazabal points out that there is no known instance of OSHA enforcement, or even threatened enforcement, against an employer who relied on the ADA to hire a worker willing to accept a risk to himself from his disability on the job. In Echazabal's mind, this shows that invoking OSHA policy and possible OSHA liability is just a red herring to excuse covert discrimination. But there is another side to this. The text of OSHA itself says its point is "to assure so far as possible every working man and woman in the Nation safe and healthful working conditions," § 651(b), and Congress specifically obligated an employer to "furnish to each of his employees employment and a place of employment which are free from recognized hazards that are causing or are likely to cause death or serious physical harm to his employees,"§ 654(a)(1). Although there may be an open question whether an employer would actually be liable under OSHA for hiring an individual who knowingly consented to the particular dangers the job would pose to him, there is no denying that the employer would be asking for trouble: his decision to hire would put Congress's policy in the ADA, a disabled individual's right to operate on equal terms within the workplace, at loggerheads with the competing policy of OSHA, to ensure the safety of "each" and "every" worker.

Nor can the EEOC's resolution be fairly called unreasonable as allowing the kind of workplace paternalism the ADA was meant to outlaw. It is true that Congress had paternalism in its sights when it passed the ADA, *see* § 12101(a)(5) (recognizing "overprotective rules and policies" as a form of discrimination). But the EEOC has taken this to mean that Congress was not aiming at an employer's refusal to place disabled workers at a specifically demonstrated risk, but was trying to get at refusals to give an even break to classes of disabled people, while claiming to act for their own good in reliance on untested and pretextual stereotypes. Its regulation disallows just this sort of sham protection, through demands for a particularized enquiry into the harms the employee would probably face. The direct threat defense must be "based on a reasonable medical judgment that relies on the most current medical knowledge and/or the best available objective evidence," and upon an expressly "individualized assessment of the individual's present ability to safely perform the essential functions of the job," reached after considering, among other things, the imminence of the risk and the severity of the harm portended. 29 C.F.R. § 1630.2(r) (2001).

Similarly, Echazabal points to several of our decisions expressing concern under Title VII, which like the ADA allows employers to defend otherwise discriminatory practices that are "consistent with business necessity," 42 U.S.C. § 2000e-2(k), with employers adopting rules that exclude women from jobs that are seen as too risky. *See, e.g.*, Dothard v. Rawlinson, 433 U.S. 321, 335 (1977); Automobile Workers v. Johnson Controls, Inc., 499 U.S. 187, 202 (1991). Those cases, however, are beside the point, as they, like Title VII generally, were concerned with paternalistic judgments based on the broad category of gender, while the EEOC has required that judgments based on the direct threat provision be made on the basis of individualized risk assessments.

Accordingly, we reverse the judgment of the Court of Appeals and remand the case for proceedings consistent with this opinion.

NOTES AND QUESTIONS

1. On remand, the Ninth Circuit held that there were material issues of fact whether Chevron's decision to reject Echazabal was based on "reasonable medical judgment," and whether Chevron properly assessed nature, severity, likelihood and imminence of harm. Echazabal v. Chevron USA, Inc., 336 F.3d 1023 (9th Cir. 2003).

2. After *Echazabal*, an employer might be even more likely to condition an offer of employment on a medical examination. However, an employer must comply with ADA rules limiting medical examinations, privacy laws, and laws prohibiting genetic discrimination. See Chapter 3, Parts C.3, D.1.b and D.5.

3. An employer asserting the direct threat defense must also show that the threat "cannot be eliminated or reduced by reasonable accommodation." In a case like *Echazabal*, there might be an issue whether the threat to an employee's health could be reduced or eliminated by personal protective gear, better ventilation, or other measures to reduce employee toxin exposure. But an employer is required to offer only accommodations that are "reasonable" and will not impose "undue hardship" on the employer. *See* 42 U.S.C. § 12111(10) and Chapter 3, Part C.6.

4. Advances in genetic science might make it possible to predict who is most susceptible to diseases that might be exacerbated by specific occupational toxins or stresses. However, the Genetic Information Nondiscrimination Act makes it illegal for an employer to collect genetic information about employees or to discriminate on the basis of genetic information. 42 U.S.C. §§ 2000ff *et seq*.

CHAPTER 6

Management and Supervision of the Workforce

A. RIGHTS AND DUTIES OF SUPERVISION

1. *Employer Control and Employee Autonomy*

When courts differentiate employees from independent contractors, they frequently cite an employer's right to supervise the details of the work as a distinguishing feature of employment. See Chapter 2.A, *supra*. But how far does the employer's right to control the "details of the work" go? Is the employer the complete master of its employees' time and activity during "working time"? What if an employer seeks to manage not only details of the "work" but also personal aspects of an employee's lifestyle and "private" activity?

The airlines and their employment of flight attendants are a good example of the long reach of employer control. Before the full impact of Title VII (prohibiting sex discrimination in employment), airlines routinely required that flight attendants must remain single. If a flight attendant married, she lost her job. She would certainly lose her job if she became pregnant, whether or not she was married. If she gained too much weight, she lost her job. She lost her job when she turned 30. She was necessarily a "she," because the airlines did not employ male flight attendants until they were required to do so by Title VII.

Resolution of a conflict between employer management of the work and an employee's management of his or her personal life begins with but does not necessarily end with the parties' contract.

a. Contract Law

Questions about the source and limits of an employer's right to supervise have been important in a number of contexts, beginning with disputes over worker status. When a court holds that a worker is an "employee," it might say the proof is in the employer's right to control the work. Under this view, if the contract does not explicitly state the employer's right to supervise, the employer's right arises implicitly by virtue of the parties' understanding that the worker is an "employee," which by definition means the worker will submit to the employer's control over details of the work. In the real world of work, however, employers and employees seldom agree to any clear or express allocation of authority. In most situations the employer has no need for a clear agreement because it has no need or use for a contractual remedy to "enforce" control. The employer is more likely to gain and preserve control by retaining the right to discharge employees at will. Employers don't sue employees for insubordination; they discipline or discharge them. An "economic realities" view of employment, exemplified by NLRB v. Hearst Publications, Inc., reproduced in Chapter 2, Part A, *supra*, acknowledges that employee submission to employer control is just as likely to result from economic power as from a contract, but in either case the employee is still an employee.

Sometimes, an employer successfully exercises control simply because it has the power to enforce its will by virtue of employment at will. Any contractual allocation of control, however, can be especially important if the contract is for a definite term or otherwise restricts termination. If the contract grants the employee a right to continued or fixed term employment in a particular position, the employer is bound to observe the contract's description of the employee's duties or limits on the employer's control of the work. *See, e.g.*, Murray v. Monroe-Gregg Sch. Dist., 585 N.E.2d 687 (Ind. App. 1992) (school district breached contract by reassigning school principal to classroom teaching position). If an employer summarily discharges an "insubordinate" employee who has a contractual right to continued employment, the employer might need to prove its right to issue the order the employee disobeyed. There is, however, wide agreement among courts that an employer retains an implicit right to control work details and make *reasonable* changes in work assignments and rules, even if an employee has a contractual right to continued employment or job protection. *See, e.g.*, Bishop v. Anchorage, 899 P.2d 149, 153 (Alaska 1995); Ehlers v. Langley & Michaels Co., 237 P. 55 (Cal. App. 1925).

Whether employment is at will or for a fixed term, an employer might have promised *not* to control certain aspects of an employee's behavior or personal life. *See, e.g.*, Goodyear Tire & Rubber Co. v. Portilla, 879 S.W.2d 47 (Tex. 1994) (employer was bound by agreement not to apply its no-nepotism policy against the plaintiff); Rulon-Miller v. Int'l Bus. Mach., 208 Cal. Rptr. 524 (Cal. App. 1984) (employer was bound by promise to respect privacy of its employees, as long as private behavior did not affect work or employer's business). In employment at will, an employer can generally revoke such a promise by reasonable advance notice. In employment for a fixed term, the employer can wait until the end of the term and then require that renewal of the employment will be conditioned on revocation of the promise.

A collective bargaining contract significantly affects an employer's right to control the work. From the start, unions have challenged an employer's right unilaterally to control the details of work. *See* M. Hill & A. Sinicropi, Management Rights: A Legal and Arbitral Analysis (1986). At the very least, collective bargaining changes the "economic realities" between an employer and its employees. Employees acting collectively can often respond more effectively to employer efforts to exercise control, and they are more likely to negotiate term contracts with clear limits on the employer's control over employees. In the case beginning the next subpart, *Kelley v. Johnson*, note that a union (acting though its president) initiated the legal challenge to the employer's "grooming" rules.

b. Appearance & Grooming: Introduction to Constitutional Rights & Discrimination Statutes

An employer might demand an employee's adherence to the employer's standards of grooming or appearance. From the employer's point of view, decisions about grooming and appearance at work are part of the "details" of the work. From an employee's point of view, grooming and appearance might be an important aspect of personal autonomy, the employer can discharge a non-conforming employee "at will" regardless of whether non-conformity is "good cause" for discharge—unless the contract or some law protects employee autonomy with respect to grooming and appearance.

KELLEY v. JOHNSON
425 U.S. 238 (1976)

Mr. Justice REHNQUIST delivered the opinion of the Court.

. . . [R]espondent's predecessor, individually and as president of the Suffolk County Patrolmen's Benevolent Association, brought this action under the Civil Rights Act of 1871, 42 U.S.C. § 1983, against petitioner's predecessor, the Commissioner of the Suffolk County Police Department. The Commissioner had promulgated Order No. 71-1, which established hair-grooming standards applicable to male members of the police force. The regulation was directed at the style and length of hair, sideburns, and mustaches; beards and goatees were prohibited, except for medical reasons; and wigs conforming to the regulation could be worn for cosmetic reasons. The regulation was attacked as violative of respondent patrolman's right of free expression under the First Amendment and his guarantees of due process and equal protection under the Fourteenth Amendment, in that it was "not based upon the generally accepted standard of grooming in the community" and placed "an undue restriction" upon his activities. . . . The District Court granted the relief prayed for [and] . . . was affirmed. . . .

Section 1 of the Fourteenth Amendment to the United States Constitution provides in pertinent part: "No State shall ... deprive any person of life, liberty, or property, without due process of law." This section affords not only a procedural guarantee against the deprivation of "liberty," but likewise protects substantive aspects of liberty against unconstitutional restrictions by the State. Board of Regents v. Roth, 408 U.S. 564(1972) ....

The "liberty" interest claimed by respondent . . . is distinguishable from the interests protected by the Court in Roe v. Wade, 410 U.S. 113 (1973); Eisenstadt v. Baird, 405 U.S. 438 (1972); Stanley v. Illinois, 405 U.S. 645 (1972); Griswold v. Connecticut, *supra*; and Meyer v. Nebraska, 262 U.S. 390 (1923). Each of those cases involved a substantial claim of infringement . . . with respect to certain basic matters of procreation, marriage, and family life. But whether the citizenry at large has some sort of "liberty" interest within the Fourteenth Amendment in matters of personal appearance is a question on which this Court's cases offer little, if any, guidance. We can . . . assume an affirmative answer for purposes of deciding this case, because we find that assumption insufficient to carry the day . . . .

Respondent has sought the protection of the Fourteenth Amendment, not as a member of the citizenry at large, but on the contrary as an employee of the police department of Suffolk County .... In Pickering v. Board of Education, 391 U.S. 563, 568 (1968), after noting that state employment may not be conditioned on the relinquishment of First Amendment rights, the Court stated that "(a)t the same time it cannot be gainsaid that the State has interests as an employer in regulating the speech of its employees that differ significantly from those it possesses in connection with regulation of the speech of the citizenry in general." ... [W]e have sustained comprehensive and substantial restrictions upon activities of both federal and state employees lying at the core of the First Amendment. CSC v. Letter Carriers, 413 U.S. 548 (1973); Broadrick v. Oklahoma, 413 U.S. 601 (1973). If such state regulations may survive challenges based on the explicit language of the First Amendment, there is surely even more room for restrictive regulations of state employees where the claim implicates only the more general . . . liberty interest protected by the Fourteenth Amendment.

The hair-length regulation here touches respondent as an employee of the county and, more particularly, as a policeman. Respondent's employer has, in accordance with its well-established duty to keep the peace, placed myriad demands upon the members of the police force, duties which have no counterpart with respect to the public at large. Respondent must wear a standard uniform, specific in each detail. When in uniform he must salute the flag. He may not take an active role in local political affairs by way of being a party delegate or contributing or soliciting political contributions. He may not smoke in public. All of these and other regulations of the Suffolk County Police Department infringe on respondent's freedom of choice in personal matters, and it was apparently the view of the Court of Appeals that the burden is on the State to prove a "genuine public need" for each and every one of these regulations ....

The promotion of safety of persons and property is unquestionably at the core of the State's police power, and virtually all state and local governments employ a uniform police force to aid in the accomplishment of that purpose. Choice of organization, dress, and equipment for law enforcement personnel is a decision entitled to the same sort of presumption of legislative validity as are state choices designed to promote other aims within the cognizance of the State's police power .... [T]he question is not, as the Court of Appeals conceived it to be, whether the State can "establish" a "genuine public need" for the specific regulation. It is whether respondent can demonstrate that there is no rational connection between the regulation and the promotion of safety ....

... Neither this Court, the Court of Appeals, nor the District Court is in a position to weigh the policy arguments in favor of and against a rule regulating hairstyles .... The constitutional issue ... is whether petitioner's determination that such regulations should be enacted is so irrational that it may be branded "arbitrary," and therefore a deprivation of respondent's "liberty" ... to choose his own hairstyle .... The overwhelming majority of state and local police of the present day are uniformed. This fact itself testifies to the recognition by those who direct those operations, and by the people of the States and localities who directly or indirectly choose such persons, that similarity in appearance of police officers is desirable. This choice may be based on a desire to make police officers readily recognizable to the members of the public, or a desire for the esprit de corps which such similarity is felt to inculcate within the police force itself .... Either one is a sufficiently rational justification for regulations so as to defeat respondent's claim based on the liberty guarantee of the Fourteenth Amendment.

NOTES AND QUESTIONS

1. If the officers in *Kelley* were employed "at will" by a private sector

employer, such as a private security service, the reasonableness of the challenged rule would be of little gravity as a legal matter. The Fifth and Fourteenth Amendments, the source of the right to "liberty" asserted in *Kelley*, do not apply to private sector employers; nor does the First Amendment, the source of some asserted employee autonomy rights (discussed below). The reasonableness of a private sector employer's infringement of an employee's liberty is important only to the extent a contract or statute protects the liberty in question.

2. Most people would probably not object to a police department's requirement that law enforcement officers wear uniforms while on duty. Such a rule clearly relates to the details of the work and serves a clear purpose, considering the extraordinary authority law enforcement officers wield and the civilian population's need to quickly identify law enforcement officers. Moreover, Fifth or Fourteenth Amendment "liberty" challenges against a public employer's dress and grooming codes nearly always fail when nothing more than a general "liberty" interest in appearance is at stake. Although Justice Rehnquist agreed in *Kelley* noted that a public employer's grooming code might be unlawful if truly "arbitrary," public employees have found it difficult to carry their burden of disproving any rational basis for a dress or grooming code. *See, e.g.,* Zalewska v. County of Sullivan, 316 F.3d 314 (2d Cir. 2003) (rule prohibiting employee from wearing skirt did not unlawfully violate liberty interest); Hottinger v. Pope County, 971 F.2d 127 (8th Cir. 1992) (ambulance department rule against facial hair did not unlawfully violate liberty interest). *But see* Pence v. Rosenquist, 573 F.2d 395 (7th Cir. 1978) (doubting whether school district had rational basis for prohibiting bus driver's mustache, but remanding for further proceedings).

3. Private sector employees have no Constitutional rights against employer dress or grooming codes, but might have claims under discrimination statutes that apply applicable to both the public and the private sector, especially if the employer's rules can be described as discriminatory on the basis of religion or sex. Title VII, for example, requires an employer to accommodate an employee's religious practices if accommodation will not cause more than a de minimis burden. *See* Chapter Three, Part C.6. If a religious practice includes particular dressing or grooming, Title VII might require an employer to accommodate the practice by granting an exception, as long as it would not impose more than a de minimis burden, as the Supreme Court held in E.E.O.C. v. Abercrombie & Fitch Stores, Inc., 135 S. Ct. 2028 (2015):

> An employer is surely entitled to have, for example, a no-headwear policy as an ordinary matter. But when an applicant requires an accommodation as an "aspec[t] of religious ... practice," it is no response that the subsequent "fail[ure] ... to hire" was due to an otherwise-neutral policy. Title VII requires otherwise-neutral policies to give way to the need for an accommodation.

Id. at 2034 (alterations in original).

4. Title VII's prohibition against discrimination on the basis of sex provides another potential basis for employee challenges to an employer's dress or grooming rules. Employer grooming codes often distinguish between permissible "male" dress and permissible "female" dress and grooming. However, as long as

an employer's grooming standards are not demeaning to one sex, do not place an unreasonably greater burden on one sex, and are based on conventional standards, courts normally defer to the employer. *Compare* Jespersen v. Harrah's Oper. Co., 444 F.3d 1104 (9th Cir. 2006) (casino did not violate Title VII by requiring female employees to wear makeup); Willingham v. Macon Tel. Pub. Co., 507 F.2d 1084 (5th Cir. 1975) (employer's rule limiting hair length of men but not women did not discriminate on the basis of sex); *with* Bradley v. Pizzaco of Neb., 939 F.2d 610 (8th Cir. 1991) (employer's no-beard policy caused illegal disparate impact against African-American men, who are more likely to suffer a painful skin disorder when forced to shave); EEOC v. Sage Realty Corp., 507 F. Supp. 599 (S.D.N.Y. 1981) (employer violated Title VII by requiring office lobby attendant to wear sexually provocative uniform). Moreover, an employer's sex-based dress and grooming standards might be some evidence that the employer unlawfully expects women to and men to follow stereotypical standards of masculine and feminine demeanor in violation of Title VII. *See* Price Waterhouse v. Hopkins, 490 U.S. 228 (1989).

c. Social, Family or Sexual Relations & Other Fundamental Liberties

Public employees are more likely to succeed in challenging work rules when they assert "fundamental" liberty interests or rights specifically enumerated in the Constitution. For example, a public employee challenging a grooming code is more likely to prevail if the code interferes with First Amendment religious rights. *See, e.g.,* Fraternal Order of Police Newark Lodge No. 12 v. City of Newark, 170 F.3d 359 (3d Cir. 1999) (police department refusal to exempt Sunni Muslims from no-beard rule violated First Amendment freedom of religion); Barrett v. Steubenville City Sch., 388 F.3d 967 (6th Cir. 2004) (school district violated teacher's "fundamental" liberty to direct his child's education by requiring him to withdraw child from private school and enroll in public school). In *Kelley*, Justice Rehnquist observed that the Court has been particularly protective of liberty interests involving "procreation, marriage, and family life." These liberty interests are bolstered by the combined support of the Fifth and Fourteenth Amendment and the privacy rights emanating from the First and Fourth Amendments. After *Kelley*, some courts have protected a public employee's liberty interests with respect to nonmarital or extramarital sexual conduct. *See, e.g.*, Wilson v. Taylor, 733 F.2d 1539, 1544 (11th Cir. 1984) (police officer's relationship with daughter of organized crime figure was protected); Briggs v. N. Muskegon Police Dep't 563 F. Supp. 585, 590 (W.D. Mich. 1983) (police department's discharge of officer for nonmarital cohabitation violated officer's right of privacy), *aff'd*, 746 F.2d 1475 (6th Cir. 1984); Shuman v. City of Philadelphia, 470 F. Supp. 449, 459 (E.D. Pa.1979) (regulations permitting inquiry into police officers' off-duty relationships violated right of privacy).

The protection of liberty interests as to intimate relationships, particularly between members of the same sex, has expanded to some degree by virtue of the Supreme Court's decision in Lawrence v. Texas, 539 U.S. 558, 571 (2003). *Lawrence* struck down a Texas law prohibiting consensual sexual conduct of two persons of the same sex. The Court held that the prosecution and conviction of same-sex partners in *Lawrence* impermissibly intruded on their liberty interests.

"The petitioners are entitled to respect for their private lives. The State cannot demean their existence or control their destiny by making their private sexual conduct a crime." 539 U.S. at 578. *See also* Obergefell v. Hodges, ___ U.S. ___, 135 S. Ct. 2584 (2015) (invalidating state laws against same sex marriage).

A public employee's right to marital and non-marital relationships is not absolute. Employers often successfully defend anti-nepotism rules restricting relationships within the workforce. A typical anti-nepotism rule prohibits employees from marrying or dating subordinates or other employees in the same department. *See, e.g.*, Vaughn v. Lawrenceburg Power Sys. 269 F.3d 703 (6th Cir. 2001). Would a rule against dating *any* employee of the same employer go too far? Dangers of jealousy, favoritism, employee conflict, public scandal, and sexual harassment are likely reasons for nepotism and no-fraternization rules. Could these arguments ever justify restricting relationships with persons *outside* the workforce? *See, e.g.*, Beecham v. Henderson County, 422 F.3d 372 (6th Cir. 2005) (county did not violate deputy clerk's First Amendment right to intimate association by discharging her for relationship with attorney married to another clerk working on the same floor); Seegmiller v. LaVerkin City, 528 F.3d 762 (10th Cir. 2008) (police officer separated from husband was lawfully reprimanded for off-duty sexual relationship with member of another department).

Public employers have also successfully defended policies restricting or prohibiting intimate relationships between employees and the persons they serve, manage, or investigate. Sylvester v. Fogley, 465 F.3d 851 (8th Cir. 2006) (state has compelling interest in preventing sexual relationships between investigating officers and victims or witnesses); Poirier v. Massachusetts Dep't of Correction, 532 F. Supp. 2d 275 (D. Mass. 2008) (state could lawfully prohibit prison guards from having intimate relationships with inmates).

As with dress and grooming codes, private sector employees who wish to challenge restrictions or discrimination on the basis of personal relations, marriage, and family life must look beyond the Constitution. Again, Title VII is one possible basis for protection if the employer's restriction or discrimination can be described as a form of race, sex or religious discrimination. *See, e.g.,* Holcomb v. Iona Coll., 521 F.3d 130 (2d Cir. 2008) (discrimination based on the basis of interracial marriage violates Title VII); Deffenbaugh-Williams v. Wal-Mart Stores, Inc., 156 F.3d 581 (5th Cir. 1998) (discrimination on the basis of interracial relationships violates Title VII); Faraca v. Clements, 506 F.2d 956 (5th Cir. 1975) (discrimination on the basis of interracial marriage violates Civil Rights Act of 1866). *See generally* Equal Employment Opportunity Commission, *Facts about Discrimination in Federal Government Employment Based on Marital Status, Political Affiliation, Status as a Parent, Sexual Orientation, and Gender Identity*, https://www.eeoc.gov/federal/otherprotections.cfm (last visited Sept. 9, 2017).

d. Free Speech and Expression

Among the fundamental liberties protected by the Constitution in the case of public employees is freedom of speech. But a public employee's exercise of free speech and expression is one of the most common sources of conflict between public employees and their employers. From an employee's point of view, the right or need to speak freely or express one's self might seem compelling even at work. From the employer's point of view, however, unrestrained speech and expression by employees can wreak havoc. The following case and the notes that follow set forth the rules for balancing the interests of public employers and their employees in free speech disputes under the First Amendment.

CITY OF SAN DIEGO v. ROE

543 U.S. 77 (2004)

PER CURIAM.

. . . Respondent John Roe, a San Diego police officer, made a video showing himself stripping off a police uniform and masturbating. He sold the video on the adults-only section of eBay, the popular online auction site. His username was "Code3stud@aol.com," a wordplay on a high priority police radio call. The uniform apparently was not the specific uniform worn by the San Diego police, but it was clearly identifiable as a police uniform. Roe also sold custom videos, as well as police equipment, including official uniforms of the San Diego Police Department (SDPD), and various other items such as men's underwear. Roe's eBay user profile identified him as employed in the field of law enforcement.

Roe's supervisor, a police sergeant, discovered Roe's activities when, while on eBay, he came across an official SDPD police uniform for sale offered by an individual with the username "Code3stud@aol.com." He searched for other items Code3stud offered and discovered listings for Roe's videos depicting the objectionable material. Recognizing Roe's picture, the sergeant printed images of certain of Roe's offerings and shared them with others in Roe's chain of command, including a police captain. The captain notified the SDPD's internal affairs department, which began an investigation. In response to a request by an undercover officer, Roe produced a custom video. It showed Roe, again in police uniform, issuing a traffic citation but revoking it after undoing the uniform and masturbating.

The investigation revealed that Roe's conduct violated specific SDPD policies, including conduct unbecoming of an officer, outside employment, and immoral conduct. When confronted, Roe admitted to selling the videos and police paraphernalia. The SDPD ordered Roe to "cease displaying, manufacturing, distributing or selling any sexually explicit materials or engaging in any similar behaviors, via the internet, U.S. Mail, commercial vendors or distributors, or any other medium available to the public." Although Roe removed some of the items he had offered for sale, he did not change his seller's profile, which described the first two videos he had produced and listed their prices as well as the prices for custom videos. After discovering Roe's failure to follow its orders, the SDPD — citing Roe for the added violation of disobedience of lawful orders — began termination proceedings. The proceedings resulted in Roe's dismissal from the police force.

Roe brought suit in the District Court pursuant to . . . 42 U.S.C. § 1983, alleging that the employment termination violated his First Amendment right to free speech. In granting the City's motion to dismiss, the District Court decided that Roe had not demonstrated that selling official police uniforms and producing, marketing, and selling sexually explicit videos for profit qualified as expression relating to a matter of "public concern" under . . . Connick v. Myers, 461 U.S. 138 (1983).

In reversing, the Court of Appeals held Roe's conduct fell within the protected category of citizen commentary on matters of public concern. Central to the Court of Appeals' conclusion was that Roe's expression was not an internal workplace grievance, took place while he was off duty and away from his employer's premises, and was unrelated to his employment.

A government employee does not relinquish all First Amendment rights otherwise enjoyed by citizens just by reason of his or her employment. *See, e.g.,* Keyishian v. Board of Regents of Univ. of State of N. Y., 385 U.S. 589, 605-606 (1967). On the other hand, a governmental employer may impose certain restraints on the speech of its employees, restraints that would be unconstitutional if applied to the general public. The Court has recognized the right of employees to speak on matters of public concern, typically matters concerning government policies that are of interest to the public at large, a subject on which public employees are uniquely qualified to comment. *See* Connick, supra; Pickering v. Board of Ed. of Township High School Dist. 205, Will Cty., 391 U.S. 563 (1968). Outside of this category, the Court has held that when government employees speak or write on their own time on topics unrelated to their employment, the speech can have First Amendment protection, absent some governmental justification "far stronger than mere speculation" in regulating it. United States v. Treasury Employees, 513 U.S. 454, 465, 475 (1995) (NTEU). We have little difficulty in concluding that the City was not barred from terminating Roe under either line of cases.

In concluding that Roe's activities qualified as a matter of public concern, the Court of Appeals relied heavily on the Court's decision in *NTEU*. . . . In *NTEU* it was established that the speech was unrelated to the employment and had no effect on the mission and purpose of the employer. The question was whether the Federal Government could impose certain monetary limitations on outside earnings from speaking or writing on a class of federal employees. The Court held that, within the particular classification of employment, the Government had shown no justification for the outside salary limitations. The First Amendment right of the employees sufficed to invalidate the restrictions on the outside earnings for such activities. The Court noted that throughout history public employees who undertook to write or to speak in their spare time had made substantial contributions to literature and art, 513 U.S., at 465, and observed that none of the speech at issue "even arguably [had] any adverse impact" on the employer, *ibid.*...

Although Roe's activities took place outside the workplace and purported to be about subjects not related to his employment, the SDPD demonstrated legitimate and substantial interests of its own that were compromised by his speech. Far from confining his activities to speech unrelated to his employment, Roe took deliberate steps to link his videos and other wares to his police work, all in a way injurious to his employer. The use of the uniform, the law enforcement reference in the Web site, the listing of the speaker as "in the field of law enforcement," and the debased parody of an officer performing indecent acts while in the course of official duties brought the mission of the employer and the professionalism of its officers into serious disrepute. 356 F.3d, at 1111 (internal quotation marks omitted) . . . .

To reconcile the employee's right to engage in speech and the government employer's right to protect its own legitimate interests in performing its mission, the *Pickering* Court adopted a balancing test. It requires a court evaluating restraints on a public employee's speech to balance "the interests of the [employee], as a citizen, in commenting upon matters of public concern and the interest of the State, as an employer, in promoting the efficiency of the public services it performs through its employees." 391 U.S., at 568.

Underlying the decision in *Pickering* is the recognition that public employees are often the members of the community who are likely to have informed opinions as to the operations of their public employers, operations which are of substantial concern to the public. Were they not able to speak on these matters, the community would be deprived of informed opinions on important public issues. The interest at stake is as much the public's interest in receiving informed opinion as it is the employee's own right to disseminate it.

Pickering did not hold that any and all statements by a public employee are entitled to balancing. To require *Pickering* balancing in every case where speech by a public employee is at issue, no matter the content … , could compromise the proper functioning of government offices. This concern prompted the Court in *Connick* to explain a threshold inquiry (implicit in *Pickering* itself) that in order to merit *Pickering* balancing, a public employee's speech must touch on a matter of "public concern." 461 U.S., at 143 (internal quotation marks omitted).

In *Connick*, an assistant district attorney, unhappy with her supervisor's decision to transfer her to another division, circulated an intraoffice questionnaire. The document solicited her co-workers' views on . . . office transfer policy, office morale, the need for grievance committees, the level of confidence in supervisors, and whether employees felt pressured to work in political campaigns. . . . *[I]d.*, at 141.

Finding that — with the exception of the final question — the questionnaire touched not on matters of public concern but on internal workplace grievances, the Court held no *Pickering* balancing was required. . . . To conclude otherwise would ignore the "common-sense realization that government offices could not function if every employment decision became a constitutional matter." *Id.*, at 143. *Connick* held that a public employee's speech is entitled to *Pickering* balancing only when the employee speaks "as a citizen upon matters of public concern" rather than "as an employee upon matters only of personal interest." 461 U.S., at 147.

Although the boundaries of the public concern test are not well defined, *Connick* provides some guidance. It directs courts to examine the "content, form, and context of a given statement, as revealed by the whole record" in assessing whether an employee's speech addresses a matter of public concern. *Id.*, at 146-147. In addition, it notes that the standard for determining whether expression is of public concern is the same standard used to determine whether a common-law action for invasion of privacy is present. *Id.*, at 143, n.5. That standard is established by our decisions in Cox Broadcasting Corp. v. Cohn, 420 U.S. 469 (1975), and Time, Inc. v. Hill, 385 U.S. 374, 387-388 (1967). These cases make clear that public concern is something that is a subject of legitimate news interest;

that is, a subject of general interest and of value and concern to the public at the time of publication. The Court has also recognized that certain private remarks, such as negative comments about the President of the United States, touch on matters of public concern and should thus be subject to *Pickering* balancing. *See* Rankin v. McPherson, 483 U.S. 378 (1987).

Applying these principles to the instant case, there is no difficulty in concluding that Roe's expression does not qualify as a matter of public concern under any view of the public concern test. He fails the threshold test and *Pickering* balancing does not come into play.

Connick is controlling precedent, but to show why this is not a close case it is instructive to note that even under the view expressed by the dissent in *Connick* from four Members of the Court, the speech here would not come within the definition of a matter of public concern. The dissent in *Connick* would have held that the entirety of the questionnaire circulated by the employee "discussed subjects that could reasonably be expected to be of interest to persons seeking to develop informed opinions about the manner in which . . . an elected official charged with managing a vital governmental agency, discharges his responsibilities." 461 U.S., at 163 (opinion of Brennan, J.). No similar purpose could be attributed to the employee's speech in the present case. Roe's activities did nothing to inform the public about any aspect of the SDPD's functioning or operation. Nor were Roe's activities anything like the private remarks at issue in *Rankin*, where one co-worker commented to another co-worker on an item of political news. Roe's expression was widely broadcast, linked to his official status as a police officer, and designed to exploit his employer's image.

The speech in question was detrimental to the mission and functions of the employer. There is no basis for finding that it was of concern to the community as the Court's cases have understood that term in the context of restrictions by governmental entities on the speech of their employees.

NOTES AND QUESTIONS

1. Courts frequently question the merit or importance of general liberty interests or require only a "rational" justification for liberties that are not "fundamental," but courts regularly take the importance of free speech for granted and demand a strong justification for any restrictions. In Rankin v. McPherson, 483 U.S. 378 (1987), a clerical employee reacted to the attempted assassination of President Reagan by commenting out loud, "If they go for him again, I hope they get him." The Court held that the defendant county constable unlawfully violated the employee's First Amendment rights by discharging her for this comment. The employee's statement, even if "inappropriate," involved a matter of public concern because, among other things, it occurred "in the course of a conversation addressing the policies of the President's administration," and was not an unlawful threat to kill the President. 483 U.S. at 386-387,. Moreover, the constable failed to show that the employee's statement had interfered in any way with her clerical work, with office harmony, or with the employer's services. 483 U.S. at 390-392. *Compare* Waters v. Churchill, 511 U.S. 661 (1994) (public hospital did not violate First Amendment if it discharged nurse for discouraging other employees from

working and told other employees she would refuse to "wipe the slate clean" in her ongoing conflict with her supervisor).

2. Social media present frequent clashes between public employee speech and public employer need for efficient and effective management of work. In Liverman v. City of Petersburg, 844 F.3d 400 (4th Cir. 2016), a police department adopted a social networking policy prohibiting comments "that would tend to discredit or reflect unfavorably upon" the department, or any other city department or city employees. The department qualified its policy as follows: "Officers may comment on issues of general or public concern (as opposed to personal grievances) so long as the comments do not disrupt the workforce, interfere with important working relationships or efficient work flow, or undermine public confidence in the officer. The instances must be judged on a case-by-case basis." Nevertheless, the department disciplined two officers for posting opinions on Facebook that police officers should be promoted based on experience. The court held that the department's social media policy was unconstitutionally overbroad. The court also held that the department's actions against the officers violated the First Amendment because the department failed to show the Facebook posts caused any *actual* disruption of the department's mission.

On the other hand, in Grutzmacher v. Howard County, 851 F.3d 332 (4th Cir. 2017), the same court upheld a city's discharge of a fire department battalion chief because of his posts that included comments about gun control and the department's social media policy. One of the chief's "gun control" posts was as follows: "lets all kill someone with a liberal ... then maybe we can get them outlawed too! Think of the satisfaction of beating a liberal to death with another liberal ... its almost poetic." Another employee responded, "pick a black [liberal], those are more scary." The chief "liked" that response. Although the chief's posts related to issues of public concern (gun control), the city presented evidence that his posts led to actual dissension in the department, caused minority firefighters to distrust him, conflicted with his responsibility to uphold department policies, and undermined "community trust" in the department by advocating violence.

Another set of questions arises from an employer's methods for *investigation* of possible violations of a social media or other employee speech policy. If an employee uses privacy controls to limit access to a Facebook page, can the employer demand access, or use surreptitious means to access the page? An exploration of such issues begins in Section B of this Chapter.

3. Protection for free speech is limited in an additional way when the speech is part of a public employee's work or service. In Garcetti v. Ceballos, 547 U.S. 410 (2006), the Supreme Court greatly diminished protection for speech "pursuant to" a public employee's job duties. In *Garcetti*, the Los Angeles County District Attorney's Office discharged Ceballos after he reported his suspicions and objections about a police officer's affidavit in support of a search warrant. Although Cebellos's speech might easily have satisfied the "public concern" test, the Court dismissed his claim under a new rule. Where a public employee's speech is *pursuant to job duty*, it is unprotected, based on the employer's interest in managing the employee's work. *Garcetti* is reproduced in Chapter 8.B.4.d *infra*, which also explores the availability of other remedies for employees who suffer retaliation for "blowing the whistle."

4. A public employer's requirement that employees support or oppose a particular party or a candidate for public office is a clear violation of the First Amendment with respect to most employees, but not all. An elected official can require loyalty among employees on whom that official relies to make policy. The test for whether a public official, acting as the employer, can remove an employee for failing to support that official, or for providing support for an opponent, depends on whether the employer official can show that party affiliation is an appropriate and reasonable requirement for effective performance of the public office in question. Thompson v. Shock, 852 F.3d 786 (8th Cir. 2017).

5. What if a public employee did *not* actually engage in protected speech, but the employer retaliates based on an *incorrect* belief that the employee did so? Despite the employer's argument that no actual "protected activity" occurred, the Supreme Court held that such an employee does have a First Amendment claim in *Heffernan v. City of Paterson*, 136 S. Ct. 1412 (2016). In *Heffernan*, a police officer alleged that he was demoted based on his supervisors' mistaken perception that he supported a disfavored political candidate. The Court stated:

> [T]o prevent the employee from engaging in political activity that the First Amendment protects . . . [is] unlawful action . . . even if, as here, the employer makes a factual mistake. . . . [The] reason for demoting Heffernan is what counts. . . . [The] harm . . . consists in large part of discouraging . . . the employee . . . and his or her colleagues[] from engaging in protected activities . . . . [D]ischarge or demotion based upon an employer's belief that the employee has engaged in protected activity can cause the same . . . harm whether that belief does or does not rest upon a factual mistake.

Id. at 1418-1419.

6. In at least one way, public sector employees are *less* protected than private sector employees as to free speech, support for a cause, or opposition to a cause. Under the Hatch Act, public employees are *prohibited* from some types of partisan political activities. 5 U.S.C. §§ 1501-1508, 7321-7326. For example, a federal, state or local government employee or official must not use his official authority or influence to interfere with or affect the result of an election, or to coerce or advise another official or employee to give anything of value for a political purpose. *Id.* §§ 1502, 7323. Many non-elective state and local government employees are prohibited from running for office in a "partisan" election. *Id.* §§ 1502, 1503. The federal government enforces the Hatch Act against state and local government officials and employees by withholding government funds in case of a violation, but many states have their own local versions of the Hatch Act. *See* United States Civil Serv. Comm'n v. Nat'l Ass'n of Letter Carriers, 413 U.S. 548 (1973) (describing what partisan political activities might be prohibited without violating public employees' First Amendment rights).

e. Statutory Protection for "Off-Duty" Conduct

Constitutional protection for public employee liberty and speech is far from absolute, and private sector employees lack any constitutional protection at all. Discrimination law applies to both public and private sectors but focuses on specific problems that can be characterized as illegal discrimination, sex discrimination. These laws fail to address the more general question whether employees should be beyond employer control with respect to matters truly disconnected from work, especially off duty conduct away from the workplace.

Congress has adopted the broad approach with respect to federal employees. *See* 5 U.S.C. § 2302, providing that a federal agency employer may not "discriminate . . . on the basis of conduct which does not adversely affect the performance of the employee or applicant or the performance of others." Even before this law, federal employees were generally protected by civil service rules that protected them from arbitrary discipline or discharge. Should similar "off-duty" protection apply to private sector employees subject to employment at will?

Several states have statutes broadly prohibiting employer discrimination based on off-duty employee conduct. See, e.g., Calif. Labor Code §§ 96(k), 98.6 (barring "demotion, suspension, or discharge from employment for lawful conduct occurring during nonworking hours away from the employer's premises"); Colo. Rev. Stat. § 24-34-402.5 (barring discharge based on "any lawful activity off the premises of the employer during nonworking hours"); N.Y. Lab. L. § 201-d (somewhat more narrowly protecting, as long as outside work hours, off of the employer's premises and without use of the employer's . . . property," the following: "political activities[,] . . . legal use of consumable products prior to the beginning [of] or after . . . work hours, and legal recreational activities")

These statutes typically prohibit discrimination based on off-duty conduct, or broad categories of off-duty conduct, subject to an employer's proof of justification. *See, e.g.,* Col. Rev. Stat. 24-34-402.5 (employer may prove a restriction bases on a "bona fide occupational requirement" for a particular job or "is necessary to avoid a conflict of interest with any responsibilities to the employer or the appearance of such a conflict"); N.Y. Lab. L. § 201-d (similar). Thus, off-duty conduct is presumed to be none of the employer's business, subject to proof that the conduct is legitimately important to the employer's business.

Other states have similar laws that limit their protections of private sector employee to *political* activities or similar matters, such as compulsion to vote or to donate in a particular way. *E.g.*, S.C. Code § 16-17-560 ("It is unlawful for a person to assault or intimidate a citizen, discharge a citizen from employment or occupation, or eject a citizen from a rented house, land, or other property because of political opinions or the exercise of political rights and privileges guaranteed to every citizen by the Constitution and laws of the United States or . . . of this State."); Minn. Stat. § 181.937 ("No employer shall engage in any reprisal against an employee for declining to participate in contributions or donations to charities or community organizations . . . ."); Tex. Election Code § 253.102(a) ("A corporation or labor organization . . . commits an offense if it uses or threatens to use physical force, job discrimination, or financial reprisal to obtain money or any other thing of value to be used to influence the result of an election or to assist an officeholder."); Wash. Rev. Code § 42.17A.495(2) ("No employer or labor organization may discriminate against an officer or employee in the terms or conditions of employment for (a) the failure to contribute to, (b) the failure in any way to support or oppose, or (c) in any way supporting or opposing a candidate, ballot proposition, political party, or political committee.").

Litigation under such statutes typically proceeds as in any other discrimination or retaliation case. The plaintiff bears the burden of proving illegal motive, i.e., retaliation for engaging in protected off-duty activity. Proof of illegal motive might be easy if the employer acted upon an express policy, such as a rule against using a competitor's product, but it might depend on circumstantial evidence, such as the lack of a credible non-retaliatory reason. Protected off-duty conduct cases also tend to present other difficult issues: How broad a range of conduct is protected? Was the employee's conduct truly within that protected range? And was the employer's action justified by the nature of its business?

COATS v. DISH NETWORK, LLC

350 P.3d 849 (Col. 2015)

JUSTICE EID delivered the Opinion of the Court.

This case requires us to determine whether the use of medical marijuana in compliance with Colorado's Medical Marijuana Amendment, Colo. Const. art. XVIII, § 14, but in violation of federal law, is a "lawful activity" under section 24–34–402.5, C.R.S. (2014), Colorado's "lawful activities statute." This statute generally makes it an unfair and discriminatory labor practice to discharge an employee based on the employee's "lawful" outside-of-work activities. § 24–34–402.5(1).

Here, petitioner Brandon Coats claims respondent Dish Network, LLC ("Dish") violated section 24–34–402.5 by discharging him due to his state-licensed use of medical marijuana at home during nonworking hours. He argues that the Medical Marijuana Amendment makes such use "lawful" for purposes of section 24–34–402.5, notwithstanding any federal laws prohibiting medical marijuana . . . .

I.

Brandon Coats is a quadriplegic and has been confined to a wheelchair since he was a teenager. In 2009, he registered for and obtained a state-issued license to use medical marijuana to treat painful muscle spasms caused by his quadriplegia. Coats consumes medical marijuana at home, after work, and in accordance with his license and Colorado state law.

Between 2007 and 2010, Coats worked for respondent Dish as a telephone customer service representative. In May 2010, Coats tested positive for tetrahydrocannabinol ("THC"), a component of medical marijuana, during a random drug test. Coats informed Dish that he was a registered medical marijuana patient and planned to continue using medical marijuana. On June 7, 2010, Dish fired Coats for violating the company's drug policy.

Coats then filed a wrongful termination claim against Dish under section 24–34–402.5 . . . . Coats contended that Dish violated the statute by terminating him based on his outside-of-work medical marijuana use, which he argued was "lawful" under the Medical Marijuana Amendment and its implementing legislation. . . .

The trial court dismissed Coats's claim. It rejected Coats's argument that the Medical Marijuana Amendment made his use a "lawful activity" for purposes of section 24-34-402.5. Instead the court found that the Amendment provided registered patients an affirmative defense to state criminal prosecution without making their use of medical marijuana a "lawful activity" within the meaning of section 24-34-402.5. As such, the trial court concluded that the statute afforded no protection to Coats and dismissed the claim without examining the federal law issue.

In a split decision, the court of appeals affirmed based on the prohibition of marijuana use under the federal Controlled Substances Act, 21 U.S.C. § 844(a) (2012) (the "CSA"). Looking to the plain language of section 24–34–402.5, the majority found that the term "lawful" means "that which is 'permitted by law.' Applying that plain meaning, the majority reasoned that to be "lawful" for purposes of section 24–34–402.5, activities that are governed by both state and federal law must "be permitted by, and not contrary to, both state and federal law." Given that the federal CSA prohibits all marijuana use, the majority concluded that Coats's conduct was not "lawful activity" protected by the statute....

In dissent, Judge Webb argued that the term "lawful" must be interpreted according to state, rather than federal, law. He argued that the majority's interpretation failed to effectuate the purpose of the statute by improperly narrowing the scope of the statute's protection. Finding that the Medical Marijuana Amendment made state-licensed medical marijuana use "at least lawful," Judge Webb concluded that Coats's use should be protected by the statute.

II.

... The "lawful activities statute" provides that "[i]t shall be a discriminatory or unfair employment practice for an employer to terminate the employment of any employee due to that employee's engaging in any lawful activity off the premises of the employer during nonworking hours" unless certain exceptions apply. By its terms the statute protects only "lawful" activities. However, the statute does not define the term "lawful." Coats contends that the term should be read as limited to activities lawful under state law. We disagree.

In construing undefined statutory terms, we look to the language of the statute itself "with a view toward giving the statutory language its commonly accepted and understood meaning." People v. Schuett, 833 P.2d 44, 47 (Colo. 1992). We have construed the term "lawful" once before and found that its "generally understood meaning" is "in accordance with the law or legitimate." See id. Similarly, courts in other states have construed "lawful" to mean "authorized by law and not contrary to, nor forbidden by law." Hougum v. Valley Memorial Homes, 574 N.W.2d 812, 821 (N.D. 1998). We therefore agree with the court of appeals that the commonly accepted meaning of the term "lawful" is "that which is 'permitted by law' or, conversely, that which is "not contrary to, or forbidden by law."

We still must determine, however, whether medical marijuana use that is licensed by the State of Colorado but prohibited under federal law is "lawful" for purposes of section 24–34–402.5. Coats contends that the General Assembly intended the term "lawful" here to mean "lawful under Colorado state law," which, he asserts, recognizes medical marijuana use as "lawful." We do not read the term "lawful" to be so restrictive. Nothing in the language of the statute limits the term "lawful" to state law. Instead, the term is used in its general, unrestricted sense, indicating that a "lawful" activity is that which complies with applicable "law," including state and federal law....

[T]he federal Controlled Substances Act prohibits medical marijuana use. The CSA lists marijuana as a Schedule I substance, meaning federal law designates it as having no medical accepted use, a high risk of abuse, and a lack of accepted safety for use under medical supervision. *Id.* at § 812(b)(1)(A)-(C). This makes the use, possession, or manufacture of marijuana a federal criminal offense, except where used for federally-approved research projects. There is no exception for marijuana use for medicinal purposes, or for marijuana use conducted in accordance with state law. 21 U.S.C. § 844(a); see also Gonzales, 545 U.S. at 29 (finding that "[t]he Supremacy Clause unambiguously provides that if there is any conflict between federal and state law, federal law shall prevail," including in the area of marijuana regulation). Coats's use of medical marijuana was unlawful under federal law and thus not protected by section 24–34–402.5.

Echoing Judge Webb's dissent, Coats argues that because the General Assembly intended section 24–34–402.5 to broadly protect employees from discharge for outside-of-work activities, we must construe the term "lawful" to mean "lawful under Colorado law." In this case, however, we find nothing to indicate that the General Assembly intended to extend section 24–34–402.5's protection for "lawful" activities to activities that are unlawful under federal law. In sum, because Coats's marijuana use was unlawful under federal law, it does not fall within section 24–34–402.5's protection for "lawful" activities.

Having decided this case on the basis of the prohibition under federal law, we decline to address the issue of whether Colorado's Medical Marijuana Amendment deems medical marijuana use "lawful" by conferring a right to such use. [The court then affirmed the lower court's dismissal of Coats' claim.]

NOTES AND QUESTIONS

1. The denial of protection for "unlawful" activity is only one of the potential limits of off-duty conduct laws. Another possible limit is a denial of protection for off-duty conduct that might unreasonably harm the employer. Suppose an off-duty employee embarrasses his employer by calling the media or the police to report work-related matters. *Compare* Marsh v. Delta Air Lines, Inc., 952 F. Supp. 1458 (D. Colo. 1997) (employee's publication of letter critical of employer in a major newspaper was not protected by Colorado's off-duty conduct statute; statute does not allow employee to "strike indiscriminate public blows against the business reputation of their employer") *with Watson v. Pub. Serv. Co.*, 207 P.3d 860, 865 (Colo. App. 2008) (off-duty conduct statute protects even conduct that is related to work, and therefore statute may protect "whistleblowing activity" in which employee lawfully reports illegal workplace activity). Whether or not "whistleblowing" is protected by an off-duty statute, whistleblowing is frequently protected by other statutes or judicial doctrines. *See* Chapter 8.B.4.d.

2. Recall that an employer—particularly in the private sector—may discipline an employee under some circumstances for romantic relationships with a co- employee. If two employees are "strictly business" at the workplace but "romantic" off-duty, is their conduct protected by an off-duty conduct statute? *See* Hudson v. Goldman Sachs & Co., 283 A.D.2d 246 (N.Y. App. Div., 1st Dep't,

2001) (no, under New York statute).

3. Given the uncertainty whether discrimination based on sexual orientation is prohibited by employment discrimination statutes, off-duty conduct statutes might be an important alternative protection against such discrimination. In *Robert C. Ozer, P.C. v. Borquez*, 940 P.2d 371, 376 (Colo. 1997), the court held that an employee might prove a violation of Colorado's off duty statute if the employer discriminated because of his *actions off duty*. However, the court reversed a verdict for the employee because the trial judge had instructed the jury that it could find for the plaintiff simply because of his sexual orientation.

4. Does a broad statute protecting all lawful off-duty activities amount to a ban on employer policies against "moonlighting," *i.e.*, policies that employees cannot work other jobs while off-duty? The answer depends on the details of the law (*i.e.*, exactly what activities does the statute protect, and what defenses does the statute grant to employers?) and facts (*i.e.*, has moonlighting actually affected the employee's performance or ability to serve the employer, or is it constitute disloyal service for a competitor?). *See, e.g.*, Michael G. Petrie, *Monitoring and Controlling Off-Duty Behavior*, 14 CONN. EMP. L. LETTER 1 (2006).

5. States have addressed a variety of other specific problems by protecting specific types of employee conduct. Many states have "company store" laws prohibiting an employer from requiring employees to buy goods from a particular store, especially the employer's own store. *See, e.g.,* Tex. Lab. Code § 54.041. Others limit employer restrictions on the use of certain products. *See, e.g.,* Conn. Gen. Stat. Ann. § 31-40s (tobacco); D.C. Code § 7-1703.03 (tobacco); Mo. Stat. § 290.145 (alcohol); Mont. Code Ann. § 39-2-313 (any lawful food or beverage). During the last decade, some states have adopted laws to protect an employee's right to store a firearm in a car parked on an employer's property. *See, e.g.*, Tex. Lab. Code § 52.061; Plona v. UPS, 2007 WL 509747 (N. D. Ohio 207) (right to store firearm in car in parking lot protected by judicially recognized public policy).

6. An important limitation of most off-duty conduct statutes and other laws protecting employee autonomy is that they apply to "employees." Non-employee workers such as independent contractors remain unprotected. In contrast, constitutional liberty or free speech rights do not typically hinge on an individual's employee status. *See* Oscar Renda Contracting, Inc. v. City of Lubbock, 463 F.3d 378 (5th Cir. 2006) (contractor may have First Amendment claim based on city's alleged retaliatory denial of his bid because of his protected speech).

f. "Concerted" Employee Activity to Address Terms and Conditions of Employment

The laws discussed above accept as a basic premise that an employer has the right and power to manage the business. An employee's Constitutional liberty and free speech or statutory rights are strongest when the employee's conduct does not interfere with the employer's management and operation of the business.

What lawful employee activity could be any more disruptive of an employer's business than a strike, picketing to discourage other workers, or a publicity campaign to discourage the public from doing business with the employer? These tactics are common tools of unions in their negotiations with employers over terms and conditions of employment. Sometimes, it makes little difference whether the employer has a legal right to discipline or discharge employees engaged in such conduct because the union has enough bargaining power to protect the employees from retaliation. Usually, especially in the present era, the union is not so powerful. Nevertheless, employees, especially in the private sector, are legally protected to some extent by Sections 7 and 8(a)(1) of the National Labor Relations Act.

Section 7 states that employees have the right to "bargain collectively ... and to engage in other concerted activities for the purpose of ... mutual aid or protection." 29 U.S.C. § 157. Section 8(a)(1) makes it an "unfair labor practice" for an employer to interfere with this right or discriminate against employees exercising this right. *Id.* § 158(a). *See also* Chapter 4.B.2. The premise of Section 7 is that employees acting collectively have the right to bargain, sometimes by very adversarial means, over the terms and conditions of employment. It is easy to see that Sections 7 and 8(a)(1) apply when employees are formally organized into a union. What if non-union employees act spontaneously or informally to challenge an employer's management with respect to employment issues?

The following decision is by the National Labor Relations Board, the agency charged with enforcement of the National Labor Relations Act. NLRB proceedings are initiated by a charge, filed with the NLRB by a union, employer or individual employee within 6 months of the alleged "unfair labor practice."

MASTEC ADVANCED TECHNOLOGIES

357 NLRB 103 (2011), *enforced,* 837 F.3d 25 (D.C. Cir. 2016)

BY CHAIRMAN LIEBMAN AND MEMBERS BECKER AND HAYES

This case presents the question of whether 26 former service technicians employed by Respondent Advanced Technologies, a division of MasTec, Inc. (MasTec), lost the protection of the Act by appearing on a television news broadcast in which statements were made about their employer and Respondent DirecTV, Inc., for which MasTec provides installation services. The technicians' participation in the newscast grew out of their opposition to a new compensation formula that MasTec implemented in response to DirecTV's dissatisfaction with MasTec's performance.

Applying the principles set forth by [NLRB v. Elec. Workers Loc. 1229 (Jefferson Standard), 346 U.S. 464 (1953)], regarding the extent to which employees' disparaging statements to third parties about their employer's product or service enjoy the Act's protection, the judge concluded that the technicians' statements were unprotected and thus that neither MasTec, by terminating its employees, nor DirecTV, by causing their termination, violated Section 8(a)(1).

. . . [T]he General Counsel challenges the judge's finding that the employees' statements were unprotected. . . . [W]e find merit in the General Counsel's position.

[Editor: The employees in this case were satellite TV installation technicians whose compensation was affected by a new employer rule reducing compensation for an employee who failed to persuade a customer to accept a telephone line hookup, which involved additional service and products non-essential to the satellite connection. After several meetings at which the employees expressed their displeasure with the rule to their employer, the employees took their problem to a local TV station. The resulting story broadcast on the local TV news was about both the pa dispute and certain sales techniques to which the pay dispute was connected. For example, one part of an interview aired on the TV news was as follows: Interviewer: "So you've basically been told to lie to customers [about the need for the phone hookup]?" Technician: "Yeah."

When the employer saw the story on the TV news, he fired several of the employees. The employees filed charges with the NLRB alleging that the employer had interfered with their right to engage in concerted activity under Section 7. An administrative law judge held that the employee's conduct was not protected. The NLRB's decision on appeal is set forth below.]

Section 7 of the Act provides, in part, that "[e]mployees shall have the right … to engage in … concerted activities for the purpose of … mutual aid or protection." However, that right is not without limitation. In *Jefferson Standard*, the Court upheld the employer's discharge of employees who publicly criticized both the quality of the employer's product and its business practices without the employees relating their complaints to any labor controversy. The Court found that the employees' conduct amounted to disloyal disparagement of their employer and was outside the Act's protection.

In cases decided since *Jefferson Standard*, "the Board has held that employee communications to third parties in an effort to obtain their support are protected where the communication indicated it is related to an ongoing dispute between the employees and the employers and the communication is not so disloyal, reckless or maliciously untrue as to lose the Act's protection." [Mountain Shadows Golf Resort, 330 NLRB 1238, 1240 (2000)].

The first prong of this test is not at issue here. The Respondents do not contest the judge's finding, with which we agree, that the employee communications here were clearly related to their pay dispute. As to the second prong of the test, we find that the judge clearly erred in finding that the employee communications and/or participation in the Channel 6 newscast were either maliciously untrue or so disloyal and reckless as to warrant removal of the Act's protection.

Statements are maliciously untrue and unprotected, "if they are made with knowledge of their falsity or with reckless disregard for their truth or falsity…. The mere fact that statements are false, misleading or inaccurate is insufficient to demonstrate that they are maliciously untrue…." [Valley Hospital Medical Center, 351 NLRB 1250, 1252-1253 (2007), *enfd. sub nom.* Nevada Service Employees Local 1107 v. NLRB, 358 Fed. Appx. 783 (9th Cir. 2009)].

None of the statements made by the technicians were maliciously untrue under these well-established legal principles. Indeed, for the most part, the statements were accurate representations of what the Respondents had instructed the technicians to tell customers. Contrary to the judge, the technicians were essentially told to lie, as certain technicians stated during the telecast. The record clearly establishes that although the Respondents may have avoided expressly using the word "lie" when suggesting ways to overcome obstacles to making receiver-phone line connections, both Respondents affirmatively encouraged the technicians to do just that. Thus, a MasTec supervisor told the technicians to say "the receiver would not work" without the connection. Similarly, DirecTV vice president Brown advised technicians to say that the hookup to the phone was "a mandatory part of the installation" and needed "for the equipment to function correctly." Indeed, Brown instructed technicians to tell customers "whatever you have to tell them" and "whatever it takes" to make the connection. The technicians would readily understand these instructions to include "lie if you have to." Brown's joking suggestion to tell customers that an unconnected receiver would "blow up" underscored that message, as it undoubtedly was meant to do. Thus, whether the Respondents' officials expressly told the technicians to lie is immaterial. They expressly encouraged technicians to make statements known by the Respondents' managers to be false and intended to deceive customers into believing, erroneously, that their satellite receivers would not work if they were not connected to a land line telephone.

Similarly, the technicians did not make maliciously false statements by failing to specify that they would be back charged only if they failed to connect 50 percent of the receivers they installed. The statements the technicians did make fairly reflected their personal experiences under the new pay scheme. Almost all of them indicated that they had failed to achieve at least a 50 percent connection rate, and some had incurred significant back-charges as a result. In any event, the failure to fully explain the 50 percent connection rule was at most an inaccuracy. There is no basis in the record to find that the technicians knowingly and maliciously withheld that information in order to mislead the viewing public.

In sum, we find that almost all of the statements made by the technicians during the Channel 6 newscast were truthful representations of what the Respondents told them to do. Any arguable departures from the truth were no more than good-faith misstatements or incomplete statements, not malicious falsehoods justifying removal of the Act's protection.

We also find that none of the technicians' statements constituted unprotected disloyalty or reckless disparagement of the Respondents' services. Statements have been found unprotected where they constitute "a sharp, public, disparaging attack upon the quality of the company's product and its business policies, in a manner reasonably calculated to harm the company's reputation and reduce its income." [NLRB v. Electrical Workers Local 1229 (Jefferson Standard), 346 U.S. 464, 472 (1953)]. The Board has stated that it will not find a public statement unprotected unless it is "flagrantly disloyal, wholly incommensurate with any grievances which they might have." [Five Star Transportation, Inc., 349 NLRB 42, 45 (2007), *enfd.* 522 F.3d 46 (1st Cir. 2008), quoting Veeder-Root Co., 237 NLRB 1175, 1177 (1978)]. Further, "[i]n determining whether an employee's communication to a third party constitutes disparagement of the employer or its product, great care must be taken to distinguish between disparagement and the airing of what may be highly sensitive issues." [Allied Aviation Service Company of New Jersey, Inc., 248 NLRB 229, 231 (1980), *enfd.* 636 F.2d 1210 (3d Cir. 1980)].

In this case, the technicians participated in the Channel 6 newscast only after repeated unsuccessful attempts to resolve their pay dispute in direct communications with the Respondents. The newscast shed unwelcome light on certain deceptive business practices, but it was nevertheless directly related to the technicians' grievance about what they considered to be an unfair pay policy that they believed forced them to mislead customers. While the technicians may have been aware that some consumers might cancel the Respondents' services after listening to the newscast, there is no evidence that they intended to inflict such harm on the Respondents, or that they acted recklessly without regard for the financial consequences to the Respondents' businesses. We therefore find that the technicians did not engage in unprotected disloyal or reckless conduct, as previously defined by Board and court precedent.

Based on the foregoing, we find that the technicians' participation in the Channel 6 newscast was protected concerted activity directly and expressly related to and in furtherance of an ongoing labor dispute. Accordingly, we reverse the judge and find that by causing the discharge of the technicians for their participation in the newscast, and by discharging them, Respondents DirecTV and MasTec, respectively, violated Section 8(a)(1) of the Act....

MEMBER BECKER, concurring.

... I write separately because I believe the Supreme Court's decisions in NLRB v. Electrical Workers Local 1229 (*Jefferson Standard*), 346 U.S. 464 (1953), Linn v. Plant Guards, 383 U.S. 53 (1966), and NLRB v. Washington Aluminum Co., 370 U. S. 9 (1962), require us to apply *Jefferson Standard* in a less expansive manner consistent with the facts of that case.

The critical fact here, as my colleagues recognize, is that the statements at issue were expressly and directly related to the labor dispute. The statements concerned what the Respondent had asked the employees to do and the resulting implications for their wages. That critical fact takes this case outside the scope of the unprotected conduct defined in *Jefferson Standard.* The Court in that seminal case repeatedly emphasized that the speech at issue was not expressly tied to a labor dispute, and that was why it could constitute cause for discharge as product disparagement or disloyalty. The Court made clear that the employees' "attack related itself to no labor practice of the company. It made no reference to wages, hours or working conditions. The policies attacked were those of finance and public relations for which management, not technicians, must be responsible. The attack asked for no public sympathy or support." 346 U.S. at 476. The Court reiterated, "While they were also union men and leaders in the labor controversy, they took pains to separate those categories. In contrast to their claims on the picket line as to the labor controversy, their handbill of August 24 omitted all reference to it. The handbill diverted attention from the labor controversy. It attacked public policies of the company which had no discernible relation to that controversy." Id. at 476. The Court concluded: "the findings of the Board effectively separate the attack from the labor controversy and treat it solely as one made by the company's technical experts upon the quality of the company's product. As such, it was as adequate a cause for the discharge of its sponsors as if the labor controversy had not been pending. The technicians, themselves, so handled their attack as thus to bring their discharge under § 10(c)." Id. at 477.

Here, in contrast, the employees' statements were expressly and intimately linked to the labor dispute. The line of product disparagement and disloyalty cases running from *Jefferson Standard* has no application. Thus, because the employees' speech was clearly concerted activity for mutual aid and protection, it was protected unless it was uttered with actual malice. That standard is consistent with Congress' intent to protect concerted activity for mutual aid and protection even if the conduct—a strike, for example—inflicts economic injury on the employer. That standard also makes sense as a matter of policy, because so long as the statements are expressly linked to the labor dispute, the public will evaluate them within that context. As the Supreme Court recognized in *Linn*, and as the consuming public understands, "Labor disputes are ordinarily heated affairs .... Both labor and management often speak bluntly and recklessly, embellishing their respective positions with imprecatory language." 383 U.S. at 58. In other words, when the statements are expressly linked to a labor dispute, the public will take them with a grain of salt. The Court's holding in Linn further supports the proposition that otherwise protected statements do not lose protection simply because they "are erroneous and defame one of the parties to the dispute." 383 U.S. at 61. Such statements are protected unless they are made with actual malice. This standard is clear and has been elaborated by the courts under both *Linn* and New York Times v. Sullivan, 376 U.S. 254 (1964). Thus, I would end the majority opinion after finding, as my colleagues do, that the statements were not made with actual malice.

My colleagues go on to analyze whether the technicians' statements here are "so disloyal … as to lose the Act's protection." Not only is that standard so vague as to chill the exercise of Section 7 rights, it is in tension with the central purpose of Section 7, which is to grant employees a right to engage in concerted activity for mutual aid and protection even when the exercise of that right might otherwise be considered disloyalty. Employees have a right to strike despite the disloyalty involved in refusing to work. Employees have a right to ask consumers to boycott their employer in support of the employees' position in a labor dispute despite the disloyalty involved in seeking to reduce their employer's business. Similarly, employees have the right to criticize their employer's product or services so long as the criticism is expressly and directly tied to a labor dispute and is not made with actual malice.

My colleagues find that the statements were not reckless, but instead a last resort to resolve a legitimate grievance. While I agree with their finding, the Supreme Court made clear in Washington Aluminum that concerted activity for mutual aid and protection need not be measured or proportional in order to be protected. Even if such activity is "unnecessary and unwise," it remains protected. 370 U.S. at 16. As in *Washington Aluminum*, the employees here "were part of a small group of employees who were wholly unorganized. They had no bargaining representative and, in fact, no representative of any kind to present their grievances to their employer. Under these circumstances, they had to speak for themselves as best they could." Id. at 14.

Finally, my colleagues draw the applicable standard from Mountain Shadow Golf Resort, 330 NLRB 1238 (2000), but there, as in *Jefferson Standard*, the handbill at issue "did not mention the problems the employees' union was having negotiating with the Respondent, and bore no indication that it was written by or on behalf of any employee of the Respondent." Id. at 1241. In other words, the statements, like those in *Jefferson Standard*, but unlike those in the instant case, were not expressly and directly tied to any labor dispute. *Mountain Shadow* is thus distinguishable on its facts and the standard it articulates is overbroad for the reasons explained above.

Because the majority, based on *Mountain Shadow*, reads *Jefferson Standard* and its progeny too broadly, I concur only in the result.

NOTES AND QUESTIONS

1. An essential requirement of protection under Section 7 is that the employee conduct in question was "concerted" rather than solitary or for purely individual purposes. It was obvious in *MasTec* that the employees acted in concert about a matter of interest to them as a group of employees. In contrast, when an employee complains but not to, with or on behalf of at least one other employee, the employee's conduct is not "concerted" employee conduct.

2. The internet and the rise of social media have spawned a wave of Section 7 cases for the NLRB. Employees frequently take to social media to complain about their supervisors, working conditions, pay, or customers. One employee's social media post might be purely solitary and unprotected, or it might be protected "concerted" activity involving communication with at least one other employee or an appeal seeking the support or approval of other employees. Another employee might join in concerted activity by "liking" or otherwise responding to the first employee's post. *See* Office of the General Counsel, National Labor Relations Board, OM 11-74 (Aug. 18, 2011).

3. In the Memorandum cited in the preceding note, the General Counsel described the following case:

> In early 2011, several of the Employer's former and current employees discovered that they owed state income taxes for 2010, related to earnings at the Employer. After this discovery, at least one employee brought the issue to the Employer's attention and requested that the matter be placed on the agenda for discussion at an upcoming management meeting with employees.
>
> ... [A] former employee posted on her Facebook page a statement, including a short-hand expletive, that expressed dissatisfaction ... that she now owed money. She also asserted that the Employer's owners could not even do paperwork correctly. One employee—Charging Party A—responded to this posting by clicking "Like." ... Two other employees commented that they had never owed money before, and one of them referred to telling the Employer that we will discuss this at the meeting. Two of the Employer's customers joined in the conversation, as did Charging Party B, who asserted that she also owed money and referred to one of the Employer's owners as "[s]uch an asshole."

The General Counsel found that the employees were engaged in protected concerted activity and that the employer violated Section 8(a)(1) by discharging them. The General Counsel also found that the employer unlawfully interfered with its employees' Section 7 rights by adopting a policy threatening discipline for engaging in "inappropriate discussions" about the company, management, and/or coworkers. In contrast, the General Counsel found that a restaurant employee was *not* engaged in protected concerted activity given the following facts:

> In February 2011, the employee had a conversation on Facebook with a

> relative. Responding to her query as to how his night at work had gone, he complained that he hadn't had a raise in five years and that he was doing the waitresses' work without tips. He also called the Employer's customers "rednecks" and stated that he hoped they choked on glass as they drove home drunk. He did not discuss his posting with any of his coworkers, and none of them responded to it.

Note that the employee in the second case conversed with a non-employee relative, not another employee. Wholly apart from the question whether his conduct was so disloyal or destructive as to lose protection, his conduct was not protected by Section 7 because it was not *concerted* employee activity.

4. The remedies available to employees under the National Labor Relations Act are very limited. Section 10 of the act authorizes awards of reinstatement and back pay, but no other compensatory damages or punitive damages or attorney's fees. The limited damages available and the unavailability of an award of attorney's fees makes private attorney action impractical in many instances. However, the prosecution of a complaint under the NLRA is by the Regional Counsel of the NLRB on behalf of the complaining party.

2. *Duties of Supervision*

a. Negligent Supervision and Third Parties

The employer and employee are not necessarily the only parties concerned with the quality and reach of an employer's supervision and management. If the employee's behavior harms a customer, invitee, passer-by or other third party, the injured party might well argue that the employer did not do enough to control the employee. Of course, the issue whether an employer was "negligent" in its supervision of its employee is usually irrelevant to an injured party who can rely on the doctrine of *respondeat superior*. *Respondeat superior* makes the employer strictly liable for the employee's accidents whether or not the employer was negligent in supervising the employee. See also Chapter 3.B, *supra*, discussing how *respondeat superior* obviates a third party's proof of employer negligence in selecting employees. But careful and competent supervision is important as a practical matter to reduce the incidence of employee accidents,.

Still, there are situations in which employer negligence is important as a legal matter in a tort suit by a third party. *Respondeat superior* does not impute liability to the employer if the employee was acting outside the scope of his employment when he caused the injury. In that case, an employer's own negligence is an alternative basis for liability. This alternative basis for employer liability is especially important in cases involving an employee's *intentional* tort. For example, it is normally plausible for an employer to say that it did not employ the employee to commit assault or battery and that such torts are outside the scope of employment. A good example is Booker v. GTE.net LLC, 350 F.3d 515 (6th Cir. 2003). There, an unnamed employee apparently sought to discourage a customer from complaining about his employer, Verizon, to the Kentucky Attorney General's office. The unnamed employee impersonated the plaintiff, an employee of the attorney general's office, by writing an email to the customer under the plaintiff's name. Among other things, the email called the customer a "grumpy, horrible man," warned that Verizon might sue him, and urged him to withdraw his complaint. The email apparently caused the plaintiff considerable trouble with her own employer, the attorney general. An investigation eventually cleared the plaintiff of any guilt, but she sued Verizon for intentional infliction of emotional distress.

The plaintiff argued for holding Verizon liable under *respondeat superior*, first by inferring that the unknown imposter was a Verizon employee, and second by finding that the imposter was seeking to further Verizon's interests by deterring a customer complaint. But the court rejected the plaintiff's reasoning. "We cannot agree that it is beneficial to Verizon's business to pacify customer complaints through … the implicit threat of lawsuits and the offensively-worded suggestion that the customer discontinue his business with Verizon." Even assuming the unknown imposter was a Verizon employee, he acted outside the scope of employment and therefore his actions could not be imputed to Verizon.

KRISTIE'S KATERING, INC. v. AMERI

72 Ark. App. 102, 35 S.W.3d 807 (2000)

SAM BIRD, Judge.

Kristie's Katering, Inc., appeals a decision of a Pulaski County jury awarding Nasser Ameri $16,000 for injuries he claimed he sustained at the hands of security guards at one of Kristie's night clubs, the Discovery Club, on July 21, 1996. Kristie's argues that the trial court erred in . . . denying Kristie's motion for judgment notwithstanding the verdict because Ameri failed to prove all the elements of his claim of negligence. . . . [W]e affirm.

At trial, Ameri testified that he had come to the United States from Yemen in 1987 for an education and graduated from UALR with a degree in computer science. He said he went to the Discovery Club every couple of weeks for an evening of dancing and entertainment. On July 21, 1996, Ameri got to the club around 1 a.m. Although he said he was not drinking, his friend, Saif, was, and Saif got into a verbal confrontation with an oriental man. Ameri said he attempted to separate the men but was unsuccessful. About that time the lights came on, and the disc jockey announced that the club was closing. Ameri testified that as he was leaving, one of the club's security guards grabbed Saif, and another security guard [identified as Charleston] grabbed him from behind with his arm around Ameri's neck. [Charleston], [t]he guard who was holding Ameri choked him while another guard hit him in the face with his fist, and his nose was broken. Ameri said he incurred medical bills of approximately sixty-three hundred dollars. . . .

On cross-examination, Ameri admitted that, about six weeks before the July 21 incident, he had had a dispute with Charleston involving another incident in the parking lot of the Discovery Club, and that Charleston had told him following the earlier dispute that, "I will get you." . . .

Two witnesses were called for the defense. Lamont Charleston testified that he had been a security guard at the Discovery Club during the period that included July 21, 1996. However, Charleston testified that he did not know Ameri, that he had never before seen Ameri, that he had never been involved in an altercation of any kind involving Ameri, and that he had not had a dispute with Ameri in the parking lot of the Discovery Club about six weeks before July 21, 1996, "because we didn't have any liability on what happened in the parking lot." . . . Although Charleston indicated that there were frequent occasions requiring security guards to expel unruly patrons from the club, they seldom involved physical altercations. He said that when a patron became unruly to the point of requiring expulsion, two security guards would "walk the person out," with one guard on each side. He said that if a patron "got physical, like throwing punches," the guards would hug them and escort them out.

Norman Jones, the president and sole shareholder in Kristie's Katering, testified that he was in charge of security at the club when Ameri was injured and that he hired the security personnel. Jones admitted that he had no formal training program for security guards, no training manuals, materials, or workbooks to inform them of their duties, and no written rules or regulations governing their conduct. However, he said, the security personnel he hired almost always had experience in the field and they all were expected to use common sense in trying to maintain calm at the club. . . .

[T]he evidence offered by Ameri and Alkhomairi relating to the incident on July 21, 1996, was clearly sufficient to enable the jury to conclude that both security guards were acting in the course of their employment by Kristie's and in furtherance of Kristie's interests. . . . [Moreover,] Ameri proceeded at trial on the theory that Kristie's was negligent in failing to monitor, properly train, or supervise its security force. . . . This theory is completely separate from the *respondeat superior* theory of vicarious liability because the cause of action is premised on the wrongful conduct of the employer, such that the employer's negligence was the proximate cause of the plaintiff's injuries. . . .

We think that the evidence that Kristie's owner provided no formal training, no training manuals, materials or workbooks, and that there existed no written rules or regulations governing the conduct of security guards in ejecting patrons, coupled with the evidence of the frequency of occurrences requiring such action, was sufficient evidence for the jury to conclude that Kristie's was negligent in its failure to provide adequate supervision of the guards. Affirmed.

ROBBINS, Chief Judge, dissenting.

. . . The majority holds that the evidence supported appellee's contention that his damages were proximately caused by appellant's negligent supervision of its employees. I disagree.

By Mr. Ameri's own testimony, his damages were caused by intentional malice on the part of the security personnel. He testified that, a month and a half prior to being attacked, he inserted himself into a hostile confrontation between Mr. Charleston and an unknown stranger, and that he was a witness against Mr. Charleston. On the night of the prior confrontation Mr. Charleston told Mr. Ameri, "We will get you." According to Mr. Ameri, the attack was motivated by revenge. With regard to attending the club, Mr. Ameri stated, "I always feel unsafe in there, because I know they're going to beat me every time."

. . . Moreover, in my view, no amount of training would likely have prevented this incident. This was not a situation where the security guards acted imprudently in dealing with an altercation. Rather, it was a situation where, by Mr. Ameri's own account, they committed a personal and intentional act of violence, which appellant could not have reasonably expected or prevented. . . . Based on Mr. Ameri's allegations, his remedy was against the employees who attacked him, but not against the employer. I would reverse.

NOTES AND QUESTIONS

1. A security guard is one type of employee whose intentional assault and battery might naturally be in the scope of employment, *provided* his intent was to further the employer's business. *See, e.g.*, Tucker v. Kroger Co., 133 Ohio App. 3d 140, 726 N.E.2d 1111 (1999) (employer would be liable for security guard's alleged wrongful detention of customer if guard was acting "to facilitate or promote firm's business"); Howard v. J. H. Harvey Co., 239 Ga. App. 677, 521 S.E.2d 691 (1999). An employee's intentional tort for purely personal reasons having nothing to do with the employer's business is generally not "in the course of employment" even if it occurred during working time and on the employer's premises. *But see* RESTATEMENT (SECOND) OF TORTS (1965) § 317 (describing special circumstances under which employer might be responsible for preventing intentional torts of employees on employer's premises or in possession of employer's chattel). If Ameri were not a guest or visitor of the Discovery Club, and if Charleston had committed the assault off duty and away from his employer's premises, there would probably be little doubt that Charleston acted outside the scope of his employment. *Respondeat superior* does not impute purely personal torts to a person who simply happens to be the tortfeasor's employer.

2. In *Kristie's Katering,* the majority found an alternative basis for the employer's liability: negligent supervision. Negligent supervision is the employer's own tort, and an employer might be liable for negligent supervision even if the employee's actions were outside the scope of employment, which is frequently the case when the employee committed an intentional tort. Moreover, while *respondeat superior* imputes only simple negligence, an employer's *gross* negligence in hiring might expose the employer to punitive damages. In these ways, the doctrine of negligent supervision serves the same functions as its sibling, the doctrine of negligent hiring. See Chapter Three, Part B, *supra.*

3. If a plaintiff alleges the employer's negligent supervision as the basis for employer liability, he must also prove a causal link between the employer's negligence and the employee's tort. Do you agree with the majority in *Kristie's Katering* that the plaintiff proved the employer was negligent in a way that caused the assault? What in particular should the employer have done to prevent the incident that lead to Ameri's injuries?

4. If Ameri added the security guard Charleston as a co-defendant in the lawsuit against Kristie's, could an attorney properly represent both Kristie's and Charleston? In thinking about this problem, it may be helpful to know that an employer owes its employee a common law duty of indemnification if the employee is sued by a third party with respect to an action the employer "authorized." RESTATEMENT (SECOND) OF AGENCY §439(d). *See also* Dunton v.

Suffolk County, 729 F.2d 903 (2d Cir. 1984) (attorney's simultaneous representation of county employer and its employee violated ABA Code of Professional Responsibility).

5. Modern technology presents a new realm of potential liability for an employer who fails to prevent an employee's use of the employer's resources to commit torts against third parties. In Doe v. XYC Corp., 887 A.2d 1156 (N.J. Super. 2005), the New Jersey court considered an employer's liability for an employee's Internet transmission of pornographic photographs of his stepdaughter. The proposed basis for the employer's liability was that the employer knew or should have known of the employee's use of an office computer for this activity. A trial court dismissed a lawsuit by the girl and her mother against the perpetrator's employer, but the Superior Court of New Jersey reversed and remanded the action for trial:

> We hold that an employer who is on notice that one of its employees is using a workplace computer to access pornography, possibly child pornography, has a duty to investigate the employee's activities and to take prompt and effective action to stop the unauthorized activity.

887 A.2d at 1158. Among other things, the court cited Restatement (Second) of Torts § 317, which provides:

> A master is under a duty to exercise reasonable care so to control his servant while acting outside the scope of his employment as to prevent him from intentionally harming others or from so conducting himself as to create an unreasonable risk of bodily harm to them, if
>
> (a) the servant (i) is upon the premises in possession of the master . . . or (ii) is using a chattel of the master, and
>
> (b) the master (i) knows or has reason to know that he has the ability to control his servant, and (ii) knows or should know of the necessity and opportunity for exercising such control.

Among the key facts as to which there was at least some evidence: (1) various supervisors were aware that the employee was using his office computer to access pornographic websites; (2) some of these supervisors instructed the employee to cease using his computer for such activities, but otherwise delayed taking substantial action against the employee even when he continued to use his computer to access pornography; (3) the employer knew the employee had recently married and had a young stepdaughter; (4) the employer had the right to inspect data on office computers used by its employees; (5) if the employer taken reasonable steps to investigate the employee's use of his office computer, it would have discovered he was using the office computer to transmit pornographic photographs of his stepdaughter. 887 A.2d at 1170.

6. Negligent training or supervision is a particularly important alternative to *respondeat superior* when the defendant is a local government employer of an employee whose alleged wrongful act or omission constituted a violation of federal constitutional rights. The Supreme Court has held that for purposes of civil rights law, a local government employer is liable only for its *own* actions. There is *no respondeat superior* liability. Monell v. Department of Social Services, 436 U.S. 658 (1978). The doctrine of negligent training or supervision is one way of holding

a local government liable for its own acts or omissions in a civil rights case. However, a local government employer's negligence must have constituted a "deliberate indifference" to the particular federal civil right that is the basis of the plaintiff's claim. Young v. City of Providence, 404 F.3d 4 (1st Cir. 2005).

7. There are other bases for holding an employer liable for an employee's tort outside the scope of employment. Section 219(2) of the Restatement (Second) of Agency adopted in 1958 stated that an employer may be liable for an employee's action outside the scope of his employment if the employee was "aided in accomplishing the tort by the existence of the agency relationship." The courts once applied this rule mainly in situations in which an employee's position created a special risk to vulnerable customers or clients who depended on his services or who were at the mercy of his access to their private rooms or property. An employer might be liable in such a situation without regard to its negligence in selecting or supervising an employee. The Second Restatement's "aided in accomplishing" rule eventually served as a model for an employer's vicarious liability for sexual harassment between employees. See Part A.2.c of this Chapter.

The "aided in accomplishing" rule provoked objections that it was too broad a rule of vicarious employer liability for intentional employee torts outside the scope of employment. *See, e.g.*, Costos v. Coconut Island Corp. 137 F.3d 46, 49 (1st Cir. 1998) The Third Restatement discarded the "aided in accomplishing" standard, replacing it with a more restrictive rule of liability. Under Section 7.05 of the Restatement (Third) of Agency, if an employer has a "special relationship" with a person (such as a vulnerable client or patient), the employer owes a duty of *reasonable care* to prevent its agent from causing that person harm.

8. If Ameri had been an employee and not a customer of Kristie's Discovery Club, the rules of liability would have been quite different. When an employee is injured in an "accident" arising out of and in the course of his employment, workers' compensation provides limited benefits regardless of fault, so an employer's negligence is unimportant and *respondeat superior* is unnecessary. But workers' compensation law also bars an employee's common law tort claim against the employer or fellow employee unless the injured employee can prove one of the exceptions to workers' compensation coverage. See Chapter Five, Parts B.2 and B.6, *supra*.

b. Abusive Supervision

An "at will" employee has no legally enforceable right to be treated, supervised, managed or instructed "fairly" or competently as long as an employer does not engage in prohibited forms of discrimination or violate statutory or constitutional liberty rights. If an employee suffers economically along with the employer because incompetent personnel management leads to a loss of job and career opportunities, there is no cause of action for such economic loss. However, an employer does not have a right to cause personal injury to its employees.

If an employee suffers a personal injury because of a work-related accident or industrial disease, it is usually irrelevant whether the employer's negligence was a cause because workers' compensation provides benefits without regard to fault. Moreover, workers' compensation benefits are the exclusive remedy as between the employee and the employer or co-employees. Suppose, however, the personal injury is not because of an "accident" or an "industrial disease," or the injury is a type for which workers' compensation benefits are not available. Can bad supervision hurt an employee in a way that is not covered by workers' compensation, but *is* covered by tort law?

GTE SOUTHWEST, INC. v. BRUCE

998 S.W.2d 605 (Tex. 1999)

Justice ABBOTT delivered the opinion of the court.

I. Facts

Three GTE employees, Rhonda Bruce, Linda Davis, and Joyce Poelstra, sued GTE for intentional infliction of emotional distress premised on the constant humiliating and abusive behavior of their supervisor, Morris Shields. Shields is a former U.S. Army supply sergeant who began working for GTE in 1971. . . .

In May 1991, GTE transferred Shields from Jacksonville to Nash, Texas, where he became the supply operations supervisor. The supply department at Nash was small, consisting of two offices and a store room. There were approximately eight employees other than Shields. Bruce, Davis, and Poelstra ("the employees") worked under Shields at the Nash facility. . . . In March 1994, the employees filed suit, alleging that GTE intentionally inflicted emotional distress on them through Shields. . . . The jury awarded $100,000.00 plus prejudgment interest to Bruce, $100,000.00 plus interest to Davis, and $75,000.00 plus interest to Poelstra.

II. The Texas Workers' Compensation Act

[The Court held that whether or not the alleged torts occurred in the scope of the plaintiffs' employment, the exclusive remedy defense of workers' compensation law did not bar the plaintiffs' common law tort claims against the employer, because the Texas Workers' Compensation Act does not provide benefits for the type of emotional distress injuries the plaintiffs suffered. For more on this aspect of workers' compensation law, see Part B.6 of Chapter 5, *supra*.]

III. Intentional Infliction of Emotional Distress

An employee may recover damages for intentional infliction of emotional distress in an employment context as long as the employee establishes the elements of the cause of action. *See* Wornick Co. v. Casas, 856 S.W.2d 732, 734 (Tex. 1993). To recover damages for intentional infliction of emotional distress, a plaintiff must prove that: (1) the defendant acted intentionally or recklessly; (2) the conduct was extreme and outrageous; (3) the actions of the defendant caused the plaintiff emotional distress; and (4) the resulting emotional distress was severe. Standard Fruit & Vegetable Co. v. Johnson, 985 S.W.2d 62, 65 (Tex. 1998). . . .

A. EXTREME AND OUTRAGEOUS CONDUCT

GTE first argues that Shields's conduct is not extreme and outrageous. To be extreme and outrageous, conduct must be "so outrageous in character, and so extreme in degree, as to go beyond all possible bounds of decency, and to be regarded as atrocious, and utterly intolerable in a civilized community." Natividad v. Alexsis, Inc., 875 S.W.2d 695, 699 (Tex. 1994) (quoting Twyman v. Twyman, 855 S.W.2d 619, 621 (Tex. 1993)); Restatement (Second) of Torts § 46 cmt. d (1965). Generally, insensitive or even rude behavior does not constitute extreme and outrageous conduct. Similarly, mere insults, indignities, threats, annoyances, petty oppressions, or other trivialities do not rise to the level of extreme and outrageous conduct. *See* Porterfield v. Galen Hosp. Corp., 948 S.W.2d 916, 920 (Tex. App. – San Antonio 1997, writ denied); Restatement (Second) of Torts § 46 cmt. d (1965).

In determining whether certain conduct is extreme and outrageous, courts consider the context and the relationship between the parties . . . "The extreme and outrageous character of the conduct may arise from an abuse by the actor of a position, or a relation with the other, which gives him actual or apparent authority over the other, or power to affect his interests." Restatement (Second) of Torts § 46 cmt. e (1965).

In the employment context, some courts have held that a plaintiff's status as an employee should entitle him to a greater degree of protection from insult and outrage by a supervisor with authority over him than if he were a stranger. *See, e.g.*, Alcorn v. Anbro Eng'g, Inc., 2 Cal. 3d 493, 468 P.2d 216, 218 n.2, 86 Cal. Rptr. 88 (1970); White v. Monsanto Co., 585 So. 2d 1205, 1209-10 (La. 1991). This approach is based partly on the rationale that, as opposed to most casual and temporary relationships, the workplace environment provides a captive victim and the opportunity for prolonged abuse. *See* Coleman v. Housing Auth. of Americus, 191 Ga. App. 166, 381 S.E.2d 303, 306 (1989).

In contrast, several courts, including Texas courts, have adopted a strict approach to intentional infliction of emotional distress claims arising in the workplace. *See, e.g.*, Miller v. Galveston/Houston Diocese, 911 S.W.2d 897, 900-01 (Tex. App. — Amarillo 1995, no writ). These courts rely on the fact that, to properly manage its business, an employer must be able to supervise, review, criticize, demote, transfer, and discipline employees. Although many of these acts are necessarily unpleasant for the employee, an employer must have latitude to exercise these rights in a permissible way, even though emotional distress results. We agree with the approach taken by these courts.

Given these considerations, Texas courts have held that a claim for intentional infliction of emotional distress does not lie for ordinary employment disputes. *Miller*, 911 S.W.2d at 900-01; *see also Johnson*, 965 F.2d at 33. The range of behavior encompassed in "employment disputes" is broad, and includes at a minimum such things as criticism, lack of recognition, and low evaluations, which, although unpleasant and sometimes unfair, are ordinarily expected in the work environment. *See, e.g., Johnson*, 965 F.2d at 33-34; *Ulrich v. Exxon Co., U.S.A.*, 824 F. Supp. 677, 687 (S.D. Tex. 1993). Thus, to establish a cause of action for intentional infliction of emotional distress in the workplace, an employee must prove the existence of some conduct that brings the dispute outside the scope of an ordinary employment dispute and into the realm of extreme and outrageous conduct.... Such extreme conduct exists only in the most unusual of circumstances.

GTE contends that the evidence establishes nothing more than an ordinary employment dispute. To the contrary, the employees produced evidence that, over a period of more than two years, Shields engaged in a pattern of grossly abusive, threatening, and degrading conduct. Shields began regularly using the harshest vulgarity shortly after his arrival at the Nash facility. In response, Bruce and Davis informed Shields that they were uncomfortable with obscene jokes, vulgar cursing, and sexual innuendo in the office. Despite these objections, Shields continued to use exceedingly vulgar language on a daily basis. Several witnesses testified that Shields used the word "f — " as part of his normal pattern of conversation, and that he regularly heaped abusive profanity on the employees. Linda Davis testified that Shields used this language to get a reaction. Gene Martin, another GTE employee, testified that Shields used the words "f — " and "motherf — er" frequently when speaking with the employees. On one occasion when Bruce asked Shields to curb his language because it was offensive, Shields positioned himself in front of her face, and screamed, "I will do and say any damn thing I want. And I don't give a s — who likes it." Another typical example is when Gene Martin asked Shields to stop his yelling and vulgarity because it upset the female employees, and Shields replied "I'm tired of walking on f — ing eggshells, trying to make people happy around here." There was further evidence that Shields's harsh and vulgar language was not merely accidental, but seemed intended to abuse the employees.

More importantly, the employees testified that Shields repeatedly physically and verbally threatened and terrorized them. There was evidence that Shields was continuously in a rage, and that Shields would frequently assault each of the employees by physically charging at them. When doing so, Shields would bend his head down, put his arms straight down by his sides, ball his hands into fists, and walk quickly toward or "lunge" at the employees, stopping uncomfortably close to their faces while screaming and yelling. The employees were exceedingly frightened by this behavior, afraid that Shields might hit them. Linda Davis testified that Shields charged the employees with the intent to frighten them. At least once, another employee came between Shields and Poelstra to protect her from Shields's charge. A number of witnesses testified that Shields frequently yelled and screamed at the top of his voice, and pounded his fists when requesting the employees to do things. Bruce testified that Shields would "come up fast" and "get up over her" — causing her to lean back — and yell and scream in her face for her to get things for him. Shields included vulgar language in his yelling and screaming. Bruce stated that such conduct was not a part of any disciplinary action against her. Further, the incidents usually occurred in the open rather than in private. Bruce testified that, on one occasion, Shields began beating a banana on his desk, and when he jumped up and slammed the banana into the trash, Bruce thought he would hit her. Afterwards, Shields was shaking and said "I'm sick."

Bruce also told of an occasion when Shields entered Bruce's office and went into a rage because Davis had left her purse on a chair and Bruce had placed her umbrella on a filing cabinet in the office. Shields yelled and screamed for Bruce to clean up her office. Shields yelled, "If you don't get things picked up in this office, you will not be working for me." He later said that Bruce and Davis would be sent to the unemployment line and "could be replaced by two Kelly girls" that were twenty years old. On another occasion, Shields came up behind Bruce and said,

"You're going to be in the unemployment line." Once he told Bruce that he had been sent to Nash to fire her. Another time, he typed "quit" on his computer and said, "That's what you can do." Davis testified that Shields threatened to "get them" for complaining about his behavior. And both Bruce and Martin testified that Shields had stated that "he was in a position to get even for what [the employees] had done." . . .

In considering whether the evidence establishes more than an ordinary employment dispute, we will also address GTE's argument that because none of Shields's acts standing alone rises to the level of outrageous conduct, the court of appeals erred in holding that, considered cumulatively, the conduct was extreme and outrageous. 956 S.W.2d at 644, 647. As already noted, the employees demonstrated at trial that Shields engaged in a course of harassing conduct directed at each of them, the totality of which caused severe emotional distress. It is well recognized outside of the employment context that a course of harassing conduct may support liability for intentional infliction of emotional distress. *See, e.g.*, Duty v. General Fin. Co., 154 Tex. 16, 273 S.W.2d 64, 65-66 (1954) (debt collection). In such cases, courts consider the totality of the conduct in determining whether it is extreme and outrageous.

Similarly, in the employment context, courts and commentators have almost unanimously recognized that liability may arise when one in a position of authority engages in repeated or ongoing harassment of an employee, if the cumulative quality and quantity of the harassment is extreme and outrageous. . . . When such repeated or ongoing harassment is alleged, the offensive conduct is evaluated as a whole. *See, e.g.*, Subbe-Hirt v. Baccigalupi, 94 F.3d 111, 114-15 (3d Cir. 1996). . . .

We agree with the overwhelming weight of authority in this state and around the country that when repeated or ongoing severe harassment is shown, the conduct should be evaluated as a whole in determining whether it is extreme and outrageous. Accordingly, we hold that the court of appeals did not err in doing so.

We now consider whether Shields's conduct, taken as a whole, amounts to extreme and outrageous conduct. . . GTE argues that the conduct complained of is an ordinary employment dispute because the employees' complaints are really that Shields was a poor supervisor with an objectionable management style. GTE also contends that the actions are employment disputes because Shields committed the acts in the course of disciplining his employees.

We recognize that, even when an employer or supervisor abuses a position of power over an employee, the employer will not be liable for mere insults, indignities, or annoyances that are not extreme and outrageous. Restatement (Second) of Torts § 46 cmt. e (1965). But Shields's ongoing acts of harassment, intimidation, and humiliation and his daily obscene and vulgar behavior, which GTE defends as his "management style," went beyond the bounds of tolerable workplace conduct. . . . The picture painted by the evidence at trial was unmistakable: Shields greatly exceeded the necessary leeway to supervise, criticize, demote, transfer, and discipline, and created a workplace that was a den of terror for the employees. And the evidence showed that all of Shields's abusive conduct was common, not rare. Being purposefully humiliated and intimidated, and being repeatedly put in fear of one's physical well-being at the hands of a supervisor is more than a mere triviality or annoyance. . . .

Occasional malicious and abusive incidents should not be condoned, but must often be tolerated in our society. But once conduct such as that shown here becomes a regular pattern of behavior and continues despite the victim's objection and attempts to remedy the situation, it can no longer be tolerated. It is the severity and regularity of Shields's abusive and threatening conduct that brings his behavior into the realm of extreme and outrageous conduct. Conduct such as being regularly assaulted, intimidated, and threatened is not typically encountered nor expected in the course of one's employment, nor should it be accepted in a civilized society. An employer certainly has much leeway in its chosen methods of supervising and disciplining employees, but terrorizing them is simply not acceptable. If GTE or Shields was dissatisfied with the employees' performance, GTE could have terminated them, disciplined them, or taken some other more appropriate approach to the problem instead of fostering the abuse, humiliation, and intimidation that was heaped on the employees. Accordingly, the trial court properly submitted the issue to the jury, and there was some evidence to support the jury's conclusion that Shields's conduct was extreme and outrageous.

B. INTENT

GTE argues that the employees failed to establish that GTE, as opposed to Shields, possessed the requisite intent to support GTE's liability. . . . Generally, a master is vicariously liable for the torts of its servants committed in the course and scope of their employment. This is true even though the employee's tort is intentional when the act, although not specifically authorized by the employer, is closely connected with the servant's authorized duties. If the intentional tort is committed in the accomplishment of a duty entrusted to the employee, rather than because of personal animosity, the employer may be liable. *See* Soto v. El Paso Natural Gas Co., 942 S.W.2d 671, 681 (Tex. App. — El Paso 1997, writ denied). Shields's acts, although inappropriate, involved conduct within the scope of his position as the employees' supervisor. . . . GTE admitted as much when it argued that Shields's acts were "mere employment disputes." GTE has cited no evidence that Shields's actions were motivated by personal animosity rather than a misguided attempt to carry out his job duties. The jury concluded that Shields's acts were committed in the scope of his employment, and there is some evidence to support this finding. Thus, GTE is liable for Shields's conduct. . . .

C. SEVERE EMOTIONAL DISTRESS

. . . The employees testified that, as a result of being exposed to Shields's outrageous conduct, they experienced a variety of emotional problems, including crying spells, emotional outbursts, nausea, stomach disorders, headaches, difficulty in sleeping and eating, stress, anxiety, and depression. The employees testified that they experienced anxiety and fear because of Shields's continuing harassment, especially his charges and rages. Each employee sought medical treatment for these problems, and all three plaintiffs were prescribed medication to alleviate the problems. An expert witness testified that each of them suffered from post-traumatic stress disorder. This evidence is legally sufficient to support the jury's finding that the employees suffered severe emotional distress. . . .

. . . We conclude that there is legally sufficient evidence to support the jury's verdict against GTE on each of the employees' claims for intentional infliction of emotional distress. . . . Accordingly, we affirm the court of appeals' judgment.

NOTES AND QUESTIONS

1. Employers routinely cause stress for employees to motivate them — demanding faster or better work, criticizing performance, or punishing conduct they find undesirable. To this extent, an employer's intentional infliction of stress is widely accepted by the courts as normal and not "outrageous," at least if the employer did not act in a way foreseeably causing extreme stress and leading to severe emotional harm. Do you agree with the Texas court that employers must be allowed greater leeway (and presumably greater license to create stress) than parties in other relationship types? Or do you agree with decisions of other courts *GTE Southwest* cited that hold employers to a higher standard of behavior because of their economic power over employees? For an argument for a higher standard of behavior, *see* Regina Austin, *Employer Abuse, Worker Resistance, and the Tort Theory of Intentional Infliction of Emotional Distress*, 41 Stan. L. Rev. 1 (1998).

2. Do you agree with the court in *GTE Southwest* that a factfinder is entitled to consider the cumulative effect of a series of separate abusive acts, or should each act be viewed in isolation? Does it matter whether employment is "at will"? If the plaintiffs were employed at will, why did they not resign and look for work elsewhere when Shields's abuse began? Would it matter if they were earning premium wages for difficult work circumstances? If an associate for a law firm endures outrageous behavior by a supervising partner over an extended period, should salary and alternative employment opportunities be factors in determining the firm's liability if the associate eventually decides to sue?

3. Whether conduct is outrageous might seem to be the perfect jury question, because a judge's position as a legal authority provides no unique advantage in knowing society's expectations. Judges, however, dismiss many "outrage" claims on summary judgment on the ground that no reasonable person could find the employer's behavior outrageous. Summary judgment might be a matter of judicial economy, a way of protecting an employer from a jury's feared pro-employee sentiment, or a means of protecting an employer's at-will prerogative against claims of unfair treatment. As the Third Circuit in *Cox v. Keystone Carbon*, 861 F.2d 390, 395 (3d Cir. 1988), noted, "it is extremely rare to find conduct in the employment context that will rise to the level of outrageousness necessary to provide a basis for recovery for the tort of intentional infliction of emotional distress." *See also* Mintz v. Bell Atl. Sys. Leasing Int'l, 905 P.2d 559, 563 (Ariz. App., Div. 1, 1995) (same quoted language as above in *Cox*).

4. Is a standard of outrageous behavior sufficiently clear for supervisors to know when they are about to cross the line? A lower standard resulting in liability for merely "unreasonable" behavior might be hazardous for a supervisor, who may be no better equipped to deal with stressful situations than a subordinate. One might think long and hard about accepting a supervisory position if any burst of temper, poor choice of words, or failure of good judgment could result in a lawsuit. Thus the "outrageous" standard imposes liability only when an actor has crossed *two* lines: a first line marking unreasonable behavior that still allows a margin of error;

and a *second* line marking the end of the margin of error and the occurrence of truly outrageous behavior.

5. There are many variations in the law of outrage from one jurisdiction to the next — perhaps even from one judge to the next. Still, there are a few useful generalizations about which courts widely agree. First, many employer actions such as discharge or disciplinary action are naturally stressful whether or not stress is an employer's purpose. However, stress standing alone does not make an otherwise normal and lawful employment action tortious. *See, e.g.*, Heller v. Pillsbury Madison & Sutro, 58 Cal. Rptr. 2d 336 (Cal. App. 1996). In *GTE Southwest* the court drew a line between "ordinary employment disputes" involving supervision, discipline, performance review, and termination, and truly "outrageous" employer conduct that may accompany an otherwise normal employer action. Another good example of this distinction is Archer v. Farmer Bros. Co., 70 P.3d 495 (Colo. App. 2002). A manager, having decided to fire an employee named Archer, was anxious to convey the message to Archer. Archer, however, was confined to bed at the home of his mother-in-law, recuperating from a possible heart attack. Not to be delayed, the manager instructed two supervisors — Henshaw and Rawson — to go to Archer to bring him the news. Henshaw evidently expressed some doubts about the timing of such a visit. The manager responded, "I don't give a ________if [Archer] is on his deathbed, if I tell you to fire him, that's what you will do, or I'll get somebody who will." Thus, Henshaw and Rawson agreed to carry out the manager's instructions.

> Henshaw and Rawson went in search of Archer, ending up at Archer's mother-in-law's home. In the twenty years Henshaw and Rawson had known Archer, they had never visited him or been invited to his home. Upon arrival at his mother-in-law's home, they entered uninvited. Neither Henshaw nor Rawson announced the purpose of their visit or asked about Archer's health. Upon entering the spare bedroom, they found Archer lying in bed, not fully clothed. Without asking Archer whether he was fit to discuss work matters or when he intended to return to work, they peremptorily announced that they had his termination papers, which they needed him to initial.

Id. at 499. Later the same evening, Archer attempted suicide. The court found that the employer's conduct and the resulting injury satisfied all the requirements for a claim of intentional infliction of emotional distress. *But see* Wornick Co. v. Casas, 856 S.W.2d 732 (Tex. 1993) (firing employee in front of co-workers and escorting her off the premises with a security guard was not outrageous).

6. A second generalization is that an employer may terminate employment at will for a good reason, bad reason, or no reason at all, as long as the employer does not have an illegal reason such as race discrimination. In theory, a lawful but "outrageous" reason should not be the basis for the tort of outrage if the courts are to preserve the employment at will doctrine. *Cf.* Texas Farm Bur. Mut. Ins. Cos. v. Sears, 84 S.W.3d 604 (Tex. 2002) (preservation of employment at will doctrine requires dismissing plaintiff's claim of discharge as a result of employer's negligent investigation). However, as will be seen in Chapter 8, the employment at will doctrine is not impregnable. Moreover, it does appear that an outrageous reason for terminating an employee may predispose a judge or jury toward finding

employer methods outrageous. *See, e.g.*, Agis v. Howard Johnson Co., 355 N.E.2d 315 (Mass. 1976) (employer announced that until he determined identity of thief, he would fire employees in alphabetical order, starting with "A").

7. A third generalization is that outrage claims are frequently based in part on conduct that constitutes some other type of tort or statutory violation. In *GTE Southwest*, for example, the employees might also have alleged assault. In the materials that follow, we consider a variety of other torts that are frequently associated with claims of outrage, including sexual harassment, false imprisonment, invasion of privacy, and retaliation. The fact that conduct is tortious does not necessarily mean that it is outrageous. Southwestern Bell Mobile Sys., Inc. v. Franco, 971 S.W.2d 52, 54-55 (Tex. 1998). However, the existence of an independent tort tends to lend support to a conclusion that the actor's behavior was outrageous. Outrage claims are also frequently associated with unlawful discrimination, although discrimination in itself is not "outrageous." *See* Wilson v. Monarch Paper Co., 939 F.2d 1138 (5th Cir. 1991).

The fact that an employer's allegedly outrageous conduct also constituted some other tort might cut both ways in some jurisdictions. Not long after *GTE Southwest*, the Texas Supreme Court held that outrage is a "gap-filling" tort designed for special situations in which no other tort remedy is available. If the conduct in question constitutes an assault, battery, defamation or other intentional tort, the outrage tort is superseded by the more specific tort. *Creditwatch, Inc. v. Jackson,* 157 S.W.3d 814 (Tex. 2005)

8. Employees subject to collective bargaining agreements can challenge disciplinary action, discharge or other ill treatment through a contractual grievance and arbitration process. However, some tort claims are preempted by the federal law of collective bargaining. Preemption depends on whether resolution of a claim requires interpretation and application of the collective bargaining agreement. For example, if the propriety of an employer's action depends on the agreement, a court will likely hold that the claim is preempted. *Compare* Humble v. Boeing Co., 305 F.3d 1004 (9th Cir. 2002) (claim of outrageous job assignments was preempted, because collective bargaining agreement addressed propriety of job assignments), *with* Cramer v. Consol. Freightways, Inc., 255 F.3d 683 (9th Cir. 2001) (claim based on employer's secret observation of employees in restrooms not preempted, because it did not implicate collective bargaining agreement).

Intentional Infliction of Emotional Distress and Workers' Compensation

Lawmakers did not have cases such as *GTE Southwest* in mind when they adopted workers' compensation laws assuring benefits for victims of work-related accidents and diseases without regard to fault. In general, workers' compensation laws bar most employee tort claims based on work-related accidents, repetitive stress, or occupational disease, Thus, employers frequently assert the workers' compensation exclusive remedy defense against claims of intentional infliction of emotional distress. *See, e.g.*, Gibbs v. Am. Air., Inc., 87 Cal. Rptr. 2d 554 (Cal. App. 1999); Webster v. Dodson, 522 S.E.2d 487 (Ga. App. 1999); Helland v. Kurtis A. Froedtert Mem. Lutheran Hosp., 601 N.W.2d 318 (Wis. 1999).

As *GTE Southwest* illustrates, however, the exclusive remedy defense is not absolute. It is subject to a number of exceptions, depending on the facts and local variations in the law. Most importantly, workers' compensation laws usually allow an injured employee to sue his employer for the employer's own *intentional* tort. The intentional tort of a fellow *employee*, such as the supervisor in *GTE*, is not necessarily the *intentional* tort of the employer, even if *respondeat superior* would have imputed liability to the employer for the fellow employee's negligence. As discussed earlier, employees' intentional torts — particularly physical torts such as assault — are generally not within the scope of employment for *respondeat superior* purposes unless the use of force is part of the job or the employer authorized or ratified the intentional tort. If the employer was merely negligent in its lack of oversight of a supervisor tortfeasor, the employer's fault would still be based on mere negligence, not intent. *But see* Hart v. Nat'l Mortgage & Land Co., 235 Cal. Rptr. 68 (Cal. App. 1987) (employer knew of supervisor's actions and ratified these actions by failing to discipline the supervisor).

A manager might exercise so much control or authority over an employer's business that a court views him as the employer's "alter ego" (or in some jurisdictions, a "vice principal") as to actions in furtherance of the employer's business. If so, his intent is the intent of the employer. In a section omitted from the above *GTE* excerpts, the court found that Shields's position at GTE made him a "vice principal under Texas law, so that his intentional tort was the intentional tort of GTE. 998 S.W.2d at 618; *see also* Gunderson v. Harrington, 632 N.W.2d 695 (Minn. 2001) (owner of employer was employer's alter ego for purposes of workers' compensation law); Nelson v. Winnebago Indus., Inc., 619 N.W.2d 385 (Iowa 2000) (supervisor who assaulted and killed employee was not "alter ego" of employer, and therefore workers' compensation law barred wrongful death claim).

An employee might also avoid the exclusive remedy defense by showing that an intentional tort was not an "accident" arising out of and in the course of employment. *See, e.g.*, Toothman v. Hardee's Food Sys., Inc., 710 N.E.2d 880 (Ill. App. 1999) (employer's strip search of employee was not an "accident"); Archer v. Farmer Bros. Co., 70 P.3d 495 (Colo. App. 2002) (employee did not suffer distress in course of employment, because he was on sick leave when supervisor caused distress by visiting him at bedside to tell him he was fired). Of course, if the tort did not arise out of or occur in the course of employment, it may be difficult to find a basis for imputing an act of an individual tortfeasor to the employer.

A third exception to the exclusive remedy defense relates to the nature of the injury. In *GTE*, the court held that workers' compensation law did not bar employees' tort claims because their purely psychic injuries were not compensable under Texas workers' compensation law. *See also* Nassa v. Hook-SupeRx, Inc., 790 A.2d 368 (R.I. 2002) (injury to reputation not compensable, and therefore exclusive remedy defense did not bar defamation action). However, depending on local workers' compensation law and the circumstances and symptoms of an employee's distress, a tort claim might in fact be compensable. Moreover, the exclusive remedy defense is a bar in some states regardless of whether the underlying injury is compensable, if no other exceptions apply. *See, e.g.*, Lewis v. Northside Hosp., Inc., 599 S.E.2d 267 (Ga. App. 2004).

c. Discriminatory Harassment

The employer in *GTE* was liable for its supervisor's abusive supervision only because his conduct was "outrageous." The tort rule limiting liability to "outrageous" conduct causing severe emotional distress licenses a great deal of very bad conduct that is too typical to be "outrageous" and not harmful enough to cause *severe* emotional distress—even if it makes work especially difficult or intolerable for the victim. The unavailability of compensatory damages is not the only problem. If an employer is not liable for misbehavior of managers, supervisors or fellow employees, it also has limited incentives for preventing misbehavior. Abuse or the condonation of abuse might be bad for morale, but it is mainly bad for the morale of the victims, not the workforce as a whole. Moreover, upper management might willingly participate in or tolerate abusive conduct that is motivated by a pervasive culture of bias against a minority.

If abusive conduct is not sufficiently outrageous or emotionally damaging to be tortious, discrimination law might provide a better remedy, provided the abuse is "because of" a protected characteristic like race, religion, sex or national origin, and provided a supervisor's or fellow employee's misconduct can be attributed or imputed to the employer. If abusive conduct is discrimination, the standard for unlawful abuse is not whether it is "outrageous" or causes severe emotional injury, it is whether the abuse materially affected the *terms and conditions* of employment.

It did not take long after the enactment of Title VII for courts to recognize that hostile or offensive "harassment" can be an employer's act of discrimination *provided* the harassment was by a supervisor or other agent of the employer and motivated by discriminatory bigotry or animus. *See, e.g.*, Rogers v. EEOC, 454 F.2d 234 (5th Cir. 1971) (national origin harassment). Of course, much harassment is by fellow employees whose offensive conduct is not in the scope of duty and not naturally imputed to the employer. Early court decisions embraced the common law approach for *intentional* torts in this situation. An employee's intentional torts, especially if motivated by a personal dispute, are generally outside the scope of employment and not imputed to the employer. RESTATEMENT (SECOND) OF TORTS (1965) § 317. A supervisor's intentional harassment of a subordinate might be imputed to the employer if the harassment was within the scope of the supervisor's duties of supervision and management of personnel. A non-supervisory employee, however, is not acting in the scope of his duties when he intentionally harasses another employee. Thus, employer liability for a non-supervisor's intentional and discriminatory harassment of another employee depends on proof of the employer's own negligence, such as failing to prevent harassment of which it was aware. *See* Dickerson v. U.S. Steel Corp., 439 F. Supp. 55, 75 (E. D. Penn. 1977).

"Sexual" harassment has been a special problem for the law of discrimination because a sexual harasser's motivation might be quite different from the animus typical of racial or other discriminatory harassment. Some sexual harassers are motivated not by hatred or low regard for their victims but by sexual attraction. Arguably, a male supervisor who annoys a particular female employee by his unwelcome sexual advances is not "discriminating" against women as a class. Moreover, this type of sexual harasser is not "supervising" or acting in the scope of his duties. Instead, he is acting for a purely personal motivation. The fact that his sexual advances occurred at work and during work time is simply a coincidence. This sort of reasoning led many courts in early cases to reject or question whether unwelcome sexual advances could be treated as the employer's sex discrimination. *See, e.g.*, Corne v. Bausch & Lomb, Inc., 390 F. Supp. 161 (D. Ariz. 1975), *vacated*, 562 F.2d 55 (9th Cir. 1977); Miller v. Bank of Am., 418 F. Supp. 233 (N.D. Cal. 1976), *rev'd*, 600 F.2d 211 (9th Cir. 1979).

The first courts to recognize sexual harassment as a form of sex discrimination relied on the "quid pro quo" theory, in which a plaintiff alleges that submission to a supervisor's sexual advances was a "condition of employment," and that the supervisor terminated her from employment or denied job benefits because she resisted. *See, e.g.*, Tomkins v. Public Serv. Elec. & Gas Co., 568 F.2d 1044 (3d Cir. 1977); Barnes v. Costle, 561 F.2d 983 (D.C. Cir. 1977). The discriminatory character of the supervisor's actions was obvious to most courts in these early cases, because the "condition" of sexual submission was not one the supervisor would likely have required of a male, and because the supervisor's action had direct economic impact on the victim. An obvious shortcoming of the quid pro quo theory was that sexual advances standing alone, without any job-related "bargaining" or retribution, were not "discriminatory" no matter how offensive. Heelan v. Johns-Manville Corp., 451 F. Supp. 1382 (D. Colo. 1978).

An alternative but initially much more controversial theory was "offensive atmosphere harassment" or "hostile environment." A plaintiff relying on this theory does not allege that any job benefit was conditioned on sexual submission. Instead, she alleges that conduct motivated by sexual attraction is "because of sex," and that sexual advances can create a hostile working environment just as disturbing as harassment motivated by class-based hatred. The Supreme Court endorsed this hostile environment theory in Meritor Savings Bank v. Vinson, 477 U.S. 57 (1986). In the same case, the Court also rejected the employer's argument that Title VII reaches only discriminatory actions causing economic loss, such as termination or demotion causing a loss of pay. Even actions causing only psychological harm can constitute unlawful discrimination under the act. Congress reinforced this conclusion in 1991 when it amended the act to permit the recovery of compensatory damages, including damages for emotional distress, and punitive damages.

The Court's *Meritor Savings Bank* decision left a number of important issues unresolved, including the rules for holding an employer liable for one employee's sexual harassment of another. The Court declined to decide whether the employer in *Meritor Savings Bank* was liable for the supervisor's conduct if sexual harassment had in fact occurred. It doubted whether a rule of absolute liability for employers would be appropriate even if the harasser was a supervisor, but otherwise it left this issue to be addressed in some future case.

BURLINGTON INDUSTRIES, INC. v. ELLERTH

524 U.S. 742 (1998)

Justice KENNEDY delivered the opinion of the Court.

We decide whether, under Title VII of the Civil Rights Act of 1964, 78 Stat. 253, as amended, 42 U.S.C. § 2000e et seq., an employee who refuses the unwelcome and threatening sexual advances of a supervisor, yet suffers no adverse, tangible job consequences, can recover against the employer without showing the employer is negligent or otherwise at fault for the supervisor's actions.

I

Summary judgment was granted for the employer, so we must take the facts alleged by the employee to be true. . . . The employer is Burlington Industries, the petitioner. The employee is Kimberly Ellerth, the respondent. From March 1993 until May 1994, Ellerth worked as a salesperson in one of Burlington's divisions in Chicago, Illinois. During her employment, she alleges, she was subjected to constant sexual harassment by her supervisor, one Ted Slowik.

In the hierarchy of Burlington's management structure, Slowik was a mid-level manager. Burlington has eight divisions, employing more than 22,000 people in some 50 plants around the United States. Slowik was a vice president in one of five business units within one of the divisions. He had authority to make hiring and promotion decisions subject to the approval of his supervisor, who signed the paperwork. According to Slowik's supervisor, his position was "not considered an upper-level management position," and he was "not amongst the decision-making or policy-making hierarchy." Slowik was not Ellerth's immediate supervisor. Ellerth worked in a two-person office in Chicago, and she answered to her office colleague, who in turn answered to Slowik in New York.

Against a background of repeated boorish and offensive remarks and gestures which Slowik allegedly made, Ellerth places particular emphasis on three alleged incidents where Slowik's comments could be construed as threats to deny her tangible job benefits. In the summer of 1993, while on a business trip, Slowik invited Ellerth to the hotel lounge, an invitation Ellerth felt compelled to accept because Slowik was her boss. When Ellerth gave no encouragement to remarks Slowik made about her breasts, he told her to "loosen up" and warned, "you know, Kim, I could make your life very hard or very easy at Burlington."

In March 1994, when Ellerth was being considered for a promotion, Slowik expressed reservations during the promotion interview because she was not "loose enough." The comment was followed by his reaching over and rubbing her knee. Ellerth did receive the promotion; but when Slowik called to announce it, he told Ellerth, "you're gonna be out there with men who work in factories, and they certainly like women with pretty butts/legs."

In May 1994, Ellerth called Slowik, asking permission to insert a customer's logo into a fabric sample. Slowik responded, "I don't have time for you right now, Kim . . . — unless you want to tell me what you're wearing." Ellerth told Slowik she had to go and ended the call. A day or two later, Ellerth called Slowik to ask permission again. This time he denied her request, but added something along the lines of, "are you wearing shorter skirts yet, Kim, because it would make your job a whole heck of a lot easier."

A short time later, Ellerth's immediate supervisor cautioned her about returning telephone calls to customers in a prompt fashion. In response, Ellerth quit. She faxed a letter giving reasons unrelated to the alleged sexual harassment we have described. About three weeks later, however, she sent a letter explaining she quit because of Slowik's behavior.

During her tenure at Burlington, Ellerth did not inform anyone in authority about Slowik's conduct, despite knowing Burlington had a policy against sexual harassment. In fact, she chose not to inform her immediate supervisor (not Slowik) because "it would be his duty as my supervisor to report any incidents of sexual harassment." On one occasion, she told Slowik a comment he made was inappropriate.

In October 1994, after receiving a right-to-sue letter from the Equal Employment Opportunity Commission (EEOC), Ellerth filed suit in the United States District Court for the Northern District of Illinois, alleging Burlington engaged in sexual harassment and forced her constructive discharge, in violation of Title VII. The District Court granted summary judgment to Burlington. . . . The Court of Appeals en banc reversed in a decision which produced eight separate opinions and no consensus for a controlling rationale. . . . The disagreement revealed in the careful opinions of the judges of the Court of Appeals reflects the fact that Congress has left it to the courts to determine controlling agency law principles in a new and difficult area of federal law. We granted certiorari to assist in defining the relevant standards of employer liability.

II

At the outset, we assume an important proposition yet to be established before a trier of fact. . . . The premise is: A trier of fact could find in Slowik's remarks numerous threats to retaliate against Ellerth if she denied some sexual liberties. The threats, however, were not carried out or fulfilled. Cases based on threats which are carried out are referred to often as quid pro quo cases, as distinct from bothersome attentions or sexual remarks that are sufficiently severe or pervasive to create a hostile work environment. The terms quid pro quo and hostile work environment are helpful, perhaps, in making a rough demarcation between cases in which threats are carried out and those where they are not or are absent altogether, but beyond this are of limited utility.

"Quid pro quo" and "hostile work environment" do not appear in the statutory text. The terms appeared first in the academic literature, *see* C. MacKinnon, Sexual Harassment of Working Women (1979); . . . and were mentioned in this Court's decision in Meritor Savings Bank, FSB v. Vinson, 477 U.S. 57 (1986). . . .

In *Meritor*, . . . [w]e distinguished between quid pro quo claims and hostile environment claims, and said both were cognizable under Title VII, though the latter requires harassment that is severe or pervasive. The principal significance of the distinction is to instruct that Title VII is violated by either explicit or constructive alterations in the terms or conditions of employment and to explain the latter must be severe or pervasive. The distinction was not discussed for its bearing upon an employer's liability for an employee's discrimination. On this question *Meritor* held, with no further specifics, that agency principles controlled.

Nevertheless, as use of the terms grew in the wake of *Meritor*, they acquired their own significance. The standard of employer responsibility turned on which type of harassment occurred. If the plaintiff established a quid pro quo claim, the Courts of Appeals held, the employer was subject to vicarious liability. [citations omitted]. The rule encouraged Title VII plaintiffs to state their claims as quid pro quo claims, which in turn put expansive pressure on the definition. The equivalence of the quid pro quo label and vicarious liability is illustrated by this case. The question presented on certiorari is whether Ellerth can state a claim of quid pro quo harassment, but the issue of real concern to the parties is whether Burlington has vicarious liability for Slowik's alleged misconduct, rather than liability limited to its own negligence. . . .

When a plaintiff proves that a tangible employment action resulted from a refusal to submit to a supervisor's sexual demands, he or she establishes that the employment decision itself constitutes a change in the terms and conditions of employment that is actionable under Title VII. For any sexual harassment preceding the employment decision to be actionable, however, the conduct must be severe or pervasive. Because Ellerth's claim involves only unfulfilled threats, it should be categorized as a hostile work environment claim which requires a showing of severe or pervasive conduct. For purposes of this case, we accept the District Court's finding that the alleged conduct was severe or pervasive. The case before us involves numerous alleged threats, and we express no opinion as to whether a single unfulfilled threat is sufficient to constitute discrimination in the terms or conditions of employment.

When we assume discrimination can be proved, however, the factors we discuss below, and not the categories quid pro quo and hostile work environment, will be controlling on the issue of vicarious liability.

III

We must decide, then, whether an employer has vicarious liability when a supervisor creates a hostile work environment by making explicit threats to alter a subordinate's terms or conditions of employment, based on sex, but does not fulfill the threat.

We turn to principles of agency law, for the term "employer" is defined under Title VII to include "agents." 42 U.S.C. § 2000e(b). In express terms, Congress has directed federal courts to interpret Title VII based on agency principles. Given such an explicit instruction, we conclude a uniform and predictable standard must be established as a matter of federal law. We rely "on the general common law of agency, rather than on the law of any particular State, to give meaning to these terms." Community for Creative Non-Violence v. Reid, 490 U.S. 730, 740 (1989). . . . As *Meritor* acknowledged, the Restatement (Second) of Agency (1957) (hereinafter Restatement) is a useful beginning point for a discussion of general agency principles. 477 U.S., at 72. . . .

A

Section 219(1) of the Restatement sets out a central principle of agency law: "A master is subject to liability for the torts of his servants committed while acting in the scope of their employment."

An employer may be liable for both negligent and intentional torts committed by an employee within the scope of his or her employment. Sexual harassment under Title VII presupposes intentional conduct. While early decisions absolved employers of liability for the intentional torts of their employees, the law now imposes liability where the employee's "purpose, however misguided, is wholly or in part to further the master's business." W. Keeton, D. Dobbs, R. Keeton, & D.

Owen, Prosser and Keeton on Law of Torts § 70, p. 505 (5th ed. 1984) (hereinafter Prosser and Keeton on Torts). In applying scope of employment principles to intentional torts, however, it is accepted that "it is less likely that a willful tort will properly be held to be in the course of employment and that the liability of the master for such torts will naturally be more limited." F. Mechem, Outlines of the Law of Agency § 394, p. 266 (P. Mechem 4th ed. 1952). The Restatement defines conduct, including an intentional tort, to be within the scope of employment when "actuated, at least in part, by a purpose to serve the [employer]," even if it is forbidden by the employer. Restatement §§ 228(1)(c), 230. For example, when a salesperson lies to a customer to make a sale, the tortious conduct is within the scope of employment because it benefits the employer by increasing sales, even though it may violate the employer's policies. *See* Prosser and Keeton on Torts § 70, at 505-506.

As Courts of Appeals have recognized, a supervisor acting out of gender based animus or a desire to fulfill sexual urges may not be actuated by a purpose to serve the employer. . . . The harassing supervisor often acts for personal motives, motives unrelated and even antithetical to the objectives of the employer. . . . There are instances, of course, where a supervisor engages in unlawful discrimination with the purpose, mistaken or otherwise, to serve the employer. E.g., Sims v. Montgomery County Comm'n, 766 F. Supp. 1052, 1075 (M.D. Ala. 1990) (supervisor acting in scope of employment where employer has a policy of discouraging women from seeking advancement and "sexual harassment was simply a way of furthering that policy"). . . .

The general rule is that sexual harassment by a supervisor is not conduct within the scope of employment.

B

Scope of employment does not define the only basis for employer liability under agency principles. In limited circumstances, agency principles impose liability on employers even where employees commit torts outside the scope of employment. The principles are set forth in the much-cited § 219(2) of the Restatement:

> (2) A master is not subject to liability for the torts of his servants acting outside the scope of their employment, unless:
>
> (a) the master intended the conduct or the consequences, or (b) the master was negligent or reckless, or
>
> (c) the conduct violated a non-delegable duty of the master, or
>
> (d) the servant purported to act or to speak on behalf of the principal and there was reliance upon apparent authority, or he was aided in accomplishing the tort by the existence of the agency relation.

Subsection (a) addresses direct liability, where the employer acts with tortious intent, and indirect liability, where the agent's high rank in the company makes him or her the employer's alter ego. None of the parties contend Slowik's rank imputes liability under this principle. There is no contention, furthermore, that a nondelegable duty is involved. *See* § 219(2)(c). So, for our purposes here, subsections (a) and (c) can be put aside.

Subsections (b) and (d) are possible grounds for imposing employer liability on account of a supervisor's acts and must be considered. Under subsection (b), an employer is liable when the tort is attributable to the employer's own negligence. § 219(2)(b). Thus, although a supervisor's sexual harassment is outside the scope of employment because the conduct was for personal motives, an employer can be liable, nonetheless, where its own negligence is a cause of the harassment. An employer is negligent with respect to sexual harassment if it knew or should have known about the conduct and failed to stop it. Negligence sets a minimum standard for employer liability under Title VII; but Ellerth seeks to invoke the more stringent standard of vicarious liability.

Section 219(2)(d) concerns vicarious liability for intentional torts committed by an employee when the employee uses apparent authority (the apparent authority standard), or when the employee "was aided in accomplishing the tort by the existence of the agency relation" (the aided in the agency relation standard). . . .

C

As a general rule, apparent authority is relevant where the agent purports to exercise a power which he or she does not have, as distinct from where the agent threatens to misuse actual power. . . . In the usual case, a supervisor's harassment involves misuse of actual power, not the false impression of its existence. Apparent authority analysis therefore is inappropriate in this context. If, in the unusual case, it is alleged there is a false impression that the actor was a supervisor, when he in fact was not, the victim's mistaken conclusion must be a reasonable one. Restatement § 8, Comment c ("Apparent authority exists only to the extent it is reasonable for the third person dealing with the agent to believe that the agent is authorized"). When a party seeks to impose vicarious liability based on an agent's misuse of delegated authority, the Restatement's aided in the agency relation rule, rather than the apparent authority rule, appears to be the appropriate form of analysis.

D

We turn to the aided in the agency relation standard. In a sense, most workplace tortfeasors are aided in accomplishing their tortious objective by the existence of the agency relation: Proximity and regular contact may afford a captive pool of potential victims. Were this to satisfy the aided in the agency relation standard, an employer would be subject to vicarious liability not only for all supervisor harassment, but also for all co-worker harassment, a result enforced by neither the EEOC nor any court of appeals to have considered the issue. . . . The aided in the agency relation standard, therefore, requires the existence of something more than the employment relation itself.

At the outset, we can identify a class of cases where, beyond question, more than the mere existence of the employment relation aids in commission of the harassment: when a supervisor takes a tangible employment action against the subordinate. . . . A tangible employment action constitutes a significant change in employment status, such as hiring, firing, failing to promote, reassignment with significantly different responsibilities, or a decision causing a significant change in benefits. . . .

When a supervisor makes a tangible employment decision, there is assurance the injury could not have been inflicted absent the agency relation. A tangible employment action in most cases inflicts direct economic harm. As a general proposition, only a supervisor, or other person acting with the authority of the company, can cause this sort of injury. A co-worker can break a co-worker's arm as easily as a supervisor, and anyone who has regular contact with an employee can inflict psychological injuries by his or her offensive conduct. . . . But one co-worker (absent some elaborate scheme) cannot dock another's pay, nor can one co-worker demote another. Tangible employment actions fall within the special province of the supervisor. The supervisor has been empowered by the company as a distinct class of agent to make economic decisions affecting other employees under his or her control.

Tangible employment actions are the means by which the supervisor brings the official power of the enterprise to bear on subordinates. A tangible employment decision requires an official act of the enterprise, a company act. The decision in most cases is documented in official company records, and may be subject to review by higher level supervisors. The supervisor often must obtain the imprimatur of the enterprise and use its internal processes. For these reasons, a tangible employment action taken by the supervisor becomes for Title VII purposes the act of the employer. Whatever the exact contours of the aided in the agency relation standard, its requirements will always be met when a supervisor takes a tangible employment action against a subordinate. In that instance, it would be implausible to interpret agency principles to allow an employer to escape liability, as *Meritor* itself appeared to acknowledge.

Whether the agency relation aids in commission of supervisor harassment which does not culminate in a tangible employment action is less obvious. Application of the standard is made difficult by its malleable terminology, which can be read to either expand or limit liability in the context of supervisor harassment. On the one hand, a supervisor's power and authority invests his or her harassing conduct with a particular threatening character, and in this sense, a supervisor always is aided by the agency relation. . . . On the other hand, there are acts of harassment a supervisor might commit which might be the same acts a coemployee would commit, and there may be some circumstances where the supervisor's status makes little difference. . . .

Although *Meritor* suggested the limitation on employer liability stemmed from agency principles, the Court acknowledged other considerations might be relevant as well. *See* 477 U.S., at 72 ("common-law principles may not be transferable in all their particulars to Title VII"). For example, Title VII is designed to encourage the creation of anti-harassment policies and effective grievance mechanisms. Were employer liability to depend in part on an employer's effort to create such procedures, it would effect Congress' intention to promote conciliation rather than litigation in the Title VII context. . . . To the extent limiting employer liability could encourage employees to report harassing conduct before it becomes severe or pervasive, it would also serve Title VII's deterrent purpose. . . . As we have observed, Title VII borrows from tort law the avoidable consequences doctrine, *see* Ford Motor Co. v. EEOC, 458 U.S. 219, 232, n.15 (1982), and the considerations which animate that doctrine would also support the limitation of employer liability in certain circumstances.

In order to accommodate the agency principles of vicarious liability for harm caused by misuse of supervisory authority, as well as Title VII's equally basic policies of encouraging forethought by employers and saving action by objecting employees, we adopt the following holding in this case and in Faragher v. Boca Raton, 524 U.S. 775 (1998), also decided today. An employer is subject to vicarious liability to a victimized employee for an actionable hostile environment created by a supervisor with immediate (or successively higher) authority over the employee. When no tangible employment action is taken, a defending employer may raise an affirmative defense to liability or damages, subject to proof by a preponderance of the evidence, *see* Fed. Rule Civ. Proc. 8(c). The defense comprises two necessary elements: (a) that the employer exercised reasonable care to prevent and correct promptly any sexually harassing behavior, and (b) that the plaintiff employee unreasonably failed to take advantage of any preventive or corrective opportunities provided by the employer or to avoid harm otherwise. While proof that an employer had promulgated an anti-harassment policy with complaint procedure is not necessary in every instance as a matter of law, the need for a stated policy suitable to the employment circumstances may appropriately be addressed in any case when litigating the first element of the defense. And while proof that an employee failed to fulfill the corresponding obligation of reasonable care to avoid harm is not limited to showing any unreasonable failure to use any complaint procedure provided by the employer, a demonstration of such failure will normally suffice to satisfy the employer's burden under the second element of the defense. No affirmative defense is available, however, when the supervisor's harassment culminates in a tangible employment action, such as discharge, demotion, or undesirable reassignment.

IV

Relying on existing case law which held out the promise of vicarious liability for all quid pro quo claims, Ellerth focused all her attention in the Court of Appeals on proving her claim fit within that category. Given our explanation that the labels quid pro quo and hostile work environment are not controlling for purposes of establishing employer liability, Ellerth should have an adequate opportunity to prove she has a claim for which Burlington is liable.

Although Ellerth has not alleged she suffered a tangible employment action at the hands of Slowik, which would deprive Burlington of the availability of the affirmative defense, this is not dispositive. In light of our decision, Burlington is still subject to vicarious liability for Slowik's activity, but Burlington should have an opportunity to assert and prove the affirmative defense to liability.

For these reasons, we will affirm the judgment of the Court of Appeals, reversing the grant of summary judgment against Ellerth. On remand, the District Court will have the opportunity to decide whether it would be appropriate to allow Ellerth to amend her pleading or supplement her discovery.

NOTES AND QUESTIONS

1. The motivation for the sexual harassment described in *Burlington Industries* was arguably different from the sort of bigotry typical of race, national origin or religious harassment. Nevertheless, *Burlington Industries* is now the

roadmap for employer liability for harassment in general. *See, e.g.*, Tademy v. Union Pacific Corp., 614 F.3d 1132 (10th Cir. 2008) (racial harassment).

2. Eight years after *Burlington Industries*, in 2006, the American Law Institute issued a new Restatement (Third) of Agency. Section 7.05 discards the "aided in accomplishing" rule in favor of a more limited rule of vicarious liability. Under the revised rule, a principal may be liable for an agent's actions harming a third party if the principal has a "special relationship" with the third party. But this rule requires proof of the principal's failure to exercise reasonable care, i.e., its "negligence," in failing to protect the third party from the agent's tort.

3. *Burlington Industries* envisions two types of cases in which employers can be liable for employees' sexual harassment of other employees: (1) cases involving a "tangible employment action" against an employee; and (2) "hostile environment" without a tangible employment action. For a tangible employment action, the employee's usual remedy will include back pay and, where appropriate, reinstatement. For a hostile environment claim, the usual remedy will consist mainly of emotional distress damages. Each type of claim, however, has a different set of rules for holding employers liable for harassers' actions.

4. The rule of employer liability for a tangible employment action is relatively simple. If a "supervisor" takes a tangible employment action against an employee in the course of harassment, such retaliating against the employee for resisting advances, or to demonstrate power, the employer is *strictly* liable for the action and the harassment. At best, employer effort to prevent harassment will protect it from punitive damages. *See* Kolstad v. Am. Dental Ass'n, 527 U.S. 526 (1999) (good faith defense to Title VII punitive damages).

5. The rules of employer liability in a hostile environment case without a tangible adverse action are closer to the rules of fault-based tort law. If the employee has not suffered an adverse, tangible job action, such as discharge, demotion, or denial of promotion, the employer might still be liable for failing to prevent harassment by a *supervisor* even if the supervisor acted for "personal" motivations. As the Court observed in a companion case decided the same day, Faragher v. Boca Raton, 524 U.S. 775 (1998),

> It is by now well recognized that hostile environment sexual harassment by supervisors (and, for that matter, coemployees) is a persistent problem in the workplace. . . . An employer can, in a general sense, reasonably anticipate the possibility of such conduct occurring in its workplace, and one might justify the assignment of the burden of the untoward behavior to the employer as one of the costs of doing business, to be charged to the enterprise rather than the victim.

Id. at 797-798. Thus, an employer is presumptively at fault for hostile atmosphere harassment by a supervisor. However, this liability is qualified: The employer can assert the affirmative defense described in *Burlington Industries*.

6. In *Burlington Industries*, the Court described an employer's affirmative defense for a supervisor's hostile environment harassment in two parts: "[T]he employer exercised reasonable care to prevent and correct promptly any sexually harassing behavior, *and* . . . the plaintiff employee unreasonably failed to take advantage of any preventive or corrective opportunities provided by the employer

or to avoid harm otherwise." (emphasis added).

Note that this two part test is stated in the conjunctive. The employer remains liable for the supervisor's harassment unless it proves the employee acted unreasonably by failing to use available remedies. Of course, the employer must also prove it created and made internal remedies available to the employee. The employee cannot be faulted if there was no internal remedy, or if circumstances created by the employer deterred the employee from using the remedy (e.g., because the employer required the employee to file a grievance with the harasser). *See* Wyatt v. Hunt Plywood Co., 297 F.3d 405, 409 (5th Cir. 2002) ("the employer is vicariously liable unless the employer can establish both prongs of the conjunctive *Ellerth/Faragher* affirmative defense"); Indest v. Freeman Decorating, Inc., 168 F.3d 795, 797 (5th Cir. 1999) (Weiner, dissenting) ("Indest quickly reported Arnaudet's behavior, thereby defeating the only affirmative defense potentially available"). As a practical matter, this might mean an employer cannot avoid vicarious liability for a single instance or brief period of a supervisor's harassment if the employee complained reasonably and promptly. However, such an employee might have a difficult time persuading a court that one or a few incidents, unless extreme, caused much injury if the employer responded quickly and effectively prevented further harassment.

7. Assuming the employee unreasonably failed to report harassment, what constitutes proof of the second prong of the defense—that "the employer exercised reasonable care to prevent and correct promptly any sexually harassing behavior"? Merely proving the existence of an anti-harassment policy and reporting system might not be enough. The employer's track record of responding to complaints can be important to whether it was reasonable for the employee to fail to make a timely internal complaint. Moreover, if the employee did act reasonably by making an internal complaint, the employer will still be liable not only for harm she suffered before the complaint, but also for any subsequent harm she suffered because the employer failed to take reasonable steps to prevent further harassment.

8. What do you make of Ellerth's statement that she decided not to report Slowick's conduct to her direct supervisor because "it would be his duty as my supervisor to report any incidents of sexual harassment"? It is not unusual for an employee to procrastinate in filing a formal internal charge against a supervisor or a fellow employee. Is it "unreasonable"? If an employee tells one supervisor about another supervisor's harassment, but insists she does not want to make a formal complaint, what should the first supervisor do?

9. Does *Burlington Industries* require the establishment of formal sexual harassment policies and procedures that are too burdensome for a small employer? First, recall that Title VII applies only to employers with more than 15 employees. Second, the companion *Faragher* case suggested that expectations would vary depending on the size and sophistication of the employer. In commenting on the inadequacy of the City of Boca Raton's sexual harassment policy, the Court stated:

> Unlike the employer of a small work force, who might expect that sufficient care to prevent tortious behavior could be exercised informally, those responsible for city operations could not reasonably have thought that precautions against hostile environments in any one of many departments in far-flung locations could be effective without communicating some formal

policy against harassment, with a sensible complaint procedure.

524 U.S. at 808.

10. The employer is *vicariously* liable for hostile atmosphere harassment under the rules described in the preceding notes *only* if the harasser was a "supervisor," but definitions of "supervisor" vary, and most of the definitions are sufficiently vague to leave plenty of room for disagreement. In *Ellerth*, the Court offered no suggestions for determining who qualifies as a supervisor for purposes of harassment law. The Court finally addressed the problem in *Vance v. Ball State University*, 570 U.S. 421 (2013). holding that a person qualifies as a supervisor "when the employer has empowered that employee to take tangible employment actions against the victim, i.e., to effect a 'significant change in employment status, such as hiring, firing, failing to promote, reassignment with significantly different responsibilities, or a decision causing a significant change in benefits.'" *Id.* at 431 (*quoting Ellerth*, 524 U.S. at 761). This definition omits many persons who have the power to make work difficult for another employee. A person who assigns an employee's tasks, oversees and directs the employee's work, evaluates the employee's performance, and is regarded by other employees as a leader and example might not be a "supervisor" for purposes of harassment law.

11. *Burlington Industries* involved harassment by a supervisor or a person of "immediate (or successively higher) authority over" the claimant. What if the actor is higher than a supervisor, perhaps the owner or chief executive officer of the employer entity? According to the Court, there is a "class of an employer organization's officials who may be treated as the organization's proxy," such as owners, partners, and corporate officials. 524 U.S. at 789. In the case of hostile atmosphere harassment by these "proxies" or alter egos, it appears that the employer is strictly liable and without the availability of an affirmative defense. Ackel v. National Comm'ns, Inc., 339 F.3d 376, 383-384 (5th Cir. 2003).

12. At the other end of the spectrum are harassers who are just fellow employees. An employer is vicariously liable for harassment by such non-supervisors. Instead, employer liability is based on negligence according to rules analogous to the common law doctrine of negligent supervision. Proving negligence is likely to depend on the same types of facts that might relate to the employer's affirmative defense against liability for a supervisor's harassment. Did the employer have a well-known policy? Did it provide an effective procedure for complaints, investigation, and remedies? Did the claimant invoke the procedure? As a practical matter, this means the claimant bears the burden of proving employer negligence if the harasser is a fellow employee, but the employer bears the burden of disproving negligence if the harasser is a supervisor.

13. If harassment is one of the "costs of doing business, to be charged to the enterprise rather than the victim," as the Court stated in *Faragher*, should an employer also be liable for harassment by customers or other visitors to the employer's workplace? *See* Lockard v. Pizza Hut, Inc., 162 F.3d 1062 (10th Cir. 1998) (yes, if employer was aware of customers' harassment and failed to take reasonable actions to prevent or remedy it).

What Is Unlawful Harassment?

Harassment is unlawful only if it is "because of" the victim's membership in a class protected by anti-discrimination law. There can be an issue whether harassment was because of unlawful discriminatory intent whenever the harassing words or conduct do not overtly or intrinsically signal bias. Offensive conduct might be for reasons other than bigotry. It might be a coincidence that the harasser and victim are of different classes. *See, e.g.*, Wyninger v. New Venture Gear, Inc., 361 F.3d 965 (7th Cir. 2004) (vulgar conduct targeting both genders was not because of sex and was not illegal sexual harassment).

Distinguishing discriminatory from nondiscriminatory harassment has been a special challenge in cases involving alleged *sexual* harassment. Harassment can be "because of sex" in many different ways. Since Title VII prohibits "reverse" discrimination, harassment is illegal even if the harasser is female and the victim is male. *See, e.g.*, Jones v. U.S. Gypsum, 81 Fair Empl. Prac. Cases 1695 (N.D. Iowa 2000). Harassment can even be illegal if harasser and the victim are of the same sex, provided the harasser acted "because of sex." Wrightson v. Pizza Hut of Am., Inc., 99 F.3d 138 (4th Cir. 1996). On the other hand, the requirement that harassment must be "because of sex" does not mean sexual harassment must be motivated by sexual attraction or misogyny to qualify as sex discrimination. Any harassment that is part of a pattern of treating men differently from women might be "because of sex." In Oncale v. Sundowner Offshore Servs., Inc., 523 U.S. 75 (1998), the Supreme Court considered a male employee's claim based on a pattern of severe harassment by other men assigned to the same oil platform. According to Oncale, on several occasions he "was forcibly subjected to sex-related, humiliating actions . . . in the presence of the rest of the crew." The harassers physically assaulted Oncale in a sexual manner, and one harasser threatened him with rape. *Id.* at 77. The Supreme Court held that the plaintiff had stated a claim under Title VII and that the employer was not entitled to summary judgment:

> [H]arassing conduct need not be motivated by sexual desire to support an inference of discrimination on the basis of sex. A trier of fact might reasonably find such discrimination, for example, if a female victim is harassed in such sex-specific and derogatory terms by another woman as to make it clear that the harasser is motivated by general hostility to the presence of women in the workplace. A same-sex harassment plaintiff may also, of course, offer direct comparative evidence about how the alleged harasser treated members of both sexes in a mixed-sex workplace. Whatever evidentiary route the plaintiff chooses to follow, he or she must always prove that the conduct at issue was not merely tinged with offensive sexual connotations, but actually constituted "discrimina[tion]... because of... sex."

Id. at 80-81.

The Court's reasoning in *Oncale* might but does not necessarily mean that Title VII prohibits harassment on the basis of sexual *orientation*, as where a male employee harasses another male employee for being homosexual. For discussion of the differing opinions and caselaw on that issue, *see* note 3 on p. 135, *supra*.

The "because of sex" requirement creates other conceptual difficulties when harassment grows out of a consensual relationship between employees. Suppose a supervisor favors his or her paramour and gives less favorable treatment to other employees. Do the disfavored employees have a viable sex discrimination claim? According to the EEOC, "Where employment opportunities or benefits are granted because of an individual's submission to the employer's sexual advances or requests for sexual favors, the employer may be held liable for unlawful sex discrimination against other persons who were qualified for but denied that employment opportunity or benefit." 29 C.F.R. § 1604.11(g); *see also* Miller v. Dep't of Corr., 115 P.3d 77 (Cal. 2005). For a different view, *see* DiCintio v. Westchester County Med. Ctr., 807 F.2d 304 (2d Cir. 1986), which held that this rule applied only when the favored employee's "submission" was involuntary. Dismissing a claim by male employees that their supervisor preferred a woman with whom he had a mutually consensual relationship, the court explained that the plaintiffs "were not prejudiced because of their status as males; rather, they were discriminated against because [the supervisor] preferred his paramour." *Id.* at 308; *see also* Thomson v. Olson, 866 F. Supp. 1267, 1272 (D.N.D. 1994), *aff'd*, 56 F.3d 69 (8th Cir. 1995) ("The proscribed differentiation under this provision must be a distinction based on a person's sex, not on his or her sexual affiliations").

Another variation on the "because of sex" problem occurs when a consensual relationship turns bad and one of the parties retaliates, harasses, or ceases favoring the other. Are the aggressor's actions "because of sex," or because of the termination of the relationship? *See* Babcock v. Frank, 729 F. Supp. 279, 287-288 (S.D.N.Y. 1990) (Title VII protection is not withdrawn merely because harassment victim and perpetrator had past consensual sexual relationship); Perks v. Town of Huntington, 251 F. Supp. 2d 1143, 1156 (E.D.N.Y. 2003) (same).

The Severity of Harassment and Its Consequences.

Another question in harassment law is how to determine whether harassment is sufficiently hostile or offensive to violate Title VII. If the plaintiff employee has suffered a "tangible" employment loss such as discharge, demotion, or the denial of promotion, the answer is clearly "yes" because the employer has taken an action that affected the employee's "compensation, terms, conditions, or privileges of employment." 42 U.S.C. § 2000e-2(a)(1). The issue is more difficult when hostile environment harassment does not result in a tangible employment action. The Supreme Court has emphasized that Title VII is not a code of "civility." Oncale v. Sundowner Offshore Servs., Inc., 523 U.S. 75 (1998). But what rules or standards will aid employers, employees, and the courts in distinguishing merely rude behavior from unlawful behavior?

The solution to this problem began to evolve in *Meritor Savings Bank.* There, the Court observed that Title VII prohibits discrimination "with respect to . . . compensation, terms, conditions, or privileges of employment."

> Of course, . . . not all workplace conduct that may be described as "harassment" affects a "term, condition, or privilege" of employment within the meaning of Title VII. . . . For sexual harassment to be actionable, it must be sufficiently *severe or pervasive*" to *alter* the conditions of [the victim's] employment and create an *abusive* working environment."

477 U.S. at 67 (emphasis added), *quoting* Rogers v. E.E.O.C., 454 F.2d 234, 238

(5th Cir. 1972).

The requirement that harassment must be severe *or* pervasive to be illegal under Title VII suggests a sliding scale. A single incident cannot be "pervasive" and thus will not constitute illegal harassment unless it is "severe." *See, e.g.*, Jones v. U.S. Gypsum, 81 Fair Empl. Prac. Cases 1695 (N.D. Iowa 2000) (single episode in which female employee allegedly struck male supervisor in genital area may be severe enough to constitute unlawful harassment). On the other hand, a continuing pattern of less severe incidents might combine to constitute "pervasive" harassment. Harris v. Forklift Sys., Inc., 510 U.S. 17 (1993). Obviously, each case depends on its unique facts. *Id.* at 22 (abusive work environment "is not, and by its nature cannot be, a mathematically precise test").

The Court revisited the question of what constitutes a hostile work environment in *Harris*. The question in that case was whether a plaintiff must show a serious effect on psychological well-being, and the Court said no:

> Title VII comes into play before the harassing conduct leads to a nervous breakdown. A discriminatorily abusive work environment, even one that does not seriously affect employees' psychological well-being, can and often will detract from employees' job performance, discourage employees from remaining on the job, or keep them from advancing in their careers. Moreover, even without regard to these tangible effects, the very fact that the discriminatory conduct was so severe or pervasive that it created a work environment abusive to employees because of their race, gender, religion, or national origin offends Title VII's broad rule of workplace equality. . . .
>
> So long as the environment would reasonably be perceived, and is perceived, as hostile or abusive, there is no need for it also to be psychologically injurious.

Id. at 22.

The Court also held in *Harris* that a plaintiff must show that harassment was *objectively* and *subjectively* severe or pervasive. *Id.* at 21-22. Thus, a factfinder must find not only that the plaintiff actually perceived the harassment as severe or pervasive, but also that a reasonable person would agree with that perception.

An objective approach to harassment requires a factfinder to look at the entire context of alleged harassment. There may be cases in which a plaintiff was honestly and severely offended by conduct, but the conduct was not objectively offensive. In *Oncale*, the Court added the following note of caution:

> In same-sex (as in all) harassment cases, [the] inquiry requires careful consideration of the social context in which particular behavior occurs and is experienced by its target. A professional football player's working environment is not severely or pervasively abusive, for example, if the coach smacks him on the buttocks as he heads onto the field — even if the same behavior would reasonably be experienced as abusive by the coach's secretary (male or female) back at the office. The real social impact of workplace behavior often depends on a constellation of surrounding circumstances, expectations, and relationships which are not fully captured by a simple recitation of the words used or the physical acts performed. Common sense, and an appropriate sensitivity to social context, will enable courts and juries to distinguish between simple teasing or roughhousing

> among members of the same sex, and conduct which a reasonable person in the plaintiff's position would find severely hostile or abusive.

523 U.S. at 81-82.

At some point, conduct is so severe or pervasive that the doctrine of hostile environment intersects with the doctrine of tangible employment actions. In Pennsylvania State Police v. Suders, 542 U.S. 129 (2004), the Supreme Court held that an employee's resignation in the face of a hostile environment of sexual harassment constitutes a "constructive discharge" if "working conditions become so intolerable that a reasonable person in the employee's position would have felt compelled to resign," for purposes of recovering back pay.

The Requirement that Alleged Sexual Harassment Must Be Unwelcome.

Harassment because of bigotry or misogyny is normally objectively offensive to the target. Sexual advances or innuendo, on the other hand, might not be offensive to the target. A person who purposely encourages or enjoys such attention has not been unlawfully harassed even if a reasonable person might be offended by the same conduct. But the problem is much more complex than it might seem. In *Meritor Savings Bank*, the plaintiff conceded that she appeared to consent to a sexual relationship with her supervisor only because she feared losing her job. The district court held that the plaintiff could not have suffered unlawful harassment because her submission to sexual advances was "voluntary." The Supreme Court, however, rejected any rule that would automatically bar the claim of a plaintiff who had yielded to a supervisor's demands.

> [T]he fact that sex-related conduct was "voluntary," in the sense that the complainant was not forced to participate against her will, is not a defense to a sexual harassment suit brought under Title VII. The gravamen of any sexual harassment claim is that the alleged sexual advances were "unwelcome." 29 CFR § 1604.11(a) (1985). While the question whether particular conduct was indeed unwelcome presents difficult problems of proof and turns largely on credibility determinations committed to the trier of fact, the District Court in this case erroneously focused on the "voluntariness" of respondent's participation in the claimed sexual episodes. The correct inquiry is whether respondent by her conduct indicated that the alleged sexual advances were unwelcome, not whether her actual participation in sexual intercourse was voluntary.

477 U.S. at 68. Thus, a plaintiff's conduct that might seem to have permitted or even to have invited attention, such as dressing in a sexually provocative way, does not foreclose the possibility that the attention she received was unwelcome and offensive. On the other hand, such conduct by the plaintiff may be relevant to the question whether the alleged harassment was unwelcome and offensive. *See, e.g.*, Burns v. McGregor Elec. Indus., 955 F.2d 559 (8th Cir. 1992) (plaintiff's nude modeling for motorcycle magazines, which other employees brought to workplace, was relevant to whether harassment by co-employees was "welcome").

NOTES AND QUESTIONS

1. Conduct that constitutes both harassment under Title VII and a tort under

state law presents the question whether a plaintiff is free to choose which remedy she will pursue. The question is important for several reasons, including the plaintiff's desire to maximize the recovery. Damages under Title VII (and many analogous state laws) are "capped," 42 U.S.C. § 1981a, while the rules for damages under state tort law may be more generous. Plaintiffs frequently assert both statutory discrimination and tort claims in the same case, but some state courts hold that local discrimination laws supersede and bar tort claims based on the same conduct. *Compare, e.g.*, Waffle House, Inc. v. Williams, 313 S.W.3d 796 (Tex. 2010) (if the gravamen of claim is sexual harassment cognizable under state or federal discrimination statute, tort action is preempted), *with* B.C. v. Steak N Shake Oper., Inc., 512 S.W.3d 276 (Tex. 2017) (discrimination law did not preempt tort claim based on sexual assault by supervisor).

2. Employers have adopted a variety of policies to prevent harassment. Some of these policies, such as rules against intimate relations between employees or restrictions on employee speech, come with some cost to employee autonomy. For public sector employers, there is some question whether an employer's overzealous enforcement of sexual harassment policies violates Constitutional privacy or free speech rights. *Compare* O'Rourke v. City of Providence, 235 F.3d 713 (1st Cir. 2001) (rejecting city's contention that male firefighters' reading of pornography in public spaces of fire station was protected by First Amendment) *with* Johnson v. County of Los Angeles Fire Dep't, 865 F. Supp. 1430 (C.D. Cal. 1994) (invalidating department policy insofar as it prohibited male firefighter from "merely seeking to read and possess Playboy quietly and in private . . . [and] not seeking to expose the contents of the magazine to unwitting viewers"; upholding policy insofar as it prohibited displaying nude pictures). *Cf.* Saxe v. State Coll. Area Sch. Dist., 240 F.3d 200 (3d Cir. 2001) (school district harassment policy was unconstitutionally overbroad). *See generally* E. Volokh, *What Speech Does "Hostile Work Environment" Harassment Law Restrict?* 85 Geo. L.J. 627 (1997).

Private sector employers enjoy greater latitude in steering the passage between Title VII compliance and employee rights of autonomy, because they are not subject to the Constitutional restraints upon public employers. On the other hand, a private sector employer's overzealous efforts to prevent harassment might violate other rights. *See* Wal-Mart Stores, Inc. v. Canchola, 64 S.W.3d 524 (Tex. App. 2001) (employer's sexual harassment investigation constituted intentional infliction of emotional distress against accused employee), *rev'd*, 121 S.W.3d 735 (Tex. 2003) (method of investigating accused employee was not outrageous). Would a rule against supervisor-subordinate "fraternization" violate a state statute prohibiting discrimination based on off-duty conduct? *See, e.g.,* Colo. Rev. Stat. § 24-34-402.5 (protecting off-duty conduct if both lawful and off-premises, subject to defense that restriction is "reasonably and rationally related to the employment activities and responsibilities").

PROBLEMS

1. An employer client has come to you for advice concerning its proposal to ban "fraternization" between supervisors and employees, and to prohibit "dating" between any two employees. Is the proposal a good idea? Does it matter

whether the employer is in the public sector or the private sector?

2. Until recently, the Mack City Fire Department had employed only male firefighters. This year, the department employed its first female firefighter, Brenda Blaze. When Blaze arrived at Station No. 30 for her first day of work, she noticed that the station's firefighters had decorated the walls in the sleeping quarters, dining area, and recreation area with pictures from Playboy, Penthouse, and similar magazines. A few pictures were particularly pornographic. When Blaze complained to the captain that the pictures made her feel uncomfortable, the captain replied, "Lady, we don't have to change the way we are just because you showed up. The boys like their pictures and always have. If you don't like that, you can put in a request to transfer." Has Blaze suffered unlawful sexual harassment?

3. Suzie Tips worked as a waitress at Hoover's, a bar/restaurant whose usual clientele were male businessmen from the nearby office buildings. Tips and the other waitresses wore the same employer-provided uniform, which the employer had selected because it would likely appeal to male customers. Tips's mainly male customers were frequently boisterous, overly friendly, and flirtatious. She was the regular object of compliments (sometimes crude), requests for dates, sexual innuendo, and inappropriate touching (including efforts to hug and kiss). Tips always handled such matters with aplomb and managed to resist eager customers without offense. One day, however, after the restaurant had closed and only Tips and the manager/bartender Tad Swizler were left to clean up, Swizler suddenly grabbed Tips from behind and attempted to kiss her. Tips pushed Swizler away and immediately left the restaurant. The next day, she did not report to work. Instead, she called Swizler to inform him that she was frightened by what happened, and that she was resigning. Tips then filed a sexual harassment charge with the EEOC against Hoover's (a nationwide chain of restaurants), seeking back pay to compensate her for her loss of income between her resignation and her next job. Is Tips entitled to back pay for sexual harassment under Title VII?

B. INTRUSIVE INVESTIGATION OF EMPLOYEES

1. Interrogation

An employer's supervision and management of the workforce requires a constant exchange of information between the employer and its employees. In this section, we consider a potentially treacherous form of information gathering: Interrogation of an employee to investigate possible wrongdoing.

Questioning an employee about possible wrongdoing is implicitly threatening, because the employee could lose her job if she is guilty. Of course, when an employer has reason to believe misconduct has occurred, it is entitled to ask questions. But what if the employee denies wrongdoing?

When an employer continues to interrogate in the face of an employee's denial, the purpose of further interrogation is to test the credibility of the employee's denial by exploring or confronting other facts, to obtain evidence that might implicate *other* employees, or to overcoming that employee's resistance to telling what the employer believes is the truth. In the latter case, interrogation is not a mere interview. It is a psychological assault against the employee. If such interrogation goes too far, it may invite tort claims such as the intentional infliction of emotional distress (outrage).

If an employee asserts the tort of outrage, it may seem the employer enjoys the benefit of a very wide margin for error because the employee can prevail only if the employer's conduct was "outrageous." See section A.2.b of this chapter, *supra*. In the context of interrogation, however, drawing a line between rude or misguided versus outrageously bad can be a difficult task. Even judges sympathetic to the employee's point of view would likely agree that an employer has a legitimate business interest in investigating the cause of a theft or loss of property. They might also agree that an employer need not take the employee's initial denial of wrongdoing as the final word. At some point, however, an employer's effort to "break" an employee crosses the line. In finding the right balance between the employer's legitimate business interests and the employee's personal integrity, it may be helpful to remember that both the employer and the employee have a range of options when an employee is firm in her denial of guilt.

The employer has three options. First, it can accept that the employee has nothing more to say and assume her innocence. Second, it can accept that the employee has nothing more to say, disbelieve her, and discipline or discharge her (perhaps referring the matter to the police in the case of suspected criminal misconduct). Third, it can persist in the interrogation, hoping that further questioning might lead the employee to confess. The employer might prefer the third option because either of the first two options risks an error in firing or not firing the employee. The employer might also worry that without a confession, it risks allegations of discrimination or wrongful discharge. Continued interrogation might finally corner the employee with her own words or overwhelm her resistance.. At some point, however, interrogation may begin to look more like coercion, especially if the employer suggests it has already determined the employee's guilt and needs only the employee's written confession.

The employee has two options. First, she can endure further questioning, hoping to persuade the employer of her innocence and preserve her job. Second, she can terminate the interrogation by leaving, risking discharge. However, more than the loss of a job may be at stake. Termination under suspicion of theft could taint the employee's employment record and hurt her future job prospects.

KELLY v. WEST CASH & CARRY BLDG. MATERIALS STORE

745 So. 2d 743 (La. App. 1999)

BYRNES, Judge.

The plaintiff, Burnetta Kelly was arrested and fired from her job as assistant head cashier at West Cash & Carry Building Materials Store (West), a retail outlet, based on allegations that she assisted an unidentified man to remove merchandise from the store without payment. The charges were ultimately dropped and similar allegations were rejected by the State of Louisiana Office of Employment Security. Plaintiff filed a petition alleging false arrest and imprisonment . . . and infliction of emotional distress. . . .

Pursuant to a motion for summary judgment, the plaintiff's claims were dismissed in their entirety. We affirm. . . .

West hired plaintiff as a cashier in October of 1995. . . . Shortly before she was terminated, Mr. Edward Knight, the store general manager, promoted her to . . . assistant head cashier. Early on July 2, 1996, Mr. Knight held an employee meeting at which he informed the employees that merchandise was missing and that it was suspected that an employee might have allowed a customer to leave without paying. After the meeting, cashier Marshia Jimenez informed Mr. Knight that she witnessed a suspicious incident on June 30, 1996, when an unknown man was allowed to leave the store without a receipt because plaintiff vouched for him. Another cashier, Jill Fourcade, confirmed this to Gary Heflin, the Consumer Marketing Director. Ms. Kelly was summoned to Mr. Knight's office . . . .

Plaintiff alleges that when she was summoned to Mr. Knight's office for questioning she was wrongfully detained against her will. Plaintiff's brief contends that she "was held against her will in the office . . . for approximately three hours" where she was interrogated until the police came and arrested her.

The affidavit of Burnetta Kelly made the following assertions . . . :

> 17. Then I was told that Mr. Knight ordered me to report to his office. Immediately, I reported to Mr. Knight's office about 10 a.m.
>
> 18. When I reported to his office on the morning of July 2, 1996, about 10 a.m., Mr. Knight, Gary Heflin and Keith Yeager accused me of stealing a lawn mower and other merchandise from the store by helping a man on June 30, 1996.
>
> 19. I told Mr. Knight, Gary Heflin and Keith Yeager that I did not steal any merchandise from the store on June 30, 1996 or any other time. I told Mr. Knight, Gary Heflin and Keith Yeager that I did not help anyone steal any merchandise from the store on June 30, 1996 or any other time. I told them that I did not tell Marshia Jimenez, Jill Fourcade or any other employee to allow anyone to take any merchandise out of the store on June 30, 1996 or any other time. Mr. Knight and Gary Heflin told me to confess and they would not call the police. I told them I was not confessing to anything I did not do.
>
> 20. I was kept in Mr. Knight's office from 10 a.m. to about 1 p.m. At one point during the questioning I stood and walked near the closed door. But, Mr. Knight ordered me to sit down in the chair. I sat down and they continued to question me.
>
> 21. When my husband arrived and came in the office, he told me that I did not have to stay there and take this. But, Mr. Knight told him that I could not leave. Mr. Knight and Gary Heflin ordered my husband to leave. My husband left the office without me.
>
> 22. Through all of this, I was scared and felt sick to my stomach. I felt myself trembling and could not sit still. I could not understand what was happening to me. My father came in the office trying to find out what had happened. But, the police came in and arrested me.

The affidavit of Terrence L. Kelly, the plaintiff's husband, relates . . . "During the time the store management held Burnetta in the office, Burnetta appeared frightened, her eyes were watery, she looked visibly shaken and physically ill.

Burnetta looked sad like she was physically drained. Burnetta did not look like she could handle being accused of a crime and held in the room." . . .

Significantly, Ms. Kelly testified that she never asked to leave the room and that the door to the room was never locked. Ms. Kelly did not state in her deposition as she did in her later affidavit that at one time she got up and was ordered to sit back down. . . .

Ms. Kelly's testimony and affidavit and her husband's affidavit are significant for what they fail to say. There is no testimony or affidavit suggesting that there was any physical impediment preventing her departure, or any threat of physical force preventing Ms. Kelly's freedom of movement. . . .

False imprisonment is the unlawful and total restraint of the liberty of the person. Crossett v. Campbell, 122 La. 659, 48 So. 141 (1908). Submission to the mere verbal direction of an employer, unaccompanied by force or by threats, does not constitute false imprisonment. Moen v. Las Vegas Intern. Hotel, Inc., 90 Nev. 176, 521 P.2d 370 (1974); Mullins v. Rinks, Inc., 27 Ohio App. 2d 45, 272 N.E.2d 152 (1971); White v. Levy Brothers, Inc., 306 S.W.2d 829 (Ky. 1957). And there is no false imprisonment where an employer declines to terminate an interview of his employee if no force or threat of force is used. *Id.* False imprisonment may not be predicated on a person's unfounded belief that he was restrained. *Id.* Apprehension that one might in the future lose one's job or be prosecuted for theft is not the force or the threat of force necessary to establish false imprisonment. *Moen, supra.* Bare words are insufficient to effect an imprisonment if the person to whom they are spoken is not deprived of freedom of action. Ford Motor Credit Co. v. Gibson, 566 S.W.2d 154 (Ky. 1977); Grayson Variety Store, Inc. v. Shaffer, 402 S.W.2d 424 (Ky. 1966).

In Dominguez v. Globe Discount City, Inc., 470 S.W.2d 919 (Tex. Civ. App. 1971), the plaintiff was ordered about by a security guard, which if anything should carry a greater inference of force than would an order from one's employer. But the *Dominguez* court noted that there was never any physical force and that the plaintiff was never touched by the security guard. The plaintiff did not testify that the guard threatened her or exercised any physical restraint. The court found no false imprisonment. . . .

It is in the nature of the employer-employee relationship that the employer may give orders to the employee restricting his liberty of movement. Such does not constitute a "restraint of liberty" in the sense of false imprisonment. In Weiler v. Herzfeld-Phillipson Co., 189 Wis. 554, 208 N.W. 599 (Wis. 1926), a case remarkably similar to the instant case the court noted that:

> In the instant case an employer summoned to his office an employe[e] for an interview concerning matters coming to the attention of the employer casting doubt upon the fidelity of the employe[e]. The office was small, but it was a regularly established office of the employer. The interview was somewhat prolonged, but during the entire period the time of the employe[e] belonged to the employer. She was compensated for every minute of the time spent by her in the office. Her time was under the employer's direction and control. The subject of the interview was the conduct of the plaintiff in the discharge of her duties as an employe[e]. The only evidence of restraint imposed upon the plaintiff was her own testimony that upon two occasions

> during the interview she asked [her employer] if she could leave the room, and he replied, "Why no, what do you want to go out for"; that she got up, and he said, "Sit down." Upon one occasion she asked if she could telephone to her husband, and he said "No"; that her husband had nothing to do with the matter.
>
> . . . [The door] was not locked from the inside, and the door could readily be opened by turning a knob. While the interview was somewhat long, we know of no standard by which the length of such interviews within the bounds of propriety may be definitely fixed.
>
> . . . There is the further evidence that he threatened to call the patrol and send her to jail if she did not confess. We cannot express our entire approval of this conduct on the part of Mr. Carter. It savors too much of third degree methods. It was one of the means adopted by Carter to coerce a confession from the plaintiff. It amounted to intimidation, and tended to deprive the plaintiff of her own free will. That, however, bears only upon the value of her confession as evidence. It has nothing to do with the question of whether she was falsely imprisoned. The socalled confession might have been made because she feared that, otherwise, she would be sent to jail. That fact might render her confession involuntary, but it would not make her presence in the room false imprisonment.

Plaintiff in the instant case was allowed more freedom under interrogation by her employer than was the *Weiler* plaintiff. The West executives allowed Mrs. Kelly to make a number of phone calls and receive visits from family members.

Mr. Knight testified that the plaintiff was always free to leave. In the trial court, plaintiff's opposition to the summary judgment motion focused on allegations that plaintiff was detained in Knight's office for three hours in contravention of LSA-C.Cr.P. art. 215 which limits the authority of a merchant to detain someone for questioning for the suspected "theft of goods," "for a length of time, not to exceed sixty minutes." The defendants counter that the plaintiff was questioned in Knight's office for less than sixty minutes. However, this fact, although contested, is not material, because we have found that management's questioning of plaintiff did not constitute an imprisonment. It does not matter if an employee is ordered by her employer to subject herself to interrogation for more than the sixty minutes allowed in LSA-C.Cr.P. art. 215 when the only impediment to her freedom of movement is the psychological force of her employer's orders unaccompanied by any actual or physical restraint.

At a trial on the merits, the burden would be on the plaintiff to prove that she was falsely arrested or imprisoned. An essential element of such a tort is proof of total restraint. The defendants offered sufficient evidence of a lack of total restraint to shift the summary judgment burden to the plaintiff and prevent plaintiff from resting on mere allegations. LSA-C.C.P. art. 966C(2). Plaintiff offered no evidence of any actual or threatened total or partial physical restraint — and for the restraint to constitute an imprisonment it must be total. Crossett v. Campbell, *supra.* Accordingly, we find no basis for reversing the trial court judgment as regards plaintiff's claim for false arrest or imprisonment. . . .

Any emotional distress plaintiff experienced would have been as an element of damage arising out of her claims for false imprisonment and arrest, defamation and malicious prosecution. Her emotional distress under the facts alleged in this case do not give rise to a cause of action separate and apart from her claims for false imprisonment/arrest, defamation, and malicious prosecution. Therefore, there is no need to consider plaintiff's claim for intentional and/or negligent infliction of emotional distress separately. . . .

NOTES AND QUESTIONS

1. If Kelly refused to confess after prolonged and evidently fruitless interrogation, why did the employer instruct her to remain? If an employer is convinced of an employee's guilt and chooses to call the police, may it forcibly hold the employee to prevent her departure before the police arrive to make a formal arrest? Many states have "citizen's arrest" laws that permit one person to forcibly detain another under certain circumstances, but exercising this right is risky because circumstances do not always justify detention and might lead to false imprisonment liability. In many states, an employer's "probable cause" to believe an employee committed a crime may be a defense against false imprisonment, provided the employer observed the requirements of local law for forcibly detaining a person. Jackson v. Kmart Corp., 851 F. Supp. 469 (M.D. Ga. 1994) (employee's indictment for theft created rebuttable presumption under Georgia law that employer had cause to detain employee based on reasonable belief that employee was shoplifting); Silvera v. Home Depot U.S.A., 189 F. Supp. 2d 304 (D. Md. 2002); Etienne v. Wal-Mart Stores, Inc., 186 F. Supp. 2d 129 (D. Conn. 2001); Weatherholt v. Meijer Inc., 922 F. Supp. 1227, 1231 (E.D. Mich. 1996).

But why might an employer detain a *regular employee* for the police to make an arrest? In *Kelly*, the employer did not "arrest" Kelly but it used its authority as an employer to delay her departure. Would the employer have been reasonable in fearing Kelly would flee to avoid arrest and prosecution??

2. A recurring issue in cases involving employee interrogation is whether the employer's actions constituted an "arrest" or forcible detention. Appearances can be ambiguous to the employee, and ambiguity may be part of the employer's strategy. If an employer denies an employee's request to leave or instructs the employee to remain in a room, by what authority does it make this instruction? Perhaps the employee understands she has a "right" to leave but that the employer has a right to fire her for insubordination. Why did Kelly not leave with her husband? Is it likely she believed she could save her job by voluntarily remaining in the office until the police arrived? Could she reasonably have believed the employer was exercising any extra-supervisory power over her?

3. An employer might purposely create circumstances that resemble an arrest. If so, does evidence of this employer strategy matter for purposes of determining whether there has been a false imprisonment or outrageous conduct by the employer? *See* Johnson v. Federal Express Corp., 147 F. Supp. 2d 1268 (M.D. Ala. 2001) (fact issue regarding wrongful detention, where interrogators followed plaintiff to the restroom, allowed her to talk by telephone with husband and an attorney only in their presence, told her interrogation would stop if she confessed, and denied her permission to pick up daughter from school, leaving daughter to walk home in rain to an empty house).

An employee's age or relative sophistication may be important in determining the effect of an employer's demand that the employee not leave. *Compare* Cuellar v. Walgreens Co., 2002 WL 471317 (Tex. App. 2002) (unpublished) (two-hour interrogation of 22-year-old former newspaper reporter with some college education, who did not appear intimidated by employer, was not false imprisonment), *with* Smithson v. Nordstrom, Inc., 664 P.2d 1119 (Or. App. 1983) (noting that plaintiff was age 19, and finding other evidence sufficient for intentional infliction of emotional distress claim from employer interrogation).

As the *Smithson* case suggests, if a factfinder is "outraged" by the employer's conduct, it might dismiss a false imprisonment claim but uphold a claim for intentional infliction of emotional distress.

4. In false imprisonment/outrage cases involving interrogation, there are a number of factors that appear to weigh heavily in the outcome of the issue whether the employer unlawfully detained the employee. As noted above, the age and sophistication of the detainee are two factors. Another is the duration of the interrogation. *See, e.g.*, Johnson v. Federal Express Corp., 147 F. Supp. 2d 1268 (M.D. Ala. 2001) (issue of fact regarding false imprisonment claim, where among other things interrogation lasted more than seven hours); Crump v. P&C Food Markets, Inc., 576 A.2d 441 (Vt. 1990) (upholding jury verdict for intentional infliction of emotional distress, based in part on three-hour interrogation without break for rest or food); Adams v. Wal-Mart Stores, Inc., 324 F.3d 935 (7th Cir. 2003) (confinement in manager's office for "several minutes" not false imprisonment); Turner v. Holbrook, 278 F.3d 754 (8th Cir. 2002) (two interrogations, one for five minutes, and one for twenty minutes, not unlawful). *But see* Cellamare v. Milbank, Tweed, Hadley & McCloy LLP, 2003 WL 22937683 (E.D.N.Y. 2003) (four hours of interrogation "does not rise to anything more than a lengthy interview"); Lee v. Bankers Trust Co., 1998 WL 107119 (S.D.N.Y. 1998) (five hours of interrogation not false imprisonment).

5. The existence and purpose of a physical impediment created by the employer is particularly important to the issue of false imprisonment. Adams v. Wal-Mart Stores, Inc., 324 F.3d 935 (7th Cir. 2003) (confinement in manager's office for "several minutes," including three to five minutes in which door was locked, not false imprisonment, because locking of door was apparently "accidental"); Arrington v. Liz Claiborne, Inc., 688 N.Y.S.2d 544 (N.Y. App. Div. 1999) (plaintiffs "belief" that door was locked insufficient to show physical restraint); Palmer v. GTE California, Inc., 2002 WL 120567 (Cal. App. 2002) (unpublished) (supervisor kept foot against the door to prevent employee from leaving conference room — false imprisonment).

6. Interrogators may use varied techniques to frighten and intimidate an employee, such as claiming to have independent evidence of the employee's guilt or threatening to call the police if the employee does not confess. Are such techniques a "detention" or an outrage? *Compare* Kelly *and* McKinney v. K Mart Corp., 649 F. Supp. 1217 (D. W. Va. 1986) (raising voice, calling employee a "liar," slamming hand on the table, not enough to constitute intentional infliction of emotional distress) *with* Hall v. May Dep't Store, 637 P.2d 126 (Or. 1981) (upholding verdict for employee based on evidence employer insisted it had "proof" of her guilt and threatened to have her arrested if she did not confess).

7. In contrast with many other situations in which an employer's vicarious liability for an employee's intentional torts is doubtful, an employer is almost certainly liable for intentional torts committed by managers and security personnel to extract an employee's confession. Courts appear to have little difficulty finding that the interrogators acted in furtherance of the employer's business and in the scope of their employment. *See, e.g.*, Silvera v. Home Depot U.S.A., Inc., 189 F. Supp. 2d 304 (D. Md. 2002).

8. Interrogation is a common but not exclusive context for an employee's possibly wrongful detention. Other cases have arisen out of a "security lock-in" or the use of force to prevent employees from leaving early. Barstow v. Shea, 196 F. Supp. 2d 141 (D. Conn. 2002) (material issue of fact as to claim that employer wrongfully detained employee by blocking doorway to prevent her from leaving workplace for medical treatment); Miraliakbari v. Pennicooke, 561 S.E.2d 483 (Ga. App. 2002) (supervisor's threat to fire employee if she left early to tend to her son's medical emergency did not constitute tort of outrage or false imprisonment); Richardson v. Costco Wholesale Corp., 169 F. Supp. 2d 56 (D. Conn. 2001) (employees failed to show false imprisonment from security "lock-ins" in which store exits were locked during certain hours, because employees could have left through emergency exit, although that would have resulted in disciplinary action).

The ultimate form of wrongful detention in employment is involuntary servitude. *See, e.g.*, Manliguez v. Joseph, 226 F. Supp. 2d 377 (E.D.N.Y. 2002) (domestic employee alleged employers locked her inside apartment, forced her to work 18½ hours per day, confiscated her passport, prohibited her from communicating with people outside, fed her stale leftovers, denied her personal hygiene items, and attempted to sever her ties with her mother abroad); *see also* 18 U.S.C. § 1584 ("Whoever knowingly and willfully holds to involuntary servitude or sells into any condition of involuntary servitude, any other person for any term, or brings within the United States any person so held, shall be fined under this title or imprisoned not more than 20 years, or both.").

9. Public employers are usually safe from tort liability by reason of sovereign immunity. However, a public employee might still file a civil rights action to challenge a detention or interrogation.

First, forcible detention of a public employee by a public employer is a "seizure," unlawful under the Fourth Amendment unless it is "reasonable." *See* McGann v. Ne. Illinois Reg'l Commuter R.R. Corp., 8 F.3d 1174 (1993) (employees whose cars were stopped in employer parking facility established issue of fact whether they were "seized" in violation of Fourth Amendment, for purposes of determining validity of subsequent consent to search).

Second, a public employer's interrogation of a public employee under threat of adverse action presents a Fifth Amendment problem if the interrogation relates to conduct that might constitute a criminal offense. If the employee asserts the "Fifth" and refuses to answer questions, would the employer violate the Fifth Amendment by discharging the employee?

Ordinarily, a public employer has the same right as a private employer to ask questions, demand information, and discipline the employee for refusing to answer, subject to the employee's right to privacy as to unreasonably intrusive questions, and subject to civil service or other statutory or contractual job protection.

Questions related to the employee's work or the employer's business or mission are not likely to violate employee privacy or contract rights. Patrick v. City of Chicago, 662 F. Supp. 2d 1039, 1058 (N.D. Ill. 2009). However, an employee's suspected misconduct might also constitute a crime. If so, there is a real chance any answers will be used as evidence in a criminal prosecution. In this situation, the public employer wears two hats: one as an employer with the power to manage its operations and discipline employees, and another as the "state" with the power to prosecute and punish criminal behavior by penal sanctions. The Fifth Amendment limits the public employer only in the latter capacity. Thus, the public employer may demand answers and discharge the employee for refusing to answer. But if the employee asserts the Fifth Amendment, the employer must acknowledge this right and the employee will be entitled to "use immunity" with regard to his or her answers in a subsequent criminal prosecution. *See* Uniformed Sanitation Men Ass'n v. Comm'r of Sanitation, 392 U.S. 280 (1968); Patrick v. City of Chicago, 662 F. Supp. 2d 1039, 1058 (N.D. Ill. 2009).

10. Neither public nor private sector employees have a right to the presence of an attorney or other representative in dealing with an employer in disciplinary matters, unless a contract or statute provides otherwise. *Cf.* Porterfield v. Mascari II, Inc., 823 A.2d 590 (Md. 2003) (employee lawfully discharged for refusing to sign disciplinary notice until after consulting attorney). A major exception to this rule arises from the law of collective bargaining, as set forth in the next section.

2. *Interrogation and the Law of Collective Bargaining*

When employees elect to deal with their employer through collective bargaining, their choice has important implications for the employer's investigation of employee misconduct and administration of discipline. One of the most important implications is that a collective bargaining agreement is very likely to create a contractual grievance and arbitration procedure permitting employees to challenge disciplinary action. The creation of this disciplinary review procedure and the union's involvement in the procedure are designed to assure that disciplinary action is fair and in accordance with the contract.

The union's involvement is not limited to the post-disciplinary action review. A union representative may also be involved in the employer's pre-disciplinary interrogation of an employee during the course of an initial investigation. In NLRB v. J. Weingarten, Inc., 420 U.S. 251 (1975), an employer refused to grant an employee's request for the attendance of a union representative in an investigatory interrogation. The employer continued the interrogation and eventually determined that the employee was innocent. Nevertheless, the union charged the employer with violating the employee's right under section 7 of the National Labor Relations Act to act in concert with other employees for mutual aid and protection. The Court agreed with the union that the employer violated section 7 by proceeding with the interrogation after denying the employee's request for union assistance.

> The action of an employee in seeking to have the assistance of his union representative at a confrontation with his employer clearly falls within the literal wording of § 7 that "(e)mployees shall have the right . . . to engage in . . . concerted activities for the purpose of . . . mutual aid or protection." This

> is true even though the employee alone may have an immediate stake in the outcome; he seeks "aid or protection" against a perceived threat to his employment security. The union representative whose participation he seeks is, however, safeguarding not only the particular employee's interest, but also the interests of the entire bargaining unit by exercising vigilance to make certain that the employer does not initiate or continue a practice of imposing punishment unjustly. The representative's presence is an assurance to other employees in the bargaining unit that they, too, can obtain his aid and protection if called upon to attend a like interview. . . .
>
> The Board's construction also gives recognition to the right when it is most useful to both employee and employer. A single employee confronted by an employer investigating whether certain conduct deserves discipline may be too fearful or inarticulate to relate accurately the incident being investigated, or too ignorant to raise extenuating factors. A knowledgeable union representative could assist the employer by eliciting favorable facts, and save the employer production time by getting to the bottom of the incident. . . . [H]is presence need not transform the interview into an adversary contest. . . .[R]espondent would defer representation until the filing of a formal grievance challenging the employer's determination of guilt after the employee has been discharged or otherwise disciplined. At that point, however, it becomes increasingly difficult for the employee to vindicate himself, and the value of representation is correspondingly diminished. The employer may then be more concerned with justifying his actions than re-examining them.

420 U.S. at 260-264. Thus, in denying the employee her right to the assistance of a union representative at an interview she reasonably believed might result in disciplinary action, the employer unlawfully interfered with the right of its employees to engage in concerted activity for mutual aid and protection.

Ordinarily, an employee must request her *Weingarten* right. Absent such a request, an employer has no duty to invite a union representative to attend the meeting. An employer has no duty to inform or remind an employee of her *Weingarten* right. New Jersey Bell Tel. Co., 300 NLRB 42 (1990). Collective bargaining agreements, however, sometimes place an affirmative duty on the employer to arrange for the attendance of a union representative without any request by an employee. If an employee invokes *Weingarten* right, the employer has two options. It can suspend the interview until a union representative arrives, or it can terminate the interview altogether and complete its investigation by other means. Either way, the employer is still free to make a decision whether the employee has engaged in misconduct and whether to administer discipline.

The employer's effort to continue the interview without a union representative after the employee requested one is a clear violation of the NLRA, but the remedy for the employee is frequently uncertain. If the employer takes disciplinary action against the employee, there may be a question whether the employer was motivated to retaliate against the employee for invoking *Weingarten* or for refusing to answer questions without a union representative. If so, the employee might be entitled to reinstatement and back pay or reversal of other disciplinary action. However, if the employer would have taken the same action irrespective of the employee's assertion of *Weingarten* rights, the remedy will be limited to an order to cease further violations and will not include any individual relief. Structural Composites Indus., 304 NLRB 729 (1991).

A lingering issue after *Weingarten* was whether employees in a *nonunion* setting are entitled to assert *Weingarten* rights by demanding the assistance of a co-worker at an interrogation. The NLRB has wavered on this issue. Seven years after the Supreme Court's *Weingarten* decision, the NLRB extended the doctrine to nonunion workplaces in Materials Research Corp., 262 NLRB 1010 (1982). Only three years later, however, the board reversed course. In Sears, Roebuck & Co., 274 NLRB 230 (1985), the board overruled *Materials Research* and held that *Weingarten* does *not* apply in the absence of a certified or recognized union.

Fifteen years after *Sears*, the board reversed itself again: Epilepsy Found. of Northeast Ohio, 331 NLRB 676 (2000), *enf'd in relevant part*, 268 F.3d 1095 (D.C. Cir. 2001), returned to the *Materials Research* holding that nonunion employees enjoy *Weingarten* rights. Below is the latest holding on the issue.

IBM CORP.

341 NLRB 1288 (2004)

. . . On October 15, 2001, the Respondent, prompted by allegations of harassment contained in a letter it received from a former employee, interviewed each of the Charging Parties. None of them requested the presence of a witness during the October 15 interviews. On October 22, the Respondent's manager, Nels Maine, denied Charging Party Bannon's request to have a coworker or an attorney present at an interview scheduled for the next day. On October 23, Maine interviewed each of the Charging Parties individually after denying each employee's request to have a coworker present during the interview. All three employees were discharged approximately a month after the interviews. [The Charging Parties filed charges with the NLRB, alleging that the Respondent's actions interfered with their rights under section 7, in violation of section 8(a)(1) of the NLRA, 29 U.S.C. § 158(a).]

[An administrative law] judge found . . . that Bannon, Schult, and Parsley each asked to have a coworker present during their October 23 interviews and that the Respondent denied their requests. The judge next observed that the Board, in Epilepsy Foundation, 331 NLRB 676 (2000), *enf'd in relevant part*, 268 F.3d 1095 (D.C. Cir. 2001), *cert. denied*, 536 U.S. 904 (2002), had extended to unrepresented employees the *Weingarten* right to have a witness present during an investigatory interview that the employees reasonably believed might result in discipline. Applying *Epilepsy Foundation*, the judge concluded that the Respondent violated Section 8(a)(1) of the Act by denying the Charging Parties' requests to have a coworker present during their October 23 interviews. . . .

After careful reexamination of . . . *Epilepsy Foundation*, we find that national labor relations policy will be best served by overruling existing precedent and returning to the earlier precedent of [E.I. DuPont & Co., 289 NLRB 627 (1988)], which holds that *Weingarten* rights do not apply in a nonunion setting. . . .

. . . The years after the issuance of *Weingarten* have seen a rise in the need for investigatory interviews, both in response to new statutes governing the workplace and as a response to new security concerns raised by terrorist attacks on our country.

Employers face ever-increasing requirements to conduct workplace investigations pursuant to federal, state, and local laws, particularly laws addressing workplace discrimination and sexual harassment. We are especially cognizant of the rise in the number of instances of workplace violence, as well as the increase in the number of incidents of corporate abuse and fiduciary lapses. Further, because of the events of September 11, 2001 and their aftermath, we must now take into account the presence of both real and threatened terrorist attacks. Because of these events, the policy considerations expressed in *DuPont* have taken on a new vitality. Thus, . . . [w]e hold that the *Weingarten* right does not extend to the nonunion workplace.

1. Coworkers do not represent the interests of the entire work force. In *Weingarten*, the Supreme Court emphasized that a union representative accompanying a unit employee to an investigatory interview represents and "safeguards" the interests of the entire bargaining unit . . . because the unit employees have selected a union as their bargaining representative and the union has delegated to its officials the authority to act on its behalf for the entire unit. The union's officials are bound by the duty of fair representation to represent the entire unit. . . .

A coworker in a nonunion setting, on the other hand, has no such obligation to represent the entire work force. There is no legally defined collective interest to represent, because there is no defined . . . bargaining unit, [and] typically no designated representative. Rather, the choice of a representative is done on an ad hoc basis and the identity of the representative may change from one employee interview to the next. . . . It is speculative to find that a coworker would think beyond the immediate situation in which he has been asked to participate and look to set precedent. A coworker has neither the legal duty nor the personal incentive to act in the same manner as a union representative.

2. Coworkers cannot redress the imbalance of power between employers and employees. In *Weingarten*, the Supreme Court recognized that one of the purposes of the Act is to protect workers in the exercise of concerted activities for their mutual aid or protection. The presence of a union representative at a meeting with an employer puts both parties on a level playing field. . . .

Additionally, a union representative has a different status in his relationship with an employer than does a coworker. The union representative typically is accustomed to dealing with the employer on a regular basis concerning matters other than those prompting the interview. Their ongoing relationship has the benefit of aiding in the development of a body of consistent practices concerning workplace issues. . . .

Unlike a union representative a coworker chosen on an ad hoc basis does not have the force of the bargaining unit behind him. A coworker does not usually have a union representative's knowledge of the workplace and its politics. Because the coworker typically is chosen on an ad hoc basis, he has no "official status." . . . [A] coworker is far less able to "level the playing field," for there is no contract from which he derives his authority and he typically has no other matters to discuss with an employer.

3. Coworkers do not have the same skills as a union representative. The Supreme Court in *Weingarten* recognized the unique skills that a union representative brings to an investigatory interview: a "knowledgeable" union representative can facilitate the interview by "eliciting favorable facts," clarifying issues, and eliminating extraneous material, all of which save the employer valuable production time. A union representative is accustomed to administering collective-bargaining agreements and is familiar with the "law of the shop" . . . A union representative's experience allows him to propose solutions to workplace issues and thus try to avoid the filing of a grievance by an aggrieved employee.

A coworker is unlikely to bring such skills to an interview primarily because he has no experience as the statutory representative of a group of employees. [A] coworker, with enthusiasm but with no training or experience in labor relations matters, could actually frustrate or impede the employer's investigation because of his personal or emotional connection to the employee being interviewed.

Finally, an employee being interviewed may request as his representative a coworker who may, in fact, be a participant in the incident requiring the investigation, as a "coconspirator." It can hardly be gainsaid that it is more difficult to arrive at the truth when employees involved in the same incident represent each other. . . .

4. The presence of a coworker may compromise the confidentiality of information. Employers have the legal obligation, pursuant to a variety of federal, state, and local laws, administrative requirements, and court decisions, to provide their workers with safe and secure workplace environments. . . . An employer must take steps to prevent sexual and racial harassment, to avoid the use of toxic chemicals, to provide a drug-free and violence-free workplace, to resolve issues involving employee health matters, and the like. Employers may have to investigate . . . substance abuse allegations, improper computer and internet usage, and allegations of theft, violence, sabotage, and embezzlement.

Employer investigations into these matters require discretion and confidentiality. The guarantee of confidentiality helps an employer resolve challenging issues of credibility involving these sensitive, often personal, subjects. The effectiveness of a fact-finding interview in sensitive situations often depends on whether an employee is alone. . . .

Union representatives, by virtue of their legal duty of fair representation, may not, in bad faith, reveal or misuse the information obtained in an employee interview. A union representative's fiduciary duty to all unit employees helps to assure confidentiality for the employer.

A coworker, however, is under no similar legal constraint. A coworker representative has no fiduciary duty to the employee being questioned or to the workplace as a whole. Further, it is more likely that a coworker representative in casual conversation among other coworkers and friends in the workplace, could inadvertently "let slip" confidential, sensitive, or embarrassing information. Not only is this upsetting to the employee directly affected, it also interferes with an employer's ability to conduct an effective internal investigation. . . .

We recognize that many of these same concerns exist in a unionized setting as well. However, the dangers are far less when the assisting person is an experienced union representative with fiduciary obligations and a continuing interest in having an amicable relationship with the employer. . . .

Our examination and analysis of all these factors lead us to conclude that, on balance, the right of an employee to a coworker's presence in the absence of a union is outweighed by an employer's right to conduct prompt, efficient, thorough, and confidential workplace investigations. It is our opinion that limiting this right to employees in unionized workplaces strikes the proper balance between the competing interests of the employer and employees. . . .

In sum, employees have the right to seek such representation; they cannot be disciplined for asserting those rights. Electrical Workers Local 236, 339 NLRB No. 156, slip op. at 2 (2003). *See also* E. I. DuPont & Co., 289 NLRB 627, 630 fn. 15 (1988). Our only holding is that the nonunion employer has no obligation to accede to the request, i.e., to deal collectively with the employees. . . .

[W]e find that the Charging Parties were not entitled to the presence of a coworker during the interviews . . . . Accordingly, we dismiss the complaint.

Members LIEBMAN and WALSH, dissenting.

. . . [T]he majority has simply failed to make the case that a nonunion employer cannot conduct an effective investigation if employees are entitled to coworker representation during interviews. . . . If employers' obligation to conduct effective investigations is an overriding concern, then even the right to a union representative should be foreclosed (a radical step we hope the majority forswears). . . .

If and when the right to representation raises legitimate concerns, they can and should be addressed by refining the right, case-by-case. For example, our colleagues have suggested that an investigation could be impeded if the employer were compelled to permit representation by a coworker involved in the same incident being investigated (a so-called "coconspirator"). That concern could be addressed specifically, by permitting an employer to deny an employee's request for representation by a possible coconspirator, under appropriate circumstances.

. . . [M]odest as the *Weingarten* right is, it brings a measure of due process to workplace discipline, particularly in nonunion workplaces, where employees and their representatives typically are at-will employees . . . . "[T]he presence of a coworker gives an employee a potential witness, advisor, and advocate in an adversarial situation, and, ideally, militates against the imposition of unjust discipline by the employer." *Epilepsy Foundation* , 268 F.3d at 1100. Needless to say, unjust discipline can provoke labor disputes. Because a purpose of the Act is to provide a vehicle for employee voice and a system for resolving workplace disputes, this due process requirement furthers the goals of the Act. . . .

NOTES AND QUESTIONS

1. When the Supreme Court approved the *Weingarten* doctrine for union-represented employees, it was deferring to the special experience and expertise of the board in regulating industrial relations:

> It is the province of the Board, not the courts, to determine whether or not the "need" exists in light of changing industrial practices and the Board's cumulative experience in dealing with labor management relations. For the Board has the "special function of applying the general provisions of the Act to the complexities of industrial life," and its special competence in this field is the justification for the deference accorded its determination . . . . [T]he Board's construction here, while it may not be required by the Act, is at least

> permissible under it. . . .

420 U.S. at 266 (citations omitted). If *Weingarten* is a "permissible" rather than mandatory construction of the act, it might follow that *either* of the board's opposite views of the applicability of *Weingarten* in nonunion settings is a permissible interpretation of the act. *See also* E. I. DuPont & Co., 289 NLRB 627, 628 (1988) ("[T]he holding in *Materials Research* represented a permissible construction of the Act, but not the only permissible construction.").

2. The *Weingarten* doctrine is only one of the ways the National Labor Relations Act might restrict investigation and interrogation of employees, and some of the act's restrictions indisputably apply even when a union has not yet achieved representative status. First, an employer must not interrogate or otherwise investigate employees in a way that might interfere with their rights to join or form a union or to engage in other concerted activity. Rossmore House, 269 NLRB 1176 (1984), *aff'd sub nom.* Hotel Employees Local 11 v. NLRB, 760 F.2d 1006 (9th Cir. 1985). For example, questioning an employee about his support for a union or for the cause of collective bargaining might be unlawful interrogation regardless of whether any union presently represents the employee. Second, if an employer is investigating and preparing its defense against a charge in an NLRB proceeding, its interviews of its own employees are subject to the so-called *Johnnie's Poultry* rules:

> [T]he employer must communicate to the employee the purpose of the questioning, assure him that no reprisal will take place, and obtain his participation on a voluntary basis; the questioning must occur in a context free from employer hostility to union organization and must not be itself coercive in nature; and the questions must not exceed the necessities of the legitimate purpose by prying into other union matters, eliciting information concerning an employee's subjective state of mind, or otherwise interfering with the statutory rights of employees.

Johnnie's Poultry, 146 NLRB 770, 775 (1964), *enf. denied on other grounds,* 344 F.2d 617 (8th Cir. 1965).

3. *Investigatory Polygraph Examinations*

In Chapter 3 we examined the use of a "lie detector" in employee selection, when an employer is investigating an applicant's background, honesty and character. The Employee Polygraph Protection Act (EPPA) prohibits nearly any use of a lie detector for employee selection in the private sector. However, the act permits an employer's use of a *polygraph* test in connection with "an ongoing investigation involving economic loss or injury to the employer's business," provided the employer and the examiner observe a number of safeguards designed to protect the rights of the employee-examinee. 29 U.S.C. § 2006(d)(1). The "economic loss or injury" exception authorizes only a polygraph test and not any other form of lie detector test. Moreover, this exception does not allow a wide-ranging fishing expedition for information about employees. The employer must examine only those employees who had access to the lost or injured thing, and who are the object of "reasonable suspicion" of involvement in the loss or injury. 29 U.S.C. §§ 2006(d)(2), (3). If an employee refuses to take the test, the employer must not discharge or discipline the employee "without additional supporting evidence." If the employee agrees to take the test, he enjoys a number of procedural rights, including advance written notice of the examination, advance notice of the questions, and limitations on the scope of the questioning.

BLACKWELL v. 53RD-ELLIS CURRENCY EXCH.

852 F. Supp. 646 (N.D. Ill. 1994)

PLUNKETT, District Judge.

. . . Plaintiff Yvonne Blackwell ("Blackwell") is a Chicago resident who was employed by 53rd-Ellis Currency Exchange, Inc. as a cashier from approximately October 15, 1990, until she was fired on April 4, 1991. . . . Defendant Sidney R. Miller ("Miller") is the principal owner and president of 53rd-Ellis. Miller acted in his capacity as president in all of his dealings with Plaintiff. . . . [A]round February 1991, a notary seal was discovered missing from 53rd-Ellis. In approximately mid-March, Miller made a general statement to all of the employees that each would be required to take a polygraph test ("test") in conjunction with certain missing notary seals and cash shortages.

Plaintiff received written notice about taking the test on March 20, 1991, when she signed a one page statement acknowledging that she and the other employees were requested to submit to the test. According to Plaintiff, the statement was signed "maybe a day or two" after Miller made the general announcement about the test. Plaintiff took a polygraph test on March 21, 1991. Lee McCord ("McCord"), a polygraph examiner, administered the test and verbally informed Plaintiff immediately after the test that she had passed. Miller also informed Plaintiff that she had passed when she arrived at work later that same afternoon.

Plaintiff's employment with 53rd-Ellis was terminated on April 4, 1991. When she arrived at work that morning, Plaintiff was informed by the manager, Deborah Garrett ("Garrett"), that Miller had fired her. . . . According to Miller's deposition testimony, Plaintiff was fired because she cashed several forged checks; misrepresented the verification of a thirteen hundred dollar cashier's check to Miller; failed to perform tasks requested of her by Garrett; and acted uncivilly toward Miller by being "sassy to [him] a couple of times when [he] asked her to do something."

Plaintiff's complaint against Defendants alleges substantive and procedural violations of the Employee Polygraph Protection Act of 1988 ("EPPA"), 29 U.S.C. § 2001 et seq. . . . Plaintiff seeks reinstatement to her former position of employment at 53rd-Ellis, actual and punitive damages in amounts to be determined at trial, the costs of this action, and reasonable attorneys' fees. Plaintiff seeks summary judgment solely on the issue of liability. . . .

The EPPA generally prohibits most private employers' use of polygraph tests either for pre-employment screening or for random testing during the course of employment. 29 U.S.C. § 2002. Section 2006 spells out six exemptions from the general prohibition on administering polygraph tests. The exemption at issue here . . . , subsection (d) of section 2006 states . . . [that] a private employer is entitled . . . to administer a polygraph test if (1) the test is given in connection with an "ongoing investigation" involving economic loss, such as theft, to the employer's business; (2) the employee had "access" to the property in question; (3) the employer has a "reasonable suspicion" that the employee was involved in the incident under investigation; (4) the employer signs a statement containing the required information and provides it to the employee prior to testing; and (5) the limitations set forth in section 2007 are met. . . .

Plaintiff first argues that the dictates of section 2006(3) have not been met because Defendants did not have a "reasonable suspicion" that Plaintiff was involved in the incident or activity under investigation. Plaintiff asserts that Defendants lacked the requisite reasonable suspicion about her . . . because all employees were asked to submit to the test, other employees had access to the missing items, and no specific allegations have been made that Plaintiff more than any other employee was involved in the disappearance of the missing items. Defendant's response seems to be that all employees were requested to take the test because all employees had access to the missing items. Whether Plaintiff can prevail on this issue turns on the interpretation of "reasonable suspicion."

The EPPA does not define the term "reasonable suspicion." The statute merely states that an employer may request an employee to submit to a polygraph test if, inter alia, "the employer has a reasonable suspicion that the employee was involved in the incident or activity under investigation." 29 U.S.C. § 2006(3). Thus, we look to the legislative history of the Act and the interpretive regulations promulgated by the Department of Labor. . . .

. . . Congress intended "reasonable suspicion" to refer to

> some observable articulable basis in fact *beyond the predicate loss and access required for testing*. This could include such factors as the demeanor of the employee or discrepancies which arise during the course of an investigation. And while access alone does not constitute a basis for reasonable suspicion, the totality of the circumstances surrounding such access, such as its unauthorized or unusual nature, may constitute an additional factor.

H.R. Conf. Rep. No. 659, 100th Cong., 2d Sess. 12-13, *reprinted in* 1988 U.S.C.C.A.N. 751 (emphasis added).

The regulations promulgated by the Department of Labor provide further insight into the term's meaning. Regulation 801.12(f)(1) mirrors the language found in the legislative history that reasonable suspicion refers to an "observable, articulable basis in fact which indicates that a particular employee was involved in, or responsible for, an economic loss." 29 C.F.R. § 801.12(f)(1). The regulation further emphasizes that "[a]ccess in the sense of possible or potential opportunity, standing alone, does not constitute a basis for 'reasonable suspicion.' "[6] *Id.*

The regulations illustrate the limited circumstances in which reasonable suspicion may be predicated on access alone.

> [I]n an investigation of a theft of an expensive piece of jewelry, an employee authorized to open the establishment's safe no earlier than 9 A.M., in order

[6] 29 C.F.R. § 801.12(f)(1) further states that "[i]nformation from a co-worker, or an employee's behavior, demeanor, or conduct may be factors in the basis for reasonable suspicion. Likewise, inconsistencies between facts, claims, or statements that surface during an investigation can serve as a sufficient basis for reasonable suspicion." *Id.*

> to place the jewelry in a window display case, is observed opening the safe at 7:30 A.M. In such a situation, the opening of the safe by the employee one and one-half hours prior to the specified time may serve as the basis for reasonable suspicion. On the other hand, in the example given, if the employer asked the employee to bring the piece of jewelry to his or her office at 7:30 A.M., and the employee then opened the safe and reported the jewelry missing, such access, standing alone, would not constitute a basis for reasonable suspicion that the employee was involved in the incident unless access to the safe was limited solely to the employee. If no one other than the employee possessed the combination to the safe, and all other possible explanations for the loss are ruled out, such as a break-in, the employer may formulate a basis for reasonable suspicion based on sole access by one employee.

29 C.F.R. § 801.12(f)(2). The employer has the burden of establishing that the specific individual to be tested is "'reasonably suspected' of involvement in the specific economic loss or injury for the requirement in section [200]7(d)(3) to be met." 29 C.F.R. § 801.12(f)(3).

Defendants have failed to establish that there is a genuine issue regarding the requisite "reasonable suspicion" that Plaintiff was involved in the missing notary seals and/or the cash shortages . . . . [R]easonable suspicion was premised solely upon the fact that Plaintiff had access to the missing notary seals and to the cash. Defendants do not . . . argue that Plaintiff had sole access.

The fact that Plaintiff had access to the missing items is not enough. The legislative history of the EPPA and the Department of Labor's regulations state in no uncertain terms that mere access is not enough to establish the reasonable suspicion required under 29 U.S.C. § 2006(d)(3). Because . . . mere access to stolen items is as a matter of law an insufficient foundation for reasonable suspicion under the EPPA, Defendants have not met their burden under Rule 56 to "designate specific facts" that show that there is a genuine issue of fact.

Plaintiff is entitled to summary judgment on the issue of liability. The EPPA exemption for on-going investigations into economic loss or injury to business is only available if the employer fulfills every one of the requirements set forth in section 2006. Defendants have not shown that there is a genuine issue for trial on the issue of reasonable suspicion. . . .

Plaintiff also is entitled to summary judgment based on the insufficiency of the statement given her by Defendant 53rd-Ellis prior to administration of the polygraph test. Section 2006(d)(4) provides that an employer is required to sign a statement given to the employee prior to the test which "sets forth with particularity the specific incident . . . being investigated and the basis for testing particular employees," and contains "an identification of the specific economic loss . . . to the business of the employer," a statement that the employee had access to the property in question, and a statement describing the basis for the employer's "reasonable suspicion" that the employee was involved in the theft. 29 U.S.C. § 2006(d). Regulation 801.12(g)(2) requires that the statement "be received by the employee at least 48 hours" prior to the time of the examination. 29 C.F.R. § 801.12(g)(2).

There is no evidence even suggesting that these requirements might have been met. The only notice provided by Defendants to Plaintiff prior to . . . the test is a statement that she and the other employees were requested to submit to the test. . . . Defendants admit that the statement does not set forth all of the information required under 29 U.S.C. § 2006(d)(4) . . . [and] that written notice was given 24 hours in advance rather than the requisite forty-eight.

There is no dispute about Defendants' failure to furnish Plaintiff with a statement meeting the requirements of subsection 2006(d)(4). . . . Accordingly, Plaintiff is entitled to summary judgment on this basis as well.

NOTES AND QUESTIONS

1. The court vacated its opinion for unstated reasons at 873 F. Supp. 103.

2. If Blackwell "passed" the unlawfully administered polygraph but was lawfully terminated for being "sassy," what remedy might she have obtained under the act? *See* 29 U.S.C. § 2005(c)(1): "An employer who violates this chapter shall be liable . . . for such legal or equitable relief as may be appropriate, including, *but not limited to*, employment, reinstatement, promotion, and the payment of lost wages and benefits." *See also* Mennen v. Easter Stores, 951 F. Supp. 838 (N.D. Iowa 1997) ($15,000 in damages for emotional distress based on unlawful administration of lie detector test *and* unlawful demotion). Even if an employee was not "injured" in a way for which legal or equitable relief may be appropriate, the Secretary of Labor may seek to collect a civil penalty of up to $10,000.

3. If an employer unlawfully conducts a polygraph and then discharges an employee based in part on the results, must the court award the employee reinstatement and lost pay? What if the employer had other evidence sufficient to justify requesting and conducting an examination? *See* Worden v. SunTrust Banks, Inc., 549 F.3d 334 (4th Cir. 2008) (employee need only prove unlawful test result was "factor" in discharge; employer avoids liability by proving it would have made same decision regardless of test); Mennen, 951 F. Supp. at 855-856.

4. If an employer has sufficient cause to ask an employee to take a polygraph test, and the employee refuses or fails a properly administered test, the employer may then rely *in part* on the results of the test in taking disciplinary action *provided* the employer has "additional supporting evidence." But the act further provides that the evidence required to establish grounds to conduct a test in the first instance may serve as the "additional supporting evidence" needed for adverse employment action. 29 U.S.C. § 2007(a)(1). Does this mean an employer always has sufficient "supporting evidence" to discharge or otherwise discipline an employee if it had enough evidence to justify *asking* the employee to take a test?

5. If several employees had access to missing items and the employer suspects one employee in particular because he "looks like he's hiding something," does the employer have reasonable cause to ask this employee to take a polygraph test? *See* 29 C.F.R. § 801.12(f)(1) ("employee's behavior" and "demeanor" may be "factors in the basis for reasonable suspicion"). If that employee refuses to take the test or he fails the test, may the employer discharge him?

6. In addition to the statutory requirements for investigatory polygraph use, 29 U.S.C. § 2007 lists other requirements, mainly as to the scope and procedure of the examination and the communication of important information to the examinee.

First, the act restricts the scope and manner of the examination by requiring that "the examinee is not asked questions in a manner designed to degrade, or needlessly intrude on, such examinee" and that the examination must not include questions relating to religion, race, politics, sexual behavior, or union affiliation or support. *Id.* § 2007(b)(1). The examiner must not conduct the test if there is "sufficient written evidence by a physician that the examinee is suffering from a medical or psychological condition or undergoing treatment that might cause abnormal responses during the actual testing phase." *Id.* § 2007(b)(1).

Second, an examinee has the right to terminate an examination at any time. *Id.* § 2007(b)(1).

Third, the act enumerates additional examinee rights during the pretest phase, actual test phase, and post-test phase. In the pretest phase, the examinee's rights include the right to reasonable advance notice of the date, time, and location of the test; of his right to consult with an attorney or employee representative (such as a union); of the type of test and of certain techniques the examiner might use; and of the examinee's statutory rights. The employer must also provide the examinee an opportunity to review all examination questions in advance. *Id.* § 2007(b)(2). During the test phase, the examiner must not ask "any question relevant during the test that was not presented in writing for review to such examinee before the test." *Id.* § 2007(b)(3). In the post-test phase, if an employer takes any adverse employment action it shall first "further interview the examinee on the basis of the results of the test," and shall provide the examinee "a written copy of any opinion or conclusion rendered as a result of the test, and a copy of the questions asked during the test along with the corresponding charted responses." *Id.* § 2007(b)(4).

Finally, an examination is not exempt from prohibition unless the examiner fulfilled certain professional qualifications, conducted the test for at least 90 minutes, conducted no more than five examinations on the same calendar day, and rendered his opinion in a form prescribed by the act. *Id.* §§ 2007(b)(5), (c).

7. How strict should the courts be in applying the EPPA's procedural requirements? In Wiltshire v. Citibank, 653 N.Y.S.2d 517 (N.Y. Sup. Ct. 1996), the court assumed the employer had complied with all requirements except one. The employer's written notice to the employee of the grounds for suspicion was not sufficiently particularized. The employer argued that the employee previously learned of the necessary facts from other conversations. Nevertheless, the court held that the employer violated the act and was liable for wrongful discharge.

> In essence Citibank is arguing for a rule that would permit substantial compliance with the requirements of a written statement. The court finds that the law is to the contrary. Literal compliance with the provisions of 29 U.S.C. § 2006(d) is required to take an employer out of the basic prohibition on using polygraphs provided in the EPPA.

Id. at 524.

8. As noted earlier, the act's ongoing investigation exception authorizes an employer's use of a "polygraph" but not any other kind of "lie detector" technology. A polygraph is an instrument that "records, continuously, visually, *permanently*, and simultaneously changes in cardiovascular, respiratory, *and* electrodermal patterns." 29 U.S.C. § 2001(4) (emphasis added). Other "lie detectors" — which are not authorized — include a wide range of existing and

possible future technology including a "deceptograph, voice stress analyzer, psychological stress evaluator, *or any other similar device (whether mechanical or electrical)* that is used, or the results of which are used, *for the purpose of rendering a diagnostic opinion regarding the honesty or dishonesty* of an individual." *Id.* § 2001(3) (emphasis added). If an employer reviewed a video recording in an effort to verify an employee's account of some loss or accident at the workplace, would the video camera, recorder, and monitor be "lie detectors"?

In Veazey v. Communications & Cable of Chicago, Inc., 194 F.3d 850 (7th Cir. 1999), the employer interrogated the plaintiff about an offensive anonymous phone message left on the voicemail of another employee. When the plaintiff denied responsibility, the employer asked the plaintiff to speak into a tape recorder to make a "voice exemplar" the employer could compare against the offensive message. The plaintiff refused, and the employer discharged him. In a wrongful discharge lawsuit, the plaintiff argued that the tape recorder was a potential "lie detector," and that the employer had violated the EPPA by failing to follow the requirements of the act in requesting a voice recording. The district court granted the employer's motion to dismiss, but a divided panel of the Seventh Circuit reversed. The court distinguished use of a device to "directly gauge a person's truthfulness" from use of a device *indirectly* to determine whether the person's statement is true. The former is use of a lie detector. The latter is not. Thus, a device used to analyze DNA samples at the scene of a crime is not used as a lie detector if it only verifies certain facts that may or may not be consistent with a person's statement. In this instance, the device is used "indirectly" to determine the truthfulness of the person's statement. On the other hand, an audio recorder could be used as a "lie detector" if used to record an interview and then to analyze voice stress as a direct gauge of truthfulness. *Id.* at 860 n.9. *See also* Theisen v. Covenant Med. Ctr., Inc., 636 N.W.2d 74 (Iowa 2001).

9. *Veazey* suggests a practical problem for enforcement of the EPPA: the problem of surreptitious use of lie detector technology. There are several widely marketed "portable" lie detector devices that rely on voice stress analysis. Advertisers claim the devices are useful for detecting lies in face-to-face conversations or in telephone conversations.

10. Remember that the EPPA does not apply to public sector employers and employees. However, public sector employees may assert constitutional rights against the administration of lie detector tests or the use of test results. See Chapter 3.D.4, *supra*. In addition, many states have statutes, in some cases long pre-dating the EPPA, that authorize, prohibit, or restrict the use of lie detectors, and some of these statutes may protect state and local government employees. *See, e.g.*, R.I. Gen. Laws § 28-6.1-1 ("No employer . . . shall either orally or in writing request, require, or subject any employee to any lie detector tests as a condition of employment or continued employment.").

PROBLEM

Sleuth Solutions, Inc., recently received a grievance by one of its employees, Sue Mohr, alleging that her supervisor Harry Razor sexually harassed her by implying she would not get any promotions unless she submitted to him sexually. Razor, a fifteen-year employee with no record of sexual harassment, denied the charge, saying "I never said anything of the sort." Mohr, who was only recently hired, insisted her charge was true, although there were no witnesses to what she alleged to have been a private conversation. Sleuth suggested to both parties that they submit to a polygraph examination. When Razor declined, Sleuth announced that it had determined that the sexual harassment charge was true, and it fired Razor. Does Razor have a claim under the EPPA?

4. *Investigatory Searches*

An employer's investigatory search of an employee's person or property is subject to the same Fourth Amendment and common law "invasion of privacy" protections that apply to a background investigation of a job applicant. See Chapter 3.D.1.b, *supra*. Both the Fourth Amendment (in the case of public employment) and the common law of privacy protect an applicant or employee's reasonable expectations of privacy against unreasonable search by an employer.

Chapter 3 presented rules for an employer's "search" of applicants. The abstract rules for a search of current employees are generally the same as the rules for a search of applicants. However, the context for an employer's search of current employees is entirely different. Current employees have different expectations of privacy, employers have different reasons for searching current employees, and current employees are much more vulnerable to intrusive searches.

An applicant arrives as a stranger to the employer, and the employer has a compelling interest in learning about the applicant's general background, lifestyle, and values before deciding whether to establish an employment relationship. The applicant likely expects at least some investigation, but he can withdraw his application without a great loss if he finds an investigation objectionable. Thus, courts have been comparatively permissive of employer intrusion in the hiring context. *See, e.g.,* Baughman v. Wal-Mart Stores, Inc., 592 S.E.2d 824 (W. Va. 2003) ("Employers regularly perform pre-employment background checks, seek references, and require pre-employment medical examinations, etc., that are far more intrusive than what would be considered tolerable for existing employees without special circumstances.").

A current employee, on the other hand, is no stranger to the employer. The employer has less reason to continue to pry into the employee's personal life to gauge the employee's qualifications if it has already hired the employee. Moreover, the employee does not arrive at work each day expecting further background inspection. Nevertheless, there are at least two important reasons why an employer may need — and its current employees may foresee — an investigation of current employees: (1) general oversight of work or (2) investigation of work-related wrongdoing. A current employee's expectation of privacy is further diminished because he is under the oversight of the employer throughout the working day and his personal items and data are stored at the worksite or mixed with the employer's property. If an employer demands to search a current employee, the current employee may find it much harder to withhold consent than if he were an applicant. Quitting or being "fired" for resisting an investigatory search is likely to be much more painful than merely withdrawing a job application.

Two important sources of protection for employees against intrusion are the

Fourth Amendment right against unreasonable search (for public sector employees) and the tort law doctrine of invasion of privacy (for private sector employees).

O'CONNOR v. ORTEGA

480 U.S. 709 (1987)

Justice O'CONNOR announced the judgment of the Court and delivered an opinion in which THE CHIEF JUSTICE, Justice WHITE, and Justice POWELL join.

This suit . . . presents two issues concerning the Fourth Amendment rights of public employees. First, we must determine whether the respondent, a public employee, had a reasonable expectation of privacy in his office, desk, and file cabinets at his place of work. Second, we must address the appropriate Fourth Amendment standard for a search conducted by a public employer in areas in which a public employee is found to have a reasonable expectation of privacy.

I

Dr. Magno Ortega, a physician and psychiatrist, held the position of Chief of Professional Education at Napa State Hospital (Hospital) . . . for 17 years, until his dismissal from that position in 1981. . . . Dr. Ortega had primary responsibility for training young physicians in psychiatric residency programs.

In July 1981, Hospital officials, including Dr. Dennis O'Connor, the Executive Director of the Hospital, became concerned about possible improprieties in Dr. Ortega's management of the residency program. In particular, the Hospital officials were concerned with Dr. Ortega's acquisition of an Apple II computer for use in the residency program. The officials thought that Dr. Ortega may have misled Dr. O'Connor into believing that the computer had been donated, when in fact the computer had been financed by the possibly coerced contributions of residents. Additionally, the Hospital officials were concerned with charges that Dr. Ortega had sexually harassed two female Hospital employees, and had taken inappropriate disciplinary action against a resident.

On July 30, 1981, Dr. O'Connor requested that Dr. Ortega take paid administrative leave during an investigation of these charges. . . . Dr. Ortega . . . was [also] requested to stay off Hospital grounds for the duration of the investigation. . . . Dr. Ortega remained on administrative leave until the Hospital terminated his employment on September 22, 1981.

Dr. O'Connor selected several Hospital personnel to conduct the investigation, including an accountant, a physician, and a Hospital security officer. Richard Friday, the Hospital Administrator, led this "investigative team." . . . Mr. Friday made the decision to enter Dr. Ortega's office. The specific reason for the entry into Dr. Ortega's office is unclear from the record. The petitioners claim that the search was conducted to secure state property. Initially, petitioners contended that such a search was pursuant to a Hospital policy of conducting a routine inventory of state property in the office of a terminated employee. At the time of the search, however, the Hospital had not yet terminated Dr. Ortega's employment; Dr. Ortega was still on administrative leave. Apparently, there was no policy of inventorying the offices of those on administrative leave. Before the search had been initiated, however, petitioners had become aware that Dr. Ortega had taken the computer to his home. Dr. Ortega contends that the purpose of the search was to secure evidence for use against him . . . .

The resulting search of Dr. Ortega's office was quite thorough. The investigators entered the office a number of times and seized several items from Dr. Ortega's desk and file cabinets, including a Valentine's Day card, a photograph, and a book of poetry all sent to Dr. Ortega by a former resident physician. These items were later used in a proceeding before a hearing officer of the California State Personnel Board to impeach the credibility of the former resident, who testified on Dr. Ortega's behalf. The investigators also seized billing documentation of one of Dr. Ortega's private patients under the California Medicaid program. The investigators did not otherwise separate Dr. Ortega's property from state property because, as one investigator testified, "[t]rying to sort State from non-State, it was too much to do, so I gave it up and boxed it up." Thus, no formal inventory of the property in the office was ever made. Instead, all the papers in Dr. Ortega's office were merely placed in boxes, and put in storage for Dr. Ortega to retrieve.

Dr. Ortega commenced this action . . . under 42 U.S.C. § 1983, alleging that the search of his office violated the Fourth Amendment. . . .

II

The Fourth Amendment protects the "right of the people to be secure in their persons, houses, papers, and effects, against unreasonable searches and seizures. . . ." Our cases establish that Dr. Ortega's Fourth Amendment rights are implicated only if the conduct of the Hospital officials at issue in this case infringed "an expectation of privacy that society is prepared to consider reasonable." United States v. Jacobsen, 466 U.S. 109, 113 (1984). . . . Because the reasonableness of an expectation of privacy, as well as the appropriate standard for a search, is understood to differ according to context, it is essential first to delineate the boundaries of the workplace context. The workplace includes those areas and items that are related to work and are generally within the employer's control. At a hospital, for example, the hallways, cafeteria, offices, desks, and file cabinets, among other areas, are all part of the workplace. These areas remain part of the workplace context even if the employee has placed personal items in them, such as a photograph placed in a desk or a letter posted on an employee bulletin board.

Not everything that passes through the confines of the business address can be considered part of the workplace context, however. An employee may bring closed luggage to the office prior to leaving on a trip, or a handbag or briefcase each workday. While whatever expectation of privacy the employee has in the existence and the outward appearance of the luggage is affected by its presence in the workplace, the employee's expectation of privacy in the contents of the luggage is not affected in the same way. The appropriate standard for a workplace search does not necessarily apply to a piece of closed personal luggage, a handbag or a briefcase that happens to be within the employer's business address.

Within the workplace context, this Court has recognized that employees may have a reasonable expectation of privacy against intrusions by police. *See* Mancusi v. DeForte, 392 U.S. 364 (1968). As with the expectation of privacy in one's home, such an expectation in one's place of work is "based upon societal expectations that have deep roots in the history of the Amendment." Oliver v. United States, *supra*, 466 U.S., at 178, n.8. Thus, in Mancusi v. DeForte, *supra*, the Court held that a union employee who shared an office with other union employees had a privacy interest in the office sufficient to challenge successfully the warrantless search of that office. . . .

Given the societal expectations of privacy in one's place of work expressed in both *Oliver* and *Mancusi*, we reject the contention made by the Solicitor General and petitioners that public employees can never have a reasonable expectation of privacy in their place of work. Individuals do not lose Fourth Amendment rights merely because they work for the government instead of a private employer. The operational realities of the workplace, however, may make some employees' expectations of privacy unreasonable when an intrusion is by a supervisor rather than a law enforcement official. Public employees' expectations of privacy in their offices, desks, and file cabinets, like similar expectations of employees in the private sector, may be reduced by virtue of actual office practices and procedures, or by legitimate regulation. Indeed, in *Mancusi* itself, the Court suggested that the union employee did not have a reasonable expectation of privacy against his union supervisors. 392 U.S., at 369. The employee's expectation of privacy must be assessed in the context of the employment relation. An office is seldom a private enclave free from entry by supervisors, other employees, and business and personal invitees. Instead, in many cases offices are continually entered by fellow employees and other visitors during the workday for conferences, consultations, and other work-related visits. Simply put, it is the nature of government offices that others — such as fellow employees, supervisors, consensual visitors, and the general public — may have frequent access to an individual's office. We agree with Justice Scalia that "[c]onstitutional protection against unreasonable searches by the government does not disappear merely because the government has the right to make reasonable intrusions in its capacity as employer," but some government offices may be so open to fellow employees or the public that no expectation of privacy is reasonable. . . . Given the great variety of work environments in the public sector, the question whether an employee has a reasonable expectation of privacy must be addressed on a case-by-case basis.

The Court of Appeals concluded that Dr. Ortega had a reasonable expectation of privacy in his office, and five Members of this Court agree with that determination. (Scalia, J., concurring in judgment . . . and Blackmun, J., joined by Brennan, Marshall, and Stevens, JJ., dissenting). . . . But regardless of any legitimate right of access the Hospital staff may have had to the office as such, we recognize that the undisputed evidence suggests that Dr. Ortega had a reasonable expectation of privacy in his desk and file cabinets. The undisputed evidence discloses that Dr. Ortega did not share his desk or file cabinets with any other employees. Dr. Ortega had occupied the office for 17 years and he kept materials in his office, which included personal correspondence, medical files, correspondence from private patients unconnected to the Hospital, personal financial records, teaching aids and notes, and personal gifts and mementos. The files on physicians in residency training were kept outside Dr. Ortega's office. Indeed, the only items found by the investigators were apparently personal items because, with the exception of the items seized for use in the administrative hearings, all the papers and effects found in the office were simply placed in boxes and made available to Dr. Ortega. Finally, we note that there was no evidence that the Hospital had established any reasonable regulation or policy discouraging employees such as Dr. Ortega from storing personal papers and effects in their desks or file cabinets, although the absence of such a policy does not create an expectation of privacy where it would not otherwise exist.

On the basis of this undisputed evidence, Dr. Ortega had a reasonable expectation of privacy at least in his desk and file cabinets.

III

Having determined that Dr. Ortega had a reasonable expectation of privacy in his office, the Court of Appeals simply concluded without discussion that the "search . . . was not a reasonable search under the fourth amendment." 764 F.2d, at 707. But as we have stated in *T.L.O.*, "[t]o hold that the Fourth Amendment applies to searches conducted by [public employers] is only to begin the inquiry into the standards governing such searches. . . . [W]hat is reasonable depends on the context within which a search takes place." New Jersey v. T.L.O., 469 U.S., at 337. Thus, we must determine the appropriate standard of reasonableness applicable to the search. A determination of the standard of reasonableness applicable to a particular class of searches requires "balanc[ing] the nature and quality of the intrusion on the individual's Fourth Amendment interests against the importance of the governmental interests alleged to justify the intrusion." United States v. Place, 462 U.S. 696 (1983); Camara v. Municipal Court, 387 U.S., at 536-537. In the case of searches conducted by a public employer, we must balance the invasion of the employees' legitimate expectations of privacy against the government's need for supervision, control, and the efficient operation of the workplace.

"[I]t is settled . . . that 'except in certain carefully defined classes of cases, a search of private property without proper consent is "unreasonable" unless it has been authorized by a valid search warrant.'" Mancusi v. DeForte, 392 U.S., at 370 (quoting Camara v. Municipal Court, *supra*, 387 U.S., at 528-529). There are some circumstances, however, in which we have recognized that a warrant requirement is unsuitable. In particular, a warrant requirement is not appropriate when "the burden of obtaining a warrant is likely to frustrate the governmental purpose behind the search." Camara v. Municipal Court, *supra*, at 533. . . . In Marshall v. Barlow's, Inc., 436 U.S. 307 (1978), for example, the Court explored the burdens a warrant requirement would impose on the Occupational Safety and Health Act regulatory scheme, and held that the warrant requirement was appropriate only after concluding that warrants would not "impose serious burdens on the inspection system or the courts, [would not] prevent inspections necessary to enforce the statute, or [would not] make them less effective." 436 U.S., at 316. . . .

The legitimate privacy interests of public employees in the private objects they bring to the workplace may be substantial. Against these privacy interests, however, must be balanced the realities of the workplace, which strongly suggest that a warrant requirement would be unworkable. While police, and even administrative enforcement personnel, conduct searches for the primary purpose of obtaining evidence for use in criminal or other enforcement proceedings, employers most frequently need to enter the offices and desks of their employees for legitimate work-related reasons wholly unrelated to illegal conduct. Employers and supervisors are focused primarily on the need to complete the government agency's work in a prompt and efficient manner. An employer may have need for correspondence, or a file or report available only in an employee's office while the employee is away from the office. Or, as is alleged to have been the case here, employers may need to safeguard or identify state property or records in an office in connection with a pending investigation into suspected employee misfeasance.

[R]equiring an employer to obtain a warrant whenever the employer wished to enter an employee's office, desk, or file cabinets for a work-related purpose would seriously disrupt the routine conduct of business and would be unduly burdensome. Imposing unwieldy warrant procedures in such cases upon supervisors, who would otherwise have no reason to be familiar with such procedures, is simply unreasonable. In contrast to other circumstances in which we have required warrants, supervisors . . . are hardly in the business of investigating the violation of criminal laws. Rather, work-related searches are merely incident to the primary business of the agency. Under these circumstances, the imposition of a warrant requirement would conflict with "the common-sense realization that government offices could not function if every employment decision became a constitutional matter." Connick v. Myers, 461 U.S. 138, 143 (1983).

Whether probable cause is an inappropriate standard for public employer searches of their employees' offices presents a more difficult issue. For the most part, we have required that a search be based upon probable cause, but as we noted in New Jersey v. T.L.O., "[t]he fundamental command of the Fourth Amendment is that searches and seizures be reasonable, and although 'both the concept of probable cause and the requirement of a warrant bear on the reasonableness of a search, . . . in certain limited circumstances neither is required.'" 469 U.S., at 340 (quoting Almeida-Sanchez v. United States, 413 U.S. 266, 277 (1973) (Powell, J., concurring)). . . . [T]he appropriate standard for administrative searches is not probable cause in its traditional meaning. Instead, an administrative warrant can be obtained if there is a showing that reasonable legislative or administrative standards for conducting an inspection are satisfied.

. . . [I]t is important to recognize the plethora of contexts in which employers will have an occasion to intrude to some extent on an employee's expectation of privacy. Because the parties in this case have alleged that the search was either a noninvestigatory work-related intrusion or an investigatory search for evidence of suspected work-related employee misfeasance, we undertake to determine the appropriate Fourth Amendment standard of reasonableness only for these two types of employer intrusions and leave for another day inquiry into other circumstances.

The governmental interest justifying work-related intrusions by public employers is the efficient and proper operation of the workplace. Government agencies provide myriad services to the public, and the work of these agencies would suffer if employers were required to have probable cause before they entered an employee's desk for the purpose of finding a file or piece of office correspondence. Indeed, it is difficult to give the concept of probable cause, rooted as it is in the criminal investigatory context, much meaning when the purpose of a search is to retrieve a file for work-related reasons. Similarly, the concept of probable cause has little meaning for a routine inventory conducted by public employers for the purpose of securing state property. . . . To ensure the efficient and proper operation of the agency, therefore, public employers must be given wide latitude to enter employee offices for work-related, noninvestigatory reasons.

We come to a similar conclusion for searches conducted pursuant to an investigation of work-related employee misconduct. Even when employers conduct an investigation, they have an interest substantially different from "the normal need for law enforcement." New Jersey v. T.L.O., *supra*, 469 U.S., at 351 (Blackmun, J., concurring in judgment). Public employers have an interest in ensuring that their agencies operate in an effective and efficient manner, and the work of these agencies inevitably suffers from the inefficiency, incompetence, mismanagement, or other work-related misfeasance of its employees. Indeed, in many cases, public employees are entrusted with tremendous responsibility, and the consequences of their misconduct or incompetence to both the agency and the public interest can be severe. [P]ublic employers are not enforcers of the criminal law; instead, public employers have a direct and overriding interest in ensuring that the work of the agency is conducted in a proper and efficient manner. In our view, therefore, a probable cause requirement for searches of the type at issue here would impose intolerable burdens on public employers. The delay in correcting the employee misconduct caused by the need for probable cause rather than reasonable suspicion will be translated into tangible and often irreparable damage to the agency's work, and ultimately to the public interest. . . . Additionally, while law enforcement officials are expected to "schoo[l] themselves in the niceties of probable cause," *id.*, at 343, no such expectation is generally applicable to public employers, at least when the search is not used to gather evidence of a criminal offense. It is simply unrealistic to expect supervisors in most government agencies to learn the subtleties of the probable cause standard. . . .

Balanced against the substantial government interests in the efficient and proper operation of the workplace are the privacy interests of government employees in their place of work which, while not insubstantial, are far less than those found at home or in some other contexts. . . . Government offices are provided to employees for the sole purpose of facilitating the work of an agency. The employee may avoid exposing personal belongings at work by simply leaving them at home.

In sum, . . . "special needs, beyond the normal need for law enforcement make the . . . probable-cause requirement impracticable," 469 U.S., at 351 (Blackmun, J., concurring in judgment), for legitimate work-related, noninvestigatory intrusions as well as investigations of work-related misconduct. A standard of reasonableness will neither unduly burden the efforts of government employers to ensure the efficient and proper operation of the workplace, nor authorize arbitrary intrusions upon the privacy of public employees. . . . [I]ntrusions on the constitutionally protected privacy interests of government employees for noninvestigatory, work-related purposes, as well as for investigations of work-related misconduct, should be judged by the standard of reasonableness under all the circumstances. [B]oth the inception and the scope of the intrusion must be reasonable. . . .

Ordinarily, a search of an employee's office by a supervisor will be "justified at its inception" when there are reasonable grounds for suspecting that the search will turn up evidence that the employee is guilty of work-related misconduct, or that the search is necessary for a noninvestigatory work-related purpose such as to retrieve a needed file. Because petitioners had an "individualized suspicion" of misconduct by Dr. Ortega, we need not decide whether individualized suspicion is an essential element of the standard of reasonableness that we adopt today. The search will be permissible in its scope when "the measures adopted are reasonably related to the objectives of the search and not excessively intrusive in light of . . . the nature of the [misconduct]." 469 U.S., at 342.

IV

In the procedural posture of this case, we do not attempt to determine whether the search of Dr. Ortega's office and the seizure of his personal belongings satisfy the standard of reasonableness we have articulated in this case. No evidentiary hearing was held in this case because the District Court acted on cross-motions for summary judgment, and granted petitioners summary judgment. The Court of Appeals, on the other hand, concluded that the record in this case justified granting partial summary judgment on liability to Dr. Ortega.

We believe that both the District Court and the Court of Appeals were in error because summary judgment was inappropriate. The parties were in dispute about the actual justification for the search, and the record was inadequate for a determination on motion for summary judgment of the reasonableness of the search and seizure. . . . On remand, therefore, the District Court must determine the justification for the search and seizure, and evaluate the reasonableness of both the inception of the search and its scope.[12*]

[Omitted: concurring opinion of Justice Scalia, and dissenting opinion of Justice BLACKMUN, joined by Justices BRENNAN, MARSHALL, and STEVENS.]

NOTES AND QUESTIONS

1. Dr. Ortega's lawsuit was far from over when the Supreme Court delivered its opinion. His case eventually went to trial where Dr. Ortega, having dismissed his lawyer, proceeded pro se. At the close of the evidence the district court granted a directed verdict in favor of the defendants and dismissed Dr. Ortega's claims. Dr. Ortega rehired his lawyer and filed another appeal, resulting in yet another reversal, remand, and retrial. In the second trial, a jury awarded Dr. Ortega $376,000 in compensatory damages and $60,000 in punitive damages. Seventeen years after the search that led to the lawsuit, the Ninth Circuit Court of Appeals affirmed the verdict. Ortega v. O'Connor, 146 F.3d 1149 (9th Cir. 1998).

2. Justice Scalia, the "swing" vote, concurred with the plurality in remanding the case for further proceedings, but he differed from the plurality in some important respects. First, he criticized the plurality's "case-by-case" approach to Fourth Amendment protection of a public employee's office, which

---

[12*]We have no occasion in this case to reach the issue of the appropriate standard for the evaluation of the Fourth Amendment reasonableness of the seizure of Dr. Ortega's personal items. . . . Finally, we do not address the appropriate standard when an employee is being investigated for criminal misconduct or breaches of other nonwork-related statutory or regulatory standards.

depends on how "open" the office is to fellow employees or the public. 480 U.S. at 729-730. According to Justice Scalia, this "formulation of a standard [is] so devoid of content that it produces rather than eliminates uncertainty in this field." *Id.* Second, Justice Scalia agreed with the four dissenting Justices that Dr. Ortega had a reasonable expectation of privacy with respect to his *office*, and not just the desk and cabinets, regardless of whether his office was "open" to others. "It is privacy that is protected by the Fourth Amendment," he reminded the Court, "not solitude," and he pointed to the Court's earlier rulings permitting public employees and other persons to assert a Fourth Amendment right against warrantless police searches of space shared with others. *Id.*

Justice Scalia substantially agreed with the majority with respect to the ultimate question whether the search of Dr. Ortega's desk and cabinets was necessarily unlawful. Even if an employee has a reasonable expectation of privacy with respect to some space or item, the Fourth Amendment does not absolutely foreclose a public employer's search, and the lawfulness of a search for legitimate work-related or investigatory purposes will be tested by a standard of reasonableness, with no requirement of a warrant or "probable cause." In the words of Justice Scalia, the fifth vote on this point, "I would hold that government searches to retrieve work-related materials or to investigate violations of workplace rules — searches of the sort that are regarded as *reasonable and normal* in the private-employer context — do not violate the Fourth Amendment." 480 U.S. at 732.

3. Like Justice Scalia, the four dissenting Justices (Blackmun, Brennan, Marshall, and Stevens) found that Dr. Ortega had a Fourth Amendment right against an unreasonable search of his office, as well as his desk and cabinets, notwithstanding that his office may have been open to others. 480 U.S. at 737-741. Their other disagreement with the plurality and Justice Scalia related to the standard for testing the lawfulness of a public employer's search under the Fourth Amendment when an employee proves a reasonable expectation of privacy. The dissenters were not prepared to abandon the requirement of a warrant or "probable cause." They found the plurality's adoption of a "reasonable" cause standard too lenient without a better developed record supporting the application of such a standard. 480 U.S. at 741-748.

4. *City of Ontario v. Quon*, 560 U.S. 746 (U.S.,2010), applied the *O'Connor v. Ortega* balancing test to a police department's investigatory search of text messages a police officer sent on a department-issued pager:

> [S]ince *O'Connor* ... the threshold test for determining the scope of an employee's Fourth Amendment rights has not been clarified further. Here, though they disagree on whether Quon had a reasonable expectation of privacy, both petitioners and respondents start from the premise that the *O'Connor* plurality controls. It is not necessary to resolve whether that premise is correct. The case can be decided by determining that the search was reasonable even assuming Quon had a reasonable expectation of privacy.

Id. at 757. *Quon* is discussed further in the discussion of electronic surveillance in part B.6 of this chapter.

5. Lower courts appear to have followed the lead of the plurality with respect to the reasonableness of an employee's expectation of privacy in a workplace office,

frequently finding that an employer's day-to-day access to an employee's office and its contents eliminates the employee's claim of Fourth Amendment protection. *See, e.g.*, Gossmeyer v. McDonald, 128 F.3d 481 (7th Cir. 1997) (employee had no reasonable expectation of privacy with respect to office, cabinet, desk and storage units, even though she purchased some of the furniture herself, because the office and furniture stored mainly work-related material). *But see* Varnado v. Dep't of Emp. and Training, 687 So. 2d 1013 (La. App. 1996) (employee had reasonable expectation of privacy as to office, desk and filing cabinets; employer's search was unreasonable in inception, manner, and scope).

6. The Fourth Amendment applies to public sector employers but not private sector employers. Private sector employees, however, may find similar protection under the common law doctrine of invasion of privacy. *See, e.g.*, Sowards v. Norbar, Inc., 605 N.E.2d 468 (Oh. App. 1992) (employee had reasonable expectation of privacy in motel room that employer regularly reserved for its employees, and employer unlawfully invaded employee's privacy by searching the room to look for documents relating to the employee's suspected misconduct); K-Mart Corp. Store No. 7441 v. Trotti, 677 S.W.2d 632 (Tex. App. 1984) (evidence supported employee's reasonable expectation of privacy in locker she used on employer's premises, for purposes of invasion of privacy claim against employer).A version of the common law of privacy frequently applied by the state courts includes a requirement that the intrusion must have been one that would be highly offensive to a reasonable person and involved what should have remained the private affairs of the employee. RESTATEMENT (SECOND) OF TORTS § 652B (1977). How does this compare with the Fourth Amendment?

7. The new Restatement of Employment Law includes a number of provisions important to "invasion of privacy" or intrusion by an employer into the private affairs of its current employees. That Restatement begins by identifying potential privacy interests, depending on an employee's "reasonable expectation" under the circumstances: (1) the "physical person, including bodily functions;" (2) personal possessions; (3) physical and electronic locations; and (4) information of a "personal nature." RESTATEMENT OF THE LAW, EMPLOYMENT LAW § 7.02. Other provisions address reasons why an employee may or may not reasonably expect privacy with respect to these matters. *Id.* §§ 7.03 – 7.05. But an employer is liable for intruding against the employee's reasonably expected privacy only if the intrusion "would be highly offensive to a reasonable person under the circumstances." *Id.* at § 7.06. Whether an intrusion is "highly offensive" requires balancing the nature, manner and scope of the intrusion against "the employer's legitimate business interests or the public's interests in intruding." *Id.* Thus, a final determination whether a private sector employer's intrusion is tortious requires consideration of all the same factors important to whether a public sector employer's "search" violates the Fourth Amendment.

8. Perhaps the most extreme and degrading search or intrusion is a strip search. Should an employer ever be entitled to demand a strip search of an employee? *See, e.g.*, Leverette v. Bell, 247 F.3d 160 (4th Cir. 2001) (no Fourth Amendment violation by body cavity search of prison guard based on tip from reliable informant that employee would be bringing contraband into prison); Kirkpatrick v. City of Los Angeles, 803 F.2d 485 (9th Cir. 1986) (police

department's strip searches of officers, conducted at police station, violated officers' Fourth Amendment rights); Matthews v. Stewart, 207 F. Supp. 2d 496 (M.D. La. 2001) (restaurant manager allegedly conducted strip and body cavity search of restaurant employee; invasion of privacy claim dismissed for lack of federal court jurisdiction); Bodewig v. K-Mart, Inc., 635 P.2d 657 (Or. App. 1981) (reversing summary judgment for employer and finding issue of fact whether employer's strip search of employee constituted unlawful invasion of privacy).

9. The *O'Connor* plurality speaks of searches based on suspected "work-related misconduct" and searches for a "work-related purpose such as to retrieve a needed file." What if an investigatory search is not based on individualized suspicion of misconduct, but is part of a "random" search to *deter* theft or other misconduct? A public employer needs neither a warrant nor "probable cause" to search a particular employee, or employee property, but the purpose must still pass a "reasonableness" test. A goal of deterring wrongdoing by random, suspicionless searches will not pass this test, absent special circumstances. Nat'l Fed'n of Fed. Employees v. Vilsack, 681 F.3d 483 (D.C. Cir. 2012); True v. Nebraska, 612 F.3d 676 (8th Cir. 2010). Special circumstances might include exceptional risks to public safety. *See, e.g.*, Thomson v. Marsh, 884 F.2d 113 (4th Cir. 1989) (upholding random search by drug testing of employees at chemical weapons facility). An employee's advance consent by accepting or continuing employment with notice of the public employer's random search policy may tip the scales in favor of allowing random search if safety or theft-prevention goals, standing alone, might be insufficient to justify the search. United States v. Gonzalez, 300 F.3d 1048 (9th Cir. 2002) (upholding random, suspicionless search of employee backpack pursuant to employer's clear notice regarding searches of persons exiting particular facility).

10. Under either Fourth Amendment or invasion of privacy analysis, an employee's advance consent to a search might bar his claim that the search was unlawful. As compared with job applicants, current employees may be in a somewhat better position to claim that submission to an employer's demand for permission to conduct a search was not "voluntary." In jurisdictions with a strong employment at will doctrine, the threat of discharge standing alone is unlikely to vitiate the employee's consent. However, the threat of discharge might be combined with other coercive circumstances to tip the scales in the employee's favor. Addington v. Wal-Mart Stores, Inc., 105 S.W.3d 369 (Ark. App. 2003), is one example of the cumulative effect of coercive factors. In *Addington*, the employee signed a written consent to his employer's search for stolen company property at the employee's home. The employee signed the consent after consulting with an attorney. Nevertheless, the court overruled summary judgment for the employer, and remanded the case for further proceedings:

> [S]everal particulars here . . . create a fact question . . . of whether Addington's consent was voluntarily given: [Wal-Mart's] threat [to report its suspicions to] the IRS; the fact that Addington declined to consent three times, yet [Wal-Mart's loss prevention officer] and [a county deputy] remained on the premises [of Addington's home]; Addington's fear that he would lose his job if he did not consent; mention of the media . . . ; and the fact that Addington agreed to go to his home in the first place only to allow Womack to look at the light poles. . . . [B]efore signing the consent, Addington took

> the opportunity to consult with counsel. However, while Addington's consultation with an attorney before signing the consent form is certainly a factor to be considered in determining the voluntariness of his actions, we do not deem it conclusive. By that point, Addington had already refused to consent three times and had been subjected to the other coercive actions. The totality of the circumstances, in particular the fact that Addington declined to consent three times before succumbing, leads us to conclude that a fact question remains as to whether his consent was voluntarily given.

Id. at 380. *See also* Bodewig v. K-Mart, Inc., 635 P.2d 657 (Or. App. 1981) (fact issue of consent to strip search by "youthful" part-time employee in "subservient" position alleging she believed she had no choice and would be fired for refusing).

11. An employer might gain an employee's implied consent by posting a rule or regulation making it clear that submission to certain searches are a condition of continued employment. One might also say that the advance notice eliminates any reasonable expectation of privacy. Prior to *O'Connor*, some federal courts had held that public employees have no reasonable expectation of privacy with respect to areas the employer's regulations have designated as territory subject to occasional inspection. *See, e.g.*, United States v. Speights, 557 F.2d 362, 364-365 (3d Cir. 1977). *O'Connor* appears to reinforce this rule by the plurality's statement that "Public employees' expectations of privacy in their offices, desks, and file cabinets . . . may be reduced by virtue of actual office practices and procedures, or by legitimate regulation." *See also* Brambrinck v. City of Philadelphia, 1994 WL 649342 (E.D. Pa. 1994) (upholding search of police officers' lockers in view of department regulation permitting such search).

The effect of a clearly posted employer rule might be negated by the employer's mixed signals about employee privacy. In Haynes v. Office of Attorney General, 298 F. Supp. 2d 1154 (D. Kan. 2003), the court held that a terminated employee had sufficiently demonstrated a likelihood of success on the merits in his Fourth Amendment claim for purposes of a preliminary injunction limiting other persons' access to his private files on a work computer, and granting him access to make copies of his private files. The employer had a clearly posted policy purporting to negate any expectation of privacy in the computer system, but the employee alleged he was told he could put personal information in a private computer file so that no one could access it, employees were allowed to use computers for private communications, employees were given passwords to prevent other persons from accessing their files, and the employer had not previously monitored private files of any employee.

12. The Restatement of Employment Law takes a strong position in the case of an employer's actual *termination* of an employee for refusing to submit to an intrusion that, absent voluntary consent, would be unlawful. Section 7.07 states that "an employer who discharges an employee for refusing to consent to a wrongful employer intrusion … is subject to liability for wrongful discharge in violation of well-established public policy." RESTATEMENT OF THE LAW, EMPLOYMENT LAW § 7.07. The discharge is unlawful under the Restatement view only if the intrusion would have been unlawful without advance consent after considering the overall circumstances and weight of the employer or public interest in the intrusion. Thus, even under this view, discharge for resisting intrusion will

not always support a wrongful discharge claim.

But what if the employee consents, in writing or by submitting to an intrusion in the face of an express or implicit threat of termination? Does consent bar a claim that the intrusion was unlawful? As a practical matter, a remedy for wrongful discharge might not strengthen the employee's resolve to resist even if the employee knows discharge would be unlawful. The Restatement of Employment Law is less than clear with respect to whether consent makes an otherwise unlawful intrusion lawful if the employer makes consent "mandatory" or threatens discharge: it describes and favors a "predominant" view that consent obtained by threat of discharge is not voluntary with respect to an otherwise unlawful intrusion; but it also concedes a wide divergence of views on the matter. RESTATEMENT OF THE LAW, EMPLOYMENT LAW § 7.06, comment h.

Divergent outcomes in cases addressing the problem of consent by current employees are not surprising. First, as a practical matter an employer's "threat" will not always be obvious. In employment at will, any employer instruction or order carries with it an implicit understanding that the employer can terminate an employee, perhaps for resisting the intrusion or perhaps for suspicion that the employee is guilty of the misconduct that is the reason for the investigation. At the very least, an employee is likely to understand that resisting the employer's request will hurt the employee's standing in the workplace. Not surprisingly, some of the cases cited by the Restatement in support of invalidating consent given under threat of discharge involve cases in which the threat was explicit or with special force. *See, e.g.*, Wal-Mart Stores, Inc. v. Lee, 74 S.W.3d 634 (Ark. 2002) (consent invalid where, among other things, the consent form was presented by police officer). Second, the offensiveness of the intrusion is a likely factor for a court in rejecting consent, especially if the intrusion was so offensive that voluntary consent is naturally suspect or public policy would not tolerate the intrusion. *See, e.g.*, Bodewig v. K-Mart, Inc., 635 P.2d 657 (Or. App. 1981) (invalidating employee consent to disrobe in front of customer after customer accused employee of theft). Finally, some cases invalidating consent do so in part because the employer's intrusion exceeded the scope of the consent, or because the employee could not have appreciated that nature and depth of the employer's intrusion when he or she gave the consent. *See, e.g.*, O'Brien v. Papa Gino's of Am., Inc., 780 F.2d 1067, 1072 (1st Cir. 1986) (consent to investigation of drug use was not consent to polygraph use).

13. Under the Fourth Amendment, an individual's consent to a search of certain property is invalid if it is preceded by an illegal "seizure," unless the consent was in fact "sufficiently an act of free will to purge the primary taint" of the unlawful seizure. Wong Sun v. United States, 371 U.S. 471, 486 (1963). In McGann v. Ne. Illinois Regional Commuter R.R. Corp., 8 F.3d 1174 (1993), the court applied this rule in public employment to hold that employees might not be bound by consents to an employer search of their cars because they were unable to leave the parking facility without passing through a checkpoint for searches.

Investigatory and Random Substance Abuse Tests

A substance abuse test is a kind of search covered by the Fourth Amendment, and might also constitute invasion of privacy. As discussed in connection with employee selection in Chapter 3, Part D.3, drug and alcohol testing of applicants or current employees is subject to the usual general principles regarding the reasonableness of expectations of privacy, the examinee's consent, the employer's need for intrusion, and the manner of intrusion. There are, however, some unique features of drug testing of current employees that require additional comment.

First, legislatures, regulatory agencies, and courts frequently view substance abuse testing as a relatively slight and permissible intrusion in the employment context when conducted for legitimate reasons and according to certain safeguards. Many legislatures have enacted statutes restricting the administration of substance abuse tests by employers, but some of these statutes also have the effect of legitimizing substance abuse testing that complies with the regulatory scheme. Congress and some federal agencies have adopted the same approach in regulating transportation and other industries in which public safety is a major concern. *See, e.g.*, Omnibus Transp. Employee Testing Act of 1991, 49 U.S.C. § 5331. As for the workforce as a whole, Congress has neither authorized nor prohibited substance abuse testing, but it has encouraged employers to adopt "drug-free workplace" programs to discourage illegal drug use by employees. 41 U.S.C. §§ 701-07.

Second, as is true in for the law of "searches" in general, a court's analysis of a search by substance abuse testing is likely to differ when the examinee is a current employee rather than an applicant: A current employee is not a stranger as to whom the employer needs a background investigation. Thus, in the absence of special circumstances, there is no compelling reason for random, suspicionless, or periodic across-the-board testing of current employees. However, an employer may have good reason to require a substance abuse test based on an employee's work-related accident or behavioral problems. Local workers' compensation law may provide an extra motivation for an employer's demand for a test after a work-related accident because an employee's work under the influence of alcohol or a controlled substance may disqualify him from receiving workers' compensation benefits. Regardless of the reason for an employer's demand for a test, a current employee may find it difficult to deny consent for a test if the consequence would be discharge.

A watershed case regarding substance abuse testing of current employees is Skinner v. Railway Labor Executives' Ass'n, 489 U.S. 602 (1989), where the Supreme Court upheld investigatory testing of railroad employees. Although the railroads were private sector employers, the Court considered the legality of the testing under the Fourth Amendment because federal transportation regulations required the testing. The regulations required testing after every "major train accident" or "impact accident," as defined in the regulations, and after any "train incident" causing a fatality to an on-duty employee. 489 U.S. at 609. The Court found a persuasive reason for testing current employees based on heightened public safety concerns in the transportation industry and a proven correlation between substance abuse and railroad accidents. Indeed, the Court believed that the importance of public safety was so obvious that employees must naturally anticipate some safety-based intrusions on their privacy. 489 U.S. at 627.

Arguably, the tests required by the regulations in *Skinner* were not purely "investigatory" because an accident might occur under circumstances that would raise no suspicion that an employee's substance abuse was a contributing factor. To a certain extent, therefore, testing was random as well as investigatory. Nevertheless, the Court found the testing regimen neither overbroad nor overly intrusive. After balancing the respective interests of the public and railroad employees, the Court held that the needs for safety and the *deterrence* of substance abuse justified testing of railroad employees without individualized suspicion:

> By ensuring that employees in safety-sensitive positions know they will be tested upon the occurrence of a triggering event, the timing of which no employee can predict with certainty, the regulations significantly increase the deterrent effect of the administrative penalties associated with the prohibited conduct, . . . increasing the likelihood that employees will forgo using drugs or alcohol while subject to being called for duty.

Id. at 629-630.

Following *Skinner*, the lower courts have approved purely random substance abuse testing in a number of safety-sensitive occupations, especially occupations that present a risk of mass disaster. *See* Thomson v. Marsh, 884 F.2d 113 (4th Cir. 1989) (civilian employees at chemical weapons facility); Teamsters v. Dep't of Transp., 932 F.2d 1292, 1304 (9th Cir. 1991) (commercial truck drivers); IBEW Local 1245 v. Skinner, 913 F.2d 1454, 1458 (9th Cir. 1990) (employees in operational, maintenance, or emergency response functions on gas pipelines). Congress has now authorized testing employees in federally regulated transportation industries. *See* 49 U.S.C. § 5331 (mass transit), 49 U.S.C. § 20140 (railroads), 49 U.S.C. § 31306 (commercial motor vehicles), 49 U.S.C. § 45102 (aviation). But courts and state legislatures have prohibited random, suspicionless testing when the work in question presents less risk of catastrophe. Loder v. City of Glendale, 927 P.2d 1200 (Cal. 1997) (suspicionless testing of general workforce violated Fourth Amendment); Jones v. Graham County, 677 S.E.2d 171 (N. C. App. 2009) (school district employees); Petersen v. City of Mesa, 207 Ariz. 35, 83 P.3d 35 (2004) (firefighters); Anchorage Police Dep't Employees Ass'n v. Anchorage, 24 P.3d 547 (Alaska 2001) (police officers).

Private sector employees might also assert the common law of privacy, but in doing so they must overcome two major impediments: (1) consent, if they allowed the testing that caused their discharge; and (2) the employment at will doctrine, which relieves the employer of having to defend its reason for discharging an employee. *Compare* Bellinger v. Weight Watchers Gourmet Food Co., 756 N.E.2d 1251 (Ohio App. 2001) (employment at will doctrine precluded employee's claim that employer improperly required drug test and discharged employee based on result) *with* Borse v. Piece Goods Shop, Inc., 963 F.2d 611 (3d Cir. 1992) (under some circumstances, discharging private sector at-will employee for refusal to consent to drug or alcohol testing might violate public policy of Pennsylvania), *and* Benson v. AJR, Inc., 599 S.E.2d 747 (W. Va. 2004) (employment for fixed term was not "at will," and fact issue precluded summary judgment as to whether employer's administration of random drug test and discharge of plaintiff based on test result breached the contract).There is one situation in which even suspicion-based drug testing might constitute illegal "retaliation" under federal law. In late 2016 near the end of the Obama Administration, the Department of Labor adopted regulations to require employers to implement systems for reporting work-related accidents to the Occupational Safety and Health Administration. 29 C.F.R. § 1904.35(b). Naturally, the effectiveness of such a reporting system depends on the willingness of employees to report the accidents they observe or suffer. While an employer might require a drug test of the reporting employee as part of a good faith investigation of the accident, the employer must not use drug testing to retaliate against an employee for reporting an accident. The Department explained as follows:

> Regardless of whether an adverse action is taken pursuant to a disciplinary policy, post-accident drug testing policy, or employee incentive program, OSHA's ultimate burden is to prove that the employer took the adverse action because the employee reported a work-related injury or illness, not for a legitimate business reason. Determining in a particular case whether a violation occurred and whether there is enough evidence to substantiate the violation will be a fact-specific inquiry.

U.S. Dep't of Labor, Memorandum: Interpretation of 1904.35(b)(1)(i) and (iv) (Oct. 19, 2016), https://www.osha.gov/recordkeeping/finalrule/index.html

The Reasonableness of the Method of Testing: The Problem of Direct Observation

The reasonableness of a search by testing depends in part on the reasonableness of the employer's chosen method. An otherwise justifiable test is unreasonable if its method is needlessly intrusive or so inaccurate that the intrusion yields no significant benefit to the employer.

Courts approving employer-mandated substance abuse testing have typically assumed that a test can be performed in a manner that is both minimally intrusive and also accurate. In fact, the collection of a sample for substance abuse testing by urinalysis is generally no more intrusive than a routine medical examination, and laboratory analysis of the sample is widely regarded as sufficiently accurate to justify this intrusion. But what if the sample delivered to the laboratory is not genuine or has been "tainted?" There is a substantial black market in substances and devices designed to "beat" a drug test. A quick search on the internet for "drug test" and "beat" or "cheat" reveals a thriving business, including the sale of "synthetic" urine and chemicals which, if ingested, promise to "cleanse" the urinary system. If any of these products actually work, this fact would throw into question whether urinalysis in the routine, nonintrusive manner is accurate enough to be "reasonable." Thus, some employers have changed the collection procedure to make it more accurate by deterring cheating. But making the test more accurate is likely to make it more intrusive.

BNSF RAILWAY CO. v. DEPARTMENT OF TRANSPORTATION

566 F.3d 200 (D.C. Cir. 2009)

[Concerned about the problem of cheating in urinalysis-based drug tests, the Department of Transportation adopted new rules for testing in the transportation industry. Department regulations had already required drug testing of certain employees. The new rules required testing to include "partial disrobing" and "direct observation" of urination of employees who previously tested positive and were returning after a suspension. A railroad and a labor union challenged the rule under the Administrative Procedure Act (APA) and the Fourth Amendment.]

Prior to the rulemaking at issue . . . , employers had the option of conducting return-to-duty and follow-up tests using so-called "direct observation," a procedure that requires a same-gender observer to "watch the urine go from the employee's body into the collection container." Concerned that employers were underutilizing this option, especially in light of evidence of a growing proliferation of products that facilitate cheating on drug tests, . . . the Department promulgated a regulation requiring transportation industry employers to use direct observation for all return-to-duty and follow-up testing. Procedures for Transportation Workplace Drug and Alcohol Testing Programs ("Direct Observation Rule"). The regulation also requires that immediately prior to all direct observation tests, employees must raise their shirts above the waist and lower their lower clothing so as to expose their genitals and allow the observers to verify the absence of any cheating devices. 49 C.F.R. § 40.67(i) (2008).

The Department marshaled and carefully considered voluminous evidence of the increasing availability of a variety of products designed to defeat drug tests. It cited congressional testimony describing the ready availability, through Internet sales, of hundreds of different cheating products, the most elaborate of which is a "prosthetic device that looks like real human anatomy, color-matched," that can be used to deliver synthetic or drug-free urine. The Department also relied on a Government Accountability Office (GAO) report indicating that existing drug testing protocols were inadequate to prevent cheating. . . . GAO undercover investigators were able to adulterate their urine specimens even at testing sites that followed then-existing procedures. [T]he Department determined it was "not practicable" to ignore the cheating problem.

Petitioners dispute none of this evidence. Instead, they fault the Department for failing to provide direct evidence that employees are actually using cheating devices. Acknowledging that it had no statistics on the rates of actual use of such devices, the Department inferred their use from the anecdotal evidence of their availability. *Id.* at 62,913. As any successful use of cheating devices would not show up in statistics, the Department reasoned, it was "illogical" to require statistical evidence of cheating. *Id.* Given that people presumably buy cheating devices to use them, we think this approach quite reasonable . . . .

Finally, petitioners complain that the Department failed to consider less intrusive alternatives. They point out that some commenters suggested that the Department test hair and saliva rather than urine. As the Department explained, however, the Omnibus Testing Act required it to use only testing methods approved by the Department of Health and Human Services, which "ha[d] not approved any specimen testing except urine." *Id.* at 62,917; *see also* 105 Stat. 917, 955, 957, 959, 963. And although commenters suggested other safeguards such as further training of collection personnel and pursuit of additional legislative authority, the Department responded — gain reasonably in our view — that it was pursuing these approaches as well but that they could not substitute for the efficacy of direct observation. Direct Observation Rule, 73 Fed. Reg. at 62,916-17 . . . .

Thus, the Department acted neither arbitrarily nor capriciously in concluding that the growth of an industry devoted to circumventing drug tests, coupled with returning employees' higher rate of drug use and heightened motivation to cheat, presented an elevated risk of cheating . . . that justified the mandatory use of direct observation. We thus turn to petitioners' argument that the Department's suspicionless use of direct observation for returning employees, as well as the partial disrobing requirement, runs afoul of the Fourth Amendment . . . .

The government's interest in transportation safety is "compelling," to say the least. *Skinner*, 489 U.S. at 628. "Employees subject to the tests discharge duties fraught with such risks of injury to others that even a momentary lapse of attention can have disastrous consequences." *Id.* Petitioners dispute the extent of the cheating problem, but as discussed above, the Department permissibly found it to be great indeed . . . . And although the effectiveness of a search compared to available alternatives may be relevant to the government's interest in conducting the search, *see Delaware v. Prouse*, 440 U.S. 648, 659 (1979), there is no per se requirement that the government use the least intrusive practicable means, *Vernonia*, 515 U.S. at 663. . . . [W]e have little difficulty concluding that direct observation furthers the government's interest in effective drug testing.

Petitioners argue that the unannounced nature of follow-up tests diminishes the need for direct observation testing. We think the Department's contrary assessment was reasonable . . . . Though the precise dates of follow-up tests are unannounced, returning employees know they will have to face at least six such tests over the first year of their return to work. §40.307(d). Armed with such foreknowledge, returning employees can easily obtain and conceal cheating devices, keeping them handy even for unannounced follow-up tests. The government thus has a strong interest in conducting direct observation . . . .

The other side of the balance is trickier. Individuals ordinarily have extremely strong interests in freedom from searches as intrusive as direct observation urine testing. In this case, however, those interests are diminished because the airline, railroad, and other transportation employees subject to direct observation perform safety-sensitive duties in an industry that is "regulated pervasively to ensure safety." *Skinner*, 489 U.S. at 627. That said, when the Supreme Court recognized the diminished nature of transportation employees' privacy interests and found suspicionless drug testing permissible, it stressed that the tests at issue in that case required no direct observation. *Id.* at 626. . . .

According to the Department, returning employees have diminished privacy interests for reasons over and above their performance of safety-sensitive duties in a pervasively regulated industry. . . [A]ll have violated the Department's drug regulations by either refusing to take a test or testing positive . . . . Of course, this does not mean, as the Department claims, that returning employees are akin to convicted offenders on probation or parole; after all, the latter are subject to penal sanctions imposed after criminal process. . . . That said, we have little trouble concluding that employees who have intentionally violated a valid drug regulation, at least in the relatively recent past, *see* § 40.307 (providing a five-year time limit on follow-up tests), have less of a legitimate interest in resisting a search intended to prevent future violations of that regulation . . . .

We turn, then, to balancing the individuals' interest with the government's. Although weighing the strength of each is necessarily imprecise, we think that the employees' prior misconduct is particularly salient, especially compared to their choice to work in a pervasively regulated industry. It's one thing to ask individuals seeking to avoid intrusive testing to forgo a certain career entirely; it's a rather lesser thing to ask them to comply with regulations forbidding drug use. True, direct observation is extremely invasive, but that intrusion is mitigated by the fact that employees can avoid it altogether by simply complying with the drug regulations. On the other side of the balance, the Department has reasonably concluded that the proliferation of cheating devices makes direct observation necessary to render these drug tests — needed to protect the traveling public from lethal hazards — effective. Weighing these factors, we strike the balance in favor of permitting direct observation testing in these circumstances . . . .

Petitioners also claim that the partial disrobing requirement amounts to a strip search. As they acknowledge, however, the balancing inquiry remains the same regardless of how one characterizes the search. *See* Bell v. Wolfish, 441 U.S. 520, 559-560 (1979) (analyzing cavity search by balancing interests). . . . [W]e recognize the intrusiveness of the partial disrobing requirement, but find it only somewhat more invasive than direct observation, which already requires employees to expose their genitals to some degree. Because of this, and because the Department has permissibly found the requirement necessary to detect certain widely-available prosthetic devices, we conclude that it represents a reasonable procedure for situations posing such a heightened risk of cheating . . . .

We emphasize the limited nature of our holding. Because petitioners bring a facial challenge, we consider only "whether the tests contemplated by the regulations can ever be conducted." *Skinner*, 489 U.S. at 632 n. 10. We thus express no view on either the merits of any as-applied challenge to this rule or the constitutionality of any other rule.

NOTES AND QUESTIONS

1. Drug use can also be tested by hair sample analysis, which is less invasive but requirees removal of 80 to 120 strands of hair cut close to the scalp. A disadvantage is that the portion of a strand of hair affected by drug use requires a few days to grow above the scalp. Thus, a test based on a hair sample will not reveal very recent drug use. The black market for products designed to beat drug tests includes chemicals alleged to cleanse hair of any trace of drug use.

2. Blood analysis is the most accurate but expensive method of drug testing. Drawing blood requires more expensive equipment and trained personnel. Drawing blood can also be painful and involves some risk of injury.

Tests Revealing Lawful Use of Drugs

An employer's drug test usually targets unlawful drugs, but the employer or laboratory might cast a wider net and test for drugs that are lawful, perhaps always lawful or perhaps lawful under some circumstances but not under other circumstances. Can the employer lawfully discharge an employee who tests positive for drug use that is arguably "lawful?"

NOFFSINGER v. SSC NIANTIC OPERATING CO.

273 F. Supp. 3d 326 (D. Conn. 2017)

JEFFREY ALKER MEYER, United States District Judge

Connecticut is one of a growing number of States to allow the use of marijuana for medicinal purposes. Connecticut likewise bars employers from firing or refusing to hire an employee who uses medical marijuana in compliance with the requirements of Connecticut law. By contrast, federal law categorically prohibits the use of marijuana even for medical purposes.

This lawsuit calls upon me to decide . . . if federal law precludes enforcement of a Connecticut law that prohibits employers from firing or refusing to hire someone who uses marijuana for medicinal purposes. I conclude that the answer to that question is "no" and that a plaintiff who uses marijuana for medicinal purposes in compliance with Connecticut law may maintain a cause of action against an employer who refuses to employ her for this reason. Accordingly, I will largely deny defendant's motion to dismiss this lawsuit.

Background

. . . Connecticut is one of 29 States that have "comprehensive public medical marijuana and cannabis programs," and an additional 16 States have more limited programs allowing for the use of "low THC, high cannabidiol" products for particular medical reasons. Ibid.

The range of state statutes provide different rights and remedies to medical marijuana users. While all protect qualified users from state criminal prosecution, many also include broader protections "stating that medical marijuana patients are not to be subject to 'penalty,' 'sanction,' or may not be 'denied any right or privilege.'" Elizabeth Rodd, *Light, Smoke, and Fire: How State Law Can Provide Medical Marijuana Users Protection from Workplace Discrimination*, 55 B.C. L. REV. 1759, 1768 (2014). Several States—including Connecticut—provide explicit protection against employment discrimination on the basis of the medicinal use of marijuana in compliance with state law.

Notwithstanding the proliferation of state marijuana-use statutes, federal law stands to the contrary. The federal Controlled Substances Act classifies marijuana as a Schedule I substance, meaning that Congress has decided that "marijuana has no medicinal value." Kathleen Harvey, *Protecting Medical Marijuana Users in the Workplace*, 66 CASE W. RES. L. REV. 209, 211 (2015). [C]ourts around the country are now confronted with the question of how these permissive state laws may reconcile—if at all—with federal law.

In 2012, Connecticut enacted the Palliative Use of Marijuana Act (PUMA), Conn. Gen. Stat. § 21a–408 et seq. PUMA permits the use of medical marijuana for "qualifying patients" with certain debilitating medical conditions. The law exempts such patients, their primary caregivers, and prescribing doctors from state criminal penalties that would otherwise apply to those who use or distribute marijuana. It also sets forth a framework for a system of licensed dispensaries and directs the Department of Consumer Protection to adopt implementing regulations. Most importantly for purposes of this case—and in contrast to medical marijuana laws in many other States—PUMA includes a provision that explicitly prohibits discrimination against qualifying patients and primary caregivers by schools, landlords, and employers. See Conn. Gen. Stat. § 21a–408p(b).

Plaintiff's complaint alleges the following facts, which I accept as true for the purposes of this motion to dismiss. In 2012, plaintiff Katelin Noffsinger was diagnosed with posttraumatic stress disorder (PTSD). In 2015, her doctors recommended medical marijuana to treat her PTSD. She registered with the state Department of Consumer Protection as a qualifying patient under PUMA. After receiving her registration certificate, plaintiff began taking one capsule of Marinol, a synthetic form of cannabis, each night as prescribed.

When she started taking Marinol, plaintiff was employed as a recreation therapist at Touchpoints, a long-term care and rehabilitation provider. In July 2016, plaintiff was recruited for a position as a director of recreational therapy at Bride Brook, a nursing facility in Niantic, Connecticut. After a phone interview, plaintiff interviewed in person on July 18 with Lisa Mailloux, the administrator of Bride Brook. During the interview, Mailloux offered plaintiff the position, and plaintiff accepted the offer the following day. . . . Mailloux contacted plaintiff to set up a meeting . . . to complete paperwork and a routine pre-employment drug screen. Mailloux also instructed plaintiff to give notice to Touchpoints so that plaintiff could begin working at Bride Brook on August 3. Plaintiff informed Touchpoints that her last day would be August 2.

On July 25, . . . plaintiff disclosed her disability of PTSD and explained that she was taking prescription marijuana as a "qualifying patient" under PUMA. Plaintiff showed Mailloux her registration certificate and explained that she took Marinol, but only in the evening before bed, and therefore she was never impaired during the workday. Plaintiff also offered to provide additional medical documentation, but Mailloux did not request it. Mailloux continued to process plaintiff's pre-employment documents and gave plaintiff a packet of documents to . . . bring back when she returned for orientation on August 3. . . . [P]laintiff provided defendant with a urine sample to be used as part of the pre-employment drug test.

On August 2, the day before plaintiff was scheduled to start work at Bride Brook, the drug testing company used by Bride Brook called plaintiff to inform her that she had tested positive for cannabis. Plaintiff immediately called Mailloux and left a voice message in which she informed Mailloux of her call with the drug testing company and asked a question about the upcoming orientation session. Later that day, Mailloux called plaintiff back to inform her that Bride Brook was rescinding plaintiff's job offer because she had tested positive for cannabis. In the meantime, plaintiff's former position at Touchpoints had already been filled, so she was not able to remain employed there.

On August 22, 2016, plaintiff filed a complaint . . . alleging three causes of action: (1) a violation of PUMA's anti-discrimination provision, Conn. Gen. Stat. § 21a–408p(b)(3), (2) a common law claim for wrongful rescission of a job offer in violation of public policy, and (3) negligent infliction of emotional distress. . . .

DISCUSSION

Preemption

Defendant's principal argument for dismissal is that PUMA is preempted by three different federal statutes: the Controlled Substances Act, the Americans with Disabilities Act, and the Food, Drug, and Cosmetic Act. . . .

The U.S. Constitution's Supremacy Clause provides that "the Laws of the United States ... shall be the supreme Law of the Land ... any Thing in the Constitution or Laws of any State to the Contrary notwithstanding." U.S. Const. art. VI, cl. 2. . . . Congress may preempt a state law . . . expressly ("express preemption"), or it may preempt state law implicitly in circumstances where it is clear that Congress intended to occupy an entire regulatory field ("field preemption"). Congress may also preempt state law where state law stands as an obstacle to the objectives of Congress ("obstacle preemption") or where simultaneous compliance with both federal and state law is impossible ("impossibility preemption"). In general, a federal statute will not be found to preempt claims arising under state law unless Congress's intent to do so is "clear and manifest." Wyeth v. Levine, 555 U.S. 555, 565 (2009).

Defendant argues that the Controlled Substances Act, Americans with Disabilities Act, and Food, Drug, and Cosmetic Act each invalidate PUMA under a theory of obstacle preemption.

A defendant making an argument under obstacle preemption faces a heavy burden. "The mere fact of 'tension' between federal and state law is generally not enough to establish an obstacle supporting preemption, particularly when the state law involves the exercise of traditional police power." Madeira v. Affordable Hous. Found., Inc., 469 F.3d 219, 241 (2d Cir. 2006). Rather, obstacle preemption precludes only those state laws that create an "actual conflict" with an overriding federal purpose and objective. *See* Mary Jo C. v. N.Y. State & Local Ret. Sys., 707 F.3d 144, 162 (2d Cir. 2013). . . . [T]here is no preemption unless "the repugnance or conflict is so direct and positive that the two acts cannot be reconciled or consistently stand together." In re MTBE Prods. Liab. Litig., 725 F.3d 65, 102 (2d Cir. 2013).

1. Controlled Substances Act

Defendant first argues that PUMA is preempted by the Controlled Substances Act, 21 U.S.C. § 801 et seq. ("CSA"). Specifically, defendant contends that by "affirmatively authoriz[ing] the medical use, possession, cultivation, sale, dispensing, and distribution of marijuana," PUMA "stands as an impermissible obstacle to the basic purpose of the CSA." ... "The main objectives of the CSA were to conquer drug abuse and to control the legitimate and illegitimate traffic in controlled substances." Gonzales v. Raich, 545 U.S. 1, 12 (2005). To carry out these goals, "Congress devised a closed regulatory system making it unlawful to manufacture, distribute, dispense, or possess any controlled substance except in a manner authorized by the CSA." *Id.* at 13. The CSA classifies marijuana as a Schedule I substance, which indicates the drug's "high potential for abuse," and the CSA allows no exceptions for medical use.

The CSA, however, does not make it illegal to employ a marijuana user. Nor does it purport to regulate employment practices . . . . [It] explicitly indicates that Congress did not intend for the CSA to preempt state law "unless there is a positive conflict between that provision of this subchapter and that State law so that the two cannot consistently stand together." 21 U.S.C. § 903.

Defendant argues that PUMA stands as an obstacle to the CSA because it affirmatively authorizes the very conduct—marijuana use—that the CSA prohibits. But this argument is overbroad . . . . I must focus on PUMA's specific anti-employment discrimination provision rather than the statute as a whole. . . .

[D]efendant relies heavily on Emerald Steel Fabricators, Inc. v. Bureau of Labor & Indus., 230 P.3d 518 (Ore. 2010), in which the Oregon Supreme Court determined that Oregon's medical marijuana statute was preempted by the CSA. Factually, the context in *Emerald Steel* is quite similar to this case: a plaintiff was fired by his employer one week after disclosing his status as a state-law-authorized user of medical marijuana. Legally, however, *Emerald Steel* is different, because Oregon's medical marijuana statute contains no provision explicitly barring employment discrimination. The very different question presented in *Emerald Steel* was whether the CSA more generally preempted a provision of Oregon law that authorized the use of medical marijuana. Here, by contrast, the question is whether the CSA preempts a provision that prohibits an employer from taking adverse action against an employee on the basis of the employee's otherwise state-authorized medicinal use of marijuana.

. . . Other factually similar cases are even more distinguishable, because they have been decided on statutory interpretation grounds rather than on preemption grounds. *See, e.g.*, Coats v. Dish Network, LLC, 350 P.3d 849 (Colo. 2015) (plaintiff was not protected under statute that prohibited employer from terminating employee due to employee's participating in "lawful" activities off the premises of the employer during non-working hours, because court interpreted "lawful" to mean lawful under both state and federal law); Casias v. Wal-Mart Stores, Inc., 695 F.3d 428, 435–36 (6th Cir. 2012) (Michigan's medical marijuana statute, which provides protection against disciplinary action by a "business," does not impose restrictions on private employers, as a matter of textual interpretation); Stanley v. Cty. of Bernalillo Comm'rs, 2015 WL 4997159, at *5 (D.N.M. 2015) (citing additional cases in which courts have "rejected the plaintiff's claims that state anti-discrimination laws prohibit private employers from terminating employees for state-authorized medical marijuana usage as a matter of statutory interpretation, and not on federal-preemption grounds").

Although most cases dealing with the CSA's preemption of state medical marijuana statutes have come out in favor of employers, these cases have not concerned statutes with specific anti-discrimination provisions; courts and commentators alike have suggested that a statute that clearly and explicitly provided employment protections for medical marijuana users could lead to a different result. Indeed, one court recently held that the CSA does not preempt the anti-discrimination-in-employment provision of Rhode Island's medical marijuana statute. *See* Callaghan v. Darlington Fabrics Corp., 2017 WL 2321181, at *13–14 (R.I. Super. 2017).

Like the provision at issue in *Callaghan*, § 21a–408p(b)(3) of PUMA regulates the employment relationship, an area in which States "'possess broad authority under their policy powers to regulate.'" Arizona, 567 U.S. at 404 (*quoting* De Canas v. Bica, 424 U.S. 351, 356 (1976)). Given that the CSA nowhere prohibits employers from hiring applicants who may be engaged in illegal drug use, defendant has not established the sort of "positive conflict" between §

21a–408p(b)(3) and the CSA that is required for preemption under the very terms of the CSA. See 21 U.S.C. § 903. Nor does any tension between § 21a–408p(b)(3) and the CSA rise to the level of the "sharp" conflict required to establish obstacle preemption under the case law. The CSA does not preempt § 21a–408p(b)(3).

2. Americans with Disabilities Act

Defendant next contends that PUMA's anti-discrimination employment provision is preempted by the Americans with Disabilities Act, 42 U.S.C. § 12101 et seq. ("ADA"). The ADA of course protects the rights of persons with disabilities to be free from discrimination, including discrimination in the employment context. Given the ADA's remedial purpose to protect employees from discrimination, it may seem odd to suppose that the ADA of all statutes should be understood to preclude the States from fighting employment discrimination of any kind.

Defendant nevertheless fashions its somewhat counterintuitive ADA preemption argument from a provision of the ADA—42 U.S.C. § 12114—that was crafted in order to make clear that the ADA does not extend its protections to persons who use illicit drugs or alcohol. . . I draw the following conclusions from these various sub-provisions of § 12114.

First and most importantly, the ADA explicitly provides that an employer "may prohibit the illegal use of drugs and the use of alcohol at the workplace by all employees." 42 U.S.C. § 12114(c)(1). But the facts of this case do not involve any use of marijuana by plaintiff at the workplace, and PUMA explicitly declines to authorize such workplace use. See Conn. Gen. Stat. §§ 21a–408p(b)(3), 21a–408a(b)(2). And the fact that the ADA does not further provide that an employer may prohibit an employee from the illegal use of drugs outside of the workplace is a powerful indication that the ADA was not meant to regulate non-workplace activity, much less to preclude the States from doing so or to preclude the States from prohibiting employers from taking adverse actions against employees who may use illegal drugs outside the workplace (and whose drug use does not affect job performance).

Second, although the ADA refers to and contemplates employers' use of drug testing, it does so for a limited purpose to make clear that such use of drug testing is not itself a violation of the ADA. See 42 U.S.C. § 12114(b). Other than making clear what conduct does not violate the ADA, the ADA is not an employer's Magna Carta to engage in drug testing of all employees. That is why § 12114(d)(2) provides that the ADA does not "encourage, prohibit, or authorize" drug testing . . . . The fact that the ADA allows an employer to use drug testing without fear of facing liability under the ADA does not additionally and exorbitantly mean that the ADA was intended to categorically preclude the States from preventing an employer from taking adverse action against someone who fails any kind of a drug test.

Defendant relies heavily on the wording of § 12114(c)(4), which as noted above provides that an employer "may hold an employee who engages in the illegal use of drugs or who is an alcoholic to the same qualification standards for employment or job performance and behavior that such entity holds other employees, even if any unsatisfactory performance or behavior is related to the drug use or alcoholism of such employee." . . . [D]efendant argues that its drug testing of plaintiff was a "qualification standard" that it was free under the ADA to impose . . . . I cannot agree with defendant's understanding that a drug test is itself a "qualification standard" within the meaning of this sub-provision, because the wording of this sub-provision further states that the "qualification standard" must be job-performance/behavior-related. There is no suggestion in this case that plaintiff's medicinal use of marijuana adversely would affect her job performance. . . .

My conclusion that the ADA does not preempt PUMA's anti-discrimination employment provision is reinforced by consideration of the ADA's preemption "savings clause":

> Nothing in this chapter shall be construed to invalidate or limit the remedies, rights, and procedures of any Federal law or law of any State or political subdivision of any State or jurisdiction that provides greater or equal protection for the rights of individuals with disabilities than are afforded by this chapter.

42 U.S.C. § 12201(b). The evident intent of Congress was to allow the States to enact greater protections for parties like plaintiff who may suffer from a disability such as plaintiff's post-traumatic stress disorder . . . .

The ADA is an anti-discrimination statute that exempts the use of illegal drugs from its scope of protection. Beyond doing so, the ADA does not preclude the States from regulating employers who discriminate against employees who engage in the medicinal use of drugs in compliance with state law.

At most, defendant presents a convincing case that plaintiff could not seek relief under the ADA for defendant's rescission of her job offer. *See, e.g.*, James v. City of Costa Mesa, 700 F.3d 394, 405 (9th Cir. 2012) ("We hold ... that the ADA does not protect medical marijuana users who claim to face discrimination on the basis of their marijuana use."). But the question here is not whether the ADA affords plaintiff relief. It is whether the ADA precludes Connecticut from granting plaintiff relief. I conclude that defendant has not shown a conflict between the ADA and PUMA that would justify preemption.

3. Federal Food, Drug, and Cosmetic Act

[The court held that the Food, Drug, and Cosmetic Act did not preempt PUMA]

Count One—Private Right of Action under PUMA

[The court concluded that although PUMA does not expressly grant employees a right to seek judicial remedies for a violation of the rule against discrimination, PUMA does imply the existence of a cause of action.]

Conclusion

For the reasons explained above, defendant's motion to dismiss is denied as to Count One (violation of Conn. Gen. Stat. § 281–408p(b)(3)).

NOTES AND QUESTIONS

1. Coats v. Dish Network, LLC, 350 P.3d 849 (Colo. 2015), one of the cases cited in *Noffsinger*, involved a different kind of challenge to drug testing: a state "off-duty conduct" statute. The employee in *Coats* tested positive for marijuana

use, and the employer discharged the employee even though the use of marijuana is not prohibited by Colorado law. The employee sued for wrongful discharge under the Colorado "off-duty" conduct statute, but the court rejected his claim. The Colorado law protects only *lawful* off-duty conduct, but marijuana use is still unlawful under federal law. *Coats* is reproduced in section A.1 of this chapter.

2. Some states have repealed their local laws against sale, possession or use of marijuana, making the use of marijuana lawful for purposes of state law. Other states have declared the use of marijuana lawful for a prescribed medical treatment but not for recreation. Under any of these or other varieties of state marijuana laws, the sale, possession or use of marijuana remains unlawful under *federal* law.

3. Some drugs are lawful if used with a doctor's lawful prescription. Use without or in excess of a lawful prescription is unlawful. An employer might test for such drugs because it seeks to investigate an unlawful use of prescription drugs, the lawful use of prescription drugs that might affect work performance or safety, or a use of drugs that reveals underlying medical conditions the employer believes should disqualify the worker. The use of a powerful painkiller might be evidence of lawful treatment of pain and the existence of a medical condition such as arthritis, or it might reveal opioid addiction and the unlawful use of prescription drug. Either way, the employer might fear that the painkiller or the underlying medical condition will affect job performance or safety. The use of a prescribed anti-depressant might be perfectly lawful, but it might also reveal to the employer that the employee is depressed, and the employer might believe that depression will affect the employee's performance or safety. Employer drug testing under these circumstances is subject to all of the rules discussed above. Perhaps more importantly, the employer is subject to the Americans with Disabilities Act.

BATES v. DURA AUTOMOTIVE SYSTEMS, INC.

767 F.3d 566 (6th Cir. 2014)

COOK, Circuit Judge.

In 2007, Dura Automotive Systems, Inc., ("Dura") began testing employees at its manufacturing facility in Lawrenceburg, Tennessee, for substances appearing in both illegal drugs and in prescription medications packaged with warnings about operating machinery. Plaintiffs-appellees, none of whom has a disability under the Americans with Disability Act ("ADA"), worked at the facility and took prescribed medications for a variety of conditions. After these employees tested positive, Dura directed the employees to disclose their medications to Freedom From Self ("FFS"), a third-party company hired to administer the drug tests. . . . Dura warned plaintiffs to discontinue using the offending medications. After retests came back positive, Dura terminated the plaintiffs' employment.

Plaintiffs . . . claim[] that Dura violated ADA § 102(d)(4)(A), 42 U.S.C. § 12112(d)(4)(A), which prohibits employers from requiring "medical examination[s]" or "mak[ing] inquiries of an employee as to whether such employee is an individual with a disability ... unless such examination or inquiry is shown to be job-related and consistent with business necessity." The claim reduces to two essential inquiries: (1) whether the employer performed or authorized a medical examination or disability inquiry ("the regulated conduct"); and if so, (2) whether the exam/inquiry was job-related and consistent with business necessity ("the justification"). . . .

I.

Dura manufactures glass windows for cars, trucks, and buses at its Lawrenceburg facility. Between the end of 2006 and early 2007, Dura received reports of employees' drug and alcohol abuse. The facility experienced some property damage and a few workplace accidents attributable to employees' use of illegal and prescription drugs.

In response, Dura implemented a new substance-abuse policy, which … policy prohibited employees from "being impaired by or under the influence" of alcohol, illegal drugs, or legal drugs—including prescription medications and over-the-counter drugs—to the extent that employees' use of such drugs endangered others or affected their job performance. Dura reserved the right to enforce its policy via employee drug testing.…

In May 2007, Dura ordered a plant-wide drug screening …. Dura instructed FFS to test for twelve substances—amphetamines, barbiturates, benzodiazepines, cocaine, ecstasy, marijuana, methadone, methamphetamine, opiates, oxycodone, phencyclidine, and propoxyphene—some of which appear in prescription medications. FFS conducted the urinalysis testing in private at the facility's technology center and reported to Dura representatives Mark Jent and Lindy Boots. Following the results of the "instant panel" test, Boots and/or Jent sent home those employees who tested positive.

FFS [medical review officers, or "MROs"] questioned employees about medical explanations, sometimes requesting prescription information or documentation from the employee's physician. If the MRO determined that the employee had a valid reason for the non-negative result, including use of prescription medications, the MRO changed the final test result to negative. FFS forwarded these results to Dura, but Dura disregarded the MRO's revisions, opting instead to prohibit any employee use of machine-restricted drugs.

… Dura instructed positive-testing employees to bring their medications to FFS for documentation. Affected employees produced their medications to FFS [, which] identified the medications packaged with machine-operation warnings and reported those to Dura. Dura then informed the employees that it would terminate them if they continued to use these medications.

All [plaintiffs-appellees] but Toungett tested positive during the plant-wide screening, and Toungett tested positive during a "random" retest performed a few days after he informed Dura about a doctor appointment for back pain. Plaintiffs-appellees' machine-restricted medications included oxycodone, Cymbalta, Didrex, Lortrab (acetaminophen/hydrocodone), Soma, and Xanax. Though Dura warned most of these employees to discontinue using the machine-restricted medications, it called Long back to work to complete a project, only to terminate him after a "random" retest that targeted other positive-testing employees. Dura terminated the other plaintiffs-appellees after positive retests with the exception of Wade, who discontinued her medication. . . .

No one pressed plaintiffs-appellees for their underlying medical conditions, and Dura denies questioning them directly about their medications. Dura acknowledges, however, that [FFS] disclosed plaintiffs-appellees' machine-restricted medications, and ... admitted that Dura had a "blanket policy" of terminating employees who tested positive for such medications….

II.

B. The Regulated Conduct of 42 U.S.C. § 12112(d)(4)(A): Medical Examinations & Disability Inquiries

Whether Dura's drug-testing constituted a "medical examination" or "disability inquiry" under (d)(4) presents a close question because the ADA leaves these terms undefined. . . . Specifically, this provision states:

> A covered entity shall not require a medical examination and shall not make inquiries of an employee as to whether such employee is an individual with a disability or as to the nature or severity of the disability, unless such examination or inquiry is shown to be job-related and consistent with business necessity.

This broad protection reflects Congress's effort to "curtail all questioning that would serve to identify and exclude persons with disabilities from consideration for employment." Griffin v. Steeltek, Inc., 160 F.3d 591, 594 (10th Cir.1998).

Dura argues that its drug-testing protocol sought no information about employees' physical or mental health, or even employees' general use of medications, but only whether the employees ingested illegal drugs or prescription medications with machine-operation warnings. Looking to the statutory language, one can easily imagine a medical examination consisting of a urine test to determine whether a patient has a health condition, but Dura's testing, implemented by a third-party firm to avoid unnecessary disclosure to Dura, defies easy classification. A different ADA provision exempts testing for "*illegal* use of drugs" from the prohibition on medical examinations, but that provision offers little guidance here, because Dura's screening for *prescribed* medications exceeded its parameters. [Emphases added.]*See* 42 U.S.C. § 12114(d)(1) ("[A] test to determine the illegal use of drugs shall not be considered a medical examination.").

1. Medical Examination

The relevant EEOC guidance defines "medical examination" as "a procedure or test that seeks information about an individual's physical or mental impairments or health," and identifies several factors bearing on this determination:

> (1) whether the test is administered by a health care professional; (2) whether the test is interpreted by a health care professional; (3) whether the test is designed to reveal an impairment or physical or mental health; (4) whether the test is invasive; (5) whether the test measures an employee's performance of a task or measures his/her physiological responses to performing the task; (6) whether the test normally is given in a medical setting; and, (7) whether medical equipment is used.

EEOC, Enforcement Guidance: Disability–Related Inquiries and Medical Examinations of Employees Under the Americans with Disabilities Act (ADA)

Part B.2 (July 27, 2000) (hereinafter "DRI & ME Guidance"). "In many cases, a combination of factors will be relevant ... ," but in others "one factor may be enough." *Id.* Examples ... include vision tests, blood pressure and cholesterol screening, range-of-motion tests, and diagnostic procedures such as x-rays, CAT scans, and MRIs. The guidance also identifies two qualifying urine tests: (1) to discover alcohol use, and (2) to detect disease or genetic markers. . . .

If the ADA prohibits urinalysis testing for the use of ... alcohol, the [district] court reasoned, it must ban testing for other legal substances, like prescription medications. While this logic has facial appeal—especially given alcohol's association with vice and medicine with virtue—it fails here.

First, the guidance itself gives contrary instructions on alcohol testing. *See* DRI & ME Guidance Part 13.2 n. 31 (cross-referencing n. 26, which states that employers "may maintain and enforce rules prohibiting employees from being under the influence of alcohol in the workplace and may conduct alcohol testing for this purpose" upon reasonable suspicion); *but see* EEOC, Enforcement Guidance: Preemployment Disability–Related Questions & Medical Examinations (Oct. 10, 1995) (hereinafter "Preemployment Guidance") (explaining that an employer cannot give alcohol tests to job applicants because such tests "are medical, and there is no statutory exemption") [emphasis added]. The ADA's allowance that employers "*may* require that employees shall not be under the influence of alcohol ... at the workplace," 42 U.S.C. § 12114(c)(2), further cautions against extending the guidance's alcohol-testing example to these circumstances.

Second, . . . [b]y permitting testing as to the "illegal use of drugs," 42 U.S.C. § 12114(d)(1)—as opposed to the use of illegal drugs—the exemption contemplates circumstances where employees abuse medications not prescribed to them. So, while the illegality of use bears on whether the employer may invoke the drug-testing exception, the legality of a substance does not settle the medical-examination question. For that, we turn to the EEOC's definition and the medical-examination factors.

The first, second, sixth, and seventh factors . . . tip the scales toward medical examination because FFS administered urine-based tests in a quasi-medical setting, with medical equipment, and health professionals interpreted the results. The fifth factor (task performance/physiological response) appears inapplicable. The fourth factor (invasiveness), meanwhile, offers little guidance. Though a urine sample certainly intrudes on a private bodily function neither plaintiffs-appellees nor the EEOC argues that Dura's tests were invasive, and we have recognized in other legal contexts that urine tests typically "are not invasive of the body." Norris v. Premier Integrity Solutions, Inc., 641 F.3d 695, 699 (6th Cir. 2011). That said, the EEOC's Preemployment Guidance suggests that the "drawing of blood, urine or breath" may demonstrate invasiveness.

That brings us to the third factor, "arguably the most critical": whether the test is designed to reveal an impairment or the employee's health. The Preemployment Guidance ... add[s] an eighth factor: whether "the employer [is] trying to determine the applicant's physical or mental health or impairments." This emphasis on a diagnostic purpose aligns with the EEOC definition of medical-examination and links that term to its sister term, disability inquiries. The "uncovering of [health] defects at an employer's direction is the precise harm that

§ 12112(d)(4)(A) is designed to prevent." *Kroll*, 691 F.3d at 819.

Here, Dura denies using its drug-testing protocol to reveal impairments or health conditions. . . . [T]he evidence shows that Dura abstained from asking plaintiffs about their medical conditions, and only one plaintiff suggested that Dura directly asked her to identify the medications she was taking. . . . Importantly, the plaintiffs-appellees offer no evidence showing how FFS's urinalysis or post-test reporting of machine-restricted medications revealed information to Dura about plaintiffs-appellees' medical conditions. The urine test itself revealed only the presence of chemicals—amphetamines, barbiturates, benzodiazepines, cocaine, ecstasy, marijuana, methadone, methamphetamine, opiates, oxycodone, phencyclidine, and propoxyphene. No one suggests that the consumption of prescription medications containing these chemicals constitutes protected medical information (or even an "impairment") under the EEOC definition of medical examination.

FFS's post-test reporting, meanwhile, disclosed to Dura only the machine-restricted medications. ... Although some prescription medications may reveal more than meets the eye because of brand-name recognition and ubiquitous marketing campaigns, an employer might struggle to discern medical conditions from the prescription drugs discovered here, which included a number of prescription pain relievers. Arguably, this attenuated testing protocol—with a narrow focus on substances containing machine-operation restrictions, as opposed to all prescription drugs—reflects Dura's effort to avoid obtaining information about employees' medical conditions and to avoid discriminating against all employees who take prescription drugs.

Of course, an employer cannot hire a third party to discriminate on its behalf. ... But, viewing the evidence in its favor, we cannot say as a matter of law that Dura used FFS's drug tests to seek information about plaintiffs-appellees' medical conditions, or even that such revelations likely would result.

Still, much depends on Dura's credibility. Inconsistencies between Dura's written and actual drug-testing policies and its disparate treatment of individual employees may evince a pernicious motive. For instance, one plaintiff (Bates) claims that Dura asked her directly about her prescription medications and fired her for not reporting them, and Dura allowed another plaintiff (Long) to return to work despite testing positive. If credited, a jury could reject Dura's explanation as a pretext for screening out potentially disabled employees. Moreover, plaintiffs-appellees may present evidence that the disclosure of machine-restricted medications typically reveals confidential health information....

This fact-sensitive inquiry presents a genuine issue of fact inappropriate for judgment as a matter of law...

2. Disability Inquiries

So too with § 12112(d)(4)(A)'s prohibition on "inquiries ... as to whether [an] employee is an individual with a disability or as to the nature or severity of the disability"—what the EEOC has termed "disability-related inquiries." [D]isability-related inquiries "may include ... asking an employee whether s/he currently is taking any prescription drugs or medications, [or did] in the past, or monitoring an employee's taking of such drugs or medications." DRI & ME Guidance Part B.1....

The guidance defines disability-related inquiry as "a question (or series of questions) that is likely to elicit information about a disability." DRI & ME Guidance Part B.1. Conversely, the guidance explains that "[q]uestions that are not likely to elicit information about a disability are not disability-related inquiries and, therefore, are not prohibited under the ADA." *Id.* Examples of permissible inquiries include asking about an employee's general well-being, a non-disability impairment such as a broken limb, and alcohol or illegal-drug use. EEOC Guidance Part B.1.

Dura denies asking employees about their general prescription-drug usage. Viewing the evidence in its favor, Dura's third-party-administered test revealing only machine-restricted medications differs from directly asking employees about prescription-drug usage or monitoring the same, per the guidance example.

Next, the EEOC guidance lists prescription inquiries as conduct that "may" constitute a disability-related inquiry; it does not state a categorical rule. *Id.*; see also id. Question 8 (explaining that an employer "[g]enerally" may not "ask all employees what prescription medications they are taking" because such questioning "is not job-related and consistent with business necessity"). … [T]he Preemployment Guidance gives this nuanced instruction:

> May an employer ask applicants about their lawful drug use?
>
> No, if the question is likely to elicit information about disability. Employers should know that many questions about current or prior lawful drug use are likely to elicit information about a disability, and are therefore impermissible at the pre-offer stage. . . .

[A] jury could reasonably conclude that Dura implemented a drug-testing policy in a manner designed to avoid gathering information about employees' disabilities.... A drug test that requires positive-testing employees to disclose medications to a third party, who then relays only machine-restricted medications to the employer, need not reveal information about a disability....

3. Conclusion

… Accepting the EEOC's fact-bound definitions of "medical examination" and "disability-related inquiry" as reasonable, we conclude that a reasonable jury could decide these issues either way. We therefore vacate the district court's judgment and remand for a trial on the regulated-conduct issue: whether Dura's drug testing constituted a medical examination or disability inquiry....

III.

B. The Justification Under 42 U.S.C. § 12112(d)(4)(A): The Jury's Adverse Verdict

… The jury found Dura's drug tests neither job related nor a matter of business necessity. Our remand of the regulated-conduct issue does not disturb this finding. We therefore consider Dura's challenge to the weight of the evidence….

The EEOC instructs that

> a disability-related inquiry or medical examination of an employee may be job-related and consistent with business necessity when an employer has a reasonable belief, based on objective evidence, that: (1) an employee's ability

to perform essential job functions will be impaired by a medical condition; or (2) an employee will pose a direct threat due to a medical condition.

DRI & ME Guidance. This "reasonable belief ... must be based on objective evidence obtained, or reasonably available to the employer, prior to making a disability-related inquiry or requiring a medical examination. Such a belief requires an assessment of the employee and his/her position and cannot be based on general assumptions." *Id.* [A]n employer "[g]enerally" may not "ask all employees what prescription medications they are taking," because such an inquiry "is not job-related and consistent with business necessity," but . . . the questioning may be necessary for "employees in positions affecting public safety." DRI & ME Guidance.

Dura presented some evidence at trial supporting its drug testing—e.g., testimony and video evidence of the "congested" nature of the Lawrenceburg facility and numerous hazards there, including machinery, glass, chemicals, and forklifts. Nonetheless, plaintiffs-appellees also presented evidence consistent with a reasonable jury conclusion that Dura's showing fell short of the high standard for job relatedness and business necessity. For example, Jent testified that Dura neglected to make individualized risk determinations of jobs, tools, and work stations in the facility. Jent and Boots also admitted that they failed to consider the plaintiffs' abilities or the risk that they posed by taking medications. The jury could infer from this evidence that Dura lacked a reasonable belief, based on objective evidence, that plaintiffs-appellees' medications impaired their abilities to do their jobs or made them dangerous to others. . . .

Because the evidence supported the jury's conclusion, we affirm the district court's denial of a new trial on the (d)(4) justification issue.

IV.

For the above reasons, we … reverse the district court's conclusion that Dura's drug-testing protocol constituted either a medical examination or disability inquiry . . . as a matter of law…. On remand, the jury shall first decide whether Dura's drug testing constituted a medical examination or disability inquiry, relying on … the relevant EEOC guidance.

JULIA SMITH GIBBONS, Circuit Judge, dissenting.

It is … undisputed that FFS implemented a "blanket policy" of terminating employees who tested positive for medications carrying a machine-restriction warning. Some of the terminated employees provided Dura with doctor's notes stating that the use of their prescription medication did not affect work performance. Dura, however, refused to allow these employees to return to work unless they discontinued their medications regardless of whether the medications had any real likelihood of affecting their ability to perform the job safely. That Dura categorically disregarded medical advice in such a manner is compelling evidence that its drug-testing program was designed to discover and then to discriminate against employees with health conditions.…

[I]f, as Dura claims, the protocol was designed only to disclose machine-restricted medications for safety purposes, then Dura had absolutely no reason to disregard any of plaintiffs' doctors who ensured Dura that the employees could perform their jobs safely notwithstanding their use of machine-restricted medications. This leads to the inescapable conclusion that Dura's drug tests, far from being designed to ferret out employees who could not safely operate machinery, were actually designed to reveal impairments ....

Because Dura's drug-testing protocols did not disclose which precise impairments its employees had, only that they had impairments, the majority reasons that its conduct was lawful. But nothing in the statute, the EEOC's guidance, or our case law counsels so narrow an interpretation. Congress prohibited medical examinations unless job related and justified by a business necessity.... There is no business justification for an employer to inquire into whether its employees are impaired if the employer is going to disregard the nature and limitations of that impairment.

I would affirm the district court's grant of judgment as a matter of law.

NOTES AND QUESTIONS

1. The plaintiffs appear to have conceded for purposes of the appeal in *Bates* that they were not "disabled." Alleging disability might seem to admit that an underlying impairment or its medicinal treatment "substantially limits" a plaintiff in a "major life activity." 42 U.S.C. 12102(1)(A). The employer might then argue that if the condition or treatment is disabling, the employee is unqualified for the job. A plaintiff might respond that despite his disabling condition, he *can* perform the job with "reasonable accommodation." 42 U.S.C. 12111(8), (9), (10), 12112(a). A plaintiff can also allege that he is not disabled and needs no accommodation, but the employer "regards" him as disabled. 42 U.S.C. 12102(1)(C). In 2008, Congress amended the ADA to emphasize and expand the "regarded as" prong of the anti-discrimination rule, but the events giving rise the claims in *Bates* preceded the effective date of the amendments.

2. Approximately 17 percent of Americans use prescription psychiatric drugs. Anti-depressants are the most commonly prescribed psychiatric drugs. Sarah Miller, *1 in 6 Americans Takes Psychiatric Drugs*, SCIENTIFIC AMERICAN (Dec. 13, 2016). Use of painkillers is even more typical. In a one year period, 35 percent of Americans used prescribed pain killers. A higher number—about 38 percent—used pain killers when non-prescription use is included. Christopher Ingraham, *Prescription Painkillers Are More Widely Used Than Tobacco, New Federal Study Finds*, WASH. POST (Sept 20, 2016). According to the American Society of Addiction Medicine, in 2012, "259 million prescriptions were written for opioids, which is more than enough to give every American adult their own bottle of pills." American Society of Addiction Medicine, Opioid Addiction 2016 Facts & Figures, https://www.asam.org/docs/default-source/advocacy/opioid-addiction-disease-facts-figures.pdf.

5. *Surveillance*

Supervision requires watching: to train and instruct employees, to verify that they complete their work properly, to encourage employees to use time productively, and to prevent misconduct or unsafe activity. Indeed, many of the duties employers owe to employees and third parties require oversight of employee work.

Occupational health and safety law requires an employer to be vigilant against preventable employee misconduct that could result in serious injury or death. The law of discrimination makes an employer responsible for preventing and investigating sexual harassment between employees. The law of *respondeat superior* imputes any employee negligence to the employer, and the employer might be liable for intentional employee torts if it has failed in its duty to supervise.

Employees might find a supervisor's observation annoying, inhibiting, or even humiliating, but "excessive" observation is unlikely to violate legally enforceable employee rights unless the employer offensively intrudes upon a normally private space, such as a restroom, or unlawfully discriminates or retaliates by targeting an employee for extra surveillance. *Compare* Roberts v. Houston Indep. Sch. Dist., 788 S.W.2d 107 (Tex. App. 1990) (teacher lacked reasonable expectation of privacy against overt videotaping of her performance in classroom) *with* Anderson v. Davila, 125 F.3d 148 (3d Cir. 1997) (employer's "uncalled for surveillance" of employee was part of illegal retaliatory harassment in violation of federal civil rights laws), *and* Fieldcrest Cannon, Inc. v. NLRB, 97 F.3d 65 (4th Cir. 1996) (employer's surveillance of employees unlawfully interfered with their efforts to form a union, in violation of NLRA).

An employer's ability to watch employees is amplified tremendously by modern technology. Video cameras and monitors allow for continuous, possibly surreptitious observation from distances or angles that would be impossible in the case of direct, human observation. Moreover, a camera can record an employee's activity even while no supervisor is present, and a supervisor can view a preserved record long after the recorded event. Could observation and recording by a video camera convert otherwise lawful watching into something unlawfully intrusive?

Video cameras are now ubiquitous in many settings — stores, banks, medical facilities, and even parking lots and public roads — and they serve many legitimate purposes, from security to traffic control. A frequent complaint against video camera monitoring is that a camera is more intrusive and threatening than human observation, because it never tires and never blinks. Video monitoring may be particularly discomfiting when it targets an individual in a place from which the individual cannot easily escape. Indeed, in some contexts video monitoring can be hurtful even when it records nothing more than what the observer might see with the naked eye. Goosen v. Walker, 714 So. 2d 1149 (Fla. App. 1998) (upholding injunction against "stalking" of a neighbor by videotaping); Wolfson v. Lewis, 924 F. Supp. 1413 (E.D. Pa. 1996) (enjoining journalists' videotaping and other surveillance of petitioner's home that was designed to force petitioner to grant interview). What limits, if any, must an employer respect in using video cameras to enhance its otherwise normal observation of employees and their workplace?

VEGA-RODRIGUEZ v. PUERTO RICO TELEPHONE CO.

110 F.3d 174 (1st Cir. 1997)

SELYA, Circuit Judge.

As employers gain access to increasingly sophisticated technology, new legal issues seem destined to suffuse the workplace. This appeal raises such an issue. In it, plaintiffs-appellants Hector Vega-Rodriguez (Vega) and Amiut Reyes-Rosado (Reyes) revile the district court's determination that their employer, the Puerto Rico Telephone Company (PRTC), may monitor their work area by means of continuous video surveillance without offending the Constitution. Because the red flag of constitutional breach does not fly from these ramparts, we affirm.

I. Factual Surveillance

. . . The Executive Communications Center (the Center) is located in the penthouse of the PRT's office complex in Guaynabo, Puerto Rico. . . . For security reasons, access to the Center is restricted; both the elevator foyer on the penthouse floor and the doors to the Center itself are inaccessible without a control card.

PRTC employs Vega, Reyes, and others as attendants (known colloquially as "security operators") in the Center. They monitor computer banks to detect signals emanating from alarm systems at PRTC facilities throughout Puerto Rico, and they alert the appropriate authorities if an alarm sounds. . . . The work space is completely open and no individual employee has an assigned office, cubicle, work station, or desk.

PRTC installed a video surveillance system at the Center in 1990 but abandoned the project when employees groused. In June of 1994, the company reinstated video surveillance. Three cameras survey the work space, and a fourth tracks all traffic passing through the main entrance to the Center. None of them cover the rest area. The surveillance is exclusively visual; the cameras have no microphones or other immediate eavesdropping capability. Video surveillance operates all day, every day; the cameras implacably record every act undertaken in the work area. A video monitor, a switcher unit, and a video recorder are located in the office of the Center's general manager, Daniel Rodriguez-Diaz, and the videotapes are stored there. PRTC has no written policy regulating any aspect of the video surveillance, but it is undisputed that no one can view either the monitor or the completed tapes without Rodriguez-Diaz's express permission.

Soon after PRTC installed the surveillance system (claiming that it was desirable for security reasons), the appellants and several fellow employees protested. They asserted, among other things, that the system had no purpose other than to pry into employees' behavior. When management turned a deaf ear, the appellants filed suit in Puerto Rico's federal district court. They contended that the ongoing surveillance constitutes an unreasonable search prohibited by the Fourth Amendment, [and] violates a constitutionally-conferred entitlement to privacy . . . PRTC moved for dismissal and/or summary judgment, and the individual defendants moved for summary judgment. The district court found merit in these submissions and entered judgment accordingly. . . .

III. The Fourth Amendment

PRTC is a quasi-public corporation. . . . It is, therefore, a government actor . . . , subject to . . . the Fourth Amendment . . . "right of the people to be secure in their persons . . . against unreasonable searches." . . .

A. Privacy Rights and the Fourth Amendment

Intrusions upon personal privacy do not invariably implicate the Fourth

Amendment. Rather, such intrusions cross the constitutional line only if the challenged conduct infringes upon some reasonable expectation of privacy. *See* Smith v. Maryland, 442 U.S. 735, 740 (1979). To qualify under this mantra, a privacy expectation must meet both subjective and objective criteria: the complainant must have an actual expectation of privacy, and that expectation must be one which society recognizes as reasonable. *See* Oliver v. United States, 466 U.S. 170, 177 (1984). . . . Determining the subjective component of the test requires only a straightforward inquiry into the complainant's state of mind, and, for purposes of this appeal, we are willing to assume arguendo that the appellants, as they profess, had some subjective expectation of privacy while at work. We turn, then, to the objective reasonableness of the asserted expectation of privacy. . . .

B. PRIVACY RIGHTS AND BUSINESS PREMISES

Generally speaking, business premises invite lesser privacy expectations than do residences. . . . Still, deeply rooted societal expectations foster some cognizable privacy interests in business premises. . . . The Fourth Amendment protections that these expectations entail are versatile; they safeguard individuals not only against the government qua law enforcer but also qua employer. *See* National Treasury Employees Union v. Von Raab, 489 U.S. 656, 665 (1989).

The watershed case in this enclave of Fourth Amendment jurisprudence is O'Connor v. Ortega, 480 U.S. 709 (1987). *O'Connor*'s central thesis is that a public employee sometimes may enjoy a reasonable expectation of privacy in his or her workplace vis-à-vis searches by a supervisor or other representative of a public employer. Withal, *O'Connor* recognized that "operational realities of the workplace," such as actual office practices, procedures, or regulations, frequently may undermine employees' privacy expectations. *Id.* at 717 (plurality op.). . . .

C. PRIVACY INTERESTS IN THE APPELLANTS' WORKPLACE

We begin with first principles. It is simply implausible to suggest that society would recognize as reasonable an employee's expectation of privacy against being viewed while toiling in the Center's open and undifferentiated work area. PRTC did not provide the work station for the appellants' exclusive use, and its physical layout belies any expectation of privacy. Security operators do not occupy private offices or cubicles. They toil instead in a vast, undivided space — a work area so patulous as to render a broadcast expectation of privacy unreasonable. *See O'Connor*, 480 U.S. at 717-18. The precise extent of an employee's expectation of privacy often turns on the nature of an intended intrusion. *See id.* at 717-18; *id.* at 738 (Blackmun, J., dissenting). In this instance the nature of the intrusion strengthens the conclusion that no reasonable expectation of privacy attends the work area. Employers possess a legitimate interest in the efficient operation of the workplace, *see id.* at 723, and one attribute of this interest is that supervisors may monitor at will that which is in plain view within an open work area. Here, moreover, this attribute has a greater claim on our allegiance because the employer acted overtly in establishing the video surveillance: PRTC notified its work force in advance that video cameras would be installed and disclosed the cameras' field of vision.[4] Hence, the affected workers were on clear notice from the outset that any movements they might make and any objects they might display within the work area would be exposed to the employer's sight.

The appellants concede that, as a general matter, employees should expect to be under supervisors' watchful eyes while at work. But at some point, they argue, surveillance becomes unreasonable. In their estimation, when surveillance is electronic and, therefore, unremitting — the camera, unlike the human eye, never blinks — the die is cast. In constitutional terms, their theory reduces to the contention that the Fourth Amendment precludes management from observing electronically what it lawfully can see with the naked eye. This sort of argument has failed consistently under the plain view doctrine, and it musters no greater persuasiveness in the present context.[5] *See* 1 LaFave, *supra,* § 2.7(f). When all is said and done, employees must accept some circumscription of their liberty as a condition of continued employment. *See* INS v. Delgado, 466 U.S. 210, 218 (1984).

Once we put aside the appellants' theory that there is something constitutionally sinister about videotaping, their case crumbles. If there is constitutional parity between observations made with the naked eye and observations recorded by openly displayed video cameras that have no greater range, then objects or articles that an individual seeks to preserve as private may be constitutionally protected from such videotaping only if they are not located in plain view. *See Taketa*, 923 F.2d at 677. In other words, persons cannot reasonably maintain an expectation of privacy in that which they display openly. Justice Stewart stated the proposition in no uncertain terms three decades ago: "What a person knowingly exposes to the public, even in his own home or office, is not a subject of Fourth Amendment protection." Katz v. United States, 389 U.S. 347, 351 (1967). Consequently, no legitimate expectation of privacy exists in objects exposed to plain view as long as the viewer's presence at the vantage point is lawful. *See* Horton v. California, 496 U.S. 128, 133, 137 (1990); *Oliver*, 466 U.S. at 179. And the mere fact that the observation is accomplished by a video camera rather than the naked eye, and recorded on film rather than in a supervisor's memory, does not transmogrify a constitutionally innocent act into a constitutionally forbidden one.[6] *See* 1 LaFave, *supra*, § 2.7(f) (stating that

---

[4] While this circumstance bears heavily on both the subjective and objective reasonableness of an employee's expectation of privacy, we do not mean to imply that an employer always can defeat an expectation of privacy by pre-announcing its intention to intrude into a specific area. *See, e.g., Smith*, 442 U.S. at 740 n.5 (hypothesizing that "if the Government were suddenly to announce on nationwide television that all homes henceforth would be subject to warrantless entry," individuals still might entertain an actual expectation of privacy regarding their homes, papers, and effects). . . . In cases in which notice would contradict expectations that comport with traditional Fourth Amendment freedoms, a normative inquiry is proper to determine whether the privacy expectation is nonetheless legitimate.

[5] We caution, however, that cases involving the covert use of clandestine cameras, or cases involving electronically-assisted eavesdropping, may be quite another story.

[6] It is true . . . that human observation is less implacable than video surveillance. But we can find no principled basis for assigning constitutional significance to that divagation. Both methods — human observation and video surveillance — perform the same function. Thus, videotaping per se does not alter the constitutional perspective in any material way.

individuals can record what is readily observable from a nonintrusive viewing area).

The bottom line is that since PRTC could assign humans to monitor the work station continuously without constitutional insult, it could choose instead to carry out that lawful task by means of unconcealed video cameras not equipped with microphones, which record only what the human eye could observe.

D. THE APPELLANTS' OTHER FOURTH AMENDMENT ARGUMENTS

The appellants trot out a profusion of additional asseverations in their effort to convince us that continuous video surveillance of the workplace constitutes an impermissible search. First, invoking Orwellian imagery, they recite a catechism pasted together from bits and pieces of judicial pronouncements recognizing the intrusive nature of video surveillance. These statements are taken out of context. Without exception, they refer to cameras installed surreptitiously during the course of criminal investigations. . . . Concealed cameras which infringe upon the rights of criminal defendants raise troubling constitutional concerns — concerns not implicated by the employer's actions in this case.

By like token, the appellants' attempts to analogize video monitoring to physical searches are unavailing. The silent video surveillance which occurs at the Center is less intrusive than most physical searches conducted by employers. PRTC's stationary cameras do not pry behind closed office doors or into desks, drawers, file cabinets, or other enclosed spaces, but, rather, record only what is plainly visible on the surface. Sounds are not recorded; thus, the cameras do not eavesdrop on private conversations between employees. And while the Court occasionally has characterized the taking of pictures as a search, it is a constitutionally permissible activity if it does not transgress an objectively reasonable expectation of privacy. *See, e.g.*, Dow Chem. Co. v. United States, 476 U.S. 227, 238-39 (1986) (upholding a search by aerial camera when the photographs taken were limited to the outline of the surveilled plant's buildings and equipment, even though the photos revealed more detail than could be seen by the human eye).

Next, the appellants complain that while at work under the cameras' unrelenting eyes they cannot scratch, yawn, or perform any other movement in privacy. This complaint rings true, but it begs the question. "[T]he test of legitimacy is not whether a person chooses to conceal assertedly 'private' activity," but whether the intrusion is objectively unreasonable. *Oliver*, 466 U.S. at 182-83. . . .

Finally, the appellants tout the potential for future abuse, arguing, for example, that PRTC might expand video surveillance "into the restrooms." Certainly, such an extension would raise a serious constitutional question. *See, e.g.*, People v. Dezek, 308 N.W.2d 652, 654-55 (Mich. App. 1981) (upholding a reasonable expectation of privacy against video surveillance in restroom stalls). But present fears . . . and potential privacy invasions do not constitute searches within the purview of the Fourth Amendment. . . .

We have said enough on this score. The appellants have failed to demonstrate the existence of an issue of material fact sufficient to withstand summary judgment on their Fourth Amendment claim. Because they do not enjoy an objectively reasonable expectation of privacy against disclosed, soundless video surveillance while at work, they have no cause of action under the Fourth Amendment.[7]

IV. THE RIGHT OF PRIVACY

In addition to their Fourth Amendment claim, the appellants contend that the Constitution spawns a general right, in the nature of a privacy right, to be free from video surveillance in the workplace. We do not agree.

Although the Constitution creates no free-floating right to privacy . . . specific guarantees may create protectable zones of privacy. *See* Paul v. Davis, 424 U.S. 693, 712-13 (1976); Roe v. Wade, 410 U.S. 113, 152-53 (1973). Thus, the appellants' privacy claim cannot prosper unless it is anchored in an enumerated constitutional guaranty.

The Fourth Amendment obviously is unavailable for this purpose. *See supra* Part III(C) & (D). . . . The appellants' privacy claim thus hinges upon a right to privacy which has its origin in the Fourteenth Amendment's concept of personal liberty. Such privacy rights do exist, but they have been limited to fundamental rights that are implicit in the concept of an ordered liberty. *See Paul*, 424 U.S. at 713. On the facts of this case, the right to be free from disclosed video surveillance while at work in an open, generally accessible area does not constitute a fundamental right.

The courts have identified two clusters of personal privacy rights recognized by the Fourteenth Amendment. One bundle of rights relates to ensuring autonomy in making certain kinds of significant personal decisions; the other relates to ensuring the confidentiality of personal matters. *See* Whalen v. Roe, 429 U.S. 589, 598-600 (1977); Borucki v. Ryan, 827 F.2d 836, 840 (1st Cir. 1987). PRTC's monitoring does not implicate any of these rights.

The autonomy branch of the Fourteenth Amendment right to privacy is limited to decisions arising in the personal sphere—matters relating to marriage, procreation, contraception, family relationships, child rearing, and the like. . . . [W]orkplace surveillance cannot be shoehorned into any of these categories. Because the appellants do not challenge a governmental restriction imposed upon decisionmaking in uniquely personal matters, they cannot bring their claim within the reach of the "autonomy" cases.

The appellants' argument is no stronger under the confidentiality bough of the Fourteenth Amendment right to privacy. Even if the right of confidentiality has a range broader than that associated with the right to autonomy, . . . that range has not extended beyond prohibiting profligate disclosure of medical, financial, and other intimately personal data. Any data disclosed through PRTC's video surveillance is qualitatively different, if for no other reason than that it has been revealed knowingly by the appellants to all observers (including the video cameras). This information cannot be characterized accurately as "personal" or "confidential."

VI. CONCLUSION

. . . Because the appellants do not have an objectively reasonable expectation

---

[7] In light of this conclusion, we need not reach the question of whether the intrusion attributable to PRTC's video monitoring is reasonable . . . . *See O'Connor*, 480 U.S. at 725.

of privacy in the open areas of their workplace, the video surveillance conducted by their employer does not infract their federal Constitutional rights.

NOTES AND QUESTIONS

1. Common law privacy claims against video monitoring by private sector employers generally have fared no better than the Fourth Amendment claims in *Vega-Rodriguez,* at least when the employees had advance knowledge of monitoring that did not involve an especially private part of the workplace, such as a restroom. *See, e.g.*, Marrs v. Marriott Corp., 830 F. Supp. 274 (D. Md. 1992); Sacramento County Deputy Sheriffs' Ass'n v. County of Sacramento, 59 Cal. Rptr. 2d 834 (Cal. App. 1996) .

2. What if an employer's monitoring of the workplace is surreptitious? Surreptitious monitoring is usually to investigate employee misconduct or to watch for the possibility of employee misconduct rather than to protect the business or its employees from outsiders. In some situations, investigatory monitoring cannot be effective unless it is surreptitious. If the examined employee later discovers the camera, can he claim a reasonable expectation of being free of video monitoring at the workplace? Does it matter whether the camera observed only what a supervisor or fellow employee could have seen?

Surreptitious video surveillance might be a tort or a violation of the Fourth Amendment, but not necessarily. As for other types of employer intrusion, the reasonableness of an employee's expectation of privacy against such observation depends on a mix of facts including the "openness" or accessibility of that part of the workplace, the angle or magnification of the recording, and nature of the activity under observation. *See, e.g.,* Cowles v. State, 23 P.3d 1168 (Alaska 2001) (even if employee worked in area observable by customers at ground level, she could reasonably expect not being observed by camera directly above her). An observed individual might reasonably expect some degree of privacy against surreptitious surveillance even in a space available to, or observable by, others. *Compare* Chadwell v. Brewer, 59 F. Supp. 3d 756 (W.D. Va. 2014) (plaintiff had reasonable albeit diminished expectation of privacy against video surveillance in shared office area) *with* Thompson v. Johnson County Cmty. Coll., 930 F. Supp. 501 (D. Kan. 1996) (plaintiffs lacked reasonable expectation against surreptitious video surveillance of locker room that was also storage room accessible to and used by many others). Even if an employee has some reasonable expectation of privacy in an observed space, employer actions might nevertheless be reasonable, especially if the employer uses the surveillance to investigate theft or other wrongdoing. In *Thompson*, the court held that surreptitious surveillance of a locker room was reasonable to investigate reports that an employee might be stealing from the lockers and bringing weapons to work. *See also* Brannen v. Kings Loc. Sch. Dist. Bd. of Educ., 761 N.E.2d 84 (Ohio App. 2001); Hernandez v. Hillsides, Inc., 211 P.3d 1063 (Cal. 2009). In general, the stronger an employee's expectation of privacy, the greater the demand for justification and reasonableness in the intrusion. Chadwell v. Brewer, 59 F. Supp. 3d 756, 764-65 (W.D. Va. 2014) (tentatively concluding that video surveillance of employee office was justified by his record of drinking at work and his submission to second-chance agreement).

3. An employer does not necessarily *watch* a video transmission or

recording, surreptitious or otherwise. The employer might review a recording only on those occasions when something wrong has happened and the video recording can reveal the identity of the wrongdoer. *Not* watching the recording might seem like an effective defense against an employee's invasion of privacy claim, but the employee might reply that the *sense* of being watched can constitute an injury in itself. *See* RESTATEMENT (SECOND) OF TORTS § 652B, comment b ("The intrusion itself makes the defendant subject to liability, even though there is no publication or other use of any kind of the photograph or information outlined"). *See also* Hernandez v. Hillsides, Inc., 48 Cal. Rptr. 3d 780 (Cal. App. 2006) (employees stated claim for invasion of privacy based on surreptitious video monitoring, even if they could not prove surveillance system recorded their images or that employer actually viewed video), *rev'd on oth. grounds*, 211 P.3d 1063 (Cal. 2009).

4. An employer watching or otherwise using a video recording may create an unlawful intrusion even if the original recording was lawful. Suppose an employer justifiably uses a camera for investigation and records an employee undressed in a locker room. Viewing and presenting the video can be an intrusion in itself. *See, e.g.,* Gillespie v. City of Battle Creek, 100 F. Supp. 3d 623 (W.D. Mich. 2015) (displaying video can be unlawful where portion showing female employee undressed was displayed to investigatory group with male employees).

5. An employer's most serious potential liability for video recording might be an employee's unauthorized use of a recording or of the camera. *See, e.g.,* Doe v. B.P.S. Guard Servs. Inc., 945 F.2d 1422 (8th Cir. 1991) (*respondeat superior* liability where guards used security cameras to videotape fashion models in dressing room); Stien v. Marriott Ownership Resorts, Inc., 944 P.2d 374 (Utah 1997) (dismissing lawsuit by wife of employee whose videotaped interview was edited and played as joke at company party; resulting videotape was insufficiently offensive to a reasonable person). But an employee's surreptitious surveillance of another may be insufficiently within the scope of employment for *respondeat superior* liability. Sometimes employees surreptitiously record to bolster their own claims of harassment by others or to make a record of a dispute with the employer. *See, e.g.*, Fox v. Pittsburg State Univ., 257 F. Supp. 3d 1112 (D. Kan. 2017).

6. When an employer takes surveillance beyond the workplace and watches employees at their home or in their personal life, the balance of interests may tip in employees' favor, especially if surveillance results in physical trespass of employee property. Issues about the lawfulness of employer surveillance of off-duty, off-premises employee activity frequently arise in connection with an employer's investigation of an employee's injury or disability claim. *Compare* McLain v. Boise Cascade Corp., 533 P.2d 343, 346 (Or. 1975) (employee's injury claim constituted waiver of expectation of privacy against reasonable investigation of claim, and employer's videotaping of employee's activity observable by any passerby was reasonable), *and* Claverie v. L.S.U. Med. Ctr. in New Orleans, 553 So. 2d 482 (La. App. 1989) (surveillance of employee going to and from home, to investigate his use of sick leave, did not violate his right to privacy), *with* Association Servs., Inc. v. Smith, 549 S.E.2d 454 (Ga. App. 2001) (fact issues regarding possible trespass precluded summary judgment against employee).

7. Some state statutes regulate video surveillance in general, including in employment, usually based on principles analogous to those of the Fourth Amendment or privacy common law. Such statutes typically permit monitoring of

persons who have consented or have no reasonable expectation of privacy because they are not in a "private place" or are subject to other circumstances defeating such an expectation. *See, e.g.*, Ariz. Rev. Stat. Ann. § 13-3018; Cal. Civ. Code § 1708.8; N.H. Stat. Ann. § 644:9; Tenn. Code Ann. § 39-13-605.

8. Does an employer ever have a *duty* to engage in video monitoring? Would an employer violate a duty by *failing* to use a video camera to investigate a pattern of racially or sexually motivated "pranks" against an employee? Cf. Williams v. Port Huron Sch. Dist., 455 Fed. Appx. 612 (6th Cir. 2012) (school district's use of video surveillance in effort to identify perpetrators of racial harassment was evidence of efforts to investigate and prevent harassment).

PROBLEM

Phillip Files's employer, Peyton, PLC, provided him with his own office and a computer, but company policy stated that "office computers are for business use, and any personal use is prohibited." Peyton also periodically issued reminders to employees that it "reserves the right to monitor employee computer usage." Nevertheless, Files used his computer for occasional personal uses, such as emailing personal correspondence, and checking financial markets, weather, and traffic. Files was sure his supervisor Sam Hazard knew of his personal use because Hazard sometimes visited Files' office when a non-work-related website was clearly visible on the computer monitor. Files also understood that Hazard and other employees with whom Files corresponded by email were making personal use of their computers when they sent or received non-work-related emails to him.

After Files was passed over for a promotion, Hazard worried that Files might start looking for another job, and that Files might even take confidential data with him. One evening, after Files had left work for home, Hazard and one of the company's computer technicians accessed Files's computer data folders and files to see if he was collecting and organizing confidential data, and to see if they could find any evidence that Files was looking for a job. As they searched Files's folders, they found one named "personal data." They opened the folder and examined some of the files. They found no evidence that Files was looking for a job or that Files was collecting confidential data, but they did find a draft of a romantic message Files had written to Hazard's wife. The next day, Hazard confronted Files about the message, and announced that Files was terminated effective immediately. Did Hazard or his employer, Peyton, unlawfully invade Files' privacy?

Employee Communications and Transmitted or Stored Data

A person with no reasonable expectation of privacy against visual observation of his workplace might nevertheless expect privacy with respect to what he *says* in the workplace. Walker v. Darby, 911 F.2d 1573 (11th Cir. 1990). When we speak, we usually have some sense of who is listening. Normally prudent people are careful to say what is appropriate for the audience. For example, a person might tell an off-color joke in the presence of a trusted colleague without fear that the colleague will use the incident to accuse the speaker of insensitivity, bias or poor judgment. But if the conversation is captured surreptitiously and recorded by the employer's audio recorder, the speaker loses control over the size and identity of the audience. Audio surveillance can occur in combination with video surveillance, and depending on the circumstances either aspect of the surveillance might be more intrusive than the other. A cautious employer, however, will not use a video camera that records sound. Thus, in some of the video surveillance cases described above, employees were unable to prove a violation of their communicative privacy because the employers used cameras without an audio recording capability. *See, e.g.*, Thompson v. Johnson County Comm. Coll., 930 F. Supp. 501 (D. Kan. 1996).

Speaking is only one of many forms of communication subject to employer surveillance. All forms of communication, including transmitted or stored data such as e-mails or computer files, are subject to the same privacy and Forth Amendment rights that limit an employer's visual or video surveillance, but with two additional concerns. First, usual employer justifications for intrusive visual or video surveillance might not support audio or other communication surveillance in a particular case. Second, audio and electronic communication or data surveillance is more likely subject to special federal and state statutes, especially the Electronic Communications Privacy Act and Stored Communications Act.

The Fourth Amendment and the Law of Privacy. Surveillance of a person's communications including stored or transmitted electronic data can be a "search" subject to the Fourth Amendment and tort law. In City of Ontario v. Quon, 560 U.S. 746 (2010), the Supreme Court applied the Fourth Amendment to Quon's claim that his city employer unlawfully inspected the content of text messages he sent and received on a pager the city supplied for his work as a police officer. Notwithstanding written policies that warned employees their pager messages were subject to an "audit," the Court assumed for the sake of argument that Quon had a reasonable expectation of privacy with respect to the content of personal text messages. Quon's alleged expectation of privacy was based on the city's practice permitting officers to use their pagers for personal purposes and avoid an audit provided they reimbursed the city for messages in excess of a monthly limit.

The audit that led to the city inspection of text messages was for the purpose of reevaluating a formula by which the city charged officers for all messages above a certain limit. Quon's use of his pager routinely exceeded the monthly limit even if the city counted only messages during work hours. Thus, in order to determine whether his work-time messages were truly work-related and whether it would be fair to charge him for these messages, the investigators examined the content of the messages. It was the city's inspection of the content of Quon's personal messages that provoked his Fourth Amendment search challenge.

The Court held that the city's search of Quon's messages did not violate the Fourth Amendment because it was reasonable. The search was justified in its inception by a "work-related purpose": to reevaluate the formula for charging officers for text messages above their limit. Also, the search was reasonably performed and consistent with its purpose. It was not "excessively intrusive" because, for example, the city examined only a limited sample of messages to determine Quon's actual work needs. The Court rejected an argument that the city had to prove it investigated in the "least intrusive" manner practicable, fearing that such an approach would invite too much judicial retrospective analysis and interference with day-to-day operations of public employers.

Could non-employees who sent Quon messages have asserted their own

Fourth Amendment claims? Three non-employee "senders" did join Quon's lawsuit. However, they evidently conceded that their claims depended entirely on whether the city had violated *Quon's* Fourth Amendment rights. The Court did not interpret their claims to be independent of Quon's claims. Since the Court had rejected Quon's claims, it rejected the senders' dependent claims as well.

The Electronic Communications Privacy Act and Stored Communications Act. The older of these sibling statutes is the Electronic Communications Privacy Act (ECPA), 18 U.S.C. §§ 2510-2520, which is a descendent of the Wiretap Act. Today, it applies mainly to technologically enhanced eavesdropping on face-to-face communications and interception of electronic communications — particularly telephone communications. The Stored Communications Act (SCA), 18 U.S.C. §§ 2701-2712, applies mainly to unauthorized "accessing" of stored electronic communications — such as e-mail — and other electronic data. Both statutes include civil causes of action for a person whose communications have been "intercepted" or whose data has been "accessed." Neither statute is designed particularly for employment relations. However, considering that so much of our communication occurs at or during work and that employee communications might be relevant to an employer's disciplinary investigation, supervision of work, or other business purposes, it is not surprising that the ECPA and SCA are frequently invoked in disputes between employers and employees.

The ECPA does not apply unless there is a "wire" communication (e.g., telephone call) or an "oral or electronic communication" to protect. Thus, the ECPA would not apply to the surreptitious reading of another person's letter because a letter is not "oral" or "electronic." Next, the ECPA requires an "interception" of a covered communication. To "intercept," a person who is *not a party* to the communication must use an "electronic, mechanical, or other device." 18 U.S.C. § 2510(4). Since a party to a conversation cannot "intercept" a communication sent by or intended for him, the ECPA does not apply to a party's own surreptitious recording of his conversation, but some local laws do apply to such activity. Smith v. Cincinnati Post & Times-Star, 475 F.2d 740 (6th Cir. 1973); Lane v. Allstate Ins. Co., 14 Nev. 1176, 969 P.2d 938 (1998). In the employment context, employees have frequently relied on the ECPA in challenging an employer's use of a device such as a microphone, tape recorder, or extension line of a telephone system to record or eavesdrop on communications between employees or between employees and other third parties. In Walker v. Darby, 911 F.2d 1573 (11th Cir. 1990), for example, the plaintiff employee alleged that the employer had secretly placed a microphone at his desk to eavesdrop on his conversations with other employees. The Eleventh Circuit held that the employee stated a claim under the ECPA.

The definition of "intercept" also requires an "aural or other acquisition" of a communication. 18 U.S.C. § 2510(4). The interceptor's "aural" acquisition is by listening to a conversation with his ear aided by the device. "Other acquisition" is likely to be by recording a communication. In the view of most courts, "acquisition" and interception are complete with the recording regardless of whether the interceptor listens to the record. *See* Arias v. Mutual Cent. Alarm Serv., 202 F.3d 553, 557-558 (2d Cir. 2000) (discussing alternative views).

It might already be evident that the ECPA's rules do not necessarily follow the contours of the Fourth Amendment or the common law of privacy. For example, an employer who places his ear against a closed door to listen to a private conversation might be violating the law of privacy but not the ECPA because he has not used a "device." On the other hand, if the employer does use a "device" to listen to the conversation, he might violate the ECPA regardless of whether his intrusion is "reasonable" under the law of privacy. The employer's defense under the ECPA is not that his interception was "reasonable" but that his actions fit within one of the express exceptions of the act.

One of the most important defenses for an employer's interception of employee communications is an exception for interception in the "ordinary course of business." To understand this exception, imagine a typical setting: A supervisor picks up a phone on a shared line to listen to an employee's conversation with another party. In the absence of an exception, the supervisor's action is an interception because he has used a device — the phone — and he has acquired the communication by listening to it. Another typical setting is an employer's recording of employee telephone conversations. In the absence of an exception, this action is an interception because the employer has used a device — the recording equipment — to acquire conversations by recording them. The exception that might apply in both these settings is the "ordinary course of business" exception. The exception is found in the statutory definition of "device" (an instrument used to intercept) that excludes

> any telephone . . . instrument, equipment or facility, or any component thereof . . . furnished to the subscriber or user by a provider of wire or electronic communication service . . . and being used by the subscriber or user in the ordinary course of its business or furnished by such subscriber or user for connection to the facilities of such service and used in the ordinary course of its business.

18 U.S.C.A. § 2510(5). In short, employer use of an extension line or recorder is not use of a "device" to intercept and acquire employee telephone communications if the employer or its service provider supplied the device and the employer used it in the ordinary course of the employer's business. The requirement that the employer or its service provider furnished the device has the effect of denying the exemption to a rogue employee who might attach his own device to the employer's system. The other key requirement for the exemption — that the employer used the device in the ordinary course of its business — raises more difficult issues.

Under what circumstances and for what purposes would listening to or recording employee telephone conversations be in the "ordinary course" of employer business? For businesses that provide or sell goods or services over the telephone, monitoring employee calls might be as much a part of supervision as visual oversight of employees in any other type of work. For other businesses, recording calls might be a security precaution to permit the retrieval of emergency information or the investigation of the handling of an emergency. *See Arias, supra.*

An employer might also listen to or record telephone conversations of employees to investigate possible misconduct. It remains uncertain whether investigatory eavesdropping qualifies as "the ordinary course of business." It might be argued that the business of an employer is something other than investigating its own employees. *But see Arias, supra* (security service may continuously record of employee calls to deter criminality). Moreover, some courts have held that *surreptitious* interception is *never* the ordinary course of business. *See, e.g.*, George v. Carusone, 849 F. Supp. 159 (D. Conn. 1994). *Contra Arias, supra*; Deal v. Spears, 980 F.2d 1153 (8th Cir. 1992); Briggs v. Am. Air Filter Co., 455 F. Supp. 179 (N.D. Ga. 1978), *aff'd*, 630 F.2d 414 (5th Cir. 1978).

Regardless of whether an employer's initial interception of communications is in the ordinary course of business for purposes of the exception, the employer may not lawfully exploit the opportunity to listen to more than is necessary for its purpose. *Compare* Dillon v. Massachusetts Bay Transp. Auth., 729 N.E.2d 329 (Mass. App. 2000) (recording all personal calls on employer's system was an unavoidable consequence of a legitimate business practice), *with* Ali v. Douglas Cable Comm'ns, 929 F. Supp. 1362, 1380 (D. Kan. 1996) (employer may intercept personal calls only to extent necessary to investigate unauthorized calls or determine whether calls are personal), *and* Deal v. Spears, 980 F.2d 1153 (8th Cir. 1992) (recording 22 hours of personal calls exceeded investigatory needs).

If an employer "intercepting" employee telephone calls cannot claim the benefit of the ordinary course of business exemption, can it escape liability by obtaining the express or implied consent of employees in advance? The act does provide that interception is not unlawful if one or more parties to the communication consents. 18 U.S.C. § 2511(d). However, employee consent and the scope of consent are frequently in doubt. An employer does not prove consent merely by showing that the employee knew of the employer's capability to intercept, or that the employer had threatened to intercept in the future. Deal v. Spears, 980 F.2d 1153, 1157 (8th Cir. 1992). Moreover, although an employee's knowledge of an employer's practice of recording calls might constitute implied consent to such a practice, such consent would not necessarily permit an employer to continue to listen to a call it knew was personal. Indeed, even if the employer prohibited personal calls, an employer might still violate the law if it listened to a personal call for longer than necessary to determine that the call violated the employer's policy. Watkins v. L.M. Berry & Co., 704 F.2d 577 (2d Cir. 2000). *See also* Williams v. Poulos, 11 F.3d 271 (1st Cir. 1993) (notice of monitoring of calls would not necessarily constitute notice that employer would record calls).

E-mail and similar electronic communications present another batch of problems, The ECPA and its concept of "interception" do not apply easily to e-mail and other forms of electronic communication that were not envisioned in the days of the original Wiretap Act. In contrast with telephone or direct oral communication, email communication is not instantaneous. Like the conveyance of a letter through the mail, the transmission of email takes place in stages over a period of time. At one moment it is in the possession of the sender or his facility; then it is in the temporary possession of an intermediary such as the post office or service provider; then it is "stored" in the intended recipient's mailbox; and finally it is received and read by the intended recipient. The recipient might then dispose of the message or store it for future reference. The message is vulnerable to "acquisition" by a third party at any point in this process.

In fact, according to a 2003 American Management Association survey, 52 percent of responding employers engage in some form of monitoring of employee email. An additional 13 percent answered "don't know" if their email was being monitored. Employers who monitor employee email typically perform key word or key phrase searches of email or computer files. Most had policies for employee use of the employer's computer system to send or receive email, and about 22 percent had terminated at least one employee for "email infractions." About 5 percent had been involved in a lawsuit "triggered" in some way by an email. The most serious worries about employee email are that the computer system or business operations will be disrupted by non-business email or by viruses attached to email. American Management Association, *E-Mail Practices* (2003), at http://www.amanet.org/research/pdfs/Email_Policies_Practices.pdf.

Are employers "intercepting" e-mail when they monitor or acquire it? "Interception" suggests a third-party action taking place during or simultaneous with transmission of the message and before the message's intended receipt. But e-mail is most vulnerable to acquisition by a third party, such as an employer, when it is in a "*stored*" state. An e-mail is stored in several places during its transmission: In the sender's computer, in a server of a service provider (which might be the sender's employer or a third party), in a server of the recipient's service provider (which might be the recipient's employer or a third party) and finally in the recipient's computer. The e-mail might continue to be stored in one or more of these locations long after it is received and read by the intended recipient.

FRASER v. NATIONWIDE MUTUAL INSURANCE CO.

352 F.3d 107 (3d Cir. 2003)

AMBRO, Circuit Judge.

. . . This dispute stems from [Nationwide Mutual Insurance Company's] September 2, 1998 termination of [Richard] Fraser's [Independent Insurance] Agent's Agreement (the "Agreement"). It provided that Fraser sell insurance policies as an independent contractor for Nationwide on an exclusive basis. The relationship was terminable at will by either party.

The parties disagree on the reason for Fraser's termination. Fraser argues Nationwide terminated him because he filed complaints with the Pennsylvania Attorney General's office regarding Nationwide's allegedly illegal conduct, including its discriminatory refusal to write car insurance for unmarried and new drivers. . . . Nationwide argues, however, that it terminated Fraser because he was disloyal. It points out that Fraser drafted a letter to two competitors—Erie Insurance Company ("Erie") and Zurich American Insurance ("Zurich") . . . to determine whether Erie and Zurich would be interested in acquiring the policyholders of the agents in [an association of independent agents headed by Fraser]. Fraser claims that the letters only were drafted to get Nationwide's attention and were not sent. (Were the letters sent, however, they would constitute a violation of the "exclusive representation" provision of Fraser's Agreement with Nationwide.)

When Nationwide learned about these letters, it claims that it became concerned that Fraser might also be revealing company secrets to its competitors. It therefore searched its main file server — on which all of Fraser's e-mail was lodged — for any e-mail to or from Fraser that showed similar improper behavior.[2]

[2] Nationwide's associate general counsel (Randall Orr) testified that he directed a systems

Nationwide's general counsel testified that the e-mail search confirmed Fraser's disloyalty. Therefore, on the basis of the two letters and the e-mail search, Nationwide terminated Fraser's Agreement. It is this search of his e-mail that gives rise to Fraser's claim for damages under the Electronic Communications Privacy Act of 1986 ("ECPA"), 18 U.S.C. § 2510. . . .

The [District] Court granted summary judgment … [against] all counts….

Fraser argues that, by accessing his e-mail on its central file server without his express permission, Nationwide violated Title I of the ECPA, which prohibits "intercepts" of electronic communications such as e-mail. The statute defines an "intercept" as "the aural or other acquisition of the contents of any wire, electronic, or oral communication through the use of any electronic, mechanical, or other device." 18 U.S.C. § 2510(4). Nationwide argues that it did not "intercept" Fraser's e-mail within the meaning of Title I because an "intercept" can only occur contemporaneously with transmission and it did not access Fraser's e-mail at the initial time of transmission.

On this matter of statutory interpretation . . . , we agree with Nationwide. Every circuit court to have considered the matter has held that an "intercept" under the ECPA must occur contemporaneously with transmission. *See* United States v. Steiger, 318 F.3d 1039, 1048-49 (11th Cir. 2003); Konop v. Hawaiian Airlines, Inc., 302 F.3d 868 (9th Cir. 2002); Steve Jackson Games, Inc. v. U.S. Secret Serv., 36 F.3d 457 (5th Cir. 1994); *see also* Wesley College v. Pitts, 974 F. Supp. 375 (D. Del. 1997), *summarily aff'd*, 172 F.3d 861 (3d Cir. 1998).

The first case to do so, *Steve Jackson Games*, noted that "intercept" was defined as contemporaneous in the context of an aural communication under the old Wiretap Act, . . . and that when Congress amended the Wiretap Act in 1986 (to create what is now known as the ECPA) to extend protection to electronic communications, it "did not intend to change the definition of 'intercept.'" *Steve Jackson Games*, 36 F.3d at 462. Moreover, the Fifth Circuit noted that the differences in definition between "wire communication" and "electronic communication" in the ECPA supported its conclusion that stored e-mail could not be intercepted within the meaning of Title I. A "wire communication" under the ECPA was (until recent amendment by the USA Patriot Act, *see* note 8) "any aural transfer made in whole or in part through the use of facilities for the transmission of communications by the aid of wire, cable, or other like connection between the point of origin and the point of reception . . . *and such term includes any electronic storage of such communication*." 18 U.S.C. § 2510(1) (emphasis added) (superseded by USA Patriot Act).[8] By contrast, an "electronic communication" is defined as "any transfer of signs, signals, writing, images, sounds, data, or intelligence of any nature transmitted in whole or in part by a wire, radio, electromagnetic, photoelectronic or photooptical system . . . but *does not include . . . any wire or oral communication*." 18 U.S.C. § 2510(12) (emphasis added). Thus, the Fifth Circuit reasoned that because "wire communication" explicitly included

---

expert to perform the search in … [Orr's] presence. The systems expert opened e-mail written to or by Fraser if the e-mail headers (i.e., the to, from, and re: lines) contained relevant information.

[8] The USA Patriot Act § 209, 115 Stat. 272, 283 (2001), amended the definition of "wire communication" to eliminate electronic storage from the definition of wire communication.

electronic storage but "electronic communication" did not, there can be no "intercept" of an e-mail in storage, as an e-mail in storage is by definition not an "electronic communication." *Steve Jackson Games*, 36 F.3d at 461-62.

Subsequent cases, cited above, have agreed with the Fifth Circuit's result. While Congress's definition of "intercept" does not appear to fit with its intent to extend protection to electronic communications, it is for Congress to cover the bases untouched. We adopt the reasoning of our sister circuits and therefore hold that there has been no "intercept" within the meaning of Title I of ECPA.

Fraser also argues that Nationwide's search of his e-mail violated Title II of the ECPA [also known as the Stored Communication Act (SCA)]. That Title creates civil liability for one who "(1) intentionally accesses without authorization a facility through which an electronic communication service is provided; or (2) intentionally exceeds an authorization to access that facility; and thereby obtains, alters, or prevents authorized access to a wire or electronic communication while it is in electronic storage in such system." 18 U.S.C. § 2701(a). The statute defines "electronic storage" as "(A) any temporary, intermediate storage of a wire or electronic communication incidental to the electronic transmission thereof; and (B) any storage of such communication by an electronic communication service for purposes of backup protection of such communication." *Id.* § 2510(17).

The District Court granted summary judgment in favor of Nationwide, holding that Title II does not apply to the e-mail in question because the transmissions were neither in "temporary, intermediate storage" nor in "backup" storage. Rather, according to the District Court, the e-mail was in a state it described as "post-transmission storage." We agree that Fraser's e-mail was not in temporary, intermediate storage. But to us it seems questionable that the transmissions were not in backup storage — a term that neither the statute nor the legislative history defines. Therefore, while we affirm the District Court, we do so through a different analytical path, assuming without deciding that the e-mail in question was in backup storage.

18 U.S.C. § 2701(c)(1) excepts from Title II seizures of e-mail authorized "by the person or entity providing a wire or electronic communications service." There is no circuit court case law interpreting this exception. However, in Bohach v. City of Reno, 932 F. Supp. 1232 (D. Nev. 1996), a district court held that the Reno police department could, without violating Title II, retrieve pager text messages stored on the police department's computer system because the department "is the provider of the 'service'" and "service providers [may] do as they wish when it comes to accessing communications in electronic storage." *Id.* at 1236. Like the court in *Bohach*, we read § 2701(c) literally to except from Title II's protection all searches by communications service providers. Thus, we hold that, because Fraser's e-mail was stored on Nationwide's system (which Nationwide administered), its search of that e-mail falls within § 2701(c)'s exception to Title II. . . .

We affirm the . . . grant of summary judgment in favor of Nationwide....

NOTES AND QUESTIONS

1. As the court noted in *Fraser*, the SCA (also sometimes known as Title II of the ECPA) applies to accessing of electronic communications in "temporary,

intermediate storage of a wire or electronic communication incidental to the electronic transmission." The court expressed some uncertainty whether the stored emails accessed by Nationwide fell within this definition of "electronic storage." The solution might lie in a key part of the subpart (A) definition of electronic storage in Section 2510(17): A stored communication is not in "electronic storage" for purposes of the SCA unless the storage is "incidental to the electronic transmission." Once the transmission is complete in the sense that the recipient has viewed the email, any subsequent storage is no longer "incidental to transmission." If this interpretation is correct, the "accessing" of electronic communications is analogous to the "interception" of wire or oral communications: It must occur during the process of transmission, and later accessing is not within the scope of the SCA. Bohach v. City of Reno, 932 F. Supp. 1232 (D. Nev. 1996). *See also* Anzaldua v. Ne. Ambulance & Fire Prot'n Dist., 793 F.3d 822 (8th Cir. 2015) (draft of email never sent and copy of "sent" email were not in storage subject to the SCA).

But Subpart (B) of Section 2510(17) defines an additional type of protected electronic storage: "any storage of such communication by an electronic communication service for purposes of *backup* protection of such communication" (emphasis added). The meaning of "backup protection" in this context is not clear, but at the very least it raises the possibility that a copy of an e-mail left on the service provider's server is protected even after the transmission is complete. *See* Theofel v. Farey-Jones, 359 F.3d 1066, 1075 (9th Cir. 2004) (subpart (B) extends protection to copy of e-mail in post-transmission phase). If so, an employee's e-mail left on an employer's server might continue to be in protected "electronic storage" even after the intended recipient has opened and read the email. Shefts v. Petraki, 2011 WL 5930469 (C.D .Ill. 2011) (employer's search of post-transmission copies of e-mail constituted accessing of electronic storage).

2. There is a further requirement for SCA protection of a stored communication. The storage must be in a covered "facility." 18 U.S.C. § 2701(a). The courts have generally distinguished a "facility" from a "device." A storage facility is the facility a communications or internet services provider uses to store customer communications for the purpose of facilitating communications by its customers. If you check your Google or Yahoo email or post messages or comments on Facebook, you are accessing a storage facility. A personal device, such as a cell phone, tablet, laptop computer or desktop computer, might store many electronic communications but it is not a "facility" for providing communications services. Garcia v. City of Laredo, 702 F.3d 788 (5th Cir. 2012). Thus, if an employer, searches data on an employee's cell phone without the employee's permission or authorization, the employer will not have violated the SCA. *Id.* Of course, the employer might well have committed a tort of trespass, invasion of privacy, or intentional infliction of emotional distress.

3. Stored telephone messages were once treated as "communications" that might be "intercepted" in violation of the ECPA if retrieved by a non-party to the communication. Under the current version of the ECPA and SCA, however, a stored "wire communication" such as a telephone message stored on a service provider's telephone message system is included in the definition of "electronic storage" and is addressed mainly by the SCA. 18 U.S.C. § 2510(17). Thus, if the message is in temporary storage incidental to transmission and waiting for the

intended recipient to access it for the first time, access to that record is subject to the SCA. A stored telephone message might also be protected if it remains in storage by the service provider "for purposes of backup protection of such communication."

4. If a communication is in electronic storage in a facility subject to the SCA, the next question is whether a third party accessed the communication without authorization. The answer might depend on *which* facility was accessed. In the case of e-mail, a communication might be stored in multiple facilities and devices. In workplace situations, the employer's own server might be one of the storage facilities. If so, it is easy for the employer to inspect the message by accessing its own facility.. But is the employer always "authorized" to access all data on its own server? What does *Fraser* suggest? *See also* Bohach v. City of Reno, 932 F. Supp. 1232 (D. Nev. 1996) (for SCA purposes, employer could authorize its own search of any communications on its own server for its own communication system). In *Bohach*, the court also held that the employees had no reasonable expectation of privacy for Fourth Amendment purposes with respect to messages stored on the employer's facility. To the extent there is any question about an employer's authority to access its own system, the employer's express notice to employees and other evidence of employee consent to access may rebut a claim that the employer's access to a particular employee message was unauthorized. Shefts v. Petrakis, 758 F.Supp.2d 620 (C.D.Ill.2010).

5. If an employer seeks access to an employee's stored communications on a facility the employer does not own or control, such as a third party facility providing personal email services for the employee, the employer must obtain the authorization of the employee. Using surreptitious means to obtain an employee's login information to gain access without the employee's authorization would be a clear violation of the SCA. Pure Power Boot Camp v. Warrior Fitness Boot Camp, 587 F. Supp. 2d 548 (S.D.N.Y. 2008); Konop v. Hawaiian Airlines, Inc., 411 B.R. 678 (D. Hawai'i 2009), *aff'd* 401 Fed. Appx. 242 (9th Cir. 2010). If an employee does give login information and authorization to another employee or the employer for "one time" access or some limited purpose, further accessing in excess of that authorization is in violation of the SCA. Anzaldua v. Northeast Ambulance & Fire Prot'n Dist., 793 F.3d 822 (8th Cir. 2015).

It follows that authorization must be knowing and voluntary. Suppose an employer provides an employee with a laptop or other portable device that the employee subsequently uses to access her personal email account with a third party provider. Typically, the employee must return the device to the employer when employment terminates. In Lazette v. Kulmatycki, 949 F. Supp. 2d 748 (N.D. Ohio 2013), an employee returned such a device to her employer but forgot to delete the connection between the device and her personal email account. The court held that the employer's subsequent use of the device to access the former employee's personal email was unauthorized access in violation of the SCA.

6. What has been said about email accounts is also generally true of social media accounts, which involve storage of data in the facilities of service providers such as Facebook or LinkedIn. An important difference between email and social media is that many communications via social media are naturally directed at a much wider audience. Depending on the user's selection of privacy controls,

communications can be to one person, a limited audience or to the world, including the user's employer. An employer violates no law by inspecting posts on an employee's publicly accessible social media. However, if an employee limits access, an employer must not use unlawful means to circumvent the privacy controls. Making unauthorized use of the employee's login information to the social media site would violate the SCA: the employer would be accessing communications on a third party storage facility without authorization. But an employer might obtain surreptitious access simply by asking authorized associates of the employee to supply reports or images of the employee's posts. In Ehling v. Monmouth-Ocean Hospital Service Corp., 872 F. Supp. 2d 369 (D.N.J. 2012), the court held that an employer did not violate the SCA by using the targeted employee's co-employees to report the employee's social media posts. However, the court denied the employer's motion to dismiss because the employer may have committed the tort of invasion of privacy.

Employees frequently use social networking websites to complain about their employment or to respond to or support other employees' work-related comments. If the employer lawfully visits an employee's webpage and sees disparaging comments about employment conditions, can the employer discipline or threaten the employee because of the disparaging comments? Communications that are not private might still constitute protected "concerted activity" under Section 7 of the National Labor Relations Act. For more on this topic, *see* Office of the General Counsel, NLRB, Memorandum OM 11-74 (August 18, 2011), reproduced in Chapter 4, Part B.2.

7. Conduct that does not violate the ECPA or SCA might violate other laws, including the Fourth Amendment or tort law. Moreover, some states have enacted statutes that are more protective of communications than the ECPA or the SCA. *See, e.g.*, Borchers v. Franciscan Tertiary Province of Sacred Heart, Inc., 962 N.E.2d 29 (Ill. App. 2011) (tort claim); 19 Del.C. § 705 (regulating any "monitoring" of employee e-mail on the employer's own system).

8. If an employee lacks legal protection as to e-mails sent, received or stored with employer devices or facilities, it might follow that employee e-mail communications with her attorney through such devices or facilities are not subject to the attorney-client privilege. *See* Holmes v. Petrovich Development Co., 119 Cal.Rptr.3d 878 (Cal. App. 2011).

9. Employer monitoring and regulation of employee e-mail and other communications is limited by laws against discrimination or protected employee conduct. In Gallup, Inc., 334 NLRB 366 (2001), the employer evidently had not regulated employee use of office computers to send email until it was confronted by a union organizing campaign. Suddenly, the employer issued a number of new rules including one prohibiting the use of email for nonbusiness solicitation (which would have included soliciting employees to join or support the union). The NLRB held that the timing of the rule evidenced discriminatory intent and that the rule unlawfully interfered with employee rights to organize or join a union, in violation of Section 7 of the National Labor Relations Act.

10. Is an office computer dedicated to one employee's use analogous to the desk dedicated to Dr. Ortega in *O'Connor v. Ortega*, reproduced in Part B.6 of this chapter? In that Fourth Amendment "search" case, the U.S. Supreme Court held that an employee may have a reasonable expectation of privacy with respect to the

contents of a desk, subject to a reasonable search by the employer for various legitimate business purposes. If a computer is analogous to a desk, an employee might have a reasonable expectation of privacy with respect to a personal file saved on the computer dedicated to his or her use.

Such was the employee's argument in an invasion of privacy case, McLaren v. Microsoft Corp., 1999 WL 339015 (Tex. App. — Dallas 1999), where an employer investigating the employee's alleged sexual harassment inspected files left on the computer assigned to the employee. The court held that the employee's expectation of privacy was limited because the computer was not assigned to him for the purpose or convenience of storing personal items. Neither did the court accept the employee's argument that his expectation of privacy was strengthened by his creation of a password protected "personal" folder for the files in question. In any event, the court held that the employer's search was not "offensive" for tort law purposes because the search was part of a legitimate investigation of sexual harassment allegations against the employee.

11. A separate kind of employer regulation of employee computer use involves regulation of the websites an employee might visit. *See* Urofsky v. Gilmore, 216 F.3d 401 (4th Cir. 2000) (rejecting professors' First Amendment challenge against state legislation restricting state employees from accessing sexually explicit material on computers owned or leased by the state).

PROBLEM

Reread the facts in the previous problem on p. 607. Suppose that immediately after Sam Hazard discovered the draft of Files's message to Mrs. Hazard, Sam Hazard and the computer technician checked Files's email "inbox" and discovered an email Mrs. Hazard had sent only minutes earlier. Sam Hazard read the email, and it confirmed his worst suspicions. Did Sam Hazard or his employer violate any laws with respect to the privacy of such communications?

6. *Third Party Investigations of Alleged Wrongdoing: The Fair Credit Reporting Act and Fair and Accurate Credit Transactions Act*

One other law potentially limiting employer investigation of employees is the Fair Credit Reporting Act, which regulates an employer's use of "consumer reports" and "investigative consumer reports" an employer obtains from a third-party "consumer reporting agency." See Chapter 3.D.2. Under the act, an employee has a right to advance notice of the employer's intention to obtain a consumer report, a right to notice if the employer's adverse action against the employee is based on the contents of a consumer report, and a right to invoke the act's procedure for disputing and correcting a consumer reporting agency's information.

The employer must also obtain an employee's written authorization before accessing a credit report with respect to the employee. The requirement of employee authorization raises many of the same issues surrounding consent for other employer investigation or examination of employees. In Kelchner v. Sycamore Manor Health Center, 135 Fed. Appx. 499 (3d Cir. 2005), the Third Circuit held that the FCRA did not prohibit an employer from imposing a new condition of employment that every employee sign a "blanket authorization" for the employer to obtain an investigative credit report on the employee.

A "consumer reporting agency" might seem an unlikely party to an internal disciplinary matter. However, by its terms the FCRA appears to apply to an increasingly common scenario in disciplinary investigations of employees: the hiring of an independent outsider such as an attorney to conduct an investigation of sexual harassment or other alleged wrongdoing. An outside lawyer or investigator in this scenario might be a "consumer reporting agency" who "for monetary fees . . . regularly engages in whole or in part in the practice of assembling or evaluating" covered information "for the purpose of furnishing consumer reports to third parties." 15 U.S.C. § 1681a. *See* Hartman v. Lisle Park Dist., 158 F. Supp. 2d 869 (N.D. Ill. 2001) (finding that attorney was not a consumer reporting agency, but noting FTC's position to the contrary). If the FRCA applied to such an investigation in the same matter that it applies to background checks by traditional consumer reporting agencies, the investigated employee would have a right of access to the data and sources of data in the investigator's report to the employer.

In 2003, Congress enacted the Fair and Accurate Credit Transactions Act, 15 U.S.C. § 1681a(x)(1), amending the FCRA in a way that might be interpreted to confirm that outside investigators of disciplinary matters are covered agencies. However, the amendment also provides special treatment for an investigator's report "made to an employer in connection with an investigation of (i) suspected misconduct relating to employment; or (ii) compliance with Federal, State, or local laws and regulations, the rules of a self-regulatory organization, or any preexisting written policies of the employer. . . ." 15 U.S.C. § 1681a(x)(1).

For investigations and reports that fall within this special category for employer investigations, the amended act relieves employers and independent investigators of many of their usual FCRA duties. However, the act still imposes a limited obligation on the employer:

> After taking any adverse action based in whole or in part on [an employer investigatory report], the employer shall disclose to the [employee] a summary containing the *nature and substance* of the communication upon which the adverse action is based, except that the *sources* of information acquired solely for use in preparing . . . [the] report need *not* be disclosed.

15 U.S.C. § 1681a(x)(2) (emphasis added). The usefulness of an employee's right to the "nature and substance" of the report is quite limited, because the employee lacks the usual FCRA remedies for challenging inaccuracies in a report. Moreover, an employee might be subject to an employer's right to discharge at will regardless of whether the investigator's report provides a fair and accurate basis for discharge.

C. NEGLIGENT INVESTIGATION

Suppose the flaw in the employer's investigation is not unlawful intrusion but *inaccuracy*. As discussed in Chapter 3, employers generally owe *potential* employees no duty of care in employee selection; an employer has a right to be wrong or negligent in selecting employees. The mere fact that the employer relied on inaccurate information or conclusions is ordinarily of no legal consequence. Is an employer similarly free of any duty of care in investigating a current employee and evaluating the information before making a decision?

MISSION PETROLEUM CARRIERS, INC. v. SOLOMON

106 S.W.3d 705 (Tex. 2003)

Justice JEFFERSON delivered the opinion of the court.

Mission Petroleum Carriers, Inc. terminated Roy Solomon, an at-will employee, for failing a random drug test. Solomon sued Mission, contending that it breached a common-law duty by not exercising ordinary care in the manner it collected his urine specimen for testing. . . .

Mission required its 520 truck drivers to submit to random drug testing pursuant to DOT regulations. As authorized by these regulations, Mission used its own employees to collect the drivers' urine samples for testing by outside laboratories. On April 3, 1997, Roy Solomon … was randomly selected to provide a urine sample for drug testing. . . .

A Medical Review Officer (MRO), charged with ensuring the accuracy of the test results, informed Solomon that he had tested positive for THC metabolite. Solomon told the MRO that the positive result could not possibly be accurate because he had never used marijuana. Solomon denied taking medication or any other product that might have caused the THC metabolite to appear in his sample. He did not, however, suggest that the results might have been compromised by Mission's faulty collection procedures. Following his discussion with the MRO, Solomon called Mission and requested a retest. Mission [which had reserved half of Solomon's urine sample for retesting if necessary] sent the second sample to a different laboratory for analysis. On April 9, 1997, when the second test also confirmed the presence of THC metabolite, Mission terminated Solomon's employment.

The next day, Solomon applied for truck-driving positions at Coastal Transport and MCX Trucking. The DOT regulations require a prospective employer to review the applicant's test results from previous employers for the preceding two years from the date of the application. Consequently, as part of each employment application, Coastal Transport and MCX Trucking asked Solomon to sign a consent form authorizing Mission to release those drug test results. Mission reported Solomon's test results to Coastal and MCX after Solomon consented to the disclosure. *See id.* § 382.405(f); *see also* 62 Fed. Reg. 16380 (1997) (employers may only release test results with the informed written consent of the employee). Neither Coastal Transport nor MCX Trucking hired Solomon. . . .

Solomon['s] negligence claim [against Mission, based on its collection and handling of his urine sample] proceeded to trial. Solomon testified that he had never smoked marijuana. [Solomon's evidence also showed that Mission violated DOT regulations by (1) relying on Solomon's immediate supervisor to collect the sample; (2) removing the collection container from its sealed kit out of Solomon's presence; (3) failing to restrict access to the collection site; and (4) failing to accept and seal the sample during Solomon's continuous observation.]

The jury found that Mission's negligence proximately caused Solomon's injuries and awarded Solomon past and future damages for medical care, loss of earning capacity, and mental anguish totaling $802,444.22. The jury also assessed $100,000 in exemplary damages on a finding that Mission acted with malice. . . . The court of appeals affirmed,

. . . . [W]e begin by addressing whether an employer owes a duty to an at-will employee to use reasonable care when collecting an employee's urine sample for drug testing pursuant to DOT regulations. The existence of a duty is a question of law. When considering whether there is a basis for imposing a duty, we consider various factors, "including the risk, foreseeability, and likelihood of injury weighed against the social utility of the actor's conduct, the magnitude of the burden of guarding against the injury, and the consequences of placing the burden on the defendant." [Greater Houston Transp. Co. v. Phillips, 801 S.W.2d 523, 525 (Tex. 1990).] With these factors in mind, we consider whether Solomon has presented a basis for imposing a common-law duty of reasonable care on employers when conducting in-house urine specimen collection pursuant to DOT regulations.

In SmithKline Beecham Corp. v. Doe, this Court addressed the related question of whether an independent drug testing laboratory, hired by an employer to test prospective employees, owes a duty to warn those employees that certain substances, if ingested prior to a drug test, could cause a positive test result. Emphasizing that we were deciding only the narrow question presented, we concluded that the testing laboratory owed no duty to warn the person tested or to investigate the reason for a positive result. We declined to address any duty the employer may owe to an employee and expressly reserved the question whether a laboratory may be liable for performing drug tests negligently. *Id.* at 351. . . .

Courts in other jurisdictions are split on whether a testing laboratory owes a duty to third-party employees when collecting or analyzing urine samples. Courts in New York, Illinois, and Wyoming have utilized risk/utility balancing tests, applying many of the factors we articulated in *Phillips*, to hold that laboratories obtaining specimens as part of an employer's substance abuse testing program owe a duty of care to employees submitting specimens.[6] On the other hand, courts in Texas and Ohio reject a laboratory's duty of care, emphasizing generally that drug-testing companies have a direct relationship only with the employer and not the employee.[7] Courts in Louisiana and Pennsylvania are divided.[8] Each of these cases, however, involves third-party collection of urine for drug testing, an issue not before this Court. We must answer, then, whether an employer owes a duty of care when the employer itself collects the employees' urine samples.

We are not aware of any cases recognizing the duty that Solomon advocates

---

[6] *See, e.g.*, Santiago v. Greyhound Lines, Inc., 956 F. Supp. 144, 152-53 (N.D.N.Y. 1997); Stinson v. Physicians Immediate Care, Ltd., 646 N.E.2d 930, 934 (Ill. App. 1995); Duncan v. Afton, Inc., 991 P.2d 739, 745 (Wyo. 1999).

[7] *See, e.g.*, Frank v. Delta Airlines, Inc., 2001 WL 910386 (N.D. Tex. Aug. 3, 2001); Hall v. United Labs, Inc., 31 F. Supp. 2d 1039, 1043 (N.D. Ohio 1998); *Willis*, 61 F.3d at 316. . . .

[8] *Compare* Elliott v. Lab. Specialists, Inc., 588 So. 2d 175, 176 (La. Ct. App. 1991) *with* Herbert v. Placid Ref. Co., 564 So. 2d 371, 374 (La. Ct. App. 1990); *compare also* Sharpe v. St. Luke's Hosp., 573 Pa. 90, 821 A.2d 1215, 1221 (2003) *with* Caputo v. Compuchem Labs, Inc., 1994 WL 100084 (E.D. Pa. Feb. 23, 1994).

here. In fact, we have located only one case directly addressing what duty an employer owes when the employer itself collects employees' urine samples. In Bellinger v. Weight Watchers Gourmet Food Co., 756 N.E.2d 1251, 1257 (Oh. App. 2001), an employer terminated an employee for failing a random drug test. The employee claimed that his employer breached a duty to perform the drug test in a competent manner because it failed to follow the company's drug and alcohol policy. The court, however, disagreed. It held that because the plaintiff was an at-will employee, his employer was entitled to discharge him whether or not he was subject to a drug test; therefore, the employer did not owe the employee a duty to perform the test in a competent manner. *Id.* at 1257.

Other courts have similarly refused to impose a common-law tort duty requiring an employer's agent to comply with DOT protocol when the agent collects samples for drug testing. In Carroll III v. Federal Express Corp., 113 F.3d 163 (9th Cir. 1997), an outside drug-test administrator for Federal Express allegedly violated several DOT collection protocols and chain-of-custody requirements when collecting the employee's urine sample, resulting in a "false positive" test result. The plaintiff argued that Federal Express's drug-testing policy created an implied obligation that he would not be terminated except for a positive drug test "that was untainted by error." *Id.* at 167. The court, however, rejected the plaintiff's invitation to recognize an implied obligation to ensure error-free testing. *Id.* . . .

The New York Court of Appeals in [Hall v. United Parcel Serv.,555 N.E.2d 273 (N.Y. 1990)] refused to recognize a cause of action based on allegations that an employee's polygraph test, which was negligently administered, resulted in an innocent employee's termination for theft. *Hall*, 555 N.E.2d at 278. The court deferred to state and federal legislative initiatives as the more appropriate avenue for addressing legitimate concerns about the consequences of an employer's use of questionable test results. *Id.* at 277-78. Moreover, the court noted that the Federal Employee Polygraph Protection Act of 1988, 29 U.S.C. § 2001, which creates a private cause of action for certain violations of the Act, greatly diminished the need to recognize a new common-law tort remedy for negligently conducted polygraph tests. *Id.*

Although these opinions inform our consideration of the issue, they rest largely on analysis of wrongful termination claims. We recognize that Solomon does not contest Mission's right to terminate him. Instead, he asserts that Mission had a duty not to destroy his future employment prospects. We must consider, then, whether imposing that duty is consistent with the comprehensive federal regulatory scheme already in place and with our common law in related areas.

Congress has not given employees a private cause of action under the DOT regulations at issue here. *See* Parry v. Mohawk Motors of Mich., Inc., 236 F.3d 299, 308 (6th Cir. 2000). . . . Nevertheless, like the Polygraph Protection Act, the DOT regulations impose stringent rules for administering and disclosing drug test results and levy civil penalties for violation of these rules. . . . In addition, employees have significant avenues of redress when employers fail or refuse to follow DOT protocol in collecting urine samples. . . . [F]or example, employers cannot require employees to sign consent or release forms with respect to any part of the drug testing, including collection, when the employer fails to follow statutory requisites for collecting the specimen. *See* 62 Fed. Reg. 16380 (1997). When employers do not follow DOT protocol, employees can refuse to initial the seal on the specimen bottle and can refuse to sign the Federal Drug Testing Custody and Control Form. *See id.* Without this form, the Medical Review Officer (MRO) cannot verify the drug test. *See* 49 C.F.R. § 40.33(a), (c).

The regulations anticipate that positive test results do not necessarily confirm that the employee is guilty of drug use. . . . For that reason, the DOT regulations require not only that an independent MRO review the test results, but also provide the MRO with the authority to examine the procedures by which the sample was collected, including interviewing the employee to determine if positive results can be explained by factors other than drug use. *Id.* § 40.33. . . . If an employee chooses not to initial or sign the seal or Custody and Control Form, the MRO cannot confirm the chain of custody and must contact the employee to discuss the positive result. 49 C.F.R. § 40.33(a), (c). And even if the chain of custody is confirmed, the MRO cannot verify a positive test result if aware that the urine sample was not obtained in accordance with the DOT protocols. *Id.* § 40.33(b). These protections reduce the risk of harm and likelihood of injury to an employee whose employer negligently collects urine samples for drug testing. Solomon did not attempt to utilize these avenues of redress.

On the day Solomon was first employed, Mission gave him explicit guidelines not only implementing but also supplementing the DOT regulations. Under these guidelines, Solomon could have requested that the positive test result be reported by the MRO as negative. . . . Instead, he (1) signed the Custody and Control Form . . . and (2) did not disclose to the MRO Mission's alleged malfeasance during the collection . . . . [N]othing on the face of the sample would have suggested to the MRO that the chain of custody was breached; indeed, Solomon himself certified that the chain of custody was unbroken.

Solomon also could have complained and initiated administrative proceedings challenging Mission's specimen-collection regimen. *See* §§ 386.12, 386.1. An Associate Administrator for the Federal Highway Administration is charged with investigating alleged violations of the regulations and determining if employers have complied with the statutory requirements. 49 C.F.R. §§ 386.1, 386.21. Upon finding violations, the Associate Administrator has the authority to compel compliance, assess civil penalties, or both. *Id.* § 386.1. . . . The DOT regulations also give the Associate Administrator authority to fashion relief to the complainant and "assure that the complainant is not subject to harassment, intimidation, disciplinary action, discrimination, or financial loss" for having filed the complaint. 49 C.F.R. § 386.12. . . .

Applying the *Phillips* risk/utility factors here, we agree there is a serious risk that an employee can be harmed by a false positive drug test. However, the risk is reduced by the protection DOT regulations afford to the employees. . . . Without these protections, the risk of harm resulting from a negligently conducted urinalysis test would be great. But here, the DOT regulations strike an appropriate balance between the need for efficient drug testing and the requirement that each employee have the means to insist on the integrity of the process. While the regulations do not create a private cause of action for an employer's breach of DOT protocols, employees are entitled to compel compliance by invoking regulations already in place. Those regulations serve both as an incentive for employers to carefully abide by those protocols and as a safe harbor for employees whose test results are tainted by unacceptable breaches of collection procedures. . . .

We must also balance any risk to employees against the burden it could place on our employment-at-will doctrine. . . . We recently refused to limit the scope of the doctrine by declining to recognize a cause of action for negligent investigation of an at-will employee's alleged misconduct. Tex. Farm Bureau Mut. Ins. Cos. v. Sears, 84 S.W.3d 604, 606 (Tex. 2002). Solomon attempts to distinguish this case from a negligent discharge or a negligent investigation cause of action. He argues that the negligent act in question was the mechanical function of urine collection conducted by Mission's safety department, not a personnel decision to determine Solomon's employment status. He contends that the urine collection process was implemented to ensure safe roadways and not to determine an employee's employment status.

We agree that the employment-at-will doctrine is not directly implicated here because Solomon has not sued for wrongful discharge. But we must consider his claim in its overall context. Because Solomon's complaint concerns the process by which Mission chose to terminate him, it goes to the core of at-will employment. The exception Solomon advocates here could quickly swallow the rule.

The court of appeals based its decision to impose a duty in part on the fact that Mission's negligently conducted test caused Solomon damages beyond mere termination of his employment. The court of appeals reasoned that because the DOT regulations require each new employer to inquire about any prior positive drug test results and compelled Solomon to consent to their disclosure before assuming a safety sensitive position, Solomon was effectively denied a career as a truck driver. The court of appeals failed to acknowledge, however, that any process used to discover employee misconduct or to evaluate employee effort is, in effect, an "investigation." Background checks, coworker interviews, electronic surveillance, finger or voice print analysis, expense-report audits, and performance reviews are all "investigations," conducted by employers, that may result in job termination. . . . If a duty of care were to arise every time the harm to an employee transcends the employment agreement, the employment-at-will doctrine would be undermined because an employer's basis for termination would have to be justified by a reasonable investigation, which is contrary to the doctrine. Just as we have consistently preserved the doctrine of employment-at-will from encroachment by other liability theories, we decline Solomon's invitation to adopt a new theory of liability for negligent drug testing.

We reverse the court of appeals' judgment and render judgment that Solomon take nothing.

[Concurring opinions omitted.]

NOTES AND QUESTIONS

1. The lower court's opinion includes additional background facts that may explain the jury's verdict and award of punitive damages. Among other things, the supervisor who handled the collection container admitted "that he had received a ten-year deferred adjudication for an unspecified offense and that he was subject to random drug testing by his probation officer." 37 S.W.3d at 485.

2. As the Texas Supreme Court's opinion and discussion of authorities in *Mission Petroleum* suggests, employees have been somewhat more successful in asserting negligence claims against independent third parties who perform examinations for employers. *See, e.g.*, Ishikawa v. Delta Air Lines, 149 F. Supp. 2d 1246 (D. Or. 2001) (analogizing examinee employees to third party beneficiaries of a contract between the employer and the laboratory). For more on the difference between an employer's duty of care and an independent examiner's duty of care, see Chapter 3.D.1.a.

3. Even if a court holds that an employer or third-party examiner owed a duty of care to an employee, the employee still faces a major evidentiary challenge: *proving* the test result was a false positive and that negligence caused the false positive. *See, e.g.*, O'Connor v. SmithKline Bio-Science Labs., Inc., 631 N.E.2d 1018 (Mass. App. 1994) (employee proved laboratory's negligence but failed to prove negligence caused employee's positive test result). Solomon evidently persuaded the jury on the issue of causation. First, even Solomon's supervisor testified that he was "shocked" that Solomon tested positive. 37 S.W.3d at 485. Second, a psychiatrist and therapist who treated Solomon for depression following his discharge testified that they did not find Solomon "to possess any of the characteristics that they associated with drug abusers." *Id.* Third, a hair-follicle test nearly three months after Solomon's discharge showed he was not a "persistent" user of marijuana, although it could not disprove occasional or isolated use. Fourth, Mission Petroleum's violations of drug testing protocol and the supervisor's personal drug testing obligation might have led the jury to infer that Solomon's sample was "switched" or tainted somewhere in the collection process.

4. The effects of an employer's negligent investigation or erroneous conclusions are compounded in some situations by statutory reporting requirements for certain types of suspected employee misconduct. See Tex. Civ. Prac. & Rem. Code § 81.003 (making prospective employer liable for failure to contact applicant's former employer about record of "sexual exploitation,", and making former employer liable for failure to report applicant's suspected "sexual exploitation" to an inquiring prospective employer); Tex. Health & Safety Code ch. 253 (employee misconduct registry for employees of certain health facilities).

PROBLEM

Texas Law prohibits a mental health services provider from engaging in "sexual exploitation" of patients. *See* Tex. Civ. Prac. & Rem. Code §§ 81.001 et seq. "Sexual exploitation" includes "sexual contact" or other conduct that "can reasonably be construed as being for the purposes of sexual arousal or gratification." *Id.* § 81.001(5). The same law provides that the former employer of a provider is liable to a victim of sexual exploitation if it received a request for information about the provider from a subsequent employer, and failed to disclose that it "knows of the occurrence of sexual exploitation" by the provider. *Id.* § 81.0013. The law provides no means for a provider to challenge or appeal an employer's determination that the provider has committed "sexual exploitation."

Sheila Kunstler was a counselor for Green Meadows Academy, a private school where she worked with troubled teenagers. Under the law, she qualified as a "mental health services provider." Kunstler worked part time and shared an office with an academic counselor. One day after Kunstler left for home, the academic counselor who shared the office, Suzie Sparks, found a file Kunstler left on the desk. Sparks opened the file and saw a sexually suggestive poem a student wrote to Kunstler. Sparks showed the principal the poem. Fearing Kunstler was guilty of "sexual exploitation," the principal immediately discharged Kunstler (who was employed at will). Had the principal inquired further, she would have learned the poem's author was emotionally disturbed and had a habit of writing fantasies about sexual experiences with teachers and other authority figures.

Kunstler applied for work with other schools and various employers in the mental health care industry, but each prospective employer contacted Green Meadows about Kunstler's record, and each time Green Meadows reported that it believed Kunstler may have engaged in an act of sexual exploitation of a patient.

Based only on the materials included in this chapter, does Kunstler have any claim against Green Meadows based on the manner in which the school investigated her conduct and concluded she was guilty of sexual exploitation? This hypothetical is repeated in Chapter 8 for purposes of additional legal principles.

CHAPTER 7

Accommodating Personal, Family, and Civic Needs

A. INTRODUCTION

Sooner or later, every employee confronts the challenge of fitting personal, family, and community needs into a daily schedule dominated by work. When employees work a 40-hour week, about 36 percent of their waking hours are under their employers' direction and control. Adding time to prepare for and commute to work, and meal and break times with practical restrictions on employee freedom, "work time" is more likely in the neighborhood of 45 percent of waking hours. Overtime can easily push work time past 50 percent. The remaining hours are for rest, recreation, social life, personal needs, and non-work-related obligations.

Whether or not half an employee's waking hours is sufficient for personal pursuits, an employer's need for work on particular days and times is often inflexible. Employer coordination of work requires dedicated and predictable attendance according to a schedule. The employee, on the other hand, may need time for matters that cannot be scheduled. Illness and family emergencies cannot be postponed. Some employee needs can be scheduled, but doctors' appointments, parent-teacher conferences, and civic duties such as jury service are frequently limited to the hours an employer expects the employee to be at work.

What are an employee's rights in such a conflict? Is an employee missing work for personal, family, or other non-work reasons subject to discharge? Must the employer pay for time off it grants the employee? Will time off for an extended period affect an employee's right to benefits such as health insurance?

Lurking in the background are the employment at will doctrine and the common law of contracts. If an employee misses a day of work to care for a sick child, it may not matter whether he or she had a good excuse for not coming to work. The employer can terminate him or her for any reason, and the reason might be a single absence. If the employer continues the employment when the employee returns the next day, it need not pay for the missed day or hour, unless a contract or statute requires paid leave and the missed time qualifies for this benefit.

Resolving conflict between demands of the job and other employee needs and obligations is actually much more complicated because of a pastiche of laws, some of which were introduced in earlier chapters. Title VII, the Pregnancy Discrimination Act, the Americans with Disabilities Act, and state and federal workers' compensation laws all have a part to play. The leading role, however, is given to the Family and Medical Leave Act (FMLA), 29 U.S.C. §§ 2601-2654, a relatively recent federal law that establishes an employee right to limited, unpaid leave for reasons related to the health of an employee and his family. In 2008, Congress amended the FMLA to provide additional rights to unpaid leave in the event an employee's family member is called to active duty in the Armed Services.

The FMLA is the nearest thing in U.S. law to a basic law of sick leave and family leave, but it does not apply to all conflicts employees confront. It provides leave only for an employee to deal with his own "serious health condition," to care for an ill family member, or to spend time at home with a recently born or placed adoptive or foster child. The act works differently depending on whether the employee needs to attend to his own illness or the illness of a family member. For some conflicts, other laws may be more important than the FMLA.

B. PERSONAL NEEDS

Excused time off from regularly scheduled hours, with or without pay, is largely a matter of contract and takes many different forms, including paid vacation, paid holidays, paid or unpaid sick leave, paid or unpaid disability leave, paid or unpaid maternity/paternity leave, and paid or unpaid personal leave without limitation as to purpose. An unexcused absence is simply one the employer did not approve in advance or that does not qualify under the employer's policy for excused leave, and the employer might have a policy that counts unexcused absences toward progressive discipline or eventual discharge. An employer could also treat questions of attendance on a case-by-case basis because an employer is not required to have a uniform policy for every employee as long as the employer does not unlawfully discriminate. The FMLA and some state laws do establish a floor below which employer policies must not fall, but the floor is quite low and leaves considerable room for employer discretion, restriction, and innovation.

Employers have such wide latitude in designing paid or unpaid leave policies that it is difficult even to generalize about the amount or sufficiency of personal leave the average U.S. employee enjoys. It appears, however, that the United States compares poorly with other industrialized nations on this score, and that significant numbers of U.S. workers are without any guaranteed leave at all. Most surveys of employee leave policies focus on paid or unpaid "sick leave," because employee illness is the most common cause of unavoidable conflict between work and personal needs. According to one such survey, about 39 percent of U.S. workers in the private sector are without paid sick leave. U.S. Bureau of Labor Statistics, *On Paid Sick Leave*, Program Perspectives, Vol. 2, Issue 2 (March 2010). Presumably, the employers of many of these employees "excuse" at least some number of *unpaid* absences for good cause. The lack of paid sick leave falls hard on the poor, who may have compelling need for leave but lack savings to afford an unpaid day away from work. If the employer lacks even an unpaid leave or absence policy, an employee who misses work even for good reason might lose more than a day's pay. He might lose his job.

Sick leave is not the only solution for employee illness. An employee who has exhausted sick leave, or had none to begin with, might have a number of paid vacation days. However, more than a quarter of civilian employees in the U.S. do not qualify for paid vacations. Bureau of Statistics, Department of Labor, The Economics Daily (June 1, 2017). Since its enactment in 1993, the FMLA has required a covered employer to provide up to 12 weeks of *unpaid* leave per year for personal or family medical reasons. 29 U.S.C. § 2612(a)(1). An employer may choose one of four methods for determining the 12-month period during which an employee may take FMLA leave: (1) the calendar year; (2) any fixed 12-month period such as a fiscal year or a year starting on an employee's "anniversary"; (3) the 12-month period measured forward from the date an employee's first FMLA leave begins; or (4) a "rolling" 12-month period measured backward from the date an employee takes FMLA leave. 29 C.F.R. § 825.200(b). FMLA leave might be continuous or intermittent, or in the form of reduced hours of work, depending on the circumstances. 29 U.S.C. § 2612(b). An employer cannot discharge an employee for seeking or taking FMLA leave from work, and the employer must restore the employee to the same or an equivalent position when the employee returns from leave if the employee did not exceed the 12-week limit. *Id.* §§ 2614(a), 2615.

The FMLA protects an employee from the loss of his job due to illness, but the employee still bears the cost of missed work because an employer need not pay for FMLA leave. 29 U.S.C. § 2612(c).[1] Moreover, if the employer offers sick leave or vacation pay benefits, the employer may "substitute" these benefits for FMLA leave. *Id.* § 2612(d). In other words, an employer can require an employee to use vacation time or paid sick leave for a condition covered by the FMLA, and the employee's use of these benefits counts against his 12 weeks of annual FMLA leave. If the employer provides group health plan benefits, the employee's coverage under the plan continues during his FMLA leave, but the employee may have to reimburse the employer for the cost of continued coverage if the employee fails to return to his position after FMLA leave. *Id.* § 2614(c).

Many employees are not protected at all by the FMLA. The act exempts employers with fewer than 50 employees, and even the largest of employers may claim an exemption for a specific worksite employing fewer than 50 employees within 75 miles of the site. *Id.* § 2611(2)(B), (4). The act also denies coverage of recently hired or part-time employees because an employee must work for at least 12 months before becoming eligible for leave, and must have worked at least 1,250 hours in the year preceding a request for leave. *Id.* § 2611(2)(A). For state government employees, there are Eleventh Amendment complications.

"Highly compensated" employees are another group with significantly diminished FMLA rights. The employer can deny job restoration rights to these employees if necessary "to prevent substantial and grievous economic injury to the operations of the employer." *Id.* § 2614(b). "Highly compensated" is relative. An employee is "highly compensated" if among the highest paid 10 percent of the employer's employees within a 75-mile radius of the site where he or she works. *Id.* § 2614(b)(2). Employees of "local educational agencies" serving in an "instructional capacity" form one more group subject to special rules. *Id.* § 2618.

The FMLA protects employees as to a limited range of personal needs, primarily involving the health of the employee or his or her family. For leave to attend to the employee's own health condition, the basic qualification for FMLA leave is that the employee must have a "*serious* health condition" that disables the employee from performing the job. *Id.* § 2612(a)(1)(D) (emphasis added).

---

[1] The Fair Labor Standards Act ordinarily limits an employer's right to "dock" an exempt *salaried* employee's pay for a partial-day absence. *See* Chapter 4.C.1.b, *supra*. However, the FMLA authorizes docking salary for partial-day *FMLA* leave. 29 U.S.C. § 2612(c).

MILLER v. AT&T CORP.

250 F.3d 820 (4th Cir. 2001)

WILKINS, Circuit Judge:

AT&T Corporation (AT&T) appeals orders . . . finding it liable for violating Kimberly Miller's rights under the Family and Medical Leave Act (FMLA) of 1993, 29 U.S.C.A. §§ 2601-2654 (West 1999), and awarding back pay and attorneys' fees. . . . AT&T contends that it did not violate the FMLA because the illness for which Miller sought FMLA leave — an episode of the flu — was not a serious health condition as defined by the Act and implementing regulations; that if Miller's flu was a serious health condition under the applicable regulations, those regulations are contrary to congressional intent . . . ; and that . . . Miller failed to comply with AT & T's procedures for the granting of FMLA leave. . . . [N]one of AT&T's challenges warrants reversal, and we therefore affirm.

I.

A. THE FAMILY AND MEDICAL LEAVE ACT

The FMLA entitles an eligible employee to as many as 12 weeks of unpaid leave per year for "a serious health condition that makes the employee unable to perform the functions of the position of such employee." 29 U.S.C.A. § 2612(a)(1)(D). The Act defines "serious health condition" as an illness, injury, impairment, or physical or mental condition that involves —

(A) inpatient care in a hospital, hospice, or residential medical care facility; or

(B) continuing treatment by a health care provider.

Id. § 2611(11). Thus, as is relevant here, an eligible employee is entitled to FMLA leave for an illness that incapacitates the employee from working and for which the employee receives "continuing treatment," a term the FMLA does not define.

The FMLA grants the Secretary of Labor authority to promulgate regulations implementing the Act. *See id.* § 2654. Pursuant to this authority, the Secretary promulgated the following regulation:

> A serious health condition involving continuing treatment by a health care provider includes . . . :
>
> (i) A period of incapacity (i.e., inability to work . . .) of more than three consecutive calendar days . . . that also involves:
>
> (A) Treatment two or more times by a health care provider . . . ; or
>
> (B) Treatment by a health care provider on at least one occasion which results in a regimen of continuing treatment under the supervision of the health care provider.

29 C.F.R. § 825.114(a)(2) (2000). The regulations further provide that "treatment" "includes (but is not limited to) examinations to determine if a serious health condition exists and evaluations of the condition." 29 C.F.R. § 825.114(b) . . . .

B. AT &T'S ATTENDANCE AND LEAVE POLICIES

AT&T considers satisfactory attendance to be a condition of employment, and it expects all employees to be at work on time on scheduled work days and to remain at their posts during scheduled hours. . . . Absences are either "chargeable" or "non-chargeable," and only chargeable absences are considered in determining whether an employee's attendance is satisfactory. Absences covered by the FMLA are considered non-chargeable. . . .

C. MILLER'S EMPLOYMENT

Miller was employed by AT&T as an account representative from September 1990 until her termination in March 1997. In November 1994, Miller's supervisor, Steve Snedegar, engaged Miller in a serious discussion about her attendance record. Snedegar warned Miller that continued absences could result in the issuance of a letter of warning, and he encouraged her to make use of FMLA leave. . . . [Nevertheless, over the course of the next two years, Miller accumulated nine more chargeable absences, despite additional warnings that she might be discharged for unsatisfactory attendance if she incurred additional chargeable absences.] . . .

On December 26, 1996, Miller began feeling ill while at work. She completed her shift that day but was too ill to work on the 27th. The following day, Miller sought treatment at an urgent care center. Dr. T. Donald Sommerville diagnosed Miller as suffering from the flu and determined that she was severely dehydrated. He also conducted a blood test, which revealed that Miller's white blood cell and platelet counts were significantly lower than normal. After administering intravenous fluids, Dr. Sommerville directed Miller to take over-the-counter medications to alleviate her symptoms and to return on December 30 for reevaluation. On December 30, Dr. Sommerville examined Miller and conducted another blood test, which revealed that Miller's white blood cell and platelet counts were still low, although the platelet level had improved and Miller felt better. After consulting a hematologist, Dr. Sommerville directed Miller to return two weeks later for a third blood test. By the time of the third test, Miller's white blood cell and platelet counts had returned to normal.

At the conclusion of her initial visit on December 28, Miller was given a work-excuse slip for December 28 through the 31st. On December 31, Miller telephoned the urgent care center and requested a work-excuse slip for January 1, explaining that she was feeling better but needed an additional day off work. The urgent care center granted this request.

Miller subsequently requested FMLA leave for December 27 through January 1. . . . AT & T denied Miller's request for FMLA leave on February 26, 1997. Maxine M. Condie, RN, a division manager with the Health Affairs Office, determined that Miller's illness was not covered by the FMLA because (1) the flu is not generally considered to be the type of condition for which an employee is entitled to FMLA leave; and (2) the information submitted by Miller did not demonstrate that she received treatment on two or more occasions.

On March 12, Attendance Administrator Kathy Collison learned that Miller's FMLA request had been denied. . . . Collison recommended termination to Miller's immediate supervisor, Nan Hensley. After reviewing Miller's attendance record and consulting with various others, including Snedegar, Hensley decided to fire Miller. Miller was terminated on March 20, 1997. . . .

Miller filed this action in August 1998, alleging, as is relevant here, that

AT&T violated her rights under the FMLA by denying her request for FMLA leave for the December 27–January 1 absences. Following discovery, the district court granted summary judgment to Miller on the issue of liability, holding that Miller's flu constituted a serious health condition and that she had provided adequate certification of her need for FMLA leave. . . .

II.

A.

We turn first to AT&T's contention that Miller's flu was not a "serious health condition" under the Act and regulations. First, AT&T contends that Miller cannot satisfy the regulatory criteria for a serious health condition because she did not receive "treatment" on two or more occasions.[9] . . . AT&T asserts that Miller's second visit to Dr. Sommerville — during which he conducted a physical examination and drew blood — did not constitute "treatment" because Dr. Sommerville simply evaluated Miller's condition. However, this assertion is contradicted by the regulations, which define "treatment" to include "examinations to determine if a serious health condition exists and evaluations of the condition." 29 C.F.R. § 825.114(b). Under this definition, Miller's second visit to Dr. Sommerville clearly constituted "treatment."

AT&T next argues that even if Miller satisfies the regulatory criteria for a "serious health condition," the regulations nevertheless specifically exclude the flu and other minor illnesses from coverage under the FMLA. AT&T points to the following regulatory language:

> Ordinarily, unless complications arise, the common cold, *the flu*, ear aches, upset stomach, minor ulcers, headaches other than migraine, routine dental or orthodontia problems, periodontal disease, etc., are examples of conditions that do not meet the definition of a serious health condition and do not qualify for FMLA leave.

29 C.F.R. § 825.114(c) (2000) (emphasis added). According to AT&T, this regulation establishes that absent complications, the flu is never a serious health condition even if the regulatory test is satisfied. . . . We disagree.

There is unquestionably some tension between subsection (a), setting forth objective criteria for determining whether a serious health condition exists, and subsection (c), which states that certain enumerated conditions "ordinarily" are not serious health conditions. Indeed, that tension is evidenced by Miller's illness. Miller was incapacitated for more than three consecutive calendar days and received treatment two or more times; thus, she satisfied the regulatory definition of a serious health condition under subsection (a). But, the condition from which Miller suffered — the flu — is one of those listed as being "ordinarily" not subject to coverage under the FMLA. AT&T urges us to resolve this tension by holding that subsection (c) essentially excepts the enumerated ailments from FMLA coverage even when an individual suffering from one of those ailments satisfies the regulatory criteria of subsection (a).

Miller, in contrast, urges us to defer to the position taken by the Secretary of Labor in a 1996 opinion letter:

---

[9] AT&T does not dispute that Miller . . . was incapacitated for three or more consecutive days.

> The FMLA regulations . . . provide examples, in section 825.114(c), of conditions that ordinarily, unless complications arise, would not meet the regulatory definition of a serious health condition and would not, therefore, qualify for FMLA leave. . . . Ordinarily, these health conditions would not meet the [regulatory criteria]. . . . If, however, any of these conditions met the regulatory criteria for a serious health condition, . . . then the absence would be protected by the FMLA.
>
> . . . Complications, per se, need not be present to qualify as a serious health condition if the regulatory . . . tests are otherwise met. The regulations reflect the view that, ordinarily, conditions like the common cold and flu (etc.) would not be expected to meet the regulatory tests, not that such conditions could not routinely qualify under FMLA where the tests are, in fact, met in particular cases.

Opinion Letter FMLA-86, 1996 WL 1044783 (Dec. 12, 1996). . . .

Whenever possible, this court must reconcile apparently conflicting provisions. That is not difficult to do here. 29 C.F.R. § 825.114(c) provides that "ordinarily" the flu will not qualify as a serious health condition. Presumably, this is because the flu (and the other conditions listed in the regulation) ordinarily will not meet the objective criteria for a serious health condition, inasmuch as such an illness normally does not result in an inability to work for three or more consecutive calendar days or does not require continuing treatment by a health care provider. Section 825.114(c) simply does not automatically exclude the flu from coverage under the FMLA. Rather, the provision is best read as clarifying that some common illnesses will not ordinarily meet the regulatory criteria and thus will not be covered under the FMLA.

B.

AT&T's next challenge to liability concerns the validity of the regulations themselves. The company argues that if Miller's flu was a serious health condition pursuant to the regulations, those regulations are invalid as contrary to congressional intent. AT&T primarily attacks the regulatory definition of "treatment," maintaining that a mere evaluation of a patient's condition should not qualify as treatment. However, AT&T also makes a more general challenge to the regulations, maintaining that Congress did not intend for the FMLA to cover relatively minor illnesses such as the flu.

In enacting the FMLA, Congress explicitly granted the Secretary of Labor authority to promulgate regulations implementing the Act. *See* 29 U.S.C.A. § 2654. Regulations promulgated pursuant to such an express delegation of authority "are given controlling weight unless they are arbitrary, capricious, or manifestly contrary to the statute." Chevron U.S.A. Inc. v. Natural Res. Def. Council, Inc., 467 U.S. 837, 844 (1984). Particularly when a regulatory choice "represents a reasonable accommodation of conflicting policies that were committed to the agency's care by the statute, we should not disturb it unless it appears from the statute or its legislative history that the accommodation is not one that Congress would have sanctioned." *Id.* at 845 (internal quotation marks omitted). . . .

Congress enacted the FMLA in response to concern regarding, inter alia, "inadequate job security for employees who have serious health conditions that prevent them from working for temporary periods." 29 U.S.C.A. § 2601(a)(4); *see* S. Rep. No. 103-3, at 11-12, *reprinted* in 1993 U.S.C.C.A.N. 3, 13-14 (noting that "[j]ob loss because of illness has a particularly devastating effect on workers who support themselves and on families where two incomes are necessary to make ends meet or where a single parent heads the household"). Congress did not intend to create a federal sick leave program but rather aspired to create a workable "minimum labor standard for leave" that would balance the needs of employees and the interests of employers. S. Rep. No. 103-3, at 4, *reprinted in* 1993 U.S.C.C.A.N. at 6; *see id.* at 4-5, *reprinted in* 1993 U.S.C.C.A.N. at 6-7. . . .

We first consider AT&T's contention that the regulatory definition of "treatment" is overly broad because it includes mere evaluations of an employee's condition. Nothing in the legislative history discusses the "continuing treatment" requirement, and Congress elected not to provide a statutory definition of that term. There is thus nothing upon which to base a conclusion that the regulatory definition of treatment, which allows for situations in which a health care provider determines that an illness requires continued monitoring but not aggressive treatment, is contrary to congressional intent. *Cf.* S. Rep. No. 103-3, at 29, *reprinted in* 1993 U.S.C.C.A.N. at 31 (noting that serious health conditions typically "involve either inpatient care or continuing treatment *or supervision* by a health care provider, and frequently involve both" (emphasis added)).

We note also that AT&T's challenge to the regulatory definition of "treatment" overlooks the fact that the "treatment" requirement does not stand alone. Consistent with the statutory language, the regulations require that treatment be accompanied by a period of incapacity of at least three consecutive days. It is apparent that the requirement that the employee be incapacitated will suffice to weed out those claims that are based on nothing more than multiple visits to a physician for a minor health complaint.

We next consider AT&T's more general argument that, to the extent the regulations permit FMLA coverage for the flu and similar illnesses, those regulations contravene the legislative purpose underlying the FMLA. In support of this claim, AT&T points to the following passage from the Senate Report:

> The term "serious health condition" is not intended to cover short-term conditions for which treatment and recovery are very brief. *It is expected that such conditions will fall within even the most modest sick leave policies.* Conditions or medical procedures that would not normally be covered by the legislation include minor illnesses which last only a few days and surgical procedures which typically do not involve hospitalization and require only a brief recovery period. Complications arising out of such procedures that develop into "serious health conditions" will be covered . . . . Examples of serious health conditions include but are not limited to heart attacks, heart conditions requiring heart bypass of [sic] valve operations, most cancers, back conditions requiring extensive therapy or surgical procedures, strokes, severe respiratory conditions, spinal injuries, appendicitis, pneumonia, emphysema, severe arthritis, severe nervous disorders, injuries caused by serious accidents on or off the job, ongoing pregnancy, miscarriages, complications or illnesses related to pregnancy, such as severe morning sickness, the need for prenatal care, childbirth and recovery from childbirth.

> All of these conditions meet the general test that either the underlying health condition or the treatment for it requires that the employee be absent from work on a recurring basis or for more than a few days for treatment or recovery. They also involve either inpatient care or continuing treatment or supervision by a health care provider, and frequently involve both.

S. Rep. No. 103-3, at 28-29, *reprinted in* 1993 U.S.C.C.A.N. at 30-31 (emphasis added); *see* Bauer v. Dayton-Walther Corp., 910 F. Supp. 306, 310 (E.D. Ky. 1996) ("Congress sought to parse out illnesses which it believed should be treated under sick leave policy from those much more serious illnesses that implicate the protections of the FMLA."), *aff'd*, 118 F.3d 1109 (6th Cir. 1997).

AT&T is correct, of course, that the legislative history indicates that in enacting the FMLA Congress was focused on "major" illnesses, such as cancer, rather than relatively minor ailments. But, the passage in the Senate Report on which AT&T relies is not reflected in the statutory language. *See Thorson*, 205 F.3d at 380. Rather, the FMLA defines "serious health condition" broadly "and does not include any examples of conditions that either do or do not qualify as FMLA 'serious health conditions.'" *Id.* Consistent with the statutory language, the regulations . . . establish a definition of "serious health condition" that focuses on the effect of an illness on the employee and the extent of necessary treatment rather than on the particular diagnosis. This policy decision is neither unreasonable nor manifestly inconsistent with Congress' intent to cover illnesses that "require[ ] that the employee be absent from work on a recurring basis or for more than a few days for treatment or recovery" and involve "continuing treatment or supervision by a health care provider." S. Rep. No. 103-3, at 29, *reprinted in* 1993 U.S.C.C.A.N. at 31. It is possible, of course, that the definition adopted by the Secretary will, in some cases — and perhaps even in this one — provide FMLA coverage to illnesses that Congress never envisioned would be protected. . . .

IV.

In sum, we conclude that AT&T violated Miller's rights under the FMLA when it denied her request for leave for the December 27–January 1 absence. Miller's flu satisfied the regulatory criteria for a serious health condition. . . .

[Dissenting opinion of Chief District Judge HILTON omitted.]

NOTES AND QUESTIONS

1. Department of Labor regulations recognize some other categories of "serious health conditions" not discussed in *Miller*. One is "incapacity or treatment for such incapacity due to a *chronic* serious health condition." A "chronic serious health condition" is a condition that:

> (i) Requires periodic visits (defined as at least twice a year) for treatment by a health care provider, or by a nurse under direct supervision of a health care provider;
>
> (ii) Continues over an extended period of time (including recurring episodes of a single underlying condition); and
>
> (iii) May cause episodic rather than a continuing period of incapacity (e.g.,

> asthma, diabetes, epilepsy, etc.).

29 C.F.R. § 825.102. Examples include asthma, diabetes, and epilepsy. *Id.*

2. Was Congress's decision to guarantee leave only for "serious" health conditions the right approach? Why not for all incapacitating health conditions?

3. Note that the definition of "serious health condition" is based on not only the *effect* of the illness but also the amount and nature of *treatment*. Could a seriously ill employee lose protection by failing to go to the doctor? *See* Seidle v. Provident Mutual Life Ins. Co., 871 F. Supp. 238 (E.D. Pa. 1994) (excerpted below) (telephone call alone did not count toward requirement of "treatment two or more times" to establish "continuing treatment") But the FMLA and *Seidle* predate internet-based online appointments — often known as "telemedicine" or "virtual providers." Consider the following description of one "virtual provider:"

> KRH Care Anywhere connects patients to a medical provider through a smartphone, tablet, or computer via an internet connection.... KRH Care Anywhere is staffed by board-certified physicians and nurse practitioners. ... Patients are charged a flat fee of $45 for each visit. No appointment is necessary, and there is no time limit on visits. Any prescriptions ... will be called in to the patient's pharmacy."

"Kalispell Regional Medical Center Launches Internet Consults," *Montana Living* (June 2, 2017). Nevertheless, it is unclear whether such appointments qualify as episodes of "continuing treatment" under current regulations. "The requirement ... for treatment by a health care provider means an *in-person visit* to a health care provider." 29 C.F.R. § 825.115(a)(3) (emphasis added).

4. Given the way Congress and the Department of Labor have defined "serious health condition," one cannot always be sure at the outset whether an illness will be serious or not. An employer who believes an employee's illness is not serious and who fires the employee at the beginning of an absence might be gambling. If later developments show the illness was serious, the employer will have violated the FMLA. Caldwell v. Holland of Texas, Inc., 208 F.3d 671 (8th Cir. 2000). *But see* Phillips v. Quebecor World RAI Inc., 450 F.3d 308 (7th Cir. 2006) (duration of employee's absence, standing alone, was not enough to place employer on notice that reason for absence might be a serious health condition, even though employee was later determined to be suffering from brain tumor).

5. It would be difficult to administer the FMLA if the law did not recognize some employee duties, because an employee has the best knowledge about his prospective need for leave. Thus, to gain the protection of the act, the employee must provide an employer with enough information for the employer to make a determination whether the employee's absence will be FMLA leave. The employee might have to provide this information many days in advance if he is able to foresee his need for leave for a pending medical treatment or other covered event. 29 U.S.C. § 2612(e). Recall, however, that the Americans with Disabilities Act *prohibits* an employer from inquiring too deeply into an employee's health conditions. *See* 42 U.S.C. § 12112(d)(4). Can these two laws be reconciled?

6. There are times an employer is in a better position than the employee to perceive the seriousness of an employee's condition. With a mental or emotional illness, for example, the employee's condition may prevent his or her awareness

of her condition even though it is obvious to the employer. In this situation, some courts have found the employer had "constructive notice" of the employee's need for FMLA leave. *See* Stevenson v. Hyre Elec. Co., 505 F.3d 720 (7th Cir. 2007).

7. If an employee has a flu not "serious" enough for FMLA coverage, the employer might still be well advised to excuse his or her absence. "Presentism" of sick employees can be even more costly to employers than absences. If the employer excuses the employee for a non-serious health condition, can the employer count the missed time against the employee's FMLA leave? Arguably, an employer who grants time off for non-serious conditions and counts such time against FMLA leave is merely exercising its right to provide a sick leave policy more generous than the FMLA. *See* 29 C.F.R. § 825.700 ("[N]othing in the Act is intended to discourage employers from adopting or retaining more generous leave policies."). However, an employee might be surprised to learn that staying home a few days for a "cold" has cost his or her job if a subsequent serious health condition requires more than the remainder of his or her FMLA leave.

Department of Labor regulations suggest a partial solution. First, use of paid leave such as vacation or sick leave to recover from illness does not count against the employee's FMLA leave if the illness does not qualify under the FMLA. 29 C.F.R. § 825.207(e). It is the employer's duty to designate leave as FMLA leave if it believes there are grounds for doing so, and to notify the employee of this designation. *Id.* § 825.300(d). "If there is a dispute between an employer and an employee as to whether leave qualifies as FMLA leave, it should be resolved through discussions between the employee and the employer. Such discussions and the decision must be documented." *Id.* § 825.301(c). What if the employer and employee disagree whether leave for flu counts against FMLA leave?

8. Many states have enacted sick leave laws or variations of the FMLA that might provide employees broader rights. A few states and local governments even require covered employers to provide a minimum number of *paid* sick leave days. *State and Local Paid Sick Leave Laws*, Workplace Fairness: Know your Rights,, https://www.workplacefairness.org/paid-sick-leave; National Partnership for Women and Families, State and Local Action on Paid Sick Days (May 2013), http://go.nationalpartnership.org/site/DocServer/PSD_Tracking_Doc_Nov_2011_Final.pdf?docID=1922.

9. If an employee's injury or illness is work-related, his rights to disability pay and job restoration might be affected by workers' compensation law. Workers' compensation law protects an employee from loss of income due to a work-related injury or illness. Unlike the FMLA, workers' compensation laws do not typically require an employer to "hold" an injured employee's job until he or she can return. Instead, the usual rule is that employers must not discriminate or retaliate against employees with workers' compensation claims. Thus, if an employee exhausts FMLA leave as a result of a work-related injury, his or her right to restoration to his or her old job, or any other job, might become a question of whether denial of restoration is illegal discrimination. *See* Swearingen v. Owens-Corning Fiberglass Corp., 968 F.2d 559 (5th Cir. 1992). *Swearingen* and workers' compensation retaliation are discussed in Chapter 5.B.5.

10. U.S. employment law generally does not require employers to provide disability benefits for non-work-related illness or injury. As of 2014, only about a

third of employees in the private sector had access to employer-sponsored long-term disability plans, and a little more than a third had access to short-term disability plans. Bureau of Statistics, Department of Labor, *Disability Insurance Plans: Trends in Employee Access and Employer Costs*, PAY & BENEFITS (Feb. 2015), https://www.bls.gov/opub/btn/volume-4/disability-insurance-plans.htm. A few states — including New York, California, Hawaii, New Jersey, and Rhode Island — have established short-term disability systems that operate in a manner similar to an unemployment compensation system and are financed by payroll taxes or deductions. Society for Human Resource Management, *Which States Require an Employer to Have a Short-Term Disability Plan*? (Sept. 18, 2015), https://www.shrm.org/resourcesandtools/tools-and-samples/hr-qa/pages/stateswithstd.aspx.

11. Another potential source of a right to leave is the Americans with Disabilities Act. An employee who has exhausted FMLA leave might be a "disabled" person entitled to "reasonable accommodation," including continuous or intermittent time off or scheduling adjustments to deal with a disabling condition. *See* Criado v. IBM Corp., 145 F.3d 437, 444 (1st Cir. 1998). An important limitation of the ADA is that employee must prove a "disability," as the term is defined in the ADA. 29 U.S.C. § 12102(2). A temporary condition, such as a short-term injury or illness from which an employee will recover, is not necessarily a "disability" for purposes of the ADA. *See* 42 U.S.C. §12102(3)(B).

If an employee's condition is a "disability" under the ADA, the ADA has important implications when the employee exhausts FMLA leave but is not fully recovered or does not expect a full recovery. First, the employer might be required to accommodate the employee's condition by offering extended leave beyond the FMLA requirements, but only if doing so would not cause the employer "undue hardship." In determining whether extended leave would be an undue hardship, the EEOC allows consideration of the combined burdens of the initial 12-week FMLA leave and any ADA "accommodation" leave. 29 C.F.R. § 1630.2(p). Holding a job open may be out of the question if a disability is permanent or indefinite. A second implication of the ADA is that the employer might be required to accommodate a partial disability by extended intermittent leave, a reduced working schedule, or reassignment to a less demanding position. *See* 42 U.S.C. § 12111(9)(B); 29 C.F.R. § 1630.2(o)(2)(ii). *But see* Hoskins v. Oakland County Sheriff's Dep't, 227 F.3d 719, 730 (6th Cir. 2000) (ADA does not require employer to create a new position or redesign an old one for a disabled employee).

12. The FMLA's enforcement provisions resemble those of the Fair Labor Standards Act. The FMLA authorizes the Secretary of Labor to investigate employee complaints and bring an action against an employer if settlement efforts fail. 29 U.S.C. § 2617(b). However, an individual employee can file a lawsuit without filing a complaint with the Secretary. Like the FLSA, the FMLA authorizes not only reinstatement and back pay but also "liquidated damages" equal to the back pay or other damages. 29 U.S.C. § 2617(a)(1). The employer's liability for liquidated damages is subject to a defense of "good faith."

13. The FMLA defines "employer" to include any "public agency." 29 U.S.C. §§ 2611(4)(A)(iii), (4)(B). However, application of the FMLA to state government employees is limited by states' Eleventh Amendment immunity from money

damages in federal court. Congress can override the Eleventh Amendment to implement some later Amendments, such the Fourteenth Amendment and its Equal Protection Clause. However, in Coleman v. Court of Appeals of Maryland, 566 U.S. 30 (2012), the Supreme Court held that the self-care provisions of the FMLA do not implement the Equal Protection Clause. Thus, a state employee's self-care claim remains subject to the Eleventh Amendment. However, the clash between the FMLA and the Eleventh Amendment has a different outcome when a state employee seeks damages for a violation of the *family* care provisions. Family care issues are discussed in the next section of this chapter.

14. Illness is not the only personal reason for which an employee might want a leave of absence. A few state laws recognize and grant protected leave for other personal needs. *See, e.g.*, Ariz. Rev. Stat. § 13-4439 (leave for victims of crime to attend legal proceedings); Danny v. Laidlaw Transit Servs, Inc., 165 Wash.2d 200, 193 P.3d 128 (Wash. 2008) (recognizing employer duty to accommodate employee need for time to deal with consequences of domestic violence).

PROBLEMS

1. Julie Lombard was a waitress for Sally's Steakhouse, a nationwide chain of restaurants employing hundreds of employees and offering up to seven days of annual paid sick leave. One Monday morning, Lombard awoke with severe back pain. Barely able to rise from bed, she called her supervisor to say she was in too much pain to work that day. Thinking the pain would go away, Lombard did not see a doctor immediately. Instead, she took aspirin and rested at home. Her back was no better the next day, and only slightly better the day after that. By the weekend had arrived, she had missed five work days. She felt better the next Monday and reported to work. Do her absences qualify as FMLA leave?

2. Assume Lombard filed a workers' compensation claim and received continuing treatment and disability benefits. Nevertheless, her back was no better after she had exhausted all her FMLA leave. If she eventually recovers enough to return to work, will she have any legally enforceable right to reinstatement?

3. If Lombard's recovery is less than complete and she can no longer work in the position of a waitress (because her back is not strong enough to lift and carry trays of food and drinks), what obligations, if any, might Sally's Steakhouse have if Lombard seeks re-employment at the end of her FMLA leave?

C. FAMILY OBLIGATIONS

Parenthood is a good predictor of employment. About 82 percent of all families (with and without children) have at least one employed member. For families with children, the rate rises to over 90 percent. For married couples with children, the rate is nearly 97 percent. Bureau of Labor Statistics, Department of Labor, *Employment Characteristics of Families* (Apr. 20, 2004), at http://www.bls.gov/news.release/famee.nr0.htm. The relationship between parenthood and employment is not surprising, because parenthood sharpens the need for income. Many individuals probably try to postpone parenthood until they are employable or have a relationship with an employable person.

Income, however, is only one of the ingredients for effective parenthood. Parenthood requires considerable physical and emotional effort, and on-duty time as a parent is not easily scheduled (if it can be "scheduled" at all) around work.

Two-parent households are at a distinct advantage over one-parent households in bearing the economic, physical, and emotional burdens of parenthood, if only because they are better able to share these burdens between two adults. Moreover, the classic division of household labor (one primary caretaker and one income-earner) might be a practical option for a two-parent household. Nevertheless, both parents are employed in approximately 60 percent of married-couple households with children, and within these households neither parent is entirely relieved of the challenge of accommodating conflicting demands of work and parenthood. *Id.* The challenge is even greater for single parents.

The burden of balancing work and family responsibilities tends to fall disproportionately on mothers, who are still more likely than fathers to act as primary caretakers of children. Caring for a very young preschool child can be a full-time job in itself. Nevertheless, nearly 53 percent of married mothers of children under the age of one are employed. For unmarried mothers of children under the age of one, the rate of employment is over 56 percent. *Id.*

In addition to day-to-day needs children have for their parents, children get sick. A child with a day care provider may need full-time parental attention when ill, or even when not seriously ill, because day care providers may exclude mildly ill children to avoid contagion or additional burdens. Older schoolchildren may need care when too sick for school; school-aged children average over three days of health-related absence per year. National Partnership for Women and Families, *Get Well Soon: Americans Can't Afford to Be Sick* (June 2004), p. 1, http://www.nationalpartnership.org/site/DocServer/GetWellSoonReport.pdf?docID=342.

Minor children are not employees' only source of family obligation. Employees may have adult children, spouses, or parents whose health problems require assistance. There are over 44 million individual caregivers of related adults in the United States; about 48 percent of these caregivers have full-time jobs. National Alliance for Caregiving and AARP, *Caregiving in the U.S.* (April 2004).

Employees who bear caregiving responsibilities enjoy limited protection under "sex discrimination" laws such as Title VII or more specialized "family status" or "family responsibility" discrimination laws enacted by some state and local governments. A sex discrimination law would prohibit an employer from failing to hire or promote "mothers" based on an assumption that mothers are more likely than fathers to be distracted by family responsibilities. And a state or local "parenthood" discrimination law would prohibit an employer from refusing to hire either mothers or fathers based on an assumption that parents are more likely than non-parents to be distracted by family responsibilities. Stephanie Bornstein & Robert Rathmell, The Center for Work Life Law, *Caregivers As a Protected Class?* (December 2009) (listing state and local laws). But discrimination laws standing alone do not necessarily address the impact of an employer's non-discriminatory application of a rule limiting absences from work. Parents might actually need additional leave to bear their family responsibilities.

A simple sick leave policy is of little use for accommodating parental or adult caregiver needs if it does not provide time off for caregiving other than self-care.

By one estimate, only 13 percent of private sector workers were entitled to paid *family* leave from their employment as of 2016. Dep't of Labor, Bureau of Labor Statistics, The Economics Daily, (Nov. 4, 2016), https://www.bls.gov/opub/ted/2016/13-percent-of-private-industry-workers-had-access-to-paid-family-leave-in-march-2016.htm. Other job benefits that might aid caregivers are rare. As of 2006, only 10 percent of private sector employees had access to employer-provided funds for child care or employer-sponsored child care facilities. Bureau of Labor Statistics, U.S. Dep't of Labor, Employee Benefits Survey, Table 40 (March 2016), https://www.bls.gov/ncs/ebs/benefits/2016/ownership/private/table40a.pdf.

The FMLA offers a partial solution. As its name suggests, it is not just a medical leave act for employee self care. It is also a family leave act, although it applies to a limited range of family needs. The same 12 weeks of annual leave that are available for self care may also be used in three other types of situations. First, an employee may use FMLA leave to attend to the medical needs of a minor child. Second, the employee may use FMLA leave to care for an adult child, spouse, or parent. Third, the employee may use FMLA leave to spend time at home with a newly born or newly placed child. 29 U.S.C. § 2612(a)(1). There are important differences in the application and impact of the FMLA for each type of leave.

1. *Sick Child Leave*

As noted earlier, the act guarantees unpaid leave for an employee's "serious" health condition. Illnesses that do not qualify as "serious" are not excusable absences under the act. Congress's expectation was that less serious illnesses would be covered by existing, employer-established sick leave plans. However, the FMLA "serious" health condition standard also applies to determining whether a parent's need for child care leave qualifies for FMLA leave. Thus, a parent's need for sick child leave does not qualify unless the *child* has a "serious" health condition. The "serious" health condition threshold is especially important if the employer lacks a *family* leave policy. It is one thing to tell an employee her illness is non-serious and he or she must come to work. It is another to tell the employee a two-year-old child's illness is non-serious and he or she must come to work.

SEIDLE v. PROVIDENT MUT. LIFE INS. CO.

871 F. Supp. 238 (E.D. Pa. 1994)

WEINER, District Judge.

[The plaintiff was discharged for four unexcused absences after staying home with her four-year-old son, Terrance, whose illness began with a fever and an earache. Late in the night when Terrance's illness began, the plaintiff called a doctor's office number and spoke with "Donna," who recommended aspirin and scheduled an appointment for the next day. The next day the doctor diagnosed Terrance's earache and prescribed antibiotics. Terrance's fever and any pain from the earache ended after about one day, but Terrance remained tired, listless, and without appetite for the remainder of the week. According to the plaintiff, Terrance's day care center would have refused to allow his attendance because he still had a runny nose. After missing about four days of work (in addition to an excused personal absence), the plaintiff finally returned Terrance to the day care center and attempted to return to work, but the employer discharged her. The plaintiff sued under the FMLA, and the employer moved for summary judgment, arguing Terrance's condition was not a "serious health condition."

Terrance's earache did not require "*inpatient care* in a hospital, hospice, or residential medical care facility," and therefore his condition was "serious" only if it required "*continuing treatment* by a health care provider." 29 U.S.C. § 2611(11) (emphasis added). However, the Department of Labor's regulations provide, in relevant part, that a non-chronic condition cannot qualify under the "continuing treatment" prong unless the condition requires absence from work or school for more than *three days*. The regulations also define "continuing care" of a non-chronic condition, in relevant part, as *two or more visits* to a health care provider or his assistant, or two or more treatments or a regimen of continuing treatment under the supervision of a health care provider. 29 C.F.R. § 825.115. — ED.]

Plaintiff claims that Terrance had a "serious health condition" [as defined by the Department of Labor in 29 C.F.R. § 825.114(a)(2)]. That section requires that Terrance both undergo a period of incapacity requiring absence from his day care center for more than three days and be under the continuing treatment of a physician. Unfortunately for plaintiff, she cannot establish either prong.

First, although Terrance did not attend his day-care center for four calendar days (October 12-15), his incapacity (otitis media) required him to be absent for only three calendar days. . . . As of the evening of October 14th, Terrance had been free of fever for 48 hours. Therefore, Terrance should have been able to attend his day-care center on October 15th. However, plaintiff herself testified that Terrance did not attend his day care center on the fourth day, October 15th, because of the day-care center's policy prohibiting children with a "runny nose" from attending. There is no evidence that Terrance had more than a runny nose on October 15, 1993. A runny nose can hardly be classified as an incapacity. Nor does the fact that Terrance may have been "listless" and without a good appetite on October 15th make him incapacitated. Therefore, Terrance was not absent from his day-care center for more than three days because of an incapacity.

Even if the evidence can be construed as demonstrating that Terrance was absent from his day-care center for more than three days because of an incapacity, the evidence does not show that the period of incapacity involved "continuing treatment by (or under the supervision of) a health care provider" as that phrase is defined in the Regulations. Plaintiff cannot meet the definition of "continuing treatment by a health care provider" contained in § 825.114(b)(1) since Terrance was treated on just one occasion by Dr. Johnston on October 12, 1993.[5] For this same reason, plaintiff also cannot meet the first part of the definition contained in § 825.114(b)(2). Plaintiff, however, contends that she has met the alternative

[5] Plaintiff argues that Terrance was treated two or more times by a health care provider based on what she terms "three physician contacts" — the "telephone consultation" with "Donna" at 2:00 A.M. on October 12, 1993, Dr. Johnston's examination of Terrance on October 12, 1993 and the "recommended return visit within two weeks." The plain language of the Regulations, however, speaks only of actual treatments, not "contacts" such as telephone consultations or recommended visits. . . .

definition contained in § 825.114(b)(2) — that Terrance was treated for an illness by a health care provider on at least one occasion which result[ed] in a regimen of continuing treatment under the supervision of the health care provider — for example, a course of medication or therapy — to resolve the health condition.

As noted above, Terrance was indeed treated by Dr. Johnston on one occasion. Dr. Johnston also prescribed Amoxicillin and directed plaintiff to administer the antibiotic to Terrance for a period of ten days. However, at no time did Terrance take the medication under the continuing supervision of Dr. Johnston. The undisputed record reveals that following Terrance's examination by Dr. Johnston on October 12th, Terrance had no further contact with Dr. Johnston either in person or by telephone. Although Dr. Johnston instructed plaintiff to bring Terrance back for a follow-up examination in two weeks to ensure that the ear infection had been resolved, plaintiff never scheduled such an examination or even communicated with Dr. Johnston's office by telephone. Instead, it was plaintiff, with no continuing supervision from Dr. Johnston, who administered and supervised Terrance's course of medication. Thus, we conclude that Terrance did not undergo continuing treatment by a health care provider. . . .

In conclusion, we find that Terrance did not have a "serious medical condition" from October 12-15, 1993 as defined by Congress in the FMLA and by the Department of Labor in the Regulations. No matter where our sympathies may lie, the Court is duty bound to carry out the edict of the FMLA as mandated by Congress. Accordingly, plaintiff is not entitled to the protection of the FMLA and her termination by the defendant did not violate the FMLA.

NOTES AND QUESTIONS

1. Remember that even if an employee's need qualifies for FMLA leave, the act does not require the employer to pay for the employee-parent's time on leave. However, at least three states, including California, Washington, and New Jersey, provide benefits to replace part of an employee's lost income during family leave. The California benefit program is administered by the state and funded by employee payroll deductions. Cal. Ins. Code §§ 3300-3306.

2. Illness is not the only occasion when an employee's sense of parental duties may conflict with work. Parental attendance at teachers' conferences and school activities may be helpful to a child's well-being, but these needs are not covered by the FMLA. California is one state that has extended a right to leave for up to 40 hours in each year for such occasions. Cal. Lab. Code § 230.8. *See also* 820 Ill. Comp. Stat. §§ 147/1 to 147/49; Mass. Gen. L. 149, 52D.

3. Sheila Jones was taking care of her neighbor's daughter while the neighbor was away on business. The neighbor's daughter became sick. Is Sheila entitled to FMLA leave? *See* 29 U.S.C. § 2611(12) (regarding care for children as to whom the employee stands "in loco parentis").

4. If an employer unlawfully denies an employee's request for leave to care for a sick child, the employer's liability to the employee may include the cost of providing alternative care arrangements. 29 U.S.C. § 2617(a)(1)(A)(i)(II).

5. The fact that the burden of child care falls disproportionately on women has important implications for the ability of state employees to obtain FMLA

remedies. Recall that state employees face an Eleventh Amendment problem when they sue their employers for money damages. *See* note 14 in part B.7 of this chapter, *supra*. A state's Eleventh Amendment immunity can be overcome, however, in the case of a federal cause of action enacted by Congress to implement the Fourteenth Amendment, which among other things prohibits the states from engaging in actions that deny "equal protection." In Nevada Dep't of Human Resources v. Hibbs, 538 U.S. 721 (2003), the Supreme Court held that the FMLA's dependent family care provisions are sufficiently connected with the goals of the Fourteenth Amendment to constitute a valid waiver of Eleventh Amendment immunity. In short, the dependent family care provisions promote equal employment opportunity for women. Thus, in contrast with a suit for money damages against a state under the *self*-care provisions of the FMLA, a suit against a state for money damages under the dependent family care provisions may proceed in a federal court.

2. *Leave to Care for Adult Family Members*

A seriously ill *adult* family member does not always require the personal care of the employee family member. Seriously ill adults can often take care of themselves. For this reason, the FMLA provides that an employee is not entitled to FMLA leave to care for an adult child unless the adult child is "incapable of self-care because of a mental or physical disability." There are two separate components to this requirement. First, the adult child must be incapable of "self-care." According to the Department of Labor, an adult child is incapable of "self-care" if he is unable to perform three or more "activities of daily living" (ADLs) or "instrumental activities of daily living" (IADLs). ADLs include grooming, bathing, dressing, and eating. IADLs include cooking, cleaning, shopping, taking public transportation, paying bills, maintaining a residence, or using a telephone. While the department's formula for testing the degree of incapacity may seem overly technical, nearly any serious illness requiring the employee parent's aid is likely to interfere with some ADLs and IADLs. In most situations, the more important question will be whether the situation satisfies the second requirement: The adult child's incapacity is *because of* a mental or physical *disability*. 29 C.F.R. § 825.113.

The requirement that a "disability" must be the cause of the adult child's incapacity is potentially troublesome. The FMLA does not specifically refer to the Americans with Disabilities Act or the ADA's definition of "disability," but it is certainly plausible that when Congress enacted the FMLA in 1993 they may have expected that "disability" would have the same definition under both laws. The Department of Labor evidently assumed as much, and it issued regulations defining "disability" and incorporating by reference the EEOC's definition of "disability" for purposes of the ADA. The difficulty with this approach is revealed in cases such as Navarro v. Pfizer Corp., 261 F.3d 90 (1st Cir. 2001).

In *Navarro*, the plaintiff employee learned that her adult daughter in Germany was experiencing pregnancy complications. The daughter had no disability before or apart from her pregnancy. However, a doctor recommended bed rest, and the pregnant daughter was unable to care for her other children. The plaintiff requested leave to assist her daughter, but the employer denied the request. The plaintiff departed for Germany anyway, and the employer discharged her. In her FMLA lawsuit, the employer argued that the employee's situation was not covered by the FMLA because her adult daughter did not have a "disability" that prevented her from caring for herself. Indeed, the EEOC's definitions of ADA terms and ADA case law tended to confirm the employer's position, because pregnancy and other short-term conditions do not necessarily constitute disabilities for purposes of the ADA. *See* 42 U.S.C. § 12102(3)(B). The district court agreed with the employer and dismissed the plaintiff's claim.

The First Circuit reversed. The court had no difficulty finding that the daughter had a serious health condition. It was also clear that the daughter was incapable of self-care because she was confined to bed. The pivotal question was whether the daughter had a "disability" that caused her incapacity, and the daughter's only potential disability was her pregnancy with its complications. The court of appeals held that the daughter's condition *was* a disability, if only for purposes of the FMLA. Assuming *arguendo* the correctness of the district court's view that a temporary condition is not a "disability" under the ADA, the court of appeals found that the FMLA required a more expansive concept of disability.

> The FMLA's primary purposes are "to balance the demands of the workplace with the needs of families, to promote the stability and economic security of families, and to promote national interests in preserving family integrity." 29 U.S.C. § 2601(b)(1). Those objectives would be frustrated by reading the implementing regulations through the prism of the EEOC's interpretive guidance, for this would impose a rigid requirement that an employee must prove that an impairment is long-lasting before it can qualify as substantially limiting (and, thus, furnish the basis for FMLA leave).

Id. at 101-102. In conclusion, the court held that "an impairment of modest duration" might be a "disability" for FMLA purposes. *Id.* at 102. The court was also satisfied that the adult daughter's condition presented at least an issue of fact whether the employee was entitled to FMLA leave.

NOTES AND QUESTIONS

1. For employee leave to care for a seriously ill spouse or parent, the FMLA does *not* require proof that the spouse or parent is incapacitated by "disability." 29 U.S.C. §§ 2611(7), (13). Why do you suppose Congress took a more lenient approach to leave to care for a spouse or parent than an adult child?

2. Congress did not list grandparents among the relatives whose needs can be grounds for employee FMLA leave. Was this an oversight? Bauer v. Dayton-Walther Corp., 910 F. Supp. 306, 307 & n.12 (E.D. Ky. 1996) (FMLA does not require leave to care for grandparents), *aff'd*, 118 F.3d 1109 (6th Cir. 1997).

PROBLEMS

1. Linda Carson's elderly mother had a case of the flu. Her mother was generally able to care for herself, but Linda was worried that her mother might be at special risk because of her age. Linda decided to stay home with her mother, and she took her mother to the doctor for an examination. The doctor prescribed medicine to relieve the symptoms of the flu and advised Linda to bring her mother back in a week if her mother was still sick. Linda missed one more day but decided

to return to work by the third day when it appeared that her mother was recovering. By the end of the week, Linda's mother was sufficiently well recovered that neither Linda nor her mother made a second appointment with the doctor. Did Linda's absences qualify for FMLA leave?

2. Suppose it was not Linda's mother but Linda's adult daughter who was sick. How might this affect your answer?

3. Suppose it was Linda's two-year-old daughter who was sick. How might this affect your answer?

3. *Is Leave Needed for Care?*

The FMLA grants an employee a right to leave "in order to care for" a medically dependent family member. 29 U.S.C. § 2612(a)(1)(C). Leave merely to be with a sick family member does not necessarily satisfy this requirement. Moreover, it might be implicit that the right to leave is dependent on a *need* for the employee to provide care at a time when he is ordinarily scheduled to work. The employee's assistance in providing care might not really be needed if, for example, others are already providing the care, or the employee and his family member could manage things differently to avoid a work-family conflict. The requirement that leave must be "needed" is also suggested by 29 U.S.C. § 2613(b)(4)(A), which provides that an employer is entitled to require an employee to present the certification of a health care provider showing, among other things, that the employee "is needed to care" for the family member.

FIOTO v. MANHATTAN WOODS GOLF ENTERS., LLC

270 F. Supp. 2d 401 (S.D.N.Y. 2003)

MCMAHON, District Judge.

On April 4, 2003, after a three day trial, a jury returned a verdict in favor of plaintiff on two claims against defendants. Count I alleges that defendants violated the Family and Medical Leave Act (FMLA), 29 U.S.C. § 2612(a)(1)(C), by firing plaintiff from his job as sales manager at Manhattan Woods Golf Club after he took a day off work to be present while his dying mother underwent emergency brain surgery. Count II alleges a breach of contract growing out of the same conduct. The jury awarded plaintiff damages in the amount of $126,825.00 for defendants' violation of FMLA, and in the amount of $74,375.00 for their breach of contract.

Defendants — who moved to dismiss the FMLA claim at the close of plaintiff's case (a motion on which I reserved decision) — now renew their motion for judgment as a matter of law. . . .

FMLA provides that an eligible employee is entitled to take up to twelve weeks of unpaid leave "[i]n order to care for the spouse, or a son, daughter, or parent, of the employee, if such spouse, son, daughter, or parent has a serious health condition." 29 U.S.C. § 2612(a)(1)(C). According to the Department of Labor, the "to care for" requirement may be satisfied by the provision of either physical or psychological care. The regulation states:

> (A) The medical certification provision that an employee is "needed to care for" a family member encompasses both physical and psychological care. It includes situations where, for example, because of a serious health condition, the family member is unable to care for his or her own basic medical, hygienic, or nutritional needs or safety, or is unable to transport himself or herself to the doctor, etc. The term also includes providing psychological comfort and reassurance which would be beneficial to a child, spouse or parent with a serious health condition who is receiving inpatient or home care.
>
> (B) The term also includes situations where the employee may be needed to fill in for others who are caring for the family member, or to make arrangements for changes in care, such as transfer to a nursing home.

29 C.F.R. § 825.116.

As the language of the statute and the regulation make clear, FMLA does not provide qualified leave to cover every family emergency. FMLA leave is only available when an employee is needed "to care for" a family member. FMLA does not cover absences that do not implicate giving physical or psychological care for a relative. And while the statute has been broadly construed — for example, one court has found that assisting in making medical decisions constituted giving "care" to a relative for FMLA purposes, *see* Brunelle v. Cytec Plastics, 225 F. Supp. 2d 67 (D. Me. 2002) — merely visiting a sick relative does not fall within the statute's parameters. The employee must be involved in providing some sort of on-going care for his relative in order to qualify for FMLA leave. As Magistrate Judge Lefkow stated in Cianci v. Pettibone Corp., 1997 WL 182279 (N.D. Ill. Apr. 8, 1997), a case in which the plaintiff claimed that FMLA had been violated when she was denied an extended leave to visit her ailing mother in Italy, "However sympathetic plaintiff's request to visit her ailing mother may have been and however unfair or uncaring the company's response, the evidence before this court indicates that it is not the type of leave to which she is statutorily entitled." *Id.* at *7. . . .

The trial record shows that on July 15, 2000 plaintiff telephoned his employer to let the club know that he would not be coming to work that day . . . . He testified as follows:

> My mother had been hospitalized for about ten days, and the cancer they had discovered had spread to her brain, and she was going to have brain surgery that day. I didn't know what time the surgery was going to be, I knew it was going — that she was being prepped early in the morning. So I was just calling in early to let them know it was a very serious surgery, that I had been warned there was a good chance that my mother wasn't going to get through it and to be there.

The record is completely barren about the condition of plaintiff's mother prior to her surgery. It also includes nothing about what plaintiff did at the hospital, except for the fact that plaintiff did not see her after surgery:

> I was already upset before I [returned to work the next morning] because I hadn't seen my mother following her surgery. I knew that it went okay, but I was already kind of upset; and when I got this [memo terminating my employment] it was just like getting kicked in the solar plexus.

There is a paucity of law on the subject of what constitutes the provision of physical or psychological care to a sick relative. *Cianci* stands for the proposition — readily derived from the words of the statute — that FMLA leave is not available to accommodate mere visitation with a sick relative. Our sister court in Maine, however, has twice ruled that the concept of "psychological care" includes providing even a minimal level of comfort to a sick relative.

In Plumley v. Southern Container Inc., 2001 WL 1188469 (D. Me. Oct. 9, 2001), plaintiff testified that he spent time with his father while the father was hospitalized. The plaintiff's father testified that his son was present with him and that the son's presence was comforting and reassuring. Magistrate Judge Cohen concluded (albeit in dicta) that this sufficed to meet the threshold of "psychological care" for FMLA purposes, which includes providing "psychological comfort and reassurance which would be beneficial to a . . . parent with a serious health condition who is receiving inpatient . . . care." *Id.* at *9 (quoting 29 C.F.R. § 825.116).

A year later, in Brunelle v. Cytec Plastics Inc., 225 F. Supp. 2d 67 (D. Me. 2002), plaintiff was the son of a man who was critically burned in a fire. Plaintiff's father remained hospitalized for several months, enduring several surgeries in what ultimately proved a futile effort to save his life. During that period, the plaintiff kept vigil at his father's bedside. According to the testimony of the father's physician, Brunelle helped doctors make decisions concerning his father's care. Chief Judge Hornby, adopting a decision by Magistrate Judge Cohen, concluded that Brunelle satisfied FMLA's "to care for" requirement.

I have no difficulty taking the same view of the law that was taken by the Maine courts. By the very terms of the FMLA regulations, a child's offering comfort and reassurance to a bedridden parent qualifies as "caring for" the parent. Moreover, I will assume for purposes of this motion that assisting in the making of medical decisions on behalf of that parent also qualifies as "providing physical or psychological care" within the meaning of FMLA regulations. Indeed, it seems to me that making medical decisions on behalf of an ailing parent is far more than psychological, and qualifies as assisting in the physical care of the parent.

Unfortunately for Fioto, the record is completely devoid of any evidence that Fioto was needed to provide either physical or psychological care for his mother, even under this extremely generous reading of FMLA.

Insofar as psychological care is concerned, the jury knew only that plaintiff went to the hospital and did not see his mother after her surgery. It was not told whether he saw his mother prior to surgery, or whether his mother was conscious or unconscious when plaintiff arrived at the hospital. The jury did not even know whether plaintiff's mother was aware that he was on the way to the hospital, or was capable of being aware of his imminent arrival. It is entirely possible that his mother was aware of her son's presence at the hospital and felt succored and reassured by it. It is equally possible that she never even knew he was there. Indeed, it is possible that defendant's [sic] mother was unconscious for some period prior to her surgery — counsel's assertion in his memorandum of law that Mr. Fioto's mother fell into a coma after her surgery has no evidentiary support. Because the language of the statute does not guarantee employees FMLA leave to visit an ailing parent, it was incumbent on plaintiff to demonstrate that he was doing something — anything — to participate in his mother's care. It would not have taken much to meet the very loose "psychological care" standard. . .

In short, while it is entirely possible that plaintiff did some or all of the kinds of things that qualify as "taking care of" his mother, it is equally possible that he did none of them. In order to return a verdict in his favor, the jury necessarily engaged in speculation. . . .

It is beyond question that Lee's behavior following plaintiff's wholly understandable taking of a single day for an important personal reason was uncaring and unfeeling — indeed, it was unreasonable and, as the jury quite properly concluded, a violation of Fioto's contract. But that does not make it a FMLA violation.

Defendants' motion for judgment as a matter of law on plaintiff's "breech" of contract claim is denied. Defendants assert, without any support, that the FMLA and contract claims "are one and the same." This, with respect, is utter nonsense. . . . The letter of agreement called for plaintiff to be employed beginning April 19, 1999. The letter also provided that plaintiff could be terminated only for "reasonable cause." . . .

[I]t is obvious that the jurors concluded that Lee did not have "reasonable cause" to fire Fioto within the meaning of the letter of agreement. . . . The Clerk of the Court is directed to enter judgment in favor of plaintiff on Count II, in the amount of $74,375.00, plus interest at the statutory rate from the date of the breach (July 16, 2000), and to dismiss Count I. . . .

NOTES AND QUESTIONS

1. *Fioto* offers several cautionary tales: First, failure to present a complete factual record at trial can be fatal to one's claim (as in any other kind of case). Second, many worthy reasons for taking leave to be with a sick or disabled adult relative might not be covered by the FMLA if the leave was not "needed to care for" the relative. Third, an employee with no FMLA claim might still have a claim based on contract terms. Many employees, however, are not as fortunate as Mr. Fioto in having contracts providing job security. If Mr. Fioto had been an employee at will, the court probably would have dismissed his contract claim.

2. Even if a medically dependent family member needed an employee's care, there might be a question whether caring for the family member required the employee's absence from work. In Gradilla v. Ruskin Mfg., 320 F.3d 951 (9th Cir. 2003), for example, Mr. Gradilla's wife depended on him to administer the correct dosage of medication to calm her if her heart raced too fast and to care for her if she had a traumatic episode. One day Mrs. Gradilla learned that her father had died in Mexico. She asked Mr. Gradilla to accompany her to the funeral (because of her medical condition, she could not have traveled without him) and he agreed. When he returned, his employer fired him.

Mr. Gradilla filed suit under the California Family Rights Act (CFRA), Cal. Govt. Code § 12945.2, which is the California version of the FMLA The court held that Mr. Gradilla's leave was unprotected. Mr. Gradilla may have been giving needed care to Mrs. Gradilla, but the CFRA does not require an employer to grant leave "whenever the family member with a serious health condition chooses to travel for non-medical reasons." While the Gradillas might understandably have felt compelled to make the journey, the court rejected Mr. Gradilla's invitation to consider the "worthiness" of non-medically related travel on a case-by-case basis. *See also* Pang v. Beverly Hosp., Inc., 79 Cal. App. 4th 986, 94 Cal. Rptr. 2d 643 (Cal. App. 2000) (employee failed to prove she was "needed" for FMLA purposes, or that her assistance was "warranted" for purposes of California law, to move her disabled mother to a new home, where the move was not for a medical purpose, and evidence failed to show the move was necessary on that particular day).

PROBLEM

Fred Driver learned that his father was suffering from serious depression after the death of his wife (Fred's mother), and his father was having trouble managing his personal affairs because of his depression. Assume the father's depression qualified as a serious medical condition. Fred Driver's sister Mary (the father's daughter) lived only a few miles from the father and was able to look out for the father, but the father was not nearly as close to Mary as to Fred, and Fred believed (and the father agreed) that Fred's presence would be of greater emotional comfort to the father. Unfortunately, the father lived about 500 miles from Fred. If Fred chooses to visit his father for ten weeks to help him through depression, will Fred's absence qualify for FMLA leave?

4. *Leave for Newborn or Newly Placed Children*

The FMLA rules for leave to spend time with newborn or newly placed children are relatively straightforward in comparison with the rules for other types of leave. A parent (including an adoptive or foster parent) is entitled to use FMLA leave on the occasion of the birth or placement of a child without regard to any health difficulties and without showing that leave is "needed" to care for the child, because the purpose of the leave is to promote the parent-child bonding and adjustment process. An employee parent may begin leave at any time during the first year of the child's birth or placement, but the leave must be concluded within that one-year period unless state law or the employer's policy permits leave for a longer period. 29 C.F.R. § 825.201. The act appears to permit an employee parent to take leave to spend time with a new child even if the other parent is already at home with the child or has used leave from another employer to spend time with the child. However, if both employees work for the same employer, the employer can limit the parents to an aggregate of 12 weeks of leave for this purpose. *Id.* In this situation, each parent retains the balance of their FMLA leave entitlement for other purposes, such as sick leave. *Id.*

5. *Discrimination on the Basis of Pregnancy or Childbirth*

Title VII, which prohibits discrimination on the basis of sex or pregnancy, *might* lead to an employer's duty to "accommodate" pregnancy or childbirth under certain circumstances. Many employers grant work leave, light duty or other accommodations for some types of "disabilities" to comply with the Americans with Disabilities Act or to reduce workers' compensation disability costs of work-injured employees struggling to return to work. If an employer accommodates "disabled" or work-injured employees but *not* employees affected by pregnancy or childbirth, has the employer engaged in illegal pregnancy or sex discrimination under Title VII? In Young v. United Parcel Serv., Inc., 135 S. Ct. 1338 (2015), the Supreme Court held that an employer who grants light duty or leave from work for work-related injuries, but who denies the same accommodation to employees affected by pregnancy or childbirth, *might* be engaging in illegal pregnancy discrimination.

An accommodation policy that differentiates between pregnancy or childbirth versus "disability" or work-related injury is not necessarily *illegal* discrimination. The employer might have a "legitimate, nondiscriminatory" reason" for such a difference in treatment. But the employer's reason "normally cannot consist simply of a claim that it is more expensive or less convenient to add pregnant women" to a policy of accommodation. *Id.* at 1354. Whether the difference in treatment is illegal will depend on a comparison of the significance of the resulting burden for pregnant workers and the strength of the employer's justification for excluding pregnancy from its policy. *Id.*

After *Young* a number of courts have allowed claims, especially by pregnant police officers, that exclusion of pregnancy from an accommodation policy is illegal pregnancy discrimination. *See, e.g.,* Hicks v. Tuscaloosa, 870 F.3d 1253, 1260–61 (11th Cir. 2017) (plaintiff proved illegal discrimination by policy that granted "alternative duty" for some conditions but not pregnancy); Legg v. Ulster County, 820 F.3d 67, 74 (2d Cir. 2016) (issue of fact whether policy illegally accommodated some conditions but not pregnancy).

6. *Time Off for Breastfeeding*

Section 4207 of the Patient Protection and Affordable Care Act of 2010 amended the Fair Labor Standards Act to require an employer to accommodate an employee's need to breastfeed her infant by providing a reasonable amount of uncompensated time and a private place, other than a restroom, to express milk. *See* 29 U.S.C. § 207(r). Employers with fewer than 50 employees are not subject to this provision if compliance would cause an undue hardship.

In addition, some courts have applied *Young*, discussed in the immediately preceding section, to hold that an employer illegally discriminates on the basis of pregnancy or childbirth in violation of Title VII by failing to extend its existing accommodation policy to employees needing breastfeeding accommodations, such as time off during a shift or reassignment to a different work station. Hicks v. Tuscaloosa, 870 F.3d 1253, 1260–61 (11th Cir. 2017).

7. *Leave When Family Members Are Called to Active Duty*

Members of the uniformed services have long enjoyed protection for their need for prolonged — sometimes very prolonged — absence from work to fulfill their reserve and active military duties. Rights of reserve and active duty leave for service members are discussed in section D of this chapter, *infra*. In 2008, Congress recognized that an employee service member's call to active duty also places special demands on the service member's family members, who might find themselves suddenly responsible for the service member's children or other affairs. As amended in 2008, the FMLA provides unpaid leave rights for a service member's spouse, parents, children or "next of kin" based on a qualifying "exigency" arising out of the fact that the service member has been called to active duty. 29 U.S.C. § 2612(a)(1)(E). The Department of Labor has issued detailed regulations defining "qualifying exigency." 29 C.F.R. § 825.126. If the service member is injured, the family member's right to leave is extended to 26 weeks in a 12-month period. 29 U.S.C. §§ 2611(15), 2612(a)(3). As in the case of family care leave, an employer may require certification of the "need for leave" requested by an employee to assist or care for a service member. 29 C.F.R. § 825.309.

A number of states have also enacted their own family military leave laws. *See, e.g.*, 820 Ill. Comp. Stat. 151/1 et seq.

D. RESTORATION, NONINTERFERENCE, AND NONDISCRIMINATION

The FMLA grants employees the right to unpaid leave for qualified reasons. This right would mean nothing except for a corollary: the employee has the right to be "restored" to the employee's pre-leave job or an "equivalent" job.

There are many ways an employer might prevent an employee's enjoyment of these rights. First, the employer might deny the employee's request for leave, expressly or implicitly threatening discharge if the employee takes leave. The employer could also take other steps to interfere, such as by misrepresenting the law or facts to the employee, or imposing arbitrary and burdensome procedural requirements for requesting leave. The employer could adopt policies or policies that make leave costly, such as by suspending eligibility for health insurance, suspending or voiding seniority, or reducing an employee's prospects for promotion or layoff protection. Any of these measures would tend to interfere with, restrain or deny an employee's right to FMLA leave.

If the employee does take leave despite the employer's interference or denial of permission, the employer has at least two other ways to interfere. First, the employer might refuse to accept the employee's request to return after leave. Second, the employer might reinstate the employee but fail to "restore" the employee to the same or an equivalent position. If the employer restores the employee to a different position, the new position might result in loss of compensation or prestige, or cause extra burden or inconvenience.

The FMLA addresses any adverse action affecting an employee's quest for rights of leave and restoration under a provision titled "*interference* with rights." 29 U.S.C. § 2615(a)(1) (emphasis added). Section 2615(a)(1) states that an employer must not "interfere with, restrain or deny" the rights guaranteed by the FMLA—mainly taking leave and being restored after leave. It is sometimes said that this provision establishes the "interference" or "entitlement" theory. Smith v. Diffee Ford-Lincoln-Mercury, Inc., 298 F.3d 955, 960 (10th Cir. 2002). But as the next case illustrates, Congress's use of the terms "interfere", "restrain" or "deny" (all titled acts of "interference") is somewhat unusual and has confused courts because *most* employments laws use the terms "discriminate" or "retaliate" to describe an employer's adverse actions caused by an employee's protected status or assertion of legal rights. Moreover, the use of the word "interference" might imply important rules for the employer's violation.

To compound the confusion, the FMLA uses the term "discriminate" in another provision, 29 U.S.C. § 2615(a)(2), to describe adverse action against an employee for an entirely *different* kind of conduct: "opposing" a violation of the FMLA such as by speaking against an employer's violation of the law (as opposed to requesting or taking leave or returning from leave). Most other employment statutes use the term "retaliate" to describe employer action to punish opposition to violations of the law. Thus, it is sometimes said that section 2615(a)(2) establishes a "discrimination-retaliation" theory to protect employees from retaliation for opposing violations. *Smith, supra.*

Congress added to the confusion when it described adverse action against yet another type of employee conduct: participating in or aiding an enforcement proceeding. 29 U.S.C. § 2615(b). Congress titled adverse action because of *this* type of employee conduct "interference" rather than "discrimination" or "retaliation." Such employer action does tend to "interfere" with the *proceeding* and ultimately with availability of rights of leave. It might seem appropriate, however, to apply "discrimination-retaliation" theory rather than "interference theory" to an aggrieved employee's section 2615(b) claim.

At first glance, it may seem inconsequential whether an employer action is "interference" or "discrimination." However, these words have their own histories and implied meanings. The following case illustrates one court's effort to bring clarity to the confusion and determine the effect of Congress's choice of words for adverse action against different types of employee conduct.

BACHELDER v. AMERICA WEST AIRLINES, INC.

259 F.3d 1112 (9th Cir. 2001)

Penny Bachelder claims that her employer, America West Airlines, violated the Family and Medical Leave Act of 1993 ("FMLA" or "the Act") when it terminated her in 1996 for poor attendance. . . . [She] appeals from the district court's . . . finding, after a bench trial, that, in deciding to fire her, America West did not impermissibly consider FMLA-protected leave that she took in 1994 and 1995. . . .

Bachelder began working for America West as a customer service representative in 1988. From 1993 until her termination in 1996, she was a passenger service supervisor, responsible for several gates at the Phoenix Sky Harbor Airport. . . .

On January 14, 1996, one of America West's managers had a "corrective action discussion" with Bachelder regarding her attendance record. Among the absences that concerned the company were several occasions on which Bachelder had called in sick and [two] FMLA leaves. Bachelder was advised to improve her attendance at work and required to attend pre-scheduled meetings at which her progress would be evaluated.

In February 1996, Bachelder was absent from work again for a total of three weeks. . . . Bachelder's attendance was flawless in March 1996, but in early April, she called in sick for one day to care for her baby, who was ill. Right after that, on April 9, Bachelder was fired. The termination letter her supervisor prepared gave three reasons for the company's decision: (1) Bachelder had been absent from work 16 times since being counseled about her attendance in mid-January; (2) she had failed adequately to carry out her responsibilities for administering her department's Employee of the Month program; and (3) her personal on-time performance and the on-time performance in the section of the airport for which she was responsible were below par.

In due course, Bachelder filed this action, alleging that America West impermissibly considered her use of leave protected by the FMLA in its decision to terminate her. . . . Following the trial, the district court found that America West had not considered Bachelder's 1994 and 1995 FMLA-protected leaves in making the firing decision, and entered judgment for America West. . . .

II. Discussion

The FMLA creates two interrelated, substantive employee rights: first, the employee has a right to use a certain amount of leave for protected reasons, and second, the employee has a right to return to his or her job or an equivalent job after using protected leave. 29 U.S.C. §§ 2612(a), 2614(a). . . .

Implementing this objective, Congress made it unlawful for an employer to "interfere with, restrain, or deny the exercise of or the attempt to exercise, any right provided" by the Act. 29 U.S.C. § 2615(a)(1). The regulations explain that this prohibition encompasses an employer's consideration of an employee's use of FMLA-covered leave in making adverse employment decisions:

> [E]mployers *cannot use the taking of FMLA leave as a negative factor in employment actions*, such as hiring, promotions or disciplinary actions; nor can FMLA leave be counted under "no fault" attendance policies.

29 C.F.R. § 825.220(c) (emphasis added). We find, for the following reasons, that this rule is a reasonable interpretation of the statute's prohibition on "interference with" and "restraint of" employee's rights under the FMLA.

Section 2615's language of "interference with" and "restraint of" the exercise of the rights it guarantees to employees largely mimics that of § 8(a)(1) of the National Labor Relations Act. *See* 29 U.S.C. § 158(a)(1) (providing that it is an unfair labor practice for an employer "to interfere with, restrain, or coerce employees in the exercise of the rights guaranteed" by § 7 of the NLRA). Like the NLRA, the FMLA entitles employees to engage in particular activities — under the FMLA, taking leave from work for FMLA-qualifying reasons — that will be shielded from employer interference and restraint. . . .

Because the FMLA's language so closely follows that of the NLRA, the courts' interpretation of § 8(a)(1) of the NLRA helps to clarify the meaning of the statutory terms "interference" and "restraint." The Supreme Court has held that, for example, an employer's award of preferential seniority rights to striker replacements interferes with employees' rights under the NLRA, NLRB v. Erie Resistor Corp., 373 U.S. 221, 231 (1963) (observing that the practice's "destructive impact upon the strike and union activity cannot be doubted"), as does an employer's threat to shut down its plant in retaliation if its employees should elect to form a union. NLRB v. Gissel Packing Co., 395 U.S. 575, 616-20 (1969). Similarly, this circuit has held — giving just a few examples — that literature distributed by an employer indicating that job losses will be inevitable if employees vote to form a union "interferes" with employees' rights, NLRB v. Four Winds Indus. Inc., 530 F.2d 75, 78-79 (9th Cir. 1976), as does an employer's surveillance of its employees meeting with a union organizer outside the workplace. California Acrylic Indus. Inc. v. NLRB, 150 F.3d 1095, 1099 (9th Cir. 1998). . . .

As a general matter, then, the established understanding at the time the FMLA was enacted was that employer actions that deter employees' participation in protected activities constitute "interference" or "restraint" with the employees' exercise of their rights. Under the FMLA as under the NLRA, attaching negative consequences to the exercise of protected rights surely "tends to chill" an employee's willingness to exercise those rights: Employees are, understandably, less likely to exercise their FMLA leave rights if they can expect to be fired or otherwise disciplined for doing so. The Labor Department's conclusion that employer use of "the taking of FMLA leave as a negative factor in employment actions," 29 C.F.R. § 825.220(c), violates the Act is therefore a reasonable one.

The pertinent regulation uses the term "discrimination" rather than "interfere" or "restrain" in introducing the "negative factor" prohibition. *See* 29 U.S.C. § 2615(a)(1); 29 C.F.R. § 825.220(c).[10] In the case before us and in similar cases, the issue is one of *interference* with the exercise of FMLA rights under § 2615(a)(1), not retaliation or discrimination: Bachelder's claim does not fall under the "anti-retaliation" or "anti-discrimination" provision of § 2615(a)(2), which prohibits "*discriminat[ion]* against any individual for opposing any practice made unlawful by the subchapter" (emphasis added); nor does it fall under the anti-retaliation or anti-discrimination provision of § 2615(b), which prohibits discrimination against any individual for instituting or participating in FMLA proceedings or inquiries. By their plain meaning, the antiretaliation or anti-discrimination provisions do not cover visiting negative consequences on an employee simply because he has used FMLA leave. Such action is, instead, covered under § 2615(a)(1), the provision governing "Interference [with the] Exercise of Rights."

The regulation we apply in this case, 29 C.F.R. 825.220, implements all the parts of 29 U.S.C. § 2615. As noted, the particular provision of the regulations prohibiting the use of FMLA-protected leave as a negative factor in employment decisions, 29 C.F.R. 825.220(c), refers to "discrimination," but actually pertains to the "interference with the exercise of rights" section of the statute, § 2615(a)(1), not the anti-retaliation or anti-discrimination sections, §§ 2615(a)(2) and (b). While the unfortunate intermixing of the two different statutory concepts is confusing, there is no doubt that 29 C.F.R. 825.220(c) serves, at least in part, to implement the interference with the exercise of rights section of the statute.

Consequently, our analysis is fairly uncomplicated. Much as it should be obvious that the "FMLA is not implicated and does not protect an employee against disciplinary action based upon [ ] absences" if those absences are not taken for one

[10] Some of the case law applying § 2615 erroneously uses the term "discriminate" to refer to interference with exercise of rights claims. This semantic confusion has led many courts to apply anti-discrimination law to interference cases, instead of restricting the application of such principles — assuming they are applicable to FMLA at all — to "anti-retaliation" or "anti-discrimination" cases under §§ 2615(a)(2) and (b)....

of the reasons enumerated in the Act, *Rankin*, 246 F.3d, at 1147 (8th Cir. 2001), the FMLA is implicated and does protect an employee against disciplinary action based on her absences if those absences are taken for one of the Act's enumerated reasons.

America West contends for quite a different approach, arguing that we should apply a *McDonnell Douglas*-style shifting burden-of-production analysis, familiar from anti-discrimination law, to determine whether the company illegally "retaliated" against Bachelder for using leave that was protected by the FMLA. *See* McDonnell Douglas Corp. v. Green, 411 U.S. 792 (1973). The *McDonnell Douglas* approach is inapplicable here, however.

The regulation promulgated by the Department of Labor, 29 C.F.R. 825.220(c), plainly prohibits the use of FMLA-protected leave as a negative factor in an employment decision. In order to prevail on her claim, therefore, Bachelder need only prove by a preponderance of the evidence that her taking of FMLA-protected leave constituted a negative factor in the decision to terminate her. She can prove this claim, as one might any ordinary statutory claim, by using either direct or circumstantial evidence, or both. No scheme shifting the burden of production back and forth is required.[11]

In the case before us, there is direct, undisputed evidence of the employer's motives: America West told Bachelder when it fired her that it based its decision on her sixteen absences since the January 1996 corrective action discussion. If those absences were, in fact, covered by the Act, America West's consideration of those absences as a "negative factor" in the firing decision violated the Act. The pivotal question in this case, then, is only "whether the plaintiff has established, by a preponderance of the evidence, that [s]he is entitled to the benefit [s]he claims." *Diaz*, 131 F.3d at 713.

[The court concluded that the absences in question were covered by the act.] America West nonetheless contends that "Bachelder's termination could not have been for her exercise of FMLA rights in 1996 because . . . she and [America West] believed she had exhausted all of her FMLA leave." Whether either America West or Bachelder believed at the time that her February 1996 absences were protected by the FMLA is immaterial, however, because the company's liability does not depend on its subjective belief concerning whether the leave was protected.

First, the employer's good faith or lack of knowledge that its conduct violated the Act is, as a general matter, pertinent only to the question of damages under the FMLA, not to liability. An employer who violates the Act is liable for damages equal to the amount of any lost wages and other employment-related compensation, as well as any actual damages sustained as a result of the violation, such as the cost of providing care, and interest thereon. 29 U.S.C. § 2617(a)(1)(A). The employer is also liable for liquidated damages equal to the amount of actual damages and interest, unless it can prove that it undertook in good faith the conduct that violated the Act and that it had "reasonable grounds for believing that [its action] was not a

[11] In contrast, the "anti-retaliation" provisions of FMLA prohibit "[discrimination] against any individual for opposing any practice made unlawful by this subchapter," (a)(2), and discrimination against any individual for instituting or participating in FMLA proceedings, (b), prohibitions which are not at issue in this case. 29 U.S.C. § 2615(a)(2). Whether or not the *McDonnell Douglas* anti-discrimination approach is applicable in cases involving the "anti-retaliation" provisions of FMLA, is a matter we need not consider here.

violation" of the Act. 29 U.S.C. § 2617(a)(1)(A)(iii). Under such circumstances, it is within the district court's discretion to limit damages to only the amount of actual damages and interest thereon. *Id.* An employer who acts in good faith and without knowledge that its conduct violated the Act, therefore, is still liable for actual damages regardless of its intent.

Second, it is the employer's responsibility, not the employee's, to determine whether a leave request is likely to be covered by the Act. Employees must notify their employers in advance when they plan to take foreseeable leave for reasons covered by the Act, *see* 29 U.S.C. § 2612(e), and as soon as practicable when absences are not foreseeable. *See* 29 C.F.R. § 825.303(a). Employees need only notify their employers that they will be absent under circumstances which indicate that the FMLA might apply:

> The employee need not expressly assert rights under the FMLA or even mention the FMLA, but may only state that leave is needed [for a qualifying reason]. The employer should inquire further of the employee if it is necessary to have more information about whether FMLA leave is being sought by the employee, and obtain the necessary details of the leave to be taken. In the case of medical conditions, the employer may find it necessary to inquire further to determine if the leave is because of a serious health condition and may request medical certification to support the need for such leave.

29 C.F.R. § 825.302(c). In short, the employer is responsible, having been notified of the reason for an employee's absence, for being aware that the absence may qualify for FMLA protection.

Bachelder provided two doctor's notes to America West regarding her absences in February 1996. The company was therefore placed on notice that the leave might be covered by the FMLA, and could have inquired further to determine whether the absences were likely to qualify for FMLA protection.

Finally, America West argues that Bachelder failed to show that the other two reasons it initially put forward for firing her — her failure adequately to administer the Employee of the Month program and her unsatisfactory on-time performance — were pretextual. As we have already explained, however, there is no room for a *McDonnell Douglas* type of pretext analysis when evaluating an "interference" claim under this statute. The question here is not whether America West had additional reasons for the discharge, but whether Bachelder's taking of the 1996 FMLA-protected leave was used as a negative factor in her discharge. We know that the taking of the leave for the period in question was indeed used as a negative factor because America West so announced at the time of the discharge and does not deny that fact now. Moreover, America West does not seriously contend that, even though it considered an impermissible reason in firing Bachelder, it would have fired her anyway for the other two reasons alone. Even had it made such an argument, of course, the regulations clearly prohibit the use of FMLA-protected leave as a negative factor at all. Therefore no further inquiry on the question whether America West violated the statute in discharging Bachelder is necessary.

III. Conclusion

Because we hold that Bachelder's February 1996 absences were protected by the

FMLA, and because America West used these absences as a negative factor in its decision to fire her, we reverse the district court's . . . judgment for America West, direct the court to grant Bachelder's cross-motion for summary judgment as to liability, and remand for further proceedings.

NOTES AND QUESTIONS

1. As the court notes in *Bachelder*, the act's provision making it unlawful to "interfere with, restrain, or deny" the exercise of FMLA rights is modeled after section 8(a)(1) of the National Labor Relations Act (NLRA), 29 U.S.C. § 158(a)(1). Section 8(a)(1) makes it unlawful for an employer to "interfere with, restrain, or coerce" employees in the exercise of NLRA rights. "Interference" has a prospective orientation: it describes action that *deters* or impedes protected conduct from continuing or happening in the future. Interference might include actions that have not yet resulted in immediate harm to a particular employee, such as where an employer tells all employees in advance it will grant no FMLA leave. Employer "discrimination," on the other hand, is a response to a particular employee or group's *present* status or record, and it includes retaliation against a particular employee for what the employee has done in the *past*. But NLRA precedents also regard discrimination and retaliation as forms of "interference" because of the *signal* these acts send to all employees about their prospective exercise of rights. *See* R. Gorman, Basic Text on Labor Law, 137-138 (1982).

2. The court in *Bachelder* held that "interference" claims do not always require proof intent to retaliate on the basis of FMLA leave. Thus, an employer still unlawfully "interferes" if it takes adverse action against an employee based on a *mistaken* belief that the employee is not entitled to leave.

An "interference" claim *does* require proof of retaliatory motive if the employer asserts a reason *other than* FMLA leave for an adverse action. The employee must then prove that the employer's asserted reason is a pretext, and that the real reason was the FMLA leave. The plaintiff can prove "pretext" with the same types of evidence used in other types of discrimination claims — for example, showing that the employer's explanation is untruthful, or that the employer acted more favorably toward others who were similar to the plaintiff except for their lack of a record of FMLA leave. *See* Grace v. USCAR, 521 F.3d 655, 670 (6th Cir. 2008); Donald v. Sybra, Inc., 667 F.3d 757, 762 (6th Cir. 2012).

3. There are other situations in which an "interference" claim will likely require proof of illegal intent, especially if the employer asserts a legitimate reason for an act that might tend to interfere with prospective exercise of FMLA rights. Suppose, for example, an employer transfers a pregnant employee from an FMLA-covered facility to an uncovered facility (recall that coverage is facility by facility). The transfer will interfere with that employee's exercise of FMLA rights, but the transfer is lawful if it is for a legitimate business reason and not because of an intent to interfere. *See* 29 C.F.R. § 825.220(b)(3). Of course, the employee might prove that the asserted business reason is a "pretext."

4. An employer might like to reward employees for "perfect attendance" or for *not* using leave time. Could the employer's refusal to grant a perfect attendance reward to an employee who used FMLA leave constitute unlawful interference

even if the employer did not "intend" to interfere? After all, denying eligibility for the reward could discourage or "restrain" employees from using FMLA rights regardless of the employer's intent. The Department of Labor's regulations confirm this view. 29 CFR §§ 825.215, .220. *But see* Chubb v. City of Omaha, 424 F.3d 831 (8th Cir. 2005) (employer policy granting additional hours of leave to any employee who did not take more than 40 hours of sick leave in a year did not unlawfully interfere with FMLA rights).

If NLRA precedent is the right guide, "unintentional" interference with rights is lawful if the employer's legitimate business purpose outweighs the overall impact of its action on the willingness or ability of employees to enjoy their rights. *See* R. Gorman, Basic Text on Labor Law, 137-138 (1982).

5. Not all courts follow the *Bachelder* distinction between adverse action because of an employee attempt to exercise FMLA rights (employer "interference" under Section 2615(a)(1)) and adverse action because of employee "opposition" to employer violations of the law (employer "discrimination" or "retaliation" under Section 2615(a)(2)). The Eighth Circuit has thus far reluctantly adhered its own earlier precedents that the *opposition* clause, Section 2615(a)(2), applies when adverse action is because the employee *exercised* FMLA rights. Under this view, an employee suffering adverse action because of FMLA leave must *always* prove employer intent to retaliate. Lovland v. Employers Mut. Cas. Co., 674 F.3d 806, 811 (8th Cir. 2012) (reaffirming that circuit's rule "whatever the merits" of the argument that this approach is wrong).

6. If the employer in *Bachelder* had proved it would have terminated Bachelder anyway, even without considering her FMLA-protected absences, would it have defeated her FMLA claim? Is the issue one of liability, or damages? *See* Richardson v. Monitronics Int'l, Inc., 434 F.3d 327 (5th Cir. 2005) (applying the same "mixed motive" analysis used in Title VII cases).

7. In another common type of interference case, the employer fails to restore an employee to her job when the employee returns from FMLA leave. The employer must reinstate the employee immediately upon her return, with an allowance of two business days if the employee returns earlier than expected. 29 C.F.R. § 825.312(e); *see* Hoge v. Honda of Am. Mfg., Inc., 384 F.3d 238 (6th Cir. 2004) (rejecting employer's argument that it should have a "reasonable time" to arrange for the employee's return to the workforce). *See also* Harrell v. U.S. Postal Serv., 415 F.3d 700 (7th Cir. 2005) (employer may not impose rules or conditions for return to work that are more burdensome than what the FMLA requires).

8. The employer must restore the employee to same position or "an equivalent position with equivalent employment benefits, pay, and other terms and conditions of employment." 29 U.S.C. § 2614(a)(1). The Department of Labor's regulations add that equivalent "terms and conditions" include "substantially similar duties and responsibilities [entailing] substantially equivalent skill, effort, responsibility, and authority." 29 C.F.R. § 825.215(a).

9. The FMLA does not require an employer to restore an employee to "any right, benefit, or position of employment other than any right, benefit or position to which the employee would have been entitled had the employee not taken the leave." 29 U.S.C. § 2614(a)(3)(B). Thus, if the employer eliminated the employee's position as a result of a legitimate reorganization or reduction in force,

the employer is not obligated to restore the employee to her job. Sylvester v. Dead River Co., 260 F. Supp. 2d 181 (D. Me. 2003). *See also* Rice v. Sunrise Express, Inc., 209 F.3d 1008 (7th Cir. 2000) (employee retains ultimate burden of proving she would have been restored to employment but for protected leave).

E. CIVIC DUTIES

Employees also have civic duties that may interfere with work. Jury duty, voting, and military service are three duties particularly likely to conflict with employment. Of these three, military service causes the most severe conflict.

1. *Military Service*

a. Overview

In general, an employee's military service can lead to two types of conflict with employment. First, an employee might enlist in active duty or receive a call to active duty in a military service, requiring continuous, extended leave, possibly for over a year. An employee who departs for active duty does not necessarily expect to return to the same employment at the end of military duty, but a right to re-employment might be important, especially if the active duty is involuntary.

Second, an employee might be a member of the National Guard or one of the military reserves, and periodic training and service duties may conflict with the employee's work schedule on a regular basis throughout the year. As of 2010, there were about 1,103,000 reservists in the U.S. uniformed military services. U.S. Census Bureau, 2012 Statistical Abstract, Table 513, http://www.census.gov/compendia/statab/2012/tables/12s0513.pdf. A reservist frequently sacrifices earnings as well as time during his reserve duties, because reserve pay may be less than what the employee would earn in his regular employment, and it is not always possible to fulfill reserve duty outside of regular working hours. No federal law requires an employer to compensate an absent service member for lost earnings, but approximately 50 percent of employees in the private sector are eligible for military leave pay if they miss regular work and suffer a difference in pay for reserve duties. Bureau of Statistics, Department of Labor, *News Release: Employee Benefits in Private Industry* (Sept. 17, 2003), at http://www.bls.gov/news.release/ebs2.t03.htm.

For most employers, the most important legal obligations to accommodate military service are the result of the Uniformed Services Employment and Reemployment Rights Act of 1994 (USERRA). 38 U.S.C. §§ 4301-4333. The act applies to employee service in any of the "uniformed services," including the Army, Navy, Marine Corps, Air Force, Coast Guard, Public Health Service commissioned corps, reserve components of these services, and the Army National Guard and Air National Guard. USERRA covers nearly all employees, including part-time and probationary employees, and virtually all U.S. employers, public and private, regardless of size. 38 U.S.C. § 4303.

Given the substantial and sometimes expensive duties USERRA imposes on employers, an employer might be motivated to discriminate against applicants or employees who are associated with the uniformed services, who are subject to the possibility of reserve or active duties, or who are assertive about their rights under the act. Therefore, the act begins by prohibiting an employer from discriminating on the basis of service, or retaliating against employees who assert rights or participate in the enforcement of the act. 38 U.S.C. § 4311. Beyond this general antidiscrimination rule, the act affects the employer-employee relationship in two types of situations: an employee's extended leave on active duty, and an employee's occasional short-term reserve or national guard duty.

Re-employment Rights. An employee who leaves civilian employment for voluntary or involuntary duty, active or reserve, is entitled to re-employment upon returning, if the employee gave the employer notice he or she was leaving for active duty in one of the uniformed services, the service continued for a *cumulative* period usually not exceeding five years, the service discharge was not dishonorable or subject to other punitive conditions, and the employee reported back to the civilian job in a timely manner. 38 U.S.C. §§ 4304, 4312. *See* Vega Colon v. Wyeth Pharm., 625 F.3d 22 (1st Cir. 2010) (USERRA protection for employee who had not yet applied for active duty when he informed his employer of intent to return to military service). The speed with which an employee must return to work varies with the duration of the USERRA leave. For short-term leaves (under 31 days), as is typical of reserve duty, an employee must report back to work by "the first regularly scheduled work period after the end of the calendar day of duty, plus time required to return home safely and an eight hour rest period." 38 U.S.C. § 4312(e)(1)(A). When an employee's USERRA leave is for 181 days or more (as is common for active duty), the employee must "apply for reemployment no later than 90 days after completion of military service." *Id.* § 4312(e)(1)(D). In some cases, an employer's duty goes beyond merely restoring the pre-leave job: if the employee would have advanced to another position but for USERRA leave, the employer might be required to offer that position with the same status and seniority as if he or she were never absent. *Id.* § 4313.

Protection of Other Employment Rights and Benefits. USERRA also has important effects on an employee benefit rights, seniority, and other job rights during USERRA leave. *Id.* §§ 4316-4318. The rules vary according to the rights in question, but the general purpose of the rules is to prevent service leave from causing a loss of job rights and minimize the employee's employment sacrifice.

b. Rights and Benefits of Employment: How Does Military Leave "Count"?

One of the basic rules of USERRA is nondiscrimination on the basis of uniformed service. Section 4311(a) states that a person "shall not be denied initial employment, reemployment, retention in employment, promotion, or any benefit of employment" because he is or has applied to be a member of a uniformed service. *See also* 38 U.S.C. § 4311(b) (prohibiting discrimination because a person has sought to enforce rights under USERRA). Clearly, an employer who refuses to hire or rehire a person, or who discharges a person because the employer fears the complications of accommodating that person's uniformed service obligations would be violating the rule against discrimination.

A more difficult question is whether an employer "discriminates" if he treats an employee's absence for military service as time not worked. Requiring employers to pay employees for time on military leave would be a considerable and probably unintended burden. However, compensation is not the only benefit or right that could be affected by an employee's absence. Nearly any other benefit, including vacation time, pensions, medical insurance, or eligibility for promotion could be affected by whether time is counted "time worked" or "time not worked." Is it "discrimination" to treat an employee's absence due to uniformed service leave as time not worked, for purposes of any particular benefit? Note that section 4311, titled "Discrimination against persons who serve in the uniformed services," states that a person "shall not be denied . . . any *benefit* of employment" because of uniformed service (emphasis added).

A more specific benefits provision is 38 U.S.C. § 4316, which provides one rule for "seniority" rights, another for non-seniority rights and benefits.

The rule for seniority-based rights is in section 4316(a). A typical seniority-based right would be a rule for layoffs in reverse order of seniority, so that more senior employees are less likely affected by layoffs. Another such rule might be eligibility for promotion based on seniority, or preference in requesting certain assignments. Under section 4316(a), an employee who is absent for uniformed service continues to accumulate seniority as if he were actually at work. One might say he is constructively at work, for purposes of accumulating seniority.

Section 4316(b) states a different rule for employment rights that are *not* seniority-based: a person absent because of uniformed service "shall be . . . deemed to be on furlough or leave of absence," and he is entitled to the same non-seniority-based rights and benefits "as are generally provided by the employer . . . to employees having similar seniority, status, and pay who are on furlough or leave of absence" for reasons other than uniformed service leave.

In sum, there are three rules affecting the way employers count absence due to uniformed leave: (1) a general rule against discrimination; (2) a rule requiring continued accumulation of seniority during uniformed service leave; and (3) a rule that absence for uniformed service leave is to be treated like leave for other purposes, in determining an employee's non-seniority-based rights and benefits.

ROGERS v. CITY OF SAN ANTONIO

392 F.3d 758 (5th Cir. 2004)

DENNIS, Circuit Judge:

Plaintiffs, fifteen employees of the San Antonio fire department, who are members of either the United States military reserves or the National Guard ("Uniformed Services"), brought this civil action under the Uniform Services Employment and Reemployment Rights Act of 1994 ("USERRA") against the City of San Antonio, Texas. . . . The plaintiffs contend that the City violated USERRA by denying them employment benefits because of their absences from work while performing their military duties in the Uniformed Services. More specifically, the employees assert that the City's Collective Bargaining Agreement ("CBA") and policies regarding military leave of absence deprive them of straight and overtime pay, opportunities to earn extra vacation leave and vacation scheduling flexibility, and opportunities to secure unscheduled overtime work and job upgrades. Plaintiffs assert that under USERRA § 4311(a) "the City, in implementing these employment practices, unlawfully discriminates against them by deeming them 'absent' from work whenever they are on leave fulfilling their military reserve duties, as opposed to viewing them as 'constructively present at work.'" The City contends that, because § 4316(b)(1) provides that persons absent from civilian employment by reason of military service are entitled only to such non-seniority rights and benefits as the employer provides to employees when they are on non-military leaves of absence, plaintiffs cannot recover since they were treated equally as to such rights with all employees absent on non-military leave.

[T]he overtime policy the plaintiffs challenged was as follows: In accordance with special rules of the Fair Labor Standards Act applicable to firefighters, 29 U.S.C. § 207(k); 29 C.F.R. § 553.201, the city and the union agreed to a special 21-day work period with 159 regular hours at a regular rate. The firefighters actually worked 168 hours per work period, and in accordance with the special FLSA rules, they earned an overtime rate for nine of these hours. Only hours *actually worked* counted for purposes of determining whether a firefighter had worked more than 159 hours in a 21-day work period, but as long as a firefighter worked his regularly scheduled hours, he was sure to earn pay at an overtime rate for the 160th through 168th hours of a regular work period, and additional overtime pay for hours in excess of 168. On the other hand, if a firefighter was absent from scheduled working time, the general rule was that hours of absence would not count toward his entitlement to premium overtime pay.

An important exception, negotiated by the union on the firefighters' behalf, was to count some vacation time and certain other leave time as if a firefighter had actually worked, for overtime purposes. Whenever a firefighter had "lost" 27 hours of overtime pay he would have earned but for vacation or other eligible leave, his subsequent hours of vacation and eligible leave would count as if he had actually worked, for overtime purposes. Thus, the loss of overtime pay due to vacation and other eligible leave was "capped" at 27 hours. Absences due to *military* leave were not included in this exception. Hours of absence for military leave were simply hours not worked, either before or after an employee reached the 27-hour lost overtime "cap."]

Plaintiffs assert that under USERRA § 4311(a), "the City, in implementing these employment practices, unlawfully discriminates against them by deeming them 'absent' from work whenever they are on leave fulfilling their military reserve duties, as opposed to viewing them as 'constructively present at work.'" The City contends that, because § 4316(b)(1) provides that persons absent from civilian employment by reason of military service are entitled only to such non-seniority rights and benefits as the employer provides to employees when they are on non-military leaves of absence, plaintiffs cannot recover since they were treated equally as to such rights with all employees absent on nonmilitary leave.

FACTS

Plaintiffs are employed by the City fire department in its Fire Suppression division and Emergency Medical Services division ("Firefighters"). The CBA between the

City and the employees' Union governs the working conditions of all City firefighters. Plaintiffs, as members of the Uniformed Services ("reservists"), typically must take leave of absence for military training a minimum of one weekend per month and one annual two week session. Reservists may volunteer or be ordered to take military leave to perform extra duties. In order to be promoted, reservists must meet the same educational requirements as a fulltime active member of the Uniformed Services, such as officer training courses.

. . . The district court granted the employees' motion [for summary judgment] as to liability on substantially all claims and denied the City's cross- motion. . . . The City appealed. . . .

ANALYSIS

1.

A. USERRA Overview

. . . USERRA is the most recent in a series of laws protecting veterans' employment and reemployment rights dating from the Selective Training and Service Act of 1940. USERRA's immediate precursor, the Veterans' Reemployment Rights Act (VRRA), was enacted as § 404 of the Vietnam Era Veterans' Readjustment Assistance Act of 1974. "Congress emphasized [1] USERRA's continuity with the VRRA and its intention to clarify and strengthen that law. [2] Federal laws protecting veterans' employment and reemployment rights for the past fifty years had been successful." [3] "[T]he large body of case law that had developed under those statutes remained in full force and effect, to the extent it is consistent with USERRA."[9]

. . . In construing a precursor to USERRA, the Supreme Court in Fishgold v. Sullivan Drydock and Repair Corp., 328 U.S. 275 (1946), invented the "escalator" principle in stating that a returning service member "does not step back on the seniority escalator at the point he stepped off. He steps back on at the precise point he would have occupied had he kept his position continuously during the war." *Id.* at 284-285. Although *Fishgold* was mainly a seniority case, the escalator principle applies to the employment position, and rate of pay, as well as the seniority rights to which the returning service member is entitled.

Thus, USERRA requires that the service member be reemployed in the escalator job position comparable to the position he would have held had he remained continuously in his civilian employment. 38 U.S.C. § 4313. After service of 90 days or less, the person is entitled to reinstatement in the position of employment in which she or he would have been but for the interruption of employment by uniformed service. *Id.* at § 4313(a)(1)(A). If the service period was longer than 90 days, the service member is entitled to reemployment in the escalator position, but the employer may also reinstate the member in any position of like seniority status and pay for which he is qualified. 38 U.S.C. § 4313(a)(2)(A). If the service member is unable to qualify for either the escalator position or a comparable position, despite reasonable employer efforts, he is entitled to reemployment in a position that is the nearest approximation to the

[9] 20 C.F.R. Pt. 1002, Federal Register, Vol. 69, No. 181, p. 56286 (2004) ("Proposed Regulation").]

escalator position. *Id.* at § 4313(a)(2)(A), (B).

A person who is reemployed under USERRA is entitled to the seniority and other rights and benefits determined by seniority that the person had on the date of the beginning of service plus the additional seniority and rights and benefits that he or she would have attained if the person had remained continuously employed. *Id.* at § 4316(a). This section states the basic escalator principle as it applies to seniority and seniority-based rights and benefits. An employer is not required to have a seniority system. USERRA requires only that employers who do have a seniority system restore the returning service member to the proper place on the seniority ladder. An employee's rate of pay after an absence from work due to uniformed service is also determined by application of the escalator principle.

USERRA does not grant escalator protection to service members' nonseniority rights and benefits but provides only that the employer treat employees absent because of military service equally with employees having similar seniority, status, and pay who are on comparable non-military leaves of absence under a contract, agreement, policy, practice, or plan in effect at any time during that uniformed service. § 4316(b)(1).

B. *Legislative History and Jurisprudence*

The nation's first peacetime draft law, the Selective Training and Service Act of 1940 was designed to provide reemployment for veterans returning to civilian life in positions of "like seniority, status, and pay." The Reserve Forces Act of 1955, "provided that employees returning from active duty for more than three months in the Ready Reserve were entitled to the same employment rights as inductees, with limited exceptions." Monroe v. Standard Oil Co., 452 U.S. 549 (1981).

In 1960, these reemployment rights and benefits were extended to National Guardsmen. A new section, VRRA § 2024(d), was also enacted in 1960 to protect employees who had military training obligations lasting less than three months. This section provide[d] that employees must be granted a leave of absence for training and, upon their return, be restored to their positions "with such seniority, status, pay, and vacation" as they would have had if they had not been absent for training.

VRRA § 2024(d) did not, however, protect reservists from discrimination by their employers in the form of discharges, demotions, or other adverse conduct between leaves of absence for training. In the years following its enactment discriminatory employment practices intensified. Congress responded with legislation codified as VRRA § 2021(b)(3) which, in pertinent part, provided that "[a]ny person who [is employed by a private employer] shall not be denied retention in employment or any promotion or other incident or advantage of employment because of any obligation as a member of a reserve component of the Armed Forces."

. . . In West v. Safeway Stores, Inc., the Fifth Circuit construed § 2021(b)(3) "to require that employers, in applying collective bargaining agreements, treat reservists as if they were constructively present during their reserve duty in similar contexts." 609 F.2d at 150. The employee, a meat cutter, had contended that, since the collective bargaining agreement guaranteed a 40 hour work week and because the only reason that he was not receiving a 40 hour work week was due to his National Guard obligations, he was being denied an advantage of employment. The court agreed and held that the employer must provide him with his guaranteed 40 hour work week despite the fact that the collective bargaining agreement specifically provided that an employee's absence for weekend reserve or National Guard duty was excluded or negated from the guarantee.

The Sixth Circuit in a virtually identical situation, involving a 40 hour work week guarantee, however, disagreed with West, holding that § 2021(b)(3) merely required that reservists be treated no differently than other employees who are absent for non-military reasons. [Monroe v. Standard Oil Co., 613 F.2d 641, 646 (6th Cir. 1980), *aff'd*, 452 U.S. 549 (1981).] . . . Thus, the court held, . . . the employer was required to do no more than grant him a leave of absence without pay to comply with his military reserve obligation. Further, the court found "nothing in the legislative history or the statute to support judicial invalidation of nondiscriminatory conditions precedent to employee benefits and adhere[d] to [its] belief that conditional benefits are protected by § 2021(b)(3) only to the extent that the conditions have been actually satisfied." *Id.* at 647.

The Supreme Court granted *certiorari* in *Monroe*, affirmed the Sixth Circuit's decision, and substantially agreed with its reasoning. 452 U.S. 549. The Supreme Court concluded that the "legislative history . . . indicates that § 2021(b)(3) was enacted for the significant but limited purpose of protecting the employee-reservist against discrimination like discharge and demotion," by reason of reserve status. *Id.* at 559. Further, the Court found nothing in § 2021(b)(3) or its legislative history to indicate that Congress even considered imposing an obligation on employers to provide a special work-scheduling preference, but rather that the history suggests that Congress did not intend employers to provide special benefits to employee reservists not generally made available to other employees. *Id.* at 561. . . .

After the Supreme Court's decision in *Monroe*, the Third Circuit, in Waltermyer v. Aluminum Co. of America, 804 F.2d 821 (3d Cir. 1986), addressed whether a National Guardsman was entitled to pay for a holiday that occurred during his leave of absence for a two-week military training period. . . . The [collective bargaining] agreement provided that full-time employees would receive pay for designated holidays if, during the payroll week in which the holiday occurs, the employee is at work; on a scheduled vacation; on a layoff under specified conditions; performing jury service; a witness in a court of law; qualified for bereavement pay; or absent because of personal illness and certain sick leave conditions apply. *Id.* at 822. . . . The court noted the similarities between the characteristics of absence from work required by the military obligation at issue and the absences of the exempted categories, viz., the absences were not generally of extended duration; and they were for reasons beyond the control of the absent employee. *Id.* at 825. Therefore, the court concluded, "relieving [National Guard members] on military leave from the work requirement merely establishes equality for National Guardsmen and reservists, not preferential treatment." *Id.* at 825. Thus, the court concluded, the plaintiff Guardsman had established his right to holiday pay under § 2021(b)(3). Significantly, however, the court indicated that a scheduled vacation, which also was exempted from the work requirement, was not comparable to military leave. The court observed: "We realize a planned vacation is different from the other exceptions on the list. Vacation is earned time away from work, and this exception merely recognizes that an employee should not be prejudiced, in the form of lost holiday pay, for taking an earned vacation." *Id.* at 825 n.3.

The Senate report on the bill that became § 4316(b)(1) stated that it "would codify court decisions that have interpreted current law as providing a statutorily-mandated leave of absence for military service that entitles service members to participate in benefits that are accorded other employees. *See Waltermyer*, 804 F.2d 821." S. Rep. 103-158 (October 18, 1993). . . .

The House Report declared that the bill had the same purpose and effect. . . . H.R. Rep. 103-65(I) (April 28, 1993). The House Report elaborated:

> The Committee intends to affirm the decision in Waltermyer v. Aluminum Co. of America, 804 F.2d 821 (3d Cir. 1986) that, to the extent the employer policy or practice varies among various types of non-military leaves of absence, the most favorable treatment accorded any particular leave would also be accorded the military leave, regardless of whether the non-military leave is paid or unpaid. Thus, for example, an employer cannot require servicemembers to reschedule their work week because of a conflict with reserve or National Guard duty, unless all other employees who miss work are required to reschedule their work. . . . However, servicemembers are not entitled to receive benefits beyond what they would have received had they remained continuously employed.

Id.

. . . While new § 4316(b)(1)'s legislative history clearly reflects the intent to specifically guarantee reservists equality of on-leave benefits, the history of § 4311(a) shows an intent to continue and strengthen the anti-discrimination provision but not the specific goal of guaranteeing parity of benefits. . . . Further, the brief legislative history of the bill that became § 4311(a) reflects no intention to prohibit neutral labor contracts from treating employees on military leave equally with those on non-military leave with respect to the loss of benefits due to absence from work. . . .

C. Section 4316(b)(1) Governs This Case

Section 4316(b)(1) of USERRA provides that an employee who is absent from employment for military service is deemed to be on leave of absence and "entitled to such rights and benefits not determined by seniority . . . generally provided by the employer to employees having similar seniority, status, and pay who are on furlough or leave of absence under a contract, agreement, policy, practice or plan. . . ." . . . Congress sought by § 4316(b)(1) to guarantee a measure of equality of treatment with respect to military and non-military leaves and to strike an appropriate balance between benefits to employee-service persons and costs to employers. USERRA does not authorize the courts to add to or detract from that guarantee or to restrike that balance.

For these reasons, we conclude that the district court erred in deciding that § 4311(a), rather than § 4316(b)(1), must be applied in this case. . . .

The district court decided that "[s]ection 4316 is inapplicable to this case [, because] it only applies to a person who is reemployed under this chapter or who is absent on furlough or leave of absence." The district court stated that § 4316 "is specifically tailored to apply to a reservist or veteran returning to employment from active duty rather than reservists . . . away for relatively short periods [for] drilling and training[.]" Furthermore, the court stated, "the anti-discrimination provisions [§ 4311(a-c)] were specifically added 'to protect the rights of reservists which had been found to be inadequately protected' under the provision cited by the City [§ 4316] . . . . We believe that the district court was mistaken in each of its reasons for deciding that § 4311(a) must be applied in this case. . . .

First, § 4316(b)(1) is fully applicable to reservists' short absences from civilian employment for weekend drills or two-week annual training. In USERRA, the term "service in the uniformed services" . . . includes "active duty, active duty for training, initial active duty for training, inactive duty training, full-time National Guard duty," medical examinations to determine fitness for duty, and performance of funeral honors duty. [38 U.S.C. § 4303(13).] The term "uniformed services" means "the Armed Forces, the Army National Guard and the Air National Guard when engaged in active duty for training, inactive duty training, or full-time National Guard duty[.]" 38 U.S.C. § 4303(16). Thus, both of these terms apply to members of the uniformed services who participate in inactive duty training for weekend drills and two-week annual training. Consequently, § 4316(b)(1), which applies to "a person who is absent from a position of employment by reason of service in the uniformed services" is fully applicable to reservists during their weekend and two-week military duty sessions.

Second, "reemployment" is not formally defined in § 4303, but §§ 4312-4313, providing for USERRA reemployment rights and positions, plainly apply to "any person whose absence from a position of employment is necessitated by reason of service in the uniformed services." 38 U.S.C. § 4312. As noted in the previous paragraph, the terms "service in the uniformed services" and "uniformed services" apply to "inactive duty training," which refers to reservists and their two week and weekend training periods. Further, USERRA makes specific provisions for the reemployment of a person whose period of service in the uniformed services was less than 31 days. 38 U.S.C. § 4312(e)(1)(A); 4313(a)(1). Thus, a reservist who returns to his or her job after weekend drill is "reemployed" just as much as one who is reinstated after a period of service of two years.

. . . Finally, as we have noted, *West* and its "constructively present" theory of interpretation was disapproved by the Supreme Court in *Monroe* and legislatively overruled in the codification of *Monroe* and *Waltermyer* by USERRA § 4316(b)(1).

2.

Applying § 4316(b)(1) to the summary judgment record in this case, we conclude that the district court's judgment must be reversed and summary judgment granted for the City on the following claims: (1) lost straight-time pay; (2) lost overtime opportunities; and (3) missed upgrading opportunities. From our review of the record we have determined that there is no type of nonmilitary leave available to any employee under which an employee can accrue or receive the foregoing kinds of benefits. Hence, insofar as the record shows, there is no type of leave under which these benefits may accrue that is comparable to any military leave.

We further conclude that the district court's summary judgment with respect to: (1) bonus day leave; (2) perfect attendance leave; and (3) the twenty-seven hour cap on lost overtime must be reversed and the case remanded for further proceedings on these claims. There are genuinely disputable issues as to the material facts of whether involuntary non-military leaves, not generally for extended durations, for jury duty, bereavement, and line of duty injury leave (provided that the employee returns to work in the following shift), under which employees may accrue or receive bonus day leave and perfect attendance leave benefits, are comparable to each plaintiff's military leaves taken for service in the uniformed services. For the same reason, there is a disputable issue as to whether sick leave, under which employees receive the benefit of the twenty-seven hour cap for the first shift of sick leave they use, is comparable to military leave. Thus, we reverse and remand on this claim also.

NOTES AND QUESTIONS

1. The Fifth Circuit in *Rogers* appears to have viewed the lost overtime "cap" as a kind of "benefit" — thus the issue whether the cap was subject to the general rule against discrimination with regard to benefits, or the rule that an employer must treat service leave the same as other similar forms of leave. But what if the cap is simply part of the formula for determining a firefighter's wages? *See* 38 U.S.C. § 4303(2) (defining "benefits").

2. The Fifth Circuit's solution in *Rogers* is for the district court, on remand, to compare the city's treatment of uniformed service leave with its treatment of other "comparable" forms of leave. The court appears to have been particularly interested in a comparison between uniformed service leave (always counted as absent) and sick leave (sometimes counted as present) for purposes of the lost overtime cap. On the other hand, the court appears to have agreed with *Waltermyer* that vacation time, which is "earned time away from work," is not "comparable" to uniformed service leave. Are you persuaded by this distinction?

3. Another example of a potential problem caused by uniformed service leave involves an employee's missed opportunity to work overtime. Overtime opportunities are often prized by employees, and an employer can distribute these opportunities in a variety of ways. For example, an employee who declines or is unable to accept a specific overtime opportunity when it is his turn for an opportunity might not receive another opportunity until the employer has made offers to all the other employees on the list. In Carney v. Cummins Engine Co., 602 F.2d 763 (7th Cir. 1979), the court applied one of USERRA's predecessor laws in holding that an employer must not penalize an employee for missing an overtime opportunity because of uniformed service leave. Thus, upon returning from uniformed service leave, the employee was entitled to an overtime opportunity as if he had neither declined nor failed to accept an opportunity during his uniformed service leave. *See also* 38 U.S.C. § 4303(2) (defining "benefit" to include "the opportunity to select work hours"). Is the answer the same under the current version of USERRA, as described in *Rogers*? Does the policy in question involve potential discrimination under section 4311, or does section 4316 provide the appropriate rule?

4. Recall that under the FMLA, an employer can require an employee to use paid vacation time as part of the employee's FMLA leave. The decision whether to

do so rests with the employer. The vacation time rule under USERRA is different. Under 38 U.S.C. § 4316(d), it is the employee who decides whether to treat service leave as paid vacation time. Thus, he can use his accrued vacation benefits to maintain his stream of compensation from his civilian employer, or he can save all his accrued vacation benefits for a subsequent paid vacation.

5. USERRA and the FMLA differ in some other important ways when it comes to "benefits" affected by protected leave. As noted earlier, USERRA is particularly protective for employees when it comes to seniority. An employee's seniority continues to accrue during uniformed service leave as if he were not on leave at all. In contrast, the FMLA provides that an employee has no right to the accrual of seniority during FMLA leave. 29 U.S.C. § 2614(a)(3).

6. Since USERRA's treatment of seniority rights is so much more generous than its treatment of non-seniority rights, it may be tempting for an employee to argue that any right or benefit based on a measurement of time is based on seniority. However, the usual meaning of "seniority" is not so broad. Section 4303(12) of USERRA defines "seniority" as "longevity in employment together with any benefits of employment which accrue with, or are determined by, longevity in employment." Department of Labor regulations specify three essential features of a protected seniority right: (1) the right is "a reward for *length of service* rather than a form of short-term compensation for work performed"; (2) it is "reasonably certain that the employee would have received the right or benefit if he or she had remained continuously employed during the period of service"; and (3) "it is the employer's *actual* custom or practice to provide or withhold the right or benefit as a reward for length of service." 20 C.F.R. § 1002.212 (emphasis added).

7. The Fair Labor Standards Act is another law that may affect the way an employer treats uniformed service absences, particularly for an exempt "salaried" worker whose compensation is not based on a measurement of time shorter than a week. If an employer reduces an exempt, salaried employee's salary for a week to reflect an absence of less than a week for uniformed service or jury service, the employer might undermine its claim that the employee is an exempt "salaried" worker. 29 C.F.R. § 541.602(b)(3). However, the Department of Labor takes the position that the employer *can* offset the employee's uniformed service pay, witness fees, or jury service fees against the employee's salary for the week. *Id.*

8. USERRA's provisions with respect to employee health care benefits are analogous to COBRA, requiring an employer to offer an employee continued participation in a group health plan during his leave, but permitting the employer to charge the cost of continued coverage to the employee. 38 U.S.C. § 4317. *See also* 38 U.S.C. § 4316(b)(4) (employer may require an employee on uniformed service leave to bear the costs of other continued benefits "to the extent employees on furlough or leave of absence are so required").

9. As for pension benefits, USERRA provides that qualified leave will be treated as service with the employer for purposes of determining accrual and nonforfeitability of benefits, and that leave will not count as a "break in service." 38 U.S.C. § 4318.

10. USERRA does not preempt state laws providing greater or additional rights, and a number of states have adopted such laws. *See, e.g.*, Cal. Military and

Veterans Code § 394; N.Y. Military Law §§ 317-318.

11. Other federal laws, including the Vietnam Era Veterans' Readjustment Assistance Act (VEVRAA), 38 U.S.C. §§ 4211-4215, require federal agencies and federal contractors to grant hiring preferences to eligible veterans. *See also* 38 U.S.C. §§ 4314, 4315. A number of states have adopted their own veterans' preferences laws, especially with respect to employment in state agencies. *See, e.g.*, Tex. Gov. Code §§ 657.001-657.009.

PROBLEM

Charlie Sojourner is employed as a professor. His employment contract provides that every six years he will be eligible for a one-semester "sabbatical" from teaching in order to devote his time to other scholarly pursuits. During one six-year period, he was absent for one year as a result of a number of FMLA leaves, and for another year as a result of a military leave. If the school's general rule is to subtract time not actually served (to the extent the law permits the school to subtract such time), how long will it be before Sojourner can take his sabbatical?

2. *Jury Duty*

The call for jury service affects a much wider swath of the workforce for periods that can be much less predictable than USERRA leave. Only a few states require an employer to continue an employee's pay for any amount of time during jury service, but about 70 percent of employees in private industry have paid jury leave benefits with their employers. Bureau of Statistics, Department of Labor, *News Release: Employee Benefits in Private Industry* (Sept. 17, 2003), at http://www.bls.gov/news.release/ebs2.t03.htm. Considering the generally low rate of juror pay provided by the court system, the lack of employer paid benefits for some jurors may have important implications not only for employers and employees but also for the jury system. Some commentators have worried that underpaid jurors will allow their frustrations to affect their participation in the justice system. *See, e.g.,* H. Mooney, W. Chen & S. Kraik, *A Jury of Our Peers: Is That Right?*, 71 Def. Counsel J. 106, 112 (2004). One study shows that persons called to jury service are much more likely be "no shows" if they are not eligible for paid leave from their employers. T. Eades, *Revisiting the Jury System in Texas: A Study of the Jury Pool in Dallas County*, 54 S.M.U. L. Rev. 1813 (2001). Moreover, the burden of undercompensated jury service weighs disproportionately on the working poor and minorities. According to a study of the jury system in Dallas, Texas, 17 percent of African Americans and 19 percent of Hispanic Americans received no pay from their employers while serving on a jury, but only 5.4 percent of Caucasian Americans served without pay from their employers.

If an employer discriminates or retaliates against an employee for failing to avoid jury service, such as by replacing the employee and refusing to rehire him after his service, federal law provides a remedy in the case of federal jury service, and most states have enacted laws to provide a remedy in the case of state court jury service. *See, e.g.*, 28 U.S.C. § 1875; D.C. Code Ann. § 11-1913(a); Iowa Code Ann. § 607A.45; Miss. Code Ann. § 13-5-23; Mo. Rev. Stat. § 494.460(1); Tenn. Code Ann. § 22-4-108(F)(1). Even in the absence of a protective statute, many courts hold that employer discrimination on the basis of jury service is a violation of public policy. *See, e.g.*, Nees v. Hocks, 272 Or. 210, 536 P.2d 512 (1975); Reuther v. Fowler & Williams, Inc., 255 Pa. Super. 28, 386 A.2d 119 (1978).

CHAPTER 8

Employment Security

A. INTRODUCTION

SCOTT A. MOSS & PETER H. HUANG, *HOW THE NEW ECONOMICS CAN IMPROVE EMPLOYMENT DISCRIMINATION LAW, AND HOW ECONOMICS CAN SURIVIVE THE DEMISE OF THE "RATIONAL ACTOR"*

51 William & Mary L. Rev. 183 (2009)

There is overwhelming empirical evidence that life satisfaction does not adapt to . . . an unemployment spell, including data from several large-scale national and multinational surveys. Unemployment has a long-term scarring psychological effect. . . . [O]ne fifteen-year longitudinal study found that, on average, people who suffer unemployment never fully returned to their former levels of life satisfaction, even after becoming re-employed. Past unemployment scars . . . because it increases fears of future unemployment. . . . This proposed explanation of scarring draws support from empirical findings that even when employed, people during recessions experience fear and upset about the prospect of unemployment, so unemployment rates decrease average happiness even for those still employed.

Unemployment . . . also worsens mental and physical health outcomes. The nonmonetary costs of unemployment far exceeded the monetary costs in numerous large-scale studies . . . based on United States General Social Survey (GSS) data, Britain Household Panel Survey (BHPS) data, Dutch data, German Socio-Economic Panel (GSEP) data, Italian data, Swedish data, and Swiss data . . . The effects of unemployment cut across not only nations, but social classes. One study found no evidence that social capital moderates the negative effects. . . .

The robust empirical finding that most people fail to adapt emotionally to unemployment is all the more surprising given the overwhelming data that people do adapt to most positive and negative events alike. . . . [However,] to adapt to loss, people must be able to make sense of it. . . . [T]hose who lose jobs due to discrimination are less likely to adapt than those who lose jobs for other reasons. They may understand that discrimination occurs, but that understanding makes it harder, not easier, to make sense of. . . This interpretation draws support from the literature on dignitary harms. . . . People feel particularly harmed by discrimination because of the animosity and hatred it expresses, and the illegitimacy of discrimination makes the loss harder to make sense of, which in turn magnifies the dignitary harms and subjective losses from unemployment. . . .

The Employment at Will Doctrine

Do employees have a right against unfair discharge? Studies of employee perceptions about job security indicate they have a strong sense of legal entitlement to job security, at least in the sense that an employer cannot be unfair in selecting employees for discharge or layoff.[1] Employee beliefs are affected, no doubt, by their general awareness of laws against illegal discrimination and retaliation. When it comes to legal remedies against merely "unfair" discharge, however, the confidence employees have in their rights may be misplaced. By one estimate, 85 percent of all nonunion employment contracts leave employees subject to an employer's right to discharge "at will."[2]

The origin of the employment at will doctrine, and the question whether its existence in the United States was accidental or inevitable, are matters much in dispute.[3] By some accounts, a proper historical understanding of the doctrine begins with a look at an older "English" rule favoring employment for fixed terms of a year. The English rule presuming fixed annual terms appears to have its origin in the Statute of Labourers, 23 Edw. III (1349), and the Statute of Artificers, 5 Eliz. c. 4 (1562). Parliament enacted these feudal-era laws in response to labor shortages and wage inflation caused by deadly epidemics. The Statute of Labourers prohibited unemployment. It provided that every worker "shall be bound to serve him that doth require him;" with a preference favoring the local lord's call to duty. The law also forbade a worker to quit before the end of the "term agreed." Violation of this rule exposed the worker to imprisonment.

The Statute of Artificers, enacted more than two centuries later, was a bit more evenhanded. It required employment for an annual term, and the master as well as the servant was subject to punishment for breaching this obligation. For a master, however, there was no risk of imprisonment. A master's penalty for untimely discharge of a servant was about 40 shillings. Still another 200 years later, Blackstone described the situation as follows:

> If the hiring be general without any particular time limited, the law construes it to be a hiring for a year . . . throughout all the revolutions of the respective seasons, as well when there is work to be done, as when there is not.[4]

The rule described by Blackstone was merely a *presumption* in favor of an annual term, because the parties could agree to a shorter or longer term. For most employments in a feudal, agricultural society, there were practical reasons for presuming an annual term. Otherwise, a master might exploit his servant's services during the work-intensive planting or harvesting season only to discharge the

---

[1] Frank S. Forbes & Ida M. Jones, *A Comparative, Attitudinal and Analytical Study of Dismissal of At-Will Employees Without Cause*, 37 Lab. L.J. 157, 165-166 (1986); Pauline T. Kim, *Bargaining with Imperfect Information: A Study of Worker Perceptions of Legal Protection in an At-Will World*, 83 Cornell L. Rev. 105 (1997).

[2] J. Houlte Verkerke, *An Empirical Perspective on Indefinite Term Employment Contracts: Resolving the Just Cause Debate*, 1995 Wis. L. Rev. 837, 867-870.

[3] A sampling of the vast literature on the subject includes Deborah A. Ballam, *Exploding the Original Myth Regarding Employment-at-Will: The True Origins of the Doctrine*, 17 Berkeley J. Empl. & Lab. L. 91 (1996); Mayer G. Freed & Daniel D. Polsby, *The Doubtful Provenance of "Wood's Rule" Revisited*, 22 Ariz. St. L.J. 551 (1990); Jay Feinman, *The Development of the Employment at Will Doctrine*, 20 Am. J. Legal Hist. 118, 120 (1976); Andrew P. Morriss, *Exploding Myths: An Empirical and Economic Reassessment of the Rise of Employment-at-Will*, 59 Mo. L. Rev. 679 (1994).

[4] 1 William Blackstone, Commentaries 413 (1765).

servant during a seasonal lull.[5] Even in England, however, not all jobs were subject to the "annual term" presumption. The character of the work, the nature of the worker's profession and other circumstances might lead to a different kind of presumption.[6] Of course, a fixed term of employment provided very limited job security. The master could decline to renew the term "at will," and his decision might be as surprising and disappointing to the worker on the 365th day as on any other day of the year. English courts began to recognize that a more important rule for the protection of either party was the amount of "notice" due in advance of termination. Requisite notice periods varied according to the contract and the occupation or industry, and ranged from a few weeks to a few minutes (the latter notice period in some industries saving labor strikers from criminal prosecution).[7]

In the United States, the law of job security seems to have been uncertain before the end of the nineteenth century. The American legal system initially viewed job security primarily as a choice between two presumptions: one favoring an annual term; another favoring no term, leaving the parties free to terminate at will. An important change occurred as of about 1877, when a legal treatise writer named Horace Wood wrote, "With us the rule is inflexible, that a general or indefinite hiring is prima facie a hiring at will, and if the servant seeks to make it out a yearly hiring, the burden is upon him to establish it by proof."[8] Wood's description eventually became the clearly dominant view of American courts.

An important implication of the presumed right to terminate "at will" was that neither party's reason for terminating the relationship was important as far as the law was concerned. In contrast, if parties agreed to employment for a fixed term, their agreement implied that the employer could not discharge the employee and the employee could not resign before the end of the term without "good" or "just" cause.[9] But even in fixed term employment either party remained free not to renew employment at the end of each fixed term.

Fixed term agreements, which are one alternative to employment at will, have never been a completely satisfactory way to achieve long-term employment security for most employees. Extending the term for more than a year is difficult to the extent it requires the parties to fix other important aspects of the relationship, such as the rate of pay and particular duties, far into the future. Moreover, as much as an employee might value job security, he might be reluctant to bind himself to the same employer for a long term if he must forgo future opportunities for better work and better pay. In any event, the end of a fixed term of any duration leaves the parties in much the same position as they occupy in a relationship at will.[10] The

[5] *See* Jay Feinman, *The Development of the Employment at Will Doctrine*, 20 Am. J. Legal Hist. 118, 120 (1976).

[6] *Id.* at 120-122.

[7] *Id.*

[8] Wood, Master & Servant (1877), § 134, p. 272.

[9] Williams v. Luckett, 26 So. 967 (Miss. 1899); Carson v. McCormick Harvesting Mach. Co., 36 Mo. App. 462 (Mo. App. 1889); Knutson v. Knapp, 35 Wis. 86 (Wis. 1874). Employees can also breach a fixed term agreement by resigning. *See, e.g.*, Handicapped Children's Educ. Bd. v. Lukaszewski, 332 N.W.2d 774 (Wis. 1983); Equity Ins. Mgrs. v. McNichols, 755 N.E.2d 75 (Ill. 2001).

[10] *See* Gilmartin v. KVTV-Channel 13, 985 S.W.2d 553 (Tex. App. 1998); McKinney v. Statesman Pub. Co., 56 P. 651 (Or. 1899).

more important issue in modern times has been whether an employer could have a *perpetual* duty not to discharge an employee without just cause, and whether a contract might impose this duty on the employer without prohibiting an employee from resigning without cause.

For most of the century following Wood's declaration, employees asserting a contractual right to lifetime job security faced at least two obstacles. The first was the judiciary's skepticism that an employer would actually assent to such a duty or could reasonably be understood to assent to such a duty.[11] The second was the judiciary's doubt that an employer could be bound to an employee for life or until retirement without the employee's reciprocal promise to remain in the employer's service for an equal term. In the view of many judges, a lack of obligation on the part of the employee rendered the employer's promise of job security unenforceable for lack of consideration according to a doctrine of "mutuality."[12]

In one situation, however, courts were likely to deem a promise of lifetime job security to be enforceable: Where the employer's promise was in exchange for an employee's release of claims for personal injuries resulting from an industrial accident.[13] The employee in such an exchange gave something substantially more than his mere continuation of service. He had relinquished his right to damages that included his loss of earning capacity, and it was particularly credible that the parties intended and understood that the employee should receive in return more than the usual employment at will.

A more important example and precedent for long-term contractual job security arrangements in the early twentieth century was the emerging system of collective bargaining. By the 1930s, it was increasingly common for unions to negotiate provisions prohibiting discharge without just cause and awarding seniority protection against layoffs. Although union contracts usually ran from one fixed term to another, the practical effect of a just cause provision in an ongoing collective bargaining relationship was long term job security until the worker retired or the employer ceased its business. By the Wagner Act in 1937, a few courts had held a promise of job security enforceable against an employer in the context of collective bargaining even though employees remained free to resign.[14]

---

[11] Chesapeake & Potomac Tel. Co. of Baltimore City v. Murray, 84 A.2d 870 (Md. 1951); St. Louis, B & M Ry. v. Booker, 5 S.W.2d 856, 858 (Tex. Civ. App. 1928).

[12] *See, e.g.*, Meadows v. Radio Indus., Inc., 222 F.2d 347 (7th Cir. 1955); Louisville & N.R. Co. v. Bryant, 92 S.W.2d 749 (Ky. App. 1936); Skagerberg v. Blandin Paper Co., 266 N.W. 872 (Minn. 1936); Combs v. Standard Oil Co. of Louisiana, 59 S.W.2d 525, 526 (1933); Hazen v. Cobb, 117 So. 853, 855 (Fla. 1928); Arentz v. Morse Dry Dock & Repair Co., 164 N.E. 342 (N.Y. 1928); St. Louis, I.M. & S. Ry. Co. v. Mathews, 42 S.W. 902 (Ark. 1897); Lord v. Goldberg, 22 P. 1126 (1889). *Cf.* Fry v. Howes, 25 Pa. C.C. 493 (Pa. Com. Pl. 1901) (contract binding employee to a fixed one-year term, but not binding employer, lacked mutuality); Jennings v. Bethel, 17 Ohio C.D. 239 (Ohio Cir. Ct. 1904) (same).

[13] Lake Erie & W. Ry. Co. v. Tierney, 19 Ohio C.D. 83 (1905); Rhodes v. Cheasapeake & O. Ry. Co., 39 S.E. 209 (W. Va.1901); Smith v. St. Paul & D.R. Co., 62 N.W. 392 (Minn. 1895); Penn. Co. v. Dolan, 6 Ind. App. 109, 32 N.E. 802 (1892). *But see* East Line & R.R. Co. v. Scott, 10 S.W. 99 (Tex. 1888) (construing such a settlement as creating option for employee to fix a mutually binding term of employment if and when he returned to work).

[14] *See, e.g.*, McGlohn v. Gulf & S.I.R.R., 174 So. 250 (Miss. 1937); Rentschler v. Missouri Pac. R. Co., 253 N.W. 694 (Neb. 1934); Johnson v. Am. Ry. Express Co., 161 S.E. 473 (S.C. 1931); St. Louis, B.&M. Ry. v. Booker, 5 S.W.2d 856 (Tex. Civ. App. 1928).

Upholding the enforceability of such an employer promise may have been essential to labor peace. If organized employees could not protect each other through contractual grievance and arbitration procedures, they might have resorted to strikes to challenge each discharge.[15] Any remaining doubts about just cause provisions in union contracts were eliminated as a practical matter by the Wagner Act's clear endorsement of collective bargaining and the establishment of the NLRB to regulate and enforce collective bargaining duties. By 1979, about 80 percent of collective bargaining agreements required just cause for discharge.[16]

Yet another precedent for long-term protection against discharge without cause was the emerging civil service system, built on statutory or regulatory terms of employment rather than private contract. Federal employees began to enjoy civil service protection against discharge without just cause under President McKinley in 1897.[17] By 1979, over 90 percent of federal civilian employees enjoyed civil service protection against any "adverse action" by their employer, and at least half of state and local government employees enjoyed similar protection.[18]

B. OVERCOMING THE PRESUMPTION

1. *Employer Promises of Job Security*

TOUSSAINT v. BLUE CROSS & BLUE SHIELD OF MICHIGAN

292 N.W.2d 880 (Mich. 1980)

LEVIN, Justice.

Charles Toussaint was employed in a middle management position with Blue Cross and Walter Ebling was similarly employed by Masco. After being employed five and two years, respectively, each was discharged. They commenced actions against their former employers, claiming that the discharges violated their employment agreements which permitted discharge only for cause. A verdict of $72,835.52 was rendered for Toussaint and a verdict of $300,000 for Ebling whose discharge left him ineligible to exercise a stock option. Different panels of the Court of Appeals reversed *Toussaint* and affirmed *Ebling*.

I

In Lynas v. Maxwell Farms [273 N.W. 315 (1937)], this Court said that "(c)ontracts for permanent employment or for life have been construed by the courts on many occasions. In general, it may be said that in the absence of distinguishing features or provisions or a consideration in addition to the services to be rendered, such contracts are indefinite hirings, terminable at the will of either party." . . .

Lynas indicates, our colleague states, and we agree, that the "general" rule there set forth concerning the terminability of a hiring deemed to be for an

---

[15] *See* Dennis Nolan & Roger Abrams, *American Arbitration: The Early Years*, 35 U. Fla. L. Rev. 373 (1983).

[16] Peck, *Unjust Discharges from Employment: A Necessary Change in the Law,* 40 Ohio St. L.J. 1, 8 (1979).

[17] *See Developments — Public Employment*, 97 Harv. L. Rev. 1611, 1614-1633 (1984).

[18] Peck, *Unjust Discharges from Employment*, *supra*, 40 Ohio St. L.J. at 8-9.

indefinite term is not a substantive limitation on the enforceability of employment contracts but merely a rule of "construction." . . . Both Toussaint and Ebling inquired regarding job security when they were hired. Toussaint testified that he was told he would be with the company "as long as I did my job." Ebling testified that he was told that if he was "doing the job" he would not be discharged. Toussaint's testimony, like Ebling's, made submissible to the jury whether there was an agreement for a contract of employment terminable only for cause.

Toussaint's case is, if anything, stronger because he was handed a manual of Blue Cross personnel policies which reinforced the oral assurance of job security. It stated that the disciplinary procedures applied to all Blue Cross employees who had completed their probationary period and that it was the "policy" of the company to release employees "for just cause only."

Our colleague acknowledges that, apart from an express agreement, an employee's legitimate expectations grounded in an employer's written policy statements have been held to give rise to an enforceable contract. He states, however, that the cases so holding are distinguishable because they concern deferred compensation (termination pay, death benefits and profit-sharing benefits) that "the employers should reasonably have expected would induce reliance by the employee in joining or remaining in the employer's service." He does not explain why an employer should reasonably expect that a promise of deferred compensation would induce reliance while a promise of job security would not.

II

Masco and Blue Cross contend . . . where one party (the employer) obligates himself to continue the relationship as long as the other desires and the other (the employee) reserves the right to terminate at will, there is no mutuality of obligation and so the agreement must fail for lack of consideration. So explained, the *Lynas* "rule" for which the employers contend appears to be a principle of substantive contract law rather than a rule of construction.

The enforceability of a contract depends, however, on consideration and not mutuality of obligation. The proper inquiry is whether the employee has given consideration for the employer's promise of employment. The "rule" is useful, however, as a rule of construction. Because the parties began with complete freedom, the court will presume that they intended to obligate themselves to a relationship at will. To the extent that courts have seen the rule as one of substantive law rather than construction, they have misapplied language and principles found in earlier cases where the courts were merely attempting to discover and implement the intent of the parties.

A

If no definite time is expressed, the court must construe the agreement. Early cases took several approaches. Some followed the English rule that the term was presumed to be a year. Others looked to the period of payment and designated that the term. If payment was monthly, the contract was monthly, renewable each month as the relationship continued. Other courts, including the Michigan Court, assessed or allowed a jury to assess the evidence and determine the intent of the parties.

In Franklin Mining Co. v. Harris this Court concluded that the jury could find that the hiring, although for an indefinite term, was "for at least a year." Harris testified that he hesitated to give up his existing position, apparently a permanent one, for uncertain employment, that he told the agent negotiating the employment for the company that "the Franklin mine management changed so often he did not know what might happen," that the agent replied, "there was no fear of that; he would see the plaintiff all right. . . ."

Shortly thereafter, Horace Gay Wood wrote in his treatise on master-servant relations: "With us the rule is inflexible, that a general or indefinite hiring is prima facie a hiring at will, and if the servant seeks to make it out a yearly hiring, the burden is upon him to establish it by proof. A hiring at so much a day, week, month or year, no time being specified, is an indefinite hiring, and no presumption attaches that it was for a day even, but only at the rate fixed for whatever time the party may serve."[12]

Franklin Mining was one of the four American cases cited by Wood as authority. To the extent the issue of the term of employment was even present in these cases, the juries were permitted to determine the duration of the contract from written or oral communications between the parties, usages of trade, the type of employment, and other circumstances. Like many rules, however, Wood's rule was quickly cited as authority for another proposition. Some courts saw the rule as requiring the employee to prove an express contract for a definite term in order to maintain an action based on termination of the employment. The "rule" was applied in cases where the claim was one of "permanent" or lifetime employment, a term of employment inherently indefinite . . . .

In all events, the issue in all these cases was whether, assuming a contract for "permanent" employment, that employment was terminable at the will of the employer, not whether, as here, assuming an employment contract for an indefinite term, the employment must be terminable at will so that the employer could not enter into a legally enforceable agreement to terminate the employment only for cause.

The court's task in the cited cases was to construe "permanent" consistent with the circumstances surrounding the formation of the contract; where the parties appeared to intend only steady employment, the general rule that the relationship is terminable at will was applied. No authority is cited by Blue Cross, Masco or our colleague for the proposition that where an employer has agreed that an employee hired for an indefinite term shall not be discharged except for cause the employer may, nevertheless, terminate the employment without cause.

B

The amici curiae argue in support of the employers that permitting the discharge of employees hired for an indefinite term only for cause will adversely affect the productivity and competency of the work force.

Employers are most assuredly free to enter into employment contracts terminable at will without assigning cause. . . . [However,] [w]e see no reason why an employment contract which does not have a definite term — the term is "indefinite" — cannot legally provide job security. When a prospective employee inquires about job security and the employer agrees that the employee shall be

[12] Wood, Master & Servant (1877), § 134, p. 272.

employed as long as he does the job, a fair construction is that the employer has agreed to give up his right to discharge at will without assigning cause and may discharge only for cause (good or just cause). The result is that the employee, if discharged without good or just cause, may maintain an action for wrongful discharge. . . .

Where the employment is for a definite term — a year, 5 years, 10 years — it is implied, if not expressed, that the employee can be discharged only for good cause and collective bargaining agreements often provide that discharge shall only be for good or just cause. There is, thus, no public policy against providing job security or prohibiting an employer from agreeing not to discharge except for good or just cause. That being the case, we can see no reason why such a provision in a contract having no definite term of employment with a single employee should necessarily be unenforceable and regarded, in effect, as against public policy and beyond the power of the employer to contract.

Toussaint and Ebling were hired for responsible positions. They negotiated specifically regarding job security with the persons who interviewed and hired them. If Blue Cross or Masco had desired, they could have established a company policy of requiring prospective employees to acknowledge that they served at the will or the pleasure of the company and, thus, have avoided the misunderstandings that generated this litigation. . . . It may indeed not be practicable to enter into a written contract in many kinds of hirings, and there is a risk that a claimed oral promise of job security may be false. Most lawsuits, civil and criminal, however, depend largely, often entirely, on testimonial evidence. Only a few kinds of claims cannot be proven solely by testimony. A promise of job security is not a claim barred unless in writing.

III

We have already indicated that we do not agree with our colleague's conclusion in *Toussaint* that "the record is wholly devoid of evidence, direct or circumstantial, to justify the conclusion that the parties agreed that the manual would become the plaintiff's contract of employment." . . . We do not, however, rest our conclusion that the jury could properly find that the Blue Cross policy manual created contractual rights solely on Toussaint's testimony concerning his conversation with the executive who interviewed and hired him.

While an employer need not establish personnel policies or practices, where an employer chooses to establish such policies and practices and makes them known to its employees, the employment relationship is presumably enhanced. The employer secures an orderly, cooperative and loyal work force, and the employee the peace of mind associated with job security and the conviction that he will be treated fairly. No pre-employment negotiations need take place and the parties' minds need not meet on the subject;[25] nor does it matter that the employee knows nothing of the particulars of the employer's policies and practices or that the employer may change them unilaterally. It is enough that the employer chooses, presumably in its own interest, to create an environment in which the employee believes that, whatever the personnel policies and practices, they are established

[25] It was therefore unnecessary for Toussaint to prove reliance on the policies . . . in the manual.

and official at any given time, purport to be fair, and are applied consistently and uniformly to each employee. The employer has then created a situation "instinct with an obligation."[26] . . .

We hold that employer statements of policy, such as the Blue Cross Supervisory Manual and Guidelines, can give rise to contractual rights in employees without evidence that the parties mutually agreed that the policy statements would create contractual rights in the employee, and, hence, although the statement of policy is signed by neither party, can be unilaterally amended by the employer without notice to the employee, and contains no reference to a specific employee, his job description or compensation, and although no reference was made to the policy statement in pre-employment interviews and the employee does not learn of its existence until after his hiring. . . .

The Blue Cross Manual . . . promised that the company would conduct itself in a certain way with the stated objective of achieving fairness. . . . Since Blue Cross published and distributed a 260-page manual establishing elaborate procedures promising "(t)o provide for the administration of fair, consistent and reasonable corrective discipline" and "to treat employees leaving Blue Cross in a fair and consistent manner and to release employees for just cause only," its employees could justifiably rely on those expressions and conduct themselves accordingly. Recognition that contractual obligations can be implicit in employer policies and practices is not confined to cases where compensation is in issue. . . . The right to continued employment absent cause for termination may, thus, because of stated employer policies and established procedures, be enforceable in contract just as are rights so derived to bonuses, pensions and other forms of compensation as previously held by Michigan courts.

One amicus curiae argues that large organizations regularly distribute memoranda, bulletins and manuals reflecting established conditions and periodic changes in policy. These documents are drafted "for clarity and accuracy and to properly advise those subject to the policy memo of its contents." If such memoranda are held . . . to form part of the employment contract, large employers will be severely hampered by the resultant inability to issue policy statements.

An employer who establishes no personnel policies instills no reasonable expectations of performance. Employers can make known to their employees that personnel policies are subject to unilateral changes by the employer. Employees would then have no legitimate expectation that any particular policy will continue to remain in force. Employees could, however, legitimately expect that policies in force at any given time will be uniformly applied to all. If there is in effect a policy to dismiss for cause only, the employer may not depart from that policy at whim simply because he was under no obligation to institute the policy in the first place. Having announced the policy, presumably with a view to obtaining the benefit of improved employee attitudes and behavior and improved quality of the work force, the employer may not treat its promise as illusory . . . .

The amici curiae and employers express fears that enforcing contracts requiring cause for discharge will lead to employee incompetence and inefficiency.

---

[26] Wood v. Lucy, Lady Duff-Gordon, 118 N.E. 214 (1917); McCall Co. v. Wright, 117 N.Y.S. 775 (N.Y. App. 1909).

First, no employer is obliged to enter into such a contract. Second, those who do, we agree, must be permitted to establish their own standards for job performance and to dismiss for non-adherence to those standards although another employer or the jury might have established lower standards. . . . The employer's standard of job performance can be made part of the contract. Breach of the employer's uniformly applied rules is a breach of the contract and cause for discharge. In such a case, the question for the jury is whether the employer actually had a rule or policy and whether the employee was discharged for violating it. . . .

Additionally, the employer can avoid the perils of jury assessment by providing for an alternative method of dispute resolution. A written agreement for a definite or indefinite term to discharge only for cause could, for example, provide for binding arbitration on the issues of cause and damages.

. . . The question of cause for discharge was thus properly one for the jury. It was for the jury to resolve the factual issues whether there was a contract and . . . whether there was cause for discharge. . . .

We affirm Ebling and remand Toussaint to the trial court with instructions to reinstate the verdict.

NOTES AND QUESTIONS

1. Employers frequently issue policy manuals describing the employer's expectations of employees, rules of conduct, job benefits available to employees, and, as *Toussaint* illustrates, assurances about job security. If policies do not constitute contracts, what else might they be? *See* Chapter 4.B.1.

Long before *Toussaint*, courts had easily accepted that employer "policies" and "general rules" could be enforced as contracts insofar as the rules or policies described compensation and benefits. Anthony v. Jersey Central Power & Light Co., 143 A.2d 762 (N.J. Super. 1958); Cowles v. Morris & Co., 161 N.E. 150 (Ill. 1928). However, when an employer policy in a handbook or manual assures employees that the employer will treat them fairly and not discharge them without cause, courts were more likely to reject an employee's argument that the policy was part of a contract. *See, e.g.*, Trader v. People Working Cooperatively, Inc., 663 N.E.2d 335, 337-338 (Ohio App1994); Reynolds Mfg. Co. v. Mendoza, 644 S.W.2d 536 (Tex. App. 1982); Salazar v. Amigos Del Valle, Inc., 754 S.W.2d 410 (Tex. App. 1988).Why might courts be more hesitant to grant that an employer policy is part of the contract of employment when the policy addresses matters of discipline and job security rather than compensation and benefits?

2. *Toussaint*'s holding that an employee need not prove "reliance" on a particular handbook provision is consistent with the modern rule of contracts that "bargained for exchange" makes a promise enforceable with or without reliance. *See* Chapter 4.B.1. If a promise was the result of an express or implied bargain, it is unnecessary for the promisee to prove he acted differently and to his detriment because of the promise. For example, if the employer handed a policy manual to the employee in the course of a job interview and said, "look this over as you decide whether to accept our job offer," it might be clear that the policy manual was part of the resulting employment "bargain" even if the employee failed to read the provision on disciplinary discharge before accepting the job. *See* Woolley v.

Hoffmann-La Roche, Inc., 491 A.2d 1257, 1268 n.10 (N.J. 1985), *modified*, 499 A.2d 515 (N.J. 1988) ("[E]mployees neither had to read [the manual], know of its existence, or rely on it to benefit from its provisions any more than employees in a plant that is unionized have to read or rely on a collective-bargaining agreement in order to obtain its benefits."). But employers do not always present policy manuals in this fashion. In a dissenting opinion in *Toussaint*, Justice Ryan wrote,

> [t]he record bears no evidence that during Mr. Toussaint's several preemployment interviews any reference was made either to the Manual or Guidelines, or even to the subject of a written employment contract. Mr. Toussaint did not learn of the existence of the Manual and Guidelines until they were handed to him after he was hired....

292 N.W.2d at 906. How did the majority in *Toussaint* reach the conclusion that the handbook became part of the Toussaint's bargain with his employer?

3. In the absence of other circumstances showing an employee "bargained for" an employer's policies, some courts are inclined to require the employee to prove actual reliance on the policies in accepting or continuing employment. *See, e.g.*, Bulman v. Safeway, Inc., 27 P.3d 1172 (Wash. 2001). While it might seem easy for an employee merely to assert he "relied" on the handbook, he must have known of the policy to rely on it. *Id. See also* Continental Air Lines, Inc. v. Keenan, 731 P.2d 708 (Colo. 1987) (employee can state a claim by showing *either* bargained-for exchange *or* reliance with respect to employer's discharge policy).

4. The Restatement (Third) of Employment Law adopts the view that standardized employer "policies" are promises forming a binding contract:

> Policy statements by an employer in documents such as employee manuals, personnel handbooks, and employer policy directives that are provided or made accessible to employees, whether by physical or electronic means, and that, reasonably read in context, establish limits on the employer's power to terminate the employment relationship, are binding on the employer until modified or revoked.

RESTATEMENT OF THE LAW, EMPLOYMENT LAW § 2.05; *id.* § 2.05

The Restatement's commentary notes that court decisions supporting this approach are split as to the rationale. Some courts treating "policies" as binding describe the policies as unilateral contracts based on an exchange of consideration, while others use the concept of "estoppel" based on the promisee's reasonable and substantial "reliance." *Id.* § 2.05 cmt. b. The Restatement appears to favor the latter. The choice between these doctrines could be very important depending on an employee's ability to prove he acted differently because of reasonable and substantial reliance on a policy. Moreover, damages for "reliance" tend to be less than damages based on loss of expectation in a contract based on an exchange of consideration. *See* Stephen F. Befort, *Employee Handbooks and Policy Statements: From Gratuities to Contracts and Back Again*, 21 Emp. Rts. & Emp. Pol. J. __ (forthcoming 2018).

5. In determining whether an employer's statement of policies was part of the employment contract, is it important whether the employer issued the statement for general distribution? What if the employer issued the policy statement to supervisors, but employees became aware of the policy? That was the situation in

Woolley v. Hoffman-LaRoche, Inc., 491 A.2d 1257 (N.J.1985), where the court held that a manual issued to supervisors became part of the employment contract for nonsupervisors. *Id.* at 1265. *Accord* Huey v. Honeywell, Inc., 82 F.3d 327 (9th Cir. 1996) (employees were informed of company's disciplinary procedures through supervisors). But many courts hold that a handbook is not part of an employee's contract unless the employer provided the handbook in a context that suggested the handbook was part of a bargain with the employee. *See, e.g.*, Lytle v. Malady, 579 N.W.2d 906, 912 (Mich. 1998); Morosetti v. Louisiana Land and Exploration Co., 564 A.2d 151 (Pa. 1989); Labus v. Navistar Int'l Transp. Corp., 740 F. Supp. 1053, 1062 (D.N.J. 1990); Boone v. Frontier Refining, Inc., 987 P.2d 681 (Wy. 1999); Sabetay v. Sterling Drug, Inc., 506 N.E.2d 919 (N.Y. 1987).

6. If an employer promises lifetime job security, what *kind* of job is the employer promising over the life of the employment? Does a promise of job security constitute any guarantee against disappointments or unpleasing changes in employment? The Supreme Court of New Jersey considered this problem in Woolley v. Hoffman-LaRoche, Inc., 491 A.2d 1257 (N.J. 1985):

> The lack of definiteness concerning the other terms of employment—its duration, wages, precise service to be rendered, hours of work, etc., does not prevent enforcement of a job security provision. The lack of terms (if the complete manual is similarly lacking) can cause problems of interpretation about these other aspects of employment, but not to the point of making the job security term unenforceable. . . . If there is a problem arising from indefiniteness, in any event, it is one caused by the employer. It was the employer who chose to make the termination provisions explicit and clear. If indefiniteness as to other provisions is a problem, it is one of the employer's own making from which it should gain no advantage.

Id. at 1269.

What if an employer, having promised not to discharge without cause, takes a lesser disciplinary action against an employee without cause? *See* Scott v. Pacific Gas & Elec. Co., 904 P. 2d 834 (Cal. 1995) (implied promise not to discharge without just cause also barred wrongful demotion). What if the employer merely denies the employee the annual raise he expected?

7. If an employer promises not to discharge or discipline without just cause, is the employee required to exhaust the employer's internal dispute resolution procedure before challenging a disciplinary action by a lawsuit? Yes, according to O'Brien v. New England Telephone & Telegraph, 664 N.E.2d 843 (Mass. 1996):

> O'Brien did not follow the grievance procedure, and that omission … is fatal to her claim that NET violated the terms of her employment. O'Brien knew of the grievance procedure (she had notice of it in any event) and had used it successfully. She cannot assert a right against unfair treatment under one part of her employment contract and fail to follow procedures set forth in another part …. The grievance procedure was not optional ….

Id. at 849.

It is now common for employers to establish a system of arbitration of employment disputes of all kinds, including wrongful discharge. Whether an employer's arbitration procedure is part of the employment contract, whether the employee must exhaust the procedure before seeking judicial relief, and whether an arbitration result is binding against an employee is discussed in Chapter 10.

8. Note that Toussaint and Ebling relied not only on written promises but also oral promises of job security. Oral promises are not only more likely to be disputed; they are also more likely to raise an issue under the Statute of Frauds.

OHANIAN v. AVIS RENT A CAR SYSTEM, INC.

779 F.2d 101 (2d Cir. 1985)

CARDAMONE, Circuit Judge:

Defendant Avis Rent A Car System (Avis) appeals from a judgment entered on a jury verdict in the Eastern District of New York (Weinstein, Ch. J.) awarding $304,693 in damages to plaintiff Robert S. Ohanian for lost wages and pension benefits arising from defendant's breach of a lifetime employment contract made orally to plaintiff. The jury also awarded Ohanian $23,100 in bonuses and moving expenses that did not depend on the oral contract. Avis argues that the alleged oral contract is barred by the statute of frauds, is inadmissible under the parol evidence rule and, in any event, that the evidence is insufficient to establish a promise of lifetime employment. . . . [W]e affirm.

Plaintiff Ohanian began working for Avis in Boston in 1967. Later he was appointed District Sales Manager in New York, and subsequently moved to San Francisco. By 1980 he had become Vice President of Sales for Avis's Western Region. Robert Mahmarian, a former Avis general manager, testified that Ohanian's performance in that region was excellent. During what Mahmarian characterized as "a very bad, depressed economic period," Ohanian's Western Region stood out as the one region that was growing and profitable. According to the witness, Ohanian was directly responsible for this success.

In the fall of 1980, Avis's Northeast Region—the region with the most profit potential—was "dying." Mahmarian and then Avis President Calvano decided that the Northeast Region needed new leadership and Ohanian was the logical candidate. They thought plaintiff should return to New York as Vice President of Sales for the Northeast Region. According to Mahmarian, "nobody anticipated how tough it would be to get the guy." Ohanian was happy in the Western Region, and for several reasons did not want to move. First, he had developed a good "team" in the Western Region; second, he and his family liked the San Francisco area; and third, he was secure in his position where he was doing well and did not want to get involved in the politics of the Avis "World Headquarters," which was located in the Northeast Region. Mahmarian and Calvano were determined to bring Ohanian east and so they set out to overcome his reluctance. After several phone calls to him, first from then Vice President of Sales McNamara, then from Calvano, and finally Mahmarian, Ohanian was convinced to accept the job in the Northeast Region. In Mahmarian's words, he changed Ohanian's mind

> [on] the basis of promise, that a good man is a good man, and he has proven his ability, and if it didn't work out and he had to go back out in the field, or back to California, or whatever else, fine. As far as I was concerned, his future was secure in the company, unless—and I always had to qualify—

> unless he screwed up badly. Then he is on his own, and even then I indicated that at worst he would get his [severance] because there was some degree of responsibility on the part of management, Calvano and myself, in making this man make this change.

Ohanian's concerns about security were met by Mahmarian's assurance that "[u]nless [he] screwed up badly, there is no way [he was] going to get fired . . . [he would] never get hurt here in this company." Ohanian accepted the offer and began work in the Northeast Region in early February 1981. . . .

Seven months after Ohanian moved to the Northeast Region, he was promoted to National Vice President of Sales and began work at Avis World Headquarters in Garden City, New York. He soon became dissatisfied with this position and in June 1982, pursuant to his request, returned to his former position as Vice President of Sales for the Northeast Region. A month later, on July 27, 1982, at 47 years of age, plaintiff was fired without severance pay. He then instituted this action. . . .

Defendant's principal argument is that the oral contract that the jury found existed is barred under the statute of frauds, § 5-701 (subd. a, para. 1) of the General Obligations Law. Section 5-701 provides in relevant part:

> Every agreement, promise or undertaking is void, unless it or some note or memorandum thereof be in writing, and subscribed by the party to be charged therewith, or by his lawful agent, if such agreement, promise or undertaking . . . [b]y its terms is not to be performed within one year from the making thereof or the performance of which is not to be completed before the end of a lifetime.

It has long been held that the purpose of the statute is to raise a barrier to fraud when parties attempt to prove certain legal transactions that are deemed to be particularly susceptible to deception, mistake, and perjury. *See* D & N Boening, Inc. v. Kirsch Beverages, 472 N.E.2d 992 (N.Y. 1984). The provision making void any oral contract "not to be performed within one year" is to prevent injustice that might result either from a faulty memory or the absence of witnesses that have died or moved. *See id.*; 2 Corbin on Contracts § 444, at 534 (1950).

The fact that inconsistent theories have been advanced to explain the statute's enactment perhaps sheds light on modern courts' strict construction of it. Parliament enacted An Act for Prevention of Frauds and Perjuries in 1677 that required certain contracts to be evidenced by a signed writing. One theory for its enactment was that evidence of oral contracts tended to be susceptible to perjury and inherently unreliable. *See, e.g.*, Burns v. McCormick, 135 N.E. 273 (N.Y. 1922) (Cardozo, J.) (passage of the statute of frauds was necessary because of the "peril of perjury . . . latent in the spoken promise"). This view is premised on the theory that an interested plaintiff will testify untruthfully about the existence of an oral contract. Another view derives from the fact that in a seventeenth century jury trial the parties and all others interested in the outcome were incompetent to testify as witnesses. T. Plucknett, A Concise History of the Common Law, 55-56 (2d ed. 1936). To overcome that hurdle, so this theory goes, parties desiring legal protection for their transactions had to embody them in documents whose contents and authenticity were easily ascertainable. *Id.* at 56.

Whatever may be the fact with regard to the history of the statute, and whatever may have been the difficulties arising from proof that all sides agree brought about the enactment of the statute of frauds over 300 years ago, it is an anachronism today. The reasons that prompted its passage no longer exist. And, far from serving as a barrier to fraud—in the case of a genuinely aggrieved plaintiff barred from enforcing an oral contract—the statute may actually shield fraud.

In fact, New York courts perhaps also believing that strict application of the statute causes more fraud than it prevents, have tended to construe it warily. . . . It was long ago established that

> [i]t is not the meaning of the statute that the contract must be performed within a year. . . . [I]f the obligation of the contract is not, by its very terms, or necessary construction, to endure for a longer period than one year, it is a valid agreement, although it may be capable of an indefinite continuance.

Trustees of First Baptist Church v. Brooklyn Fire Ins. Co., 19 N.Y. 305, 307 (1859). Therefore, a contract to continue for longer than a year, that is terminable at the will of the party against whom it is being enforced, is not barred by the statute of frauds because it is capable of being performed within one year. *See* North Shore Bottling Co. v. C. Schmidt & Sons, Inc., 239 N.E.2d 189 (N.Y. 1968). Similarly, it has been held that a contract which provides that either party may rightfully terminate within the year falls outside the statute. Blake v. Voigt, 31 N.E. 256 (N.Y. 1892); *see* 2 Corbin on Contracts § 449, at 564.

When does an oral contract not to be performed within a year fall within the strictures of the statute? A contract is not "to be performed within a year" if it is terminable within that time only upon the breach of one of the parties. *Boening*, 472 N.E.2d 992. That rule derives from logic because "[p]erformance, if it means anything at all, is 'carrying out the contract by doing what it requires or permits' . . . and a breach is the unexcused failure to do so." *Id.* (citing Blake v. Voigt, 31 N.E. 256). The distinction is between an oral contract that provides for its own termination at any time on the one hand, and an oral contract that is terminable within a year only upon its breach on the other. The former may be proved by a plaintiff and the latter is barred by the statute.

Avis contends that its oral agreement with Ohanian is barred by the statute of frauds because it was not performable within a year. . . . What defendant fails to recognize is that under New York law "just cause" for termination may exist for reasons other than an employee's breach. . . . [J]ust cause for dismissing Ohanian would plainly include any breach of the contract, such as drinking on the job or refusing to work, since the agreement contemplates plaintiff giving his best efforts. But . . . just cause can be broader than breach and here there may be just cause to dismiss without a breach. To illustrate, under the terms of the contract it would be possible that despite plaintiff's best efforts the results achieved might prove poor because of adverse market conditions. From defendant's standpoint that too would force Avis to make a change in its business strategy, perhaps reducing or closing an operation. That is, there would be just cause for plaintiff's dismissal. But if this is what occurred, it would not constitute a breach of the agreement. Best efforts were contemplated by the parties, results were not. Defendant was anxious to have plaintiff relocate because of his past success, but plaintiff made no guarantee to produce certain results. Thus, this oral contract could have been terminated for just cause within one year, without any breach by plaintiff, and is therefore not barred by the statute of frauds. . . .

Avis says that inasmuch as the evidence of an oral promise of lifetime employment was insufficient as a matter of law, that issue should not have gone to the jury. It relies on Brown v. Safeway Stores, Inc., 190 F. Supp. 295 (E.D.N.Y. 1960), as support for this argument. Defendant can draw little solace from *Brown*. In that case the claimed assurances were made in several ways including meetings of a group of employees—the purpose of which was not to discuss length of employment—or during casual conversation. *Id.* at 299-300. The conversations were not conducted in an atmosphere, as here, of critical one-on-one negotiation regarding the terms of future employment. Further, in *Brown* the district court found as a matter of fact that the alleged promise of lifetime employment was never made. In contrast, in the instant case the evidence was ample to permit the jury to decide whether statements made to Ohanian by defendant were more than casual comments or mere pep talks delivered by management to a group of employees. All of the surrounding circumstances—fully related earlier—were sufficient for the jury in fact to find that there was a promise of lifetime employment to a "star" employee who, it was hoped, would revive a "dying" division of defendant corporation. . . .

Accordingly, the judgment appealed from is affirmed.

WYATT, District Judge, dissenting:

Believing that the oral lifetime employment contract as claimed by plaintiff is void under the New York Statute of Frauds, I am compelled to dissent. . . .

The "oral employment contract" . . . was a "lifetime employment contract" which he could terminate at any time, but which Avis could terminate only for "just cause." . . . [T]he words "just cause" were never used. . . . Ohanian was guaranteed his job for life "unless he totally screws up" and . . . would not be fired "unless you screwed up badly." "Just cause" was the legal term selected by counsel for Ohanian as a translation of the words actually used: "totally screws up" and "screwed up badly."

. . . [T]here is no indication in the record that counsel for Ohanian ever argued that Ohanian could be terminated "if adverse market conditions . . . would force Avis to make a change in its business strategy" or "for reasons other than the plaintiff's breach," as the majority now holds. To the contrary, Ohanian has always insisted that he was induced to leave California only by an oral contract giving him lifetime job security unless he "totally screws up."

Ohanian therefore has never claimed that Avis had any right to fire him except for a breach by him of the oral contract. . . . Although neither party ever made the claim in this Court or in the trial court, the majority now holds that under the oral contract here in suit "there may be just cause to dismiss without a breach" by Ohanian. For this reason, the majority rejects the application of the Statute of Frauds and affirms the judgment against Avis. There being no evidence that the oral employment contract gave Avis any right to dismiss Ohanian unless he "screwed up badly," unless "he totally screws up," the Statute of Frauds in my view makes the oral contract void; the majority seems clearly wrong. . . .

The Statute of Frauds does not seem to be an "anachronism" for such cases . . . . The oral lifetime employment contract was . . . in a telephone conversation between him in California and Mahmarian for Avis in New York. The conversation was not recorded; no memoranda were made. The only testimony was, and could only be, that of Ohanian and Mahmarian. Not only was Ohanian a witness hostile to Avis, but, Mahmarian, whose testimony was given by deposition on November 9, 1983, had himself been dismissed by Avis on August 4, 1982, a few days after Ohanian was dismissed, and was presumably hostile to Avis. Thus, Avis was at the mercy of Ohanian and Mahmarian in the sense that no person and no writing was available to confirm or contradict them; they alone had made the claimed oral contract and there was no writing. . . . I would hold that ... the oral lifetime employment contract claimed by Ohanian is void for being unwritten.

NOTES AND QUESTIONS

1. A key assumption of the majority's reasoning in *Ohanian* is that the employer could have fulfilled its promise by employing Ohanian only so long as there was enough business to justify his employment. In other words, a layoff for legitimate economic reasons even within the first year of employment would not have breached the alleged oral promise. In this regard, it appears that fixed term agreements are more secure for employees in one way: A fixed term agreement is binding on the employer even in the event of adverse economic conditions. Grappone v. City of Miami Beach, 495 So. 2d 838 (Fla. App. 1986). In contrast, a promise not to discharge an employee except for just cause over an indefinite term appears to permit an employer to eliminate an employee's job for legitimate economic or business management reasons. Guz v. Bechtel Nat'l, Inc., 8 P.3d 1089, 1102-1103 (Cal. 2000).

2. If the Statute of Frauds does not require a writing in the case of a promise of employment for life or until retirement, must a promise of employment for a shorter fixed term, such as two years, be in writing? Consider the following footnote from the Michigan court's opinion in *Toussaint, supra*.

> There is indeed a practical difference between definite and indefinite hirings. A contract for a definite term has been generally regarded to be within the section of the statute of frauds concerning an "agreement that, by its terms, is not to be performed within 1 year from the making thereof," while an agreement for an indefinite term is generally regarded as not being within the proscription of the statute of frauds. . . . Employers are thus protected from an entirely oral agreement for a definite term in excess of one year but are not so protected against jury resolution of a claim of an oral agreement for an indefinite term.

292 N.W. at 891 n.24. What if an employer makes an oral promise of employment for two years, provided there is sufficient business for the work?

3. Following *Ohanian*, a number of courts questioned the validity of its interpretation of New York law. *See, e.g.*, Burke v. Bevona, 866 F.2d 532, 537 (2d Cir. 1989); Cucchi v. New York City Off-Track Betting Corp., 818 F. Supp. 647, 653 (S.D.N.Y. 1993) ("All of the [New York] Appellate Division cases, that our research has uncovered . . . hold that oral assurances that an employer will only

terminate an employee for cause are not a sufficient basis for finding that the employer has expressly agreed to limit its right to fire an employee at will.").

4. The question whether the Statute of Frauds applies to oral promises of long-term job security divides courts outside New York too, depending not only on local law but also on the precise wording of the alleged oral promise. For recent cases applying the Statute of Frauds in wrongful discharge cases, *see* McInerney v. Charter Golf, Inc., 680 N.E.2d 1347 (1997) (promise of lifetime employment unenforceable); Wior v. Anchor Indus., 669 N.E.2d 172 (Ind. 1996) (oral promise of "twenty-plus years" of employment was unenforceable; also discussing the unenforceability of promises of permanent or lifetime employment); Montgomery County Hosp. Dist. v. Brown, 965 S.W.2d 501 (Tex. 1998) (Statute of Frauds did not apply to oral promise not to discharge without cause, but promise was unenforceable for other reasons); Shaw v. Maddox Metal Works, Inc., 73 S.W.3d 472, 480 (Tex. App. 2002) (discussing Texas rule that promise of lifetime employment implies employment until expected retirement age and is subject to Statute of Frauds).

Do the outcomes in these cases depend too much on the exact wording and completeness of an oral promise the employer may have made years ago? *See* Rath v. Selection Research, Inc., 519 N.W.2d 503 (Neb. 1994) (issue of fact precluded summary judgment based on Statute of Frauds, because record showed that employee sometimes recalled employer's oral statement as a promise of "lifetime" employment, sometimes as a promise of 50 years employment, and sometimes as a promise of employment until age 65; and the Statute might bar some forms of the promise but not others).

5. Considering that Ohanian could have resigned and terminated his employment in less than a year without breaching his contract, is there an alternative reason for holding that the employer's alleged promise was not barred by the Statute of Frauds? Wouldn't Avis have performed its promise in less than a year, for purposes of the Statute of Frauds, if Ohanian had resigned six months after the promise? Judge Wyatt considered and rejected this argument in another part of his dissent. According to Judge Wyatt, an employee cannot avoid the Statute of Frauds by relying on his own right to terminate at will. It is the alleged *promisor's* right to terminate within a year that counts, for purposes of the Statute of Frauds. *See* Blake v. Voight, 31 N.E. 256 (N.Y. 1892); North Shore Bottling v. Schmidt & Sons, 239 N.E.2d 189 (N.Y. 1968).

6. An employee seeking to enforce an oral promise might circumvent the Statute of Frauds by alleging promissory estoppel, not breach of contract. Daup v. Tower Cellular, Inc., 566, 737 N.E.2d 128, 136 (Ohio App. 2000); United Parcel Serv. Co. v. Rickert, 996 S.W.2d 464 (Ky. 1999). Promissory estoppel, however, requires an employee to prove he relied on the employer's promise. For Ohanian, this requirement might have been no obstacle, because the promise of job security apparently was decisive in inducing him to leave his position in San Francisco to accept a difficult assignment in the Northeast. For other employees, proof of reliance might be more difficult. The mere facts that an employee accepted and continued employment might not be enough to prove he acted differently because of an alleged oral promise. *See, e.g.*, Trabing v. Kinko's, Inc., 57 P.3d 1248 (Wyo. 2002); Barnell v. Taubman Co., 512 N.W.2d 13 (Mich. App. 1993). *See also* James

v. W. New York Computing Sys., Inc., 710 N.Y.S.2d 740 (N.Y. App. Div. 2000) (requiring proof that nonenforcement of oral promise would be "unconscionable").

In some states, promissory estoppel provides no relief from the Statute of Frauds. In these states, an oral promise subject to the Statute is unenforceable under either a contract or promissory estoppel theory. Urologic Surgeons, Inc. v. Bullock, 117 S.W.3d 722, 728 (Mo. App. 2003); McInerney v. Charter Golf, Inc., 680 N.E.2d 1347 (Ill. 1997). Still other states permit a plaintiff to overcome the Statute of Frauds by alleging promissory estoppel only under special circumstances. *See, e.g.*, Shedd v. Gaylord Ent. Co., 118 S.W.3d 695 (Tenn. App. 2003) (promissory estoppel claim permitted "where to enforce the statute of frauds would make it an instrument of hardship and oppression, verging on actual fraud"); Choi v. McKenzie, 975 S.W.2d 740 (Tex. App. 1998) (plaintiff must allege defendant promised to put the agreement in writing and sign it).

7. The Statute of Frauds is usually asserted by an employer against an employee, but sometimes, an employee asserts the Statute as a defense against enforcement of his alleged oral promise to the employer. *See, e.g.*, Skillgames, LLC v. Brody, 767 N.Y.S.2d 418 (N.Y. App. Div. 2003) (Statute of Frauds barred enforcement of employee's alleged oral promise that he would continue his employment); Treasure Valley Gastroenterology Specialists, P.A. v. Woods, 20 P.3d 21 (Idaho App. 2001) (Statute of Frauds barred enforcement of employee's alleged promise not to compete).

8. The Statute of Frauds is only one of several possible barriers to the enforcement of oral promises of job security. An employer's statement about job security may be vague or ambiguous whether oral or in writing, but uncertainty about the meaning of the statement is compounded if the employer's exact words are in doubt or the employer disputes having made the statement at all. *See, e.g.*, Lytle v. Malady, 579 N.W.2d 906, 914 (Mich. 1998) (interviewer's and supervisor's oral statements that plaintiff's job was secure and she had potential for promotion were expressions of "optimistic hope" and not binding promises); Rowe v. Montgomery Ward & Co., 473 N.W.2d 268 (Mich. 1991) (manager's alleged statement that "generally, as long as [salesmen] generated sales and were honest [they] had a job," insufficient to rebut presumption that employment was at will); Hetes v. Schefman & Miller Law Office, 393 N.W.2d 577 (Mich. App. 1986) (it was for jury to decide whether there was a contract based on employee's description of a promise that "I had a job as long as I did a good job"); Forman v. BRI Corp., 532 F. Supp. 49 (E.D. Pa. 1982) (employee proved contract based on job interviewer's statements that the job was a good one to "stay and grow" and that the employer was concerned the applicant might take job and "not stay").

9. Another issue typical of cases involving oral promises is whether the person who made the promise spoke with authority for an employer. *See, e.g.*, Krickler v. Brooklyn, 776 N.E.2d 119 (Ohio App. 2002) (mayor lacked authority to make binding promise to reclassify employee so that she would have job protection); Miksch v. Exxon Corp., 979 S.W.2d 700 (Tex. App. 1998) (issue of fact whether alleged promisor constituted "management" and had authority to modify plaintiff's at-will status); Tiranno v. Sears, Roebuck & Co., 472 N.Y.S.2d 49 (N.Y. App. Div. 1984). If an employee's direct supervisor promises to be fair in exercising his authority to discipline or recommend discharge, is the

supervisor's statement necessarily the statement of the employer?

10. The admissibility of evidence of an employer's oral promises might be affected by the parol evidence rule, which bars evidence of alleged promises either party made *before* or *contemporaneously* with the execution of a final, exclusive and written statement of the agreement. RESTATEMENT (SECOND) OF CONTRACTS §§ 209-216. The effect of the parol evidence rule in disputes over job security is discussed below in section B.2 on Employer Countermeasures.

PUGH v. SEE'S CANDIES, INC.

171 Cal. Rptr. 917 (Cal. 1981)

GRODIN, Associate Justice.

After 32 years of employment with See's Candies, Inc., in which he worked his way up the corporate ladder from dishwasher to vice-president in charge of production and member of the board of directors, Wayne Pugh was fired. Asserting that he had been fired in breach of contract and for reasons which offend public policy he sued his former employer seeking compensatory and punitive damages for wrongful termination, and joined as a defendant a labor organization which, he alleged, had conspired in or induced the wrongful conduct. The case went to trial before a jury, and upon conclusion of the plaintiff's case-in-chief the trial court granted defendants' motions for nonsuit, and this appeal followed.

. . . The defendant employer is in the business of manufacturing fresh candy at its plants in Los Angeles and South San Francisco and marketing the candy through its own retail outlets. The South San Francisco plant is operated under the name See's Candies, Inc., a wholly owned subsidiary corporation of See's Candy Shops, Inc., which operates the Los Angeles plant as well. The stock of See's Candy Shops, Inc., was held by members of the See family until 1972, when it was sold to Blue Chip Stamps Corporation. For convenience, the designation "See's" will be used to refer to both companies.

Pugh began working for See's at its Bay Area plant (then in San Francisco) in January 1941 washing pots and pans. From there he was promoted to candy maker, and held that position until the early part of 1942, when he entered the Air Corps. Upon his discharge in 1946 he returned to See's and his former position. After a year he was promoted to the position of production manager in charge of personnel, ordering raw materials, and supervising the production of candy. When, in 1950, See's moved into a larger plant in San Francisco, Pugh had responsibility for laying out the design of the plant, taking bids, and assisting in the construction. While working at this plant, Pugh sought to increase his value to the company by taking three years of night classes in plant layout, economics, and business law. When See's moved its San Francisco plant to its present location in South San Francisco in 1957, Pugh was given responsibilities for the new location similar to those which he undertook in 1950. By this time See's business and its number of production employees had increased substantially, and a new position of assistant production manager was created under Pugh's supervision.

In 1971 Pugh was again promoted, this time as vice-president in charge of production and was placed upon the board of directors of See's Northern California subsidiary, "in recognition of his accomplishments." In 1972 he received a gold watch from See's "in appreciation of 31 years of loyal service."

In May 1973 Pugh traveled with Charles Huggins, then president of See's, and their respective families to Europe on a business trip to visit candy manufacturers and to inspect new equipment. Mr. Huggins returned in early June to attend a board of director's meeting while Pugh and his family remained in Europe on a planned vacation. Upon Pugh's return from Europe on Sunday, June 25, 1973, he received a message directing him to fly to Los Angeles the next day and meet with Mr. Huggins. Pugh went to Los Angeles expecting to be told of another promotion. The preceding Christmas season had been the most successful in See's history, the Valentine's Day holiday of 1973 set a new sales record for See's, and the March 1973 edition of See's Newsletter, containing two pictures of Pugh, carried congratulations on the increased production.

Instead, upon Pugh's arrival at Mr. Huggins' office, the latter said, "Wayne, come in and sit down. We might as well get right to the point. I have decided your services are no longer required by See's Candies. Read this and sign it." Huggins handed him a letter confirming his termination and directing him to remove that day "only personal papers and possessions from your office," but "absolutely no records, formulas or other material"; and to turn in and account for "all keys, credit cards, et cetera." The letter advised that Pugh would receive unpaid salary, bonuses and accrued vacation through that date, and the full amount of his profit sharing account, but "No severance pay will be granted." Finally, Pugh was directed "not to visit or contact Production Department employees while they are on the job."

The letter contained no reason for Pugh's termination. When Pugh asked Huggins for a reason, he was told only that he should "look deep within (him) self" to find the answer, that "Things were said by people in the trade that have come back to us." Pugh's termination was subsequently announced to the industry in a letter which, again, stated no reasons.

When Pugh first went to work for See's, Ed Peck, then president and general manager, frequently told him: "if you are loyal to (See's) and do a good job, your future is secure." Laurance See, who became president of the company in 1951 and served in that capacity until his death in 1969, had a practice of not terminating administrative personnel except for good cause, and this practice was carried on by his brother, Charles B. See, who succeeded Laurance as president.

During the entire period of his employment, there had been no formal or written criticism of Pugh's work. No complaints were ever raised at the annual meetings which preceded each holiday season, and he was never denied a raise or bonus. He received no notice that there was a problem which needed correction, nor any warning that any disciplinary action was being contemplated.

Pugh's theory as to why he was terminated relates to a contract which See's at that time had with the defendant union. . . . In April of [1973], Huggins asked Pugh to be part of the negotiating team for the new union contract. Pugh responded that he would like to, but he was bothered by the possibility that See's had a "sweetheart contract" with the union. In response, someone banged on the table and said, "'You don't know what the hell you are talking about.'" Pugh said, "Well, I think I know what I am talking about. I don't know whether you have a sweetheart contract, but I am telling you if you do, I don't want to be involved because they are immoral, illegal and not in the best interests of my employees." At the trial, Pugh explained that to him a "sweetheart contract" was "a contract whereby one employer would get an unfair competitive advantage over a competitor by getting a lower wage rate, would be one version of it." He also felt, he testified, that "if they in fact had a sweetheart contract that it wouldn't be fair to my female employees to be getting less money than someone would get working in the same industry under the same manager."

. . . The presumption that an employment contract is intended to be terminable at will is subject, like any presumption, to contrary evidence. This may take the form of an agreement, express or implied, that the relationship will continue for some fixed period of time. Or, and of greater relevance here, it may take the form of an agreement that the employment relationship will continue indefinitely, pending the occurrence of some event such as the employer's dissatisfaction with the employee's services or the existence of some "cause" for termination. . . . Accordingly, "(i)t is settled that contracts of employment in California are terminable only for good cause if . . . the parties agreed, expressly or impliedly, that that employee could be terminated only for good cause." (Rabago-Alvarez v. Dart Industries, Inc., *supra*, 55 Cal. App. 3d 91, 96, 127 Cal. Rptr. 222. . . .

In determining whether there exists an implied-in-fact promise for some form of continued employment courts have considered a variety of factors in addition to the existence of independent consideration. These have included, for example, the personnel policies or practices of the employer, the employee's longevity of service, actions or communications by the employer reflecting assurances of continued employment, and the practices of the industry in which the employee is engaged. [citations omitted].

A related doctrinal development exists in the application to the employment relationship of the "implied-in-law covenant of good faith and fair dealing inherent in every contract." . . . In Cleary v. American Airlines, Inc., *supra*, 168 Cal. Rptr. 722, an employee who had been dismissed for alleged theft after 18 years of allegedly satisfactory service brought suit claiming, among other things, that his dismissal was in violation of published company policy requiring a "fair, impartial and objective hearing" in such matters, and in breach of the covenant of good faith and fair dealing. Holding that the complaint stated a cause of action on these grounds, the court reasoned:

> Two factors are of paramount importance in reaching our result. . . . One is the longevity of service by plaintiff 18 years of apparently satisfactory performance. . . . The second factor of considerable significance is the . . . adoption of specific procedures for adjudicating employee disputes such as this one . . . [which] compels the conclusion that this employer had recognized its responsibility to engage in good faith and fair dealing rather than in arbitrary conduct with respect to all of its employees. In the case at bench, we hold that the longevity of the employee's service, together with the expressed policy of the employer, operate as a form of estoppel, precluding any discharge of such an employee by the employer without good cause.

(*Id.*, at p. 722.)

If "(t)ermination of employment without legal cause (after 18 years of service) offends the implied-in-law covenant of good faith and fair dealing contained in all contracts, including employment contracts," as the court said in the above-quoted portion of *Cleary*, then a fortiori that covenant would provide protection to Pugh, whose employment is nearly twice that duration. Indeed, it seems difficult to defend termination of such a long-time employee arbitrarily, i.e., without some legitimate reason, as compatible with either good faith or fair dealing.

We need not go that far, however. In *Cleary* the court did not base its holding upon the covenant of good faith and fair dealing alone. Its decision rested also upon the employer's acceptance of responsibility for refraining from arbitrary conduct, as evidenced by its adoption of specific procedures for adjudicating employee grievances. While the court characterized the employer's conduct as constituting "(recognition of) its responsibility to engage in good faith and fair dealing" (168 Cal. Rptr. 722), the result is equally explicable in traditional contract terms: the employer's conduct gave rise to an implied promise that it would not act arbitrarily in dealing with its employees.

Here, similarly, there were facts in evidence from which the jury could determine the existence of such an implied promise: the duration of appellant's employment, the commendations and promotions he received, the apparent lack of any direct criticism of his work, the assurances he was given, and the employer's acknowledged policies. While oblique language will not, standing alone, be sufficient to establish agreement, it is appropriate to consider the totality of the parties' relationship: Agreement may be "'shown by the acts and conduct of the parties, interpreted in the light of the subject matter and the surrounding circumstances.'" (Marvin v. Marvin (1976) 557 P.2d 106) We therefore conclude that it was error to grant respondents' motions for nonsuit as to See's. . . .

NOTES AND QUESTIONS

1. Proof of an express or implied promise of job security is only the first step for an employee who alleges that his employer breached a contract by discharging him. Depending on the precise terms of the alleged promise, the employee must also prove his discharge was without just cause. It was at this stage that Pugh ultimately failed. Fifteen years after Pugh's discharge, a California court of appeals upheld judgment against Pugh based on a jury verdict in favor of See's. The jury had rendered its verdict in favor of See's after hearing testimony that Pugh was disrespectful, disloyal, and uncooperative with superiors and subordinates. Pugh v. See's Candies, Inc., 250 Cal. Rptr. 195 (1988).

2. The California Supreme Court endorsed *Pugh* in Foley v. Interactive Data Corp., 765 P.2d 373 (Cal. 1988). Outside California, the response to *Pugh*'s implied contract theory has been mixed. *See* Calleon v. Miyagi, 876 P.2d 1278, 1285-86 (Hi.1994); Porter v. Pioneer Hi-Bred Int'l, Inc., 497 N.W.2d 870, 871 (Iowa 1993).

3. If the duration of employment is a factor for determining the existence of an implied contract of job security, how many years must the employment continue before this factor weighs in favor of an implied contract? In *Foley*, the California Supreme Court decision that approved *Pugh*'s implied contract theory, the defendant employer argued that the plaintiff's period of employment was too short for an implied contract. The court replied, "six years and nine months is sufficient

time for conduct to occur on which a trier of fact could find the existence of an implied contract." 765 P.2d at 387-388. Though Foley's employment was short in comparison with Pugh's employment, Foley alleged that he received "oral assurances of job security" and "consistent promotions, salary increases and bonuses," all of which contributed to his expectation that he would not be discharged except for good cause. *Id.* at 383, 387-388.

4. If *Foley* suggests that an implied contract might evolve in as few as six years, it also appears to be the law in California that a very long term of employment, standing alone, is not enough to establish an implied contract of job security. Both Pugh and Foley alleged that their employers made oral assurances about job security. While the assurances apparently were vague and insufficient as express promises not to discharge without cause, other features of the plaintiffs' job histories, including longevity, promotions, raises and praise, supported their theories of implied contract. Could Pugh and Foley have proven implied contracts *without* oral assurances or similar communications by their employers? Consider the following statement of the Supreme Court of California in Guz v. Bechtel Nat'l Inc., 8 P.3d 1089 (Cal. 2000):

> [M]ere passage of time in the employer's service, even where marked with tangible indicia that the employer approves the employee's work, cannot alone form an implied-in-fact contract that the employee is no longer at will. Absent other evidence of the employer's intent, longevity, raises and promotions are their own rewards for the employee's continuing valued service; they do not, in and of themselves, additionally constitute a contractual guarantee of future employment security. A rule granting such contract rights on the basis of successful longevity alone would discourage the retention and promotion of employees.
>
> On the other hand, long and successful service is not necessarily irrelevant to the existence of such a contract. Over the period of an employee's tenure, the employer can certainly communicate, by its written and unwritten policies and practices, or by informal assurances, that seniority and longevity do create rights against termination at will. *The issue is whether the employer's words or conduct, on which an employee reasonably relied, gave rise to that specific understanding.*

Id. at 1104-1105 (emphasis added).

5. Aside from general assurances of managers and supervisors that an employee need not worry about arbitrary discharge, what other conduct or statements by an employer might imply a promise not to discharge without cause? Following are a few of the actions or communications that might imply contractual job security in a jurisdiction that agrees with the implied contract theory:

a. An employer's list of specific grounds for discipline. *See, e.g.*, Garcia v. Middle Rio Grande Conservancy Dist., 918 P.2d 7 (N.M. 1996); Derrig v. Wal-Mart Stores, Inc., 942 F. Supp. 49 (D. Mass. 1996). *Contra*, Eaton v. City of Parkersburg, 482 S.E.2d 232 (W. Va. 1996); Hamilton Ins. Servs., Inc. v. Nationwide Ins. Co., 714 N.E.2d 898 (Ohio 1999).

b. An employer's establishment of a probationary period of employment followed by regular or permanent employment. Wiskotoni v. Michigan Nat'l Bank-West, 716 F.2d 378 (6th Cir. 1983) (Michigan law). *Contra*, Welch v. Doss

Aviation, Inc., 978 S.W.2d 215 (Tex. App. 1998).

c. An employer's establishment of a disciplinary procedure. Trombley v. Southwestern Vermont Med. Ctr.,738 A.2d 103 (Vt. 1999). *Contra*, Wyatt v. Bell South, 998 F. Supp. 1303 (M.D. Ala. 1998); Bowen v. Income Producing Mgmt. of Okla. Inc., 202 F.3d 1282 (10th Cir. 2000).

MONTGOMERY COUNTY HOSP. DIST. v. BROWN

965 S.W.2d 501 (Tex. 1998)

HECHT, Justice:

. . . For ten years Valarie Brown was employed by the Montgomery County Hospital District as laboratory systems manager for Medical Center Hospital. After her employment terminated, Brown brought this action against the District and its president and vice president (collectively, "the District") for breach of oral and written contracts of employment. . . . The district court granted summary judgment for the District. The circumstances surrounding the termination of Brown's employment, vigorously disputed by the parties, are largely irrelevant to the contract issues before us. Given the conflict in the summary judgment record, we accept as true Brown's assertion that she did not voluntarily resign but was fired without good cause. We assume that Brown is not estopped by acceptance of her severance pay to assert that she was wrongfully terminated. And we take Brown's word that:

> At the time I was hired as well as during my employment, I was told by [the Hospital administrator] that I would be able to keep my job at the Hospital as long as I was doing my job and that I would not be fired unless there was a good reason or good cause to fire me. This representation was important to me since I was going to have to relocate from Houston to the Conroe area if I accepted the position with the Hospital.

. . . For well over a century, the general rule in this State, as in most American jurisdictions, has been that absent a specific agreement to the contrary, employment may be terminated by the employer or the employee at will, for good cause, bad cause, or no cause at all. Federal Express Corp. v. Dutschmann, 846 S.W.2d 282, 283 (Tex. 1993) (per curiam). . . . The District argues that its assurances to Brown were too indefinite to constitute an agreement limiting the District's right to discharge Brown at will. We agree.

A promise, acceptance of which will form a contract, "is a manifestation of intention to act or refrain from acting in a specified way, so made as to justify a promisee in understanding that a commitment has been made." RESTATEMENT (SECOND) OF CONTRACTS § 2(1) (1981). General statements like those made to Brown simply do not justify the conclusion that the speaker intends by them to make a binding contract of employment. For such a contract to exist, the employer must unequivocally indicate a definite intent to be bound not to terminate the employee except under clearly specified circumstances. General comments that an employee will not be discharged as long as his work is satisfactory do not in themselves manifest such an intent. Neither do statements that an employee will be discharged only for "good reason" or "good cause" when there is no agreement on what those terms encompass. Without such agreement the employee cannot reasonably expect to limit the employer's right to terminate him. An employee who has no formal agreement with his employer cannot construct one out of indefinite comments, encouragements, or assurances.

This is the rule in other states. For example, in Rowe v. Montgomery Ward & Co., 437 Mich. 627, 473 N.W.2d 268 (1991), the court held that a supervisor's assurance that employees would have their jobs "generally, as long as they generated sales and were honest" did not limit the employer's right to discharge an employee at will. *Id.* at 270. Noting that a decade earlier it had "joined the forefront of a nationwide experiment in which, under varying theories, courts extended job security to nonunionized employees," the court retreated from earlier decisions in which it had been more inclined to find an employment agreement in general assurances made by the employer. *Id.* at 269. "[C]alling something a contract that is in no sense a contract cannot advance respect for the law," the court wrote. *Id.* It concluded: "[O]ral statements of job security must be clear and unequivocal to overcome the presumption of employment at will." *Id.* at 275.

Likewise, in Hayes v. Eateries, Inc., 905 P.2d 778 (Okla. 1995), the court held that oral assurances that an employee "would be employed as long as he did an adequate job and/or performed his duties satisfactorily" did not constitute "a binding agreement that protected him from discharge except for 'just cause.'" *Id.* at 782. The court explained:

> Courts "must distinguish between carefully developed employer representations upon which an employee may justifiably rely, and general platitudes, vague assurances, praise, and indefinite promises of permanent continued employment." Only when the promises are definite and, thus, of the sort which may be reasonably or justifiably relied on by the employee, will a contract claim be viable, not when the employee relies on only vague assurances that no reasonable person would justifiably rely upon. There is, thus, an objective component to the nature of such a contract claim in the form of definite and specific promises by the employer sufficient to substantively restrict the reasons for termination.

Id. at 783 (citations omitted). . . .

The District also argues that oral promises modifying employment at will are unenforceable under the Statute of Frauds. The District is correct only if the promises cannot be performed within one year. . . . An employment contract for an indefinite term is considered performable within one year. Bratcher v. Dozier, 162 Tex. 319, 346 S.W.2d 795 (1961). It would be unusual, however, for oral assurances of employment for an indefinite term to be sufficiently specific and definite to modify an at-will relationship. . . .

Accordingly, the judgment of the court of appeals is reversed and judgment is rendered for the District.

NOTES AND QUESTIONS

1. *Montgomery County Hospital District* might be described as the antipode of *Pugh*. Does *Montgomery County Hospital District* merely restate the older common law presumption of employment at will? Or does it strengthen it?

2. What do you make of the Texas court's pronouncement that there can be no express contract of job security based merely on "statements that an employee will be discharged only for 'good reason' or 'good cause' when there is no agreement on what those terms encompass"? The standard job security clause in a collective bargaining agreement uses the same language: Employees will not be discharged without "just" or "good cause." Does the Texas court mean that *written* contracts with such terms are unenforceable? Or would the court distinguish "formal" and "informal" versions of such a promise? What facts might persuade a court that an employer "unequivocally indicate[d] a definite intent to be bound not to terminate the employee except under clearly specified circumstances"?

3. Courts in a number of other states have adopted rules similar to the one *Montgomery County Hosp. Dist.* articulates, essentially rejecting the implied contract theory of *Pugh* and perhaps reinforcing a presumption in favor of employment at will. In some but not all of these cases, the courts might be distinguishing between oral promises, as to which the courts have grown skeptical, and written promises that leave no doubt as to what the employer really said. *See, e.g.*, Sayres v. Bauman, 425 S.E.2d 226 (W. Va. 1992) (oral promise must be ascertainable and definitive to be enforceable); Brown v. Cty. of Niota, Tenn., 214 F.3d 718 (6th Cir. 2000) (describing Tennessee law as requiring a high standard of proof of an employer's specific intent to be bound by employee handbook terms).

4. Even as the Texas court adopted a strong presumption for employment at will, it *rejected* a strong application of the Statute of Frauds. Are the court's rulings on these issues inconsistent? Or is the court erecting a substitute to the Statute of Frauds?

5. One might wonder whether it is ever possible for an employee to prove a *binding* oral promise of job security in Texas or any other jurisdiction that has adopted a strong presumption of employment at will. But *Montgomery County Hosp. Dist.* does not completely shut the door against oral promises. A few years earlier the same court upheld enforcement of an oral promise in Goodyear Tire & Rubber Co. v. Portilla, 879 S.W.2d 47 (Tex. 1994). In that case, Portilla alleged Goodyear had specifically promised not to enforce its anti-nepotism rule against her. The promise was important to Portilla because Goodyear had transferred her brother to manage the store where she worked, and her family circumstances prevented her from accepting transfer to any other location. Seventeen years after the alleged oral promise, Goodyear "rediscovered" that Portilla's store assignment was in violation of the antinepotism rule. When Portilla refused to accept a transfer, Goodyear discharged her. The Texas court held that Goodyear had breached its oral promise. *See also* Mueller v. Union Pacific R.R., 371 N.W.2d 732 (Neb. 1985) (employer bound by specific promise that it would not retaliate against employee if he cooperated in investigation).

If the result in *Goodyear* seems inconsistent with the court's later decision in *Montgomery County Hosp. Dist.*, it may be important to note that Portilla's testimony about the oral promise was substantially corroborated by other evidence, including Goodyear's own records. Goodyear's 1974 audit proved it was aware that Portilla worked in a store managed by her brother, and Goodyear's records included a manager's written request for a waiver of the anti-nepotism rule with respect to Portilla. Another former manager testified that he prepared a written document granting the waiver, but the seventeen-year-old document was evidently destroyed in accordance with a document retention policy.

When the Texas court later decided *Montgomery County Hospital District*, it did not expressly overrule or reaffirm *Goodyear*. Can the two cases be reconciled?

What Is "Good" or "Just" Cause?

An employee who proves a contractual right to job security still must prove the employer breached its promise in discharging the employee. A fixed term of employment, an implied contract such as the one described in *Pugh*, and most express promises of lifetime or indefinite job security lead to the same basic question: Did the employer have "good" or "just" cause to discharge the employee?

Whether there is cause to discharge a particular employee can be intensely fact-specific. Appropriate standards of conduct and performance vary among workplaces and industries; an employee's unique individual record also may be important to what is "fair." For example, a recently hired employee's rough language toward a supervisor might be cause for discharge in one workplace, but the same language by a twenty-year veteran in another workplace might not be. Nevertheless, caselaw reveals some basic principles of "cause" for discharge.

- **Violations of law or other serious misdeeds** often qualify, *see, e.g.*, Phillips v. Am. Family Ins., 345 F. Supp. 2d 1187 (D. Kan. 2004) ("pattern of boorish behavior" that "likely constituted sexual harassment and battery" was cause for discharge). But if an employee's misconduct was unintentional or because of an honest mistake, proof of "cause" may require evidence of material harm to employer interests or loss of trust. Shapiro v. Massengill, 661 A.2d 202, 209 (Md. App. 1995).
- **Multiple violations** strengthen the argument for cause, but there is no per se rule requiring more than one violation. McDermott v. Chicago Police Bd., 58 N.E.3d 860, 871-872 (Ill. App. 2016).
- **Insubordination** can be "cause" but perhaps not if the employee was resisting an inappropriate order, Pettus v. Cole, 49 Cal.App.4th 402, 462 (Cal. App. 1996), or the employer "provoked" insubordination. Dorrance v. Hoopes, 90 A. 92, 93-94 (Md. 1914) ("provocation by the master will sometimes render excusable words or behavior which, apart from that element, would constitute a good ground of dismissal").
- **Bad attitude** sometimes suffices if it impedes the work. Paros v. Hoemako Hosp., 681 P.2d 918, 920-921 (Ariz. App. 1984) ("chronic, argumentative, hostile attitude inconsistent with performance of supervisory duties … constituted good cause"). However, judging a person's "attitude" is highly subjective and context-specific, and thus "attitude" alone often fails to be "cause." *Dorrance, supra*, 90 A. at 94.

Is an **economic need to eliminate jobs** "cause" to discharge otherwise blameless employees, who neither under-performed, committed misdeeds, nor are at fault for the economic need? Most courts, like *Ohanian, supra,* find true economic need sufficient to discharge employees with *indefinite-term* for-cause rights. *See, e.g.,* Wilde v. Houlton Reg'l Hosp., 537 A.2d 1137, 1138 (Me. 1988) ("[D]ischarge of employees for financial or other legitimate business reasons does not offend 'for cause' language .... Absent some clear indication to the contrary, a 'dismissal for cause' provision refers only to disciplinary discharge. ... [A] private employer has an essential business prerogative to adjust his work force as market forces and business necessity require."); Phillips v. Amoco Oil Co., 799 F.2d 1464, 1468 (11th Cir. 1986) (sale of business justifies discharging employee with lifetime "cause" guarantee; "even where a lifetime employment contract is legally enforceable, Alabama law provides that the contract remains in effect only as long as the employer remains in the business for which the employee was hired and needs the particular services the employee was hired to perform"); Taylor v. Nat'l Life Ins. Co., 652 A.2d 466, 472 (Vt. 1993) ("[E]conomic circumstances that necessitate employer layoffs constitute good cause for termination .... To hold otherwise would impose an unworkable economic burden upon employers to stay in business to the point of bankruptcy in order to satisfy employment contracts and related agreements terminable only for good or sufficient cause.").

Even if economic need can suffice as "cause," however, an employer may lack evidence of sufficient need to eliminate disputed positions. The Restatement of Employment Law demands not just some degree of economic decline, but a sufficiently "significant change" that "the employer no longer has a business need for the employee's services." RESTATEMENT OF THE LAW, EMPLOYMENT LAW § 2.04. Thus, even an employer's loss of a significant sales market will not provide "cause" to terminate a sales employee, *if* that employee could remain engaged in other tasks of the same sort he was hired to perform. For example, in Ryan v. Brown Motors, wartime limits on new car sales "greatly limited the opportunities" of a car dealership to make sales, "but did not destroy the field" provably enough to be "cause" to terminate sales manager, because the limits on new car sales might have increased demand for the employer's used car, car parts, and car repair services. 39 A.2d 70, 72 (1944). *Ryan* also shows that even an employer with a strong argument for economics-driven "cause" is in a weaker position if it rushes to discharge: the car dealership lost in part because it fired the employee when the new car sales limits were so new that it could not show whether its loss of new car business would be mitigated by increases used car, parts, and repair business. *Id.*

Definite-term for-cause agreements, however, often feature the opposite rule: that economic need is not "cause." They bind employers for limited durations (typically one or a few years), so many courts, on the below rationale, interpret definite-term contracts as requiring payment to the employee for the full term, even if economic circumstances eliminate the need for the employee's services.

> Unlike the "lifetime" contract in Phillips...appellant's employment contract here is for a specified and relatively short period of two years. Under these circumstances, we do not think it unreasonable to hold a company to its obligations under an employment contract, just as it would be held to its obligations under other contracts, despite its voluntary decision to get out of the business for which the obligations were incurred.

Derosa v. Shiah, 421 S.E.2d 718, 723 (Ga. 1992). *Accord* Drake v. Geochemistry & Env'tl Chemistry Research, Inc., 336 N.W.2d 666, 668 (S.D. 1983)The Restatement of Employment Law also takes this view. *See* RESTATEMENT OF THE LAW, EMPLOYMENT LAW § 2.04. Thus, "[c]hanges in the employer's business circumstances generally do not constitute 'cause' when the employment is for a definite term." *Id.* §2.04, comments b & c Reporter's Notes.

Collective Bargaining Precedents

Collective bargaining agreements typically provide that the employer will not discipline or discharge employees except for just cause, and employees can challenge their discipline or discharge through contractual grievance and arbitration procedures. Not surprisingly, therefore, the law of collective bargaining furnishes a wealth of precedents regarding just cause. However, in the collective bargaining context the ultimate decision whether there was cause for discharge rests with an arbitrator, who is not bound by the decisions of other arbitrators and whose decision is not binding on any future arbitrator. The resulting industrial "common law" of just cause is not as sure as it might have been if it were the product of a system governed by stare decisis.

Nevertheless, Professors Roger Abrams and Dennis Nolan have offered the following general principles for the collective bargaining context. First, the employer must prove the employee failed to meet his obligation to provide "satisfactory work," which includes regular attendance, obedience to reasonable work rules, a "reasonable quality and quantity of work," and the avoidance of conduct (on or off duty) that interferes with the employer's ability to operate its business.

Second, the employer must show that disciplinary action was designed to prevent or deter the same misconduct by the same employee or other employees, or to protect the employer's ability to operate its business.

Third, the employer's action must be in accordance with "industrial due process," which requires notice to the employee of expected standards of performance or conduct, a fair investigation, "progressive discipline" ("the imposition of discipline in gradually increasing degrees" for all but the most serious misconduct), "industrial equal protection" (or "like treatment of like cases" with due regard for "distinctive facts" in the employee's record), and a decision based on the "facts." R. Abrams & D. Nolan, *Toward a Theory of "Just Cause" in Employee Discipline Cases*, 1985 Duke L.J. 594, 611-612 (1985). An arbitrator is the ultimate authority as to whether these requirements are satisfied in any particular case.

It is not clear whether the collective bargaining model of "just cause" is entirely suitable in a case involving the breach of an individual contract of employment. An arbitrator decides the issue of just cause in the collective bargaining context because the employer and union have selected the arbitrator for that purpose and have agreed to be bound by his findings of fact and his judgment. However, when the claimant is an individual employee and his claim is based on an alleged contract other than a collective bargaining agreement, there may be a question whether the employer intended to submit to *de novo* review and independent reconsideration by a jury or any other third party.

Procedure and Judicial Review for the Issue of Just Cause

As noted in the immediately preceding section, an employer promising not to discharge an individual employee except for just cause is not necessarily submitting to the independent and *de novo* exercise of judgment of a third party such as an arbitrator, jury or judge. The precise words of the employer's alleged promise might suggest something less than full, independent reconsideration. For example, an employer might promise employment as long as an employee's performance is "satisfactory" to the employer. If the employee alleges he was discharged in violation of a promise stated in this fashion, most courts state the issue as whether the employer was *honestly* dissatisfied, not whether the employer acted "unreasonably" in a judge or jury's view. *See, e.g.*, Silvestri v. Optus Software, Inc., 814 A.2d 602 (N.J. 2003).

An employer might also qualify a promise of job security by prescribing the procedure for determining cause. In Thomas v. John Deere Corp., 517 N.W.2d 265 (Mich. App. 1994), the court held that the same employer statements that promised no discharge except for cause also reserved the employer's right to make its decision according to a specified procedure. The promise was not hollow, the court observed. The requirement of a procedure for management review of discharge decisions "protects defendant's employees from some risks . . . such as being fired rashly in a fit of pique, and being fired only because of a personality conflict with an immediate supervisor that does not affect job performance."

If the employer's promise is not qualified as it was in *Thomas* or *Silvestri*, most courts agree that alleged cause for discharge is subject to judicial review in much the same way that "material breach" is reviewed by a court in any other contract case. To the extent "cause" depends on fact issues about which reasonable minds might disagree, the ultimate decision maker may be a jury. *See, e.g.*, Toussaint v. Blue Cross & Blue Shield of Michigan, *supra*, 292 N.W.2d at 895. Moreover, an employer's honest and good faith belief that it had cause to discharge is no defense if its promise of job security was unqualified and a judge or jury determines that there was in fact insufficient cause for discharge. *See* Scribner v. Worldcom, Inc., 249 F.3d 902 (9th Cir. 2001); Marcy v. Delta Air., 166 F.3d 1279 (9th Cir. 1999) (applying Montana's Wrongful Discharge from Employment Act).

An important issue on which courts differ is whether a judge or jury owes any measure of deference to an employer's exercise of managerial judgment. The issue tends to be especially important in discharge actions involving upper- or middle-level managers (who seem to constitute the majority of plaintiffs in individual contract cases), because an employer's standards for evaluating such personnel are bound to be more subjective than the sort of standards that govern the productivity and performance of factory workers in the collective bargaining setting.

In *Toussaint* (in a passage omitted from the previously reproduced opinion), the court considered but ultimately rejected the deferential view. The court began by observing that a jury's precise role might vary depending on the employer's alleged cause for discharge and the employee's rebuttal.

> Where the employer claims that the employee was discharged for specific misconduct — intoxication, dishonesty, insubordination — and the employee claims that he did not commit the misconduct alleged, the question is one of fact for the jury: did the employee do what the employer said he did? Where the employer alleges that the employee was discharged for one reason — excessive tardiness — and the employee presents evidence that he was really discharged for another reason — because he was making too much

money in commissions — the question also is one of fact for the jury.

> Where an employee is discharged for stated reasons which he contends are not "good cause" for discharge, the role of the jury is more difficult to resolve. If the jury is permitted to decide whether there was good cause for discharge, there is the danger that it will substitute its judgment for the employer's. If the jurors would not have fired the employee for doing what he admittedly did, or they find he did, the employer may be held liable in damages although the employee was discharged in good faith and the employer's decision was not unreasonable. . . . Nevertheless, . . . [w]here the employee has secured a promise not to be discharged except for cause, he has contracted for more than the employer's promise to act in good faith or not to be unreasonable. . . .
>
> In addition to deciding questions of fact and determining the employer's true motive for discharge, the jury should, where such a promise was made, decide whether the reason for discharge amounts to good cause: is it the kind of thing that justifies terminating the employment relationship? Does it demonstrate that the employee was no longer doing the job?

292 N.W.2d at 896.

In contrast, the California Supreme Court adopted a deferential approach, at least for *implied* contracts of job security, in Cotran v. Rollins Hudig Hall Int'l., 948 P.2d 412 (Cal. 1998).

> The proper inquiry for the jury . . . is not, "Did the employee in fact commit the act leading to dismissal?" It is "Was the factual basis on which the employer concluded a dischargeable act had been committed reached honestly, after an appropriate investigation and for reasons that are not arbitrary or pretextual?"

948 P.2d at 421-422. In adopting this deferential standard for reviewing an employer's decision, the court reasoned as follows:

> [A] standard permitting juries to reexamine the factual basis for the decision to terminate for misconduct—typically gathered under the exigencies of the workaday world and without benefit of the slow-moving machinery of a contested trial—dampens an employer's willingness to act, intruding on the "wide latitude" [which is] a reasonable condition for the efficient conduct of business. . . .
>
> Equally significant is the jury's relative remoteness from the everyday reality of the workplace. The decision to terminate an employee for misconduct is one that not uncommonly implicates organizational judgment and may turn on intractable factual uncertainties, even where the grounds for dismissal are fact specific. If an employer is required to have in hand a signed confession or an eyewitness account of the alleged misconduct before it can act, the workplace will be transformed into an adjudicatory arena and effective decisionmaking will be thwarted. Although these features do not justify a rule permitting employees to be dismissed arbitrarily, they do mean that asking a civil jury to reexamine in all its factual detail the triggering cause of the decision to dismiss—including the retrospective accuracy of the employer's comprehension of that event—months or even years later, in a context distant from the imperatives of the workplace, is at odds with

> . . . the need for a sensible latitude for managerial decisionmaking and . . . an optimum balance point between the employer's interest in organizational efficiency and the employee's interest in continuing employment.

948 P.2d at 420-421. Concurring, Justice Mosk added that "the majority's definition of 'good cause' is a 'default' definition that applies only in the absence of more specific contractual provisions." 948 P.2d at 423-424. In other words, in Justice Mosk's view, a court might find that the terms of any particular express or implied promise of job security call for a less deferential view.

PROBLEMS

1. ABC Consulting has an employee policy manual that states in its preface,

> These are policies that we seek to live by, and we expect our employees to live by them too. The company reserves the right to change or revoke any of these policies at any time.

The manual lists rules of conduct, the violation of which will lead to discipline "including, if the company deems appropriate, discharge."

Helen Sloan had been on the job at ABC Consulting for a year when her supervisor, Ken Stevens, asked her out on a date. Sloan happily accepted, but she worried that she might get in trouble for "dating my boss." Stevens assured Sloan it was okay, and that the company didn't fire employees for things like that.

Sloan and Stevens quickly became romantically involved partners. When the Vice President of Human Resources learned of the relationship, she called Sloan aside and explained the company's unwritten no-fraternization policy, which prohibited dating between a supervisor and a subordinate. Ordinarily, the VP explained, the company might offer Sloan a transfer to another department, but there were no other openings. The company couldn't let Stevens go because he was a "key" employee. Therefore, it was the company's decision to terminate Sloan. If ABC terminates Sloan, will it have breached its contract with Sloan?

2. Fred Hutchins, a chemical engineer, had worked for fifteen years at DEF Chemicals and had enjoyed regular promotions, salary increases, and bonuses. He was vaguely aware of a disciplinary procedure policy the company had issued to managers with supervisory responsibilities, but Hutchins had not received a copy of this policy because he did not supervise other employees or make disciplinary decisions. Nevertheless, he had heard from other personnel at the company that the policy required investigation, review, and a fair decision in each disciplinary case.

DEF had enjoyed special tax concessions from the city for years as part of the city's effort to preserve jobs and develop new business. However, Hutchins's wife Tara won election to the city council on a promise to end DEF's special tax treatment, arguing that it was depriving the city of much needed revenue. As a newly elected member of the council, Tara Hutchins eventually succeeded in carrying out her pledge. On the day the city withdrew its tax concessions to DEF, DEF's president summarily discharged Fred Hutchins, accusing him of "disloyalty." Has DEF breached its contract with Fred Hutchins?

2. *Employer Countermeasures*

a. Disclaimers

One might wonder whether the employers in *Toussaint, Ohanian, Pugh,* or *Montgomery County Hosp. Dist.* really believed they had committed themselves to judicial enforcement of their assurances about job security, or whether they expected judicial review of their disciplinary discharge decisions. Their denial of contractual liability suggests they did not expect to be bound. On the other hand, perhaps they intended to be bound, and their denial of any potential liability was a lawyer's after-the-fact strategy.

If an employer chooses at will employment relations, is it enough for the employer to do nothing—to *not* promise anything? Even courts that endorse the implied contract theory of job security usually require proof of some kind of employer assurance of security. Strictly speaking, the presumption of employment at will reigns in nearly every state, although the presumption is clearly weaker in some states than others. In theory, if an employer says and does nothing to imply a promise of job security, it has preserved its right to discharge at will.

As a practical matter, however, an employer cannot always count on its ability to control everything its managers and supervisors may say to an employee. Nor can an employer assume an employee will not misunderstand what he has seen or heard. Indeed, a practical consequence of cases like *Pugh* is that the usual presumption of employment at will is reversed, at least in the case of long term employees. Thus, if an employer is determined to preserve its right to terminate employees at will, it must take positive steps to negate an implied promise of job security. *See also* Peter Stone Partee, *Reversing the Presumption of Employment at Will*, 44 Vand. L. Rev. (1991) and Cass Sunstein, *Switching the Default Rule*, 26 N.Y.U. L. Rev. 106 (2002) (discussing the merits of reversing a presumption and forcing one party to speak with greater clarity about an otherwise unstated issue).

Indeed, it is now routine for employers to include a clear affirmation of employment at will on documents an employee might sign during the hiring process or the first days of employment. Application forms, employee handbooks and other personnel forms contain the ubiquitous language of employment at will. The effectiveness of these affirmations depends partly on the parol evidence rule, which limits either party's proof of a promise contradicting a final, written statement of the contract. The effectiveness of the parol evidence rule depends partly on whether the parties have adopted a "complete" integration or only a "partial" integration. A partial integration bars proof of only a contradictory term; a *completely* integrated written agreement purports to be the exclusive statement of the contract and bars proof of *any* extrinsic term, even a consistent but supplementary term. *See* RESTATEMENT (SECOND) OF CONTRACTS §§ 209-218. For reasons described earlier, completely integrated agreements are rare, if even possible, in the employment context. *See* Chapter 4.B.1.

A more likely situation is that the parties have made a "partial integration," a final written statement about one aspect of their relationship, such as their agreement that employment is at will. Under the parol evidence rule, a partial integration bars proof of any term or promise that *contradicts* the integrated document. Proof of a term that merely *supplements* or explains the parties' agreement, however, is not barred by a partial integration. Ringle v. Bruton, 86 P.3d 1032, 1037-1038 (Nev. 2004). Thus, an employer might seek to avoid allegations of job security by requiring the employee to acknowledge a document that includes an affirmation of employment at will. If such a document is a partial integration, it might bar the employee's effort to prove a promise of job security. Nel v. DWP/Bates Technology, LLC, 579 S.E.2d 842 (Ga. App. 2003); Matter of Liquidation of New York Agency and Other Assets of Bank of Credit & Commerce Int'l, S.A., 642 N.Y.S.2d (N.Y. App. Div. 1996).

An important limitation of the parol evidence rule is that it bars proof only of terms or promises a party made *prior to or contemporaneously with* the integrated agreement. It does not bar proof of a subsequent promise modifying the original agreement. If an employee alleges the employer assured him of job security a year after the employee signed an acknowledgment of employment at will, the parol evidence rule will not bar the employee from testifying about the alleged assurance.

GUZ v. BECHTEL NAT'L, INC.
100 Cal. Rptr. 2d 352 (Cal. 2000)

BAXTER, J.

. . . Plaintiff John Guz, a longtime employee of Bechtel National, Inc. (BNI), was released at age 49 when his work unit was eliminated and its tasks were transferred to another Bechtel office. Guz sued BNI and its parent, Bechtel Corporation (hereinafter collectively Bechtel), alleging . . . breach of an implied contract to be terminated only for good cause. . . . The trial court granted Bechtel's motion for summary judgment and dismissed the action. In a split decision, the Court of Appeal reversed. The majority found that Bechtel had demonstrated no grounds to foreclose a trial on any of the claims asserted in the complaint.

. . . At the outset, Bechtel insists that the existence of implied contractual limitations on its termination rights is negated because Bechtel expressly disclaimed all such agreements. Bechtel suggests the at-will presumption of Labor Code 2922 was conclusively reinforced by language Bechtel inserted in Policy 1101, which specified that the company's employees "have no . . . agreements guaranteeing continuous service and may be terminated at [Bechtel's] option." As Bechtel points out, Guz concedes he understood Policy 1101 applied to him.

This express disclaimer, reinforced by the statutory presumption of at-will employment, satisfied Bechtel's initial burden, if any, to show that Guz's claim of a contract limiting Bechtel's termination rights had no merit. But neither the disclaimer nor the statutory presumption necessarily foreclosed Guz from proving the existence and breach of such an agreement.

Cases in California and elsewhere have held that at-will provisions in personnel handbooks, manuals, or memoranda do not bar, or necessarily overcome, other evidence of the employer's contrary intent, particularly where other provisions in the employer's personnel documents themselves suggest limits on the employer's termination rights. [Citations omitted.] The reasoning, express or implied, is that parol evidence is admissible to explain, supplement, or even contradict the terms of an unintegrated agreement, and that handbook disclaimers should not permit an employer, at its whim, to repudiate promises it has otherwise made in its own self-interest, and on which it intended an employee to rely.

We agree that disclaimer language in an employee handbook or policy manual does not necessarily mean an employee is employed at will. But even if a handbook disclaimer is not controlling in every case, neither can such a provision be ignored in determining whether the parties' conduct was intended, and reasonably understood, to create binding limits on an employer's statutory right to terminate the relationship at will. Like any direct expression of employer intent, communicated to employees and intended to apply to them, such language must be taken into account, along with all other pertinent evidence, in ascertaining the terms on which a worker was employed. We examine accordingly the evidence cited by Guz in support of his implied contract claim.

[The court found that Guz's 20 years of employment, steady raises, promotions and good performance reviews were not sufficient, standing alone, to create an implied contract of job security. The court also found that a corporate official's deposition testimony that there was an unwritten corporate policy regarding job security did not establish an implied contract, because there was no evidence employees were aware of this unwritten policy.]

. . . In sum, if there is any significant evidence that Guz had an implied contract against termination at will, that evidence flows exclusively from Bechtel's written personnel documents. It follows that there is no triable issue of an implied contract on terms broader than the specific provisions of those documents. In reviewing the Court of Appeal's determination that Bechtel may have breached contractual obligations to Guz by eliminating his work unit, we must therefore focus on the pertinent written provisions.

As Bechtel stresses, Policy 1101 itself purported to disclaim any employment security rights. However, Bechtel had inserted other language, not only in Policy 1101 itself, but in other written personnel documents, which described detailed rules and procedures for the termination of employees under particular circumstances. Moreover, the specific language of Bechtel's disclaimer, stating that employees had no contracts "*guaranteeing* . . . continuous service" (italics added) and were terminable at Bechtel's "option," did not foreclose an understanding between Bechtel and all its workers that Bechtel would make its termination decisions within the limits of its written personnel rules. Given these ambiguities, a fact finder could rationally determine that despite its general disclaimer, Bechtel had bound itself to the specific provisions of these documents.

. . . Bechtel's written personnel documents—which, as we have seen, are the sole source of any contractual limits on Bechtel's rights to terminate Guz—imposed no restrictions upon the company's prerogatives to eliminate jobs or work units, for any or no reason, even if this would lead to the release of existing employees such as Guz. . . . Policy 1101 confirmed that Bechtel was free to "reorganiz[e]" itself, or to "change[ ] . . . job requirements," and to "initiate[ ]" employee "terminations . . . caused by" this process, so long as Bechtel provided the requisite advance notice.

The RIF Guidelines set forth more detailed procedures for selecting individual layoff candidates, and for helping such persons obtain jobs elsewhere within the company. But the RIF Guidelines, like the Policies, neither stated nor implied any limits on Bechtel's freedom to implement the reorganization itself. . . . [Moreover], [w]hatever rights Policy 1101 gave an employee threatened with replacement on account of his or her individual poor performance, we see nothing in Bechtel's personnel documents which, despite Bechtel's general disclaimer, limited Bechtel's prerogative to eliminate an entire work unit, and thus its individual jobs, even if the decision was influenced by a belief that the unit's work would be better performed elsewhere within the company.

Accordingly, we conclude the Court of Appeal erred in finding, on the grounds it stated, that Guz's implied contract claim was triable. . . . The Court of Appeal did not address Guz's second theory, i.e., that Bechtel also breached its implied contract by failing, during and after the reorganization, to provide him personally with the fair layoff protections, including force ranking and reassignment help, which are set forth in its Policies and RIF Guidelines. This theory raises difficult questions, including what the proper remedy, if any, should be if Guz ultimately shows that Bechtel breached a contractual obligation to follow certain procedural policies in the termination process. . . . On remand, the Court of Appeal should confront this issue and should determine whether Guz has raised a triable issue on this theory.

NOTES AND QUESTIONS

1. As *Guz* suggests, if an employer includes a disclaimer in its policy manual, a court might still have to reconcile an apparent contradiction between the disclaimer and other policy provisions. *See* Rice v. Walmart Stores, Inc., 12 F. Supp. 2d 1207 (D. Kan. 1998) (denying summary judgment for employer despite handbook disclaimer, in part because handbook included other provisions that seemed to contradict the disclaimer); McGinnis v. Honeywell, Inc., 110 N.M. 1, 791 P.2d 452 (1990) (allowing jury to consider actual practice despite disclaimer). *But see* Dore v. Arnold Worldwide, Inc., 139 P.3d 56 (Cal. 2006) (employer's "90 day assessment" and "annual review" policies did not contradict or render ambiguous its "at will" proviso).

2. The parol evidence rule gives a disclaimer a certain effect with respect to prior or contemporaneous extrinsic promises. However, an employee's proof of an implied contract often depends on statements and events *subsequent* to the disclaimer. The parol evidence rule would not bar proof of subsequent statements or events. However, the disclaimer may still have important weight as evidence of what the employer intended and the employee could reasonably have understood.

California cases after *Guz* suggest that courts must balance the weight of evidence supporting an implied promise against the employer's disclaimer. In some cases courts have found evidence sufficient to overcome otherwise clear disclaimers. In *Stillwell v. Salvation Army*, 84 Cal.Rptr.3d 111 (Cal. App. 2008), for example, a court upheld a jury verdict for an employee despite a written agreement providing that employment was at will. While the court agreed that an employer's written policies should be the "central focus" of a dispute over job security, the court confirmed that an at-will proviso will not always bar or overcome other evidence implying an agreement to limit disciplinary discharge. The employee in *Stillwell* adduced four types of evidence in rebuttal of the at will proviso: (1) managers repeatedly assured him of continued employment and fairness; (2) he had served in a long and distinguished career with the employer; (3) the employer followed a custom of terminating employees only for cause; and (4) he had been instructed not to terminate other employees without prior performance warnings and an opportunity for improvement.

3. An employer's solution to the problem of alleged subsequent promises (promises postdating the written disclaimer) might be a provision requiring that any modification of "at will" status or other terms of employment must be in writing and signed by an authorized manager. *See, e.g.*, Solomon v. Walgreen Co., 975 F.2d 1086 (5th Cir. 1992); Kovacs v. Electronic Data Sys. Corp., 762 F. Supp. 161 (E.D. Mich. 1990). *Cf.* Andrews v. Southwest Wyoming Rehab. Ctr., 974 P.2d 948 (Wyo. 1999) (disclaimer plus no oral modification clause barred implied contract claim); HeartSouth, PLLC v. Boyd, 865 So. 2d 1095 (Miss. 2003) (provision requiring amendments to be in writing barred employer's claim that employee renewed expired agreement not to solicit employer's customers).

In some jurisdictions, however, a no oral modification clause provides a porous defense at best. Indeed, the common law of contracts granted little effect to such a clause. *See* Beatty v. Guggenheim Exploration Co., 122 N.E. 378, 381 (N.Y. 1919) (Cardozo, J.) ("Those who make a contract may unmake it. The clause which forbids a change may be changed like any other."). *See also* EMI Music Marketing v. Avatar Records, Inc., 317 F. Supp. 2d 412 (S.D.N.Y. 2004) (no oral modification clause does not bar claim based on subsequent agreement that has been partly performed in a way unequivocally referable to the oral modification); Shaw v. Burchfield, 481 So. 2d 247, 253 (Miss. 1985) (no-oral-modification clause would not have precluded evidence of subsequent oral modification of the contract, but plaintiff failed to prove such a modification). *But see* Avery Wiener Katz, *The Economics of Form and Substance in Contract Interpretation*, 104 Colo. L. Rev. 496, 508 (2004) ("[W]hile the common law of contracts does not recognize no-oral modification clauses as an official formal device, the presence of such a clause certainly raises the bar of persuasion for anyone who subsequently tries to claim that a contract has been so modified.").

4. Employers have used many types of documents during or after the hiring process to declare "at will" employment and disclaim any promise of job security. According to the Restatement (Second) of Contracts § 211, a person's apparent manifestation of assent to a writing is binding if he "has reason to believe that like writings are regularly used to embody terms of agreement of the same type." In *Ohanian, supra*, the employer inserted a disclaimer in an expense reimbursement form it required the plaintiff to submit for his relocation expenses. In a paragraph omitted from this book's reproduction of the court's opinion, the court dismissed the employer's parol evidence rule argument based on the disclaimer, because "strong evidence in the record" supported the jury's finding "that the writing was not intended to be a contract." 779 F.2d at 108-109. *Cf.* Ronnie Loper Chevrolet-GEO v. Hagey, 999 S.W.2d 81 (Tex. App. 1999) ("employment card" filled out by employee after accepting employment, which served among other things to provide employee's personal history information, and which included a declaration that employment was at will, did not override specific prior agreement of employment for a fixed term).

5. There are really two kinds of disclaimers. An employer might simply disclaim that an employee has any right of job security. In other words, the employer reaffirms the traditional presumption of employment at will. But an employer anxious to avoid a contrary implied promise arising from other policy statements might insert a much broader disclaimer, denying that an entire policy manual or handbook is a "contract." The goal of the broad disclaimer appears to be to head off an employee's invitation for a court to consider the policy manual in its entirety and resolve apparent contradictions in favor of an implied promise of job security. The Michigan court upheld a broad, no-contract disclaimer in Lytle v. Malady, 579 N.W.2d 906 (1998), finding that the disclaimer defeated any contractual effect with respect to other policy provisions appearing to require cause for discharge.

6. A broad disclaimer denying the contractual effect of policies can backfire if the employer hopes to rely on policies as proof of *employee* duties. *See, e.g.*, Heurtebise v. Reliable Business Computers, Inc., 550 N.W.2d 243 (Mich. 1996) (disclaimer negated employee's obligation to submit disputes to arbitration under employer's dispute resolution policy).

7. Assuming a disclaimer has any effect, whether under the parol evidence rule or for purposes of interpretation, are there any formal requirements for the disclaimer? Should courts be wary of employer disclaimers of job security in the same way they are wary of merchant disclaimers of warranty? *See* Worley v. Wyo. Bottling Co., 1 P.3d 615 (Wyo. 2000) (disclaimer ineffective to preclude implied promise because it did not occupy a paragraph of its own, but was blended into a paragraph covering several topics without bolding, capitalization, or use of other means to highlight its importance); Nicosia v. Wakefern Food Corp., 643 A.2d 554 (N.J. 1994) (broad disclaimer that policies were "not contractual" and "subject to change" were insufficiently clear to overcome implications of discipline and termination procedure); Jones v. Central Peninsula Gen. Hosp., 779 P.2d 783 (Alaska 1989) (handbook disclaimer not sufficiently clear and conspicuous).

Not all courts agree that a disclaimer must satisfy any special standard of conspicuousness. In Anderson v. Douglas & Lomason Co., 540 N.W.2d 277 (Iowa 1995), the Iowa court found that such a rule only begged the question and invited more litigation. The Iowa court proposed a more lenient two-part test, which is "similar to our consideration of handbook language in general." *Id.* at 288. First, is the disclaimer clear in its terms? Second, is it clear in its coverage? In *Anderson*, the disclaimer appeared at the end of a 53-page handbook, two inches below the preceding paragraph, evidently without any special typeface:

> This Employee Handbook is not intended to create any contractual rights in favor of you or the Company. The Company reserves the right to change the terms of this handbook at any time.

Id. Applying its two-part test, the court found this disclaimer reasonably clear in its denial of intent to create a contract, and unequivocal in its application to the entire handbook, including disciplinary procedures. Accordingly, the court rejected the employee's breach of contract claim based on the handbook.

8. In several states that have adopted a strong version of the presumption of employment at will, a disclaimer might be unnecessary to prevent an implied promise of job security. In any event, the courts of such states are much more likely

to uphold the effect of a disclaimer without regard to its clarity or conspicuousness, and despite other employer "policies" regarding discipline and discharge. *See, e.g.*, Williams v. First Tennessee Nat'l Corp., 97 S.W.3d 798 (Tex. App. 2003).

b. Modification or Revocation

IN RE CERTIFIED QUESTION (BANKEY v. STORER BROADCASTING CO.)

443 N.W.2d 112 (Mich. 1989)

GRIFFIN, Justice.

Pursuant to MCR 7.305(B), the United States Court of Appeals for the Sixth Circuit has certified, and we have agreed to answer, the following question:

> Once a provision that an employee shall not be discharged except for cause becomes legally enforceable under *Toussaint v. Blue Cross & Blue Shield of Michigan*, 408 Mich. 578 [579]; [292 N.W.2d 880] (1980), as a result of an employee's legitimate expectations grounded in the employer's written policy statements, may the employer thereafter unilaterally change those written policy statements by adopting a generally applicable policy and alter the employment relationship of existing employees to one at the will of the employer in the absence of an express notification to the employees from the outset that the employer reserves the right to make such a change?

We answer in the affirmative. An employer may, without an express reservation of the right to do so, unilaterally change its written policy from one of discharge for cause to one of termination at will, provided that the employer gives affected employees reasonable notice of the policy change.

I

In its order certifying the question, the Court of Appeals for the Sixth Circuit set forth the following facts:

> Kenneth Bankey was employed as a salesman for Storer Broadcasting Company for thirteen years until he was discharged on March 23, 1981. The reason given by Storer Broadcasting was poor job performance. On July 15, 1982, Mr. Bankey filed a complaint in the Michigan Circuit Court for the County of Oakland alleging that throughout his employment with Storer, there existed a policy that Storer would not terminate its employees without just cause, and that in reliance upon that policy he remained in Storer's employ for more than twelve years. On August 24, 1982, Storer Broadcasting removed the case from the Circuit Court for Oakland County to the United States District Court for the Eastern District of Michigan on the basis of diversity jurisdiction pursuant to 28 USC 1332. This case is controlled by the substantive law of the State of Michigan.

Mr. Bankey successfully argued in the district court that his employment relationship with Storer was controlled by [a] 1980 Personnel Policy Digest [issued by Storer] which expressly states that "an employee may be . . . discharged for cause." In January, 1981, Storer revised its Digest to eliminate any "for cause" requirement for discharge of its employees. The January 1981 Digest states that "[e]mployment is at the will of the company." The district court found as a matter of law that the 1980 Digest created a "for cause" employment contract and that once such a contract is established under *Toussaint*, the employer cannot unilaterally alter the employment relationship as to existing employees to permit discharge at will. The court's ruling on this issue was made following the defendant's motion for directed verdict at the close of plaintiff's case.

A jury awarded Mr. Bankey $55,000 in damages on his claim that Storer had breached its obligation not to discharge without cause. Storer's appeal in the United States Court of Appeals for the Sixth Circuit precipitated the certified question.

II

This Court granted the request to answer the certified question in order to resolve some of the uncertainty concerning the scope of what has come to be known as the *Toussaint* "handbook exception" to the employment-at-will doctrine. *Toussaint* modified the presumptive rule of employment-at-will by finding that a written discharge-for-cause employment policy may become legally enforceable in contract. . . . Do handbook provisions setting forth a personnel policy of termination for cause support only a limited expectation that the employer will adhere to that policy while it is in effect as official company policy? Or, may an employee legitimately expect that discharge for cause has become a permanent feature of his employment contract with the company?

III

. . . In a brief submitted in connection with our consideration of the certified question, Storer asserts that an employer may unilaterally change or adopt new personnel policies without having explicitly reserved the right to do so because only a unilateral contract is formed when an employee is hired for an indefinite period. Storer reasons that when an employee continues to work following an employer's unilateral change in policy, the employee's continued employment signifies acceptance of, and provides the necessary consideration for, a new unilateral contract. A unilateral contract is one in which the promisor does not receive a promise in return as consideration. 1 Restatement Contracts, §§ 12, 52, pp. 10-12, 58-59. In simplest terms, a typical employment contract can be described as a unilateral contract in which the employer promises to pay an employee wages in return for the employee's work. In essence, the employer's promise constitutes the terms of the employment agreement; the employee's action or forbearance in reliance upon the employer's promise constitutes sufficient consideration to make the promise legally binding. In such circumstances, there is no contractual requirement that the promisee do more than perform the act upon which the promise is predicated in order to legally obligate the promisor. *Toussaint, supra*, pp. 630-631, 292 N.W.2d 880 (separate opinion of Ryan, J.).

In a typical situation, where employment is for an indefinite duration, the unilateral contract framework provides no answer to the question: When will the act bargained for by the employer be fully performed? The answer to that question depends on the characterization of the "act" for which the promise is exchanged. If the "act" is simply a day's work (for a day's wage), then Storer's argument makes sense: The employer's offer is renewed each day, and each day's performance by the employee constitutes a new acceptance and a new consideration. But such a characterization can be strikingly artificial. Few employers and employees begin each day contemplating whether to renew or modify the employment contract in effect at the close of work on the previous day.

In his brief, plaintiff Bankey does not clearly state whether he relies on unilateral or a bilateral contract theory. He simply argues that any unilateral attempt by Storer to change an existing discharge-for-cause policy can be no more than a proposal for modification of the contract for which mutual assent would be required. However, Bankey admonishes us that there must be a "meeting of the minds" upon all essential points to constitute a valid contract. . . .

The major difficulty with such an argument as applied to the question before us is that the contractual obligation which may not be modified without mutual assent, under Bankey's theory, could have arisen without mutual assent under *Toussaint*'s own terms: "We hold that employer statements of policy . . . can give rise to contractual rights in employees without evidence that the parties mutually agreed that the policy statements would create contractual rights in the employee. . . ."*Toussaint, supra*, 408 Mich. pp. 614-615, 292 N.W.2d 880. Under circumstances where "contractual rights" have arisen outside the operation of normal contract principles, the application of strict rules of contractual modification may not be appropriate.

IV

While a majority of jurisdictions now recognize some type of "handbook exception" to the employment-at-will doctrine, there is no clear consensus as to either the legal theory supporting the handbook exception or the scope of the exception. Some of the cases suggest that enforceability of a handbook policy turns on an individual employee's reliance upon its provisions, though the extent to which detrimental reliance or promissory estoppel is a necessary element is not always made clear. Other courts have employed the unilateral contract theory to find an offer and acceptance of handbook provisions as terms of an employment contract.

The issue now before us—whether a written discharge-for-cause policy may be modified by the employer without explicit reservation at the outset of the right to do so—has been addressed by two other courts. In Chambers v. Valley Nat'l Bank, 3 IER Cases 1476 (Ariz. 1988); a bank employee hired in 1971 claimed that her layoff in 1987 breached a contractual obligation created by the bank's personnel manual. In 1984, following adoption by the Arizona Supreme Court of a handbook exception to the employment-at-will doctrine, the bank revised its manual and disclaimed any obligation to discharge only for cause. The United States District Court for the District of Arizona held that, given the 1984 disclaimer, the plaintiff could not reasonably have relied thereafter on the handbook as creating a contract guaranteeing discharge only for cause. The court characterized the disclaimer as an offer of modification of a unilateral contract which the plaintiff accepted by continuing to work for the bank.

In Thompson v. Kings Entertainment Co., 653 F. Supp. 871 (E.D. Va. 1987), the plaintiff employee painted signs at a Virginia theme park. In 1980, three years after he was hired, the plaintiff was given a personnel manual which included a discharge-for-cause provision. Subsequently, the theme park changed ownership, and in July, 1985, a new manual providing for employment at will was distributed. In August, 1985, the plaintiff was discharged, and he thereafter filed a diversity action in federal court, contending that the 1980 manual and various representations of his employer rebutted the presumption of employment at will. His employer argued that even if the 1980 manual created a discharge-for-cause contract, distribution in 1985 of the new manual served to reinvoke plaintiff's employment-at-will status. . . . [T]he federal district court . . . rejected the employer's motion for summary judgment, finding that the effect of the 1985 manual on plaintiff's status turned on whether he had accepted the change of status and received consideration for it. The court held that acceptance could not be inferred merely from plaintiff's continuing to work, and remanded the case for a jury determination of the questions of acceptance and consideration. . . .

V

Without rejecting the applicability of unilateral contract theory in other situations, we find it inadequate as a basis for our answer to the question as worded and certified by the United States Court of Appeals. We look, instead, to the analysis employed in *Toussaint* which focused upon the benefit that accrues to an employer when it establishes desirable personnel policies. Under *Toussaint*, written personnel policies are not enforceable because they have been "offered and accepted" as a unilateral contract; rather, their enforceability arises from the benefit the employer derives by establishing such policies.

> While an employer need not establish personnel policies or practices, where an employer chooses to establish such policies and practices and makes them known to its employees, the employment relationship is presumably enhanced. The employer secures an orderly, cooperative and loyal work force, and the employee the peace of mind associated with job security and the conviction that he will be treated fairly. No pre-employment negotiations need take place and the parties' minds need not meet on the subject; nor does it matter that the employee knows nothing of the particulars of the employer's policies and practices *or that the employer may change them unilaterally*. It is enough that the employer chooses, presumably in its own interest, to create an environment in which the employee believes that, whatever the personnel policies and practices, they are established and official at any given time, purport to be fair, and are applied consistently and uniformly to each employee. The employer has then created a situation "instinct with an obligation."

Toussaint, supra, 408 Mich. p. 613, 292 N.W.2d 880 (emphasis added).

Under the *Toussaint* analysis, an employer who chooses to establish desirable personnel policies, such as a discharge-for-cause employment policy, is not seeking to induce each individual employee to show up for work day after day, but rather is seeking to promote an environment conducive to collective productivity. The benefit to the employer of promoting such an environment, rather than the traditional contract-forming mechanisms of mutual assent or individual detrimental reliance, gives rise to a situation "instinct with an obligation." When, as in the question before us, the employer changes its discharge-for-cause policy to one of employment-at-will, the employer's benefit is correspondingly extinguished, as is the rationale for the court's enforcement of the discharge-for-cause policy.

Even though a discharge-for-cause policy may be modified or revoked, while such a policy remains in effect, "the employer may not treat its promise as illusory" by refusing to adhere to the policy's terms. *Toussaint*, p. 619, 292 N.W.2d 880. It has been suggested that if such a policy is revocable, it is of no value, and thus is the equivalent of an illusory promise. Of course, a permanent job commitment would be highly prized in the modern work force. However, it does not follow that anything less than a permanent job commitment is without meaning or value. Indeed, the prevalence of job security provisions in collective bargaining agreements that typically expire after only a few years attests to the fact that such commitments need not be permanent to have value.

Furthermore, it is important to recognize that even though an employment policy is revocable, the *Toussaint* approach to employer obligation promotes stability in employment relations in two significant ways: by holding employees accountable for personnel policies that "are established and official at any given time," and by requiring that such policies be "applied consistently and uniformly to each employee." *Toussaint* holds that an employee may "legitimately expect" that his employer will uniformly apply personnel policies "in force at any given time." *Id.*

It is one thing to expect that a discharge-for-cause policy will be uniformly applied while it is in effect; it is quite a different proposition to expect that such a personnel policy, having no fixed duration, will be immutable unless the right to revoke the policy was expressly reserved. The very definition of "policy" negates a legitimate expectation of permanence. "Policy" is defined as "a definite course or method of action selected (as by a government, institution, group, or individual) from among alternatives and in the light of given conditions to guide and usu[ally] determine present and future decisions; . . . a projected program consisting of desired objectives and the means to achieve them. . . ." Webster's Third New International Dictionary, Unabridged Edition (1964). In other words, a "policy" is commonly understood to be a flexible framework for operational guidance, not a perpetually binding contractual obligation. In the modern economic climate, the operating policies of a business enterprise must be adaptable and responsive to change.

Were we to answer the certified question by holding that once an employer adopted a policy of discharge-for-cause, such a policy could never be changed short of successful renegotiation with each employee who worked while the policy was in effect, the uniformity stressed in *Toussaint, supra*, pp. 613, 619, 624, 292 N.W.2d 880, would be sacrificed. If an employer had amended its handbook from time to time, as often is the case, the employer could find itself obligated in a variety of different ways to any number of different employees, depending on the modifications which had been adopted and the extent of the work force turnover. Furthermore, were we to answer the certified question as plaintiff Bankey requests, many employers would be tied to anachronistic policies in perpetuity merely because they did not have the foresight to anticipate the Court's *Toussaint* decision by expressly reserving at the outset the right to make policy changes.

While we hold today that an employer may make changes in a written discharge-for-cause policy applicable to its entire work force or to specific classifications without having reserved in advance the right to do so, we caution against an assumption that our answer would condone changes made in bad faith —for example, the temporary suspension of a discharge-for-cause policy to facilitate the firing of a particular employee in contravention of that policy. The principles on which *Toussaint* is based would be undermined if an employer could benefit from the good will generated by a discharge-for-cause policy while unfairly manipulating the way in which it is revoked. Fairness suggests that a discharge-for-cause policy announced with flourishes and fanfare at noonday should not be revoked by a pennywhistle trill at midnight. We hold that for the revocation of a discharge-for-cause policy to become legally effective, reasonable notice of the change must be uniformly given to affected employees.

We emphasize that our answer today is necessarily limited by the wording of the certified question which asks whether an employer under the circumstances set forth may unilaterally change from a discharge-for-cause to an employment-at-will policy.[17]

We answer the certified question in the affirmative. An employer may, consistent with *Toussaint*, unilaterally change a written discharge-for-cause policy to an employment-at-will policy even though the right to make such a change was not expressly reserved from the outset.

NOTES AND QUESTIONS

1. *Bankey* is an example of what is widely regarded as the "majority" rule permitting an employer unilaterally to modify or revoke a job security policy it unilaterally issued, without any requirement that the employer must supply additional consideration for the modification or revocation. *See also* Asmus v. Pacific Bell, 999 P. 2d 71, 78 (2000).

2. There is an alternative "minority" position that imposes a more substantial limit on the employer's unilateral modification or revocation of its policy. According to the minority rule, the employer must provide additional consideration for an employee's agreement to the change in policy, and the consideration must be something more than continued employment (which the employer already owes under its original policy). *See, e.g.*, Demasse v. ITT Corp., 984 P.2d 1138 (Ariz. 1999). What might constitute "consideration" for this purpose? Should a court examine the sufficiency of consideration to make sure that cancellation of job security is "fair"?

3. How important is it in *Bankey* that Storer Broadcasting System's alleged duty not to discharge without cause emanated from a policy manual? Would the court have permitted Storer to implement a new "at will" policy if it had made an *express* promise of job security in a formal, individual contract of employment with Bankey? What if Bankey had a fixed term of employment? *See* McCaskey v. Cal. State Automobile Ass'n, 118 Cal. Rptr. 3d 34 (Cal. App. 2010) (fixed term

---

[17] Our answer might be different, for example, if the employer's change in policy purported to affect employee benefits already accrued or "vested." In such cases, an employee's expectation that changes in policy for the future will not affect entitlements already vested or accrued finds support in our case law. Ottawa Co. v. Jaklinski, 377 N.W.2d 668 (Mich. 1985).

contract barred employer's unilateral modification).

According to Justice Levin, writing separately in *Bankey*, "Where . . . the employment contract arises not from statements in a policy manual but from an express contract or representation, a change in policy cannot change the contract because the contract is not based on a policy statement but on express agreement or a representation." 443 N.W.2d at 121 n.2. Does Justice Levin's approach suggest a hierarchy of promises, some more binding than others? Justice Levin offered the following example of a promise not so easily revoked: "If an employee accepts an offer of employment as long as the employee does the job, the contract is that he will be employed as long as he does the job because the contract arose out of an *express* agreement." *Id.*

4. If an employer's policy expressly *limits* the employer's right to modify, is the employer bound by its own limit? In *Asmus, supra*, the court noted that Pacific Bell once included the following statement in its "Management Employment Security Policy":

> It will be Pacific Bell's policy to offer all management employees who continue to meet our changing business expectations employment security through reassignment to and retraining for other management positions, even if their present jobs are eliminated.
>
> This policy *will be maintained* so long as there is no change that will materially affect Pacific Bell's business plan achievement.

999 P.2d at 73 (emphasis added). About five years later, after warning that the company might reconsider its policy, Pacific Bell announced it was cancelling its policy effective in six months. Subsequently terminated employees filed suit challenging Pacific Bell's action. The California Supreme Court held that Pacific Bell's cancellation of the policy was effective.

> An employer may unilaterally terminate a policy that contains a specified condition, if the condition is one of indefinite duration, and the employer effects the change after a reasonable time, on reasonable notice, and without interfering with the employees' vested benefits.

999 P.2d at 73.

5. By how much time must an employer's notice predate its reversal of a policy under the courts' reasoning in *Asmus* and *Bankey*? Writing separately from the majority in *Bankey*, Justice Levin worried that a "one rule fits all" approach might lead to disturbing results:

> Since the notice is to be given "uniformly," it may be contended that a middleaged employee who worked for twenty years under the discharge-for-cause policy is entitled to no more notice than a young entry-level employee who has worked for one month before the change in policy. . . . Most employees to whom job security may be important do not have the desire, mobility or ability to conduct a search for a discharge-for-cause employer during even a generous "reasonable notice" time span, especially if the employee does not expect that the employer may be considering discharging the employee after the "reasonable notice" expires.

443 N.W.2d at 122 n.3.

PROBLEMS

1. When Main Street Bank announced its plan to acquire First City Bank, employees at First City worried than some of them might be laid off when Main Street combined the administrative operations of both banks. Some of First City's employees began actively searching for positions elsewhere. To discourage employees from "jumping ship" while they were still needed, First City and Main Street announced two policies: (1) Main Street would continue to adhere to First City's job security policies, which included a provision that employees would not be discharged "without cause"; and (2) any First City employee whose job was "eliminated" in the course of corporate reorganization would be transferred to another position with Main Street with at least the same rate of pay. Because of this announcement, John Apple and Elsa Orange decided not to look elsewhere — they stayed with First City and then with Main Street after the acquisition was complete.

The acquisition did not immediately affect Apple's or Orange's jobs, and they remained in the same positions for the next two years. Near the end of the second year, Main Street issued a notice that it was "revoking" the job security/ job elimination policy in six months, and that all employment would be "at will." Main Street also announced that "in lieu of" the job security/job elimination policy, it was amending its severance pay policy to increase severance benefits by one week's pay for any employee whose termination was the result of "job elimination." Apple and Orange began to investigate alternative job opportunities, but job openings in their field were scarce.

a. Six months later, and a few days after the new policy took effect, Main Street informed Apple that he had been selected for layoff. Does Apple's layoff constitute a breach of contract?

b. On the same day it informed Apple of his prospective layoff, Main Street also informed Orange that it was terminating her employment for unsatisfactory performance. Main Street denied her request for severance pay on the grounds that it had terminated her employment for cause. Assuming Orange could successfully dispute that her termination was for good cause, does her termination constitute a breach of contract?

2. When Walter Pear applied for work at Main Street Bank, he filled out an application form that included the following language at the bottom of the front page: ALL EMPLOYMENT AT MAIN STREET BANK IS "AT WILL" AND MAY BE TERMINATED BY EITHER PARTY WITH TWO WEEKS' ADVANCE NOTICE. During his job interview, Pear mentioned that he was concerned about the layoffs the bank had experienced during the past few years, and the interviewer responded, "The Bank is past all that. This is a very successful organization and we wouldn't be hiring if jobs weren't secure." Pear also mentioned that his wife was pregnant, and that he might need a little time off in a few weeks. The interviewer replied, "this is a very family-friendly place. I'm sure it will be no problem." The Bank offered Pear a job and Pear accepted.

During his first month on the job Pear received a call at the office that his wife had gone into labor. Pear left work to take his wife to the hospital despite his supervisor's protest that Pear was needed at the office that day, and Pear took the next day off to be with his wife and new baby. When Pear finally returned to work, his supervisor fired him (as a recently hired employee, Pear did not qualify for FMLA leave). Is Pear's termination a breach of contract?

3. *Should Job Security Depend on Express Agreement of the Parties?*

STEWART J. SCHWAB, *LIFE-CYCLE JUSTICE: ACCOMMODATING JUST CAUSE AND EMPLOYMENT AT WILL*

92 Mich. L. Rev. 8 (1993)

A. THE SPECIFIC HUMAN-CAPITAL STORY

The key feature of the career employment relationship is that both sides are locked into it. The easiest explanation for lock-in comes from a human-capital story that emphasizes "asset specificity." Under the basic human-capital model, workers become more productive as they learn the ways of the firm. Because the gains exceed the costs of training, these firm-specific skills are worth learning. In contrast to general skills, however, these skills are not useful to other firms.

The issue becomes whether the employer and employee can decide how to share the costs and benefits so that this desirable training will occur. This issue can be resolved in a number of ways. . . . The best solution is for the employer and worker to share both the costs and benefits of firm-specific training.

In the training period at the firm, the worker accepts less than the outside wage [equaling productivity based on general skills], thereby paying for some of the training, but the employer pays him more than his productivity during the training period, thereby paying for some of the training. After training, the worker receives more than the outside wage, thereby reaping some of the benefits of training, but the employer does not pay the worker for his full productivity, thereby allowing the employer to reap some of the benefits of training. . . .

In practice, these higher post-training wages take the form of seniority based wages and late-vesting pensions, which induce workers to stay with the firm after training. Compared with the life cycle of otherwise similar workers, the model predicts that workers who receive substantial on-the-job training will receive higher pay in later years. Considerable empirical evidence supports this steep age-earnings profile of career employees and its relationship to training early in the career.

A critical part of this simple human-capital story is the self-enforcing feature of the relationship. Because the parties share the costs and benefits of training throughout the employee's work life, both parties want to continue the relationship. The employer pays employees less than their full value later in their career. This protects employees from discharge because a discharge would harm the employer as well. The late-career wage exceeds, however, the outside wage the employee could receive, thereby discouraging the employee from quitting.

B. THE EFFICIENCY-WAGE STORY AND THE POTENTIAL FOR OPPORTUNISM

Gary Becker's human-capital theory explained why wages rise with seniority, but puzzles arose that caused commentators to question the theory that workers would receive less than their value late in their career. . . . A final puzzle stems from studies that suggest that workers' pay relative to others in their job grade increases with seniority but their relative productivity does not. This evidence conflicts with Becker's hypothesis that productivity increases faster than wages. . . . To explain the puzzles, economists have developed an efficiency-wage model. The basic insight behind efficiency-wage models is that workers often work harder when the job pays more. High "efficiency wages" increase worker effort by making the job more valuable to the worker. Because workers want to keep the valuable job, they will work hard to avoid being dismissed. In effect, high wages increase the penalty for being dismissed—a dismissed worker forgoes the large payout. . . .

. . . The implicit contract promises large payouts for senior workers, but it promises this reward only for hard-working employees. The firm recognizes that day-to-day monitoring of a worker's effort may be difficult, but over a period of years the firm hopes to spot and weed out shirkers. The threat of being fired before the large payoff keeps employees working hard. Because employees work harder than otherwise, the firm can afford the higher compensation. Large law firms epitomize this model.

A related literature emphasizes that firms may conduct internal tournaments to induce high effort by junior and midlevel management employees. Tournaments are especially likely when firms cannot monitor actual effort or output but can evaluate relative performance. A firm may (implicitly) tell an incoming class of workers that the best worker will win the grand prize of C.E.O. A single prize may be insufficient inducement, however, so the firm may (implicitly) offer several runner-up prizes of cushy vice-president jobs for those who try hard but fail. This model likewise suggests an implicit agreement whereby firms pay late-career employees more than their current productivity. . . .

. . . The critical point of the expanded story is that the implicit contract is not always self-enforcing. [After a certain point], firms pay late-career employees more than they currently produce. At this point, late-career employees become vulnerable to opportunistic firing because the general self-interest check on arbitrary firings does not exist; firing such a worker does not hurt the employer but is instead in its immediate economic interest. One can see a role for law in improving this situation. By policing against opportunism, the law can make the employment relationship more secure for and valuable to both sides. To understand fully the role law can play, we must examine the concept of opportunism more closely.

C. Contracting Problems in Career Employment

One solution to the problem of opportunism is for the parties entering into career employment to negotiate detailed contracts, enforceable by courts, that specify appropriate behavior by both sides. Unfortunately, three contracting challenges make detailed contracts an unsatisfactory solution. First, the parties cannot easily anticipate the future contingencies, or states of the world, that will influence the relationship. Will demand for the product stay strong? Will the firm shift its focus from the employee's specialty to other areas that require more general skills? While all predictions of the future are difficult, anticipating events twenty or thirty years in advance is an exceptional challenge for employers and employees.

Second, even if parties can anticipate a future event, they may have difficulty specifying in detail the appropriate contractual response, particularly when one party has access to relevant information that the other cannot easily observe. A key element in the employment relationship is whether the employee is working hard, or, from the employee's perspective, whether the employer is dismissing him for failure to work hard or for an unfair, opportunistic reason. When monitoring is difficult, two alternatives emerge. First, the parties may decide not to make any part of the contract contingent on difficult-to-monitor behavior. An at-will clause would accomplish this goal by making worker efforts irrelevant to the permissibility of discharge. Alternatively, the parties may write a vague "best efforts" or "good faith" clause for the contingency. While this solution invites later court or arbitrator supervision over the meaning of the terms, that supervision may be preferable to contractual language that straitjackets parties' future options.

Finally, having anticipated a future problem and specified the contractual response, a party may be unable to prove a breach in court. Economists term this problem an unverifiable contract. Unverifiability is particularly problematic when the contractual language is vague — as it will often be in relational contracts. Both employer and employee might know that the employee is not working as hard as "best efforts" require, but the employer cannot assemble sufficient objective evidence to convince a court or arbitrator of this fact. If the parties cannot turn to outside enforcement, they must develop self-enforcing mechanisms for any agreement to be effective. But, as we have seen, career employment contracts — particularly those following the efficiency-wage model — are not fully self-enforcing.

D. POTENTIAL FOR OPPORTUNISM

In the absence of enforceable, detailed contracts that regulate behavior, parties to a long-term relationship become vulnerable to opportunism. They cannot easily leave the relationship because they would have to repeat the investments or forgo their value. The existence of "sunk costs" for one party creates a potential for opportunistic behavior by the other side. A firm can pay workers less than they are worth or treat them more harshly than the initial agreement contemplated, knowing they cannot easily move. The employees can produce less than their skills allow, knowing the employer cannot easily replace them.

The law can sometimes help monitor opportunistic behavior, thereby increasing the parties' overall gains from the relationship. If the law can enforce promises not to exploit the other side's vulnerability, the parties can more confidently invest and the relationship will be more rewarding to both sides. The law has limits, however, because the contractual language often will be general and vague, as we have seen. More importantly, because both employer and employee are investing, both can be exploited. A legal rule favoring one side would leave much opportunism by the other unchecked. To curb opportunism adequately, courts must engage in difficult, case-by-case assessments or create more flexible presumptions. . . .

1. EMPLOYER VULNERABILITY TO SHIRKING

As the human-capital model indicates, employers make heavy investments in recruiting and training workers. To ensure an adequate return on their investment, employers want workers to stay and produce for them after training. Some scholars focus on employer recruitment and training costs in emphasizing employer vulnerability to employees quitting, but this is not the true problem of opportunism. The basic human-capital model suggests that employers can adopt delayed-payment schemes to discourage quitting, thus making the contract self-enforcing. Late-vesting pensions and seniority-based wages can tell workers: "If you stick around, you will do well."

The greater risk to employers comes from employee shirking. The efficiency-wage model highlights the shirking problem. Even if pensions and seniority wages discourage workers from quitting, an employer still faces problems when workers stay. Workers often do not work as hard as they would under a fully specified and monitored contract. . . . A fully specified optimal contract would designate an optimal level of effort. Workers would agree to exert this effort because they prefer the higher wages that accompany it to an easier work life; the employer would agree because the greater productivity is worth the higher wages. Once hired, however, an employee may shirk from this optimal effort if employers have difficulty monitoring or replacing workers. Indeed, it is irrational for workers to work up to "optimal" levels if they prefer coasting a little. Workers know that the employer will have to spend money to catch shirkers and that, if it fires a shirker, the employer will have to recruit and train a replacement. As long as workers perform better than a rookie would — considering the costs of monitoring, recruiting, and training — the firm must accept less than optimal efforts from its workers.

Much of the debate over at-will employment addresses whether parties can write effective contracts to overcome the shirking problem. To put it bluntly, the real question is whether the threat of firing for cause is sufficient to deter substandard performance by workers. Proponents of at will emphasize the unverifiability of the performance standard in many employment contracts. The employer may know the worker is shirking but cannot convince a court or arbitrator that the conduct amounts to shirking. Oliver Williamson has emphasized the difficulty in distinguishing a consummate performance from a perfunctory performance: "Consummate cooperation is an affirmative job attitude whereby gaps are filled, initiative is taken, and judgment is exercised in an instrumental way. Perfunctory cooperation involves working to rules and in other respects performing in a minimally acceptable way." One problem employers have in documenting a "perfunctory performance" is that particular instances of misconduct often seem trivial. Concluding that they add up to a significant problem requires acknowledging that the whole problem exceeds the sum of the parts. The heart of the employment-at-will argument is that proving cause under what is essentially an unverifiable agreement against shirking places too great a burden on employers, preventing them from effectively using efficiency wages to deter shirking.

Some may argue that commentators overstate this shirking problem because the employee's desire for a good reputation deters shirking. Even if shirking is possible in a just-cause world, this counterargument runs, benefits accrue to employees with a reputation for hard work. Not only may the incumbent employer reward hard work with promotions and pay raises, but employees with good reputations are most attractive to outside employers. Nevertheless, this reputation argument, in both its inside and outside reputation forms, ignores several important facts. First, an individual worker with a good inside reputation may not reap major rewards. As we saw, employers often establish pay and promotion ladders that do not depend on current individual productivity in order to discourage quits with promises of big paydays in the future. In such internal labor markets, pay scales attach to jobs rather than workers, and seniority rather than merit often determines who gets the jobs. Promoting individual workers simply because of individual hard work may not be worth the disruptions in the general progression system. In these internal labor markets, then, unusually good effort may not be rewarded even though unusually bad effort is punished by firing. Second, an employee may find it hard to acquire a good outside reputation if his skills are firm-specific. An academic whose publications are useful to many potential employers can obtain an outside reputation. Indeed, some might argue that the major inside job of the academic is to acquire an outside reputation. An engineer working on a classified defense project finds it more difficult—and therefore has less incentive—to obtain an outside reputation for hard work. The reluctance of employers to give candid references, itself a response to defamation law, exacerbates the difficulty for employees seeking to establish outside reputations.

A second response to the shirking argument involves a quick comparative law lesson. In the rest of the industrialized world, at-will employment is unknown, yet workers manage to work hard without the threat of firing. As Jack Beermann and Joseph Singer lament, why does our society assume it can trust employers not to abuse the power of arbitrary firings while it refuses to trust employees protected by just cause? Of course, one can overdramatize the comparative lesson. Industrial tribunals in Europe, having found a dismissal to be unjust, usually award modest severance pay that rarely exceeds six months duration. Further, commentators of "Eurosclerosis" would caution against using Europe as a model for productive labor markets.

Ultimately, the verifiability problem involves a question of degree, and the problem is greater for some jobs than for others. To the degree that clear contracts against shirking are difficult to write, monitor, and enforce, opportunistic behavior by employees will remain a threat.

2. EMPLOYEE VULNERABILITY

As both the human-capital and efficiency-wage models emphasize, employees invest heavily as they pursue a career with a single employer. First, they obtain training that is more useful for their own employer than it would be elsewhere—what economists term job-specific human capital. Second, they join the company's career path. This path, as we have seen, ties pay, promotions, and benefits to seniority and generally forbids lateral entry. A major cost of pursuing a career with one firm is that one forgoes other ladders and must start over at the bottom if one leaves the firm. Additionally, as they plan for a lifetime with an employer, workers put down roots, establish networks of friends in the workplace and the community, buy homes within commuting distance of the job, and build emotional ties to the community.

Losing these investments, roots, and ties can be devastating. Many studies document how even impersonal plant closings lead to increases in "cardiovascular deaths, suicides, mental breakdowns, alcoholism, ulcers, diabetes, spouse and child abuse, impaired social relationships, and various other diseases and abnormal conditions." Being singled out and fired may be even more devastating.

Because of these tremendous costs, no employee wants to lose his job involuntarily. Further, these investments, roots, and ties are sunk costs that trap the worker in his current firm, inhibiting him from departing voluntarily. Even if the career does not proceed as anticipated, the employee is reluctant to quit because the job remains preferable to alternative jobs. Such trapped workers are vulnerable to opportunism. The employer might pay them less than the implicit contract requires or work them harder, knowing they cannot easily quit.

By itself, this potential for opportunism does not justify a just-cause standard. Employers want such exploited workers to stay, not to leave. Only when conditions become so intolerable that the employee prefers to quit for another job might termination law come into play. In the economist's framework, this situation occurs when the employer has appropriated all the gains from the relationship, making the career no longer better than alternative jobs. Lawyers label these intolerable conditions a constructive discharge.

Defenders of at will contend that employer self-interest protects productive employees from discharge. An employer hurts itself by arbitrarily terminating a productive worker or by causing him to quit because it wastes the recruiting and training investment in the employee. To avoid its own sunk-cost losses, an employer wants to keep good workers and fire only workers who fall below the standard of new entrants. . . .

While employers can make mistakes, the self-enforcing feature should minimize firing of productive workers. Employees do not need the grand and expensive apparatus of the law for further protection, claim at will's defenders. Indeed, its very expense harms employees as well as employers, for wages will inevitably fall as terminations become more expensive.

Opponents of at-will employment remain skeptical. A major concern is that an employer is not a monolith but rather a hierarchy of high-level managers and low-level supervisors. Often low-level supervisors make the decision to fire, and the factors influencing their decisions are often not perfectly aligned with the profit-maximizing interest of shareholders. Thus, while shareholders may not want employees to be fired arbitrarily, supervisors might. Personality conflicts and power trips may lead supervisors to fire valuable and productive employees. Again, one can overstate the dangers of front-line supervisors running amok. The firm has incentives voluntarily to reduce supervisor mistakes so long as the gains in employee satisfaction outweigh the costs of supervising the supervisors. Just-cause advocates cannot make their point simply by showing that agency costs exist. They must show further that employers will not take cost-effective steps to ensure that they treat their employees fairly.

One check on such opportunism—emphasized in the efficiency-wage literature—is the employer's concern for its reputation. If word gets out that an employer routinely fires older workers, it will be harder for the employer to recruit entrants into career jobs. Perhaps more damaging than its outside reputation is its inside reputation with fellow employees when older, productive workers are fired. This loss of collegiality may encourage other workers to quit. Problematically for the employer, the most productive workers likely have the greatest opportunities for moving elsewhere.

In many situations, reputation is unlikely to check fully the employer's incentive to fire late-career workers. Young job entrants cannot easily assess an employer's reputation for how it handles senior workers. Great problems arise in passing on knowledge of a firm's opportunistic firings between generations of workers. These problems are particularly acute in small or new firms, where much of the workforce works. Finally, a reputation for harsh personnel policies may not greatly harm declining firms that are not hiring many new workers.

Because reputation is not a full check on opportunism, firms must compensate workers for the risk that the delayed bonanza may not accrue. Early-career wages, or the late-career bonuses and pensions, must be higher than they would have to be were reputations more secure. Court scrutiny of opportunistic firings may offer another method of policing long-term contracts. Such thirdparty scrutiny may allow employers to offer efficiency-wage contracts at lower overall cost. The danger, of course, is that court intervention will diminish the employer's flexibility in firing workers whose shirking a court cannot verify. The question is whether court intervention can be limited to opportunistic firings, rather than to a broader supervision against unfair firings in general.

NOTES AND QUESTIONS

1. As Professor Schwab points out, the termination of employment can cause a significant loss to either party—employee or employer—depending on the timing and circumstances of the termination. By what contractual devices do employers seek to protect themselves and discourage employees from resigning?

In addition to some of the devices we have seen in previous chapters, employers sometimes require employees to sign agreements restricting resignation or post-employment competitive activity. The effect and enforcement of such agreements is addressed in Chapter 9.

2. How well do any of the contract theories described in previous sections of this chapter address the "life cycle" risks described by Professor Schwab?

3. The Age Discrimination in Employment Act prohibits employers from discriminating against employees over the age of 40. How does the ADEA compare with the "implied contract" theory of cases such as *Pugh* in addressing employee life-cycle risks? To the extent an implied contract theory depends on an employee's longevity, does the ADEA render that theory superfluous?

4. Montana abrogated the employment at will doctrine by statute in 1987, replacing it with a rule against "wrongful discharge." Discharge is "wrongful" if:

a. it was in retaliation for the employee's refusal to violate public policy or for reporting a violation of public policy;

b. the discharge was not for good cause and the employee had completed the employer's probationary period of employment; or

c. the employer violated the express provisions of its own written personnel policy.

Mont. Code Ann. § 39-2-904(1). In the absence of a specific employer policy, the "probationary" period for new employees is six months. *Id.* . *See generally* Leonard Bierman & Stuart A. Youngblood, *Interpreting Montana's Pathbreaking*

Wrongful Discharge from Employment Act: A Preliminary Analysis, 53 Mont. L. Rev. 53 (1992). *See also* Corrada Betances v. Sea-Land Serv., Inc., 248 F.3d 40 (1st Cir. 2001) (describing Puerto Rican statute requiring severance pay to employees discharged without "good cause").

If an employer in Montana hires an employee for a fixed one-year term, and declines "without cause" to renew the employee's employment at the end of the term, has the employer violated Montana's wrongful *discharge* statute? *See* Mont. Code Ann. § 39-2-912; Farris v. Hutchinson, 838 P.2d 374 (Mont. 1992) (no).

5. There is a lively debate whether job protection statutes such as the Montana law raise unemployment by making employers fearful of hiring hard-to-fire employees. Professor Richard Epstein warns that "where an employer might have been more willing to take risky employees under an at-will rule, he will now be less willing to do so under the for-cause rule because any subsequent demotion or dismissal will be an open invitation to a lawsuit." Richard Epstein, *In Defense of the Contract at Will*, 51 U. Chi. L. Rev. 947, 953, 972 (1984). *See also* Andrew P. Morriss, *Bad Data, Bad Economics, and Bad Policy: Time to Fire Wrongful Discharge Law*, 74 Tex. L. Rev. 1901, 1902 (1996).

On the other hand, Professor Ann McGinley argues that U.S. jurisdictions or other nations with job security laws have not seen diminished employer enthusiasm for hiring or a rise in unemployment:

> Studies in Great Britain of management attitudes have shown that only eight percent of firms surveyed expressed reluctance to hire additional staff because of the job protection laws .... Instead of failing to hire ..., employers reacted to the job security laws passed in Britain in the 1970s by taking greater care in selection of persons to hire. The laws have ... led to the establishment of internal procedures. Companies with internal procedures have a lower rate of suits filed against them .... [O]nly approximately 10% of British employees dismissed for reasons other than layoffs file unfair dismissal suits. In Montana, the only state to have passed legislation requiring just cause for discharge, the unemployment rate has declined from 7.4% in 1987 when the Montana Wrongful Discharge Act was passed to 5.5% in 1995.

Ann C. McGinley, *Rethinking Civil Rights and Employment at Will: Toward a Coherent National Discharge Policy*, 57 Ohio St. L.J. 1443, 1522-23 (1996). In fact, since enacting job protection Montana's unemployment rate has remained, as it was before, about 1% lower than he national average, and comparable to unemployment in two neighboring states:[19]

---

19 Chart created from data at: U.S. Bureau of Labor Statistics, *Annual Unemployment Rates by State* (online at https://www.icip.iastate.edu/tables/employment/unemployment-states) (last accessed Jan. 1, 2018).

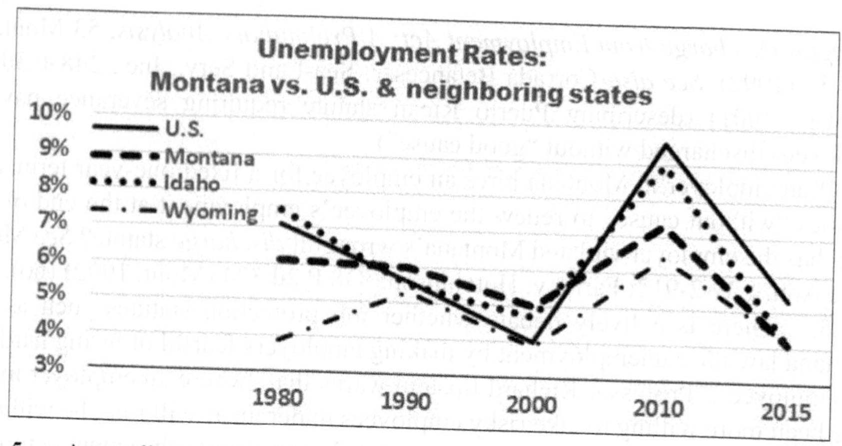

5. According to the Restatement of Contracts, "Every contract imposes upon each party a duty of good faith and fair dealing in its performance and its enforcement." RESTATEMENT (SECOND) OF CONTRACTS § 205. A recurring question in employment law has been whether the requirement of "good faith" limits an employer's reasons for terminating "at will" employment. To put the question another way, is a bad faith motivation for terminating employment a violation of the "covenant" of good faith implied in every contract, including employment contracts? If so, when does an unreasonable motivation for discharge constitute "bad faith" or a lack of "good faith?" Answering this question has proven difficult because there is no precise definition of "good faith." However, cases applying the duty of good faith have involved some identifiable fact patterns. In one fact pattern, courts have applied the duty of good faith to prevent one party from unexpectedly recapturing or appropriating a thing of value that was all or part of the intended consideration for the other party's performance of a contract.

WAKEFIELD v. NORTHERN TELECOM, INC.

769 F.2d 109 (2d Cir. 1985)

WINTER, Circuit Judge:

This is an action by a salesman against his former employer for damages arising out of the termination of the employment relationship. A jury awarded the plaintiff, Wilfred Wakefield, $111,079.87 on a breach of contract claim. Northern Telecom, Inc. ("NTI"), the employer, appeals. . . .

Wilfred Wakefield . . . began working as a salesman for Danray, Inc. in 1975, selling Danray's telephone switching systems. In 1978, commissions on sales of Danray equipment were governed by a "Sales Incentive Plan" that stated it would be in effect from January 1, 1978 to December 31, 1978.

In January, 1978, NTI, . . . a wholly owned subsidiary of Northern Telecom Ltd., and sells switching systems similar to Danray's, acquired Danray. On October 26, 1979, Danray discharged 57 employees, one of which was Wakefield. . . .

The district court applied New Jersey law to Wakefield's breach of contract claim. NTI argues that this was error, and that the district court should have applied the substantive law of New York. We need not decide this issue, because New Jersey and New York contract law do not differ so far as the legal issues before us are concerned.

Wakefield's claim is that NTI breached its contract to pay him commissions on sales of switching equipment by dismissing him after he had performed services that assured a number of sales in the future. The parties agree that the NTI commission plan constituted a binding contract, although they dispute the precise terms of the plan in effect at the pertinent times. NTI claims the relevant contract is the 1978 Danray Sales Incentive Plan, which NTI adopted after the takeover. Paragraph J of the Plan provided that

> In order to receive incentive compensation under this Plan, the participant must be a Danray employee on the date the incentive compensation is to be paid pursuant to the Plan. It will be Danray's policy to ensure a fair, equitable and prompt payment of any incentive due an employee whose employment is terminated or who is transferred to a non-sales position.

NTI argues that this provision on its face defeats Wakefield's claim for commissions because Wakefield was not an NTI employee at the time the commissions in question became payable. . . .

Wakefield offers a . . . theory that would, if legally and factually supported, permit recovery whether or not Paragraph J was in effect at the pertinent time. That theory is that NTI fired him precisely in order to avoid paying him commissions on sales that were completed but for formalities. A termination so motivated, he argues, violates an implied covenant of good faith and fair dealing.

NTI responds . . . by arguing that Wakefield was an at-will employee, terminable by NTI for any reason at any time. It notes that the New York Court of Appeals has squarely held that the implied covenant of good faith does not give rise to a contract action for the wrongful discharge of an at-will employee under New York law, Murphy v. American Home Products, Inc., 448 N.E.2d 86, 91 (N.Y. 1983), since the contrary result would be wholly inconsistent with the very nature of the contract . . . New Jersey law leads to the same result. Pierce v. Ortho Pharmaceutical Corp., 417 A.2d 505, 512 (N.J. 1980). . . .

Wakefield may not, therefore, recover for his termination *per se.* However, the contract for payment of commissions creates rights distinct from the employment relation, and, whether or not Paragraph J is still effective, obligations derived from the covenant of good faith implicit in the commission contract may survive the termination of the employment relationship.

Implied contractual obligations may coexist with express provisions which seemingly negate them where common expectations or the relationship of the parties as structured by the contract so dictate. Zilg v. Prentice-Hall, Inc., 717 F.2d 671 (2d Cir.1983), *cert. denied,* 466 U.S. 938 (1984) (publisher must make good faith initial promotional efforts notwithstanding contract clause vesting in it the sole determination as to number of volumes printed and amount of advertising expenditures). A covenant of good faith should not be implied as a modification of an employer's right to terminate an at-will employee because even a whimsical termination does not deprive the employee of benefits expected in return for the employee's performance. ... Where, however, a covenant of good faith is necessary to enable one party to receive the benefits promised for performance, it is implied by the law as necessary to effectuate the intent of the parties. Thus, in

Zilg, an obligation on the publisher's part to make a good faith initial effort to promote a book was implied from the contractual structure in which the author gave the publisher exclusive rights to publish it. *See also* Onderdonk v. Presbyterian Homes, 425 A.2d 1057 (N.J. 1981). . . .

Paragraph J . . . cannot be read to enable the defendant to terminate an employee for the purpose of avoiding the payment of commissions which are otherwise owed. Such an interpretation would make the performance by one party the cause of the other party's non-performance. *See* Association Group Life, Inc. v. Catholic War Veterans, 293 A.2d 382 (N.J. 1972) (per curiam). Commission agreements are customarily used in circumstances in which agents or employees cannot be directly supervised and their performance cannot be effectively monitored or measured apart from concrete results. In such circumstances, an unfettered right to avoid payment of earned commissions in the principal or employer creates incentives counterproductive to the purpose of the contract itself in that the better the performance by the employee, the greater the temptation to terminate.

Implying this obligation into the contract by no means deprives Paragraph J . . . of meaning. Employees who leave NTI voluntarily or who are terminated for reasons other than a desire to avoid payment of earned commissions, including reasons which are mistaken or arbitrary, have no right to further commissions. Thus, if NTI demonstrates that Wakefield's discharge was part of a legitimate reduction in force or motivated by dissatisfaction with him, justified or not, Paragraph J, if effective, would operate to bar payment of commissions to Wakefield. . . .

[The court found it necessary to remand the case for another trial with respect to Wakefield's implied duty of good faith claim, because the trial court had failed to submit to the jury an issue with respect to continuing efficacy of Paragraph J, and the jury's verdict may have been based on an erroneous interpretation of the express terms of contract]. We conclude that the district court's charge on NTI's implied obligation of good faith was also erroneous. The heart of that instruction was that Wakefield had to prove

> that NTI did not act in good faith, but terminated him for reasons which were known or should have been known to be invalid, mere pretext, or resulted from a delegation of authority so that the recommendation with respect to the plaintiff's discharge was entrusted to a superior who was not disinterested or objective.

At no point did the instructions limit Wakefield's recovery to a discharge motivated by a desire to avoid paying commissions otherwise owed. Rather, they imported notions of wrongful discharge into the implied obligation of good faith and thus imposed upon NTI a generalized duty not to discharge Wakefield wrongfully, a duty which does not exist under New York or New Jersey law.[3]

We thus remand for a new trial. To summarize, Wakefield . . . may attempt to prove that NTI's desire to avoid paying him commissions that were virtually

[3] This error was aggravated by a charge on damages which instructed the jury to award Wakefield all the commissions he "would have earned" had he remained in NTI's employ. To the extent this language suggested that he might recover more than the commissions earned before his termination, it had to have been based upon a wrongful discharge theory rather than a breach of the agreement to pay vested commissions. . . .

certain to become vested was a substantial motivating factor in the decision to discharge him. If the discharge was otherwise motivated, he may not recover on the good faith theory.

NOTES AND QUESTIONS

1. Another early case applying the implied duty of good faith in a dispute over deferred compensation is Fortune v. National Cash Register Co., 364 N.E.2d 1251 (Mass. 1977). There, the court held that an employer breached the implied duty of good faith by terminating the plaintiff to defeat the vesting of his right to sales commissions for work he had already performed. The court upheld a jury verdict for the amount of the commissions. *See also* K Mart Corp. v. Ponsock, 732 P.2d 1364 (Nev. 1987) (affirming jury finding that employer dismissed employee "to save having to pay him retirement benefits"); Hall v. Farmers Ins. Exch., 713 P.2d 1027 (Okla. 1985) (employer wrongfully and in bad faith discharged employee in order to deprive employee of renewal premiums); Mitford v. de Lasala, 666 P.2d 1000 (Alaska 1983) (employer violated covenant of good faith by discharging him to interfere with his right to share of profits).

But not all states agree that an implied duty of good faith imposes any limit on an employer's right to discharge at will, even under circumstances such as those in *Wakefield. See, e.g.,* Melnick v. State Farm Mut. Auto. Ins. Co., 749 P.2d 1105 (N.M. 1988); Frichter v. Nat'l Life & Acc. Ins. Co., 620 F. Supp. 922, 927 (E.D. La. 1985) (interpreting Louisiana law).

The Restatement of Employment Law chooses the path of *Wakefield* and *Fortune* in endorsing an employer's implied duty of good faith "not to terminate or seek to terminate the employment relationship or effect other adverse employment action for the purpose of: (1) preventing the vesting or accrual of an employee right or benefit; or (2) retaliating against the employee for refusing to consent to a change in earned compensation or benefits. " *Id.* § 3.05.

2. In the case of deferred benefits under a plan covered by the Employee Retirement Income Security Act (ERISA), there is a federal remedy for an employer's interference with an employee's benefit rights. *See* 29 U.S.C. § 1140. The ERISA remedy preempts any similar claim under state law. Ingersoll-Rand Co. v. McClendon, 498 U.S. 133 (1990).

3. *Wakefield*, *Fortune*, and *McLendon* involved an employee's loss of limited components of the compensation or "consideration" for which he or she had rendered performance to the employer. In light of Professor Schwab's article, *supra*, on the life cycle of employment, is there a broader view of the "benefit" for which an employee renders service exclusively to the employer over the long term? Is the right to security in the later years of an employee's long service part of the deferred compensation for which employee works ? Such was the view of an intermediate California court in Cleary v. American Airlines, 168 Cal. Rptr. 722 (Cal. App. 1980): "As a result of this covenant [of good faith], a duty arose on the part of the employer . . . to do nothing which would deprive plaintiff . . . of the benefits of the employment bargain—benefits described in the complaint as having accrued during the plaintiff's 18 years of employment." Stated in this fashion, an implied duty of good faith resembles the implied contract theory of

Pugh. *See also* Kuhl v. Wells Fargo Bank, N.A., 281 P.3d 716 (Wyo. 2012). Whether a theory of good faith offers better protection than *Pugh*'s implied contract depends in part on whether it is more effective in overriding "disclaimers" and other employer countermeasures that limiting an implied contract.

GUZ v. BECHTEL NAT'L, INC.

24 Cal. 4th 317, 8 P.3d 1089, 100 Cal. Rptr. 2d 352 (Cal. 2000)

[The facts are set forth in another portion of this court's opinion at p. 705, *supra*.]

The sole asserted basis for Guz's implied covenant claim is that Bechtel violated its established personnel policies when it terminated him without a prior opportunity to improve his "unsatisfactory" performance, used no force ranking or other objective criteria when selecting him for layoff, and omitted to consider him for other positions for which he was qualified. Guz urges that even if his contract was for employment at will, the implied covenant of good faith and fair dealing precluded Bechtel from "unfairly" denying him the contract's benefits by failing to follow its own termination policies.

Thus, Guz argues, in effect, that the implied covenant can impose substantive terms and conditions beyond those to which the contract parties actually agreed. . . . The covenant of good faith and fair dealing, implied by law in every contract, exists merely to prevent one contracting party from unfairly frustrating the other party's right to receive the benefits of the agreement actually made. (E.g., Waller v. Truck Ins. Exchange, Inc. (1995) 900 P.2d 619.) The covenant thus cannot "'be endowed with an existence independent of its contractual underpinnings.'" (*Ibid.*, quoting Love v. Fire Ins. Exchange (1990) 271 Cal. Rptr. 246.) It cannot impose substantive duties or limits on the contracting parties beyond those incorporated in the specific terms of their agreement.

Labor Code section 2922 establishes the presumption that an employer may terminate its employees at will, for any or no reason. A fortiori, the employer may act peremptorily, arbitrarily, or inconsistently, without providing specific protections such as prior warning, fair procedures, objective evaluation, or preferential reassignment. Because the employment relationship is "fundamentally contractual" (*Foley, supra*, 254 Cal. Rptr. 211, 765 P.2d 373), limitations on these employer prerogatives are a matter of the parties' specific agreement, express or implied in fact. The mere existence of an employment relationship affords no expectation, protectible by law, that employment will continue, or will end only on certain conditions, unless the parties have actually adopted such terms. Thus if the employer's termination decisions, however arbitrary, do not breach such a substantive contract provision, they are not precluded by the covenant.

The same reasoning applies to any case where an employee argues that even if his employment was at will, his arbitrary dismissal frustrated his contract benefits and thus violated the implied covenant of good faith and fair dealing. Precisely because employment at will allows the employer freedom to terminate the relationship as it chooses, the employer does not frustrate the employee's contractual rights merely by doing so. In such a case, "the employee cannot complain about a deprivation of the benefits of continued employment, for the agreement never provided for a continuation of its benefits in the first instance." (Hejmadi v. AMFAC, Inc. (1988) 249 Cal. Rptr. 5.)

Of course, as we have indicated above, the employer's personnel policies and practices may become implied-in-fact terms of the contract between employer and employee. If that has occurred, the employer's failure to follow such policies when terminating an employee is a breach of the contract itself.

A breach of the contract may also constitute a breach of the implied covenant of good faith and fair dealing. But insofar as the employer's acts are directly actionable as a breach of an implied-in-fact contract term, a claim that merely realleges that breach as a violation of the covenant is superfluous.

To the extent Guz's implied covenant cause of action seeks to impose limits on Bechtel's termination rights beyond those to which the parties actually agreed, the claim is invalid. To the extent the implied covenant claim seeks simply to invoke terms to which the parties did agree, it is superfluous. Guz's remedy, if any, for Bechtel's alleged violation of its personnel policies depends on proof that they were contract terms to which the parties actually agreed. The trial court thus properly dismissed the implied covenant cause of action.[18]

NOTES AND QUESTIONS

1. The theory rejected by the California court in *Guz*—that lack of good cause necessarily equates with bad faith toward a long term employee—appears to remain viable in at least two states: Alaska and Wyoming. *See* Kuhl v. Wells Fargo Bank, N.A., 281 P.3d 716 (Wyo. 2012); Wilder v. Cody Country Chamber of Commerce, 868 P.2d 211 (Wyo. 1994); Becker v. Fred Meyer Stores, Inc., 335 P.3d 1110 (Alaska 2014).

2. The preceding materials focused on two strands of the theory of good faith, one which applies if an employer recaptures or appropriates employee compensation as in *Wakefield,* and a second which applies when the employer deprives an employee of a long-term "benefit" of job security in the latter part of his career cycle.

A third strand of the theory of good faith applies when an employer exercises its right to terminate "at will" in order to achieve a goal that is against the public interest or in violation of public policy. An early example is Monge v. Beebe Rubber Co., 316 A.2d 549 (N.H. 1974), where the plaintiff alleged that her employer discharged her for refusing to submit to her supervisor's sexual advances. At the time, Title VII was not yet widely interpreted to prohibit sexual harassment in employment. Thus, in the absence of a tortious assault or battery, Monge's cause of action depended on contract law. The court held that "termination by the employer of a contract of employment at will which is motivated by bad faith or malice . . . is not in the best interest of the economic system or the public good. . . ." 316 A.2d at 551. Subsequently, the same court

---

[18] We do not suggest the covenant of good faith and fair dealing has no function whatever in the interpretation and enforcement of employment contracts. As indicated above, the covenant prevents a party from acting in bad faith to frustrate the contract's actual benefits. Thus, for example, the covenant might be violated if termination of an at-will employee was a mere pretext to cheat the worker out of another contract benefit to which the employee was clearly entitled, such as compensation already earned. We confront no such claim here.

clarified in Howard v. Dorr Woolen Co., 414 A.2d 1273 (N.H. 1980), that this implied prohibition against "bad faith" applies "only to a situation where an employee is discharged because he performed an act that public policy would encourage, or refused to do that which public policy would condemn." 414 A.2d at 1274. *See also* Willard v. Khotol Services Corp., 171 P.3d 108 (Alaska 2007). The public policy theory, which is based on public interests in the performance of a contract and which operates in most states independently of the theory of good faith between contracting parties, is described in greater detail later in section B.4.d, of this Chapter, *infra.*

3. Closely related to the "public policy" group of cases is a fourth group in which the implied duty of good faith serves as a "gap filler" remedy for behavior that deserves condemnation but falls outside the bounds of traditional tort or contract remedies. Such cases resemble "public policy" cases but lack a court's emphasis on public interests apart from the injured party's private interests. Facts like those in *Monge*, described above, would fit as easily within this "gap filler" class of cases as within the "public policy" class of cases. Another example of a "gap filler" application of good faith is Luedtke v. Nabors Alaska Drilling, Inc., 834 P.2d 1220 (Alaska 1992), where the court held that an employer breached an at will employment contract by administering a surprise mandatory drug test and by disciplining an employee who failed the test.

4. To the extent an implied duty of good faith limits an employer's prerogatives, is a violation of the duty a breach of contract? Or is it a tort, exposing the employer to liability for emotional distress and exemplary damages? Precedent for the latter theory might be found in insurance law, which holds an insurer liable in tort for the bad faith denial of insurance coverage to an insured. However, in Foley v. Interactive Data Corp., 765 P.2d 373 (Cal. 1988) (en banc), the Supreme Court of California rejected the insurance law analogy and held that a breach of the implied duty of good faith in employment relations is simply a breach of contract. Thus, an employee's remedy is limited to the usual measures of damages available in a breach of contract case. *But see* K Mart Corp. v. Ponsock, 732 P.2d 1364 (Nev. 1987) (imposing tort liability on employer for bad faith discharge to interfere with the accrual of plaintiff's pension).

4. Extracontractual Remedies

a. Promissory Estoppel

ROBERTS v. GEOSOURCE SERVS., INC.

757 S.W.2d 48 (Tex. App. 1988)

LEVY, Justice.

This is an appeal from a summary judgment adjudicating an employment contract. In October, 1983, while an employee of Huthnance Drilling Company ("Huthnance"), appellant, Bobby Wayne Roberts, an oil drilling worker living in Louisiana, sought overseas employment with appellee, Geosource Drilling Services, Inc. ("Geosource"). An interview was arranged for October 3, 1983, in

Houston, Texas, between Roberts and appellee, Thomas J. Sturm ("Sturm"), who hired personnel for Geosource, to determine whether Geosource would employ Roberts. Sturm found him to be suitably qualified and immediately so informed Roberts. Roberts was then sent to Geosource's doctor for a physical examination and to have his vaccinations updated. He filled out various employment-related forms, read and signed Geosource's Drilling Service Employment Agreement, hereinafter referred to as "the contract," and turned his passport over to Geosource.

Sturm was aware that Roberts was employed by Huthnance and was due to report back to work on October 4, 1983, for an offshore assignment. Sturm also executed the contract that Roberts had signed, and informed Roberts that he, Roberts, would be leaving from Monroe, Louisiana, for Peru, South America, on or about October 14, 1983. Roberts was further informed that he would be notified in three or four days about the flight number, time of departure, and how the tickets would be sent to him.

Relying upon Sturm's oral promises and the written contract, Roberts thereafter contacted Huthnance and terminated his employment with the company, informing his boss that he had another job. A few days later, Sturm contacted Roberts and told him that he was not going to be employed by Geosource after all, and that the corporation had found someone better qualified to fill its position. Roberts then filed suit against Geosource and Sturm seeking recovery for anticipatory breach, breach of a written employment contract, detrimental reliance upon oral and written representations, wrongful discharge, and fraud. Geosource and Sturm moved for and received the summary judgment from which this appeal is taken.

Appellant urges in his second point of error that there was no evidence to support appellee's motion for summary judgment as to appellant's claim for breach of contract, detrimental reliance, wrongful discharge, and anticipatory breach. Appellant adds in his fourth point of error that the trial court erred in refusing to grant his motion for partial summary judgment on the issue of anticipatory breach of employment contract.

For the doctrine of "detrimental reliance" to be available, Roberts must show the existence of a promise "designedly made to influence the conduct of the promisee, tacitly encouraging the conduct, which conduct, although not necessarily constituting any actual performance of the contract itself, is something that must be done by the promisee before he could begin to perform, and was a fact known to the promisor." Wheeler v. White, 398 S.W.2d 93, 96 (Tex. 1965). . . .

Perhaps more succinct is the Texas Supreme Court's recent formulation of the requisites of its doctrinal sibling, "promissory estoppel": (1) a promise, (2) the promisor's foreseeability of the promisee's reliance thereon, and (3) substantial reliance by the promisee to his detriment. English v. Fischer, 660 S.W.2d 521, 524 (Tex. 1983). We have here the three elements of "promissory estoppel" articulated by the Texas Supreme Court in English v. Fischer: (1) Sturm's promise of employment; (2) Sturm's foreseeing Roberts' relying on his promise; and (3) Roberts' consequent quitting his job with Huthnance and preparing for an overseas job, at his expense and to his detriment. Sturm's undisputed oral promise clearly imposed a duty on Geosource to employ Roberts—but not for a fixed duration—and that duty was breached by Geosource. It is no answer that the parties' written contract was for an employment-at-will, where the employer foreseeably and intentionally induces the prospective employee to materially change his position to his expense and detriment, and then repudiates its obligations before the written contract begins to operate.

If the appellant/promisee acts to his detriment in reliance upon the promise of employment, or parts with some legal right or sustains some legal injury as the inducement for the employment agreement, we hold that there is sufficient consideration to bind the employer/promisor to its promise. . . .

Appellees have failed to prove that there is no genuine issue of material fact or that they are entitled to judgment as a matter of law. We conclude that appellant Roberts has, in his claim of detrimental reliance upon Geosource's promise of employment, raised genuine issues of material fact, which should have precluded appellees' receiving their summary judgment. . . .

Appellant's fourth point of error asserting that the trial court erred in refusing to grant his motion for partial summary judgment on the issue of anticipatory breach of employment contract is overruled for the same reason: issues of material fact exist (e.g., Did Sturm offer employment to Roberts? Did Roberts quit his employment with Huthnance in reliance upon Sturm's offer? What damages, if any, did Roberts sustain as a result of such reliance? etc.) arising out of differing interpretations of the inducements and contract in question, which are for the jury to decide. Any significant fact issue precludes a summary judgment.

It is unnecessary for us to discuss any of the other points of error. Appellant's second point of error is sustained, the summary judgment is reversed, and the cause is remanded.

NOTES AND QUESTIONS

1. Doesn't an employee always "rely" on an employer's job offer when he accepts the offer and begins to take actions necessary to begin the employment? At the very least, he ceases his efforts to find employment anywhere else and misses other opportunities. If any amount of reliance on an offer of employment at will were sufficient to create a right against the employer, then employment at will would always begin with some sort of reliance-based duty. And what if the employer actually employs an employee for a brief period of employment at will and then fires the employee? Are frustrated applicants who have not worked at all in a better position to sue than employees who have worked for at least a day?

Looking at the matter with these sorts of questions in mind, many courts have simply dismissed the idea that promissory estoppel converts an offer of employment at will into any kind of employer obligation. *See, e.g.*, Clark v. Collins Bus. Corp., 736 N.E.2d 970 (Ohio App. 2000); Heinritz v. Lawrence Univ., 535 N.W.2d 81, 83-84 (Wis. 1995) (rejecting promissory estoppel claim where plaintiff, having accepted defendant's offer of employment at will, resigned from another job only to learn that defendant had withdrawn its offer because of "insurance problems" relating to plaintiff's disabled child).

Even within Texas, several courts have expressed skepticism about the rule and the result in *Roberts*. *See, e.g.*, Collins v. Allied Pharmacy Mgmt., Inc., 871 S.W.2d 929, 937 (Tex. App. 1994) ("In our opinion, *Roberts* was wrongly decided;

no Texas cases have cited it and we decline to follow it."). *Accord,* Robert J. Patterson, P.C. v. Leal, 942 S.W.2d 692, 694-695 (Tex. App. 1997).

2. The Restatement suggests some solutions to the worry that a promissory estoppel exception will swallow the whole of employment at will: "A promise which the promisor *should reasonably expect* to induce action or forbearance on the part of the promisee or a third person and which does induce such action or forbearance is binding *if injustice can be avoided only by enforcement of the promise.*" RESTATEMENT (SECOND) OF CONTRACTS § 90. Thus, a court might first ask whether the employer was on notice of the extent to which the employee might suffer irreversible damage if the employer revoked an offer the employee had already accepted. Second, a court might endeavor to draw a line between those cases in which detrimental reliance is so substantial that "justice" demands enforcement, and those where detrimental reliance is not so substantial. Cashdollar v. Mercy Hosp. of Pittsburgh, 595 A.2d 70, 73 (Pa. Super. 1991) (plaintiff "resigned from his position at Fairfax Hospital, sold his house in Virginia and moved his pregnant wife and two-year-old child to Pittsburgh"); Peck v. Imedia, Inc., 679 A.2d 745 (N.J. Super. 1996) (plaintiff sold her business); Ravelo v. County of Hawaii, 658 P.2d 883, 887-888 (1983) (police officer and spouse quit their jobs, moved and changed their children's school).

3. Aside from miscommunication, confusion, and changes in business plans, what other reasons might an employer have for revoking a job offer? In Comeaux v. Brown & Williamson Tobacco Co., 915 F.2d 1264 (9th Cir. 1990), the employer extended an offer to the plaintiff without explaining that employment was subject to a background check. After the employee accepted the offer, the employer investigated and became troubled by the plaintiff's credit history, and it withdrew its offer. Applying California law, the court reversed summary judgment for the employer and remanded for trial on the plaintiff's promissory estoppel claim:

> A party may not protect itself from liability under a contract by asserting that a heretofore hidden term is somehow part of the agreement. Comeaux reasonably thought he had bargained for and obtained an opportunity to begin work if he met the explicit conditions set forth by B & W. We would, under these assumptions, hold that B & W is liable to Comeaux for those damages Comeaux incurred in reliance on B & W's promise of employment.

Id. at 1271.

Many employers now make job offers expressly conditional on completion of further investigation. Should an express condition or disclaimer bar a promissory estoppel claim? Would it be reasonable for an employee to rely on a job offer that the employer, from the very beginning, has described as conditional or subject to termination at will? *See* McDonald v. Mobil Coal Producing, Inc., 789 P.2d 866 (Wyo. 1990) (interpreting disclaimer on job application as applying to termination after beginning of employment, not before beginning of employment).

4. What is the remedy for the breach of a promise of a job that an employer could have terminated at will? In contracts law a prevailing plaintiff ordinarily recovers his expectation interest. A prevailing employee's expectation interest is ordinarily based on the compensation he would have earned but for the employer's breach of contract. To award a disappointed job applicant his expectation interest

with respect to "at will" employment requires some speculation as to how long he would have served the defendant employer. *See* Cashdollar v. Mercy Hosp. of Pittsburgh, 595 A.2d 70 (N. J. Super. 1991) (awarding damages based on the court's estimate that it would have taken approximately seven years to "accomplish the objectives" of the job).

Damages for promissory estoppel might be less generous but easier to calculate. The Restatement indicates that the remedy for promissory estoppel might be based on the reliance interest instead of the expectation interest, depending on the circumstances and the jurisdiction. RESTATEMENT (SECOND) OF CONTRACTS § 90. Indeed, Courts applying promissory estoppel in the case of a revoked job offer have taken a variety of approaches to the question of damages. Some courts have limited the plaintiff to his reliance interest, i.e., the expenses he incurred in reliance on the employer's offer of employment. *See, e.g.*, Comeaux v. Brown & Williamson Tobacco Co., 915 F.2d 1264, 1271 (9th Cir. 1990); Peck v. Imedia, Inc., 679 A.2d 745 (N.J. Super. 1996). Reliance expenses would certainly include the plaintiff's relocation expenses. Would it also include compensation he lost by reason of his resignation from other "at will" employment? Grouse v. Group Health Plan, Inc., 306 N.W.2d 114, 116 (Minn. 1981) ("[T]he measure of damages is not so much what he would have earned from respondent as what he lost in quitting the job he held and in declining at least one other offer of employment elsewhere."). *Accord*, Toscano v. Greene Music, 21 Cal. Rptr. 3d 732 (Cal. App. 2004). *But see* Ford v. Trendwest Resorts, Inc., 43 P.3d 1223 (Wash. 2002) (awarding only nominal damages).

5. A long-term employee might also invoke the doctrine of promissory estoppel when the employer discharges the employee in violation of an alleged promise of job security or a promise not to discharge for a particular reason. *See, e.g.*, Tiernan v. Charleston Area Med. Ctr., Inc., 575 S.E.2d 618 (W. Va. 2002) (employer allegedly promised not to discharge employees for speaking to newspaper reporters about employment policies). A promissory estoppel claim might avoid a statute of frauds defense or some other bar to enforcing the promise as a contract, but it requires proof of reliance. A promissory estoppel claim might also fail for one of the other reasons that contract claims often fail, such as the indefiniteness of the promise, the promisor's lack of authority, or an employer disclaimer.

b. Fraudulent Inducement

STEWART v. JACKSON & NASH

976 F.2d 86 (2d Cir. 1992)

WALKER, Circuit Judge:

Victoria A. Stewart . . . is an attorney admitted to practice law in the State of New York. Prior to October 1988, she was employed in the environmental law department of the New York law firm of Phillips, Nizer, Benjamin, Krim & Ballon. Ronald Herzog, a partner in the firm of Jackson & Nash, . . . contacted Stewart while at Phillips, Nizer regarding the possibility of employment with his firm.

Herzog allegedly "represented to Stewart that Jackson had recently secured a large environmental law client, that Jackson was in the process of establishing an environmental law department, and that Stewart would head the environmental law department, and be expected to service the firm's substantial existing environmental law client." Stewart asserts that, in reliance on these representations, she resigned her position with Phillips, Nizer in October 1988 and the following month began work at Jackson & Nash.

Upon her arrival, Stewart alleges that Jackson & Nash put her to work primarily on general litigation matters. When she inquired about the promised environmental work, Herzog repeatedly assured her that it would be forthcoming and "also consistently advised [her] that she would be promoted to a position as head of Jackson's environmental law department." The major environmental law client and substantial environmental case work, however, never materialized. Finally, in May 1990, a Jackson & Nash partner allegedly informed Stewart that "Jackson had never 'really' had this 'type' of work, nor had [it], in fact, secured an environmental law client." Jackson & Nash dismissed Stewart on December 31, 1990. Jackson & Nash . . . asserts that it engaged in a year-long effort to acquire environmental work but concedes that it failed to achieve this end.

Count I of Stewart's complaint, filed April 11, 1991, alleges that Jackson & Nash fraudulently induced her to enter into and remain in its employ. Stewart asserts that she took the position with the firm in reliance on its knowing misrepresentations, as outlined above. She claims that her "career objective— continuing to specialize in environmental law—was thwarted and grossly undermined during her employment with Jackson," and that she suffered "loss of professional opportunity, loss of professional reputation" and damage to her "career growth and potential." . . .

The district court found that Stewart's fraud claim arose from her termination from the firm and dismissed Count I on the authority of *Murphy v. American Home Prod. Corp.,* 448 N.E.2d 86 (N.Y. 1983). *Murphy* held that because at-will employees "may be freely terminated . . . at any time for any reason or even for no reason," they can neither challenge their termination in a contract action nor "bootstrap" themselves around this bar by alleging that the firing was in some way tortious. *Id.* at 89, 91. . . .

We find *Murphy* distinguishable. In *Murphy,* the plaintiff, an at-will employee of the defendant, claimed that he had been fired in a tortious manner. He alleged that his firing "'was deliberately and viciously insulting, was designed to and did embarrass and humiliate plaintiff and was intended to and did cause plaintiff severe mental and emotional distress thereby damaging plaintiff.'" *Id.* 448 N.E.2d at 88 (quoting from complaint). These tort allegations, springing as they do directly from the termination itself, are a transparent attempt to restate the forbidden contractual challenge in the guise of tort.

Stewart's alleged injuries, on the other hand, commenced well before her termination and were, in several important respects, unrelated to it. . . . Jackson & Nash's misrepresentations caused Stewart, a budding environmental lawyer, to leave a firm with an environmental practice and spend two years at one in which she was largely unable to work in her chosen specialty. The resulting damage to her career development was independent of her later termination . . . [and] began while she was still at the firm. . . . Although *Murphy* precludes an award of damages for injuries caused by her termination, it does not prevent her from recovering for injuries that resulted from her reliance on the defendants' false statements. . . .

Appellees Jackson & Nash urge a second ground for dismissal . . . that Stewart's alleged injuries, both pre-termination and termination-related, result in substance from broken contractual promises regarding the terms and conditions of her employment. Such broken promises, they contend, cannot support a fraud claim because "[t]he fraudulent breach of a contract does not give rise to an action for fraud. Thus, where the only fraud charged relates to a breach of the contract and not to its inducement or making, no action for fraud is alleged." 60 N.Y.Jur.2d *Fraud & Deceit* § 19 at 455-456 (1987) . . . Appellees' argument boils down to an assertion that Stewart's claim is nothing more than a contract action which, since it is based on an oral agreement, is not enforceable under New York's Statute of Frauds. . . .

Stewart contends that the firm's misrepresentations are actionable under a theory of fraud in the inducement. She correctly points out that under New York law "[i]t is elementary that where a contract or transaction was induced by false representations, the representations and the contract are distinct and separable. . . . Thus, fraud in the inducement of a written contract is not merged therein so as to preclude an action for fraud." 60 N.Y.Jur.2d *Fraud & Deceit* § 206 at 740 (1987) (citing cases).

Stewart alleges four misrepresentations: (1) "Jackson had recently secured a large environmental law client"; (2) "Jackson was in the process of establishing an environmental law department"; (3) "Stewart would head the environmental law department"; and (4) "[Stewart would] be expected to service the firm's substantial existing environmental law client."

As to representations (1) and (2), we find dispositive the New York Court of Appeals' distinction between a prospective business partner's "promissory statement[s] as to what will be done in the future," which give rise only to a breach of contract claim, and his or her false "'representation[s] of present fact,'" which give rise to a separable claim of fraudulent inducement. Deerfield Commun. v. Chesebrough-Pond's, 502 N.E.2d 1003, 1004 (N.Y. 1986) (citations omitted) (quoting Citibank v. Plapinger, 485 N.E.2d 974 (N.Y. 1985)). In the case of Coolite Corp. v. American Cyanamid Co., 384 N.Y.S.2d 808 (N.Y. App.1976), for example, defendant Cyanamid, a manufacturer of light sticks, represented to Coolite that it had fully tested its product and had developed a means of correcting the product's defects. Coolite, allegedly in reliance on these statements, contracted to become the exclusive distributor of the light sticks. Coolite later found the product not to be of merchantable quality and sued for fraudulent misrepresentation. The Appellate Division let the fraud claim stand on the grounds that "Cyanamid's representations . . . were representations of fact and not merely promises of future action." 384 N.Y.S.2d at 810.

In this case Jackson & Nash's declarations that it "had recently secured a large environmental law client" and "was in the process of establishing an environmental law department" were not future promises but representations of present fact. Under *Coolite,* these representations support a claim for fraudulent inducement which is distinct and separable from any contract action.

In paragraphs thirty-six and thirty-seven of her complaint Stewart amplifies her allegations regarding representation (3). She asserts that Jackson & Nash informed her that she "would be promoted to a position as head of Jackson's environmental law department . . . [although], upon information and belief, *at the time Jackson made the aforesaid representations to Stewart, it knew that it did not intend to make her the head of its environmental law department.*" (Emphasis added). While representation (3) appears, initially, to be a future promise (Stewart *would* be made head of the department), the new York Court of Appeals has explained that

> [w]hile [m]ere promissory statements as to what will be done in the future are not actionable, . . . it is settled that, *if a promise was actually made with a preconceived and undisclosed intention of not performing it, it constitutes a misrepresentation of material existing fact* upon which an action for recision [based on fraudulent inducement] may be predicated.

Sabo v. Delman, 143 N.E.2d 906, 908 (N.Y. 1957) (emphasis added). Stewart's assertion that Jackson & Nash, at the time it made the promise, "knew that it did not intend" to fulfill it, makes representation (3) an allegation of present fact which gives rise to a claim of fraudulent inducement. . . .

To the extent that representation (4)'s pledge that Stewart would "be expected to service the firm's substantial existing environmental law client" goes beyond representation (1)'s statement of the existence of an environmental law client, it is a future promise and would not be actionable.

In sum, we hold that representation (1) is a representation of present fact and that (2) and (3) included both elements of present fact and future promise. To the extent the representations were of present fact, they are actionable. . . . Count I of Stewart's complaint, alleging fraudulent inducement, survives Jackson & Nash's motion to dismiss.

NOTES AND QUESTIONS

1. As the court observed in *Stewart*, there is tension between an employee's fraudulent inducement claim and the employment-at-will rule. Some courts agree with the argument of Jackson & Nash that an employer's promise of a job to continue at-will cannot be a fraudulent inducement even if the employer made the promise intending to "break" it, because a promise to perform "at will" promises nothing at all. According to this argument, any amount of employment under any circumstances—perhaps even no employment at all—would still constitute all that the employer had really promised. To put it another way, it is no lie to promise something you intend not to deliver, if what you promised was nothing at all. Ikemiya v. Shibamoto Am., Inc., 444 S.E.2d 351, 351-53 (Ga. Ct. App. 1994) ("fraud cannot be predicated on a promise . . . unenforceable at the time it is made"). Nevertheless, most states do allow for the possibility of a fraudulent inducement claim based on a promise of a job—even "at will"—if the promisor had already formed an intent not to provide the described job at the very moment he was making the promise. Courts that allow for such a claim might still stop short of awarding "expectation" damages based on the plaintiff's loss of the promised job. What alternative measure of damages did Stewart seek to prove? How will she prove such damages?

2. Fraudulent inducement to leave one job or opportunity to accept another is not so much a novel claim as just one scenario for common-law fraud. Liability for fraud requires "a misrepresentation of fact, opinion, intention or law for the purpose of inducing another to act or to refrain from action in reliance upon it," and liability includes damages for "pecuniary loss caused . . . by [the other party's] justifiable reliance upon the misrepresentation." RESTATEMENT (SECOND) OF TORTS § 525 (1977).

a. **Misrepresentation of Fact, Opinion, Intention, or Law**. What if Jackson & Nash did *not* commit the clearest of its misrepresentations, that it "had recently secured a large environmental law client," but *did* represent that (a) it was "in the process of establishing an environmental law department" and (b) Stewart would "head the environmental law department?" What facts would show that either (a) or (b) was a "misrepresentation of fact, opinion, intention, or law"? Compare Manon v. Solis, 142 S.W.3d 380, 385 (Tex. App. 2004) (judgment for defendant law firm based on jury's finding that plaintiff lawyer failed to prove defendant law firm *did not intend* to fulfill stated intentions to give her certain assignments, work hours, and support staff).

A knowing misstatement about *present fact* can clearly be the basis for fraudulent inducement, and a promise the speaker *does not intend to keep* can be the basis for fraudulent inducement in most states. But what about an opinion or *prediction*?

Recruiters tend to exhibit optimism. They often state opinions or feelings they have or pretend to have (*e.g.*, that opportunities are "wonderful") or they make optimistic predictions, which are statements about *future* facts they *expect* or pretend to expect to occur even if these facts are not entirely within their control. Can an opinion or prediction be the basis for fraudulent inducement? *See* Elizaga v. Kaiser Found. Hosps. Inc., 487 P.2d 870 (Or. 1971) (upholding plaintiff's verdict because "[m]aking a promise with the knowledge that it probably cannot be performed or with reckless disregard whether the promisor can or cannot perform can be . . . fraud"); Wildes v. Pens Unlimited, Co., 389 A.2d 837, 839-840 (Me. 1978) (plaintiff was "clearly at the mercy of the defendant insofar as any representations made regarding . . . employment opportunities and remuneration," and therefore defendant's representations "could well have been justifiably understood as being of fact not mere opinion"). Nevertheless, courts tend to especially skeptical of fraudulent inducement claims based entirely on predictions or statements of opinion because of the great difficultly of proving the defendant only pretended to have the opinion or to believe the prediction.

b. Reasonable Reliance. Like promissory estoppel, fraudulent inducement requires proof that the plaintiff acted differently and suffered a detriment because of the false statement. Moreover, the plaintiff's reliance must have been "justifiable" or "reasonable." What facts might support or undercut Stewart's claim that she reasonably relied on the firm's misrepresentations?

c. Causation. A newly hired employee's loss of employment might be caused by an employer's misrepresentation about work it stated would be available in its business. But what if the employee remained employed under circumstances different from those the defendant had described? In Geary v. Hunton & Williams, 257 A.D.2d 482, 482 (N.Y. App. Div. 1999), the plaintiff sought to recover what he would have earned if the defendant's banking litigation practice was as substantial as the defendant had represented. The court rejected his claim: "[P]laintiff admits that he gained substantial experience in banking litigation while employed by defendant, and therefore plaintiff's reliance on [the alleged misrepresentations] could not have been the cause of plaintiff's failure to meet his career goals." The court also noted that the plaintiff "was terminated not because defendant did not have enough banking litigation . . . but because he raised concerns about the ethical propriety of a partner's billing practices."

3. In most jurisdictions, fraud complaints must satisfy a special standard of "particularity." *See e.g.*, Fed. R. Civ. Pro. 9(b); W. Va. R. Civ. P. 9(b); N.Y. Civ. Prac. L. & R. § 3016(b). This means, among other things, that a plaintiff's complaint must state the defendant's misrepresentations with particularity. *See, e.g.,* McGovern v. T.J. Best Bldg. & Remodeling, 927 (N.Y. App. 1997) (dismissing complaint for "fail[ure] to identify which of the named defendants made the alleged misrepresentations and/or . . . when such representations were made, i.e., plaintiffs have not demonstrated with . . . particularity who said what and when"). Moreover, in a few states a plaintiff must prove fraud by "clear and convincing evidence." *See, e.g.*, Clarke v. Wallace Oil Co., 284 A.D.2d 492, 493 (N.Y. App. Div. 2001).

4. Some states have enacted fraudulent inducement statutes specifically applicable to employment agencies or employers that misrepresent working conditions or fail to disclose the existence of a strike. *See, e.g.*, Cal. Lab. Code § 970; Colo. Rev. Stat. § 8-2-104. These statutes tend to restate rather than modify the elements of common law fraudulent inducement, but some statutes add a criminal penalty. *See, e.g.*, Cal. Lab. Code § 970 (misdemeanor).

c. Third Party Tortious Interference

An employer might discharge an employee because of some third party's reasons rather than the employer's own reasons. The employer might feel compelled to comply with the third party's desire to discharge the employee if the third party exercises control over the employer or if good relations with the third party are important to the employer's business. Under special circumstances a third party's "interference" with the employment can be either of two closely related torts: (1) third party interference with a contractual relation, or (2) third party interference with prospective business relations. The former requires a contract with which the third party "interfered." The latter requires no contract, only a "prospective" relation or prospective continuation of a relation that is not bound by contract to continue.

POPESCU v. APPLE INC.

1 Cal. App. 5th 39 (Cal. App. 2016)

MÁRQUEZ, J.

Plaintiff Dan Popescu sued Apple Inc. (Apple) for damages after he was fired by his employer, Constellium Rolled Products Ravenswood, LLC (Constellium). He alleged that between August and October of 2011, Apple took affirmative steps to convince Constellium to terminate him in retaliation for his resistance to Apple's alleged illegal anti-competitive conduct. The court sustained Apple's demurrer to Popescu's first amended complaint (Complaint) without leave to amend....

PROCEDURAL BACKGROUND

Popescu, an Arizona resident, alleged1 that he is "an aluminum engineering manager who developed cutting edge alloys for high-tech customers." The gist of his action is that he "objected to Apple's unlawful trade practices," and that Apple therefore "convinced [his] employer to terminate him for cause on a trumped up basis," thereby "blackball[ing] Popescu from his profession."

In 2000, Popescu was working for Alcoa, Inc. (Alcoa). He was hired that year by Algroup Alusuisse (Algroup), an aluminum supplier that is Alcoa's largest competitor. Algroup hired Popescu because he had expertise "in marketing value-added aluminum substrates directly to end users in high-tech industries." ...

Popescu alleged that he was "a stellar and highly valued employee [who] survived a series of corporate transactions" that resulted in his employment by Constellium. In a June 2009 written employment agreement, Constellium reaffirmed Popescu's severance provision in his prior agreement with Algroup....

In March 2011, the business unit president of Constellium Global ATI (of which Constellium is a subdivision) designated Popescu to lead in the pursuit of a relationship with Apple in the latter's goal of using an aluminum alloy for its iPhone products. Popescu was designated the project lead because of his "expertise and performance."

Popescu and a team of engineers from Constellium commenced work on the Apple custom alloy project.... While development was progressing, Apple insisted that Constellium sign a "'Development Agreement'" containing "restrictive terms," including provisions that (a) Apple was not obligated to purchase any developed products or to use Constellium as its supplier, and (b) Constellium, for an effective period of five years, "would [be] precluded ... from supplying alloy to any manufacturer of consumer electronics." Apple advised Constellium that Constellium's competitors (other elite aluminum alloy suppliers) had already signed such an agreement. Popescu objected to the agreement and refused to sign it on Constellium's behalf.

Popescu alleged that he subsequently attended a meeting with Apple in Cupertino on August 30, 2011. The Apple engineers with whom Popescu had worked for months were silent, while their superiors, who were new to the project, led the meeting and "were visibly upset that the nearly complete custom alloy had outpaced the execution of the Development Agreement." Apple representatives insisted that Constellium sign the Development Agreement, which included an additional restrictive term that required Constellium to transfer its intellectual property interests in the custom aluminum alloy to Apple. Popescu again refused to sign the agreement on behalf of Constellium.

Popescu alleged that Apple wanted to use the executed Development Agreement to restrict competition in the smartphone market. He alleged that by "lock[ing] up [the elite aluminum] suppliers with the [R]estrictive Development Agreement, Apple would be free to ... prevent its competitors from developing a smartphone with a comparable aluminum alloy body. "Apple saw Popescu as an obstacle to the Development Agreement, so he was an obstacle to the larger scheme to restrict competition in smartphones."

Popescu also alleged that, during the August 30 meeting, he had inadvertently activated the recording feature of his Livescribe Smartpen (the recording incident). Apple's attorney noticed that the meeting was being recorded, confiscated the Smartpen, and the meeting continued. After the meeting, Apple insisted that Constellium commence an investigation into the recording incident. Apple also requested that Constellium terminate Popescu, but his supervisors resisted. Apple then appealed to the executive management of the private equity firm that owned Constellium, after which Popescu was terminated for cause....

After Popescu was terminated, Constellium signed the Development Agreement.... Popescu alleged that as a result of his termination and Constellium's execution of the Development Agreement, Apple was able to misappropriate Constellium's aluminum alloy trade secrets. He alleged that the Development Agreements signed by Constellium and other elite aluminum suppliers—which agreements were "naked output contracts ... in which a firm bargains for another's entire output on the condition that the seller does not deal with the firm's rivals"—had anticompetitive effects in the global marketplace because "Apple's competitors [were] denied a potentially efficiency-increasing resource while the public [was] denied a better, more durable smartphone." He also alleged that Apple's anticompetitive actions negatively impacted elite aluminum suppliers, consumer electronics companies (including smartphone manufacturers), and smartphone consumers.

In the first cause of action, Popescu alleged a claim for contract interference. He ... alleged that (1) Apple was aware of his contract; (2) it intentionally induced Constellium to terminate his employment; (3) as a result of Apple's actions, Constellium terminated him, purportedly for cause, on October 28, 2011; and (4) he was damaged as a result of Apple's conduct.

In the second cause of action, Popescu alleged a purported claim for business interference. He claimed (1) he had an employment relationship with Constellium under which there was a probability he would receive future economic benefits; (2) he had intended to work for at least 10 more years at the time his employment was terminated; and (3) had it not been for Apple's actions, it was extremely likely he would have stayed employed with Constellium as he had planned....

Apple filed a demurrer to the Complaint ... asserting that the first and second claims failed to state facts sufficient to constitute causes of action.... The court sustained the demurrer without leave to amend....

II. Order Sustaining Demurrer To Contract Interference Claim

Five elements must be alleged to support a claim for intentional interference with contractual relations (contract interference). They are "(1) a valid contract between plaintiff and a third party; (2) defendant's knowledge of this contract; (3) defendant's intentional acts designed to induce a breach or disruption of the contractual relationship; (4) actual breach or disruption of the contractual relationship; and (5) resulting damage." Pacific Gas & Electric Co. v. Bear Stearns & Co. 791 P.2d 587 (Cal. 1990). It is not a requirement that "the defendant's conduct be wrongful apart from the interference with the contract itself." Quelimane Co. v. Stewart Title Guaranty Co., 960 P.2d 513 (Cal. 1998).

Furthermore, a plaintiff need not establish that the primary purpose of the defendant's actions was to disrupt the contract. The tort is shown even where "'the actor does not act for the purpose of interfering with the contract or desire it but knows that the interference is certain or substantially certain to occur as a result of his [or her] action.'" *Ibid.* quoting Rest.2d Torts, § 766, com. j, p. 12....

Apple relies on Applied Equipment Corp. v. Litton Saudi Arabia Ltd., 869 P.2d 454 (Cal. 1994), to argue it has no liability for contract interference because, "while [it] was not [Popescu's] employer, [Apple nevertheless] [']was not a stranger ['] to his 'at-will' employment" arrangement with Constellium. Apple contends that Popescu alleged that Apple "contracted with Constellium to develop a proprietary aluminum extruding process. This research and development [process] would represent a significant investment of time and resources by Apple. Apple therefore had a legitimate economic interest in making sure the individuals Constellium staffed the project with would not cause Apple any harm." Apple relies on the following language in *Applied Equipment*: "'It has long been held that a stranger to a contract may be liable in tort for intentionally interfering with the performance of the contract.' However, ...[o]ne contracting party owes no general tort duty to another not to interfere with performance of the contract; its duty is simply to perform the contract according to its terms. The tort duty not to interfere with the contract falls only on strangers—interlopers who have no legitimate interest in the scope or course of the contract's performance." 869 P.2d 454.

We do not read the foregoing language from *Applied Equipment* (as asserted by Apple) to immunize a noncontracting party from tort liability because the noncontracting party has a "legitimate interest in the scope or course of the contract's performance." ... The court did not address whether a tort claim for contract interference or conspiracy could be made against a noncontracting party who had a "legitimate interest" in the contract, let alone hold that such a claim could never be asserted as a matter of law....

An extension of *Applied Equipment*'s holding to immunize a third party from tortious interference claims simply because the third party asserts some economic or other interest in a contract would significantly undercut the tort itself and the public policy underlying it. As noted recently by the Ninth Circuit Court of Appeals: "To shield parties with an economic interest in the contract from potential liability would create an undesirable lacuna in the law between the respective domains of tort and contract. A party with an economic interest in a contractual relationship could interfere without risk of facing either tort or contract liability. This result is particularly perverse as it is those parties with some type of economic interest in a contract whom [sic] would have the greatest incentive to interfere with it. Such a result would hardly serve the established goal of protecting 'a formally cemented economic relationship ... from interference by a stranger to the agreement.'" United Nat. Maintenance, Inc. v. San Diego Convention Center, Inc., 766 F.3d 1002, 1007 (9th Cir. 2014), *quoting* Della Penna v. Toyota Motor Sales, U.S.A., Inc., 902 P.2d 740, 750 (Cal. 1995) 902 P.2d 740....

We conclude that Apple, even as a third party having some interest in the manner in which Popescu performed his employment agreement with Constellium, is not immune from tort liability for interfering with his contract. We next address whether the trial court correctly found that Popescu alleged an at-will employment relationship with Constellium, and, if so, whether his contract interference claim was precluded as a matter of law....

[Editor: Apple then argued that Popescu could not have a contract interference claim against Apple because Popescsu was an "at will" employee and his termination was not a breach of contract. Apple cited Reeves v. Hanlon, 95 P.3d 513 (Cal. 2004), for the proposition that an at-will employee cannot maintain a contract interference claim. The court of appeals agreed with Apple that Popescu was employed at will notwithstanding his contract right to substantial severance pay in the event of involuntary termination for reasons other than misconduct. However, the court of appeals disagreed that Popescu's at will status or the California Supreme Court's decision in *Reeves* compelled dismissal of Popescu's contract interference claim.]

In *Reeves*, the plaintiffs, a law firm and one of its partners, alleged that the defendants, attorneys who left the firm, unlawfully lured the plaintiffs' employees to join the defendants' new firm. *Reeves*, 95 P.3d 513.... It was undisputed that the nine employees who left the law firm, including six who went to work for the defendants, were the plaintiffs' at-will employees.... The Supreme Court noted initially that it has been recognized historically that a contract interference claim may be based upon disruption of an at-will contract under the theory that "[a] third party's 'interference with an at-will contract is actionable interference with the contractual relationship' because the contractual relationship is at the will of the parties, not at the will of outsiders." 95 P.3d 513, *quoting PG & E, supra*, 791 P.2d 587.... But it observed that this state's public policy has long been "that '[a] former employee has the right to engage in a competitive business for himself and to enter into competition with his former employer, even for the business of ... his former employer, provided such competition is fairly and legally conducted.' *Ibid. quoting* Continental Car-Na-Var Corp. v. Moseley, 148 P.2d 9 (Cal. 1944). Further, the court noted that "'it is not ordinarily a tort to hire the employees of another for use in the hirer's business,'" subject to the exception that liability will be imposed "if unfair methods are used in interfering in such advantageous relations." *Reeves*, 95 P.3d 513, *quoting* Buxbom v. Smith (Cal. 1944), 145 P.2d 305.)

Based upon these policy considerations, the court concluded that "[w]here no unlawful methods are used, public policy generally supports a competitor's right to offer more pay or better terms to another's employee, so long as the employee is free to leave." *Reeves,* 95 P.3d 513. Accordingly, the court held ... to recover for a defendant's interference with an at-will employment relation, a plaintiff must plead and prove that the defendant engaged in an independently wrongful act—i.e., an act 'proscribed by some constitutional, statutory, regulatory, common law, or other determinable legal standard'—that induced an at-will employee to leave the plaintiff." 95 P.3d 513.... In other words, our high court did not negate the contract interference claim involving an at-will employment agreement entirely; it merely subjected it to an additional "independent wrongful act" requirement.

The trial court appears to have concluded that *Reeves* held that a plaintiff, in all circumstances, may only pursue a contract interference claim based upon an at-will employment relationship if "the defendant engaged in an independently wrongful act." As noted above, however, the Supreme Court based its conclusion that interference with an at-will employment relationship was not actionable without an independent wrongful act upon the dual public policy considerations of employee freedom of movement and a business's right to legitimately compete in the marketplace. Those underlying policy considerations are specific to the typical employment contract interference claim at issue in *Reeves*: where the defendant company (current employer) has induced an employee to breach an at-will employment contract he or she had with the plaintiff company (former employer and competitor of the defendant). By contrast, the claim here is an atypical one in which the defendant company (not a prospective employer) allegedly induced an employer (Apple's business partner, not its competitor) to breach an at-will employment agreement. . . . Under these circumstances, neither policy consideration that animated our high court's holding in *Reeves* is present....

We hold that *Reeves*'s additional requirement of pleading and proof of an independently wrongful act in contract interference claims involving at-will employment contracts does not apply where, as here, the employee is the alleged victim of a third party's conduct in inducing its business partner to terminate his or her employment contract. Accordingly, since Popescu alleged each of the five elements of a contract interference claim, it was error to sustain the demurrer to the first cause of action.

III. Order Sustaining Demurrer to Business Interference Claim

The elements of the tort of intentional interference with prospective economic advantage (business interference) are "(1) an economic relationship between the plaintiff and some third party, with the probability of future economic benefit to the plaintiff; (2) the defendant's knowledge of that relationship; (3) intentional acts on the part of the defendant designed to disrupt the relationship; (4) actual disruption of the relationship; and (5) economic harm to the plaintiff proximately caused by the acts of the defendant. Youst v. Longo, 729 P.2d 728 (Cal. 1987). The business interference tort "is considerably more inclusive than actions based on contract or interference with contract, and is thus not dependent on the existence of a valid contract." (Buckaloo v. Johnson, 537 P.2d 865 (Cal. 1975), *disapproved on other grounds in Della Penna*, 902 P.2d 740.

Although business interference is related to contract interference, our high court has noted that a distinction must be made between the two, and "a greater solicitude [must be afforded] to those relationships that have ripened into agreements." *Della Penna*, 902 P.2d 740. Based upon this distinction, a plaintiff alleging business interference must also plead and prove "that the defendant's interference was wrongful 'by some measure beyond the fact of the interference itself.'" 902 P.2d 740 [fn. omitted].

[In] Korea Supply Co. v. Lockheed Martin Corp. 63 P.3d 937 (Cal. 2003), the court explained that wrongful conduct is sufficient to support a business interference claim if it is proscribed by "some constitutional, statutory, regulatory, common law, or other determinable legal standard" where it amounts to "independently actionable conduct." The court explained that this requirement serves to "distinguish [ ] lawful competitive behavior from tortious interference." It also clarified the intent element of the tort, concluding that a plaintiff is not required to plead and prove a defendant's specific intent to disrupt the plaintiff's prospective economic advantage. Rather, the plaintiff may either plead specific intent, or, alternatively, "plead that the defendant knew that the interference was certain or substantially certain to occur as a result of its action." 63 P.3d 937....

Apple argues that Popescu did not allege any conduct that was independently wrongful because "[t]here is simply no law prohibiting an individual or entity from reporting an employee's unlawful conduct to his/her employer." By itself, Apple's conduct as alleged by Popescu of requesting that Constellium investigate the recording incident was not independently wrongful. And we will assume for purposes of this discussion that Apple's alleged exertion of additional pressure upon Constellium by contacting its majority shareholder to request that it terminate Popescu's employment for cause was not independently wrongful to support a business interference claim. But Popescu alleged in the Complaint that Apple's conduct in persuading Constellium to terminate him was interconnected with Apple's larger goal of requiring Constellium to sign the Development Agreement and "thereby complete its fraud of Constellium, further misappropriate its trade secrets, obtain non-trade secret information and materials, and restrict competition in the smartphone market." Apple describes these allegations as Popescu's having "concoct[ed] a fanciful anticompetitive scheme ... result[ing] in his termination." But in considering a demurrer, the factual allegations of the Complaint are deemed to be true....

Accepting the allegations of the Complaint as true for purposes of demurrer, Popescu adequately alleged independently wrongful conduct. He alleged that Apple's conduct in persuading Constellium to terminate Popescu—by removing him as an obstacle to execution of the Development Agreement—was connected with its effort to misappropriate Constellium's trade secrets. This same alleged conduct, combined with Apple's successfully obtaining the execution of similar Development Agreements from other aluminum alloy manufacturers, was alleged to have the anticompetitive purpose and effect of denying Apple's smartphone competitors an aluminum alloy resource, and denying consumers "a better, more durable smartphone." Popescu therefore alleged independently wrongful conduct by Apple, including (1) a violation of the Sherman Antitrust Act (15 U.S.C. § 10); (2) a violation of the Cartwright Act (Bus. & Prof. Code, § 16720 et seq.); (3) a Development Agreement that amounts to an unlawful restraint of trade (Bus. & Prof. Code, § 16600); (4) a violation of the Uniform Trade Secrets Act (Civ. Code, § 3426 et seq.); and (5) a scheme intending to defraud Constellium....

Apple's argument that Popescu has not alleged that its conduct directed toward Constellium was independently wrongful appears to be based upon the assumption that the wrongful conduct must be wrongful toward the plaintiff. But the California Supreme Court has held to the contrary: "[W]e find no sound reason for requiring that a defendant's wrongful actions must be directed toward[ ] the plaintiff seeking to recover for this tort. The interfering party is liable to the interfered-with party 'when the independently tortious means the interfering party uses are independently tortious only as to a third party. Even under these circumstances, the interfered-with party remains an intended (or at least known) victim of the interfering party—albeit one that is indirect rather than direct.'" *Korea Supply*, 63 P.3d 937, *quoting Della Penna*, 902 P.2d 740 (conc. opn. of Mosk, J.).

Accordingly, the trial court erred in sustaining the demurrer to the second cause of action....[W]e express no view as to the likelihood that Popescu will be able to establish that Apple intentionally interfered with his employment relationship with Constellium or that Apple's conduct was independently wrongful.

The judgment is reversed with directions to the trial court that it ... enter a new order overruling the demurrer to the first and second causes of action and granting Apple, Inc. leave to answer the Complaint.

NOTES AND QUESTIONS

1. When an "at will" employee invokes the doctrine of intentional interference with a contract, an important question of law at the outset is whether it is possible for any party to "interfere with a contract" that continues only at the will of the contracting parties. One contracting party's termination of an "at will" contract is not a breach of contract. If an employer does not breach a contract by terminating the employment, can the terminated employee sue a third party who caused the termination? *Popescu* presents one answer to this question. For an opposing view, see El Paso Healthcare System, Ltd. v. Murphy, 518 S.W.3d 412 (Tex. 2017) and McHenry v. Lawrence, 886 N.Y.S.2d 492 (N.Y. App. Div. 2009).

2. If interference causing the breach of an existing contract can be tortious without the commission of an independently wrongful or improper act, could a customer be liable for honestly complaining about an employee if the complaint caused the employer to discharge the employee? Courts following the *Popescu* approach often hold that a third party might have a conditional privilege to interfere based on a legitimate interest in the matter. The third party does not have a privilege to act maliciously. *See* Sterner v. Marathon Oil Co., 767 S.W.2d 686 (Tex. 1989) (if third party commits tort by interfering with an at will contract, third party can assert "legal justification," but intent to retaliate against employee for earlier personal injury lawsuit was not a sufficient legal justification); Sheets v. Birky, 54 N.E.3d 1064 (Ind. App. 2016); Koehler v. Packer Group, Inc., 53 N.E.3d 218 (Ill. App. 2016).

If Apple had a right, privilege or legal justification to report or complain to Constellium about Popescu's conduct, how might its conduct have exceeded that right, privilege or justification? If Apple had a legitimate reason to complain about Popescu's conduct, how would you have advised Apple to proceed?

3. In states where a third party commits no tort simply by causing termination of "at will" employment, a discharged employee's potential alternative claim against the third party is for tortious interference with a *prospective* contract or business relation. *See* El Paso Healthcare System, Ltd. v. Murphy, 518 S.W.3d 412 (Tex. 2017) and McHenry v. Lawrence, 886 N.Y.S.2d 492 (N.Y. App. Div. 2009). However, as the court observed in *Popescu*, tortious interference with a prospective contract or business relation requires something more than "interference." The third party's reason for and means of interference are particularly important. The plaintiff must prove that the third party committed some independently wrongful act. Lewis-Gale Medical Center, LLC v. Alldredge, 710 S.E.2d 716 (Va. 2011). One frequently asserted "independently wrongful act" is a third party's retaliation against an employee for questioning or reporting possibly illegal business activities of the third party. *See, e.g.*, Duty v. Boys and Girls Club of Porter County, 23 N.E.3d 768 (Ind. App. 2014). *See also* United

States Fidelity & Guarantee Co. v. Millonas, 89 So. 732 (Ala. 1921) (workers' compensation carrier unlawfully caused employer to discharge employee after employee refused to abandon his claim for benefits).

4. Apple was clearly a "third party" to the contract with which it allegedly interfered. In many cases, however, a defendant's "third party" status is a principal issue. The persons most likely to have interfered—supervisors and fellow employees—likely acted in the scope of their employment, and in this sense their actions were the actions of the employer and not the actions of a third party. Community Health Systems Professional Services, 525 S.W.3d 671 (Tex. 2017); Lanzer v. Louisville, 75 N.E.3d 752 (Oh. App. 2016); Sims v. Software Solutions Unlimited, Inc., 939 P.2d 654 (Or. App. 1997). *But see* Yaindl v. Ingersoll-Rand Co., 422 A.2d 611 (Pa. Super. 1980) (manager from one division unlawfully interfered with plaintiff's employment in another division of the same company); Creel v. Davis, 544 So. 2d 145 (Ala. 1989) (allowing recovery by employee of one subsidiary against employee of another subsidiary).

5. There may be some situations in which a supervisor carrying out a typical employment action such as evaluating, disciplining, or discharging an employee is acting as a "third party" to that employee's contract. For example, a supervisor might be acting as a third party if he acted for personal profit or other selfish motives not associated with the furtherance of the employer's business. Community Health Systems Professional Services, 525 S.W.3d 671 (Tex. 2017) (if defendant was both a corporate agent, plaintiff" must prove agent "acted in a fashion so contrary to the corporation's best interests that his actions could only have been motivated by personal interests"); Trimble v. City & County of Denver, 697 P.2d 716, 720-721, 725-727 (1985); AVGraphics, Inc. v. NYSE Group, Inc., 881 N.Y.S.2d 361 (Table) (N.Y. Super. Ct. 2009) (manager who caused plaintiff's discharge interfered as a third party where he was motivated by personal hostility rather than for organizational purposes). Even a non-supervisory employee can act as a "third party" if he sabotages another's employment for revenge or other malicious purpose.

However, even if a supervisor is partly motivated by a personal grudge or self-interest in "interfering" with an employee's employment, most courts deem his actions to be in the scope of his employment for purposes of the law of tortious interference as long as it can be said that he was motivated at least in part to serve the employer's interests. *See, e.g.,* Thompson v. Memphis Light, Gas and Water, 416 S.W.3d 402 (Tenn. App. 2011) (proof of co-employee's spite, jealousy, or poor judgment is not enough to prove co-employee acted in role of third party). Moreover, courts generally reject a plaintiff's demand for an objective analysis of the reasonableness of a supervisor's estimation of what is in his employer's interests. *See* Sims v. Software Solutions Unlimited, Inc., 939 P.2d 654 (Or. App. 1997) (plaintiff's allegation that supervisor discharged her because she was a "troublemaker" indicated supervisor was acting to protect employer's interests and foreclosed any issue whether the supervisor was motivated "solely" by self-interest).

It may be particularly difficult for a plaintiff to persuade a fact finder that a supervisor acted solely for personal purposes if the employer presents a joint defense with the supervisor or otherwise condones the supervisor's action at trial.

In Powell Industries, Inc. v. Allen, 985 S.W.2d 455 (Tex. 1998), the court dismissed an employee's tortious interference claim against a manager with the comment that "[a] corporation is a better judge of its own best interests than a jury or court," and "if a corporation does not complain about its agent's actions, then the agent cannot be held to have acted contrary to the corporation's interests." *Id.*

6. A dilemma posed by a theory of tortious interference by a supervisor is that success on such a claim might defeat the most likely basis for imputed employer liability. To succeed on the tortious interference claim, the plaintiff ordinarily must prove the supervisor acted *outside* the scope of his authority for entirely self-serving reasons and not to serve the employer's business. But success on this issue usually means losing any basis for the employer's imputed liability.

In Cappiello v. Ragen Precision Industries, Inc., 471 A.2d 432 (N.J. Super. 1984), however, the plaintiff succeeded where most plaintiffs fail: He proved the individual defendants acted outside the scope of their authority as corporate managers, and the court *still* imputed liability to the employer. The plaintiff alleged, and the jury found, that the individual defendants had conspired to terminate the plaintiff to appropriate his right to certain commissions about to come due on sales the plaintiff had arranged. The jury awarded damages, including punitive damages, against the corporate employer as well as the individual defendants. On appeal, the court upheld the verdict against the corporate employer. The court emphasized two facts. First, one of the individual defendants was the corporate president, a person "so high in authority as to be fairly considered executive in character" and his action might properly be deemed to be the action of the employer (even though he acted for his own economic benefit). Second, since the employer "here has participated in a single defense with its executives in an effort to retain plaintiff's commissions, we can well find a specific ratification of the individual defendant's actions." *Id.* at 437.

d. Discharge for an Illegal Reason

i. Overview

At one time it might have been said that in the absence of any contractual limit, the employment at will doctrine permits an employer to discharge an employee for any reason at all, and that there can be no "illegal" reasons. In Coppage v. Kansas, 236 U.S. 1 (1915), for example, the U.S. Supreme Court invoked a "constitutional freedom of contract" to strike down a state law that would have prohibited an employer from discharging an employee for being a member of a union. The law had clearly changed by 1937 when the U.S. Supreme Court decided N.L.R.B. v. Jones & Laughlin Steel Corp., 301 U.S. 13 (1937), upholding the Wagner Act's regulation of collective bargaining, including provisions that had the effect of prohibiting an employer from discharging employees because of their support for a union. Since *Jones & Laughlin Steel Corp.*, employment at will has been qualified by the rule that an employer must not discharge an employee for an "illegal" reason. Congress declared another set of employer motivations illegal in the Civil Rights Act of 1964, prohibiting discrimination on the basis of race, color, national origin, religion, and sex. Since that time, Congress and the state legislatures have gradually extended the list of illegal reasons to discriminate or retaliate against employees.

The trial of a case of alleged discharge for an illegal reason is fundamentally different from the trial of a case of alleged discharge without just cause. To begin with, proof of an absence of "just cause" requires application of the parties' contract, while proof of "illegal" intent requires application of a particular statute or public policy. More importantly, in a "just cause" case the employer bears the burden of proof as *practical* matter because the employer must explain and prove a "cause" that is "fair" or "just," while the plaintiff need only create sufficient suspicion in the mind of the fact-finder that the employer's explanation was false or not fair. The plaintiff in a "just cause" case is not required to identify or prove some ulterior motive. If the employer was simply wrong, the plaintiff prevails.

In contrast, in an illegal discharge case the employee must identify and prove the employer's usually secret illegal intent, typically a *specific* intent, such as to discriminate against the employee on the basis of race or to retaliate against the employee for "blowing the whistle" against illegal activity. It will not be enough for the plaintiff to prove the discharge was unfair or without reasonable cause. Discharge without just cause is not necessarily illegal.

As discussed in Chapter 3.C.2 in connection with the law of illegal discrimination, an illegal discharge case might proceed initially in a manner similar to a contractual unfair discharge case. The employer accused of illegal intent will articulate a lawful reason for the discharge. The employee will seek to prove the employer's reason is *not* the true cause of the discharge. Successful rebuttal of the employer's explanation makes it more likely—and possible to infer—that the real cause was illegal intent. But that inference is permissive, not mandatory, even if the employer's explanation is completely rebutted. Employers sometimes assert a "wrong" explanation for a discharge simply because they are mistaken about the facts, embarrassed about arbitrary and unfair discipline, or have something other than illegal intent to hide, such as incompetence. *See* St. Mary's Honor Ctr. v. Hicks, 509 U.S. 502 (1993) (plaintiff who rebutted employer's explanation for discharge in alleged illegal discriminatory discharge case was not entitled to judgment as a matter of law; fact finder might still find based on other evidence that there was yet another lawful cause for discharge).

ii. Discharge Undermining Public Policy

Much has already been said about the various reasons and ways an employer might "discriminate" on the basis of an employee's personal characteristics such as race, or "retaliate" against the employee's exercise of employee rights such as seeking workers' compensation benefits. The primary subject of this section is an employer's use of its power to discharge employees to prevent enforcement of the law or thwart public interests beyond "employee rights," such as protection of public safety, the environment, or financial integrity.

An early case frequently cited as an example of the public danger of unbridled employer discretion to discharge employees is Payne v. Western & Atlantic R. Co., 81 Tenn. 507 (1884). The plaintiff in *Payne* was a merchant who alleged that the defendant railroad sought to destroy his business by issuing an order that any of its employees who did business with the plaintiff would be discharged. The court upheld dismissal of the merchant's claim against the railroad. Wholly apart from the question whether a third party like the plaintiff merchant could challenge the railroad's authority to discharge its own employees, the majority doubted that the employer's exercise of its power to discharge was unlawful merely because it was harmful to other members of the community like the plaintiff. *Id.* at 5-6. Justice Freeman dissented:

> The principle of the majority opinion will justify employers, at any rate allow them to require employees to trade where they may demand, to vote as they may require, or do anything not strictly criminal that employer may dictate, or feel the wrath of employer by dismissal from service. Employment is the means of sustaining life to himself and family to the employee, and so he is morally though not legally compelled to submit. . . . Perfect freedom in all legitimate uses is due to capital, and should be zealously enforced, but public policy and all the best interests of society demands it shall be restrained within legitimate boundaries, and any channel by which it may escape or overleap these boundaries, should be carefully but judiciously guarded. For its legitimate uses I have perfect respect, against its illegitimate use I feel bound, for the best interests both of capital and labor, to protest.

Id. at 16.

In *Payne*, the railroad allegedly used its power to discharge employees to enforce cooperation in a business strategy harmful to another member of the community, and possibly harmful to the whole community. The strategy was also harmful to employees because it depended on the employer's right to discharge at will to enforce the boycott. From the community's point of view, the case was not just about employer freedom of contract, it was also about free competition. Even the majority admitted, "Great loss may result" from the employer's action.

There are many ways an employer engaged in an otherwise lawful business might seek to maximize profits at the expense of the community — by avoiding taxes, cheating consumers or investors, avoiding responsibility for the costs of pollution, or failing to correct conditions hazardous to the public. Nearly any of these strategies requires the cooperation or acquiescence of employees. At the very least, an employer engaged in harmful conduct needs its employees to look the other way, especially if the employer's conduct is criminal or violates legally enforceable rights of other members of the community. The risk that an employee might "blow the whistle" by reporting illicit employer activity to the government or injured third parties would make the activity too risky unless the employer is confident that employees who learn of the activity will not report it. The employer might even be confident enough to demand more than silence. It might require employees actively to assist in conduct harmful to the community. But some employees may have feelings of loyalty or duty to the community that are greater than their feelings of loyalty to the employer or its managers. For this reason, an explicit or implicit threat of discharge may be essential to an employer's illegal conduct.

While the majority in *Payne* recognized the "great loss" the railroad's conduct might cause, the railroad's conduct was not illegal when the court decided its opinion. Today, such conduct might violate federal or state unfair trade practice laws. The merchant Payne might have a remedy against the railroad today, but what about an employee who was discharged for breaching the employer's edict by shopping at Payne's store? Is it enough that the state or injured members of the community can sue or prosecute the employer?

Arguably, an employee discharged for blowing the whistle or refusing to cooperate in illicit activity is no worse off than an employee discharged for any other unfair reason. However, the public's ability to discover, prosecute, and remedy violations depends to some extent on the willingness of employees to uphold the law even at the risk of losing a job. In Petermann v. Teamsters Local 396, 344 P.2d 25 (Cal. 1959), an employee alleged his employer discharged him for testifying truthfully and refusing to obey his employer's instruction to commit perjury before a state legislative committee. The California court became one of the first to recognize the need for a special exception to employment at will.

> The threat of criminal prosecution would, in many cases, be a sufficient deterrent upon both the employer and employee, the former from soliciting and the latter from committing perjury. However, . . . to more fully effectuate the state's declared policy against perjury, the civil law, too, must deny the employer his generally unlimited right to discharge an employee whose employment is for an unspecified duration, when the reason for the dismissal is the employee's refusal to commit perjury. . . . To hold that one's continued employment could be made contingent upon . . . a felonious act at the instance of his employer would be to encourage criminal conduct upon the part of both the employee and employer and would serve to contaminate the honest administration of public affairs.

Id. at 27.

The public's interest in protecting employee whistleblowers has grown over time with the emergence of the regulated economic system. Beginning with New Deal legislation such as the Fair Labor Standards Act, Congress has augmented nearly every federal employment law by prohibiting retaliatory job actions against employees who oppose or report violations of those laws. The Fair Labor Standards Act, for example, makes it illegal for an employer

> to discharge or in any other manner discriminate against any employee because such employee has filed any complaint or instituted or caused to be instituted any proceeding under or related to this chapter, or has testified or is about to testify in any such proceeding. . . .

29 U.S.C. §215(a)(3). A more modern anti-retaliation provision is section 704 of Title VII of the Civil Rights Act of 1964, 42 U.S.C. §2000e-3(a):

> It shall be an unlawful employment practice for an employer to discriminate against any of his employees or applicants for employment . . . because he has opposed any practice made an unlawful employment practice by this subchapter, or because he has made a charge, testified, assisted, or participated in any manner in an investigation, proceeding, or hearing under this subchapter.

These early anti-retaliation laws protected employees who asserted personal rights as employees or who aided in the enforcement of employment laws, but they did nothing to protect employees acting to uphold other public interests. Inspired perhaps by *Petermann* and other judicial exceptions to the employment at will doctrine, Congress and the state legislatures began to provide anti-retaliation protection for employees acting to uphold many *non*-employment laws, including environmental, financial and public safety laws. A typical example is the Clean Air Act, which makes it illegal for an employer to "discharge . . . or otherwise discriminate against any employee" for commencing or assisting "in any manner" a proceeding under the act. 42 U.S.C. § 7622(a). Two of the most recent examples are the Sarbanes-Oxley Act, which adds protection for employees who oppose or report fraud against investors, and the Dodds-Frank Wall Street Reform and Consumer Protection Act, which provides protection and rewards for employees who report or oppose violations of laws relating to financial securities, consumer finance, or commodities exchanges. 7 U.S.C. § 26, 12, U.S.C. § 5567, 15 U.S.C. § 78u-6, and 18 U.S.C.A. § 1514A. But Congress and state legislatures have not consistently added anti-retaliation protection to their laws. For example, the Immigration and Reform and Control Act, 8 U.S.C. 1324a, which prohibits employers from employing undocumented workers, has no anti-retaliation provision for employees who report such violations. *See also* Wiersum v. U.S. Bank, N.A., 785 F.3d 483 (11th Cir. 2015) (National Bank Act, which provides that bank officers serve "at pleasure" of a covered bank, preempted alleged whistleblower claim under state law).Thus, whether an employee is protected for acting to uphold public policy might depend on the jurisdiction in which she was employed, the industry or occupation in which she was employed, the specific "policy" she sought to uphold, and the manner of her opposition.. .

Should Congress and the state legislatures enact a statute, or should the courts declare a common law rule, broadly protecting employees who act in any manner to uphold any public interests or oppose any wrongful conduct? Would it be possible to declare a rule sufficiently covering the gamut of "public policy" interests and all the varieties of oppositional conduct without protecting too much oppositional conduct?

BANAITIS v. MITSUBISHI BANK, LTD.
129 Or. App. 371, 879 P.2d 1288 (Or. 1994)

LANDAU, Judge.

Defendants appeal from a judgment awarding plaintiff compensatory damages on his claim for wrongful discharge against defendant The Bank of California, N.A. (BanCal), and on his claim for interference with a contractual relationship against defendant Mitsubishi Bank, Ltd. (MBL). Plaintiff crossappeals a judgment notwithstanding the verdict that deprived him of a jury award of punitive damages against both defendants. We affirm on the appeal and reverse on the cross-appeal.

We state the facts in the light most favorable to plaintiff. Plaintiff, a former vice president of BanCal, began working for the bank in 1980. MBL is a financial institution in the "Mitsubishi Group," a collection of related companies in Japan. In 1984, MBL acquired directly 13 percent of the stock in BanCal. It then acquired a holding company that held the balance of BanCal's stock. MBL transferred a number of its officers from Tokyo to manage the bank. One of those officers, Tanaka, remained an MBL employee, but was given a title at BanCal. Tanaka was plaintiff's supervisor from late 1986 until plaintiff's termination.

BanCal had a policy of keeping its customers' financial information confidential. It stated that policy in its employee policy manual, and each year employees were required to certify that they understood the policy. An employee who breached the confidentiality policy was subject to immediate dismissal.

When MBL acquired BanCal, a number of BanCal's customers expressed concern that MBL would acquire information from BanCal that would be used by other members of the Mitsubishi Group for competitive advantage. Some customers stopped doing business with BanCal. Others demanded written confidentiality agreements that would insure that their financial information would not be disclosed to MBL.

In the fall of 1986, an employee of MBL telephoned plaintiff and asked him to supply a "comparison chart on [BanCal's] grain company customers." The comparison chart that MBL requested contains information that shows the relative financial positions of five large grain shippers, including each company's cash on hand, accounts receivable, inventory of grain, accounts and notes payable, long-term indebtedness, net worth, cost of goods, operating expenses, profit and inventory turnover. Knowledge of that information would give a competitor an advantage in the marketplace. Plaintiff refused the MBL employee's request for the chart, explaining that disclosure of the information was against bank policy, against the law and unethical. When the MBL employee explained that he sought the information for MBL's internal use only, plaintiff responded that he would not release the information without written authorization from the bank's president.

In September, 1986, the manager of MBL's Portland office made a similar request of plaintiff, this time asking for confidential financial information about a particular customer, Schnitzer Steel Industries, Inc. (Schnitzer). Schnitzer was one of the BanCal customers that had demanded express promises from BanCal that confidential information would not be disclosed to MBL or any member of the Mitsubishi Group. Plaintiff again refused MBL's request.

Soon after that, in February, 1987, Tanaka wrote a performance evaluation that falsely accused plaintiff of not meeting his 1986 budget. In June, 1987, Tanaka falsely accused plaintiff of going to New York on business without approval. Tanaka also accused plaintiff of being dishonest and questioned his integrity. In August, 1987, BanCal put plaintiff on probation for 90 days, based on another evaluation that reiterated the earlier falsehoods and added new false charges.

Plaintiff's probation was over in mid-November, but BanCal did not dismiss him. Meanwhile, plaintiff informed BanCal's Human Resources Department that he could not stay at the bank and offered to negotiate a smooth departure. On December 16, while negotiations continued, plaintiff told his staff at a breakfast meeting that he would be leaving the bank soon. He had anticipated that he would continue to work at least through December 31, 1987, so that he would receive the full value of the bank's contributions to his pension fund for 1987. However, Tanaka and BanCal's Human Resources Department accelerated his departure date to December 30, 1987, thus depriving him of those pension benefits. Plaintiff received notice of that decision in a letter handdelivered by Tanaka. Plaintiff then was instructed that he had 30 minutes to "clean out his desk." He protested that he could not possibly complete the task that quickly, so he was allowed to remove his things the next day after working hours. Other employees were instructed to watch him while he packed.

Plaintiff commenced this action on December 12, 1989. He alleged a claim against BanCal for wrongful discharge and a claim against MBL for interference with a contractual relationship. The complaint included demands for punitive damages against both defendants.

At the close of the evidence at trial, defendants moved for directed verdicts.... The trial court denied the motions, and the jury returned a verdict for plaintiff, awarding plaintiff compensatory and punitive damages against both defendants....

In the first assignment of error, BanCal contends that the trial court erred in denying its motion for directed verdict, because plaintiff failed to produce evidence of a prima facie case for wrongful termination. BanCal concedes, for the purpose of the motion, that it deliberately made plaintiff's working environment so unpleasant that he had to leave, and that it did so in retaliation for his withholding BanCal's confidential customer information from MBL. According to BanCal, that does not constitute wrongful termination, because plaintiff was an at-will employee, and the reason for his discharge does not fall within any exception to the general rule that at-will employees may be discharged at any time, for any reason.

In general, an employer may discharge an employee at any time, for any reason, unless doing so violates a contractual, statutory or constitutional requirement. Patton v. J.C. Penney Co., 719 P.2d 854 (Or. 1986). There are exceptions to the general rule. A cause of action will lie against an employer who discharges an employee for performing a public duty, or fulfilling a societal obligation such as serving on a jury, Nees v. Hocks, 536 P.2d 512 (Or. 1975), or refusing to commit a potentially tortious act of defamation. Delaney v. Taco Time Intl., 681 P.2d 114 (Or. 1984). An employer also may be held liable for discharging an employee for pursuing private statutory rights that are directly related to the employment, such as resisting sexual harassment by a supervisor, Holien v. Sears, Roebuck and Co., 689 P.2d 1292 (Or. 1984), or filing a claim for workers' compensation benefits. Brown v. Transcon Lines, 588 P.2d 1087 (Or. 1978).

In this case, plaintiff contends that his termination for refusing to disclose confidential information falls within the "societal obligation" or "public duty" exception to the at-will rule. According to plaintiff, there is a public duty to avoid disclosing valuable, confidential customer financial information held by a bank. That public duty, he argues, is evidenced by a host of state and federal statutes that generally protect business information from discovery by or disclosure to the public or to government agencies. In particular, plaintiff relies on federal and state public records statutes, rules of civil procedure and various criminal statutes, all of which protect against disclosure of confidential financial information.

BanCal argues that plaintiff's refusal to divulge the requested information implicates no societal obligation or public duty. It argues that none of the statutes on which plaintiff relies specifically applies to the disclosure of customer financial information held by a bank. Without such statutes, "carefully tethered" to the specific conduct at issue, BanCal contends, there can be no societal obligation or public duty.

We first address the parties' arguments concerning the standard that we must apply in determining whether a societal obligation or public duty is implicated. In deciding the question whether an employer could be held liable for discharging an employee for serving on a jury, the Supreme Court in Nees v. Hocks, *supra*, looked to the provisions in the Oregon Constitution preserving the right of jury trials, to various statutes describing exemptions from jury service and consequences for neglecting to show up for jury service, and to caselaw from other jurisdictions concerning the importance of jury duty. The court concluded:

> These actions by the people, the legislature and the courts clearly indicate that the jury system and jury duty are regarded as high on the scale of American institutions and citizen obligations. . . . [W]e hold that the defendants are liable for discharging plaintiff because she served on the jury.

536 P.2d 512.

The constitutional provisions on which the court relied, as well as the statutes and the caselaw, do not impose an obligation of jury service. Nevertheless, the court drew on them as indicia of the public policy that it found to be the basis for liability.

Likewise, in Delaney v. Taco Time Intl., *supra*, in which the Supreme Court considered whether an employer could be found liable for discharging an employee who refused to sign a false performance evaluation, the court relied on two provisions of the Oregon Constitution, Article I, sections 8 and 10. Neither of those provisions prohibits a person from defaming another. Nevertheless, the court concluded that "[t]hese two sections indicate that a member of society has an obligation not to defame others." 681 P.2d 114. . . .

In short, there is no requirement, as BanCal contends, that a specific statute has been violated before we may conclude that a societal obligation or a public duty has been implicated. We must review all the relevant "evidence" of a particular public policy, whether that be expressed in constitutional and statutory provisions or in the caselaw of this or other jurisdictions. We turn, then, to the issue of whether discharging an employee for refusing to disclose a customer's confidential financial information falls within the societal obligation exception to the at-will rule. We conclude that it does.

Numerous statutes reflect a legislative recognition of the important public policy of protecting from disclosure confidential commercial and financial information. The Federal Right to Financial Privacy Act of 1978, 12 U.S.C. § 3401 et seq., prohibits, with certain exceptions, the disclosure of a customer's records by a financial institution to a government authority without the customer's consent. The Federal Freedom of Information Act, 5 U.S.C. § 552, similarly exempts from disclosure by public agencies any "commercial or financial information" that is privileged or confidential. 5 U.S.C. § 552(b)(4). The Oregon Public Records Act, ORS 192.501(2), likewise exempts from disclosure any

> compilation of information which is not patented, which is known only to certain individuals within an organization and which is used in a business it conducts, having actual or potential commercial value, and which gives its user an opportunity to obtain a business advantage over competitors who do not know or use it.

In a related vein, ORCP 36 C(7) authorizes courts to issue protective orders to avoid disclosure of "a trade secret or other confidential . . . commercial information." *See also* FRCP 26(c)(7). Various criminal statutes reflect a public interest in protecting the confidentiality of commercial financial records. ORS 165.095(1) provides that a person who "misapplies" property entrusted to a financial institution commits a crime. Removal or disclosure of a bank's files or other property is a Class C felony. ORS 708.715.

At common law, the courts in a number of jurisdictions have recognized a bank's duty not to divulge to a third party, without the customer's consent, any information relating to the customer acquired through the keeping of the customer's account. As the Idaho Supreme Court said in Peterson v. Idaho First National Bank,, 367 P.2d 284 (Idaho 1961): "It is inconceivable that a bank would at any time consider itself at liberty to disclose the intimate details of its depositors' accounts. Inviolate secrecy is one of the inherent and fundamental precepts of the relationship of the bank and its customers or depositors." 367 P.2d 284. . . . Consistent with that rule, BanCal's own internal policy prohibits the disclosure of confidential customer financial information.

Those statutory provisions, rules and common law principles reflect a common concern for the protection of valuable commercial financial information, particularly when that information has been entrusted to a bank. Permitting a bank to discharge with impunity its employee for refusing to disclose confidential customer financial information would violate that public policy and compromise the protections that the statutes, rules and common law duties were designed to afford.

BanCal acknowledges the foregoing authorities. It also concedes that they concern the type of confidential customer financial information that is involved in this case. It nevertheless maintains that most of the statutory provisions only establish limitations on the authority of governmental agencies—not banks—to disclose that confidential customer financial information. It also insists that the authorities that do concern the disclosure of information entrusted to banks only give rise to private remedies and, therefore, cannot be evidence of important public policies.

BanCal's arguments rest on an incorrect characterization of the standard we apply in discerning the existence of a societal obligation or public duty. As we have said, it is not necessary that a statute specifically regulate the conduct that precipitated the discharge. We review statutes and other authorities for evidence of a substantial public policy that would, as the Supreme Court said in Nees v. Hocks, *supra*, be "thwarted" if an employer were allowed to discharge its employee without liability. 536 P.2d 512. . . . The trial court did not err in denying BanCal's motion for a directed verdict.

. . . In the fourth assignment of error, MBL argues that the trial court erred in denying its motion for a directed verdict on the intentional interference with contractual relations claim. According to MBL, because it owned BanCal, MBL was effectively a party to the employment contract between BanCal and plaintiff, and, as a result, MBL cannot be held liable for interfering with a contract between plaintiff and itself. . . .

The rule in Oregon is that a party to a contract cannot be held liable for interference with that contract. Lewis v. Oregon Beauty Supply Co., *supra*, 733

P.2d 430. The Oregon courts, however, have never held that a parent company's mere ownership of stock in a subsidiary completely shields the parent from liability for interfering with a contract between the subsidiary and a third party. . . . MBL does not own BanCal outright; it owns only 13 percent of BanCal's stock. The rest of BanCal's stock is owned by an intermediary holding company, and there is no conclusive evidence that MBL either controls the holding company or controls BanCal through its control of the holding company. Ownership of stock, by itself, is insufficient to establish actual control of a corporation. . . . On the record before us, it simply cannot be said that, as a matter of law, MBL was a party to plaintiff's employment contract with BanCal. The trial court did not err in denying the motion for a directed verdict on the intentional interference claim.

[The court held that the record supported the jury's award of punitive damages, and that the trial court erred in granting the defendants' motion for judgment notwithstanding the verdict on punitive damages.]

[R]emanded for reinstatement of jury verdict awarding punitive damages.

NOTES AND QUESTIONS

1. In 1997, Banaitis and the defendants entered into a settlement agreement to resolve all their disputes. In accordance with the agreement, the defendant banks paid a total of $8,728,559. From this amount the banks paid $3,864,012 directly to Banaitis's attorney, leaving Banaitis $4,864,547. Oregon law requires a plaintiff who recovers punitive damages to share a portion with the state, and Oregon's share of Banaitis' damages came to $150,000. Then there was the Internal Revenue Service's claim. Banaitis's income tax issues with the IRS are described in Banaitis v. Commissioner of Internal Revenue, 340 F.3d 1074 (9th Cir. 2003).

2. Several state and federal employment statutes take some variation of the *Banaitis* approach: general protection of employee oppositional conduct in support of a broad range of potential public interests instead of specialized protection on a statute by statute basis. In 1989, Congress enacted the Whistleblower Protection Act to protect federal employees—but only federal employees—who report violations of "any law," any "gross mismanagement," any "gross waste of funds," any "abuse of authority," or any "substantial and specific danger to public health and safety." 5 U.S.C. § 1213. A few state legislatures or courts have declared similarly broad laws protecting public employees in most cases, and sometimes private sector employees as well. *See, e.g.*, N.J. Stat. Ann. § 43:19-3.3 A frequent argument against protection of employees acting by "any" means in support of "any" public policy or "any" public interest is that such a law would be difficult to administer and invite too many claims by employees seeking by their own means to impose their own views of "public policy" and "public interest" on their employers. Another argument is that overbroad protection makes it too easy for employees to preempt expected disciplinary action by engaging in last minute, plausibly protected conduct. Compare *Banaitis* with McGowan v. Medpace, Inc., 42 N.E.3d 256 (Ohio App. 2015) (discussing Ohio's common law public policy exception to employment at will doctrine, and holding that whistleblower is protected only if employee had affirmative duty to report alleged wrongdoing, or if law allegedly violated was for protection of public health and safety). Thus, Congress and many state legislatures

or courts have continued the narrow approach, adding anti-retaliation protection to specific laws or policies believed to be so vital to the public interest that employees should be specially encouraged and protected or rewarded for specific conduct (e.g., "reporting") to aid enforcement or assure compliance.

3. One more objection to whistleblower protection is that a whistleblower might unreasonably disclose private, potentially personal and confidential information or trade secrets. Colorado has responded to this concern for state employees by creating a "whistleblower review agency." A state employee gains maximum protection for whistleblowing by first sending information to the review agency for a determination whether it is properly disclosed by the employee. Col. Rev. Stat. § 24-50.5-101 et seq.

4. Courts declaring common law exceptions to the employment at will doctrine were once the vanguard of the movement to protect employee action in the public interest. How might the judiciary's power to mold and expand employment law be affected by a legislature's enactment of a specialized anti-retaliation provision to a particular regulatory statute?

AUSTIN v. HEALTHTRUST, INC.

967 S.W.2d 400 (Tex. 1998)

OWEN, Justice.

We have been requested in this case to create a judicial exception to the employment-at-will doctrine by recognizing a cause of action for private whistleblowers. Because the Legislature has been so proactive in promulgating statutes that prohibit retaliation against whistleblowers in many areas of the private sector, we decline to recognize a common-law cause of action....

I

This case was decided by summary judgment. The parties included in the trial court record only the facts necessary to resolve the legal issue of whether a private whistleblower cause of action exists under the common law. Therefore, our account of the facts is brief, and we set forth only the factual allegations asserted by Austin, against whom summary judgment was rendered.

Lynda Gail Austin worked as an emergency room nurse at Gulf Coast Medical Hospital for approximately fifteen years. In July 1992, she noticed that another emergency room nurse, Clay Adam, appeared to be under the influence of drugs. Austin learned shortly thereafter that Adam had been distributing prescription medication to patients without authorization from a physician. Austin relayed this information to her supervisor, Patrick Lilley. She also submitted a written report to Lilley detailing Adam's conduct and actions. Lilley instructed Austin to keep the information to herself, and she complied.

Austin alleges that Lilley subjected her to extreme scrutiny after she reported Adam's conduct. Then, on December 1, 1992, Lilley fired Austin and asked her to leave the premises. Upon learning that Lilley was a family friend of Adam, Austin brought this suit against HealthTrust Inc.—The Hospital Company, the Gulf Coast Medical Foundation d/b/a Gulf Coast Medical Center, and Lilley (hereinafter

HealthTrust). Austin alleges that she was discharged in retaliation for reporting Adam's unlawful, dangerous, and unethical activities.

HealthTrust moved for summary judgment, asserting that Austin failed to state a cognizable claim under Texas law. The trial court granted the motion. The court of appeals affirmed, holding that Texas does not recognize a common-law cause of action for retaliatory discharge of a private employee who reports the illegal activities of others in the workplace. We affirm.

II

This is not the first time that the Court has been urged to recognize a private whistleblower cause of action. In Winters v. Houston Chronicle Publishing Co., 795 S.W.2d 723, 723 (Tex. 1990), Richard Winters, who worked as an at-will employee for the Chronicle, was discharged after reporting suspected illegal activities of his fellow employees to his superiors. We declined to further modify the employment-at-will doctrine by permitting a suit for retaliation. In so doing, we observed that the Legislature had already enacted numerous measures to protect employees who report illegal activity in the workplace. *Id.* at 724.

Since *Winters*, several courts of appeals have contemplated whether to recognize a private whistleblower cause of action. In Thompson v. El Centro Del Barrio, 905 S.W.2d 356 (Tex. App. 1995), a private nonprofit corporation allegedly fired an employee for reporting coworkers who were misusing public money. Concluding that the issue was better left to the Legislature or this Court, the court of appeals refused to recognize a cause of action. *Id.* at 359. Similarly, in Burgess v. El Paso Cancer Treatment Center, 881 S.W.2d 552, 554, 556 (Tex. App. 1994), the court of appeals held that there was no cause of action for an employee who was discharged after reporting an alleged conspiracy among fellow employees to replace new parts from radiation machines with defective used parts. . . .

Austin urges us to embrace a cause of action that is more narrowly tailored than those that were under consideration in *Winters* and *Thompson*. Taking a page from the concurring opinion in *Winters*, Austin advocates a private whistleblower cause of action in cases in which the conduct or activity that was reported would have "a probable adverse effect upon the public." *Winters*, 795 S.W.2d at 725 (Doggett, J., concurring). Our review of legislative action in the employment-at-will area leads us to conclude that it would be unwise for this Court to expand the common law because to do so would essentially eclipse more narrowly-crafted statutory whistleblower causes of action. Prior to *Winters*, and in the eight years that have followed, the Legislature has enacted a variety of private remedies and has declined to create a cause of action that would have general applicability.

As recently as the 1995 legislative session, an amendment to the Labor Code was proposed that would have created a "Whistleblower Act" for all private employees. The proposed bill, like the cause of action Austin proposes here, would have prohibited an employer from terminating an employee "who in good faith reports activities within the workplace that constitute a violation of law or would otherwise have a probable adverse effect on the public." This version of the bill was rejected in legislative committee. An amended bill was then proposed that deleted protection for reports of activities that would have a "probable adverse effect on the public" in favor of the requirement that the reported activity "constitute a violation of law." However, the Legislature did not pass the modified bill.

Rather than create a one-size-fits-all whistleblower statute, the Texas Legislature has instead opted to enact statutes that protect specific classes of employees from various types of retaliation. For example, section 554.002 of the Government Code protects public employees from retaliation for reporting, in good faith, the employing governmental entity's or fellow employees' violations of law to an appropriate law enforcement agency. Tex. Gov't Code § 554.002. Similarly, a physician cannot be retaliated against for reporting to the State Board of Medical Examiners the acts of another physician that pose a continuing threat to the public welfare. Tex. Rev. Civ. Stat. Ann. art. 4495b, § 5.06(d), (q) (Vernon Supp. 1998). The Legislature has also enacted a statute that prohibits retaliation against nursing home employees who report abuse or neglect of a nursing home resident. Tex. Health & Safety Code § 242.133. Additionally, employers who use hazardous chemicals may not retaliate against employees for reporting a violation of the Hazard Communication Act. *Id.* § 502.017; *see also* Tex. Agric. Code § 125.013(b) (prohibiting retaliation against agricultural laborer for reporting a violation of the Agricultural Hazard Communication Act). Nor can employers retaliate against employees for opposing or reporting discriminatory practices in the workplace. Tex. Lab. Code § 21.055; *see also* Tex. Lab. Code § 411.082 (prohibiting employer from retaliating against employee for using the Workers' Compensation Commission's toll-free telephone service to report, in good faith, an alleged violation of an occupational health or safety law); Tex. Loc. Gov't Code § 160.006 (preventing county employee from being subject to retaliation for exercising a right or participating in a grievance procedure established under Chapter 160 of the Local Government Code).

Moreover, the Legislature has enacted specific statutes to address the retaliation that Austin alleges she suffered in the present case. Registered nurses, such as Austin, are required by law to report another registered nurse who "has exposed or is likely to expose a patient or other person unnecessarily to a risk of harm" or who "is likely to be impaired by chemical dependency." Tex. Rev. Civ. Stat. Ann. art. 4525a, § 1 (Vernon Supp. 1998). The report must be in writing and submitted to the Board of Nurse Examiners. *Id.*; *see also* Clark v. Texas Home Health, Inc., 971 S.W.2d 435 (Tex. 1998), which we decide today. Any nurse who files a report pursuant to the statute is protected from retaliation:

> A person has a cause of action against an individual, organization, agency, facility, or other person that suspends or terminates the employment of the person or otherwise disciplines or discriminates against the person reporting under this article.

Tex. Rev. Civ. Stat. Ann. art. 4525a, § 11(a) (Vernon Supp. 1998). Although article 4525a was in effect when Austin reported Adam's conduct to Lilley, Austin has not alleged that she filed a report with the Board of Nurse Examiners or that she was fired for doing so. She has not pursued any cause of action under the statute.

Beyond the protections provided by article 4525a, the Legislature has recently enacted another specific whistleblower statute for any hospital employee who reports illegal activity. *See* Tex. Health & Safety Code § 161.134. Section 161.134 of the Health and Safety Code provides a specific cause of action against a hospital-employer who has retaliated against an employee for reporting a violation of the law to a supervisor. While this statute was not in effect at the time Austin was discharged and she cannot avail herself of its provisions, it nevertheless is another factor this Court must consider in determining whether to create a broader common-law cause of action.

Aside from the aforementioned whistleblower statutes, the Legislature has created numerous other restrictions on and exceptions to the employment at-will doctrine. *See, e.g.*, Tex. Lab. Code § 451.001 (prohibiting retaliation for filing a workers' compensation claim in good faith); Tex. Lab. Code § 101.052 (prohibiting denial of employment based on union membership or nonmembership); Tex. Gov't Code § 431.006 (prohibiting discharge because of active duty in the state military forces); Tex. Civ. Prac. & Rem. Code § 122.001 (prohibiting discharge because of jury service); Tex. Lab. Code § 21.051 (prohibiting discrimination based on race, color, disability, religion, national origin, age, or sex); Tex. Fam. Code § 158.209 (prohibiting discrimination based on withholding order for child support); Tex. Health & Safety Code § 592.015 (mandating that mentally retarded individuals receive equal employment opportunities); Tex. Elec. Code § 276.004 (subjecting employer to criminal liability for prohibiting employee from voting); Tex. Elec. Code § 276.001 (creating felony offense for employer who retaliates against employee for voting a certain way); Tex. Elec. Code § 161.007 (creating criminal liability for employer who prohibits or retaliates against employee for attending a political convention as a delegate); Tex. Lab. Code § 52.041 (subjecting employer to fine for coercing employee to purchase certain merchandise); Tex. Health & Safety Code § 81.102 (limiting an employer's ability to require employee to undergo test for AIDS virus); Tex. Rev. Civ. Stat. Ann. art. 4512.7, § 3 (Vernon Supp.1998) (prohibiting discrimination against health care employee for refusing to perform or participate in an abortion).

In enacting statutes that prohibit certain conduct in the employment area, the Legislature has carefully balanced competing interests and policies. This has resulted in statutes not only with diverse protections, but also with widely divergent remedies and varying procedural requirements. For example, some whistleblower statutes allow recovery of exemplary damages while other statutes limit recovery to lost wages. . . . The period of limitations varies from statute to statute. . . . And some statutory schemes require exhaustion of administrative remedies before filing suit, . . . while others allow the employee to proceed directly to court. . . .

Unlike the Legislature, we cannot craft statutes of limitation that vary depending upon the area of employment. Nor can the Court establish an administrative scheme. Were we to create a broad-based whistleblower cause of action, it would in large part eviscerate the specific measures the Legislature has already adopted.

We do not doubt that significant public policy interests are advanced when employers are prohibited from discriminating against employees who report violations of the law. However, the Legislature has enacted specific statutes to redress wrongful termination. While we are not bound by the Legislature's policy decisions when we consider whether to create a common-law whistleblower action, "the boundaries the Legislature has drawn do inform our decision." Ford Motor Co. v. Miles, 967 S.W.2d 377, 383 (Tex. 1998). Accordingly, rather than recognize a common-law cause of action that would effectively emasculate a number of statutory schemes, we leave to the Legislature the task of crafting remedies for retaliation by employers. . . .

For the foregoing reasons, we affirm the judgment of the court of appeals.

GONZALEZ, Justice, concurring.

. . . I agree that the facts of Lynda Gail Austin's discharge, like in *Winters*, do not provide the appropriate situation for us to broaden the exceptions to at-will employment. Since Austin's firing, the Legislature has enacted a whistleblower statute that provides a remedy to any hospital employee who has been discharged for reporting illegal activity to his or her employer. Tex. Health & Safety Code Ann. § 161.134 (Vernon Supp. 1998). Even though Austin was unable to benefit from this enactment, she was not without a remedy. In fact, as the Court points out, under a statute that went into effect in 1987, Austin, as a registered nurse, was required by law to report another registered nurse that she suspected had exposed or was "likely to expose a patient or other person unnecessarily to a risk of harm," or who "is or is likely to be impaired by chemical dependency. . . ." Tex. Rev. Civ. Stat. art. 4525a, § 1(a) (Vernon Supp. 1998). While the record does not reflect whether Austin reported her suspicions to the Board of Nurse Examiners as required, there is no doubt she would have then had a civil cause of action if she was suspended, terminated, or otherwise disciplined or discriminated against. *Id.* § 11(a). Accordingly, this is not a compelling scenario of injustice that requires us to modify the long-standing employment-at-will doctrine.

However, such a compelling situation may present itself in the future, and when it does, it will be incumbent on this Court to once again, as we did in *Sabine Pilot*, carry its "burden and the duty of amending [the doctrine] to reflect social and economic changes." *Sabine Pilot*, 687 S.W.2d at 735 (Kilgarlin, J., concurring).

NOTES AND QUESTIONS

1. Even if Austin had invoked the Texas nurse whisleblower statute as the basis for her claim, her claim evidently would have failed because she was an "internal" whistleblower and not an "external" whistleblower. In other words, the statute clearly required that an employee must file a report with the Board of Nurse Examiners to gain protection. Reporting to a supervisor might not be enough. On the other hand, on the same day the Texas Supreme Court decided *Austin*, it also decided Clark v. Texas Home Health, Inc., 971 S.W.2d 435 (Tex. 1998), and held that an employer unlawfully violated the nurse whistleblower law by firing nurses before they could make their report to the board. The court distinguished that case from *Austin* by noting that the employer knew the plaintiff nurses' official complaint to the board was "imminent."

2. Are the arguments for a court to defer to a legislature equally compelling whether the legislature has acted a little versus not at all? In *Austin*, it could be said that the Texas Legislature had already acted within the realm of Austin's cause of action. The Legislature had not entirely overlooked the situation of nurses such as Austin. In contrast, in the New York case of Murphy v. American Home Prods.

Corp., 448 N.E.2d 86 (N.Y. 1983), there was no statute addressing the circumstances of the plaintiff employee's claim and little danger of upsetting the legislature's balance of policies and interests for a particular category of cases. Nevertheless, the New York court deferred to the legislature's inaction. Like the Texas court in *Austin,* the New York court believed the preliminary investigation and groundwork needed for such an important law, and the determination of precise rules of coverage and remedies, would be better performed by the legislature. *Id.* at 90-91.

Not all courts defer to a legislature, especially if the legislature's approach seems to have fallen short. *See, e.g.*, Collins v. Elkay Mining Co., 371 S.E.2d 46 (W. Va. 1988) (permitting tort action for refusal to falsify mine safety reports, where court deemed existing administrative remedy inadequate); Hodges v. S.C. Toof & Co., 833 S.W.2d 896 (Tenn. 1992) (allowing common law remedies despite statutory remedies under jury service statute); Flanker v. Willamette Industries, Inc., 967 P.2d 295 (Kan. 1998) (state court applying its own remedy after finding OSHA's administrative scheme for protecting whistleblowers to be inadequate).

3. In general, states can be classified in three groups based on the breadth of common-law wrongful discharge actions based on "public policy."

Broad view: The *Banaitis* case is a leading example of an approach allowing a common-law cause of action for termination contravening any public policy implied or supported by other laws, including laws not directly on-point – such as the laws and rules *Banaitis* cited about financial privacy that did not specifically make unlawful the act that the bank asked the employee to do.

Narrow view: *Austin* presents the case for a narrow approach, based partly on the argument that a legislature is the superior forum for designing anti-retaliation law, and partly on the argument that a court should hesitate to invent common law anti-retaliation causes of action if the legislature has already shown its awareness of the problem by enacting limited protection or by choosing not to enact any protection at all. *See also* Murphy v. Am. Home Prods. Corp., 448 N.E.2d 86 (N.Y. 1983) (deferring to legislature's inaction in granting anti-retaliation protection to employees). Included within this group are state courts that simply confine common law anti-retaliation causes of action to very limited situations for which there is clear precedent. See, e.g., McGowan v. Medpace, Inc., 42 N.E.3d 256 (Ohio App. 2015) (common-law public policy claim requires proof that whistleblowing was required by affirmative duty to report wrongdoing, or was to uphold a law for the protection of public health and safety).

Middle view: Courts in this group remain willing to extend an existing common-law public policy theory or adopt a new one rather than deferring to legislative inaction, but they might demand very clear proof of the policy the employee sought to uphold, usually in statutes, administrative regulations or ethics codes. *See, e.g.,* Kempfer v. Automated Finishing, Inc., 564 N.W.2d 692, 698 (Wis. 1997) (requiring "fundamental and well-defined public policy as evidenced by existing law," and finding expression of such a policy in an administrative rule against performing services as a nurse without requisite qualifications); Rocky Mtn. Hosp. v. Mariani, 916 P.2d 519, 526 (Colo. 1996) ("clear mandate of public policy" was established by professional ethics code for accountants); Gen'l

Dynamics Corp. v. Superior Ct., 876 P.2d 487, 497, 502 (Cal. 1994) (requiring that "public policy at issue must be one that is not only fundamental but is clearly established"; finding sufficient "a mandatory ethical obligation prescribed by professional rule or statute" allegedly violated by firing an attorney for refusing to violate an ethical duty").

4. The Restatement of Employment Law adopts the "middle view." It requires a "well-established public policy." RESTATEMENT OF EMPLOYMENT LAW § 5.01. But the Restatement allows evidence of policy from a broad range of sources including statutes, local ordinances, judicial decisions, administrative regulations, administrative agency decisions or orders, and professional or occupational codes of conduct. *Id.* § 5.03.

5. In some states, legislatures have authorized their courts to declare public policy—at least within certain limits—for purposes of a retaliation cause of action. The New Jersey Conscientious Employee Protection Act protects an employee from retaliation for opposing a violation of "a clear mandate of public policy concerning the public health, safety or welfare or protection of the environment." N.J. Stat. Ann. § 34:19-3. As interpreted by the New Jersey courts, a "clear" mandate need not be a rule adopted by a legislative body. The New Jersey law allows proof of policy based on tort law declared by the courts, or a rule of ethics declared by an established professional organization. *See* Smith-Bozarth v. Coalition Against Rape and Abuse, Inc., 747 A.2d 322 (N. J. Super. 2000); Barratt v. Cushman & Wakefield of New Jersey, Inc., 675 A.2d 1094 (N.J. 1996).

6. Should an employee have the right to protect his or her own personal safety, even by insubordination, if the employee is not protecting the "public?" An employee who refuses to perform dangerous work might be protected by federal law if the circumstances of the work violate the Occupational Safety and Health Act and present a significant risk of serious personal injury. See Chapter 5.C.3.a. However, not all self-protection involves a refusal to work under the OSHA work refusal rule. In Ray v. Wal-Mart Stores, 359 P.3d 614 (Utah 2015), two employees alleged that their employer had wrongfully discharged them in for engaging in active "self-defense" against armed shop-lifters, in violation of the employer's disengagement rule. The employees alleged that they reasonably believed they could not safely disengage under the circumstances. The court held that the employees stating a cause of action for wrongful discharge, finding that Utah's "right of self-defense" was a "clear and substantial public policy" justifying an exception to the employment at will doctrine.

7. Many employers now demand that employees sign agreements not to serve any competitor after the termination of employment. All states now have laws, statutory or common law, restricting such non-competition agreements. *See* Chapter 9.B.2. If the an employer discharges an employee for refusing to accept an *unenforceable* promise not to compete, should the employee be able to sue the employer for wrongful discharge in violation of public policy? *Compare, e.g.,* Edwards v. Arthur Andersen LLP, 189 P.3d 285 (Cal. 2008) (termination of employee for refusing to sign illegal non-competition agreement constitutes wrongful termination in violation of public policy) *with* Madden v. Omega Optical, Inc., 683 A.2d 386 (Vt. 1996) (regardless of whether agreement employer demanded was enforceable, termination for refusing to sign the agreement did not

violate public policy) *and* Tatge v. Chambers & Owen, Inc., 579 N.W.2d 217 (Wisc. 1998) (if noncompetition agreement is unreasonable it is void, but termination for refusal to sign void agreement is not wrongful discharge against public policy).

8. If an employer retaliates by wrongful discharge in violation of public policy, is the employee's cause of action based on an implied term of his contract, or is it a tort? If the claim grows out of an implied contractual right to comply with the law, the employee is limited to the usual contract law remedies, such as lost wages and benefits, and possibly reinstatement. On the other hand, if the claim is based on tort law, the employee's recovery might include punitive damages and damages for emotional distress. Most courts that have considered the question have concluded that a wrongful discharge in violation of public policy is a tort. Foley v. Interactive Data Corp., 765 P.2d 373 (Cal. 1988) (en banc) (tort); Pierce v. Ortho Pharmaceutical Corp., 417 A.2d 505 (N.J. 1980) (tort); Porter v. City of Manchester, 849 A.2d 103 (N.H. 2004) (tort); Dunwoody v. Handskill Corp., 60 P.3d 1135 (Or. App. 2003) (tort). *But see* Brockmeyer v. Dun & Bradstreet, 335 N.W.2d 834 (Wis. 1983) (contract).

The Restatement of Employment Law agrees with the majority view that "wrongful discharge in violation of public policy" is a "tort claim" yielding "tort liability." RESTATEMENT OF THE LAW, EMPLOYMENT LAW § 5.01.

9. Are tort or contract-based remedies enough to encourage employee defense of public interests? The False Claims Act, first enacted in 1863 to punish contractors who sold defective goods or committed other fraud against the U.S. government, provides an extra reward for employee and non-employee whistleblowers. Under the current version of the act, an individual whistleblower who brings the fraud to light or prosecutes a qui tam claim on the government's behalf is entitled to an amount ranging from 15 to 30 percent of the "proceeds of the action." 31 U.S.C. § 3730. The recently federal enacted Dodds-Frank Wall Street Reform and Consumer Protection Act adopts this bounty approach for whistleblowing with respect to violations of a wide range of financial regulations. 7 U.S.C. § 26, 12 U.S.C. § 5567, 15 U.S.C. § 78u-6. Awards under these whistleblower bounty laws sometimes far exceed the recoverable damages the whistleblower suffered as a result of a retaliatory discharge. However, the "bounty" or award approach is likely to be practical only for employees who uphold the law by "whistleblowing," and only when the whistleblower's action results in a significant financial recovery for the public. *See, e.g.*, 7 U.S.C. § 26 (whistleblower entitled to award of 10-30 percent of "monetary sanctions" imposed on wrongdoer).

Protected Conduct: An Employee's Means of Supporting Public Policy

By what means might an employee act in support of public policy? Are all means equally deserving of protection? For lawmakers, defining the conduct to be protected has been as difficult as defining "public policy." A broad approach might grant protection to *any* form of conduct reasonable or appropriate under the circumstances. Washington law illustrates a variation of this approach. It protects any reasonable employee conduct "discouraging" a violation of public policy. *See* Gardner v. Loomis Armored Inc., 913 P.2d 377 (Wash. 1996). But many retaliation laws are much more specific about the types of conduct deserving protection.

Some retaliation laws, especially older ones, protect mainly "whistleblowing," or making a report about an employer or manager's violations of the law. Some whistleblower laws by their express terms apply only to "external" whistleblowing to outside law enforcement authorities, leaving "internal" whistleblowers unprotected. If so, an employee who complains first to her own supervisors and managers might have no protection against retaliation. She is protected only if and when she has made a report to outside authorities. Section 15 of the Fair Labor Standards Act is an example of a law that might deny protection to internal whistleblowers. It protects an employee who has "filed any complaint or instituted . . . a proceeding" under the act. 29 U.S.C. § 215(a)(3). Some courts interpret this provision to protect only external whistleblowers. *See* Ball v. Memphis Bar B Q, 228 F.3d 360 (4th Cir. 2000); Groce v. Eli Lilly & Co., 193 F.3d 496 (7th Cir. 1999). The Supreme Court dodged the issue in Kasten v. Saint Gobain Performance Plastics, Corp., 563 U.S. 1 (2011), although its opinion there suggests an expansive interpretation of section 215 that might support protection for internal whistleblowing. At the other end of the spectrum, some states *require* an internal complaint to the employer as a first step toward protection. Failure to bring alleged illegality to the attention the employer might be fatal to a later retaliation lawsuit. *See e.g.*, N.Y. Lab. Code § 740 (McKinney); Me. Rev. Stat. Ann. tit. 26, § 833.

Any specific definition of the means of protected activity might leave some important activity unprotected. Investigation of wrongdoing often begins with suspicion of wrongdoing, but whistleblower laws protecting "reporting" of wrongdoing do not necessarily protect an employee who reports concerns, suspicions or doubts. Nor is asking questions necessarily protected by a law that protects reporting. *See, e.g.*, City of South Houston v. Rodriguez, 425 S.W.3d 629 (Tex. App. 2014) (asking for meeting to discuss concerns about possible wrongdoing" did not constitute a "report" of wrongdoing within meaning of applicable whistleblower law).

Naturally, if the whistleblower cause of action is the result of court-made law, a court may be more inclined to discard any technical distinction between internal and external whistleblowing. *See, e.g.*, Himmel v. Ford Motor Co., 342 F.3d 593 (6th Cir. 2003). *But see* Wiltsie v. Baby Grand Corp., 774 P.2d 432, 433 (1989) (declining to extend common law doctrine to internal whistleblower).

The law and media tend to focus on whistleblowing as the usual means by which employees support public policy, but there are other ways of promoting the public interest that, depending on circumstances, might be equally or even more deserving of legal protection. Here are some other forms of conduct for which some courts and legislatures have sometimes granted protection:

a. Compliance with the Law. Recall that in *Banaitis*, the plaintiff refused to comply with his employer's instructions to turn over confidential customer information. Refusing to obey an employer by continuing certain conduct or failing to cease certain conduct may be insubordination from the employer's point of view, but if the employer's instructions are illegal, the employee's insubordination might be in the public interest. *See, e.g.*, Woodson v. AMF Leisureland Ctr., Inc., 842 F.2d 699 (3d Cir. 1988) (refusing order to serve drink to intoxicated patron in violation of local law); Sabine Pilot Serv. v. Hauck, 687 S.W.2d 733 (Tex. 1985) (refusing to dump water pollutants in violation of environmental law). This category includes action that the employee took in the absence of employer instructions but that subsequently provoked an employer's retaliation. *See, e.g.*, Thompson v. St. Regis Paper Co., 685 P.2d 1081 (1984) (instituting accounting program to comply with Foreign Corrupt Practices Act); Wagner v. City of Globe, 722 P.2d 250 (1986) (police officer discovered illegally detained person in jail, brought the detainee before magistrate, and sought detainee's release).

b. Participation in Democratic Governance and Defense. A successful democracy depends on the participation of its citizens. As noted in Chapter 7, an employer cannot discharge employees for taking time away from work to fulfill certain public duties such as jury duty or military service. *See also* Bowman v. State Bank of Keysville, 331 S.E.2d 797 (Va. 1985) (cause of action for discharge to influence voting); Nees v. Hock, 536 P.2d 512 (Or. 1975) (non-statutory cause of action for discharge in retaliation for employee's jury service). When the government compels certain service, such as jury duty or military service, the argument for job protection is particularly strong. Recall that one of the first public policy cases, Petermann v. International Bhd. of Teamsters, Local 396, 344 P.2d 25 (Cal. App. 1959), discussed above, involved an employee's compliance with a subpoena in an investigation probing his employer's corruption. But what if an employee was not subpoenaed but appeared voluntarily before a court or investigatory committee? Can an employee provide more public service than is required by law, perhaps at some cost or inconvenience to his employer, and still claim job protection? Of course, the best advice for an employee facing such a dilemma is to request and obtain a subpoena in advance if possible.

Should it matter whether employee conduct fits within one category or another if the conduct reasonably advances or protects the public interest? Consider, for example, *Wagner v. City of Globe*, noted above, in which a police officer discovered a wrongfully detained person in the city jail. Realizing the grounds for the detainee's arrest were illegal, the officer took the initiative to bring the detainee before a magistrate to gain the detainee's release. His actions angered other officials who evidently would have been pleased to keep the detainee behind bars, and they fired the police officer/rescuer. The court that heard the officer's wrongful discharge claim had little difficulty finding a public interest in preventing illegal imprisonment. The court's struggle was in categorizing the officer's conduct. Local precedent strongly supported the rights of "whistleblowing" employees but said nothing of a general right to take other actions to comply with the law or prevent illegality. To avoid appearing to create new law, the court chose to style the case as a whistleblower case, although the "fit" was far from perfect.

Another example of the importance of categorizing employee conduct is Ed Rachal Found. v. D'Unger, 207 S.W.3d 330 (Tex. 2006), where the plaintiff alleged he was discharged for reporting certain criminal activity to the police. Unfortunately, Texas has no whistleblower protection statute for the private sector and no common law whistleblower doctrine. On the other hand, Texas does recognize a cause of action for discharge for refusing to commit an illegal act. A lower court squeezed the plaintiff's claim into the latter category by noting that a failure to report a felony might constitute "criminal misprision." By reporting the crime, the plaintiff was disobeying the employer's instruction to commit the crime of not reporting a crime. The Texas Supreme Court disagreed, holding that its limited public policy rule "protects employees who are asked to *commit* a crime, not those who are asked not to *report* one." *Id.* at 332.

PROBLEM

Which of the following cases should be protected from employer retaliation? In each case, consider the strength and clarity of policy the employee sought to uphold, and his action in upholding the policy.

1. An employee who drives a delivery truck for his employer fails to make a crucial delivery on time, because he drove no faster than the posted speed limit (55 mph) despite his employer's instruction to "hurry."

2. An employee suspects (correctly, as it turns out) that the shoes her employer sells in its retail establishment are made by oppressive child labor in violation of the international law of "human rights." She refuses to stock the store's shelves with these shoes.

3. An employee discovers a misstatement in a financial report the employer filed with a government agency. Without mentioning the matter to her supervisor, the employee calls the government agency and reports her suspicion that her employer has committed "fraud."

4. An employee pleads in his complaint that before he was discharged, he was aware the employer was violating air pollution laws. He further pleads that before his discharge he mentioned the violation to other employees, and that his discharge for unsatisfactory performance was a pretext for retaliation for "whistleblowing."

5. A secretary suspects her supervisor has been making excessive claims for reimbursement of travel expenses. She reports her concerns to higher management. Neither hearing nor seeing any further response from the company, she begins to scrutinize and investigate other expenses claimed by her supervisor.

iii. Employee Action Pursuant to Employment Duty

For some employees, acting in the public interest is part of the job description. A police officer enforces the law. An inspector or auditor looks for and reports violations of regulatory standards. An EEO officer assures compliance with rules of non-discrimination, reasonable accommodation and perhaps affirmative action. If an employer disciplines such an employee because of a disagreement over the manner or zealousness of his or her performance or exercise of judgment, might the employer have unlawfully retaliated against the employee's protected conduct?

A related problem concerns the employee whose job is to advocate for, defend, or counsel the employer in the event the employer is challenged by law enforcement authorities. Obviously, this category of employees includes attorneys, but it might also include other professionals or persons expected to advise, assist, or speak for the employer. Should the law uphold and protect such an employee's right to serve the public interest *first*, ahead of the interest or instructions of his employer?

The next case involves a public employee's First Amendment claim and not a claim under a whistleblower or other public policy cause of action. For a public employee acting in the public interest, the First Amendment could be an important source of protection, particularly if the employee lacks civil service protection and his "protected conduct" involves speech, such as whistleblowing. First Amendment law has rules and limitations quite different from those of public policy–based wrongful discharge law or anti-retaliation statutes. However, there is also much common ground, including the problem of the employee whose allegedly protected conduct is within the scope of his duty to his employer.

GARCETTI v. CEBALLOS

547 U.S. 410 (2006)

Justice KENNEDY delivered the opinion of the Court.

It is well settled that "a State cannot condition public employment on a basis that infringes the employee's constitutionally protected interest in freedom of expression." Connick v. Myers, 461 U.S. 138 (1983). The question presented by the instant case is whether the First Amendment protects a government employee from discipline based on speech made pursuant to the employee's official duties.

I

Respondent Richard Ceballos has been employed since 1989 as a deputy district attorney for the Los Angeles County District Attorney's Office. During the period relevant to this case, Ceballos was a calendar deputy in the office's Pomona branch, and in this capacity he exercised certain supervisory responsibilities over other lawyers. In February 2000, a defense attorney contacted Ceballos about a pending criminal case. The defense attorney said there were inaccuracies in an affidavit used to obtain a critical search warrant. The attorney informed Ceballos that he had filed a motion to traverse, or challenge, the warrant, but he also wanted Ceballos to review the case. According to Ceballos, it was not unusual for defense attorneys to ask calendar deputies to investigate aspects of pending cases.

After examining the affidavit and visiting the location it described, Ceballos determined the affidavit contained serious misrepresentations. . . . He relayed his findings to his supervisors, petitioners Carol Najera and Frank Sundstedt, and followed up by preparing a disposition memorandum. . . .

Based on Ceballos' statements, a meeting was held to discuss the affidavit. Attendees included Ceballos, Sundstedt, and Najera, as well as the warrant affiant and other employees from the sheriff's department. The meeting allegedly became heated, with one lieutenant sharply criticizing Ceballos for his handling of the case.

Despite Ceballos' concerns, Sundstedt decided to proceed with the prosecution, pending disposition of the defense motion to traverse. The trial court held a hearing on the motion. Ceballos was called by the defense and recounted his observations about the affidavit, but the trial court rejected the challenge to the warrant.

Ceballos claims that in the aftermath of these events he was subjected to a series of retaliatory employment actions. The actions included reassignment from his calendar deputy position to a trial deputy position, transfer to another courthouse, and denial of a promotion. . . . [He] sued . . . , asserting, as relevant here, a claim under . . . 42 U.S.C. § 1983. He alleged petitioners violated the First and Fourteenth Amendments by retaliating against him based on his memo . . . .

Petitioners moved for summary judgment, and the District Court granted their motion. Noting that Ceballos wrote his memo pursuant to his employment duties, the court concluded he was not entitled to First Amendment protection for the memo's contents. . . .

The Court of Appeals for the Ninth Circuit reversed, holding that "Ceballos's allegations of wrongdoing in the memorandum constitute protected speech under the First Amendment." . . . [The Ninth Circuit] relied on Circuit precedent rejecting the idea that "a public employee's speech is deprived of First Amendment protection whenever those views are expressed, to government workers or others, pursuant to an employment responsibility." [361 F.3d] at 1174-1175.

We granted certiorari, and we now reverse.

II

. . . [Pickering v. Board of Ed. of Township High School Dist. 205, Will Cty., 391 U.S. 563 (1968)] provides a useful starting point in explaining the Court's doctrine. . . . *Pickering* and the cases decided in its wake identify two inquiries to guide interpretation of the constitutional protections accorded to public employee speech. The first requires determining whether the employee spoke as a citizen on a matter of public concern. If the answer is no, the employee has no First Amendment cause of action based on his or her employer's reaction to the speech. If the answer is yes, then the possibility of a First Amendment claim arises. The question becomes whether the relevant government entity had an adequate justification for treating the employee differently from any other member of the general public. This consideration reflects the importance of the relationship between the speaker's expressions and employment. A government entity has broader discretion to restrict speech when it acts in its role as employer, but the restrictions it imposes must be directed at speech that has some potential to affect the entity's operations.

To be sure, conducting these inquiries sometimes has proved difficult. This is the necessary product of "the enormous variety of fact situations in which critical statements by teachers and other public employees may be thought by their superiors . . . to furnish grounds for dismissal." *Id.*, at 569. The Court's overarching objectives, though, are evident.

When a citizen enters government service, the citizen by necessity must accept certain limitations on his or her freedom. Government employers, like private employers, need a significant degree of control over their employees' words and actions; without it, there would be little chance for the efficient provision of public services. *Cf. Connick, supra*, at 143 ("[G]overnment offices could not function if every employment decision became a constitutional matter"). Public employees, moreover, often occupy trusted positions in society. When they speak out, they can express views that contravene governmental policies or impair the proper performance of governmental functions.

At the same time, the Court has recognized that a citizen who works for the government is nonetheless a citizen. The First Amendment limits the ability of a public employer to leverage the employment relationship to restrict, incidentally or intentionally, the liberties employees enjoy in their capacities as private citizens.

So long as employees are speaking as citizens about matters of public concern, they must face only those speech restrictions that are necessary for their employers to operate efficiently and effectively.

The Court's employee-speech jurisprudence protects, of course, the constitutional rights of public employees. Yet the First Amendment interests at stake extend beyond the individual speaker. The Court has acknowledged the importance of promoting the public's interest in receiving the well-informed views of government employees engaging in civic discussion. Pickering again provides an instructive example. The Court characterized its holding as rejecting the attempt of school administrators to "limi[t] teachers' opportunities to contribute to public debate." 391 U.S., at 573. It also noted that teachers are "the members of a community most likely to have informed and definite opinions" about school expenditures. *Id.*, at 572. The Court's approach acknowledged the necessity for informed, vibrant dialogue in a democratic society. It suggested, in addition, that widespread costs may arise when dialogue is repressed. The Court's more recent cases have expressed similar concerns. *See, e.g.,* San Diego v. Roe, 543 U.S. 77, 82 (2004) (per curiam) ("Were [public employees] not able to speak on [the operation of their employers], the community would be deprived of informed opinions on important public issues. The interest at stake is as much the public's interest in receiving informed opinion as it is the employee's own right to disseminate it" (citation omitted)).

The Court's decisions, then, have sought both to promote the individual and societal interests that are served when employees speak as citizens on matters of public concern and to respect the needs of government employers attempting to perform their important public functions. Underlying our cases has been the premise that while the First Amendment invests public employees with certain rights, it does not empower them to "constitutionalize the employee grievance." *Connick*, 461 U.S., at 154.

III

With these principles in mind we turn to the instant case. Respondent Ceballos believed the affidavit used to obtain a search warrant contained serious misrepresentations. He conveyed his opinion and recommendation in a memo to his supervisor. That Ceballos expressed his views inside his office, rather than publicly, is not dispositive. Employees in some cases may receive First Amendment protection for expressions made at work. Many citizens do much of their talking inside their respective workplaces, and it would not serve the goal of treating public employees like "any member of the general public," *Pickering*, 391 U.S., at 573, to hold that all speech within the office is automatically exposed to restriction.

The memo concerned the subject matter of Ceballos' employment, but this, too, is nondispositive. The First Amendment protects some expressions related to the speaker's job. *See, e.g., ibid.* As the Court noted in *Pickering*: "Teachers are, as a class, the members of a community most likely to have informed and definite opinions as to how funds allotted to the operation of the schools should be spent. Accordingly, it is essential that they be able to speak out freely on such questions without fear of retaliatory dismissal." 391 U.S., at 572. The same is true of many other categories of public employees.

The controlling factor in Ceballos' case is that his expressions were made pursuant to his duties as a calendar deputy. That consideration — the fact that Ceballos spoke as a prosecutor fulfilling a responsibility to advise his supervisor about how best to proceed with a pending case — distinguishes Ceballos' case from those in which the First Amendment provides protection against discipline. We hold that when public employees make statements pursuant to their official duties, the employees are not speaking as citizens for First Amendment purposes, and the Constitution does not insulate their communications from employer discipline.

Ceballos wrote his disposition memo because that is part of what he, as a calendar deputy, was employed to do. It is immaterial whether he experienced some personal gratification from writing the memo; his First Amendment rights do not depend on his job satisfaction. The significant point is that the memo was written pursuant to Ceballos' official duties. Restricting speech that owes its existence to a public employee's professional responsibilities does not infringe any liberties the employee might have enjoyed as a private citizen. It simply reflects the exercise of employer control over what the employer itself has commissioned or created. *Cf.* Rosenberger v. Rector and Visitors of Univ. of Va., 515 U.S. 819, 833 (1995) ("[W]hen the government appropriates public funds to promote a particular policy of its own it is entitled to say what it wishes"). Contrast, for example, the expressions made by the speaker in *Pickering*, whose letter to the newspaper had no official significance and bore similarities to letters submitted by numerous citizens every day.

Ceballos did not act as a citizen when he went about conducting his daily professional activities, such as supervising attorneys, investigating charges, and preparing filings. In the same way he did not speak as a citizen by writing a memo that addressed the proper disposition of a pending criminal case. When he went to work and performed the tasks he was paid to perform, Ceballos acted as a government employee. The fact that his duties sometimes required him to speak or write does not mean his supervisors were prohibited from evaluating his performance.

This result is consistent with our precedents' attention to the potential societal value of employee speech. Refusing to recognize First Amendment claims based on government employees' work product does not prevent them from participating in public debate. The employees retain the prospect of constitutional protection for their contributions to the civic discourse. This prospect of protection, however, does not invest them with a right to perform their jobs however they see fit.

Our holding likewise is supported by the emphasis of our precedents on affording government employers sufficient discretion to manage their operations. Employers have heightened interests in controlling speech made by an employee in his or her professional capacity. Official communications have official consequences, creating a need for substantive consistency and clarity. Supervisors must ensure that their employees' official communications are accurate, demonstrate sound judgment, and promote the employer's mission. Ceballos' memo is illustrative. It demanded the attention of his supervisors and led to a heated meeting with employees from the sheriff's department. If Ceballos' superiors thought his memo was inflammatory or misguided, they had the authority to take proper corrective action.

Ceballos' proposed contrary rule, adopted by the Court of Appeals, would commit state and federal courts to a new, permanent, and intrusive role, mandating judicial oversight of communications between and among government employees and their superiors in the course of official business. This displacement of managerial discretion by judicial supervision finds no support in our precedents. When an employee speaks as a citizen addressing a matter of public concern, the First Amendment requires a delicate balancing of the competing interests surrounding the speech and its consequences. When, however, the employee is simply performing his or her job duties, there is no warrant for a similar degree of scrutiny. To hold otherwise would be to demand permanent judicial intervention in the conduct of governmental operations to a degree inconsistent with sound principles of federalism and the separation of powers.

The Court of Appeals based its holding in part on what it perceived as a doctrinal anomaly. The court suggested it would be inconsistent to compel public employers to tolerate certain employee speech made publicly but not speech made pursuant to an employee's assigned duties. This objection misconceives the theoretical underpinnings of our decisions. Employees who make public statements outside the course of performing their official duties retain some possibility of First Amendment protection because that is the kind of activity engaged in by citizens who do not work for the government. The same goes for writing a letter to a local newspaper, *see Pickering*, 391 U.S. 563, or discussing politics with a co-worker, *see Rankin*, 483 U.S. 378. When a public employee speaks pursuant to employment responsibilities, however, there is no relevant analogue to speech by citizens who are not government employees.

The Court of Appeals' concern also is unfounded as a practical matter. The perceived anomaly, it should be noted, is limited in scope: It relates only to the expressions an employee makes pursuant to his or her official responsibilities, not to statements or complaints (such as those at issue in cases like *Pickering* and *Connick*) that are made outside the duties of employment. If, moreover, a government employer is troubled by the perceived anomaly, it has the means at hand to avoid it. A public employer that wishes to encourage its employees to voice concerns privately retains the option of instituting internal policies and procedures that are receptive to employee criticism. Giving employees an internal forum for their speech will discourage them from concluding that the safest avenue of expression is to state their views in public. . . .

IV

Exposing governmental inefficiency and misconduct is a matter of considerable significance. As the Court noted in *Connick*, public employers should, "as a matter of good judgment," be "receptive to constructive criticism offered by their employees." 461 U.S., at 149. The dictates of sound judgment are reinforced by the powerful network of legislative enactments — such as whistle-blower protection laws and labor codes — available to those who seek to expose wrongdoing. *See, e.g.*, 5 U.S.C. § 2302(b)(8); Cal. Govt. Code Ann. § 8547.8 (West 2005); Cal. Lab. Code Ann. § 1102.5 (West Supp. 2006). Cases involving government attorneys implicate additional safeguards in the form of, for example, rules of conduct and constitutional obligations apart from the First Amendment. *See, e.g.*, Cal. Rule Prof. Conduct 5-110 (2005) ("A member in government service shall not institute or cause to be instituted criminal charges when the member knows or should know that the charges are not supported by probable cause"); Brady v. Maryland, 373 U.S. 83, 83 (1963). These imperatives, as well as obligations arising from any other applicable constitutional provisions and mandates of the criminal and civil laws, protect employees and provide checks on supervisors who would order unlawful or otherwise inappropriate actions.

We reject, however, the notion that the First Amendment shields from discipline the expressions employees make pursuant to their professional duties. Our precedents do not support the existence of a constitutional cause of action behind every statement a public employee makes in the course of doing his or her job. The judgment of the Court of Appeals is reversed, and the case is remanded for proceedings consistent with this opinion. . . .

[Dissenting opinions of Justices STEVENS, SOUTER, GINSBURG, and BREYER omitted.]

NOTES AND QUESTIONS

1. Although it may not be clear from the majority's opinion in *Garcetti*, remanding the case left the lower courts to ponder whether Ceballos's speech other than his disposition memorandum might be protected, and whether other protected speech, if any, caused the adverse actions he alleged. 547 U.S. at 441 (Souter, dissenting). In what ways might Ceballos have exercised his right of free speech in a way not "pursuant to his duty?"

2. Lower courts have interpreted *Garcetti* to deny protection only to speech directly within the *scope* of and pursuant to the employee's duties. Speech that *concerns* an employee's duties but is not truly pursuant to the job remains protected. *Compare* Cory v. Basehor, 631 F. App'x 526, 530 (10th Cir. 2015) (no protection for police officer who reported unsafe practices within department; report not only concerned his own duty but was made "within the scope" of duty) *with* Seifert v. Wyandotte Cty., 779 F.3d 1141 (10th Cir. 2015) (sheriff's deputy's testimony regarding prisoner's mistreatment by federal officers concerned deputy's work, but was not pursuant to his duty, because testifying was not routine part of job, and testimony was against a different employer).

3. Should the "pursuant to duty" defense recognized by the Court in *Garcetti* for First Amendment cases apply equally to claims under other protected conduct laws, such as a public policy-based wrongful discharge claim? Even before *Garcetti*, some courts applying a variety of anti-retaliation laws denied protection to employees whose alleged reporting or other protected conduct was pursuant to their job duties. *See, e.g.*, Sassé v. Dep't of Labor, 409 F.3d 773 (6th Cir. 2005) (federal environmental whistleblower provision); Claudio-Gotay v. Becton Dickinson Caribe, Ltd., 375 F.3d 99, 102 (1st Cir. 2004) (FLSA retaliation provision); EEOC v. HBE Corp., 135 F.3d 543, 554 (8th Cir. 1998) (Title VII retaliation provision); Huffman v. Office of Pers. Mgmt., 263 F.3d 1341, 1352 (Fed. Cir. 2001) (federal Whistleblower Act); Rinehimer v. Luzerne County Cmty.

Coll., 539 A.2d 1298 (Pa. Super. 1988) (Pennsylvania law).

After *Garcetti*, courts might be even more likely to recognize the "pursuant to duty" defense in retaliation cases. *See, e.g.*, Cook v. CTC Comm'ns Corp., 2007 WL 3284337 (D.N.H. 2007) (USERRA anti-retaliation provision); Schuman v. Dianon Sys. Inc., 43 A.3d 111 (Conn. 2012); Lumsden v. Foster Farms, LLC, 2008 WL 496137 (W.D. Wash. 2008) (Washington public policy wrongful discharge law). *See generally* Nancy Modesitt, *The Garcetti Virus*, 80 U. Cin. L. Rev. 161 (2011). Some courts have pushed back against this development, rejecting an employer's "pursuant to duty" defense for various federal or state anti-retaliation laws. See, e.g., DeMasters v. Carilion Clinic, 796 F.3d 409 (4th Cir. 2015) (interpreting Title VII's anti-retaliation provision); Igwe v. City of Miami, 208 So.3d 150 (Fla. App 2016) (interpreting Florida whistleblower law); Lippman v. Ethicon, 119 A.3d 215 (N.J. 2015) (interpreting New Jersey's "conscientious employee" law); Lodis v. Corbis Holdings, 292 P.3d 779 (Wash. App. 2013) (interpreting Washington's discrimination law).

4. How might a "pursuant to duty" rule apply to conduct other than whistleblowing, reporting, or complaining? Could the defense apply in the case of a quality control inspector discharged for doing his job too well and rejecting too much work? What about a waste disposal employee discharged for refusing to carry out an instruction to dump toxic waste in violation of the law?

5. Whether or not a court adopts the "pursuant to duty" rule for a retaliation cause of action, special duties of an employee's position might be important in determining the reasonableness of the employee's allegedly protected conduct. Oppositional conduct that would be reasonable for some types of employees might be not be reasonable for others. In Rinehimer v. Luzerne County Community College, 539 A.2d 1298 (Pa. Super. 1988), for example, the court held that a college board of trustees did not wrongfully discharge its president who sought to "clean house," in view of the unreasonable manner in which he demanded a public audit of financial improprieties, and in view of his responsibility for leadership and protection of the institution's relationship with its students and the community.

The call of public duty poses a special dilemma for employees whose job duties include counseling the employer in matters of potential civil or criminal liability, representing the employer, or serving as the employer's voice. To the extent society values such service, an employee's higher public duty might be to preserve his employer's confidences, take lawful actions designed to minimize the employer's liability or embarrassment, and to avoid actions not mandated by law but likely to exacerbate the employer's liability. The in-house attorney is one category of employee whose unique professional duties—particularly to preserve client confidences—might prevent a court from granting a cause of action against retaliation for whistleblowing. *See* Balla v. Gambro, Inc., 584 N.E.2d 104 (Ill. 1991) (declining to extend public policy exception to attorney fired for whistleblowing). *But see* General Dynamics Corp. v. Superior Court, 876 P.2d 487 (Cal. 1994) (granting cause of action under certain circumstances); Wieder v. Skala, 609 N.E.2d 105 (N.Y. 1992) (granting cause of action to associate who insisted that his firm report misconduct of another associate); Wily v. Coastal States Mgmt. Co., 939 S.W.2d 193 (Tex. App. 1996) (granting cause of action to in-house counsel).

6. Many anti-retaliation laws protect only "employees." What about applicants? A whistleblower who recovers back pay might be discouraged to learn that he or she still faces retaliation—possibly lawful retaliation—by prospective employers who have learned of past whistleblowing. *Compare* Vander Boegh v. EnergySolutions, Inc., 772 F.3d 1056 (6th Cir. 2014) (applicant lacked standing to sue prospective employer under anti-retaliation provision of federal energy law), *with* Baines v. Walgreen Company, 863 F.3d 656 (7th Cir. 2017) (employer who refused to rehire former employee because of former employee's past protected conduct violated Title VII). However, an employer's post-employment retaliation by interfering with an employee's future job prospects is sometimes the basis for a tort claim for third party intentional interference with prospective contract, with the former employer in the role of a "third party." See section B.4.c of this chapter.

iv. Employee Good Faith

Employees who oppose illegal conduct are frequently mistaken about the law or the facts. Some mistakes are understandable considering how uncertain the law and facts can be even for lawyers and judges. But does the public have an interest in protecting employee work stoppages or conflicts that do not in fact uphold the law?

A related question concerns an employee's motive. An employee's allegedly protected conduct might be to serve some personal interest or motive, such as spite, rather than the public interest. Indeed, employers frequently complain that retaliation laws permit opportunistic employees to invent their own protected status. An employee who knows adverse action is imminent might place a call to a law enforcement authority simply to create a record that will be useful for suing the employer or threatening a lawsuit if the employer discharges the employee. The employee might even report illegal conduct in which he willingly participated in the past. How should the courts respond to conduct motivated by malice or other self-interest rather than civic duty?

WICHITA COUNTY v. HART

917 S.W.2d 779 (Tex. 1996)

SPECTOR, Justice, delivered the opinion of the court, in which all justices join.

. . . Allen Hart and Ernie Williams worked as deputies in the Wichita County Sheriff's Department. In February 1989, Hart and Williams told an investigator for the county's district attorney's office and an agent for the Federal Bureau of Investigation that they believed Sheriff Thomas Callahan had broken the law. The investigator spoke with Callahan on May 1, 1989. Callahan fired Hart that day and Williams two days later.

Hart and Williams sued the county, contending that the sheriff fired them in retaliation for reporting a violation of law. [The jury eventually rendered a verdict in favor of the plaintiffs. However, the court held that the trial court had erred in denying the defendant county's motion to transfer venue, and that the jury's verdict and trial court judgment must be reversed on this ground.]

Because we remand this case and in the interest of judicial economy, we also consider the proper definition of "good faith" as used in the [Texas] Whistleblower

Act. . . . Under the Whistleblower Act, a "state agency or local government may not suspend or terminate the employment of or discriminate against a public employee who in *good faith* reports a violation of law to an appropriate law enforcement authority." Tex. Gov't Code § 554.002 (emphasis added). The Whistleblower Act does not define "good faith." The trial court submitted the following definition to the jury: "'Good faith' means honesty in fact in the conduct concerned. A report of a violation of law may be in good faith even though it is incorrect, as long as the belief is not unreasonable." The county had proposed the following definition:

> "Made in good faith" means (1) that the employee undertook to report the activities in the workplace in good faith rather than as a result of some less admirable motive such as malice, spite, jealousy, or personal gain and (2) the employee had reasonable cause to believe that the activities reported were a violation of law.

Id. The court of appeals held that the trial court did not abuse its discretion by denying the county's proposed instruction, noting that "the focus of the good faith requirement is the employee's belief that the reported conduct violates the law."

The U.S. Supreme Court also grappled with this issue when it considered whether school officials could receive immunity from damages in a civil rights action brought under section 1983 by expelled students. *See* Wood v. Strickland, 420 U.S. 308, 321-22 (1975) (construing 42 U.S.C. § 1983). The district court had instructed the jury that officials could only be held liable if they had acted with complete malice when carrying out the expulsions. *Id.* at 314. . . . The Court, facing what it described as a showdown between "an 'objective' versus a 'subjective' test of good faith," held that "the appropriate standard necessarily contains elements of both [tests]. The official himself must be acting sincerely and with a belief that he is doing right, but an act . . . can[not] be . . . justified by ignorance or disregard of settled, indisputable law. . . ." *Id.*

Although the *Wood* Court's discussion of "good faith" came in an official immunity context, we believe that its balancing of public and private concerns illustrates an appropriate approach for "good faith" in the whistleblower context. The Whistleblower Act protects public employees who attempt to report illegal activity. At the same time, public employers must preserve their right to discipline employees who make either intentionally false or objectively unreasonable reports. Therefore, we agree with the rationale used by the *Wood* Court that an appropriate explanation of "good faith" can accommodate both subjective and objective components. Today, we adopt the following definition, which we believe achieves a fair balance between the competing interests: "Good faith" means that (1) the employee believed that the conduct reported was a violation of law and (2) the employee's belief was reasonable in light of the employee's training and experience. The first part of the definition embodies the "honesty in fact" part of the trial court's definition in this case. This element ensures that employees seeking a remedy under the Whistleblower Act must have believed that they were reporting an actual violation of law. The second part of the definition ensures that, even if the reporting employee honestly believed that the reported act was a violation of law, an employer that takes prohibited action against the employee violates the

Whistleblower Act only if a reasonably prudent employee in similar circumstances would have believed that the facts as reported were a violation of law.

Hart and Williams urge us to adopt a standard that would determine the reasonableness of a report without regard to the reporting employee's training or experience. They note that none of the courts of appeals that have considered the "good faith" issue have concluded that trial courts should use different standards for different employees. . . . However, we believe that a workable, fair standard to determine if a report was made in "good faith" must take into account differences in training and experience. A police officer, for example, may have had far more exposure and experience in determining whether an action violates the law than a teacher or file clerk.

The county, on the other hand, urges us to adopt a definition of good faith that revolves around an employee's subjective motive in making the report. The county argues that the Legislature modeled the Whistleblower Act on other whistleblower statutes and that the Act should therefore be construed in accordance with interpretations that courts outside our state have given "good faith." However, the Legislature passed the Whistleblower Act for the "protection of public employees who report a violation of law" and did not include language indicating that the reporting employee's motivation in and of itself should obviate the Act's protection. Furthermore, no clear consensus has emerged from other courts on the issue of whether motivation is relevant to "good faith." *Compare* Fiorillo v. U.S. Dep't of Justice, 795 F.2d 1544, 1550 (Fed. Cir. 1986) ("[T]he primary motivation of the employee must be the desire to inform the public on matters of public concern, and not personal vindictiveness."), *and* Wolcott v. Champion Int'l Corp., 691 F. Supp. 1052, 1059 (W.D. Mich. 1987) ("Those availing themselves of [a whistleblower act's] protection should be motivated, at least in part, by a desire to inform the public about violations of laws and statutes, as a service to the public as a whole.") (citation omitted), *with* LaFond v. General Physics Serv. Corp., 50 F.3d 165, 173 (2d Cir. 1995) (holding that a plaintiff met his prima facie burden of showing "that he engaged in a protected activity" by merely reporting "suspected violations of federal law"), *and* Melchi v. Burns Int'l Sec. Servs., Inc., 597 F. Supp. 575, 583 (E.D. Mich. 1984) ("The Court believes it is reasonable to conclude that the Michigan legislature . . . meant to bring within the Act's protections an employee's subjective good faith belief that he was reporting a violation of law.").

We believe the definition we adopt today meets many of the concerns that the county and amici curiae express. For example, an employee motivated almost entirely by malice when making the report may honestly, though falsely, believe that a violation of law has occurred, but only if a reasonable person with the same level of training and experience would have made the report will the employee enjoy the relief the Whistleblower Act provides. On the other hand, we do not believe that we should adopt an absence of malice standard for "good faith." The fact that an employee harbors malice toward an individual should not negate the Whistleblower Act's protection if the employee's report of a violation of law was honestly believed and objectively reasonable given the employee's training and experience.

. . . Therefore, we reverse the judgment of the court of appeals and remand the case to the trial court. We also hold that the appropriate definition for "good faith" as used in the Whistleblower Act is that (1) the employee believed that the conduct reported was a violation of law and (2) the employee's belief was reasonable in light of the employee's training and experience.

NOTES AND QUESTIONS

1. Not all courts have been equally sympathetic to an employee who acted upon a good faith but mistaken understanding of the facts or law. *See, e.g.*, Remba v. Federation Employment & Guidance Serv., 545 N.Y.S.2d 140 (1989) (employee unprotected; employer's conduct was not actually illegal), *aff'd*, 559 N.E.2d 655 (N.Y. 1989). However, in Harp v. Charter Communications, Inc., 558 F.3d 722 (7th Cir. 2009), the court adopted an approach similar to that in *Hart* and applied a combined objective-subjective standard of good faith with respect to an employee's Sarbanes-Oxley Act whistleblower claim.

2. Assuming an employee's self-serving motivations do not bar his entitlement to protection for whistleblowing, what about his own participation in the very scheme against which he blew the whistle? *See* Paolella v. Browning-Ferris, Inc., 158 F.3d 183 (3d Cir. 1998) (employee's participation in illegal activity did not bar his claim); Jacobs v. Universal Development Corp., 62 Cal. Rptr. 2d 446 (Cal. App. 1997) (employee's initial acquiescence in illegal activity does not bar wrongful discharge claim).

3. An employee must also be reasonable in his manner of opposing illegal employer conduct. Some forms of opposition are needlessly and inappropriately disruptive of an employer's legitimate interests. As noted earlier, some state statutes explicitly require that under certain circumstances an employee must report a suspected illegality to the employer and provide the employer a reasonable opportunity to investigate and remedy the problem before the employee may report the illegality to outside authorities. Courts have sometimes denied protection to employees who report or otherwise oppose illegal conduct in a way calculated to harm to the employer. In particular, "going public" with an issue has led to mixed results for whistleblowers. Employees who appeal to the media or the public in disputes about discrimination are frequently deemed to be protected under Title VII's broad anti-retaliation rule for employees who have "opposed" a violation of Title VII. *See, e.g.*, Wrighten v. Metro. Hosps., Inc., 726 F.2d 1346, 1355-1356 (9th Cir. 1984). On the other hand, a direct appeal to the public in other types of disputes might not be protected if a court deems such action unreasonable or premature or if the anti-retaliation rule in question protects only a report to law enforcement authorities. *See, e.g.*, City of Beaumont v. Bouillion, 896 S.W.2d 143 (Tex. 1995) (no cause of action for employees' discharge after they called press conference to disclose alleged illegalities).

v. The Employee's Prima Facie Case and the Problem of Employer Knowledge

When courts consider the requirements for a plaintiff's proof of an employer's illegal retaliation, they frequently consult the federal law of employment discrimination that has evolved under Title VII. *See, e.g.,* In re Montplaisir, 787 A.2d 178 (N.H. 2001) (outlining the respective burdens of proof under both "pretext" and "mixed motive" models for a whistleblower case). Thus, a plaintiff must first establish at least a minimum set of facts that could lead a reasonable person to infer that the employer was motivated by illegal retaliatory intent. However, the *McDonnell Douglas* formula for a minimum set of facts evidencing illegal intent needs substantial modification in this context. In *Montplaisir*, the New Hampshire court offered a typical statement of the law:

> To establish a prima facie case of retaliation, the employee must demonstrate that: (1) she engaged in an act protected by the whistleblowers' protection statute; (2) she suffered an employment action proscribed by the whistleblowers' protection statute; and (3) there was a causal connection between the protected act and the proscribed employment action.

Id. at 182. The third element, "a causal connection," begs the question. What minimum set of facts would suffice to show a causal connection? Obviously, direct evidence such as an employer's statement, "I'm firing you for blowing the whistle!" would satisfy the need for proof of a causal connection. However, employees increasingly lack this sort of evidence because employers know they are liable for retaliation. What *circumstantial* evidence would suffice?

In a race discrimination case, the plaintiff might succeed by showing he was replaced by a person of a different race. In contrast, proof of a whistleblower's replacement with a newly hired individual who had not yet blown the whistle appears to add nothing to the evidence of employer intent. A more likely fact completing the plaintiff's proof is that the employer made its decision quite soon after the plaintiff's protected activity. However, there is no consensus whether even this fact suffices to establish a prima facie case. *Compare* West v. General Motors Corp., 665 N.W.2d 468 (Mich. 2003) ("Plaintiff must show something more than merely a coincidence in time between protected activity and adverse employment action.") *with* Little v. Windermere Relocation, Inc., 301 F.3d 958, 970 (9th Cir. 2002) (discharge within "minutes" of reporting rape completed the minimum requirements for a prima facie case of retaliation).

A court might also demand evidence that the employer or its decision maker knew the plaintiff had engaged in protected activity. For some courts, proof of an employer's knowledge is a necessary part of any prima facie case. *See, e.g.*, Marsaglia v. University of Texas, El Paso, 22 S.W.3d 1 (Tex. App. 1999). According to some courts, a plaintiff must prove more than the fact that his conduct was known by anyone in the employer's management. He must prove the knowledge of the ultimate decision maker who took or approved the adverse action. In *Marsaglia*, for example, it was clear that some officials of the employer institution knew of the plaintiff's protected activity, but the plaintiff could not prove the ultimate decision maker had this knowledge. The court upheld dismissal of the plaintiff's claim for failing to present a prima facie case.

In Staub v. Proctor Hospital, 562 U.S. 411 (2011), the Supreme Court rejected an argument that a plaintiff in a USERRA action must prove the ultimate decision maker's knew of the protected conduct. The Court held that a plaintiff may prevail by showing that others in the organization knew of his conduct, were motivated to retaliate, and "caused" an adverse action by their recommendations or reports to the ultimate decision maker.

vi. Adverse Retaliatory Action

How far should courts go in intervening in the day-to-day relations between an employer and its employees for the sake of insulating employees from adverse consequences of protected conduct? An employee's whistleblowing or other protected conduct may chill relations between him and some managers, but if the employee retains his job does the balance of pubic versus private interests favor judicial abstinence? If a court does intervene, will it find an effective remedy for hostility or coolness?

In *Garcetti, supra*, Ceballos complained that his employer retaliated against him by reassigning him, transferring him, and denying a promotion, but Ceballos kept his job. The Court assumed for the sake of argument that any of the alleged adverse employment actions might be sufficiently harmful to justify a legal remedy —provided those actions were motivated by unlawful retaliatory intent. However, the vast majority of public policy–based retaliation lawsuits—particularly in the private sector—involve termination. Perhaps this is because the judicial process is not particularly suitable for disputes involving lesser retaliatory actions. Moreover, to the extent courts have been reluctant to recognize new causes of action for wrongful discharge, they have been especially reluctant to recognize new causes of action for lesser employment actions.

In some areas of employment law, courts and administrative agencies have a long history of addressing whether certain employment actions are sufficiently "adverse" to justify a legal remedy. The National Labor Relations Act and Title VII are two examples. Both laws have goals that could not be achieved if employers could simply "harass" minorities and union members by an endless stream of insults and indignities to deter them from continuing employment or achieving their organizational goals. For each of these laws, however, Congress established an administrative agency — the NLRB for the NLRA and the EEOC for Title VII — to facilitate investigation, mediation, and correction of relatively "minor" acts of discrimination that might otherwise seem too small to justify judicial action. Still, even under Title VII the courts have searched for a practical threshold for judicial intervention against discrimination. Consider the following statement of this problem in Washington v. Illinois Department of Revenue:

> Title VII does not define "discrimination." . . . Lack of a definition leaves unresolved the question *how important* a difference must be to count as "discrimination." Suppose a supervisor regularly smiles or nods when a member of his own religious faith walks by, but does not change expression when an adherent of another faith passes through the office. Does this difference in treatment violate Title VII's prohibition on religious discrimination? Courts have resisted the idea that federal law regulates matters of attitude or other small affairs of daily life — not just because of the maxim *de minimis non curat lex* (the law does not bother with trifles), but because almost every worker feels offended or aggrieved by many things that happen in the workplace, and sorting out which of these occurred because of race, sex, religion, national origin, or a complaint about any of these would be an impossible task. Even in an all-white, all-male, labor force where all workers share one religious faith, everyone feels put upon or slighted occasionally; if these cannot be attributed to discrimination, neither can most

of the other disappointments people encounter at work.

420 F.3d 658, 660 (7th Cir. 2005).

Assuming the court's statement of the problem in *Washington* is correct, there are two restraints against seemingly irremediable "trifles" designed to discriminate against minorities or women. First, the availability of an administrative scheme such as that provided by the EEOC makes it possible to address some relatively minor acts of discrimination that a federal or state court might tend to regard as de minimis. Second, small but persistent differences in an employer's attitude toward minorities or women could eventually affect the statistical composition of an employer's workforce in ways that might expose the employer to discriminatory "pattern or practice" class action liability.

Considering the foregoing, does the problem of relatively "minor" acts of *retaliation* differ from the problem of relatively minor acts of discrimination against minorities?

BURLINGTON NORTHERN & SANTA FE RY. v. WHITE

548 U.S. 53 (2006)

Justice BREYER delivered the opinion of the Court.

Title VII of the Civil Rights Act of 1964 forbids employment discrimination against "any individual" based on that individual's "race, color, religion, sex, or national origin." 42 U.S.C. § 2000e-2(a). A separate section of the Act—its anti-retaliation provision—forbids an employer from "discriminat[ing] against" an employee or job applicant because that individual "opposed any practice" made unlawful by Title VII or "made a charge, testified, assisted, or participated in" a Title VII proceeding or investigation. § 2000e-3(a).

The Courts of Appeals have come to different conclusions about the scope of the Act's anti-retaliation provision, particularly the reach of its phrase "discriminate against." Does that provision confine actionable retaliation to activity that affects the terms and conditions of employment? And how harmful must the adverse actions be to fall within its scope?

We conclude that the anti-retaliation provision does not confine the actions and harms it forbids to those that are related to employment or occur at the workplace. We also conclude that the provision covers those (and only those) employer actions that would have been materially adverse to a reasonable employee or job applicant. In the present context that means that the employer's actions must be harmful to the point that they could well dissuade a reasonable worker from making or supporting a charge of discrimination.

I

A

This case arises out of actions that supervisors at petitioner Burlington Northern & Santa Fe Railway Company took against respondent Sheila White, the only woman working in the Maintenance of Way department at Burlington's Tennessee Yard. . . .

[Burlington hired White in June, 1997 and initially assigned her to drive a forklift. Within a few months she filed an internal complaint and then an EEOC complaint about sex discrimination in the Maintenance of Way Department. Her complaint to the EEOC alleged among other things that Burlington had reassigned her to less desirable general labor duty in retaliation for her internal complaints about sex discrimination. Two months later, White filed a second EEOC retaliation complaint alleging that her supervisor "had placed her under surveillance and was monitoring her daily activities." Not long after White's second complaint, her supervisor suspended her for alleged insubordination. White filed an internal grievance, which resulted in her reinstatement with backpay, but this incident led White to file a third retaliation complaint with the EEOC. White exhausted administrative remedies before the EEOC and then filed this Title VII action based on unlawful retaliation. A jury found in her favor and awarded $43,500 in compensatory damages. The District Court entered judgment in favor of White based on the jury verdict, and the Sixth Circuit affirmed. — ED.]

II

Title VII's anti-retaliation provision forbids employer actions that "discriminate against" an employee (or job applicant) because he has "opposed" a practice that Title VII forbids or has "made a charge, testified, assisted, or participated in" a Title VII "investigation, proceeding, or hearing." § 2000e-3(a). No one doubts that the term "discriminate against" refers to distinctions or differences in treatment that injure protected individuals. . . . But different Circuits have come to different conclusions about whether the challenged action has to be employment or workplace related and about how harmful that action must be to constitute retaliation.

Some Circuits have insisted upon a close relationship between the retaliatory action and employment. The Sixth Circuit majority in this case, for example, said that a plaintiff must show an "adverse employment action," which it defined as a "materially adverse change in the terms and conditions" of employment. 364 F.3d, at 795 (internal quotation marks omitted). . . . The Fifth and the Eighth Circuits have adopted a more restrictive approach. They employ an "ultimate employment decisio[n]" standard, which limits actionable retaliatory conduct to acts "'such as hiring, granting leave, discharging, promoting, and compensating.'" Mattern v. Eastman Kodak Co., 104 F.3d 702, 707 (C.A.5 1997); *see* Manning v. Metropolitan Life Ins. Co., 127 F.3d 686, 692 (C.A.8 1997).

Other Circuits have not so limited the scope of the provision. The Seventh and the District of Columbia Circuits have said that the plaintiff must show that the "employer's challenged action would have been material to a reasonable employee," which in contexts like the present one means that it would likely have "dissuaded a reasonable worker from making or supporting a charge of discrimination." Washington v. Illinois Dep't of Revenue, 420 F.3d 658, 662 (C.A.7 2005); *see* Rochon v. Gonzales, 438 F.3d 1211, 1217-1218 (C.A.D.C. 2006). And the Ninth Circuit, following EEOC guidance, has said that the plaintiff must simply establish "'adverse treatment that is based on a retaliatory motive and is reasonably likely to deter the charging party or others from engaging in protected activity.'" Ray v. Henderson, 217 F.3d 1234, 1242-1243 (C.A.9 2000). . . .

We granted certiorari to resolve this disagreement. To do so requires us to decide whether Title VII's anti-retaliation provision forbids only those employer actions and resulting harms that are related to employment or the workplace. And we must characterize how harmful an act of retaliatory discrimination must be in order to fall within the provision's scope.

A

Petitioner and the Solicitor General both argue that the Sixth Circuit is correct to require a link between the challenged retaliatory action and the terms, conditions, or status of employment. They note that Title VII's substantive anti-discrimination provision protects an individual only from employment-related discrimination. They add that the anti-retaliation provision should be read in pari materia with the anti-discrimination provision. And they conclude that the employer actions prohibited by the anti-retaliation provision should similarly be limited to conduct that "affects the employee's 'compensation, terms, conditions, or privileges of employment.'"

. . . We cannot agree. The language of the substantive provision differs from that of the anti-retaliation provision in important ways. Section 703(a) sets forth Title VII's core anti-discrimination provision in the following terms:

> "It shall be an unlawful employment practice for an employer—
>
> "(1) to fail or refuse to *hire* or to *discharge* any individual, or otherwise to discriminate against any individual with respect to his *compensation, terms, conditions, or privileges of employment*, because of such individual's race, color, religion, sex, or national origin. . . . (emphasis added).

Section 704(a) sets forth Title VII's anti-retaliation provision in the following terms:

> "It shall be an unlawful employment practice for an employer to *discriminate* against any of his employees or applicants for employment . . . because he has opposed any practice made an unlawful employment practice by this subchapter, or because he has made a charge, testified, assisted, or participated in any manner in an investigation, proceeding, or hearing under this subchapter." § 2000e-3(a) (emphasis added).

The underscored words in the substantive provision—"hire," "discharge," "compensation, terms, conditions, or privileges of employment,"—explicitly limit the scope of that provision to actions that affect employment or alter the conditions of the workplace. No such limiting words appear in the anti-retaliation provision. Given these linguistic differences, the question here is not whether identical or similar words should be read in pari materia to mean the same thing. . . . Rather, the question is whether Congress intended its different words to make a legal difference. We normally presume that, where words differ as they differ here, "'Congress acts intentionally and purposely in the disparate inclusion or exclusion.'" Russello v. United States, 464 U.S. 16, 23 (1983).

There is strong reason to believe that Congress intended the differences that its language suggests, for the two provisions differ not only in language but in purpose as well. The anti-discrimination provision seeks a workplace where individuals are not discriminated against because of their racial, ethnic, religious, or gender-based status. The anti-retaliation provision seeks to secure that primary objective by preventing an employer from interfering (through retaliation) with an employee's efforts to secure or advance enforcement of the Act's basic guarantees. The substantive provision seeks to prevent injury to individuals based on who they are, i.e., their status. The anti-retaliation provision seeks to prevent harm to individuals based on what they do, i.e., their conduct.

To secure the first objective, Congress did not need to prohibit anything other than employment-related discrimination. . . . But one cannot secure the second objective by focusing only upon employer actions and harm that concern employment and the workplace. Were all such actions and harms eliminated, the anti-retaliation provision's objective would not be achieved. An employer can effectively retaliate against an employee by taking actions not directly related to his employment or by causing him harm outside the workplace. *See, e.g.*, Rochon v. Gonzales, 438 F.3d, at 1213 (FBI retaliation against employee "took the form of the FBI's refusal, contrary to policy, to investigate death threats a federal prisoner made against [the agent] and his wife"); Berry v. Stevinson Chevrolet, 74 F.3d 980, 984, 986 (C.A.10 1996) (finding actionable retaliation where employer filed false criminal charges against former employee who complained about discrimination). A provision limited to employment-related actions would not deter the many forms that effective retaliation can take. . . .

Title VII depends for its enforcement upon the cooperation of employees who are willing to file complaints and act as witnesses. "Plainly, effective enforcement could thus only be expected if employees felt free to approach officials with their grievances." Mitchell v. Robert DeMario Jewelry, Inc., 361 U.S. 288, 292 (1960). Interpreting the anti-retaliation provision to provide broad protection from retaliation helps assure the cooperation upon which accomplishment of the Act's primary objective depends.

For these reasons, we conclude that . . . [t]he scope of the anti-retaliation provision extends beyond workplace-related or employment-related retaliatory acts and harm. We therefore reject the standards applied in the Courts of Appeals that have treated the anti-retaliation provision as forbidding the same conduct prohibited by the anti-discrimination provision and that have limited actionable retaliation to so-called "ultimate employment decisions."

B

The anti-retaliation provision protects an individual not from all retaliation, but from retaliation that produces an injury or harm. As we have explained, the Courts of Appeals have used differing language to describe the level of seriousness to which this harm must rise before it becomes actionable retaliation. We agree with the formulation set forth by the Seventh and the District of Columbia Circuits. In our view, a plaintiff must show that a reasonable employee would have found the challenged action materially adverse, "which in this context means it well might have 'dissuaded a reasonable worker from making or supporting a charge of discrimination.'" *Rochon*, 438 F.3d, at 1219 (quoting *Washington*, 420 F.3d, at 662).

We speak of material adversity because we believe it is important to separate significant from trivial harms. Title VII, we have said, does not set forth "a general civility code for the American workplace." Oncale v. Sundowner Offshore

Services, Inc., 523 U.S. 75, 80 (1998); *see Faragher*, 524 U.S., at 788 (judicial standards for sexual harassment must "filter out complaints attacking 'the ordinary tribulations of the workplace, such as the sporadic use of abusive language, gender-related jokes, and occasional teasing'"). An employee's decision to report discriminatory behavior cannot immunize that employee from those petty slights or minor annoyances that often take place at work and that all employees experience. *See* 1 B. Lindemann & P. Grossman, Employment Discrimination Law 669 (3d ed. 1996) (noting that "courts have held that personality conflicts at work that generate antipathy" and "'snubbing' by supervisors and co-workers" are not actionable under § 704(a)). The anti-retaliation provision seeks to prevent employer interference with "unfettered access" to Title VII's remedial mechanisms. *Robinson*, 519 U.S., at 346. It does so by prohibiting employer actions that are likely "to deter victims of discrimination from complaining to the EEOC," the courts, and their employers. *Ibid.* And normally petty slights, minor annoyances, and simple lack of good manners will not create such deterrence.

We refer to reactions of a reasonable employee because we believe that the provision's standard for judging harm must be objective. An objective standard is judicially administrable. It avoids the uncertainties and unfair discrepancies that can plague a judicial effort to determine a plaintiff's unusual subjective feelings. We have emphasized the need for objective standards in other Title VII contexts, and those same concerns animate our decision here. *See, e.g., Suders*, 542 U.S., at 141 (constructive discharge doctrine); Harris v. Forklift Systems, Inc., 510 U.S. 17, 21 (1993) (hostile work environment doctrine).

We phrase the standard in general terms because the significance of any given act of retaliation will often depend upon the particular circumstances. Context matters. "The real social impact of workplace behavior often depends on a constellation of surrounding circumstances, expectations, and relationships which are not fully captured by a simple recitation of the words used or the physical acts performed." *Oncale, supra*, at 81-82. A schedule change in an employee's work schedule may make little difference to many workers, but may matter enormously to a young mother with school age children. *Cf., e.g., Washington, supra*, at 662 (finding flex-time schedule critical to employee with disabled child). A supervisor's refusal to invite an employee to lunch is normally trivial, a nonactionable petty slight. But to retaliate by excluding an employee from a weekly training lunch that contributes significantly to the employee's professional advancement might well deter a reasonable employee from complaining about discrimination. *See* 2 EEOC 1998 Manual § 8, p. 8-14. Hence, a legal standard that speaks in general terms rather than specific prohibited acts is preferable, for an "act that would be immaterial in some situations is material in others." *Washington, supra*, at 661.

III

Applying this standard to the facts of this case, we believe that there was a sufficient evidentiary basis to support the jury's verdict on White's retaliation claim. . . . The jury found that two of Burlington's actions amounted to retaliation: the reassignment of White from forklift duty to standard track laborer tasks and the 37-day suspension without pay.

Burlington does not question the jury's determination that the motivation for these acts was retaliatory. But it does question the statutory significance of the harm these acts caused. . . .

First, Burlington argues that a reassignment of duties cannot constitute retaliatory discrimination where, as here, both the former and present duties fall within the same job description. . . . We do not see why that is so. Almost every job category involves some responsibilities and duties that are less desirable than others. Common sense suggests that one good way to discourage an employee such as White from bringing discrimination charges would be to insist that she spend more time performing the more arduous duties and less time performing those that are easier or more agreeable. That is presumably why the EEOC has consistently found "[r]etaliatory work assignments" to be a classic and "widely recognized" example of "forbidden retaliation." 2 EEOC 1991 Manual § 614.7, pp. 614-31 to 614-32.

To be sure, reassignment of job duties is not automatically actionable. Whether a particular reassignment is materially adverse depends upon the circumstances of the particular case, and "should be judged from the perspective of a reasonable person in the plaintiff's position, considering all the circumstances.'" *Oncale*, 523 U.S., at 81. But here, the jury had before it considerable evidence that the track labor duties [to which White was reassigned] were "by all accounts more arduous and dirtier"; that the "forklift operator position required more qualifications, which is an indication of prestige"; and that "the forklift operator position was objectively considered a better job and the male employees resented White for occupying it." 364 F.3d,at 803 (internal quotation marks omitted). Based on this record, a jury could reasonably conclude that the reassignment of responsibilities would have been materially adverse to a reasonable employee.

Second, Burlington argues that the 37-day suspension without pay lacked statutory significance because Burlington ultimately reinstated White with backpay. Burlington says that "it defies reason to believe that Congress would have considered a rescinded investigatory suspension with full back pay" to be unlawful, particularly because Title VII, throughout much of its history, provided no relief in an equitable action for victims in White's position. . . .

We do not find Burlington's last mentioned reference to the nature of Title VII's remedies convincing. After all, throughout its history, Title VII has provided for injunctions to "bar like discrimination in the future," Albemarle Paper Co. v. Moody, 422 U.S. 405, 418 (1975) (internal quotation marks omitted), an important form of relief. 42 U.S.C. §2000e-5(g). And we have no reason to believe that a court could not have issued an injunction where an employer suspended an employee for retaliatory purposes, even if that employer later provided backpay. In any event, Congress amended Title VII in 1991 to permit victims of intentional discrimination to recover compensatory (as White received here) and punitive damages, concluding that the additional remedies were necessary to "'help make victims whole.'" West v. Gibson, 527 U.S. 212, 219 (1999) (quoting H.R.Rep. No. 102-40, pt. 1, pp. 64-65 (1991), U.S. Code Cong. & Admin. News 1991, pp. 549, 602-603); *see* 42 U.S.C. §§ 1981a(a)(1), (b). We would undermine the significance of that congressional judgment were we to conclude that employers could avoid liability in these circumstances.

Neither do we find convincing any claim of insufficient evidence. White did receive backpay. But White and her family had to live for 37 days without income. They did not know during that time whether or when White could return to work. Many reasonable employees would find a month without a paycheck to be a serious hardship. And White described to the jury the physical and emotional hardship that 37 days of having "no income, no money" in fact caused. ("That was the worst Christmas I had out of my life. No income, no money, and that made all of us feel bad. . . . I got very depressed"). Indeed, she obtained medical treatment for her emotional distress. A reasonable employee facing the choice between retaining her job (and paycheck) and filing a discrimination complaint might well choose the former. That is to say, an indefinite suspension without pay could well act as a deterrent, even if the suspended employee eventually received backpay. *Cf. Mitchell*, 361 U.S., at 292 ("[I]t needs no argument to show that fear of economic retaliation might often operate to induce aggrieved employees quietly to accept substandard conditions"). Thus, the jury's conclusion that the 37-day suspension without pay was materially adverse was a reasonable one.

IV

For these reasons, the judgment of the Court of Appeals is affirmed.
[Concurring opinion of Justice ALITO omitted].

NOTES AND QUESTIONS

1. As *White* illustrates, the question whether a law against retaliation provides a remedy for lesser forms of retaliation or non-employment actions depends in part on statutory interpretation. With Title VII compare the Texas Whistleblower Act, Tex. Gov. Code § 554.002, prohibiting a retaliatory "personnel action." The same law defines "personnel action" as "an action that affects a public employee's compensation, promotion, demotion, transfer, work assignment, or performance evaluation."

A statute can also make it clear whether a court is authorized or required to award compensatory damages for non-economic injury, such as emotional distress caused by actions short of discharge. In contrast, when a plaintiff employee invokes a common law cause of action it may be unclear whether a court should grant a remedy for injuries involving actions short of discharge. *See, e.g.,* Dargart v. Ohio Dep't of Transp., 2005 WL 2065179 (Ohio Ct. Cl. 2005) (unpublished) (questioning whether Ohio's public policy cause of action is available to employee who has not suffered discharge); Davis v. Board of Regents for Oklahoma State University, 25 P.3d 308 (Okla. Civ. App. 2001) (no cause of action for retaliatory demotion); Trosper v. Bag'N Save, 734 N.W.2d 704 (Neb. 2007) (retaliatory demotion states cause of action under Nebraska public policy exception to employment at will; one Justice dissenting).

2. If White had resigned in response to continuing harassment, would she be able to collect damages for lost pay as if she had been discharged? Under certain circumstances, an employee who resigns may invoke the doctrine of "constructive discharge." The U.S. Supreme Court has considered the doctrine of constructive discharge in the context of sexual harassment. In Pennsylvania State Police v.

Suders, 542 U.S. 129 (2004), the Court held that an employer constructively discharges an employee if it creates or permits working conditions so intolerable that a reasonable person would feel compelled to resign.

3. Is it unlawful retaliation for an employer to refuse to hire a job applicant who was a whistleblower against a prior employer? *See* In re Campbell, 2008 WL 3891132 (App. Div. N.J. 2008) (unpublished) (job applicant not protected from retaliation); Baker v. Campbell County Board of Education, 180 S.W.3d 479 (Ky. App. 2005) (public policy cause of action does not extend to refusal to hire); Vasquez v. Ritchey, 973 S.W.2d 406 (Tex. App. 1998) (statutory retaliation claim depended on "employee" status at time of retaliation, and applicant would not qualify as an employee).

4. A vengeful employer might retaliate not only against the employee who engaged in protected conduct but also against that person's relatives or other associates. Can the victim of such collateral retaliation sue for retaliation if he or she did not participate in any protected conduct? In Thompson v. North American Stainless, L.P., 562 U.S. 170 (2011), the Supreme Court held that an employer unlawfully retaliated against the fiancée of an employee who had engaged in protected conduct under Title VII by complaining about gender discrimination, and that the fiancée had his own cause of action under Title VII's anti-retaliation provision even though he had not engaged in protected conduct.

e. Other Employer Torts in the Course of Discharge

Many of the tort law doctrines and statutory employee rights discussed in Chapter 6, Management and Supervision of the Workforce, might be implicated in any wrongful discharge action, particularly when the discharge followed supervision or investigation that exceeded the bounds of the law. Tortious infliction of emotional distress, also known as the tort of "outrage," figures prominently in wrongful discharge cases. However, discharging an employee is not tortious merely because it causes distress. *See, e.g.*, Parsons v. United Techs. Corp., 700 A.2d 655 (Conn. 1997). Even some particularly humiliating aspects of the termination process are not necessarily tortious. In *Parsons*, for example, the court held that escorting a summarily discharged employee out of work was not tortious.

Escorting an employee from the workplace with a security guard and in full view of other employees may be humiliating to the employee, but there is a plausible explanation for the employer's action. The employer might fear the security risk posed by a furious or vengeful employee. On the other hand, if an employer humiliates an employee in a *purely gratuitous* and "outrageous" fashion, its right to discharge the employee is no defense to its liability for the tort of outrage. For example, an employer eager to terminate an employee might take action designed to force the employee to "resign" in a misguided effort to avoid a discrimination claim, a severance pay claim, or impairment of the employer's unemployment compensation rating. In Wilson v. Monarch Paper Co., 939 F.2d 1138 (5th Cir. 1991), the employer attempted first to induce the plaintiff Wilson's resignation by a relatively small offer of severance pay. Wilson refused the offer. The employer then began a persistent course of severely humiliating actions against Wilson, including posting a sign at the workplace that read "Wilson is old," and assigning the former executive to janitorial duties, evidently for the purpose of driving him from the workforce. The harassment accomplished that goal and more. Wilson was eventually hospitalized for severe depression. A jury verdict for Wilson on his tort claim awarded punitive damages and damages for emotional distress totaling $3 million. The Fifth Circuit affirmed.

Could an employer's motive or intent *standing alone* ever be "outrageous" if its conduct is not outrageous and its intent is not prohibited by a discrimination statute, anti-retaliation law, or other wrongful discharge law? Such cases appear to be extremely rare, not because it is rare for employers to act arbitrarily or unreasonably but because the requirement of "outrageous" conduct sets a very high threshold. One of the rare cases is Agis v. Howard Johnson Co., 355 N.E.2d 315 (Mass. 1976). In *Agis,* one of the employer's managers believed that "there was some stealing going on" and that one of the employees must be guilty. The manager was unable to pinpoint the culprit, so he resorted to group pressure. He announced that he would begin to fire the employees one at a time in alphabetical order until the culprit stepped forward and confessed. Hearing no confession, the manager terminated Agis on the spot. The trial court dismissed Agis's tort claim against the employer, but the Supreme Court of Massachusetts reversed. The court found that there was an issue of fact whether the employer had committed the tort of outrage, and it remanded the case for a jury trial on this issue.

One other tort employees frequently assert in the context of discharge is defamation or other injury to reputation and employability. Section D of this chapter addresses the tort of defamation and the civil rights doctrine of "stigmatization."

C. JOB SECURITY IN THE PUBLIC SECTOR

In comparison with private sector employees, public sector employees are much more likely to enjoy substantive and procedural protection against discharge without cause. Most federal employees, for example, have a right to appeal adverse actions to an independent body, the Merit Systems Protection Board. 5 U.S.C. §§ 7501-7543. An employee who believes he is the victim of a retaliatory "prohibited personnel practice" may also seek an investigation by the Office of the Special Counsel. 5 U.S.C. §§ 1211-1219. More than half of all state and local government employees enjoy protection under civil service commission laws, academic tenure systems, and other local job security practices of public employers. Peck, *Unjust Discharges from Employment: A Necessary Change in the Law*, 40 Ohio St. L.J. 1, 8-9 (1979). As discussed in Chapter 6, public sector employees at all levels also enjoy the protection of the U.S. Constitution, which among other things limits a public sector employer's power to discharge employees in violation of their rights to equal protection or their First or Fourth Amendment rights.

Under the Fifth and Fourteenth Amendments to the U.S. Constitution, public sector employees may also have certain procedural due process rights above and beyond what statutory or contractual job security arrangements provide. If a public employer's termination of an employee's employment affects the employee's "property" or "liberty" interests, due process requires "some kind of prior hearing." Board of Regents of State Colleges v. Roth, 408 U.S. 564, 569-570 (1972). Not all public employees are entitled to procedural due process. The right to "some kind of prior hearing attaches only if the employee has "property interest" in employment by virtue of a statutory or contractual requirement of "cause" for discharge. Determining the existence of a property interest in employment involves many of the same issues courts consider in private sector litigation of express or implied contracts for job security. *See, e.g.*, Calhoun v. Gaines, 982 F.2d 1470 (10th Cir. 1992) (even without formal system of tenure, university professor might have reasonable expectation of job security based on contract, agreements, or policy manuals and procedures). In some states the doctrine of sovereign immunity limits an employee's ability to recover monetary relief from the government even when the government has breached a contract. A theory that a state or local government or its agents acted without due process in depriving an employee of his "property" interest in his job provides the basis for an alternative remedy under federal civil rights law.

If an employee has a "property interest" in his or her public employment, the employee is entitled to a pretermination "hearing." In Cleveland Bd. of Education v. Loudermill, 470 U.S. 532 (1985), the Court described the right to hearing in the employee disciplinary context as follows:

> The point is straightforward: the Due Process Clause provides that certain substantive rights—life, liberty, and property—cannot be deprived except pursuant to constitutionally adequate procedures.... "While the legislature may elect not to confer a property interest in [public] employment, it may not constitutionally authorize the deprivation of such an interest, once conferred, without appropriate procedural safeguards." Arnett v. Kennedy, 416 U.S., at 167 (Powell, J., concurring in part and concurring in result in part). In short, once it is determined that the Due Process Clause applies, "the question remains what process is due." Morrissey v. Brewer, 408 U.S. 471, 481 (1972).
>
> We have described "the root requirement" of the Due Process Clause as being "that an individual be given an opportunity for a hearing *before* he is deprived of any significant property interest." Boddie v. Connecticut, 401 U.S. 371, 379 (1971) (emphasis in original). This principle requires "some kind of a hearing" prior to the discharge of an employee who has a constitutionally protected property interest in his employment. Board of Regents v. Roth, 408 U.S., at 569-570. . . . Even decisions finding no constitutional violation in termination procedures have relied on the existence of some pretermination opportunity to respond. For example, in *Arnett* six Justices found constitutional minima satisfied where the employee had access to the material upon which the charge was based and could respond orally and in writing and present rebuttal affidavits. *See also* Barry v. Barchi, 443 U.S. 55, 65 (1979) (no due process violation where horse trainer whose license was suspended "was given more than one opportunity to present his side of the story").
>
> [T]he pretermination "hearing," though necessary, need not be elaborate. We have pointed out that "[t]he formality and procedural requisites for the hearing can vary, depending upon the importance of the interests involved and the nature of the subsequent proceedings." Boddie v. Connecticut, 401 U.S., at 378.... "[S]omething less" than a full evidentiary hearing is sufficient prior to adverse administrative action. Mathews v. Eldridge, 424 U.S., at 343.

> ... It should be an initial check against mistaken decisions — essentially, a determination of whether there are reasonable grounds to believe that the charges against the employee are true and support the proposed action....
>
> The essential requirements of due process ... are notice and an opportunity to respond. The opportunity to present reasons, either in person or in writing, why proposed action should not be taken is a fundamental due process requirement. The tenured public employee is entitled to oral or written notice of the charges against him, an explanation of the employer's evidence, and an opportunity to present his side of the story....

470 U.S. at 541-46.

Although the pretermination hearing required under *Loudermill* "need not be elaborate," it must be more than pro forma. In Cotnoir v. University of Maine Sys., 35 F.3d 6 (1st Cir. 1994), university officials conducted an investigation into certain alleged improprieties involving the plaintiff Cotnoir. After receiving an investigatory report on the matter, the university president invited Cotnoir to a meeting "so that you might further clarify your role in this series of events," and warned him "that disciplinary action may result from my investigation of your participation in this serious academic matter." At Cotnoir's meeting with the university president, the president asked a series of questions but did not show the investigatory report to Cotnoir and evidently did not explain the substance of the evidence against Cotnoir.

The university subsequently terminated Cotnoir's employment and Cotnoir sued under section 1983 for the violation of his property right in his employment without the pretermination hearing required by due process. In an interlocutory appeal from the district court's denial of summary judgment based on official immunity, the court held that if the facts alleged by Cotnoir were true, it was unreasonable for university officials to believe they had satisfied the pretermination requirements of due process. In particular, the court found that (1) the university president's warning that Cotnoir might be subject to disciplinary action did not sufficiently forewarn him that the university might *terminate* his employment; and (2) the university president's questioning of Cotnoir did not constitute the requisite explanation of the evidence against him. The court therefore held that the individual defendants were not entitled to assert qualified immunity at the summary judgment stage.

What if a public employer unlawfully terminates an employee without a pretermination hearing, but a fair *post*-termination hearing subsequently upholds the termination? Is a plaintiff entitled to damages or any other remedy under these circumstances? *See* Koopman v. Water Dist. No. 1 of Johnson County, Kansas, 41 F.3d 1417 (10th Cir. 1994) (upholding jury award of nominal damages of $1, but also awarding attorney's fees, in absence of evidence that plaintiff's emotional distress resulted from denial of due procedural process rather than termination); Lum v. City and County of Honolulu, 963 F.2d 1167 (9th Cir. 1992) (upholding award of $8,000 for embarrassment and humiliation arising from denial of pretermination hearing, despite post-termination hearing that lawfully upheld plaintiff's discharge); Brewer v. Chauvin, 938 F.2d 860, 864 (8th Cir. 1991) (plaintiff entitled to back pay "from the date of his discharge to the earliest date the discharge could have taken effect had the proper procedures been followed," plus punitive damages if denial of due process was reckless or indifferent).

D. MITIGATING THE IMPACT OF TERMINATION OF EMPLOYMENT

1. *The Employee's Reputation: Defamation and Stigmatization*

a. Common Law Defamation

The law of defamation applies to relations between employers and their current or former employees in much the same fashion as it applies to other relationships. Moreover, termination of employment, especially if based on disciplinary reasons, is fertile ground for actual or alleged defamation.

There are at least five likely occasions for an employer's communication of defamatory statements about an employee in connection with a disciplinary discharge: (1) intrafirm communications during investigation of alleged misconduct and the firm's decision to discharge; (2) discussions with other employees outside the scope of the investigation or decision; (3) discussions with persons outside the firm interested in the employee's sudden discharge, such as customers or community members; (4) reports to a former employee's prospective employers who inquire about his job history; and (5) testimony at unemployment compensation hearings, grievance hearings, or other post-discharge proceedings.

In each of these situations, a former employee alleging defamation must prove publication of a defamatory statement to some third party, and in many instances he must overcome the employer's defenses that the defamatory statement was in fact "true," or that the employer had a "privilege" to make the communication to other parties sharing a legitimate interest in the matter.

The initial hurdle plaintiff employees face is to prove an employer's "publication" of a defamatory statement to a third party. Even if an employee has reason to believe the employer has accused the employee of something bad, it is often difficult to prove the employer stated the accusation to someone who would qualify as a third party. Consider first the matter of intrafirm communications. If more than one supervisor, manager, investigator, or witness within the firm participated in an investigation or decision, one might argue that they "published" defamatory statements to each other. Courts tend to be protective of such communications, however, and with good reason, because an employer cannot carefully and completely investigate a disciplinary matter unless participants in the investigation can speak and report to each other without fear of defamation liability. A few courts simply treat the firm as a single entity that is talking to itself, not to a third party. *See, e.g.*, Halsell v. Kimberly-Clark Corp., 683 F.2d 285, 288-289 (8th Cir. 1982). If there is no "publication" to a third party, the inquiry ends right there. Most courts, however, regard intrafirm communications as publications between different persons, but the communications are cloaked with a qualified privilege that protects the publishers from liability as long as they acted without "malice." *See, e.g.*, Raiola v. Chevron U.S.A., Inc., 872 So. 2d 79 (Miss. App. 2004) (qualified privilege for supervisor's statement in course of employer's internal review proceeding); Chambers v. Am. Trans Air, Inc., 577 N.E.2d 612,

616 (Ind. App. 1991).

Communications beyond the circle of intrafirm investigators, witnesses and decision makers might be privileged too, depending on a court's determination whether the communications are the sort that ought to be encouraged based on the parties' shared interest in the employee's situation. A court might be less inclined to accept at face value the employer's mere assertion of "shared interests" in making defamatory statements to employees outside the investigatory circle, or to customers or other members of the community. As one moves from the inner circle to the outer circle, one finds decisions either granting a privilege or denying a privilege, based on the particular circumstances. *See, e.g.,* High v. A.J. Harwi Hardware Co., 115 Kan. 400, 223 P.264 (1924) (communications between employer and customers were privileged); Austin v. Inet Tech., Inc., 118 S.W.3d 491 (Tex. App. 2003) (manager's explanation of the plaintiff's discharge to one of plaintiff's friends was privileged, because the friend was a fellow employee and had asked the manager why the company had terminated the plaintiff); DeWald v. Home Depot, 2000 WL 1207124 (Tex. App. 2000) (unpublished) (employer's statement to other employees "to make an example of [the plaintiff] and intimidate other employees" was not privileged).

A plaintiff employee who seeks to persuade a court that the communication was not privileged might find himself boxed into a corner. A supervisor who defames an employee for no legitimate business reason might be acting outside the scope of his authority, and the employer might not be liable for the communication. *Cf.* Counts v. Guevara, 328 F.3d 212 (5th Cir. 2003) (remanding case under Federal Employees Liability Reform and Tort Compensation Act for further proceedings to determine whether manager was acting in the scope of his authority when he made certain statements at a company retirement party).

There is one situation in which the employer's communications enjoy an *absolute* privilege regardless of malice in most states: The communications were part of a judicial or quasi-judicial proceeding, such as an unemployment compensation hearing to determine whether an employee claimant is disqualified from receiving benefits by reason of "misconduct."

Communications that are not privileged, such as an employer's needless disparagement of an employee in the community or industry, can still present a practical problem for the former employee. He still faces the difficulty of proving the communication occurred at all. When an employee is discharged suddenly and not in connection with a general reduction in force, other employees and members of the community may draw their own conclusions. Even if the employee's reputation is damaged, there might be no way of proving the employer was the source of any particular communication. Perhaps the mere fact of the discharge caused the injury, but discharge, standing alone, is not a publication of a defamatory statement.

CHURCHEY v. ADOLPH COORS CO.

759 P.2d 1336 (Colo. 1988)

MULLARKEY, Justice.

The petitioner, Diana K. Churchey, filed a civil action stating three claims for relief against her former employer, Adolph Coors Company: wrongful discharge, defamation, and outrageous conduct. The trial court granted Coors' motions for summary judgment on all claims. The court of appeals affirmed. . . .

[The facts leading to Churchey's discharge involve a convoluted series of miscommunications between Churchey, Coors officials, and medical personnel. In defending its decision to discharge, Coors evidently argued that Churchey took advantage of the situation and deceived company personnel in taking time off without permission. Churchey argued she was innocent of any intent to deceive.

The problem began when Churchey visited her own doctor during an excused absence, and the doctor diagnosed her eye infection as conjunctivitis. The company required Churchey to visit a company nurse to verify Churchey's condition, and the nurse confirmed Churchey's conjunctivitis but instructed Churchey to return to work the following day. Overnight, Churchey's condition worsened. Instead of going to work the next day, she visited her own doctor and a specialist, and these doctors diagnosed her condition as maxillary sinusitis in addition to conjunctivitis. They instructed Churchey not to return to work for at least another five days.

When Churchey called a supervisor to explain her worsened condition and her doctors' diagnosis, she apparently did not tell the supervisor that a company nurse had previously instructed her to return to work, and the company later regarded this omission as "dishonesty." Nevertheless, the supervisor required Churchey to return to the company's medical center to verify her condition.

When Churchey eventually visited a company doctor, the doctor made an error that became very important. In contrast with the opinion of Churchey's own doctors, the company doctor believed Churchey was well enough to return to work *immediately*. However, he signed a document that, for unexplained reasons, appeared to show Churchey was not required to return to work for several more days. He handed Churchey this document, and according to her testimony, she interpreted it to conform to her own doctors' opinion: She should not return to work for several days. Churchey went home and did not report to work that day. The company fired her for not only for unexcused absence, but for "dishonesty."]

Churchey's first claim, defamation, is based on the fact that Coors terminated her for "dishonesty." A cause of action for defamation requires, at a minimum, publication of a false statement of defamatory fact. *See generally* Prosser & Keeton on the Law of Torts § 113 (W. Keeton, D. Dobbs, R. Keeton & D. Owen, 5th ed. 1984). The statement that Churchey was "dishonest" is clearly defamatory and Coors has not disputed this. However, in its answer, Coors denied that the statement was false.

Truth is an affirmative defense to an allegation of defamation. . . . Neither the trial court nor the court of appeals addressed the truth of the statement because each disposed of the defamation claim on publication grounds. . . .

The record before us discloses that a jury trial was demanded by the plaintiff and that there are sharp factual conflicts between the parties on the issue of dishonesty. Churchey has contended from the beginning that she followed the personnel policies to the best of her ability and that she was not dishonest. She asserts that her failure to appear for work cannot constitute an act of dishonesty and that she did not deceive either her supervisors or the medical personnel. Coors contends that Churchey was dishonest when, on two separate occasions, she failed to tell her supervisors that Coors' medical personnel had instructed her to return to work and that, on the second occasion, she lied to the Coors' physician. . . .

Given the disputes of fact in the record and the varying inferences that can be drawn from those facts, we cannot say as a matter of law that Churchey was "dishonest." We must leave that for the jury to decide. . . . Therefore, for purposes of reviewing the summary judgment we accept as true Churchey's allegation that the statement was false. . . .

We next turn to the issue of publication. The statement that Churchey was "dishonest" may have been made and published during the discussions that the Coors' supervisory personnel had about her conduct. *See generally* Prosser & Keeton, *supra*, § 113, at 798-99 (publication may be made to anyone, even agent of defendant). Any such publication, however, was subject to a qualified privilege, . . . *see generally* Prosser & Keeton, *supra*, § 115, at 828-29 (communication to protect common interest), and Churchey does not base her claim on those communications.

Instead, in her amended complaint, she asserts that publication occurred because she "has been forced to repeat the reason for her discharge to prospective employers to her damage and detriment, an event which was or should have been foreseeable by the Defendant and is, accordingly, attributable to the Defendant." This theory of publication has not been addressed previously in Colorado. The trial court recognized the general rule that a defamatory remark must be published to someone other than the defamed person to create a cause of action for defamation. *See generally* Prosser & Keeton, *supra*, § 113, at 797. However, it concluded that the exceptions set forth in the Restatement (Second) of Torts section 577 comments k and m (1977) were the law in Colorado. Comment k to section 577 of the Restatement, *supra* ("comment k"), provides as follows:

> *k. Intentional or negligent publication.* There is an intent to publish defamatory matter when the actor does an act for the purpose of communicating it to a third person or with knowledge that it is substantially certain to be so communicated. . . .

It is not necessary, however, that the communication to a third person be intentional. If a reasonable person would recognize that an act creates an unreasonable risk that the defamatory matter will be communicated to a third person, the conduct becomes a negligent communication. A negligent communication amounts to a publication just as effectively as an intentional communication. . . .

In this court, Churchey argues that comment k correctly states the law in Colorado and that, under the theory set forth in that comment, her allegations of publication were sufficient. . . . The text of comment k explains that conduct which creates an unreasonable risk that defamatory matter will be published to one other than the defamed person amounts to publication. The circumstances alleged by Churchey do fall within this special situation, so the question of whether comment k correctly states the law is squarely before us. Although this is a question of first impression in Colorado, many other jurisdictions have ruled on this issue and have developed two formulations of the exception. Both formulations permit a defendant to be held liable for certain foreseeable "self-publication," i.e., when the defendant communicates a defamatory statement only to the plaintiff and the plaintiff publishes it to other people. The first approach imposes liability if the defendant knew or could have foreseen that the plaintiff would be compelled to repeat the defamatory statement; the second imposes liability if the defendant knew or could have foreseen that the plaintiff was likely to repeat the statement.

We agree with the former approach, as set forth by the California Court of Appeal: when "the originator of the defamatory statement has reason to believe that the person defamed will be under a *strong compulsion* to disclose the contents of the defamatory statement to a third person," the originator is responsible for that publication. McKinney v. County of Santa Clara, 110 Cal. App. 3d 787, 796, 168 Cal. Rptr. 89, 93-94 (1980) (emphasis added). In *McKinney*, the court explained that:

> The rationale for making the originator of a defamatory statement liable for its foreseeable republication is the strong causal link between the actions of the originator and the damage caused by the republication. This causal link is no less strong where the foreseeable republication is made by the person defamed operating under a strong compulsion to republish the defamatory statement and the circumstances which create the strong compulsion are known to the originator of the defamatory statement at the time he communicates it to the person defamed.

Id., 110 Cal. App. 3d at 797-98, 168 Cal. Rptr. at 94. . . .

The trial court followed those jurisdictions which have recognized a more literal interpretation of comment k, holding that it is sufficient if a reasonably prudent person would have expected the plaintiff to republish the communication. *See* Grist v. Upjohn Co., 16 Mich. App. 452, 168 N.W.2d 389, 405-06 (1969) (publication may occur when originator of statement "intends or has reason to suppose that in the ordinary course of events the matter will come to the knowledge of some third person"). . . .

We believe that the trial court's broad construction of the foreseeable selfpublication exception would impose unreasonable liability on defendants for harm they did not cause directly and would discourage some communications which, on balance, should be encouraged. When the originator of the statement reasonably can foresee that the defamed person will be compelled to repeat a defamatory statement to a third party, there is a strong causal link between the originator's actions and the harm caused to the defamed person; this causal connection makes the imposition of liability reasonable. If publication could be based on the defamed person's freely-made decision to repeat a defamatory remark, however, the defendant would be held liable for damages which the plaintiff reasonably could have avoided. In other contexts, we have held that "one may not recover damages for an injury which he might by reasonable precautions or exertions have avoided." Valley Dev. Co. v. Weeks, 147 Colo. 591, 596, 364 P.2d 730, 733 (1961). In the case of a voluntary self-publication, the plaintiff could have avoided the damage to his or her reputation, as well as emotional distress and any other harm, simply by declining to repeat the defendant's statement. In addition, . . . , both employers and employees have significant interests in open communication about job-related problems. Imposing liability for self-publication which is "likely" but not compelled would unnecessarily deter such communication. For these reasons, we reject the trial court's interpretation of comment k.

. . . In this case, Churchey's amended complaint alleged that Coors was or should have been able to foresee that she would be forced to repeat the reason for her discharge. Coors never submitted affidavits or other evidence on this issue, nor did it argue that compelled self-publication was not foreseeable. Therefore, the trial court should have accepted Churchey's allegation of foreseeability as true for purposes of Coors' summary judgment motion. . . . Summary judgment should not have been granted based on the lack of evidence of foreseeability.

We now turn to Coors' assertion that the trial court's judgment should be affirmed because Coors had a qualified privilege to reveal to Churchey the reason for her termination. Determining when a qualified privilege should protect a communication is a question of law requiring the court to balance the interests protected by a privilege and the interests served by allowing a defamation action. For example, in Dominguez v. Babcock, 727 P.2d 362 (Colo. 1986), we held that a memorandum by faculty members setting forth their reasons for requesting that a department head be reassigned was subject to a qualified privilege "because it was published by persons having a common interest in the subject matter to persons sharing that interest." *Id.* at 365. After balancing the interests of the defamed person in the protection of his reputation against the interests of others in allowing the publication, we concluded that the interest in permitting coworkers to comment was of sufficient importance to merit the protection of a qualified privilege. *Id.* at 366.

In our view, the interests of employers and employees in assuring that employees know the reasons for their discharges and are not fired based on mistaken beliefs outweigh any harm which the knowledge of a negative reason may cause an employee. Therefore, an employer's communication to an employee of its reasons for discharging that employee is subject to a qualified privilege. This conclusion is supported by the existence of other qualified privileges in the employment context, such as the qualified privilege applicable to inter-office memoranda, *Abrahamsen*, 177 Colo. at 427, 494 P.2d at 1289, the qualified privilege protecting the right of corporate officers to communicate with one another about their employees' conduct, Denver Pub. Warehouse Co. v. Holloway, 34 Colo. 432, 83 P. 131 (1905), and the qualified privilege of an employer to explain the reasons for an employee's discharge to other employees, Patane v. Broadmoor Hotel, Inc., 708 P.2d 473 (Colo. Ct. App. 1985).

However, this conclusion does not mean that Coors was entitled to summary judgment. Once the court determines as a matter of law that a qualified privilege applies to the defendant's communication, the plaintiff has the burden of showing that, as a matter of fact, the defendant "publishe[d] the material with malice, that is, knowing the matter to be false, or act[ed] in reckless disregard as to its veracity."[3] *Dominguez*, 727 P.2d at 366. . . .

Coors has not demonstrated the absence of any material issue of fact which would justify summary judgment in its favor on the question of malice. To the contrary, some evidence in the record may support Churchey's contentions that her

[3] This is the standard for nonmedia defendants. . . .

supervisors recklessly disregarded the truth when, based on their belief that Churchey had not followed a leave of absence policy, they stated that she had been dishonest, because (1) on its face, that policy did not apply to her; (2) they failed to determine what constituted dishonesty under the personnel manual; and (3) they failed to verify the underlying facts by contacting Churchey or her physicians. . . . She also asserts that Coors used the dispute over her absence as a pretext for terminating her employment. Each of these assertions, if supported by evidence, would be relevant to the issue of Coors' malice. On remand, therefore, Churchey must be permitted to introduce evidence in order to meet her burden of proving that Coors made the communication with malice. . . .

In summary, we conclude that the element of publication can be established by self-publication if the plaintiff proves that it was foreseeable to the defendant that the plaintiff would be under a strong compulsion to publish the defamatory statement. We also recognize that a qualified privilege protects an employer's statements to an employee of the reasons for that employee's termination; such a privilege may be overcome by a showing of "malice," i.e., a showing that the employer knew the statement was false or acted in reckless disregard as to its veracity. Because Coors failed to show that there was no material issue of disputed fact as to Churchey's defamation claim, summary judgment in favor of Coors was incorrect.

ERICKSON, Justice, concurring in part and dissenting in part:

. . . After reviewing [Restatement (Second) of Torts § 577] comment k and the supporting illustrations . . . I believe that the comment was not intended to govern "compelled self-publication," which the majority defines as compelled publication by the defamed party.

. . . The unduly broad language of comment k is limited by the following illustrations:

> 4. A and B engage in an altercation on the street where there are a number of pedestrians. During the course of the quarrel, A in a loud voice accuses B of larceny, the accusation being overheard by a number of passers-by. A has published a slander.
>
> 5. A, a cartoonist, while working at his desk in an office building represents B, a member of the editorial staff, in a ludicrous attitude. A leaves the cartoon on his desk, where it can easily be seen by numerous people who pass by the desk. A stenographer subsequently sees the cartoon. A has published a libel.
>
> 6. A writes a defamatory letter to B and sends it to him through the mails in a sealed envelope. A knows that B is frequently absent and that in his absence his secretary opens and reads his mail. B is absent from his office and his secretary reads the letter. A has published a libel.

Based on the illustrations, comment k addresses negligent publication by the defamer and not voluntary publication by the defamed person. Comment m is the only comment in the Restatement (Second) of Torts dealing with voluntary publication by the defamed person. Comment m provides:

> One who communicates defamatory matter directly to the defamed person, who himself communicates it to a third person, has not published the matter

> to the third person if there are no other circumstances. If the defamed person's transmission of the communication to the third person was made, however, without an awareness of the defamatory nature of the matter and if the circumstances indicated that communication to a third party would be likely, a publication may properly be held to have occurred.

Comment m observes that communication of defamatory matter by the defamed person does not generally constitute publication and discusses only one exception to the rule. The majority concedes, and I agree, that the exception contained in comment m does not apply in this case because Churchey was aware of the defamatory nature of the statement at the time she communicated it to third parties. . . . Accordingly, I would affirm the trial court's granting of summary judgment on Churchey's claim for defamation.

NOTES AND QUESTIONS

1. In the year following the court's decision in *Churchey*, the Colorado Legislature overruled the court and barred the doctrine of compelled self-publication in Colorado. *See* Colo. Rev. Stat. Ann. §§ 13-25-125.5.

2. Since the decision in *Churchey*, the theory of compelled self-publication has had, at best, a mixed reception in the courts. A few states recognize the doctrine. *See, e.g.*, Rivera v. Costco Wholesale Corp., 2017 WL 3405305 (Cal. App. 2017) (describing the doctrine but finding it inapplicable to the facts of that case); Munsell v. Ideal Food Stores, 494 P.2d 1063 (Kan. 1972). However, most courts have rejected the doctrine, typically fearing it would constitute too easy a circumvention of the employment-at-will doctrine. *See, e.g.,* Cweklinsky v. Mobil Chem. Co., 837 A.2d 759 (Conn. 2004); Atkins v. Indus. Telecomm'ns Ass'n, 660 A.2d 885 (D.C. 1995); Gonsalves v. Nissan Motor Corp. in Hawaii, Ltd., 58 P.3d 1196 (Haw. 2002); White v. Blue Cross & Blue Shield of Massachusetts, Inc., 809 N.E.2d 1034 (Mass. 2004); Wieder v. Chem. Bank, 608 N.Y.S.2d 195 (N.Y. App. Div. 1994); Sullivan v. Baptist Mem. Hosp., 995 S.W.2d 569 (Tenn. 1999); Gonzales v. Levy Strauss & Co., 70 S.W.3d 278 (Tex. App. 2002).

3. Would the doctrine of compelled self-publication mean the virtual end of employment at will? Could an employer arbitrarily and unfairly discharge an employee in a manner that would avoid liability for compelled self-publication?

4. A theory of compelled self-publication is one way to overcome the difficulty of proving publication in the employment context. Another solution is illustrated by Frank B. Hall v. Buck, 678 S.W.2d 612 (Tex. App. 1984), where the plaintiff was suspicious that his former employer was making defamatory statements to prospective employers with whom he sought work. The plaintiff hired a private detective to pose as someone performing a background check on the plaintiff. The court held that the former employer's defamatory statement to the detective constituted publication. *See also* Chambers v. American Trans Air, Inc., 577 N.E.2d 612 (Ind. App. 1991).

5. Employer-controlled computer networks create a new potential for publication of defamatory statements. In Mars, Inc. v. Gonzalez, 71 S.W.3d 434 (Tex. App. 2002), a worker (characterized as an independent contractor) wrote a disparaging email about one of the employer's supervisors and sent the email to a

number of employees. The main issue was whether the employer "published" the defamation by the distribution of the unauthorized message on its email system. A majority of the court rejected the claim, finding no publication by the employer. The author was a contractor not acting on behalf of the employer, and the employer acted to remove the message from its system when it discovered it (two employees entered each account, changed passwords, and deleted the message over the course of a day). The dissent argued that the employer may have published the message by not immediately shutting down its system and deleting the message from every computer. By not shutting down the system, the employer risked the chance that employees would continue to read the message during the course of the day.

6. Many employers attempt to avoid liability for defamation by adopting limited disclosure policies. Typically, company personnel are required to redirect all inquiries about former employees to a personnel office that provides minimal information, such as the start and end dates of a former employee's employment. If an employer carefully limits the information it discloses about an employee, might that not signal to prospective employers that there is some problem with the employee? *See* Saucedo v. Rheem Mfg. Co., 974 S.W.2d 117 (Tex. App. 1998) (employer's manner of declining to answer questions was not defamatory).

7. Most courts resist the notion that an employer could be liable for *failing* to disclose important information to the former employee's prospective employers. Nevertheless, there are at least a handful of cases in which injured parties have sued a tortfeasor's former employer, alleging that a failure to disclose information about the tortfeasor's dangerous propensities was a proximate cause of injury. . Courts are generally reluctant to hold an employer liable for failing to forward adverse information about a former employee to prospective employers. *See, e.g.,* San Benito Bank & Trust Co. v. Landair Travels, 31 S.W.2d 312 (Tex. App. 2000); Louviere v. Louviere, 839 So. 2d 57 (La. App. 2002); Moore v. St. Joseph Nursing Home, Inc., 459 N.W.2d 100 (Mich. App. 1990); Doe v. McLean County Unit Dist. No. 5 Bd. of Directors, 593 F.3d 507 (7th Cir 2010). A court is far more likely to hold a former employer liable for forwarding positive information it knows to be false or misleading. *See, e.g.,* Kadlec Med. Ctr. v. Lakeview Anesthesia Assocs., 527 F.3d 412 (5th Cir. 2008) (employer hospital had no duty to disclose doctor's drug addiction to prospective employer, but individual defendants who recommended doctor were liable for negligent misrepresentation); Randi W. v. Muroc Joint Unified Sch. Dist., 929 P.2d 582 (Cal. 1997) (writer of letter of recommendation liable for failing to disclose applicant teacher's record of sexual conduct with students).

8. Employers do not always accuse employees of specific acts of moral turpitude. They are just as likely to state opinions about an employee's personality or damn him by faint praise. If an employer states an opinion about an employee, such as that the employee is difficult to work with, the result might be just as a statement of a particular fact. If the opinion implies the existence of undisclosed, defamatory facts, the statement of opinion might be defamatory in itself. *See* Falls Sporting News Publ'g Co., 834 F.2d 611 (6th Cir. 1987).

9. Apart from the question whether an opinion is defamatory, some statements are so powerful they are libel per se, and the law presumes damages. Other statements are defamatory but less powerful. They are not libel per se, and

a plaintiff must prove actual damage. *See, e.g.*, Columbia Valley Reg. Med. Ctr. v. Bannert, 112 S.W.3d 193 (Tex. App. 2003) (statements regarding an employee's "lack of discipline" and "affront to professionalism" were not libelous per se); Free v. American Home Assurance Co., 1995 WL 324642 (Tex. App. 1995) (employer's statements that plaintiff was a "lightweight" who "lacked a comprehensive grasp of what was necessary to handle large accounts," and who was inclined to "vacillate" and "procrastinate," naturally injured the plaintiff in his occupation and branded the plaintiff an incompetent).

10. Do urinalysis and other investigatory tests "speak" and "defame" if they show a "positive" result? If the test result was in fact "positive," a statement to that effect is literally "true" and the defendant is likely to assert the truth defense. Washington v. Naylor Indus. Servs., Inc., 893 S.W.2d 309 (Tex. App. 1995) (statement that employee "failed" drug test or tested "positive" was true, and thus not defamatory, even though employee passed subsequent confirmation test). *But see* Tyler v. Macks Stores of N.C., Inc., 275 S.C. 456, 272 S.E.2d 633 (1980) (employer's act of discharging employee after polygraph examination might constitute insinuation to others that employee was guilty of wrongdoing).

11. To overcome employers' reluctance to speak frankly about their former employees, a prospective employer sometimes requires an applicant to sign an authorization for a former employer to provide information about the applicant, and the employee's release promising not to sue the former employer for its response to the request for information. The courts have generally upheld the effectiveness of such a release if the employee later sues for a defamatory evaluation. *See, e.g.*, Eitler v. St. Joseph Reg. Med. Ctr. South Bend Campus, Inc., 789 N.E.2d 497 (Ind. App. 2003) (enforcing the release and granting it the effect of an absolute privilege); Bagwell v. Peninsula Reg. Med. Ctr., 106 Md. App. 470, 665 A.2d 297 (1995) (upholding effectiveness of release, where plaintiff admitted he knew contents of documents being disclosed pursuant to the release); Wolf v. Williamson, 889 P.2d 1177 (Mont. 1995).

Can an employee knowingly consent to a communication without knowing what the communication will be? According to Restatement (Second) of Torts § 583 comment d, advance consent may be binding if the consenting party *"has reason to know* that [the communication] may be defamatory. In such a case, by consent to its publication, he takes the risk that it may be defamatory." (emphasis added). If an employee resigned to look for other work believing he left on good terms, would his consent to the former employer's evaluation bar his defamation suit if a former supervisor responded in an unexpectedly disparaging way?

12. Are there better ways of balancing the public's interest in the free exchange of information about employees and an individual employee's interest in protecting his reputation and employability? From state to state, one finds statutory variations that alter the law by a matter of degrees. A few states have century-old "service letter" laws and "anti-blacklisting" laws that were probably designed to prohibit discrimination against union activists but which, as written, appear to prohibit any defamatory statement from one employer to another. Service letter laws typically permit a discharged employee to demand the employer's truthful, written explanation for his discharge. These laws do not necessarily provide a useful remedy to a defamed employee. *See* CRSS, Inc. v. Runion, 992

S.W.2d 1 (Tex. App. 1995) (service letter law enforceable only by a criminal prosecution and not by private cause of action). However, a service letter law might require an employer to take a clear position, disclosed to the employee at the time of discharge about the cause of discharge. If the letter differs from an employer's subsequent statements to prospective employers, it might make the employer's later assertion of privilege more difficult.

13. Employees have sometimes attempted, largely without success, to assert a theory of negligent investigation based on the sorts of facts that frequently accompany a defamation claim. In states with a strong employment-at-will doctrine, the courts have been unwilling to hold that an employer breaches any duty in performing an incomplete or incompetent investigation. See Chapter 6.C, *supra*. However, a cursory investigation might be some evidence of callous disregard for the truth, for purposes of proving malice and overcoming the employer's privilege to publish its conclusions.

b. Stigmatization by a Public Entity

Employees defamed by a public employer face additional hurdles: sovereign immunity of the employer government, and official immunity of the individuals who caused the publication. For many public employees, the lack of a defamation remedy is largely offset by procedural safeguards providing a hearing before a civil service commission or other neutral body. However, not all public employees have the protection of civil service laws. Moreover, even under a civil service system it is possible that a public employer will lawfully terminate an employee but wrongly disparage or "stigmatize" the employee with false accusations.

The seminal case regarding defamation or "stigmatization" in public employment is Board of Regents v. Roth, 408 U.S. 564 (1972), where the Supreme Court held that even if a public employee lacks a "property interest" in employment, the employer wrongfully deprives the employee of a "liberty" interest in gaining other employment if the employer publicly disparages the employee without advance notice and an opportunity for a hearing "appropriate to the nature of the case." *Id.* at 570 n.7. In *Roth*, an untenured professor claimed he was "stigmatized" in his academic career when a university decided not to renew his employment for the next academic year. The university did not make any particular charge against the professor in connection with its decision. The Court rejected the professor's claim that he was entitled to a name-clearing hearing:

> The State, in declining to rehire the respondent, did not make any charge against him that might seriously damage his standing and associations in his community. It did not base the nonrenewal of his contract on a charge, for example, that he had been guilty of dishonesty, or immorality. Had it done so, this would be a different case. For "(w)here a person's good name, reputation, honor, or integrity is at stake because of what the government is doing to him, notice and an opportunity to be heard are essential." [citations omitted]. In such a case, due process would accord an opportunity to refute the charge before University officials. In the present case, however, there is no suggestion whatever that the respondent's "good name, reputation, honor, or integrity" is at stake.

408 U.S. at 573-574. In contrast, in Putnam v. Keller, 322 F.3d 541 (8th Cir. 2003), a public university accused an instructor of misappropriating school funds and other misconduct. The university even banned the instructor from the campus. The court held that the university had stigmatized the instructor, depriving him of a liberty interest, and that due process required the instructor's opportunity for a name-clearing hearing.

Stigmatization cases involve many of the same issues as defamation cases, including whether the defendant published a disparaging charge, whether a statement was sufficiently damaging to the employee's reputation to require judicial relief, and whether the statement was "true." *See, e.g.*, McCullough v. Wyandanch Union Free Sch. Dist., 187 F.3d 272 (2d Cir. 1999) (employer's policy of providing limited information to prospective employers did not, standing alone, stigmatize a former employee); Mascho v. Gee, 24 F.3d 1037 (8th Cir. 1994) (charges of unsatisfactory performance or general misconduct are not sufficiently stigmatizing to constitute a deprivation of an employee's liberty interest); Fraternal Order of Police v. Tucker, 868 F.2d 74, 82 (3d Cir. 1989) (press release about discharge of police officers was not misleading).

An employee who lacks statutory or contract protection against unjust discharge but who successfully demands a name-clearing hearing is not necessarily entitled to reinstatement if he "prevails" at the name-clearing hearing. As the label "name-clearing" suggests, the hearing serves only to "clear" the employee's reputation and preserve his liberty interest. The employee's right to reinstatement must be based on a property interest, such a statutory or contractual right to job security. *Roth, supra*, 408 U.S. at 573 n.12.

What if the employer, being ordered to conduct a hearing, conducts the hearing and then reaffirms its charges against the employee? Justice Brennan wrote as follows in his concurring opinion in Codd v. Velger, 429 U.S. 624 (1977):

> A determination of truthful material would preclude an award of damages for false stigmatization of plaintiff's reputation. Nonetheless, because of petitioners' failure to satisfy *Roth*'s requirement of a pretermination due process hearing, respondent still would have suffered deprivation of an established constitutional right. As with any infringement of an intangible constitutional right, . . . a jury should be permitted to decide whether to fix and award damages perhaps only nominal for the very denial of a timely due process forum where a stigmatized individual could participate in the process of attempting to clear his name.

429 U.S. at 630 n.3. *See also* Rosenstein v. City of Dallas, 876 F.2d 392 (5th Cir. 1989) (affirming an award of damages for mental anguish, harm to reputation and career, and punitive damages, but reversing an award of damages for the loss of a job with the defendant employer in the absence of a property interest in the employment); Brady v. Gebbie, 859 F.2d 1543 (9th Cir. 1988) (affirming $300,000 jury verdict for damages resulting from denial of right to a hearing).

A public employee seeking an award of damages in any due process case faces considerable "immunity" obstacles. The Eleventh Amendment grants states immunity from money damages in a federal court. Local governments do not enjoy Eleventh Amendment immunity. However, the doctrine of *respondeat superior* does not apply to public employers in federal civil rights matters, and therefore the wrongful act of an individual official is not necessarily imputed to the local government. The local government will be liable in money damages under federal law only if it can be said that the wrongful act was the local government's act, such as where the act was pursuant to its policy or the actor was a policy making individual whose actions constituted the actions of that government entity. Monell v. Dep't of Soc. Servs. of City of New York, 436 U.S. 658 (1978). The immunity of the state or local government employer from money damages under federal law might leave the individual defendant official as the only party financially responsible for the plaintiff's damages, but individual public officials are protected by qualified official immunity unless it can be said that the wrongful act was in violation of a clearly established rule of Constitutional law. Davis v. Scherer, 468 U.S. 183 (1984).

PROBLEM

See the problem at the end of Chapter 6.. Does Kunstler have any potential claim against the State of Texas based on these facts? If so, what remedy might she have?

2. *Unemployment Compensation*

a. An Overview of the Unemployment Compensation System

The U.S. unemployment compensation system was created by the Social Security Act of 1935 as one of the cornerstones of the Roosevelt Administration's New Deal, about the same time as the Wagner Act (the National Labor Relations Act) and the Fair Labor Standards Act. The system is administered as a partnership between the federal and state governments, and many of the details of the system are therefore determined at the local level within the minimum requirements of federal law. The federal aspect of the system prevents a "race to the bottom" that might occur if states reduced or eliminated unemployment compensation taxes to draw business away from their neighbors. The state aspect of the system allows for some measure of variation and experimentation. Richard W. Fanning, Jr., *The Federal-State Partnership of Unemployment Compensation*, 29 U. Mich. J.L. Ref. 475, 475-477 (1995).

Unemployment compensation provides temporary wage replacement for unemployed workers who have a "strong attachment" to the labor market, which means that they qualify for benefits under a set of rules that tend to favor those who have worked in regular, full-time, permanent employment and in traditional "employer-employee" relationships. Conversely, many "contingent" workers, including many independent contractors, temporary employees, and part-time employees may be excluded from coverage and denied benefits. The states generally provide regular unemployment compensation benefits for up to 26 weeks for qualified, unemployed claimants. The actual amount and duration of any individual's benefits are based on that individual's recent earnings history.

The system is financed primarily by federal and state taxation of the employer's payroll. The current federal tax rate is 6.2 percent of the first $7,000 of an employee's wages. However, an employer may credit state unemployment compensation taxes against most of the federal tax, so the actual federal tax rate may be as little as 0.8 percent, with state taxes making up the difference. A state pays its tax receipts to the U.S. Treasury Department, and the funds are credited to the Unemployment Trust Fund. The state may withdraw money from the fund to make benefit payments.

Not all employers within the same state pay the same tax rate. An employer's rate may be higher or lower because of its individual experience rating, which is a product of the level of claims made by that employer's former employees. As the level of claims by employees terminated by an employer goes up, the employer's tax rate goes up. The experience rating system tends to shift a greater share of the cost of the system to employers who experience a high rate of turnover in their workforce. It also provides some incentive for an employer *not* to terminate employees. As will be discussed further below, an employer also has an incentive to dispute a former employee's eligibility for benefits, because a terminated employee who is disqualified from receiving benefits will not affect the employer's experience rating.

The federal government uses the federal portion of the payroll tax to provide additional funds for the administration of the system and to pay for the federal share (one-half) of the cost of the Extended Benefits program. The Extended Benefits program provides an additional 13 weeks of benefits to claimants who have exhausted their regular benefits. However, extended benefits are payable only when the level of unemployment reaches a certain trigger point in a particular state. From time to time, and especially during major recessions, Congress has provided for additional benefits on an ad hoc basis.

Although the details of benefit eligibility vary from state to state, in general an employee is eligible if he (1) has satisfied the earnings history requirements by working as an employee in work that is not excluded from coverage (e.g., he is not an independent contractor); (2) is available for and able to work (e.g., he is not disabled or enrolled as a full-time student); (3) is actively seeking work; and (4) was not at fault in causing the termination of his employment (e.g., he did not resign, and he was not fired for "misconduct").

There are two other federal unemployment benefits programs worthy of note. First, Trade Readjustment Allowance (TRA) benefits are available to workers whose jobs were affected by foreign competition and who have exhausted their unemployment compensation benefits. The Federal Trade Act authorizes TRA benefits for workers who were laid off or whose hours were reduced because their employer was adversely affected by increased imports from other countries. The North American Free Trade Agreement-Transitional Adjustment Assistance (NAFTA-TAA) program provides TRA benefits for workers who were laid off or whose hours were reduced because their employer was adversely affected by increased imports from Mexico or Canada or because their employer shifted production to Mexico or Canada.

Second, The Disaster Relief and Emergency Assistance Act provides benefits to individuals whose employment or *self*-employment has been lost or interrupted as a direct result of a major disaster declared by the President. This program pays benefits only to individuals who are not eligible for regular unemployment compensation benefits.

b. Disqualification by Misconduct

An underlying theory of the unemployment compensation program is that benefits should be payable only to claimants who are not at fault in their loss of employment. Thus, state statutes defining eligibility for benefits usually provide that a claimant may be disqualified from receiving benefits because of "misconduct."

Alleged misconduct is one of the most common grounds for disqualification, and one of the most frequently litigated issues. Marshall H. Tanick & Brian R. Dockendorf, *Is There Gold in Those Hills? Shifting Contours of Unemployment Compensation Law*, Bench and Bar of Minnesota, p. 17, 19-20 (Nov. 2003) (estimating that misconduct cases constitute 25 percent of all contested cases in Minnesota and a larger portion of those involving appellate court review).

GREENBERG v. DIRECTOR, EMPLOYMENT SECURITY DEPARTMENT

53 Ark. App. 295, 922 S.W.2d 5 (Ark. App. 1996)

STROUD, Judge.

Appellant, Esther Greenberg, applied for unemployment compensation benefits after she was discharged by her employer, Checkbureau, Inc., for poor job performance. The Arkansas Employment Security Department determined that appellant was entitled to benefits under Ark. Code Ann. § 11-10-514 (Supp. 1995) because she was discharged from her last work for reasons other than misconduct. Checkbureau appealed that determination to the Arkansas Appeal Tribunal, which affirmed the Department's finding. Checkbureau then appealed the Tribunal's decision to the Board of Review, and the Board reversed the Tribunal's findings and found that appellant was disqualified for benefits because she was guilty of misconduct connected with her work. We reverse.

A person is disqualified from benefits if she is discharged from her last work for misconduct in connection with the work. Ark. Code Ann. § 11-10-514(a)(1) (Supp. 1995). "Misconduct," for purposes of unemployment compensation, involves: (1) disregard of the employer's interest, (2) violation of the employer's rules, (3) disregard of the standards of behavior which the employer has a right to expect of his employees, and (4) disregard of the employee's duties and obligations to his employer. . . . There is an element of intent associated with a determination of misconduct. In Willis Johnson Co. v. Daniels, 269 Ark. 795, 601 S.W.2d 890 (Ark. App. 1980), this Court stated that:

> Mere inefficiency, unsatisfactory conduct, failure of good performance as the result of inability or incapacity, inadvertencies, ordinary negligence or good faith errors in judgment or discretion are not considered misconduct for unemployment insurance purposes unless it is of such a degree or recurrence as to manifest culpability, wrongful intent, evil design, or an intentional or substantial disregard of an employer's interests or an employee's duties and obligations.

Whether the employee's acts are willful or merely the result of unsatisfactory conduct or unintentional failure of performance is a fact question for the Board . . . .

After reviewing the evidence in the present case, we cannot conclude that the Board's finding is supported by substantial evidence. The employer stated that appellant was discharged for poor job performance, and the evidence showed that appellant was incompetent as a legal secretary. She failed to properly spell-check documents, failed to mark dates on her employer's calendar, and failed to include important documents with a letter sent to an opposing party. In addition, the employer had documented instances of absenteeism and tardiness.

The Board found that appellant's failure to mark her employer's calendar on at least two occasions and her failure to include certain documents in a letter sent to an insurance company indicated an intentional disregard of the employer's interests. We hold that a reasonable mind would not accept this evidence as adequate to support the conclusion that appellant's conduct was of such a degree or recurrence as to manifest culpability, wrongful intent, evil design, or an intentional or substantial disregard of her employer's interests or her duties and obligations. The case is reversed and remanded to the Board for such further proceedings as may be necessary to determine the appellant's eligibility for benefits and the amount and duration of those benefits.

Reversed and remanded.

COOPER, Judge, dissenting.

. . . The majority opinion notes that the appellee, employed as a legal secretary, failed to properly spell-check documents, failed to mark dates on her employer's calendar, and failed to include important documents with a letter sent to an opposing party.

What the majority opinion does not reveal is that these were not isolated instances. The record shows that the appellant repeatedly failed to spell-check documents as she typed. The appellant claimed to have spell-checked the documents and blamed the recurrent errors on a computer malfunction. However, an employer representative testified that he watched as the appellant spell-checked a document which she claimed to have spell-checked previously, and observed that the computer stopped at the errors he had noted on his printed copy. Nor was the failure to mark dates on her employer's calendar an isolated event. The record shows that, despite being repeatedly instructed that her first priority was to ensure that scheduled court appearances were marked on her employer's calendar, the employer missed two court hearings because the appellant failed to mark his calendar. The majority fails altogether to note evidence that the appellant repeatedly made errors in billing clients, and that such errors continued to occur even after the problem was brought to the appellant's attention.

The Board specifically found that the appellant was discharged for misconduct in connection with the work, reasoning that the instances of the appellant's failure to follow specific instructions were so numerous that her actions indicated more than a mere inability to perform the work in a satisfactory manner. This conclusion that recurrent negligence may warrant a finding of misconduct is supported by our decisions.

PERRY v. GADDY

48 Ark. App. 128, 891 S.W.2d 73 (Ark. App. 1995)

PITTMAN, Judge.

Appellant appeals the Board of Review's denial of unemployment compensation benefits in accordance with Ark. Code Ann. § 11-10-514 (1987) upon finding appellant was discharged for misconduct in connection with the work. Appellant argues that the decision is not supported by substantial evidence.

. . . Mere inefficiency, unsatisfactory conduct, failure of good performance as a result of inability or incapacity, inadvertence, and ordinary negligence or good faith errors in judgment or discretion are not considered misconduct for unemployment insurance purposes unless they are of such degree or recurrence as to manifest culpability, wrongful intent, evil design, or an intentional or substantial disregard of an employer's interests or of an employee's duties and obligations. Shipley Baking Co. v. Stiles, 17 Ark. App. 72, 703 S.W.2d 465 (1986).

Appellant testified that she had worked for appellee for twelve years, initially as a claims examiner and then as a claims processor from 1983 to 1993. She maintained an adequate level of performance until 1991. The testimony was that appellant's average error rate in processing claims was 3.7% in 1991 and 4.7% in 1992, which exceeded appellee's requisite 3.0% error rate. Appellant's November 1991 performance review states that she had an average 4% error rate for the previous six months, and her supervisor commented that she felt that appellant had become relaxed or bored with her position. In appellant's October 1992 performance evaluation, her supervisor rated appellant's performance as inadequate. From August 1992 to January 1993 appellant received four warnings prior to her termination in February 1993 for excessive errors.

A mere failure to perform one's job because of an inability to do so is insufficient to establish misconduct for purposes of unemployment insurance. Here, appellant had the ability to perform her job as the record states that she worked as a claims processor for ten years, was described by her supervisor in a 1991 evaluation as a "great asset" until her error rate exceeded the 3% standard, and was able to bring her error rate below 3% in August 1992 after an August 17, 1992, reprimand.

In reaching its decision, the Board noted the testimony of appellant's supervisor that appellant made the same mistakes repeatedly and that each time appellant was given instructions for correction of her mistakes. The record indicates that appellant's error rate exceeded the 3% standard seven out of the eight months immediately preceding her termination. Appellant argues that there is no evidence that she intended harm to appellee's interest. The Board held that appellant's recurring negligence established misconduct.

From our review of the record, there is substantial evidence to support the Board's findings and decision. Therefore, we affirm the Board's decision that appellant was discharged . . . for misconduct in connection with the work.

NOTES AND QUESTIONS

1. The same court, applying the same law, reached opposite results for the

claimants in *Greenberg* and *Perry*. Was Perry's "misconduct" so much worse than Greenberg's that Greenberg should receive benefits, but Perry should be disqualified? What differences in facts might explain the different outcomes?

2. Is "misconduct," for purposes of unemployment compensation law, the same as "good cause" for the termination of employment in a breach of contract case? *See* Mercer v. Ross, 701 S.W.2d 830 (Tex. 1986):

> If the legislature had intended that mere inability to perform duties required disqualification from benefits it could have stated so. Any employee who is unable to do his job to the satisfaction of his employer lowers profits and to the extent of the time and materials needed to correct mistakes, places in jeopardy the property of his employer or the customer; however, that is not the standard. Mere inconvenience or additional cost incurred by the employer or his customers is not applicable, and [the Texas Employment Commission] is not required to address it.

Id. at 831.

3. The difference between the issue of "misconduct" in an unemployment compensation proceeding and the issues of "good cause" or nondiscrimination in other types of employment litigation is one reason why courts are wary of applying the doctrine of collateral estoppel to prevent either party from re-litigating issues relating to the cause of the termination after one or the other has prevailed in the unemployment compensation proceeding. Other reasons for not granting collateral estoppel effect to findings of fact in unemployment compensation proceedings include the lack of pre-hearing discovery, the inapplicability of the usual rules of evidence, the purposely expedited and informal character of the proceedings, and the comparative insignificance of the proceeding to the employer. *See* Rue v. K-Mart Corp., 713 A.2d 82 (Pa. 1998).

4. The rule in most states is that misconduct disqualifies a claimant only if the misconduct is "in connection with" the work. Nevertheless, employers sometimes assert that off-duty conduct having no direct impact on attendance or performance can be a form of disqualifying misconduct. In Collingsworth General Hosp. v. Hunnicutt, 988 S.W.2d 706 (Tex. 1998), the employee was a housekeeping supervisor with 25 years of service for the employer hospital. One day the employee received a call at her home from a woman who was having an affair with the employee's husband. Provoked by the call, the employee went to the home of the other woman to confront her, and the ensuing argument deteriorated into a physical fight. At some point the employee took a box cutter from her pocket and slashed the other woman. The employee was indicted for aggravated assault, a third-degree felony, and she pleaded guilty in return for deferred adjudication. Although the employer was familiar with the employee's arrest (she had reported it to the employer), it took no action against her until it learned of her guilty plea, and then it terminated her. The court held that the employee was guilty of disqualifying misconduct:

> In reaching our conclusion that Hunnicutt's misconduct was "connected with" her work at the Hospital, the Hospital's role as a public service health care provider is of paramount importance. It is vital . . . that its employees abstain from physically harming others, regardless of whether . . . on-duty or off-duty. Hunnicutt agreed that "part of the concern that a hospital has

> towards its patients is to maintain and have their trust" and that "part of the responsibility that a hospital has towards its patients [is] their safety." The Hospital administrator testified that Hunnicutt's conduct caused him concern about "the safety of the patients and the employees." . . . Hunnicutt's violent and harmful conduct—whether on-duty or off-duty—is so inimical to the very purpose and function of the Hospital that it would have adversely impacted the Hospital's interests to continue her employment. Therefore, it would not be unreasonable, arbitrary, or capricious to conclude that Hunnicutt's termination is "connected with" her work at the Hospital. . . . Hunnicutt's unemployment is her own fault.

Id. at 709-710.

5. Another approach to off-duty misconduct is described by the Washington Supreme Court in Nelson v. Department of Employment Sec., 655 P.2d 242, 244 (Wash. 1982). A key difference between the Washington approach and the Texas approach is that Washington law asks whether an employee engaged in off-duty misconduct with *intent* or *knowledge* that the employer's interest would suffer. *Accord* Rucker v. Price, 915 S.W.2d 315 (Ark. App. 1996).

MATTER OF FRANCIS

56 N.Y.2d 600, 435 N.E.2d 1086, 450 N.Y.S.2d 471 (N.Y. 1982)

MEMORANDUM.

. . . There is substantial evidence in the record to support the finding of the Unemployment Insurance Appeal Board that claimant was an alcoholic. Although no medical evidence was presented, there was documentary evidence that claimant had been intoxicated at work, that he suffered from "black-outs," and that he had been hospitalized on several occasions and for a period of 28 days in one instance in connection with his alcoholism. Evaluation reports on him indicate that his employer considered him to be an alcoholic and attempted to enlist him in various self-help programs. While claimant did not admit, when he testified, that he was an alcoholic, he did admit that he drank every day and that he had need for counseling. We cannot say, on the basis of the record before us, that the failure to present medical evidence precluded the appeal board from finding that the claimant was an alcoholic.

The appeal board, having reached the conclusion that petitioner was an alcoholic, acted within its discretion in denominating his discharge to be the result of his illness, rather than his own misconduct.

Thus, while the claimant is not automatically barred from qualifying for unemployment insurance benefits, the matter must be remitted to the Appellate Division with directions to remand to the Unemployment Insurance Appeal Board for determination as to claimant's "availability for, and capability of employment" pursuant to section 527 of the Labor Law.

NOTES AND QUESTIONS

1. If eligibility for benefits is based on "fault," can there be instances when "misconduct" is excused because it was caused by factors that were not the

employee's fault? Is the New York rule that misconduct is excused by alcoholism an appropriate application of the concepts of misconduct and fault? *See also* Gardner v. State Unemployment Appeals Comm'n 682 So. 2d 122 (Fla. App. 1996) (misconduct excused by alcoholism). What if the employee's misconduct was caused by addiction to illegal drugs?

Not all states agree with the New York approach. Leibbrand v. Employment Sec. Dep't, 27 P.3d 1186 (Wash. App. 2001) (upholding Washington law providing that alcoholism shall not be a defense to misconduct). In deciding whether alcoholism is an excuse, should the employee's willingness to participate in a rehabilitation program be a factor? *See* Reigelsberger v. Employment App. Bd., 500 N.W.2d 64 (Iowa 1993) (driver fired for refusing to undergo alcoholism treatment was guilty of misconduct and thus was not entitled to unemployment compensation benefits). The employee in *Reigelsberger* was an employee driver. Is that relevant?

The Americans with Disabilities Act provides that alcoholism and drug addiction may be "disabilities," but an employee *currently* using illegal drugs is not necessarily protected under the act. Thus, an employer may prohibit employees from being under the influence of alcohol or illegal drugs at the workplace. Moreover, an employer can require an alcoholic or illegal drug user to observe the same standards of job performance and behavior that it requires of other employees "even if unsatisfactory performance or behavior is related to drug use or alcoholism." 42 U.S.C. §§ 12114(a), (b).

2. The court's decision that Francis was not guilty of misconduct does not necessarily mean he receives benefits. He must also be *available* for work; if his alcoholism renders him unfit or unable to work, he is not eligible for unemployment compensation, but might be eligible for public disability benefits.

3. An incarcerated employee's absence from work might violate the employer's absence control policy, and courts generally agree that excessive absence is a form of misconduct. But absence is not always because of an employee's fault. Should incarceration excuse the employee's misconduct? *Compare* Magma Copper Co., San Manuel Div. v. Arizona Dep't of Economic Sec., 625 P.2d 935 (Ariz. 1981) (incarceration for fewer than 24 hours was not grounds for disqualification from benefits, where employee gave employer notice that he was incarcerated and would not be reporting to work), *and* Fleming v. Director, Arkansas Employment Sec. Dep't, 40 S.W.3d 820 (Ark. App. 2001) (claimant not disqualified where charges that led to his incarceration were ultimately dismissed), *with* Weavers v. Daniels, 613 S.W.2d 108 (Ark. App. 1981) (employee disqualified where absence was due to incarceration for public intoxication, in view of recurring, unexcused absences without advance notice).

4. Claimants sometimes assert a constitutional right in support of their "misconduct" that was the cause of their discharge. Even if a claimant could not have asserted the constitutional right against his former private sector employer in a wrongful discharge lawsuit, the claimant might still be entitled to unemployment compensation benefits if treating his actions or speech as "misconduct" and denying benefits would interfere with the claimant's rights under the Constitution. A claimant might also assert his constitutional right not to be disqualified from benefits if he resigned or refused an offer of work in the exercise of constitutional rights. Thomas v. Review Bd. of Indiana Employment Sec. Div., 450 U.S. 707

(1981) (state could not disqualify claimant who resigned from his job because of religious-based objections to manufacture of armaments); Sherbert v. Verner, 374 U.S. 398 (1963) (state could not disqualify claimant for refusing offer of job that required work on Saturday, in violation of her religious beliefs). *But see* Employment Div., Dep't of Human Resources of Oregon v. Smith, 494 U.S.872 (1990) (upholding denial of benefits to claimants who were discharged from employment for use of peyote, a controlled substance, even though the claimants used peyote as part of a religious ceremony, because state is permitted to prohibit the use of such substances despite alleged First Amendment rights of religious practitioners); Texas Employment Comm'n v. Hughes Drilling Fluids, 746 S.W.2d 796 (Tex. App. 1988) (claimant who was discharged from "at will" private sector employment for refusing to submit to drug testing was disqualified from receiving benefits; rejecting Fourth Amendment claim).

Does an employer have a constitutional right to discharge an employee without bearing the financial cost of paying for the employee's constitutional right? *See* Bishop Leonard Reg. Catholic Sch. v. Unemployment Compensation Bd. of Rev., 593 A.2d 28 (Pa. 1991) (teacher's marriage to divorced man in violation of Catholic school policy was disqualifying willful misconduct).

5. Employees who engage in strikes, who refuse to cross picket lines, or who are laid off because of the consequences of a strike create other complications for unemployment compensation law. *See* Baker v. General Motors Corp., 478 U.S. 621 (1986) (upholding Michigan law that denied benefits to claimants who were laid off because of a strike and who provided "financing" for the strike other than by their payment of regular union dues); New York Tel. Co. v. New York State Dep't of Labor, 440 U.S. 519 (1979) (federal collective bargaining law does not preempt state law authorizing benefits for claimants who are on strike against their employer); Ohio Bur. of Employment Servs. v. Hodory, 431 U.S. 471 (1977) (upholding Ohio statute disqualifying claimant if his unemployment was "due to a labor dispute other than a lockout at any factory . . . owned or operated by the employer by which he is or was last employed"). *See generally* James K. Bradley & Daniel R. Schuckers, *Toward a Unified Theory of Unemployment Compensation Eligibility for Replaced Striking Employees*, 61 U. PITT. L. REV. 499 (2000).

c. Disqualification Because of Resignation

A claimant who voluntarily resigned from employment is disqualified from receiving benefits, subject to some important exceptions. In general, a resignation will not cause disqualification unless it was truly voluntary. Thus, if an employer tells an employee, "quit or be fired," the employee can resign and a court is likely to hold that the termination was a "constructive" discharge or involuntary termination. *See, e.g.*, Madisonville Consolidated Indep. Sch. Dist. v. Texas Employment Comm'n, 821 S.W.2d 310 (Tex. App. 1991).

Even in the case of voluntary resignation, a state may have one of several possible exceptions to disqualification. One rule permits a claimant to receive benefits if his resignation was for good cause "connected with the employment." Tex. Lab. Code §§ 207.045, .046. Under this rule, the cause for resignation must have something to do with the job or the working conditions. Causes personal to the claimant do not qualify. Thus, the claimant is entitled to resign without disqualification if a court agrees it was reasonable for him to resign in the face of oppressive working conditions or a sudden reduction in pay or benefits. American Petrofiuna Co. v. Texas Employment Comm'n, 795 S.W.2d 899 (Tex. App. 1990). *But see* Allegheny Valley Sch. v. Pennsylvania Unemployment Compensation Bd. of Rev. 697 A.2d 243 (Pa. 1997) (if employer had good cause to demote employee, employee who resigned in response is still disqualified).

A second approach permits an employee to resign for at least some non-work-related reasons and still qualify for benefits. *See, e.g.*, Reep v. Comm'r of Dep't of Employment & Training, 593 N.E.2d 1297 (Mass. 1992) (no disqualification after resignation to relocate with living mate). Some courts emphasize, however, that a non-work-related cause must satisfy a more demanding standard, such as a "necessitous and compelling" test. Total Audio-Visual Sys., Inc. v. Dep't of Labor, Licensing and Reg.,758 A.2d 124 (Md. 2000). Moreover, the employee must ordinarily bear the burden of persuading the tribunal that the cause for resignation was indeed "necessitous and compelling." *See, e.g.*, Sturpe v. Unemployment Comp. Bd. of Rev., 823 A.2d 239 (Pa. 2003) (former airline employee failed to establish necessitous and compelling reason for resigning to join her husband in Ohio, where maintenance of separate households by claimant and her husband predated move to Ohio by husband by at least six years, and there was no evidence of economic hardship or insurmountable commuting problems).

WIMBERLY v. LABOR & INDUS. REL. COMM'N OF MISSOURI

479 U.S. 511 (1987)

Justice O'CONNOR delivered the opinion of the Court.

. . . In August 1980, after having been employed by the J.C. Penney Company for approximately three years, petitioner requested a leave of absence on account of her pregnancy. Pursuant to its established policy, the J.C. Penney Company granted petitioner a "leave without guarantee of reinstatement," meaning that petitioner would be rehired only if a position was available when petitioner was ready to return to work. Petitioner's child was born on November 5, 1980. On December 1, 1980, when petitioner notified J.C. Penney that she wished to return to work, she was told that there were no positions open.

Petitioner then filed a claim for unemployment benefits. The claim was denied by the Division of Employment Security (Division) pursuant to Mo. Rev. Stat. § 288.050.1(1) (Supp. 1984), which disqualifies a claimant who "has left his work voluntarily without good cause attributable to his work or to his employer." A deputy for the Division determined that petitioner had "quit because of pregnancy," and therefore had left work "voluntarily and without good cause attributable to [her] work or to [her] employer." . . .

The Federal Unemployment Tax Act (Act), 26 U.S.C. § 3301 et seq., enacted originally as Title IX of the Social Security Act in 1935, 49 Stat. 639, envisions a cooperative federal-state program of benefits to unemployed workers. . . . The Act establishes certain minimum federal standards that a State must satisfy in order for a State to participate in the program. *See* 26 U.S.C. § 3304(a). The standard at issue in this case, § 3304(a)(12), mandates that "no person shall be denied compensation under such State law solely on the basis of pregnancy or termination of pregnancy."

Apart from the minimum standards reflected in § 3304(a), the Act leaves to state discretion the rules governing the administration of unemployment compensation programs. . . . State programs, therefore, vary in their treatment of the distribution of unemployment benefits, although all require a claimant to satisfy some version of a three-part test. First, all States require claimants to earn a specified amount of wages or to work a specified number of weeks in covered employment during a 1-year base period in order to be entitled to receive benefits. Second, all States require claimants to be "eligible" for benefits, that is, they must be able to work and available for work. Third, claimants who satisfy these requirements may be "disqualified" for reasons set forth in state law. The most common reasons for disqualification under state unemployment compensation laws are voluntarily leaving the job without good cause, being discharged for misconduct, and refusing suitable work. . . .

The treatment of pregnancy-related terminations is a matter of considerable disparity among the States. Most States regard leave on account of pregnancy as a voluntary termination for good cause. Some of these States have specific statutory provisions enumerating pregnancy-motivated termination as good cause for leaving a job, while others, by judicial or administrative decision, treat pregnancy as encompassed within larger categories of good cause such as illness or compelling personal reasons. A few States, however, like Missouri, have chosen to define "leaving for good cause" narrowly. In these States, all persons who leave their jobs are disqualified from receiving benefits unless they leave for reasons directly attributable to the work or to the employer.

Petitioner does not dispute that the Missouri scheme treats pregnant women the same as all other persons who leave for reasons not causally connected to their work or their employer, including those suffering from other types of temporary disabilities. . . . She contends, however, that § 3304(a)(12) is not simply an antidiscrimination statute, but rather that it mandates preferential treatment for women who leave work because of pregnancy. According to petitioner, § 3304(a)(12) affirmatively requires States to provide unemployment benefits to women who leave work because of pregnancy when they are next available and able to work, regardless of the State's treatment of other similarly situated claimants.

Contrary to petitioner's assertions, the plain import of the language of § 3304(a)(12) is that Congress intended only to prohibit States from singling out pregnancy for unfavorable treatment. The text of the statute provides that compensation shall not be denied under state law "solely on the basis of pregnancy." The focus of this language is on the basis for the State's decision, not the claimant's reason for leaving her job. Thus, a State could not decide to deny benefits to pregnant women while at the same time allowing benefits to persons who are in other respects similarly situated: the "sole basis" for such a decision would be on account of pregnancy. On the other hand, if a State adopts a neutral rule that incidentally disqualifies pregnant or formerly pregnant claimants as part of a larger group, the neutral application of that rule cannot readily be characterized as a decision made "solely on the basis of pregnancy." For example, under Missouri law, all persons who leave work for reasons not causally connected to the work or the employer are disqualified from receiving benefits. To apply this law, it is not necessary to know that petitioner left because of pregnancy: all that is relevant is that she stopped work for a reason bearing no causal connection to her work or her employer. Because the State's decision could have been made without ever knowing that petitioner had been pregnant, pregnancy was not the "sole basis" for the decision under a natural reading of § 3304(a)(12)'s language. . . .

Even petitioner concedes that § 3304(a)(12) does not prohibit States from denying benefits to pregnant or formerly pregnant women who fail to satisfy neutral eligibility requirements such as ability to work and availability for work. *See* U.S. Code Cong. & Admin. News 1976, pp. 5997, 6015 ("Pregnant individuals would . . . continue to be required to meet generally applicable criteria of availability for work and ability to work"); H.R. Rep. No. 94-755, p. 50 (1975). Nevertheless, she contends that the statute prohibits the application to pregnant women of neutral disqualification provisions. But the statute's plain language will not support the distinction petitioner attempts to draw. The statute does not extend only to disqualification rules. It applies, by its own terms, to any decision to deny compensation. In both instances, the scope of the statutory mandate is the same: the State cannot single out pregnancy for disadvantageous treatment, but it is not compelled to afford preferential treatment. . . .

The Senate Report also focuses exclusively on state rules that single out pregnant women for disadvantageous treatment. In Turner v. Department of Employment Security, *supra,* this Court struck down on due process grounds a Utah statute providing that a woman was disqualified for 12 weeks before the expected date of childbirth and for 6 weeks after childbirth, even if she left work for reasons unrelated to pregnancy. The Senate Report used the provision at issue in *Turner* as representative of the kind of rule that § 3304(a)(12) was intended to prohibit. . . . S. Rep. No. 94-1265, at 19, 21, U.S. Code Cong. & Admin. News 1976, pp. 6013, 6015.

In short, petitioner can point to nothing in the Committee Reports, or elsewhere in the statute's legislative history, that evidences congressional intent to mandate preferential treatment for women on account of pregnancy. There is no hint that Congress disapproved of, much less intended to prohibit, a neutral rule such as Missouri's. Indeed, the legislative history shows that Congress was focused only on the issue addressed by the plain language of § 3304(a)(12): prohibiting rules that single out pregnant women or formerly pregnant women for disadvantageous treatment. . . . Because § 3304(a)(12) does not require States to afford preferential treatment to women on account of pregnancy, the judgment of the Missouri Supreme Court is affirmed. . . .

NOTES AND QUESTIONS

1. Things might have worked out differently for Ms. Wimberly if the law was then as it is now. Today, depending on her eligibility for protection under the Family and Medical Leave Act, the amount of statutory "leave" she had when she began maternity leave, and the duration of her maternity leave, her employer might

have been required to restore her to her job. If the employer had denied reinstatement, it might have violated the FMLA unless it could have asserted some defense. Under many unemployment compensation laws today, Ms. Wimberly would have regained her eligibility for benefits as soon as she became "available" for work. *See, e.g.*, Tex. Lab. Code § 207.045.

2. Personal and family conflicts lead to many issues under laws disqualifying claimants because of discharge for "misconduct" (e.g., excessive absenteeism); voluntary resignation (e.g., to have a baby); or unavailability for work (e.g., a claimant's disability or the disability of a dependent). Unemployment compensation tribunals have grown more sympathetic in recent years, frequently refusing to treat some family and personal health conflicts as disqualifying events. *See, e.g.*, Dep't of Corrections v. Stokes, 558 So. 2d 955 (Ala. Civ. App. 1990) (resignation to deal with personal mental health problem caused or aggravated by work was for good cause); McCourtney v. Imprimis Tech., Inc., 465 N.W.2d 721 (Minn. App. 1991) (absences to care for sick child were not misconduct). *But see* In re Williams, 574 N.Y.S.2d 416 (N.Y. App. Div. 1991) (claimant unable to search for work because of difficulty finding babysitter was unavailable and disqualified). *See generally* Martin H. Malin, *Unemployment Compensation in a Time of Increasing Work-Family Conflicts*, 29 U. Mich. J.L. Ref. 131 (1995).

Specific provisions in unemployment compensation laws now address many of these work-family conflicts. *See, e.g.*, Tex. Lab. Code § 207.045 (employee resigning or discharged because of need to care for child, or to relocate with spouse).

3. After misconduct and resignation, a third major ground for disqualification is unavailability for work. A claimant must be available to work in the sense that he would be able to work if offered a job, and he must be seeking work in good faith. A claimant unable to work for reasons of health, family conflicts, or other circumstances is generally not "available," and is disqualified. In some instances, the effects of disqualification for lack of availability are mitigated by eligibility for workers' compensation benefits, disability benefits or other social welfare benefits. However, a worker might be "unavailable" for work and still not be eligible for any other social welfare benefits. *See, e.g.*, Knox v. Unemployment Compensation Bd. of Rev., 12 Pa. Commw. 200, 315 A.2d 915 (1974) (laid-off employee awaiting recall, and telling prospective employers of his expected recall, is disqualified on grounds of unavailability). In the case of laid-off employees awaiting recall, some states now permit the employee to receive benefits pending recall if the employer has provided a definite recall date.

3. *Collective Terminations*

a. Overview

Layoffs affecting an entire class of employees can cause harm beyond the individuals who lose their jobs. A significant reduction in force can cause severe damage to the local community. Local retailers may suffer a significant decline in business. Property values may decline because of a sudden exodus of residents and the lack of demand for residences. Unions, schools and places of worship might suffer a decline in enrollment or membership. For these reasons, local communities or organizations had sometimes asserted often novel legal theories to prevent or delay employer reductions in force. Lawsuits seeking to enjoin eliminations of jobs typically included one of more of three types of claims: (1) the employer promised employees it would preserve their jobs; (2) the employer promised the community it would maintain job-creating operations; and (3) the community or employees have a property interest in the employer's operations. Whether for lack of evidence of an enforceable contract, the unreasonableness of reliance on an alleged promise, or the practical difficulties of recognizing and enforcing the promise or a property interest, such lawsuits have invariably failed. *See, e.g.*, Local 1130, United Steelworkers of Am. v. U.S. Steel Corp., 631 F.2d 1264 (6th Cir. 1980); Charter Township of Ypsilanti v. Gen'l Motors Corp., 506 N.W.2d 556 (Mich. App. 1993) (employer "hyperbole and puffery" in negotiating with township for tax abatement to keep manufacturing operation in the community was not an enforceable promise to maintain operations at that location for any definite period of time; and township did not reasonably rely on employer's representations); Marine Transport Lines, Inc. v. Int'l Org. of Masters, Mates & Pilots, 636 F. Supp. 384, 391 (S.D.N.Y. 1986); Abbington v. Dayton Malleable, Inc., 561 F. Supp. 1290 (S.D. Ohio 1983).

Employees have sometimes, but without much success, challenged plant closings under laws against discrimination or ERISA's noninterference provision where the facility selected for closing has a disproportionate number of older or minority workers. For more on these issues, *see* Chapter 4.D.2.e.

Collective bargaining provides employees at least some opportunity to negotiate rules against restructuring, but the typical collective bargaining agreement has a term of only three years, and even within such a term there are limits to a union's ability to compel an employer to discuss rules, let alone to agree to rules, confining the employer's right to restructure its business and eliminate job-creating work. *See, e.g.*, NLRB v. First Nat'l Maintenance Corp., 452 U.S. 666 (1981) (employer was not required to negotiate with union over a decision to close a part of its business). As a legal and practical matter, unions can be more effective in negotiating the "effects" of employer restructuring, such as by seeking transfer rights or severance pay for employees.

b. The Worker Adjustment and Retraining Notification Act

In 1988, Congress enacted the Worker Adjustment and Retraining Notification Act (WARN Act), which does not restrict an employer's restructuring decisions but does require advance notice to employees, unions, and affected communities. Advance notice, it is hoped, will help employees better prepare for their pending unemployment, begin their search for new opportunities, alert the union (if any) of the need to seek "effects" bargaining for transfer rights and severance pay, and alert local governments of the need to direct unemployment and retraining services and business development programs to the affected community. The act is not limited to employer restructuring resulting in the permanent loss of employment. It also applies to temporary layoffs such as those caused by periodic recessions or other business cycles.

If a layoff is covered by the act, the employer must give 60 days' advance notice. Notice is to each of the affected employees or their union, if there is one; to the chief elected official of the local government within which the closing or layoff occurs; and to the state (or an entity designated by the state). An employer who fails to provide required advance 60-day notice is liable to affected employees for their compensation and benefits for each day of the violation.

Layoffs Covered by the Act. The WARN Act applies only to "mass layoffs" and "plant closings" of a certain magnitude, measured in part by the number of employees affected and in part by the portion of a workforce affected. First, it applies only to employers of at least 100 full-time employees. 29 U.S.C. § 2101(a)(1). Even a complete shutdown of an employer of fewer than 100 employees is not covered, regardless of its actual impact on the local community.

Second, the act applies only to "mass layoffs" or "plant closings." A plant closing is a temporary or permanent shutdown of a "single site," or of one or more facilities or operating units within a single site, if the shutdown results in an "employment loss" for 50 or more full-time employees at the site over any 30-day period. 29 U.S.C. § 2101(a)(3). In contrast, a "mass layoff" might occur even when no particular site or discrete part thereof is entirely closed. A mass layoff is one that, in any 30-day period at a single "site," results in "employment loss" for 50 employees and one-third of the workforce, or for 500 employees whether or not they constitute one-third of the workforce. 29 U.S.C. § 2101(a)(3).

In some instances, an employer's significant layoffs over time might never trigger the act's notification provisions because they occurred as a steady, measured flow and not as a sudden flood. On the other hand, a steady drum-beat of layoffs that never reaches the notification threshold might alert employees and local communities as effectively as an official WARN Act notice.

An "employment loss" that counts toward the thresholds entitling employees to notice is not limited to a complete separation from employment. The act defines "employment loss" as "(A) an employment *termination*, other than a discharge for cause, voluntary departure, or retirement, (B) a *layoff exceeding 6 months*, or (C) *a reduction in hours* of work of more than 50 percent during each month of any 6-month period." 29 U.S.C. § 2101(a)(6). An employee does not suffer an "employment loss" if the employer offers him a transfer to another job "within a reasonable commuting distance," or if the employee actually accepts a transfer regardless of the distance. 29 U.S.C. § 2101(b)(2).

Employees who are laid off on a temporary basis can suffer more than one "employment loss" over time, triggering more than one notification requirement. In Graphic Communications Int'l Union, Local 31-N v. Quebecor Printing Corp., 252 F.3d 296 (4th Cir. 2001), the employer first notified the employees of a pending temporary layoff, and 60 days later it laid the employees off. A few days after the layoff, the employer decided to close the plant, making the previously announced temporary layoff "permanent." Thinking the employees had already received all the WARN Act notice they were due, and that they could suffer no further "employment loss," the employer simply informed the laid off employees that the plant was closing immediately and that they were terminated from employment, with attendant loss of dental insurance, life insurance, and seniority recall rights. In the ensuing WARN Act litigation, the court held that the change from temporary layoff to permanent termination was a new "employment loss" entitling the employees to an additional 60 days' advance notice under the act.

Exemptions Under the Act. There are three exemptions that might relieve an employer from providing a full 60 days' advance notice of the covered event:

(1) *Actively seeking capital or business (faltering business).* The employer was "actively seeking capital or business which, if obtained, would have enabled the employer to avoid or postpone the shutdown and the employer reasonably and in good faith believed that giving the notice required would have precluded the employer from obtaining the needed capital or business."

(2) *Unforeseeable circumstances.* The plant closing or mass layoff was "caused by business circumstances that were not reasonably foreseeable as of the time that notice would have been required."

(3) *Natural disaster.* The plant closing or mass layoff was due to "any form of natural disaster, such as a flood, earthquake. . . ."

29 U.S.C. § 2102(b). An employer relying on one of these exceptions must give as much notice as practicable under the circumstances, together with a "brief statement" of the basis for the shortened notice.

WILSON v. AIRTHERM PRODUCTS, INC.

436 F.3d 906 (8th Cir. 2006)

BOWMAN, Circuit Judge.

Former employees of Airtherm Products, Inc. (API) sued API for failing to notify them of a plant closing as required by the Worker Adjustment and Retraining Notification Act (WARN Act), 29 U.S.C. §§ 2101-09 (2000), before API sold its business to Airtherm LLC (ALLC). Concluding that API violated the WARN Act by terminating its employees' employment without guaranteeing that ALLC would hire the employees after the sale was concluded, the District Court granted summary judgment to the former employees and awarded damages in the amount of $515,661.92. . . . [W]e conclude that the WARN Act's sale-of-business exclusion, 29 U.S.C. § 2101(b)(1), protected API from liability in the circumstances of this case. Therefore, we reverse.

I.

API formerly engaged in the business of manufacturing heating and air conditioning products. In 2000, ALLC's parent company, Mestek, Inc., which also manufactured heating and air conditioning products, became interested in purchasing API's business. When Mestek formed ALLC as a subsidiary for the purchase of API, Mestek decided to use the name Airtherm because that name had value in the heating and air conditioning market. On May 24, 2000, API and ALLC executed an Asset Purchase Agreement (Purchase Agreement) for the sale of API's manufacturing business to ALLC. Under the Purchase Agreement, ALLC agreed to offer employment to all of API's employees. An exhibit appended to the Purchase Agreement contained a list of API's employees. Closing was scheduled for June 30, but the parties did not close the sale on or before that date. On August 21, API and ALLC executed the First Amendment to Asset Purchase Agreement (Amended

Purchase Agreement). The Amended Purchase Agreement replaced the section of the Purchase Agreement that included ALLC's promise to offer employment to all of API's employees with a section that included the following promise: "Effective on the next working day following the Closing Date, [ALLC] (a) shall offer employment to all salaried and clerical employees of [API] in St. Louis and Arkansas; and (b) shall offer employment to employees within the bargaining unit represented by the [union]." The Amended Purchase Agreement also changed the closing date from June 30 to August 25. The Amended Purchase Agreement added provisions under which ALLC agreed to indemnify API for WARN Act violations and API agreed to notify the union in writing about the decision to close the manufacturing plant and allow the union to request bargaining over the effects of the plant closure. Specifically, API agreed to allow ALLC to approve the contents of the letter to the union, and once approved, ALLC promised to indemnify API for any liability under the WARN Act.

On August 22, ALLC assured API in writing that ALLC would "hire a substantial number of [API's] current employees" such that "[t]he jobs of fewer than 50 people will be affected by termination." The letter also included an "Employment Application Schedule" to be posted for API's employees so they would know that ALLC would accept applications from the employees on Monday, August 28, and on Tuesday, August 29. In an August 23 letter from API's attorney to the union representing some of API's employees, API stated that it was "in the process of being sold" to ALLC and notified the union that it was exercising its rights under the labor agreement's "Severance Allowance" clause "to close the plant, terminate the bargaining unit employees, and pay all eligible employees their severance pay." The letter also stated, "It is [API's] understanding that after any sale is concluded [ALLC] will begin taking applications for employment on Monday, August 28, 2000, at 8:30 A.M. It is hoped that all of [API]'s current employees will make application for employment with [ALLC]."

The sale closed on August 25, the same day API terminated the employment of its employees. By September 25, ALLC had hired "a substantial number of former [API] employees." In March 2001, a number of API's former employees, including those hired by ALLC, sued API for failing to give notice of a plant closing under the WARN Act. The District Court granted summary judgment to the employees. In deciding this appeal, we do not address the majority of issues raised by API or the employees. Instead, we focus solely on the District Court's interpretation and application of the WARN Act's sale-of-business exclusion.

II.

The WARN Act requires an employer to provide written notice to employees at least sixty days before a plant closing. 29 U.S.C. § 2102(a)(1). The purpose of the notice requirement is to provide "workers and their families some transition time to adjust to the prospective loss of employment, to seek and obtain alternative jobs and, if necessary, to enter skill training or retraining that will allow these workers to successfully compete in the job market." 20 C.F.R. § 639.1(a) (2005). Although the notice requirement may seem straightforward, its application often depends on the WARN Act's technical definitions. For instance, the WARN Act defines plant closing as "the permanent or temporary shutdown of a single site of employment

. . . result[ing] in an employment loss . . . during any 30-day period for 50 or more [full-time] employees." 29 U.S.C. § 2101(a)(2). The WARN Act defines an employment loss as "an employment termination, other than a discharge for cause, voluntary departure, or retirement." *Id.* § 2101(a)(6)(A).

Critical to this case, however, is the WARN Act's exclusion of sales of businesses from what constitutes an employment loss:

> In the case of a sale of part or all of an employer's business, the seller shall be responsible for providing notice for any plant closing . . . up to and including the effective date of the sale. After the effective date of the sale of part or all of an employer's business, the purchaser shall be responsible for providing notice for any plant closing. . . . Notwithstanding any other provision of this chapter, *any person who is an employee of the seller* (other than a part-time employee) *as of the effective date of the sale shall be considered an employee of the purchaser immediately after the effective date of the sale.*

Id. § 2101(b)(1) (emphasis added). This sale-of-business exclusion stresses that the WARN Act does not automatically require a seller of a business to give notice to its employees that their employment will be terminated as a result of the sale. The regulations explain, "Although a technical termination of the seller's employees may be deemed to have occurred when a sale becomes effective, WARN notice is only required where the employees, in fact, experience a covered employment loss." 20 C.F.R. § 639.6. Therefore, we must apply the sale-of-business exclusion to the facts of this case to determine whether API — as the seller — was required to give notice to its employees of a looming employment loss due to a plant closing.

The plain language of the sale-of-business exclusion supports API's contention that the WARN Act did not require it to provide notice to its employees of a plant closing. Even though a seller of a business technically terminates the employment of its employees—it would be difficult to imagine a sale of a business as a going concern where the seller does not terminate the employment of its employees—the WARN Act does not focus on technical terminations. *See id.* Instead, the WARN Act creates a system that allocates notice responsibility between the seller of the business and the buyer of the business, and only the party actually causing employment loss due to a plant closing is required to provide WARN Act notice. As long as the seller's employees are employed by the seller on the effective date of the sale, those employees automatically are considered to be employees of the buyer "immediately after the effective date of the sale" for purposes of the WARN Act. 29 U.S.C. § 2101(b)(1).

In addition to the WARN Act's plain language strongly suggesting that API, as the seller of a business, had no WARN Act responsibility to provide notice of a plant closing in the circumstances of this case, our Circuit's recent decision in *Smullin* also supports API's position. 420 F.3d at 836-41. Similar to what happened in this case, the seller in *Smullin* terminated the employment of its employees on a Friday, the day it sold its Arkansas manufacturing plant as a going concern to the buyer. Over the weekend, the buyer interviewed and hired forty-four of the plant's sixty-eight employees. On the following Monday, the plant continued operating under the buyer's ownership. The seller's former employees sued the seller for violating the WARN Act by terminating the employment of all sixty-eight employees without proper notification. The district court granted summary judgment to the seller, and the Circuit affirmed. *Id.* at 837.

Writing for the Court, Chief Judge Loken recognized that fewer than fifty employees suffered an employment loss because the buyer immediately hired all but twenty-four of the seller's employees. Thus, the Court concluded that "WARN Act notices were required only if the buyer's hiring must be ignored," which forced the Court to consider § 2101(b)(1)'s sale-of-business exclusion. *Id.* at 838. The plaintiffs argued that the sale-of-business exclusion did not apply "because the sale took the form of a sale of assets, and the plant's employees were terminated by [the seller] with no right to be rehired by the buyer." *Id.* at 839. Rejecting this argument, the Court stated that the sale-of-business exclusion "clearly connotes any transaction that transfers all or part of the employer's overall operations as a going concern." *Id.* Expounding on "this functional, common sense approach," i.e., asking whether the sale of the business involves merely the sale of assets or whether it is a sale of a business as a going concern, the Court noted that this approach "is consistent with the purposes of the WARN Act because the buyer of a going concern is likely to retain a substantial proportion of the employees of the on-going business." *Id.* The Court further opined that "defining the exclusion in this generic fashion promotes compliance with the [WARN] Act because buyers and sellers know when a transaction is intended to transfer a going concern and can determine who must give the WARN Act notice if a covered employment loss is likely to occur." *Id.*

Thus, the Court recognized that when a case involves simply a sale of assets, . . . as opposed to the sale of a business as a going concern, the seller retains the WARN Act notice requirement because the seller is the party actually closing the plant that results in employment losses for fifty or more employees. *Smullin*, 420 F.3d at 839-40. Because the plant in *Smullin* was sold as a going concern, the sale fell within § 2101(b)'s sale-of-business exclusion, so that any potential notice requirement fell on the buyer's shoulders, regardless of the seller's technical termination of its employees' employment that occurred by reason of the sale itself. *Id.* at 841. Because the seller did not owe a duty under the WARN Act and because the buyer did not take any action that violated the WARN Act, the Court held that neither the buyer nor the seller violated the WARN Act. *Id.*

There can be no doubt that employees are entitled to notice under the WARN Act when a qualified plant closing occurs. *See* 20 C.F.R. § 639.4(c) ("Affected employees are always entitled to notice; at all times the employer is responsible for providing notice."). The essential question is whether the seller or the buyer is considered the employer for WARN Act purposes. When the sale of a business as a going concern is involved, the sale-of-business exclusion creates a presumption that the buyer is the employer for WARN Act purposes if the seller still employs its employees on the day of the sale. Unless something indicates otherwise, the sale of a business as a going concern typically will not involve a qualified plant closing with resultant employment loss unless and until the buyer makes such a decision.

In this case, any potential WARN Act notification requirement belonged to ALLC, the buyer of API's business as a going concern. It is undisputed that API did not terminate its employees' employment until August 25, 2000, the date of the sale. We also deem it obvious that API did not close its Arkansas manufacturing plant before August 25. Indeed, API had every reason to believe that the sale of its business would not result in a plant closing, as defined by the WARN Act, because ALLC gave every indication that it was buying API as a going concern. For example, Mestek, Inc., ALLC's parent company, formed ALLC to purchase API, thus keeping the Airtherm name for continuity of operations. In May 2000, ALLC agreed in the Purchase Agreement to hire all of API's employees. Until the Amended Purchase Agreement was executed four days before the sale closed, API absolutely had no reason to believe the sale of its business would result in a plant closing affecting fifty or more employees. When the Amended Purchase Agreement changed the section dealing with the hiring of all of API's employees, ALLC concomitantly promised API that ALLC would hire a substantial number of API's employees such that fewer than fifty employees would lose their jobs as a result of the sale of the business.

In the face of ALLC's assurances, why would API notify its employees of a plant closing? There is no good answer to that question. A simple reading of the WARN Act—with an eye toward its purpose—prescribes that no such notice was required. Indeed, if API had given WARN Act notice to its employees in the face of ALLC's assurances, one could imagine a situation in which no employee would remain by the time the closing date arrived. ALLC, as the buyer of API's business as a going concern, certainly would not be enthused by a vacant labor pool at the time of closing. Thus, the sale-of-business exclusion and our precedent dictate that ALLC became the employees' employer for WARN Act purposes once the sale of API's business became final. Any WARN Act notice responsibilities fell on ALLC, and not on API.

The District Court asked, "[D]oes the 'sale of business' exception apply in cases like this, where assets are sold but the employees are not immediately or actually transferred to the buyer as part of the sale?" This question misses the mark because "nothing in [the] WARN [Act] requires a seller to insist upon a contract term guaranteeing its employees continued employment with the buyer." Int'l Alliance of Theatrical & Stage Employees & Moving Picture Mach. Operators, AFL-CIO v. Compact Video Servs., Inc., 50 F.3d 1464, 1468 (9th Cir.), *cert. denied*, 516 U.S. 987 (1995). Similarly, it is presumed that a sale of a business as a going concern involves the hiring of the seller's employees unless something indicates otherwise. Focusing on whether the seller terminated its employees' employment is not the proper focus when analyzing potential WARN Act violations involving the sale of a business as a going concern. Instead, the WARN Act takes a "functional, common sense approach," *Smullin*, 420 F.3d at 839, attempting to determine who actually effects the plant closing. An example might illustrate why the District Court's question lacked the proper focus. Assume that API terminated its employees' employment on the day of the sale of its business as a going concern without guaranteeing that its employees would gain employment with ALLC. But ALLC had assured API that ALLC would hire a substantial number of API's employees such that fewer than fifty employees would suffer an employment loss under the WARN Act. On the day after the sale, ALLC hired all of API's employees, including every employee that had been laid off by API over the past ten years. If we were to apply the District Court's and the plaintiffs' interpretation of the WARN Act, we would be required to hold API liable for failing to give WARN Act notice to its employees regardless of the fact that all of API's employees were hired by the buyer. The WARN Act does not compel such an absurd result. Without the benefit of *Smullin*, the District Court wrongly focused on API's technical termination of its employees' employment on the day of the sale rather than focusing on whether there was a sale of a business as a going concern and on what API and ALLC anticipated as to employee hiring.

III.

For the reasons stated, we reverse the grant of summary judgment to the plaintiffs and remand to the District Court to enter judgment in API's favor.

NOTES AND QUESTIONS

1. *Wilson* suggests a distinction between the sale of a business as a going concern—continuing its operations with little or no interruption after a change of ownership—versus a sale of assets in which operations cease and assets are distributed to one or more other business operations. In the case of a sale of assets, there may be a real employment loss triggering the employees' right to WARN Act notice. The duty to give such notice will rest with the seller, because the buyer will not have become the employer of the employees.

Unfortunately, the nature of the transaction might not become clear until it is too late for employees to receive effective WARN Act notice. In Burnsides v. MJ Optical, Inc., 128 F.3d 700 (8th Cir. 1997), for example, the seller engaged in negotiations for the sale of a failing business. During most of the negotiations, the seller evidently assumed that the buyer would continue the employment of the employees, in addition to taking assets. However, a few days before the closing, the buyer insisted that while it would purchase certain assets, it would not continue operations at the seller's plant. On the day of the closing, the seller terminated the employees, and the buyer did not rehire them.

The employees sued the seller and the buyer for failing to give notice, but the court rejected the claim against the buyer. "Even if this case involves the "sale of part or all of an employer's business" within the meaning of § 2101(b), responsibility for giving notice never passed to [the buyer] because the plant closing occurred on the sale's effective date. Through the end of that day, the employees were still employed by [the seller]." 128 F.3d at 703.

The duty to provide notice was owed by the seller, but the seller had the benefit of the affirmative defense with respect to a plant closing "caused by business circumstances that were not reasonably foreseeable [when the sixty-day] notice would have been required." 29 U.S.C. § 2101(b)(2)(A). The court held that the buyer's last minute refusal to take over operations of the facility constituted unforeseeable circumstances. However, § 2102(b)(3) provides that in a case of unforeseeable circumstances, an employer "shall give as much notice as is practicable and . . . a brief statement of the basis for reducing the notification period." The seller had given its employees neither the four days advance notice that might have been possible, nor a "brief statement" explaining the lack of sixty days' notice. The court therefore remanded the case for further proceedings to determine the seller's possible liability to the employees.

2. The unforeseeable circumstances defense has engendered considerable

litigation under the WARN Act. Employers frequently accumulate knowledge of trouble over a long period of time before they are certain of the result. The WARN Act does not require an employer to be an especially accurate prognosticator. *See* 20 C.F.R. § 639.9(b)(1)-(2) ("employer must exercise . . . commercially reasonable business judgment . . . in predicting the demands of its particular market," but is not required "to accurately predict general economic conditions that also may affect demand for its products or services"). Still there are likely to have been multiple events that were signals of trouble. The earliest signals of pending trouble may have occurred with plenty of time for an employer to give 60-day notice. How optimistic is an employer entitled to be in ignoring bad news for WARN Act purposes? *See* Halkias v. Gen'l Dynamics Corp., 137 F.3d 333 (5th Cir. 1998) (cancellation of contract to build aircraft was not a foreseeable probability until Secretary of Defense directed Navy to show cause why contract should not be canceled due to cost overrun, even though employer knew of possible cancellation and layoffs months earlier, because Navy and Secretary had previously expressed unwavering support for the contract).

3. Why might an employer be so reluctant to speak forthrightly with employees about their prospects when an employer realizes there is a grave risk that he will need to close a facility or reduce his workforce? With respect to the faltering business defense, Department of Labor regulations state as follows:

> The employer must be able to objectively demonstrate that it reasonably thought that a potential customer or source of financing would have been unwilling to provide the new business or capital if notice were given, that is, if the employees, customers, or the public were aware that the facility, operating unit, or site might have to close. This condition may be satisfied if the employer can show that the financing or business source would not choose to do business with a troubled company or with a company whose workforce would be looking for other jobs.

29 C.F.R. § 639.9(a)(4).

4. If employees surmise what their employer has concealed, is their actual knowledge an excuse for the employer's failure to provide official WARN Act notice? *See* Local 1239 v. Allsteel, Inc., 9 F. Supp. 2d 901 (N.D. Ill. 1998) (no).

5. The WARN Act does not preempt state laws or other sources of more generous leave or severance "except that the period of notification required by this chapter shall run concurrently with any period of notification required by contract or by any other statute." 29 U.S.C. § 2105. A number of states have enacted their own plant closing laws, sometimes applying to a broader range of workforce reductions, and sometimes requiring substantially more notice or imposing other responsibilities on an employer. *E.g.*, Cal. Lab. Code §§ 1400-1408 (extending notice requirements to smaller layoffs); Mass. Gen. Laws Ann. ch. 149 § 182 (applying to "[a]ny person utilizing financing issued, insured, or subsidized by a quasi-public agency of the commonwealth" and requiring 90 days' notice and reemployment assistance); Me. Rev. Stat. Ann. tit. 26, § 625-B (requiring one week's severance pay for each year of employment).

CHAPTER 9

Protecting the Employer's Interests

A. IMPLIED EMPLOYER RIGHTS AND EMPLOYEE DUTIES

Courts frequently describe employment as a unilateral contract in which an employer makes promises of compensation and benefits, and an employee accepts these promises by working. The unilateral model is useful for some purposes, especially for the majority of employees who work for an indefinite duration and are free to resign at any time. Whether or not an employee makes any express promise, however, the employee owes some implied duties to the employer in connection with the employee's access to, and use and management of the employer's resources and relationships with clients and other personnel. These duties tend to become especially critical toward the end of the employment, when the employer's and employee's interests can diverge quite dramatically.

1. The Employee's Implied Duty of Loyalty

If employment at will is a unilateral contract—an employer's promise to pay in exchange for an employee's service—the employee owes no contractual duties. The employee has not promised to work. If the employee fails to provide service, serves poorly, or annoys the employer or other employees, the employer can discharge the employee and revoke its offer to pay, but the employer cannot sue the employee for breach of contract. If the employee negligently or intentionally damages employer property, the employer's cause of action against the employee is in tort, not contract. The employee has made no promise unless employment was for a fixed term and included the employee's promise to serve for the fixed term.

The unilateral model of employment at will works well enough for many purposes but overlooks the possibility of implied contractual duties an employee owes. An employer might reasonably expect the employee, in return for access to the employer's resources, to promise not to use these resources to serve interests detrimental to the employer. If the employee owes such an implied duty of "loyalty," the consequence of a breach could be more than termination. A disloyal employee might be liable to the employer for damages caused by a breach.

JET COURIER SERV., INC. v. MULEI

771 P.2d 486 (Colo. 1989)

LOHR, Justice.

. . . Jet is an air courier company engaged principally in supplying a specialized transportation service to customer banks. Jet provides air and incidental ground courier service to carry canceled checks between banks to facilitate rapid processing of those checks through the banking system. Shortened processing time enables the banks at which the checks are cashed to make use of the funds sooner.

Because the sums involved are large, substantial amounts of daily interest are at stake. As a result, the ability to assure speedy deliveries is essential to compete effectively in the air courier business.

In 1981 Jet was an established family-owned corporation headed by Donald W. Wright. The principal offices of the corporation were in Cincinnati, Ohio. Jet had no office in Denver. Anthony Mulei at that time was working in Denver for another air courier service in a management capacity. Mulei had worked in the air courier business for a number of years and was very familiar with it. He had numerous business connections in the banking industry in Denver and other cities. On February 18, 1981, Wright and Mulei agreed that Mulei would come to work for Jet and would open a Denver office and manage Jet's Western Zone operations from that office. They orally agreed that Mulei would be vice president and general manager for the Western Zone and would have autonomy in matters such as the solicitation of business, the operation of the business, and personnel policies. . . .

Mulei performed services as agreed and was successful in significantly increasing the business of Jet in the Western Zone as well as other areas of the United States. . . . [However], Mulei became progressively dissatisfied with his inability to resolve [a] bonus issue and with what he believed to be intrusions into his promised areas of autonomy in personnel and operational matters. Toward the end of 1982 he began to look for other work in the air courier field and sought legal advice concerning the validity of the noncompetition covenant in his employment contract.

In the course of seeking other employment opportunities and while still employed by Jet, Mulei began to investigate setting up another air courier company that would compete with Jet in the air courier business. In January 1983, Mulei spoke with John Towner, a Kansas air charter operator who was in the business of supplying certain air transportation services, about going into business together. In February 1983, Mulei met with Towner and two Jet employees to discuss setting up this new business and obtaining customers. . . .

[American Check Transport, Inc. (ACT)] was incorporated on February 28, 1983. Mulei was elected president at the first shareholders meeting. On behalf of Jet, Wright fired Mulei on March 10, 1983, when Wright first learned of Mulei's organization of a competing enterprise. On that same day Mulei caused ACT to become operational and compete with Jet. Five Denver banks that had been Jet customers became ACT customers at that time. Additionally, when Mulei was fired, three of the four other employees in Jet's Denver office also left Jet and joined ACT. All of Jet's ground carriers in Denver immediately left Jet and joined ACT. All nine of Jet's pilots in Denver either quit or were fired. Jet was able to maintain its Denver operations only through a rapid and massive transfer of resources, including chartered aircraft and ground couriers, from Jet's other offices.

Mulei filed suit against Jet in Denver District Court on March 10, 1983, the same day he was fired, seeking principally to recover unpaid compensation. . . . Jet counterclaimed for breach of contract, breach of fiduciary duty, and civil conspiracy and sought damages and other relief. Jet also filed a separate suit in Denver District Court against ACT . . . alleging a civil conspiracy among Towner, Mulei, ACT, Towner's air charter company, and others to harm Jet's business interests and seeking damages and injunctive relief.

The two cases were consolidated for trial. The district court concluded that . . . Mulei was entitled to salary and bonus compensation totaling $93,740.34 plus a fifty-percent statutory penalty of $46,870.17 pursuant to section 8-4-104, as well as vacation pay, attorney fees in connection with the compensation and penalty claims, interest, and costs. The district court also concluded that Mulei did not violate his duty of loyalty to Jet. . . . The court of appeals affirmed the district court's judgment. . . .

Whether an employee's actions in preparation for competing with his employer constitute a breach of the employee's duty of loyalty is an issue of first impression for this court. We derive guidance in determining the nature of an employee's duty of loyalty from the Restatement (Second) of Agency and from the decisions of other jurisdictions applying the standards found in the Restatement.

Section 387 of the Restatement (Second) of Agency provides that "[u]nless otherwise agreed, an agent is subject to a duty to his principal to act solely for the benefit of the principal in all matters connected with his agency." Rest. (2d) Agency § 387 (1957). . . . Underlying the duty of loyalty arising out of the employment relationship is the policy consideration that commercial competition must be conducted through honesty and fair dealing. "Fairness dictates that an employee not be permitted to exploit the trust of his employer so as to obtain an unfair advantage in competing with the employer in a matter concerning the latter's business." [Maryland Metals, Inc. v. Metzner, 282 Md. 31, 382 A.2d 564, 568 (1978).]

Thus, one facet of the duty of loyalty is an agent's "duty not to compete with the principal concerning the subject matter of his agency." Rest. (2d) Agency § 393. A limiting consideration in delineating the scope of an agent's duty not to compete is society's interest in fostering free and vigorous economic competition. In attempting to accommodate the competing policy considerations of honesty and fair dealing on the one hand and free and vigorous economic competition on the other, courts have recognized "a privilege in favor of employees which enables them to prepare or make arrangements to compete with their employers prior to leaving the employ of their prospective rivals without fear of incurring liability for breach of their fiduciary duty of loyalty." *Maryland Metals*, 382 A.2d at 569. . . .

Given the employee's duty of loyalty to and duty not to compete with his employer and the employee's corresponding privilege to make preparations to compete after termination of his employment, the issue here is whether Mulei's pre-termination meetings with Jet's customers and his co-employees to discuss ACT's future operations constituted violations of his duty of loyalty or whether these meetings were merely legally permissible preparations to compete.

. . . The court of appeals affirmed the trial court's holding that Mulei's pretermination meetings with customers did not violate a duty of loyalty since ACT did not become operational and commence competing with Jet until after Mulei left Jet's employ. This reasoning fails to accord adequate scope to the duty of loyalty outlined in the Restatement and the cases cited above. While still employed by Jet, Mulei was subject to a duty of loyalty to act solely for the benefit of Jet in all matters connected with his employment. Rest. (2d) Agency § 387. Jet was entitled to receive Mulei's undivided loyalty. The fact that ACT did not commence operations and begin competing with Jet until after Mulei's departure from Jet is not dispositive. Instead, the key inquiry is whether Mulei's meetings amounted to solicitation, which would be a breach of his duty of loyalty. Generally, under his privilege to make preparations to compete after the termination of his employment, an employee may advise current customers that he will be leaving his current employment. *See* Maryland Metals, Inc. v. Metzner, 382 A.2d 564, 569 n.3 (Md. 1978); Crane Co. v. Dahle, 576 P.2d 870, 872-73 (Utah 1978). . . . However, any pre-termination solicitation of those customers for a new competing business violates an employee's duty of loyalty. Rest. (2d) Agency § 393 comment e.

. . . The trial court concluded that Mulei did not violate a duty of loyalty to Jet. In its findings of fact, the trial court stated that

ACT was able, through the solicitation of [Mulei] before and after termination, to acquire business of certain banks, some of which had agreements with Jet.

Based on these findings and the record before us, we are unable to determine whether Mulei's pre-termination meetings with Jet's customers amounted to impermissible solicitation or were merely allowable preparations for competition. We cannot determine, for instance, whether Mulei specifically solicited Jet's customers before he was fired by Jet. . . . Accordingly, this case must be returned to the trial court for retrial to determine whether under the standards governing an employee's duty of loyalty set forth in this opinion, Mulei's pretermination meetings with Jet's customers amounted to impermissible solicitation in violation of his duty of loyalty to Jet.

We next consider whether the court of appeals erred in concluding that Mulei's meetings with Jet employees did not breach his duty of loyalty. An employee's duty of loyalty applies to the solicitation of co-employees, as well as to the solicitation of customers, during the time the soliciting employee works for his employer. Generally, an employee breaches his duty of loyalty if prior to the termination of his own employment, he solicits his co-employees to join him in his new competing enterprise. Rest. (2d) Agency § 393 comment e. . . .

. . . In concluding that there was no breach of Mulei's duty of loyalty, the court of appeals relied on its previous decision in Electrolux Corp. v. Lawson, 654 P.2d 340 (Colo. App. 1982). . . . In *Electrolux*, . . . [t]he court of appeals read the Restatement (Second) of Agency § 393 comment e as imposing liability for breach of an employee's duty not to compete only when "he causes his fellow employees to breach a contract." 654 P.2d at 341. Because the Electrolux workers' employment contracts were terminable at will, their resignations did not constitute a breach of their employment contracts. Thus, reasoned the court of appeals, since there was no breach of any employment contracts there was no breach of the manager's duty not to compete. *Id.*

Comment e to section 393 of the Restatement notes that the "limits of proper conduct with reference to securing the services of fellow employees are not well marked." The comment goes on to state that an "employee is subject to liability if, before or after leaving the employment, he causes fellow employees to break their contracts with the employer." Rest. (2d) Agency § 393 comment e. However, the Restatement neither implies nor explicitly states . . . that causing co-employees to break their contracts is the only instance where an employee will be liable for breaching his duty of loyalty by soliciting co-employees. For instance, the Restatement notes that "a court may find that it is a breach of duty for a number of the key officers or employees to agree to leave their employment simultaneously and without giving the employer an opportunity to hire and train replacements." *Id.* . . . [W]e conclude that a court should focus on the following factors in determining whether an employee's actions amount to impermissible solicitation of co-workers. A court should consider the nature of the employment relationship, the impact or potential impact of the employee's actions on the employer's operations, and the extent of any benefits promised or inducements made to co-workers to obtain their services for the new competing enterprise. No single factor is dispositive; instead, a court must examine the nature of an employee's preparations to compete to determine if they amount to impermissible solicitation. Additionally, an employee's solicitation of coworkers need not be successful in order to establish a breach of his duty of loyalty. Rest. (2d) Agency § 469 comment a (agent breaches duty of loyalty by acting in competition with principal even though agent's conduct does not harm principal).

Under this flexible approach, traditional actions by departing employees, such as the executive who leaves with her secretary, the mechanic who leaves with his apprentice, or the firm partner who leaves with associates from her department, would not give rise to a breach of the duty of loyalty unless other factors, such as an intent to injure the employer in the continuation of his business, were present.

. . . Again, based on the trial court's findings and the record before us, we are unable to determine whether Mulei's pre-termination meetings with his Jet co-employees were permissible preparations for competition or whether these actions constituted solicitation of co-employees that amounted to a breach of his duty of loyalty. Accordingly, this case must be returned to the trial court for retrial for the additional purpose of determining whether under the standards of an employee's duty of loyalty set forth in this opinion, Mulei's pre-termination meetings with Jet co-employees amounted to impermissible solicitation in violation of his duty of loyalty.

The trial court concluded that Mulei did not violate any duty of loyalty to Jet in part because he "continued to operate the Western Zone on a profitable, efficient and service-oriented basis." Mulei now contends that this finding regarding his profitable operation of Jet's Western Zone precludes a determination that he breached any duty of loyalty to Jet. We disagree.

. . . We conclude that these same principles are applicable here. The key inquiry in determining whether Mulei breached his duty of loyalty is not whether Jet's Western Zone was profitable. Instead, the focus is on whether Mulei acted solely for Jet's benefit in all matters connected with his employment, and whether Mulei competed with Jet during his employment, *see* Rest. (2d) Agency §§ 387, 393, giving due regard to Mulei's right to make preparations to compete. Accordingly, the fact that Mulei operated Jet's Western Zone efficiently and profitably does not preclude a determination that he breached his duty of loyalty to Jet by his pre-termination actions.

Neither does the fact that Jet failed to make the agreed-upon quarterly bonus payments excuse Mulei from being subject to a duty of loyalty to Jet. . . . Assuming, without deciding, that Jet's nonpayment amounted to a material breach of Mulei's employment agreement, then Mulei had the option of renouncing his authority and leaving Jet's employ. *See* Rest. (2d) Agency § 415 comment a. However, there is no evidence in the record indicating that Mulei renounced his authority; instead, the record shows he continued to act for Jet and to operate the Western Zone despite Jet's failure to make the quarterly bonus payments. If the trial court finds on retrial that Mulei did not renounce his agency/employment relation with Jet, then he had a duty to continue that relationship and a corresponding duty of loyalty. *See id.* §§ 387, 415. Thus, Jet's breach of the employment agreement would not excuse Mulei from being subject to a continuing duty of loyalty to act solely for Jet's benefit in all matters connected with his employment until the time his employment with Jet was terminated on March 10, 1983. . . .

In order to provide guidance to the trial court on remand in the event it determines that Mulei breached his duty of loyalty to Jet, we consider the remaining issues on which we granted certiorari.

Jet argues that Mulei would not be entitled to any compensation or bonus payments for the period in which he was disloyal. We agree.

The general rule is that an employee is not entitled to any compensation for services performed during the period he engaged in activities constituting a breach of his duty of loyalty even though part of these services may have been properly performed. Rest. (2d) Agency § 469 ("agent is entitled to no compensation for conduct . . . which is a breach of his duty of loyalty").

. . . However, if Mulei breached any duty of loyalty, he could still recover compensation for services properly rendered during periods in which no such breach occurred and for which compensation is apportioned in his employment agreement. Rest. (2d) Agency §§ 456, 469. Apportioned compensation is that paid to an agent or employee that is allocated to certain periods of time or to the completion of specified items of work. Rest. (2d) Agency § 456 comment b.

Mulei's employment contract provided that his salary was to be paid on a monthly basis, and that his bonus was to be calculated and paid on a quarterly basis. Applying the principles outlined above, if on retrial the trial court concludes that Mulei breached his duty of loyalty to Jet, then Mulei would be entitled to compensation for services properly performed during periods in which no such breach occurred and for which compensation is apportioned in the employment agreement. Moreover, under this apportionment approach, Mulei would not be entitled to any salary compensation for any month during which he engaged in acts breaching his duty of loyalty, nor would he be entitled to any bonus payments for any quarter during which he engaged in acts breaching his duty of loyalty. . . .

[W]e reverse that portion of the court of appeals' judgment affirming the trial court's conclusion that Mulei did not breach his duty of loyalty to Jet. . . . We remand the case to the court of appeals for further remand to the district court with directions to reinstate and retry Jet's counterclaim for breach of duty of loyalty. . . .

NOTES AND QUESTIONS

1. In the original trial of Mulei's and Jet Courier's respective claims against each other, the trial court dismissed Jet Courier's claims and awarded Mulei

$202,000 based on Jet Courier's failure to pay compensation and bonuses due under the terms of the employment contract. After the Colorado Supreme Court reversed and remanded for further consideration of Jet Courier's claims related to Mulei's alleged disloyalty, the parties reached a settlement in which Jet Courier paid Mulei an amount substantially less than Mulei's original judgment. Mulei v. Jet Courier Serv., Inc., 860 P.2d 569 (Colo. App. 1993).

2. The court in *Jet Courier* distinguishes an employee's lawful pre-departure preparation to compete from active, disloyal competition, such as by solicitation of customers and fellow employees. When an employee is starting a new business from scratch, lawful preparation might include nearly anything necessary to form the business and make it ready to compete as soon as the employee resigns. *See, e.g.*, Harllee v. Professional Serv. Indus., Inc., 619 So. 2d 298 (Fla. App. 1992) (opening bank account, obtaining office space and telephone service were permissible acts of preparation); Mercer Mgmt. Consulting, Inc. v. Wilde, 920 F. Supp. 219 (D.D.C. 1996) (no breach of duty in incorporating business, arranging for office space, meeting with accountant).

3. If it is neither wise nor practical to prohibit an employee from preparing to compete, should the law at least require the employee to disclose his plans to his employer? *Compare* Crawford & Co. v. M. Hayes & Assocs., L.L.C., 13 Fed. Appx. 174, 177 (4th Cir. 2001) (no breach of duty in failing to disclose competitive business plans, provided employee took no other actions inimical to employer's interest), *and* Western Med. Consultants, Inc. v. Johnson, 835 F. Supp. 554 (D. Or. 1993) (no breach of duty in failure to disclose plans), *with* Bancroft-Whitney Co. v. Glen, 411 P.2d 921 (Cal. 1966) (corporate officer breached fiduciary duty by failing to disclose his preparations to compete, based on "particular circumstances" that included soliciting employees after recommending that employer should defer raising their salaries).

4. Solicitation of customers is one way a departing employee might breach his duty to his employer. In *Jet Courier*, however, the court suggests an employee is entitled to "advise current customers that he will be leaving his current employment" even before he has given the same notice to his own employer, provided he does not actively "solicit" customers. When does an employee, in communicating with customers, cross the line between mere disclosure of future plans and disloyal "solicitation"? *See* Mercer Mgmt. Consulting, Inc. v. Wilde, 920 F. Supp. 219 (D.D.C. 1996) ("the Court finds unreasonable and unrealistic the proposition that any client contact prior to leaving one's employment and starting a competing business constitutes a breach of one's fiduciary duty" in the absence of "overt solicitation . . . or other improper actions"); Nilan's Alley, Inc. v. Ginsburg, 430 S.E.2d 368 (Ga. App. 1993) (salesman did not breach duty when he inquired of customers whether they would consider continuing to place orders through him if he changed his employment; conversations were mere preparation for postemployment competition and not direct competition).

Would it be disloyal solicitation for an employee to tell customers he will be leaving to form a new business or join an established one, and that his purpose is to provide better service?

5. Pre-departure solicitation of fellow employees is another matter. On the whole, courts appear to be more reluctant to find a breach of duty in pre- departure

communication with a fellow employee than with a customer. In the case of a customer, for example, it seems clear that solicitation is improper even if the customer's relationship with the employer is "at will" and the solicitation causes no breach of contract with the employer. The employee's breach of duty is in *competing* whether or not he "interferes" with his employer's customer contracts. The question whether an employee breaches any duty to his employer by soliciting *fellow employees* for their participation in a competing enterprise is more difficult to answer.

The Restatements of Agency and Torts offer two different answers to the question whether a person may solicit the services of another person's "at will" employee. Section 768 of the Restatement (Second) of Torts states that a competitor ordinarily commits no tort by soliciting an "at will" employee of another employer, provided the competitor does not use wrongful means, and acts at least partly for legitimate competitive reasons and not to create an unlawful restraint of trade. But a prospectively departing employee's position, unlike other prospective competitors, owes the employer a duty of loyalty as long as he or she remains employed. The employee's actions are more appropriately judged under section 393 of the Restatement (Second) of Agency. However, as the court notes in *Jet Courier Service*, that Restatement's view of interference with "at will" employment relations is ambiguous. The contractual status of solicited employees appears to be an important factor but not the only factor in determining whether a departing employee may lawfully recruit them. *But see* Sun Life Assur. Co. of Canada v. Coury, 838 F. Supp. 586, 590-591 (S.D. Fla. 1993) ("Without an employment contract, section 393 of the Restatement is inapplicable."). Moreover, even if solicitation of an at-will employee *could* be a breach of the solicitor's duty of loyalty, it is not *necessarily* a breach. *See* Restatement (Second) of Agency § 393 cmt. e; Crawford & Co. v. M. Hayes & Assocs., L.L.C., 13 Fed. Appx. 174 (4th Cir. 2001) (unpublished) (no breach of duty where defendant discussed planned post-employment plans with subordinate mid-level managers, and six of these managers later joined defendant in her new business).

6. When courts find a breach of duty of loyalty because of fellow employee solicitation, they frequently emphasize the harm caused by the additional loss of a team of defecting employees, especially if the defectors were so numerous or important that their sudden departure significantly impaired the employer's business. *See, e.g.*, Veco Corp. v. Babcock, 611 N.E.2d 1054 (Ill. App. 1993) (defendants believed their mass exodus would cripple their employer, and used this predicted scenario to solicit employer's customers in advance of their departure); Augat, Inc. v. Aegis, Inc., 565 N.E.2d 415 (Mass. 1991) (general manager breached duty by seeking to hire key managers away from employer); Duane Jones Co. v. Burke, 117 N.E.2d 237 (N.Y. 1954) (defendant employees breached duty by inducing a "mass exodus" of a majority of employer's key personnel).

7. Would it be appropriate or realistic to prohibit an employee from soliciting a close personal friend or associate to join in forming a new venture or moving to a competing employer? *See, e.g.*, Western Med. Consultants, Inc. v. Johnson, 835 F. Supp. 554 (D. Or. 1993) (departing employee did not breach duty by hiring receptionist who was her sister and roommate). *But see* Hill v. Names & Addresses, Inc., 571 N.E.2d 1085 (Ill. App. 1991) (employee breached duty of

loyalty by soliciting her assistant to join her prospective new employer).

8. There are other ways a departing employee might violate his employer's trust even without pre-departure solicitation of customers and employees. *See, e.g.*, Alagold Corp. v. Freeman, 20 F. Supp. 2d 1305 (M.D. Ala. 1998) (employee continued to access and learn confidential information about his employer's business for two months after accepting employment and an advance payment of compensation from competitor); Koontz v. Rosener, 787 P.2d 192 (Colo. App. 1989) (salespersons listed some properties for short periods, and failed to list other properties, so that properties would be free for listing by competing agency after their resignation); Platinum Mgmt., Inc. v. Dahms, 666 A.2d 1028 (N.J. Super. 1995) (employee delayed appointments with customers until after his resignation and beginning of employment with a competitor); FryeTech, Inc. v. Harris, 46 F. Supp. 2d 1144 (D. Kan. 1999) (after employer designated certain equipment to be dismantled and sold for scrap, employees deceptively acquired the equipment for use in their new competing business).

9. The departing and subsequently competing employee is the most common, but not the only occasion for an employer to invoke the duty of loyalty. Another potential situation for application of the duty of loyalty is the "lost opportunity" case: An employee, particularly an upper management official with elevated fiduciary duties, may not secretly compete with his employer for business opportunities, such as by acquiring the same property the employer had sought to acquire. *See* Regal-Beloit Corp. v. Drecoll, 955 F. Supp. 849 (N.D. Ill. 1996). For another, but ultimately unsuccessful application, see the discussion of union "salts" who accept employment for the purpose of organizing an employer's employees, at p. 44-45, *supra*. *But see* Food Lion, Inc. v. Capital Cities/ABC, Inc., 194 F.3d 505 (4th Cir. 1999) (television reporters who obtained employment with grocery store for purpose of surreptitious investigation of grocery violated duty of loyalty, because their intent in maintaining duel employment was to act against the interests of the plaintiff employer).

10. Even if an employee's conduct falls short of breaching the duty of loyalty, the mere fact that the employee is preparing to compete may constitute "cause" for discharge. *See. e.g.*, Long v. Vertical Techs., Inc.,, 439 S.E.2d (N.C.App.1994); Stokes v. Dole Nut Co., 48 Cal. Rptr. 2d 673 (Cal. App. 1995).

2. *Inventions, Trade Secrets and Other Property Interests*

a. The Employer's Shop Right

The usual rule is that an invention is the property of the person who conceived and developed it. Standing alone, the fact that the inventor is someone's employee has no bearing on his ownership of the invention unless the inventor was employed for the very purpose of inventing such things for his employer. In the latter case, the invention belongs to the employer, as would any other thing the employer engaged and paid the employee to make. Standard Parts Co. v. Peck, 264 U.S. 52 (1924). It is not uncommon, however, for an employee hired for nearly any other purpose to have an idea or invent something that relates to his work and is useful to his employer. When the employee invents outside the purpose of his employment but with the support and encouragement of the employer, the parties' respective rights in the invention may lie somewhere between exclusive employee/inventor ownership and exclusive employer ownership.

McELMURRY v. ARKANSAS POWER & LIGHT CO.

995 F.2d 1576 (Fed. Cir. 1993)

RICH, Circuit Judge.

Max C. McElmurry and White River Technologies, Inc. (WRT) appeal the February 10, 1992 Judgment of the U.S. District Court . . . that AP&L holds "shop rights" to certain subject matter claimed in U.S. Patent No. 4,527,714, titled "Pressure Responsive Hopper Level Detector System" (Bowman patent), and thus, as a matter of law, AP&L had not infringed any claim of the Bowman patent. For the reasons set forth below, we affirm. . . .

AP&L hired Harold L. Bowman, the patentee, as a consultant on October 24, 1980, to assist in the installation, maintenance and operation of electrostatic precipitators at AP&L's White Bluff Steam Electric Station (White Bluff) located near Redfield, Arkansas. . . . Prior to April of 1982, the precipitator hoppers at White Bluff employed a level detector system using a nuclear power source (K-ray system) to detect the level of fly ash in the hoppers.

AP&L was not satisfied with the K-ray system. As a result, in the early part of 1982, Bowman discussed with a Mr. Richard L. Roberts, an AP&L employee, replacing the K-ray system with a new level detector, an initial design of which they drew on a napkin. . . .

AP&L considered the proposed level detector and, during a power outage in March of 1982, ordered its installation on one hopper at White Bluff for testing purposes. . . . When this system proved successful, AP&L ordered that the level detectors be installed on the remaining one hundred and twelve (112) precipitator hoppers at White Bluff. All costs associated with the installation and testing of the level detector . . . at White Bluff, including materials and working drawings, were paid by AP&L.

. . . In November of 1982, Bowman formed White Rivers Technology, Inc. . . . Bowman filed a patent application on the level detector on February 18, 1983, and the patent-in-suit issued on July 9, 1985. At some point prior to its issuance, Bowman assigned his patent rights to WRT.

. . . In 1985, based upon the success of the level detector on the precipitator hoppers at White Bluff and ISES, [AP&L] implemented a plan to install the level detector on fourteen (14) hydroveyer hoppers at ISES. [Bowman's company, WRT, bid on the project, but AP&L selected other contractors because WRT was not the low bidder.] In soliciting bids on the hydroveyer project, AP&L provided the contractors with specifications prepared by AP&L showing the work to be performed. . . .

On April 25, 1990, WRT brought suit against AP&L for patent infringement based on AP&L's solicitation of and contracting with a party other than WRT to install Bowman's patented level detector on the hydroveyer hoppers at ISES. The district court granted summary judgment in favor of AP&L on the basis that AP&L

had acquired a "shop right" in the level detector claimed in the Bowman patent. . . . WRT then appealed to this court.

A "shop right" is generally accepted as being a right that is created at common law, when the circumstances demand it, under principles of equity and fairness, entitling an employer to use without charge an invention patented by one or more of its employees without liability for infringement. *See generally* D. Chisum, Patents, § 22.02[3] (1985 rev.); C.T. Dreschler, Annotation, *Application and Effect of "Shop Right Rule" or License Giving Employer Limited Rights in Employee's Inventions and Discoveries*, 61 A.L.R.2d 356 (1958); P. Rosenberg, Patent Law Fundamentals, § 11.04, 11-20 (1991). However, as recognized by several commentators, the immense body of case law addressing the issue of "shop rights" suggests that not all courts agree as to the doctrinal basis for "shop rights," and, consequently, not all courts agree as to the particular set of circumstances necessary to create a "shop right."

For example, many courts characterize a "shop right" as being a type of implied license, and thus the focus is often on whether the employee engaged in any activities, e.g., developing the invention on the employer's time at the employer's expense, which demand a finding that he impliedly granted a license to his employer to use the invention. Other courts characterize a "shop right" as a form of equitable estoppel, and thus the focus is often on whether the employee's actions, e.g., consent or acquiescence to his employer's use of the invention, demand a finding that he is estopped from asserting a patent right against his employer. Neither characterization appears to be inherently better than the other, and the end result under either is often the same, given that the underlying analysis in each case is driven by principles of equity and fairness, and given that the courts often analyze a "shop right" as being a combination of the two even though they may characterize it in name as one or the other.

It is thus not surprising that many courts adopt neither characterization specifically, instead choosing to characterize a "shop right" more broadly as simply being a common law "right" that inures to an employer when the circumstances demand it under principles of equity and fairness. These courts often look to both the circumstances surrounding the development of the invention and the facts regarding the employee's activities respecting that invention, once developed, to determine whether it would be fair and equitable to allow an employee to preclude his employer from making use of that invention. This is essentially the analysis that most courts undertake regardless of how they characterize "shop rights."

In view of the foregoing, we believe that the proper methodology for determining whether an employer has acquired a "shop right" in a patented invention is to look to the totality of the circumstances on a case by case basis and determine whether the facts of a particular case demand, under principles of equity and fairness, a finding that a "shop right" exists. In such an analysis, one should look to such factors as the circumstances surrounding the development of the patented invention and the inventor's activities respecting that invention, once developed, to determine whether equity and fairness demand that the employer be allowed to use that invention in his business. A factually driven analysis such as this ensures that the principles of equity and fairness underlying the "shop rights" rule are considered. Because this is exactly the type of analysis that the district court used to reach its decision, we see no error in the district court's analysis justifying reversal.

To reach its decision, the district court looked to the discussion of "shop rights" set forth in the often-cited [United States v. Dubilier Condenser Corp., 289 U.S. 178 (1933)], in which the Court said:

> Where a servant, during his hours of employment, working with his master's materials and appliances, conceives and perfects an invention for which he obtains a patent, he must accord his master a nonexclusive right to practice the invention. [citation omitted] This is an application of equitable principles. Since the servant uses his master's time, facilities and materials to attain a concrete result, the latter is in equity entitled to use that which embodies his own property and to duplicate it as often as he may find occasion to employ similar appliances in his business.

289 U.S. at 188-89. . . .

Applying *Dubilier* . . . to the facts of this case, the district court properly found that AP&L had acquired a "shop right" in Bowman's patented level detector which entitled AP&L to duplicate the level detector for use in its business. Bowman developed the patented level detector while working at AP&L and suggested it to AP&L as an alternative to the K-ray system. AP&L installed the level detector on one hundred and twenty eight (128) precipitator hoppers at White Bluff with Bowman's consent and participation. Bowman also consented to, and participated at least in part in, the installation of the level detector on one hundred and twenty eight (128) precipitator hoppers at ISES. In addition, the level detectors on half of the hoppers at ISES were installed by a contractor other than WRT, with Bowman's and WRT's knowledge and consent. All costs and expenses associated with the testing and implementation of the level detector on the hoppers at White Bluff and ISES were paid by AP&L.

Furthermore, Bowman never asserted that AP&L was precluded from using the level detector without his permission or that AP&L was required to compensate him for its use. . . . WRT argues that Bowman's consent or acquiescence after he had assigned his rights in the Bowman application to WRT is irrelevant. Even if this were true, Bowman's actions at White Bluff prior to this assignment justify the district court's finding that a "shop right" was created. Nevertheless, WRT, of which Bowman was a part owner during the relevant time period, acquiesced both to AP&L's continued use of the level detector at White Bluff and ISES and to the installation of the level detector by outside contractors at ISES. This lends further support to the district court's decision.

WRT also argues that, even if AP&L had acquired a "shop right" to use the patented level detector, AP&L somehow exceeded the scope of that right when it allegedly "carelessly and casually disseminated the design and specifications of the patented device to private contractors." WRT argues that, by putting information of this nature on the open market, AP&L rendered the patent "worthless" and robbed Bowman of the "fruit of his labor." We find these arguments unpersuasive for two reasons.

First, WRT has failed to explain how AP&L's mere dissemination of specifications of the patented level detector constituted patent infringement.

Clearly, it did not. The owner of a patent right may exclude others from making, using or selling the subject matter of a claimed invention. 35 U.S.C. §§ 154 and 271. AP&L's dissemination of information obviously does not fall into any of these categories. Even so, it is also unclear how disseminating specifications of the level detector after it was patented rendered the Bowman patent "worthless." The owner of the Bowman patent still retained the right to exclude all others than AP&L from practicing the claimed invention.

Second, we find no error in the district court's holding that AP&L's "shop right" entitled it to duplicate the level detector and to continue to use it in its business. Such a conclusion clearly finds support in the law. H.F. Walliser & Co. v. F.W. Maurer & Sons Co., 17 F.2d 122, 124 (E.D. Pa. 1927). Furthermore, AP&L's "shop right" was not limited to AP & L's use of level detectors that AP&L itself had manufactured and installed. Quite to the contrary, we find that AP&L's "shop right" entitled it to procure the level detector from outside contractors. Schmidt v. Central Foundry Co., 218 F. 466, 470 (D.N.J. 1914), *aff'd on other grounds*, 229 F. 157 (3d Cir. 1916). . . .

NOTES AND QUESTIONS

1. The shop right doctrine is a matter of state law, but it remains relatively uniform from state to state owing to its origins in pre-*Erie* decisions of the U.S. Supreme Court. United States v. Dubilier Condenser Corp., 289 U.S. 178, 188 (1933); M'Clurg v. Kingsland, 42 U.S. (1 How.) (1843).

2. In contrast, the law of copyright is a matter of federal law. Generally, the owner of a copyright "is the party who actually creates the work, that is, the person who translates an idea into a fixed, tangible expression entitled to copyright protection." Cmty. for Creative Non-Violence v. Reid, 490 U.S. 730, 737 (1989). However, the copyright for a "work made for hire" vests with the employer or the party who commissioned the work. 17 U.S.C. § 201(b). The Copyright Act defines a "work made for hire" as "a work prepared by an employee within the scope of his or her employment." 17 U.S.C. § 101. *See also* Restatement (Second) of Agency § 228 (listing factors relevant for determining whether a work was "made for hire"). Copyright law has gained additional importance and prominence in the information technology era, because computer software is work subject to copyright. *See, e.g.*, PFS Distrib. Co. v. Raduechel, 332 F. Supp. 2d 1236 (S.D. Iowa 2004) (applying the work made for hire rule in an ownership dispute between an employer and former employee).

A key difference between copyright law and patent law is that copyright law does not recognize an employer's "shop right." *See* Avtec Sys., Inc. v. Peiffer, 21 F.3d 568 (4th Cir. 1994). *See also* Rochelle Cooper Dreyfuss, *The Creative Employee and the Copyright Act of 1976*, 54 U. Chi. L. Rev. 590, 639 (1987).

3. The employer's shop right is not necessarily limited to *employee* inventions. An independent contractor might also be subject to the shop right if an invention is a result of work for the employer, the employer provided resources for the invention's development, and the contractor acquiesced in or induced the employer to use the invention in its business. *See, e.g.*, Crowe v. M & M/Mars, a Div. of Mars Inc., 577 A.2d 1278 (N.J. Super. 1990); Neon Signal Devices, Inc. v.

Alpha-Claude Neon Corp., 54 F.2d 793, 794 (W.D. Pa. 1931).

4. The difference between an employee and an independent contractor is much more important in copyright law. Under the Copyright Act, when an employee produces copyrightable work "in the scope of his employment," the work is "made for hire" and the employer is deemed the author. 17 U.S.C. §§ 101, 201. Moreover, "unless the parties have expressly agreed otherwise in a written instrument signed by them, [the employer] owns all of the rights comprised in the copyright." *Id. See* Shaul v. Cherry Valley-Springfield Cent. Sch. Dist., 363 F.3d 177 (2d Cir. 2004) (tests, quizzes, and homework problems teacher wrote outside normal class hours were works made for hire). In *Shaul*, the court relied on the "work made for hire" doctrine to hold that the employer school district did not violate the teacher's property or privacy interests in seizing the materials as part of an investigation of the teacher's alleged misconduct.

In contrast, when an independent contractor produces work for an employer, the independent contractor rather than the employer usually is deemed the author and holds the copyright in the absence of a written agreement to the contrary. 17 U.S.C. § 201; Community for Creative Non-Violence v. Reid, 490 U.S. 730 (1989). *But see* 17 U.S.C. § 101 (regarding "collective" works and certain other works included within the definition of works "made for hire").

5. When an employer and employee dispute their respective rights to an invention, there are often difficult issues of fact and problems of proof about the scope of the employment and the means of invention. If the employer discovers the employee's invention only after the employment has terminated, there could be another issue: *When* did the employee conceive the invention? Even if it were possible to be certain of the date of any stage in the development of the invention, the invention did not necessarily occur to the employee all at one moment. The employee may have begun to conceive the invention during his employment and perfected the invention after his employment. *See, e.g.*, Jamesbury Corp. v. Worcester Valve Co., 443 F.2d 205 (1st Cir. 1971) (former employee's invention did not occur during employment, for purposes of agreement to assign inventions to employer, where employee did not put idea in tangible, written form until two weeks after leaving employment).

One way an employer might address these problems in advance is to require an employee to sign an agreement assigning to the employer a right to all employment-related inventions, regardless of whether the employee was hired to invent or for any other purpose. To deal with uncertainty about the timing of an invention and the threat of an employee's postemployment exploitation of the employer's confidential information in pursuit of an invention, the agreement might even include a "holdover" clause, requiring the employee to assign to the employer any inventions the employee conceives for some period of time *after* the employment. The enforceability of such agreements is addressed in section B of this chapter, *infra*.

PROBLEMS

Wanda Merlin was a production manager for a factory owned by Ace Food Processing Co. when she began to conceive the idea of a new kind of resealable flap for food packaging. Her idea was based partly on her education and her varied experience with other employers, and partly on the additional knowledge she had gained about the food packaging process in her work for Ace. Merlin perfected her idea working mainly at home after hours with her tools and supplies she acquired on her own (including surplus or scrap materials she acquired with permission from Ace), but from time to time she called various personnel at the factory for advice. The plant manager, Will Honor, was aware of Merlin's efforts, and he frequently referred her to other specialists at the company for further consultation. From time to time, Honor encouraged Merlin by reminding her that the company rewarded creative and useful ideas with substantial bonuses.

When Merlin was fully satisfied with her invention, she filed for and obtained a patent. At Honor's suggestion she also presented her idea to Ace's Product Development Committee. The committee's response was favorable, but after the meeting, the committee chair confided to Merlin that the company's difficult financial condition made it likely that the company would postpone production and use of the new resealable flap for at least a year and perhaps longer.

As the calendar year ended, Merlin waited to see if her annual bonus would reflect her efforts in designing the resealable flap. She was gravely disappointed to learn Ace decided to forgo all bonuses because of a continuing financial crisis.

Frustrated at Ace's unwillingness to reward her for her invention or to begin production and use of her resealable flap, Merlin contacted one of Ace's rivals, Diamond Foods. Merlin and Diamond negotiated an agreement in which Merlin licensed Diamond's use and production of the resealable flap for Diamond's food packaging, in return for a substantial royalty. Within a few months Diamond's products were arriving at grocery stores in packages with the new resealable flap. When Honor saw that Merlin's invention was being used by a competitor, he fired Merlin. Spurred by competition from Diamond, Ace then accelerated its introduction of Merlin's resealable flap for its own products.

1. Does Merlin have a claim for unpaid compensation, based on contract or restitution/quantum meruit, for Diamond's use of her invention?

2. Would Ace have a viable counterclaim against Merlin for breaching her duty of loyalty?

b. The Employer's Trade Secrets

The modern firm might be imagined as a repository of information. The firm discovers, collects, organizes, and preserves information, and puts the information to productive use. Some information is intrinsically valuable, like a secret formula or process known to no one outside the firm. Other information is widely available outside the firm and has little intrinsic value, like the name and address of a customer, but there may be significant value in the way the firm assembles the information, associates it with other information, and makes it useful and accessible to employees. Information might have real value like any other tangible or intangible asset, depending partly on its usefulness, and partly on the cost other persons would incur to discover or organize the same information.

In collecting information, organizing it and putting it to use, the firm necessarily makes the information available to employees, and herein lies a dilemma. Unlike physical assets, information is "nonrivalrous," which means that more than one person can possess it at the same time. Once the employer discloses information to an employee, the employer cannot repossess the information from the employee the way it might repossess a physical asset. And whenever an employee gains possession of the firm's valuable information, there is a risk of "spillover." The employee might leave the firm and disclose the information to an outsider, such as a competitor. The new employer might then possess and use the information without having to pay for it, and the firm that bore the cost of discovering or collecting the information will lose the competitive advantage the information once provided. The risk of spillover can harm an employer even if no employee actually discloses the information to outsiders. The mere fact that an employee *could* disclose the information to others may tempt the employee to demand premium compensation as the price for silence. The greater the number of employees who know the information, the more expensive it might be for the employer to prevent spillover. *See generally* Dan L. Burk, *Intellectual Property and the Firm*, 71 U. Chi. L. Rev. 3 (2004).

Protection against spillover is important for an employer to have incentive to bear the costs of discovering and organizing information. Patent law provides protection for patentable inventions, but not all useful information is patentable. An employer could require employees to sign long-term "no resignation" contracts, but employees are likely to demand a steep increase in compensation in exchange for such mobility restraints. In any event, the public interests in competition, free commerce, and labor mobility would not be well served if all employers sought maximum contractual restraints against employee resignation.

The law of "trade secrets" provides an alternative source of protection for employers. Trade secret law has evolved to protect those who invest in the development of valuable information without unnecessarily immobilizing the labor market. The common law defined "trade secret" as a confidential formula, process, or other compilation of information that a person developed and used in his business, and that gave him an advantage over competitors who lacked the information. Peabody v. Norfolk, 98 Mass. 452, 458 (1868); Restatement (First) of Torts § 757 (1939). An employee's duty of loyalty barred him from disclosing or misusing his employer's trade secrets in competition with the employer, even after the employment had ceased. In enforcing the duty not to misuse or disclose, courts frequently relied on an employee's express agreement, if there was one, or described the duty as part of an employee's "implied contract." Most courts, however, regarded the duty as a natural incident of employment, with or without an employee's express agreement. O. & W. Thum Co. v. Tloczynski, 72 N.W. 140 (Mich. 1897); Little v. Gallus, 38 N.Y.S. 487 (N.Y. App. Div. 1896).

The law of trade secrets is now governed in most states by the Uniform Trade Secret Act, which identifies two essential elements of a "trade secret." First, the information must have "independent economic value" derived from its "not being generally known to, and not being readily ascertainable by proper means by, other persons." Uniform Trade Secrets Act § 1. Second, the party claiming the trade secret must prove it used "reasonable" effort to preserve the secrecy of the information. *Id. See also* Rockwell Graphic Sys., Inc. v. DEV Indus., Inc., 925 F.2d 174 (7th Cir. 1991).

A trade secret need not be something that could qualify for patent or copyright protection. 3M v. Pribyl, 259 F.3d 587, 595-596 (7th Cir. 2001). Indeed, much trade secret litigation by employers against former employees and other defendants involves matters that clearly would not qualify for patent or copyright protection, such as supplier or customer lists. *See, e.g.*, Yeti by Molly, Ltd. v. Deckers Outdoor Corp., 259 F.3d 1101 (9th Cir. 2001) (supplier list); Dicks v. Jensen, 768 A.2d 1279 (Vt. 2001) (customer list could be trade secret).

Moreover, as noted above, a collection of information can be valuable not because any specific piece of information is unknown to others, but because the information is organized and presented in a way that makes it more useful and accessible. In 3M v. Pribyl, 259 F.3d 587 (7th Cir. 2001), for example, a manufacturer of resin sheeting sought an injunction against a group of former employees and their new business to prevent their use of certain production and process manuals and notes they had acquired in their employment with the plaintiff employer. On appeal from a jury verdict for the plaintiff employer, the defendants argued that the manuals and notes did not constitute a trade secret because all the information was otherwise available to the rest of the industry. Conceding that no single bit of information was secret, the court nevertheless held that the compilation of information was a trade secret.

> There is no doubt that within the 500-plus pages of manuals at issue, there are a host of materials which would fall within the public domain. For example, 3M's instructions on how to clean the area around its machines, and how to properly assemble a cardboard box, surely cannot be considered independent trade secrets . . . . Yet, when all the cleaning procedures, temperature settings, safety protocols, and equipment calibrations are collected and set out as a unified process, that compilation, if it meets the other qualifications, may be considered a trade secret.
>
> Contrary to defendants' suggestion, 3M is not attempting to preclude Accu-Tech from folding cardboard boxes. Rather, the company is seeking to prevent Accu-Tech from using and disclosing a process which it took the company six years and considerable income to perfect. These manuals and processes, even if comprised solely of materials available in the public domain, have been created by combining those materials into a unified system which is not readily ascertainable by other means. Thus, viewing the evidence in the light most favorable to 3M, we believe there was sufficient evidence to support the jury's finding that 3M has a trade secret in the operating procedures, quality manuals, trade manuals, process standards and operator notes for using 3M's equipment that makes resin sheeting.

Id. at 595-596.

Remember, however, that even if information might have qualified as a trade secret because of its economic value, it can fail the second part of the test if the claimant failed to use reasonable efforts to maintain its secrecy. One measure an employer can take to preserve secrecy is to require employees to acknowledge in writing that the information is a trade secret, and to agree in writing not to disclose or misuse the information. The agreement is not necessary to establish an employee's duty to protect trade secrets, but it bolsters the employer's argument that it used reasonable effort to protect the information in question, and that the information is in fact a trade secret.

Of course, a person's discovery or use of information another person claims as a trade secret is not, standing alone, unlawful. Both parties might have acquired the same information independently and without any improper means. A person's discovery or use of information is unlawful only if he "misappropriated" the information from another person who can prove that the information is his trade secret. Uniform Trade Secrets Act § 1 (defining misappropriation), § 2 (authorizing injunctive relief against misappropriation); § 3 (authorizing damages for misappropriation). *See also* Economic Espionage Act of 1996, 18 U.S.C. §§ 18312 et seq. (making misappropriation of a trade secret a federal criminal offense). In the case of a former employee, however, the misappropriation is ordinarily established by proof that the employee learned the trade secret in the course of his employment, that he reasonably should have known it was a trade secret, and that he breached his duty as an employee by improperly using the information or improperly disclosing it to others. Merrill Lynch, Pierce, Fenner & Smith Inc. v. Dunn, 191 F. Supp. 2d 1346, 1350-1351 (M.D. Fla. 2002).

Proving that an employee has actually disclosed or used a trade secret learned during employment can be a difficult matter. In most cases, the proof will have to be circumstantial. There is no clear consensus among the courts as to what constitutes sufficient circumstantial proof, and what is mere speculation. In 3M v. Pribyl, *supra*, the court upheld the jury's finding of misappropriation based mainly on the facts that (1) "it took 3M six years and countless resources in order to make its carrier tape operation efficient and profitable, [but] Accu-Tech was able to almost immediately operate its resin sheeting line effectively"; and (2) there were "significant similarities" between 3M's production methods and the defendants' production methods. 259 F.3d at 596.

PEPSICO, INC. v. REDMOND
54 F.3d 1262 (7th Cir. 1995)

FLAUM, Circuit Judge.

. . . The facts of this case lay against a backdrop of fierce beverage-industry competition between Quaker and PepsiCo, especially in "sports drinks" and "new age drinks." Quaker's sports drink, "Gatorade," is the dominant brand in its market niche. PepsiCo introduced its Gatorade rival, "All Sport," in March and April of 1994, but sales of All Sport lag far behind those of Gatorade. Quaker also has the lead in the new-age-drink category. Although PepsiCo has entered the market through joint ventures with the Thomas J. Lipton Company and Ocean Spray Cranberries, Inc., Quaker purchased Snapple Beverage Corp., a large new-age-drink maker, in late 1994. PepsiCo's products have about half of Snapple's market share. Both companies see 1995 as an important year for their products: PepsiCo has developed extensive plans to increase its market presence, while Quaker is trying to solidify its lead. . . .

William Redmond, Jr., worked for PepsiCo in its Pepsi-Cola North America division ("PCNA") from 1984 to 1994. Redmond became the General Manager of the Northern California Business Unit in June, 1993, and was promoted one year later to General Manager of the business unit covering all of California. . . . Redmond's relatively high-level position at PCNA gave him access to inside information and trade secrets. . . .

Donald Uzzi, who had left PepsiCo in the beginning of 1994 to become the head of Quaker's Gatorade division, began courting Redmond for Quaker in May, 1994. . . . On November 8, 1994, Uzzi extended Redmond a written offer for the position of Vice President-Field Operations for Gatorade and Redmond accepted. Later that same day, Redmond called William Bensyl, the Senior Vice President of Human Resources for PCNA, and told him that he had an offer from Quaker to become the Chief Operating Officer of the combined Gatorade and Snapple company but had not yet accepted it. Redmond also asked whether he should, in light of the offer, carry out his plans to make calls upon certain PCNA customers. Bensyl told Redmond to make the visits. . . . [Finally, on November 10, 1994, Redmond informed PCNA that he had decided to accept the Quaker offer and was resigning from PCNA.]

. . . PepsiCo filed this diversity suit on November 16, 1994, seeking a temporary restraining order to enjoin Redmond from assuming his duties at Quaker and to prevent him from disclosing trade secrets or confidential information to his new employer. . . .

[T]he district court conducted a preliminary injunction hearing on the same matter. . . . PepsiCo offered evidence of a number of trade secrets and confidential information it desired protected and to which Redmond was privy. First, it identified PCNA's "Strategic Plan," an annually revised document that contains PCNA's plans to compete, its financial goals, and its strategies for manufacturing, production, marketing, packaging, and distribution for the coming three years. . . . The Strategic Plan derives much of its value from the fact that it is secret and competitors cannot anticipate PCNA's next moves. PCNA managers received the most recent Strategic Plan at a meeting in July, 1994, a meeting Redmond attended. . . .

Second, PepsiCo pointed to PCNA's Annual Operating Plan ("AOP") as a trade secret. The AOP is a national plan for a given year and guides PCNA's financial goals, marketing plans, promotional event calendars, growth expectations, and operational changes in that year. . . . The AOP bears a label that reads "Private and Confidential—Do Not Reproduce" and is considered highly confidential by PCNA managers.

In particular, the AOP contains important and sensitive information about "pricing architecture"—how PCNA prices its products in the marketplace. Pricing architecture covers both a national pricing approach and specific price points for given areas. . . . As with other information contained in the AOP, pricing architecture is highly confidential and would be extremely valuable to a competitor. Knowing PCNA's pricing architecture would allow a competitor to anticipate PCNA's pricing moves and underbid PCNA strategically whenever and wherever the competitor so desired. PepsiCo introduced evidence that Redmond had detailed knowledge of PCNA's pricing architecture and that he was aware of and had been involved in preparing PCNA's customer development agreements with PCNA's California and California based national customers. Indeed, PepsiCo showed that Redmond, as the General Manager for California, would have been responsible for implementing the pricing architecture guidelines for his business unit.

PepsiCo also showed that Redmond had intimate knowledge of PCNA "attack plans" for specific markets. Pursuant to these plans, PCNA dedicates extra funds to supporting its brands against other brands in selected markets. To use a hypothetical example, PCNA might budget an additional $500,000 to spend in Chicago at a particular time to help All Sport close its market gap with Gatorade. Testimony and documents demonstrated Redmond's awareness of these plans and his participation in drafting some of them.

Finally, PepsiCo offered evidence of PCNA trade secrets regarding innovations in its selling and delivery systems. Under this plan, PCNA is testing a new delivery system that could give PCNA an advantage over its competitors in negotiations with retailers over shelf space and merchandising. Redmond has knowledge of this secret because PCNA, which has invested over a million dollars in developing the system during the past two years, is testing the pilot program in California.

Having shown Redmond's intimate knowledge of PCNA's plans for 1995, PepsiCo argued that Redmond would inevitably disclose that information to Quaker in his new position, at which he would have substantial input as to Gatorade and Snapple pricing, costs, margins, distribution systems, products, packaging and marketing, and could give Quaker an unfair advantage in its upcoming skirmishes with PepsiCo. Redmond and Quaker countered that Redmond's primary initial duties at Quaker as Vice President—Field Operations would be to integrate Gatorade and Snapple distribution and then to manage that distribution as well as the promotion, marketing and sales of these products. . . . The defendants also pointed out that Redmond had signed a confidentiality agreement with Quaker preventing him from disclosing "any confidential information belonging to others," as well as the Quaker Code of Ethics, which prohibits employees from engaging in "illegal or improper acts to acquire a competitor's trade secrets." Redmond additionally promised at the hearing that should he be faced with a situation at Quaker that might involve the use or disclosure of PCNA information, he would seek advice from Quaker's in-house counsel and would refrain from making the decision.

PepsiCo responded to the defendants' representations by pointing out that the evidence did not show that Redmond would simply be implementing a business plan already in place. . . . PepsiCo further argued that Snapple's 1995 marketing and promotion plans had not necessarily been completed prior to Redmond's joining Quaker, that Uzzi disagreed with portions of the Snapple plans, and that the plans were open to re-evaluation. . . . Moreover, PepsiCo continued, diverging testimony made it difficult to know exactly what Redmond would be doing at Quaker. Redmond described his job as "managing the entire sales effort of Gatorade at the field level, possibly including strategic planning," and at least at one point considered his job to be equivalent to that of a Chief Operating Officer. . . . Thus, PepsiCo asserted, Redmond would have a high position in the Gatorade hierarchy, and PCNA trade secrets and confidential information would necessarily influence his decisions. . . .

On December 15, 1994, the district court issued an order enjoining Redmond from assuming his position at Quaker through May, 1995, and permanently from using or disclosing any PCNA trade secrets or confidential information. . . . This appeal followed.

II.

Both parties agree that the primary issue on appeal is whether the district court correctly concluded that PepsiCo had a reasonable likelihood of success on its various claims for trade secret misappropriation and breach of a confidentiality agreement.

The Illinois Trade Secrets Act ("ITSA"), which governs the trade secret issues in this case, provides that a court may enjoin the "actual or threatened misappropriation" of a trade secret. 765 ILCS 1065/3(a). . . . A party seeking an injunction must therefore prove both the existence of a trade secret and the misappropriation. The defendants' appeal focuses solely on misappropriation; although the defendants only reluctantly refer to PepsiCo's marketing and distribution plans as trade secrets, they do not seriously contest that this information falls under the ITSA.

. . . The question of threatened or inevitable misappropriation in this case lies at the heart of a basic tension in trade secret law. Trade secret law serves to protect "standards of commercial morality" and "encourage[ ] invention and innovation" while maintaining "the public interest in having free and open competition in the manufacture and sale of unpatented goods." 2 Jager, *supra*, § IL.03 at IL-12. Yet that same law should not prevent workers from pursuing their livelihoods when they leave their current positions. . .

This tension is particularly exacerbated when a plaintiff sues to prevent not the actual misappropriation of trade secrets but the mere threat that it will occur. While the ITSA plainly permits a court to enjoin the threat of misappropriation of trade secrets, there is little law in Illinois or in this circuit establishing what constitutes threatened or inevitable misappropriation. Indeed, there are only two cases in this circuit that address the issue: Teradyne, Inc. v. Clear Communications Corp., 707 F. Supp. 353 (N.D. Ill. 1989), and AMP Inc. v. Fleischhacker, 823 F.2d 1199 (7th Cir. 1987).

In *Teradyne*, . . . Judge Zagel observed that "[t]hreatened misappropriation can be enjoined under Illinois law" where there is a "high degree of probability of inevitable and immediate . . . use of . . . trade secrets." *Teradyne*, 707 F. Supp. at 356. Judge Zagel held, however, that Teradyne's complaint failed to state a claim because Teradyne did not allege "that defendants have in fact threatened to use Teradyne's secrets or that they will inevitably do so." . . .

> [T]he defendants' claimed acts, working for Teradyne, knowing its business, leaving its business, hiring employees from Teradyne and entering the same field (though in a market not yet serviced by Teradyne) do not state a claim of threatened misappropriation. All that is alleged, at bottom, is that defendants could misuse plaintiff's secrets, and plaintiffs fear they will. This is not enough. It may be that little more is needed, but falling a little short is still falling short.

Id. at 357.

In *AMP*, we affirmed the denial of a preliminary injunction on the grounds that the plaintiff AMP had failed to show either the existence of any trade secrets or the likelihood that defendant Fleischhacker, a former AMP employee, would compromise those secrets or any other confidential business information. . . . [W]e emphasized that the mere fact that a person assumed a similar position at a competitor does not, without more, make it "inevitable that he will use or disclose . . . trade secret information" so as to "demonstrate irreparable injury." *Id.*

. . . The defendants are incorrect that Illinois law does not allow a court to enjoin the "inevitable" disclosure of trade secrets. Questions remain, however, as to what constitutes inevitable misappropriation and whether PepsiCo's submissions rise above those of the *Teradyne* and *AMP* plaintiffs and meet that standard. We hold that they do.

PepsiCo presented substantial evidence at the preliminary injunction hearing that Redmond possessed extensive and intimate knowledge about PCNA's strategic goals for 1995 in sports drinks and new age drinks. The district court concluded on the basis of that presentation that unless Redmond possessed an uncanny ability to compartmentalize information, he would necessarily be making decisions about Gatorade and Snapple by relying on his knowledge of PCNA trade secrets. It is not the "general skills and knowledge acquired during his tenure with" PepsiCo that PepsiCo seeks to keep from falling into Quaker's hands, but rather "the particularized plans or processes developed by [PCNA] and disclosed to him while the employer-employee relationship existed, which are unknown to others in the industry and which give the employer an advantage over his competitors." *AMP*, 823 F.2d at 1202. The *Teradyne* and *AMP* plaintiffs could do nothing more than assert that skilled employees were taking their skills elsewhere; PepsiCo has done much more.

Admittedly, PepsiCo has not brought a traditional trade secret case, in which a former employee has knowledge of a special manufacturing process or customer list and can give a competitor an unfair advantage by transferring the technology or customers to that competitor. . . . PepsiCo has not contended that Quaker has stolen the All Sport formula or its list of distributors. Rather PepsiCo has asserted that Redmond cannot help but rely on PCNA trade secrets as he helps plot Gatorade and Snapple's new course, and that these secrets will enable Quaker to achieve a substantial advantage by knowing exactly how PCNA will price, distribute, and market its sports drinks and new age drinks and being able to respond strategically. . . . This type of trade secret problem may arise less often, but it nevertheless falls within the realm of trade secret protection under the present circumstances.

Quaker and Redmond assert that they have not and do not intend to use whatever confidential information Redmond has by virtue of his former employment. They point out that Redmond has already signed an agreement with Quaker not to disclose any trade secrets or confidential information gleaned from his earlier employment. They also note with regard to distribution systems that even if Quaker wanted to steal information about PCNA's distribution plans, they would be completely useless in attempting to integrate the Gatorade and Snapple beverage lines.

The defendants' arguments fall somewhat short of the mark. Again, the danger of misappropriation in the present case is not that Quaker threatens to use

PCNA's secrets to create distribution systems or co-opt PCNA's advertising and marketing ideas. Rather, PepsiCo believes that Quaker, unfairly armed with knowledge of PCNA's plans, will be able to anticipate its distribution, packaging, pricing, and marketing moves. Redmond and Quaker even concede that Redmond might be faced with a decision that could be influenced by certain confidential information that he obtained while at PepsiCo. In other words, PepsiCo finds itself in the position of a coach, one of whose players has left, playbook in hand, to join the opposing team before the big game. Quaker and Redmond's protestations that their distribution systems and plans are entirely different from PCNA's are thus not really responsive.

The district court also concluded from the evidence that Uzzi's actions in hiring Redmond and Redmond's actions in pursuing and accepting his new job demonstrated a lack of candor on their part and proof of their willingness to misuse PCNA trade secrets. . . .

That conclusion also renders inapposite the defendants' reliance on Cincinnati Tool Steel Co. v. Breed, 482 N.E.2d 170 (Ill. App. 1985). In *Cincinnati Tool*, the court held that the defendant's "express denial that she had disclosed or would disclose any confidential information or that she even possessed such information" left the plaintiff without a case, one that could not be saved "merely by offering evidence that defendant used customer and price data in her work while employed by plaintiff." 482 N.E.2d at 180. . . . In the instant case, the district court simply did not believe the denials and had reason to do so.

Thus, when we couple the demonstrated inevitability that Redmond would rely on PCNA trade secrets in his new job at Quaker with the district court's reluctance to believe that Redmond would refrain from disclosing these secrets in his new position (or that Quaker would ensure Redmond did not disclose them), we conclude that the district court correctly decided that PepsiCo demonstrated a likelihood of success on its statutory claim of trade secret misappropriation. . . .

III.

Finally, Redmond and Quaker have contended in the alternative that the injunction issued against them is overbroad. They disagree in particular with the injunction's prohibition against Redmond's participation in the integration of the Snapple and Gatorade distribution systems. The defendants claim that whatever trade secret and confidential information Redmond has, that information is completely irrelevant to Quaker's integration task. . . .

While the defendants' arguments are not without some merit, the district court determined that the proposed integration would require Redmond to do more than execute a plan someone else had drafted. It also found that Redmond's knowledge of PCNA's trade secrets and confidential information would inevitably shape that integration and that Redmond could not be trusted to avoid that conflict of interest. If the injunction permanently enjoined Redmond from assuming these duties at Quaker, the defendants' argument would be stronger. However, the injunction against Redmond's immediate employment at Quaker extends no further than necessary and was well within the district court's discretion.

. . . [W]e affirm the district court's order enjoining Redmond from assuming his responsibilities at Quaker through May, 1995, and preventing him forever from disclosing PCNA trade secrets and confidential information.

NOTES AND QUESTIONS

1. The Seventh Circuit did not address whether the information at stake in *PepsiCo* actually constituted a trade secret. The trial court found that the information was a trade secret, and Redmond and Quaker did not appeal that particular finding. *See also* Whyte v. Schlage Lock Co., 125 Cal. Rptr. 2d 277 (Cal. App. 2002) (employer's strategic and marketing plans were trade secrets).

2. The inevitable disclosure doctrine remains controversial, with some courts accepting the doctrine and others rejecting it. *See, e.g.,* LeJeune v. Coin Acceptors, Inc., 849 A.2d 451 (Md. 2004) (rejecting the doctrine); Del Monte Fresh Produce Co. v. Dole Food Co., 148 F. Supp. 2d 1326 (S.D. Fla. 2001) (Florida and California law require proof of actual appropriation); EarthWeb, Inc. v. Schlack, 71 F. Supp. 2d 299 (S.D.N.Y. 1999) (adopting the doctrine).

3. A California court rejected the inevitable disclosure doctrine in Whyte v. Schlage Lock Co., 125 Cal. Rptr. 2d 277 (Cal. App. 2002), partly on the ground that an employee is ordinarily free to engage in post-employment competition, but an injunction without proof of actual misuse of a trade secret has the effect of an after-the-fact, court-imposed duty *not* to engage in post-employment competition. *Id.* at 292-293. Even if the employee had consented to such a duty in an agreement not to compete, California is one state that takes a dim view of such agreements. The enforcement of covenants not to compete is addressed in section B of this chapter, *infra.*

4. There is some precedent, especially in older cases, for extending protection to information that does not qualify as a trade secret for one reason or another. *See, e.g.,* Gloria Ice Cream & Milk Co. v. Cowan, 41 P.2d 340 (Cal. 1935). The First Restatement of Torts adopted this view, proposing that "[a]lthough given information is not a trade secret, one who receives the information in a confidential relation or discovers it by improper means may be under some duty not to disclose or use that information." Restatement (First) of Torts § 757 (1939). The more current Restatement (Third) of Unfair Competition (1995) appears to take the contrary view by offering protection only against misappropriation of trade secrets. *See* Robert Unikel, *Bridging the "Trade Secret" Gap: Protecting "Confidential Information" Not Rising to the Level of Trade Secrets,* 29 Loy. U. Chi. L.J. 841 (1998).

5. The usual rule is that a court will not issue an injunction unless money damages are an inadequate remedy. Why might an action for money damages be inadequate as a remedy for a party whose trade secrets are misappropriated?

6. For a variation on the usual injunctive remedy barring misappropriation of trade secrets, see 3M v. Pribyl, 259 F.3d 587 (7th Cir. 2001), where the court's injunction permitted the defendants to use the trade secrets in question if they paid their former employer the cost they would have incurred to develop the same information independently.

7. The remedies that trade secret law provides are still less than a patent. The trade secret claimant does not "own" the information and cannot exclude other persons from using the information if they acquire it independently. The trade

secret claimant can only exclude employees and other persons from gaining the information by misappropriation.

8. Trade secret law can work in reverse, protecting an employee from an employer's misappropriation of the *employee*'s information. *See* Bloom v. Hennepin County, 783 F. Supp. 418 (D. Minn. 1992) (physician stated claim that employer misappropriated multiple sclerosis protocol physician had developed and might constitute trade secret; "shop right" doctrine did not apply).

The Federal Defend Trade Secrets Act. The Defend Trade Secrets Act (DTSA), 18 U.S.C. §1831 et seq., enacted in 2016, creates a federal cause of action, without need for diversity jurisdiction, for misappropriation of trade secrets. It is limited to trade secrets "related to a product used in, or intended for use in, interstate or foreign commerce," leaving state law applicable to all other trade secrets. 18 U.S.C. § 1836(b)(1).

DTSA aligns closely with the Uniform Trade Secrets Act, the widespread state adoption of which makes existing state caselaw persuasive authority for federal courts interpreting the relatively new DTSA. The relief provisions of DTSA, however, includes provisions stronger than in some states. As to damages, DTSA provides not only compensatory damages for actual loss and unjust enrichment, *id.* § 1836(b)(3)(B)(i)(I)-(II), but also, where a trade secret is "willfully and maliciously misappropriated," double damages and attorney's fees, *id.* §§ 1836(b)(3)(C),(D). As to equitable relief, DTSDA authorizes injunctions to "prevent any actual or threatened misappropriation" of a trade secret, *id.* § 1836(b)(3)(A), as well as ex parte seizure of property in "extraordinary circumstances," when "necessary to prevent the propagation or dissemination of the trade secret," *id.* § 1836(b)(2)(A)(i). The breadth of available equitable relief has a key limitation, however: an injunction may be issued

> provided the order does not--
>
> (I) prevent a person from entering into an employment relationship, and that conditions placed on such employment shall be based on evidence of threatened misappropriation and not merely on the information the person knows; or
>
> (II) otherwise conflict with an applicable State law prohibiting restraints on the practice of a lawful profession, trade, or business . . . .

DTSA thereby rejects "inevitable disclosure" doctrine as a basis for preventing employees from starting new employment.

Unauthorized Accessing of Electronic Data and the CFAA. Employer data—trade secret and otherwise—is often stored electronically. To access or copy data, one must access the employer's computer. Unsurprisingly, disputes over trade secrets or other valued or confidential data often involve former employee use of a computer owed by the employer. When an employee accesses an employer's computer to misappropriate trade secrets, the employer's obvious remedies are to sue for misappropriation of trade secrets, or sue in contract for violation of an implied duty of loyalty or an express non-disclosure agreement.

However, an employer might also sue the employer under the Computer Fraud and Abuse Act (CFAA), 18 U.S.C. § 1030, which provides criminal penalties and civil liability if a person engages in unauthorized access of another person's computer. The advantages of a suit under the CFAA from the employer's point of view are twofold: (1) federal question jurisdiction to permit a lawsuit in federal court; and (2) the possible avoidance of the necessity of proving that the data in question was a "trade secret." The CFAA would also be useful to the employer if the employee altered, destroyed or otherwise damaged the data but did not "misappropriate" or use the data.

Application of the CFAA to disputes over use or copying of data in the employment context has been controversial. Frequently, the accused employee had authorization to access the computer in question for employment purposes. The employer might even have assigned the computer to the employee for work-related purposes. However, the employer alleges that the employee *exceeded* authorization by using the computer for some purpose outside the expected scope of employment. Indeed, the key provision of the CFAA declares that a person authorized to access a computer still violates the law if he or she engages in conduct that "exceeds authorized access." 18 U.S.C. § 1030. Some courts have held that an employee exceeds implied limits of authorization for purposes of the CFAA if he or she uses a computer for the purpose of breaching a duty of loyalty, such as copying data to use in future competition against the employer. *See, e.g.*, Airport Centers LLC v. Citrin, 440 F.3d 418 (7th Cir. 2006). Other courts have rejected that view. In U.S. v. Nosal, 676 F.3d 854 (9th Cir. 2012), for example, the court held that the phrase "exceeds authorized access" in the CFAA applies to acts that exceed *access* authorization, but not *use* authorization. *See also* Lane v. Brocq, 2016 WL 1271051 (N.D. Ill. 2016) (CFAA targets loss or damage to a computer or database, not alleged misappropriation of data).

The CFAA has figured in some whistleblower cases in which employees accessed employers' computers to acquire or copy data to prove illegal activities. *See* Connor C. Turpan, *Whistleblower? More Like Cybercriminal: The Computer Fraud and Abuse Act As Applied to Sarbanes-Oxley Whistleblowers*, 42 Rutgers Computer & Tech. L.J. 120, 121–23 (2016). Because the CFAA does not require proof that data was a "trade secret," some employers have argued that the CFAA applies to unauthorized accessing of a computer to acquire any kind of data if the accessing results in a harm to the employer. *See, e.g.*, Ahlers v. CFMOTO Powersports, Inc., 2014 WL 2574747 (D. Minn. 2014) (describing but rejecting employer theory that employee violated CFAA by copying data to support her allegations that employer's business practices violated the law),

c. Ownership of Social Media

One of the frontiers in property disputes between employers and employees involves ownership of social media. Social media accounts tied to an employee and built over the course of an employment relationship might have value worth fighting over in the event employment terminates. For example, a social media account might provide access to client contacts, client data or records of communications. To promote its own business, an employer might assist the employee in building the employee's account by providing staff and other resources to compose content, issue communications and update the employee's site. Who owns the account or its data when employment ends?

In Eagle v. Morgan, 2013 WL 943350 (E.D. Pa. 2013), an employee opened a LinkedIn account under her own name but used the account to promote her employer's business. She gave the employer her password and authorized the employer's staff to post communications and engage in other account maintenance. When the employment terminated, the employer accessed the employee's LinkedIn account to change the password and replace her profile with the profile of the employer's CEO. In the employee's ensuing lawsuit against the employer, the court held that the employer was liable to the employee under Pennsylvania law for unauthorized use of the employee's name, invasion of privacy, and misappropriation of identity. However, the court also found that the plaintiff had failed to prove damages.

In another case, PhoneDog v. Kravitz, 2011 WL 541561 (N.D. Cal. 2011), an employer sued a former employee based on his continued use a Twitter account allegedly belonging to the employer and containing a compilation of subscribers. The court agreed with the employer that the employer had sufficiently pleaded claims under California law for conversion and misappropriation of trade secrets. The granted the employee's motion to dismiss claims for intentional or negligent interference with prospective economic advantage on the grounds that the employer had not yet sufficiently pleaded the manner in which the former employee's continued use of the Twitter account had disrupted business relationships or caused economic harm to the employer.

B. EXPRESS CONTRACTUAL LIMITS ON RESIGNATION AND COMPETITION

As section A of this chapter suggests, an employer might have a lot at stake when employment terminates: the risk that an employee will join or form a competitor, the risk that the employee will solicit the employer's most prized customers or employees, and the risk that an employee will use inventions, trade secrets, or employer information to compete against the employer. Implied rights and duties of employment offer the employer some protection against these risks, but an employer might need or want more protection.

One reason an employer might want more protection is that the implied rights and duties of employment offer no protection for an employer's investment in employee training (except to the extent training includes transmission of trade secrets). Training costs vary tremendously depending on the nature of the work and the extent to which new employees can be expected to bring preexisting skills with them or need additional training. Even new employees with plenty of experience and preexisting skills may need weeks or months to learn the peculiarities of the employer's marketing system, products, and clients or customers. During training, an employee might not be very productive. The employer expects to recover its training costs when the employee achieves a much higher level of productivity later. But if the employee resigns soon after completing training, the employer will recoup nothing. Even worse, the employer's investment in training might benefit a competing employer who now enjoys the defecting employee's skilled services without investing in training.

1. *Express Limits on Resignation*

Employment at will leaves each party at risk of the other's decision to terminate at an inconvenient time. A fixed term contract is an incomplete solution because either party remains free to terminate at periodic intervals, perhaps with some advance notice. In any event, the continuing popularity of employment at will among employers suggests employers do not find the security of a fixed term sufficient to offset the loss of freedom to terminate. What if an employer could have it both ways, protecting itself from loss of a key employee at a bad time while simultaneously reserving its right to terminate at will? In general, an employer might follow either or both of two contract strategies to restrain an employee's untimely resignation without a fixed term: a contract provision (1) making resignation costly to the employee, or (2) limiting an employee's alternative employment opportunities. The next case involves the former.

MED+PLUS NECK & BACK PAIN CTR., S.C. v. NOFFSINGER

311 Ill. App. 3d 853, 726 N.E.2d 687 (Ill. App. 2000)

Justice INGLIS delivered the opinion of the court:

. . . On February 23, 1995, plaintiff and defendant entered into an employment agreement. The agreement provided that, for a two-year period, plaintiff would employ defendant and compensate him, for the first three months of the term, at the greater of $3,000 per month or 10% of defendant's gross billings for chiropractic services; thereafter, defendant would receive 10% of his gross billings in compensation. The agreement further contained a liquidated damages provision which stated:

> EARLY TERMINATION. The parties hereto agree that, in the event that [defendant] terminates this Agreement prior to the completion of the Subsequent Term, [plaintiff] shall be entitled to receive from [defendant] an amount which compensates [plaintiff] for the cost of training. Upon the execution of this Agreement, [defendant] shall execute and deliver to [plaintiff] a promissory note . . . in the principal amount of Fifty Thousand Dollars ($50,000). The Note shall provide that the principal amount of Fifty Thousand Dollars ($50,000) will be reduced by Two Thousand and [sic] Eighty-Three Dollars and thirty-three cents ($2,083.33) per month for each of the twenty-four (24) months of the Subsequent Term of this Agreement during which [defendant] continues to perform services for [plaintiff] under this Agreement. If this Agreement is terminated for any reason by [defendant] or [plaintiff] for cause, pursuant to section 12, hereof, the remaining outstanding balance of the Note shall become immediately due and payable. In the event that [defendant] terminates his employment with [plaintiff] after the completion of the subsequent Term, the Note shall be forgiven by [plaintiff], and the original of the Note shall be stamped "Satisfied" and returned to [defendant].

. . . On December 18, 1995, defendant resigned from plaintiff's employment. Thereafter, plaintiff filed suit against defendant alleging breach of contract and seeking to enforce the liquidated-damages provision of the employment agreement as well as seeking lost profits and training costs associated with defendant's departure. Plaintiff also sought attorney fees pursuant to the employment agreement.

The case proceeded to bench trial. Dr. David Girgenti testified that he was president and clinic director of plaintiff. He testified that the liquidated-damages clause was included to attempt to recapture the costs of training a new associate chiropractor. Girgenti testified that defendant's ability to properly complete the necessary paperwork was so lacking that he had to spend three hours a day training defendant for the first two months of defendant's employment. . . .

Dr. James Morgano and Dr. Andrew Kong testified that they were both associate chiropractors employed by plaintiff at the same time as defendant. Each testified that he observed Girgenti giving defendant very little training during the first two months of defendant's employment. Defendant testified that he received virtually no training from Girgenti. Defendant also testified that he began treating patients as soon as he was hired and was hired because he had experience in the management of a chiropractic clinic and the proper manner in which to complete the necessary paperwork.

The trial court determined that defendant breached the employment agreement[,] . . . that plaintiff failed to adequately prove the existence of damages and that the liquidated-damages provision was unenforceable as a penalty. . . . Plaintiff timely appeals and defendant timely cross-appeals.

Plaintiff initially contends that the trial court erred by refusing to award it damages for lost profits following defendant's resignation. . . . In any breach of contract case, the proper measure of damages is the amount that will place the nonbreaching party in as satisfactory a position as it would have been had the contract been fully performed. . . . The issue here is whether lost profits are recoverable in damages by a nonbreaching employer against the breaching employee. Surprisingly, neither the parties' nor our own research has uncovered any Illinois case that speaks directly to this issue. In this situation, where the nonbreaching employer is seeking damages against an employee for breaching an employment contract, the general rule is this:

> The measure of recovery is generally the extra cost of obtaining other services equivalent to those promised under the contract but not performed by the employee. However, in some cases this will not amount to full compensation to the employer, and additional recovery has been allowed. These additional damages must be foreseeable at the time the parties entered into the employment contract. Recovery may be had for the cost of training a replacement, for instance, but damages will not be awarded for lost income if there is no proof that the former employee caused any substantial portion of the loss.
>
> The employer's damages will be diminished by any amount which could have been avoided under the doctrine of avoidable consequences.

22 Am. Jur. 2d Damages § 121 (1988).

In general, therefore, an employer may not collect lost profits from a breaching employee. . . . [P]laintiff has offered no persuasive argument or binding authority to show why the general rule, that the measure of damages for breach of an employment contract by an employee is the cost of obtaining other service equivalent to that promised and not performed, should not apply in this case. We therefore hold that the trial court did not err in holding that lost profits were unavailable to plaintiff in this case.

In any event, lost profits were nevertheless unavailable in this case because plaintiff failed to produce any evidence that defendant reasonably contemplated them at the time he signed the employment contract with plaintiff. Plaintiff correctly notes that the rule in Illinois is that, in order for the trial court to award lost profits, plaintiffs must prove their losses with a reasonable degree of certainty, the wrongful act of the defendant must have caused the loss of profits, and the profits were reasonably within the contemplation of the defaulting party at the time of the contract. Milex Products, Inc. v. Alra Laboratories, Inc., 237 Ill. App. 3d 177, 190, 177 Ill. Dec. 852, 603 N.E.2d 1226 (1992). . . . The record is wholly devoid of any evidence to suggest that defendant agreed to be responsible not only for performing his employment duties but also for the profits plaintiff expected to reap from the sweat of defendant's brow. Instead, the record indicates only that plaintiff and defendant negotiated extensively about the term of the contract; no other details of the negotiations were brought out. In the absence of such evidence, the trial court properly concluded that plaintiff was not entitled to lost profits as a component of damages in this case.

. . . Plaintiff next contends that the trial court erroneously found the liquidated damages clause to be unenforceable. Whether a contractual provision is a valid liquidated damages clause or a penalty clause is a question of law. A liquidated damages provision is generally valid and enforceable when

> (1) the parties intended to agree in advance to the settlement of damages that might arise from the breach; (2) the amount of liquidated damages was reasonable at the time of contracting, bearing some relation to the damages which might be sustained; and (3) actual damages would be uncertain in amount and difficult to prove.

Grossinger, 240 Ill. App. 3d at 749, 607 N.E.2d 1337.

Additionally, the damages must be for a specific amount for a specific breach; they may not be a penalty to punish nonperformance or as a threat used to secure performance. *Grossinger*, 240 Ill. App. 3d at 750, 607 N.E.2d 1337. Plaintiff argues that the liquidated damages provision was intended to recoup its costs to train defendant in the occasion of a breach. We disagree.

The provision at issue is clearly a penalty and bears no relation to training costs at all. If defendant breached the contract on the very first day, plaintiff's cost to train him would have been almost nothing, yet defendant would be liable to pay plaintiff the full $50,000 under the liquidated damages provision. If defendant breached the contract on the last day, he would have been fully trained by plaintiff over the course of two years, yet he would be liable to pay plaintiff only $2,083 (or less) under the liquidated damages provision. Thus, the liquidated damages provision bears an inverse relation to the costs of training defendant—the more training he receives, the less he must pay under the provision. Accordingly, we find it to be a penalty clause and a mechanism designed to secure defendant's performance of the contract. The trial court correctly determined that the liquidated damages provision was unenforceable.

Plaintiff next contends that the trial court erred by failing to award actual damages after finding that the liquidated damages clause was a penalty. According to plaintiff, it was entitled to recoup its training costs for training defendant. We disagree. As stated above, the measure of damages for an employee's breach of his or her employment contract is the extra cost of obtaining replacement services. This might include the cost of training the replacement employee; however, plaintiff presented no evidence to demonstrate that it even replaced defendant, let alone the amount it expended to train defendant's replacement, if any. Accordingly, we hold that the trial court did not err in refusing to award plaintiff actual damages. . . .

NOTES AND QUESTIONS

1. The contract in *Med+Plus* limited the employee's right to resign in two different ways: (1) a prescribed term of employment; and (2) a reimbursement of training expenses clause. From the employer's point of view, what are the advantages and disadvantages of each type of provision? Why don't more employers use these types of provisions?

2. Recall that it took some time for courts to accept that an employer could be contractually bound to continue employment if the employee was not similarly bound. *See* Part A of Chapter 8, *supra.* Would a court enforce a contract that bound an employee to serve a prescribed period of time but left the employer free to terminate at will? *See* Air Am. Jet Charter, Inc. v. Lawhon, 93 S.W.3d 441 (Tex. App. 2002) (yes, provided there is other consideration for employee's promise).

3. If Med+Plus attempted to prove damages in accordance with the rules laid out by the court, how might its proof have unfolded, and how might the court have made the final calculation? For a good roadmap of proof of damages from an employee's breach of a fixed-term agreement, *see* Equity Ins. Mgrs. of Illinois, LLC v. McNichols, 755 N.E.2d 75 (Ill. App. 2001), where the court upheld an arbitrator's calculation of employer damages. In essence, the employer's damages are the costs of replacing the employee (including the cost of finding and selecting a replacement, and the compensation paid to the replacement to finish the employee's term), minus the employer's cost avoided (what the employer saved by ceasing the departing employee's compensation).

In *Equity Insurance Managers*, the employer hired a replacement for a *lower* salary. Does this mean the employer enjoyed a *gain* from the first employee's resignation? The court in *Equity Insurance Managers* also upheld an award of lost profits, finding the potential for lost profits in the event of premature resignation was "certainly foreseeable" to the parties when they negotiated their agreement. However, the arbitrator reduced lost profits to reflect some shortcoming in the employer's effort to mitigate damages by hiring a replacement.

4. As a general matter, an employer and employee can agree that the employee will reimburse the employer for training if the employee resigns before a certain date, at least if the employer really provided training and the cost charged to the employee is reasonably related to the cost or value of the training. *See* Heder v. City of Two Rivers, 295 F.3d 777 (7th Cir. 2002). Determining the value of on-

the-job training can be especially difficult if the training legitimately includes the employee's experience in carrying out his tasks.

5. A few states have laws prohibiting certain agreements requiring departing employees to repay training costs. *See, e.g.*, Colo. Rev. Stat. Ann. § 8-2-113(2) (barring "[a]ny contractual provision providing for recovery of the expense of educating and training an employee" except an employee "who has served an employer for a period of less than two years"); Conn. Gen. Stat. Ann. § 3151r (barring "employment promissory note" as condition of employment).

6. Could a repayment of training expenses agreement violate the Fair Labor Standards Act? *See* Heder v. City of Two Rivers, 295 F.3d 777 (7th Cir. 2002) (yes, because to the extent FLSA required employer to pay minimum wage and overtime for time spent in training, the act "required the City to pay—and entitles Heder to retain" compensation for time in training); Wage and Hour Opinion Letter No. FLSA2005-18 (May 31, 2005) (police officer who earned pay from police department during basic training, but resigned soon after graduation and accepted employment with another police department, was entitled to retain training pay at least up to the amount of the minimum wage, and could not be required to reimburse the first department for the full amount of training pay).

7. Deferred compensation, subject to forfeiture, is another contractual device for discouraging premature resignation, but forfeiture clauses sometimes fail, either because of ERISA (in the case of "employee pension benefit plans") or the common law of contracts. See parts D.1 and D.2.a.i of chapter 4, *supra*.

8. An alternative to money damages is specific performance, a judicial order that the defendant must perform his promise. There are at least two reasons courts do not grant such relief in the case of employment and other contracts for personal services. First, such a remedy is impractical because of the difficulty of forcing an individual to perform quality service against his will. Second, the courts have regarded specific performance of personal services as a form of involuntary servitude in violation of the Thirteenth Amendment. *See* Arthur v. Oakes, 63 F. 310, 318 (7th Cir. 1894). Starting in the late nineteenth century, however, U.S. courts began to embrace the English rule of Lumley v. Wagner, 1 De Gex, M. & G. 604; 13 Eng. L. & Eq. 252 (1852), which permits a court to issue a negative injunction prohibiting an employee from working for any other employer, where the services in question are especially unique, such as the performance of a singer or sports star. *See, e.g.*, Shubert Theatrical Co. v. Rath, 271 F. 827 (2d Cir. 1921); McCaull v. Braham, 16 F. 37 (S.D.N.Y. 1883). The immediate effect of such an injunction fails to provide the plaintiff with what he wants—the defendant's services—but the defendant might decide that completing his contract is better than unemployment. For a performer or sports star, the need to maintain celebrity and goodwill might be a more powerful motivator than a judge's contempt power.

The availability of a negative injunction has become especially important for the enforcement of another type of contractual restraint on employee resignation and competition, the covenant not to compete.

2. *Express Agreements Restricting Competition*

As noted at the beginning of the prior section, an employer can protect itself from an at will employee's resignation by either of two contract strategies: (1) making resignation costly to the employee; or (2) limiting the employee's opportunities for alternative employment. This section explores the latter strategy.

An employee's implied duty of loyalty during employment is a minimal restriction against the employee's opportunities for alternative employment after resignation. A more severe limit is an express promise not to engage in postemployment competitive activity. Such a promise, if enforceable, can protect a wide range of employer interests that might be threatened by an employee's defection to or creation of a competing firm.

a. Legitimate Justifications for an Agreement Not to Compete

An agreement not to compete can damage an employee's ability to earn a living and purse a career. It also threatens the public's interest in free commerce and labor mobility. Thus, an agreement not to compete must have a legitimate purpose sufficient to justify the imposition on employee and public interests. An employer's goal of preventing fair competition is not a legitimate purpose for an agreement not to compete. RESTATEMENT (SECOND) OF CONTRACTS § 186; RESTATEMENT OF THE LAW, EMPLOYMENT LAW § 8.07, *cmt. f.*

There are, however, some potentially legitimate purposes for an agreement not to compete. A covenant might reasonably be necessary to protect the employer's real trade secrets and confidential information. RESTATEMENT OF THE LAW, EMPLOYMENT LAW § 8.07(b). An agreement not to compete might be necessary to protect trade secrets because the duty not to misappropriate, standing alone, is not enough protection. It is often impossible for an employer to know or prove a former employee is disclosing or using trade secrets. Thus, an agreement not to serve a competitor might be the employer's only practical protection. Of course, there might be an issue whether the data in question was a "trade secret," and whether the employee really had access to trade secrets.

The Restatement lists some other employer interests that might justify an agreement not to compete. One involves the employer's investment in "customer relationships," especially relationships an employee was paid to build on the employer's behalf. *Id. See also* Corroon & Black of Illinois, Inc. v. Magner, 494 N.E. 2d 785 (Ill. App. 1986) (listing factors to consider in determining whether employer is entitled to protection of customer relationships); Moss, Adams & Co. v. Shilling, 224 Cal. Rptr. 456 (Cal. App. 1986). Note, however, that an employer might gain all the protection it needs with a "no-solicitation agreement" that simply prohibits contacts with the same customers the employee served or solicited for the employer, instead of a traditional covenant not to compete. *See, e.g.*, Gen'l Comm'l Packaging, Inc. v. TPS Package Eng'g, Inc., 126 F.3d 1131 (9th Cir. 1997). The presence or possibility of a no-solicitation agreement might undermine an employer's argument that it needed an agreement not to compete.

The Restatement also endorses protection of an employer's investment in the employee's "reputation in the market," such as by the payment of travel, entertainment or advertising expenses. RESTATEMENT OF THE LAW, EMPLOYMENT LAW § 8.07(b). Finally, the Restatement endorses an employer's use of an agreement not to compete to protect its investment in a business it purchased from the employee. It is typical for the buyer of a business to offer employment to the seller in order to assure continuity and to use the seller-employee's "know-how," but the buyer's interest in the business will be severely impacted if the seller-employee is able to reestablish a new business to compete with the very business he sold. *Id.*

Not all states endorse all of these employer interests as justifications for a noncompetition agreement. California allows only noncompetition agreements necessary to protect trade secrets or the employer's interest in a business it has purchased from an employee. *See* Muggill v. Reuben H. Donnelley Corp., 398 P.2d 147, 149 (Cal. 1965)

One other potential reason for an agreement not to compete is to protect the employer's investment in employee training, but there is no clear consensus as to what kind of "training" justifies an agreement or whether training is ever sufficient to justify such an agreement. Professor Lester describes this debate in the article that follows.

GILLIAN LESTER, *RESTRICTIVE COVENANTS, EMPLOYEE TRAINING, AND THE LIMITS OF TRANSACTION-COST ANALYSIS*

76 Ind. L.J. 49 (2001)

. . . The paradigmatic starting point for transaction cost analysis of restrictive covenants is Gary Becker's 1964 treatise on human capital, which distinguishes between general and specific training.[59] General training is equally valuable across firms. An example is the training a medical intern receives at a hospital. For the worker, general training represents a valuable asset and he should be willing to pay for it in the form of reduced wages. But some workers will find it difficult to refuse jobs offering higher wages from the outset, even if the quid pro quo is less training and consequently lower prospects for long-term career advancement. In order to attract applicants, firms that offer extensive general training may defer recouping their investment by reducing the worker's compensation only after providing some or all of the training.

The problem with this arrangement is that the worker may be tempted during the "pay-back" period—when he is receiving a wage below his marginal product—to act opportunistically. The worker may "hold up" the employer by demanding a higher wage under threat of defecting to a competitor who offers a higher wage. Restrictive covenants might reduce this temptation by preventing the employee from working for competitors for some specified period following separation. To take a simple stylized example, suppose TrainCo hires Alice, offering a salary of $30,000 per year for the first two years. During year one, TrainCo spends $5000 on training programs that enhance Alice's general skills. Alice's marginal product during the first year equals $30,000, which is below TrainCo's $35,000 outlay

[59] The ITSA definition of misappropriation relevant to this discussion is "the disclosure or use of a trade secret of a person without express or implied consent by another person who . . . at the time of disclosure or use, knew or had reason to know that the knowledge of the trade secret was . . . acquired under circumstances giving rise to a duty to maintain its secrecy . . . ." 765 ILCS 1065/2(b).

(salary plus training). In year two, the value of Alice's marginal product rises to \$35,000, exceeding TrainCo's \$30,000 salary outlay. TrainCo's total outlay of \$65,000 equals Alice's total marginal product. The problem for TrainCo is that PoachCo is willing to pay \$35,000 to recruit Alice during year two. A restrictive covenant that prevents Alice from working for a competitor for some period following separation may be an effective way to protect TrainCo's investment in training Alice. Numerous scholars have advocated reforming the law to permit such restrictions.

An elaboration on this simple story introduces a bilateral threat of opportunism. The threat of opportunism declines when both parties have made investments that depend on the parties' continued relationship. From the employee's side, training or other job-specific investments that are more useful to the firm providing them than to other firms or uses are called firm-specific human-capital investments. Familiarity with matters such as a firm's personnel practices, transaction histories, or manufacturing processes might be more valuable within the firm than outside. Where there is salient risk of job loss, a worker will be reluctant to invest in firm-specific training, knowing that it will have no value to other firms. The firm, too, worries about the loss of its investment. The worker who has received firm-specific training is more valuable to the firm than a replacement who lacks such training. In the jargon of transaction-cost economics, specific investments create a type of ex post surplus, or "quasi rents," that is, value that can be captured only within that relationship.

Although the presence of quasi rents reduces the likelihood that the relationship will break down, it does not eliminate it. Even an employee who has invested heavily in firm-specific skills may possess valuable industry-specific skills that he will be tempted to exploit elsewhere. Moreover, the parties may have a preference for avoiding the type of costly ex post bargaining (and concomitant breakdown in the relationship) that quasi rents create. As such, the parties may still wish to hedge against the breakdown of the value-optimizing relationship through reputationally enforced implicit contracts. They might, for example, implicitly agree to share the cost of training in the sense that the employer will pay the worker a wage that exceeds the value of her marginal product in the training stage, yet below what the worker could earn at another firm that offers no training. Later, the parties will share in the return to investment: the firm will pay a wage below the worker's marginal product, yet above her opportunity wage (because her specialized skills make her more valuable to the firm for which she has specific training).

Still, implicit contracting over bilateral investments may not achieve the desired equanimity. The risk of "hold up," in which each party attempts to extract a disproportionate share of quasi rents, remains a lurking threat for both parties. The employee may demand higher wages under threat of departure, or alternatively, the employer may reduce wages in the postinvestment period to a competitive level (for example, by failing to increase wages with inflation).

One might assume that reputational incentives would stem opportunism on both sides. A large firm might implicitly promise not to act opportunistically in dealing with its workers, knowing that to do so would jeopardize substantial reputational capital in the eyes of other, similarly situated workers. Yet, there is still room for opportunism if the value of exploiting the right to bind the employee equals or exceeds the present discounted value of future returns to having a good reputation. Moreover, . . . rapid structural and identity changes that characterize many modern corporations may undermine the effectiveness of reputation as a way to temper opportunism. Similarly, the threat of lost reputational capital may have only a trivial disciplining effect on the individual worker, whose trading partners (firms) may be dispersed, dissolved, or hampered from exchanging information with one another, for the reasons cited above or for other reasons.

Risk aversion about the downstream division of returns to investment may therefore lead parties to enlist the further protection of explicit contracts, including restrictive covenants, to protect their respective "shares" of the assets of the relationship.

. . . Seizing on the idea that restrictive covenants may be a way for parties to hedge against opportunism by their trading partners, legal scholars have reached different conclusions on whether the scope of protectible interests ought to be expanded. Paul Rubin and Peter Shedd, for example, believe the current rules are efficient,[76] while others, such as Michael Trebilcock, believe that the range of protectible interests ought to include training per se.[77]

. . . Rubin and Shedd's argument begins with the observation that the worker will pay for only the portion of general training that he can afford. Training involving trade secrets, for example, is a type of general training that workers often cannot afford to self-finance, and thus the only way for an employer to recapture the investment is through wage concessions by the employee. However, once a worker receives this type of training, he will have an incentive to breach the contract opportunistically and take his knowledge elsewhere for financial gain. A restrictive covenant, Rubin and Shedd argue, reduces this risk, and thereby preserves the proper ex ante incentives for the employer to invest in research and training. Viewed in this light, there appears to be a compelling case for vigorous enforcement of restrictive covenants in order to promote socially valuable activities.

The authors point out, however, that the threat of opportunism is bilateral, and thus an act that stems problems of opportunism for one party may exacerbate them for the other. As applied to this context, a worker's human capital will typically be some combination of general training for which he paid and other kinds of general training, such as trade secrets, for which he did not pay. If courts always enforce restrictive covenants, the employer may well be overprotected—an absolute injunction permits the employer to prevent the worker from using any of his skills in the service of a competitor, even skills he paid for himself. This might permit an employer to undercompensate the employee over time, essentially holding him ransom via the threat of enforcing the restrictive covenant.

How, then, should courts police these bilateral incentives for opportunism? According to Rubin and Shedd, the current judicial approach gets it right. Trade secrets might be seen as the paradigmatic example of general training financed by the employer. Therefore, courts' practice of enforcing restrictive covenants that

---

[76] Gary S. Becker, Human Capital: A Theoretical and Empirical Analysis with Special Reference to Education 40 (3d ed. 1993).

[77] Paul H. Rubin & Peter Shedd, *Human Capital and Covenants Not to Compete*, 10 J. Legal Stud. 93 (1981).

protect trade secrets is efficient. Similarly efficient, they argue, is enforcing covenants that protect customer lists only where they are not generally known, and there is evidence of effort or expenditure on the part of the employer in developing the list. This, they say, is efficient because it likely singles out human capital paid for by the employer, rather than by the employee. . . .

While thought-provoking and initially convincing, Rubin and Shedd's analysis fails on several grounds. First, it is not obvious that singling out employer investments in confidential information and relationships effectively polices bilateral opportunism. To be sure, evidence of costly investments in acquiring and maintaining the secrecy of information may support a legal inference of trade secrets. But this does not answer the question of whether trade secrets alone are worth protecting. It does not follow that absence of efforts to protect secrecy signals a lack of desire to protect an underlying investment. Even assuming we could solve the classic administrative problem of distinguishing between trade secrets and general "tools of the trade," limiting protectible interests to the former may be an underinclusive rule. . . . Absent the ability to protect these investments . . . , firms may think twice before making such substantial outlays in on-the-job general training.

. . . Perhaps the vast majority of employer investments do in fact fall within the range of interests currently deemed legitimate under the law of restrictive covenants. Even assuming this is so, it raises the question of whether courts ought to single out the types of investments they currently protect. Reliance on the fact of certain kinds of investments overlooks the possibility that behavior is endogenous to the existing rule, efficient or otherwise. In other words, employers familiar with a century of common law jurisprudence know that courts will enforce covenants protecting employers' investments in trade secrets, confidential information, and nonpublicly available customer lists and relationships, but will presumptively invalidate covenants that protect even very costly investments in human capital deemed general tools of the trade. One would predict that, over time, investment decisions will shift to reflect the contours of the legal rule. Specifically, one would expect that training will be externalized, that is, workers will be required to self-finance general training by attending college or trade-school programs.

Suppose that, contrary to the current rule, investments in general, nonconfidential training were protectible. We might expect a change in investment strategies: we might see more investment in on-the-job training, apprenticeship programs, and the like. I am not aware of any convincing empirical evidence from states that have experimented with expanding the law of restrictive covenants to protect investments in nonconfidential general training. Nor can I assert definitively that the hypothesized shift in the rule would lead to an optimal investment regime. My point for the moment is simply that Rubin and Shedd's analysis falls prey to the circularity of its assertion that the common law is efficient because it protects investments made in the shadow of a rule that likely induces those investments.

NOTES AND QUESTIONS

1. The distinction between training that involves trade secrets and

confidential information versus training that does not is important in some but not all jurisdictions. *Compare* Moore v. Midwest Distrib., Inc., 65 S.W.3d 490 (Ark. App. 2002) (appearing to limit employer use of covenant to the protection of training involving trade secrets or confidential information), *and* Vantage Tech., LLC v. Cross, 17 S.W.3d 637 (Tenn. App. 1999) (same), *with* Brunswick Floors, Inc. v. Guest, 506 S.E.2d 670 (Ga. App. 1998) (weighing cost of training to employer against impact of the covenant on the employee's ability to earn a living), *and* Dyer v. Pioneer Concepts, Inc., 667 So. 2d 961 (Fla. App. 1996) (employer is entitled to protect training that exceeds "what is usual, regular, common, or customary in the industry in which the employee is employed").

2. Still another interest for which an employer might seek contractual protection is its relationship with the rest of its employees. However, most courts are disinclined to recognize that an employer has a sufficient or legitimate interest in preserving employee relationships (especially at-will relationships) to justify prohibiting former employees from soliciting other employees. *Cf.* Heyde Cos. v. Dove Healthcare, LLC, 654 N.W. 2d 830 (Wis. 2002) (denying enforcement of contract between staffing service and its customer prohibiting customer from soliciting assigned employees for regular employment with the customer).

3. There is at least one more possible employer interest justifying a covenant not to compete or similar contractual protection: the danger that a departing "inventor" employee will take an idea for an invention, already secretly conceived, to a new or established competitor. The employer's express or implied right to employee inventions or to a "shop right" might be impossible to protect if the employer cannot prove that the employee conceived the invention during his employment. A covenant not to compete offers some protection by delaying the time when the employee can exploit his invention. But a better targeted form of protection might be a "trailer" or "holdover" agreement granting the employer an interest in the employee's *post*employment inventions. From the employee's point of view, however, a holdover agreement might seem an extreme measure. If the agreement is enforceable, even inventions conceived and developed many months after the cessation of employment without any support by the employer will belong to the employer. In Ingersoll-Rand Co. v. Ciavatta, the court described the law of holdover agreements as follows:

> In view of the competing interests involved in holdover agreements, courts have not held them void per se. Rather, the courts apply a test of reasonableness. Moreover, courts strictly construe contractual provisions that require assignment of post-employment inventions; they must be fair, reasonable, and just. Generally, a clause is unreasonable if it: (1) extends beyond any apparent protection that the employer reasonably requires; (2) prevents the inventor from seeking other employment; or (3) adversely impacts on the public. . . .

542 A.2d 879, 888-889 (N.J. 1988).

In *Ciavatta*, the court denied enforcement of the holdover clause because the employer had not hired the employee to make or improve inventions of the sort the employee had conceived in postemployment, and because the employer failed to prove that the employee had relied on the employer's trade secrets.

b. Problems in Formation

Agreements not to compete involve some unique problems of contract formation. At the outset, such an agreement requires a promise by the employee—something for which the standard unilateral contract model of employment fails to account. Moreover, there is an obvious problem of consideration in the case of an employee at will. What does the employee receive in return from the employer if the employer retains the right terminate employment at any subsequent moment?

CENTRAL ADJUSTMENT BUREAU, INC. v. INGRAM

678 S.W.2d 28 (Tenn. 1984)

DROWOTA, Justice.

I

. . . The plaintiff-employer, Central Adjustment Bureau, a . . . collector of past-due debts . . . has 25 branch offices throughout the United States, including a branch in Nashville, Tennessee. The defendants are former employees who left Central Adjustment Bureau (hereinafter CAB) in 1979 to form Ingram & Associates, a company which competed directly with CAB. All of the defendants had signed covenants not to compete with CAB. After the defendants left, CAB brought suit in Chancery Court seeking both compensatory and injunctive relief. . . .

II

The collection industry with approximately 8,000 agencies nationwide is highly competitive. Agencies operate essentially in the same manner regardless of size. Salespersons contact businesses and solicit past-due accounts for collection. Collectors then contact the debtors and attempt to collect the money owed. The agency receives a fee consisting of a percentage of the amount recovered. This percentage is generally set by agreement between the salesperson and the client.

Most clients use more than one collection agency. The primary factor in choosing an agency is the rate of return to the client, although the rate charged the client, the services available from the agency and the personal contact between a client and the agency salesperson are also factors.

. . . Defendant Henry Preston Ingram was hired on March 1, 1970, by CAB as a salesman in North Carolina with a base salary of $600.00 monthly plus commissions. A week after he began working, CAB informed him that he must sign a covenant not to compete. Ingram initially refused to sign, but under threat of termination, he signed two weeks later.

In June, 1972, CAB promoted Ingram to manager of the Nashville district. Ingram was promoted in June, 1977, to manager of the northern region of CAB. . . . The northern region which was headquartered in Nashville included Kentucky and Tennessee as well as most of the states in the midwestern, northeastern and mid-Atlantic areas of the United States. As a regional manager, Ingram was employed in the highest corporate position outside that of an officer.

Ingram resigned from CAB on February 22, 1979. At that time, he was the fifth highest paid employee at CAB. In 1978, he received more than $59,000 . . . .

[The other defendants were Goostree, initially hired as a collector in 1972, and Bjorkholm, initially hired as a salesman in 1977. At least in the case of Goostree, there was no advance warning that they would be required to sign covenants not to compete. CAB presented them covenants to sign within a few days of starting their employment. Goostree eventually rose to the level of district manager.]

The covenant was identical in each case, providing as follows:

> I, the undersigned, during the term of my employment with Central Adjustment Bureau, Inc., and/or its wholly-owned subsidiaries, and at any time within two years of termination thereof, shall not compete within the United States, either directly or indirectly, with the corporation (1) by owning, operating, managing, being employed by, . . . any person, enterprise, firm or corporation which is engaged in any business in which the corporation is engaged . . .; (2) by divulging any information pertaining to the business, trade secrets, and/or confidential data of the corporation, or make any use whatsoever of the same; or (3) by contacting any client or customer of the corporation who has been a client or customer of the corporation during the term of employment.

On January 26, 1979, Ingram filed a charter of incorporation with the State of Tennessee for a corporation by the name of Ingram Associates, Inc., the purposes of which included engaging in the debt collection business. In January or early February, 1979, Ingram applied for a license in both Kentucky and Tennessee to operate a collection agency; he opened bank accounts for Ingram & Associates in Nashville and Louisville; and he began to collect master client lists and other information from other CAB offices around the country to use in his own business. Ingram resigned from CAB on February 22, 1979; Goostree and Bjorkholm resigned in March, 1979. On March 10, 1979, Ingram, Goostree and Bjorkholm of the Nashville CAB office met . . . to finalize the formation of Ingram & Associates.

On or about March 22, 1979, Ingram & Associates began actively functioning in the collection agency business. Both prior and subsequent to this date, the new venture solicited CAB customers, making use of personal contacts gained by the defendants while employed by CAB.

. . . It is undisputed that defendant Ingram made plans and took actions prior to his resignation to acquire a proprietary interest in a collection agency, which was intended to operate in direct competition with CAB. For instance, prior to leaving CAB, defendant Ingram obtained from various CAB branch officers client information sheets deemed confidential by CAB. These sheets set forth information valuable to any competitor of CAB, including the names of the client contacts, collection, legal, accounting and special requirements of each client as well as the commission charged each client by CAB. Through its access to this and similar information, Ingram & Associates was able to make proposals to major CAB clients which undercut the CAB rate of commission. Other documents indicate that Ingram & Associates in its effort to attract clients made extensive use of the good will and personal contacts developed by the defendants while working for CAB.

III

As a general rule, restrictive covenants in employment contracts will be enforced if they are reasonable under the particular circumstances. The rule of reasonableness applies to consideration as well as to other matters such as territorial and time limitations. Di Deeland v. Colvin, 208 Tenn. 551, 554, 347 S.W.2d 483, 484 (1961). Whether there is adequate consideration to support a non-competition covenant signed during an on-going employment relationship depends upon the facts of each case.

The first question before us is whether future employment of an at-will employee constitutes consideration for a non-competition covenant. In Ramsey v. Mutual Supply Co., 58 Tenn. App. 164, 427 S.W.2d 849 (1968), Ramsey agreed to a non-competition covenant with his employer, Mutual Supply Company, "at the time of such employment." 427 S.W.2d at 850. Ramsey's employment lasted nearly two and a half years before he left to work for a competitor. When Mutual Supply brought suit to enforce the covenant, Ramsey argued that employment was not sufficient consideration. The court rejected that argument, holding

> that employment, even for an indefinite period of time, subject to termination at the option of the employer is sufficient consideration to support such a contract.

Id. 427 S.W.2d at 852.

Ramsey is thus authority for the proposition that employment is sufficient consideration for a covenant which is part of the original employment agreement. The contention is made, however, that the employee must be informed of the covenant during employment negotiations before beginning employment. It is argued that if the covenant is not presented to the employee until the first day at work or shortly thereafter, the covenant is not the subject of free bargaining. Such an argument, if accepted, threatens to vitiate any agreement between an employee already working and his or her employer. We hold that a covenant signed prior to, contemporaneously with or shortly after employment begins is part of the original agreement, and that therefore, under *Ramsey*, it is supported by adequate consideration.

For this reason, we find that there is adequate consideration to support defendant Goostree's covenant.

Even when the covenant is not signed until after employment has begun, courts in [several] states have found continued employment to be sufficient consideration. . . . *See generally* Annot. 51 A.L.R.3d 825 (1973). Some of these courts reason that the mutual promises of the parties as to continued employment form a binding bilateral contract with the promise of employment constituting sufficient consideration. Other courts, however, regard the mere promise of continued employment as not binding on the employee where the employment is one at-will. They nevertheless regard the covenant as binding if there is actual performance of the promise of continued employment.

In Thomas v. Coastal Industrial Services, 214 Ga. 832, 108 S.E.2d 328 (1959), the court stated its reasoning as follows:

> Though a promise may be nudum pactum when made because the promisee is not bound, it becomes binding when he subsequently furnishes the consideration contemplated by doing what he was expected to do.

Id. 108 S.E.2d at 329.

. . . Whether performance is sufficient to support a covenant not to compete depends upon the facts and circumstances of each case. The requirement that consideration for a non-competition covenant be reasonable remains. It is possible, for instance, that employment for only a short period of time would be insufficient consideration under the circumstances. Another factor affecting reasonableness is the circumstances under which an employee leaves. Although an at-will employee can be discharged for any reason without breach of the contract, a discharge which is arbitrary, capricious or in bad faith clearly has a bearing on whether a court of equity should enforce a non-competition covenant. *Id.*, 154 So. 2d at 155; Gibson's Suits in Chancery § 18 (6th ed. 1982).

We find that because of the length of employment of each defendant, the covenant is binding against them. Defendants Ingram and Goostree remained with CAB for seven years after signing the covenants while defendant Bjorkholm was employed for two years. Each defendant left voluntarily; there is no evidence that CAB acted in bad faith or with unclean hands. It is unnecessary at this time to say how long employment must continue before there is substantial performance. . . . The length of employment of each defendant in this case is sufficient to constitute substantial performance.

In addition, we note that defendant Ingram received numerous salary increases while employed at CAB. Beginning as a salesman, Ingram advanced until at the time of his resignation, he occupied one of the highest positions in the company. Defendant Goostree also received numerous salary increases as well as two promotions. He had risen to the position of Nashville district manager at the time he resigned from CAB in order to compete with it in the Nashville area.

Some courts which have required additional consideration other than continued employment have held that a beneficial change in an employee's status constitutes sufficient consideration to support a restrictive covenant agreed to after the initial taking of employment. In Davies & Davies Agency, Inc. v. Davies, 298 N.W.2d 127 (Minn. 1980), the employee signed the covenant after his employment began. In enforcing the covenant, the court found decisive the fact that because he had signed the covenant, he had advanced to a responsible selling position in his ten years with the firm, and had in effect taken over one aspect of the firm's business which had become identified with him.

As in *Davies & Davies*, defendants Ingram and Goostree received additional benefits above and beyond continued employment which they would not have received had they not signed the covenants. The fact of these additional benefits shows the extent to which CAB performed under its contracts with Ingram and Goostree. For this additional reason, we hold that the covenants are supported by sufficient consideration.

IV

In Allright Auto Parks, Inc. v. Berry, 219 Tenn. 280, 409 S.W.2d 361 (1966) this Court held that "the time and territorial limits involved must be no greater than is necessary to protect the business interests of the employer." In the instant case the Chancellor found that Central Adjustment Bureau had a legitimate business interest to be protected by the noncompetition covenants and that the defendants' competition damaged that interest. The record supports that finding.

The Chancellor held that although Central Adjustment Bureau had such a legitimate business interest to protect, the covenants sought to be enforced were unreasonably broad. He found that the two year limitation was unreasonable but enforced a one year limitation. He based this upon a finding that when clients of a collection agency change agencies in order to maintain a relationship with a former employee, they do so immediately and that customers seldom use only one collection agency and frequently and regularly re-evaluate their agencies.

The Chancellor further found that the restriction prohibiting contact with any customer which was a client of Central Adjustment Bureau during the defendants' entire terms of employment, was also unreasonable. He, therefore, limited the prohibition to those CAB customers who were customers as of January 1, 1979, and that, as thus altered, the covenant was reasonable and enforceable.

Finally, the Chancellor concluded that the nationwide scope of the restrictions here imposed was too broad but that, since the defendants were competing with CAB in the very area in which they had worked previously, the defendants had no cause to complain.

We agree with . . . the Chancellor . . . that the restrictions were unreasonably broad. As enforced by the Chancellor, however, the covenants were reasonable. The question before this Court is whether the Chancellor had the authority to modify a covenant not to compete which is otherwise unreasonably broad.

. . . At one time the majority of courts employed the "all or nothing at all" rule. *See* Ehlers v. Iowa Warehouse Co., 188 N.W.2d 368 (Iowa 1971). Under this rule, a court either enforces the contract as written or rejects it altogether. A covenant containing a term greater than necessary to protect the employer's interest is void in its entirety. Courts employing this rule reason that partial enforcement delegates to courts, when the covenants prove excessive, power to make private agreements. Rector-Phillips-Morse, Inc. v. Vroman, 253 Ark. 750, 489 S.W.2d 1, 4-5 (1973).

The recent trend, however, has been away from the all or nothing at all rule in favor of some form of judicial modification. Several courts have explicitly overruled their own prior case law and adopted judicial modification. *See, e.g.*, Ehlers v. Iowa Warehouse Co., *supra*; Solari Industries, Inc. v. Malady, 55 N.J. 571, 264 A.2d 53 (1970). Our research indicates some form of judicial modification has now been adopted by the majority of jurisdictions. Annot. 61 A.L.R.3d 397 (1975). We think that under appropriate circumstances, some form of judicial modification should be permitted, especially when, as in the case before us, the covenant specifically provides for modification.

Courts have taken one of two approaches in modifying restrictive covenants. The "blue pencil" rule provides that an unreasonable restriction against competition may be modified and enforced to the extent that a grammatically meaningful reasonable restriction remains after the words making the restriction unreasonable are stricken. For example, in a restriction on soliciting business clients in "Toledo, Ohio, and the United States" the court would "blue pencil" or mark out "Ohio, and the United States" leaving the covenant enforceable in Toledo. *See*, Briggs v. Butler, 140 Ohio St. 499, 45 N.E.2d 757 (1942).

The blue pencil rule has the advantage of simplicity and prevents a court from actually rewriting private agreements. On the other hand, the contract still fails if the offending provision cannot be stricken. Often a divisible term contains an integral part of the agreement so that "blue penciling" the provision emasculates the contract. The rule has been criticized as emphasizing form over substance. It has been rejected as against the weight of authority and criticized by writers such as Williston and Corbin. RESTATEMENT (SECOND) OF CONTRACTS § 184 reporter's note; 6A Corbin on Contracts, §§ 1390 and 1394 (1968); 14 Williston on Contracts, § 1647B, 1647C (3d ed. 1972).

The most recent trend, therefore, has been to abandon the "blue pencil" rule in favor of a rule of reasonableness. This rule provides that unless the circumstances indicate bad faith on the part of the employer, a court will enforce covenants not to compete to the extent that they are reasonably necessary to protect the employer's interest "without imposing undue hardship on the employee when the public interest is not adversely affected." Ehlers v. Iowa Warehouse Co., *supra*, at 370.

We are persuaded that the rule of reasonableness is the better rule. It is consistent with and an extension of the rule of reasonableness set forth in Allright Auto Parks v. Berry, *supra*. In adopting it, we do not intend a retreat from the general rule precluding courts from creating new contracts for parties. We are guided instead by the special nature of covenants not to compete already discussed. Further, as noted by two leading commentators on contracts:

> This is not making a new contract for the parties; it is a choice among the possible effects of the one that they made, establishing the one that is the most desirable for the contractors and the public at large. Partial enforcement involves much less of a variation from the effects intended by the parties than total nonenforcement would. If the arguments in favor of partial enforcement are convincing, no court need hesitate to give them effect.

Williston & Corbin, *On the Doctrine of Beit v. Beit*, 23 Conn. B.J. 40, 49-50 (1949).

We recognize the force of the objection that judicial modification could permit an employer to insert oppressive and unnecessary restrictions into a contract knowing that the courts can modify and enforce the covenant on reasonable terms. Especially when the contract allows the employer attorney's fees, the employer may have nothing to lose by going to court, thereby provoking needless litigation. If there is credible evidence to sustain a finding that a contract is deliberately unreasonable and oppressive, then the covenant is invalid. Ehlers v. Iowa Warehouse Co., *supra*, at 374. Even in the absence of evidence sufficient to support a finding of invalidity, a court may well find in the course of determining reasonableness that a contractual provision for attorney's fees is unreasonable either in whole or in part.

In the instant case, we hold that the Chancellor acted properly in enforcing the contract on reasonable terms against the defendants. We further find no credible evidence to sustain a finding of bad faith on the part of CAB or to warrant invalidation of the contractual provision on attorney's fees. . . .

BROCK, Justice, dissenting.

. . . There is simply no indication in this record whatever for a conclusion that promotions and increases in compensation, given years after the covenants not to compete were executed, were bargained for and given in exchange for those covenants. The covenants not to compete in the instant case were not bargained for at all but were merely imposed upon the employees after their employment began. I would hold that these covenants fail for lack of consideration. The majority finds consideration where there is none.

I agree with both the Chancellor and the Court of Appeals that the restrictions in these covenants were unreasonably broad. But . . . I continue to adhere to the rule that the courts of this state have no business in creating new contracts for the parties. Our proper role is to enforce a contract as written, or, if it be invalid, to reject it altogether. . . . [T]he parties are not entitled to make an agreement that they will be bound by whatever contract the courts may make for them at some time in the future, since this would confer upon the courts the power to make private agreements. I also find persuasive the following observation:

> For every covenant that finds its way to court, there are thousands which exercise an in terrorem effect on employees who respect their contractual obligations and on competitors who fear legal complications if they employ a covenator, or who are anxious to maintain gentlemanly relations with their competitors. Thus, the mobility of untold numbers of employees is restricted by the intimidation of restrictions whose severity no court would sanction. If severance is generally applied, employers can fashion truly ominous covenants with confidence that they will be pared down and enforced when the facts of a particular case are not unreasonable. This smacks of having one's employee's cake, and eating it too.

Blake, *Employee Agreements Not to Compete*, 73 Harv. L. Rev. 625, 682-83 (1960).

The policy whereby unreasonable covenants not to compete are to be modified by the courts and, as thus modified, enforced, will permit an employer to insert oppressive and unnecessary restrictions into such covenants, knowing that the courts will modify and enforce the covenants on reasonable terms. And, when such covenants contain a provision for the employer to recover attorney's fees, as they often do, the employer will have nothing to lose by going to court, thereby provoking needless litigation.

I would hold that the Chancellor erred in his attempt to so modify the unreasonable provisions of these covenants not to compete as to render them reasonable and to enforce the altered "covenants."

NOTES AND QUESTIONS

1. The problem of the timing of an employer's presentation of a covenant not to compete continues to vex the courts and state legislatures. Part of the problem, as the dissent notes, is that a newly arriving employee is already committed to the employment as a practical and emotional matter before his first day of work. If the employer first presents a covenant after the employee has already accepted an offer of employment, is the employee's promise not to compete based on a freely bargained exchange? Some states have addressed the problem by statute. An Oregon law, for example, provides as follows:

> A noncompetition agreement entered into between an employer and employee is void and shall not be enforced by any court in this state unless the agreement is entered into upon the:
>
> (a) Initial employment of the employee with the employer; or

(b) Subsequent bona fide advancement of the employee with the employer.

Or. Rev. Stat. § 653.295(1). But most states do not require an employer to present a noncompetition agreement at the time of hire. *See, e.g.,* Lucht's Concrete Pumping v. Horner, 255 P.3d 1058, 1061 (Colo. 2011) (employer's forbearance of right to terminate existing at-will employment is adequate consideration for noncompetition agreement).

2. If an employee and employer made a binding oral or otherwise informal employment agreement without any mention of a covenant, isn't the employer's later insistence on the execution of a covenant a repudiation of the original agreement? If the employee refuses to sign a covenant and the employer discharges the employee, can the employee claim breach of contract? *See* Dymock v. Norwest Safety Protective Equip. for Oregon Indus. Inc. 45 P.3d 114 (Or. 2002) (no, if employment was at will); Maw v. Advanced Clinical Comm'ns, Inc., 846 A.2d 604 (N.J. 2004) (same). *But see* D'sa v. Playhut, Inc., 102 Cal. Rptr. 2d 495 (Cal. App. 2000) (plaintiff stated claim that employer discharged him for refusing to sign covenant that violated the limits of California law).

Would a discharge following a refusal to sign a covenant be a good occasion for the application of promissory estoppel or fraudulent inducement? Should it matter whether the employee is a new hire versus a long-term employee?

3. If an employee, having already started work, signs a covenant, can the employee later assert the "preexisting duty" rule as a defense against enforcement? If the employee had a contractual right to continued employment, as in the case of employment for a fixed term, the employer's implied promise to continue the employment in exchange for the covenant is worthless—the employer already owed a duty to continue the employment. Thus, the covenant lacks consideration. But if the employment is at will, the question might be whether an employer's promise to continue employment at will is "illusory." How did the majority in *Central Adjustment Bureau* avoid this question in upholding the agreement?

4. If an employer promised not to discharge an employee except for "cause," and it later insisted on the employee's execution of a covenant, would the covenant be supported by consideration?

5. Should a court require a higher level of formality for formation of a covenant not to compete than for other types of contracts? *Compare* Harrison v. Williams Dental Group, P.C., 140 S.W.3d 912 (Tex. App. 2004) (yes; and special concerns raised by such agreements preclude recognition of employee's implied agreement to amendment of covenant); *with* Metcalfe Inv., Inc. v. Garrison, 919 P.2d 1356 (Alaska 1996) (enforcing oral agreement not to misuse customer lists).

6. If the covenant is the product of a freely bargained exchange, supported by valid consideration, a court might still deny enforcement if the covenant is "unreasonable" in scope. Reasonableness, in this context, has three possible dimensions: duration, geographic coverage, and activity. What is "reasonable" depends on what types of interests (e.g., trade secrets, training, or customer relationships) an employer is seeking to protect.

a. ***Duration***. A contractual duty not to compete is unreasonable if it continues longer than necessary to protect an employer's legitimate interests. In the case of trade secrets, for example, a court might ask how long it will take for information to become "stale." *See* Surgidev Corp. v. Eye Tech., Inc., 648 F. Supp. 661, 696 (D. Minn. 1986); Volunteer Firemen's Ins. Servs., Inc. v. CIGNA Property & Cas. Ins. Agency, 693 A.2d 1330 (Pa. Super. 1997) (upholding three-year covenant, based on finding that marketing information possessed by defendant might not become stale for three years). The accelerated pace of many high-tech industries means that much information loses its value fairly quickly.

b. *Geographic coverage*. Whether a rule of reasonableness requires a limit on geographic coverage depends on the character of the interest being protected and the nature of the market with the disputed competition. In an era of global competition, a defecting employee who takes training or trade secrets with him can cause just as much damage whether he moves to the employer next door or to an employer half a world away. If the employer seeks to protect its investment in the employee's development of business and customer relationships within a particular market, that market will usually mark the geographic borders of what is reasonable. McCart v. H & R Block, Inc., 470 N.E.2d 756 (Ind. App. 1984). However, when the employer is protecting established customer relationships, courts often prefer a substitute for geographic criteria: The covenant must go no further than to bar the former employee's contact with the customers he served for the employer, regardless of where they are located. *See, e.g.,* Robert S. Weiss & Assoc. v. Wiederlight, 208 Conn. 525, 546 A.2d 216 (1988).

c. *Activity*. A covenant could not reasonably prohibit all prospective employment, only competitive employment that threatens an employer's legitimate interests. Karpinski v. Ingrasci, 268 N.E.2d 751 (N.Y. 1971) (prohibition against defendant's practice of dentistry in designated region was overbroad, where defendant had served plaintiff only for purpose of oral surgery). Former employees possessing valuable trade secret information might pose some risk to the employer no matter what their job classification with a competitor. On the other hand, a former employee who no longer works in a sales or marketing position probably poses little risk to the employer's customer relationships.

7. Is it reasonable for an employer to discharge an employee and then enforce a covenant not to compete to prevent the employee from gaining employment in her chosen profession? The answer might depend on the wording of the covenant. *See, e.g.*, Gen'l Surgery, P.A. v. Suppes, 953 P.2d 1055 (Kan. App. 1998) (agreement prohibiting competition "should she cease employment" did not apply to involuntary discharge).

Even if the covenant clearly applies to involuntary discharge, some courts have denied enforcement of covenants following a discharge without good cause. "An employer should not be permitted to use offensively an anticompetition clause coupled with a forfeiture provision to economically cripple a former employee and simultaneously deny other potential employers his services." Post v. Merrill Lynch, Pierce, Fenner & Smith, Inc., 397 N.E.2d 358, 360-361 (N.Y. 1979). *See also* Wrigg v. Junkermier Clark, Campanella, Stevens, P.C., 265 P.3d 646 (Mont. 2011); Cent. Monotoring Serv., Inc. v. Zakinski, 553 N.W.2d 513 (S.D. 1996); Insulation Corp. v. Brobston, 667 A.2d 729 (Pa. 1995); C.R. Mohan Rao v. M. Hari Kishan Rao, 718 F.2d 219, 224 (7th Cir. 1983).

An alternative view is that involuntary termination excuses an employee's duty not to compete if the employer's manner in discharging the employee constitutes a "material breach" of one of the employer's duties. *See, e.g.,* Gulick v. A. Robert Strawn & Assocs., 477 P.2d 489, 491 (Colo. App. 1970) (employee would have been relieved of duty not to compete had employer committed a "material breach" of its own obligations, but employer's breach of duty to give 15-days advance notice of termination was "minor" and did not excuse employee from duty not to compete). If this principle is correct, remember that termination is one point in an employment relationship when an employer is frequently tempted to withhold all or part of an employee's current or deferred compensation and benefits. *See* Chapter 4.C.4.b.

8. An employee who is not fired but *resigns* is in a weaker position to claim unfairness in being compelled to comply with a reasonable and legitimate duty not to compete after resignation. However, the reason for resignation might matter. A court might still deny enforcement of an otherwise lawful covenant against an employee who resigned if the employer committed a material breach, such as by failing to pay the employee what it owes under the contract. *See, e.g.,* DeCapua v. Dine-A-Mate, Inc., 292 A.D.2d 489, 491 (N.Y. App. 2002) (employee who resigned was released from duty not to compete because of employer's breach of royalty agreement); Lantor, Inc. v. Ellis, 1998 WL 726502 (Mass. Super. Ct. 1998) (employee who resigned was released from duty not to compete because of employer's improper modification of bonus agreement).

9. Injunctive relief is likely to be the employer's favorite remedy for the enforcement of a covenant not to compete, especially if the employer can gain such relief at a quick preliminary hearing before the employee's competitive activity can cause much damage. Covenants frequently recite an employee's acknowledgment that a breach would cause irreparable harm to the employer, and that injunctive relief is appropriate. A covenant might also include some variation on a liquidated damages clause, to provide for recovery of damages without the necessity of proof. *See* Olliver/Pilcher Ins., Inc. v. Daniels, 715 P.2d 1218 (Ariz. 1986) (finding covenant unreasonable and unjustified in requiring employee to pay employer certain portion of his commissions earned from customers in the same state); Post v. Merrill Lynch, Pierce, Fenner & Smith, 397 N.E.2d 358 (N.Y. 1979) (former employee who accepted competitive employment was entitled to deferred compensation from his first employer, despite agreement that he would forfeit compensation upon accepting employment with competitor, where employer terminated employee without cause).

Enforcement of "Unreasonable" Covenants

An employer might believe it has little to lose in requiring employees to sign an unjustified or unreasonably broad covenant. Even if the covenant would be plainly unenforceable in the eyes of a court, the employer might persuade some employees otherwise. Whether or not an employer is ever called to prove the case for its covenant in a court, it might use the covenant to threaten an employee or his prospective employers. If an employee successfully challenges the covenant as unreasonably broad, some courts will reform the covenant to grant the employer the maximum allowable protection, and enforce the reformed covenant. There are, however, a few rules to restrain an employer from overreaching.

First, not all courts grant reformation. An employer who drafts badly could end up with no protection at all. Moreover, reformation is an equitable remedy; a court that might have considered reformation could deny the remedy if it believes the employer was overreaching. Data Mgmt., Inc. v. Greene, 757 P.2d 1356 (Alaska 1996) (for reformation, employer must prove it drafted in good faith).

Second, reformation permits *prospective*, not *retroactive*, enforcement. An employee is not liable for violating an unenforceable covenant. Thus, if the covenant requires reformation, the employer can recover only for damages caused *after* reformation. Perez v. Texas Disposal Sys., Inc., 53 S.W.3d 480 (Tex. App. 2001). By then, the greatest damage to the employer might already be done.

Third, an employer's extrajudicial actions, such as threatening the employee's associates and new or prospective employer, could result in the employer's liability for tortious interference with the employee's contractual and business relations if the employer had no reasonable basis for believing the covenant was enforceable. Sevier Ins. Agency v. Willis Carroon Corp., 711 So. 2d 995 (Ala. 1998); Stebbins & Roberts, Inc. v. Halsey, 582 S.W.2d 266 (Ark. 1979). Finally, some states provide statutory remedies against employers who seek enforcement of unreasonable or unjustified covenants. *See, e.g.*, Tex. Bus. & Com. Code § 15.51 (awarding employee costs, including attorneys' fees, in defending against employer's action for enforcement).

Another important wrinkle in the enforcement of a covenant not to compete is that the case is often won or lost in the hearing for a preliminary injunction—not at the later full dress trial on the merits. By the time the parties reach a trial on the merits, if they get that far, one party or the other might already have prevailed as a practical matter. If the employer prevails at the preliminary hearing, the preliminary injunction may be enough to cripple the employee's new business or chill his employment prospects. But a preliminary hearing is typically without the same careful preparation, opportunity for discovery, or presentation of witnesses or briefing that accompanies a trial on the merits. In this setting, an employer's advantage of resources for litigation and experience in dealing with such cases can be especially important. The employee's chief protection against an improvidently granted preliminary injunction is the injunction bond, which an employer must post to gain the injunction. The amount of the bond is determined by the trial court, and the amount of the bond could be a key issue because it will ordinarily be the limit of the employee's recovery for a wrongful injunction. *See* Wright Med. Tech., Inc. v. Grisoni, 135 S.W.3d 561 (Tenn. App. 2001); Ex parte Waterjet Sys., Inc., 758 So. 2d 505 (Ala. 1999); Dicen v. New Sesco, Inc., 806 N.E.2d 833 (Ind. App. 2004) (under abuse of discretion standard of review, no error in trial court's determination that $10,000 security bond was sufficient for issuance of preliminary injunction); Richard v. Behavioral Healthcare Options, Inc., 647 So. 2d 976 (Fla. App. 1994) ($100 bond was wholly inadequate).

PROBLEMS

Mack Brainard was a 55-year-old research scientist for AeroTech Industries, which designed special communications for the civilian and military aerospace industries. As a result of a business slump, the company offered early retirement from regular employment for qualified employees, and Brainard qualified. Along with other benefits of early retirement, the company's package included a part-time consultant agreement, in which the employee continued to work as a part-time employee consultant for a fee (in Brainard's case) of $2,000 per month for two years. The stated purpose of the agreement was to assure the employee would be available to provide information and advice about projects in which he had been involved before retiring. Brainard did not and had not signed a covenant not to compete, although he had signed several versions of a confidentiality agreement during his career, promising not to disclose company trade secrets.

Almost immediately after accepting early retirement, Brainard accepted employment with General Engineering, a diversified engineering company with aerospace, naval, and ground transportation divisions. General Engineering hired him for communications research in its naval division. Assume AeroTech could not prove a breach of the confidentiality agreement, and would not prevail if it sued for inevitable disclosure (local law doesn't recognize the theory). Yet AeroTech has reason to fear General Engineering will eventually use what Brainard knows to strengthen its nascent aerospace communications business.

1. Can AeroTech enforce any duty Brainard might have violated by accepting employment with General Engineering?

2. Brainard continues to earn deferred compensation from a plan that pays him a share of royalties earned on inventions to which he contributed. Under the terms of the plan, an employee forfeits his interest if he accepts employment with any company that competes with AeroTech. Can AeroTech lawfully suspend Brainard's receipt of payments from this plan?

C. INTERSTATE ENFORCEMENT PROBLEMS

The enforceability of a covenant not to compete is determined by state law, except in the rare case when a covenant violates federal antitrust law by causing an adverse impact on interstate commerce and competition in the relevant market. *See* Lektro-Vend Corp. v. Vendo Co., 660 F.2d 255 (7th Cir. 1982). The variability of state law raises the question whether a covenant enforceable where made can be enforced if the employee defects to another state where the law regards such an agreement as unenforceable, perhaps on grounds of public policy. Variations in state law also present a temptation for forum shopping. If more than one state might have some basis for jurisdiction over the dispute, either the employer or employee might race to a court in the state with the law most favorable to its position. Forum shopping, in turn, leads to jurisdictional disputes when each party seeks redress in a different state.

California figures prominently in the matter of interstate conflicts, not only because it has the largest labor market of all the states, but also because its law is particularly inhospitable to covenants not to compete. In Advanced Bionics Corp. v. Medtronic, Inc., 59 P.3d 231 (Cal. 2002), a former employee of a Minnesota company accepted new employment with a California employer, and the employee and his new California employer filed a lawsuit in California seeking a declaration that the employee's covenant not to compete with his Minnesota employer was unenforceable under California law. The Minnesota employer responded by filing its own lawsuit in Minnesota seeking to enforce the covenant. The employee and his California employer then sought and obtained the California court's order enjoining the Minnesota employer from moving forward with its Minnesota lawsuit. On appeal, the California Supreme Court held the trial court's injunction against the Minnesota proceeding improper and vacated the injunction.

In finding the trial court's injunction improper, the California Supreme Court examined a number of legal principles relevant to jurisdictional battles between courts. The "first filed" rule, which gives predominance to the jurisdiction of the first court in which a party filed suit, applies to jurisdictional battles between courts of the same "sovereign" (*e.g.*, of the same state), but does not necessarily apply—and does not apply at all under California law—to lawsuits filed in different states. Thus, the California trial court could not properly invoke the "first filed" rule as a reason to enjoin a proceeding in Minnesota. 59 P.3d at 237. Compare *Medtronic, Inc. v. Advanced Bionics Corp.*, 630 N.W.2d 438 (Minn. App. 2001) (Minnesota court in same dispute also rejecting application of the "first filed" rule but for other reasons, and upholding Minnesota court's injunction to prevent enforcement of the California trial court's injunction). As a consequence, it is possible that two lawsuits between the same parties about the same dispute might proceed simultaneously in two different states—as happened in *Advanced Bionics*. However, once either court issues a final judgment entitled to full faith and credit, that judgment will be entitled to enforcement in all other states, including the state in which the other unfinished lawsuit is still proceeding. 59 P.3d at 236. Of course, this rule is likely to lead to a race to judgment as each party seeks to expedite the proceedings in the state of its choice to achieve the first final judgment.

These jurisdictional rules are not the end of the story. Eventually, each court must decide an issue of choice of law: Does the substantive law of Minnesota govern the dispute because the parties executed the covenant in Minnesota, or does California law apply because the employer's object is to remedy a breach in California and restrain employment in California? 630 N.W.2d at 454. In *Advanced Bionics*, the employee's contract with the Minnesota employer included a "choice of law" clause choosing Minnesota law. Is such a clause effective to override the usual choice of law rules? *See* DeSantis v. Wackenhut Corp., 793 S.W.2d 670, 681-682 (Tex. 1990) (invalidating contractual choice of Florida law, where employee signed the agreement in Texas and performed his work in Texas); Hostetler v. Answerthink, Inc., 599 S.E.2d 271 (Ga. App. 2004) (invalidating contractual choice of Florida law, where employee signed the agreement in Georgia and performed his work primarily in Georgia).

Finally, there is a further public policy issue. If a Minnesota court issues an injunction against an employee's service for a California employer, will the injunction violate a fundamental public policy of California favoring labor mobility and denying effect to covenants not to complete? Public policy can be a reason to reject another state's judicial acts even under the Full Faith and Credit Act. RESTATEMENT (SECOND) OF CONFLICT OF LAWS § 90. However, not every difference in state laws is a matter of important or fundamental public policy. The reported decisions of the California and Minnesota courts observed but did not resolve the public policy issues for the parties. The courts were concerned only with the propriety of either judicial system's injunctions. However, in a concurring opinion in the California *Advanced Bionics case,* Justice Brown stated as follows:

> Relocating to California may be, for some people, a chance for a fresh start in life, but it is not a chance to walk away from valid contractual obligations, claiming California policy as a protective shield. We are not a political safe zone vis-à-vis our sister states, such that the mere act of setting foot on California soil somehow releases a person from the legal duties our sister states recognize. Rather, we give full faith and credit to the laws of our sister states, and in a case such as this one, I think doing so requires California courts to apply Minnesota law.

59 P.3d at 239.

For other examples of courts struggling to resolve interstate judicial battles over enforcement of non-competition covenants, *see* Hostetler v. Answerthink, Inc., 599 S.E.2d 271 (Ga. App. 2004) (covenant and choice of law provision signed by parties in Ohio during employment in Ohio was contrary to Georgia public policy and would not be enforced to prevent employee's new employment in Georgia; trial court should enjoin further judicial action to enforce covenant by action in other states); Keener v. Convergys Corp., 342 F.3d 1264 (11th Cir. 2003) (covenant and choice of law provision executed in Ohio during Ohio employment violated Georgia public policy and were unenforceable with respect to subsequent Georgia employment, but court could not properly enjoin other judicial actions to enforce covenant "worldwide"). In *Keener*, the court stated:

> Georgia of course is entitled to enforce its public policy interests within its boundaries and, in the circumstance that litigation over [a covenant not to compete] is initiated in Georgia, it may employ that public policy to override a contracted choice of law provision. However, Georgia cannot in effect apply its public policy decisions nationwide—the public policy of Georgia is not that everywhere.

Id. at 1269.

Would a choice of forum clause have prevented the multistate jurisdictional battle in *Advanced Bionics*? *See* In re AutoNation, Inc., 228 S.W.3d 663 (Tex. 2007) (upholding choice of forum clause, noting, however, that the effectiveness of such a clause depends on a multitude of facts).

CHAPTER 10

Resolution of Employment Disputes

A. INFORMAL ADJUSTMENT OF RIGHTS AND CLAIMS

Employment law is an assortment of common law, constitutional law, and statutes, frequently overlapping and complementary, sometimes redundant or conflicting. The interaction between different laws on the same set of facts depends on the substance, source, and enforcement scheme for each applicable law.

At the outset, employment is a contractual relation. The common law of contracts may offer at least part of the answer to nearly any question of rights and duties between the parties. One way of distinguishing other types of laws is by their effect on the contract of employment. Some laws create rights that are negotiable. Such rights can be waived or overridden by contract. For example, intellectual property laws establish rules for determining who is an author or inventor, but an employer and employee can change these rules in their contract. Similarly, some state laws that prohibit wage deductions permit a contractual authorization to deduct.

In contrast, many employment statutes are not subject to variation by contract. Some statutes are particularly clear that the rights they create are not subject to negotiation. For example, workers' compensation statutes frequently expressly forbid a waiver of rights to workers' compensation protection. *See, e.g.*, 45 U.S.C. §55 (anti-waiver provision of Federal Employer's Liability Act). Even in the absence of an explicit prohibition against waiver, such a prohibition might be implicit in a protective statute. The fact that Congress or a state legislature has enacted protective legislation sometimes reflects a legislative finding that certain rights should not depend on negotiation between employees and their more powerful employers. Rights against discrimination under Title VII fall within this category. *See* Alexander v. Gardner-Denver Co., 415 U.S. 36 (1974) (rights against discrimination cannot be waived).

In a few instances Congress has taken a middle road, leaving a limited opportunity for renegotiation, especially for employees who have designated a union to represent them in collective bargaining. The Fair Labor Standards Act, for example, authorizes an employer and union to agree to some changes in the rules of overtime pay even when the same agreement by an individual employee would be void. *See* 29 U.S.C. § 207(b). *But see* Jewell Ridge Coal Corp. v. Local No. 6167, United Mine Workers of America, 325 U.S. 161 (1944) (it is no defense to an employee's statutory right to overtime pay that he earned a high rate of compensation and was represented by a union).

Negotiation and waiver of remedies *after* an employer's breach of an employee's statutory rights is another matter. A rule that prohibited an employee from negotiating a waiver of his claim in return for a payment of money, reinstatement, or other consideration, might interfere with the efficient administration of justice by forcing all cases into costly formal adjudication. For this reason, courts tend to distinguish a waiver of a claim for a past breach from a waiver of a prospective substantive right. In Faris v. Williams WPC-I, Inc., 332 F.3d 316 (5th Cir. 2003), for example, the court considered the meaning of a Department of Labor regulation that "[e]mployees cannot waive, nor may employers induce employees to waive, their rights under FMLA." 29 C.F.R. § 825.220(d). The plaintiff employee in *Faris* argued that this provision rendered her post-termination release of an anti-retaliation claim void. The court disagreed, finding that the regulation barred only a waiver of substantive entitlements under the act and did not bar the plaintiff's settlement and release of an antecedent claim based on the employer's alleged pre-release retaliation against her. *See also* EEOC v. Cosmair, Inc., L'Oreal Hair Care Div., 821 F.2d 1085, 1091 (5th Cir. 1987) (upholding release of ADEA claim); Rogers v. Gen. Elec. Co., 781 F.2d 452 (5th Cir. 1986) (Title VII).

LYNN'S FOOD STORES, INC. v. UNITED STATES

679 F.2d 1350 (11th Cir. 1982)

GOLDBERG, Circuit Judge:

. . . After an official investigation, the Department of Labor concluded that Lynn's Food Stores, Inc. ("Lynn's") had violated FLSA provisions concerning, inter alia, minimum wage, overtime, and record-keeping. As a result, the Department of Labor determined that Lynn's was liable to its employees for back wages and liquidated damages. After the employer's unsuccessful attempts to negotiate a settlement with the Department of Labor, Lynn's approached its employees directly in an attempt to resolve the back wage claims. Specifically, Lynn's offered its employees $1000.00, to be divided among them on a pro rata basis, in exchange for each employee's agreement to waive "on behalf of himself (herself) and on behalf of the U.S. Department of Labor" any claim for compensation arising under the FLSA. Some fourteen Lynn's employees signed the agreements, thereby accepting pro rata shares of $1000.00 in exchange for back wages which, according to Department of Labor calculations, totaled more than $10,000.00. Lynn's then brought this action in district court seeking judicial approval of the settlement.

The FLSA was enacted for the purpose of protecting workers from substandard wages and oppressive working hours. Barrentine v. Arkansas-Best Freight System, 450 U.S. 728 (1981). Recognizing that there are often great inequalities in bargaining power between employers and employees, Congress made the FLSA's provisions mandatory; thus, the provisions are not subject to negotiation or bargaining between employers and employees. Brooklyn Savings Bank v. O'Neil, 324 U.S. 697 (1945). "FLSA rights cannot be abridged by contract or otherwise waived because this would 'nullify the purposes' of the statute and thwart the legislative policies it was designed to effectuate." Barrentine v. Arkansas-Best Freight System, *supra* at 1445.

There are only two ways in which back wage claims arising under the FLSA can be settled or compromised by employees. First, under section 216(c), the Secretary of Labor is authorized to supervise payment to employees of unpaid wages owed to them. An employee who accepts such a payment supervised by the Secretary thereby waives his right to bring suit for both the unpaid wages and for liquidated damages, provided the employer pays in full the back wages.

The only other route for compromise of FLSA claims is provided in the context of suits brought directly by employees against their employer under section 216(b) to recover back wages for FLSA violations. When employees bring a private action for back wages under the FLSA, and present to the district court a proposed settlement, the district court may enter a stipulated judgment after scrutinizing the settlement for fairness. *See* Schulte, Inc. v. Gangi, 328 U.S. 108; Jarrard v. Southeastern Shipbuilding Corp., 163 F.2d 960, 961 (5th Cir. 1947).

It is clear that the agreements for which Lynn's seeks judicial approval fall into neither recognized category for settlement of FLSA claims. The agreements cannot be approved under section 216(c) because they were not negotiated or supervised by the Department of Labor; and because the agreements were not entered as a stipulated judgment in an action brought against Lynn's by its employees, the agreements cannot be approved under existing case law.

Lynn's takes the position that the circumstances in which its employees signed settlement agreements essentially duplicates the adversarial context of a lawsuit brought by employees to resolve a bona fide dispute over FLSA coverage. This is precisely the position rejected by the Supreme Court in . . . *Brooklyn Savings v. O'Neil*, . . . and we take this opportunity to reject it once again.

Settlements may be permissible in the context of a suit brought by employees under the FLSA for back wages because initiation of the action by the employees provides some assurance of an adversarial context. The employees are likely to be represented by an attorney who can protect their rights under the statute. Thus, when the parties submit a settlement to the court for approval, the settlement is more likely to reflect a reasonable compromise of disputed issues than a mere waiver of statutory rights brought about by an employer's overreaching. If a settlement in an employee FLSA suit does reflect a reasonable compromise over issues, such as FLSA coverage or computation of back wages that are actually in dispute; we allow the district court to approve the settlement in order to promote the policy of encouraging settlement of litigation. But to approve an "agreement" between an employer and employees outside of the adversarial context of a lawsuit brought by the employees would be in clear derogation of the letter and spirit of the FLSA.

The facts of this case illustrate clearly why this is so. Lynn's employees had not brought suit against Lynn's for back wages. Indeed, the employees seemed unaware that the Department of Labor had determined that Lynn's owed them back wages under the FLSA, or that they had any rights at all under the statute. There is no evidence that any of the employees consulted an attorney before signing the agreements. Some of the employees who signed the agreement could not speak English.

Lynn's offered for the record a transcription of the settlement "negotiations" between its representative and its employees. The transcript was offered as proof that the employees were not "pressured" to sign the agreements, that the settlements were strictly "voluntary." Ironically, the transcript provides a virtual catalog of the sort of practices which the FLSA was intended to prohibit. Lynn's representative repeatedly insinuated that the employees were not really entitled to any back wages, much less the amounts calculated by the Department of Labor. The employees were told that when back wages had been distributed as a result of past actions taken by the Department of Labor, "Honestly, most everyone returned the checks. . . ." It was suggested that only malcontents would accept back wages owed them under the FLSA: the representative stated, "some (employees) . . . indicated informally to Mr. Lynn and to others within Lynn's Food Stores that they felt like they had been paid what they were due, and that they were happy and satisfied with the arrangements which had been made." Employees who attempted to suggest that they had been paid unfairly were told by the representative "we're not really here to debate the merits of it . . ." and that the objections would be taken up at "another time." The representative summed up the proceedings with this comment, "(t)hose who feel like they've been paid fairly, we want to give them an opportunity to say so." In sum, the transcript is illustrative of the many harms which may occur when employers are allowed to "bargain" with their employees over minimum wages and overtime compensation, and convinces us of the necessity of a rule to prohibit such invidious practices.

. . . [T]he district court was correct in refusing to approve the agreements. Accordingly, the decision of the district court is affirmed.

NOTES AND QUESTIONS

1. There is one more reason for a court to resist an employer's request for judicial approval of its self-supervised settlement of FLSA wage claims: To approve the agreement, the court must engage in the painstaking review of work records, payroll records, affidavits and other documents to determine whether the settlement is at least "fair." In essence, the employer in *Lynn's* sought to bypass Department of Labor supervision by going directly to court. Unlike the Department of Labor, however, a federal judge lacks experience, expertise or dedicated resources to evaluate wage claims. Moreover, an employer has no fiduciary duty to employees or public duty for law enforcement, leaving the court to evaluate whether the settlement is a good one. If the court determines that the settlement might be within the low end of the range of fairness, should it disapprove the settlement if employees might reasonably demand more? By refusing to approve the proposed settlement in *Lynn's*, the court effectively pushed the dispute back to investigation and settlement negotiations between Lynn's and the Department of Labor. On the other hand, when employees are represented by attorneys in litigation against the employer and those attorneys jointly petition the court to approve a settlement, as is necessary in a "collective" action, employees' interests are better represented and the court's task is more limited. *See, e.g.,* Wilson v. Maxim Healthcare Servs., Inc., 2017 WL 2988289 (W.D. Wash. 2017).

2. One reason an employer might be strongly motivated to settle a minimum wage or overtime claim without the supervision of the government is to avoid liability for liquidated damages, which have the effect of doubling the amount of the employer's back pay liability. Even if the employer pays an employee the full amount of back pay in exchange for a release, the employer's payout might be half what it would be in the event of a lawsuit or government

investigation. In Brooklyn Savings Bank v. O'Neil, 324 U.S. 697 (1945), the Supreme Court held that in the absence of a "bona fide" dispute as to the employer's liability for back pay, an unsupervised release for less than back pay plus liquidated damages is no protection for the employer against a subsequent claim for the balance due. The Court's approach bore some resemblance to the "pre-existing duty" rule in contracts law, according to which an obligee's promise not to sue lacks consideration if the obligor paid less than the undisputed portion of a debt. If it cannot reasonably be disputed that at least some amount of back pay is due, an employer's payment of that mount without the additional liquidated damages would arguably be no consideration for the employee's promise not to sue. However, in *Brooklyn Savings Bank* the Court relied mainly on public policy considerations related to Congress's purposes in providing for liquidated damages.

3. Not surprisingly, when employees are represented by attorneys, and especially when they have filed suit against the employer, the courts have been far more willing to approve a settlement of a bona fide dispute over an alleged FLSA violation. *See, e.g.*, Jarrard v. Southeastern Shipbuilding Corp., 163 F.2d 960, 961 (5th Cir. 1947) (court may approve "solemn and binding stipulated judgment entered upon disputed issues of both law and fact" in FLSA suit brought by employees); Martinez v. Bohls Bearing Equipment Co., 361 F. Supp. 2d 608 (W.D. Tex. 2005) (upholding private settlement of FLSA claim where there was a bona fide dispute over the amount of the liability).

4. Most other employment statutes permit an employee to settle a claim without the participation of a court or enforcement agency, but the employee's representation by attorney is likely an important factor. *See* Runyan v. Nat'; Cash Register Corp., 787 F.2d 1039 (6th Cir. 1986) (upholding release of ADEA claim signed by well-paid, well-educated labor lawyer with years of experience). At least one court has held that even the FLSA permits one type of claim be settled without supervision: an anti-retaliation claim. *See* Dorner v. Polsinelli, White, Vardeman & Shalton, P.C., 856 F. Supp. 1483, 1488-1489 (D. Kan. 1994).

5. Unsupervised releases of other types of employee claims are subject to the usual rules of contract, including consideration, mutual assent, and voluntariness. However, where rights under employee protective legislation are involved, courts are more likely to scrutinize the agreement for evidence of unfairness. In Smith v. Amedisys, Inc., 298 F.3d 434 (5th Cir. 2002), the Fifth Circuit described a "totality of circumstances" test that includes the following six factors for deciding whether to uphold an employee's release and settlement of a claim under Title VII: (1) the plaintiff's education and business experience; (2) the amount of time the plaintiff had to review and consider the agreement before signing; (3) the role of the plaintiff in deciding the agreement terms; (4) the clarity of the agreement; (5) whether the plaintiff was represented by or consulted with an attorney; and (6) whether the consideration the employee received exceeded the benefits to which the employee was already entitled by contract or law. *See also* Nicklin v. Henderson, 352 F.3d 1077 (6th Cir. 2003) (describing similar test).

6. Even when an employment law permits the unsupervised waiver of employee claims, the law might provide other means for assuring that public interests will be vindicated. Imagine, for example, that an employer decides to discriminate against minorities by offering to "buy" their voluntary departure. An

employee or applicant who accepts the employer's money and waives any claim might be content with the arrangement, but there could be a larger public interest at stake. Some employee protective laws grant separate rights of enforcement to a government agency — such as the EEOC under Title VII. The agency might take the position, as does the EEOC, that an individual's waiver of his own right to sue does not preclude the agency from bringing its own enforcement action.

Under Title VII, the individual's waiver might bar his receipt of back pay, damages, or reinstatement, but the EEOC can still obtain declaratory and injunctive relief to prevent the employer from continuing its discriminatory practice. *See* EEOC, Enforcement Guidance, *Enforcement Guidance on Non-Waivable Employee Rights under Equal Employment Opportunity Commission (EEOC) Enforced Statutes* (April 10, 1997), at http://www.eeoc.gov/policy/docs/waiver.html. Moreover, the EEOC takes the position that an employee's right to file a charge is nonwaivable, even if he has settled his personal claim. The commission's nonwaiver rule protects the agency's chief source of information about unlawful employer practices — complaining employees. *Id; see also* General Tel. Co. v. EEOC, 446 U.S. 318, 326 (1980).

The Older Workers' Benefit Protection Act

When Congress enacted the Age Discrimination in Employment Act in 1967, it incorporated by reference certain enforcement provisions of the FLSA, which included the FLSA's provisions restricting the unsupervised settlement of claims. A decade later, when Congress transferred enforcement authority for the ADEA from the Secretary of Labor to the EEOC, it also granted the EEOC authority to promulgate its own regulations for the interpretation and enforcement of the act. The EEOC soon took the position that the FLSA's restrictive provisions for the settlement of claims conflicted with the goal of expeditious resolution of disputes, and it issued a regulation permitting the unsupervised settlement of age discrimination claims, within certain limits. 52 Fed. Reg. 32,293 (Aug. 27, 1987).

Congress eventually adopted its own rule for the settlement of age discrimination claims, affirming that individual claimants can settle their claims without government supervision, but providing more protection for age discrimination claimants than is found in nearly any other employment statute (other than the FLSA). The Older Workers' Benefit Protection Act of 1990 (OWBPA) amends the ADEA to provide that an individual's waiver of an age discrimination claim is not "knowing and voluntary" unless, at a *minimum*,

(A) the waiver . . . is written in a manner calculated to be understood by such individual, or by the average individual eligible to participate;

(B) the waiver specifically refers to rights or claims arising under [the ADEA];

(C) the individual does not waive rights or claims that may arise after the date the waiver is executed;

(D) the individual waives rights or claims only in exchange for consideration in addition to anything of value to which the individual already is entitled;

(E) the individual is advised in writing to consult with an attorney prior to executing the agreement;

(F) . . . the individual is given a period of at least 21 days within which to consider the agreement; . . .

(G) the agreement provides that for a period of at least 7 days following the execution of such agreement, the individual may revoke . . . .

29 U.S.C.A. § 626(f)(1). The waiver is subject to additional requirements if it is part of an "exit incentive or other employment termination program offered to a group or class of employees." *See* 29 U.S.C.A. §§ 626(f)(1)(F)(ii), (H).

OUBRE v. ENTERGY OPERATIONS, INC.

522 U.S. 422 (1998)

Justice KENNEDY delivered the opinion of the Court.

. . . Petitioner Dolores Oubre worked as a scheduler at a power plant in Killona, Louisiana, run by her employer, respondent Entergy Operations, Inc. In 1994, she received a poor performance rating. Oubre's supervisor met with her on January 17, 1995, and gave her the option of either improving her performance during the coming year or accepting a voluntary arrangement for her severance. She received a packet of information about the severance agreement and had 14 days to consider her options, during which she consulted with attorneys. On January 31, Oubre decided to accept. She signed a release, in which she "agree[d] to waive, settle, release, and discharge any and all claims, demands, damages, actions, or causes of action . . . that I may have against Entergy. . . ." In exchange, she received six installment payments over the next four months, totaling $6,258.

The Older Workers Benefit Protection Act (OWBPA) imposes specific requirements for releases covering [Age Discrimination in Employment Act] claims. OWBPA, § 201, 104 Stat. 983, 29 U.S.C. §§ 626(f)(1)(B), (F), (G). In procuring the release, Entergy did not comply with the OWBPA in at least three respects: (1) Entergy did not give Oubre enough time to consider her options. (2) Entergy did not give Oubre seven days after she signed the release to change her mind. And (3) the release made no specific reference to claims under the ADEA.

Oubre . . . filed this suit . . . alleging constructive discharge on the basis of her age in violation of the ADEA and state law. Oubre has not offered or tried to return the $6,258 to Entergy, nor is it clear she has the means to do so. Entergy moved for summary judgment, claiming Oubre had ratified the defective release by failing to return or offer to return the moneys she had received. The District Court agreed and entered summary judgment for Entergy. The Court of Appeals affirmed. . . .

The employer rests its case upon general principles of state contract jurisprudence. As the employer recites the rule, contracts tainted by mistake, duress, or even fraud are voidable at the option of the innocent party. . . . The employer maintains, however, that before the innocent party can elect avoidance, she must first tender back any benefits received under the contract. *See, e.g.*, Dreiling v. Home State Life Ins. Co., 213 Kan. 137, 147-148, 515 P.2d 757, 766-767 (1973). If she fails to do so within a reasonable time after learning of her rights, the employer contends, she ratifies the contract and so makes it binding. . . . The employer also invokes the doctrine of equitable estoppel. As a rule, equitable estoppel bars a party from shirking the burdens of a voidable transaction for as long as she retains the benefits received under it. *See, e.g.*, Buffum v. Peter Barceloux Co., 289 U.S. 227, 234 (1933) (citing state case law from Indiana and New York). Applying these principles, the employer claims the employee ratified the ineffective release (or faces estoppel) by retaining all the sums paid in consideration of it. The employer, then, relies not upon the execution of the release but upon a later, distinct ratification of its terms.

These general rules may not be as unified as the employer asserts. *See generally* Annot., 76 A.L.R. 344 (1932) (collecting cases supporting and contradicting these rules); Annot., 134 A.L.R. 6 (1941) (same). And in equity, a person suing to rescind a contract, as a rule, is not required to restore the consideration at the very outset of the litigation. *See* 3 RESTATEMENT (SECOND) OF CONTRACTS, *supra*, § 384, and Comment b; RESTATEMENT OF RESTITUTION § 65, Comment d (1936); D. Dobbs, Law of Remedies § 4.8, p. 294 (1973). Even if the employer's statement of the general rule requiring tender back before one files suit were correct, it would be unavailing. The rule cited is based simply on the course of negotiation of the parties and the alleged later ratification. The authorities cited do not consider the question raised by statutory standards for releases. . . .

In 1990, Congress amended the ADEA by passing the OWBPA. The OWBPA provides: "An individual may not waive any right or claim under [the ADEA] unless the waiver is knowing and voluntary. . . . [A] waiver may not be considered knowing and voluntary unless at a minimum" it satisfies certain enumerated requirements, including the three listed above. 29 U.S.C. § 626(f)(1).

The statutory command is clear: An employee "may not waive" an ADEA claim unless the waiver or release satisfies the OWBPA's requirements. The policy of the OWBPA is likewise clear from its title: It is designed to protect the rights and benefits of older workers. The OWBPA implements Congress' policy via a strict, unqualified statutory stricture on waivers, and we are bound to take Congress at its word. Congress imposed specific duties on employers who seek releases of certain claims created by statute. Congress delineated these duties with precision and without qualification: An employee "may not waive" an ADEA claim unless the employer complies with the statute. Courts cannot with ease presume ratification of that which Congress forbids.

The OWBPA sets up its own regime for assessing the effect of ADEA waivers, separate and apart from contract law. The statute creates a series of prerequisites for knowing and voluntary waivers and imposes affirmative duties of disclosure and waiting periods. The OWBPA governs the effect under federal law of waivers or releases on ADEA claims and incorporates no exceptions or qualifications. The text of the OWBPA forecloses the employer's defense, notwithstanding how general contract principles would apply to non-ADEA claims.

The rule proposed by the employer would frustrate the statute's practical operation as well as its formal command. In many instances a discharged employee likely will have spent the moneys received and will lack the means to tender their return. These realities might tempt employers to risk noncompliance with the OWBPA's waiver provisions, knowing it will be difficult to repay the moneys and relying on ratification. We ought not to open the door to an evasion of the statute by this device.

Oubre's cause of action arises under the ADEA, and the release can have no effect on her ADEA claim unless it complies with the OWBPA. In this case, both sides concede the release the employee signed did not comply with the requirements of the OWBPA. Since Oubre's release did not comply with the OWBPA's stringent safeguards, it is unenforceable against her insofar as it purports to waive or release her ADEA claim. As a statutory matter, the release cannot bar her ADEA suit, irrespective of the validity of the contract as to other claims.

In further proceedings in this or other cases, courts may need to inquire whether the employer has claims for restitution, recoupment, or setoff against the employee, and these questions may be complex where a release is effective as to some claims but not as to ADEA claims. We need not decide those issues here, however. It suffices to hold that the release cannot bar the ADEA claim because it does not conform to the statute. Nor did the employee's mere retention of moneys amount to a ratification equivalent to a valid release of her ADEA claims, since the retention did not comply with the OWBPA any more than the original release did. The statute governs the effect of the release on ADEA claims, and the employer cannot invoke the employee's failure to tender back as a way of excusing its own failure to comply.

We reverse the judgment of the Court of Appeals and remand the case for further proceedings consistent with this opinion.

NOTES AND QUESTIONS

1. The OWBA applies only to age discrimination claims under the ADEA, not to claims under other discrimination or employment statutes. Plaintiffs seeking to avoid the effect of releases under other employment laws have often urged courts to adopt the OWBPA as a model for determining whether a release is knowing and voluntary. In general, the courts have rejected the invitation. Chaplin v. NationsCredit Corp., 307 F.3d 368 (5th Cir. 2002) (rejecting the rules of the OWBPA with respect to an employee's released claims under ERISA); Adams v. Moore Bus. Forms, Inc., 224 F.3d 324 (4th Cir. 2000) (rejecting the rules of the OWBPA with respect to an employee's released claims under Virginia discrimination law).

2. In a concurring opinion, Justice Breyer emphasized his own view that a defective waiver under the OWBPA is voidable, not void:

> That the contract is voidable rather than void may prove important. For example, an absolutely void contract, it is said, "is void as to everybody whose rights would be affected by it if valid." 17A Am. Jur. 2d, Contracts § 7, p. 31 (1991). Were a former worker's procedurally invalid promise not to sue absolutely void, might it not become legally possible for an employer to decide to cancel its own reciprocal obligation, say, to pay the worker, or to provide ongoing health benefits — whether or not the worker in question ever intended to bring a lawsuit? It seems most unlikely that Congress, enacting a statute meant to protect workers, would have wanted to create — as a result of an employer's failure to follow the law — any such legal threat to all workers, whether or not they intend to bring suit. To find the contract voidable, rather than void, would offer legal protection against such threats.

522 U.S. at 432.

3. If an employee is not required to "disgorge" the payment she received for her release as a condition precedent for filing suit, might she still be liable to the employer for the amount of the payment? Could the employer assert the amount it paid as a counterclaim or offset against any eventual liability to the employee? *See* Kulling v. Grinders for Indus., Inc., 185 F. Supp. 2d 800 (E.D. Mich. 2002) (plaintiffs were not required to tender back any part of payments for their defective releases, nor would court offset amount of payments against employer's liability for ADEA violations, where payments covered not only release of ADEA claims but also claims under other laws).

4. The "disgorgement" or "tender back" rules may still apply to an employee's attempt to avoid the effect of a release of claims under a law other than the ADEA. *See, e.g.*, Jackson v. BellSouth Telecomm'ns, 372 F.3d 1250 (11th Cir. 2004) (employee was required to tender back amount employer paid for release as condition for filing lawsuit after allegedly invalid release of claim under 42 U.S.C. § 1981). *But see* Brown v. S. Burlington, 393 F.3d 337 (2d Cir. 2004) (employee did not necessarily ratify release tainted by misrepresentation even though he did not offer to return payment he received until after filing False Claims Act suit).

5. A frequent question in determining the effect of a release of claims by an employee is whether a release of "any and all claims," or similar language, is sufficient to put the employee on notice that he is waiving a claim under any particular law. The OWBPA takes a clear position in the case of age discrimination claims under the ADEA: The release is ineffective to waive the employee's ADEA claim unless it "specifically refers to rights or claims arising under" the ADEA.

Applying the same approach with respect to every type of claim might be impractical. An employer offering severance pay in exchange for a release of claims might find it difficult to anticipate and list every federal and state employment statute under which the parties might have a dispute. In general, courts hold that it is not necessary for a release to specify each statute (other than the ADEA) as to which the release might apply. *See, e.g.*, Chaplin v. NationsCredit Corp., 307 F.3d 368 (5th Cir. 2002) (waiver of "any and all" claims was sufficient for waiver of plaintiffs' claims under ERISA for unpaid severance pay benefits); Stroman v. West Coast Grocery Co., 884 F.2d 458 (9th Cir. 1989) (release of "any and all claims" barred claim under Title VII).

PROBLEMS

During an ongoing reduction in force, Dwindle & Wayne Manufacturing selected employee James Clame for involuntary layoff. The company offered him a check for $5,000 in severance pay in return for Clame's "voluntary resignation" and a waiver of "any and all claims" arising out of Clame's employment with Dwindle & Wayne. Clame, who had expected the layoff and believed he had no claim against the company, signed the waiver and accepted the $5,000 check.

a. A few days after his discharge, Clame filed a claim for unemployment compensation benefits. The company filed a statement with the unemployment compensation agency opposing the claim, arguing that Clame's waiver barred his claim for benefits. Is the company correct?

b. A few months later, Clame contacted the company's human resources office about the status of his annual bonus. Clame believed that because he was involuntarily laid off, he was entitled to a "pro rata" share of the amount of the bonus he would have earned for the whole year. Does Clame's waiver bar his claim for a part of the bonus?

B. OVERLAPPING REMEDIES AND PROCEEDINGS

1. *Time Limits for Formal Action*

In comparison with the statutes of limitations in many other fields of the law, the statutes of limitations for employment laws are typically quite short. Title VII, for example, requires a complaining party to file a charge with the EEOC before filing a judicial lawsuit, and he must file his EEOC charge within 180 days after the alleged act of discrimination (the effect of deferral procedures in some states can stretch the time for filing an EEOC charge to as many as 300 days). Many other employment statutes require judicial or administrative action in an even shorter period of time. *See, e.g.*, 15 U.S.C. § 2622(b)(1) (30-day time limit for charge under whistleblower provision of the Toxic Substances Control Act). The compressed time for initiating an administrative or judicial action makes it especially important to know exactly when the clock begins to run.

INTERNATIONAL UNION OF ELEC., RADIO & MACH. WORKERS, AFL-CIO, LOCAL 790 v. ROBBINS & MYERS, INC.

429 U.S. 229 (1976)

Mr. Justice REHNQUIST delivered the opinion of the Court.

Petitioners seek review of a decision of the Court of Appeals for the Sixth Circuit holding that a claim brought by petitioner Dortha Guy under Title VII of the Civil Rights Act of 1964 was barred by her failure to file a charge with the Equal Employment Opportunity Commission (EEOC) within the statutory limitations period. They present three contentions: The existence and utilization of grievance procedures postpone the date on which an allegedly discriminatory firing took place; the existence and utilization of grievance procedures toll the running of the limitations period which would otherwise begin on the date of the firing; and the 1972 amendments to Title VII, Equal Employment Opportunity Act of 1972, 86 Stat. 103 (Mar. 24, 1972), extending the limitations period from 90 to 180 days, apply to the charge in this case.

I

Respondent Robbins & Myers, Inc. (hereinafter respondent), terminated the employment of petitioner Guy on October 25, 1971, and assigned as its reason for doing so her failure to comply with procedures contained in the collective-bargaining agreement pertaining to leaves of absence. Two days later petitioner caused a grievance alleging an "unfair action" of the company in firing her to be filed on her behalf in accordance with the provisions of the collective-bargaining agreement then in force between petitioner Local 790 of the International Union of Electrical, Radio and Machine Workers (Local 790) and respondent. That agreement's dispute-resolution procedure, which is to be commenced within "five (5) working days of the commission of the act originating the grievance," consists of three grievance steps followed by one arbitration step. Guy's grievance was processed through the third step of the grievance procedure where it was denied on November 18, 1971, with the finding that her termination had been in accordance with the provisions of the collective-bargaining agreement.

On February 10, 1972, a date 84 days after the denial of her grievance at the third stage, but 108 days after the date of her discharge, Guy, who is black, filed a charge of racial discrimination with the EEOC directed against both respondent and Local 790. The EEOC in November 1973, issued its determination and "right to sue" letter, finding that there was "no reason to believe that race was a factor in the decision to discharge" Guy. Her suit in the United States District Court for the Western District of Tennessee under 42 U.S.C. § 2000e5, was met by a motion to dismiss on the ground, inter alia, that it was barred because of her failure to file a charge with the EEOC within 90 days of her discharge, § 706(d), 42 U.S.C. § 2000e-5(d). The District Court dismissed her action, and the Court of Appeals affirmed that judgment by a divided vote. . . .

II

[P]etitioners Guy and Local 790 assert that the complaint with the EEOC was timely filed . . . because the date "the alleged unlawful employment practice occurred" is the date of the conclusion of the collective-bargaining agreement's grievance-arbitration procedures. Until that time, we are told, the October 25 discharge of Guy (although itself an "occurrence" allowing immediate resort to the EEOC) was "tentative" and "non-final," and remained so until she terminated the grievance and arbitration process, at which time the "final" occurrence transpired. As a consequence, according to petitioners, the unfavorable termination of the grievance procedures, making the discharge "final," constituted an "occurrence" enabling Guy to start the 90-day period running from that date.

While the parties could conceivably have agreed to a contract under which management's ultimate adoption of a supervisor's recommendation would be deemed the relevant statutory "occurrence," this was not such a contract. For all that appears Guy was fired as of October 25, 1971 . . . . She stopped work and ceased receiving pay and benefits as of that date. Unless the grievance procedures resulted in her reinstatement, she would not be entitled to be paid for the period during which the grievance procedures were being implemented. . . .

III

We think that petitioners' arguments for tolling the statutory period for filing a claim with the EEOC during the pendency of grievance or arbitration procedures under the collective-bargaining contract are virtually foreclosed by our decisions in Alexander v. Gardner-Denver Co., 415 U.S. 36 (1974), and in Johnson v. Railway Express Agency, 421 U.S. 454 (1975). In *Alexander* we held that an arbitrator's decision pursuant to provisions in a collective-bargaining contract was not binding on an individual seeking to pursue his Title VII remedies in court. We reasoned that the contractual rights under a collective-bargaining agreement and the statutory right provided by Congress under Title VII "have legally independent origins and are equally available to the aggrieved employee," 415 U.S., at 52, and for that reason we concluded:

> (I)n instituting an action under Title VII, the employee is not seeking review of the arbitrator's decision. Rather, he is asserting a statutory right independent of the arbitration process.

Id., at 54.

One Term later, we reaffirmed the independence of Title VII remedies from other pre-existing remedies available to an aggrieved employee. In Johnson v. Railway Express Agency, we held that the timely filing of a charge with the EEOC pursuant to § 706 of Title VII did not toll the running of the statute of limitations applicable to an action, based on the same facts, brought under 42 U.S.C. § 1981. In reaffirming the independence of Title VII remedies from other remedies, we noted that such independence might occasionally be a two edged sword, but "in the face of congressional emphasis upon the existence and independence of the two remedies," we were disinclined "to infer any positive preference for one over the other, without a more definite expression in the legislation Congress has enacted," 421 U.S., at 461.

Petitioners insist that notwithstanding these decisions, equitable tolling principles should be applied to this litigation, and that the application of such principles would toll the 90-day period pending completion of the grievance procedures. This is so, they say, because here the "policy of repose, designed to protect defendants," Burnett v. New York Central R. Co., 380 U.S. 424 (1965), is "outweighed (because) the interests of justice require vindication of the plaintiff's rights."

But this is quite a different situation from *Burnett, supra*. There the plaintiff in a Federal Employers' Liability Act action had asserted his FELA claim in the state courts, which had concurrent jurisdiction with the federal courts, but he had the misfortune of filing his complaint in an Ohio State court where venue did not lie under Ohio law. This Court held that such a filing was sufficient to toll the statutory limitations period, even though the state-court action was dismissed for improper venue and a new complaint ultimately filed in the United States District Court. The Court said:

> Petitioner here did not sleep on his rights but brought an action within the statutory period in the state court of competent jurisdiction. Service of process was made upon the respondent notifying him that petitioner was asserting his cause of action.

Id., at 429.

Here petitioner Guy in the grievance proceedings was not asserting the same statutory claim in a different forum, nor giving notice to respondent of that statutory claim, but was asserting an independent claim based on a contract right, Alexander v. Gardner-Denver Co., *supra*, 415 U.S. at 53-54. *Burnett* cannot aid this petitioner, *see* Johnson v. Railway Express Agency, *supra*, 421 U.S. at 467, and n.14.

Petitioners advance as a corollary argument for tolling the premise that substantial policy considerations, based on the central role of arbitration in labor-management relations . . . also dictate a finding that the Title VII limitations period is tolled in this situation. Similar arguments by the employer in Alexander v. Gardner-Denver Co., urging the superiority and preeminence of the arbitration process were rejected by us in that case, and we find the reasoning of that case controlling in rejecting this claim made by petitioners.

Petitioners also advance a related argument that the danger of possible conflict between the concurrent pursuit of both collective-bargaining and Title VII remedies should result in tolling the limitations period for the latter while the former proceeds to conclusion. Similar arguments to these, albeit relating to 42 U.S.C. § 1981 and not to private labor agreements, were, however, raised and rejected in *Johnson*. We think the language we used in that case is sufficient to dispose of this claim:

> (I)t is conceivable, and perhaps almost to be expected, that failure to toll will have the effect of pressing a civil rights complainant who values his § 1981 claim into court before the EEOC has completed its administrative proceeding. One answer to this, although perhaps not a highly satisfactory one, is that the plaintiff in his § 1981 suit may ask the court to stay proceedings until the administrative efforts at conciliation and voluntary compliance have been completed. But the fundamental answer to petitioner's argument lies in the fact presumably a happy one for the civil rights claimant that Congress clearly has retained § 1981 as a remedy against private employment discrimination separate from and independent of the more elaborate and time consuming procedures of Title VII.

421 U.S., at 465-466.

Petitioners contend at some length that tolling would impose almost no costs, as the delays occasioned by the grievance-arbitration process would be "slight," noting that the maximum delay in invoking the three-stage grievance procedure (although not including the arbitration step) under the collective-bargaining agreement in force in this case would be 35 days. But the principal answer to this contention is that Congress has already spoken with respect to what it considers acceptable delay when it established a 90-day limitations period, and gave no indication that it considered a "slight" delay followed by 90 days equally acceptable. In defining Title VII's jurisdictional prerequisites "with precision," Alexander v. Gardner-Denver Co., 415 U.S., at 47, Congress did not leave to courts the decision as to which delays might or might not be "slight." . . .

IV

Guy filed her charge with the EEOC on February 10, 1972, 108 days after her October 25, 1971, discharge. On March 24, 1972, the Equal Employment Opportunity Act of 1972, extended to 180 days the time within which to file a claim with the EEOC, § 706(e). Petitioners contend that this expanded limitations period should apply to Guy's charge as the occurrence she was complaining of took place within 180 days of the enactment of the 1972 amendments. We agree.

Section 14 of the Equal Employment Opportunity Act of 1972:

> The amendments made by this Act to section 706 of the Civil Rights Act of 1964 shall be applicable with respect to charges pending with the Commission on the date of enactment of this Act and all charges filed thereafter.

. . . We thus resolve against petitioners their first two contentions, but resolve the third in their favor. The judgment of the Court of Appeals for the Sixth Circuit is therefore reversed, and the cases are remanded for further proceedings . . . .

NOTES AND QUESTIONS

1. Many employers now have grievance and dispute adjustment procedures for nonunion employees. In Delaware State College v. Ricks, 449 U.S. 250 (1980), the Supreme Court extended the principles of *Robbins & Myers* to the nonunion setting, clarifying the rules for determining when a cause of action accrues for a discharged employee. The *Ricks* plaintiff was a professor who filed an internal grievance against the university for its denial of his tenure application. In accordance with the university's usual procedure, the administration granted Ricks a "terminal year" contract to let him continue his employment while searching for an alternative position elsewhere. The university ultimately denied his grievance. Over a year after the university had formally denied his tenure application, Ricks filed his EEOC charge. Ricks argued that his charge was timely because the act of discrimination did not occur until the university finally terminated his employment at the end of his terminal year or, alternatively, that no discrimination occurred until the university denied his grievance. The Court rejected both arguments.

> It appears that termination of employment at Delaware State is a delayed, but inevitable, consequence of the denial of tenure. In order for the limitations periods to commence with the date of discharge, Ricks would have had to allege and prove that the manner in which his employment was terminated differed discriminatorily from the manner in which the College terminated other professors who also had been denied tenure. But no suggestion has been made that Ricks was treated differently from other unsuccessful tenure aspirants. Rather, in accord with the College's practice, Ricks was offered a 1-year "terminal" contract, with explicit notice that his employment would end upon its expiration.
>
> In sum, the only alleged discrimination occurred — and the filing limitations periods therefore commenced — at the time the tenure decision was made and communicated to Ricks. That is so even though one of the effects of the denial of tenure — the eventual loss of a teaching position — did not occur until later. The Court of Appeals for the Ninth Circuit correctly held, in a similar tenure case, that "[t]he proper focus is upon the time of the *discriminatory acts*, not upon the time at which the consequences of the acts became most painful." Abramson v. University of Hawaii, 594 F.2d 202, 209 (1979) (emphasis added); *see* United Air Lines, Inc. v. Evans, 431 U.S., at 558. It is simply insufficient for Ricks to allege that his termination "gives present effect to the past illegal act and therefore perpetuates the consequences of forbidden discrimination." *Id.* at 557.

449 U.S. at 257.

2. The lower federal and state courts applying other employment laws have generally adopted the same distinction between a "discriminatory act" and "effects" of the act for purposes of determining when an employee's cause of action accrued and the period of limitations began to run. *See, e.g.*, Schindley v. Ne. Texas Cmty. Coll., 13 S.W.3d 62 (Tex. App. 1999) (alleged retaliatory action

against whistleblower occurred when university informed her that grant funding her work would cease on future date and that employment would end on same day).

3. Congress has provided an extension of the time for filing an EEOC charge in one important situation: deferral to state employment discrimination proceedings. *See* 42 U.S.C. § 2000e-5(c)-(e). If a state qualifies as a "deferral" state by virtue of its employment discrimination law, a complainant must first file a charge with the appropriate state authority. Frequently, by virtue of a series of work-sharing agreements, the EEOC will accept a charge on behalf of, and transmit it to, the state authority. The EEOC must then defer to the state agency by allowing it the first (but not unlimited) opportunity to process the charge. To accommodate the additional proceedings required in a deferral state, Title VII allows additional time for the complainant to reach the EEOC. In general, a complainant has 300 days to file with the EEOC in a deferral state. *See* EEOC v. Comm'l Office Prods. Co., 486 U.S. 107 (1988).

4. A sometimes useful theory for extending the time for filing a charge under some employment statutes is the "continuing violation theory," which describes the employer's violation as a series of interconnected acts over time, rather than as a single discrete action occurring at a particular moment. The continuing violations theory is particularly useful in cases of alleged harassment when the harassment involves a continuing course of unlawful action. *See* Clark v. State, 754 N.Y.S.2d 814 (N.Y. App. 2003); Shepherd v. Hunterdon Dev'tl Ctr., 803 A.2d 611 (N.J. 2002). Where the doctrine applies, a charge is timely if at least one act of the continuing course of conduct occurred within the limitations period.

2. *Duplicative Remedies*

a. Federal Preemption of State Law

Federal employment laws frequently include specific provisions regarding their preemptive effect on state and local laws, and they usually take one of two different approaches. First, some federal employment laws completely preempt state or local law from the same field. The Employee Retirement Income and Security Act (ERISA), for example, preempts state laws "insofar as they may now or hereafter relate to" an ERISA plan. 29 U.S.C. § 1144(a). See Chapter 4.D.3, *supra*. Second, some laws preempt in one direction but not the other. They preempt state and local laws that would diminish employee rights, but do not preempt state and local laws that augment employee rights. Title VII, for example, provides that

> Nothing in this subchapter shall be deemed to exempt or relieve any person from liability, duty, penalty, or punishment provided by any present or future law of any State or political subdivision of a State, other than any such law which purports to require or permit the doing of any act which would be an unlawful employment practice under this subchapter.

42 U.S.C. § 2000e-7. Thus, a state could prohibit discrimination on the basis of characteristics not covered by Title VII (e.g., sexual orientation), prohibit employer actions not actionable under Title VII (e.g., harassment not sufficiently severe under Title VII), or award more relief than is available under Title VII.

Still, a state's effort to enhance employee rights could run into problems under this second type of preemption rule. Granting rights to one group of employees may have the effect of diminishing the rights of other employees. For example, a state law that required more affirmative action than is required under federal employment law might be preempted by federal law to the extent it permitted or required reverse discrimination in violation of Title VII. *But see* California Fed. Sav. & Loan Ass'n v. Guerra, 479 U.S. 272 (1987) (pre-FMLA California law requiring unpaid leave for pregnancy, but not requiring leave for other disabling conditions, did not discriminate in violation of Title VII).

Not all federal employment laws include express provisions delineating the extent of their preemption or accommodation of state laws. If a federal law is silent on the issue of preemption, it will likely still have preemptive force to the extent of any conflict between state law and the policy expressed by the federal law. Federal collective bargaining law is one area of employment law in which the courts have developed rules of federal preemption without much guidance from Congress. There are two federal laws of collective bargaining that have particularly important implications for state employment law.

The National Labor Relations Act is the first of these laws. The NLRA grants employees the right of "concerted" activity, governs the appointment of employee bargaining representatives, and prohibits certain "unfair labor practices" by employers or unions. It may also preempt state laws that would interfere with federal labor policy and tip the balance of power between employers and employees. *See* Sears, Roebuck & Co. v. San Diego Carpenters Dist. Council, 436 U.S. 180 (1978); San Diego Building Trades Council v. Garmon, 359 U.S. 236 (1959). The details of federal preemption under the NLRA are quite complex and are beyond the limited scope of this book.

Another federal law of collective bargaining of particular importance is section 301 of the Labor Management Relations Act, 29 U.S.C. § 185, which preempts state law by making enforcement of a collective bargaining agreement a matter of federal law. The agreement itself is a private contract, and standing alone it could not "preempt" a properly enacted statute. However, section 301 requires the application of federal substantive law to the interpretation of a collective bargaining agreement and the resolution of disputes under the agreement. Textile Workers Union v. Lincoln Mills, 353 U.S. 448 (1957).

Nearly every collective bargaining agreement provides that an employer shall not discharge an employee except for "just cause." Suppose an employer discharges an employee for a reason that is both "unjust" in the contractual sense and wrongful under a state law, such as a prohibition against retaliating for certain protected conduct. The next case addresses whether the availability of relief under a collective bargaining agreement precludes relief under state law.

LINGLE v. NORGE DIVISION OF MAGIC CHEF, INC.

486 U.S. 399 (1988)

Justice STEVENS delivered the opinion of the Court.

In Illinois an employee who is discharged for filing a worker's compensation claim may recover compensatory and punitive damages from her employer. The question presented in this case is whether an employee covered by a collective-bargaining agreement that provides her with a contractual remedy for discharge without just cause may enforce her state-law remedy for retaliatory discharge. The Court of Appeals held that . . . the state tort remedy was pre-empted by § 301 of the Labor Management Relations Act, 1947, 29 U.S.C. § 185. We disagree.

I

Petitioner was employed in respondent's manufacturing plant in Herrin, Illinois. On December 5, 1984, she notified respondent that she had been injured in the course of her employment and requested compensation for her medical expenses pursuant to the Illinois Workers' Compensation Act. On December 11, 1984, respondent discharged her for filing a "false worker's compensation claim."

The union representing petitioner promptly filed a grievance pursuant to the collective-bargaining agreement that covered all production and maintenance employees in the Herrin plant. The agreement protected those employees, including petitioner, from discharge except for "proper" or "just" cause, and established a procedure for the arbitration of grievances. The term grievance was broadly defined to encompass "any dispute between . . . the Employer and any employee, concerning the effect, interpretation, application, claim of breach or violation of this Agreement." Ultimately, an arbitrator ruled in petitioner's favor and ordered respondent to reinstate her with full backpay.

Meanwhile, on July 9, 1985, petitioner commenced this action against respondent by filing a complaint in the Illinois Circuit Court for Williamson County, alleging that she had been discharged for exercising her rights under the Illinois workers' compensation laws. Respondent removed the case to the Federal District Court on the basis of diversity of citizenship, and then filed a motion praying that the court either dismiss the case on pre-emption grounds or stay further proceedings pending the completion of the arbitration. Relying on our decision in Allis-Chalmers Corp. v. Lueck, 471 U.S. 202 (1985), the District Court dismissed the complaint. It concluded that the "claim for retaliatory discharge is 'inextricably intertwined' with the collective bargaining provision prohibiting wrongful discharge or discharge without just cause" and that allowing the state-law action to proceed would undermine the arbitration procedures set forth in the parties' contract. [The Court of Appeals affirmed.]

II

Section 301(a) of the Labor Management Relations Act of 1947, 29 U.S.C. § 185(a), provides:

> Suits for violation of contracts between an employer and a labor organization representing employees in an industry affecting commerce as defined in this Act, or between any such labor organizations, may be brought in any district court of the United States having jurisdiction of the parties, without respect to the amount in controversy or without regard to the citizenship of the parties.

. . . In Teamsters v. Lucas Flour Co., 369 U.S. 95 (1962), we were confronted with a straightforward question of contract interpretation: whether a collective-bargaining agreement implicitly prohibited a strike that had been called by the union. The Washington Supreme Court had answered that question by applying state-law rules of contract interpretation. We rejected that approach, and held that § 301 mandated resort to federal rules of law in order to ensure uniform interpretation of collective-bargaining agreements, and thus to promote the peaceable, consistent resolution of labor-management disputes.

In Allis-Chalmers Corp. v. Lueck, 471 U.S. 202 (1985), we considered whether the Wisconsin tort remedy for bad-faith handling of an insurance claim could be applied to the handling of a claim for disability benefits that were authorized by a collective-bargaining agreement. We began by examining the collective-bargaining agreement, and determined that it provided the basis not only for the benefits, but also for the right to have payments made in a timely manner. We then analyzed the Wisconsin tort remedy, explaining that it "exists for breach of a 'duty devolv[ed] upon the insurer by reasonable implication from the express terms of the contract,' the scope of which, crucially, is 'ascertained from a consideration of the contract itself.'" *Id.*, at 216 (quoting Hilker v. Western Automobile Ins. Co., 235 N.W. 413, 415 (Wis. 1931)). Since the "parties' agreement as to the manner in which a benefit claim would be handled [would] necessarily [have been] relevant to any allegation that the claim was handled in a dilatory manner," 471 U.S., we concluded that § 301 pre-empted the application of the Wisconsin tort remedy in this setting.

Thus, *Lueck* faithfully applied the principle of § 301 preemption developed in *Lucas Flour*: if the resolution of a state-law claim depends upon the meaning of a collective-bargaining agreement, the application of state law (which might lead to inconsistent results since there could be as many state-law principles as there are States) is pre-empted and federal labor-law principles — necessarily uniform throughout the Nation — must be employed to resolve the dispute.

III

Illinois courts have recognized the tort of retaliatory discharge for filing a worker's compensation claim, and have held that it is applicable to employees covered by union contracts. "[T]o show retaliatory discharge, the plaintiff must set forth sufficient facts from which it can be inferred that (1) he was discharged or threatened with discharge and (2) the employer's motive in discharging or threatening to discharge him was to deter him from exercising his rights under the Act or to interfere with his exercise of those rights." Horton v. Miller Chemical Co., 776 F.2d 1351, 1356 (CA7 1985) (summarizing Illinois state-court decisions), *cert. denied*, 475 U.S. 1122 (1986). Each of these purely factual questions pertains to the conduct of the employee and the conduct and motivation of the employer. Neither of the elements requires a court to interpret any term of a collective-bargaining agreement. To defend against a retaliatory discharge claim, an employer must show that it had a nonretaliatory reason for the discharge; this purely factual inquiry likewise does not turn on the meaning of any provision of a collective-bargaining agreement. Thus, the state-law remedy in this case is "independent" of the collective-bargaining agreement in the sense of "independent" that matters for § 301 pre-emption purposes: resolution of the state-law claim does not require construing the collective-bargaining agreement.[7]

The Court of Appeals seems to have relied upon a different way in which a state-law claim may be considered "independent" of a collective-bargaining agreement. The court wrote that "the just cause provision in the collective-bargaining agreement may well prohibit such retaliatory discharge," and went on to say that if the state-law cause of action could go forward, "a state court would be deciding precisely the same issue as would an arbitrator: whether there was 'just cause' to discharge the worker." The court concluded, "the state tort of retaliatory discharge is inextricably intertwined with the collective-bargaining agreements here, because it implicates the same analysis of the facts as would an inquiry under the just cause provisions of the agreements." We agree with the court's explanation that the state-law analysis might well involve attention to the same factual considerations as the contractual determination of whether Lingle was fired for just cause. But we disagree with the court's conclusion that such parallelism renders the state-law analysis dependent upon the contractual analysis. For while there may be instances in which the National Labor Relations Act pre-empts state law on the basis of the subject matter of the law in question, § 301 pre-emption merely ensures that federal law will be the basis for interpreting collective-bargaining agreements, and says nothing about the substantive rights a State may provide to workers when adjudication of those rights does not depend upon the interpretation of such agreements.[9] In other words, even if dispute resolution pursuant to a collective-bargaining agreement, on the one hand, and state law, on the other, would require addressing precisely the same set of facts, as long as the state-law claim can be resolved without interpreting the agreement itself, the claim is "independent" of the agreement for § 301 pre-emption purposes.

. . . In sum, we hold that an application of state law is pre-empted by § 301 of the Labor Management Relations Act of 1947 only if such application requires the interpretation of a collective-bargaining agreement.[12]

The judgment of the Court of Appeals is reversed.

NOTES AND QUESTIONS

1. Lingle's pursuit of a wrongful discharge lawsuit in a state court might

---

[7] ... Petitioner points to the fact that the Illinois right to be free from retaliatory discharge is nonnegotiable and applies to unionized and nonunionized workers alike. While ... most state laws that are not pre-empted by § 301 will grant nonnegotiable rights that are shared by all state workers, ... neither condition ensures nonpreemption. ... [A] State could create a remedy that, although nonnegotiable, nonetheless turned on the interpretation of a collective-bargaining agreement for its application. Such a remedy would be pre-empted by § 301....Conversely, a law could cover only unionized workers but remain unpreempted if no collective-bargaining agreement interpretation was needed to resolve claims brought thereunder.

[9] Whether a union may waive its members' individual, non-pre-empted state-law rights, is, likewise, a question distinct from that of whether a claim is pre-empted under § 301, and is another issue we need not resolve today.

[12] A collective-bargaining agreement may, of course, contain information such as rate of pay and other economic benefits that might be helpful in determining the damages to which a worker prevailing in a state-law suit is entitled. Although federal law would govern the interpretation of the agreement to determine the proper damages, the underlying state-law claim, not otherwise preempted, would stand.

seem redundant because she had already obtained an arbitrator's award of full back pay and reinstatement. However, the state court lawsuit offered the possibility of an additional award: punitive damages and perhaps damages for emotional distress. *See* Kelsay v. Motorola, Inc., 384 N.E.2d 35 (Ill. 1979).

2. Employees covered by a collective bargaining agreement frequently find that an employer's alleged breach of some statutory or common law duty might also be viewed as a breach of the collective bargaining agreement. For example, any wrongful discharge in violation of a discrimination or anti-retaliation law is also likely to constitute discharge without just cause in violation of the agreement. As *Lingle* illustrates, an employee might then pursue either or both remedies, *provided* the statutory or common law cause of action can be resolved independently of the collective bargaining agreement. But if an employee's claim is based on a contract right, and the employee has no contract apart from the collective bargaining agreement, he cannot avoid section 301 preemption merely by stating his claim in terms of state law. Bartholomew v. AGL Res., Inc., 361 F.3d 1333 (11th Cir. 2004).

3. When an employee whose employment was governed by a collective bargaining agreement files a complaint against his employer in a state court, the employer might well remove the action to federal court (on federal question grounds), and then seek dismissal based on federal preemption. A plaintiff might seek to avoid removal by relying on the well-pleaded complaint rule, which permits a plaintiff to allege state law and omit any mention of federal law as the basis for his claim even if he could have pleaded a claim under federal law. Moreover, the well-pleaded complaint rule ordinarily prevents removal even if the defendant asserts a defense under federal law — including the defense of preemption. *See, e.g.*, Caterpillar, Inc. v. Williams, 482 U.S. 386, 394-395 (1987); Kline v. Security Guards, Inc., 386 F.3d 246 (3d Cir. 2004). However, if the plaintiff's claim clearly involves a collective bargaining agreement, a federal court might apply the "complete preemption" doctrine, which acts as an exception to the "well pleaded complaint" rule. The complete preemption doctrine permits a federal court to look beyond the face of the plaintiff's pleading in certain cases — including many section 301 preemption cases — for purposes of removal jurisdiction. *See, e.g.*, Vera v. Saks & Co., 335 F.3d 109 (2d Cir. 2003); United Assoc. of Journeymen & Apprentices v. Bechtel Power Corp., 834 F.2d 884, 887-888 (10th Cir. 1987). *See also* Chapter 4.D.3.

4. It is rare, but not impossible, for an employee who is a member of a collective bargaining unit to have a viable claim under an individual contract of employment. Individual bargaining and contract formation is ordinarily barred by the creation of a collective bargaining unit, and an individual contract is ordinarily superseded by a collective bargaining agreement. See Chapter Four, Section B.2, *supra*. Thus, breach of contract claims by unionized employees are nearly always preempted by section 301. *But see* Caterpillar, Inc. v. Williams, 482 U.S. 386 (1987) (no preemption of plaintiffs' state breach of contract claim based on allegation that employer promised them job security while they held non-union management positions and before the employer downgraded them to bargaining unit positions).

5. Collective bargaining agreements typically govern an employee's right

to compensation. If the employer fails to pay the amount due under the contract, the employee's claim is for the breach of the agreement, and section 301 preempts a state breach of contract claim. Vera v. Saks & Co., 335 F.3d 109 (2d Cir. 2003). However, an employee might also seek statutory penalties under state law for the employer's failure to pay wages due. In Livadas v. Bradshaw, 512 U.S. 107 (1994), the Court held that such a claim is not preempted.

> The only issue raised by Livadas's claim, whether Safeway "willfully fail[ed] to pay" her wages promptly upon severance, Cal. Lab. Code Ann. § 203 (West 1989), was a question of state law, entirely independent of any understanding embodied in the collective-bargaining agreement between the union and the employer. There is no indication that there was a "dispute" in this case over the amount of the penalty to which Livadas would be entitled, and *Lingle* makes plain in so many words that when liability is governed by independent state law, the mere need to "look to" the collective-bargaining agreement for damages computation is no reason to hold the state-law claim defeated by § 301.

512 U.S. at 124-125. *But see* Antol v. Esposto, 100 F.3d 1111 (3d Cir. 1996) (section 301 preempted employee's claim against corporate officers under state wage payment law, where there was a dispute over the amount due under the terms of the collective bargaining agreement, and claim against the individual defendants would have circumvented and undermined the arbitration process).

6. In general, a tort claim based on an employer's violation of a duty that exists independently of the collective bargaining agreement is not preempted by section 301. *See, e.g.*, Kline v. Security Guards, Inc., 386 F.3d 246 (3d Cir. 2004) (common law invasion of privacy claim, based on employer's video surveillance of entrance where employees clocked in, was not preempted by section 301). *Accord*, Cramer v. Consolidated Freightways, Inc., 255 F.3d 683 (9th Cir. 2001). *But see* Mock v. T.G. & Y. Stores Co., 971 F.2d 522 (10th Cir. 1992) (torts that arise out of alleged wrongful discharge are preempted by section 301).

7. A question left open by the Supreme Court in footnotes 7 and 9 of its decision in *Lingle* is whether a union can "waive" employee rights under a state law by negotiating an agreement that purports to negate the state law. *See also* Makray v. Sara Lee Corp., 736 F. Supp. 793 (N.D. Ill. 1990) (likewise raising the issue without answering it). If so, section 301 might preempt an employee's effort to enforce the state law in a state court. If the waiver only substitutes arbitration for a state judicial or administrative forum, and the contract restates the same substantive right, it might be argued that employees have lost little and gained much. Antol v. Esposto, 100 F.3d 1111 (3d Cir. 1996) (section 301 barred proceedings under state law to determine wages owed to plaintiffs). However, most courts are reluctant to concede that a collective bargaining agreement could eliminate substantive rights under state law. Cramer v. Consolidated Freightways, Inc., 255 F.3d 683 (9th Cir. 2001) (agreement could not have permitted employer to violate privacy rights under state law); Beckwith v. United Parcel Service, 703 F. Supp. 138 (D. Me. 1988) (no section 301 preemption of state law restricting wage deductions). *But see* Medrano v. Excel Corp., 985 F.2d 230 (5th Cir. 1993) (section 301 preempted employee's claim that employer's application of collective bargaining agreement constituted violation of state law).

b. Statutory Preemption of Common Law Remedies

Preemption issues can arise even across a single level of government, because the statutes a legislature enacts may conflict or overlap with judge-made common law. Both legislatures and judges have been especially active in making new law for employers and employees, and it is not uncommon to find areas of redundancy and conflict in the law. Some statutes anticipate this problem by stating that they do or do not provide the "exclusive remedy" for any action that would constitute a violation of the statute. Still, an exclusive remedy provision may leave unresolved questions about the scope of legislative preemption. Moreover, legislatures often fail to express any intention whether to replace or merely supplement the common law. A court might need to decide whether the existence of a comprehensive administrative enforcement scheme and a specific set of remedies implicitly supersedes the common law.

GOTTLING v. P.R. INC.

61 P.3d 989 (Utah 2002)

HOWE, Justice.

We granted this interlocutory appeal to decide whether the trial court correctly ruled that an at will employee who claims to have been discriminated against by her employer and who is unable to seek relief under the Utah Anti-Discrimination Act can pursue a civil action for wrongful termination in contravention of an alleged public policy against sex discrimination.

BACKGROUND

Plaintiff Toby Gottling alleges that her employer, defendant P.R. Incorporated, terminated her because she refused to maintain a sexual relationship with P.R. Incorporated's owner, defendant Kelly Peterson. The Utah Anti-Discrimination Act (UADA or the Act) provides an administrative remedy for discrimination, retaliation, or harassment by an employer on the basis of sex, race, color, pregnancy, age, religion, national origin, or disability. Utah Code Ann. §§ 34A-5-101 to -108 (1999). The remedy is limited, however, to those persons who work for an employer of fifteen or more employees (large employers). *See* Utah Code Ann. §§ 34A-5-102(8)(a)(iv) (defining "employer" for the purposes of the act as a "person employing 15 or more employees within the state for each working day in each of 20 calendar weeks or more in the current or preceding calendar year"). Because P.R. Incorporated — along with the majority of Utah employers — employs less than fifteen people, Gottling may not look to the UADA for relief from P.R. Incorporated's alleged discrimination. *See* Burton v. Exam Ctr. Indus. & Gen. Med., 2000 UT 18, ¶ 25, 994 P.2d 1261 (Durham, J., dissenting) (stating that as recently as 1999, 69.7% of Utah employers were small employers).

Seeking an alternative remedy, Gottling brought this action asserting a common law tort cause of action previously unrecognized by this court. Relying on our case law forbidding the termination of an at will employee in contravention of a clear and substantial public policy, Gottling alleged that P.R. Incorporated wrongfully terminated her in contravention of a public policy against sex discrimination. . . .

P.R. Incorporated answered Gottling's complaint by denying her allegations and asserting the affirmative defenses that (1) Gottling's cause of action was preempted by the UADA; [and] (2) Gottling had failed to exhaust her administrative remedies under the UADA. . . . [The trial court granted summary judgment in favor of Gottling against these affirmative defenses.] We subsequently granted P.R. Incorporated's petition for interlocutory appeal. . . .

ANALYSIS

P.R. Incorporated contends that Gottling cannot pursue a wrongful termination action based on the contravention of an alleged public policy against sex discrimination because (1) the UADA preempts all common law employment discrimination remedies and (2) Utah does not have a public policy against sex discrimination. . . .

I. PREEMPTION

A.

We have long held that "where a conflict arises between the common law and a statute or constitutional law, the common law must yield," Hansen v. Utah State Ret. Bd., 652 P.2d 1332, 1337 (Utah 1982) because "the common law cannot be an authority in opposition to our positive enactments." In re Garr's Estate, 86 P. 757, 761 (1906). In fact,

> [t]he rule of the common law that statutes in derogation thereof are to be strictly construed has no application to the statutes of this state. The statutes establish the laws of this state respecting the subjects to which they relate, and their provisions and all proceedings under them are to be liberally construed with a view to effect the objects of the statutes and to promote justice.

Utah Code Ann. § 68-3-2 (1999). Consequently, like an ordinance, the common law is invalid "if it intrudes into an area which the [l]egislature has preempted by comprehensive legislation intended to blanket a particular field." State v. Hutchinson, 624 P.2d 1116, 1121 (Utah 1980) (analyzing a statute's preemptive effect on a county ordinance).

Whether legislation is intended to blanket a particular field — and thereby preempt existing or developing common law — is obviously a question of legislative intent. In short, we must decide if the legislature, with its broad lawmaking power, intended to exercise that power and to occupy the field in such a way as to exclude the contemporaneous application and development of the common law. Generally, when answering this question we apply the two-tiered analysis for determining preemptive intent established by the United States Supreme Court. We recently summarized this analytical framework as follows:

> [i] Sometimes courts, when facing the pre-emption question, find language in the . . . statute that reveals an explicit [legislative] intent to pre-empt [common] law. [ii] More often, explicit pre-emption language does not appear, or does not directly answer the question. In that event, courts must consider whether the . . . statute's "structure and purpose," or nonspecific statutory language, nonetheless reveal a clear, but implicit, preemptive intent. [a] A . . . statute,

> for example, may create a scheme of [statutory] regulation "so pervasive as to make reasonable the inference that [the legislature] left no room for the [common law] to supplement it." [b] Alternatively, [statutory] law may be in "irreconcilable conflict" with [the common] law. Compliance with both . . . , for example, may be a "physical impossibility," or, [c] the [common] law may "stand as an obstacle to the accomplishment and execution of the full purpose and objectives of [the legislature]."

Gilger, 997 P.2d 305 (quoting Barnett Bank of Marion County v. Nelson, 517 U.S. 25, 31 (1996)). . . . Thus, where a statute's plain language or its structure and purpose demonstrate a legislative intent to preempt an area of the law, the statute becomes the only source of law in that area, and the development and application of common law principles necessarily ceases.

B.

Turning to the UADA, we find that the plain language of section 34A-5-107(15) reveals an explicit legislative intention to preempt all common law remedies for employment discrimination. This section provides: "The procedures contained in this section are the exclusive remedy under state law for employment discrimination based upon race, color, sex, retaliation, pregnancy, childbirth, or pregnancy-related conditions, age, religion, national origin, or disability." § 34A-5-107(15). The language of this "exclusivity provision" unambiguously indicates that the UADA preempts "common law causes of action" for employment discrimination based on the "specific grounds" it lists. *Retherford* [v. AT&T Communications of Mountain States, Inc.], 844 P.2d at 961 (holding that the UADA preempts common law causes of action for retaliation).

In declaring the UADA to be the "exclusive remedy under state law for employment discrimination," section 34A-5-107(15) makes no distinction between actions against large and small employers. It might be argued that, as used in this section, the phrase "employment discrimination" refers solely to discrimination by large employers because only large employers are subject to the remedial provisions of the UADA. This argument fails, however, because the UADA does not define the phrase "employment discrimination," and therefore, we must read the phrase literally, according to its ordinary and accepted meaning. Ordinarily, the phrase "employment discrimination" denotes discrimination by an employer, regardless of the employer's size. It is in this general sense that the phrase is used in section 34A-5-105(7)(a)(i), where the Anti-Discrimination and Labor Advisory Council is directed to "make recommendations" to the Labor Commission and the Division of Anti-Discrimination and Labor "regarding issues" including "employment discrimination."

We assume that the legislature used the phrase "employment discrimination" advisedly. Elsewhere, the UADA refers to "discriminatory or prohibited employment practices," which are narrowly defined as those activities specified as discriminatory in section 34A-5-106(1)(a) to (f), each of which requires an "employer" within the meaning of section 34A-5-102(8)(a)(iv). *See* § 34A-5-106(1). The legislature could have used the phrase "discriminatory or prohibited employment practices" in section 34A-5-107(15) and thereby have limited the UADA's preemptive effect to common law actions for discrimination against large employers. Nevertheless, it chose to use the undefined, more expansive term. That choice, combined with the use of the word "exclusive" and the lack of any other qualifying language, explicitly reveals the legislature's intent to preempt all other state law causes of action for employment discrimination.

C.

Even if the UADA lacked an explicit statement of preemptive intent, our holding that it preempts common law remedies for employment discrimination would not change because a clear preemptive intent can be implied from the statute's structure and purpose. The UADA was designed "to prohibit discrimination in employment," and it utilizes a variety of tools to accomplish that goal. Not only does it create an administrative remedy for those alleging to have been discriminated against by large employers, the UADA also provides a remedy to those discriminated against by employment agencies, labor organizations, and persons who aid, incite, compel, or coerce to commit "discriminatory or prohibited employment practices." § 34A-5-106(1)(b) to (e). In addition, the UADA "creates a substantial bureaucratic system to implement its aims." *Burton*, 994 P.2d 1261 (Durham J., dissenting). It establishes both the Utah Division of Anti-Discrimination and Labor and the Utah Anti-Discrimination and Advisory Council. §§ 34A-5-104 to -105. It delegates the power to receive, investigate, and pass upon complaints. § 34-5-104(2)(b). . . . Such a detailed and far-reaching approach to the problem of discrimination, encompassing a wide variety of methods, clearly manifests the legislature's intent to completely blanket the field of employment law in Utah.

In addition to evidencing an intent to preempt the field of employment discrimination law in general, the structure of the statute also shows that the legislature intended its preemption of common law employment discrimination actions to apply to employees of small employers. Despite establishing a comprehensive legislative scheme, including a directive that five representatives of the general public sit on the Anti-Discrimination Advisory Committee, *see* § 34A-5-105(1)(a)(v), the UADA specifically exempts small employers from its administrative remedy. *See* § 34A-5-102(8)(a)(iv). The obvious nature of this category of employers — encompassing a majority of employers in Utah — leaves little doubt that its exclusion was intentional. . . . Moreover, the UADA creates an elaborate remedial process requiring that

> [a] covered employee alleging discrimination must assert his claim within 180 days of the alleged discrimination. . . . The charge is filed at the UADD and is handled administratively. Emphasis in the administrative process is placed on conciliation and voluntary resolution. The UADA mandates that the administrative agency "attempt a settlement between the parties by conference, conciliation, or persuasion." If the claimant is successful, the relief provided includes reinstatement, back pay and benefits, and attorney fees, but no compensatory or punitive damages may be awarded. This is all done without charge by the administrative agency.

Burton, 994 P.2d 1261 (internal citations omitted). It would be illogical to suppose that the legislature intended to provide the benefit of this timely and cost-effective procedure to large employers while, at the same time, intending to subject small employers to a civil tort action in which they would be vulnerable to a longer statute of limitations, damages, attorney fees and, possibly, a jury trial. Indeed, "it appears . . . that the policy reflected in the careful legislative designation of those liable and those not liable under the Act cannot coexist with the imposition by courts of different standards of . . . damage exposure for some of those the legislature has decided should not be liable under the Act." *Gilger*, 997 P.2d 305. Accordingly, we conclude that the structure and purpose of the UADA clearly exhibits an implicit intent to preempt common law causes of action for employment discrimination by both large and small employers. . . .

D.

. . . The available legislative history does not reflect precisely why the legislature ultimately chose to eliminate small employer liability. It does, however, reveal that the UADA was modeled after Title VII of the Civil Rights Act of 1964, which contains a similar exemption for small employers. . . . Congress included the small business exception in Title VII to protect the intimate relationships associated with small employers and to shield them from the heavy costs of defending against discrimination claims. Tomka v. Seiler Corp., 66 F.3d 1295, 1314 (2d Cir. 1995) (citing Miller v. Maxwell's Int'l Inc., 991 F.2d 583, 587 (9th Cir. 1993); Birkbeck v. Marvel Lighting Corp., 30 F.3d 507, 510 (4th Cir. 1994) (stating that the purpose of exempting small employers is to reduce burden on small businesses). We have assumed therefore that the small business exception in the UADA was modeled after its federal counterpart and arose from similar concerns about the effect of the UADA on small businesses. *See Burton*, 994 P.2d 1261 (recognizing that the reasons for the small business exemption in federal litigation are applicable to the UADA).

E.

. . . In its ruling, the trial court . . . suggested that the legislature could not have meant to preempt common law actions against small employers because it would be "inequitable" to find that "small employers are granted a license to discriminate and their employees have no recourse available to them." However, the "'legislature need not "strike at all evils at the same time," Semler v. Dental Examiners, 294 U.S. 608, 610, and . . . "reform may take one step at a time, addressing itself to the phase of the problem which seems most acute to the legislative mind," Williamson v. Lee Optical Co., 348 U.S. 483, 489.'" Greenwood v. City of North Salt Lake, 817 P.2d 816, 821 (Utah 1991) (quoting Katzenbach v. Morgan, 384 U.S. 641, 657 (1966)). Moreover, new statutory schemes, in certain circumstances, may preclude formerly available common law causes of action, despite leaving some individuals without a remedy. *See, e.g.*, Masich v. United States Smelting, Ref. & Mining Co., 191 P.2d 612, 624-25 (1948) (upholding legislation abrogating a common law right to recover for work-related injury). In this case, the legislature has not taken away an existing right, but has simply indicated its intent to preempt the creation of a new one.

We hold therefore that because the UADA preempts all common law causes of action for discrimination, retaliation, or harassment by an employer on the basis of sex, race, color, pregnancy, age, religion, national origin, or disability, the trial court erred by recognizing a common law cause of action against a small employer for wrongful termination in contravention of a public policy against sex discrimination.

. . . The summary judgment of the trial court is reversed, and the complaint is dismissed for failure to state a cause of action.

NOTES

1. A more typical setting for an issue of legislative preemption of the common law is when a plaintiff adds a tort claim to a statutory discrimination claim. Title VII and many state discrimination laws permit but "cap" damages for emotional distress and punitive damages. *See* 42 U.S.C. § 1981a. A plaintiff might hope to avoid these damages caps by alleging a tort claim, such as the intentional infliction of emotional distress. *See, e.g.*, Hoffmann-La Roche Inc. v. Zeltwanger, 144 S.W.3d 438 (Tex. 2004) (Texas statute prohibiting employment discrimination superseded common law remedy for intentional infliction of emotional distress); Tate v. Browning-Ferris, Inc., 833 P.2d 1218 (Okla. 1992) (no preemption of tort claims); Annotation, *Preemption of Wrongful Discharge Cause of Action by Civil Rights Laws*, 21 A.L.R.5th 1 (collecting cases addressing the question whether a discrimination statute preempts a tort claim arising out of an act of discrimination).

2. A plaintiff might also assert a tort claim in an effort to avoid dismissal for failure to fulfill the administrative prerequisites for the statutory cause of action. In the *Hoffmann-La Roche* case, *supra*, the Texas court held that any claim that might be presented as a statutory discrimination claim is subject to the same administrative prerequisites — namely the filing of a discrimination charge with the local civil rights agency within the prescribed time limits. Thus, the plaintiff's common law claim for intentional infliction of emotional distress arising out of sexual harassment was barred by the Texas antidiscrimination statute. The court acknowledged that a plaintiff might still have a separate tort claim based on conduct that did not constitute "sexual harassment," but the conduct that might have qualified as such in *Hoffmann-La Roche* was not sufficiently "outrageous," standing alone, to constitute a tort.

c. Multiple Forums and the Problem of Issue Preclusion

Recall that in *Lingle, supra*, an employee challenged her discharge under a collective bargaining agreement, and simultaneously sued the employer in state court for unlawful retaliation under state workers' compensation law. The Supreme Court held that section 301 did not preempt the employee's state statutory claim. Suppose, however, the arbitrator had *rejected* Lingle's grievance and found that the company discharged her for good cause. Would the arbitrator's award preclude her subsequent retaliation lawsuit, under either res judicata or collateral estoppel?

In Alexander v. Gardner-Denver Co., 415 U.S. 36 (1974), the U.S. Supreme Court held that an employee's resort to a grievance and arbitration procedure established by a collective bargaining agreement did not preclude the employee's Title VII lawsuit even if the arbitrator ruled that the employer had cause to discharge the employee.

> [T]he factfinding process in arbitration usually is not equivalent to judicial factfinding. The record of the arbitration proceedings is not as complete; the usual rules of evidence do not apply; and rights and procedures common to civil trials, such as discovery, compulsory process, cross-examination, and

> testimony under oath, are often severely limited or unavailable. And as this Court has recognized, "(a)rbitrators have no obligation to the court to give their reasons for an award." United Steelworkers of America v. Enterprise Wheel & Car Corp., 363 U.S., at 598. Indeed, it is the informality of arbitral procedure that enables it to function as an efficient, inexpensive, and expeditious means for dispute resolution. This same characteristic, however, makes arbitration a less appropriate forum for final resolution of Title VII issues than the federal courts.

415 U.S. at 49-50, 57-58; *see also* Bell v. Conopco, Inc., 186 F.3d 1099 (8th Cir. 1999) (employee's voluntary submission of discrimination issue to arbitrator under collective bargaining agreement did not preclude his later assertion of statutory discrimination claim in a judicial forum); Taylor v. Lockheed Martin Corp., 113 Cal. App. 4th 380, 6 Cal. Rptr. 3d 358 (2003) (arbitrator's decision that employer discharged employee for just cause did not preclude employee's later judicial whistleblower action). *But see* Bell v. Conopco, Inc., 186 F.3d 1099, 1102 (8th Cir. 1999) (arbitrator's award may be admitted in evidence and is entitled to as much weight as court deems appropriate).

In other contexts, where fact issues before an arbitrator and a court are truly identical, courts have sometimes held that relitigation of such issues is precluded as a matter of collateral estoppel. *See, e.g.*, Brock v. Lucky Stores, Inc., 23 Fed. Appx. 709 (9th Cir. 2001). The Supreme Court's rejection of collateral estoppel and approval of relitigation of the employee's claim in *Alexander* was based partly on the importance of judicial control over civil rights enforcement, partly on the lack of clear agreement by the employee or the union that the arbitration would encompass a statutory discrimination claim and partly on the Court's doubts about the arbitration. The lack of clear consent to arbitrate a statutory claim is particularly characteristic of collective bargaining agreements, because such agreements usually require arbitration only of *contract* claims, and a union is likely to present a grievance as a contract claim. Moreover, the issues whether an employee was discharged for "just cause" in compliance with the contract, and whether the employer unlawfully discriminated in violation of a law against discrimination, are not necessarily the same. The answer to both questions could be "yes" if the employer had a reasonable cause to discharge but would have been more forgiving of the same misconduct by a non-minority employee.

Still, there are times when the fact issues relating to discrimination are truly identical to the issues presented by an employee's discharge grievance, or when the employee or the union consented in the underlying agreement or in the course of arbitration to arbitrate the statutory discrimination claim. If so, are the lesser formality of arbitration and the importance of judicial enforcement of civil rights still sufficiently compelling to deny the application of collateral estoppel? As explained in the immediately following section of this chapter, after *Alexander* the Supreme Court has overcome many of its doubts about arbitration, at least where the parties have clearly agreed to arbitration of a discrimination claim. And when an employer requires an individual, nonunion employee to agree to arbitration, the employer-drafted agreement will likely cover any discrimination or other statutory claim the employee might have.

Of course, arbitration is not the only alternative forum that might lead to questions of issue preclusion. The frequent duplication of federal employment laws by state lawmakers sometimes leads to multiple enforcement proceedings. For example, an employee might claim his discharge violated separate state and federal laws, splitting those claims between separate state and federal courts. In Kremer v. Chemical Const. Corp., 456 U.S. 461 (1982), the Court held that a New York state court's decision, which was entitled to res judicata effect under state law, was entitled to the same effect in a federal court under 28 U.S.C.A. § 1738.

Civil service commissions created for the protection of public employees present another alternative forum in which to challenge adverse employment actions. However, civil service proceedings can vary substantially with respect to formality and procedural safeguards. The effect of such proceedings on judicial relitigation of the same adverse employment action depends on the quality of the proceedings and the details of local law. *Compare* Castillo v. City of Los Angeles, 111 Cal. Rptr. 2d 870 (Cal. App. 2001) (commission's decision reaffirming discharge precluded employee's discrimination claim in judicial proceeding) *with* Long v. Lewis, 723 A.2d 1238 (N.J. Super. 1999) (merit system board proceedings did not bar plaintiff from pursuing statutory discrimination claim in separate judicial forum; board was not forum "of equal jurisdiction," and it lacked equivalent remedial power).

C. ARBITRATION AS A FINAL RESOLUTION OF STATUTORY CLAIMS

Arbitration of labor disputes has been common for at least a century in the collective bargaining context, but it is only recently that employers have considered it a useful alternative to burgeoning litigation with individual employees. Employer interest in arbitration of individual employee disputes was sparked by the Supreme Court's decision in Gilmer v. Interstate/Johnson Lane Corp., 500 U.S. 20 (1991), which held that an employee might be bound by an agreement to submit a statutory discrimination claim to arbitration, and that pursuant to the parties' agreement, the arbitrator's award might constitute the final resolution of the matter and bar further judicial proceedings. From 1995 to 1997, the percentage of employers adopting arbitration policies for employment disputes increased from 10 percent to 19 percent. From 1997 to 2001, the number of employment cases filed with the American Arbitration Association (AAA) increased 60 percent. Theodore Eisenberg & Elizabeth Hill, *Arbitration and Litigation of Employment Claims: An Empirical Comparison*, 58 Disp. Res. J. 44 (2004). By 2007, various studies indicated that from 15 to 25 percent of employers had adopted mandatory arbitration policies. Alexander Colvin, *Empirical Research on Employment Arbitration*, 12 Employee Rights & Employment Policy Journal 405, 411 (2007).

The Supreme Court's conclusion in *Gilmer* that arbitration proceedings could completely supplant judicial proceedings might appear directly to contradict the Court's earlier decision in Alexander v. Gardner-Denver Co., 415 U.S. 36 (1974), which held that an employee was *not* foreclosed from initiating a federal lawsuit after losing in a collective bargaining arbitration proceeding. However, the effect of an arbitration award depends on the agreement of the parties. In collective bargaining, arbitration is the usual manner of resolving *contractual* disputes. There is no reason to assume that the presence of an arbitration provision in a collective bargaining agreement constitutes an agreement to refer other types of disputes (such as those based on statutory discrimination claims) exclusively to arbitration. Arbitration provisions in union agreements often *permit* the arbitration of discrimination claims (especially where the agreement itself prohibits discrimination), but *Alexander* holds that the mere amenability of arbitration to a discrimination claim does not constitute an agreement that arbitration will be the final and exclusive method of resolving such a claim.

In the years since *Alexander*, the Court has clearly become more approving of arbitration as a means of resolving civil rights disputes, provided the parties to such disputes have agreed that arbitration will take the place of judicial remedies. In Wright v. Universal Maritime Service Corp., 525 U.S. 70 (1998), the Court held that in the context of a collective bargaining agreement, an arbitration provision will not be interpreted to require arbitration and to waive judicial remedies for statutory discrimination claims unless such an intention is "clear and unmistakable." 525 U.S. at 79-80. A "particularly" clear agreement is necessary in this context, because a union's submission of an employee's grievance to arbitration is otherwise ambiguous, at best, insofar as the employee's or union's consent to submit the statutory claim in addition to the breach of contract claim.

Arbitration agreements between employers and individual employees may stand on a different footing. Although an arbitration agreement between a single employee and his employer might be limited to the resolution of contractual disputes, an employer's more likely purpose would be arbitration of all claims, contractual and otherwise. Indeed, the greatest impetus for arbitration in individual employee relations, from the employer's point of view, is the nonjudicial resolution of statutory claims.

After the Supreme Court's decision in *Gilmer* upholding contractual arbitration for the final and exclusive resolution of federal civil rights claims, another major development promoting arbitration of individual employee disputes was the Court's application of the Federal Arbitration Act to the employment context in Circuit City Stores, Inc. v. Adams, 532 U.S. 105 (2001). Before *Circuit City*, it was uncertain whether the FAA applied to employment disputes because of a provision denying coverage of "contracts of employment of seamen, railroad employees, *or any other class of workers* engaged in foreign or interstate commerce." 9 U.S.C. § 1. In *Circuit City*, the Court interpreted this phrase to apply only to workers in the transportation industry, with the effect that contracts of other employees are subject to the FAA. As a result of this extension of the FAA, state law regarding arbitration of employment disputes is subject to a key provision of the FAA tending to preempt state laws that might otherwise discourage arbitration. According to section 2 of the act,

> [a] written provision . . . to settle by arbitration a controversy thereafter arising out of such contract or transaction, or the refusal to perform the whole or any part thereof, or an agreement in writing to submit to arbitration an existing controversy arising out of such a contract, transaction, or refusal, shall be valid, irrevocable, and enforceable, *save upon such grounds as exist at law or in equity for the revocation of any contract.*

(Emphasis added.)

Despite the courts' widespread endorsement of arbitration, it is still possible for an agreement to arbitrate to fail "upon such grounds as exist at law or in equity for the revocation of any contract." Grounds for the revocation of "any contract" include unconscionability. However, the FAA's requirement that a court should apply the same rules applicable to "any contract" suggests a rule of equality for arbitration contracts. In other words, arbitration contracts are not to be regarded as inherently more suspect than other types of contracts.

The case that follows was a dispute between consumers and a telecommunications service provider. However, the court's discussion of the application of the doctrine of unconscionability in a case governed by the FAA is important to the future of judicial review and enforcement of arbitration agreements in employment.

AT&T MOBILITY LLC v. CONCEPCION

563 U.S. 333 (2011)

[The Concepcions filed a class action alleging false advertising by AT&T. AT&T sought to compel arbitration under a clause of the service agreement that required arbitration and required claims to be filed in an "individual capacity, and not as a plaintiff or class member in any purported class or representative proceeding." The District Court and Ninth Circuit, applying California law, held the agreement unconscionable for precluding the right to pursue a claim as a class action.]

We have described [Section 2] as reflecting both a "liberal federal policy favoring arbitration," and the "fundamental principle that arbitration is a matter of contract". . . . In line with these principles, courts must place arbitration agreements on an equal footing with other contracts, and enforce them according to their terms.

The final phrase of § 2, however, permits arbitration agreements to be declared unenforceable "upon such grounds as exist at law or in equity for the revocation of any contract." This saving clause permits agreements to arbitrate to be invalidated by "generally applicable contract defenses, such as fraud, duress, or unconscionability," but not by defenses that apply only to arbitration or that derive their meaning from the fact that an agreement to arbitrate is at issue . . . . The question in this case is whether § 2 preempts California's rule classifying most collective-arbitration waivers in consumer contracts as unconscionable. We refer to this rule as the *Discover Bank* rule. [*See* Discover Bank v. Superior Court, 113 P.3d 1100 (2005)].

Under California law, courts may refuse to enforce any contract found "to have been unconscionable at the time it was made," or may "limit the application of any unconscionable clause." Cal. Civ. Code Ann. § 1670.5(a) (West 1985). A finding of unconscionability requires "a 'procedural' and a 'substantive' element, the former focusing on 'oppression' or 'surprise' due to unequal bargaining power, the latter on 'overly harsh' or 'one-sided' results." *Armendariz v. Foundation Health Pyschcare Servs., Inc.*, 6 P.3d 669, 690 (2000); accord, *Discover Bank,* 113 P.3d, at 1108.

In *Discover Bank,* the California Supreme Court applied this framework to class-action waivers in arbitration agreements and held as follows:

> "[W]hen the waiver is found in a consumer contract of adhesion in a setting in which disputes between the contracting parties predictably involve small amounts of damages, and when it is alleged that the party with the superior bargaining power has carried out a scheme to deliberately cheat large numbers of consumers out of individually small sums of money, then . . . the waiver becomes in practice the exemption of the party 'from responsibility for [its] own fraud, or willful injury to the person or property of another.' Under these circumstances, such waivers are unconscionable under California law and should not be enforced." *Id.*, 113 P.3d, at 1110 . . . .

The Concepcions argue that the *Discover Bank* rule, given its origins in California's unconscionability doctrine and California's policy against exculpation, is a ground that "exist[s] at law or in equity for the revocation of any contract" under FAA § 2. Moreover, they argue that even if we construe the *Discover Bank* rule as a prohibition on collective-action waivers rather than simply an application of unconscionability, the rule would still be applicable to all dispute-resolution contracts, since California prohibits waivers of class litigation as well. *See America Online, Inc. v. Superior Ct.*, 108 Cal.Rptr.2d 699, 711–713 (2001).

When state law prohibits outright the arbitration of a particular type of claim, the analysis is straightforward: The conflicting rule is displaced by the FAA. *Preston v. Ferrer,* 552 U.S. 346, 353 (2008). But the inquiry becomes more complex when a doctrine normally thought to be generally applicable, such as duress or, as relevant here, unconscionability, is alleged to have been applied in a fashion that disfavors arbitration. In *Perry v. Thomas,* 482 U.S. 483 (1987), for example, we noted that the FAA's preemptive effect might extend even to grounds traditionally thought to exist "'at law or in equity for the revocation of any contract.'" *Id.,* at 492, n. 9 (emphasis deleted). We said that a court may not "rely on the uniqueness of an agreement to arbitrate as a basis for a state-law holding that enforcement would be unconscionable, for this would enable the court to effect what . . . the state legislature cannot." *Id.,* at 493, n. 9.

An obvious illustration of this point would be a case finding unconscionable or unenforceable as against public policy consumer arbitration agreements that fail to provide for judicially monitored discovery. The rationalizations for such a holding are neither difficult to imagine nor different in kind from those articulated in *Discover Bank.* A court might reason that no consumer would knowingly waive his right to full discovery, as this would enable companies to hide their wrongdoing. Or the court might simply say that such agreements are exculpatory — restricting discovery would be of greater benefit to the company than the consumer, since the former is more likely to be sued than to sue . . . . And, the reasoning would continue, because such a rule applies the general principle of unconscionability or public-policy disapproval of exculpatory agreements, it is applicable to "any" contract and thus preserved by § 2 of the FAA. In practice, of course, the rule would have a disproportionate impact on arbitration agreements; but it would presumably apply to contracts purporting to restrict discovery in litigation as well.

Other examples are easy to imagine. The same argument might apply to a rule classifying as unconscionable arbitration agreements that fail to abide by the Federal Rules of Evidence, or that disallow an ultimate disposition by a jury (perhaps termed "a panel of twelve lay arbitrators" to help avoid preemption). Such examples are not fanciful, since the judicial hostility towards arbitration that prompted the FAA had manifested itself in "a great variety" of "devices and formulas" declaring arbitration against public policy. Robert Lawrence Co. v. Devonshire Fabrics, Inc., 271 F.2d 402, 406 (C.A.2 1959). . . .

Although § 2's saving clause preserves generally applicable contract defenses, nothing in it suggests an intent to preserve state-law rules that stand as an obstacle to the accomplishment of the FAA's objectives. . . . The overarching purpose of the FAA, evident in the text of §§ 2, 3, and 4, is to ensure the enforcement of arbitration agreements according to their terms so as to facilitate streamlined proceedings. Requiring the availability of classwide arbitration interferes with fundamental attributes of arbitration and thus creates a scheme inconsistent with the FAA . . . .

The point of affording parties discretion in designing arbitration processes is to allow for efficient, streamlined procedures tailored to the type of dispute. It can be specified, for example, that the decisionmaker be a specialist in the relevant field, or that proceedings be kept confidential to protect trade secrets. And the informality of arbitral proceedings is itself desirable, reducing the cost and increasing the speed of dispute resolution.

California's *Discover Bank* rule similarly interferes with arbitration. Although the rule does not *require* classwide arbitration, it allows any party to a consumer contract to demand it *ex post.* The rule is limited to adhesion contracts, but the times in which consumer contracts were anything other than adhesive are long past.[6] The rule also requires that damages be predictably small, and that the consumer allege a scheme to cheat consumers. The former requirement, however, is toothless and malleable (the Ninth Circuit has held that damages of $4,000 are sufficiently small, *see* Oestreicher v. Alienware Corp., 322 Fed. Appx. 489, 492 (2009) (unpublished)), and the latter has no limiting effect, as all that is required is an allegation. Consumers remain free to bring and resolve their disputes on a bilateral basis under *Discover Bank,* and some may well do so; but there is little incentive for lawyers to arbitrate on behalf of individuals when they may do so for a class and reap far higher fees in the process. And faced with inevitable class arbitration, companies would have less incentive to continue resolving potentially duplicative claims on an individual basis.

Although we have had little occasion to examine classwide arbitration, our decision in Stolt-Nielsen S.A. v. AnimalFeeds International Corp., 559 U.S. 662 (2010) is instructive. In that case we held that an arbitration panel exceeded its power under § 10(a)(4) of the FAA by imposing class procedures based on policy judgments rather than the arbitration agreement itself or some background principle of contract law that would affect its interpretation.. We then held that the agreement at issue, which was silent on the question of class procedures, could not be interpreted to allow them because the "changes brought about by the shift from bilateral arbitration to class-action arbitration" are "fundamental." *Id.* at 686. This is obvious as a structural matter: Classwide arbitration includes absent parties,

[6] Of course States remain free to take steps addressing the concerns that attend contracts of adhesion — for example, requiring class-action-waiver provisions in adhesive arbitration agreements to be highlighted. Such steps cannot, however, conflict with the FAA or frustrate its purpose to ensure that private arbitration agreements are enforced according to their terms.

necessitating additional and different procedures and involving higher stakes. Confidentiality becomes more difficult. And while it is theoretically possible to select an arbitrator with some expertise relevant to the class-certification question, arbitrators are not generally knowledgeable in the often-dominant procedural aspects of certification, such as the protection of absent parties. The conclusion follows that class arbitration, to the extent it is manufactured by *Discover Bank* rather than consensual, is inconsistent with the FAA.

First, the switch from bilateral to class arbitration sacrifices the principal advantage of arbitration — its informality — and makes the process slower, more costly, and more likely to generate procedural morass than final judgment. "In bilateral arbitration, parties forgo the procedural rigor and appellate review of the courts in order to realize the benefits of private dispute resolution: lower costs, greater efficiency and speed, and the ability to choose expert adjudicators to resolve specialized disputes." 559 U.S., at 686. But before an arbitrator may decide the merits of a claim in classwide procedures, he must first decide, for example, whether the class itself may be certified, whether the named parties are sufficiently representative and typical, and how discovery for the class should be conducted.

Second, class arbitration *requires* procedural formality. The AAA's rules governing class arbitrations mimic the Federal Rules of Civil Procedure for class litigation. And while parties can alter those procedures by contract, an alternative is not obvious. If procedures are too informal, absent class members would not be bound by the arbitration. For a class-action money judgment to bind absentees in litigation, class representatives must at all times adequately represent absent class members, and absent members must be afforded notice, an opportunity to be heard, and a right to opt out of the class. At least this amount of process would presumably be required for absent parties to be bound by the results of arbitration.

We find it unlikely that in passing the FAA Congress meant to leave the disposition of these procedural requirements to an arbitrator. Indeed, class arbitration was not even envisioned by Congress when it passed the FAA in 1925; as the California Supreme Court admitted in *Discover Bank,* class arbitration is a "relatively recent development." 113 P.3d, at 1110. And it is at the very least odd to think that an arbitrator would be entrusted with ensuring that third parties' due process rights are satisfied.

Third, class arbitration greatly increases risks to defendants. Informal procedures do of course have a cost: The absence of multilayered review makes it more likely that errors will go uncorrected. Defendants are willing to accept the costs of these errors in arbitration, since their impact is limited to the size of individual disputes, and presumably outweighed by savings from avoiding the courts. But when damages allegedly owed to tens of thousands of potential claimants are aggregated and decided at once, the risk of an error will often become unacceptable. Faced with even a small chance of a devastating loss, defendants will be pressured into settling questionable claims . . . .

Arbitration is poorly suited to the higher stakes of class litigation. In litigation, a defendant may appeal a certification decision on an interlocutory basis and, if unsuccessful, may appeal from a final judgment as well. Questions of law are reviewed *de novo* and questions of fact for clear error. In contrast, 9 U.S.C. §10 allows a court to vacate an arbitral award *only* where the award "was procured by corruption, fraud, or undue means"; "there was evident partiality or corruption in the arbitrators"; "the arbitrators were guilty of misconduct in refusing to postpone the hearing . . . or in refusing to hear evidence pertinent and material to the controversy[,] or of any other misbehavior by which the rights of any party have been prejudiced"; or if the "arbitrators exceeded their powers, or so imperfectly executed them that a mutual, final, and definite award . . . was not made." The AAA rules do authorize judicial review of certification decisions, but this review is unlikely to have much effect given these limitations; review under § 10 focuses on misconduct rather than mistake. And parties may not contractually expand the grounds or nature of judicial review. *Hall Street Assocs.,* 552 U.S., at 578. We find it hard to believe that defendants would bet the company with no effective means of review, and even harder to believe that Congress would have intended to allow state courts to force such a decision.

The Concepcions contend that because parties may and sometimes do agree to aggregation, class procedures are not necessarily incompatible with arbitration. But the same could be said about procedures that the Concepcions admit States may not superimpose on arbitration: Parties *could* agree to arbitrate pursuant to the Federal Rules of Civil Procedure, or pursuant to a discovery process rivaling that in litigation. Arbitration is a matter of contract, and the FAA requires courts to honor parties' expectations. But what the parties in the aforementioned examples would have agreed to is not arbitration as envisioned by the FAA, lacks its benefits, and therefore may not be required by state law.

The dissent claims that class proceedings are necessary to prosecute small-dollar claims that might otherwise slip through the legal system. But States cannot require a procedure that is inconsistent with the FAA, even if it is desirable for unrelated reasons. Moreover, the claim here was most unlikely to go unresolved. As noted earlier, the arbitration agreement provides that AT & T will pay claimants a minimum of $7,500 and twice their attorney's fees if they obtain an arbitration award greater than AT & T's last settlement offer. The District Court found this scheme sufficient to provide incentive for the individual prosecution of meritorious claims that are not immediately settled, and the Ninth Circuit admitted that aggrieved customers who filed claims would be "essentially guarantee[d]" to be made whole, 584 F.3d, at 856, n. 9. Indeed, the District Court concluded that the Concepcions were *better off* under their arbitration agreement with AT & T than they would have been as participants in a class action, which "could take months, if not years, and which may merely yield an opportunity to submit a claim for recovery of a small percentage of a few dollars." . . .

The judgment of the Ninth Circuit is reversed, and the case is remanded for further proceedings consistent with this opinion.

NOTES AND QUESTIONS

1. *Concepcion* is a consumer contract case, and the general principles discussed by the Court might well apply to employment contracts as well. However, there is at least one distinguishing feature of employment contracts. The NLRB held in In re D.R. Horton, 357 NLRB No.184 (2012), that an employer unlawfully interferes with its employees' rights to engage in "concerted activity"

under section 7 of the National Labor Relations Act by adopting or maintaining a mandatory arbitration policy that precludes class or collective action. But the *Horton* decision has divided the federal courts. *Compare* Lewis v. Epic Systems Corporation, 823 F.3d 1147 (7th Cir. 2016) (mandatory employment agreement requiring employees to bring wage-and-hour claims only by individual arbitration violated right of employees to engage in concerted activity) *with* D.R. Horton, Inc. v. N.L.R.B, 737 F.3d 344 (5th Cir. 2013) (upholding employer's requirement that employees agree to individual arbitration of claims and waive right to class or collective action). As of the date of publication of this edition, the *Lewis* case is presently pending before the U.S. Supreme Court, and the Court's decision is expected in 2018.

2. Would the Court have upheld the denial of class or collective arbitration of disputes if AT&T's policies had not been so generous to prevailing complainants? What if the denial of class or collective action could be shown to preclude the vindication of rights? *See* In Re American Express Merchants' Litig., 667 F.3d 204 (2d Cir. 2012) (class action waiver clause in credit card agreement was unenforceable because "enforcement of the clause would effectively preclude any action seeking to vindicate . . . statutory rights," in light of plaintiffs' expert evidence that pursuing their statutory claims individually, rather than through class arbitration, would not be economically feasible).

3. Other potential causes of unconscionability or violation of public policy include an agreement's restrictions on discovery, allocation of costs or limits on remedies. *See* In re Poly-America, L.P., 262 S.W.3d 337 (Tex. 2008). The extent to which *Concepcion* affects analysis of these issues remains uncertain. A single agreement drafted for all types of claims might be unconscionable for some but not for others. Cost allocation rules may be unconscionable for some employees and types of disputes but not for others. Limitations on remedies may be unconscionable for some wrongs but not for others, depending on the remedies commanded by a legislature. Limits on discovery may be unconscionable in some cases but not others depending on the difficulties of investigating and proving particular claims. *See* In re Poly-America, L.P., 262 S.W.3d 337 (Tex. 2008); Fitz v. NCR Corp., 118 Cal. App. 4th 702, 13 Cal. Rptr. 3d 88 (2004); Brown v. Wheat First Sec., Inc., 257 F.3d 821 (D.C. Cir. 2001); Circuit City Stores, Inc. v. Adams, 279 F.3d 889 (9th Cir. 2002).

An arbitration agreement may be especially vulnerable to attack as unconscionable if its procedural rules are asymmetrical, with one set of rules for the employer and another for the employee. *See* Little v. Auto Stiegler, Inc., 63 P.3d 979 (Cal. 2003). A rule that allowed the employer, but not an employee, to appeal an arbitrator's decision would likely be unconscionable, at least if such a rule was not the product of genuine bargaining. The *Little* case illustrates that even facially uniform rules may be asymmetrical in effect. In *Little*, the employer-drafted agreement allowed appeal only if the arbitrator issued an award for an amount exceeding $50,000. On its face, the rule applied equally to the employer and the employee. However, as a practical matter the appeal threshold allowed the employer to appeal in nearly any wrongful discharge case the employer "lost" but precluded an employee appeal in any case the employee "lost." The court found this rule to be substantively unconscionable.

4. Even a "fair" arbitration agreement may fail for lack of mutual assent under traditional contract formation rules. The fact that the agreement is one of adhesion raises two arguments against enforcement. First, allowing an employer to exercise such coercive force against employees arguably is inconsistent with the protective purpose of many employment laws. The EEOC initially took this position as to claims under laws it enforces (Title VII, ADEA, and ADA). Federal courts, however, have generally adopted the opposite view. *See, e.g.*, E.E.O.C. v. Luce, Forward, Hamilton & Scripps, 345 F.3d 742 (9th Cir. 2003). The EEOC now appears to assume the effectiveness of such agreements. *See* EEOC, Office of Legal Counsel, Informal Discussion Letter (May 20, 2008), available online at http://www.eeoc.gov/eeoc/foia/letters/2008/ada_mandatory_arbitration.html (last visited September 28, 2012)

Another argument against an arbitration agreement as a mandatory condition of employment is that an employer's express or implicit threat to discharge or deny employment constitutes duress or renders the agreement "procedurally unconscionable." However, for an arbitration policy to be effective from the employer's point of view, the policy must be uniform for all, much like many other employment policies. Moreover, procedural unconscionability, standing alone, is generally insufficient to render a contract voidable in the absence of "substantive unconscionability" in the terms of the contract, and *Concepcion* makes it clear that an agreement to arbitrate is not per se substantively unconscionable.

5. Still another traditional contract formation argument against an arbitration agreement is lack of consideration In a typical arbitration agreement the employer's promise to submit to arbitration and to be bound by the results satisfies the requirement of consideration for the employee's agreement to submit to arbitration. *See, e.g.,* Walters v. A.A.A. Waterproofing, Inc., 85 P.3d 389 (Wash. App. 2004); In re Halliburton Co., 80 S.W.3d 566 (Tex. 2002), *cert. denied sub nom.* Myers v. Halliburton Co., 537 U.S. 1112 (2003). However, if the employer has not promised to be bound by arbitration or to arbitrate its own claims, or if it remains free unilaterally to change the terms of arbitration, a court might hold the employer has given no real promise or other consideration in return for the employee's promise, especially in those jurisdictions that reject that continued "employment at will" can constitute consideration for an employee's promise. *See, e.g.,* Mendivil v. Zanios Foods, Inc., 357 S.W.3d 827 (Tex. App. — El Paso 2012).

6. One argument against the applicability of an otherwise valid arbitration agreement is that it may cover disputes with only the one named "employer" in the contract – not with other corporate or natural persons affiliated with the named employer. *See, e.g.,* Belnap v. Iasis Healthcare, 844 F.3d 1272, 1294-98 (10th Cir. 2017) (where arbitration agreement referred to disputes "between" the signatories, neither the nonsignatory parent of the corporate defendant, nor the other nonsignatory defendants, could compel arbitration under the agreement).

7. The usual standard for judicial review of an arbitral decision is quite limited. The Federal Arbitration Act discourages such judicial review; otherwise, the efficiency and convenience of arbitration might be undermined. The act lists only the following limited grounds for a court to vacate an arbitrator's award:

(1) where the award was procured by corruption, fraud, or undue means;

(2) where there was evident partiality or corruption in the arbitrators, or either of them;

(3) where the arbitrators were guilty of misconduct in refusing to postpone the hearing, upon sufficient cause shown, or in refusing to hear evidence pertinent and material to the controversy; or of any other misbehavior by which the rights of any party have been prejudiced; or

(4) where the arbitrators exceeded their powers, or so imperfectly executed them that a mutual, final, and definite award upon the subject matter submitted was not made.

9 U.S.C.A. § 10. Courts have recognized two additional grounds: where an award was (1) arbitrary and capricious, or (2) against public policy. Brown v. Rauscher Pierce Refsnes, Inc., 994 F.2d 775, 779 (11th Cir. 1993). Even these grounds are not invitations to reverse an arbitrator who decides a case differently than a court would. Gingiss Int'l, Inc. v. Bormet 58 F.3d 328 (7th Cir. 1995) (fact or legal error, even if clear or gross, is not grounds for annulling arbitral decision).

Could an employer include a provision for greater judicial scrutiny of an arbitration award? In Hall St. Assocs. L.L.C. v. Mattel, 552 U.S. 576 (2008), the Supreme Court held that the Federal Arbitration Act bars a contractual expansion of the grounds for judicial review of arbitration awards.

8. A valid, binding arbitration agreement bars the employee from filing a lawsuit but does not bar (a) an employee from filing a charge of discrimination with the Equal Employment Opportunity Commission (EEOC) or (b) the EEOC from filing a lawsuit seeking either systemic relief or individual relief for the charging party, the Supreme Court held in E.E.O.C. v. Waffle House:

> [W]henever the EEOC chooses from among the many charges filed each year to bring an enforcement action in a particular case, the agency may be seeking to vindicate a public interest, not simply provide make-whole relief for the employee, even when it pursues entirely victim-specific relief. To hold otherwise would undermine the detailed enforcement scheme created by Congress simply to give greater effect to an agreement between private parties that does not even contemplate the EEOC's statutory function.

534 U.S. 279, 296 (2002). Yet the possibility of an EEOC lawsuit may not meaningfully undermine or circumvent an arbitration agreement because so few such suits are filed. In 2003, the EEOC received 81,293 charges, but filed only 361 "merits" lawsuits – fewer than one-half of one percent. EEOC, *Charge Statistics* (March 8, 2004), at http://www.eeoc.gov/stats/ charges.html.

TABLE OF CASES & OTHER AUTHORITIES

(only principal cases, administrative rulings, and article excerpts)

INDEX